Foragers and Farmers of the Northern Kayenta Region

John Blake Sr. excavating a Pueblo III pit house on the Rainbow Plateau, August 1997.

Foragers and Farmers of the Northern Kayenta Region

Excavations along the Navajo Mountain Road

PHIL R. GEIB

with a contribution by
Jim Collette

THE UNIVERSITY OF UTAH PRESS
Salt Lake City

The interpretations presented in this report are those of the author and in no way reflect those of the Navajo Nation or Navajo people.

Copyright © 2011 by The University of Utah Press. All rights reserved.

 The Defiance House Man colophon is a registered trademark of the University of Utah Press. It is based upon a four-foot-tall, Ancient Puebloan pictograph (late PIII) near Glen Canyon, Utah.

15 14 13 12 11   1 2 3 4 5

LIBRARY OF CONGRESS CATALOGING-IN-PUBLICATION DATA

Geib, Phil R.
  Foragers and farmers of the northern Kayenta region : excavations along the Navajo Mountain road / Phil R. Geib ; with contribution by Jim Collette.
       p. cm.
  Includes bibliographical references.
  ISBN 978-1-60781-003-2 (alk. paper)
  1. Navajo Indians — Navajo Mountain Region (Utah and Ariz.) — Antiquities. 2. Navajo Indians — Arizona — Kayenta Region — Antiquities. 3. Navajo Mountain Road Archaeological Project. 4. Excavations (Archaeology) — Navajo Mountain Region (Utah and Ariz.) 5. Paleo-Indians — Navajo Mountain Region (Utah and Ariz.) 6. Hunting and gathering societies — Navajo Mountain Region (Utah and Ariz.) 7. Agriculture, Prehistoric — Navajo Mountain Region (Utah and Ariz.) 8. Social archaelogy — Navajo Mountain Region (Utah and Ariz.) 9. Navajo Mountain Region (Utah and Ariz.) — Antiquities. 10. Kayenta Region (Ariz.) — Antiquities. I. Collette, Jim. II. Title.
  E99.N3G355 2010
  979.2'59 — dc22   2010004265

Printed and bound by Sheridan Books, Inc., Ann Arbor, Michigan.

To

Dorothy Richards Geib
for always being there

and

J. Richard Ambler
for getting me started in archaeology

Contents

List of Figures	ix
List of Tables	xv
Acknowledgments	xix

1. Introduction — 1
   - Project Location — 1
   - The Project — 4
   - Project Methods — 12

2. Background for the Navajo Mountain Road Archaeological Project — 21
   - The Kayenta Region — 21
   - Previous Research — 24
   - Synopsis of Regional Prehistory — 25
   - Environment — 48

3. Synopsis of the Navajo Mountain Road Archaeological Project Sites — 64
   - The Pits (AZ-J-14-17) — 64
   - Ditch House (AZ-J-14-21) — 72
   - Wolachii Bighan (AZ-J-14-20) — 74
   - Hólahéi Scatter (AZ-J-14-23) — 75
   - Pee Wee Grande (AZ-J-14-26) — 77
   - Windy Mesa (AZ-J-14-28) — 79
   - The Slots (AZ-J-14-30) — 82
   - Polly's Place (AZ-J-14-31) — 83
   - Naaki Hooghan (AZ-J-14-11) — 85
   - Tres Campos (AZ-J-14-12) — 87
   - Panorama House (AZ-J-14-34) — 90
   - Big Bend (AZ-J-14-13) — 92
   - Ko' Lanhi (AZ-J-14-35) — 95
   - Blake's Abode (AZ-J-14-36) — 97
   - Scorpion Heights (AZ-J-14-37) — 97
   - Camp Dead Pine (AZ-J-14-52) — 101
   - Mountainview (AZ-J-14-38) — 102
   - Hammer House (AZ-J-14-16) — 103
   - Mouse House (AZ-J-3-7) — 107
   - Sin Sombra (AZ-J-3-6) — 109
   - Hillside Hermitage (AZ-J-3-14) — 110
   - Kin Kahuna (AZ-J-3-8) — 112
   - Dune Hollow (AZ-J-2-2) — 114
   - Hymn House (AZ-J-2-3) — 116
   - Modesty House (AZ-J-2-5) — 118
   - Water Jar Pueblo (AZ-J-2-58) — 118
   - Sapo Seco (AZ-J-2-6) — 121
   - Bonsai Bivouac (AZ-J-2-55) — 122
   - Three Dog Site (UT-B-63-39) — 124
   - Hanging Ash (UT-B-63-14) — 128
   - UT-B-63-19 — 128
   - UT-B-63-38 — 131
   - Tsé Haal'á (UT-B-63-30) — 132
   - Atlatl Rock Cave (AZ-J-14-41) — 135

4. Summary and Interpretation of Archaic Period Forager Remains — 140
   - The NMRAP Archaic Site Sample — 141
   - NMRAP Archaic Chronology — 145
   - Archaic Settlement — 160
   - Subsistence Range and Territory — 183
   - Paleoindian Remains and Archaic Beginnings — 193
   - Settlement Continuity and the Middle Archaic — 193
   - Conclusions — 204

5. Summary and Interpretation of Basketmaker II Remains — 206
   - The NMRAP Basketmaker Site Sample — 207
   - Northern Kayenta Region Basketmaker Chronology — 210
   - Farming and Foraging — 222
   - Basketmaker Settlement — 234

Architecture	255	7. Conclusion	374
Basketmaker Origins	263	Research Issues	375
Basketmaker II–III Transition	279	A Middle Holocene Bottleneck?	375
Conclusions	286	Forager Territories	377
		Agricultural Transition	378
6. Summary and Interpretation of Puebloan Remains, *with Jim Collette*	290	Puebloan Craft Production and Exchange	382
		Social Issues	385
The NMRAP Puebloan Site Sample	291	Final Thoughts	389
Chronology	294		
Puebloan Architecture	313	Appendix: Contents of Supplemental Documents	391
Puebloan Settlement Types and Patterning	333	References Cited	393
Puebloan Mobility	368	Index	419
Regional Settlement History and Population Trends	370		

Figures

1.1. The Four Corners region showing prehistoric Puebloan "cultural" areas and the general location of the Navajo Mountain road. 2
1.2. The Navajo Mountain Road Archaeological Project study area in the northern Kayenta region. 3
1.3. Excavation under way at Modesty House on the central portion of the Rainbow Plateau. 13
2.1. Map of the core Kayenta region of northeast Arizona and southeast Utah. 22
2.2. Map of the northern Kayenta region and adjoining terrain. 23
2.3. General cultural-temporal framework used for this report. 26
2.4. Examples of Oshara tradition points from the southern Kaibito Plateau around Tuba City, Arizona. 31
2.5. Cowboy Cave depositional units and radiocarbon dates in relation to chronological divisions for the northern Colorado Plateau. 34
2.6. Actual intervals of Archaic period forager occupation for the N16 project area relative to the general chronological framework and chief cultural-temporal diagnostics for the northern Colorado Plateau. 35
2.7. Western Basketmaker II cultural-temporal phases relevant to the northern Kayenta region. 42
2.8. Demographic profiles for six localities of the northern Kayenta region. 46
2.9. Demographic profile for the entire northern Kayenta region and for the northern mesas excluding Upper Piute Canyon and Dzil Nez Mesa. 47
2.10. Schematic cross section along the N16 right-of-way plus three orthogonal sections. 50
2.11. View from the high divide between Navajo and Piute canyons. 51
2.12. View into a part of Upper Piute Canyon from its western rim. 51
2.13. View to the southwest of Navajo Mountain from the northern part of the Rainbow Plateau near Hawkeye Natural Bridge. 52
2.14. Examples of the silicified sandstone that outcrops on Navajo Mountain. 59
2.15. Two rim sherds of unfired Tsegi Orange Ware bowls found nested together in the trash midden at Long House. 61
2.16. Mineralized log within the Petrified Forest Member of the Chinle Formation exposed in Lower Piute Canyon. 62
3.1. Location of the N16 right-of-way showing the 33 sites excavated by the Navajo Mountain Road Archaeological Project. 69
3.2. The Pits site plan showing topography, work effort, and excavated features. 70
3.3. Ditch House site plan showing topography, work effort, and excavated features. 73
3.4. Wolachii Bighan site plan showing topography, work effort, and excavated features. 75
3.5. Hólahéi Scatter site plan showing topography, work effort, and excavated features. 76
3.6. Pee Wee Grande site plan showing topography, work effort, and excavated features. 78
3.7. Windy Mesa site plan showing topography, work effort, and excavated features. 80
3.8. The Slots site plan showing topography, work effort, and excavated features. 82
3.9. Polly's Place site plan showing topography, work effort, and excavated features. 84
3.10. Naaki Hooghan site plan showing topography, work effort, and excavated features. 86

3.11. Tres Campos site plan showing topography, work effort, and excavated features. 88
3.12. Panorama House site plan showing topography, work effort, and excavated features. 91
3.13. Big Bend site plan showing topography, work effort, and excavated features. 93
3.14. Ko' Lanhi site plan showing topography, work effort, and excavated features. 96
3.15. Blake's Abode site plan showing topography, work effort, and excavated features. 98
3.16. Scorpion Heights site plan showing topography, work effort, and excavated features. 99
3.17. Camp Dead Pine site plan showing topography, work effort, and excavated features. 102
3.18. Mountainview site plan showing topography, work effort, and excavated features. 104
3.19. Hammer House site plan showing topography, work effort, and excavated features. 105
3.20. Mouse House site plan showing topography, work effort, and excavated features. 108
3.21. Sin Sombra site plan showing topography, work effort, and excavated features. 109
3.22. Hillside Hermitage site plan showing topography, work effort, and excavated features. 111
3.23. Kin Kahuna site plan showing topography, work effort, and excavated features. 113
3.24. Dune Hollow site plan showing topography, work effort, and excavated features. 115
3.25. Hymn House site plan showing topography, work effort, and excavated features. 117
3.26. Modesty House site plan showing topography, work effort, and excavated features. 119
3.27. Water Jar Pueblo site plan showing topography, work effort, and excavated structures. 120
3.28. Sapo Seco site plan showing topography, extent of mechanized work effort, and excavated structures. 122
3.29. Bonsai Bivouac site plan showing topography, work effort, and excavated features. 123
3.30. Plan map of Three Dog Site showing topography, work effort, and excavated features. 125
3.31. Hanging Ash site plan showing topography, work effort, and excavated structures. 129
3.32. UT-B-63-19 site plan showing topography, work effort, and excavated structure. 130
3.33. UT-B-63-38 site plan showing topography and work effort. 132
3.34. Tsé Haal'á site plan showing topography, work effort, and excavated features. 133
3.35. Atlatl Rock Cave site plan showing topography and exterior features. 136
4.1. Distribution of Navajo Mountain Road Archaeological Project Archaic sites by principal temporal component. 143
4.2. Array of all but the oldest of the 59 radiocarbon dates from Navajo Mountain Road Archaeological Project Archaic sites. 147
4.3. Comparison of radiocarbon determinations on sagebrush and wood charcoal from single features at Navajo Mountain Road Archaeological Project Archaic sites. 152
4.4. Plot of the 10 obsidian-hydration dates from the Archaic component of The Pits. 157
4.5. Plot of the 12 obsidian-hydration dates from Hólahéi Scatter. 159
4.6. Averages of the two internally consistent groups of obsidian-hydration dates from Hólahéi Scatter. 159
4.7. Plots of Navajo Mountain Road Archaeological Project Archaic sites organized by density of grinding tools, faunal bone, and debitage. 168
4.8. Plan map of the lower late Archaic component of Three Dog Site showing examples of the basin hearths and the density of debitage recovered from 1-×-1-m units. 169
4.9. Plan map of the late Archaic component of Tsé Haal'á showing examples of the basin hearths. 170
4.10. Interior of Atlatl Rock Cave from its mouth prior to looting. 172
4.11. Stratigraphic exposures at Three Dog Site and Tsé Haal'á showing the vastly different depositional contexts. 174
4.12. Bone beads and other artifacts recovered

from the late Archaic component of Three Dog Site.	175
4.13. Projectile points recovered from Tsé Haal'á.	175
4.14. Frequency of debitage raw material for the late Archaic components of Tsé Haal'á and Three Dog Site.	176
4.15. Frequency of general types of flaked facial tools for the Navajo Mountain Road Archaeological Project Archaic sites identified as hunting camps.	177
4.16. Projectile points recovered from several of the Navajo Mountain Road Archaeological Project Archaic hunting camps.	178
4.17. Distribution of inferred settlement types by temporal period for Navajo Mountain Road Archaeological Project Archaic sites and three caves with excavation data.	182
4.18. Scanning electron microscope images of transport wear on obsidian artifacts from Hólahéi Scatter.	187
4.19. Frequency of obsidian debitage within the lithic assemblages of Navajo Mountain Road Archaeological Project Archaic sites.	188
4.20. Hypothetical annual logistic range of Archaic foragers.	191
4.21. Hypothetical annual logistic range of Archaic foragers, with the foraging territories configured as ellipses.	192
4.22. Plainview-like point base from the surface of Locus B at Sapo Seco.	193
4.23. Frequency distribution of Archaic radiocarbon dates for the northern Kayenta region.	196
4.24. Frequency distribution of Archaic radiocarbon dates from the Kaibito Plateau.	198
4.25. Frequency distribution of all Archaic radiocarbon dates for the northern Kayenta region and the Kaibito Plateau.	199
5.1. Distribution of Navajo Mountain Road Archaeological Project Basketmaker sites by inferred settlement type.	209
5.2. Array of all 75 of the Navajo Mountain Road Archaeological Project Basketmaker radiocarbon dates.	214
5.3. Comparison of radiocarbon determinations on sagebrush, maize cupules, a pinyon cone scale, and pinyon bark from various Basketmaker features at Ditch House.	215
5.4. Comparison of radiocarbon determinations on sagebrush, maize cupules, and ricegrass seeds from Basketmaker hearths at Three Dog Site.	216
5.5. Comparison of averaged radiocarbon determinations on burned timber, juniper seeds, and maize from Panorama House.	217
5.6. Stratigraphically consistent series of accelerator mass spectrometry radiocarbon assays on maize from superimposed features at Kin Kahuna.	218
5.7. Array of 89 Basketmaker radiocarbon dates for the northern Kayenta region.	220
5.8. Sum of the probability distributions of all 89 Basketmaker dates for the northern Kayenta region.	220
5.9. Frequency distribution of Basketmaker radiocarbon dates for the northern Kayenta region.	221
5.10. Archaic and Basketmaker radiocarbon date distributions for the northern Kayenta region.	224
5.11. Maize ubiquity values for Basketmaker and Puebloan flotation samples of the Navajo Mountain Road Archaeological Project.	227
5.12. Maize ubiquity values through time for Navajo Mountain Road Archaeological Project Basketmaker habitations.	228
5.13. Examples of Basketmaker II primary habitations partially excavated by the Navajo Mountain Road Archaeological Project.	237
5.14. Distribution of dated features at Kin Kahuna illustrating feature accretion through time.	239
5.15. The Mountainview site, a Basketmaker primary habitation with Obelisk Utility.	240
5.16. Map of a large unexcavated primary habitation outside the N16 right-of-way that has an artifact assemblage similar to Mountainview.	241
5.17. Sin Sombra, a Basketmaker II secondary habitation.	242
5.18. Blake's Abode, a Basketmaker II secondary habitation.	243
5.19. Polly's Place, a Basketmaker II secondary habitation with two noncontemporaneous structures.	243
5.20. Panorama House, a Basketmaker II	

	secondary habitation with two noncontemporaneous structures.	244
5.21.	Slab-lined ramp entryways to probable Basketmaker II houses on Piute Mesa.	248
5.22.	Maps of the Desha Caves.	250
5.23.	Comparison of Navajo Mountain Road Archaeological Project Basketmaker house configurations through time.	256
5.24.	Typical example of a deflector in a Basketmaker II house of the N16 project area.	257
5.25.	The earliest pithouse at Kin Kahuna (Structure 5) showing the twin postholes that supported the roof.	258
5.26.	Structure 1 at Kin Kahuna showing a four-post roof-support arrangement.	258
5.27.	Close-up of the hearth and low partition of upright slabs in the house at Mountainview.	259
5.28.	Array of large bell-shaped storage features at The Pits.	260
5.29.	Typical cross sections of large bell-shaped storage pits at Basketmaker sites.	261
5.30.	Frequency distribution of all Archaic and Basketmaker radiocarbon dates available from the northern Kayenta region.	265
5.31.	Frequency of feature types on early Archaic, late Archaic, and Basketmaker sites.	266
5.32.	A heel fragment of a four-warp wickerwork sandal from Desha Cave 1.	267
5.33.	Idealized outlines for western Basketmaker and Elko dart points.	268
5.34.	A western Basketmaker dart point preform and hafted dart point from Cache 1 of Sand Dune Cave.	268
5.35.	A mountain sheep horn flaking tool thought to have been used as an indirect percussion punch recovered from Atlatl Rock Cave.	270
5.36.	A western Basketmaker dart point preform recovered from Structure 3 of Kin Kahuna, AZ-J-3-8.	271
5.37.	Dart points recovered from Navajo Mountain Road Archaeological Project Basketmaker II sites.	272
5.38.	Examples of drills recovered from Kin Kahuna.	273
5.39.	Examples of ornaments, gaming pieces, and other miscellaneous artifacts recovered from Navajo Mountain Road Archaeological Project Basketmaker sites but not from Archaic sites.	276
5.40.	Examples of manos recovered from Archaic and Basketmaker sites showing the change through time in size and general morphology.	277
5.41.	Grinding surface area recorded as an approximate square-centimeter value for Archaic and Basketmaker manos.	277
5.42.	Examples of metates recovered from Basketmaker sites.	278
5.43.	Arrow-sized projectile points recovered from Mountainview.	282
5.44.	Production sequence of arrow-sized projectile points as reconstructed by pressure-flaked bifaces recovered from Mountainview.	283
5.45.	Dart and arrowpoint preforms from Mountainview at similar stages of reduction showing the contrast in flake scars that result from different reduction tools and techniques.	284
5.46.	Arrow-sized projectile point recovered from the floor of a shallow structure at The Pits.	284
6.1.	Distribution of Navajo Mountain Road Archaeological Project Puebloan sites by inferred settlement type.	293
6.2.	Graphic representation of the utility of radiocarbon dating for the Puebloan period.	297
6.3.	Calibration results for the average of two statistically equivalent dates from the Puebloan component at Windy Mesa in relation to a tree-ring date and the ceramic-based temporal assignment.	298
6.4.	Mean ceramic dating of the Navajo Mountain Road Archaeological Project Puebloan sites organized from oldest to youngest.	301
6.5.	Dating of Navajo Mountain Road Archaeological Project Puebloan sites with large ceramic assemblages.	302
6.6.	Temporal ordering of Puebloan sites from oldest to youngest based on mean ceramic dating and the seriation curve.	303
6.7.	Plan map of Ditch House showing the structures and other features derived from three separate occupations of this single location.	308

6.8. Examples of excavated Puebloan living rooms ordered by temporal interval. 314
6.9. Two Puebloan living rooms excavated to floor. 315
6.10. Scatter plot of Puebloan living room depths from shallowest to deepest. 315
6.11. Floor of Structure 16 at Sapo Seco after excavation. 317
6.12. Photo and illustration of Structure 3 at Hammer House. 318
6.13. Stick-impressed mortar chunks from Structure 8 at Sapo Seco. 319
6.14. All excavated Puebloan kivas ordered by temporal interval. 320
6.15. The kiva at Sapo Seco, excavated during its construction up to 35 cm into Navajo Sandstone. 321
6.16. The Structure 5 kiva at Three Dog Site, associated with both the middle and late Pueblo III components. 322
6.17. Small kivas at the late Pueblo III sites of Water Jar Pueblo and Sapo Seco. 323
6.18. Hypothetical roof construction method for Kayenta Anasazi kivas. 323
6.19. Well-preserved roof of a kiva at the late Pueblo II site of AZ-K-25-24. 324
6.20. Kiva at the middle Pueblo II site of Hammer House showing its numerous floor features. 325
6.21. Examples of excavated Puebloan mealing rooms ordered by temporal interval. 328
6.22. Mealing room (Structure 11) at the late Pueblo III component of Three Dog Site. 328
6.23. Examples of changing room function for Structure 20 at Three Dog Site. 331
6.24. Examples of excavated Puebloan granaries. 332
6.25. Structure 6 at Sapo Seco, an example of an activity/storage room. 334
6.26. Examples of excavated Puebloan activity/storage rooms at secondary habitations. 334
6.27. Middle Pueblo II primary habitations excavated within the N16 right-of-way. 335
6.28. Examples of middle to late Pueblo III primary habitations excavated within the N16 right-of-way. 340
6.29. Plan map of Hymn House, a middle Pueblo III primary habitation that illustrates a room cluster. 341
6.30. The structures at Hymn House after full excavation. 341
6.31. Plan map of the two superimposed architectural units at Three Dog Site. 343
6.32. Plan map of the main architectural unit at Sapo Seco, a late Pueblo III primary habitation that illustrates a unit pueblo type of arrangement. 345
6.33. Plan map of the main architectural unit at Water Jar Pueblo, a late Pueblo III primary habitation. 346
6.34. Plan map of Sapo Seco showing all loci at a late Pueblo III primary habitation. 349
6.35. Examples of Puebloan secondary habitations excavated within the N16 right-of-way. 358
6.36. Structure 2 of the middle Pueblo III component of Modesty House, excavated during its construction up to 32 cm into the Navajo Sandstone bedrock. 361
6.37. View of the divide between Piute and Navajo canyons looking north from The Slots. 362
6.38. Recycled pipe fragment of black scoria from Tres Campos. 364
6.39. Navajo Mountain Road Archaeological Project Puebloan secondary habitations ordered according to an assessment of occupation duration and building for duration. 365
6.40. The relative population trends placed in approximate geographic position. 371
6.41. Frequency of Puebloan residential components by temporal interval for the N16 right-of-way. 372
6.42. Frequency of Puebloan structures by temporal interval for the N16 right-of-way. 372

Tables

1.1. Personnel and Consultants on the Navajo Mountain Road Archaeological Project — 5
1.2. Summary of the Navajo Mountain Road Archaeological Project Site Sample — 6
2.1. Monthly Climate Summaries for Two Weather Stations That Bracket the Navajo Mountain Road Archaeological Project Area — 53
2.2. Length of Freeze-Free Season Probabilities for the Two Weather Stations That Bracket the Navajo Mountain Road Archaeological Project Area — 54
3.1. Summary of the 33 Sites Excavated During the Navajo Mountain Road Archaeological Project — 65
3.2. Summary of Pertinent Information for Each Site by Component Based on Data-Recovery Excavations — 68
4.1. Summary of Archaic Sites Excavated During the Navajo Mountain Road Archaeological Project — 142
4.2. Comparison of Macrobotanical Recovery from Early Archaic Contexts of Navajo Mountain Road Archaeological Project Open Sites and Atlatl Rock Cave — 144
4.3. Comparison of Macrobotanical Recovery from Early and Late Archaic Contexts of Navajo Mountain Road Archaeological Project Open Sites and from Buried Late Archaic Contexts — 145
4.4. List of Radiocarbon Dates from Navajo Mountain Road Archaeological Project Archaic Sites — 148
4.5. Comparison of Radiocarbon Determinations on Sagebrush and Wood Charcoal from Single Features at Navajo Mountain Road Archaeological Project Archaic Sites — 151
4.6. Radiocarbon Dates on Two Samples of Sagebrush Collected in 2002 — 154
4.7. Obsidian-Hydration Results for 10 Flakes from The Pits and 15 Flakes from Hólahéi Scatter — 156
4.8. Obsidian-Hydration Results for 10 Flakes from The Pits (AZ-J-14-17) Grouped by Obsidian Source and Arranged from Oldest to Youngest — 157
4.9. Summary Data for the Navajo Mountain Road Archaeological Project Archaic Sites or Components as well as the Inferred Settlement Role — 166
4.10. Density of Various Remains Recovered from Navajo Mountain Road Archaeological Project Archaic Sites — 167
4.11. Ordering of the Archaic Sites by the Five Density Measures of Remains from Highest to Lowest — 167
4.12. Faunal Bone Recovered from the Late Archaic Components of Tsé Haal'á and Three Dog Site — 173
4.13. General Kinds of Flaked Facial Tools Recovered from the Late Archaic Components of Tsé Haal'á and Three Dog Site — 175
4.14. Technological Flake Types for the Late Archaic Components of Tsé Haal'á and Three Dog Site — 176
4.15. Proportions of Identified Technological Flake Types for the Navajo Mountain Road Archaeological Project Archaic Sites Identified as Hunting Camps — 178
4.16. Proportions of Debitage Raw Material from Navajo Mountain Road Archaeological Project Archaic Sites — 185

4.17. Count and Weight Representation of Technological Flake Types for Obsidian Debitage from Navajo Mountain Road Archaeological Project Archaic Sites — 185
4.18. Technological Flake Type Proportions and Mean Weights for Obsidian Debitage from Navajo Mountain Road Archaeological Project Archaic Sites — 186
4.19. Summary Results for X-Ray Fluorescence Chemical Sourcing of Obsidian from Navajo Mountain Road Archaeological Project Archaic Sites — 189
5.1. Summary Data for the Navajo Mountain Road Archaeological Project Basketmaker Sites or Components as well as the Inferred Settlement Role — 208
5.2. List of Radiocarbon Dates from Navajo Mountain Road Archaeological Project Basketmaker Sites — 212
5.3. Comparison of Radiocarbon Dates on a Maize Cob (PN1045.3) from a Bell-Shaped Pit in the Floor of Structure 5 at Kin Kahuna — 219
5.4. Comparison of Radiocarbon Dates on Maize Kernels (PN623.4), Part of a Maize Offering in a Bell-Shaped Storage Pit at The Pits — 219
5.5. Characteristics of the Flotation Analysis Sample for Navajo Mountain Road Archaeological Project Basketmaker and Puebloan Sites — 226
5.6. Summary of *Zea mays* Remains Recovered from Flotation Samples of Navajo Mountain Road Archaeological Project Basketmaker and Puebloan Sites — 226
5.7. Comparison of Measurements on Maize Kernels from Preceramic and Ceramic Basketmaker Contexts of Atlatl Rock Cave — 229
5.8. Potential Subsistence Remains of "Wild" Plants Recovered from Flotation Samples of Navajo Mountain Road Archaeological Project Basketmaker Sites — 230
5.9. Rank Order of Taxa from Eight Coprolites from Desha Cave 1 — 231
5.10. Macrobotanical Remains Observed in Dry-Screened Matrix Samples from Basketmaker Layers at Atlatl Rock Cave — 232
5.11. Grinding Area for Whole Archaic and Basketmaker Manos Recovered by the Navajo Mountain Road Archaeological Project — 277
6.1. Summary Information for Navajo Mountain Road Archaeological Project Puebloan Sites — 292
6.2. Tree-Ring Dates for Navajo Mountain Road Archaeological Project Puebloan Sites — 294
6.3. Radiocarbon Determinations for Navajo Mountain Road Archaeological Project Puebloan Sites — 298
6.4. Mean Date and Mean Date Range by Sherd Count and Weight for Navajo Mountain Road Archaeological Project Puebloan Sites, Along with Occupation Median as Derived by Seriation and Subjective Temporal Assignment — 300
6.5. Comparison Among Several Middle and Late Pueblo II Sites of the N16 Project Area Using Ratios of Black Mesa Black-on-white to Sosi and Dogoszhi Black-on-white Combined and Medicine Black-on-red to Tusayan Black-on-red — 305
6.6. Count and Weight of Identified Ceramic Types by Ware for the Middle Pueblo III and Mixed Ceramic Assemblages at Ditch House — 309
6.7. Comparison Among Several Late Pueblo III Sites on the Rainbow Plateau of the Ratio of Tusayan Black-on-white to Kayenta Black-on-white and Tusayan Polychrome to Kayenta and Kiet Siel (Whiteline) Polychromes — 312
6.8. Summary of the 83 Structures Excavated at Navajo Mountain Road Archaeological Project Puebloan Sites — 313
6.9. Summary Data for Puebloan Living Structures Excavated Within the N16 Right-of-Way — 316
6.10. Summary Data for Puebloan Kivas Excavated Within the N16 Right-of-Way — 321
6.11. Summary Data for Puebloan Mealing Rooms Excavated Within the N16 Right-of-Way — 329
6.12. Comparison Among Navajo Mountain

Road Archaeological Project Primary Habitations with Comparable Levels of Investigation Using Overall Artifact and Bone Counts, Counts per Structure, and Ratios of Certain Artifact Classes ... 336

6.13. Comparison Among Navajo Mountain Road Archaeological Project Secondary Habitations with Comparable Levels of Investigation Using Overall Artifact and Bone Counts, Counts per Structure, and Ratios of Certain Artifact Classes ... 359

6.14. Changing Order of Secondary Habitations According to the Frequency of Recovered Sherds, Debitage, Formal Flaked Tools, and Grinding Tools ... 365

Acknowledgments

Concerning our work along the Navajo Mountain road (N16), Jim Collette once quipped, "It's not just a job, it's a career!" At times his remark almost seemed true. Begun with a phase of limited testing during the summer of 1991, the project progressed in fits and spurts and then slowly crept along until the completion of the contract report late in 2007. The bulk of actual excavation took place in five field seasons: 1992, 1994, 1995, 1997, and 1999. Although I accomplished several other important works during that decade and a half, most notably the Kaiparowits Plateau Survey and the final report on Bighorn Cave, the N16 project has always been there lingering in the back of my mind. Thus, it is with a great deal of relief that I am penning these acknowledgments and freeing myself of this burden.

Anyone who has overseen an excavation project of any real size knows full well the stages one commonly goes through—the initial excitement about starting the work, the thrill and toil of the actual excavations, the tedium of analysis and descriptive writing, punctuated by the occasional a-ha moments and discoveries, and ultimately the point where you just want the damn thing over with. For me though, the final stage of pushing the baby out the door can be the hardest; it is difficult to let go, to just say enough is enough, for there is always more that could be done, something else that would improve the report.

For a project of this scale and especially one that extended over more than a decade, there are many, many people deserving thanks and recognition for their help and contributions. Indeed it might prove impossible to recall everyone, so please don't feel slighted if somehow your name was omitted. Trust me—it wasn't done on purpose; it's simply that I'm older now than when the project began and "senior moments" have started.

Foremost I thank Miranda Warburton, who wore many hats on the project. Not only did she serve as the principal investigator and as the primary lithic analyst (among other roles), she also offered me the job with the Navajo Nation Archaeology Department (NNAD) that allowed me the opportunity to excavate along the Navajo Mountain road. Ever since the early 1980s when I learned that the N16 road was scheduled for paving all the way to the new boarding school at the northeast foot of the mountain, I wanted to be involved with any archaeological excavation that would take place in advance of construction. Miranda's offer of working for NNAD ensured that my dream would come true, and instead of merely being involved, I had the good fortune to be able to direct the entire undertaking. Of course this job was not without a few headaches, but these are faded or lost behind the many wonderful memories of the fieldwork and the project accomplishments. Thanks Miranda for everything over the years.

Second on my list are the field crew and especially Tory Clark, Jim Collette, and Kim Spurr—key crew chiefs during all or most phases of the project. Their involvement proved invaluable in a myriad of ways, not the least of which was helping to write many of the site descriptions included herein. Tory was a key force behind keeping the project structured—she devised the various forms and provenience system that we employed and worked hard to make sure that the entire crew knew the procedures and filled things out properly. She and Jim also created most of the site and feature maps for the first few years of excavation and created the templates and high standards for the maps of ensuing years. Jim wrote the project field manual that provided our guide to deviate from; unfortunately he edited out most of his dry wit from the final version. Ever the great organizer, Kim was a godsend for logistics and keeping the field operations humming smoothly. She also served a vital role in helping to edit the entire contract report, ensuring that it was quite clean before submitting the document to our technical editor.

At this point I should add that the interpretations presented in this report are solely mine and in no way reflect those of the Navajo Nation or Navajo people. In particular, the use of the term Puebloan, which is interchangeable with Anasazi, has no necessary bearing on ethnic affiliations in the present. I recognize that 10 of the 70 Navajo clans have Puebloan origins, thus it is conceivable that the ancestors of some of the founders of these 10 clans might have been affiliated with some of the sites that are reported in this document.

Other crew chiefs on the project who helped immensely include Ted Neff, Mick Robins, and Terry Samples, with the former two also assisting with a few site descriptions. Also contributing greatly in the field with both excavation and notes were Peter Bungart, Stewart Deats, Chris Dixon, Roger Stash, and Jonathan Till. Many others helped in the field in various capacities, all of which are listed in Table 1.1. Most of these were Navajos from the local communities of Inscription House and Navajo Mountain, but there were also many students from the NNAD at Northern Arizona University (NAU) training program. The stalwart local workers who formed the core of our excavation team throughout most of the project included Wilson Begay (now deceased), John Blake, Jacky Chief (Henry), Keith King, Leander King, Willie Navajo, Elaine Smith (Manheimer), and Bruce Whitehat. Greg Holiday was the backhoe operator for about half of the project, and although he had some rocky moments, he was a most interesting fellow and became quite the talented potter. To all I want to express my heartfelt thanks for a job well done, even under the occasional trying conditions.

Before moving on I want to give special acknowledgment to John Blake of Inscription House, a person who has been excavating prehistoric sites since at least the early 1960s, when he worked with Al Ward at Inscription House Ruin for the Museum of Northern Arizona (MNA). Since his first "dig," John has been employed as a field archaeologist at every opportunity, working on most of MNA's large projects in the 1960s and 1970s and then working on the Black Mesa Archaeological Project during its entire 15-year run. He began excavating sites on the Navajo Mountain road in 1985, when he worked for P-III Associates, on the southern portion that traverses the Shonto Plateau. In 1992 he began working for NNAD and continued in this capacity off and on until 2003; his last major effort was the final phase of N16 excavations at the foot of Navajo Mountain. John is a superlative excavator, someone with a sixth sense of the dirt. Even in his sixties he could outshovel any teenager and could do so without damaging features. John is always ready to pitch in and lend a helping hand. I never heard him say a disparaging word about anyone or ever complain. He could find humor in the smallest things and at almost any time. I am happy to recognize a man who found true enjoyment in fieldwork, who never tired of excavation.

Fieldworkers in a very real sense have the best part of the job, so perhaps even more deserving of thanks are the poor souls stuck in the office attending to all the sundry chores done behind the scenes that are absolutely essential to project completion. The administrative staff typed up the seemingly endless forms (purchase requisitions, employment forms, journal vouchers, etc.) and tracked them through the tribal bureaucracy, which is often like herding cats. They saw to it that personal time was called in and that paychecks were mailed out. They kept abreast of budget problems and paid the bills. And this is just for starters. This staff consisted at various times of Lanita Collette, Bunni Hardy, Sandy Ketchum, Laura Nez, Sharon Sanders, Yolanda Yazzie, and Orlinda Yazzie. The other key person in the office was the individual in charge of overseeing the lab where all the artifacts were processed, photos were developed and labeled, and analysis data were keyed into the computer and edited. This job was filled for most of the time by David Ortiz, with Lanita Collette starting in the position and establishing most of the protocols and database structures; Stewart Deats and Kerry Thompson also had this job at various times. Many others helped in the lab, both students and staff, all of whom are listed in Table 1.1.

The field effort for this project involved camping in the Navajo Mountain area for months on end, something that was really no hardship given the lovely scenery; clean, clear air; and generally peaceful solitude. We appreciate the hospitality of the Navajo Mountain community for letting us temporarily squat on their land and drink their water, fresh from the slopes of the mountain. I hope they realize now that archaeology was never the reason that delayed the paving of N16, that archaeology was the fall guy for a myriad of other reasons behind the endless foot-dragging and lack of progress. Today the road is totally paved, although it took more than eight years after we finished all of our work, and the drive of jarring bumps, washboard ruts, and twisting turns that used to consume an hour or more now passes in minutes, and one arrives at the foot of Navajo Mountain in what seems like no time.

All the analytical specialists for this project deserve praise for their efforts, but a few must be singled out. Peter Koehler is one of them. It was a great pleasure helping Peter find and collect pack rat middens from on and around Navajo Mountain. I have wonderful memories of those trips, but I also recall probably the coldest night I've ever spent sleeping outside in the open. It was also a great pleasure to work with Susie Smith, the pollen analyst for the project. She always had a smile and willingly answered my persistent questions about pollen and plants. Kirk Anderson worked in the field on N16 only during the first phase of testing, but as always it was both educational and fun. Just that brief interval greatly helped my understanding of soils and strata for the entire project. I also want to thank Darden Hood and Ron Hatfield of Beta Analytic for agreeing to include two of the project radiocarbon samples in their internal quality control study. Finally, I must mention Miranda Warburton again for the countless hours she spent analyzing flakes and for putting up with me as we argued about analysis procedures and individual artifacts—it was great fun now that it's all said and done (I still have Kerry Thompson's list of memorable lines that we uttered).

There are a number of archaeologists to whom I owe a debt of gratitude for helping in various ways on this project or generally in archaeology. First on this list is Dick Ambler, who taught me much of what I know about Kayenta archaeology and fieldwork in general. Indeed, it was on a field trip with Dick in 1977 that I fell in love with the Navajo Mountain area. At the time I couldn't have imagined that I would have the good fortune to be able to live and work in the area on two separate occasions (in the early 1980s for NAU and then in the 1990s for NNAD). Next is Carl Phagan, my first instructor in archaeology and then boss when I helped him run two separate field schools in Ohio. I hope some of his keen critical thinking has rubbed off over the years, although he might think not enough. Other "senior" archaeologists whom I have learned much from in more recent years include R. G. Matson, Stan Ahler, Jeff Dean, Lex Lindsay, Joel Janetski, and Doug McFadden. R. G. has constantly provided a use-

Most of the 1994 NMRAP excavation crew during an end-of-work retreat in Piute Canyon. Front row from left: Kim Spurr and Elaine Manheimer; back row from left: Phil Geib, Keith King, Wilson Begay, Jim Collette, Bruce Whitehat, and John Blake. Photo by Tory Clark.

ful sounding board for ideas about Basketmaker II and the Archaic. Jeff and Lex Lindsay both visited on several occasions while we were excavating sites along N16 and shared their extensive experience in Kayenta archaeology, as did Dick Ambler and George Gumerman on one occasion each.

The thorough comments of Bill Lipe and R. G. Matson were a huge help in revising the draft version of this manuscript as I tried to transform it from a contract report into the published version. Unfortunately I was not able to attend to all of their input because of time limitations and other obligations.

Finally, I want to give a huge hand of praise to Louella Holter, technical editor at the Bilby Research Center at NAU. This report and most other papers and reports that I have prepared over the years have greatly benefited from her expertise. Working with her has slowly improved my writing, but she can always find room for more.

CHAPTER 1

Introduction

During the 1990s, archaeologists from the Navajo Nation Archaeology Department (NNAD) excavated all or portions of 33 prehistoric sites (58 components) that lay within the right-of-way (ROW) for the proposed paving of the Navajo Mountain road (Navajo Route 16 or N16) in northeast Arizona and southeast Utah (Figure 1.1). Known as the Navajo Mountain Road Archaeological Project (NMRAP), this contract work proved far more rewarding than I could have imagined. The excavations provided an informative sample of remains from a cross section of prehistory for the northern Kayenta region. The 58 separate temporal components that were investigated ranged from the early Archaic, some 9,000 years ago, up until shortly before final Puebloan abandonment of the area at about AD 1300. This sample included 16 sites/components from forager use of the area during the early and late Archaic periods, 17 sites/components from the initial farmer presence in the area known as Basketmaker, and 25 sites/components from later Puebloan use of the area. In addition, NNAD archaeologists tested Atlatl Rock Cave, a dry shelter with stratified cultural deposits from the Puebloan period back to the early Archaic. This sample allowed examination of a number of topics regarding long-term human adaptive responses to the changing environment of the Colorado Plateau, including changes wrought by humans themselves.

Project results were documented in a five-volume contract report of limited distribution (Geib and Spurr 2007), with some highlights published in Geib and Spurr 2000, 2002. The findings clearly merited a wider audience, but publication of the entire contract report would have been impractical. Hence, I decided to present what amounts to a detailed overview of the project by including synthetic summaries for the three major temporal periods represented by the site sample: Archaic, Basketmaker, and Puebloan. These are revised versions of concluding chapters in volume 5 of the contract report. The substantive results that these three chapters are based on—the site descriptions that constitute volumes 2–4 of the contract report and the analysts' reports of volume 5—are available digitally and should be consulted by those interested in the specifics. Chapter 3 of this report presents a capsule summary of each of the sites so that readers know something about them and the excavations on which interpretations are based. This introductory first chapter presents background material about the project including a synopsis of the site sample and research orientation and an overview of field and laboratory methods. Chapter 2 characterizes the Kayenta region, summarizing previous archaeological research and the prehistoric sequence and describing the environment of the project area. The final chapter presents a summary and interpretation of NMRAP findings within the context of Kayenta archaeology and Colorado Plateau prehistory more generally.

PROJECT LOCATION

The Navajo Mountain road traverses in a south–north direction portions of the physiographic features known as the Shonto and Rainbow plateaus in northeast Arizona (Coconino and Navajo counties) and southeast Utah (San Juan County [Figure 1.2]). The land is held in trust status for the Navajo Nation by the Bureau of Indian Affairs (BIA). Long known as one of the roughest roads on the Navajo Reservation, N16 begins at Arizona State Highway 98 in the central portion of the Shonto Plateau and heads northward past Inscription House, Arizona, ending at the small community of Rainbow City, Utah, at the northeast foot of Navajo Mountain, a distance of about 60 km. In connecting the Shonto Plateau to the Rainbow Plateau, N16 runs along the one sinuous artery of land linking these two geographic features—a high and rugged expanse of slickrock that is deeply dissected on

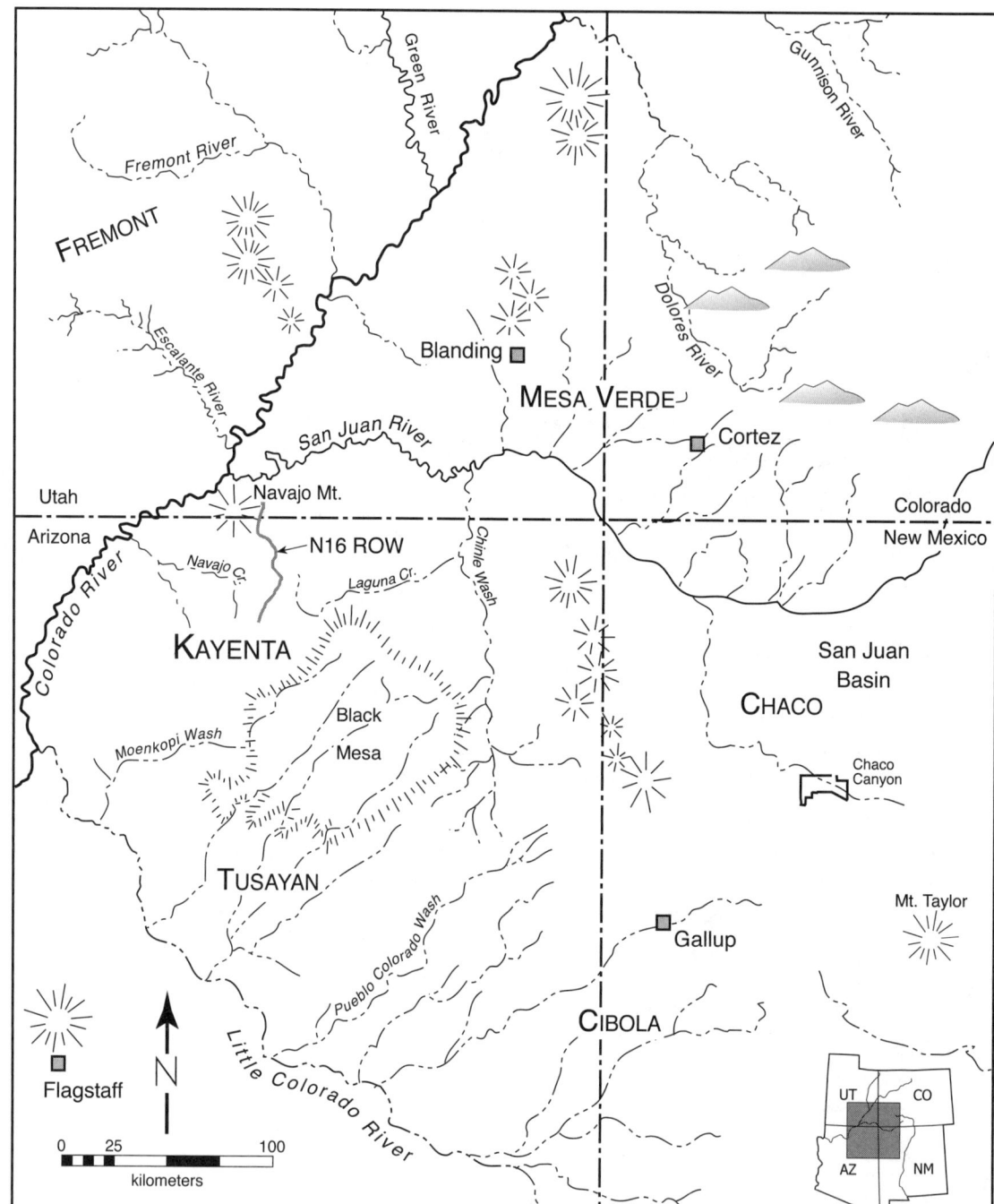

FIGURE 1.1. The Four Corners region of the Colorado Plateau showing prehistoric Puebloan "cultural" areas and the general location of the Navajo Mountain road, N16, within the northern Kayenta region.

the east by the upper reaches of Piute Canyon and on the west by the labyrinthine canyons of Navajo Creek. This connecting artery is an extension of a ridge at the northwestern edge of the Shonto Plateau. The road parallels a route pioneered by Hubert Richardson in the 1920s to start a trading business at the foot of Navajo Mountain (Richardson 1986). This historic track doubtless followed a course that natives had used for millennia. Richardson's original road has been improved over the years, but prior to any legally mandated archaeological compliance work.

In planning and funding road construction, the BIA Branch of Roads divided the ROW into six segments of varying lengths. The southernmost two segments (1–2) were realigned and paved in the late 1980s, and significant archaeological sites within that portion of the ROW were excavated by P-III Associates (Schroedl 1989). The

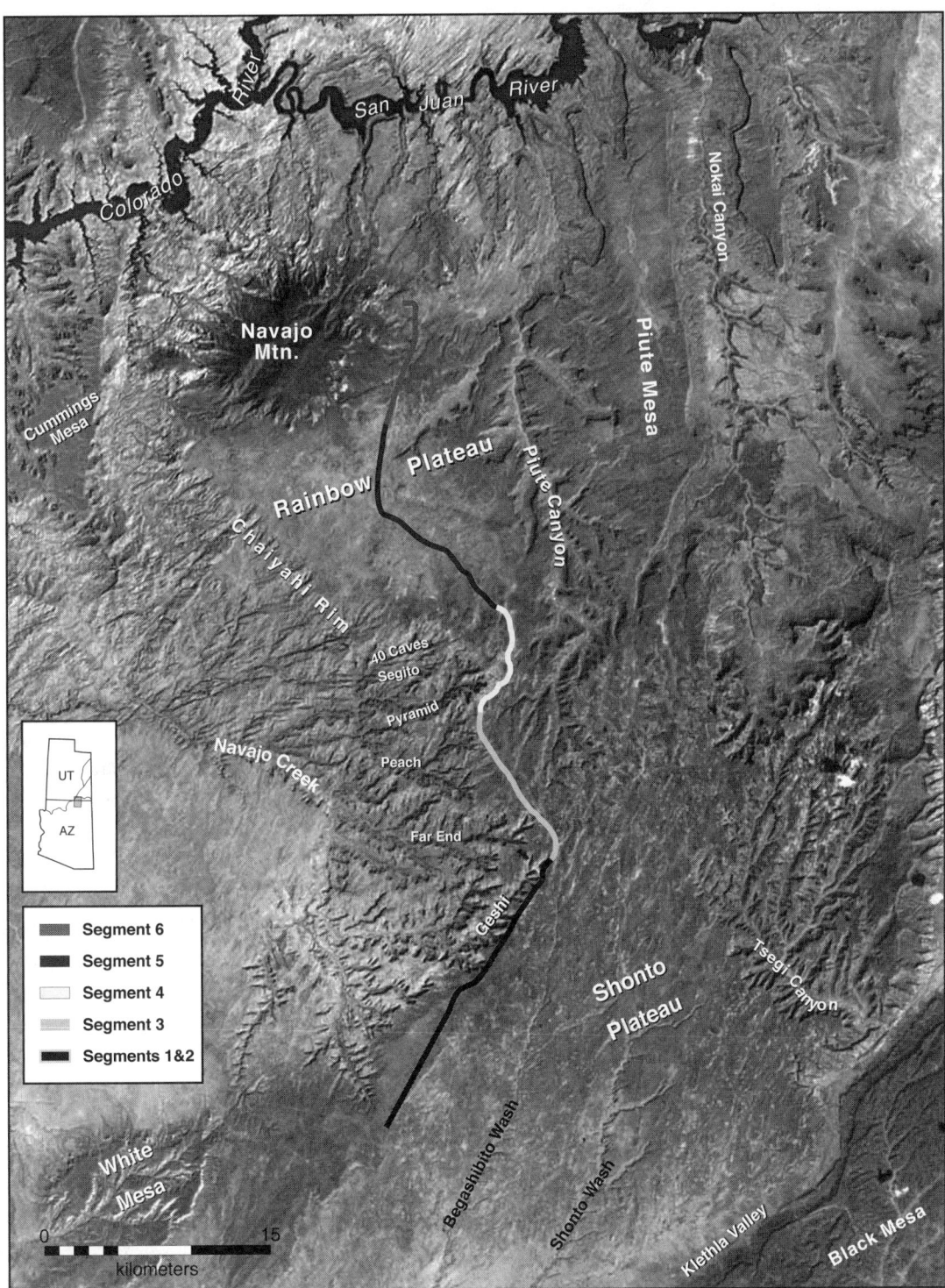

FIGURE 1.2. The Navajo Mountain Road Archaeological Project study area in the northern Kayenta region as seen in a Landsat 5 Satellite Thematic Mapper image with 30-m ground resolution. The Navajo Mountain Road, N16, extends from the northwest edge of the Shonto Plateau along a dissected slickrock divide between the canyons of Navajo and Piute creeks and onto the Rainbow Plateau, ending at the northeast foot of Navajo Mountain.

remaining four segments of the N16 ROW (3–6), which total approximately 43 km in length, were the focus of the NMRAP. Segment 3 begins about 8 mi north of Inscription House near the junction of a graded road to Shonto, Arizona, at an elevation of 2,152 m (7,060 ft). This segment extends northward along the divide between Piute and Navajo creeks. In this segment the road climbs to its maximum elevation of 2,234 m (7,330 ft). Segment 4 continues along this same divide and onto the southeast edge of the Rainbow Plateau, ending at an elevation of 1,950 m (6,400 ft). Segment 5 traverses the sagebrush-covered flats of the Rainbow Plateau at an average elevation of 1,842 m (6,040 ft) up to the Arizona–Utah border. Segment 6 extends from this border to the entrance of the Navajo Mountain Boarding School, reaching a low point of about 1,706 m (5,600 ft) near the end of the road.

The project area consists of horizontally uplifted exposures of Triassic and Jurassic sandstones and siltstones from the Glen Canyon Supergroup. The general physiography is controlled by various monoclines and synclines, creating an incised pattern of plateaus, mesas, and canyons. Navajo Mountain, a classic Tertiary laccolith that still supports a deflected veneer of sedimentary country rock along its flanks, punctuates the area. The area is considered arid to semiarid, with precipitation extremes ranging from 11 cm at the lowest elevation to 68 cm at the top of Navajo Mountain. Generally, the region receives 30–58 cm of precipitation with about a 50/50 winter–summer dominance (Anonymous 1975; NOAA 1975). Clear nights, low humidity, and generally high altitude cause wide temperature fluctuations; yearly extremes can range from daily highs in the 90s–low 100s at lower elevations to lows of less than 0°F on Navajo Mountain and in cold-air drainages. Vegetation ranges from a sky island, spruce-dominated, subalpine community on top of Navajo Mountain (3,166 m) to a blackbrush–grassland community at the lowest elevations, primarily below 1,600 m in the lower canyons and benches adjacent to Glen Canyon. Pinyon–juniper woodland (ca. 2,000–1,600 m) is the predominant vegetation across most of the area, with a sagebrush–saltbush community on flats and drainage basins. Ponderosa pine and Douglas fir are encountered in a transitional community on Navajo Mountain (ca. 2,900–2,000 m) but also occur in some of the mesic canyons throughout the area, with Douglas fir quite common on north-facing canyon walls within the pinyon–juniper woodland and ponderosa pine as sporadic isolated stands, especially within south-draining canyons at the south edge of the study area (Begashibito Wash).

THE PROJECT

Archaeological investigations along N16 were conducted by the NNAD Branch Office located on the campus of Northern Arizona University (NAU), in Flagstaff, Arizona. Miranda Warburton served as principal investigator, with me as the project director; Table 1.1 lists the many other personnel on the project. The BIA sponsored and funded the N16 archaeological investigations, with the Navajo Nation Historic Preservation Department (NNHPD) acting as contract administrator for the BIA. The research conducted by the NNAD on this project was solely concerned with prehistoric archaeological remains along the N16 ROW. Traditional cultural properties, sacred and ceremonial areas, and historic sites were explicitly excluded from the scope of NMRAP; these resources were addressed under a separate project (Newton et al. 1995).

The NMRAP had a long and involved history that need not be repeated in detail here. Fieldwork involved site reassessment, examination of small realignments and spot field checks, significance testing (22 sites), extent testing (48 sites), and data recovery (33 sites). Work began in 1991 with the initial testing of sites along Segment 3 and extended into 1999 with the final data-recovery excavations for Segment 6. Several years of analysis and writing followed, with the final contract report completed at the end of 2007 (Geib and Spurr 2007). NNAD-NAU did not resurvey the entire ROW, but in the process of reevaluating sites and checking realignments 16 new properties were discovered, especially those of Basketmaker II and Archaic temporal affiliation. It is evident that the original survey of the N16 ROW (Popelish 1984) frequently overlooked preceramic remains; hence, the results presented here stand in marked contrast to those for the southern two segments of the ROW, which only concerned sites of Puebloan or more recent age (Schroedl 1989).[1]

The 33 sites subjected to data-recovery excavations for the NMRAP lay within the 43-km-long and 61-m-wide construction corridor of Segments 3–6 of the Navajo Mountain road. These 33 sites were excavated according to a data-recovery plan approved in 1994 (Geib et al. 1993). Twenty-two of these 33 sites were fully excavated, in that virtually the entire site occurred within the N16 ROW; 11 of the 33 sites were partially excavated because those portions that extended outside the ROW were off limits and for some sites this left significant remains unstudied. The 33 sites represent a sample (51%) winnowed from a total of 65 prehistoric sites recorded within the ROW. Twenty-one of the sites were ultimately evaluated as not eligible to the National Register, principally because of distur-

TABLE 1.1. Personnel and Consultants on the Navajo Mountain Road Archaeological Project

Role	Name
Principal Investigator	Miranda Warburton
Project Director	Phil R. Geib
Crew Chiefs	Richard Boston, Peter Bungart, Victoria H. Clark, Jim Collette (né Huffman), L. Theodore Neff, Michael Robins, Kimberly Spurr
Assistant Crew Chiefs	Stewart Deats, Chris Dixon, Roger Henderson, Kim Mangum (née Tsosie), Roger Stash, Terry Samples, Jonathan Till, Nathaniel Todia
Crew Members	Ettie Anderson, Shirlene Atene, Wilson N. Begay, G. Stewart Benally, Erickson Bitsinnie, Lee Black Jr., John H. Blake, Virginia Graymountain, Sarah Grey, Jacqueline Henry (née Chief), Vicky N. Johnson, Geraldine S. King, Keith King, Leander King, Willie Navajo, Alfred Smith, Elaine Manheimer (née Smith), Phillip J. Reed, Rory T. Tomasiyo Sr., Leo Tsinnijinnie, Bruce Whitehat
Backhoe Operators	Lee Black Sr., Gregory Holiday, Leander King, Calvin Little
Camp Guard	Leonard B. King
Students	Darsita (Oozie) Ryan, Robert Begay, Roxanne Begay, Cheryl Mizell-Begay, Kilroy Klitso, Nathan Lefthand, Alfred Livingstone, Ora Marek, Lanell T. Poseyesva, Jocelyn Salt, Harriett Sandoval, Kerry Thompson, Carissa Tsosie, Neomie Tsosie, Tim Wilcox, Rachael Willie, Natasha Yazzie
Administrative Staff	Lanita Collette, Veronica (Bunni) Hardy, Alexandra (Sandy) Ketchum, Laura Nez, Sharon Sanders, Yolanda Wesley, Olivia Yazzie, Orlinda Yazzie
Graphics Specialists	Tim Wilcox, Kim Mangum, Dan Boone
Lab Directors	Lanita Collette, Stewart Deats, David Ortiz, Kerry Thompson
Lab Assistants	Tonia Anderson, Judy Begay, Judith Breen, Anderson Dyer, Esther Masayesva
Ceramic Analysts	Kelley A. Hays-Gilpin, Janet Hagopian, Jim Collette
Faunal Analysts	John Goodman, Karen Quanbeck, Kari Schmidt
Lithic Analysts	Stewart Deats, Phil Geib, Michael Robins, Kerry Thompson, Miranda Warburton
Electron Microprobe Analyst	Kimberly Spurr
Pollen Analyst	Susan Smith
Macrobotanical Analysts	Andrea Hunter, Meredith Matthews
Pack Rat Midden Analyst	Peter Koehler
Shell Analyst	Authur Vokes
Geomorphologists	Kirk Anderson, John Ponczynski
Dating Specialists	Beta Analytic, Laboratory of Tree-Ring Research, NSF–Arizona Accelerator Mass Spectrometry Laboratory
Technical Editor	Louella Holter

bance from past road construction and maintenance. Determinations of noneligibility were made for seven sites based on surface evidence alone, another seven using the findings from significance testing, and the final seven after conducting extent testing. Of the 44 register-eligible sites within the ROW, 11 were not treated by data recovery for a variety of reasons. At three of these the portions within the ROW were peripheral to the main concentrations of remains and lacked scientific value. At seven sites, the portions within the ROW were significant, but they occurred near the edge of the construction corridor in areas where the ROW could be constricted so as to preserve the remains in place. The final site of the 11 occurred entirely within the fenced compound (northeast corner) of the Navajo Mountain Boarding School at Rainbow City. As such, it clearly would not be impacted by road construction because all activity would be confined to the area outside of this compound.

During fall 1993 a small crew conducted limited work at Atlatl Rock Cave located about 1 km east of the N16 ROW. Named after an associated petroglyph panel depicting oversized atlatls, the cave contains dry stratified cultural deposits dating back to around 9,000 years ago. Large-scale looting of this previously pristine cave during 1993 prompted the study. Criminals systematically destroyed nearly 60 m^3 of cultural deposits and at least 21 storage cists plus other features. Using funds made available by the NNHPD, courtesy of Alan Downer, NNAD archaeologists conducted emergency backfilling of the massive looter holes, as well as limited study of intact deposits and features. During a five-day field session, a small crew managed to gain an understanding of the

TABLE 1.2. Summary of the Navajo Mountain Road Archaeological Project Site Sample

Component Class	Frequency	Site Numbers
Archaic Residential Camps	4	UT-B-63-30, UT-B-3-38, UT-B-63-39 (2, both late Archaic)
Archaic Temporary Camps	12	AZ-J-14-12, AZ-J-14-13 (2, early and late Archaic), AZ-J-14-17, AZ-J-14-23, AZ-J-14-26, AZ-J-14-28, AZ-J-14-31, AZ-J-2-2, AZ-J-2-6, AZ-J-2-55, AZ-J-3-7
Basketmaker Primary Habitations	4	AZ-J-14-13, AZ-J-14-17, AZ-J-14-38, AZ-J-3-8
Basketmaker Secondary Habitations	9	AZ-J-14-12, AZ-J-14-21, AZ-J-14-31, AZ-J-14-34, AZ-J-14-35, AZ-J-14-36, AZ-J-14-37, AZ-J-3-6, UT-B-63-39
Basketmaker II Temporary Camps	4	AZ-J-14-26, AZ-J-14-28, AZ-J-2-55, AZ-J-3-7
Puebloan Primary Habitations	12	AZ-J-14-11, AZ-J-14-16, AZ-J-14-21, AZ-J-14-28, AZ-J-2-3, AZ-J-2-6, AZ-J-2-58, AZ-J-3-8, AZ-J-3-14, UT-B-63-14, UT-B-63-39 (2, middle Pueblo III and late Pueblo III)
Puebloan Secondary Habitations	9	AZ-J-14-12, AZ-J-14-21, AZ-J-14-30, AZ-J-2-2, AZ-J-2-5 (2, Pueblo II and middle Pueblo III), AZ-J-2-55, AZ-J-3-7, UT-B-63-19
Puebloan Temporary Camps	4	AZ-J-14-17, AZ-J-14-20, AZ-J-14-26, AZ-J-14-52
Component Total	58	(Site Total = 33)

depositional sequence, sample features and strata from the major episodes of cultural use, profile the stratigraphic sections provided by looter broadside cuts, and backfill the site, returning it close to its previous appearance. This work was not strictly part of the NMRAP, and no project funds were spent on the effort, but the site is reported in the supporting documents online (SD vol. 2, chap. 2) because of its significance to the overall NMRAP research focus. Because the recovered remains from this site were not analyzed as part of the NMRAP, this site is seldom included in data tables.

The Site Sample

The 33 sites excavated by the NMRAP are a diverse lot regarding both temporal placement and inferred function. The sites range in age from the early Archaic, roughly 7200 cal. BC, up through the final Anasazi abandonment of the region shortly before AD 1300. Fourteen of the sites had two or more components, so in all NNAD excavated 58 components, as summarized in Table 1.2. Nineteen of the sites are single component, or at least only a single component extended into the ROW. By general temporal period there are 16 Archaic sites or components, 17 Basketmaker sites or components, and 25 Puebloan sites or components.

Only three of the Archaic sites were partially exposed on the surface from natural erosion; the other Archaic sites or components were buried and hidden from view. The buried Archaic sites were found either because prior road construction had sectioned and exposed them or because the Archaic remains fortuitously occurred under a Basketmaker or Puebloan site that was trenched. The Archaic archaeological record thus appears to be largely obscured from view, at least that portion of it containing intact features. Because the Archaic record was largely unknown prior to preparation of the data-recovery plan, few research topics were specifically focused on these resources, though the overall general approach was applicable. We also lacked prior knowledge about the function or age of the sites, something that we can now specify with greater accuracy. The sample consists mainly of temporary camps, likely used briefly and for specific purposes. At least some of them appear hunting related; others may have served in plant processing, and still others were perhaps the remains from simple overnight stays. At least three of the late Archaic components (two at one site) appear to have functioned as residential camps. Most of the Archaic sites date to the early portion of this period, before about 5000 cal. BC. At least five components date to the late Archaic after about 1500 cal. BC but before 800 cal. BC; these sites lack domesticates. Providing basic documentation of chronology, lithic assemblage variability, and subsistence remains for the Archaic components is a significant contribution of the NMRAP. The only Archaic sites previously investigated in the Kayenta region are two caves near Navajo Mountain (Lindsay et al. 1968) and a few open sites on Black Mesa (Parry and Smiley 1990).

The 17 Basketmaker sites or components include a greater diversity in site function than for the Archaic, with three primary habitations, nine secondary habitations, and five temporary camps. The distinction between primary and secondary residential sites is based on the nature of trash middens, the presence of large food-storage features at the former but absence at the latter, and, to a lesser extent, the details of house construction. Primary habitations are thought to have functioned as the principal residential location for a family group. They contain large bell-shaped storage pits or other food-storage features and have extensive and rich midden deposits and living structures that are relatively substantial. Secondary residential sites appear to have functioned as living quarters for a moderately short duration. They contain structures, but ones that are often smaller and shallower than those at the primary residential sites. Trash middens are small and relatively artifact poor, although they might contain an abundance of burned rock. Perhaps the most important distinction is the lack of large food-storage features. The Basketmaker sites all date to an interval between about 400 cal. BC (shortly thereafter) to cal. AD 500, overlapping the introduction of pottery. One Basketmaker site with an assemblage of Obelisk Utility pottery is well dated to between cal. AD 220 and 350 and appears to represent a good example of a Basketmaker II–III transitional habitation. No open Basketmaker II habitations have been studied within 40 km (25 mi) of the project area, so the investigation of these sites provides important new information regardless of research focus. The excavated sample of Basketmaker II sites provides an important complement to the information on this initial farming adaptation provided by the Black Mesa Archaeological Project (BMAP [e.g., Smiley 2002a]).

Puebloan sites or components are the most numerous, although the extent of excavation at a few of these was quite limited and recovery was poor at a secondary habitation that turned out to have been largely destroyed by past road construction. Prior to late Pueblo II, scant Puebloan sites are known on the Rainbow Plateau (e.g., Ambler et al. 1993; Lindsay et al. 1968). There is a marked increase beginning around AD 1100, and by mid– to late Pueblo III sites occur in great abundance. It is not surprising, therefore, that 13 of the 25 Puebloan components are Pueblo III in age. Three of the primary habitations are late Pueblo III or Tsegi phase, but evidently they were abandoned before the large sites of the region such as Segazlin Mesa (Lindsay et al. 1968). The Tsegi phase is perhaps better known than any phase in the Kayenta region, but much remains to be learned or examined in greater detail. The Pueblo III sites in the N16 ROW typify those that have been little studied to date—single- or extended-family habitations, some grouped closely together to form larger pithouse hamlets. Eight of the sites are middle Pueblo III in age, including both primary and secondary habitations. These sites are especially important because they date to the interval just before the larger pueblos started to form and thus are critical to understanding organizational changes leading to late Pueblo III aggregation. The two middle Pueblo II habitations are another important addition to the local database. Previously the earliest excavated residential sites for this northern portion of the Kayenta Anasazi region dated to the late Pueblo II period (Small Jar Pueblo and UT-V-13-19 [Geib et al. 1985; Lindsay et al. 1968]). Other Pueblo II sites of interest are two that functioned as secondary habitations; these were located near each other on the divide between Piute and Navajo canyons. The Pueblo I period is also virtually unknown for the Rainbow and Shonto plateaus, so excavation of the single camp site from this interval is also a contribution.

It is the nature of a phased project such as this, which proceeds from survey, to significance testing, to extent testing, to data recovery, that each successive phase of work provides new and more complete observations that change the sum of our knowledge about each site. The descriptions, interpretations, and evaluations presented in reports documenting the most recent phase of work totally supersede all such information in previous documentation. Therefore, this final concluding report should be consulted as the "final word" on the 33 excavated sites; there are bound to be discrepancies with reports from previous work phases concerning such basic matters as site size, site function, and temporal affiliation.

Research Issues

The research design for the NMRAP was mostly written in 1992, finalized in 1993, and approved by NNHPD and the Advisory Council in early 1994 (Geib et al. 1993). This plan is presented in Appendix J of the digital material largely unchanged from the original version, but here I present an abstracted version omitting most of the literature review and the extraneous and tedious cultural resource management wording. The general philosophy of the project was one that I learned from Dick Ambler and arose from the anticipated total destruction of archaeological sites within the N16 ROW. Basically, it was incumbent upon NNAD archaeologists to excavate the sites thoroughly, documenting all findings in a detailed manner and recovering as much artifactual and nonartifactual remains as possible so that future investigators could hypothetically "return" to the destroyed sites for additional information as analytic techniques become more refined and questions change. Obviously, limited time and money constrained the amount of work that could be performed in the field and the laboratory, so the work effort focused on a limited number of relevant research issues. Further limiting the number of research issues we could profitably examine were the kinds of sites within the N16 ROW—their character, age, information potential, and position relative to the ROW. Moreover, except for the late Pueblo III period (e.g., Geib et al. 1985; Hobler 1974; Lindsay et al. 1968; Schroedl 1989; Stein 1984), the prehistory of the territory crossed by N16 was not well known. The sample of excavated sites from earlier Pueblo periods was exceedingly limited, and the sample of excavated preceramic sites consisted of several caves and no work since the 1970 excavation of Dust Devil Cave (Ambler 1996).

The NMRAP research design (see SD, Appendix J) identified six broad and overlapping research issues subsumed under the domains of economic specialization and social differentiation. The economic issues were those of agricultural transition, subsistence specialization, and craft production and exchange, and the issues of social differentiation were those of social organization, social status, and gender. Though not exhaustive, these issues provided a comprehensive structure of inquiry to focus and organize field investigations and to structure analytic procedures. Each of the six research issues was developed in the plan along with a discussion of relevant data classes—material remains or field documentation—and the links between specific data classes and research issues where appropriate. Comparable amounts of information for each research issue were not expected to be forthcoming from the NMRAP excavations, and, indeed, were not recovered, but by considering them from the inception of the project, NNAD crews were poised to retrieve the maximum amount of relevant observations and remains. The nature and amount of expected remains, combined with the time and expense of acquiring those remains, led to certain study priorities: we expended more effort on some aspects of the archaeological record than others but gathered field and laboratory observations and materials in such a way that future researchers may avail themselves of them.[2] Temporal and functional differences, differential preservation and integrity, and variable locations relative to the proposed N16 ROW all contributed to a given site's research potential. As it turned out, the information recovered by the NMRAP was most relevant to economic issues, as is so often the case.

The research plan was heavily weighted toward issues pertinent to the Puebloan cultural sequence of the Kayenta region from Basketmaker II through Pueblo III. There were quite a few aceramic sites, or components thereof, within the N16 ROW, many of which belong to the Basketmaker II period. Several sites or components turned out to be Archaic in age, but this was not known at the time the research plan was authored. We were not, therefore, in a good position to propose research issues for Archaic sites beyond immediate questions of chronology and site function. Such basic documentation of Archaic remains, even in the narrow N16 ROW, could help clarify our understanding of hunter-gatherer lifeways and adaptation on the Colorado Plateau and was sufficient reason for excavation and analysis of Archaic period sites. Moreover, our understanding of the adoption of agriculture is dependent upon detailed knowledge of the Archaic period.

Agricultural Transition

One central concern of the NMRAP was the transition from a hunting-gathering economy to an agriculturally based one, a shift that involved both economic and social organizational change. Documenting the chronological and spatial aspects of initial domesticate use improves our knowledge of this complex and still poorly understood process. Archaeological research into the adoption of agriculture is a quickly changing field, and a vast amount of new information and discoveries accumulated between the time that the NMRAP research plan was authored and the final contract report was submitted. The NMRAP contributed significantly in this regard for the Kayenta region.

The picture now emerging for the Southwest is one of widespread and relatively early (ca. 2100 cal. BC) use of domesticates and recalls earlier, poorly supported claims for the antiquity of maize (e.g., Dick 1954; Irwin-Williams 1973). This is far different from the picture during the early 1980s, when Berry (1982, 1985) concluded that agriculture on the Colorado Plateau was no older than about 200 BC, a conservative estimate based on the then-limited number (nine) of direct dates on maize specimens and three adequately dated pithouse villages that yielded maize. Since then, maize cobs and kernels from both open and sheltered sites across the southern portion of the Colorado Plateau have been directly dated to as early as 3,680 rcybp (see review of dates in Huber 2005; Huckell 2006:Table 7-1). For the Kayenta region in particular, maize is well represented by as early as about 600 BC (Smiley et al. 1986) southeast of the N16 study area. This early maize is associated with Basketmaker II material culture, including remains excavated by Kidder and Guernsey (1919; Guernsey and Kidder 1921) from White Dog Cave and related shelters—sites and remains that defined Basketmaker II culture. Even earlier directly dated maize (ca. 1000 BC) is associated with Basketmaker II material culture at Three Fir Shelter on Black Mesa (Smiley and Parry 1992), with one maize cob yielding an outlying assay of 3610 BP (Smiley 1994:Table 1).

The introduction of corn and other domesticates to the Colorado Plateau is linked to the debate over Anasazi origins. Some archaeologists maintain that agriculture was adopted by Archaic populations already residing on the Colorado Plateau and that the Anasazi culture crystallized with the advent of this agricultural lifestyle. This model of in situ development has a long history: Kidder (1927, 1962 [1924]) advocated it in two early important syntheses of Southwestern archaeology, and more recently, Irwin-Williams (1967, 1973, 1979) championed it with her Oshara sequence. Another aspect of Irwin-Williams's model was the notion that domesticates initially had a minor effect on local hunter-gatherers, what Minnis termed the "monumental nonevent" (1985:310). The opposing view holds that "there was no lineal, in situ relationship between the Plateau Archaic and Basketmaker II" (Berry 1982:33), that agriculture was introduced along with an influx of new populations, specifically San Pedro phase agriculturalists out of the southern basin and range (Berry 1982; Berry and Berry 1986; Matson 1991, 2002; Morris and Burgh 1954).

Matson's (1991:305–316, 2002) detailed evaluation partially supports the intrusion model within the Kayenta and western Mesa Verde (Cedar Mesa and Red Rock Plateau) regions, where the "western" variant of Basketmaker II culture is located. In other portions of the Colorado Plateau, however, such as the eastern Mesa Verde region where the "eastern" or Los Pinos variant of Basketmaker II is found, Matson contends that the in situ model of Anasazi origins might apply. He (1991:314) was careful to point out that our current understanding is contingent on limited empirical evidence from the time interval when agriculture first appeared on the Colorado Plateau and during which the entity known as Basketmaker II became archaeologically visible.

Identifying the means of agricultural introduction (diffusion or migration) to the Colorado Plateau does not explain the process (O'Connell et al. 1982:230), but it certainly has an important bearing on our efforts at explanation. The NMRAP excavations contribute important information about the advent of food production for this portion of the Colorado Plateau. The work documents a series of Archaic sites including several late Archaic sites lacking agriculture, sites that date to the interval when maize was present on the Colorado Plateau. The material culture of the late Archaic sites is dissimilar from that present at subsequent Basketmaker II sites of the area; thus cultural continuity between the Archaic foragers and the first farmers of the area seems unlikely. This is discussed in detail in chapters 4 and 5 of this report.

Subsistence Specialization

Prehistoric subsistence strategies can vary between those that are quite generalized and those that that are highly specialized, and each can have important implications for understanding Southwest prehistory (Leonard 1989:498–499). Archaic hunter-gatherers are typically viewed as generalists, as illustrated by Jennings's (1968, 1973) Desert Archaic model, in which people exploit a wide variety of available subsistence resources. In contrast, the traditional archaeological view of Puebloan farmers as heavily reliant on the corn-beans-squash triad serves as an example of a specialized subsistence strategy, where a few resources out of many are disproportionally represented. The extent to which Puebloan groups were subsistence specialists is pivotal in many larger issues such as fluctuations in group interaction, population aggregation, and regional abandonment.

A key variable in establishing the location of a group along the generalist/specialist continuum is the degree to which they are involved in food production. Agriculture is the principal means by which humans increased the amount of food that could be produced in a given acreage (also turkey husbandry), but burning and other manipulation practices can also achieve this result, and most modern human groups, including hunter-gatherers, are active managers of their subsistence resources (Smith 2001). Food production and extraction are not mutually exclusive strategies, and prehistoric populations probably practiced a complex mix of both to satisfy their energy needs, yet the use of domesticates represented a significant step toward increased specialization. This first step happened as early as ca. 2100 cal. BC across portions of the Colorado Plateau, but the extent of agricultural dependence at this early time is unknown. Late Basketmaker II (ca. AD 100–400) populations on Cedar Mesa were apparently as dependent on maize as the Pueblo II and III populations of this mesa (Matson 1991; Matson and Chisholm 1991). Nevertheless, the degree to which the Basketmaker groups of the Kayenta region relied on food production for subsistence remained to be demonstrated. The NMRAP excavations contributed significant new data to this issue (see chapter 5), and this evidence is bolstered by and mutually supportive of stable isotope measurements from human bones (Coltrain et al. 2007).

Also of interest was the extent to which the subsistence strategy of Kayenta Puebloan groups became more specialized through time given the apparent increase in population density. A number of different subsistence models, some conflicting, some complementary, have been proposed for prehistoric Puebloans generally and for Kayenta populations specifically (e.g., Gasser 1982; Minnis 1989; Plog and Powell 1984; Powell 1983). The common conception of the Kayenta Anasazi as primarily food producers (farmers) has been questioned (e.g., Powell 1983:132–133; Schroedl 1989:809), because pollen and macrobotanical remains from feces, middens, structures, and features reveal that many plants other than the corn-beans-squash triad were exploited. Yet these other plants do not necessarily signify generalized foraging. It is essential to discriminate between gathered plants that are ecologically wild and those that thrive in humanly disturbed habitats, especially agricultural fields. Heavy use of weedy species is likely an extension of an agricultural adaptation and in this sense reflects a degree of productive specialization. Ecologically wild plants are considered low yield (Stiger 1977:50) because humans cannot intervene to enhance their production (this is not necessarily true with Opuntia). Minnis (1980:385, 1989:558) argued that some wild resources (e.g., pinyon) are not so much low yielding as they are erratic and unpredictable, both temporally and spatially. Both Stiger (1977) and Gasser (1982) saw an increased use of high-yield plants at the expense of low-yield plants from Pueblo II to late Pueblo III. A similar trend was observed at Rainbow City (Geib and Casto 1985), although the site sample was not very large. An increase in high-yield plants during the Puebloan sequence differs from the issue of subsistence diversification criticized by Leonard (1986, 1989).

Another issue with regard to subsistence specialization concerns the contribution through time of animal resources, both wild and domesticated. Certain evidence of specialization is provided by turkey (*Meleagris gallopavo*) remains—the one domesticated animal apparently eaten regularly by Puebloan populations. The extent to which wild animals were exploited by a group might relate more to the nature of their principal subsistence base. An ethnographic study of subsistence farmers outside of the Southwest (Werner et al. 1979) showed that, irrespective of the availability of animal protein, people spent more time hunting and fishing and consumed more protein when gardening was highly productive and satisfied basic caloric requirements than when garden productivity was low. In the Kayenta area, a considerable amount of small game could have been procured as an embedded part of agriculture. Fields provide considerably more forage for rabbits and certain rodents than undisturbed habitats, thereby increasing their populations and concentrating individuals within the very settings that farmers periodically visit anyway (Linares 1976; Semé 1984). Apart from turkey husbandry, the relation of animal consumption to subsistence specialization is poorly understood and problematic. These animals could be procured with traps or throwing sticks with little extra effort. In this scenario, an increase in the number of small mammal taxa might indicate intensification of agricultural pursuits and expansion of land devoted to fields, thereby providing an indirect measure of specialization. Conversely, the types of animals actually procured might better reflect the nature of the larger procurement area of a given settlement and the varied animal life it supported. Aspects of Puebloan subsistence are reported in chapter 6.

Craft Production and Exchange

The acquisition and processing of resources into tools, containers, ornaments, and other crafts are a central aspect of prehistoric economy. Craft production is also closely tied to exchange, or the transfer of material items among individuals or social groups. The emergence of specialized craft production and evidence for increased exchange are clearly important for understanding prehistoric society and are implicated in general explanations of cultural change in the Southwest (e.g., Cordell and Plog 1979). The unequal distribution of particular resources is a traditional explanation for the rise of craft specialization and exchange (cf. Arnold 1980, 1985). Craft specialization might also be fostered by social reasons, such as to promote intercommunity dependency or to maintain alliances (Cordell and Plog 1979:421). Whatever the underlying causes, unequal availability of natural resources provides an initial point of departure for examining the issue of craft production and exchange; moreover, it is important to thoroughly evaluate environmental constraints and possibilities prior to invoking social explanations.

The NMRAP attempted to examine craft production and exchange at both the intra- and interregional level. The first step toward evaluating this possibility is an assessment of the natural resources available within the local area. At first glance the bedrock geology of the Kayenta region appears to be geologically quite uniform, consisting in large part of sandstone of the three formations of the Glen Canyon Group. Nevertheless, there is significant intraregional variability, especially with regard to resources critical in the production of pottery and stone artifacts. Previous studies aimed at describing potentially usable raw materials available from the Kayenta region (e.g., Deutchman 1980; Foust et al. 1989; Geib and Ambler 1985; Geib and Callahan 1987; Green 1985; Turner and Cooley 1960) provided a basis for postulating certain patterns of craft production and exchange that were tested with the N16 site sample. For example, Turner and Cooley (1960) argued for extensive trade of flaked-stone tools or raw materials within the Kayenta region because most populations did not have ready access to material sources for producing flaked lithic tools such as bifaces (knives and projectile points). The Kayentans who resided along or close to the San Juan and Colorado rivers, however, did have access to nodules of high-quality chert and other siliceous material. As a result, these groups exchanged either the raw materials or the finished products to populations living to the south, such as those of Tsegi Canyon (Turner and Cooley 1960). Today we know that siliceous rock sources are not so limited as Turner and Cooley supposed (see especially Green 1985, 1986), yet most of these other siliceous resources are poorly suited to the production of bifaces due to small nodule size and poor fracture qualities (numerous fracture planes or coarse texture). As a result, it is still reasonable to hypothesize that Kayentans close to sources of good-quality stone for flaked implements might have specialized in tool production. As concerns the N16 ROW, the sites closest to the best sources of quality flakeable stone in Glen Canyon contained far more flaking debris, including a fair amount from biface reduction. Consequently there is some indication for the specialized production of facially thinned tools such as knives and projectile points. Yet these sites also contained more abundant large-mammal bone (deer and mountain sheep), suggesting that the greater evidence for biface production is perhaps related to hunting; after all, meat was likely a more valuable exchange item than flaked-stone tools (see chapter 6).

Rock suitable for the production of maize-grinding tools is also not ubiquitous within the Kayenta region. Although there is no shortage of sandstone, much of it is poorly suited to grinding hard maize kernels due to either friability (Navajo and Wingate sandstones) or fine grain size (sandstones of the Kayenta Formation). The best rock for maize-grinding tools comes from various Upper Jurassic and Cretaceous formations that crop out on and around Black Mesa, White Mesa, and the northwest portion of the Rainbow Plateau (Navajo Mountain and Cummings Mesa). Evidence for production of grinding tools in the Navajo Mountain area consists of abundant flaking and pecking debris at some habitations (e.g., Geib et al. 1985:192, Figure 65) and the common recovery of mano and metate blanks at most sites (e.g., Geib et al. 1985:379, Table 98; Lindsay et al. 1968:292-293). The NMRAP excavations also recovered solid evidence of mano and metate production from sites near Navajo Mountain, whereas sites farther south, away from good sources of sandstone, lacked such evidence. Exchange of grinding tools seems likely, with tools being traded south from production loci around Navajo Mountain (see chapter 6).

Regarding ceramics, there appear to be some clear patterns in the distribution of pottery-quality clays that are useful in understanding ceramic production and distribution patterns (Geib and Callahan 1987). Sources of pottery-quality clay in the northern Kayenta region are notably sparse and basically are restricted to the Chinle Formation. Some clay from this formation seems well suited for the production of Tsegi Orange Ware, and the limonitic clay necessary for producing the characteristic red slip (or paint) of this ware is also obtainable from the formation. As of yet, no light-firing clays, from which Tusayan White Ware and Tusayan Gray Ware were made, are known to occur within the northern Kayenta region. Such high-quality, light-firing clays are, however, plentiful on and around Black Mesa to the south. As part of the NMRAP, NNAD archaeologists conducted further clay sampling of the region and experimented with properties for the purposes of assessing vessel production possibilities (see SD vol. 5, chap. 2, and Appendix H3). Another part of the NMRAP was a chemical characterization of the volcanic ash used as temper within a portion of Tusayan White Ware to investigate patterns in the exchange of this pottery (see SD vol. 5, chap. 4).

Social Issues

A trend toward differentiation in the social realm—a phenomenon closely linked to increased production and economic specialization—is reflected in the material record of the prehistoric Southwest. This trend is evident in the increasingly patterned, but diverse, kinds of structures and features, lithic and ceramic artifacts, and settlement types. The NMRAP research plan discussed three social issues important to understanding Kayenta cultural change—organization, status, and gender. The archaeological examination of these or other social issues is notoriously difficult and multifaceted. The NMRAP excavations were more productive in acquiring data for inferences about organization than either status or gender (see chapter 6).

The study of Kayenta social organization formally began in the 1960s with the efforts of Jeffrey Dean (1969, 1970) and Alexander Lindsay Jr. (1969). Both authors examined the composition and structure of many individual late Pueblo III (Tsegi phase) sites with regard to units of residence and how they articulate to form different community patterns. From their architectural studies they inferred various aspects of late Pueblo III social organization. Because information from earlier time periods was lacking, these authors were unable to provide a dynamic, developmental perspective on Kayenta social organization. As Dean has observed, "Perhaps the most important implication of the present study for Kayenta Branch archaeology is that our knowledge of the Tsegi Phase contrasts so sharply with our knowledge of earlier periods of the Kayenta sequence" (1969:197). In many respects Dean's statement is still true, as he (with Gumerman) admits: "This critical period [AD 1150–1250] in Western Anasazi prehistory is still poorly known due to a paucity of excavated sites…. [This] lack of excavated sites limits what can be said about social organization" (Gumerman and Dean 1989:120, 122). The BMAP added considerably to basic data on many aspects of Kayenta Anasazi lifeways prior to the Tsegi phase, including two preliminary studies of Pueblo II social organization (Clemen 1976; Phillips 1972). Nevertheless, the occupation on northern Black Mesa ended at about AD 1150, so there is still an important data gap. Moreover, it is unclear to what extent findings from Black Mesa can be extrapolated to other portions of the Kayenta region. The NMRAP site sample is a good spatial and temporal complement to that studied by the BMAP. Whereas Anasazi occupation of northern Black Mesa ended during late Pueblo II, significant occupation of the Shonto and Rainbow plateaus was just beginning. Anasazi habitations in the N16 corridor included five sites that overlap in time with those of Black Mesa and 20 that span the period from late Pueblo II to late Pueblo III (see chapter 6). Additionally, the N16 sample included 12 Basketmaker habitations, thereby providing an important data set for making inferences about social organization during the start of the Anasazi sequence (cf. Lipe 1970:93–104). A causal link has not yet been made between Basketmaker subsistence strategy and degree and kind of social organization. Was increasing sedentism in the northern Kayenta area driven by environmental conditions that changed to favor lowland agricultural strategies, and did this process favor increased social integration (Gumerman and Dean 1989:115)? Or did increasing social competition, driven by some individuals' access to long-distance trade routes, promote surplus production by some households, which in turn drove agricultural intensification and growth of focal villages (Lightfoot and Feinman 1982)?

Project Methods

Field

The NMRAP field methods were designed to yield large artifactual samples, to disclose and expose features and activity areas within the N16 ROW, and to provide for detailed recording in a timely and cost-efficient manner. They were also designed to avoid discovery situations during road construction by thoroughly investigating the area of each site within the ROW. Uniform field methods help to achieve comparability of data, and to this end we developed a detailed field manual for the project (Huffman 1993). Standardized documentation is equally important; thus recording procedures and forms were also developed and used at all sites. Though excavation and recording methods were consistent, the specific excavation strategy for each of the NMRAP sites, such as the extent of hand excavation vs. mechanical stripping, necessarily varied somewhat. Variation resulted in part based on site character, age, depositional context, prior disturbances, and the information potential of each site or site portion within the ROW. Specific excavation strategies for each of the sites are presented in the site descriptions in volumes 2–4 of the online supporting documents. At many sites we had to retrieve relevant information from a sample of features and remains; this occurred at several sites because they lay just partially within the N16 ROW and at others because the existing Navajo Mountain road or other developments had destroyed portions.

All sites were mapped with either a total station or a transit and stadia rod. An arbitrary horizontal and vertical datum was established at each site and usually designated as N100/E100 with an elevation of 10 m. A metric

Figure 1.3. Excavation under way at Modesty House on the central portion of the Rainbow Plateau; Willie Navajo and Elaine Smith (squatting) are working on the deflated trash scatter with Bruce Whitehat (in the white cap) and an unidentified individual exposing the Pueblo III structure at the site (photo courtesy of Courtney White).

grid aligned to magnetic north was laid out over each site. Except for the sampling of trash middens, crews judgmentally selected portions of sites for hand excavation, mechanical stripping, and backhoe trenching. Extent testing allowed crews to identify the areas of each site in the ROW that would be most informative and contain all, or most, features and cultural deposits. These portions, which were designated the "main site areas," became the focus of data-recovery efforts. Hand excavation focused on those portions of each main site area where extent testing exposed features or artifact concentrations. Mechanical excavation techniques, consisting of horizontal stripping and trenching, were used extensively around these hand-excavated areas to disclose features not identified during testing. Complete excavation of all structures and thorough sampling of extramural features were critical to site interpretation. Hand excavation and screening of the cultural deposit around most structures and other features documented associations among material remains and between such remains and features. Occupation surfaces and their associated features and artifactual and nonartifactual remains provide information for analyzing relationships among artifacts, and among artifacts and features, and for reconstructing activity areas and the differential use of site space.

The excavation emphasis at nearly all sites was horizontal exposure of large surface areas of cultural deposition using 1-×-1-m units for horizontal provenience and natural stratigraphy for vertical control (Figure 1.3). This approach exposed features in plan view while simultaneously recovering samples of associated nonperishable remains that might be spatially patterned. Noncultural strata that overlay single-component sites or that separated cultural deposits of different time periods at multiple-component sites were removed by the most efficient means possible without damaging cultural deposits or features. At some sites this involved simply shoveling off the overburden by hand, whereas at other sites a backhoe stripped overburden to a depth previously determined by hand-excavated test units. A backhoe was also used at most sites toward the end of all horizontal hand excavation to mechanically strip the remainder of each site, thereby exposing features without artifact recovery. All excavation was restricted to the N16 ROW except in a few instances when a feature straddled this arbitrary line and the bulk of it lay within the ROW.

The maximum unit of horizontal provenience during hand excavation of screened cultural deposits was a 1-×-1-m square. These were designated by their north and east extent along the grid system, with the north coordinate listed first followed by the east coordinate (e.g., N100–101/E115–116). Materials collected from each layer of each unit were assigned individual provenience numbers. Even though 1-m squares were the maximal unit of horizontal provenience during hand excavation, these units were often grouped together and excavated simultaneously as blocks of variable size and shape to achieve horizontal exposure as needed to define related features emanating from an original occupation surface. Notes were taken on a block of space and usually in conjunction with a known feature to eliminate unnecessary paperwork. After excavating the cultural stratum from a site to define features in plan view, these features were then used to provide additional horizontal control for further excavation. Materials recovered from all features were provenienced by feature number as well as horizontal placement along the grid. All piece-plotted artifacts or other samples were designated in relation to the grid.

Vertical control during excavation was by natural stratigraphic units or dispositional layers that had been defined at each site based on extent-testing profiles. Arbitrary divisions of natural strata were not used. The strata within features in nearly all cases differed from those of a site as a whole, and in most cases stratification was unknown, or poorly known, prior to data recovery. Stratigraphic control for any feature was therefore established by sectioning the feature (in halves or quarters) to provide one or two profiles. Fill from the initially excavated section(s) of features was vertically subdivided according to natural breaks seen in plan view. The remaining fill was removed following natural strata using the profile(s) as an extra guide. Elevations of floors, features, strata, and the like were made relative to the arbitrary 10-m elevation established at each site and usually marked at the site datum (N100/E100). These measurements were expressed as actual elevations (e.g., 8.75 m, 11.21 m) rather than measurements below or above the datum. Elevations were made either with a transit or by a nylon string and line level.

In all cases where cultural fill was removed from hand-excavated 1-×-1-m units, the sediment was passed through either ¼-in or ⅛-in mesh screens. These two mesh sizes can result in both different rates of artifact recovery and the recovery of different types of remains, such that site interpretation can be affected. Examples include the overall underestimation of small animal exploitation because most animal bones smaller than those from a rabbit routinely pass through a ¼-in screen (e.g., Grayson 1984:168–169; Shaffer 1992; Shaffer and Sanchez 1994) and the loss of pressure-flaking debris (e.g., Towner and Warburton 1990:317). The consequences of the latter were amply illustrated during significance testing at AZ-J-14-23 (Geib 1992), where all but two of the 24 flakes recovered from two test units, including 12 obsidian flakes and one of Chuska chert (Narbona Pass), would have gone into the backdirt had ¼-in mesh been used instead of ⅛-in mesh. Notwithstanding the potential misinterpretation of site function, in this instance the site might have been inappropriately dismissed as not eligible to the National Register.

A concern over screen-size biases, however, had to be weighed against an increase in excavation costs; ⅛-in mesh greatly slowed the screening process, especially when the sediment was wet or consolidated. The choice of mesh size depended in part on site type and period of occupation. As a general guideline, ¼-in mesh was the standard screen size for the majority of hand excavation at ceramic-period habitations. Routine use of ⅛-in mesh at these sites was restricted to a sample of the trash middens and screening the floor fill of structures and the in situ fill of smaller features. At preceramic sites ⅛-in mesh was the standard screen size for all hand-excavation efforts. At some preceramic sites (those of Basketmaker II temporal affiliation), crews switched to ¼-in mesh if they found that little was actually recovered from the ⅛-in mesh.

Not all sediment was screened. Examples of instances when screens were not employed are (1) all mechanical excavation including the removal of noncultural structural fill; (2) hand removal of known sterile overburden and structural fill down to roof or wall fall or 10 cm above floor, whichever came first; and (3) shovel stripping the trash midden in search of human burials after the midden had been sampled. During any of these instances, and especially the latter, a grab sample of artifacts was collected that included large sherds, worked sherds, grinding tools or other large stone artifacts (cores, hammerstones), any patterned flaked-stone tools (projectile points and drills), and other unusual or rare artifacts such as ornaments.

A backhoe was used during data recovery for several

tasks, principally to mechanically strip deposits peripheral to the main site areas (i.e., around the portions excavated by hand). In related fashion, sterile overburden was mechanically stripped from deeply buried sites or portions thereof so that hand excavation of cultural deposits could proceed. Additional trenching was done at many sites during data recovery to search for buried structures or features not found during extent testing. A backhoe was also used to remove erosional fill from deep, large pit structures. Finally, all excavated areas were filled in or flattened subsequent to completion of data recovery, as road construction was several years away and some excavation produced deep holes that were potentially hazardous to people and livestock.

Small Features

Small features consisted of pits, hearths, cists, postholes, and the like, excluding burials and structures of any kind. After exposing small features in plan view, their outlines were mapped if outlines seemed definite. Except for postholes, these features were bisected along an axis, preferably using the grid system. One of the halves was excavated following natural levels. The sediment of this portion was screened, but analytical samples were generally not saved (unless the feature was quite small) until after profiling the feature to determine its fill sequence and potential function. If the feature fill was related to cultural processes or was illustrative of feature use, a profile of the fill was drawn at an appropriate scale (usually 1 in to 20 or 25 cm) and documented on print film. Then flotation, pollen, ^{14}C, and other appropriate samples were removed from the remaining half according to the natural strata revealed in profile. After completion of excavation, a plan view was drawn, as was a cross section that ran perpendicular to the previous profile; finishing photos were also taken. If necessary the feature was then subfloored. A feature recording form ensured standard collection of relevant information.

Postholes that were not part of an identified structure were assigned their own feature number; postholes that formed an obvious alignment were treated as a single feature. Possible postholes were cut in half so that they could be viewed in profile to confirm that they were indeed post molds and not rodent holes or other natural phenomena.

Structures

Once exposed in plan view, structures and other large features were marked into quadrants so that opposing quarters could be excavated to obtain orthogonal profiles of the fill. The lines of bisection generally paralleled the grid axes, unless it was more informative to parallel the orientation of a structure, for instance, to include an entrance or kiva recess. The fill was removed from opposing quadrants following natural stratigraphic breaks down to 10 cm above the floor (floor fill). Unless the fill was primary (e.g., trash layers) or represented an important postoccupation deposit (roof or wall fall), all sediment was shoveled out without screening. All material from the roof or wall fall layer to the floor was screened through ¼-in mesh. Shallow, small (ca. 25 cm² or less) soundings (sondages) were used at various intervals to establish vertical location relative to the floor, and the last of these was sunk through the floor to expose it in profile. In situ materials (e.g., grinding tools or slabs on roof fall) or other informative remains (e.g., burned beams) encountered during this process were mapped according to their location relative to the quadrants and the grid system. Other materials recovered during this process were provenienced by feature number, quadrant, and stratum.

Until reaching the maximum depth of the feature, a distance of at least 10 cm was maintained between the excavation and probable walls as evidenced by the plan view outline; walls were most easily located and traced at maximum depth and then followed upward to the ground surface. When the walls were exposed in both quadrants, both right-angled profiles were drawn and photographed. Any needed column samples (pollen, flotation, sedimentological) were removed from the profiles at this time.

Following drawing and sampling, the fill from remaining quadrants was removed down to roof/wall fall or floor fill (10 cm above floor) without screening unless primary cultural deposits were encountered. Again, in situ materials or other informative remains encountered during this process were mapped according to their location relative to the quadrants and the grid system. Other materials recovered during this process were provenienced by feature number and stratum.

For large or deep structures accessible by a backhoe, fill from remaining quadrants was removed mechanically. When all sediment had been removed down to 10 cm above the floor, then the floor itself was exposed. The fill from floor exposure was screened with ⅛-in mesh. Materials that lacked floor contact were provenienced by feature, quadrant, and natural level, and floor contact remains were point provenienced. Appropriate pollen samples were collected during the process of floor exposure to limit modern contamination. A planimetric map of the structure was prepared showing all floor features, floor-contact artifacts, pollen sampling areas, and other information as appropriate.

Floor and wall features were excavated according to the procedures outlined earlier for small features. The structure and its floor and wall features were documented with print film. If more than one floor was present, each was sequentially exposed and documented with particular emphasis placed on determining associations between the floor features and the different floors. At least two cross sections were drawn for each structure, one of which included the entryways on semisubterranean structures or ventilators on subterranean structures. As a final procedure, the floors and walls of each structure were cut through to learn about construction details or remodeling events and to search for other features. A structure recording form ensured the standard collection of relevant information, with liberal use of cameras for photo documentation.

Trash Middens

Trash middens were sampled intensively to recover the types and quantities of remains necessary to address the NMRAP research issues. Although an adequate sample of certain classes of remains (e.g., debitage and sherds) might be recovered from just several 1-×-1-m units, other classes of remains (projectile points, manos, and ornaments) require a considerable volume of sediment to be excavated. Also, even for data classes recovered in abundance, such as sherds, a sample size adequate for technological study is usually inadequate to address research issues that concern style, because the bulk of recovered sherds can be identified only to the ware level. Large samples of typable ceramics are required for useful seriation studies; thus a comprehensive excavation program was necessary.

During the first two years of data recovery crews sampled trash middens by a simple random method, but in the final two years they switched to a systematic sample approach. The earlier method involved defining a sample frame of 1-×-1-m units over trash middens and then selecting for excavation a simple random sample of these units (using a table of random numbers). Sampling fraction was not standardized among sites (e.g., 20%, 5%, or 1% sample) because a large number of factors had to be considered, such as midden size and density of remains. The technique implemented starting with Segment 5 involved excavating every 1-×-1-m unit of a given interval, such as every other unit or every fourth unit. In both sampling approaches, half of all midden sample units were screened with ⅛-in mesh to provide a sample of small remains, while the other half were screened with ¼-in mesh. Bulk flotation samples and pollen samples were collected as appropriate.

After the midden had been sampled, crews rapidly shovel stripped the remainder of the trash deposits to search for human remains. This technique was preferable to backhoe stripping because it vastly reduced the chance of damaging burials. A common burial practice in the Kayenta region is shallow placement of the individual within a trash midden, so that by the time a pit outline was observable (after removal of the trash deposit) mechanical stripping would have disturbed the skeletal remains. Shovel stripping the midden also enabled us to increase the sample of potentially underrepresented items such as grinding tools, hammerstones and cores, and worked sherds. Artifacts recovered in this manner were provenienced to the midden in general.

Human Burials

Prehistoric human burials were anticipated at several of the sites within the N16 ROW, and field crews made a concerted effort to locate all burials to ensure that none would be disturbed during road construction, but in the end just two sites contained human remains: AZ-J-3-8 and AZ-J-2-6. All human remains and associated grave goods found during NMRAP were treated in accordance with the Navajo Nation Policy for the Protection of Jishchaa': Gravesites, Human Remains, and Funerary Items. In accordance with those guidelines, upon discovery of human remains (whether prehistoric or historic), all excavation within a 3-m radius of the remains was halted, and workers immediately took steps to preserve and protect the remains in situ. NNHPD was contacted as soon as possible about the discovery and initiated consultation with relevant tribes. The treatment for burials was decided upon by NNHPD on a case-by-case basis. All burials within the N16 ROW were carefully excavated and reburied at the edge of the ROW in an area that was purposefully set aside and will not be subject to future disturbance. All associated mortuary objects were also reinterred with the human remains.

Special Samples

Flotation samples were collected from all hearths, pits containing in situ fill, floor fill, and primary trash deposits. Such samples varied in size depending on the dimensions, nature, and content of the features but generally were at least 4 liters; different size samples were standardized in the lab. Flotation samples were generally taken only from productive-looking contexts (charcoal rich) rather than from sterile layers or units, although a few such samples were taken for control purposes.

Pollen samples were collected from cultural deposits and features and from noncultural strata exposed in trench or unit profiles. Grinding tools found in primary contexts were wrapped in plastic for future pollen washes, and all whole (or broken in situ) ceramic vessels were also wrapped in plastic for pollen and possible flotation analysis. Specific areas of structural floors, such as under and around floor-contact artifacts, next to hearths and pits, or at systematic intervals, were sampled to assess patterned use of interiors; composite floor samples were obtained to facilitate interstructure comparison. Floor palynological samples cannot necessarily be distributed at predicted strict intervals, due to potential rodent, root, and insect disturbance, but workers tried to collect sediment to adequately characterize the pollen spectra within each structure. For control purposes, modern (composite pinch technique) pollen samples from the vicinity of several sites were taken to obtain a picture of the modern pollen rain.

Any burned structural timbers potentially suitable for tree-ring dating were saved. As necessary, these samples were wrapped in string and soaked in a paraffin–gasoline solution to stabilize them. Carbonized corn and other domesticates from trash middens or features were saved for possible radiocarbon dating as well as macrobotanical analysis. Charcoal was saved from hearths for radiocarbon dating of preagricultural-period sites, although annual plant remains, when available, took priority over charcoal. In this regard, flotation samples from preagricultural sites were processed to recover carbonized annual plant remains for possible accelerator mass spectrometry (AMS) dating.

Provenience Numbers and List

The crew assigned sequential provenience numbers in the field to all recovered artifacts and samples. The artifacts or samples from any single provenience unit, such as the cultural stratum of a 1-×-1-m unit or the floor surface of a house, were segregated by general artifact material class (e.g., ceramic, stone, bone) or type of sample (pollen, flotation, radiocarbon), bagged separately, and assigned bag numbers. The bag numbers (BN) were sequentially numbered within each provenience number (PN). For each PN and BN, NNAD crews recorded information that included codes for specimen type and sample type, a written description of bag contents, horizontal provenience on the grid system, feature number, a code for context type (midden, cultural stratum, floor fill, floor surface), stratum number, cultural component, mesh size, the initials of the excavator(s), date of recovery, and comments that provided additional provenience information not covered in previous data columns. For ease of computer manipulation the PN list was entered into a database program along with the addition of temporal assignment and report designation for features. In some cases, such as artifacts point plotted on the floor of a house, the PN and BN provide individual identification numbers for artifacts. In cases where numerous artifacts were grouped together within a single PN and BN, such as with flaked-stone tools from a midden layer of a 1-×-1-m unit, sequential item numbers within bag numbers were assigned in the laboratory.

Laboratory

All collections from the NMRAP, except those from burial contexts, were transported back to the laboratory in Flagstaff for processing and analysis. The laboratory facilitated the flow of N16 materials and information between the office and the field and provided for the care and processing of artifacts and nonartifactual samples. A laboratory manual prepared for NMRAP gave specific guidelines regarding treatment of artifacts and nonartifactual samples. The manual was available to all lab, field, and analytical personnel to ensure consistent and careful treatment of all materials. General laboratory procedures are described below, along with brief outlines of analysis methods, but details about how various material remains were analyzed are presented in volume 5 and the appendixes of the Web-posted supporting documentation.

During each session of fieldwork, materials were curated in the field camp in storage tubs. An initial check of bags for correct information and care of fragile items was performed in the field. At the end of each fieldwork session, all artifacts and nonartifactual samples, except mortuary items and human bones, were taken to the main laboratory in Flagstaff. Upon arrival at the lab, all materials were recorded on a tracking sheet that followed the progress of materials from initial receipt to final disposition. Provenience information, bag contents, and number of artifacts were recorded on this sheet during initial check-in. The sheet was initialed at each stage of processing and analysis. If a collected item was discarded at any point (as a nonartifact or worthless sample), this was also recorded.

Remains had been separated in the field according to material class such as ceramic, stone, bone, and samples of various type. Ceramic and stone artifacts were washed and rebagged after check-in with the following exceptions: sherd scrapers and knives, unfired pottery, materials with fugitive pigments, polishing stones, whole grinding tools from primary-use contexts, whole vessels, and any other items specifically identified for special handling by field personnel. Bone, shell, and any perishables or botanical remains were not washed. After initial processing, artifacts were placed in boxes separated by site number, and for sites with a large volume of artifacts, they were also separated by artifact or sample type. A label was placed on the exterior of the box to identify the contents. The label included project name and number, site number, box contents, and processing stages completed (washing, initial inventory, basic analysis, intensive analysis).

Prior to any artifact analysis per se, an initial inventory of artifacts and samples was completed. After this, artifacts and nonartifactual samples were checked out to specific analysts, and basic analyses were completed. As warranted, selected items were subjected to more intensive forms of analysis. After all analyses were completed, artifacts and other specimens were returned to the lab to be curated until transfer to the final repository (see note 2).

A computerized database for all information regarding artifacts and samples collected during NMRAP was maintained at the laboratory. Paradox was used both for database management and as an analytical tool. As soon as artifacts were checked into the lab, provenience log and tracking sheet information was entered into the database. This provided easy, organized access to information for both lab personnel and analysts. When artifacts were checked out to specific analysts, a printout and disk with all pertinent information about the artifacts accompanied the materials. Analysts, in turn, provided computerized versions of the results of their analyses for inclusion in the master database.

Ceramic Artifacts

All vessels and potsherds of sufficient size were accorded a basic analysis (unmodified sherds less than 1.5 cm in maximum dimension were not examined), which consisted of classification according to the traditional ware and type system, identification of vessel form and part, temper type, presence of sooting or other surface deposits, presence of postfiring modification, a lot number (number of sherds that can be identically coded), and aggregate weight (Hays-Gilpin 1994). An additional data field, "variety," was coded within some types, and for some temper categories a secondary descriptive code was recorded. More detailed analysis was completed for certain kinds of pottery artifacts: whole and reconstructible vessels, modified sherds, and miscellaneous clay and pottery artifacts such as figurines, pipes, and beads. Large rim sherds and handles from selected proveniences were studied for certain formal and stylistic features. Kelley Hays-Gilpin and Janet Hagopian conducted most of the basic analysis and all of the more detailed studies. Burial assemblages were analyzed and photographed in the field and not brought back to the lab.

Analysis of the elemental composition of volcanic ash temper in Tusayan White Ware sherds was undertaken by Kimberly Spurr using the electron microprobe at Northern Arizona University (see Freestone 1982). Sherds with ash temper and samples of volcanic ash from known sources were analyzed to find out if ash-tempered Tusayan White Ware sherds from N16 sites were manufactured in the Cow Springs area and traded north. For further discussion of this research question, see chapter 4 of volume 5 of the Web-posted supporting documentation.

Strength testing was conducted on 20 ash-tempered Tusayan White Ware sherds and 20 sand-tempered Tusayan White Ware sherds to test the hypothesis that ash temper provides a stronger vessel wall than sand temper. The answer to this question contributed to our understanding of craft specialization and trade in the Kayenta area. Strength testing was done by Mark Neupert using techniques developed in the University of Arizona's Laboratory of Traditional Technology. The results of his analysis are presented in Appendix H1 of the Web-posted supporting documentation.

Winston Hurst, a specialist in Mesa Verde pottery, was contracted to examine all sherds that the NMRAP ceramic analysts identified as potential Mesa Verdian pottery. His report is abstracted in chapter 2 of volume 5 of the online supporting documentation, with the full report given in Appendix H2 of the Web-posted supporting documentation.

Stone Artifacts

Stone artifacts were analyzed individually to record variables pertaining to raw material, reduction technique, function, and size. Specific tools were described individually to augment the coded information. Stone artifacts were separated into several classes for analysis: debitage, flaked facial tools, cores and nodular tools, grinding tools (manos and metates), and miscellaneous stone artifacts. Analytic routines specific to each class were used to record observations. Miranda Warburton analyzed most of the flaked-stone artifact classes, assisted at various times by Kerry Thompson, Mick Robins, and me. I analyzed most grinding tools and miscellaneous stone artifacts, with Stewart Deats analyzing these artifacts from the last year of excavation.

Certain stone artifacts received three types of specialized analyses: obsidian sourcing, obsidian hydration dating, and grinding tool washes for pollen analysis. These analyses were performed by various professionals under subcontract to NNAD. Richard Hughes (Geochemical Research Laboratory) performed nondestructive X-ray fluorescence analysis of obsidian artifacts for sourcing purposes; Chris Stevenson (Diffusion Laboratory, Archaeological Services Consultants) performed obsidian hydration dating; and Susan Smith (Laboratory of Palynology, NAU) performed the pollen analysis of grinding tools.

Other Remains

Processing samples for the recovery of plant remains and their identification and interpretation were subcontracted to specialists in the appropriate fields. The methods used by these specialists are not detailed here, but in general they followed standard practice (see Pearsall 1989). All pollen samples were analyzed by Susan Smith (Laboratory of Palynology, NAU) under the direction of R. Scott Anderson. Three individuals analyzed flotation samples: for the first year of excavations (Segment 3), Andrea Hunter (NAU, Ethnobotany Laboratory) conducted the analysis; the samples from Atlatl Rock Cave were analyzed by Nancy Coulam (see SD vol. 2, chap. 2), but all subsequent work and a chapter for the final synthetic report were completed by Meredith Mathews (San Juan College). Except for the samples from Atlatl Rock Cave, NNAD personnel, either in the NMRAP field camp or back in the laboratory, conducted flotation of sediment for the recovery of macrobotanical remains. The flotation soil samples were processed using an Illinois Department of Transportation–style water-processing system (Pearsall 1989:Figures 216–219) to separate light and heavy fractions. All collected samples were processed by this method, but only samples with the greatest interpretive potential or best preservation were submitted to the analysts; both the light and heavy fractions were examined. The samples from Atlatl Rock Cave were processed by the analyst without water using nested dry screens. Plant remains were also collected in the field while screening or directly from feature contexts; these were few in number. I identified these specimens to a general level.

Several individuals identified the faunal remains recovered during the NMRAP. Karen Quanbeck conducted the analysis of remains from the first year of excavation (Segment 3) and produced a descriptive report (Quanbeck 1995). The remains from the next two field seasons were analyzed by John Goodman, but without descriptive reports. Kari Schmidt analyzed the faunal remains from Segment 6 and prepared the final report for the project, integrating the work of previous analysts to the extent possible. Unmodified marine and freshwater shell and shell artifacts were analyzed by Arthur W. Vokes, Arizona State Museum. I described avian eggshell, several specimens of which came from a few of the Pueblo III habitations.

Kimberly Spurr analyzed most of the mineral samples recovered by the project, many of which appear to have been used as sources of pigment. No perishable artifacts were recovered from NMRAP sites because all were in the open and none of the structures at any site had burned catastrophically with a household assemblage. The limited testing project at Atlatl Rock Cave resulted in the recovery of a small sample of perishable artifacts, all of which I described in a preliminary way.

The two principal chronometric dating techniques used for the NMRAP included dendrochronology and radiocarbon. Obsidian hydration was conducted on a limited basis as a test of the procedure (see SD, Appendix E, and critique in chapter 4). All likely tree-ring specimens were submitted to the Tree-Ring Laboratory, University of Arizona. Beta Analytic was the primary contractor for radiocarbon analysis; standard samples were assayed in-house, whereas tiny samples were pretreated and converted to graphic targets for AMS assay at the Lawrence Livermore National Laboratory. Several radiocarbon samples were submitted to the NSF-AMS Laboratory at the University of Arizona as a means of checking on the previous results.

The original NMRAP research plan and data-recovery plan called for geomorphic study of the excavated sites. This work was initiated during Segment 3 significance testing (Anderson 1992; see SD, Appendix G) and was carried forward during data recovery for that road segment (Ponczynski 1995). At that time it became apparent that we could learn considerably more by investing the money that would have been spent on geomorphologic work into pack rat midden research. Accordingly, Peter Koehler was contracted to conduct the research. Koehler and I conducted several field trips to the Rainbow Plateau to collect pack rat midden samples, which Koehler then processed and analyzed (see SD Appendix K). Beta Analytic conducted the radiocarbon dating for the pack rat study.

Notes

1. It is unlikely that Archaic and Basketmaker remains were absent from Segments 1 and 2 of N16, just that they went unobserved during the survey and consequently did not become part of the contracted data recovery effort.
2. The Navajo Nation Historic Preservation Department has decided to rebury all remains recovered by data-recovery projects on tribal land except for select items that community members find useful or interesting, such as whole projectile points. Consequently, future researchers might never be able to examine the objects or samples recovered by the NMRAP. As of this writing it appears that the decision to rebury, which was made after completion of all NMRAP fieldwork, will not be applied retroactively. The ultimate disposition of the collections remains in doubt.

CHAPTER 2

Background for the Navajo Mountain Road Archaeological Project

THE KAYENTA REGION

NNAD's excavations within the ROW for the Navajo Mountain road provided a wealth of archaeological information about the prehistory of the Kayenta region. This area of northeastern Arizona and southeastern Utah (Figures 2.1–2.2) played an important role in the formative stages of Southwestern archaeology. Such luminaries of the discipline as Charles Amsden, Bryon Cummings, Samuel Guernsey, Irwin Hayden, Neil Judd, Alfred Kidder, Earl Morris, Noel Morss, and Watson Smith "cut their teeth" or otherwise worked in the area. There is little doubt that Kidder's experience in the region, along with those of several others attending the first Pecos Conference, played significantly in their conception of the developmental periods that became formalized as the Pecos Classification (Kidder 1927). The orderly Kayenta pottery sequence lent itself to early formalization of standard named types (Colton and Hargrave 1937, subsequently Colton 1955, 1956, 1958), which also influenced the discipline. The wide prehistoric exchange of vessels produced by Kayenta potters, coupled with Colton's handbooks, *Pottery Types of the Southwest*, have ensured that most Southwestern archaeologists have passing familiarity with Kayenta pottery, especially the orange wares and the striking Pueblo III black-on-whites.

The Kayenta designation comes from the modern town by that name located on the Navajo Reservation in northeast Arizona. Early excavations in localities around Kayenta by Kidder and Guernsey (1919; Guernsey 1931; Guernsey and Kidder 1921), Byron Cummings (extensive antiquarian collecting that went virtually unreported), and others unearthed distinctive pottery and other associated remains, which led to the definition of an areal tradition known as the Kayenta branch (Colton 1939). Although there is much internal variability in aspects such as architecture and treatment of the dead, the pottery tradition is quite uniform across a broad area and easily separated from most other regional traditions of pottery production. It is this trait above others that serves to distinguish the prehistoric remains of the Kayenta region from those of surrounding areas. Use of the Kayenta tradition as a typological category will vary depending on perception, experience, and research orientation, and these influence where one places arbitrary lines on maps to "bound" such constructs. There is general agreement among most researchers that Puebloan remains west of about the Chinle Wash and the Pueblo Colorado Wash differ from those to the east (Dean 1996:29). How the western remains are further differentiated is open to debate, especially since there is a temporal aspect, with maximal spread of Kayenta traits (or maximal uniformity of traits) occurring during late Pueblo II, roughly AD 1100 to 1150.

Regardless, it is possible to identify a "core" Kayenta area where this archaeological culture was represented throughout the entire Puebloan sequence until AD 1300. Central to this core is the Klethla Valley, the Red Lake area, Long House Valley, Tsegi Canyon, and the Kayenta Valley along Laguna Creek. This central area contains the full sequence of Kayenta cultural development from Basketmaker II through late Pueblo III, with some areas such as Red Lake seeming to have been occupied without hiatus. The southeastern edge of the Shonto Plateau and northwestern scarp of Black Mesa are considered part of this central area given their proximity to the other localities and degree of interaction as evidenced by the movement of raw materials. The northern part of the core Kayenta region (Figure 2.2) includes the Rainbow Plateau, Cummings Mesa, Piute Canyon, Piute Mesa, and Nakai Canyon. A Kayentan presence farther north of this in Glen Canyon appears real (Lipe 1970) and tied to the expansion of populations from the south, but this lies

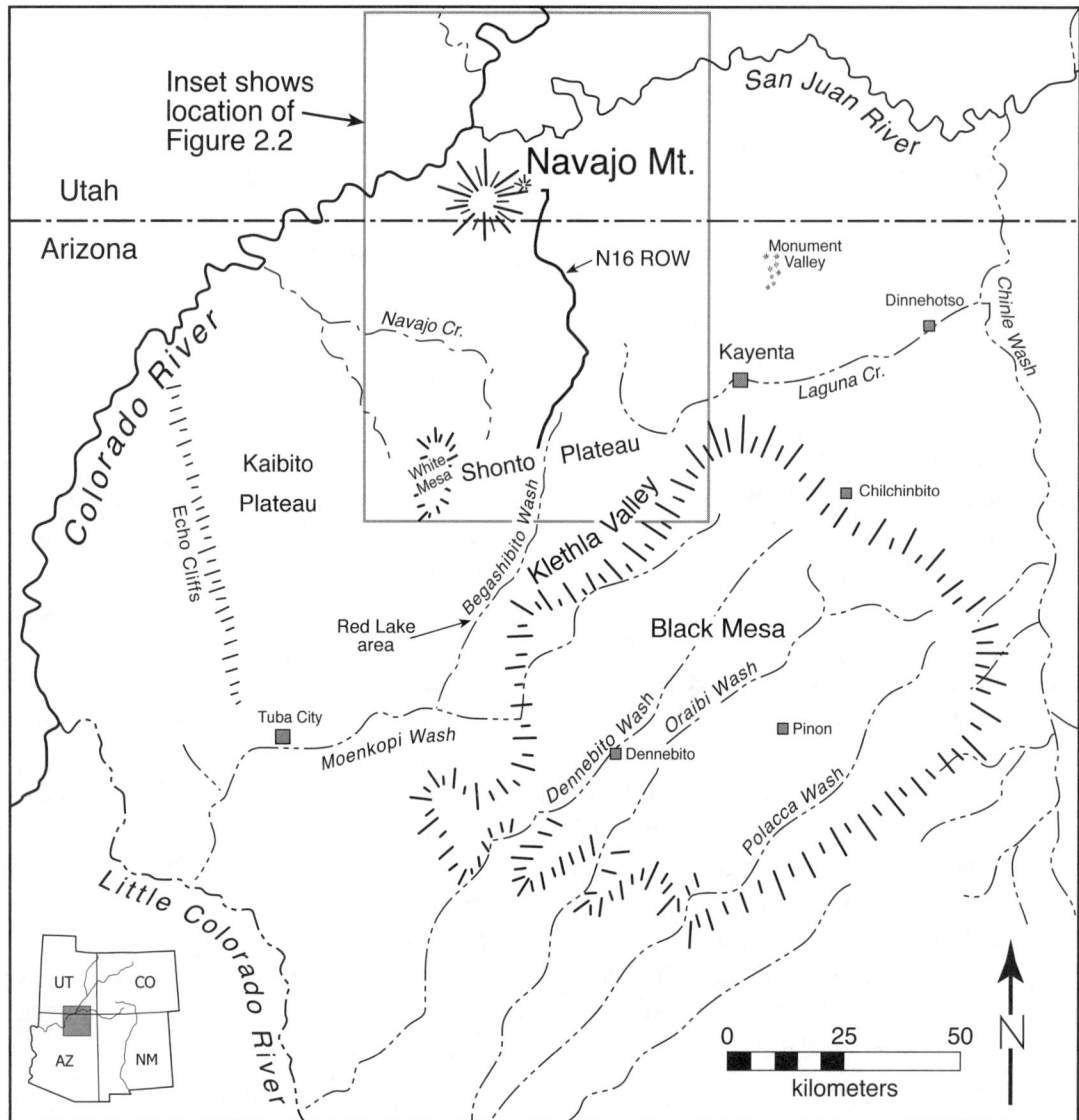

Figure 2.1. Map of the core Kayenta region of northeast Arizona and southeast Utah showing some of the major geographic features, drainages, and modern towns.

outside the core area as defined here. Puebloan occupation of the northern Kayenta region seems discontinuous, with a noticeable absence of Basketmaker III and Pueblo I habitations. The Kaibito Plateau, including White Mesa and the Tuba City–Moenave area, comprises the western portion of the core Kayenta region, while central Black Mesa south to about Pinyon and Dinnebito/Hard Rocks defines the southern part of the core area. The eastern part is less clearly defined or more gradational but includes the Chilchinbito and Rough Rock area along the northeastern foot of Black Mesa, as well as the Dinnehotso area along lower portions of Laguna Creek and Chinle Wash.

The utility of the Kayenta branch as some spatially bounded cultural tradition is only relevant to the ceramic period. During the Basketmaker II interval, the material remains found in the Kayenta region also have a large degree of unity, but this extends much farther north to include the Cedar Mesa–Comb Wash area that in the ceramic period is part of the Mesa Verde region and farther east to include Canyon de Chelly. More significantly, the Kayenta area lacks any "cultural" significance for the Archaic period, merely serving to designate some portion of the Four Corners region.

The prehistory of the Kayenta region is interesting in its own right, but aside from parochial concerns, the area is important because it presents an alternative pathway in Puebloan social development that differs in several key respects from developments in the Chaco, Mesa Verde,

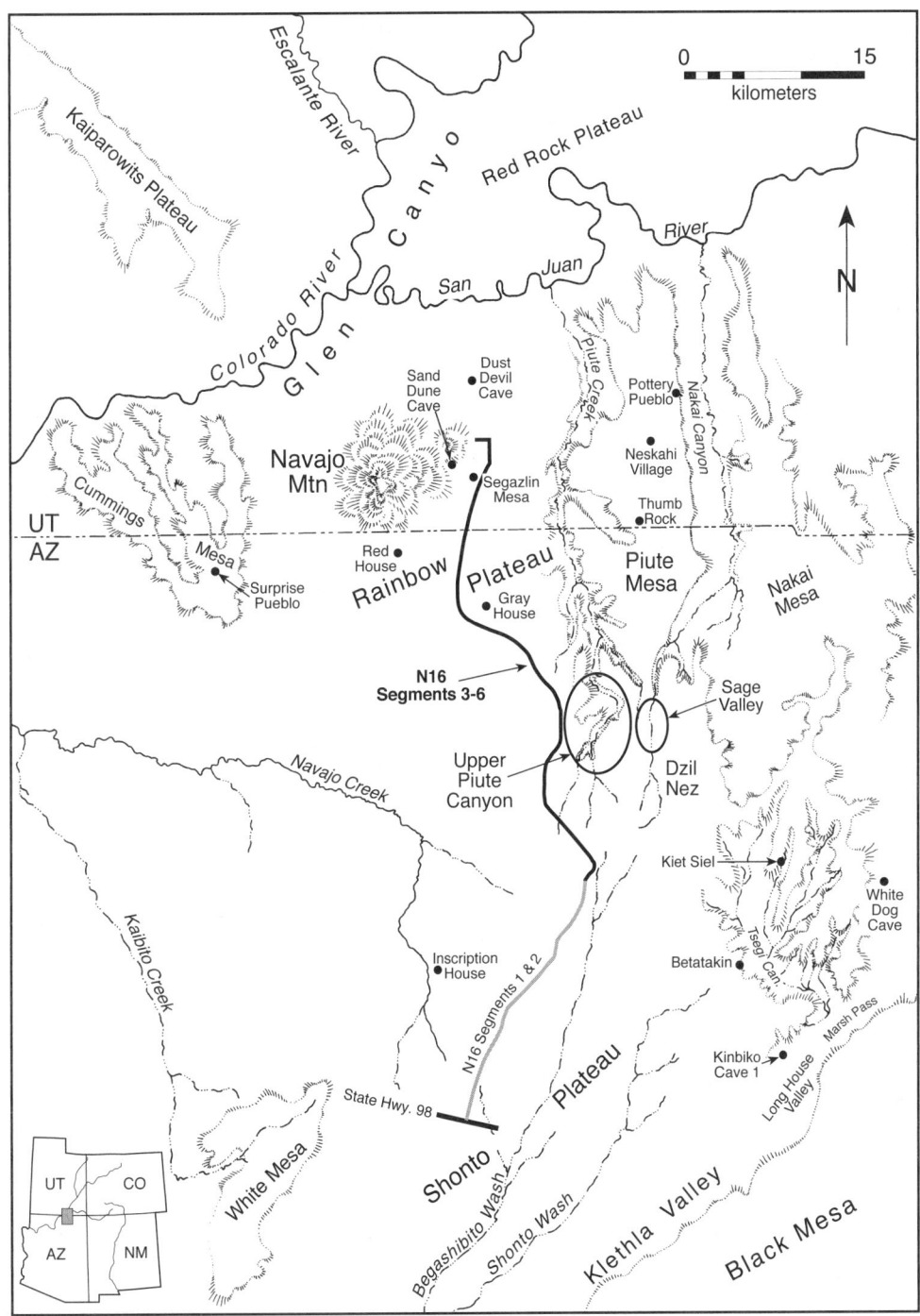

Figure 2.2. Map of the northern Kayenta region and adjoining terrain showing some of the major geographic features, drainages, and significant archaeological sites mentioned in the text. The excavated sites reported herein occur in Segments 3–6 of the Navajo Mountain Road; excavated sites in the southern two segments of this road are reported in Schroedl 1989.

and Cibola regions, including the Upper Little Colorado River. Unlike these other areas, the Kayenta region is characterized by an evident lack of significant population aggregation and settlement hierarchy until the last 50 years of permanent settlement, known as the Tsegi phase, between about AD 1250 and 1300. Missing are Chacoan great houses and aggregated Pueblo I and Pueblo II communities. For centuries the populace occupying the Kayenta region lived in settlements no larger than what could accommodate several households consisting of a large extended family (hamlets or less). Material culture and architecture changed, settlements shifted, and population grew and ebbed, but all of this without any significant alteration of an overall simple-looking social fabric. Yet in the end, despite centuries of comparative social "simplicity," the Kayenta Anasazi ended up forming aggregated communities at the very end of Pueblo III, communities that set the stage for the even more profound change represented by the large fourteenth-century villages established in the Hopi area to the south (Adams 1996).

An understanding of the processes behind the sequence of cultural change and development in the Kayenta region is far from complete. A descriptive outline of prehistoric development in the area has been assembled, but temporal and aerial coverage is still spotty. For example, the coal lease on northern Black Mesa is well known by both survey and excavation, but no comparable coverage is available from the rest of the region except for Long House Valley (Dean et al. 1978). The Tsegi phase, perhaps because of its large and visually impressive masonry pueblos, has received considerable research interest (e.g., Dean 1969, 1970, 2002; Haas and Creamer 1993, 1995; Hobler 1974; Lindsay 1969; Lindsay et al. 1968; Stein 1984), but not so the many centuries leading up to this time of rather abrupt and profound transformation (see Dean 2002). Many basic characteristics of the first farming populations of the region, founders of the Anasazi cultural sequence, remain unresolved, including the time depth, origins, and degree of subsistence specialization. Knowledge is even sketchier further back in antiquity, since the forager trace of the region is not only sparse and obscured but seldom studied.

In this context, I became immediately interested in the proposed paving of the Navajo Mountain road since this undertaking promised to be the next significant opportunity following the BMAP to conduct major excavation in the Kayenta region. Here was an excellent opportunity to greatly expand on what was currently known about the prehistory of the region, because numerous sites lay within the road ROW and excavation would be required at many of them. Cultural resource management (CRM) projects are about the only means to conduct excavation research in the area, and this undertaking promised to be of moderately large scale. The initial phase of this undertaking occurred in the 1980s when P-III Associates excavated about two dozen sites within the southernmost portion of the N16 ROW (Segments 1–2 [Schroedl 1989]). A few years later, in 1991, the BIA Branch of Roads moved forward with plans to realign and pave the remaining portion of the N16 ROW, Segments 3 through 6. These four segments totaled approximately 43 km in length, and scores of prehistoric sites lay within the proposed construction zone. The Navajo Nation Archaeology Department was subcontracted to conduct the investigations, and by happy coincidence I had been hired by NNAD a few years prior, placing me in the fortunate position to direct this project. Having missed the opportunity to excavate in the southern portion of the ROW, I relished the prospect of working within the long stretch that remained, especially since this portion of the road includes some of the most spectacular country on the Navajo Reservation. As it turned out, this undertaking was far more rewarding than I imagined, a conclusion that I trust this report helps document.

Previous Research

Summaries of previous archaeological work in the Kayenta region are available in many reports, so there is no need to reiterate the bulk of this information. Ambler (1985a), Christenson (1983), Adams (1960), Geib and Warburton (1991), Lindsay and Ambler (1963), and Powell et al. (1983), among others, provide relevant details, and the NMRAP research plan (Geib et al. 1993) summarized projects in relatively close proximity to the road ROW.

Truly scientific archaeological research in the Kayenta region began with the excavations of Kidder and Guernsey (1919; Guernsey 1931; Guernsey and Kidder 1921), who concentrated their effort in the Marsh Pass–Kayenta–Monument Valley area and never worked on the Shonto or Rainbow plateaus. Byron Cummings and his students excavated sites at various locations in the Kayenta region including the Rainbow Plateau, but regrettably he failed to publish any findings. Archaeological reconnaissances conducted in the northern Kayenta region during the 1920s and 1930s include the Bernheimer expeditions to the Rainbow Plateau and elsewhere, assisted by Earl Morris (see Adams 1960); Morss's explorations on the Shonto and Rainbow plateaus for the Peabody Museum (Morss 1931); Barrett's reconnaissance in Navajo Canyon for the Milwaukee Public Museum (West 1927); Amsden's quick survey of Upper Piute Canyon for Gila Pueblo (see Fairley 1989); reconnaissance of Upper Piute Canyon and the Rainbow Plateau during the Rainbow Bridge–Monument Valley expedition (Hargrave 1935); the excavation of two Basketmaker II caves northeast of Navajo Mountain during the Van-Bergen Expedition (Geib and

Robins 2003; Hayden 1930; Schilz 1979); and Deric Nusbaum's explorations along Begashibito Wash (Laboratory of Anthropology, Museum of New Mexico, site files). In early 1950 William Adams (1951) conducted a limited tour through the region for Walter Taylor, looking for an ideal cliff dwelling as part of Taylor's Pueblo Ecology Study (summarized in Taylor 1958).

Following the decades of exploration in the early 1900s, interest in the prehistory of the Kayenta region was kept alive in the minds of Southwestern archaeologists by a combination of at least three factors: large CRM projects, seminal dissertation research, and a few high-visibility research projects. The excitement and employment opportunities afforded by several large CRM surveys and excavations played a prominent role, especially the Museum of Northern Arizona's (MNA's) work on the Glen Canyon Project (e.g., Adams and Adams 1959; Adams et al. 1961; Ambler et al. 1964; Lindsay et al. 1968; Long 1966), followed by the Black Mesa–Lake Powell railroad corridor (Stebbins et al. 1986; Swarthout et al. 1986) and then the Black Mesa Archaeological Project, which employed hundreds of student archaeologists over the span of 17 years (Powell and Smiley 2002).

As part of the Glen Canyon Project in the early 1960s, MNA archaeologists excavated numerous sites in three highland settings of the northern Kayenta region: Cummings Mesa (Ambler et al. 1964), the Rainbow Plateau (Lindsay et al. 1968), and Piute Mesa (Hobler 1974; Stein 1984). During this period Stein (1966) conducted additional survey work on Piute and Dzil Nez mesas, and MNA initiated an extensive reconnaissance of the Navajo Canyon system (Miller and Breternitz 1958a, 1958b). In the late 1960s, MNA excavated 51 prehistoric sites for the Black Mesa–Lake Powell railroad corridor, recovering large amounts of information and quantities of artifacts (Stebbins et al. 1986; Swarthout et al. 1986). The findings of this project remain somewhat understudied and poorly integrated with previous research efforts in the region.

The late 1960s witnessed the start of a project that recovered the largest single body of data for the Kayenta region: BMAP (see Powell and Smiley 2002; Powell et al. 1983). Though northern Black Mesa is relatively distant from the N16 ROW, the BMAP data provide valuable comparative material for excavation findings along N16, especially as concerns Basketmaker II. During 17 years of fieldwork (1967–1983), the project surveyed a large block of land on northern Black Mesa, recording 1,671 prehistoric archaeological sites and excavating 188 of these (BMAP also documented 1,039 historic Navajo sites, excavating 27 of them). The project devised its own phase system keyed to ceramic types for the temporal ordering of Puebloan remains.

Significant dissertations resulting from research in the Kayenta region began with Jeffrey Dean (1969, 1970) and Alexander Lindsay (1969) and have important implications for understanding the late Pueblo III period throughout the Kayenta region. Dissertation research expanded considerably because of BMAP (e.g., Ahlstrom 1985; Gilman 1983; Green 1982; Layhe 1981; Leonard 1986; Plog 1980; Powell 1983; Smiley 1985). An intensive survey of Long House Valley (e.g., Dean et al. 1978) is the most notable "pure" research project in the region, with the resulting data used for dissertation research (Effland 1979; Harrill 1982) and most recently for computer simulations (e.g., Axtell et al. 2002; Dean et al. 2000). A project to examine the formative role of warfare in the evolution of Kayenta Anasazi social complexity also stirred some degree of interest and controversy (Haas and Creamer 1993).

The 1980s saw several informative projects in the northern Kayenta region. In 1981, NAU excavated eight sites near Rainbow City on the northeast side of Navajo Mountain (Geib et al. 1985). In conjunction with this undertaking, Ambler and field school students surveyed a several-square-kilometer area adjacent to the excavated sites (Ambler et al. 1985); another of Ambler's field school surveys concentrated on Upper Piute Canyon. The results of this survey (Fairley 1989), begun in 1980 and continuing until 1983, with additional reconnaissance by Helen Fairley and volunteers from 1983 to 1986, provide an interesting point of comparison with NMRAP findings. More recent contributions in the Kayenta region include the excavation of 16 prehistoric sites within the southernmost part of the N16 ROW (Schroedl 1989) and the excavation of 18 Archaic, Basketmaker, and Puebloan sites within the N21 ROW, the road from Red Lake to Kaibito that traverses the eastern edge of the Kaibito Plateau along the western flank of White Mesa (Bungart et al. 2004).

SYNOPSIS OF REGIONAL PREHISTORY

Previous archaeological and ethnohistorical studies in the Kayenta region, several of which have been listed above, allow the broad parameters of the cultural history to be sketched. These broad parameters as they pertain to cultural remains along the N16 road corridor are presented below according to the chronological framework shown in Figure 2.3.

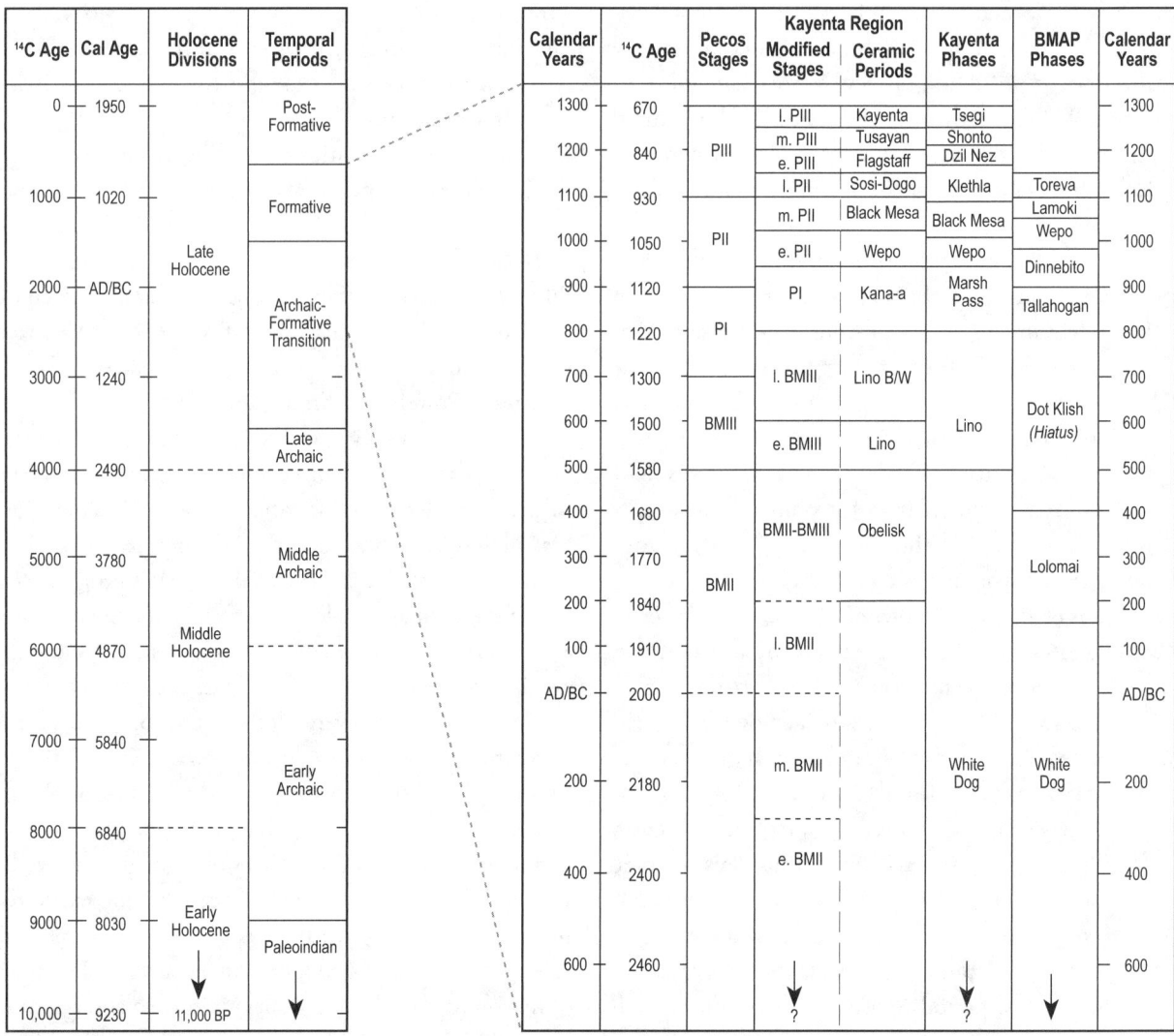

Figure 2.3. General cultural-temporal framework used for this report and by other researchers working in or near the northern Kayenta region including the traditional Pecos stages (Kidder 1927); Kayenta phases are from Ambler 1985a, 1985b, as modified from Colton 1939; Black Mesa Archaeological Project phases are from Powell and Smiley 2002, as modified from Gumerman et al. 1972.

Paleoindian

The first Native American occupation of the study area probably occurred during the Paleoindian period at the Pleistocene–Holocene boundary (ca. 11,500 BP to 9000 BP). The term *Paleoindian* is often used to mean both a lifeway and a time period. As a lifeway, Paleoindians have traditionally been defined as big-game hunters with distinctive projectile points and large-mammal associations. The extent to which plants supplemented the diet is uncertain because this early time period is mostly known from kill sites rather than base camps and also because of poor botanical preservation. Paleoindians likely lived in small nomadic family groups, traveling often in search of game or other food. On the Colorado Plateau, a Paleoindian lifeway probably did not persist much past 10,000 BP, and by around 9000 BP inhabitants evidently followed an Archaic pattern of fairly broad-spectrum foraging (Geib 1996a; see also Schroedl 1991).

Clovis and Folsom are two cultural complexes of the early Paleoindian period distinguished by point style, technology, and associated fauna: Clovis with mammoth and Folsom with an extinct form of bison. Midland points are contemporaneous and often associated with Folsom; Goshen and Plainview points can also date this early. Most other Paleoindian points postdate Folsom (Frison and Bradley 1980; Irwin-Williams et al. 1973). The late Paleoindian period is characterized by a number of different point styles, each with a somewhat different temporal and geographic distribution. Constricted-base and shouldered points such as Alberta, and those of the Cody complex, clearly postdate Folsom (Frison 1978). The radiocarbon dates for most of the Paleoindian complexes are from sites hundreds of miles from the N16 corridor, so their applicability to the study area remains to be demonstrated.

Few Paleoindian sites have been documented on the Colorado Plateau. Good examples somewhat near the N16 study area include two early sites in Utah (Davis 1985, 1989) and a late Paleoindian site surface collected by the MNA in the 1970s (Hesse et al. 1996, 1999). The latter site, which lies about 5 km south of the intersection of N16 with Arizona State Highway 98, provides the best evidence for Paleoindian occupation close to the project area. A variety of late Paleoindian projectile point types are known from surface collections in the Tuba City area.

The NMRAP excavations recovered a few hints of Paleoindian presence in the northern Kayenta region but always from later-age sites. At a late Pueblo III site on the Rainbow Plateau (Sapo Seco, AZ-J-2-6), NNAD archaeologists recovered a late Paleoindian lanceolate point with a concave base that resembles a Plainview (see Figure 4.22). A buried hearth stratigraphically below the Puebloan component and containing pressure flakes initially looked like a possible candidate to be associated with the point (SD vol. 3, chap. 12). The charcoal date on this feature of 8230 ± 50 BP seems far too recent for the point style, and none of the pressure flakes could be refit to the projectile. This point might be evidence for sporadic Paleoindian use of the Rainbow Plateau, or perhaps the Puebloan occupants of Sapo Seco collected it from elsewhere.

Another interesting find is a Folsom channel flake from the surface of a late Archaic site (Tsé Haaľá) at the foot of Navajo Mountain (SD vol. 2, chap. 16). The channel flake was of a distinctive yellow chert unique to the site assemblage. The flake, which retained a portion of the isolated platform, had been retouched on part of the ventral surface, but obvious or interpretable use-wear traces were lacking at 60× magnification. It is unlikely that a Folsom component is present at this site; indeed, the channel flake may have been collected from elsewhere by the Archaic occupants. Nonetheless, this intriguing find is another hint of a sparse Paleoindian presence in the area.

Also at the foot of Navajo Mountain from the fill of a Pueblo III structure came an end and side scraper of Chuska (Narbona Pass) chert (SD vol. 4, Figure 10.19).

This tool is made from an early-stage biface thinning flake with a heavily ground platform. The tool is patinated but shows recent flake scaring intruding the patina near the original flake platform and recent use-wear along the distal margin on the ventral side, which clearly indicates the reuse/scavenging of an earlier tool. Although not definitively a Paleoindian scraper, the patina and overall morphology of this tool make this a possibility, as does the exotic raw material, which was favored by Folsom hunters (e.g., LeTourneau 2000) and widely circulated by them.

The relationship between Archaic foragers and Paleoindians remains unknown, as does whether or not there was an occupational hiatus between the periods. For the Arroyo Cuervo region of New Mexico, Irwin-Williams is unequivocal: "The tool assemblage of these earliest Archaic cultures [Jay] differs so greatly in technology, typology and functional classes from those of the preceding Cody and other Paleo-Indian phases, that there is evidently no generic connection between them" (1973:4–5). She (1979:33, 35) subsequently extended this interpretation to the entire northern Southwest, but whether this is the case across the entire Colorado Plateau remains to be demonstrated. Irwin-Williams (1994:630–631) claimed that at the Dunas Altas site she found Jay phase materials stratigraphically above Cody (but cf. Chapin 2005) and that in addition to differences in points, there were distinctions in other artifact forms, raw materials, production technology, and the proportion of curated artifacts. Some archaeologists have considered the Jay phase of the Oshara tradition as Paleoindian (Judge 1982; Wait 1981), while others see it as Archaic, including Irwin-Williams (1973); such disagreement might point to a true transitional interval (cf. Irwin-Williams 1994:630–633). Pitblado (1994) extended Frison's (1992) Foothill–Mountain complex to southwestern Colorado, arguing that the late Paleoindian groups of this tradition were less focused on big-game hunting and instead had more generalist subsistence practices. For the northern Colorado Plateau, Schroedl (1991:11) tentatively hypothesized that a Paleoindian lifeway may have persisted at the higher elevations of Utah while an Archaic lifeway developed in the lower-elevation Canyonlands Section (cf. Reed and Metcalf 1999:68). Recent excavations at North Creek Shelter along the Upper Escalante River in southeast Utah have uncovered an early Holocene assemblage (ca. 9600–8600 cal. BC) with a distinctive set of Archaic-like stemmed points but no grinding tools that may well represent a transitional or Paleoarchaic occupation fairly close to the N16 project area (http://anthropology.byu.edu/Main%20Menu/Faculty%20Research/North%20Creek/NorthCreek1.htm).

Archaic

The term *Archaic* has both chronological and "developmental" implications, ones that seem inextricable even though this can create conceptual confusion (Cordell 1997:102–105). Archaeologists have defined the Archaic period as an extended interval of time from the end of the early Holocene to the late Holocene when most human groups had socioeconomic adaptations of fairly broad-spectrum hunting and gathering (Byers 1959; Willey and Phillips 1958). Archaic lifeways are thought to have developed in response to postglacial environmental change and the extinction of the Pleistocene megafauna. These generalist adaptations followed what are thought to have been more focal (Cleland 1966:42–45) Paleoindian hunting economies during the early Holocene and late Pleistocene. No doubt, some Paleoindian economies were more generalist (less focal) than archaeologists commonly supposed just a few decades ago. As Bruce Huckell phrases it, "The adaptive gulf between the two periods [Archaic and Paleoindian] is not so wide nor deep as we might think" (1996:306). Indeed, mobile foraging may have always been the way of life in the Great Basin; hence Jones and Beck (1999) use the term *Paleoarchaic* to refer to the terminal Pleistocene–early Holocene archaeological record. In an attempt to avoid conflating chronology with developmental criteria some researchers use a strictly chronological definition for the Archaic (e.g., Lipe and Pitblado 1999:97, 105). I agree that aspects of lifeway should be based on analysis rather than assumed by simple categorical assignment, yet even when labeled as a chronological period rather than a stage, connotations of lifeway are unavoidable when the term *Archaic* is employed.

If we conceive of the Archaic as a socioeconomic adaptation of broad-spectrum gathering and hunting, then what are the earliest traces for this on the Colorado Plateau? One piece of evidence for the presumed adaptive shift is the appearance of, or vast increase in the abundance of, seed-grinding tools. One-hand manos and grinding slabs are key markers of the Archaic because of their durability in the archaeological record; they are ubiquitous finds at temporary residential camps dating to this period. Another change in the record is evident with projectile points: not only do point styles differ, but also there is a general decline in workmanship associated with the Archaic period (at least in the Southwest). Many Archaic points are crudely shaped (perhaps expediently shaped is a better phrase), and none show the degree of control over the biface reduction process, both percussion thinning and pressure flaking, that Paleoindian points demonstrate. The dietary hallmarks of an Archaic adaptation—generalist subsistence remains like seeds and cactus pads—are subject to preservation and recovery biases but are well represented at many of the dry shelters of the region (e.g., Coulam 1988; Van Ness and Hansen 1996). Establishing when such remains first appear in the archaeological record of given areas is essential for understanding the processes involved in the development of an Archaic lifeway.

Evidence to date indicates that Archaic foragers occupied portions of the Colorado Plateau by at least 8000 cal. BC or shortly thereafter. The earliest reliable dates (those not subject to age overestimation) are two between 8,800 and 8,900 years ago on yucca leaves from Walters and Dust Devil caves, located in the heart of this vast region (Ambler 1996:Table 1; Jennings 1980:Table 3). The remains in apparent association with these dates are the archetypal residues of Archaic foragers, consisting of low-rank small seeds of diverse plants and small game (rabbits and rodents) and the technology for processing those resources, most notably numerous grinding slabs and manos. The 8000 cal. BC age estimate is in close accord with that provided by Rhode et al. (2006) for the eastern Great Basin. Based on three convincing lines of evidence, including the direct dating of human feces and pickleweed chaff from Danger Cave, they argue that an Archaic-like emphasis on small seed procurement was not established at that site until after 8700 BP. This finding can be generalized to the entire eastern Great Basin, since Danger Cave is the standard-bearer for an Archaic adaptation during the terminal Pleistocene–early Holocene.

The earliest direct date on Archaic remains for the N16 project area is 8830 ± 160 BP (Ambler 1996:Table 7), from Dust Devil Cave on the northern edge of the Rainbow Plateau. This assay is on yucca leaves lining a small storage pit (Feature 17) emanating from the bottom of Stratum IV within the cave. The calibrated two-sigma range for this date is 8300–7550 BC. There is an 8730 ± 110 BP date (Ambler 1996:Table 7) on charcoal from a hearth also originating from the bottom of Stratum IV, but the sample could overestimate the age to an unknown degree. Stratum IV of Dust Devil Cave contained abundant grinding tools, both metates (grinding slabs) and manos (Geib 1984), providing evidence for the intensive processing of low-return small seeds. The fecal specimens from Stratum IV reveal heavy reliance on such seeds, most notably dropseed (*Sporobolus* sp.), goosefoot (*Chenopodium* sp.), and sunflower (*Helianthus* sp.), along with prickly pear pads (*Opuntia* sp. [Reinhard et al. 1985; Van Ness 1986]). Bone in the feces as well as the deposits of the site indicate a focus on small game, especially cottontail (see summary in Van Ness and Hansen 1996:117–119).

Cultural-Temporal Schemes

Various researchers have devised schemes for organizing temporal and spatial variability in the material remains of foragers during the many thousands of years of the Archaic period, none of which is applicable to the entire Colorado Plateau as a whole. Despite the probable high residential mobility of Archaic foragers coupled with fluid sociality and common interaction across large areas, the plateau is not a unified region in terms of Archaic prehistory. The point styles of Irwin-Williams's (1973) Oshara tradition are widely distributed across the southern Colorado Plateau (SCP), and her phase system is commonly used by researchers working in this area, especially for the San Juan Basin. Yet the excavation of several key caves and shelters on the northern Colorado Plateau (NCP), generally north of the Colorado River, revealed distinctive projectile point styles and other traits, suggesting that the Oshara sequence has limited applicability in this area, leading Schroedl (1976) to devise an Archaic phase system for the NCP.

Continued research has only added to the impression that forager remains on northern and southern portions of the plateau contrast in several basic aspects. Geographical placement of a dividing line for this north and south distinction is somewhat arbitrary, but the line shown in Figure 1 of Geib 2000 best accords with current knowledge. This line of separation essentially groups the Canyonlands, Grand Canyon, High Plateaus, and Uinta sections as part of the NCP, with the Navajo Section and Datil-Mogollon sections as part of the SCP. Projectile points provide a principal basis for making a north–south distinction. The point sequence on the NCP as described by Holmer (1978, 1986) is markedly different from the point sequence for the SCP as represented by the Oshara tradition of the San Juan Basin (Irwin-Williams 1973, 1979). On the NCP, long-stemmed points (resembling Jay or Bajada) are poorly represented, and there is an early preference for side- or corner-notched points beginning by about 6600 cal. BC. On the SCP, stemmed points persist throughout much of the Archaic sequence from at least 8000 cal. BC until about 2500 cal. BC, and notched points are not common occurrences until after 2500 cal. BC. Sandals provide another point of contrast (Geib 2000), as do other perishables, such as split-twig figurines (Coulam and Schroedl 2004).

There is always the need for temporal order, and it is likely that spatially restricted phase systems (those based on isolative analysis [Irwin-Williams 1967]) are more likely to accurately characterize a given area than panregional ones. But there is an inherent risk of assuming that culture-historical constructs "actually reflect bounded, coherent, prehistoric groups or populations" (Wills 1988: 29). Unwarranted speculations can result, such as when projectile points do not match a given phase (see discussion in Berry and Berry 1986:279). To move discussion away from organizational constructs toward trying to understand how temporal and spatial variability informs about the processes of behavioral change it might be more informative to examine variability in all aspects of the Archaic lifeway outside of the normative assumption of phases and traditions or complexes. Providing temporal order independent of cultural content is especially useful but unfortunately is often impossible. Temporal placement based on artifact types such as Pinto points or open-twined sandals is still useful, but it carries no necessary information about social relatedness (cultural identity). Hunting with a Bajada point does not make one an Oshara tradition forager (Irwin-Williams 1973) any more than wearing an open-twined sandal makes one a Desha complex forager (Ambler 1996). Moreover, such spatial-temporal constructs lack utility when it comes to the analysis of long-term cultural change.

The Oshara Sequence. Cynthia Irwin-Williams (1973, 1979) devised the Oshara tradition based on field research between 1964 and 1969 in the Arroyo Cuervo region of northwestern New Mexico, including the excavation of at least 12 Archaic sites and the testing of other sites. The Oshara sequence included five sequential preceramic phases spanning the period from about 5500 BC to AD 400 (uncalibrated), culminating in "the formation of the central core of the relatively well-known sedentary Anasazi (Pueblo) culture" (Irwin-Williams 1979:35). There is no reason to reiterate the details of this well-known sequence, but a few issues are worth considering.

Irwin-Williams's research significantly influenced CRM work on the southern Colorado Plateau, especially within the San Juan Basin of New Mexico. Publication of the Oshara tradition in 1973 coincided with the first of many large survey and excavation projects in the San Juan Basin (the Coal Gasification Project [Reher 1977]) that made use of the Arroyo Cuervo sequence to assign chronological order to preceramic remains. Most of the dart points in the basin resembled those illustrated by Irwin-Williams, so it was a natural extension of her scheme (but see Stuart and Gauthier 1981:407). The point styles that she identified for each Oshara phase have taken on lives of their own as types, even though she did not formally name them as such. Subsequent analyses have generally verified that the point styles of the first four Oshara phases (Jay, Bajada, San Jose, and Armijo) are discrete, easily identified types of temporal utility (e.g., Moore 1994; cf. Berry 1987; Chapin 2005). Figure 2.4 illustrates examples of these projectile points according to the temporal sequence as originally proposed for the Arroyo Cuervo area; these specimens are from around the Tuba City area on the southern part of the Kaibito Plateau and the northern part of the Moenkopi Plateau. The points in this figure serve to exemplify that Oshara-like points are common to the southern portion of the Kayenta region, where point types common to the NCP are also abundantly represented. Similar projectile points are widely distributed across portions of the Colorado Plateau, especially the San Juan Basin, Rio Grande Valley, and the drainage area of the Little Colorado River. Because of this, the Oshara sequence has been commonly used to place Archaic remains within a temporal framework. Whether her phase dates apply to points found well outside the Arroyo Cuervo region remains to be adequately demonstrated. There are some indications that caution is needed, such as the dates of 8260 and 8000 BP potentially associated with Bajada and San Jose points at the Hastqin site in Arizona (Huckell 1977) and the dates of 8080 and 7810 BP associated with stemmed points identified as Bajada and San Jose at site AZ D:11:3036 on Black Mesa (Lebo and MacMinn 1984; Parry et al. 1994:Figure 9). In both cases the dates are much older than the 6800–5200 BP temporal span assigned to the Bajada phase or the 5200–3800 BP span of the subsequent San Jose phase (Irwin-Williams 1973).

Bajada points are common to northwestern New Mexico and into Arizona along the Little Colorado River (Berry 1984:62; Diggs 1982) westward to the Flagstaff area. Examples of Bajada points occur in the Kayenta region, as illustrated in Figure 2.4, particularly in the grassland environments, such as along the Lower Moenkopi Wash and tributaries or along the Lower Chinle Wash and Laguna Creek. The long stems on Bajada points serve to differentiate them from Pinto points on the NCP and in the eastern Great Basin, as illustrated in reports such as those from Sudden Shelter (Jennings et al. 1980) and Hogup Cave (Aikens 1970) or as described and illustrated by Holmer (1978, 1986). Real confusion comes with the point style for the San Jose phase. San Jose points are difficult to separate from Pinto points—that is, points classified as Pinto on the northern Colorado Plateau could be lost in assemblages of points classified as San Jose from the San Juan Basin, and vice versa (see Matson 1991:158–159). Unfortunately this is not simply an unimportant semantic argument because of the vastly different temporal spans given to Pinto and San Jose points: the former are considered early Archaic (ca. >6500 BP [e.g., Holmer 1980, 1986]), and the latter, middle Archaic (ca. <5200 BP [Irwin-Williams 1973]). Two dated San Jose sites in the San Juan Basin appear to support a middle Archaic age (ca. 5900–4000 BP) for San Jose points (Del Bene and Ford 1982:653–711, 713–778); Simmons (1982, 1986:76–79) has reported San Jose points from sites dating to the late Archaic (ca. 4000–3600 BP). It is possible that two closely similar, and often indistinguishable, point styles have considerably different temporal spans.

This age discrepancy comes to a head at intermediate places like the Kayenta region, which lies between the San Juan Basin and the northern Colorado Plateau/eastern Great Basin. A site like AZ D:11:203 on Black Mesa, with its two stemmed points (Parry and Christenson 1987:301, Plate 5a–b), well illustrates the problem. I would classify one of these (Plate 5b) as Pinto, but it might also be identified as San Jose, a possibility that both Parry et al. (1994:214) and Christenson (1987a:170) mention. If it is San Jose, then a temporal span of roughly 5200–3800 BP would be anticipated, but the radiocarbon dates on wood charcoal from two hearths are 8080 and 7810 BP (Lebo and MacMinn 1984:341; Parry et al. 1994:Table 1); these ages are in good agreement with points classified as Pinto on the NCP (Holmer 1978, 1986). The other projectile point from this site was identified by Christenson (1987a:168) as a possible Bajada point, something that Irwin-Williams (1994:602) disputed. This designation seems more appropriate than any other, but even then the dating is still wrong because the Bajada phase is roughly 6800–5200 BP. So, if we type the points in Figure 2.4 according to the Oshara tradition, which seems typologically sound, do we automatically use the temporal spans given for Oshara phases? Or, alternatively, do we assume that they are

Background for the Navajo Mountain Road Archaeological Project   31

Figure 2.4. Examples of Oshara tradition points from the southern Kaibito Plateau around Tuba City, Arizona.

roughly 2,000 years too recent, as the admittedly scant information currently suggests? Obviously a considerable amount of new excavation and dating will be required to resolve this issue to anyone's satisfaction.

The last two phases of the Oshara sequence are believed to represent the slow transition to an agricultural economy. Berry (1982:25–27) has criticized Irwin-Williams's (1973:9) position that cultigens were introduced to the Colorado Plateau during the Armijo phase (ca. 1800–800 BC) of the Oshara sequence, but there is now convincing evidence for cultigen use as early as ca. 2100 cal. BC for the Fence Lake area of New Mexico

(Huber 2005). Thus, it appears that agriculture first appeared on portions of the Colorado Plateau in the Armijo phase, as Irwin-Williams suggested. According to Hogan, "The introduction of cultigens does not appear to have caused any immediate, marked changes in settlement or subsistence strategies" (1994:172). This view accords with Irwin-Williams's (1973) notion that agriculture was initially of very limited importance to Archaic populations (cf. Berry 1982). The jury is still out about the dietary significance of maize during the initial millennia of its use, so claims one way or the other must be taken as hypotheses. Implicated in this issue is the traditional assumption that domesticates were taken up by resident hunter-gatherers in an autochthonous process. Since preceramic groups already dependent upon farming may have migrated to the Colorado Plateau, there could be different processes at work, and our conceptual frameworks should be capable of dealing with such variability.

Northern Colorado Plateau. In the mid-1970s, Jesse Jennings and students undertook the excavation of Sudden Shelter and Cowboy Cave, the two sites that have become principal reference points for reconstructions of Archaic culture history on the northern Colorado Plateau. Their importance stems partly from the sheer volume of recovered remains, which span most of the Archaic period, but also from the timely publishing of results, with reports for both sites appearing in 1980 (Jennings 1980; Jennings et al. 1980). Both sites were key in two doctoral dissertations (Holmer 1978; Schroedl 1976) that became widely used by researchers on the NCP, especially those working on large CRM surveys (e.g., Black et al. 1982; Christensen et al. 1983; Geib and Bremer 1988; Hauck 1979a, 1979b; Kearns 1982; Tipps 1988). Holmer's (1978) study of projectile points established a typology and chronology that have proven invaluable for identifying Archaic sites during survey and placing them within intervals of a few thousand years. Holmer (1986) has since slightly revised the typological system, and others have proposed additional types (e.g., Tipps 1988). Schroedl's (1976) synthetic overview of the Archaic period for the NCP included four proposed phases. Berry and Berry (1986:307–310) criticized this framework (also Gooding and Shields 1985), but others have used the phases. Nonetheless, many archaeologists working on the NCP favor Holmer's more neutral terms of *early*, *middle*, and *late* for subdividing the Archaic period. Indeed, these terms are now widely used throughout the Southwest, although they have slightly different starting and ending points, diagnostics, and meanings from one region to another (e.g., cf. Geib 1996a and Matson 1991 with Huckell 1996).

Schroedl (1976) called attention to evident differences between the Archaic archaeological records of the northern Colorado Plateau and the southern Colorado Plateau as represented by the Oshara tradition. This is most clearly seen in the projectile points. As one moves westward toward the Grand Canyon Section and northward toward the Canyonlands Section, various notched points become the predominant types during most of the documented long Archaic period. Long-stemmed points resembling Jay or Bajada occur on the NCP but are far less common than on the SCP, and none have been recovered from the Archaic layers of such sites as Sudden Shelter (Jennings et al. 1980), Joe's Valley Alcove (Barlow and Metcalfe 1993; DeBloois et al. 1979), Cowboy Cave (Jennings 1980; Schroedl and Coulam 1994), Dust Devil Cave (Ambler 1996; Geib 1984), and Old Man Cave (Geib and Davidson 1994). Various notched forms rather than stemmed ones are the common dart points throughout the Archaic sequence on the NCP, until the contracting-stem Gypsum (Gatecliff) points of the late Archaic; the latter are not a widely recognized part of the Oshara tradition.

This is not to suggest that point types common on the northern Colorado Plateau do not occur on the southern Colorado Plateau, or vice versa, because they do. As early as the late 1950s when Alice Hunt was scouring the Green River Desert, she documented examples of long-stemmed points that most researchers today would classify as Bajada and Jay (or Lake Mohave). In like fashion, point types common to the NCP occur on the SCP. Hogan (1996), for example, discusses the occurrence and dating of high side-notched points in the San Juan Basin that are virtually identical to the Sudden and San Rafael Side-notched points common to the NCP. Nonetheless, the projectile points recovered from excavated shelters of the NCP have nothing in common with the Oshara sequence. Likewise, regional surveys in Utah consistently reveal abundant projectile points that match NCP types but few if any that could be classified as Oshara types (Geib et al. 2001; Hauck 1979a, 1979b; Kearns 1982; Tipps 1988).

Schroedl (1976:57–73) delineated four phases (Black Knoll, Castle Valley, Green River, and Dirty Devil) based on cultural variation, primarily projectile points but including some perishable artifacts, as well as information on subsistence, a tabulation of radiocarbon dates (a proxy population measure), and other data. All in all, the sequence was far better substantiated than the Oshara tradition, especially after the 1980 publication of the descriptive reports for both Sudden Shelter and Cowboy Cave. A few authors have criticized the phases, most notably Berry and Berry, who characterize the scheme as "a typical case of phase-stacking to achieve the illusion of continuity" (1986:309). Schroedl (1992) addressed the Berry and Berry critique and subsequently modified the system somewhat, adding a fifth phase (Escalante) at the end of the sequence to accommodate the transitional interval after the introduction of corn but prior to the addition of pottery. Schroedl and Coulam (1994) presented a synopsis of the phases during their reevaluation of Cowboy Cave; their graphic summary is shown in Figure 2.5.

The Desha Complex. In the early 1960s, J. Richard Ambler defined the Desha complex based on excavations at Sand Dune and Dust Devil caves on the northern part of the Rainbow Plateau. The 1961 excavation of Sand Dune Cave produced sandals radiocarbon dated from 7000 to 8000 BP (Lindsay et al. 1968), providing the first solid evidence for Archaic foragers near the northern end of the N16 ROW. The Desha complex was originally characterized as having an artifact inventory that included open-twined sandals, warp-faced plain-weave sandals, elongate and shallowly side-notched projectile points, one-rod basketry, twined grass matting, worked bobcat scapulae, worked mountain sheep hyoids, and shallow-basin grinding slabs (Lindsay et al. 1968:120–121). Closest affinities were seen with the Great Basin, although no specific parallels could be found with assemblages at that time. Since then, Ambler (1996) tried to restrict the defining characteristics of the Desha complex, eliminating the warp-faced plain-weave sandals; he has also added two additional Archaic complexes. The value of the findings from these two caves is diverted by the discussion of complexes because it ends in unsatisfactory debates over what is and is not part of arbitrary archaeological constructs and no light is shed on prehistory or the processes of behavioral and cultural change. Both caves were sporadically and at times intensively used by Archaic foragers who deposited a variety of remains therein, including various types of sandals and points, all of which have much to say about past lifeways. One major contribution was the analysis of 97 human feces recovered from the early Archaic Stratum IV of Dust Devil Cave (Van Ness 1986; Van Ness and Hansen 1996).

General Temporal Divisions
In lieu of using phase systems, many researchers have opted for temporal designations with fewer implications about cultural content or other aspects of prehistoric lifeway. A tripartite division of the Archaic into early, middle, and late is commonly used throughout the Southwest (e.g., Geib 1996a; Huckell 1996; Matson 1991). Because the temporal parameters for these divisions vary slightly between authors or regions, given projectile points or other temporal diagnostics might be included in different subdivisions. For example, Huckell (1996:338–339) assigned Northern Side-notched and Gypsum points to his middle Archaic (ca. 5500–3500 BP), but most authors working on the northern Colorado Plateau would assign the former to the early Archaic (prior to 6000 BP) and the latter to the late Archaic (after about 4000 BP). This follows from Holmer's (1978) suggested tripart division of the Archaic period and the common projectile point types that he saw as characteristic of each subperiod. In the best of cases, chronometric dates allow the independent temporal analysis of each aspect of culture or variable of interest.

The Archaic temporal sequence used in this report is illustrated in Figure 2.6 along with the chief diagnostic artifacts, both projectile points and perishables. It should be realized that the lines of separation between the early, middle, and late subdivisions are not hard and fast, and different researchers may place them at slightly different positions. At least part of the basis for placing the temporal divisions in the approximate positions shown in Figure 2.6 derives from the frequency distribution of radiocarbon dates and the abandonment of several shelters.

The early Archaic starts at about 8000 cal. BC, as evidenced by the Dust Devil sequence (Ambler 1996). The early Archaic ends at 5600–5000 cal. BC, when both Cowboy and Dust Devil caves were abandoned. At this time an essentially sterile layer of dune sand started to accumulate within their confines. Projectile points common to the early Archaic consist of Elko Corner/Side-notched, Northern Side-notched, and Pinto series. Elko Corner/Side-notched is a common early Archaic point type from many stratified shelters/caves, but much to the frustration of archaeologists, these points are common throughout the entire Archaic period, so are poor temporal diagnostics (Holmer 1978, 1986). Because of this type's long duration of use, many early Archaic sites might go unrecognized. Perhaps the most distinctive artifacts of the early Archaic are sandals; open-twined and warp-faced (or plain-weave) varieties have been found in the early Archaic strata of Sand Dune, Dust Devil, and Cowboy caves (Ambler 1996; Hewitt 1980; Lindsay et al. 1968) and elsewhere in the Glen Canyon region (Geib 1996b, 2000).

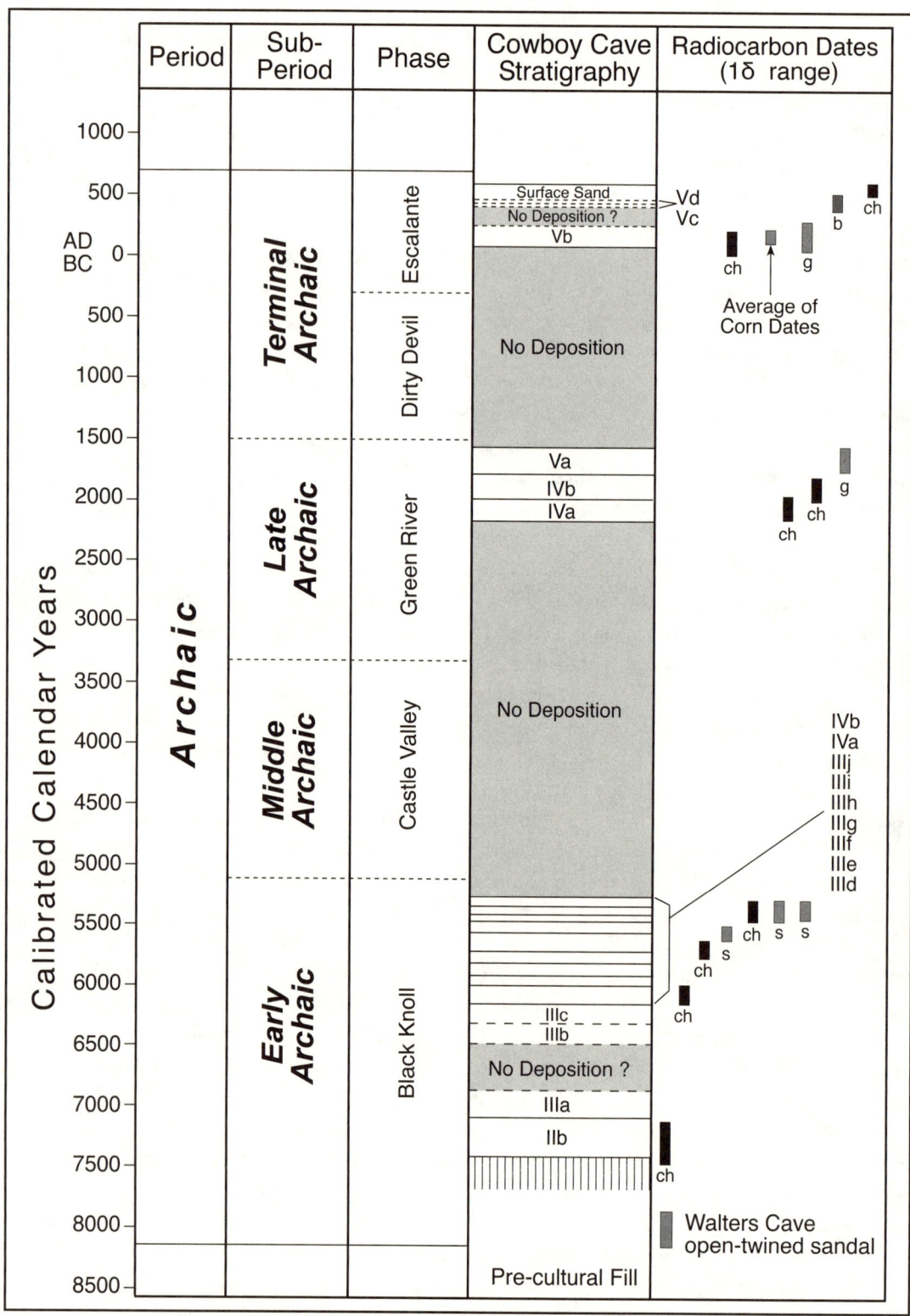

Figure 2.5. Cowboy Cave depositional units and radiocarbon dates in relation to chronological divisions for the northern Colorado Plateau (modified from Schroedl and Coulam 1994).

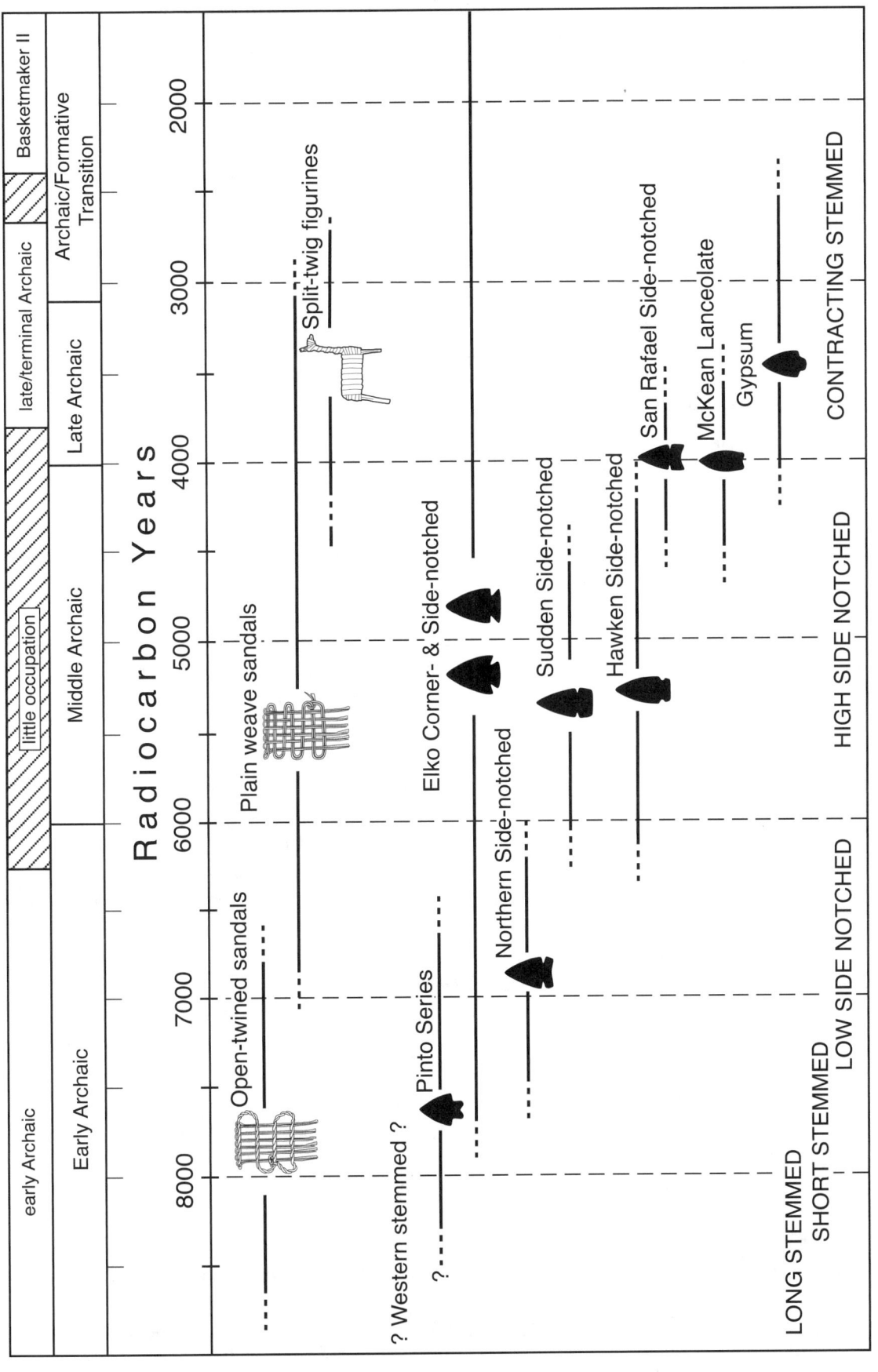

Figure 2.6. Actual intervals of Archaic period forager occupation for the N16 project area (top) relative to the general chronological framework and chief cultural-temporal diagnostics for the northern Colorado Plateau; the latter are based on excavations at various sites including those on the Rainbow Plateau.

The middle Archaic period corresponds with an apparent ca. 1,000-year gap in the radiocarbon record for the Colorado Plateau, highlighted first by Schroedl (1976: 24–25, Figure 4) and then by Berry and Berry (1986:309, Figure 14). This period corresponds with the interval when sterile eolian sand was deposited in Cowboy and Dust Devil caves. A few dates now partially fill the 1,000-year gap in the radiocarbon record (see Geib 1996a), but a population decline seems credible, with perhaps a restriction of populations to well-watered areas. The middle Archaic is characterized chiefly by high side-notched points such as Sudden and San Rafael Side-notched, the latter appearing toward the end of the middle Archaic and extending into the late Archaic.

The late Archaic has different meanings depending on the researcher and which portion of the Southwest is under discussion. Moreover, the current evidence for when maize was introduced to portions of the Colorado Plateau and the Southwest generally has greatly complicated the status of the late Archaic as a cultural-temporal designation. On the northern Colorado Plateau the late Archaic is usually recognized as that interval of the late Holocene prior to the introduction of Mesoamerican domesticates or pottery; maize on the NCP is currently no older than about the time of Christ. On the southern Colorado Plateau the late Archaic can include or not the interval when domesticates were initially used, which is now placed at around 2100 cal. BC. For example, Smiley (2002a) uses the arrival of maize on northern Black Mesa (the 3610 ± 170 BP maize date from Three Fir Shelter, Beta-26275 [Smiley 1994:Table 1]) as marking the end of the Archaic and the beginning of Basketmaker II, which he estimates may start as early as 4000 cal. BP. Because of this temporal revision, he reassigned the previously identified late Archaic (Hisatsinom phase) sites on Black Mesa—those lacking agriculture—as part of the White Dog phase of Basketmaker II. More will be said about this below, but note that designating all remains within a given temporal interval as Basketmaker II whether or not domesticates are present could obscure adaptive variability and conceal different trajectories leading to a Formative adaptation. The NMRAP excavations seem to have uncovered a good example of this because a late Archaic adaptation apparently persisted until around 800 cal. BC on the Rainbow Plateau. As reported in chapters 4 and 5 of this report (also Geib and Spurr 2000, 2002), maize on the Rainbow Plateau is no older than about 400 cal. BC.

The chief temporal diagnostics of the late Archaic on the NCP are the contracting-stem Gypsum point (Gatecliff), after about 2500 cal. BC, and split-twig figurines; both are widely distributed from southeastern Utah through northern Arizona into the southern Great Basin (Coulam and Schroedl 2004; Schroedl 1977). Gypsum points appear to be rare occurrences in the Kayenta region except close to the canyons of the Colorado River and are not widely recognized in assemblages from the SCP. Gypsum points could end prior to the introduction of agriculture into the region, as suggested by Berry and Berry (1986:309–310), but this issue remains unsettled (e.g., Eccles and Walling-Frank [1998:10.25] reported Gypsum points from a Basketmaker II site near Colorado City). On the Rainbow Plateau the terminal Archaic sites that date to around 1000 cal. BC and shortly thereafter contain Elko Corner-notched points but not Gypsum points (see chapter 4).

Archaic–Formative Transition

How we conceive of the end of the Archaic and the definitions used for denoting this are controversial, and the terms archaeologists create to discuss their subject matter often impede the exchange of ideas. Some archaeologists use the appearance of pottery to mark the end of the Archaic (e.g., Wills 1995:215), long after farming had become well established across much of the Colorado Plateau, but others use the initial appearance of domesticates (e.g., B. Huckell 1995:15–16, 117–118; Smiley 2002a, 2002b). Someone once quipped in a review that "Archaic farmers is an oxymoron." This highlights a deep divide in opinions on the issue. Pottery might be seen as a useful trait for ending the Archaic period because it is far more visible in the archaeological record than cultigens and is thought by some to mark a substantial increase in reliance on cultigens (e.g., Crown and Wills 1995). Well before pottery, however, agriculture evidently brought about significant changes in local economies, social organization, and other aspects of prehistoric lifeways (see reviews in Huckell 1996; Mabry 1998, 2005; Matson 1991).

Disagreements about when the Archaic ends also partly relate to one's conception of whether the agricultural transition was autochthonous or allochthonous (especially Berry 1982:31–33 vs. Wills 1988:150, 1995:217) and to what extent the changes wrought by the addition of cultigens were slow and minor (accretional) or sudden and far reaching (especially Minnis 1985, 1992, vs. Wills 1988 and Wills and Huckell 1994). Ending the Archaic with the appearance of domesticates follows Jennings's (1956, 1957) conception of the Archaic (the Desert culture) as lacking agriculture. Yet in Mesoamerica the Archaic period includes domesticates and a lengthy period of experimentation with food production, with domesticated squash first appearing during the early Archaic (Smith 1997). The same is true for the eastern United States, where the Archaic period encompasses a long interval of increasing human intervention in the life cycles of plants, ending in the domestication of several local species between 4,000 and 3,000 rcybp (Smith 1992). Southwestern Archaic foragers may have manipulated their environments to obtain greater yields of some plants (Winter and Hogan 1986), but the Southwest lacked an in situ transition from foraging to farming characterized by the domestication of local plants under the selective pressures from intensive foraging.

Since the North American Southwest is not a center of pristine domestication, the term *Archaic* might well have different definitional criteria and implications for processes of change than is true elsewhere. In Mesoamerica where Archaic foragers were implicated in the process of domestication there is no bright line between foraging and food-production strategies, no clear "ending" of an Archaic lifeway or "beginning" of an agricultural lifeway. The situation was very different in the Southwest, where domesticates and the practice of cultivation appeared in moderately well-developed form. Indeed, in situ Archaic foragers might have had little if anything to do with the initial spread of domesticates into the Southwest; this may have occurred instead with the movement of people who were already dependent on food production. This does not mean that everyone jumped to sustained food production, just that there is potential for discontinuity not seen in Mesoamerica. Even if Southwestern Archaic foragers adopted maize and squash to continue with their foraging lifeways (Wills 1988), doing so is entirely different from the gradual coevolution of domesticates in pristine settings, especially if they did so in the face of economic competition from food producers. I think that Berry and Berry (1986:319) made a valid point when they argued that hunter-gatherers in symbiosis or other form of social engagement with agriculturalists (or farmer-foragers) are not analyzable in the same terms as foragers alone.

To acknowledge the changed circumstances and provide a conceptual break between the Archaic and Formative periods, B. Huckell (1995:117–118) suggested reviving the term *Early Agricultural Period*. In recognition that the shift to a mixed farming-foraging economy happened at different times across the Southwest, Huckell (1996:343) retained the *late Archaic* term, resulting in the somewhat cumbersome designation of "late Archaic/early Agricultural period." Moreover, depending on where one places the arbitrary line between middle and late Archaic, it is now becoming evident that there is a middle Archaic/early Agricultural period. For this report, I use the term *Archaic–Formative transition* to refer to the interval during which domesticates were first used and subsistence economies changed from pure hunting and gathering to those that included food production based on the cultivation of corn and squash. This interval ranges between ca. 2100 cal. BC and cal. AD 500. No matter what label is favored, it is important to acknowledge variability during this interval of significant change. The shift to an agricultural economy did not happen everywhere at the same time, and a generalized hunting-gathering adaptation may have persisted up to the historic period in many areas and was always a potential survival option.

During this transitional period I use the terms *late Archaic* (or *terminal Archaic*) and *Basketmaker II* to refer to two different adaptations—one that continued to rely on foraging and another that emphasized food production. Use of domesticates on the Rainbow Plateau appears no earlier than about 400 cal. BC, and I have designated the sites at which it is found as Basketmaker II. In the central Kayenta area maize is well dated to roughly 600 cal. BC (Smiley et al. 1986), with heavy reliance occurring at about this time (Coltrain et al. 2007). There is some indication of maize use as early as 1000 cal. BC or even earlier in this area if the outlying Three Fir Shelter date is accepted (Smiley 1993; Smiley and Parry 1990). The temporal onset of Basketmaker II along the N16 ROW might change as more early corn and squash are directly dated, but current evidence indicates that it is no earlier than about 400 cal. BC (see chapter 5).

Basketmaker II Definition

Credited to discoveries by Richard Wetherill and brothers (Blackburn and Williamson 1997; McNitt 1966), initially publicized by Pepper (1902; also Prudden 1897), and corroborated and elaborated upon by Kidder and Guernsey (1919:32, 204–212; Guernsey and Kidder 1921), the term *Basketmaker* became formalized as three stages of cultural development (I–III) in Kidder's (1927) summary of the first Pecos Conference (see also Kidder 1962 [1924]). Basketmaker II was the pre-pottery, atlatl-using, initial farming stage; these early farmers created the spectacular inventory of mostly perishable remains unearthed from shelters scattered across the Four Corners region. Basketmaker I was the postulated preagricultural stage of nomadic hunting and gathering that today is known as the Archaic. Basketmaker III was characterized by the use of pottery and pithouses, but also the elaboration or refinement of perishable items such as sandals (e.g., Guernsey 1931:75–92; Hays-Gilpin et al. 1998).

Granted that the Basketmaker II concept has a long and distinguished pedigree, it is abundantly evident that this term has different meanings among archaeologists (see Matson 2006a). Precisely because of its derivation, *Basketmaker* has cultural, geographical, and lifeway connotations that are difficult to avoid—connotations that are themselves legitimate subjects of inquiry but which are difficult to examine once the label is applied. Opinions differ about what constitutes Basketmaker II, "whether it is a stage, a constellation of traits, a time period, a lifeway, an ethnic group, a geographic area, or some combination of the above" (Tipps 1995:143). Matson emphasized adaptation or lifeway, stating that "Basketmaker II, then, indicates a stage rather than a cultural or ethnic group, which I think fits well with the term's original use in the Pecos classification" (1991:123). Matson goes on to observe that "if one believes that the adoption of maize was gradual, a natural corollary would be that the first Anasazi were not fully dependent upon maize.... [W]e rejected this corollary because of recent evidence about maize reliance" (1991:309). He refers to his work on Cedar Mesa (Aasen 1984; Chisholm and Matson 1994; Matson and Chisholm 1991). Thus, Basketmaker II is not just preceramic groups merely with domesticates, first-time dabblers with corn and squash, but groups fully dependent upon domesticates. In their assessment of where the Basketmaker II diet occurs between the two ends of the dietary spectrum for Holocene populations of the Colorado Plateau—Archaic broad-spectrum hunter-gatherers or Formative maize-based horticulturalists—Chisholm and Matson argue that "Basketmaker II belongs on the 'Formative' side of this distinction" (1994:249–250).

The use of domesticates is a key defining aspect for Basketmaker II, but the degree of commitment to farming was not an explicit part of the original definition. It appears that Kidder (1962:241–244, 323–327 [1924]) viewed the stage as transitional in economy, but perhaps less midway than what some have thought in the past. According to Lipe, "Over the years a number of archaeologists have tended to treat BM [Basketmaker] II as a variant of the late Archaic, with maize farming playing a fairly minor role in subsistence" (1993:4). McGregor, for example, states that Basketmaker people "had some agriculture, but apparently extensively supplemented it with gathering and hunting" (1965:18). If Basketmaker II is Formative, then what about those groups less reliant on farming? Lipe has questioned whether "'Basketmaker II' is the most appropriate rubric for considering all of the prepottery but maize-growing manifestations in the northern Southwest?... [W]ould it be better to consider some of this material as 'Late Archaic with Maize,' and reserve 'Basketmaker II' for the more intensive maize growers?" (1994:339). He does not necessarily advocate this approach, suggesting that it may confuse matters because the issue of maize dependence would be solved largely by chronological placement rather than investigation. Perhaps the Basketmaker I label could be dusted off and reinstated with a revision of meaning, as the earliest portion of the Basketmaker interval when dependence on domesticates was substantially less than it finally became later in the Basketmaker sequence (see Matson 2006a for just this suggestion). Alternatively, we could simply recognize that there might well be temporal variability in the degree of agricultural commitment during Basketmaker II. This is certainly expectable given paleoclimatic fluctuations coupled with a variety of ecological factors, demographic patterns, an evolving social landscape, and heterogeneous cultural practices. Geographic variability likely played a part as well, for much the same reasoning, plus the diversity of settings occupied by Basketmaker II groups. Inter- and intra-annual variability in domesticate use is a predictable consequence of erratic yields, among other factors, such that evidence pertaining to specific points in time might say little about overall reliance on produced food.

The problem with the Basketmaker II label extends beyond the issue of identifying whether groups used agriculture or not or how reliant upon it they were. The term also implies historical and cultural relationships that may not be real. Evidence for the first use of agriculture on the Colorado Plateau is not uniformly associated with the material culture first described in detail by Kidder and Guernsey (1919, 1922; Guernsey and Kidder 1921) and designated by Matson (1991:122–123, 1999) as the western variant of Basketmaker II. Morris and Burgh's (1954) excavations of rockshelters in the Durango area provided some of the best samples of preceramic farming remains that differed in several key respects from those to the west but were also classified as Basketmaker. Matson (1991: 122–123, 1999) drew attention to these differences and distinguished the Basketmaker materials from the Durango and Los Pinõs areas along the Upper San Juan River and its tributaries as an eastern variant of Basketmaker II.

Yet evidence for agriculture on the Colorado Plateau may be associated with preceramic remains that are neither eastern nor western Basketmaker variants, and farther afield, away from the core region where the Basketmaker II concept was originally defined, use of the Basketmaker label for preceramic sites or components is potentially even more confusing. Principally, it might imply cultural connections or relationships where these may be lacking, such as classifying late preceramic remains in central and northern Utah as Basketmaker (e.g., Berry and Berry 1976:32–37, Figure 17; Horn 1990:51, 85–86). Considering such remains within Canyonlands National Park, Tipps argues that "the Terminal Archaic–age sites thus far discovered in Canyonlands do not typify the same stage, lifeway, cultural expression, or adaptation described by Matson (1991) for Basketmaker II" (1995:176). If this is true in Canyonlands, might not it also be true in the Four Corners region, the core area of Basketmaker II? Might there have been groups during the Archaic–Formative transition that had a Basketmaker II agricultural adaptation and cultural assemblage (western or eastern variants) as well as groups that were still essentially foragers and had a distinctive cultural assemblage? This indeed appears to be the case for the Rainbow Plateau, as argued in the chapter 4 of this volume.

Smiley (2002a, 2002b) took a different stance in the final interpretive report for the BMAP. He is explicit about his definition of Basketmaker II vis-à-vis the Archaic: "I view the Archaic both as an adaptation and a temporal period. Accordingly, I apply the term 'Archaic' only to hunter-gatherers and not early agricultural populations.... In fact, the several-millennium-long Archaic hunting-and-gathering adaptation comes to a close with the beginnings of food production" (2002b:26). The arrival of maize on Black Mesa specifically and the Colorado Plateau generally marks the beginning of Basketmaker II, which he estimates may start as early as 4000 cal. BP. This is based on acceptance of the outlier date on corn from Three Fir Shelter (3610 ± 170 BP, Beta-26275 [Smiley 1994:Table 1]) as well as the outlier corn date from Bat Cave (374070, A-4187 [Wills 1988:Table 18]). Based on this temporal revision for the beginnings of Basketmaker II, Smiley reassigned the previously identified late Archaic sites on Black Mesa—those lacking agriculture—as part of the White Dog phase of Basketmaker II: "The term, Hisatsinom, as an Archaic-period phase name, appears now obsolete in the light of recent chronological discoveries" (2002a:45). Elsewhere he states, "Sites in the period initially assigned to the Hisatsinom phase (Smiley and Andrews 1983) now appear to fall within the White Dog phase, which begins with the onset of agriculture. Accordingly, these sites are likely campsites within the phase of the White Dog settlement system" (2002b:30). The presence of 3610 BP maize at Three Fir Shelter has called into question the existence of any late Archaic manifestation on Black Mesa. Granted that early Basketmaker II farmers probably had a differentiated subsistence-settlement organization that included camps lacking agricultural remains, there could also be terminal Archaic foragers living in the region contemporaneous with Basketmaker farmers. Getting rid of the term *Hisatsinom* is welcome to avoid any implication of ethnic and linguistic affiliations between archaeological entities and historic groups. Nonetheless, blanket ascription of all remains as Basketmaker II because they fall within a given temporal interval when domesticates may have been present could mask important evidence of adaptive variability and whether different trajectories lead to a Formative adaptation.

Evidence for the first use of agriculture on the Colorado Plateau is not uniformly associated with Basketmaker II material culture as initially described by Guernsey and Kidder (1921; also Kidder and Guernsey 1919; Nusbaum 1922). For example, the two sites in the Upper Chinle Valley with early maize (Gilpin 1994) do not have a clear Basketmaker II–like cultural assemblage, although the limited nature of the excavation at these two sites might account for this. Likewise, the cultural assemblage at the Old Corn Site (Huber 2005) is not readily classified as Basketmaker. A Basketmaker II designation for the Lukachukai and Old Corn sites appears justified on an adaptive basis, although the degree of agricultural dependence remains open to question. A Basketmaker II cultural affiliation seems less well supported, but this might be explained as a consequence of early age, since remains might appear different from the well-known examples from much later (the "classic" Basketmaker materials), coupled with a lack of perishable artifacts, which are the most culturally distinctive portion of Basketmaker material culture (but see Chapter 5 and Geib 2002). The artifacts recovered from Three Fir Shelter seem typical for western

Basketmaker II (Smiley and Parry 1992), but the earliest reliable date is 2880 BP, with the rest of the reliable dates from the site earlier than 2600 BP (this excludes a direct date on a sandal that has an error term of 750 years).

As mentioned previously, my definition of Basketmaker II is based foremost on adaptation—basically the use of domesticates, with the principal archaeologically recovered trace being maize. Besides mere presence, judging from the subsistence remains recovered coupled with other less direct indicators, maize appears to have formed a substantial part of the Basketmaker diet for the project area (details in chapter 5). The truth to this claim appears borne out by the recent results of stable isotope analyses of bone collagen from western Basketmaker II burials (Coltrain et al. 2007). In essence, the adaptation was Formative in the sense used by Chisholm and Matson (1994). Evidence for the first use of agriculture on the Rainbow Plateau appears to be associated with Basketmaker II material culture as initially described by Guernsey and Kidder (1921; also Kidder and Guernsey 1919, 1922). Excavated caves on the Rainbow Plateau have produced assemblages of perishable artifacts that are no different from those of the classic Basketmaker II type sites, such as White Dog Cave and Kinboko Caves 1 and 2 (Lindsay et al. 1968; Schilz 1979; SD vol. 2, chap. 2). Open sites during this interval have yielded nonperishable remains that likewise typify the stone and bone artifacts found at the classic Basketmaker II rockshelters. Consequently, there are both adaptive and cultural grounds for referring to the preceramic agricultural sites of the N16 ROW as Basketmaker II.

The forager sites on the Rainbow Plateau that date to the Archaic–Formative transition (summarized in chapter 4) appear to be culturally distinctive from the somewhat later Basketmaker II sites in the area. This is admittedly tentative, because it is based mainly on the remains that preserve at open sites. Nonetheless, some of the nonperishable artifacts at Basketmaker II sites are distinct from those at terminal Archaic sites of the area and lack precedent in Archaic assemblages of the Colorado Plateau (see chapter 5). Basketmaker sites also appear dramatically different in character from those of the immediately preceding terminal Archaic (those dated to the interval that locally lacks domesticates). Not only does the Basketmaker archaeological record have far more visibility than that left by the terminal Archaic foragers, but Basketmaker sites contain relatively substantial houses, numerous storage facilities, dense trash accumulations, and what appears to be greater differentiation in subsistence-settlement organization. There are implications in this record for increased sedentism, lessened residential mobility, and greater population density during Basketmaker II.

In summary, *Basketmaker II* herein has both adaptive and cultural meaning and is not a simple period designation for the interval during which agriculture was first practiced but ceramics were not in use. The term *Archaic–Formative transition* provides a convenient designation for that interval, one that has no necessary implications about what was eaten, what type of footwear was worn, or other details; it only specifies that a site belongs to a given time period during which domesticates may or may not have been used. Assignment to this transitional interval is best based on chronometric dates. Other issues such as degree of maize reliance and cultural affiliation can then be investigated in their own right without becoming embroiled in definitional debate. During the Archaic–Formative transition I recognize a Basketmaker II adaptation and cultural assemblage, which on the Rainbow Plateau appears to be no older than about 400 cal. BC. Farther south in the Kayenta region this same Basketmaker II adaptation and cultural assemblage may be as old as 800 cal. BC (cf. Smiley 2002a). Also during this interval there continued to be an Archaic adaptation (continued foraging) along with a cultural assemblage that appears distinctive from Basketmaker II remains. This terminal Archaic lifeway lasted until about 800 cal. BC on the Rainbow Plateau, with the possibility for sporadic Archaic use until about 400 cal. BC.

Cultural-Temporal Schemes

Much has already been said about cultural-temporal schemes while trying to adequately define what *Basketmaker II* means for the NMRAP. Nonetheless, some additional points merit discussion. Various researchers have devised different phases to organize what is becoming an increasingly long interval for Basketmaker II. Colton (1939) created the term *White Dog focus* (or *phase*, as it is commonly known these days following Gladwin and Gladwin [1934]) with reference to the Basketmaker II remains from the Kayenta region unearthed and described by Kidder and Guernsey. The temporal parameters of this phase were undefined on the early end but often placed at about the time of Christ, with an approximation of AD 500 on the late end based on tree-ring dates from sites with early pottery. Lipe (1967, 1970) extended this phase designation to Basketmaker II remains of the Red Rock

Plateau north of the San Juan River and outside the traditionally defined Kayenta core. When Lipe did this there was still a near-total absence of chronometric dates; thus the age of Basketmaker II remains continued to be largely assumed. Subsequent work by Lipe and Matson on Cedar Mesa led to the formulation of the Grand Gulch phase, a late Basketmaker II pattern represented on Cedar Mesa by open pithouse dwellings and heavy dependence on farming—the adaptation appears to have emphasized dry farming on the mesa top (Matson 2006b provides an overview). Dating of the Cedar Mesa phase was based on a series of radiocarbon and tree-ring dates (see summary in Matson 1991:Table 3 and sidebar of pp. 90 and 92) and placed at about AD 200–400. Matson ultimately came to contrast this phase with an earlier Basketmaker II adaptation that emphasized farming and settlement in the canyons where rockshelters were used for living and storage; this he (1991:122–123) termed the White Dog phase following Colton and Lipe. This phase was seen as preceding (ancestral to) the Grand Gulch phase. The key aspect in drawing this distinction was Smiley's (1994:Table 1; Smiley et al. 1986) direct radiocarbon dating of Basketmaker II remains from the Kidder and Guernsey type sites of the Marsh Pass area. This effort showed that many of the remains previously suspected to postdate the time of Christ were actually earlier, as old as about 600 cal. BC. Thus, Colton's White Dog phase became the early portion of the Basketmaker II sequence wherever the western variant of Basketmaker II culture was recognized: the Kayenta region, Cedar Mesa, the Red Rock Plateau, and Kanab.

In the Kayenta region proper, the BMAP project proposed the Lolomai phase as the local manifestation of Basketmaker II on northern Black Mesa (Gumerman and Euler 1976:164–165). Though it was initially based on very little data, by the project's end 35 Lolomai phase sites had been excavated, providing a detailed picture of open Basketmaker II settlements for this small part of the Kayenta region. The history of dating for this phase is complicated, but in short, after a decade of thinking that the phase spanned some 1,100 radiocarbon years, from roughly 2800 to 1700 BP, Smiley (1985) demonstrated that the bulk of all radiocarbon assays for the phase were erroneous, resulting from the dating of old wood. Based on six direct dates on corn from six BMAP Basketmaker sites, Smiley argued that the phase actually had a duration of just several hundred years during the first part of the Christian era, with the interval of 1900 to 1600 cal. BP (ca. cal. AD 50–350) given in the final summary report (Smiley 2002a:50; also Smiley and Ahlstrom 1998:219).

Smiley, like Matson, distinguished between the open mesa-top settlements of the Lolomai phase and the earlier rockshelter-occupying Basketmaker II of the Kayenta region and likewise adopted Colton's term *White Dog phase* as the referent for this early expression: "I continue to apply the term, White Dog phase, to the 'classic' Basketmaker II occupation manifested in the rockshelters of the Marsh Pass region" (1998a:19). Matson and Smiley differ, however, in the temporal beginning of this phase, with a variance of some 1,000 years or more. Whereas Matson (2002; personal communication 2002) accepts that the phase is represented by at least 350 cal. BC and perhaps as early as 600 cal. BC, Smiley has it beginning substantially earlier: "The White Dog phase currently occupies the period beginning somewhere between 4000 and 3000 BP [ca. 2000–1000 cal. BC] and lasting to about 2000 BP" (1998a:19). The early estimate is based on accepting the outlier maize date of 3610 ± 170 BP from Three Fir Shelter. If this assay is eventually verified by additional dating, there is still the issue of associated cultural remains, and these should be factored in. Therefore, the outlying Three Fir Shelter maize assay does not provide sufficient cause at present to extend the White Dog phase back to around 2000 cal. BC.

The NMRAP findings reported here (see chapter 5), and summarized in a preliminary way in Geib and Spurr 2000, do not neatly correspond to this split between the earlier rockshelter-using White Dog phase and the later open-air mesa-top settlement of either the Lolomai or Grand Gulch phases. On the Rainbow Plateau and far northern Shonto Plateau, open pithouse habitations date several hundred years earlier than either the Lolomai or Grand Gulch phases, placing them within the reputed time of the White Dog phase. Moreover, Basketmaker II use of caves and rockshelters on the Rainbow Plateau is contemporaneous with the open-air settlements (Geib and Robins 2003), and indeed the shelters appear to be adjuncts of this settlement pattern—i.e., places of dry storage for adjacent open habitations. A single open habitation like Kin Kahuna (SD vol. 3, chap. 2) appears to have been occupied from the start of Basketmaker II settlement in the region at around 400 cal. BC, continuing without evident interruption until around cal. AD 400. Consequently, I lack any reasonable basis for distinguishing sequential Basketmaker II phases for the northern Kayenta region. Based on Colton's precedent I include all

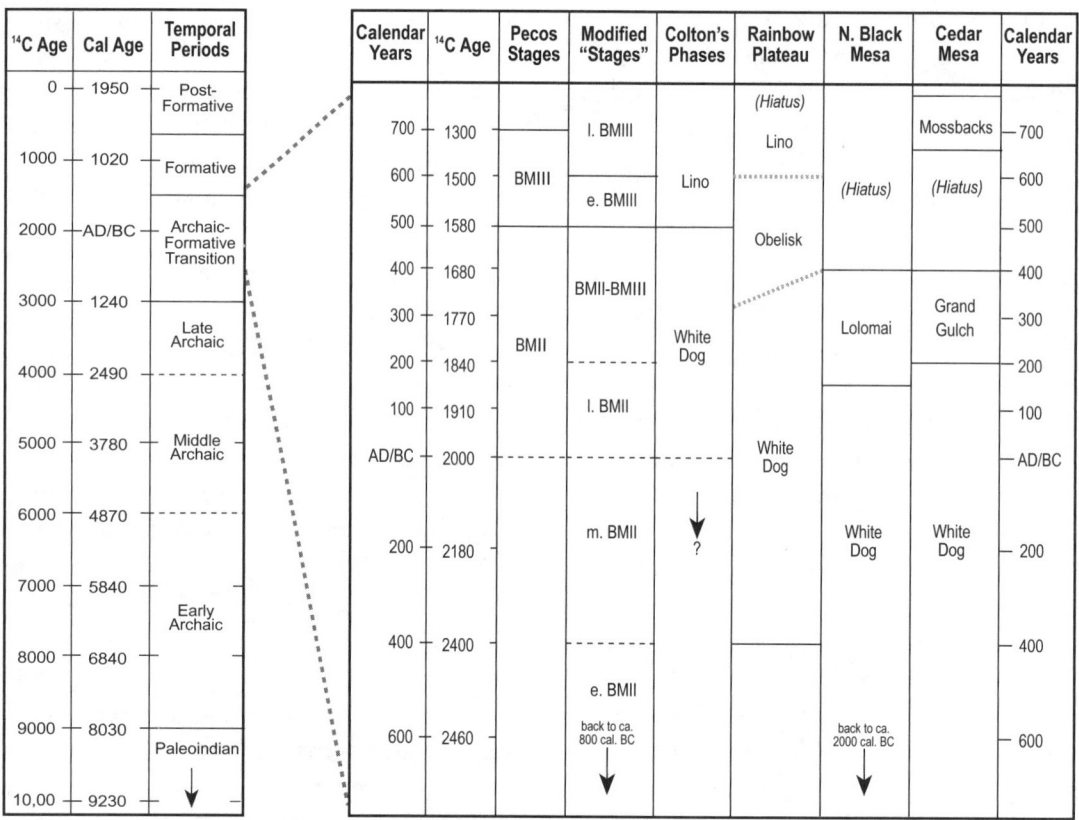

Figure 2.7. Western Basketmaker II cultural-temporal phases relevant to the northern Kayenta region, including the proposed sequence for the Rainbow Plateau; see Matson 1991, 2002, for Cedar Mesa, and Smiley 2002a for northern Black Mesa.

of the materials reported herein as part of the White Dog phase, with the possible exception of one site (Mountainview), which produced early pottery (Obelisk Utility). Mountainview is, however, contemporaneous with other Basketmaker II sites lacking pottery, so there would be temporally overlapping rather than sequential phases.

Figure 2.7 presents my current understanding of Basketmaker cultural-temporal systematics for the Kayenta region and slightly farther afield. The introduction of corn demarks the end of the Archaic and the transitional interval to the Formative period (the Archaic–Formative transition). The earliest Basketmaker II cultural expression within this transitional interval, designated the White Dog phase, is not clearly manifested until around 800 cal. BC (2600 BP). This is based on clusters of dates from Three Fir Shelter (Smiley and Parry 1992) and the earliest dates on human and artifactual remains from the classic Basketmaker type sites of the Kayenta region such as White Dog Cave and Kinboko Caves 1 and 2 (Coltrain et al. 2007; Smiley 1994:Table 1; Smiley et al. 1986). Dating might eventually show that diagnostic western Basketmaker II material extends back in time to when domesticates first appeared on the Colorado Plateau, but this has yet to be demonstrated; thus the beginning of the White Dog phase is restricted to the temporal interval when such remains are known to exist. This follows Matson's (1991) use of the term *White Dog phase*, which parallels the generally agreed-upon notion that phases delimit a spatially and temporally cohesive assemblage of materials.

On the Rainbow Plateau, the earliest Basketmaker II remains are currently no older than about 400 cal. BC; thus the initial phase of Basketmaker II settlement for this northern portion of the Kayenta region is temporally more limited and may result from the expansion of early farmers out of the Marsh Pass area or farther south. Unlike on Cedar Mesa and Black Mesa, the initial phase of Basketmaker settlement on the Rainbow Plateau during the first several centuries cal. BC appears no different from that during the first several centuries cal. AD. From the start, it involved open-air pithouse settlements in addition to natural shelters. Indeed, natural shelter use appears no more than a component of Basketmaker II settlement on the Rainbow Plateau. I classify all Basketmaker II remains on the Rainbow Plateau as part of the White Dog phase and see it as lasting until the advent of pottery production.

On both Cedar Mesa and Black Mesa the White Dog phase is followed by separate Basketmaker II phases recognized for mesa-top adaptations with open-air pithouse settlements ("proto-villages" in Smiley's [2002a:49] terminology). Neither the Grand Gulch nor the Lolomai phase is recognized for the Rainbow Plateau because open pithouse settlements date from the initiation of Basketmaker occupation in the region, contemporaneous with cave/shelter use, and there is no reliable way to distinguish a late Basketmaker II phase. This said, it is important to point out that there are Basketmaker II habitations on Piute Mesa that appear quite similar in architectural details to those of the Grand Gulch phase on Cedar Mesa (see the review in SD vol. 3, chap. 1) and which also probably date late in the Basketmaker II sequence. Also corresponding in this setting is the probable dry-farming adaptation of the Piute Mesa Basketmakers, because this was perhaps the only sure means to grow crops on this upland (see Hobler 1964:7, 12–13; Stein 1984:50–53).

A Basketmaker II–III transition is evident on the Rainbow Plateau by a continuous radiocarbon chronology, and inferred continuous population presence, that spans the interval when pottery was introduced and came into common use (see summaries in chapter 5 and in Geib and Spurr 2000). Continued settlement of the region during this interval is also evidenced by continuous cultural deposition within Atlatl Rock Cave from about cal. AD 100 to 600. Basketmaker III traits such as the bow and arrow, turkey domestication (or at least the penning of turkeys), and beans were present at this cave by about cal. AD 500. Indeed, bow and arrow use appears even earlier at several aceramic and ceramic sites of the area. I tentatively identify a phase for the Basketmaker II–III transitional interval on the Rainbow Plateau as Obelisk, after the first pottery in use at that time (Obelisk Utility). Pottery is the key diagnostic trait of this phase, but ceramics are not present at all contemporaneous sites, thus the phase is not totally sequential but involves some degree of temporal overlap with the previous White Dog phase. This phase grades into the subsequent Lino phase, and sites during the first half of the sixth century AD have a mix of Obelisk Utility and Lino Gray (good examples of this are reported by Bungart et al. [2004]).

Formative

The Formative period (ca. AD 500–1300) is a stage of cultural development characterized by a strong reliance on agriculture (see Minnis 1989), permanent or semipermanent habitations, and pottery production. Various terms referring to the Formative period occupants of the region are used in the following discussion. On a general level, *Puebloan* and *Anasazi* are used interchangeably to designate all Formative-stage populations. I include all Formative groups along the N16 ROW as part of the Kayenta branch, a regional variant of the general Puebloan cultural tradition distinguished principally by ceramics and architecture. The approximate spatial extent of this culture changed through time, but the focal area is bounded by the Colorado River and Lower San Juan River on the north, Chinle Wash on the east, Cottonwood Wash and the Little Colorado River on the south, and Marble and Grand canyons on the west. The western boundary is open to debate, because populations on the eastern margin of the Arizona Strip also share many similarities, especially between AD 1050 and 1150.

The temporal framework for the Formative period shown in Figure 2.3 presents several different subdivisions and phase schemes. Ceramic types, especially those of Tusayan White Ware, form the principal basis for temporal subdivision in the Kayenta region. Identified phases for the region, those of Colton as modified by Ambler (1985a, 1985b) or BMAP (Gumerman et al. 1972:24–27), are essentially defined by ceramics. For this reason I favor the use of ceramic periods, which I have named after the principal Tusayan White Ware types diagnostic of given intervals. For example, the interval during which Flagstaff Black-on-white was the predominant whiteware type (roughly AD 1150–1200) is known as the Flagstaff ceramic period. A site of this interval would also have Tsegi Orange Ware dominated by Tusayan Black-on-red along with early polychrome types, with Moenkopi Corrugated the predominant utilitarian type. The exception to naming ceramic periods by the predominant whiteware occurs during the Basketmaker II–III transitional period, which is designated by the utilitarian pottery type of Obelisk. Also note that the late Pueblo II ceramic period has twin diagnostics of Sosi and Dogoszhi Black-on-white, hence the designation of Sosi-Dogo.

The ceramic periods also have corresponding Pecos "stage" designations as alternative shorthand referents, usually prefixed by *early, middle and late*, or *early and late*. The Flagstaff ceramic period is also known as early

Pueblo III. These modified stage designations correspond roughly to the original temporal spans for the Pecos stages. Tree-ring dating of sites in the Kayenta Anasazi region has revealed that certain ceramic types long considered diagnostic of a given Pecos stage have temporal spans that coincide with a different stage. For example, the Pueblo II diagnostics of Sosi and Dogoszhi Black-on-white are the predominant Tusayan White Ware types during the AD 1100–1150 interval; thus Pueblo II lasts until about AD 1150.

Basketmaker III (ca. AD 500–800)

The Basketmaker III period is generally considered to be a direct outgrowth of the preceding Basketmaker II lifeway. Beans were added to the list of cultigens; two-handed manos and trough metates increased the efficiency of corn processing; the bow and arrow replaced the atlatl and spear; and plain sand-tempered pottery, occasionally decorated with black carbon paint, was manufactured. Settlement size increased, and a few communal religious structures were first built (e.g., the "great kiva" at Juniper Cove [Cummings 1953; Gilpin and Benallie 2000]). Typical dwellings were partly subterranean and slab lined, with an antechamber and central fire pit and with low wing walls extending to the house perimeter.

Basketmaker III sites are common in certain portions of the Kayenta region (Red Lake Valley and Laguna Creek, for example), but only a few sites are known from the Shonto Plateau northward, and northern Black Mesa appears unoccupied (e.g., Nichols 2002). It appears that most Kayenta Basketmaker III populations aggregated in the vicinity of well-watered alluviated valleys or canyons.

A transitional interval between Basketmaker II and Basketmaker III appears to be represented by sites with brownish firing, usually polished pottery that is classified as Obelisk Utility. A good example of a site belonging to this interval is Mountainview (AZ-J-14-38), summarized in chapter 5 (see SD vol. 3, chap. 10). This transitional interval might date as early as AD 200, and it appears to extend until around AD 500. A site in the Klethla Valley that was tree-ring dated to the AD 530s has a ceramic assemblage with a mixture of Lino Gray and Obelisk Utility (NA11,058 [Swarthout et al. 1986]; sherd assemblage at MNA examined by Kim Spurr and me). A second site in this same valley that provided tree-ring dates to the AD 550s produced mainly Lino Gray (NA8163 [Ambler and Olson 1977]). The advent of decorated pottery (Lino Black-on-white) sometime after about AD 600 serves to demarcate the late Basketmaker III interval.

Pueblo I (ca. AD 800–950)

The Pueblo I period is generally characterized by a continuation and elaboration of trends initiated during the preceding Basketmaker III period. There was increased sedentism, aggregation into larger pithouse settlements, the development of contiguous masonry and jacal surface structures, refinement of ceramic production techniques, and the addition of new ceramic styles (e.g., Kana-a Gray, Kana-a Black-on-white, and San Juan Red Wares traded from the Mesa Verde region). Habitations of this period, like those of the preceding Basketmaker III period, appear to be situated adjacent to broad, well-watered alluvial canyons and valleys. Smiley and Andrews (1983:55–56) noted that some Pueblo I (Dinnebito phase) sites on northern Black Mesa look much like Basketmaker III sites, whereas others have the construction and layout more typical of later Pueblo periods.

Pueblo I occupation is virtually unrecognized for the northern Kayenta region, and on the Rainbow Plateau and northern Shonto Plateau crossed by the N16 ROW there are no known Pueblo I habitations (those characterized by a predominance of Kana-a Black-on-white). A limited activity site excavated within the southern portion of the N16 ROW (northern Shonto Plateau) appears to have a Pueblo I age (see SD vol. 4, chap. 13), but it might also date slightly later to the early Pueblo II interval, when several substantial habitations were established along the rim of Upper Piute Canyon.

Pueblo II (ca. AD 950–1150)

Higher site density and increased territory characterize Pueblo II in the Kayenta area. Many previously unoccupied or sparsely occupied areas began to be populated in middle Pueblo II, becoming saturated by late Pueblo II. The Shonto and Rainbow plateaus are good examples of this, as well as Piute Mesa and the Kaibito Plateau. Most Pueblo II sites are small, often with one to three jacal living rooms attached to a few masonry storage rooms; most permanent habitations include a maize-grinding room and a kiva. Some larger pueblos, with five to eight living rooms, are also known. Village layout became quite uniform toward the end of the Pueblo II period, consisting of masonry room blocks used for storage with attached jacal living rooms that partly enclose a small plaza area containing a fully subterranean circular kiva and a mealing room.

Extensive excavations on northern Black Mesa resulted in the recognition of a Pueblo I–Pueblo II transitional phase, designated the Wepo phase by BMAP. The index type for this phase was a new ceramic type, Wepo

Black-on-white (Gumerman et al. 1972:247–248, Figure 10), that had previously been informally recognized as late Kana-a Black-on-white. Subsequently, archaeologists have recognized sites with the characteristic ceramic assemblage of this interval throughout the Kayenta region. Herein I consider the Wepo phase to be early Pueblo II. Some of the habitations are larger and more formally organized than during previous times, with some composed of a linear arrangement of contiguous living rooms and attached storage rooms fronting one or more pithouses or protokivas. No early Pueblo II sites were excavated in the N16 ROW, but several extended-family habitations dating to this interval are located on the east rim of Upper Piute Canyon (Fairley 1989).

By middle Pueblo II, the Kayenta also began to produce orange ware along with the continued production of white- and graywares. The replacement of San Juan Red Ware by Tsegi Orange Ware is an important temporal marker—early Pueblo II sites lack Tsegi Orange Ware and have San Juan Red Ware exclusively, whereas middle Pueblo II sites (the Black Mesa ceramic period) have a predominance of Tsegi Orange Ware with a trace of San Juan Red Ware. Black Mesa Black-on-white is diagnostic of the middle Pueblo II period from about AD 1050 to 1100, with the combination of Sosi Black-on-white and Dogoszhi Black-on-white diagnostic of late Pueblo II during the early AD 1100s (the Sosi-Dogo ceramic period). San Juan Red Ware is absent in late Pueblo II ceramic assemblages, having been replaced by Tsegi Orange Ware.

Pueblo III (ca. AD 1150–1300)
The start of Pueblo III is marked by some significant population adjustments. The vast majority of the Virgin Anasazi region west of the Kayenta region was abandoned during this time (Lyneis 1996), as was northern Black Mesa (Ahlstrom 1998a; Powell 2002). Population seems to have leveled off or declined throughout much of the Kayenta region during the start of Pueblo III. Populations apparently increased along the southern margin of the Kayenta region near Flagstaff, including the establishment of Kayenta-like communities around Wupatki (Anderson 1990). These demographic changes have been attributed largely to the onset of a severe, short-lived drought accompanied by arroyo cutting (e.g., Dean et al. 1985; Gumerman, ed. 1988). By AD 1200 populations seem to have grown again, reaching a peak at about AD 1260–1280. The Rainbow Plateau was more densely occupied during the thirteenth century than at any other time before or since.

Three Pueblo III ceramic periods are recognizable: one characterized by the predominance of Flagstaff Black-on-white (ca. AD 1150–1200), one by the predominance of Tusayan Black-on-white (ca. AD 1200–1250), and the third by the addition of Kayenta Black-on-white and "whiteline" polychromes (Kiet Siel and Kayenta Polychrome). The latter corresponds to the terminal occupation of the Kayenta region (ca. AD 1250–1300), long known as the Tsegi phase (Dean 1969, 1970; Lindsay 1969; Stein 1984), when settlements greatly increased in size (total room count and count of living rooms). Lindsay (1969:243–246) described several different basic layouts for Tsegi phase masonry sites. Pithouse villages were also common into the late Pueblo III period, and these exhibit a great deal of variation in size, layout, and construction details (see Callahan 1985:133–139). It seems that Puebloans virtually abandoned the Rainbow and Shonto plateaus shortly before AD 1300.

Formative Population Trends
In the early 1980s, J. Richard Ambler and students from NAU conducted several archaeological projects in portions of the northern Kayenta Anasazi region, both area surveys and excavations (e.g., Ambler et al. 1985; Fairley 1989; Geib et al. 1985). These projects stimulated interest in the evident ebb and flow of Puebloan populations within the region and led to an attempt at reconstructing demographic fluctuations through time for various localities and for the region as a whole. Building upon MNA's surveys and excavations for the Glen Canyon Project (Ambler et al. 1964; Lindsay et al. 1968; Stein 1966), this effort culminated in a paper presented at the Second Anasazi Symposium (Ambler et al. 1983). Unlike most previous approaches at the time (see summaries in Hassan 1981 and Layhe 1981), which tried to estimate actual numbers of people, Ambler created relative population curves. These curves are shown in Figures 2.8 and 2.9; the former illustrates trends for six separate localities of the northern Kayenta region, and the latter represents the overall pattern. Appendix F of the Web-posted supporting documentation presents Ambler et al.'s revised paper so that readers may evaluate how the curves were constructed. In brief, they were based on the frequency of every Tusayan White Ware type collected from sites in each locality, taking into account the mathematical characteristics of the temporal frequency distribution of each Tusayan White Ware type (see Ambler 1985a). Black-on-white types are the most temporally sensitive of all Kayenta pottery types, so they alone were used in the demographic calculations.

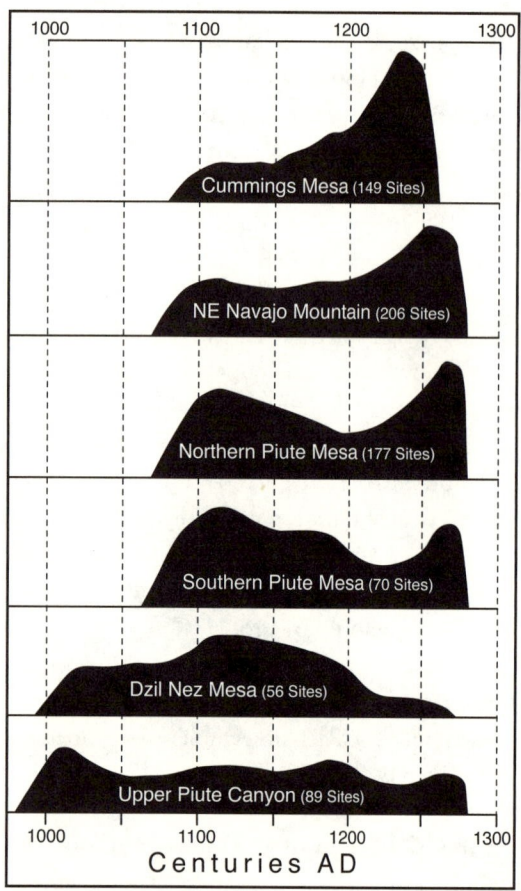

Figure 2.8. Demographic profiles for six localities of the northern Kayenta region (from Ambler et al. 1983; and Supporting Documents, Appendix F).

The method assumes that the Kayenta Anasazi made and broke pots at about the same rate per individual through time and that survey archaeologists collected a representative sample of the resulting sherds and classified them in the same way. These assumptions are no small matter, but the curves are nonetheless useful as an initial approximation of population trends for the northern Kayenta region. Indeed, several authors have reproduced the curves in discussions about the Kayenta Anasazi (e.g., Dean 1996:Figure 3.3, 2002:Figure 6.3; Gumerman and Dean 1989:Figure 15).

The curves of Figures 2.8 and 2.9 do not reflect absolute population figures, although a doubling of the height of any curve can be interpreted as a doubling of the population of that locality. Short-term fluctuations are undoubtedly obscured by the nature of the existing database as well as the method of curve creation. Beginning and ending dates for each locality are based on an assessment of the earliest and latest ceramic types and assemblages. Anasazi occupation in the northern Kayenta region ended around AD 1280, based on the lack of tree-ring dates after AD 1275 (Bannister et al. 1969; see Lindsay 1969). It is important to note that the ceramic method used by Ambler et al. fails to represent the sizable Basketmaker II population of the area or the early Basketmaker III occupation (e.g., Geib and Spurr 2000). Late Basketmaker III and Pueblo I sites are not yet reported from the study area; thus the curves begin shortly before AD 1000.

The initial thrust of Puebloans into the northern Kayenta region evidently occurred after AD 950, during early Pueblo II (the Wepo ceramic period). At this time several multifamily habitations were established within Upper Piute Canyon, mostly on the canyon rim (Fairley 1989). This initial Puebloan occupation appears intrusive because no Pueblo I sites or late Basketmaker III sites are known from Piute Canyon or the rest of the northern Kayenta region. Early Basketmaker III sites occur in and around Upper Piute Canyon (Fairley 1989; Geib and Spurr 2000; Hargrave 1935:43–44), but it is implausible that a local early Basketmaker III lifeway would have been transformed almost overnight into the full-blown Wepo phase expression present in Upper Piute Canyon. The probable planned migration into Upper Piute Canyon may have been prompted by population growth south of the Shonto divide during the 900s and consequent competition over farmlands. The unsettled, well-watered, and easily irrigable land in Upper Piute Canyon must have been quite attractive to Puebloan farmers. No other portion of the northern Kayenta region is currently known to have Wepo phase habitations. Navajo Canyon could contain similar-age sites, given the occurrence of well-watered deep alluvium and potential for subirrigation or irrigation farming just like in Upper Piute Canyon.

By middle Pueblo II (the Black Mesa ceramic period), the multifamily settlements on the rim of Piute Canyon were abandoned, and small farmsteads within the canyon became the norm (Fairley 1989). Small single-family habitation sites also occur on the highlands adjacent to Upper Piute Canyon, on both Dzil Nez Mesa and the southeast edge of the Rainbow Plateau. Hammer House and Hillside Hermitage provide examples of middle Pueblo II habitations excavated by the NMRAP (summarized in chapter 6; see SD vol. 4, chaps. 2–3). Population levels during this time appear to have remained stable, and most localities of the northern Kayenta region remained largely unoccupied until late Pueblo II. Not until around AD 1100, during the Sosi-Dogo ceramic period,

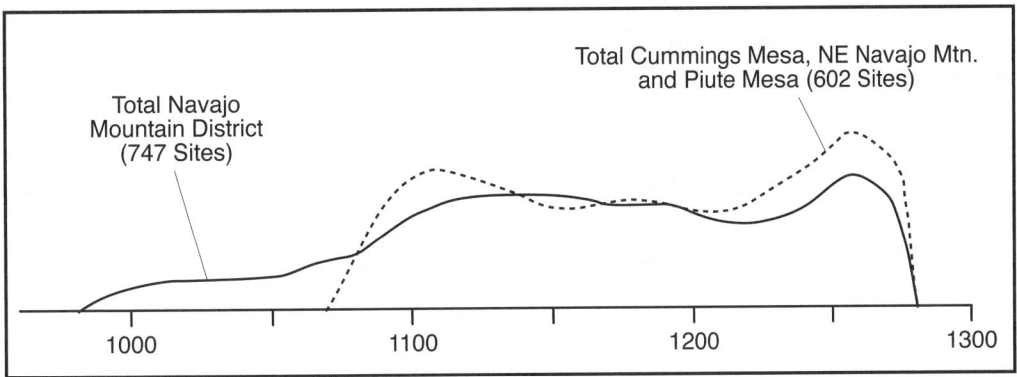

Figure 2.9. Demographic profile for the entire northern Kayenta region and for the northern mesas excluding Upper Piute Canyon and Dzil Nez Mesa (from Ambler et al. 1983; and Supporting Documents, Appendix F).

did Puebloans occupy the Navajo Mountain, Piute Mesa, and Cummings Mesa localities (Figure 2.9). Ambler et al. (SD, Appendix F) suggest that migration accounts for the seemingly sudden appearance of late Pueblo II populations on these highlands, noting that this phenomenon is also expressed farther afield at the same time—the Kaibito, Paria, Kaiparowits, and Red Rock plateaus being notable examples. Late Pueblo II farmsteads were widely scattered across all portions of the northern Kayenta region suitable for habitation. It appears that horticultural activities were practiced wherever sufficient soil and moisture were available, and the evident mesic conditions of the late 1000s and early 1100s (Dean et al. 1985; Gumerman, ed. 1988) would have increased the productive potential of the region.

Drought around AD 1150 may have resulted in an early Pueblo III population decline, but Puebloans did not totally abandon the northern Kayenta region or any specific locality (cf. Berry 1982). Indeed, Cummings Mesa appears to have experienced a population increase after about AD 1150. Population growth continued throughout the region during the entire Pueblo III interval. This increase might have resulted simply from local population growth, but influxes of groups from outside the region may have occurred. For example, much of the Arizona Strip was abandoned about this time (Lyneis 1996), and some of these migrants may have moved to the northern Kayenta region. Pueblo III was also a time of local agricultural intensification using check dams, terrace systems, grid borders, and irrigation features, including the creation of fields on the lower slopes of Navajo Mountain (Ambler et al. 1985; Lindsay 1961; Lindsay et al. 1968:184–188; Stewart and Donnelly 1943). Given the increased Pueblo III population, it appears likely that inhabitants on the Rainbow Plateau both expanded and diversified their horticultural niche. The agricultural intensification efforts may also represent the production of different crops in specialized areas.

During late Pueblo III (the Kayenta ceramic period) there was a shift toward larger nucleated settlements, a profound change from the previous settlement pattern for the area. Several diverse site layouts are evident in the nucleated villages. Some, such as Red House (Dean 2002; Hargrave 1935), Upper Desha Pueblo (Lindsay et al. 1968), Neskahi Village (Hobler 1974), and Thumb Rock Pueblo (Stein 1966), appear to be larger versions of the architecturally (and presumably socially) integrated Pueblo II and early Pueblo III "unit pueblos" and have been classified as plaza sites (Lindsay 1969; Lindsay et al. 1968). The Segazlin Mesa community, on the other hand, is a loose spatial aggregation of small extended-family courtyard pueblos (Lindsay et al. 1968), and Pottery Pueblo on Piute Mesa (Stein 1984) appears to be a physically compacted but architecturally nonintegrated agglomeration of family courtyard units. Small single-family villages also persisted until near the end of Pueblo III in the district (Geib and Ambler 1983; Geib et al. 1985; see chapter 6 of this report and SD vol. 4). As noted by Lindsay (1969:367), the variations in Tsegi phase village patterning could reflect the arrival of different traditions to the region. Lindsay (1969) and Dean (1969, 1970, 2002) have both suggested that social change from Pueblo II to Pueblo III was considerable. The appreciable diversity in social structure (as indicated by architectural patterns) during late Pueblo III in the northern Kayenta region may have resulted, at least in part, from the arrival of outside families.

Post-Formative

Post-Formative constitutes a general umbrella designation for Native American remains dating to the interval between the Puebloan abandonment of the Four Corners region around AD 1300 and the recent historic period (Geib et al. 2001). There are both behavioral and historical implications to the divisions of late Prehistoric, Protohistoric, and historic, plus a great deal of precedent for the use of those or similar terms in the archaeological literature (e.g., Wilcox and Masse 1981); these are therefore retained as temporal subdivisions of the Post-Formative period.

The late Prehistoric interval extends from AD 1300 to about AD 1500, when indirect influences from early Spanish settlers in Mexico presumably first reached the Southwest. The Protohistoric interval extends from AD 1500 to 1850, ending roughly contemporaneously with the Mormon colonization of southern Utah and the initiation of U.S. government exploratory expeditions across the southern Colorado Plateau. After 1850 the historic record for the area becomes considerably more detailed. The pioneering exploration of the Southwest by the Spanish friars Dominguez and Escalante during 1776 (Bolton 1950) provides a convenient dividing point between early (AD 1500–1775) and late (AD 1776–1850) phases of the Protohistoric interval. The historic interval of the Native American use of the region extends from 1850 to the present.

Archaeological data pertaining to the Post-Formative occupation of the Rainbow and Shonto plateaus are sparse. Occasional finds of Southern Paiute Brown Ware are generally considered indicative of a southern Numic presence, but as far as I know this pottery remains unreported from the local area. Desert Side-notched projectile points are used to identify Paiute and Ute sites in Utah, but essentially identical points were used commonly by the ancestral Hopi of Awatovi (Woodbury 1954), the Pai of north-central Arizona (Pilles 1981), and the early Navajo of the La Plata area (Gary Brown, personal communication 1990). This point type is probably best considered a widespread time marker of late Prehistoric and Protohistoric periods, rather than an ethnic diagnostic. Small quantities of Jeddito and Awatovi Yellow Ware sherds occur at some late Pueblo III Kayenta habitations and scattered campsites in the Kayenta region, including on the Rainbow Plateau (e.g., Adams et al. 1961; Lindsay et al. 1968; Lipe 1970; Sharrock et al. 1963); these have been interpreted as evidence for ancestral Hopi visits to the region for pilgrimages to shrines, trading expeditions, and big-game hunting. In a few instances, such as at site 42SA757 in Glen Canyon, where sherds of Jeddito Plain occur with probable Pueblo IV–style rock art (Sharrock et al. 1963:246–247), an ancestral Hopi presence is probable. However, at many sites it is equally plausible that Jeddito Yellow Ware represents trade items used by Southern Paiutes or Utes (Lucius 1983; Schaefer 1969).

It appears that the first post-Anasazi occupants of both the Rainbow and Shonto plateaus were Southern Paiute (Kelly 1964). These hunter-gatherers probably moved into the western and northern portion of the Kayenta region shortly after the Puebloan abandonment. Southern Paiutes are closely related by language to Southern Utes (Schroeder 1965; Stewart 1942), and perhaps these groups were not distinct ethnic entities prior to the historic era (cf. Pierson 1981:65). Summaries of Southern Paiute ethnohistory and culture have been written by Kelly (1964), Kelly and Fowler (1986), and Euler (1966). According to Kelly (1934), the San Juan Paiute is the band or dialect group of the Southern Paiute whose range included the N16 ROW. The territory of the San Juan band was delimited by the San Juan and Colorado rivers on the north; the Colorado and Little Colorado rivers on the west; the Little Colorado River on the south; and the Moenkopi Plateau, Black Mesa, and Comb Ridge on the east. Powell and Ingalls (in Fowler and Fowler 1971:104, 107) listed a total of 62 individuals in what is now known as the San Juan band in 1873, a number that was probably too low. Paiute still live around the Piute Mesa–Navajo Mountain area in a lifestyle closely resembling that of the Navajo, and they often intermarry with Navajo. Many local residents still recognize themselves as Paiute and still speak their own language, and people in the area know who is Paiute, who is Navajo, and who is both.

The historic Navajo and Paiute occupation of this area is not the subject of this report, so no further discussion is warranted. Interested readers should consult such references as Adams 1963, Bunte and Franklin 1987, Collier 1951, McPherson 1988, and Shepardson and Hammond 1970. A wider perspective on traditional Navajo history can be found in Brugge 1983, Kelley 1986, Kelley and Francis 1994, Roessel 1983, and Warburton and Begay 2002.

ENVIRONMENT

The Navajo Mountain road crosses, in a north–south direction, portions of the physiographic features known as the Shonto and Rainbow plateaus in northeast Arizona and southeast Utah. These two plateaus, remnants of a geologic uplift that began about 70 million years ago, are at the boundary between the Navajo and Canyonlands sections of the Colorado Plateau physiographic province (Hunt 1967), with Shonto Plateau part of the former and Rainbow Plateau at the south-central edge of the Canyonlands. Segments 1–2 of N16, studied previously by Schroedl (1989), are located entirely on the Shonto Plateau; the road segments for this project are on the interconnecting divide (Segments 3–4) and the Rainbow Plateau proper (Segments 5–6). The general character of the entire route for Segments 3–6 is most like the Canyonlands Section, which is known for deeply dissected terrain of cliff scarps, canyons, mesas, buttes, hogback ridges, and isolated mountains formed by intrusive laccoliths.

Segment 3 begins on a high narrow ridge between Cliff Spring Canyon, a tributary of Begashibito Wash, and the deep trench of Geshi Canyon, a tributary of Navajo Creek (Figure 2.10). This is at an elevation of 2,152 m (7,060 ft).[1] A few relict ponderosa pines occur along drainages in what is otherwise a dense pinyon–juniper forest. The road then climbs to a maximum elevation of 2,234 m (7,330 ft) next to Hill Top Well. This high point marks the divide in watersheds, with precipitation falling to the north flowing into Piute Creek and thence the San Juan River and with precipitation falling to the south draining into Cliff Spring Canyon, then into Begashibito Wash, and eventually into the Little Colorado River by way of Moenkopi Wash. Along the western side of this divide, precipitation tumbles into Far End Canyon to join Navajo Creek and finally the Colorado River, now beneath Lake Powell.

Segments 3 and 4 of the ROW take a somewhat serpentine route along the divide between Piute and Navajo creeks, slowly losing elevation along the way. The divide is mostly at an elevation between 2,234 and 2,012 m (7,200 and 6,600 ft) and is characterized by vast exposures of Navajo Sandstone slickrock, cliff escarpments, and falling dunes. Vegetated portions are covered by pinyon–juniper forest. Ridgetops have beautiful vistas of the adjoining canyons, with high mesas and mountains as a splendid backdrop (Figure 2.11). The canyons expose several geologic formations that underlie the Navajo Sandstone, including the other members of the Glen Canyon Group (Kayenta Formation and Wingate Sandstone) and the Chinle Formation (see Figure 2.12).

Segment 4 ends on the southeast edge of the Rainbow Plateau proper in a dense pinyon–juniper forest at an elevation of about 1,950 m (6,400 ft). Segments 5 and 6 then cross this plateau, reaching a low point of about 1,706 m (5,600 ft) near the end of the road at the Navajo Mountain Boarding School. Much of this area consists of broad flats covered by sagebrush, becoming pinyon- and juniper-covered ridges and narrow sagebrush-filled drainages along the foot of Navajo Mountain.

The Rainbow Plateau is a broad, generally north-sloping tableland of sandstone and siltstone lying south of the confluence of the Colorado and San Juan rivers in southeast Utah and northeast Arizona. A magma intrusion pushed up the ancient sedimentary layers on the northwest edge of the plateau, creating the magnificent dome known as Navajo Mountain (Figure 2.13). This singular, dominating topographic feature rises to a height of 3,166 m, about 1,200 m above the plateau generally and some 2,100 m above the Glen Canyon lowlands. These lowlands define the northern limits of the plateau. The south and west sides of the plateau are defined by a relatively abrupt break known as the Chaiyahi Rim, below which are the tortuous canyons that drain into Navajo and Aztec creeks. The canyon of Aztec Creek, also known as Forbidding Canyon, separates the Rainbow Plateau from the adjacent bedrock platform of Cummings Mesa. The large canyon of Piute Creek defines the eastern edge of the plateau. Most of the Rainbow Plateau ranges in elevation from about 1,650 m to 2,070 m. The highest elevations are along the southeast edge and around the lower flanks of Navajo Mountain. The northern portion of the plateau slopes toward the canyons of the San Juan and Colorado rivers.

Climate

Climatic conditions on the Rainbow and Shonto plateaus can vary considerably, but the general pattern is for a total accumulation of 23–31 cm (9–12 in) of annual precipitation (Table 2.1). Much of this occurs as snow from December through March and as heavy but short-lived rain showers from July into September. The existing weather data for the Navajo Mountain Trading Post reveal a less well-developed monsoonal pattern than is evident at the Betatakin weather station, and one with a later onset. Noted precipitation extremes for the Rainbow Plateau vary from less than 16 cm (6 in) to almost 41 cm (16 in), and this from the consecutive years of 1964 and 1965. Precipitation extremes from the Betatakin weather station are even greater—from 16 cm (6 in) in 1956 to almost 50 cm in 1982 (20 in).

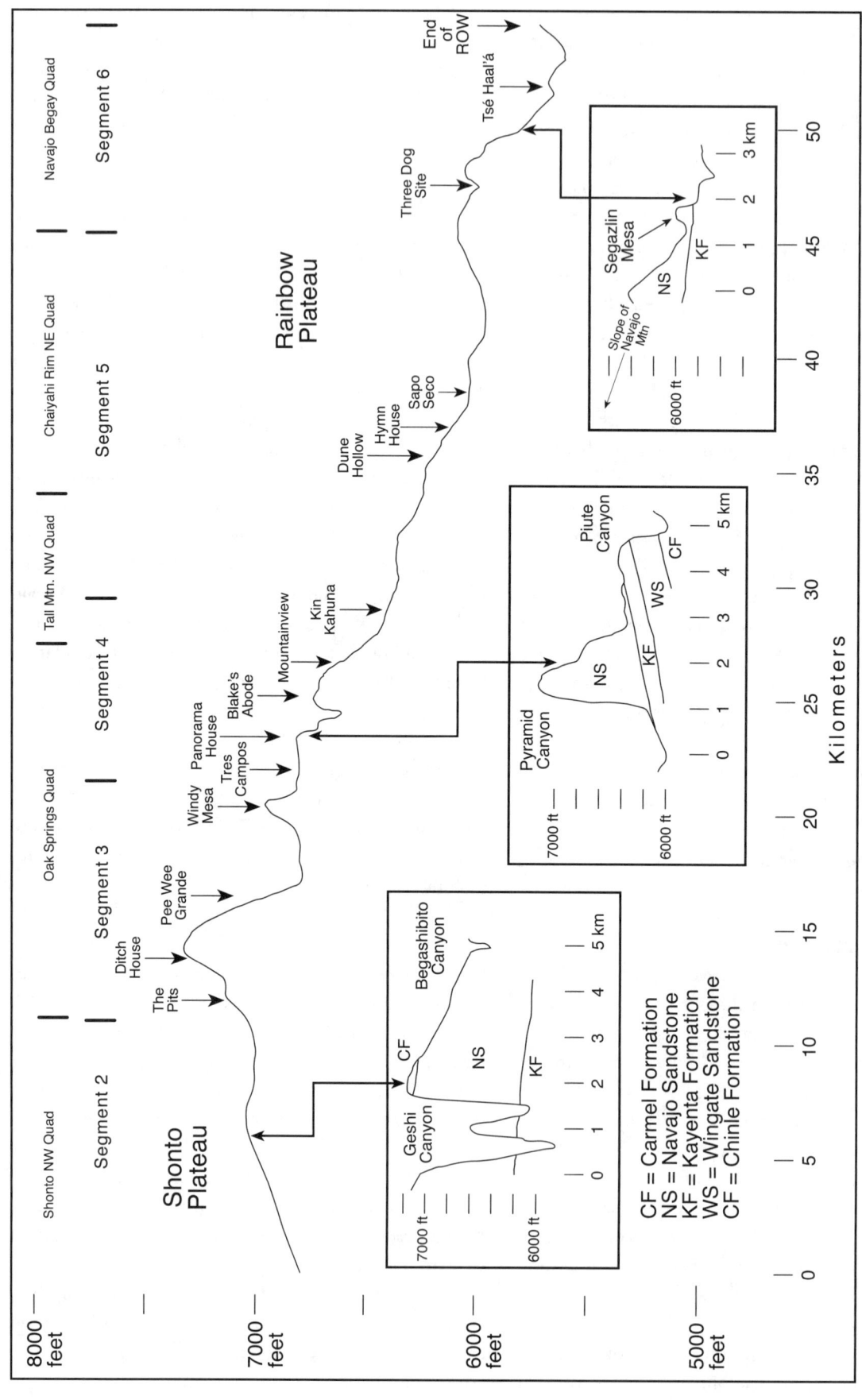

Figure 2.10. Schematic cross section along the N16 right-of-way plus three orthogonal sections (inset boxes), showing elevation in feet, bedrock geology, major topographic features and drainages, and the locations of selected sites excavated within the right-of-way; USGS 7.5 minute topographic quadrangles are listed as the top.

Figure 2.11. View from the high divide between Navajo and Piute canyons that N16 traverses looking north-northwest across Pyramid Canyon with Navajo Mountain on the horizon; Ted Neff stands in the foreground.

Figure 2.12. View into a part of Upper Piute Canyon from its western rim looking at the deep alluvium farmland that this canyon provides.

Figure 2.13. View to the southwest of Navajo Mountain from the northern part of the Rainbow Plateau near Hawkeye Natural Bridge.

The temperature for the area is quite variable day to day, day to night, seasonally, and even annually. The critical factor, at least for farmers, is the length of time between killing frosts. Table 2.2 shows that there is little difference between the Betatakin and Navajo Mountain weather stations in the length of the freeze-free season, despite the difference in elevation. This is likely a result of cold-air drainage off the slopes of Navajo Mountain past the weather station there, which was located within a narrow canyon. Microtopographic setting can have a profound effect on the length of the growing season, but in general both the Rainbow and Shonto plateaus have sufficiently long seasons to produce corn. The real problem for agriculture is the combined annual uncertainty of potentially low precipitation and unpredictable length of time between killing frosts. Together these factors make agriculture on the plateaus precarious, and coping with them must have frequently occupied the minds of past farmers. One possible response would be planting in a diversity of locations each year to spread out the risk of crop failure from drought or killing frosts.

Modern climatic records provide data that inform about high-frequency processes (Dean 1988a, 1988b), the variability that occurs on a temporal scale of less than 25 years and which people clearly recognize, put to memory, and incorporate into their behavioral strategies. High-resolution tree-ring records available for the region (Dean and Robinson 1978) provide the best proxy of this form of environmental variability. These are thought to have played a significant role in human adaptation and culture change, especially after the advent of farming (e.g., Gumerman, ed. 1988). Humans also respond to longer-term directional shifts in temperature and precipitation since these influence plant and animal distributions and densities. A case in point is the record of forager occupation during the Archaic period, a topic that is discussed in greater detail in chapter 4.

Biota

The biotic community along the entire length of the N16 ROW is the Great Basin Conifer Woodland (Brown 1982), characterized by a pinyon–juniper overstory and a variety of shrubs, grasses, and forbs. Certain grasses of economic importance in the past, such as ricegrass (*Achnatherum hymenoides*) and dropseed (*Sporobolus* spp.), are poorly represented today because of overgrazing. On sand-covered flats and drainage basins, the pinyon–juniper forest gives way to a thick cover of big sagebrush.

Local geologic, hydrologic, elevational, and topographic situations combine to create a large number of microhabitats, so the overall floral variety in the area is high.

The upper reaches and northern slopes of Navajo Mountain contain Hudsonian spruce-fir-aspen forests (Figure 2.12). Below that, ponderosa pine and Gambel's oak predominate, with understory mats of manzanita, ceanothus, and snowberry, continuing almost to the base of the mountain in sheltered locations. The lowest slopes of the mountain and much of the adjoining platform support oftentimes dense stands of pinyon and juniper, with sagebrush and grasses dominating the open valleys and flats. Descending further in elevation, below 1,525 m, sagebrush gives way to blackbrush. The deeply incised canyons, with their higher temperatures and lower precipitation, support more xeric vegetation. Numerous springs and seeps and perennially flowing streams and rivers support pockets and bands of riparian species: cottonwood, willow, common reed, cattail, and the like.

For the prehistoric people who resided on the plateaus traversed by N16, the adjacent canyons (Figure 2.13) offered a completely different set of geologic and biotic resources, and any understanding of past adaptations must take into account the broader ecological milieu. The canyons have alternately eroded and filled with alluvium during the past millennium. During periods of stability or slow aggradation the alluvium provided important farmland for prehistoric and historic agriculturalists. Periods of degradation or even rapid alluviation reduced the amount of arable land and are generally thought to have profoundly influenced the prehistoric inhabitants of the area. The canyons also provide an abundant supply of water from numerous seeps and springs for domestic purposes.

Judging from the botanical remains recovered by the work reported herein, supplemented by previous archaeological and ethnographic studies, plants of particular importance to the prehistoric inhabitants would have included pinyon (nuts and firewood), juniper (firewood and construction timber), yucca (sandals, basketry, and cordage), cactus (fruits and pads for food), ricegrass and other grasses (seeds for food), goosefoot and pigweed (greens and seeds), beeweed (greens, seeds, and rendered for carbon paint), ground-cherry (fruits), squawbush (fruits and twigs for basketry), hackberry (fruits), and mustard (seeds and greens). All of these plants are presently available in or near the project area, as they probably were in the past. Although overuse could quickly diminish the supply of

TABLE 2.1. Monthly Climate Summaries for Two Weather Stations That Bracket the Navajo Mountain Road Archaeological Project Area: the Navajo Mountain Trading Post at 1,844 m at the eastern foot of Navajo Mountain on the Rainbow Plateau and Navajo National Monument at 2,220 m on a Ridgetop Above Betatakin Ruin on the Shonto Plateau (Temperature in Fahrenheit, Precipitation in Inches)

VARIABLE	JANUARY	FEBRUARY	MARCH	APRIL	MAY	JUNE	JULY	AUGUST	SEPTEMBER	OCTOBER	NOVEMBER	DECEMBER	ANNUAL
Navajo Mountain, UT (1956–1975)													
Average Maximum Temperature	39.6	46.5	52.3	61.5	71.8	82.7	89.5	86.0	77.6	66.2	53.1	41.7	64.0
Average Minimum Temperature	13.5	20.0	24.4	31.7	41.8	49.1	58.3	56.8	46.7	36.3	26.8	16.2	35.1
Average Total Precipitation	.86	.99	.76	.42	.31	.37	.25	.89	.91	1.53	.95	.95	9.18
Average Total Snowfall	4.6	7.2	6.3	1.6	0.6	.0	.0	.0	.0	1.1	2.1	4.4	27.9
Average Snow Depth	1	0	0	0	0	0	0	0	0	0	0	1	0
Betatakin, AZ (1948–2001)													
Average Maximum Temperature	39.7	43.2	49.8	59.7	70.3	81.3	86.0	82.9	75.7	63.7	48.8	40.2	61.8
Average Minimum Temperature	20.6	23.3	27.3	33.6	42.5	52.4	58.2	56.5	50.3	40.0	28.6	21.7	37.9
Average Total Precipitation	1.08	.93	1.03	.74	.51	.42	1.34	1.69	1.07	1.20	1.04	1.09	12.14
Average Total Snowfall	11.6	9.8	8.2	4.1	.7	0	0	0	0	1.3	6.7	11.6	54.1
Average Snow Depth	4	3	1	0	0	0	0	0	0	0	1	2	1

TABLE 2.2. Length of Freeze-Free Season Probabilities for the Two Weather Stations That Bracket the Navajo Mountain Road Archaeological Project Area

STATION	TEMPERATURE (°F)	SHORTEST	90%	80%	70%	60%	50%	40%	30%	20%	10%	LONGEST
Navajo Mountain	36.5	80	99	86	123	96	100	108	140	139	155	162
	32.5	*111*	*119*	*113*	*138*	*119*	*123*	*143*	*161*	*169*	*163*	*174*
	28.5	123	158	135	163	162	177	186	186	198	191	202
	24.5	163	169	174	191	194	204	206	216	214	231	220
	20.5	186	205	199	214	213	214	223	236	243	261	254
Betatakin	36.5	78	107	112	114	123	129	135	141	149	152	162
	32.5	*111*	*128*	*139*	*146*	*149*	*156*	*160*	*163*	*165*	*171*	*177*
	28.5	143	152	160	165	170	176	178	184	189	196	209
	24.5	169	172	177	181	186	193	198	202	209	220	230
	20.5	169	191	201	208	212	221	224	230	234	249	270

Note: The percent columns give the consecutive number of days during which the minimum temperature was not below the threshold. Italics highlight the critical value of 32.5°F (freezing temperature of water and high probability of crop damage).

some species, horticultural impact would have increased the supply of others (especially the weedy forbs) by maintaining the ecological system at an early successional stage (Odum 1969).

As a result of historic grazing and hunting, animal life is not now abundant in the area, but it was probably more plentiful in prehistoric times. Judging from archaeological deposits, mountain sheep appear to have been the most common artiodactyls used and the most abundant big game in the district. They are now locally extinct but have been reintroduced to some adjoining areas such as the Kaiparowits Plateau and along the San Juan River. Deer are also reported from prehistoric contexts of the area and can still be found in remote portions of the region, with the high divide along Segments 3 and 4 known as a good place to hunt deer. Cottontails, jackrabbits, and a host of smaller mammals undoubtedly augmented the food supply and might have increased in number due to the presence of agricultural fields (e.g., Linares 1976; Rea 1978, 1997) and the reduction in predators; these animals are still common in the area. Rarely sighted today are foxes, bobcats, and mountain lions, but all have been reported from archaeological contexts. Coyotes are still relatively common, along with lizards, pinyon jays, and ravens. Birds and reptiles may have been used for subsistence, ceremonial, and decorative purposes. Fish of several species were present in the San Juan and its tributaries but were evidently rarely used by the Puebloans. Woodbury (1965) has summarized the ectoparasites, endoparasites, and diseases endemic to the region; crop and grain storage pests also made prehistoric life more difficult.

Water

Water is an essential element of daily life for all people, and after the introduction of farming it became a critical variable in the success or failure of crops. Water for domestic purposes was easier to obtain and control than that needed for farming. The latter either was precipitation based, and thus unpredictable on a yearly basis, or involved considerable work to create means of impoundment or channeling, something at which the local Puebloans excelled (see Lindsay 1961; Lindsay et al. 1968).

The most reliable and best source of domestic water comes from permanent springs, which are relatively numerous in the canyons alongside the N16 ROW for Segments 3 and 4. Upper Piute Canyon is particularly well watered, with numerous springs issuing from the contact of the Wingate and Chinle formations; some of these have an estimated volume of 50 to 100 gal per minute (Fairley 1989:44). There is a permanent flow in Upper Piute Creek for a few kilometers before the water sinks subsurface. Many of the springs have been channeled onto the deep alluvium of the canyon bottom to create rich farmland. Springs also issue from the Navajo Sandstone, usually at its base where the Kayenta Formation acts as an aquiclude, and these would have been more accessible to people living or traveling along the divide traversed by the ROW. Two springs emanating from the Navajo Sandstone that were probably of importance to the past occupants along the N16 ROW are Cliff Spring near the start of Segment 3 and Tse Ya Toe at the southeast edge of the Rainbow Plateau.

On the flats of the Rainbow Plateau in Segments 5

and 6, springs are fewer and farther away. There are a few springs up on the slopes of Navajo Mountain, such as War God, but these require some effort to get to. Perhaps one of the most important is at the location of the old Navajo Mountain Trading Post where the chapter house is still located. Other springs occur on the northern edge of the plateau in Upper Cha Canyon and Desha Creek.

Plunge pools and weathering basins provided additional sources of drinking water and were likely used for that purpose commonly. Plunge pools occur along drainages, with the Navajo Sandstone especially prone to being scoured into pools of various sizes. The hard tabular Kayenta Formation sandstone also contains such pools, like that next to site UT-B-63-30 in Segment 6. Some plunge pools can be quite large and when shaded and deep can hold water year round except in lengthy droughts. There are many good examples along the ROW of Segments 3 and 4 and several large pools in Segment 6 (next to sites UT-B-63-30 and -39) but few in the flats of Segment 5. The importance of such pools as a source of water is perhaps indicated by a large shaded plunge pool next to Sand Dune Cave that almost always contains water (Lindsay et al. 1968). Within a small alcove immediately above the pool is a jacal structure, built during late Pueblo III (site UT-B-63-7), a time of peak population. This site may have been used to monitor the water source and control its use.

Weathering basins on slickrock exposures of Navajo Sandstone were quite important because they occur in places lacking both plunge pools and springs, such as on the sagebrush flats of Segment 5. In some cases the basins can be quite small, such as examples next to site AZ-J-2-2, holding only a gallon or two, but this is adequate for a transient small group. In other cases the basins can be quite large, holding several hundred gallons and even more if improvements are made. Bathtub-size basins on Segazlin Mesa (Lindsay et al. 1968:Figure 180c) provide examples of weathering pits that were probably used frequently by the many occupants of that mesa during Pueblo III. Many of these could have been enhanced with a small amount of mortar, thus greatly increasing their capacity. One example of improving a basin with masonry and mortar is provided at AZ-J-2-10, a site located partially within the N16 ROW (Clark 1993a:22–34). Here there is an extensive and slightly sloping slickrock exposure containing numerous small catchments and one large (ca. 40 × 30 m) shallow basin that holds several thousand gallons of water. A low masonry wall roughly 122 m long and three–five courses high was built along the downslope side to help channel and impound water. The wall might be historic, though similar walls are known to be prehistoric (e.g., Kidder and Guernsey 1919:Plate 23a), but even without it the basin provides a substantial water source. Of course, the basins are more ephemeral than plunge pools and usually hold water for just a week or two following summer rains and winter snows (longer in winter because of less evaporation).

Sediments and Farming

By far, most of the surficial sediment in the general project area is very fine, brown (7.5YR5/4) sand in which little soil development has occurred. This sand is derived almost exclusively from weathering and erosion of Jurassic Navajo Sandstone, the unit that forms the bedrock for virtually the entire N16 ROW. This sediment has been deposited and reworked mainly by eolian processes into poorly defined and generally shallow sand sheets, low linear dunes, and deep falling or climbing dunes. Archaeological sites within the project area occurred exclusively within eolian sand deposits.

The soils identified at excavated NMRAP sites and referred to in the online site descriptions of volumes 2–4 were based on limited geomorphic study along Segment 3 of the N16 ROW by Kirk Anderson. His full report is presented in Appendix G of the supporting documentation because it served as the basis for the field identification of soil horizons at all sites within the project area. Key soil horizons of the NMRAP project area include surface and buried *A* horizons, cambic *B* horizons, and *C* horizons variably cemented by calcium carbonate. The oldest deposits within the area are probably late Pleistocene to early Holocene in age, designated as calcic (*Ck* or *Bk*) or argillic (*Bt*) horizons. The argillic horizons are reddish colored and contain translocated clay, making the sediment sticky and plastic when wet, properties lacking in the parent eolian sand. In calcic horizons the eolian sand is partially cemented with translocated calcium carbonate; in the project area these generally have a weak Stage I development (Gile et al. 1966), characterized by fine white carbonate filaments coating rootlets and cracks within the sediment and imparting an overall whitish discoloration to the sand.

Holocene soils are represented by weakly developed A horizons, characterized by the addition of organic matter, sometimes enriched by cultural activity (hearth charcoal and ash), and by Bw horizons, characterized by reddening and the accumulation of translocated clay. A horizons form at the earth's surface but subsequently can become buried by dune deposits or floods. The inclusion of decayed organic matter usually makes A horizons browner or grayer compared to other layers. In dry climates such as the Colorado Plateau, A horizons are generally weakly developed and difficult to detect. In areas with intensive cultural activity, A horizons can be black or gray as a result of additions of charcoal, ash, and other organic debris. Distinguishing a true A horizon developed pedogenically from a culturally enriched layer can be difficult. In this report, A horizons may be artifact rich or culturally sterile. B horizons are subsurface soil horizons that developed as a result of physical and chemical alterations. All Bw horizons identified for the project area have an increase in chroma and redder hue than the underlying parent sand and some clay content, imparting a blocky structure and plasticity when wet. The better-developed A and B soil horizons occur in flat-lying areas, especially under trees.

Although eolian sand is the principal sediment type present in the NMRAP project area, alluvial and colluvial deposits are also present. Layers of alluvial silt, sand, and gravel occur along washes, especially those flowing off of Navajo Mountain, but they are best represented in the canyons of Navajo and Piute creeks, where many meters of alluvium are present in places. Colluvium is best represented on and around the slopes of Navajo Mountain, where vast gravel and boulder fields of sandstone have eroded from the mountain.

Basketmaker and Puebloan livelihood depended upon locations suitable for the cultivation of domesticates. Despite the accumulating evidence that wild foods were used extensively by the Anasazi and formed an essential part of their diet, ultimately their existence was rooted in domesticates. It is within this context that discussions of adaptive strategies are most relevant. The importance of cultivation is strengthened by making the distinction between ecologically wild plants and ruderal genera. Weeds were important subsistence resources to the Basketmakers and Puebloans, and the disturbance caused by farming likely increased their quantity and reliability (Brush et al. 1981; Bye 1981; Nabhan and Sheridan 1982; Nabhan et al. 1977). Although species such as pinyon, prickly pear, and ricegrass were used, perhaps frequently, it seems evident that maintenance of the Kayenta lifeway was dependent upon the diverse plant foods derived from their fields and other disturbed habitats.

Opportunities for farmers on the Rainbow Plateau are diverse and include settings suitable for floodwater, dry, and irrigation farming, techniques that local Navajo and Paiute families still use. Runoff from Navajo Mountain and the high divide on the southeast edge of the plateau allows for floodwater farming in the wash bottoms, as do several of the broad washes that cross the plateau. Some of the more productive modern fields are located in such settings. Irrigation and high water table farming is possible in the canyons adjacent to the plateau and draining its northern edge. Prehistoric irrigation features occur at several locations in the area (Lindsay 1961; Lindsay et al. 1968). Extensive dune fields and large falling dunes offer dry farming opportunities during wetter years.

Soil characteristics and distributions are central to considerations of Anasazi adaptation. Numerous factors affect the formation of soils, and the dynamics of the process open up avenues of error in prehistoric reconstructions (Warren et al. 1981). Most important, soil formation is a continuous process, and present distributions do not necessarily match those of the past (Ruhe 1974). Although scientists are capable of subdividing soils on a fine scale, Hack (1942) has noted that such divisions have little relevance to Southwestern farmers. Hack found that Hopi "fields are usually located in areas of soil [sediment] accumulation so that almost no soils in which crops are grown ever have a chance to develop profiles" (1942:25). His simplified classification, based on transport mechanism and particle size, is equally applicable to the analysis and discussion of prehistoric Puebloan horticulture.

According to Hack (1942:26), sandy alluvium for floodwater farming was most important to Hopi horticulture, and this was apparently the case with Anasazi horticulture as well (Matson et al. 1988; Reher 1977:91–99). The primary reason for this preference is the greatly increased quantity of available water due to runoff. Direct evidence of prehistoric farming is quite abundant in the area around Navajo Mountain, including a diversity of techniques from hillside terracing to irrigation using springs (Lindsay 1961; Lindsay et al. 1968). Most of these intensification efforts appear to date to Pueblo III times, after about AD 1200, when population in the area reached its peak. Navajo fields today on the Rainbow Plateau are likely located in some of the same settings that Puebloans and Basketmakers farmed centuries or millennia ago. The most productive fields are located where springs can be channeled onto alluvium as in Piute Canyon. Some precipitation-dependent fields are located on sandy flats or slight slopes, but better locations are along drainages where runoff is concentrated.

Geology

The Jurassic Navajo Sandstone forms the bedrock over most of the Rainbow and Shonto plateaus (Cooley et al. 1969). There are scattered remnants of the overlying Carmel Formation on the Shonto Plateau, and the southern two segments of N16 cross a few of these (see Figure 2.10). The Kayenta Formation forms the bedrock for the northeastern portion of the Rainbow Plateau, and the northern end of N16 crosses exposures of this unit. Cretaceous formations exposed on the upper slopes of Navajo Mountain form the adjacent Cummings Mesa. The underlying Wingate Sandstone and Chinle Formation occur in the adjoining deep canyons, with Piute Canyon and the Lower San Juan River providing especially good exposures of the resource-rich Chinle Formation.

People have always relied on geologic materials for making pottery, stone tools, building materials, and mineral pigments. It is important therefore to obtain a clear understanding of the geologic resources available within a region. Cooley et al. (1969) illustrated the geologic formations exposed within the general region of the project area; descriptions of these are available from the same reference and other reports (e.g., Baars 2000). The information presented here has been gleaned from more than 20 years of working in the area, including various collection trips that delimited areas of occurrence much more precisely and provided new insights. Much of this information was previously presented by Ambler and me (Geib and Ambler 1985), but because that report had such limited distribution, the information is repeated here and updated. This information is not exhaustive because not all of the northern Kayenta region has been examined in detail.

Chert and Other Siliceous Rock

Glen Canyon Alluvial Cobbles

Cooley (1960) documented a wide variety of material types from Quaternary and Tertiary gravel of the Colorado and San Juan rivers. Predominant rock types depend on the age of the gravel, but generally they are igneous porphyry, quartzite, and chert (which includes his jasper). The alluvial cobbles are now mostly under the water of Lake Powell, but collections taken during the Glen Canyon Project are housed at MNA and are available for study. The alluvial cobble chert was used extensively for producing bifaces and other sharp implements (Turner and Cooley 1960); as a convenient referent for this resource I use the name Glen Canyon chert. The material grouped under this referent is a diverse lot but is generally quite distinctive from the other cherts available within the Kayenta region, such as Navajo chert and Owl Rock chert. Some of the material labeled as Glen Canyon chert has known primary sources such as the Honaker Trail and Paradox formations, but in cases where flakes of this material retained cortex it was evident that they came from alluvial cobbles. Alluvial cobbles of quartzite were used primarily as hammerstones if unflaked or as choppers and similar heavy-duty tools if flaked. The igneous porphyry was used on occasion for ground-stone axes or hammerstones.

Navajo Chert

Navajo Sandstone forms the bedrock across a vast portion of the Kayenta region, and within this formation occur thin freshwater limestone beds that yield a chert widely used by prehistoric groups for flaked-stone tool production. This material is generally microcrystalline and of high quality in texture, appearing quite lustrous. Two factors limit its suitability: small nodule size and numerous internal fractures and flaws. The small nodule size is partly a result of the fractures, but it is also because the chert occurs in thin seams. When found still embedded within limestone the chert is difficult to extract. The usual means of exploiting this material was to locate places where the seams had weathered out, freeing the chert from its matrix. Upon exposure the thin seams crumble along fracture planes into small angular chunks. Sometimes the chunks are so riddled with fracture planes that it is challenging to produce even a tiny usable flake. Some exposures of Navajo chert, however, are more coherent and produce almost fist-sized, check-free nodules. The color of this material is so highly variable that it is not easily characterized. Brownish colors are perhaps most common, and mottling is characteristic, but the material can range from nearly colorless and translucent (chalcedony) to black and opaque. Despite this variability, with enough experience handling nodules of the chert, the material is usually easily identified in artifacts.

Navajo chert is good for the production of sharp flakes, and the Kayenta Anasazi commonly accomplished this using bipolar reduction, which is well suited to the small angular nodules of this material. This method also has the benefit of producing flat flakes and those with square or steeply angled edges, which are particularly useful for some tasks because of their strength. For facially thinned tools such as dart points and bifaces, Navajo chert is generally less well suited than the relatively flawless chert available in large nodules from the alluvial cobble deposits of the San Juan and Colorado rivers. Nonetheless, Navajo chert was also fabricated into bifaces and projectile points, especially in portions of the Kayenta region well away from sources of chert with larger and less fractured nodules. This material was also a trade item (or at least the tools were) to Black Mesa, an area that was even more poorly endowed with lithic resources than the Shonto Plateau or Klethla Valley (Fernstrom 1980; Green 1982).

Outcrops of Navajo chert occur along portions of the N16 ROW, especially in Segments 3 and 4. Sections of the landscape crossed by Segment 5 were littered with a lag deposit of small angular nodules of Navajo chert. In Segment 6 it appears that a coarse siliceous rock designated Navajo quartz is more common within the limestone beds of the Navajo Sandstone than is the chert.

Navajo Quartz

Occasionally occurring within the limestone beds of the Navajo Sandstone on the Rainbow Plateau (and elsewhere in the Kayenta region) is a dark to light gray, grainy, siliceous material that I call Navajo quartz. The crystals are usually macroscopic, and the texture resembles quartzite, although it is obviously not metamorphic or an orthoquartzite. Limestone is often intermixed to varying degrees with this siliceous rock. This material is dense and durable and does not fracture easily, although it is flakeable. Like Navajo chert, the material is prone to split along internal flaws, resulting in angular chunks, but there are relatively flawless nodules. Several outcrops of Navajo quartz occur within a kilometer or two of the N16 ROW, with cobble- to boulder-size pieces scattered around the base of these outcrops. The pieces are usually rectangular or otherwise sharply angled. This resource appears to have been used primarily to produce pecking stones, and it accounted for almost a quarter of the debitage at several excavated habitations at the Navajo Mountain Boarding School (Geib 1985).

Owl Rock Chert

The upper part of the Chinle Formation, known as the Owl Rock Member, has thin, resistant, ledge-forming beds of limestone and calcareous siltstone. These contain bands and angular nodules of siliceous rock, varying in thickness from 5 cm to well over 1 m, which range in texture from a crystal structure that is macroscopically visible to microcrystalline. Often this variation occurs across a 1-cm section of the material. This chert usually has a highly mottled and spotted appearance, with the predominant hues being purple, light green, and tan to brown. The material is quite durable and has a conchoidal fracture but is generally ill suited to the production of thin symmetrical bifaces, principally because of its coarse mottled texture. There are of course exceptions, because some pieces of this material can be highly siliceous. Owl Rock chert is eminently suitable for the production of sharp flakes for expedient use. Its durability and nodule size make it well suited for tools such as choppers and pecking stones, and because the chert beds erode and fracture into cobble- and boulder-size pieces, large tools can be produced. This chert is easily distinguished from the colorful silicified wood and semitranslucent chert that occur within other members of the Chinle Formation. A high-quality and chalcedonic variety of colorful banded chert is available from the Chine Formation around the Bears Ears in Utah and as a lag deposit on Cedar Mesa.

Silicified Wood

No high-quality silicified wood has yet been found in Piute Canyon; the petrified wood occurring there within the Petrified Forest Member of the Chinle Formation is gray to black in color and fairly coarse. High-quality and quite colorful wood is available from this formation farther to the west around Lees Ferry.

Silicified Conglomerate and Sandstone

These resources are most commonly found in the streambeds that drain Navajo Mountain, but they also occur in the talus deposits that drape ridges and slopes around the mountain. The conglomerate is so thoroughly altered by silica-rich solutions and heat that conchoidal fracture passes through matrix and grains with minimal interference. This material is not suitable for producing grinding implements or even mauls, but it can be flaked to make choppers, large unifaces, and usable sharp flakes. Although it is moderately easy to flake, the local Puebloans seem to have used the rock most frequently for hammerstones. Sandstone on top of the mountain, mainly the Dakota, has been turned into a generally low-quality form of orthoquartzite through localized metamorphism and migrating silica. Cobbles of this material can be flaked into

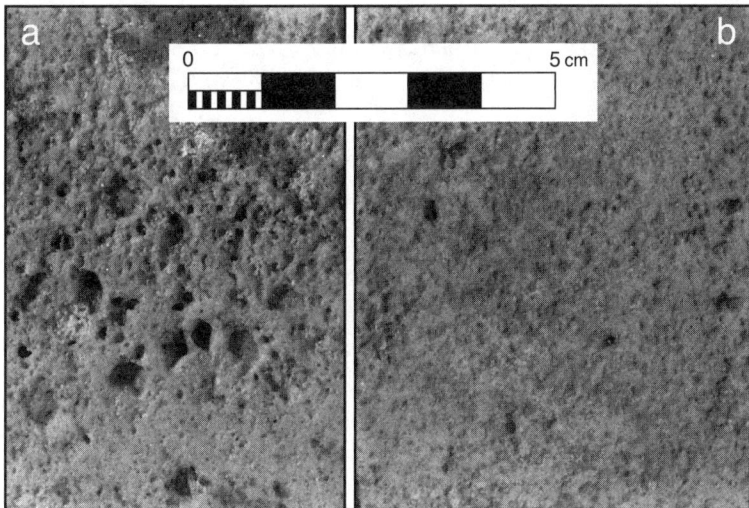

Figure 2.14. Examples of the silicified sandstone that outcrops on Navajo Mountain and is available in the talus and outwash gravel around this laccolith; both are dense medium-grain sandstone, but (a) has abundant vesicles of various size, including large pits, whereas (b) has sparse vesicles of small size.

rather crude bifaces or unifacial cobble tools such as choppers. The material was also used for pecking stones; it appears not to have been used for mauls, perhaps because its highly silicified matrix made it too brittle.

Sandstone

Navajo Mountain Sandstone

The sedimentary rock layers pushed up by the igneous intrusion that formed Navajo Mountain were affected by both heat and migrating silica-rich solutions (Condie 1964:359). This resulted in dense, well-cemented sandstones that were ideally suited for producing grinding tools and mauls (hafted hammers). Because several geologic formations were affected (from Navajo Sandstone to Dakota Sandstone), there is a great variety of textures, with grains ranging in size from fine (.125 mm) to coarse (.5 mm) to a conglomeritic variety with pebbles of chert and other rock. Much of the sandstone is vesicular (Figure 2.14), and this variety appears to have been favored for grinding implements, perhaps because the naturally pitted surface required less maintenance by pecking. Most of the sandstone is generally white to light gray in color, consisting of subangular frosted sand grains, well cemented with abundant white, primarily siliceous matrix. The sandstone is abundantly available; boulders and cobbles of the material occur in every stream draining the mountain slopes and in massive talus deposits. This was the most extensively used resource for mano and metate production by the local Kayenta Anasazi, and a Navajo woman living at the foot of Navajo Mountain (Mrs. Holgate) was making manos and metates of this sandstone through at least 2002. Beals et al., in talking about a dense light-colored sandstone used for mauls at RB568, state that "the Navajos still prize this stone for manos and say that it is brought in from somewhere near Navajo Mountain" (1945:79). Anasazi habitations close to the source of the stone contain abundant sandstone debris from the production of grinding tools by flaking and pecking (see Geib 1985:192, Figure 65). NNAD's excavations of sites at the foot of the mountain in Segment 6 likewise produced abundant sandstone production debris (see SD vol. 4, chaps. 10–11). This sandstone may also have been a source for some of the crushed sandstone used as pottery temper within Rainbow Gray, the dominant utility type on the Rainbow Plateau during Pueblo III (Callahan and Fairley 1983).

Navajo Sandstone

Navajo Sandstone is mostly eolian, cross bedded, often weakly cemented, well sorted, and fine to medium grained. Its color varies from white to light red depending on the amount of iron oxide impurities in the cement (Gregory and Moore 1931:66). Its generally friable nature makes this material a poor one for manos and metates, but it was used for unspecialized grinding and abrading implements. Due to its friability, Navajo Sandstone can be easily flaked, battered, and ground into various shapes and was thus commonly used as a source of building stone. Layers within the sandstone that are impregnated with silica or iron can be quite hard and can provide longer-lasting building blocks and better tools. Navajo Sandstone was readily available along the entire length of the N16 ROW.

Kayenta Sandstone

The Kayenta Formation consists of dark red, mainly fluvial sandstones, siltstones, and mudstones. Many portions of the Kayenta Formation have thin, even-bedded sandstones that are dense and well cemented and naturally fracture into flat slabs 2–6 cm thick. These make excellent construction stones, especially for paving floors and lining the sides of features such as mealing bins and cists. Walls made of these slabs, such as at Red House, stand tall even after hundreds of years of erosion. The slabs work well as lintels and thresholds, deflectors, and door or hatch covers. This material was used for grinding slabs (more so by Archaic foragers than the Anasazi), for small abraders, and for miscellaneous artifacts such as disks and stoppers. Outcrops of Kayenta Sandstone occur all along Segment 6 and portions of Segment 5; in Segments 3 and 4 this material could be obtained from the canyons a kilometer or two from the road ROW.

Clay

Clay was essential in pottery production both for the vessel wall (paste) and for paint (limonite-stained clay for red and kaolinite for white). Clay was also useful in house and feature construction, especially to form hard surfaces and to stabilize slabs used to line the lower walls of interior features such as mealing bins. The region traversed by the N16 ROW is clay poor because the bedrock is mostly Navajo Sandstone or Kayenta Formation; clay layers are nonexistent in Navajo Sandstone. The most readily available clay across much of the region comes from either the Carmel Formation or the underlying Kayenta Formation, which lie above and below the Navajo Sandstone, respectively. In both cases the clay is dark red and thus totally unsuitable for production of Tusayan White Ware and Tusayan Gray Ware, which contain similar if not identical light-firing clays and could not be produced from a red clay. Tsegi Orange Ware likewise could not be produced from the red clay, because it fires to a dark red or brown, not orange. The pottery that could have been made using the red clay of the Kayenta or Carmel formations is Rainbow Gray (Callahan and Fairley 1983), the local utility ware produced on the Rainbow Plateau during Pueblo III. An unfired Rainbow Gray vessel from UT-V-13-20 (Geib et al. 1985) is made of a dark red clay. In this particular case the Kayenta Formation is a more likely source than the Carmel because clay of the latter formation that is locally available from the upper slopes of Navajo Mountain and Navajo Begay contains abundant, minute gypsum crystals, which are absent in the unfired vessel. Furthermore, when the local Carmel Formation clay is fired to produce pottery, these crystals are altered into powdery anhydrite particles not observed in Rainbow Gray.

Clay more suited to pottery production comes from the Chinle Formation, with Piute Canyon providing the chief local exposure of this formation, especially the Petrified Forest Member, which consists largely of clay and mudstone. Ceramic-quality clays are generally restricted in extent, tending to grade both laterally and vertically into siltstones, a reflection of locally variable and constantly changing depositional environments. Most of the clay is bentonite, composed chiefly of montmorillonite (Allen 1930; Brown 1969). Although kaolinite has also been reported (Cadigan 1972; Schultz 1963), it occurs as sandstone matrix, rendering it useless for prehistoric potters (cf. Deutchman 1979). Ceramic-quality clays obtained from both the upper and lower parts of the Petrified Forest Member in Piute Canyon reveal a range of oxidized colors (see Geib and Ambler 1985:Table 2-2; SD, Appendix H3). I have yet to find light-firing clay suitable for the production of typical Tusayan White Ware and Tusayan Gray Ware in the Chinle Formation exposed within the Kayenta region. The oxidized colors of the Chinle clay are similar to the colors of oxidized sherds of Tsegi Orange Ware and Rainbow Gray. Strongly limonitic clay also occurs in Piute Canyon; it fires to a bright red, resembling the slip and paints on Tsegi Orange Ware. That Kayenta potters used a limonitic clay to achieve the red on Tsegi Orange Ware is demonstrated by the slip on unfired Tsegi Orange Ware Polychrome bowls (Figure 2.15; Ambler 1983). Indeed, the NMRAP excavations at Three Dog Site at the foot of Navajo Mountain recovered a small fragment of an unfired Tusayan Polychrome bowl sherd that exhibits the unmistakable limonitic clay slip (see SD vol. 5, chap. 2, and vol. 4, chap. 10).

Minerals and Pigments

Iron/Manganese

Iron/manganese occurs as a precipitate within joints and bedding planes of the Navajo Sandstone in several places along the N16 ROW. As the sandstone erodes, chunks of the hard mineral are left as a lag deposit scattered on

Figure 2.15. Two rim sherds of unfired Tsegi Orange Ware bowls (either Kiet Siel Black-on-red or Tusayan Polychrome) found nested together in the trash midden at Long House and in the collections at the Museum of Northern Arizona.

the ground surface. The chunks are usually thin and tabular but can be up to 10 cm thick; they usually have a flowstone-like appearance on at least one surface. These nodules may have been a source of the black mineral paint on Tsegi Orange Ware, though they are difficult to grind to prepare a pigment because they are so hard. Thin tabular chunks of this material were made into ornaments and disks, with several good examples coming from Basketmaker II sites (see SD vol. 3, chap. 9).

Coal

A dark gray to jet black subbituminous coal occurs sporadically immediately below the ledge-forming Sonsela Sandstone bed in Piute Canyon. This material is difficult to extract in pieces large enough to use, but given the evidence for coal ornament production at some of the Puebloan habitations around Navajo Mountain (e.g., UT-V-13-19 [Geib et al. 1985]), it seems likely that this material was exploited. Lindsay (1969:281) suggested that lignite ornaments within the Kayenta region were produced from coal outcroppings in Upper Cretaceous formations on Black Mesa, but the occurrence of lignite within the Chinle Formation exposed in Piute Canyon and unfinished and finished lignite ornaments at sites adjacent to this canyon, including those in the N16 ROW (e.g., Three Dog Site [SD vol. 4, chap. 10]), suggests that there was local procurement and production as well.[2] Archaic foragers of the region also evidently exploited this local resource, as indicated by the presence of four coal pendants with the Archaic burial at Sand Dune Cave (Lindsay et al. 1968:44, 51–52, Figure 29).

Azurite and Malachite

Trites and Hadd (1958) and also Thaden et al. (1964) reported that Shinarump-filled channel scours within the Moenkopi Formation in northern Arizona and southeastern Utah can contain abundant secondary copper minerals, including azurite and malachite. Baker (1936:99) reported finding malachite, azurite, and chrysocolla in the Shinarump conglomerate and in other outcrops of the Chinle Formation in Copper, Nokai, and Piute canyons, and Cooley (1965:11) reported their occurrence within the Monitor Butte Member at an outcrop in Glen Canyon. Malachite, chrysocolla, and small amounts of azurite also occur within a highly localized portion of the Navajo Sandstone at Coppermine and Mormon Ridge on the Kaibito Plateau (Mayo 1956). Although farther away from the NMRAP project area, the Coppermine locality contains an abundance of copper-mineralized sandstone, and it might be the chief source for the examples of material found during the project.

Travertine

Occurring within clay of the lower part of the Petrified Forest Member are thin beds of travertine (calcite) with a columnar crystalline habit. This material is ideal for pendants and spindle whorls because it occurs in thin sheets, is easily ground to shape, holds a polish, and is quite

Figure 2.16. Mineralized log within the Petrified Forest Member of the Chinle Formation exposed in Lower Piute Canyon showing the leaching of iron into the clay matrix that surrounds the log, resulting in a "limonitic" clay that can be used to produce a red slip similar to that of Tsegi Orange Ware.

durable. It could have been easily obtained while collecting clay because it is coincident with some quality clay sources.

Limonite (Goethite)

Both structureless limonite and limonite-stained clay are obtainable from the lower part of the Petrified Forest Member. Chemical analysis of a chunk of this material has shown that it is goethite (Paul Kay, personal communication 1996), but I use the less specific field term. The limonite occurs as the outer rim of richly mineralized logs replaced by iron and other minerals (Figure 2.16). These are similar to the "rods" reported by Witkind and Thaden (1963:83–89) within the Shinarump Member in the Monument Valley area or the "pods" reported by Finnell et al. (1963) within the Chinle Formation of the Deer Flat area. The iron in the mineralized logs has leached out into the surrounding clay, staining it yellow to brownish. The most intensely yellow clay fires to red, making it a probable candidate for the slip and paint of Tsegi Orange Ware. The even more iron-rich, structureless limonite could have been ground and added to clay to make a bright red slip. Both the stained clay and the raw mineral could have been used as yellow pigment for items other than pottery, such as the yellow on the petals of the remarkable flower cache from Sunflower Cave (Kidder and Guernsey 1919:145–147, Plates 60–61).

Note

1. At the junction with Arizona State Highway 98 where N16 begins, the elevation is about 1,920 m (6,300 ft).
2. It is possible that the coal worked at this site came from Cretaceous Formations on the Kaiparowits Plateau north of the Colorado River.

CHAPTER 3

Synopsis of the Navajo Mountain Road Archaeological Project Sites

As recounted in the introductory chapter, NNAD archaeologists excavated all or portions of 33 prehistoric sites that lay within the N16 ROW. Given that many of these sites had more than one temporal component, a total of 58 components were investigated. In addition, there was a limited study of Atlatl Rock Cave. Detailed site descriptions are presented in volumes 2–4 of the supporting documentation available on the Web. Site descriptions are organized by general temporal period: Archaic sites in volume 2, Basketmaker sites in volume 3, and Puebloan sites in volume 4. This presentation should make it easier for future researchers to locate temporal components of interest. Multiple-component sites are described in as many of the volumes as needed, without repeating too much redundant information such as site background and surface evidence, location and setting, excavation strategy, and stratigraphy. This information is presented in full detail only once, usually with the most significant component. The exception to this is Atlatl Rock Cave, which is described as a single unit in the Archaic volume (SD vol. 2, chap. 2). A chapter that focuses upon the temporal period around which the volume is organized introduces each of the descriptive volumes. The site descriptions provide details about artifacts and nonartifactual remains as well as the usual feature information. Volume 5 of the supporting documentation presents synthetic chapters on the analyses of the various artifacts and nonartifactual remains recovered from the excavations.

Because the primary documentation is not immediately available, it seemed appropriate to provide a capsule summary of each of the excavated sites. This way, readers will know something about the sites and the excavations upon which interpretations are based to provide a context for the ensuing temporally specific interpretive chapters. The site sketches presented here are done site by site in simple linear sequence from south to north along the N16 ROW. NNAD crews named all but two of the NMRAP sites. Site names rather than Navajo Nation site numbers are used in this and other chapters and for the site descriptions of the supporting documentation. Table 3.1 presents the concordance between names and numbers; site numbers are also given in the introduction to each site description and are presented on overall site plans. Figure 3.1 shows the locations of each of the 34 sites summarized here, and this detailed image can be used in conjunction with the small inset location figures included for each site below to help orient the reader. The numbers of structures, storage pits, pits, hearths, other features, and burials excavated at each site are listed in Table 3.2.

THE PITS (AZ-J-14-17)

The Pits (Figure 3.2) is a multiple-component site situated on a narrow ridge at an elevation of about 2,175 m (7,136 ft) between Cliff Spring Canyon to the east and the upper reach of the deeply incised Geshi Canyon to the west. The ridge is formed of Navajo Sandstone capped by a resistant layer of limestone; this cap rock is thickly mantled with eolian sand to a depth of more than 3 m. The location offers an expansive view to the south and southeast across the Shonto Plateau to the cliff scarps of Black Mesa and White Mesa on the horizon. The site occupies a level area less than 100 m wide on the ridge crest, with trash scattered down a moderately steep slope on the east side. North of the site, the ridge climbs and merges with part of a greater expanse of Navajo Sandstone that rises above the surrounding landscape. The rise divides the Shonto Plateau to the south from the Rainbow Plateau and Piute Mesa to the north.

The two principal components are preceramic, one late Archaic and the other Basketmaker II; transient use of the site during the Pueblo period left few remains and features (scattered sherds and a single hearth), and little

Table 3.1. Summary of the 33 Sites Excavated During the Navajo Mountain Road Archaeological Project

Map No.	Navajo Nation Archaeology Department Site No.	Site Name	Percent in Right-of-Way	Component No.	Temporal Affiliation(s)	Site Function(s)	Other Information
1	AZ-J-14-17	The Pits	50	3	(a) late Archaic (b) Basketmaker II (BMII) (c) Puebloan	(a) temporary camp, hunting emphasis (b) primary habitation (c) temporary camp	A major portion of the BMII component, including structures and extensive trash deposits, lies outside the right-of-way (ROW).
2	AZ-J-14-21	Ditch House	100	2	(a) Basketmaker II (b) late Pueblo II (PII), early Pueblo III (PIII) (c) mid–Pueblo III	(a) secondary habitation (b) secondary habitation (c) primary habitation	PIII component significantly impacted by existing road (structures and trash midden lost); BMII component, less so. Interpretation of the Puebloan component somewhat affected.
3	AZ-J-14-20	Wolachii Bighan	100	1	Pueblo I (PI)	temporary camp	Site partially impacted by existing road; site interpretation perhaps unaffected.
4	AZ-J-14-23	Hólahéi Scatter	100	1	Archaic	temporary camp, hunting emphasis	Site partially impacted by existing road and by deflation; site interpretation partially affected, especially temporal placement.
5	AZ-J-14-26	Pee Wee Grande	100	3	(a) early Archaic (b) Basketmaker (c) Puebloan	(a) temporary camp (b) temporary camp (c) temporary camp	Site partially impacted by existing road; site interpretation probably unaffected.
6	AZ-J-14-28	Windy Mesa	40	3	(a) early Archaic (b) Basketmaker II (c) early Pueblo III	(a) temporary camp, hunting emphasis (b) temporary camp, lithic reduction (c) primary habitation	Site partially impacted by existing road; site interpretation probably unaffected. Puebloan component mostly avoided or lying outside the ROW; data-recovery effort focused on the BMII and Archaic components. An unknown portion of the BMII component might lie outside the ROW, leaving interpretation of the portion studied open to question.
7	AZ-J-14-30	The Slots	90	1	late Pueblo II	secondary habitation	Close to total excavation, portion outside the ROW perhaps inconsequential to site interpretation.
8	AZ-J-14-31	Polly's Place	100	2	(a) early Archaic (b) Basketmaker II	(a) temporary camp (b) primary habitation	Virtually 100% excavated; portion outside is inconsequential to site interpretation.
9	AZ-J-14-11	Naaki Hooghan	90	1	late Pueblo II, early Pueblo III	secondary habitation	Virtually 100% excavated; portion outside inconsequential to site interpretation.
10	AZ-J-14-12	Tres Campos	80	3	(a) early Archaic (b) Basketmaker II (c) late Pueblo II	(a) temporary camp, hunting emphasis (b) secondary habitation (c) secondary habitation	An unknown but perhaps sizable portion of the Archaic component not impacted by existing road, though site interpretation perhaps unaffected. The BMIII component lies partially outside the ROW—a small trash midden and an extramural hearth were excavated; a burned structure just slightly in the ROW was avoided. The PII component lay totally in the ROW and was undisturbed except for deflation.

Table 3.1. (cont'd.) Summary of the 33 Sites Excavated During the Navajo Mountain Road Archaeological Project

Map No.	Navajo Nation Archaeology Department Site No.	Site Name	Percent in Right-of-Way	Component No.	Temporal Affiliation(s)	Site Function(s)	Other Information
11	AZ-J-14-34	Panorama House	20	1	Basketmaker II	secondary habitation	Most of the site lies outside the ROW; the portion excavated included a structure, part of an associated small trash deposit, and a few extramural hearths.
12	AZ-J-14-13	Big Bend	5	3	(a) early Archaic (b) late Archaic (c) Basketmaker II	(a) temporary camp (b) temporary camp (c) primary habitation	Just several features on the site periphery were investigated, all dating to the Archaic.
13	AZ-J-14-35	Ko' Lanhi	100	1	Basketmaker II	secondary habitation?	Site heavily impacted by existing and previous roads, greatly affecting site interpretations. Site might have been a secondary habitation, though no structure was found.
14	AZ-J-14-36	Blake's Abode	100	1	Basketmaker II	secondary habitation	Site partially impacted by existing road; site interpretation probably unaffected.
15	AZ-J-14-37	Scorpion Heights	90	1	Basketmaker II	secondary habitation?	Site partially impacted by existing road but significantly impacted by deflation/erosion, thus greatly affecting site interpretation.
16	AZ-J-14-52	Camp Dead Pine	100	1	late Pueblo II	secondary habitation	—
17	AZ-J-14-38	Mountain View	90	1	Basketmaker II–III	primary habitation	Virtually 100% excavated; portion of the transition outside the ROW is inconsequential to site interpretation.
18	AZ-J-14-16	Hammer House	100	1	mid–Pueblo II	primary habitation	Some disturbance by the existing road, but site interpretation was probably unaffected.
19	AZ-J-3-7	Mouse House	100	3	(a) Archaic (b) Basketmaker II (c) mid–Pueblo II	(a) temporary camp (b) temporary camp (c) secondary habitation	Puebloan component heavily impacted by existing and previous roads, greatly affecting component interpretation.
20	AZ-J-3-6	Sin Sombra	100	1	Basketmaker II	secondary habitation	—
21	AZ-J-3-14	Hillside Hermitage	100	2	(a) mid–Pueblo II (b) late Pueblo II	(a) primary habitation (b) secondary habitation	—
22	AZ-J-3-8	Kin Kahuna	40	2	(a) Basketmaker II (b) Pueblo III	(a) primary habitation (b) primary habitation	Extensive BMII habitation, over half of which is located outside the ROW; numerous features were excavated in the ROW including five structures, over 60 pits and hearths, and significant midden accumulations. The PIII component is of features within the ROW and excavated.
23	AZ-J-2-2	Dune Hollow	100	2	(a) Archaic (b) mid–Pueblo III	(a) temporary camp (b) secondary habitation	—
24	AZ-J-2-3	Hymn House	100	1	mid–Pueblo III	primary habitation	—

25	AZ-J-2-5	Modesty House	100	2	(a) late Pueblo II (b) mid–Pueblo III	(a) secondary habitation (b) secondary habitation	PIII component partially impacted by current road.

#	Site	Name	%	N	Period	Type	Notes
25	AZ-J-2-5	Modesty House	100	2	(a) late Pueblo II (b) mid–Pueblo III	(a) secondary habitation (b) secondary habitation	PIII component partially impacted by current road.
26	AZ-J-2-58	Water Jar Pueblo	100	1	late Pueblo III	primary habitation	—
27	AZ-J-2-6	Sapo Seco	90	2	(a) Archaic (b) late Pueblo III	(a) temporary camp (b) primary habitation	One portion of site (Locus B) was partially impacted by the existing road; another portion (Locus C) lay partially outside the ROW but was likely just erosional trash, so effectively the entire site was excavated.
28	AZ-J-2-55	Bonsai Bivouac	100	3	(a) Archaic (b) Basketmaker II (c) mid–Pueblo III	(a) temporary camp (b) temporary camp (c) secondary habitation	Puebloan component was heavily disturbed by grading along the current road, affecting component interpretation.
29	UT-B-63-14	Hanging Ash	58	2	(a) late Pueblo II (b) mid–Pueblo III	(a) primary habitation (b) primary habitation	The PIII component lay entirely within the ROW and was excavated; the PII component lies entirely outside the ROW (left edge) except for erosional trash of no significance.
30	UT-B-63-19		100	1	late Pueblo III	secondary habitation	A small portion of the site boundary extended outside the ROW, but only because of sparse artifacts, so effectively the entire site was excavated.
31	UT-B-63-30	Tsé Haal'á	60	1	late Archaic	residential camp	Diffuse scatter of remains extended outside the ROW (right edge) resting on bedrock or a thin veneer of sediment, but it lacked interpretive value (a noncontributing element).
32	UT-B-63-38		100	1	Archaic	residential camp	—
33	UT-B-63-39	Three Dog Site	50	4	(a–b) late Archaic (c) Basketmaker II (d) mid–Pueblo III (e) late Pueblo III	(a–b) residential camp (c) secondary habitation (d–e) primary habitation	Complex multiple-component site: the trash middens for the two Puebloan habitations are located mostly outside the ROW and may well contain human burials; the Basketmaker component might have been largely destroyed by previous road construction and may have had more features, including a structure.

Note: The sites are listed in south-to-north sequence along the right-of-way; the map numbers correspond to those shown in Figure 3.1. Site names are used throughout most of this report rather than numbers.

TABLE 3.2. Summary of Pertinent Information for Each Site (*n* = 33) by Component (*n* = 58) Based on Data-Recovery Excavations

Site No.	Temporal Period	Function	Structures	Storage Pits	Pits	Hearths	Middens	Burials
AZ-J-14-11	late Pueblo II–early Pueblo III	secondary habitation	3	0	3	2	+	0
AZ-J-14-12	early Archaic	temporary camp	0	0	0	4	0	0
AZ-J-14-12	Basketmaker II	secondary habitation	1	0	0	1	+	0
AZ-J-14-12	late Pueblo II	secondary habitation	2	0	1	1	+	0
AZ-J-14-13	early Archaic	temporary camp	0	0	0	1	0	0
AZ-J-14-13	late Archaic	temporary camp	0	0	0	7	0	0
AZ-J-14-13	Basketmaker II	primary habitation	1[a]	0	0	0	+	0
AZ-J-14-16	mid–Pueblo II	primary habitation	3	0	3	4	+	0
AZ-J-14-17	late Archaic	temporary camp	0	0	0	3	0	0
AZ-J-14-17	Basketmaker II	primary habitation	1[b]	24	0	7	+	0
AZ-J-14-17	Puebloan	temporary camp	0	0	0	1	0	0
AZ-J-14-20	Pueblo I	temporary camp	0	0	0	2	0	0
AZ-J-14-21	Basketmaker II	secondary habitation	2	2	1	1	+	0
AZ-J-14-21	late Pueblo II–early Pueblo III	secondary habitation	2	0	3	9	0	0
AZ-J-14-21	mid–Pueblo III	primary habitation	5	0	0	0	+	0
AZ-J-14-23	Archaic	temporary camp	0	0	0	0[d]	0	0
AZ-J-14-26	early Archaic	temporary camp	0	0	0	11	0	0
AZ-J-14-26	Basketmaker II	temporary camp	0	0	0	1	0	0
AZ-J-14-26	Puebloan	temporary camp	0	0	1	1	0	0
AZ-J-14-28	early Archaic	temporary camp	0	0	1	4	0	0
AZ-J-14-28	Basketmaker II	temporary camp	0	0	0	0	0	0
AZ-J-14-28	early Pueblo III	primary habitation	0[c]	0	0	4	+	0
AZ-J-14-30	late Pueblo II	secondary habitation	1	0	0	17	+	0
AZ-J-14-31	early Archaic	temporary camp	0	0	0	13	0	0
AZ-J-14-31	Basketmaker II	secondary habitation	2	0	2	5	+	0
AZ-J-14-34	Basketmaker II	secondary habitation	1	0	0	4	+	0
AZ-J-14-35	Basketmaker II	secondary habitation?	0	0	1	13	+	0
AZ-J-14-36	Basketmaker II	secondary habitation	1	0	0	3	+	0
AZ-J-14-37	Basketmaker II	secondary habitation?	0	0	0	5	+	0
AZ-J-14-38	Basketmaker II–III	primary habitation	1	0	4	15	+	0
AZ-J-14-52	late Pueblo II	temporary camp	0	0	1	1	+	0
AZ-J-2-2	early Archaic	temporary camp	0	0	0	2	0	0
AZ-J-2-2	mid–Pueblo III	secondary habitation	1	0	0	4	+	0
AZ-J-2-3	mid–Pueblo III	primary habitation	3	0	1	3	+	0
AZ-J-2-5	late Pueblo II	secondary habitation	1	0	0	1	0	0
AZ-J-2-5	mid–Pueblo III	secondary habitation	1	0	0	1	+	0
AZ-J-2-6	early Archaic	temporary camp	0	0	0	1	0	0
AZ-J-2-6	late Pueblo III	primary habitation	18	3	16	4	+	2
AZ-J-2-55	Archaic	temporary camp	0	0	0	8	0	0
AZ-J-2-55	Basketmaker II	temporary camp	0	0	0	2	0	0
AZ-J-2-55	mid–Pueblo III	secondary habitation	2	0	0	0	0	0
AZ-J-2-58	late Pueblo III	primary habitation	9	0	6	4	+	0
AZ-J-3-6	Basketmaker II	secondary habitation	1	0	0	3	+	0
AZ-J-3-7	early Archaic	temporary camp	0	0	0	2	0	0
AZ-J-3-7	Basketmaker II	temporary camp	0	0	0	4	0	0
AZ-J-3-7	mid–Pueblo II	secondary habitation	1	0	0	1	0	0
AZ-J-3-8	Basketmaker II	primary habitation	7	26	30	17	+	6
AZ-J-3-8	mid–Pueblo III	primary habitation	1	0	0	2	0	0
AZ-J-3-14	mid–Pueblo II	primary habitation	4	0	0	1	+	0
AZ-J-3-14	late Pueblo II	secondary habitation	2	0	0	0	+	0
UT-B-63-14	mid–Pueblo III	primary habitation	4	1	0	1	+	0
UT-B-63-19	late Pueblo III	secondary habitation	1	0	0	1	+	0
UT-B-63-30	late Archaic	residential camp	0	0	1	13	0	0

TABLE 3.2. (cont'd.) Summary of Pertinent Information for Each Site (*n* = 33) by Component (*n* = 58) Based on Data-Recovery Excavations

SITE NO.	TEMPORAL PERIOD	FUNCTION	STRUCTURES	STORAGE PITS	PITS	HEARTHS	MIDDENS	BURIALS
UT-B-63-38	Archaic	residential camp	0	0	0	0	0	0
UT-B-63-39	late Archaic	residential camp	0	0	0	24	0	0
UT-B-63-39	late Archaic	residential camp	1	0	0	7	0	0
UT-B-63-39	Basketmaker II	temporary camp?	0	0	2	2	0	0
UT-B-63-39	mid–Pueblo III	primary habitation	9	1	4	0	+	0
UT-B-63-39	late Pueblo III	primary habitation	11	0	15	13	+	0
Total			103	57	96	261	30	8

[a] Surface documented in the early 1980s with a sample of burned roofing material collected at that time; no Basketmaker features from this site were actually excavated as part of the Navajo Mountain Road Archaeological Project because that component is located outside the right-of-way.

[b] Additional structures lie unexcavated outside the N16 ROW.

[c] Structures lie unexcavated outside the N16 ROW.

[d] Two features thought to be hearths during excavation are now recognized as natural burns.

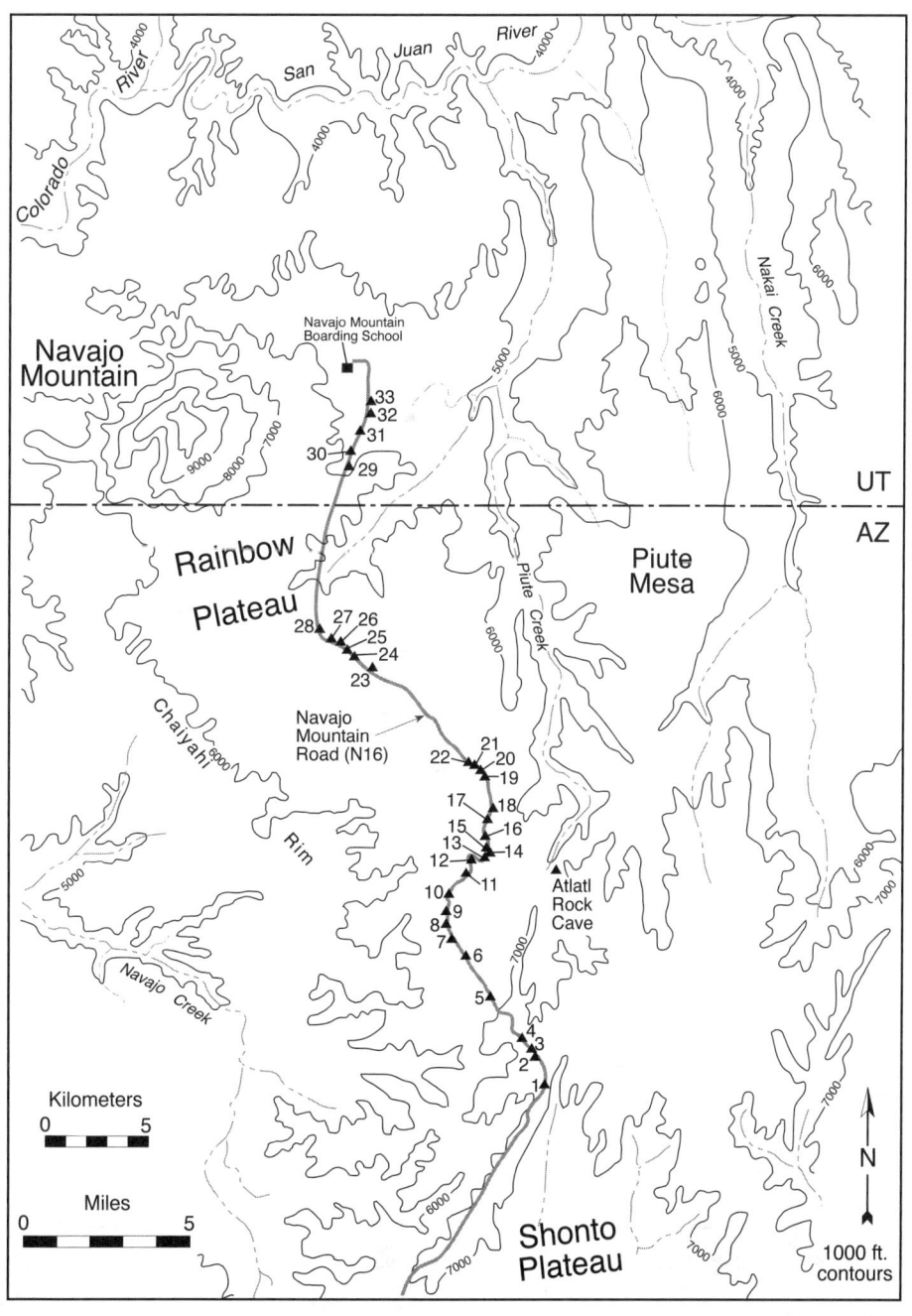

Figure 3.1. Location of the N16 right-of-way showing the 33 sites excavated by the Navajo Mountain Road Archaeological Project (see Table 3.1).

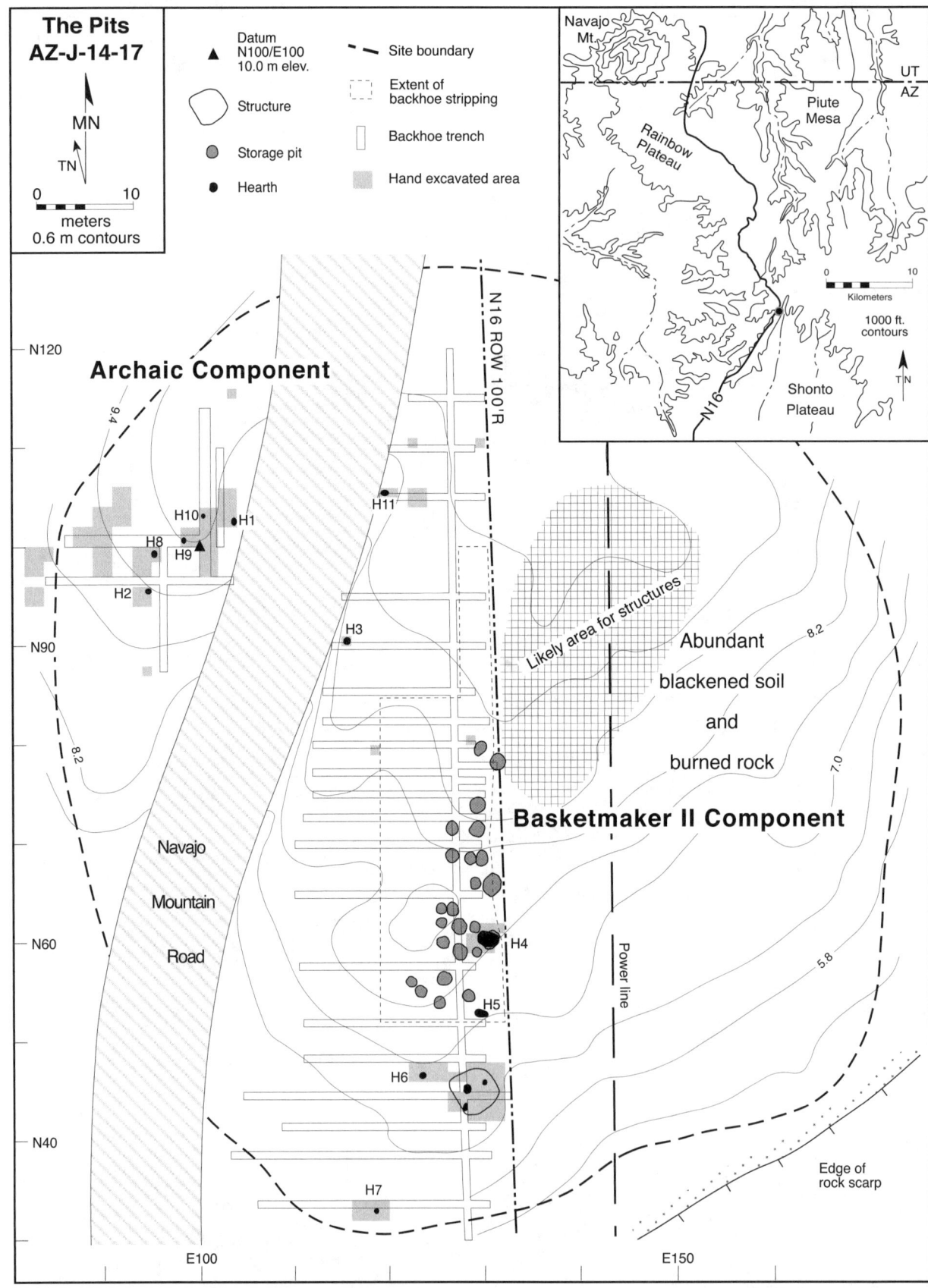

Figure 3.2. The Pits site plan showing topography, work effort, and excavated features.

can be said about this later component. The two preceramic components are spatially distinct for the most part, with the late Archaic remains clustered along the west side of the site and west of the existing Navajo Mountain road and the Basketmaker remains mostly east of the old road, on the east side of the site. Almost 40 m² of the buried cultural stratum of the Archaic component was hand excavated and screened with ⅛-in mesh; with an average stratum thickness of 10 cm, the volume of excavated cultural deposit was about 4 m³ and produced a small assemblage of bone ($n = 18$) and flaked-stone artifacts ($n = 241$). These remains were clustered around one hearth (H1) that produced a radiocarbon date of 3740 ± 60 BP on carbonized sagebrush. Two other hearths without associated remains produced earlier assays: 6030 ± 60 BP and 9780 ± 100 BP. The lithic assemblage includes a fairly high proportion of obsidian debitage (25%), most of which came from the Government Mountain source in north-central Arizona but with several flakes from the Cerro del Medio source in north-central New Mexico. The flakes of Cerro del Medio glass are larger than those of Government Mountain obsidian and were detached from a moderately large bifacial tool. Most of the flaking debris at the site, obsidian and chert, appears to be derived from late-stage biface reduction, including pressure flaking, and is probably related to refurbishing worn tool edges or modifying broken bifaces, including projectile points. On-site initial tool production appears to have been limited, except for some expedient flakes, with tools having been produced elsewhere from distant lithic sources and brought to the site in advanced stages of reduction (finished or nearly finished). The assemblage is consistent with what I would expect to find at a logistic hunting camp. The flaked-stone tools consist of dart point fragments and unifacially retouched flakes used for scraping and cutting. The sparse amount of preserved faunal bone indicates that deer and some small game animals were butchered and cooked. The lack of grinding tools and lack of subsistence plant remains appear to further support the hunting-related site function. An unknown portion of this component was destroyed by the current alignment of the Navajo Mountain road, but it seems unlikely that inclusion of this destroyed portion in data recovery would have altered findings to any great extent; rather, it may have merely bolstered the observed patterns.

The most extensive component at The Pits was a Basketmaker II habitation principally occupied between 400 and 100 cal. BC, with perhaps continued use of the site until about cal. AD 200. Temporal placement is based on 14 radiocarbon determinations on high-quality samples, mostly maize. These include five single determinations and three of multiple assays for single samples that were then averaged—two of two assays each and one of five assays. The majority of this habitation, including extensive trash deposits and what must be several living structures, lies outside the ROW and was therefore off limits to investigation. The extent of the Basketmaker II component within the ROW was totally underestimated going into data recovery. As fate would have it, a series of east–west backhoe trenches excavated during testing failed to reveal any of the numerous large storage pits of this component, and it was not until a single long north–south trench was dug during data recovery that these became known. This new trench sectioned six deep pits, revealing a previously unknown aspect of the site that became the focus of the data-recovery effort—a Basketmaker II storage pit complex. In order to efficiently locate and excavate these large deep features a backhoe was used to mechanically strip off overburden to an average depth of about 80 cm below the present ground surface. Because this pit complex was peripheral to the main area of Basketmaker trash accumulation, the loss of remains in mechanical stripping was minimal. After exposure in plan view, most pits were completely excavated, and the fill was screened; a few pits that extended outside the ROW were only partially excavated. Work at the Basketmaker II component also included hand excavation of several square meters around hearths and a shallow structure in the southern part of the site area.

Excavations within the ROW revealed a cluster of 24 bell-shaped storage pits, some quite large, arranged along the crest of a well-drained sand ridge; these features inspired the site name. The storage pits appear to have been purposefully laid out in roughly north–south and east–west alignments, perhaps to facilitate relocating them once covered. They range in size from .2 to 1.6 m³, with a combined storage capacity of 16.7 m³. The variable amounts of trash fill within the pits suggest that some of these features had been abandoned earlier than others. Reuse of some of the storage facilities as roasting pits also reveals different rates of pit abandonment. The trashy but artifact-poor fill of most pits contained abundant burned maize. Other investigated Basketmaker II features included several hearths and a surface structure that was perhaps simply covered with brush. Excavations at the Basketmaker II component recovered a small assemblage of stone artifacts (*n* = 114), faunal remains (*n* = 580), and minerals (*n* = 9). Flotation analysis produced moderately abundant macroplant remains, especially maize cob portions and kernels. Outside the N16 ROW to the east and northeast of the excavated storage pits are probable living structures along with more storage pits and associated features; the nature of the midden deposits exposed on the surface of the slope in this area is indicative of a major residential site. The Pits was a significant and important place on the landscape to several generations of Basketmaker II families; it is significant to us today because it represents a locus where considerable information about a little-known time period can be gathered. This is likely a major site, but its full research potential may never be realized. It may be destined to become like so many other parts of sites partially investigated under similar constraints, sites that are not preserved and are eventually lost through attrition.

Ditch House (AZ-J-14-21)

Ditch House (Figure 3.3) is entirely within the N16 ROW, with all of the excavated features located between the center line and the 100'L. The existing Navajo Mountain road artificially delineates the north and northeastern edges of the site, and I have little doubt but that several Puebloan houses were totally destroyed. Previous road construction and the cutting of a water lead-off ditch had eliminated portions of several Puebloan structures; a burned house exposed in the sloping profile of this ditch provided the site name.

Ditch House lies at an elevation of 2,220 m (7,280 ft), situated on a southeast-facing slope, just below a bedrock escarpment of Navajo Sandstone. The escarpment forms part of a greater ridge of Navajo Sandstone that divides the Shonto Plateau to the southeast from the Rainbow Plateau to the northwest. Vistas from the site are limited due to the dense canopy of pinyon and juniper; however, from the top of the escarpment, 12 m above Ditch House, views are commanding and to the south include White and Black mesas, with the San Francisco Peaks visible on clear days. Precipitation falling in the vicinity of Ditch House drains into a three-way divide: to the north water runs into Piute Canyon, which flows into the San Juan River; to the southeast it passes into Cliff Spring Canyon, which drains into Begashibito Wash and eventually finds its way to the Little Colorado River; to the west water tumbles into Far End Canyon, joining Navajo Canyon, and finally runs into the Colorado River, now subsumed by Lake Powell. Arable land proximal to Ditch House consists of about 40 ac of sagebrush flats located 1 km southeast of the site.

Ditch House was initially interpreted in an interim report as a small single-component settlement occupied during early–middle Pueblo III. Excavations, which totaled 208 m² by hand (plus extensive backhoe trenching and stripping), did not disclose any stratigraphic divisions that indicated separate temporal intervals, so the field crew assumed that all of the various features belonged to the same approximate time of occupancy. From the patterning of excavated features and spatial distribution of temporally sensitive ceramic types and tree-ring dates it seemed that the settlement had a few phases of construction, but there was no suspicion that some of the houses and features were substantially earlier in age. I first suspected this after the second season (1994) of N16 data recovery, during which time crews excavated Basketmaker structures at several sites. By the end of that field season it seemed highly probable that Structure 6 at Ditch House was actually Basketmaker II and not Puebloan. This house appeared unusual for a Pueblo III house, but until seeing how similar it was to other Basketmaker houses in the area there was insufficient justification to reevaluate the field findings. Subsequent radiocarbon dating of maize cupules and a pinyon cone scale from the central hearth of Structure 6 produced contemporaneous dates of just over 2,000 radiocarbon years ago, proving that the structure was Basketmaker II in age. This discovery led to the further dating of plant remains from other features, especially those that appeared atypical for Puebloan construction. First among these was the large, shallow scatter of burned rock and charcoal-stained soil initially identified as a burned rock midden and roasting area, a feature that lacked pottery but contained some maize. A radiocarbon date on carbonized sagebrush from this feature returned an assay similar to those for Structure 6. This was followed by Pit 1, which also returned an assay of almost 2,000 radiocarbon years ago. The postexcavation discovery of the Basketmaker component at Ditch House necessitated a complete reevaluation and reinterpretation of the entire site. The actual descriptive portions of the site report required minor editing rather than rewriting, with the major task being reorganization of the relevant portions so that they could be presented in the appropriate site-description volumes.

The Basketmaker II component of Ditch House is similar to other NMRAP examples of small habitations

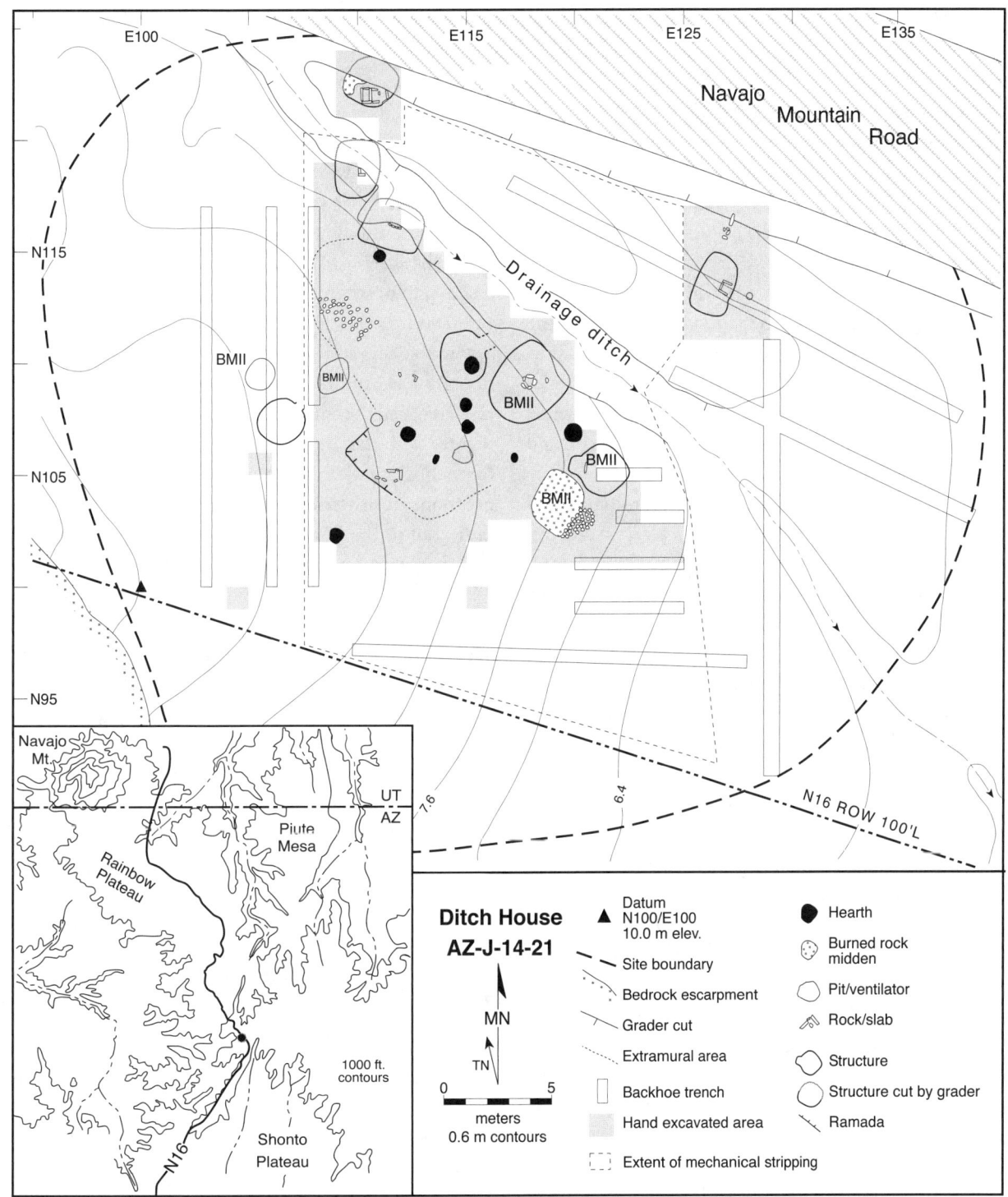

Figure 3.3. Ditch House site plan showing topography, work effort, and excavated features; those of the Basketmaker II component are designated as such, and the rest are assigned to the Puebloan component, which had two separate occupations.

lacking storage pits. It consists of one living structure, another smaller structure perhaps used as a sweat lodge, and several extramural features; absent were any substantial food-storage facilities such as bell-shaped pits or slab-lined cists. Radiocarbon dating of high-quality samples fixes the time of Basketmaker occupancy between 100 cal. BC and cal. AD 60. It seems likely that site use comprised a relatively brief interval during this span, perhaps just 10 years or less. I make this inference based on the presence of just one living structure and the absence of superimposed features. The extent of Basketmaker trash deposition and the number and superpositioning of extramural features cannot be evaluated in this instance because of the overlay of Puebloan features and trash. This also limited the number of artifacts and other remains that could be securely assigned to the Basketmaker II component (just 32 stone artifacts and two bones). The likely location of the Basketmaker trash midden would have been east of Structure 6, an area removed by the road drainage ditch, further resulting in a small artifact assemblage and less subsistence evidence. Maize remains were essentially the only subsistence-related items recovered from the few flotation samples of the Basketmaker II component. Besides the durable portions of maize cobs, kernel fragments came from two samples of differing contexts—a roasting pit and the Structure 6 hearth.

Excavated Puebloan features at Ditch House consist of seven structures, a ramada, an extramural area, six hearths, two roasting pits, three unspecified pits, two mealing bins, a mano cache, and a concentration of burned limestone. The structures contain a variety of interior features, including hearths, mealing bins, floor pits, postholes, wall niches, and ventilators. A moderate number of artifacts and nonartifactual remains were recovered considering that no formal trash midden was found, perhaps having been destroyed by prior road construction (1,792 sherds, 574 stone artifacts, and 39 faunal bones, plus three faunal artifacts). The patterning of excavated features and spatial distribution of temporally sensitive ceramic types and tree-ring dates indicate that the settlement grew during at least two construction phases. Subsequent radiocarbon dating and a closer examination of ceramic types support this interpretation. The bulk of the earlier ceramics are from an extramural activity area and less formal-looking structures in the central portion of the site area. This locus seems to have been the original focus of Puebloan occupation at Ditch House during late Pueblo II or perhaps early Pueblo III (ca. AD 1100–1200). At that time the site might have functioned as a temporary residential site, such as a field house. During middle Pueblo III (cutting dates of AD 1228), several living structures were built in the northern portion of the site area, apparently constituting a small semipermanent settlement of several families. Structures constructed toward the end of the AD 1220 decade include three living structures and a possible fourth, along with a mealing room. No doubt other structures, including a kiva, were likely associated with this habitation, but these features were destroyed by the existing alignment for the Navajo Mountain road. Other features of the middle Pueblo III occupation of Ditch House are located southwest of the structures and are partially intermixed with the earlier Puebloan features and remains. It is difficult to envision the exact layout of the middle Pueblo III settlement—whether it was simply a somewhat loose collection of living structures of several families or a more organized pithouse settlement of some sort. Charred roof and wall fall, consisting of thatch and pinyon and juniper beams and posts, overlay the floors of all Puebloan structures, and there was no accumulation of sediment, such as windblown sand or water-laid silt lenses, between the floors and the burned material. Not only had a conflagration engulfed the entire site at once, but the fire nearly coincided with the site abandonment. Despite the evidence for deliberate abandonment and the circumstance of fire, none of the structures had in-use floor assemblages; rather, all of the floors had a scavenged appearance, and all slab metates had been removed from the mealing bins.

Wolachii Bighan (AZ-J-14-20)

Wolachii Bighan (or Red Ant House) lies on the northeast side of a partially dune-covered knob of Navajo Sandstone at an elevation of 2,231 m (7,320 ft) near the rim of Upper Piute Canyon (Figure 3.4). The site commands views to the north stretching from Upper Piute Canyon to the Henry Mountains in Utah. The Navajo crew dubbed the site Wolachii Bighan due to the annoying persistence of a colony of red ants in the southern site area during excavation. Hand excavation of 37 m^2 exposed two basin hearths surrounded by a light scatter of sherds and stone artifacts along with unworked sandstone and limestone. The small sherd assemblage ($n = 122$) comes from a maximum of just five ceramic vessels or portions thereof, all jars. The stone artifact assemblage is equally skimpy, with only four lithic tools and 54 pieces of debitage. Construction and maintenance of the current Navajo Mountain road destroyed the southwest portion of the site, including perhaps a feature or two, but significant architecture and artifact-bearing midden deposits were probably not lost. I interpret the few features and artifacts documented at Wolachii Bighan as the residue from limited occupancy. The hearths seem to have been used just once, as there was no evidence that the occupants had emptied the fill of either. These meager remains could easily have been deposited during a single use episode or perhaps a few episodes within the span of a few years. Given the ceramic types present (Kana-a Gray, Lino Gray, and Kana-a Black-

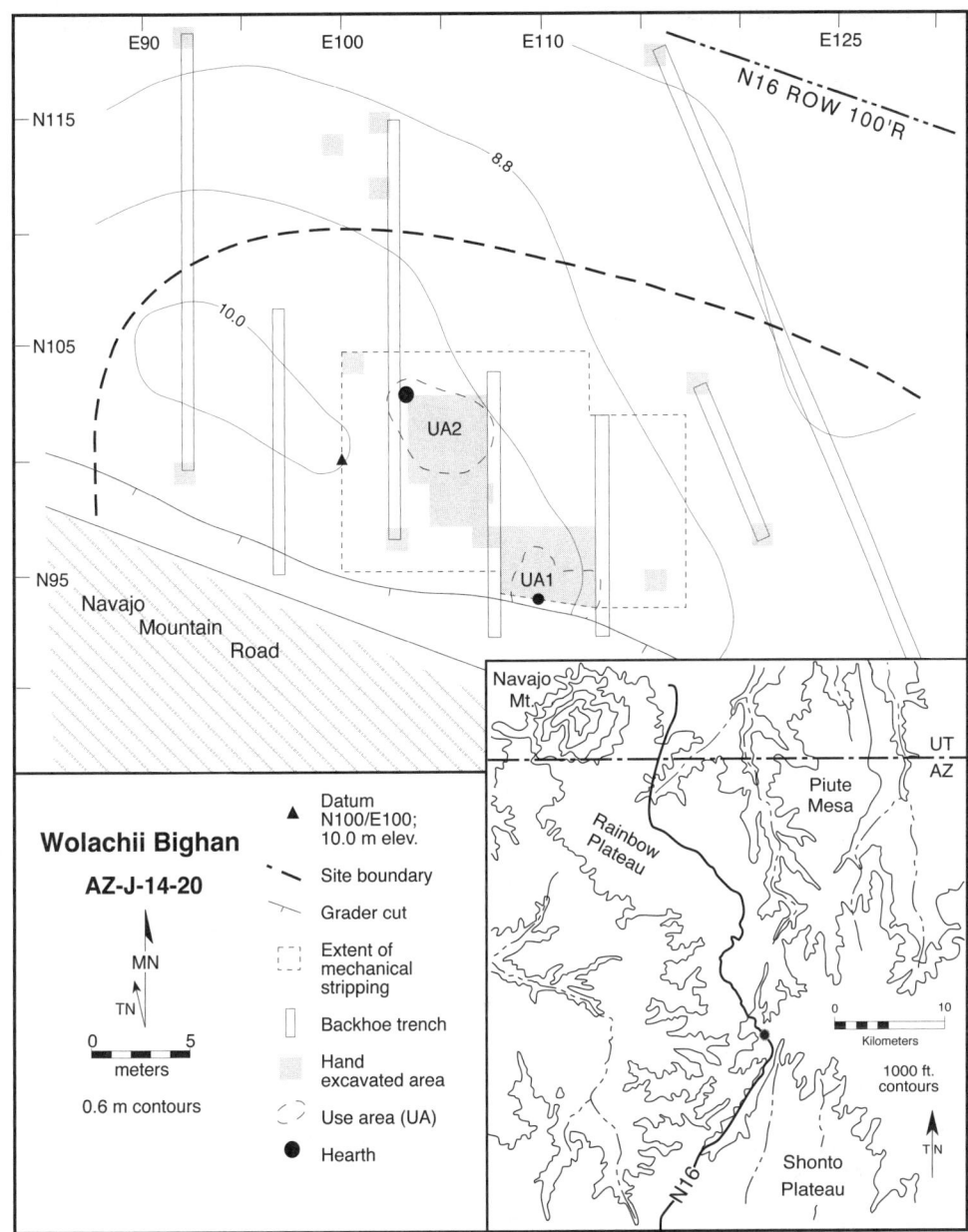

Figure 3.4. Wolachii Bighan site plan showing topography, work effort, and excavated features.

on-white), this site was occupied during Pueblo I, with occupation probably occurring sometime between about AD 700 and 900. The site was probably occupied on a limited basis related to food processing. This is the only Pueblo I site identified within the N16 ROW, although Pueblo I use of the area surrounding Wolachii Bighan is well documented. Thirty-five Pueblo I sites were recorded in nearby Upper Piute Canyon, including at least six permanent habitations (Fairley 1989:101). Additionally, several Pueblo I sites "occur in the Navajo Canyon drainage immediately to the west of upper Piute Canyon" (Fairley 1989:176; see Miller and Breternitz 1958b). None of these Pueblo I sites has been excavated.

HÓLAHÉI SCATTER (AZ-J-14-23)

Hólahéi Scatter (Figure 3.5) is a small scatter of flaked-stone artifacts and bone near the eastern edge of a limestone-capped ridge of Navajo Sandstone at an elevation of about 2,222 m (7,290 ft) along the rim of Upper Piute Canyon. The ridge provides a north–south travel corridor between the Shonto and Rainbow plateaus past the deeply entrenched canyons of Piute and Navajo

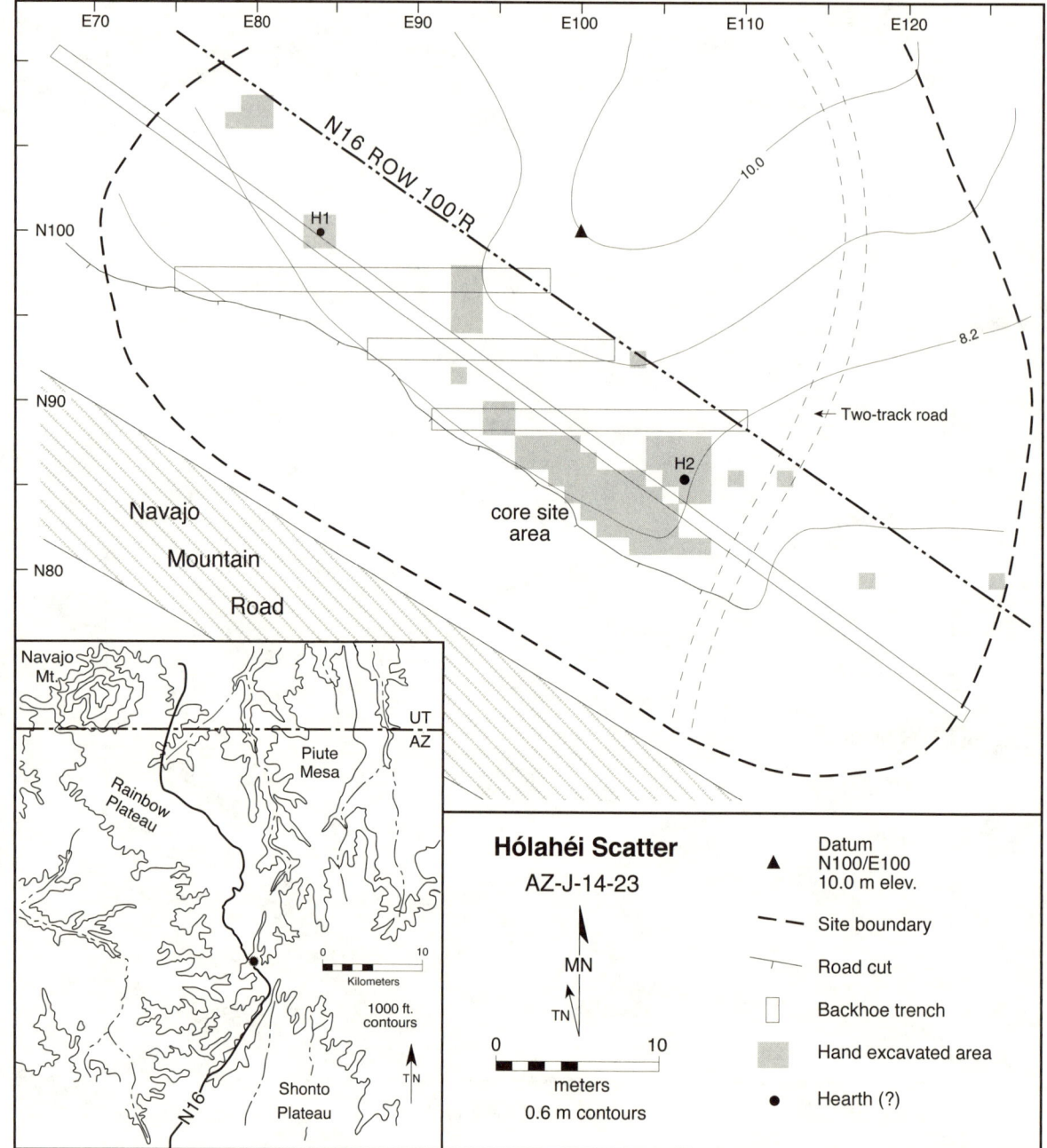

Figure 3.5. Hólahéi Scatter site plan showing topography, work effort, and excavated features.

creeks. The old alignment of N16 destroyed an unknown portion of the site but also exposed the buried remains that otherwise might have gone unrecorded. Judging from excavation units, the site lay almost entirely within the N16 ROW. Additional lithic artifacts of probable or certain Archaic age (e.g., a Gypsum point) occur north of the ROW next to the ridge scarp overlooking Piute Canyon. The remains reported here might be part of a discontinuous scatter of flaked-stone debris and tools that covers much of the ridgetop within the vicinity of Hólahéi Scatter. Nonetheless, the vast majority of artifacts and animal bone at the site occurred in a well-defined small area and seem to be the residue of a single and brief behavioral event.

All in situ prehistoric cultural materials came from a buried A horizon, with the densest concentration occurring in the southeast part of the site next to the existing roadcut (core site area). Workers excavated almost 70 m^2

of the artifact-bearing deposit by hand, screening all sediment through ⅛-in mesh, with all finds provenienced by 1-m² recovery units. Given an average thickness to the cultural layer of 15 cm, the volume of deposit removed and screened was about 10 m³. This effort recovered 866 stone artifacts and 50 small bone fragments; also revealed were two areas of in situ burning initially thought to be shallow basin hearths but now interpreted as natural burns of pinyon duff layers. Radiocarbon dates on carbonized pinyon scales and bark from the natural burns reveal that soil development occurred during the last 2,300 years, providing a minimal age for the time of artifact burial. The remains may have rested for some length of time on the ground surface prior to becoming buried and incorporated within the soil horizon. An Archaic temporal assignment is tentatively made based on the proportion of obsidian and the base portion of an untyped large stemmed projectile point with basal abrasion. Hydration rims measured on 12 obsidian flakes provided calendrical ages incompatible with the radiocarbon dates and the age of soil development, except for one flake that returned a late Archaic age. Although this one might accurately date the assemblage, there is no way of knowing whether this is the case. Bone associated with the stone artifacts at Hólahéi Scatter unfortunately lacked a collagen fraction, foiling an attempt to obtain a believable chronometric determination. Lacking this, I assign Hólahéi Scatter to a general Archaic temporal affiliation. An early Archaic designation seems supported by the basal portion of what appears to have been a large stemmed dart point. Given the conflicting chronological evidence from this site and the uncertain hearths, the Navajo term for "damned if I know!" (*hólahéi*) seemed an appropriate moniker.

I interpret Hólahéi Scatter as a temporary camp used by hunters. Bifacially flaked tools, including projectile points and likely knives, were refurbished and modified at the site, and large game was butchered and perhaps cooked. The assemblage contains numerous small obsidian pressure flakes and some percussion biface thinning flakes, mostly of chert. Judging from the overall assemblage, it looks as though late-stage bifacial tools were modified and resharpened at the site, mainly by pressure flaking but with some percussion thinning and shaping. These tools were then taken from the site; no obsidian bifaces were recovered that would account for the amount of small flakes recovered. On the basis of the stone tool assemblage, occupation of the site appears to have been of relatively short duration and related to the maintenance of hunting equipment. Any features truly associated with the remains may have been destroyed by deflation. The lithic assemblage contains a high proportion of obsidian debitage, nearly all of which originated from the Government Mountain source in north-central Arizona as revealed by X-ray fluorescence–energy-dispersive spectrometer analysis. The amount of obsidian debitage in the assemblage is best explained as a product of direct procurement by the hunters that used Hólahéi. Rather than mapping the southwest-to-northeast dimension of an annual foraging territory for the band that occupied Hólahéi Scatter, the distance from Government Mountain to the site is seen as reflecting the annual logistic hunting range for a segment of a forager band. If Hólahéi Scatter was at the far northeast side of this range, with Government Mountain at the far southwest side, then home territory for the band as a whole might have been centered around Tuba City and the Lower Little Colorado River. Regardless of this detail, I believe that the site is not part of the settlement distribution associated with forager bands local to the Navajo Mountain area.

Pee Wee Grande (AZ-J-14-26)

This multicomponent site (Figure 3.6) is situated in deep dune sand on a long narrow bedrock ridge of a slickrock slope at an elevation of 2,097 m (6,880 ft). Perched above a small valley filled with sagebrush that drains into Piute Canyon, Pee Wee Grande offers a northward view of the sagebrush flats sunken in the foreground, rugged slickrock rising in the midground, and Navajo Mountain looming on the far horizon. Excavations focused on a small area where testing revealed the presence of a buried Archaic cultural deposit containing flaked-stone artifacts and basin hearths. An area of 27 m² was excavated and screened with ⅛-in mesh, exposing several hearths and recovering 308 stone artifacts. Backhoe trenching exposed additional hearths including two that were in different stratigraphic layers above the Archaic component. The site lay completely within the N16 ROW, and its eastern edge was removed by construction of the previous Navajo Mountain road. A bulldozed swath ran northwest from the existing road through the southern site area. Both the bulldozed swath and the current road likely destroyed features once associated with Pee Wee Grande.

The Archaic component of Pee Wee Grande (Locus A) consists of a cluster of 11 basin hearths and a collection of 303 flakes, three flaked facial tools, and two cores. The features and lithic artifacts are the trace of foragers who

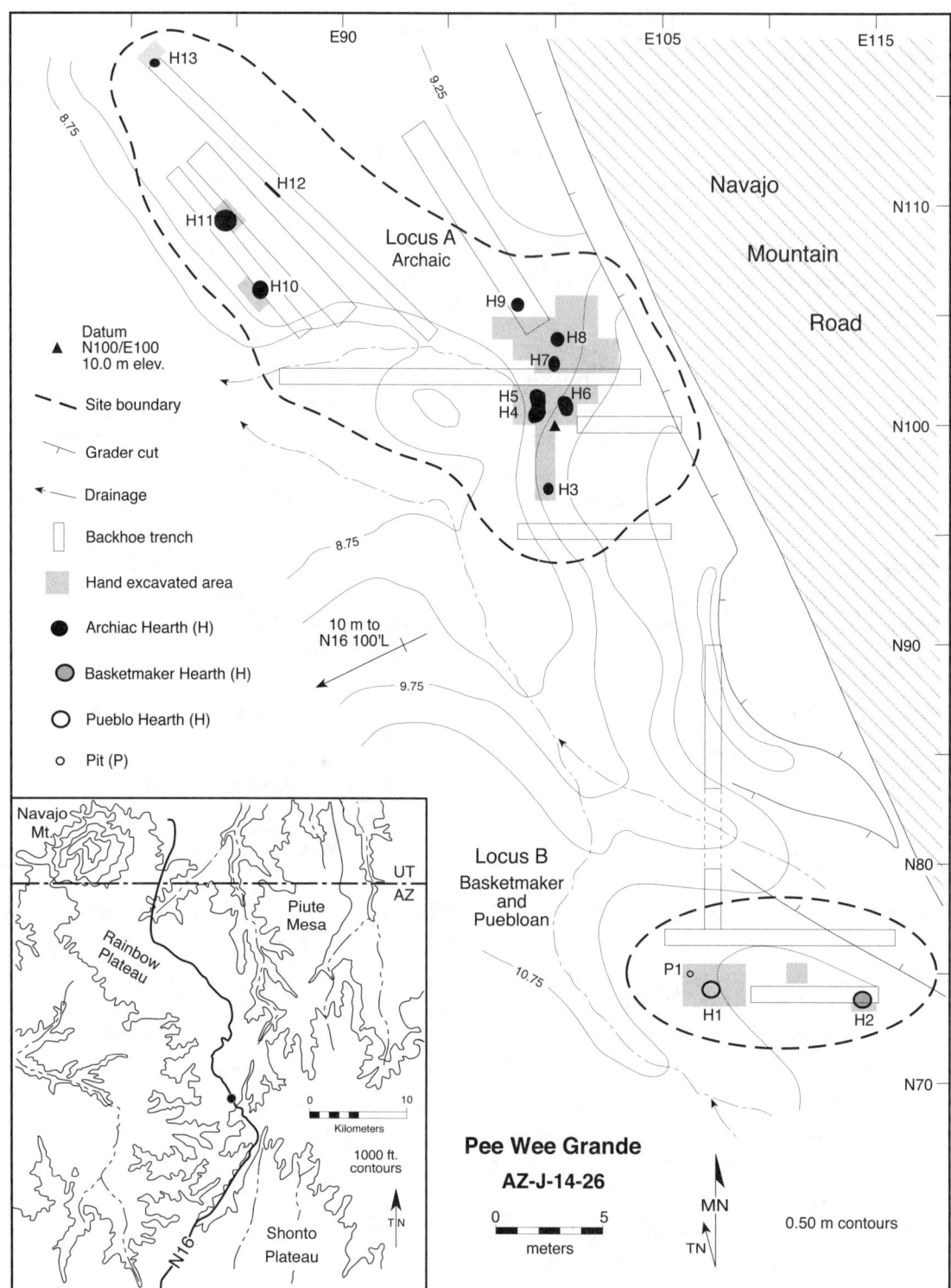

Figure 3.6. Pee Wee Grande site plan showing topography, work effort, and excavated features.

occupied the sandy ridge sometime between 7520 and 5810 cal. BC based on four radiocarbon dates that ranged between 8,230 and 7,080 radiocarbon years ago. The number of basin hearths within such a small area likely resulted from several sequential short-term use episodes, an inference that the radiocarbon results seem to support. Use of this site did not result in appreciable amounts of nonperishable artifact deposition; however, during one of these use episodes tools were required for some task, perhaps the working of wood. Several nodules of local Navajo chert were brought to the location and reduced by both percussion and pressure flaking into several mainly bifacial tools. The flaked facial tools along with two tabular core chunks were subsequently used mainly as scrapers on some semiresistant material. During the task some of the flaked facial tools were refurbished. The production and use of the tools may have been incidental to use of the hearths—i.e., making wooden artifacts while waiting for some food to cook. The used cores and three biface fragments were discarded upon site abandonment.

Limited Basketmaker and Puebloan use of the ridge slightly south of the Archaic component created three features—two basin hearths and a small circular pit (Locus B). The Basketmaker component consists of a single basin hearth filled with black, charcoal-rich sediment (Hearth 2). This may have resulted from cooking some sort of food(s), but a flotation sample provided no clue as to what this (these) could have been. No artifacts or faunal remains were associated with this feature. Lacking maize or other annual plant remains, a wood charcoal sample returned an assay of 1660 ± 50 BP (Beta-79153, –23.2‰). This sample has a calibrated age range of AD 260–440 at one sigma, but under the assumption that dead wood was likely burned, I tentatively assign Hearth 2 to the Basketmaker III period.

Several hundred years later the location was again used briefly. Another basin was dug, a fire was kindled within it, and the hot coals were then smothered by a layer of sandstone slabs (Hearth 1). Foods were probably cooked by placing them over the slabs and covering the pit for some interval. Flotation samples hint that Hearth 1 may have been used for opening green pinyon cones to free the nutritious nuts. A wood charcoal sample returned an assay of 1250 ± 70 BP (Beta-79154, assumed –25.0‰), with a calibrated age range of AD 650–960 at two sigma. Under the likely assumption that dead wood was burned, I tentatively assign Hearth 1 to the Pueblo II period. A bowl sherd of Holbrook Black-on-white found nearby on the surface has no obvious association with the hearth but is consistent with the Pueblo II inference. This is an interesting find, for sherds of this ware are rare in the northern Kayenta region and provide evidence of exchange with populations of the middle Little Colorado River region. The one artifact associated with the hearth was a used flake. A shallow, generally dish-shaped pit 50 cm northwest of Hearth 1 may have been related to the use of the thermal feature, although its specific function is unknown.

WINDY MESA (AZ-J-14-28)

Windy Mesa (Figure 3.7) is a multicomponent site situated at an elevation of 2,104 m (ca. 6,900 ft) on the top of a narrow rise that forms part of the divide between Piute and Navajo canyons. As one of the highest points around, the rise is quite exposed to the region's southwesterly winds, and gales tore across the site daily during excavation, leading to the site name (also an infamous drinking establishment in Page, Arizona). The site consists of an early Pueblo III habitation partially exposed on the surface and Basketmaker II and early Archaic cultural layers buried within separate strata underlying the Puebloan component. The Pueblo component is situated just east of the highest point of this rise on a slight east-facing slope, partially sheltered from the prevailing southwesterly wind and where accumulated sand was sufficient for the construction of deep subterranean features. With its easterly orientation, the pueblo faced a broad sagebrush-filled depression 500 m away that was likely used for dry farming and is currently being farmed by a local family. The superimposed Archaic and Basketmaker II components were located about 40 m southwest of the pueblo near the top of the rise on its southwest side. Here there was considerable exposure to the wind, although thick tree cover prior to road construction may have provided some shelter. These components had a southerly aspect, with panoramic views of the Navajo Canyon drainage and White Mesa in the distance. Piute Canyon can be viewed across the rise a short distance to the north.

Since the Puebloan habitation is only partially within the N16 ROW, it was preserved in place by constricting the construction area for the road. The data-recovery effort focused on the superimposed Basketmaker II and Archaic components and involved hand excavation within a 9-×-9-m area where testing had disclosed a buried preceramic stratum and several hearths. In this area 41 m^2 were hand excavated to sterile ground, with sediment screened through ⅛-in mesh. The Basketmaker and Archaic layers were visually distinct in profile but with a slight gradational zone; to be certain that remains from the two strata were kept separate during excavation, the crew assigned materials from the gradational layer to an intermediate layer designation. By taking into account the thickness of each stratigraphic layer and the number of excavated square meters, the crew hand excavated and screened 2.9 m^3 of the Basketmaker layer, 3.8 m^3 of the gradational layer, and 6.8 m^3 of the Archaic layer. There was less of the Basketmaker deposit because much of this

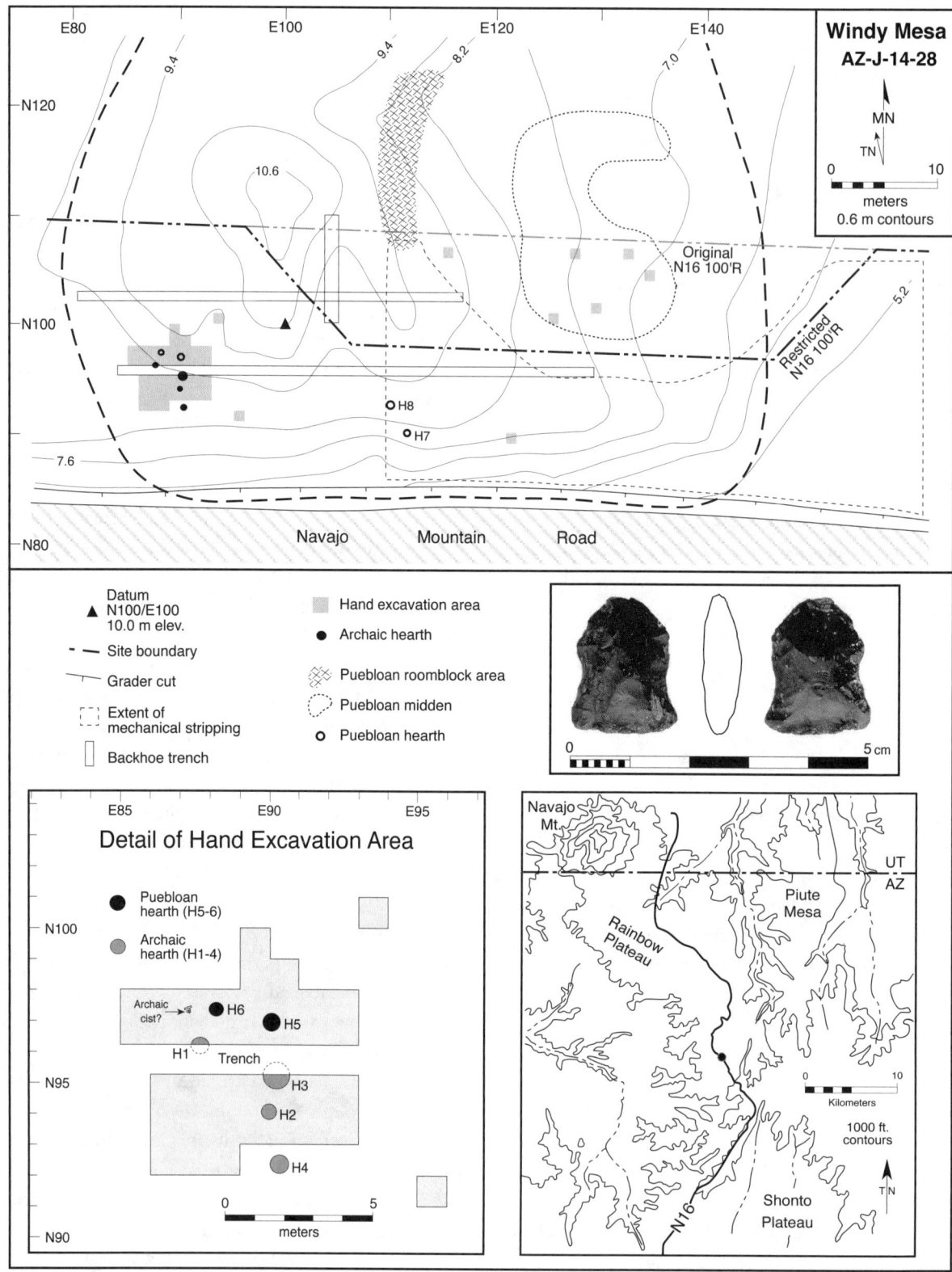

Figure 3.7. Windy Mesa site plan showing topography, work effort, and excavated features; excavation units in the Puebloan midden are from the testing phase prior to restricting the N16 right-of-way to avoid this component. Inset on right middle shows the heavily reworked obsidian projectile point recovered from the Archaic component, the base of which is heavily abraded.

layer in the area investigated was eroded, leaving a dense surface scatter of lithic artifacts, which were collected as part of the Basketmaker component. Although the ROW was reduced to avoid the Puebloan habitation, NNAD crews excavated four Puebloan hearths, two within the excavation block for the buried preceramic component and two within the mechanical stripping area around the periphery of the midden. The two hearths within the hand-excavation block were initially thought to be Basketmaker II in age, but radiocarbon dating demonstrated that both were Puebloan in age, confirmed by a near-cutting tree-ring date (+r) of AD 1132 for a charred log from one hearth.

The Archaic component at Windy Mesa consists of four basin hearths and a possible storage feature built of upright slabs. Recovered in association with these features were a few bone fragments and a small assemblage of flaked-stone artifacts, principally debitage ($n = 278$) from late-stage tool reduction but also an obsidian projectile point and two used flakes. The projectile point, which is shown in Figure 3.7, was extensively resharpened and precluded typing the point (its stem portion is heavily ground). Radiocarbon dates on wood charcoal from three hearths cover a time range of more than 2,200 radiocarbon years, from 8270 to 5990 BP. There is no inherent reason for favoring one of the dates over the others to represent the period of site occupancy; the site may have been used on a few different occasions during this time span. The use of old wood for fuel seems an unlikely explanation for the date disparity owing to the length of time involved, at least for the time separating Hearth 3 (5590 BP) from the other two (8270 BP and 7820 BP). There is no artifactual evidence to support a multiple-occupations scenario, either in the types of remains recovered or in their spatial patterning. The Archaic remains at Windy Mesa likely represent those of a temporary camp used for hunting.

The Basketmaker II component at Windy Mesa lacks features, but it has a substantial assemblage of stone artifacts, numbering close to 4,000 items, mostly debitage ($n = 3,816$, including 11 used flakes), but with 19 facial flaked tools, three core/nodular tools, and three grinding tools. It is possible that the small area investigated within the ROW represents just part of the Basketmaker II remains at this site. A few upright slabs located outside the ROW to the northwest of the excavation area provide likely evidence for features associated with this component. Also, because a portion of this component within the ROW was eroded and disturbed by road construction, some features may have been lost. Features or not, I have no doubt that a central activity for the Basketmaker II occupants was biface reduction, apparently beginning midway in the reduction sequence using edged and initially thinned bifaces and directed at the production of projectile points or point preforms. Reduction activity was quite intensive and mainly involved locally occurring Navajo chert and petrified wood that was likely procured not more than 10 km away from Piute Canyon. The Basketmaker II lithic assemblage of Windy Mesa is quite different from that of the excavated Basketmaker II habitations of the N16 ROW and clearly reflects a different settlement role and different activities. Windy Mesa may have been used as a temporary logistic camp by hunters, who, while out on their foray, replenished their tool kits with stone points.

Not much can be said about the Puebloan component owing to the limited investigation thus far, with most remains recovered from the midden during the testing phase (1,498 sherds, 1,734 flakes, 167 tools, 91 used flakes, 202 bones). Occupancy on at least a semipermanent basis is affirmed by the extensive midden, rich in artifactual and nonartifactual remains, and by the remnants of several structures. Given the amount of trash and the known area covered by structural remains, I am certain that there are at least six–eight habitation rooms associated with this component at Windy Mesa; a kiva likely occurs at the site as well. All of these features lie beyond the edge of the N16 ROW. Puebloan occupation of Windy Mesa may have begun during middle Pueblo II, before AD 1100, and may have lasted into middle Pueblo III, after AD 1200. Whether the interval reflects one long continuous occupation or a few discrete episodes cannot be specified. In general, I interpret the site as an early Pueblo III habitation. Hunting appears to have been important, as scrap bone is abundant within the midden. Turkeys were apparently raised and consumed; dogs were kept but not obviously used as food. The occupants also appear to have produced quite a few flaked-stone tools, such as bifaces and projectile points. The location of Windy Mesa may have been selected for habitation for two reasons: it is situated close to good dry-farming land in the small valley to the east, and it is at a point on the landscape that all travelers moving north–south between the Shonto and Rainbow plateaus would have passed. Thus, the occupants would have been in a favorable position for commerce and well connected to the regional flow of information and goods.

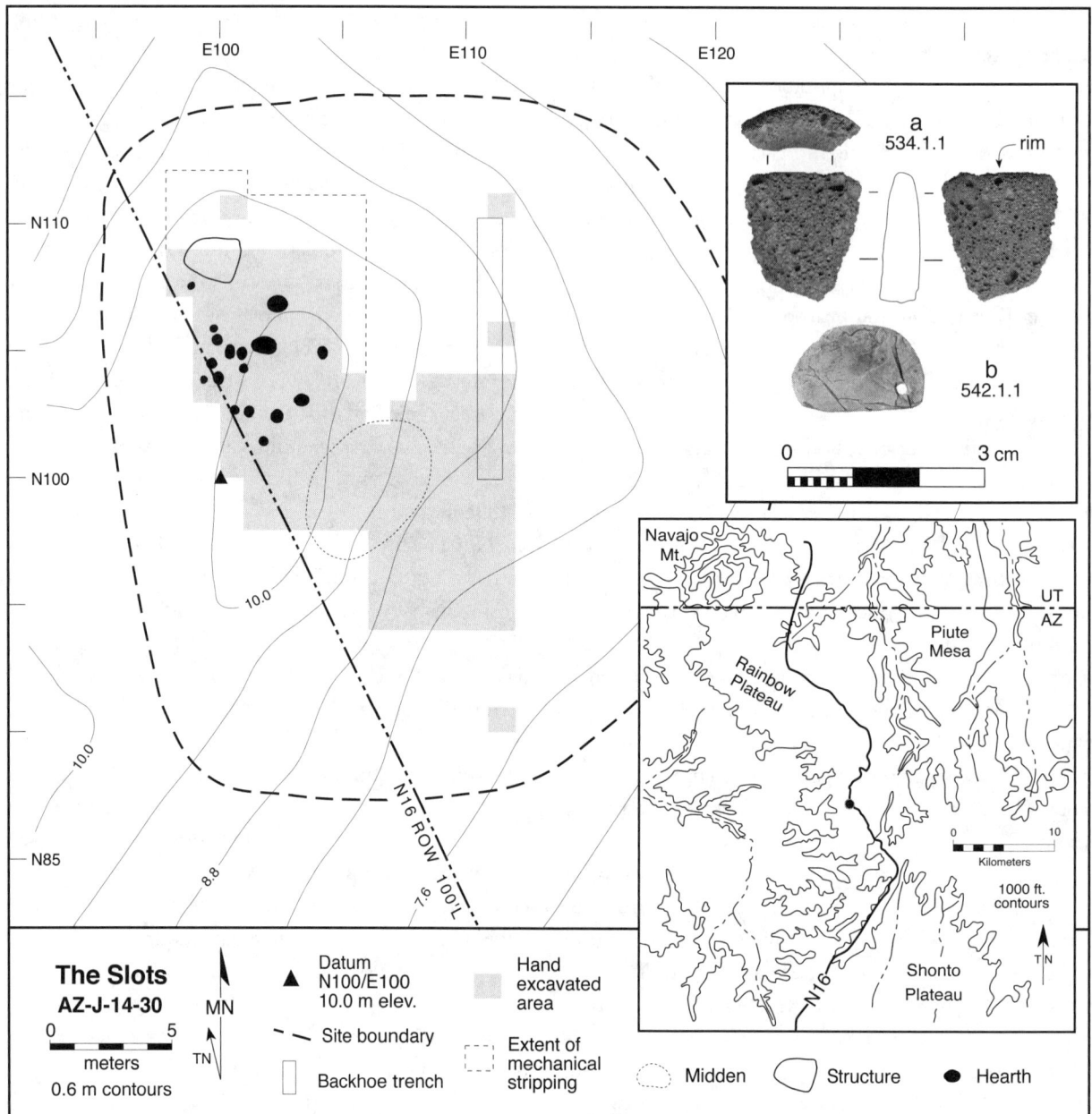

Figure 3.8. The Slots site plan showing topography, work effort, and excavated features. Inset on right top shows two miscellaneous stone artifacts from the site: (a) rim portion of a pipe made of scoria; (b) pendant of limestone.

THE SLOTS (AZ-J-14-30)

The Slots (Figure 3.8) is a small late Pueblo II temporary habitation situated on a narrow ridge of Navajo Sandstone between Upper Piute Canyon and tributaries of Peach Canyon at an elevation of 2,097 m (6,880 ft). Except to the south, this perched location affords a spectacular view in all directions, especially to the west and northwest where several steep slickrock slots descend into the upper reaches of Peach Canyon; in this direction Navajo Mountain and Cummings Mesa mark the far horizon. A deep, semistabilized eolian sand dune deposited by prevailing westerly winds occupies the site location. This dune is an extension of a large falling dune formed on the north and east sides of a bedrock prominence southwest of the site. The local dune slope was more gradual during the period of occupation, as the cultural stratum does not parallel the modern surface topography. After site abandonment, dune sand continued to accumulate, burying the cultural stratum and features up to 70 cm deep.

Due to the steep dune topography, the site was excavated in two sections, eastern (lower) and western (upper). Excavation began in the eastern section of the site by defining the trash midden. Midden deposits were exposed around the base of the recent eolian sand and extended under this deposit. Hand excavation began at the eastern edge of the deflated midden and moved westward until the intact midden deposits were buried by more than 50 cm of sterile sand. At this point a backhoe was used to mechanically strip the overburden from the western section of the midden to facilitate hand excavation. All midden deposits were screened through ⅛-in mesh. The western portion of the midden was excavated concurrently with the main activity area, which included numerous hearths. The sterile overburden was stripped off the activity area with shovels; then the cultural layer was excavated and screened through ⅛-in mesh. Hearths and other features were excavated as soon as they were defined. The structure at the northwest edge of the site was located and excavated during the final days of work; all structure fill below the roof fall (floor fill) was excavated by hand and screened through ⅛-in mesh. The area north of the structure was mechanically stripped to search for any associated features, and a deep trench was excavated through the midden area and farther north to ensure that no deeply buried deposits existed in this portion of the site.

The 19 features at the site consist of 16 small, shallow basin hearths, a large slab-lined hearth, a small midden, and a small pit structure. The basin hearths, all in close proximity to one another in the western section of the site, were probably used during a relatively short period of time. The slab-lined hearth also occurs in this area. The midden lies southeast of this activity area, the intact portion of which measures roughly 7 × 8 m and up to 30 cm thick. The small semisubterranean structure occupies the northwest end of the site. Sherds are few in number ($n = 30$) and evidently derived from a maximum of four vessels: a Sosi Black-on-white bowl and three Tusayan Corrugated jars. Stone artifacts are comparatively numerous, 1,281 in all, including a high diversity of tools and a few unusual items, such as fragments of two pipes or cloud blowers made of scoria (one shown in Figure 3.8). The small informal structure, the small midden, the scarcity of ceramics, and the near absence of grinding tools all indicate that this was not a long-term habitation; instead, it was perhaps occupied seasonally or for short intervals several times throughout a year. Subsistence remains consist of corn, seeds from weedy annuals (especially goosefoot), and a moderate amount of small-mammal bone (rabbits and hares), much of which is burned. The midden yielded fragmentary corncobs, as well as corn cupules and kernels, but the lack of areas suitable for agriculture in the immediate vicinity may indicate that the corn was brought to the site.

POLLY'S PLACE (AZ-J-14-31)

Polly's Place is a multicomponent site consisting of a temporary habitation occupied during the transitional interval between Basketmaker II and Basketmaker III and an early Archaic limited-activity camp (Figure 3.9). The site occupies a small ridge at an elevation of 2,097 m (6,880 ft) on the eastern side of the divide that separates Piute Canyon from the upper reaches of the Peach Canyon tributary of Navajo Canyon. This location is somewhat sheltered from prevailing winds, has good solar exposure, and looks out upon Piute Canyon to the east. The site lay entirely with the N16 ROW and was excavated in its entirety.

Excavation began with the Basketmaker II component and consisted largely of hand excavation in and around known features followed by backhoe stripping. Basketmaker features were excavated as they were defined and consisted of two structures, a small trash midden, and associated pits and hearths. Excavation of the underlying Archaic component proceeded by using the backhoe to strip the overburden above the buried cultural deposit. Hand excavation of the Archaic component was concentrated in the southern portion of this stripped area and around Structure 1, where seven basin hearths were revealed and subsequently excavated. Two of these were found during subfloor excavation of Structure 1; one (Hearth 6) was radiocarbon dated to verify its stratigraphic origin. After excavating 20 m² of the Archaic deposit in this portion of the site the crew reached a point of diminishing returns because almost no cultural remains were recovered and there was no variability in the hearths; no further work was done in this portion of the site. Two other hearths exposed in a backhoe trench to the southwest edge of the site were also excavated.

The Basketmaker component includes two structures, a midden between the structures, two unlined storage pits, three shallow basin hearths, a possible roasting pit, and a slab-lined hearth. Both structures have slab-lined entryways, interior hearths, and small interior storage pits. A lack of storage features such as slab-lined cists or bell-shaped pits seems significant. This lack of storage may be evidence that the site was occupied seasonally

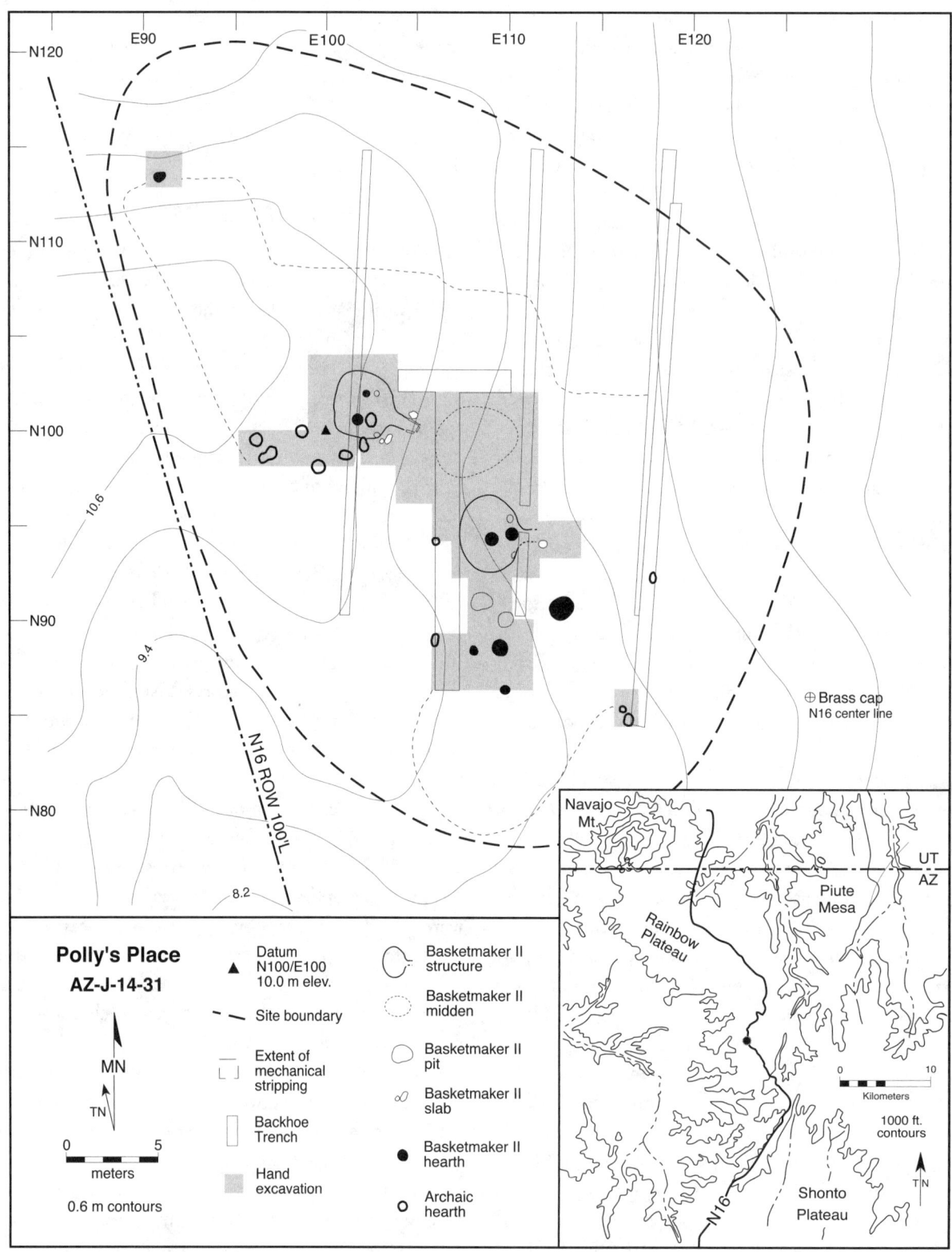

Figure 3.9. Polly's Place site plan showing topography, work effort, and excavated features.

during the growing season when food could be obtained as needed from the environment. Seasonal use is also supported by the paucity of artifacts from the site as a whole and the midden specifically, which was essentially a concentration of charcoal-stained sediment and burned rock. The low number of artifacts is also perhaps indicative of short occupation length. Recovered artifacts include just 205 flakes, 39 stone tools, and seven bones. The investment in living facilities, however, suggests that the occupants planned on more than a single episode of use. This suggests that the intended and actual use of the site may have been as a seasonally reoccupied, short-duration habitation associated with some essential annual extractive task. Pinyon nut harvesting is an obvious potential task, but the lack of pinyon remains from all contexts of the Basketmaker component makes it unlikely. What other settlement role the site may have served is not obvious. Faunal remains are poorly represented, and the flaked-stone assemblage is not what I would expect for a site related to hunting, at least not the hunting of large animals. Radiocarbon dates on mostly maize place occupancy of the site between cal. AD 340 and 540, using the overall average, but it is likely that the site was used sequentially on two separate occasions: AD 250–440 and AD 410–600, with one of the structures occupied on each occasion.

Underlying the Basketmaker II component and separated from it by a layer of sterile sand was the early Archaic component, which included 12 basin hearths of various size but few artifacts. This component is radiocarbon dated to between 7200 and 5800 cal. BC based on three assays on hearth wood charcoal. Because of a lack of contemporaneity between the dates, and the spatial separation between several of the features, the site likely was occupied on several different occasions during the early Archaic. This may have been the case even for the one hearth cluster in the west part of the site since brief sequential encampments during the span of a single generation could have created these features. I interpret the exceptional scarcity of artifacts from the Archaic component as reflecting both the temporary nature of the occupation and the likelihood that foragers used the location for tasks that did not require stone tools or did not require them to be maintained or modified. In short, the nature of the occupation was such that almost no nonperishable remains were discarded. The principal undertaking involved the use of fire within small, shallow basins, but whether they were used to process or cook certain foods or merely as campfires for heat and light during overnight stays is impossible to say. A food-processing role seems intuitively likely, but evidence in support of such an interpretation is woefully deficient. With a complete lack of bone from the Archaic stratum and the hearths, and preservation bias unlikely, faunal processing and consumption can probably be dismissed as a site activity. The flotation analysis of hearth fill was disappointing, in that only a single carbonized *Corispermum* seed was recovered. Certain plants can be processed without leaving any macrobotanical trace (e.g., prickly pear pads, banana yucca fruit, or onion and lily bulbs); thus no subsistence remains would necessarily be expected in the features themselves. The hearths also could have been used to generate hot coals for parching seeds, but with this task there is a considerable chance for accidentally spilling some seed into the fires. Several of the Archaic sites along the N21 ROW on the Kaibito Plateau likewise contained numerous hearths but few artifacts (Bungart et al. 2004). As here, the lack of artifacts at those sites was not easily accounted for; this is a topic that deserves further thought and study.

Naaki Hooghan (AZ-J-14-11)

Naaki Hooghan (Figure 3.10), a Navajo phrase meaning "two homes," is a late Pueblo II secondary habitation on the eastern end of a low, east-to-west-trending ridge overlooking a Piute Canyon tributary at an elevation of 2,079 m (6,820 ft). The site ridge is tangent to the large north–south ridge that forms the dissected slickrock divide between Navajo and Piute canyons. About 200 m northeast of the site in a minor drainage is a deep plunge pool that retains runoff throughout most of the year. The site location receives good solar warming.

Since only a very thin layer of loose eolian sand buried the remains and features, hand excavation of this site was accomplished quite efficiently. Most features become visible after only 10–15 cm of overburden were removed. Some of this effort (35 m^2) was done in testing, primarily in the area of Structure 1 and the midden. This effort continued in data recovery by expanding outward to encompass the entire midden, a second structure to the southwest, and a ramada attached to Structure 1. Four backhoe trenches helped to determine the vertical and horizontal extent of the eastern and southern portions of the site. After excavating 97 m^2 in the main site area, peripheral portions were stripped to sterile soil with a backhoe.

The features of Naaki Hooghan include two subrectangular rooms with jacal superstructures, a ramada attached to one of these houses, an extramural activity

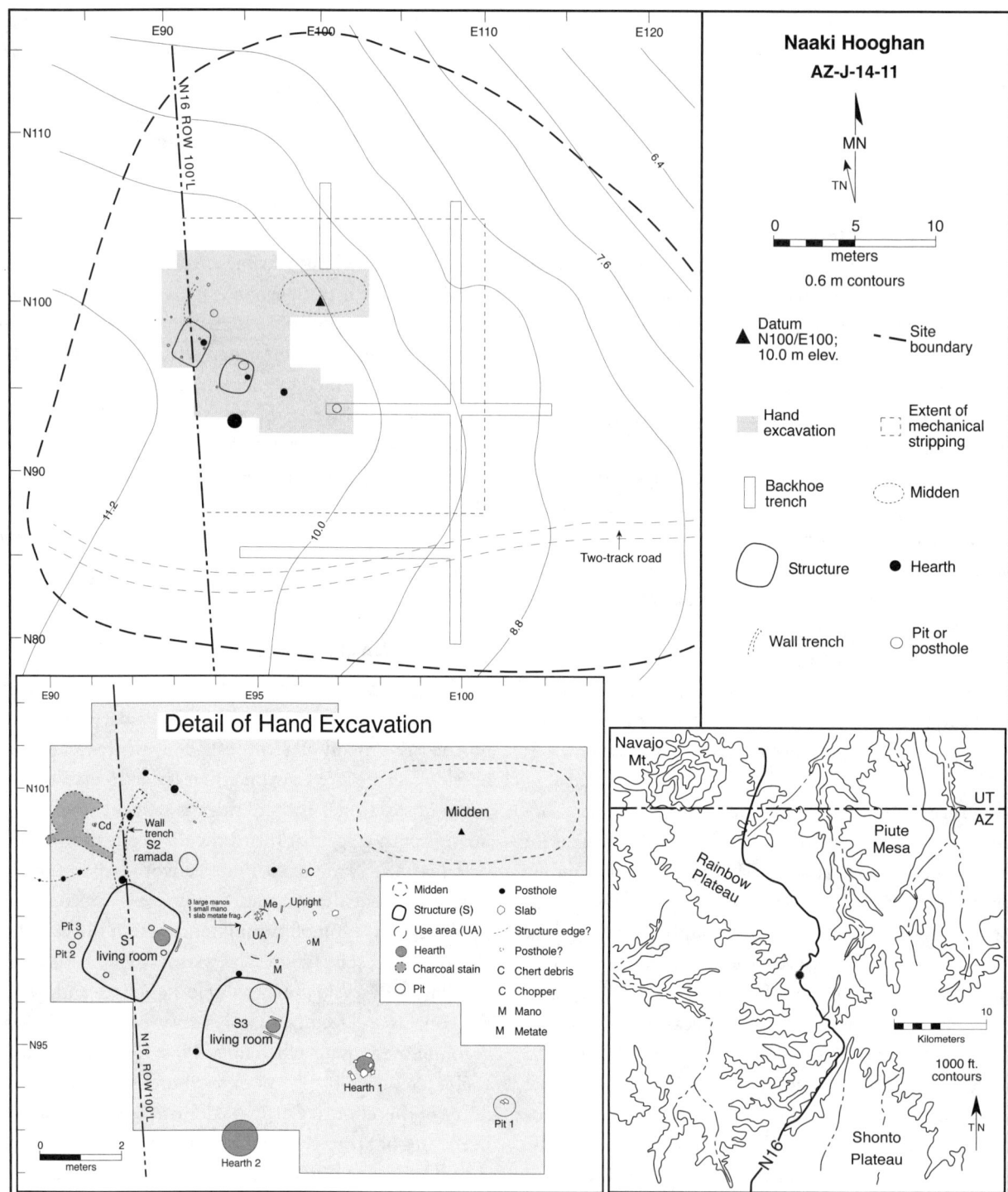

Figure 3.10. Naaki Hooghan site plan showing topography, work effort, and excavated features.

area where a mealing bin was once located, a few outside hearths and pits, and a shallow, eroded midden. The lack of specially prepared, large-volume storage features, such as cists or bell-shaped pits, is significant. Given the lack of storage I infer that the site was seasonally occupied during the growing season when food stores were unnecessary. Occupation during warmer times of the year is supported by the comparatively small, less formalized, and comparatively less-used hearths within the structures. The two houses may have provided storage using large jars, but the sherd assemblage suggests few storage jars at the site. The low number of artifacts (930 sherds, 345 stone artifacts, and 25 bones), including those with a relatively high discard rate, such as debitage, is indicative of a short occupation length. The investment in two living structures, however, suggests that the occupants planned on using the site more than once. The intended and actual use of the site, therefore, may have been as a seasonally reoccupied, short-duration habitation. An alternative that seems less in accordance with the evidence is that the occupants intended to occupy the site on a more permanent basis but then abandoned the site after living there only a short while.

Although it was evidently used as a seasonal habitation, the role of Naaki Hooghan within an overall settlement-subsistence strategy is somewhat enigmatic. Seasonal use for field tending at first seems unlikely given an apparent lack of arable land within the immediate site vicinity. Prime farmland is located in Upper Piute Canyon not too far away, but it is more likely that summer farming camps would be located closer to the fields within the canyon proper, rather than several kilometers away and more than 200 m higher in elevation. Pueblo II farmers may have planted in the deep dune sand around Naaki Hooghan as a means to diversify their field locations. Domesticates were found in analyzed flotation samples, but these could have been brought in from elsewhere. The presence of squash pollen, including aggregates, is a better indication that crops were grown in close proximity to the site. Other plant remains were found at the site, including plants most likely obtained from agricultural fields and other human-disturbed habitats, as well as wild plants such as prickly pear and pinyon. Pinyon nut harvesting is a possible additional reason that Naaki Hooghan was occupied. Based on the recovered ceramic assemblage, the approximate time of site occupancy was late Pueblo II, ca. AD 1100–1150. The site apparently was occupied for only a brief interval, probably fewer than 10 years, so occupancy during the latter part of the time range is probable. Naaki Hooghan adds to the number and diversity of late Pueblo II settlements excavated within the northern Kayenta region.

TRES CAMPOS (AZ-J-14-12)

Tres Campos (Figure 3.11) is a multicomponent site situated on the east side of the bedrock divide between the canyons of Piute and Navajo creeks overlooking the head of a tributary to Piute Canyon. The site occupies a dune of eolian sand at the foot of a north–south-trending slickrock ridge that extends off the crest of the divide. The site has an elevation of about 2,080 m, some 60 to 120 m below the crest of the divide and about 240 m above the bottom of Upper Piute Canyon's western fork. This setting affords a vista of upper slopes around the head of Piute Canyon, although the canyon bottom is out of view.

The three components at the site consist of an early Archaic temporary camp likely associated with hunting, a Basketmaker II seasonal habitation, and a Pueblo II seasonal habitation. Each component occupies largely separate areas of the site, is situated differentially relative to the ROW, and has been variably impacted by natural processes and recent development. The Archaic component may be entirely within the ROW, but the old Navajo Mountain road removed an unknown portion of this component, leaving just a small area for excavation at the eastern edge of the ROW. The current alignment of the Navajo Mountain road artificially bounds the Archaic component on the east, whereas deflation does the same to the south and west. Along the edge of the roadcut the Archaic stratum is buried, but cultural remains diminish in abundance, reflecting a rapid drop in cultural deposition going northward. Roughly 56 m^2 were excavated to investigate the Archaic component. About 21 m^2 of this exposed an intact cultural stratum; in about 8 m^2 the stratum was partially intact and partially deflated, and in the other 27 m^2 the stratum was deflated, with artifacts resting on the current ground surface. All sediment from this 56-m^2 area was screened with ⅛-in mesh. Four basin hearths associated with the Archaic component were excavated following standard procedure for small features.

The Basketmaker II component occurs near the western edge of the ROW; the two features known to be part of this component consist of a burned habitation structure and associated small trash midden; a nearby slab-lined hearth might also be associated. The ROW bisects the Basketmaker II component such that the small trash midden is within the construction area, whereas the associated structure lies mostly outside this area. The structure was preserved in place by constricting the ROW. Knowledge about this feature comes from a 1-×-2-m test unit that recovered several flakes and a burned post. The small trash midden directly east of the house is concentrated in an area about 5 × 6 m in size. Most of this area (27 m^2) was excavated, and all sediment was screened with ⅛-in mesh. A slab-lined hearth located about halfway between the Basketmaker and Puebloan components might also belong to the Basketmaker component. Because it was exposed on the surface, deflation had removed the upper

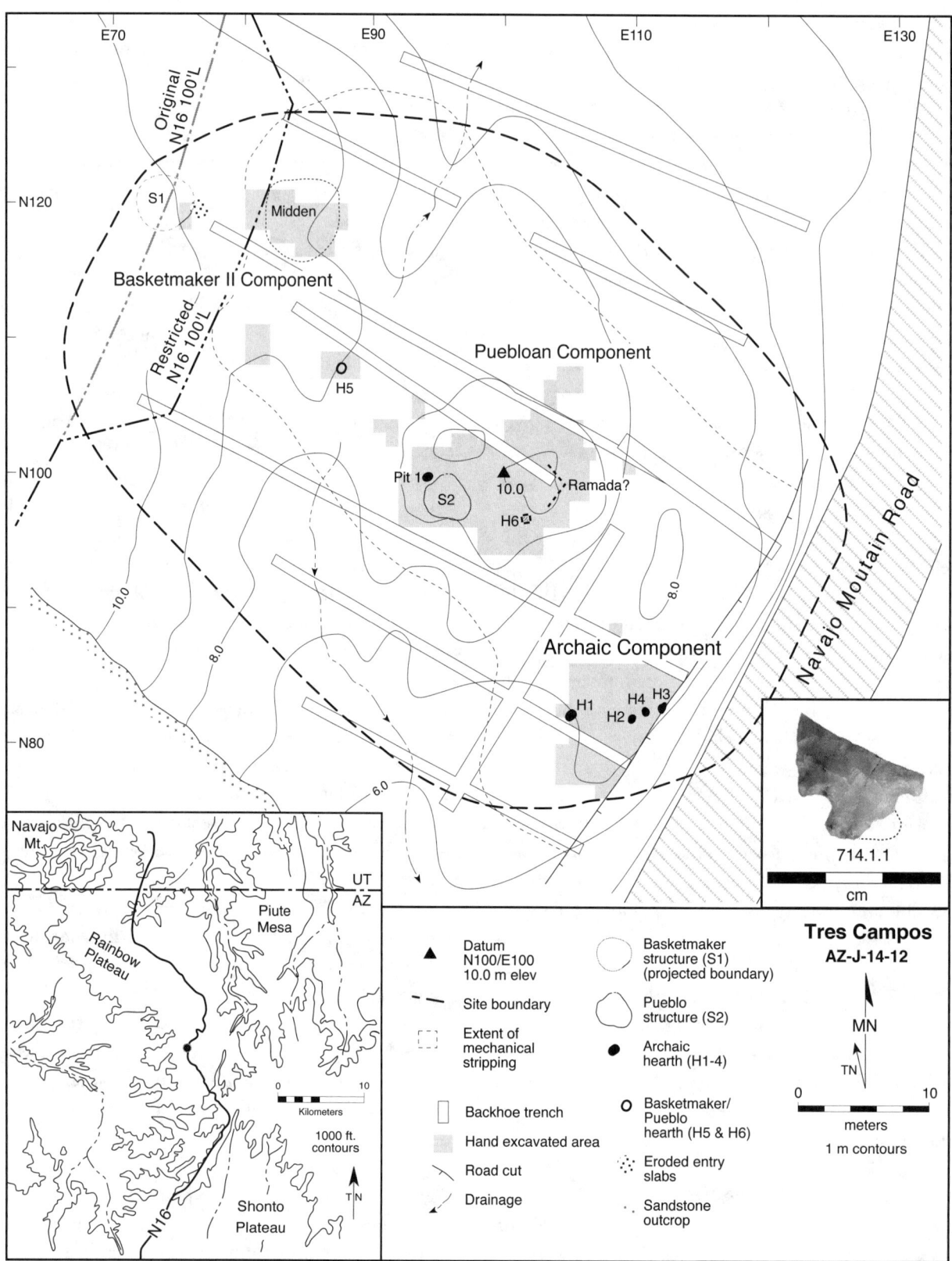

Figure 3.11. Tres Campos site plan showing topography, work effort, and excavated features. Inset on right shows an Elko Corner-notched projectile point from the Archaic component.

part of this feature and the prehistoric ground surface that the hearth originated from.

The Puebloan component occupies the top of a small sand dune near the center of the site in the center of the ROW. Dune deflation has artificially bound the Puebloan cultural stratum on the east, south, and west sides, with artifacts eroded from place and resting as a lag deposit on the surface. The stratum became progressively more buried by recent eolian sand to the north, but it pinches out quite rapidly, reflecting the limits of cultural deposition. The extent of the in situ and eroded Puebloan remains indicates that the original size of this component was probably no more than 24 m east–west × 20 m north–south. The preserved portion of this component that was excavated measures about 40 m² in size. All of the sediment from this area was screened, with at least half of it put through ⅛-in mesh. The few Puebloan features exposed during the process of horizontal exposure were excavated according to standard procedure. These features consist of a small structure, a slab-lined hearth, a pit, and traces of a possible ramada.

Excavation of the Archaic component produced a moderate density of flaked-stone artifacts ($n = 882$), much of it obsidian, and some bone ($n = 107$) in association with four basin hearths. This reflects just a portion of what the site originally contained since construction and maintenance of the existing road had removed an unknown portion of this component. Whether excavation of the entire site would have altered our interpretations seems unlikely, in that the Archaic remains lying out of context along the east side of the existing road appear no different than those recovered in situ consisting of abundant late-stage flaking debris of obsidian and extralocal chert and some small burned bone fragments. For in situ remains, artifact and bone densities are greatest around two of the basin hearths. These features (Hearths 2–3) have statistically similar radiocarbon dates, with an average two-sigma age range of 6210–5920 cal. BC. One of the hearths (4) is stratigraphically above the others and has a radiocarbon age supportive of a slightly younger age but still quite old, roughly 5300–4400 cal. BC. Hearth 1, located somewhat away from the other features and the area of greatest artifact and bone density, has two radiocarbon dates, both older than the other assays. This feature might provide evidence for initial limited use of the site during the start of the seventh millennium cal. BC.

The high incidence of extralocal materials, including much obsidian, within the stone artifact assemblage is reflective of high residential mobility. If the incidence of Government Mountain obsidian resulted from direct procurement, as seems reasonable, then the Archaic foragers occupying Tres Campos may have been near the far northern reaches of their annual range. The potential size of the annual range would vary greatly depending upon whether direct procurement was embedded within annual band movement for subsistence resources or was done more specifically for tool stone acquisition. The types of other lithic resources in the Archaic assemblage indicate that the latter appears more likely. It is also possible that the high incidence of obsidian and other nonlocal resources reflects the annual logistic territory of hunters, a territory that greatly exceeded that of the band as a whole. The flaked-stone assemblage indicates that the Archaic foragers came to Tres Campos carrying with them stone tools in the form of flake blanks, preforms, and finished items made elsewhere. These tools were further reduced or rejuvenated and resharpened at this site. Locally available raw material was also procured for expedient flake production, but most of the initial reduction of even the local material took place elsewhere. That few tools were recovered from the Archaic component suggests a limited stay by a population with a high rate of recycling and edge refurbishment but a low rate of tool discard. Three tools that were discarded are projectile point bases likely snapped in their hafts during hunting, as well as bifaces, one of which was clearly broken in production, likely of a replacement point. It appears that during the early Archaic, Tres Campos served as a temporary campsite where folks finished and resharpened hunting equipment for anticipated use elsewhere. The co-occurrence of such a stone artifact assemblage with fragmented and burned bone is best interpreted as resulting from a temporary camp associated with hunting. The lack of carbonized macrofloral remains in any of the hearths and the lack of grinding slabs seem to corroborate this interpretation.

Since the principal feature (the structure) of the Basketmaker II component was excluded from study, interpretations of this component are limited. However, the configuration and character of this component make it similar to several Basketmaker II sites excavated within the N16 ROW such as Blake's Abode, Polly's Place, Panorama House, and Sin Sombra. Temporal assignment is provided by a radiocarbon date on the outer tree rings of a burned post from the house (unfortunately this post could not be linked to the local tree-ring sequence for the area). The age of the post after calibration suggests that the site was occupied sometime between 170 cal. BC and cal. AD 140 (two-sigma range). Given the limited remains from the midden, the simple site layout with no suggestion of feature superpositioning, and the evidently finite use-life of the house as suggested by its construction, I believe that the Basketmaker component was occupied briefly, perhaps just once during a season or for short intervals during several consecutive seasons. The midden is small and limited in artifactual remains, being identified chiefly by abundant charcoal flecking and burned rock. Artifacts are limited to 122 flakes, three core tools, a flat abrader, and a small chunk of pigment. Lithic reduction seems to have emphasized unretouched flakes and nodular core tools rather than bifaces and other formal facial tools. This small assemblage is probably a reflection of both a limited occupation span and the relatively small role that stone tools played in the Basketmaker activities at this site. The presence in the midden of burned bones from large and small game indicates some degree of hunting. There was a complete lack of food-related macrobotanical remains; midden flotation samples contained only wood charcoal. The absence of floral subsistence scraps might merely be a sampling problem, in that other similar Basketmaker II sites yielded maize and occasional remains of other economic plants. The abundance of burned rock (limestone and some sandstone) in the midden suggests that some form of pit baking or stone boiling took place, and given that all of the bone is burned, animal cooking is indicated.

The Puebloan component consists of a shallow informal structure without an interior hearth, a slab-lined hearth that may have been within another structure, an extramural pit, and traces of a probable ramada. The cultural stratum filling and surrounding these features was rich with charcoal and burned rock, evidently from frequent pit baking, stone boiling, or other forms of food processing involving fire and hot stones. Given the informal nature of the structure and the lack of an interior hearth, it seems likely that the dwelling and the site as a whole were occupied during the warm months of the year. Seasonal short-term use is also indicated by the general scarcity of remains associated with food preparation and consumption—specifically the near absence of grinding tools and low proportion of utility ceramics, with few being sooted. The construction of at least one structure, and possibly a second, as well as a ramada, indicates that the occupants planned to use the site for longer than one brief episode. That this actually came to pass is suggested by the accumulation of artifacts (413 sherds, 777 stone artifacts), burned rock, and charcoal. Occupants perhaps used the site for short intervals during warmer months over a span of several years. It is difficult to estimate the number of vessels in use at the site, but they could have been counted on a single hand, and it seems likely that some of the sherds came from vessel portions rather than whole items. Portions of jars may have been brought in for use as plates or other utensils. The artifact assemblage is distinctive for its high frequency and diversity of stone artifacts, including a few unusual items such as fragments of a scoria pipe. The majority of raw material was locally obtained for reduction into expedient flake tools or simple nodular core tools. The large number of pecking stones from this component further reflects this trend. Hunting might be evidenced by a Bull Creek point and biface as well as the flaking debris from bifacial tools. Faunal remains indicate that the Puebloan occupants hunted mostly small game, mainly rabbits and a few rodents (squirrel and gopher). A single deer bone and unidentifiable fragments of large-animal bones demonstrate some hunting of larger game. Fragmentary corn kernels, cupules, and cobs were recovered from flotation samples; cobs were also collected in the field while screening the cultural stratum. Since areas suitable for agriculture appear lacking in the immediate vicinity, the site seems unlikely to have functioned as a camp for tending fields. The lack of maize pollen from the structure might support such an interpretation. Although I may have a poor notion about how Anasazi farmers rated the farming potential of landscapes, especially during times of higher population density than currently exists in the area and when conditions may have been more optimal for farming, it is worth mentioning that *no* Navajo farm plots exist in the immediate area. The ceramic assemblage is dominated by the late Pueblo II ceramic types of Sosi and Dogoszhi Black-on-white, Tusayan Black-on-red, and Tusayan Corrugated. Occupancy sometime between AD 1100 and 1150 is likely, perhaps extending somewhat later as indicated by a few later types such as Flagstaff Black-on-white (a few earlier types such as Black Mesa Black-on-white are easily accounted for by recycling or heirlooms).

Panorama House (AZ-J-14-34)

Panorama House (Figure 3.12) is a Basketmaker II habitation occupying the crest of a narrow falling dune that extends eastward from a slickrock slope on the east side of the divide between the canyons of Navajo and Piute creeks. The dune crest, at about 2,072 m in elevation, affords an excellent panorama of the colorful slickrock

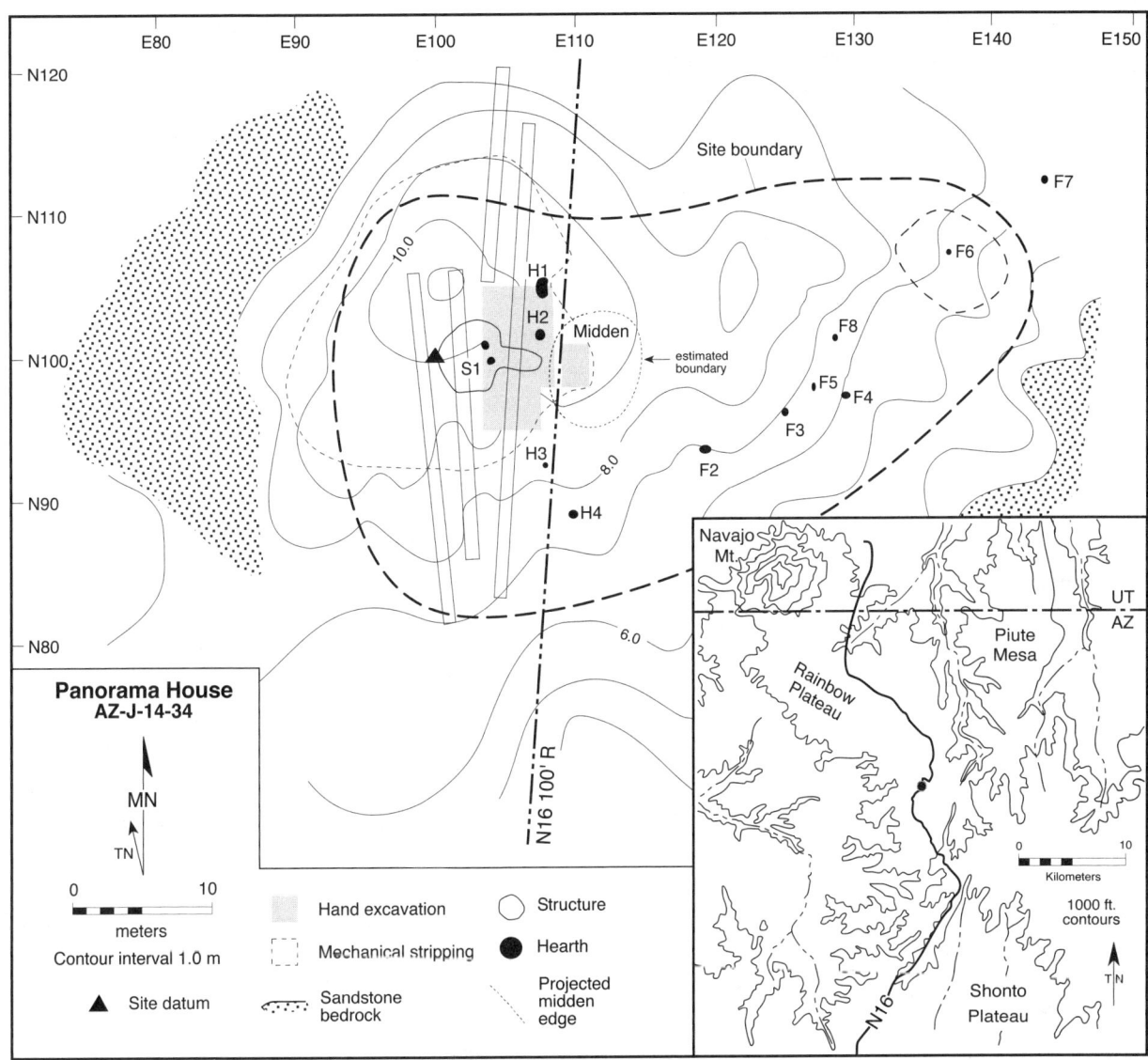

Figure 3.12. Panorama House site plan showing topography, work effort, and excavated features.

ridges and escarpments defining or bordering the head of Piute Canyon. The dune also overlooks the neighboring Basketmaker site known as Big Bend, nestled near the foot of a bedrock ridge about 400 m to the north and 30 m lower in elevation. The ridge crest where cultural features occur is buried by variable amounts of eolian sand. Remains are exposed on the wind-eroded south side of the dune ridge rather than its crest or the north side. Just a portion of the site is within the ROW, but it contains a burned structure, a few extramural hearths, and part of a small trash midden. Because the house had burned, plan definition proved easy and was accomplished by hand excavation of the cultural stratum to trace the outline of the structure and expose the prehistoric occupation surface. Sterile overburden was shoveled off initially, but when it became clear that the house was about 5 m in diameter

and that the northern half was buried by more than 1 m of recent blow sand, a backhoe was used to strip the overburden. Cultural deposits were screened with ⅛- or ¼-in mesh, with all remains provenienced by 1-×-1-m units for horizontal control. The midden was only sampled because much of it extended outside the ROW; 6 m² of the midden area was excavated and screened through ⅛-in mesh. From all the excavation units the total recovery consisted of 255 stone artifacts and 22 bones, all burned. The flaking debris seems largely derived from the production of unretouched flakes and nodular core tools rather than bifaces and other formal facial tools.

Excavations at Panorama House disclosed a burned shallow pithouse a little more than 5 m in diameter, with an eastern ramp entry partially defined by small sandstone slabs. The entry was remodeled at least once with a slight change of orientation from east-southeast to east. The house had two interior hearths, each likely corresponding with one of the entries. Burned posts from a superstructure occurred around the house perimeter and toward its center. Two central posts might have supported a north–south primary beam for the roof, as seen at Kin Kahuna. Roughly two–three steps away from the structure entry (to the east) was a small midden deposit, up to 20 cm thick. As at similar Basketmaker II sites of the N16 ROW, this midden was rich with burned rock and charcoal but comparatively artifact poor. The density of burned rock in the core portion of the midden averaged 337 pieces and 13.9 kg per square meter. This, along with the density of charcoal pieces and charcoal staining, indicates considerable processing of some sort, either pit roasting with heated stones, stone boiling, or both. Stone boiling seems most likely because no roasting pits were found in or around the structure and because most of the burned limestone had been reduced to small chunks. Experimental use of the local limestone for pit cooking and stone boiling found that the latter technique greatly fractures the limestone, reducing it into increasingly smaller chunks.

Despite intensive flotation analysis (14 samples totaling 56 liters) and considerable screening with ⅛-in mesh, just a few charred seeds (one each of goosefoot and juniper), small maize portions (cupules and a kernel fragment), and a handful of burned bones from large and small game were recovered. Few faunal remains were found in the midden or elsewhere at the site, but there is evidence for deer and large mammal exploitation. The small artifact assemblage is probably a reflection of a limited occupation span and perhaps the limited settlement role of the site. Both interpretations also seem supported by the sparse amount of subsistence-related floral and faunal remains. Maize was probably not being grown at the site, given an evident lack of suitable locations, but nearby Piute Canyon provides excellent farmland. Four statistically contemporaneous AMS assays on maize fix the time of occupancy at cal. AD 240–390 (two-sigma range). Given the limited remains from the midden, the simple site layout with no suggestion of feature superpositioning, and the finite use-life of the house as suggested by its construction, I believe that the Basketmaker component was occupied briefly for short intervals during several consecutive seasons (reuse is indicated by modification of the entry and interior hearth). The structure excavated at Panorama House occupied the highest possible elevation at the westernmost edge of the dune. This was also the western edge of the site because the slickrock slope west of the house offered no possibility for residential use. Based on the limited natural exposure of remains farther east down the dune ridge, the site likely contains at least one additional structure, similar to the one excavated, and an associated small midden. If there is another structure at this location, then it might well be like the situation at Polly's Place, where noncontemporaneous houses and associated features are grouped together simply because ideal settlement locations are quite restricted in the local setting.

Big Bend (AZ-J-14-13)

Big Bend (Figure 3.13) is a moderate-size multiple-component site occupying the top of a flat bench at an elevation of 2,048 m between two small canyons that drain into Upper Piute Creek. The bench occurs below an escarpment of sandstone slickrock that encircles the site area on three sides and provides a colorful backdrop. The site name refers to a large bend in the existing Navajo Mountain road, the tightest single curve along the entire route. There are both Archaic and Basketmaker II components at Big Bend, with the latter evidently the most extensive. Just a small and heavily damaged portion of the site is within the N16 ROW; the bulk of obvious features and refuse occur west of this corridor. Although data recovery was restricted to a peripheral portion of the site that initially seemed minimally informative, the excavated features and remains date to the late Archaic, around 3,400–3,000 radiocarbon years ago, a time poorly represented within the Kayenta region at large. This is an important interval for understanding the processes by which the practice of food production using Mesoamerican domesticates (maize and squash) spread across the Colorado Plateau.

After shovel stripping eolian sand overburden, the cultural layer from about 70 m² was excavated and screened, initially with ⅛-in mesh but then with ¼-in mesh to expedite the work since recovery was so low. The total yield from this effort was just 39 stone artifacts and three bones. Features exposed in plan were excavated by hand and appropriately sampled following standard practice. An area roughly 1,080 m² in size was mechanically stripped. This area partially overlapped the hand-excavation area, but most of it was to the northeast and east. Mechanical stripping exposed two additional hearths outside the area of hand excavation (Hearths 5–6). The remaining portions of these features were excavated and sampled.

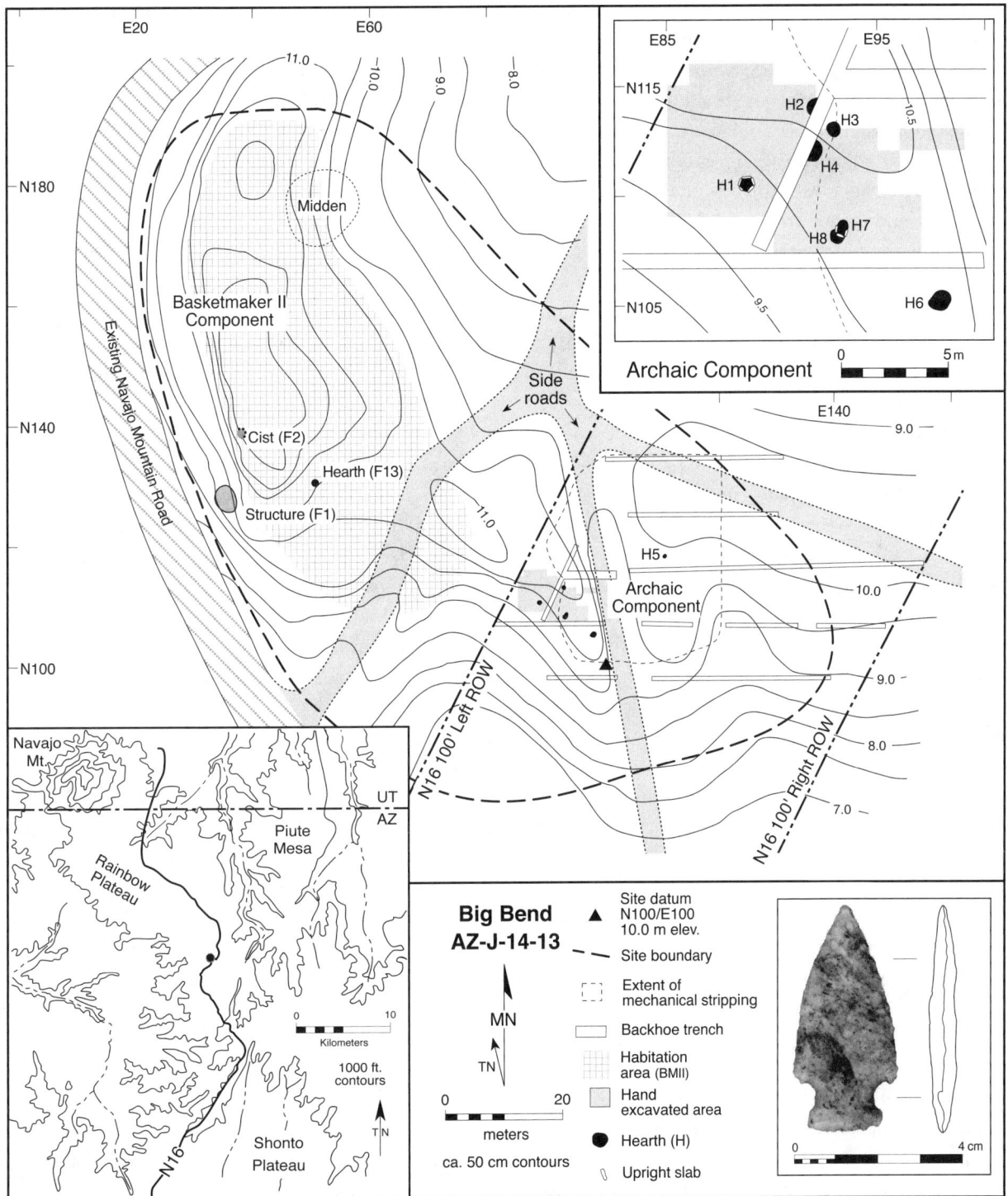

Figure 3.13. Big Bend site plan showing topography, work effort, and excavated features. Inset on bottom right shows a western Basketmaker II projectile point recovered from the burned roof fall layer of a pithouse (F1) that was exposed by road-grading along the old Navajo Mountain road; a small-diameter piece of sagebrush wood from the burned roof fall returned a radiocarbon age of 2170 ± 40 BP (Beta-135681, −17.3‰).

Foragers initially occupied the Big Bend site during the early Archaic, building a fire in Hearth 5 sometime between 6460 and 6240 cal. BC (two-sigma range). Little else can be said about the use of the site at this early time. The hearth flotation sample yielded no plant remains except wood charcoal, and no other plant or animal remains were recovered from the feature; no other features date to this interval, and there are no associated artifacts or other remains. The hearth occurs in a heavily disturbed area; thus other early Archaic features or remains may have been destroyed by earth-moving equipment during prior episodes of road construction. It also seems likely that the stratum of origin for the hearth had been removed prior to our excavation of the feature. A charcoal-stained layer that excavators found by backhoe stripping north of Hearths 2 and 3 may have represented an early Archaic cultural layer. If true, then there could be other early Archaic features and remains preserved outside the ROW under the late Archaic and Basketmaker II components. Supporting this possibility is a small basin hearth exposed in the Navajo Mountain roadcut at the far western edge of the site; lying well below (ca. 1 m) the Basketmaker II component, it is a potential candidate for an early Archaic hearth.

The Late Archaic foragers occupying Big Bend created a cluster of thermal features (Hearths 1–4 and 6–8). Calibration and averaging when appropriate of five radiocarbon dates indicate probable initial use of the site by late Archaic foragers sometime between 1690 and 1510 cal. BC, with subsequent reuse sometime between 1440 and 1260 cal. BC. Despite the evidence for multiple uses, I cannot separate the minimal artifact assemblage to associate with these dates. Most remains came from around Hearths 1, 2, and 4, but because these hearths are from each temporal group it is impossible to know to which the artifacts belong—perhaps both. It is clear that the portion of the site excavated is peripheral to the Basketmaker II component, but is it also peripheral to a larger and more complex late Archaic component? If the excavated portion was the focal area for late Archaic activity, then the few recovered remains indicate a site of limited use, one unlikely to have been residential. The scarcity of remains is further compounded by the radiocarbon evidence suggesting at least two separate use episodes during the late Archaic. It might be the case, however, that the portion excavated represents just a peripheral edge of a much more substantial late Archaic occupation, one that might have been located in the previously disturbed portion of the existing ROW or perhaps under the still-intact Basketmaker II component outside the ROW. Not knowing how extensive the late Archaic component was or is necessitates interpretative restraint.

The late Archaic component contains seven hearths of several types: two slab-lined (Hearths 1 and 7), one a deep and straight-sided roasting pit (Hearth 4), one a moderately deep and straight-sided pit that seemed little used or perhaps totally cleaned of its charcoal fill (Hearth 3), and the rest shallow basins (Hearths 2, 6, and 7). Hearth 2 yielded three fragments of a large-mammal bone, the only bone from this component, but otherwise these features did not contain any subsistence remains. Hearth 4 contained a juniper seed, but this was likely part of the fuel layer for Hearth 4, introduced with a juniper branch. The different hearth morphologies could have been used for processing different resources. The deep roasting pit (Hearth 4) certainly served to pit cook some sort of food, because it could not have provided any warmth or light. The slab-lined hearths also were likely used for cooking; the slabs serve to retain heat for internal cooking purposes, but they limit external radiation for warmth. Shallow basin hearths are effective for both warmth and cooking, but the lack of ash in these features may indicate that the coals were smothered, something more likely to happen during cooking. What resources may have been processed and perhaps consumed at the site is unknown because of the lack of subsistence remains from flotation samples. A small mano fragment from near the slab-lined Hearth 1 is scant evidence for seed processing, especially as no grinding slabs were found. The few fragments of large-mammal bone from Hearth 2 may support limited hunting, but since the bone is not burned it might be intrusive. The flaked-stone assemblage is not typical of that commonly associated with hunting, containing few pressure flakes and no projectile points or other bifacial tools or fragments. The significance of this component (along with two additional sites described later) lies in the documentation of a late Archaic presence on the Rainbow Plateau. It is important to study sites of this time period to learn where the evidence for domesticate use first appears, on what sorts of sites and in what settings, and to document the nature of the associated artifact assemblages. No maize remains came from this component.

The Basketmaker II component at Big Bend was outside the N16 ROW and therefore not included in data recovery. When it was initially recorded by NAU archaeologists in 1981, a road grader had sectioned a burned pithouse along the edge of the existing road, exposing charred roof timbers. A year later, additional road maintenance had removed a further portion of the house and exposed a burned Basketmaker II–style dart point within the roof fall layer resting on the floor (see photo inset of Figure 3.13). The point and a sample of the burned roof fall were collected at the time and added to the NAU archives. By 1983, continued road maintenance had removed all traces of the burned pithouse. When NNAD started on data recovery the projectile point and radiocarbon sample were retrieved from the NAU repository and incorporated into the existing collections that NNAD obtained from Big Bend. A radiocarbon date on a small sagebrush twig from the burned roof fall has a calibrated two-sigma date range of 380–90 BC. This radiocarbon date is toward the early end of the current Basketmaker II radiocarbon record for the Rainbow Plateau, with only eight dates that are earlier. Other features visible from the surface or in the roadcut profile include one other pithouse, hearths, several slab-lined storage cists (there might also be large storage pits), and at least one midden east of an intact structure. It seems likely that the structures and features occur in two groups and may represent two households or family units that occupied the ridge at somewhat different times. This is the general pattern for multiple-dwelling Basketmaker II sites situated on the dissected divide between Piute and Navajo canyons. Nevertheless, the presence of storage features makes this site different from excavated Basketmaker II sites in the immediate area, such as Panorama House, because they lack storage features. Because of its storage features, Big Bend may have been a primary residential site like The Pits or Kin Kahuna. The dated structure that no longer exists may be earlier than the slab-lined storage cist (Feature 2) and slab-lined pithouse/cists (Features 15 and 18) that occur to the north. Based on current dating, it appears that slab-lined storage cists in the open occurred toward the latter portion of the Basketmaker II period, after the time of Christ. The Basketmaker component may therefore consist of two separate occupations, one early and one late, with the latter likely involving some degree of permanent residence.

Ko' Lanhi (AZ-J-14-35)

Ko' Lanhi, which is Navajo for "many hearths," is a heavily disturbed, single-component Basketmaker II site that lies almost entirely within the N16 ROW on a north–south-trending stabilized sand dune (Figure 3.14) at an elevation of 1,911 m (6,720 ft). The dune has collected at the base of a sandstone cliff to the west that forms part of the high and rugged Navajo Sandstone slickrock divide between the canyons of Navajo and Piute creeks and links the Shonto and Rainbow plateaus. Past construction activity, especially for a power line, severely impacted the site, bisecting it down the center with a dozer swath that removed up to 3 m of sediment and perhaps many features, including a structure or two.

Data recovery involved hand excavation of 106 m² in three separate areas. The focus of activity (77 m²) was centered over a series of charcoal stains and revealed numerous discrete hearths. The largest of the surface stains turned out to be three discrete hearth (Hearths 1, 3, and 9). Another excavation area, 20 m² in size, lay southeast of the hearth concentration to expose an undulating but intact cultural deposit visible in the north profile of a backhoe trench. This effort thoroughly sampled the remnant of a midden-like deposit and also exposed a small pit (Pit 1). The third area of horizontal exposure, 9 m² in size, in the central east portion of the site, investigated a possible structure that turned out to be a natural soil stain. Most site matrix removed by these excavations was screened through ⅛-in mesh, with ¼-in mesh used to screen the sediment from 11 m². All small features were excavated following standard practice.

Excavations at Ko' Lanhi documented 13 hearths, one pit, and the probable fringe remnant of a midden, all part of a single Basketmaker II component. Hearth superpositioning and blurring of feature boundaries suggest that the site formed by repeated use of the location. This is also supported by the stone artifacts recovered ($n = 718$), which seem too numerous and diverse to be the accumulation of a single use episode for limited purpose. The stone artifacts are indicative of various production and maintenance tasks, with tools being used for a variety of purposes including food processing. Some of the stone artifacts, such as a pipe fragment, a calcite disk, and portions of probable iron/manganese ornaments, suggest that activities of a more esoteric nature occurred. Sediment samples from nearly all of the hearths as well as the midden remnant revealed few carbonized plant remains other than charcoal. One hearth yielded maize kernels, and eight of the 11 sampled hearths produced goosefoot seeds. The site is lacking cob fragments, but shucked kernels may have been brought to the site for consumption. Statistically contemporaneous radiocarbon determinations on maize kernels and juniper seeds from two different hearths place site occupancy during the last few centuries BC (350 cal. BC to cal. AD 10 at two sigma).

Unfortunately, the nature and extent of Ko' Lanhi are open to speculation because of the extent of prior disturbance. If at least one structure had been removed, then the settlement role inferred for the site would differ greatly

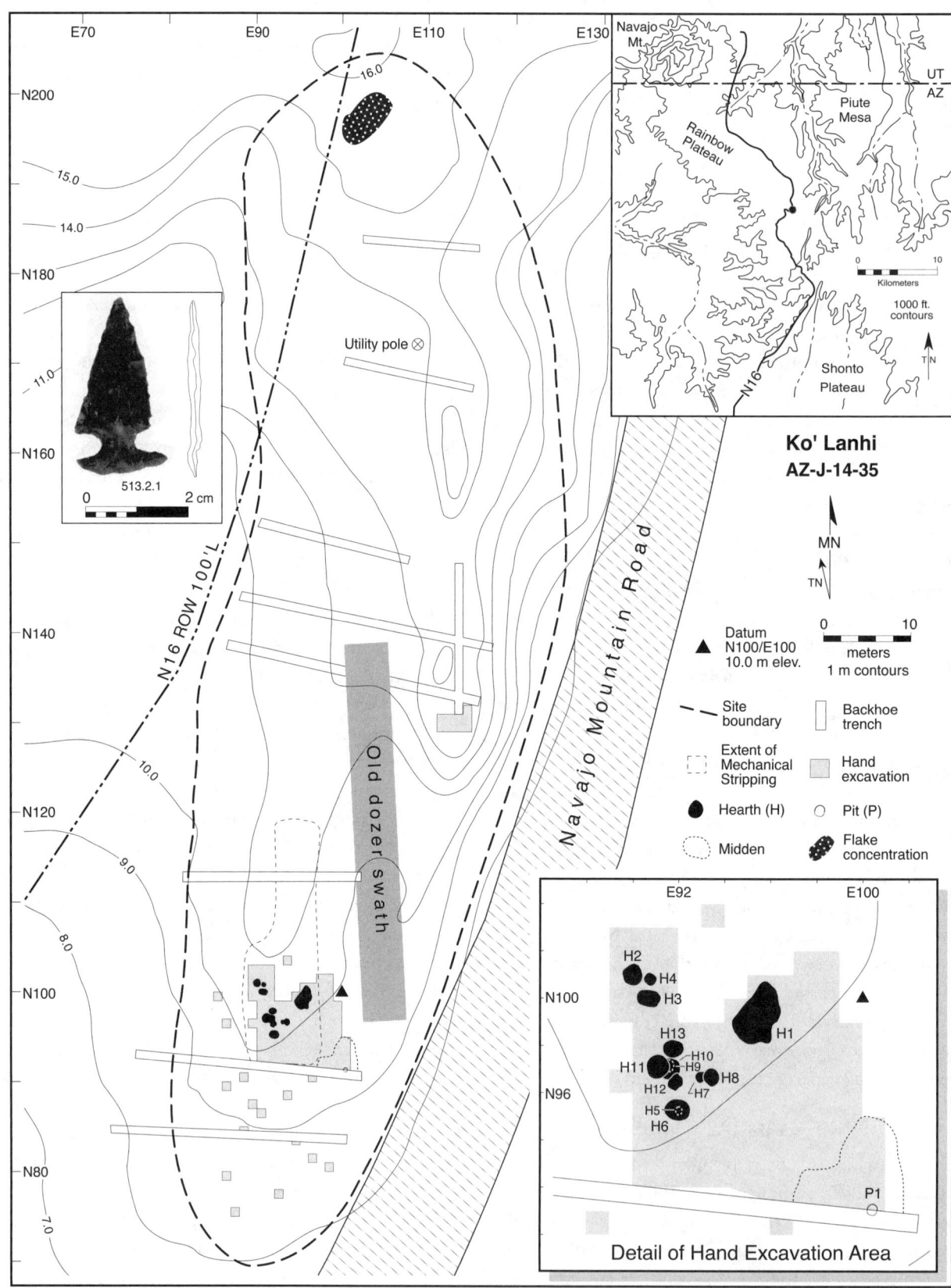

Figure 3.14. Ko' Lanhi site plan showing topography, work effort, and excavated features; inset shows a western; inset shows a western Basketmaker II projectile point recovered from the site.

than if no structures had been destroyed. Interpretation is further complicated by the quantity and types of other features and cultural remains lost to study. For example, if Ko' Lanhi was a structural site, did it have abundant remains and features including a large developed midden and storage features, or was there never much more than what excavations revealed? Of course, we shall never know, but I can make a reasonable inference on what the site was like by comparing Ko' Lanhi with other Basketmaker II sites excavated within the N16 ROW. If Ko' Lanhi had served as a major residential location such as Kin Kahuna (see below and chapter 5 of this volume), then excavations should have recovered substantially more artifacts and other remains. Even with the amount of prior disturbance, quantities of artifacts and burned rock should have littered the surface of the bladed swath to the east and southeast of the preserved features, and this was not the case. The quantity of remains is more in accord with the findings from nearby sites such as the previously described Panorama House or Blake's Abode, described next. These are single-structure sites that likely served as seasonal, short-term residences, reused during several consecutive years as domiciles for nuclear or small extended families.

Blake's Abode (AZ-J-14-36)

Blake's Abode (Figure 3.15) is a single-component Basketmaker II habitation situated on the east end of a low, east–west-trending linear dune at 2,048 m (6,720 ft) elevation. This dune formed at the base of a low cliff that is part of the slickrock divide separating Piute and Navajo canyons. Construction of the old Navajo Mountain road just west of the site had removed a small portion of a pithouse and may have destroyed additional minor features. The site was named in honor of John Blake, a resident of Inscription House who helped excavate the structure and worked on the project from the beginning.

Very little sediment covered this site, so hand excavation was done efficiently. A surface trash scatter was sampled for small artifacts and other remains by excavating 18 m² and screening the cultural matrix using ⅛-in mesh. An additional 93 m² around Structure 1 on the east side of the road and 8 m² around a suspected hearth on the west side of the road were excavated, with all sediment screened through ¼-in mesh. The structure was excavated and documented following standard practice, and then the site area was mechanically stripped to search for additional features. The backhoe work exposed three extramural hearths 9–10 m northeast of the structure, which were excavated following standard practice. The entire effort recovered a moderate stone artifact assemblage that contained 794 items, including seven whole manos and quite a few unusual or exotic items such as a pipe fragment and various ornaments. Recovery also included 70 bones, 10 of which were worked, including a gaming piece, a flat bead, and a tubular bead.

Blake's Abode consists of a single pithouse, three extramural hearths, and a light artifact scatter mainly to the southeast of the pithouse. No high-quality radiocarbon samples were obtained in the field, just samples of wood charcoal from the hearths, and unfortunately flotation analysis did not recover portions of maize or other annual plants. There were, however, pieces of carbonized pinyon bark, and two samples of this from the structure returned identical assays that, after averaging, have an age of 2150 ± 28 BP, with a calibrated two-sigma range of 360–90 BC. On-site food processing is indicated by the grinding tools within the pithouse and three extramural hearths likely used for roasting purposes. The lack of plant remains in the flotation samples does not accord with such an interpretation, but unless there were processing accidents these samples might merely reflect fuel use. The fact that maize pollen was observed in a mano pollen wash from the structure suggests that corn was used by the occupants and perhaps processed with the tool. The finding of prickly pear pollen on another mano might indicate the exploitation of this plant for its fruits or pads. Given the lack of storage facilities and the relatively shallow depth of the house, occupation during warmer months seems likely. Also, had the site been used during the winter there should have been considerably more charcoal flecking and staining in the trash disposal area in front of the house (greater hearth use within the structure). Blake's Abode may have essentially been an elaborate field house, although ideal farm areas do not seem to be close at hand. Excavated sites similar to Blake's Abode include Sin Sombra, Tres Campos, Panorama House, and Polly's Place. The site is interpreted as a short-lived, seasonal habitation. The recovered artifact assemblage reflects a range of activities, including those unrelated to subsistence.

Scorpion Heights (AZ-J-14-37)

Scorpion Heights (Figure 3.16) occupies a dune at the base of a Navajo Sandstone escarpment on the west side of Upper Piute Canyon at an elevation of 2,054 m (6,740 ft). During the time of occupation the dune crest was evidently broader, but erosion along the site's southwest side

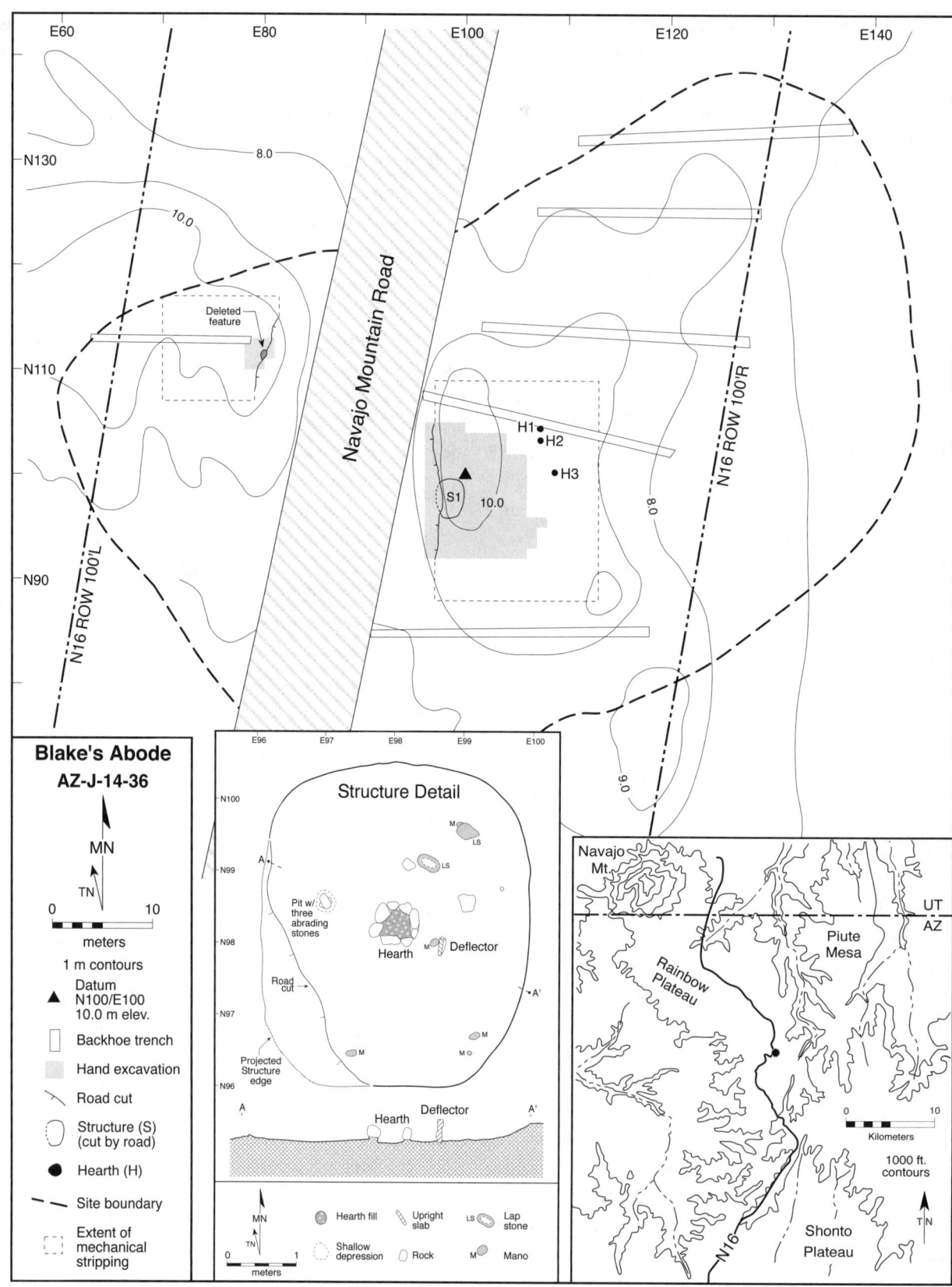

Figure 3.15. Blake's Abode site plan showing topography, work effort, and excavated features.

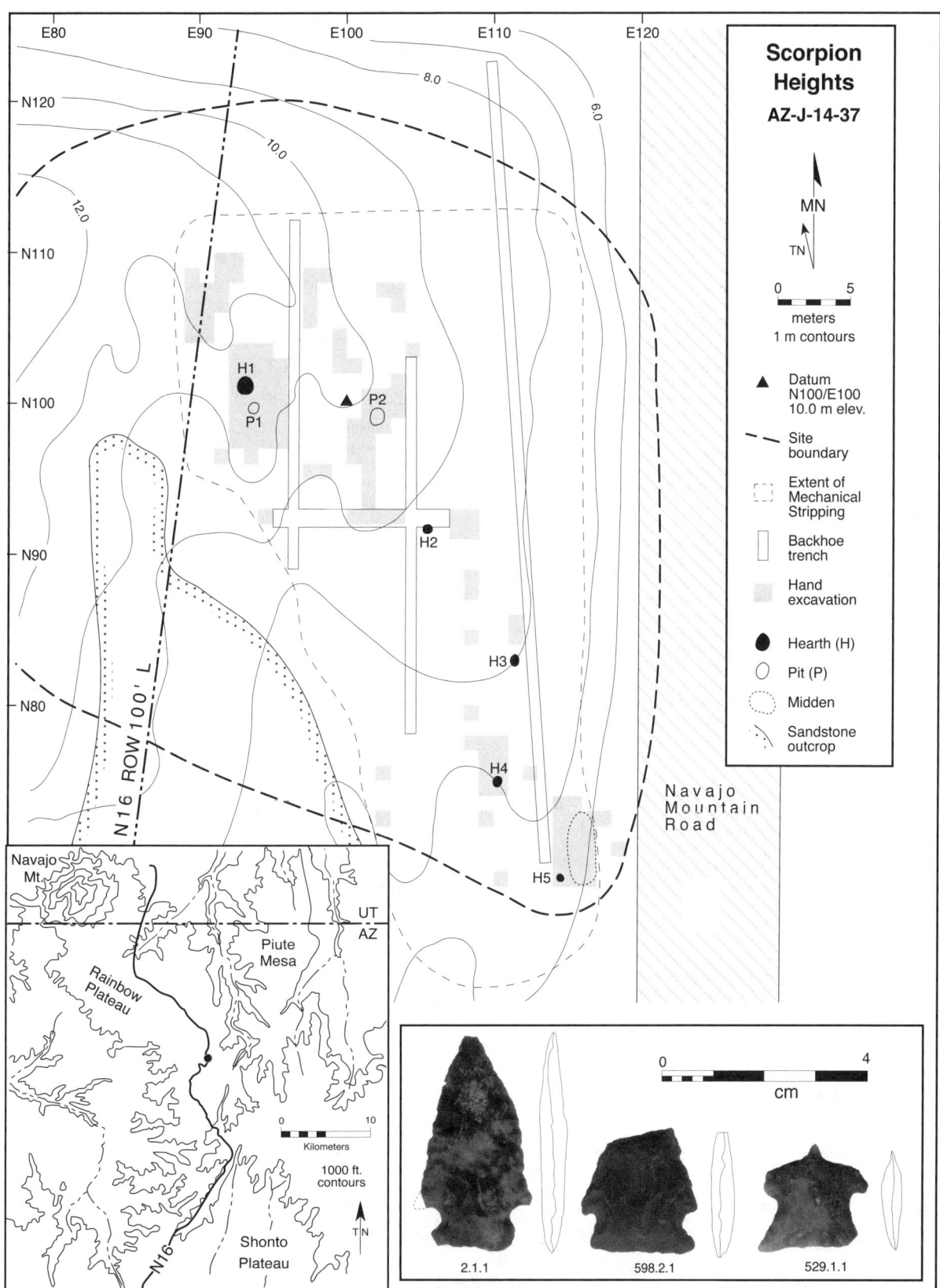

Figure 3.16. Scorpion Heights site plan showing topography, work effort, and excavated features; inset shows three projectile points recovered from the site, one of which is reworked into a drill.

removed a large amount of sand and exposed the underlying bedrock. In the process, the occupation layer across the southwestern third of the site was removed, leaving cultural remains as a lag deposit or washed away by runoff. Eolian deflation in this area likely also eradicated features, including a structure. A portion of a small midden in the southeast part of the site and perhaps other small features were removed by construction along the old Navajo Mountain road.

Data recovery began by excavating a random sample of 20 1-×-1-m units across the site area thought likely to contain buried cultural remains, with all deposits screened through ⅛-in mesh. No features were encountered in these units. Further hand excavation was done on a judgmental basis, with all sediment screened through ¼-in mesh; 77 m² were excavated in various portions in the northern part of the site, exposing two pits and a hearth, which were excavated as they were encountered following standard practice. In the southern part of the site additional horizontal exposure after sampling involved excavating 19 m² in and around a small midden deposit as well as 15 m² to the west and northwest of the midden in a search for associated features; none were located. Hearth 4 was excavated concurrently with the midden, and an additional 9 m² were excavated between the north and south artifact concentrations. No features were exposed in these units, and artifact recovery was low.

Prior to data recovery, the site was believed to be relatively undisturbed, but the work effort revealed that almost the entire site is deflated, with few areas of intact cultural deposits. Many of the artifacts existed as a lag deposit on strata below the original occupation surface, and few features remained. The work documented and sampled one midden, five hearths, and two pits, plus recovering a moderate assemblage of stone artifacts ($n = 807$) along with a few bones ($n = 11$) and minerals ($n = 2$). Although extensively impacted by eolian and alluvial erosion, the extant pattern of features and artifacts allows inferences about site layout and use. Scorpion Heights seems to be a composite of at least two and perhaps three separate use episodes that occurred during Basketmaker II. At a general level there is a north–south division that was apparent from the first recording of the site. The southern portion includes a remnant of a small trash midden along with Hearth 4 and perhaps Hearth 3. The presence of a burned rock midden remnant is the key element in suggesting that this portion of the site served as a small seasonal habitation. It is abundantly evident from the NMRAP excavations that middens of this sort occur at Basketmaker II sites with structures lacking large-volume storage, such as Blake's Abode, Panorama House, Polly's Place, and Sin Sombra. The likely location for a structure at Scorpion Heights is to the west and perhaps slightly north of the midden remnant, and this is the area where the Basketmaker occupation surface has eroded away. Since the structures at other nonstorage habitations are relatively shallow and informal, erosion could remove such a feature easily. Hearth 4 probably represented an activity area alongside the structure on its northeast side. The one radiocarbon date of cal. AD 90–395 on burned sagebrush from Hearth 4 provides an approximate age estimate for the remains from the southern portion of the site.

The northern portion of Scorpion Heights may contain slightly overlapping remains from two functionally distinct use episodes or one episode with spatial division of activities. It is perhaps impossible to prove either alternative, but I suspect the former to be more likely. The northern area can be segregated into east and west portions, with the western portion centered around Hearth 1 and the eastern portion centered between Pit 2 and Hearth 2. The quantity and type of debitage illustrate a marked difference between these areas, with the flake waste in the eastern area indicative of intensive late-stage biface production, including the reduction of bifacial blanks of white baked siltstone from northern Black Mesa. In this area, too, occurred a whole projectile point and five point bases, four of them broken across the notches and the fifth with its tip removed by an impact bending fracture. This evidence is the signature of hunters removing the broken proximal ends of points from foreshafts and rearming them with new points. This northeast portion of the site therefore would seem to have served as a temporary camp for hunters.

The west site area shows a diversity of stone tools, including all but two of the grinding tools, five of the core/nodular tools, the drills, one of the two scrapers, and five used flakes. This area also yielded most of the sparse faunal remains recovered (nine of the 11 bone fragments). This variety of remains may reflect a greater diversity of activities than for the east portion of the northern site area. The remains of the western portion are more of what I would expect for a seasonal residence. It is difficult to say what features were originally present in this area of the site besides a slab-lined hearth (Hearth 1, eroded to a concentration of horizontal slabs and rock chunks) and some sort of pit, only the bottom of which remained intact (Pit 1). It is possible that a temporary residential structure was present south of Hearth 1, having been lost to erosion. One aspect of the assemblage that gives cause for such speculation is the concentration of fragmented grinding tools found on the ground surface in this area. At other Basketmaker II temporary residential sites, grinding tools, when present, tended to occur within structures. Moreover, the metates are of the type more likely to be found at a residential site of some sort rather than simply a limited-activity camp. The lack of abundant burned rock does not accord with the speculative structure, unless it was actually located west of the hearth. This would mean that the artifacts and burned rock scattered around Hearth 1 and to the south were part of a midden. If a structure is located west of Hearth 1, it lies outside the ROW. My present best guess is that the west portion of the northern site area was used as a temporary residence. The age of the remains in both portions of the northern site area can be approximated based on the presence of Basketmaker II–style projectile points. Fine-tuning the rough age estimate provided by the points is not possible at present. It is possible that the two-sigma range of the radiocarbon date for Hearth 4 encompasses the time interval when the northern site area was occupied.

Camp Dead Pine (AZ-J-14-52)

Camp Dead Pine (Figure 3.17) is a late Pueblo II encampment on a southeast-facing slope at an elevation of 2,060 m (6,760 ft) in the midst of dense pinyon–juniper woodland near the rim of Upper Piute Canyon. The site is on the northeastern edge of the Navajo Sandstone ridgeline that separates the canyon systems of Piute and Navajo creeks and links the Rainbow and Shonto plateaus. Less than 1 km west of Camp Dead Pine is the highest point along the ridgeline, at an elevation of 2,206 m (7,236 ft), which offers commanding views of the entire region. The NMRAP field camp for two seasons, centered on the standing remains of an old lightning-struck tree, lay at the edge of the site; the camp name became the site name. Lying entirely within the N16 ROW, the entire area of Camp Dead Pine was excavated. The work effort consisted of hand excavation of 30 m² and mechanical stripping of ca. 115 m². Hand excavation was divided between a known trash area and an area several meters upslope (northwest) from the trash, where architecture and extramural features were thought likely to exist. Sediment from about half of the excavation units was screened with ¼-in mesh, with ⅛-in mesh used for the remainder. Feature exploration expanded into feature excavation as work progressed. The work recovered a modest assemblage of sherds ($n = 425$) and stone artifacts ($n = 258$).

The site consists of a use area with a mealing bin, a multipurpose pit, a basin hearth, and a burned post, with an associated trash scatter to the southeast. The post suggests that at least part of the use area was covered with a brush structure, such as a shade or ramada. The mealing bin and the emphasis on the preparation or refurbishment of core tools, such as pecking stones, indicate that grinding tools were once present and used at the site for food processing. All usable grinding implements had been removed upon abandonment, leaving only a single grinding tool fragment recycled as a heating or cover stone for roasting. The basin hearth yielded carbonized seeds including tansy mustard, which ripens in early to midsummer. Other weedy remains suggest that the occupancy may have extended into late August or September, if not later, with perhaps multiple occupations during different seasons represented. Corn was also present in both the hearth and the ashy upper fill of the bell-shaped pit. The preparation and consumption of various seeds probably made up an important activity at the site, suggesting that the site was occupied for several days and thus required meal preparation. The fairly dense, if small, trash scatter seems the result of repeated use. The combined evidence indicates that Camp Dead Pine was a seasonal field camp situated so as to take advantage of a specific resource. It is not proximal to arable land, so the resources may have been wild, such as pinyon nuts or the seeds of grass or weedy annuals. The site location is similar to other NMRAP Pueblo II limited-activity sites, such as Tres Campos and The Slots. The predominance of Owl Rock chert at the site suggests that the occupants of Camp Dead Pine frequented Piute Canyon and indeed may have had their permanent home there. The ceramic assemblage has sufficient typable pottery to provide a reasonable estimate of temporal placement. The high percentage of Sosi and Dogoszhi Black-on-white sherds indicates a late Pueblo II occupation, sometime after AD 1100 but perhaps before AD 1150; this is supported by the predominance of Tusayan Black-on-red over Medicine Black-on-red and the absence of both Flagstaff Black-on-white and polychrome sherds.

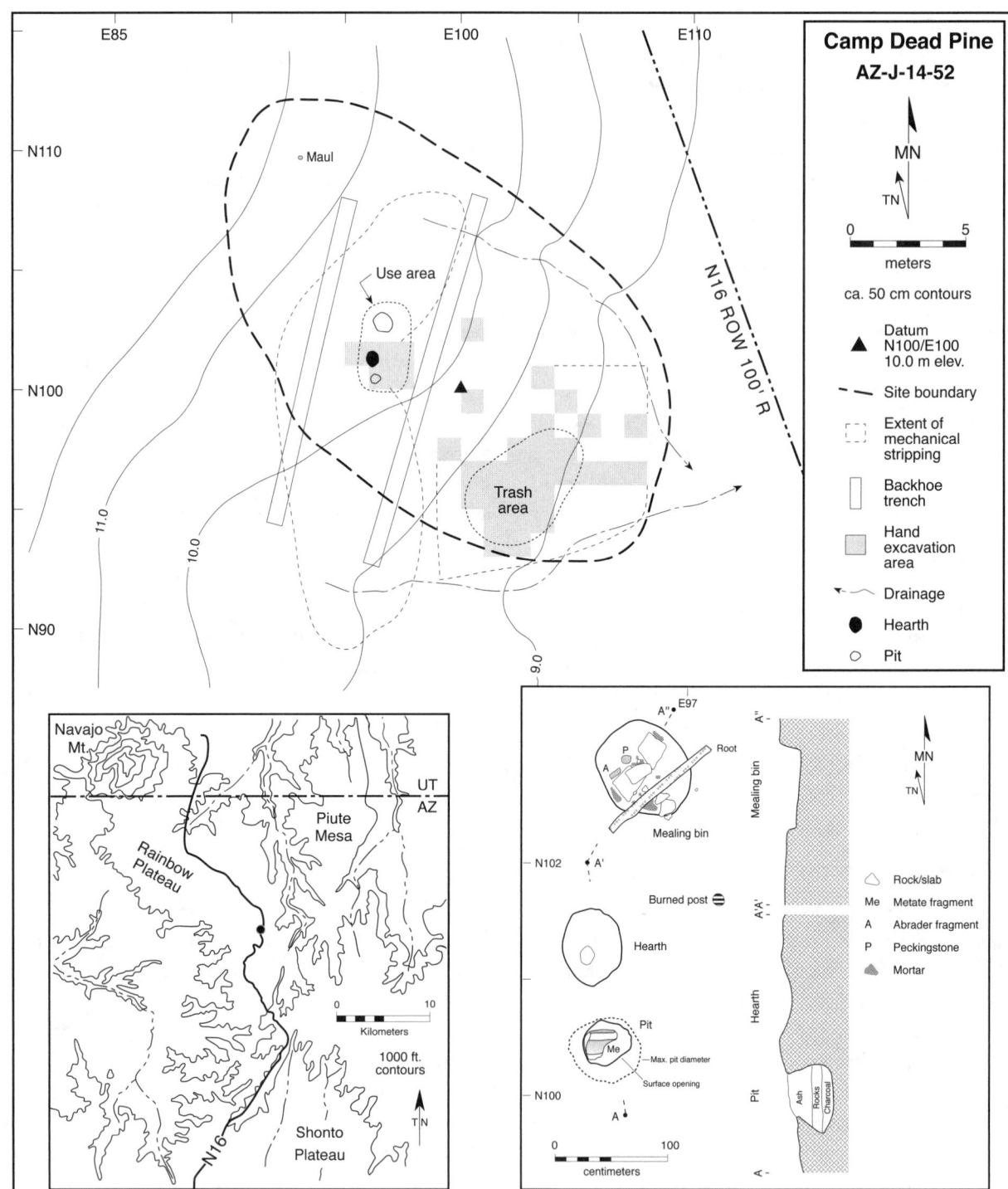

Figure 3.17. Camp Dead Pine site plan showing topography, work effort, and excavated features.

Mountainview (AZ-J-14-38)

Mountainview is an important site because it provides a sample of the technological innovations that culminated in the cultural configuration recognized as Basketmaker III (Figure 3.18). This habitation occupies a small level bench at an elevation of about 2,018 m (6,620 ft) on a prominent narrow ridge at the southeast margin of the Rainbow Plateau. As the name implies, the site has a spectacular northwest view across the plateau to Navajo Mountain and into the upper reaches of Piute Canyon to the east. The underlying bedrock ridge is an extension off the northeast end of the long, sinuous divide between the canyons of Piute and Navajo creeks. The north end of the divide, which reaches a high point of 2,207 m (7,236 ft), delimits the southeastern edge of the Rainbow Plateau. Rising a few hundred meters above the plateau, the sheer Navajo Sandstone slickrock of the divide forms a visibly obvious line of demarcation. Runoff from this slickrock flows into several northeast-trending washes that likely offered excellent floodwater farming opportunities, and two springs issue from the sandstone of this divide. Just 500 m upslope to the southwest from Mountainview is an extensive habitation with at least five structures and the same assemblage of early pottery (Obelisk Utility), so Mountainview forms part of a cluster of similar Basketmaker II–III transitional settlements.

The entire Basketmaker component lies within the N16 ROW and was excavated; a sparse scatter of Pueblo II–III sherds outside the ROW to the west appears to be associated with a nearby Puebloan habitation. Data recovery began with the removal of loose surface sand to define the known structure in plan and to determine the extent of disturbance caused by construction of a power line access road directly across the house. The entire structure except the north edge had intact floor fill, but the access road had removed most of the upper feature fill. The eastern entryway was also heavily disturbed by the road construction. After defining the house in plan view, the crew excavated it by halves, screening the upper feature fill through ¼-in mesh and the floor fill through ⅛-in mesh. A sample of small remains was recovered from 17 randomly placed 1-×-1-m units within an 89-m² sampling frame laid out across the main part of the activity area and the trash deposit east and southeast of the structure, with all cultural sediment being screened through ⅛-in mesh. The remainder of the area within the sampling frame, plus some additional area around the structure, was hand excavated, with all sediment screened through ¼-in mesh. Hand excavation south of the structure exposed an activity area that consisted of 13 hearths and one pit, while mechanical stripping northwest of the structure exposed three pits and two hearths; all of these small features were excavated following standard practice.

Excavations revealed a single pit structure, a midden, and an activity area containing 15 hearths and four pits. Six statistically contemporaneous radiocarbon dates on corn from both the structure and midden place site occupancy sometime between cal. AD 220 and 350 (two-sigma range). This main occupation involved the structure, midden, and most hearths; a single hearth (no. 14) may represent a subsequent episode of use. Botanical remains indicate that the occupants relied on domesticates and weedy species; bone indicates limited use of faunal resources, principally jackrabbit and cottontail (perhaps also deer). A single family probably occupied the site for perhaps several sequential annual seasons. Certainly more than one season is indicated by the amount of remains (393 sherds, 4,378 stone artifacts, 37 mineral/pigment specimens, and 175 faunal bones), the size of the midden, the number of hearths, and some feature superpositioning. Plain brownware pottery identified as Obelisk Utility and arrowpoints in various stages of manufacture were recovered from the structure and the midden. The occupants of Mountainview were using ceramics and the bow and arrow on the Rainbow Plateau several hundred years earlier than previously suspected. Mountainview foreshadows some of the changes that would later characterize the entire Kayenta region and beyond. Pottery would be universally used on the Colorado Plateau, as would the bow and arrow. The atlatl would be replaced by the bow and arrow, and atlatl weights would become a curiosity of the past. Upright slabs would be added to the construction of houses, including their use in wing walls to separate the hearth and back two-thirds or so from the front/entryway portion. The presence of sites similar to Mountainview on the Rainbow Plateau means that this area should prove useful for documenting the transitional interval between preceramic and early ceramic times.

Hammer House (AZ-J-14-16)

Hammer House (Figure 3.19) is a middle Pueblo II habitation located on the far southeast edge of the Rainbow Plateau at an elevation of ca. 1,992 m (6,530 ft). The site is situated just east of the old N16 alignment on the east side of a dune-covered sloping ridge just above a small, incised drainage. As such, the site was conveniently located along the north–south travel route and may have been purposely established there with this benefit in mind. The site is in a heavily treed zone of pinyon pine and juniper, with a sparse understory of sagebrush and other shrubs. Drainages from the slickrock divide to the southwest provide farmland, and the site location also afforded easy access to the excellent farmland of Piute Canyon as well as the Segito tributary of Navajo Canyon. More than 50 pecking stones covered the floor of the one semisubterranean living room at the site, which led to the official site moniker.

The site is entirely within the N16 ROW and was completely excavated; no features are believed to remain

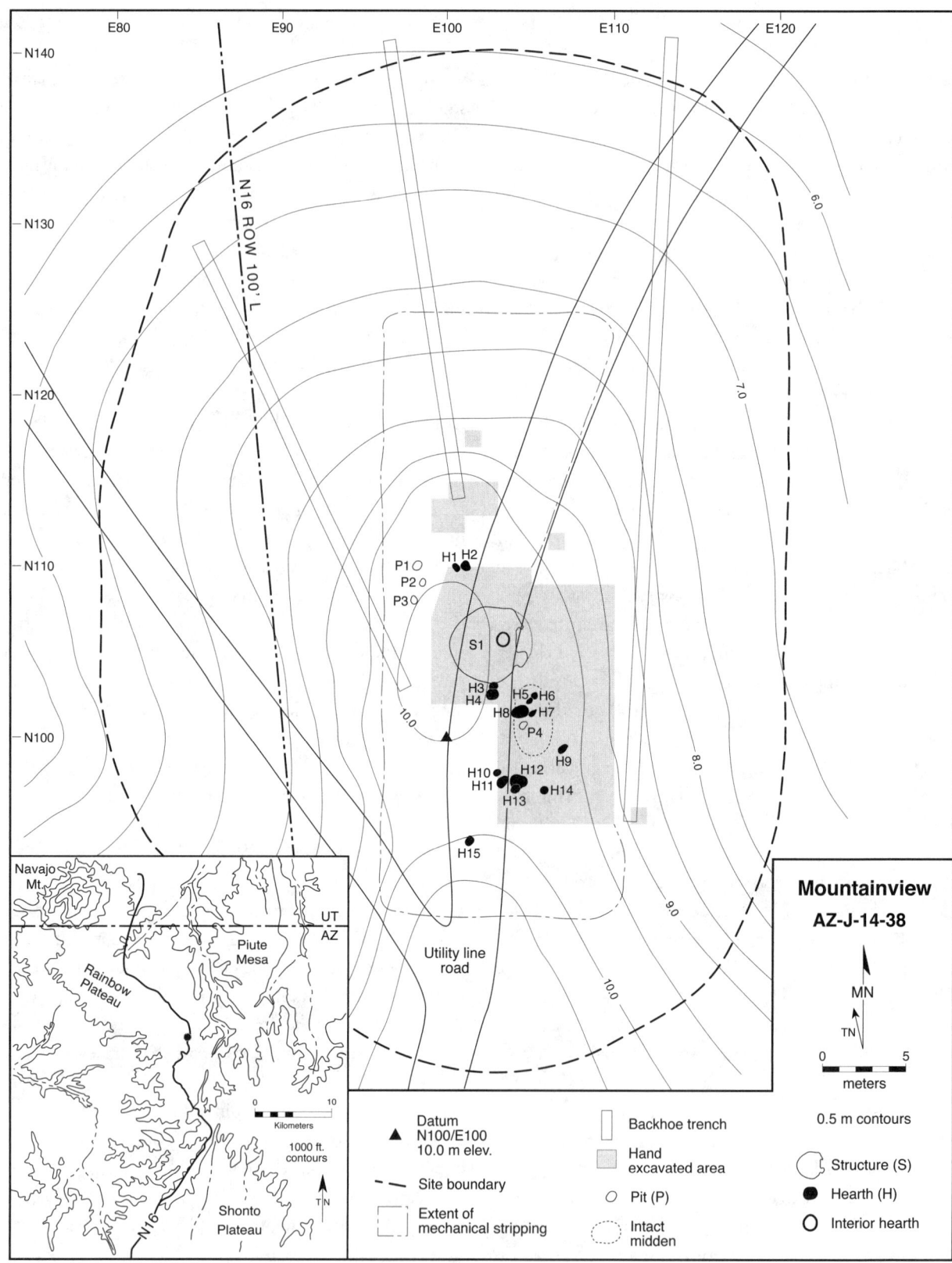

Figure 3.18. Mountainview site plan showing topography, work effort, and excavated features.

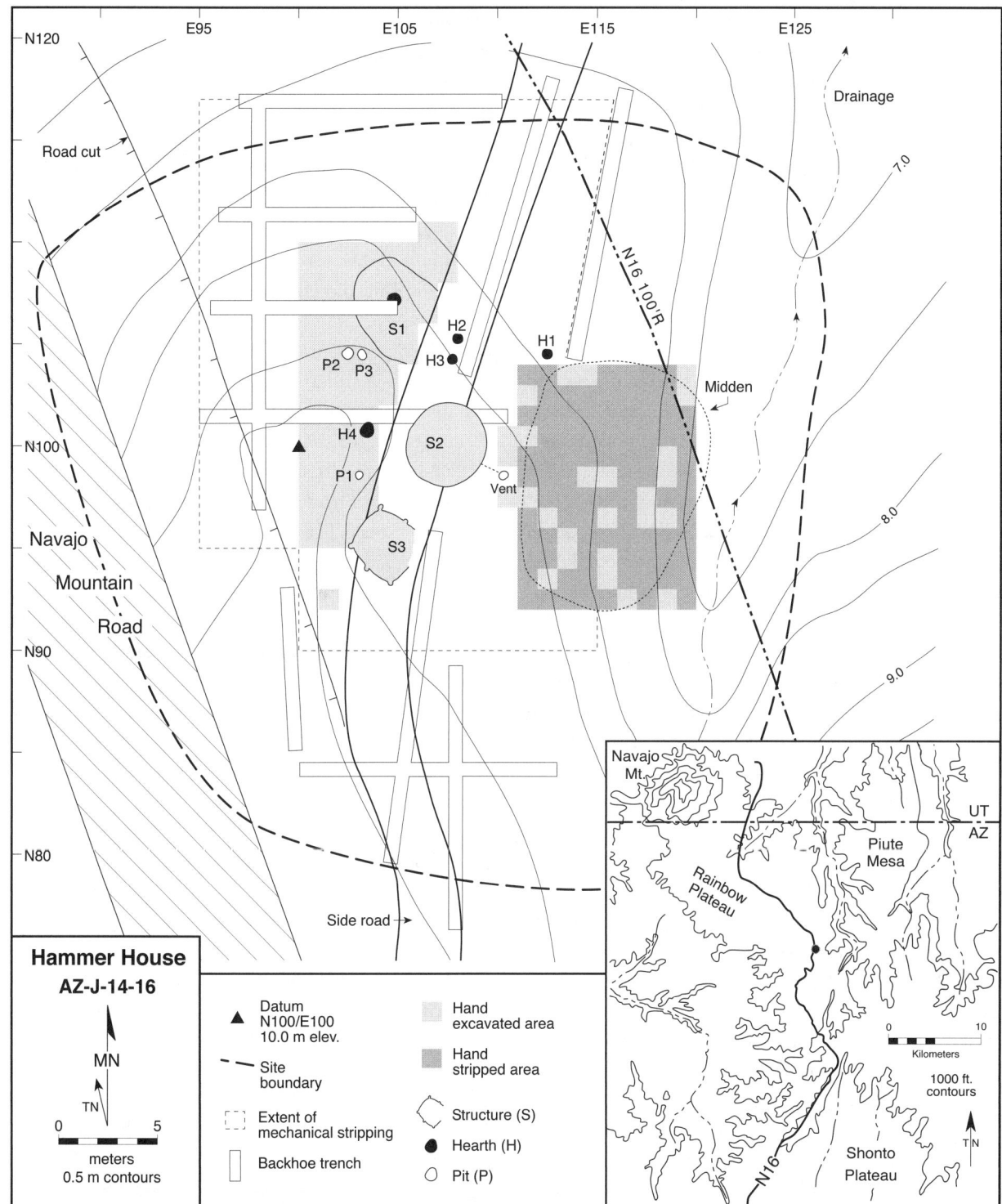

Figure 3.19. Hammer House site plan showing topography, work effort, and excavated features.

outside of the right-of-way. Construction and maintenance of the old Navajo Mountain road may have eliminated part of the site, but this seems unlikely given the location of the midden and the lack of remains or features exposed by trenching and surface stripping west of the main site area. An even earlier alignment of this road, now used for woodcutting, passed through the center of Hammer House and over the top of both the kiva and living room, removing portions of the upper walls. A 20 percent simple random sample of the midden was excavated using a 12-×-9-m sample frame (equaling 108 m²). Half of the 22 1-×-1-m midden units were screened through ⅛-in screen mesh to recover small remains, and the other half were screened through ¼-in mesh. The remainder of the midden (85 m²) was hand stripped to sterile soil in a search for burials and extramural features. An area of 76 m² from southwest to northwest of the kiva was hand excavated to sterile soil, with all sediment screened through ¼-in mesh. This process exposed a possible ramada (which included a hearth), three shallow pits, and a basin hearth. Concurrent with horizontal exposure, the crew excavated all known features, including the kiva, which was first defined in plan and then most of the erosional fill was removed by backhoe down to 15–20 cm above floor and within 10–15 cm of the walls. The remaining fill was excavated by hand and screened through ⅛-in mesh, with artifacts provenienced by 1-×-1-m units. Floor and wall features, such as the hearth, pits, and posts, were then mapped and excavated. Backhoe stripping near the end of hand excavation disclosed three extramural hearths northeast of the kiva and a pit structure just south of the kiva, which were excavated following standard procedure; the backhoe removed a small portion of the east side of this room, but it was otherwise well preserved.

Hammer House consists of a circular earthen kiva, a probable surface ramada, a small semisubterranean pithouse, a midden, and several extramural hearths and pits. Excavations recovered a sizable assemblage of remains including 2,566 sherds, 2,382 stone artifacts, 25 mineral/pigment specimens, and 354 faunal bones. The layout of Hammer House lacks formal arrangement as at some Pueblo II habitations, with the familiar room block–kiva–midden alignment, and it likewise lacks the masonry architecture (granaries) common to such sites. There is, however, the general pattern of surface or near-surface rooms and activity space grouped around the southwest, west, and northwest sides of a kiva or deep pit structure, with the midden to the east and southeast.

The site has only three structures and probably served a single nuclear family. Each room or structure was used for multiple activities, to make the most efficient use of the facilities available. No above-ground storage rooms were discovered, with food storage evidently occurring in large-volume pits within both the kiva and the semi-subterranean living room. Surface habitation units made use of jacal and expedient shade superstructures, and the kiva was a simple, earthen-walled design lacking a bench or recess. The midden seems substantial relative to the size of the site and indicates use at the level of a permanent or near-permanent habitation. Considering the size of the ceramic and lithic assemblage, it seems likely that Hammer House was occupied for more than two–three years but no more than 10 years. The site could have been repeatedly, rather than continuously, occupied, but the kiva would have made a suitable winter shelter, allowing the inhabitants to live at Hammer House on a year-round basis. The bell-shaped pits in the kiva and living room provided some means for surplus food storage; these features alone seem adequate to support a nuclear family during the lean months of winter and spring: ca. 2.3 m³ of total storage space, which, based on B. Huckell's (1995:120) estimates, might hold approximately 900 kg of maize, enough calories for a family of five for almost a year. Longer or more intensive site use might also be inferred from the number of pecking stones, which total 95. There is little quantitative information on the use-lives of pecking stones, though Dodd (1979:237–238) relates numerous ethnographic examples of using these tools to produce and maintain manos and metates. They were probably routinely used during periods of intensive grinding, and Bartlett (1933:4) mentioned that a Hopi informant used a pecking stone to refurbish grinding tools every five days. There are many factors that could affect the use-life of pecking stones, and using them as a proxy for the length of prehistoric site occupation is a problematic exercise, yet the quantity of these tools hints at some duration of occupancy.

The kiva at Hammer House has more than 70 diverse floor features, plus several hypothesized use areas. There is also evidence for reuse and remodeling, including the patching of floor pits and depressions, sealing of abandoned pits, construction of new pits over old pits, reconfiguration of loom anchors, and possible remodeling of the ashpit. This indicates that the residents of Hammer House were highly dependent on the kiva as a dedicated living area and not just a ceremonial retreat and that it acted as a sustained but evolving focal point for site activities. Perhaps there were seasonal shifts in kiva functions—used more strictly for habitation part of the year and for ritual devotion the rest of the year (perhaps during a ceremonial cycle). If so, such shifts would likely have entailed changes in interior activities and features. Maize grinding, for example, was perhaps performed in the kiva during the coldest months but then was moved to Structure 3 or outside during the warmer months. Weaving, too, might have been done in the kiva during winter, but with the onset of the growing season, as ceremonial activity increased, space requirements might have dictated that looms be dismantled and moved outside if necessary.

Mouse House (AZ-J-3-7)

Mouse House is a multicomponent Archaic, Basketmaker, and Puebloan site situated at an elevation of 1,955 m (6,410 ft) on the southeast portion of the Rainbow Plateau (Figure 3.20). The site extends across a broad, gentle northeast-trending slope situated at the base of a low ridge overlooking a small sunken flatland with both fallow and in-use Navajo farm plots. The rolling landscape consists of low ridges covered with pinyon and juniper, with sagebrush predominating along drainage basins and in lowland depressions. The wide and deep cut for the old N16 road alignment artificially bounds the site on its east side and removed a portion of the Puebloan component and perhaps features of the earlier components as well. The remains of all three components evidently lay entirely within the N16 ROW, and the work thoroughly investigated what remained at the site.

Data recovery involved excavation of known features, a mechanical search for new features, and the excavation of discoveries. Known features consisted of a possible structure with a slab-lined hearth and the basin hearths exposed in backhoe trenches. A total of 29 m² was hand excavated around the structure, with the entire cultural stratum screened through ¼-in mesh (80%) and ⅛-in mesh (20%). Areas of various dimensions were hand excavated around each of the known hearths, for a discontinuous total of 11 m². Screening of the cultural stratum around these hearths was generally begun with ⅛-in mesh but switched to ¼-in mesh as artifact recovery was minimal to absent. The mechanical search for new features included both backhoe trenching and backhoe surface stripping, which resulted in the discovery of four additional hearths. All features were hand excavated following standard practice. Artifact recovery was fairly light, consisting of 27 sherds and 43 stone artifacts but including a sandstone mortar.

Construction and maintenance of the old Navajo Mountain road partially removed features and deposits, but it appears that whatever was lost would not appreciably change the conclusion that the Puebloan component was a simple seasonal-use settlement. It consists of a partially enclosed structure (ramada) surrounded by a use area and one isolated rock-filled hearth (Hearth 1). The limited architectural, artifactual, and nonartifactual remains are believed indicative of a short-duration and perhaps warm-season occupation. That some investment was made in the construction of living and working facilities suggests that the inhabitants planned on more than a single use episode. Considering this, combined with a location proximate to land that is currently farmed and was likely productive in the past, I conjecture that the site functioned as a field house during portions of the growing season. The site appears to have been occupied during the late Pueblo II or early Pueblo III period, most likely between about AD 1150 and 1200. Use was probably limited to several years at most.

The Basketmaker II component, like the Archaic component, consists of four basin hearths clustered together on an old dune surface. Based on the average of two radiocarbon assays from two different hearths, I conclude that Basketmaker II use occurred sometime between cal. AD 80 and 340. These hearths are contemporaneous with the temporary residential site of Sin Sombra located just 100 m to the northwest. They are perhaps vestiges of a single, limited-duration use episode or closely sequential episodes, the purpose(s) of which remains unknown. The few flakes and macrobotanical remains from hearth fill give little basis for inferences about settlement role. Corn and late summer–fall seeds from two of the hearths might be taken as evidence of occupancy late in the growing season. Except for Hearth 5, which was moderately deep, the others are shallow and might have been mainly surface fires for warmth.

The Archaic component of Mouse House consisted of three or possibly four basin hearths clustered together in dune sand. Burned sagebrush from two of these features produced AMS radiocarbon ages near the end of the eighth millennium BP, and based on the average of these two dates, I conclude that the site was used sometime between 7040 and 6690 cal. BC (two-sigma range). Site use during this early interval may have occurred just once. No artifacts were found in or around these features, and

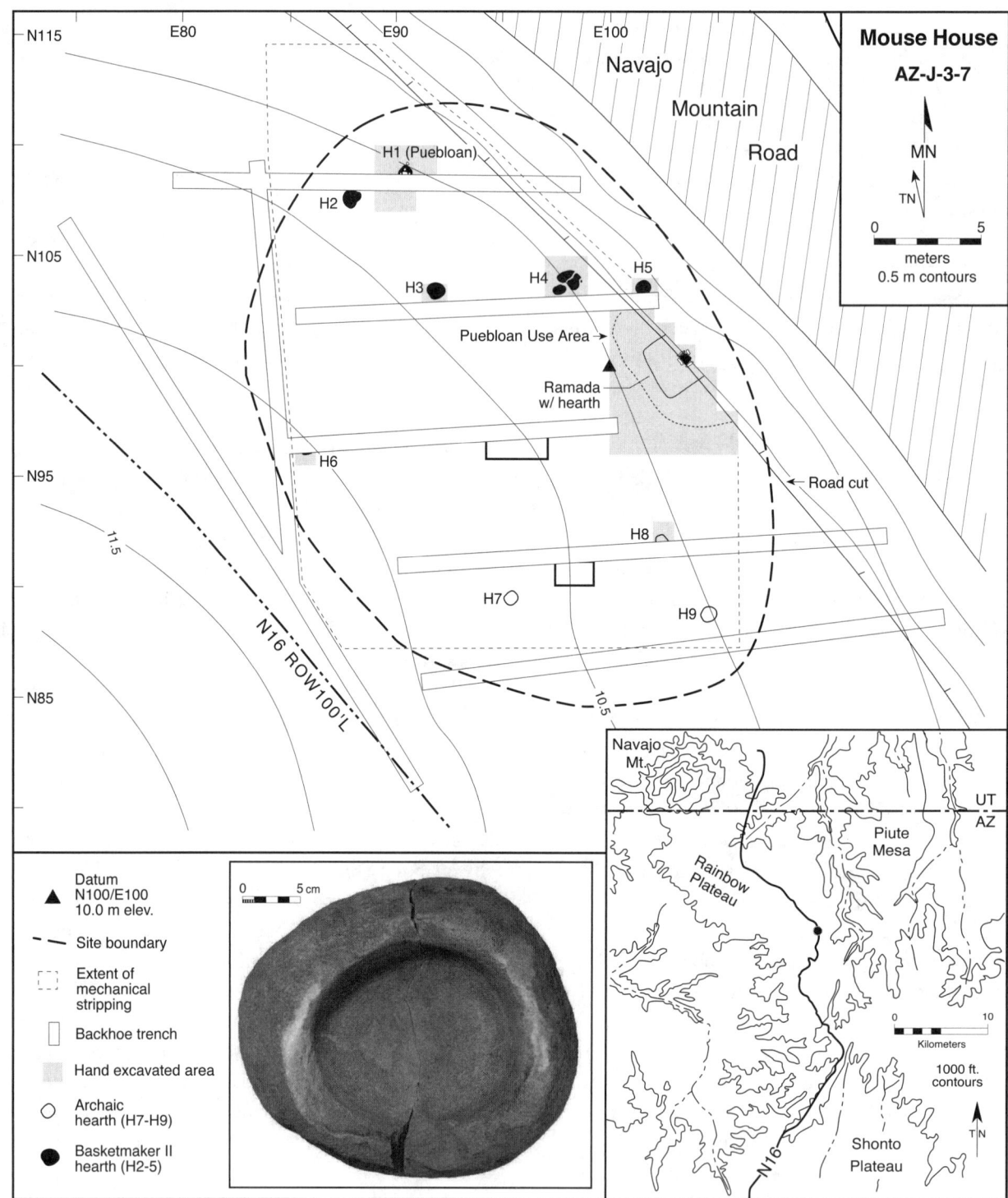

Figure 3.20. Mouse House site plan showing topography, work effort, and excavated features; inset shows a stone mortar recovered from the site.

no macrobotanical or faunal remains occurred in the fill that might indicate what the fire basins were used for. The sparse amount of recognizable fuel in the hearths probably relates to the near-exclusive burning of easily degradable sagebrush and to the 8,000 years of various agents working on the fuel by-products. That basins were built to contain the fires bespeaks more of some form of food processing (pit baking) than a need for warmth (i.e., campfires). Singly the Archaic component tells us little, and one should not expect otherwise; it is via the regional ag-

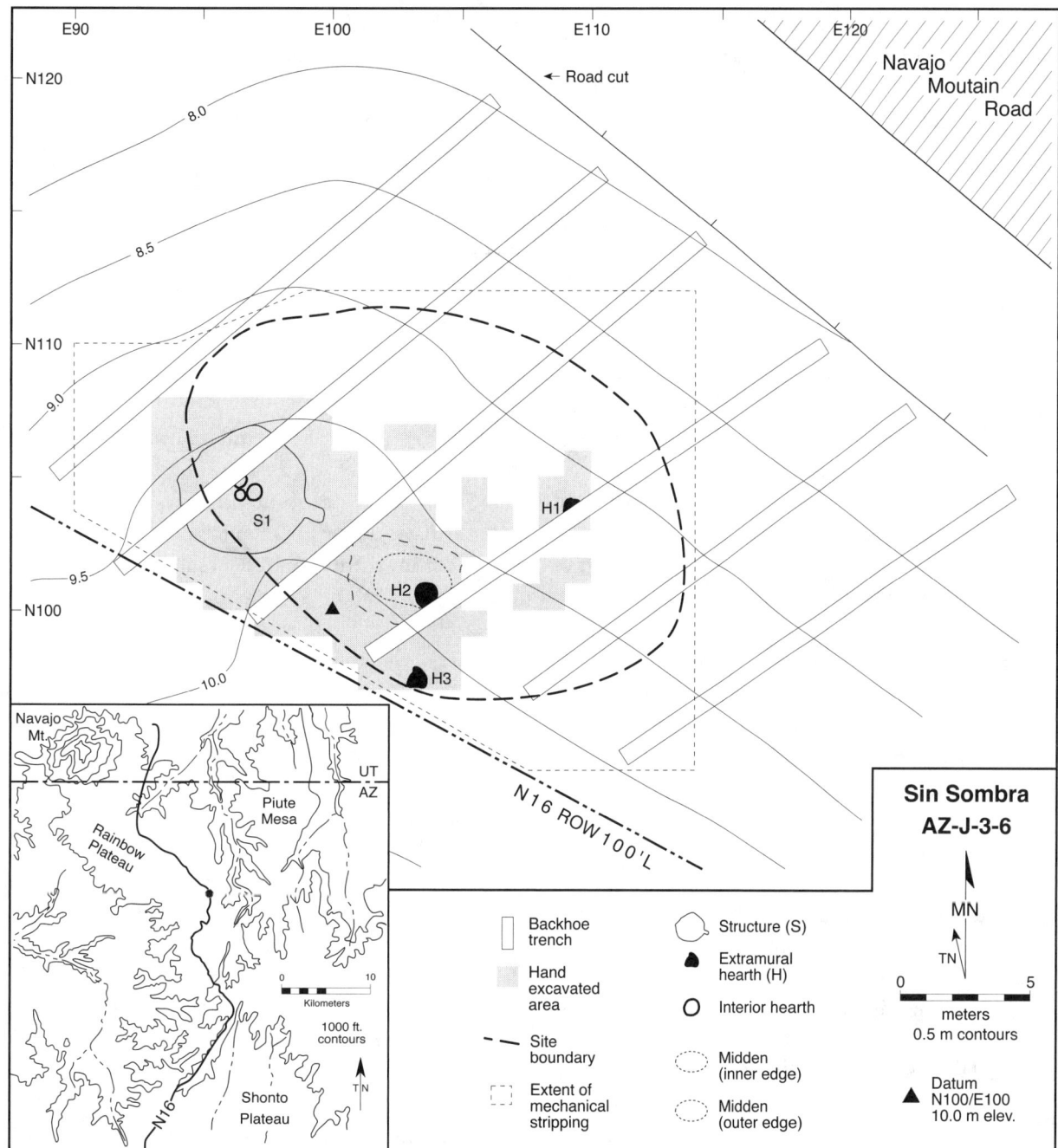

Figure 3.21. Sin Sombra site plan showing topography, work effort, and excavated features.

gregate of evidence from sites of similar and dissimilar characteristics that broader conclusions are possible.

Sin Sombra (AZ-J-3-6)

Sin Sombra is a Basketmaker II temporary residential site on a slight, east-facing slope at an elevation of 1,952 m (6,400 ft) on the southeast edge of the Rainbow Plateau (Figure 3.21). The site lies adjacent to a shallow drainage basin that local Navajo families have farmed for several generations, a drainage likely quite productive during prehistory. Although the site originally had a dense cover of pinyon pine and juniper, with a sparse understory of sagebrush and other shrubs, all vegetation was cleared by backhoe prior to excavation; hence the site name. The site was located entirely on the west side of the current N16 road against the left edge of the ROW. Data recovery began by excavating 19 randomly selected 1-×-1-m units, which constituted a 15 percent sample of a 124-m² area identified as the site core; all of the sediment from these units was screened through ⅛-in mesh. This was followed by hand excavating up to 80 m² around a small midden and the buried pithouse and screening the cultural layer through ¼-in mesh; the trash midden and floor fill of the structure were screened through ⅛-in mesh. Coincident with horizontal exposure, excavation began on all known features including the structure. Near the conclusion of feature excavation, an area of approximately 185 m² around the structure was mechanically stripped with the backhoe to search for any outlying features, which located an extramural hearth just south of the midden (Hearth 3). Excavation recovered 947 stone artifacts and 46 mammal bones.

Sin Sombra was a small Basketmaker II habitation site consisting of a shallow semicircular pithouse, a small midden just outside the short ramp entry to the house, and three extramural hearths east and southeast of the house. As these features lay only several meters from the edge of the ROW, additional features may lie outside the limits of excavation. Given what I currently know about this class of Basketmaker II site, however, any remains outside of the ROW are likely to be inconsequential. Based on the average of four radiocarbon dates on maize cupules from three principal features (structure, midden, and extramural hearth), site occupancy occurred between cal. AD 120 and 330. Sin Sombra apparently functioned as a seasonally used and relatively short-lived Basketmaker II habitation for a single small family. As it is lacking storage features, the likely time of site occupancy was summer or fall, when survival would not depend upon stored foods. Given the proximity of this site to arable land, the site may have functioned as a field house.

HILLSIDE HERMITAGE (AZ-J-3-14)

Hillside Hermitage (Figure 3.22) is located at an elevation of 1,954 m (6,410 ft) near the southeastern edge of the Rainbow Plateau. The broad interior portion of the plateau lies a short distance to the north, beyond several small ridges. The site is situated on the northeast-facing slope of a sand-covered ridge overlooking a small drainage basin to the northeast that is currently used for farming and was doubtless used for such activities in the past. The site was discovered while backhoe trenching the adjacent Basketmaker II settlement of Kin Kahuna, which exposed three structures and a midden. The site contains two loci, both occupied during the Pueblo II period and both completely within the N16 ROW; the site was excavated in its entirety. Data recovery began by clearing out the backhoe trenches and drawing profiles of the trench walls. The overburden and cultural stratum were removed by hand above Structures 3 and 5 to expose them in plan view. Additional hand stripping between these features revealed Structure 4. The midden deposit, exposed on the surface by erosion, was excavated by hand. Twenty percent of the midden deposit was screened with ⅛-in mesh, and the rest of the deposit was screened with ¼-in mesh. After hand excavation of all known features (Locus B), the entire site area was mechanically stripped with a backhoe, exposing the features at Locus A. All features in this locus were hand excavated, and the area was then completely stripped with the backhoe.

Locus A at Hillside Hermitage consisted of a small field house probably used during just a few farming seasons. The small midden and sparse trash (191 sherds, 174 stone artifacts) argue for a limited occupation span, and the lack of any thermal features or substantial charcoal accumulation in the midden implies use during the warm season. The lack of food-storage facilities is also consistent with use during the growing season, because winter survival probably hinged on stored produce. Other than the masonry along the back wall of Structure 1, the architecture at Locus A was relatively informal and insubstantial. Jacal formed most of the Structure 1 walls and perhaps part of Structure 2 as well. Brush walls and/or roof elements probably completed the Structure 2 enclosure. Interior features were limited to a few pits, possibly for storage, and two mealing bins. The presence of mealing bins in Structure 2 suggests a moderate amount of food processing for domestic purposes, an interpretation supported by the relative abundance of pecking stones and spalls. Maize occurred in all four of the flotation samples from Locus A along with other likely food items such as ground-cherry, purslane, and grass.

Excavations at Locus B revealed three pithouses and a surface structure that apparently functioned as a ramada. Northeast of the structures in the direction of the natural slope was a shallow midden with a moderate density of artifacts, including over 900 sherds and over 400 stone artifacts. The midden and the nature of the architecture suggest that Locus B functioned as a primary residence for a nuclear or perhaps a small extended family. Occupancy occurred during middle Pueblo II, sometime between AD 1050 and 1100, with AD 1060–1080 the likely time of site use. The structural types at this component appear transitional with those that occur with greater formality in late Pueblo II habitations of the region. Structure 5, for

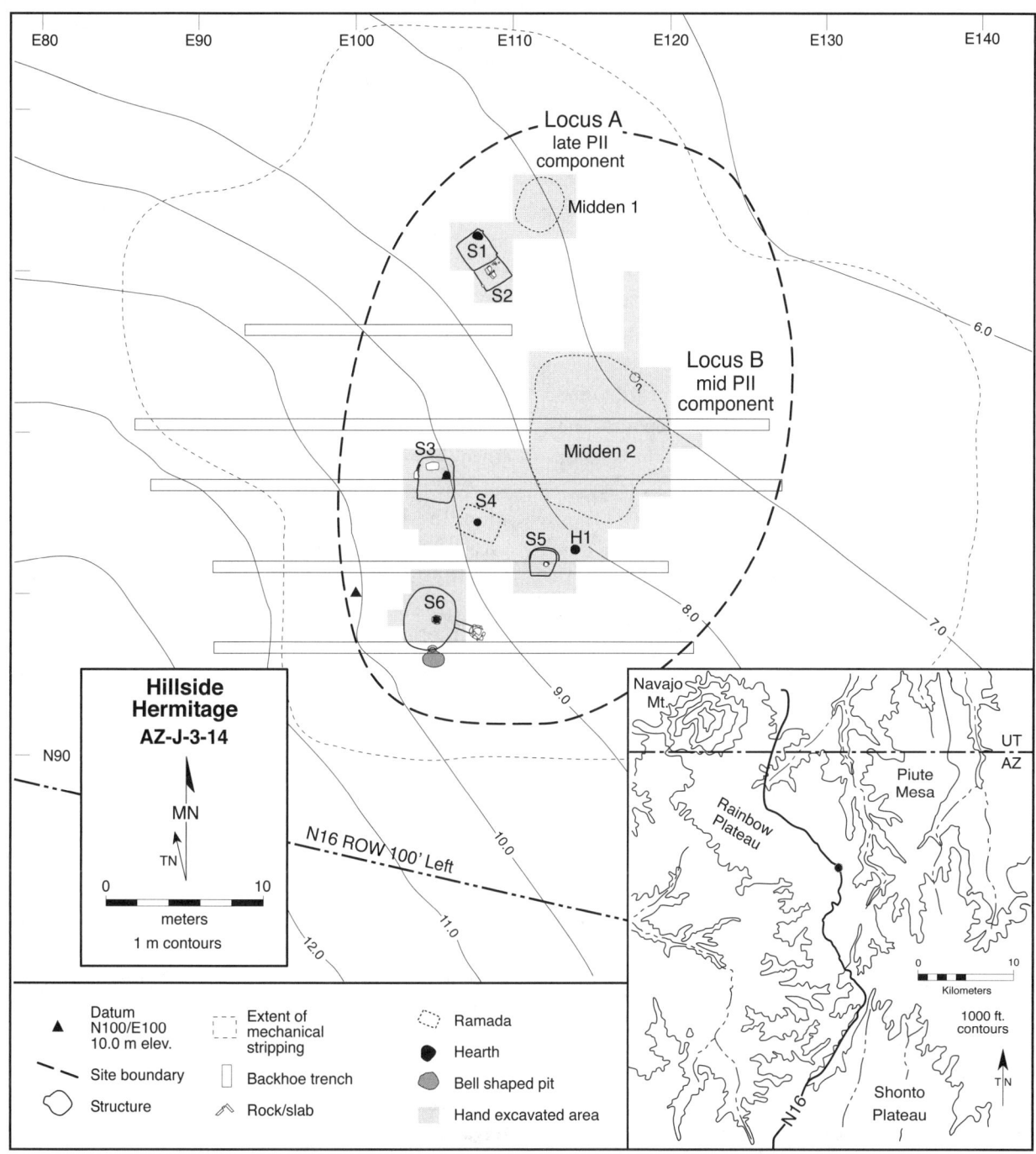

Figure 3.22. Hillside Hermitage site plan showing topography, work effort, and excavated features.

example, was the appropriate size and shape for a traditional mealing room, and the artifact assemblage strongly suggests that it was used in mealing activities, as does the single partially intact interior bin. Although its location in relation to other structures was atypical, the slope of the site, rather than traditional patterning, apparently dictated the layout of Locus B. Structure 6, at the rear of the site, appears transitional in characteristics between a pithouse and a kiva. The size, shape, ventilator, and certain floor features make this structure more typical of kivas. Its depth also sets it apart from typical Pueblo II pit structures; at 1.1 m deep, the feature was two to three times as deep as most pithouses of this period. Structure 6 was not, however, fully subterranean, as is typical for kivas in this area. It also contains a large storage pit, the only potential food-storage feature at the site.

Kin Kahuna (AZ-J-3-8)

At an elevation of about 1,957 m (6,420 ft), Kin Kahuna occupies the north portion of a sand-covered ridge overlooking the confluence of two small drainages on the southeast edge of the Rainbow Plateau (Figure 3.23). The drainage bottom to the north is still farmed by a local Navajo family and was doubtless a principal reason for site occupancy in prehistory. The site has both Basketmaker II and Puebloan components, but most Puebloan features are located outside the ROW except for a Pueblo III activity area and a light scatter of Puebloan trash. The Basketmaker component in the ROW is impressive, consisting of a half dozen living structures, 75 pits and hearths of various sizes and shapes, and extensive trash deposits. These remains represent probably less than half of the total Basketmaker component. That considerably more of the Basketmaker component lies outside the ROW is evidenced by four facts: (1) the cultural stratum thickens from north to south, reaching its maximum (ca. 20 cm thick) at the very edge of the ROW, the limit of excavation; (2) as the cultural stratum approaches the edge of the ROW it not only thickens but becomes more heavily charcoal stained and contains greater quantities of cultural debris; (3) features increase in density and superimposition from north to south, so that near the edge of the ROW features are literally one on top of the other; (4) the large depressions of Structures 4 and 5 near the edge of the ROW were entirely filled by trash disposal, implying that additional Basketmaker houses are located upslope outside the ROW.

The buried Basketmaker component was unknown prior to backhoe trenching the site area in the ROW, which was defined by erosional Puebloan trash and an isolated slab-lined hearth. These trenches sectioned several houses and numerous other features. The Basketmaker II component became the focus of data recovery at Kin Kahuna, which emphasized recovery of a sample of stone artifacts and other remains and fully documenting all features. The one suspected Puebloan hearth in the ROW was investigated and found to be part of a slightly larger activity area likely once covered by a ramada, but the scattered Puebloan remains overlying the Basketmaker II component were not sampled in any systematic fashion. Hand excavation began with two separate tasks: horizontal exposure around known Basketmaker structures (the four exposed in trenches) and excavation of a simple random sample of 1-×-1-m units from across the main site area in the ROW. The sample frame measured 915 m², and 79 units were excavated (an 8.6% sample) to provided a representative collection of Basketmaker artifacts and to search for additional features. Sediment from the first 18 sample units was screened with ⅛-in mesh, whereas sediment from the rest of the units was screened with ¼-in mesh. Known houses were exposed in plan view by excavating as many square meters as necessary to completely define their outlines beginning at the house edges seen in backhoe trenches. All sediment from this task was screened with ¼-in mesh. The erosional fill of structures was mostly removed without screening down to 10 cm above the floor (floor fill), whereas the purposeful trash accumulation in a few structures was mostly excavated and screened with ⅛- or ¼-in mesh. After the crew excavated the known structures and other features and finished the sample units, a backhoe mechanically stripped the core site area to reveal additional Basketmaker II features. The depth of stripping varied but generally did not exceed 50 cm. This depth was achieved gradually, removing about 10 cm at a time from an area of approximately 18 m² (the reach of the backhoe in a narrow arc). As features were found they were excavated entirely or partially; all features were excavated to the extent necessary to acquire basic measurements (length, width, and depth below occupation surface) and samples. Each stripping parcel was completely finished before moving on to the next parcel; thus, in this fashion the entire Basketmaker II component within the ROW was systematically explored.

Excavation of the Basketmaker II component at Kin Kahuna revealed seven pithouses, 26 storage pits, 32 other pits, 17 hearths, extensive trash deposits, and human burials (five in one pit and one in another). Because half or more of this site lies outside the ROW, obscured by shallow sand and a Puebloan component, the true size and complexity of this Basketmaker residence remain unknown. Six houses were completely excavated, whereas the seventh, which lay mostly outside the ROW, was only sectioned along its northern edge. The houses are 3–5 m in diameter and extend from .3 to 1 m in depth below the prehistoric occupation surface. Their small size (floor areas of less than 20 m²) seems barely sufficient to house a single family. All have central hearths that mostly consist of no more than fires built directly on the floor surface without prior preparation. In one case rocks placed on the floor surface helped contain the ash pile. Most houses have small upright slabs as deflectors and eastern ramp entries. The posthole pattern for three of the houses indicates that two large posts located west of center supported a primary north–south roof beam. One of the houses has

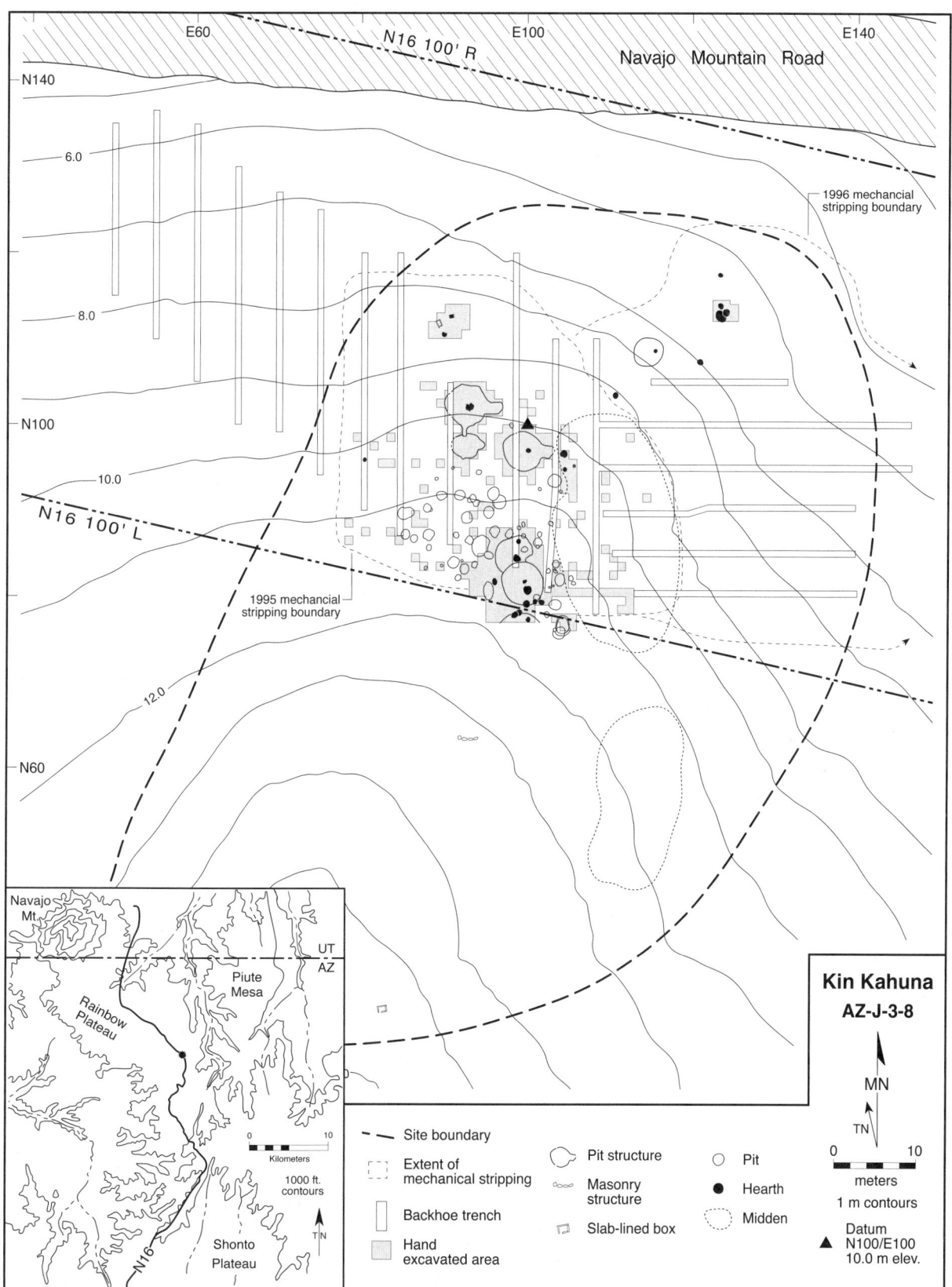

Figure 3.23. Kin Kahuna site plan showing topography, work effort, and excavated features.

four primary posts of a quadrilateral roof-support system, whereas the smallest house may have been roofed by simply leaning posts in from the edge of the pit to form a conical superstructure. Eighteen of the storage pits are bell-shaped and range in capacity from .2 to 1.6 m³ (average .6 m³), with a combined storage volume of 10.4 m³. The eight other storage pits are shallow with straight sides but still large; estimating their capacity is difficult because they might have had domed superstructures of sticks and mortar as seen in certain sheltered sites, which would have added considerable volume.

With maize radiocarbon dates ranging from about 400 cal. BC to cal. AD 400, it is clear that Basketmaker occupancy of this one location, besides being intensive, was long lived. Of the four dated houses, two may be contemporaneous, but the other two were occupied at different times. Consequently, current evidence indicates that the site never housed more than two nuclear families at any one time, making it considerably smaller than a village or even a proto-village. Evidence for long-term occupancy of this hamlet is also based on the superpositioning of structures and other features and the filling of abandoned structures and storage pits with rich midden accumulations. The oldest and deepest house (Structure 5), at slightly more than 1 m deep, had been totally trash filled, with another house partially superimposed over it, which was in turn trash filled (Structure 4). A large quantity of remains was recovered from the small fraction of the cultural stratum and midden that got sampled. This is perhaps most easily appreciated by the total counts of debitage (9,207) and bone (2,380). The density of remains within the trashy fill of Structure 5 exceeds 200 per cubic meter for flakes and 100 per cubic meter for bone.

An obvious reason for the long-duration use of this location was the prime agricultural land that lay immediately north of the site at the confluence of two small drainages. The importance of maize for the occupants of Kin Kahuna seemed obvious during excavation, because workers found corn kernels and cupules (sometimes cobs) in most features, either while digging or in sediment screening. The macrobotanical remains recovered from 72 flotation samples corroborate this inference: corn in some form was the most frequently represented plant remain, occurring in 92 percent of the samples and 97 percent of the 34 individual features that were sampled. Corn kernels occurred in 29 percent of the samples and 62 percent of the features, making it the most frequently represented seed other than goosefoot. Maize and field weeds seem to have been the most important plant resources, so settlement strategies clearly emphasized placement close to agricultural fields.

The Puebloan component of Kin Kahuna mostly lies outside the ROW. Within the ROW there was a diffuse scatter of Puebloan trash that rested upon the surface of the Basketmaker II cultural deposit. A sample of this scattered trash was recovered during the process of excavating the Basketmaker II component, but this material lacks an interpretative context and seems to be a congeries of remains from various periods, including Basketmaker II. The one portion of the Puebloan component that was investigated in its own right is an activity area consisting of several features and a lightly trash-covered use surface. The features of the activity area include a mealing bin, a rectangular slab-lined hearth, and a basin hearth built against a large upright slab. The large upright and another upright adjacent to it may have been part of a wall used as a windbreak. It seems probable that the activity area was also roofed, but excavators found no evidence for posts despite a diligent search. The few sherds associated with the activity area indicate middle to late Pueblo III use. The activity area may have served as a temporary camp associated with tending fields in the drainage bottom immediately north of the site. The activity area affords an excellent view of this farming location. While monitoring the crops, inhabitants evidently prepared food using the mealing bin and the hearths. Nearly all of the stone artifacts from the activity area relate to use of the mealing bin, principally from the production or modification of grinding tools.

Dune Hollow (AZ-J-2-2)

Dune Hollow is a multicomponent site located toward the south-central portion of the Rainbow Plateau at an elevation of 1,878 m (6,160 ft [Figure 3.24]). The local setting is a rolling landscape of dunes, bedrock exposures, and broad shallow drainages covered with sagebrush and dotted by pinyon and juniper trees. The site is positioned along the edge of a small, localized outcrop of Navajo Sandstone with the bedrock dropping out of sight, covered by eolian sand. The archaeological remains of Dune Hollow lie in the undulating eolian sand that buries the edge of the sandstone outcrop. The Archaic component consists of two basin hearths associated with a sparse scatter of flaked stone and grinding slab fragments. Charcoal from the hearths was dated to 8,000 radiocarbon years ago, placing the component within the early Archaic. Windblown sand buried the Archaic material by

Synopsis of the NMRAP Sites   115

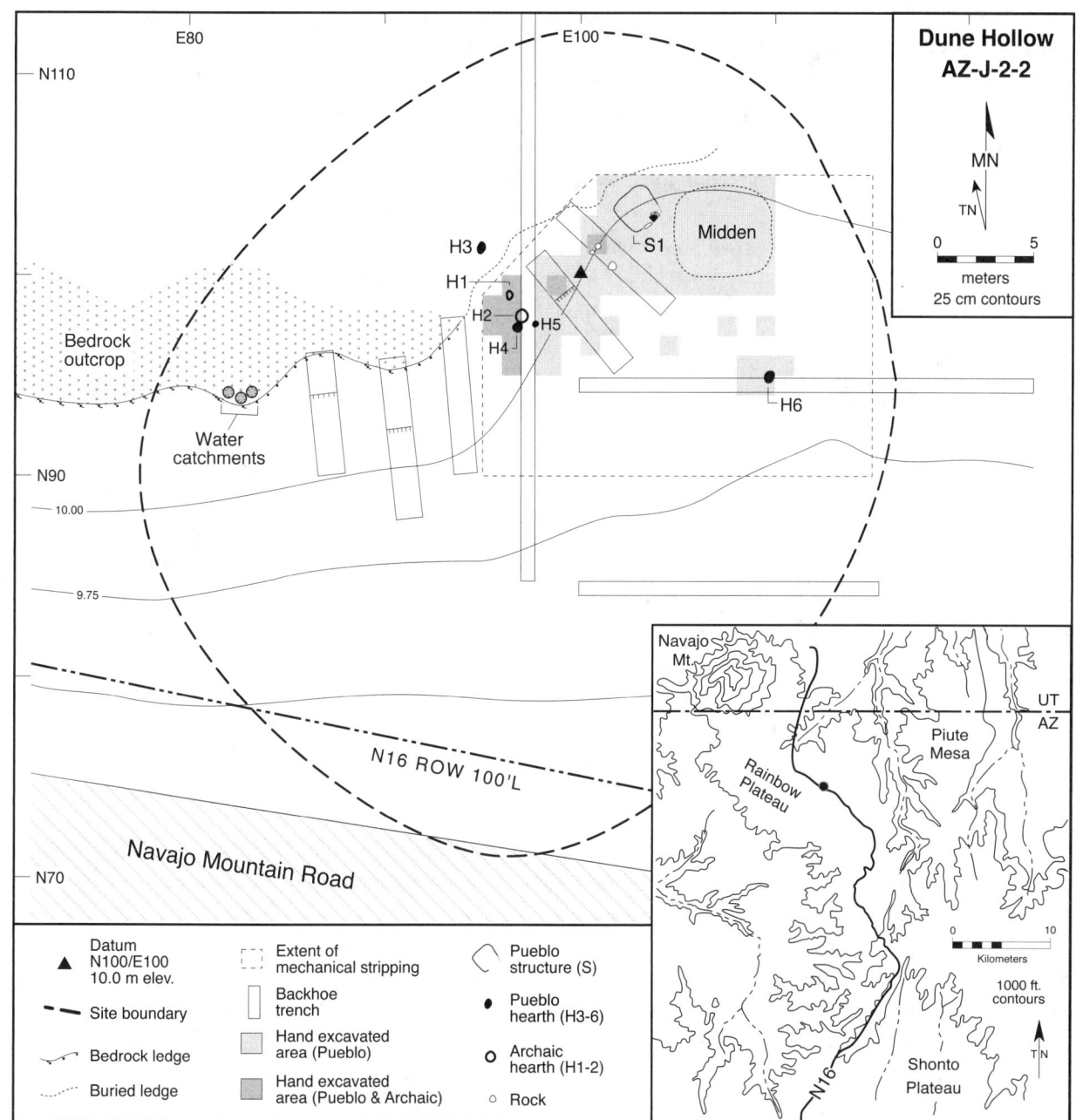

Figure 3.24. Dune Hollow site plan showing topography, work effort, and excavated features.

more than 1.4 m, whereas some of the Puebloan remains are exposed on the surface in deflated areas. The Puebloan component consists of a single structure built against the bedrock ledge, a dispersed midden, and four extramural hearths.

Data-recovery excavations at Dune Hollow had two phases; the first concentrated on the upper Pueblo component, and the second focused on the lower Archaic component. The work commenced with backhoe stripping the eolian overburden from a 15-×-20-m area, cen-

tered over the previously defined main site area (Puebloan locus). The cleared overburden consisted of numerous hummocks of windblown sand, some rising more than 1.5 m above the Puebloan occupation surface. The sand was removed to the top of where ceramics began to appear. The known structure was excavated, while horizontal excavation by hand commenced south and southwest of the room to search for additional features. Forty-one 1-×-1-m contiguous units were dug. Two extramural Pueblo hearths identified southwest of the structure were duly excavated. A second block of five 1-×-1-m units was excavated around the other known Pueblo feature, a hearth located in a test trench. No new features were found around this hearth, which was then excavated. To ensure that no features existed between the two excavation blocks, three noncontiguous 1-×-1-m units were placed in the unexcavated corridor.

Excavation of the Archaic component was somewhat less orderly, with the process evolving as new evidence was uncovered. The work effort began with the backhoe carefully stripping off about 1 m of overlying sand above the one known pre-Puebloan hearth. An area measuring approximately 4 m × 2 m was cleared over the hearth, and then hand excavation by 1-×-1-m units commenced to reveal the hearth and the immediate surroundings in plan. In total, 7 m² were hand excavated, with all sediment screened through ⅛-in mesh. A second hearth and an occasional flake were found, but generally the discoveries were minimal, and the component was believed to be of limited scope. Both hearths were excavated. Because hand excavation was slow and artifact recovery was slight, further exploration used the backhoe to trench either side of the hand-excavated area. The trenches were oriented perpendicular to the buried bedrock ledge, against which the Archaic occupation was concentrated. No new Archaic features or artifacts were discovered in any of the trenches.

The Puebloan component of Dune Hollow consists of a single small jacal structure built against a low ledge of Navajo Sandstone bedrock, a sparse and deflated scatter of trash located immediately east of the room, and four extramural basin hearths. The room has a hearth built against one wall, where it used up less of the limited floor area (less than 4 m²). Several different aspects of the site suggest seasonal use of the structure for short-term residence, perhaps while tending fields: the structure is isolated and located in a setting conducive to farming; it has an expedient construction style; and the hearth fill is distinctive from that of structure hearths used for warmth, suggesting a role in cooking rather than heating (summer use). The fuel wood in the hearth fill consists of sagebrush, with no wood of tree species identified. There are few associated remains, either in the house or in the midden, and few items associated with food processing. In particular there are no grain-grinding tools typical of Pueblo III habitations—no metates and no two-hand manos. Debitage and sherds are few in number, suggesting brief use of the site. Based on the ceramic types present, the structure was probably used sometime early in the thirteenth century.

Use of Dune Hollow by Archaic foragers appears to have been quite limited; excavations exposed two small basin hearths and recovered a small assemblage of stone artifacts and bone. The features and remains were situated in eolian sand collected along the base of a small sandstone outcrop on its southeast side. The outcrop evidently provided some protection from the elements and perhaps seasonal water in small weathering basins. AMS radiocarbon dating of sagebrush and juniper charcoal from the two hearths revealed that both are more than 8,000 radiocarbon years old, with occupation occurring sometime between 7520 and 6750 cal. BC. The limited spatial extent of the remains and proximity of the two hearths might be taken as an indication of a single use episode, but this might have simply resulted because the site setting fostered repeated use of a small area. The recovery of artifacts and bone from the entire 85-cm thickness of the dune sand that constituted the Archaic stratum seems more consistent with multiple use episodes. The artifacts consist of just 16 flakes and two tiny grinding slab fragments; there were no flaked facial-stone tools and no used flakes. The flake waste is mainly from cores or nodular core tools and not from bifacially flaked tools, as at some early Archaic lithic assemblages of the N16 ROW—assemblages that seem oriented toward hunting and were found associated with large-mammal bone. The faunal remains from Dune Hollow were equally meager and did not include large-mammal bone. There were unidentifiable bone fragments of the small size class (rabbit-sized), and all identifiable bone of this size class came from desert cottontail, an animal more likely taken by traps or with sticks and not requiring the production and maintenance of projectile points. The finding of grinding tool fragments, along with the occurrence of goosefoot seeds in the basin hearths, might support the conclusion that the site also served as a temporary camp related to seed collecting and processing. The site is currently located in an overgrazed sagebrush flat that contains few other plant species, but during the early Archaic the surrounding drainage basins may have supported abundant grasses and other important seed-producing plants such as sunflower.

Hymn House (AZ-J-2-3)

Hymn House is a middle Pueblo III habitation occupying a low bedrock rise at an elevation of 1,859 m (6,100 ft) on the south-central portion of the Rainbow Plateau (Figure 3.25). Navajo Sandstone bedrock is variably exposed on the surface or shallowly buried around the site providing for ready building stone. A broad drainage basin north-

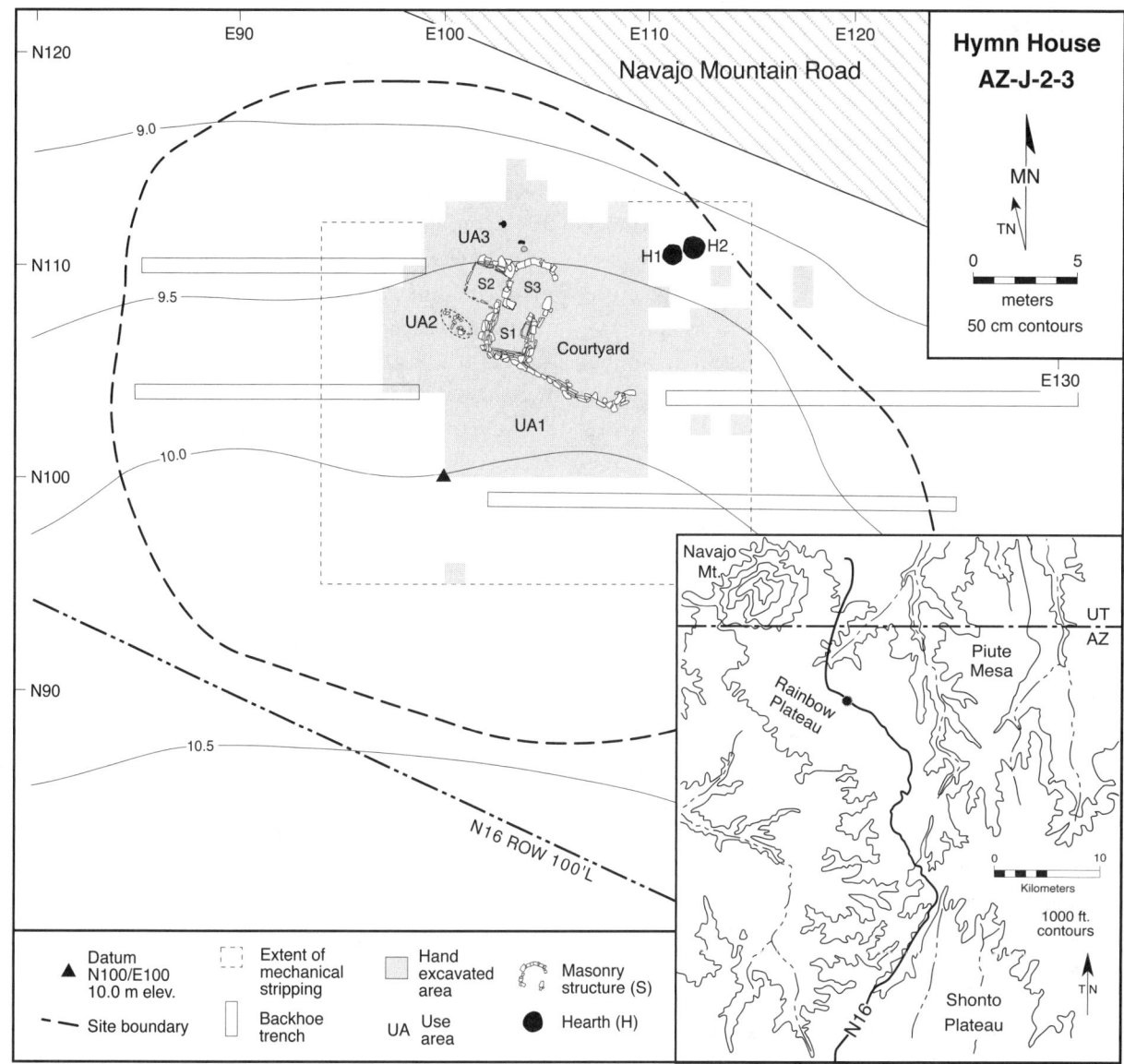

Figure 3.25. Hymn House site plan showing topography, work effort, and excavated features.

west of the site seems suitable for farming. Vistas from the site are unobstructed, with the enormous mass of Navajo Mountain monopolizing the northwestern horizon. The work effort at Hymn House consisted of horizontal exposure of the main site area (with all sediment excavated in 1-×-1-m units and screened with ¼-in mesh), hand excavation of known and newly exposed features, and mechanical stripping of the surrounding perimeter. Excavations began with the hand removal of overburden and wall fall in and around the masonry rubble. As the structures were defined in plan, hand excavation expanded out from the rooms in search of extramural features, eventually totaling 168 m². Removal of the wall fall revealed a low retaining wall bounding a broad courtyard east of the actual room block, and horizontal exposure disclosed three open activity and trash-disposal areas (Use Areas 1–3) on the south, west, and northwest sides. For the structures, fill was removed, and floors and interior features were revealed and excavated. The work effort uncovered all significant features present at Hymn House and recovered most of the nonperishable artifactual remains deposited at this site. A sparse number of artifacts might have been scattered to the north of the room block, where they were removed by construction of the existing Navajo Mountain road.

The room block at Hymn House consists of three masonry structures attached in cloverleaf fashion and connected to a courtyard partially enclosed by a low masonry retaining wall. One room with a hearth evidently served for living purposes, another for storage (a granary), and the third for general activity, including mealing. The latter opens onto the courtyard and provides an access buffer between the outside and the adjoining rooms; they could only be entered via this third room. The courtyard space contains a hearth, mealing bin, and pit. Hymn House provides an archetypal example of a Pueblo III room cluster (Dean 1969:34–35; Lindsay 1969:156–157), the distinctive grouping of architectural units that were combined to form many of the large Tsegi phase habitations, whether in the open or in alcoves. Hymn House was occupied toward the end of the middle Pueblo III period, around AD 1230 to 1260. The site lacks late Pueblo III (Tsegi phase) ceramic types such as Kayenta Black-on-white and whiteline polychromes (Kayenta and Kiet Siel). The near absence of Flagstaff Black-on-white and the low proportion of Moenkopi Corrugated place a lower temporal bracket of roughly AD 1230 (see Ambler 1985b:59). Even with a probable 30-year time bracket, occupancy of Hymn House doubtless lasted only 10 years or less given that recovered remains total less than 1,600 sherds, 300 flakes, and 100 stone tools and the lack of midden accumulation, especially dense charcoal-stained sediment. Judging from architectural investment, functionally specialized rooms including a storage room with a potential capacity of more than 3 m³, artifacts, and subsistence remains, Hymn House likely functioned as a primary residential site. Though artifacts do not occur in great quantity, there is considerable diversity, more than would be expected for a temporary residence.

Modesty House (AZ-J-2-5)

Modesty House is a small dual-component site located on a low, sand-covered rise of Navajo Sandstone at an elevation of 1,847 m (6,060 ft) overlooking the broad sagebrush flats of the central Rainbow Plateau and lying entirely within the N16 ROW. Complete excavation of the site revealed a late Pueblo II brush structure and associated hearth and a late Pueblo III pit structure, midden, and hearth (Figure 3.26). The Pueblo II features lie toward the northeast side of the site where the terrain slopes slightly to the north, with the Pueblo III features on the southwest side of the rise. The Pueblo III cultural stratum was missing in the far southwestern edge of the site, removed by construction and maintenance of the old N16 alignment.

Prior to controlled hand excavation, the overlying sterile sand was removed by hand and backhoe from much of the site. All features were exposed through hand excavation of the cultural stratum, with all sediment screened through ¼-in mesh, totaling nearly 135 m². Randomly selected units within the midden and artifact concentration at the south end of the site were screened with ⅛-in mesh, representing 30 percent and 25 percent, respectively, of these deposits. After hand excavation, all parts of the site and a 5-m buffer around all features were mechanically stripped to search for any remaining features or evidence of earlier occupations.

Both occupations of the rise were probably related to field tending; the lack of storage features or interior hearths indicated that occupancy was of limited duration and took place during warm months. The residents of Modesty House probably farmed in the deep sand dunes surrounding the site. The Pueblo II occupation might represent a single season of field tending, a scenario that would account for the lack of a midden and the sparse artifact recovery. The entire Pueblo II locus was confined to an area 5 m in diameter. The Pueblo III occupation was more substantial, covering an area 10 × 15 m, and probably represented more than one season of use. It is possible that the real difference between the two components stemmed from the degree of investment that went into construction because of differences in planned use-life, with the Pueblo III component built with the idea that it would be used for a number of seasons, but the Pueblo II component simply thrown together hastily for expedient use during a single season.

Water Jar Pueblo (AZ-J-2-58)

Water Jar Pueblo is a late Pueblo III habitation situated on the crest of a dune-covered bedrock rise at an elevation of 1,843 m (6,045 ft) near the south-central portion of the Rainbow Plateau (Figure 3.27). Rising nearly 3 m above the surrounding terrain, the site commands an excellent view of Navajo Mountain and the sagebrush-covered flats that characterize this portion of the plateau. Water Jar Pueblo was entirely within the N16 ROW and consequently was completely excavated. An overburden of eolian sand (ca. 5–30 cm) was removed by hand around the room block in the main site area to expose the cultural stratum. After clearing wall fall and excavating the cultural stratum, which was screened with ¼-in mesh, the crew exposed the basal course of masonry that defined the southern rooms, as well as smaller rocks that supported jacal walls along the northern rooms. Interior features were excavated after definition of the rooms. To the north of the room block and kiva an area was mechanically stripped

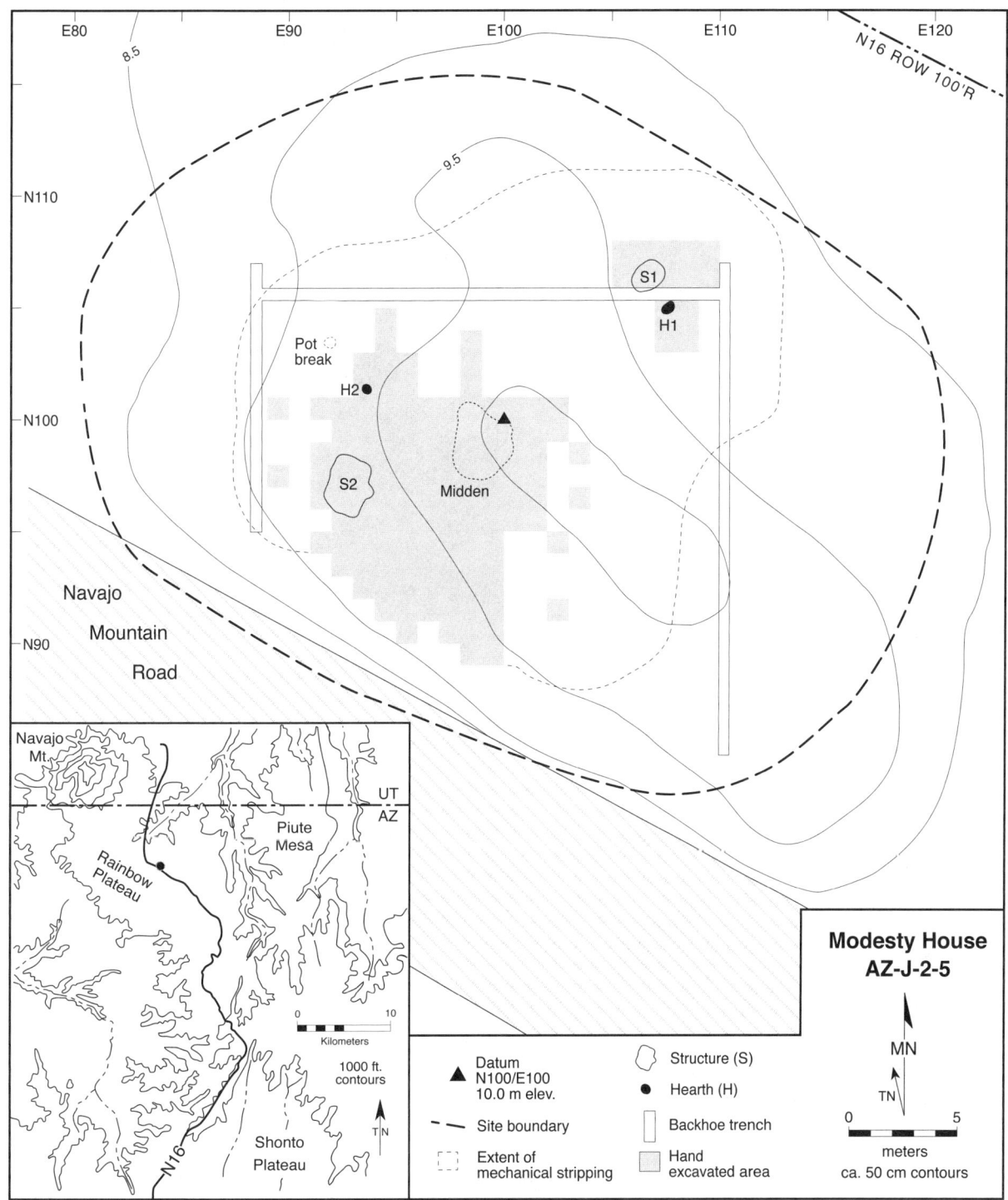

Figure 3.26. Modesty House site plan showing topography, work effort, and excavated features.

to expose buried features, which were then excavated by hand. Backhoe trenches were placed across the entire site, interspersed between the test trenches, for a maximum spacing of 7 m; most of these trenches were culturally sterile. In the midden area, the overlying eolian sand reached a meter thick and was removed with the backhoe. The entire midden deposit was excavated by hand, and a systematic sample of 50 percent was screened using ¼- and ⅛-in mesh in equal frequencies. Subsequent mechanical stripping to search for any burials or other features extended well into sterile soil or to bedrock; this activity exposed no new features.

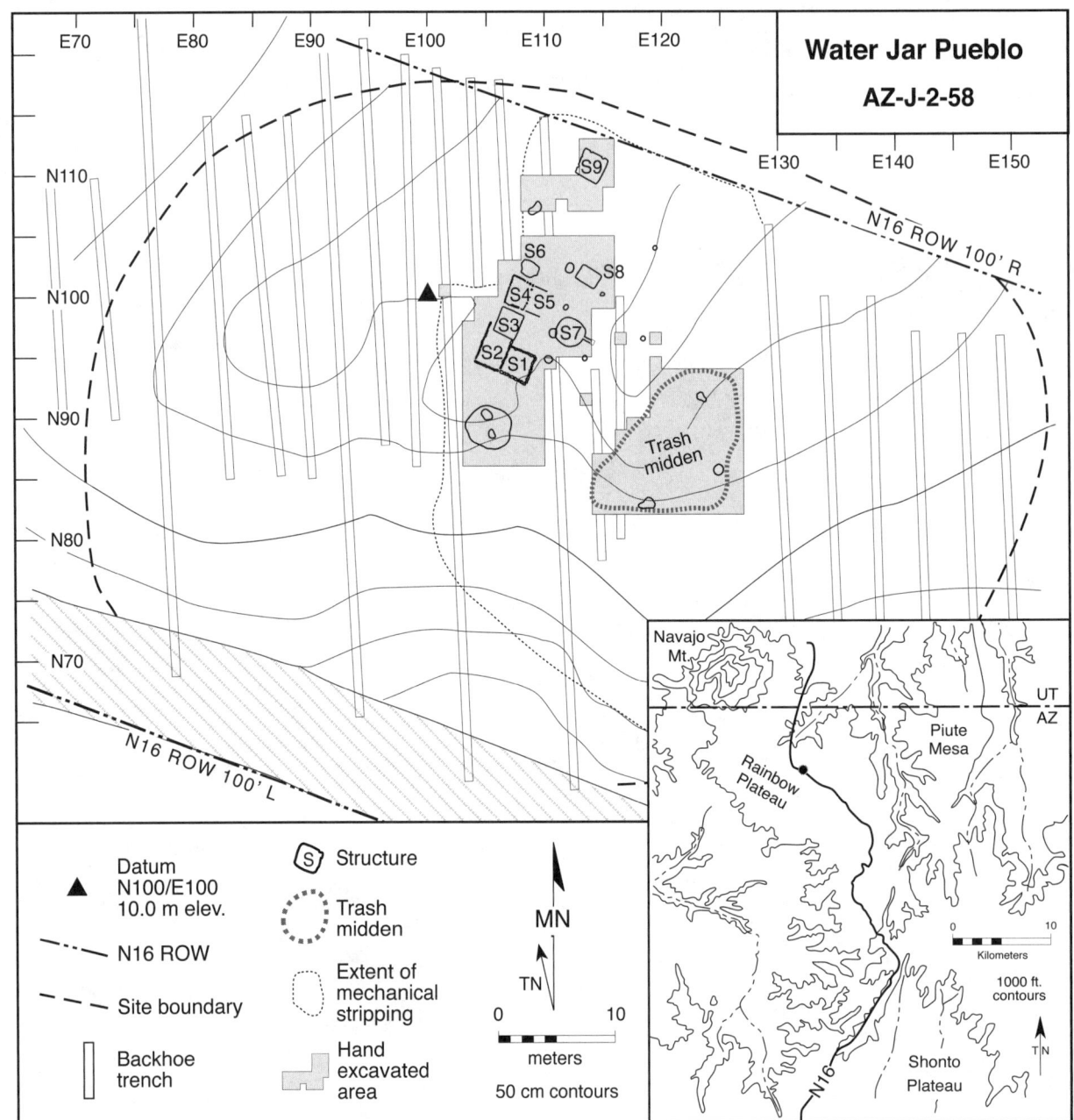

Figure 3.27. Water Jar Pueblo site plan showing topography, work effort, and excavated structures.

Water Jar Pueblo evidently began as a permanent, year-round residential site with masonry storage rooms, jacal and masonry living rooms, a kiva, and a mealing room. These structures were formally organized into a room block that, along with the mealing room, defined a small unit pueblo focused on the kiva. Two living rooms formed part of the room block, suggesting that an extended family occupied the site. Residential use lasted long enough to warrant remodeling of the kiva and at least two of the rooms as well. Ultimately the kiva was abandoned, the roof was removed, and a major portion of the room block was dismantled and scavenged of masonry. The mealing room was probably dismantled as well at this time. Subsequently, the two living rooms were modified, with one continuing to serve this purpose but the other turned into a connected activity and storage room. At this time the kiva depression became the chief area for trash disposal. Trash deposits in the kiva depression indicated that the site was used on an intermittent basis for several years, probably at least five. The modified settlement seems more substantial than a field house, and the nature of the trash in the kiva depression is more like that from a year-round habitation.

Ceramic types indicate that Water Jar Pueblo and the adjacent Sapo Seco, described next, were occupied during the same 30-year time span of roughly AD 1240–1270. It is possible that the two sites were used simultaneously, which suggests some kind of familial, clan, or other form of social relationship. Yet several lines of evidence suggest that Water Jar Pueblo was originally inhabited prior to Sapo Seco and that Locus A at the latter was the next major habitation of the Water Jar Pueblo residents. The similarity of the site layouts and features, including similar but atypical kivas (at least for late Pueblo III), suggests that the inhabitants of Water Jar Pueblo relocated to Sapo Seco and constructed the Locus A compound. The refitting of metate fragments recovered from the kivas of both sites supports this interpretation. When Water Jar Pueblo was subsequently reconfigured as a single-family homestead, without the deep pit structure, the new occupants may have been related to the former residents now living at Sapo Seco. The kivas at both Water Jar Pueblo and Sapo Seco were atypical of late Pueblo III kivas, being small in diameter, lacking a recess or any masonry lining, and lacking certain floor features but containing loom holes and sipapus. Perhaps the kivas at both sites served a somewhat more utilitarian function than their counterparts at larger contemporaneous sites.

Sapo Seco (AZ-J-2-6)

Sapo Seco consists of a loose aggregation of Pueblo III structures and a single early Archaic hearth occupying a flat expanse of sagebrush and semivegetated dune hummocks at an elevation of ca. 1,842 m (6,040 ft) on the central portion of the Rainbow Plateau. Situated between the existing Navajo Mountain road and a two-track road that branches off to a nearby windmill and water tank, the site is divided into four loci (A–D) based on perceived groupings of structures and associated primary features (Figure 3.28). All of the loci are ceramically dated to the same general period of middle to late Pueblo III, but it seems unlikely that all were strictly contemporaneous. Indeed, the trashy fill in some structures, structure and feature superimposition, and differences in time-sensitive ceramic types suggest that certain houses were built and abandoned before other houses. Data recovery involved a large amount of horizontal excavation by hand, especially at Locus A, and extensive backhoe trenching and stripping to ensure that no important features were missed. At the start, crews concentrated on excavating known features, those disclosed previously during testing, accompanied by horizontal exposure around them in search of nearby related features. An area of more than 150 m² was excavated by hand at Locus A, with considerably less at Locus B. Excavations at Loci C and D were mainly feature based, with the backhoe used to search for additional features. Following all hand excavation, the entire site area within the ROW, totaling more than 2,700 m², was thoroughly stripped with a backhoe.

The site has a total of 18 living or communal structures and 32 primary features (such as pits and hearths). Locus A is the main habitation area focal point of the settlement and was probably home to one extended family. It consists of a small pueblo of surface and semisubterranean masonry and jacal rooms built in a semicircle and centered on a kiva. The rooms, plus a jacal wall, define a courtyard that contains the kiva. There are rooms for living, mealing, storage, and general activity. Attached to the south side of the pueblo is another living room with an associated small mealing room. To the east lies a compressed but artifact-rich trash midden that was extensively sampled. At the southern edge of the site, partially impacted by the current Navajo Mountain road, is Locus B, consisting of a semisubterranean living room, a surface mealing and general activity room, and a deflated trash midden. Two burials located within a wall niche of the living room were excavated and relocated where they would not be impacted by road construction. Backhoe stripping at Locus B uncovered a buried hearth well below the ceramic-era occupation surface, adding another component to the otherwise Puebloan site; the hearth later yielded an early Archaic radiocarbon date. Locus C, northeast and east of Locus A by 10–20 m, is a loose aggregation of two mealing rooms, two living rooms, and several associated pits and hearths. Locus D, 20 m southeast of Locus A, consists of two superimposed pit structures, with the later structure built into the fill of the earlier room. A burial intruded through the floors of both houses; it was also excavated and reinterred in a safe place. Nearby are three pits, including one large feature that might be an unfinished pithouse.

As opposed to Locus A, the structures at the other three loci appear to have been occupied on a short-term, seasonal, or intermittent basis. The principal reason for this conjecture is the lack of adequate food-storage facilities for overwintering. The four loci are from the same

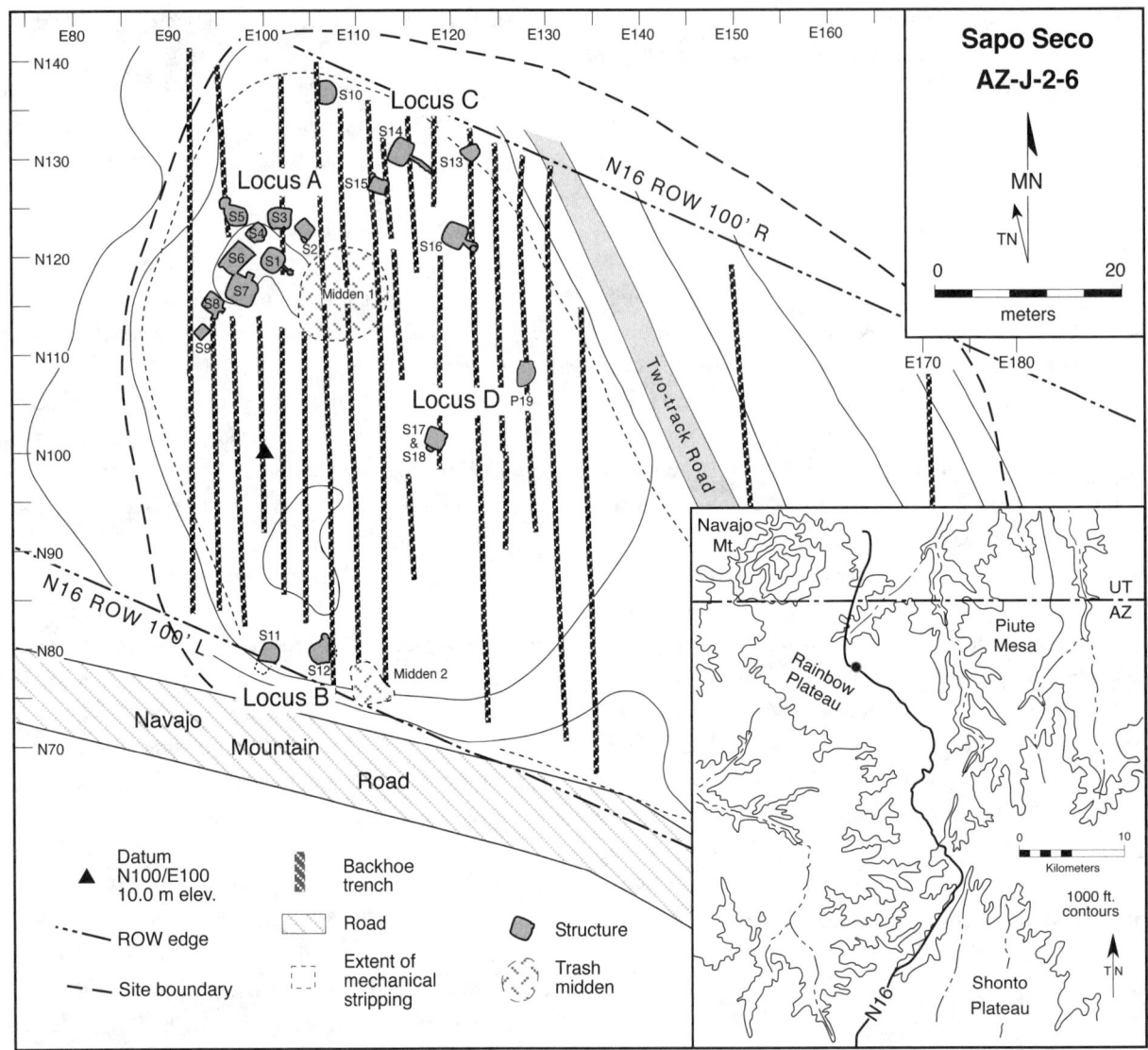

Figure 3.28. Sapo Seco site plan showing topography, extent of mechanized work effort, and excavated structures; considerable hand excavation occurred around Locus A and portions of the other loci.

general time period but may or may not have been strictly contemporaneous with each other. In fact, the lack of Kayenta Black-on-white and whiteline polychrome outside of Locus A may indicate that this locus followed the occupation of Loci B–D. If so, it is unlikely that the residents of Loci B–D would have gone on to construct the Locus A pueblo, given its architectural integration. Given the household autonomy reflected by the scattered structures of Loci B–D, any pueblo built by the occupants likely would have been one of Lindsay's (1969; Lindsay et al. 1968:365) courtyard-oriented community types. Given the possible lack of contemporaneity, it may be mere coincidence that the structures of Loci B–D are located in proximity to Locus A. Loci B–D may have been temporary residential sites that were abandoned at the time that Locus A was built. If they were occupied at the same time, at least initially, the occupants of all four loci were perhaps related by kin, clan, or some other form of social or economic association. Nonetheless, Loci B–D are expressly not part of the Locus A pueblo core.

Bonsai Bivouac (AZ-J-2-55)

Bonsai Bivouac is a multicomponent site situated at an elevation of 1,840 m (ca. 6,040 ft) on the sagebrush-covered flats near the central portion of the Rainbow Plateau (Figure 3.29). The area is marked by shifting dunes and exposures of Navajo Sandstone, with the terrain dipping slightly to the east. A shallowly buried, disturbed room block with a surrounding light scatter of artifacts make up a Puebloan component. Backhoe stripping exposed

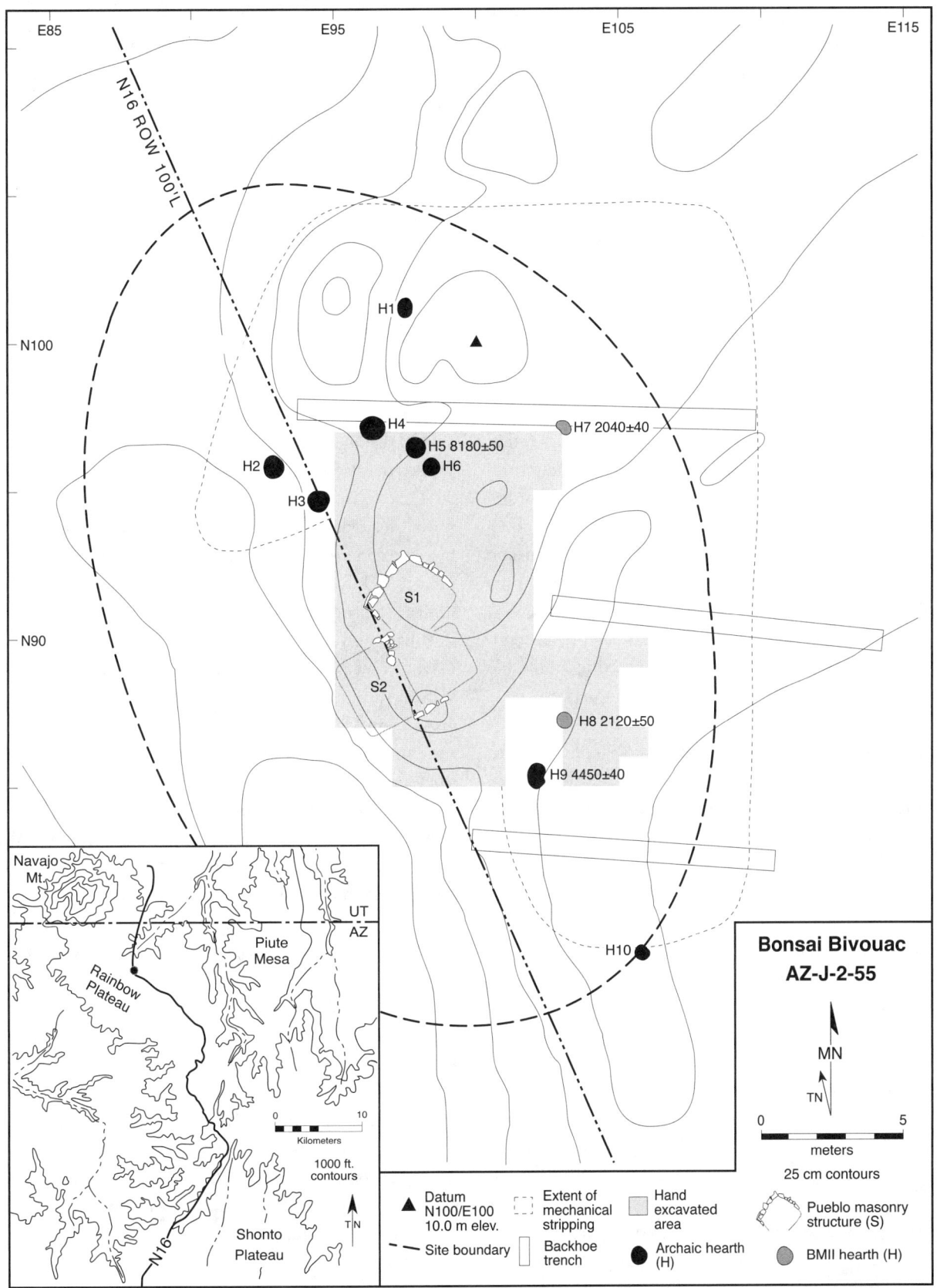

Figure 3.29. Bonsai Bivouac site plan showing topography, work effort, and excavated features.

shallow basin hearths below the Pueblo remains, which returned radiocarbon ages in the Archaic and Basketmaker II periods. Data recovery at Bonsai Bivouac involved three main tasks: (1) hand excavation of the known room block; (2) hand excavation of the cultural stratum surrounding the room block, with an emphasis to the southeast, where a midden might be buried; and (3) mechanical stripping of the greater site area.

Excavation efforts in and around the room block proved disappointing—clearing away the overlying sand revealed far less intact masonry than expected. The two rooms identified during testing became merely half of one room, accompanied by an imposing push pile of redeposited architecture. Exploratory hand excavation around and to the southeast of the intact portion of the room block was equally unsatisfactory, with no features found and only a smattering of artifacts recovered after hand excavation of 77 m², with all sediment from the cultural stratum screened through ¼-in mesh. Road grading along the existing Navajo Mountain road had collapsed and compressed the majority of the room block, leaving only half of one masonry room intact. Judging from the extent of displaced rock, mortar, and artifacts, the structure in its entirety probably included two connecting rooms. No extramural features or concentrated trash deposits were found accompanying the room block. The Pueblo component was interpreted as a seasonal habitation linked with farming. The lack of extramural features and the absence of a formal midden suggested that the site was used for only a short time, perhaps just a few years.

Mechanical excavation encompassed a roughly 10- to 15-m-wide swath radiating out from the room block to the north, northeast, east, and southeast. All sediment was removed to the level of bedrock, exposing 10 charcoal stains on or just above bedrock. The stains originated below the Pueblo surface, with some more distinct and regular than others; all were excavated, with floats collected and the remaining fill screened through ⅛-in mesh. No artifacts were recovered either from the screening of hearth fill or from the remnant portions of intact stratum around the features. The lack of artifactual remains might relate to how the features were discovered, as the backhoe might have stripped away the associated cultural stratum, but it might also be a consequence of limited activity. Charcoal from four of the stains returned dates ranging from 8,000 to 2,000 radiocarbon years ago. These charcoal stains are interpreted as evidence of brief early Archaic and Basketmaker II encampments at the site.

THREE DOG SITE (UT-B-63-39)

Located at the eastern foot of Navajo Mountain on the northern side of a narrow valley at an elevation of 1,832 m (6,010 ft), Three Dog Site was the most complex site excavated by the NMRAP. The portion of the site available for investigation was arbitrarily bounded on the eastern side by the N16 ROW, which cut across the recess of a kiva and part of an adjoining mealing room. The majority of the extensive Puebloan midden was excluded from study because it lay outside the ROW. The old N16 alignment bounded excavations to the west; the road truncated that edge of the site and destroyed an unknown number of Basketmaker features and perhaps Archaic deposits and features. The road only minimally affected the Puebloan features and cultural deposits in the main site area, primarily through construction of a drainage ditch that crossed the slope south of the room block.

Despite its relatively small areal extent, the site produced rich assemblages of cultural remains grouped into five components spanning more than two millennia (Figure 3.30). The earliest use was by late Archaic foragers who built a series of unlined hearths on a gravelly sand surface as eolian sand started to accumulate as a climbing dune. Intermittent use of the location as the sand built up resulted in additional Archaic hearths and associated lithic artifacts and faunal remains within the deep sand. Activity during the Basketmaker II period produced several small features associated with an activity area; road construction in the 1970s destroyed a probable associated structure. After a hiatus of nearly a millennium, the dune was reoccupied during the middle Pueblo III period by families that built two household units, each consisting of one or two shallow living rooms and a mealing room centered around a kiva. After perhaps one decade or less the architecture was remodeled to produce a more formalized pueblo with a series of connected, semisubterranean and surface rooms of masonry and jacal. The final layout retained two architectural units with mealing rooms and courtyards but only one kiva. Additional room alignments extended perpendicular to the core room block, producing bounded space around the large kiva and northern courtyard. The southern courtyard was apparently enclosed on only two sides. Each courtyard was associated with mealing and storage rooms in addition to living rooms.

Excavation of this site was a complicated affair because of the partially overlying components, with late Pueblo III rooms constructed over or within those from

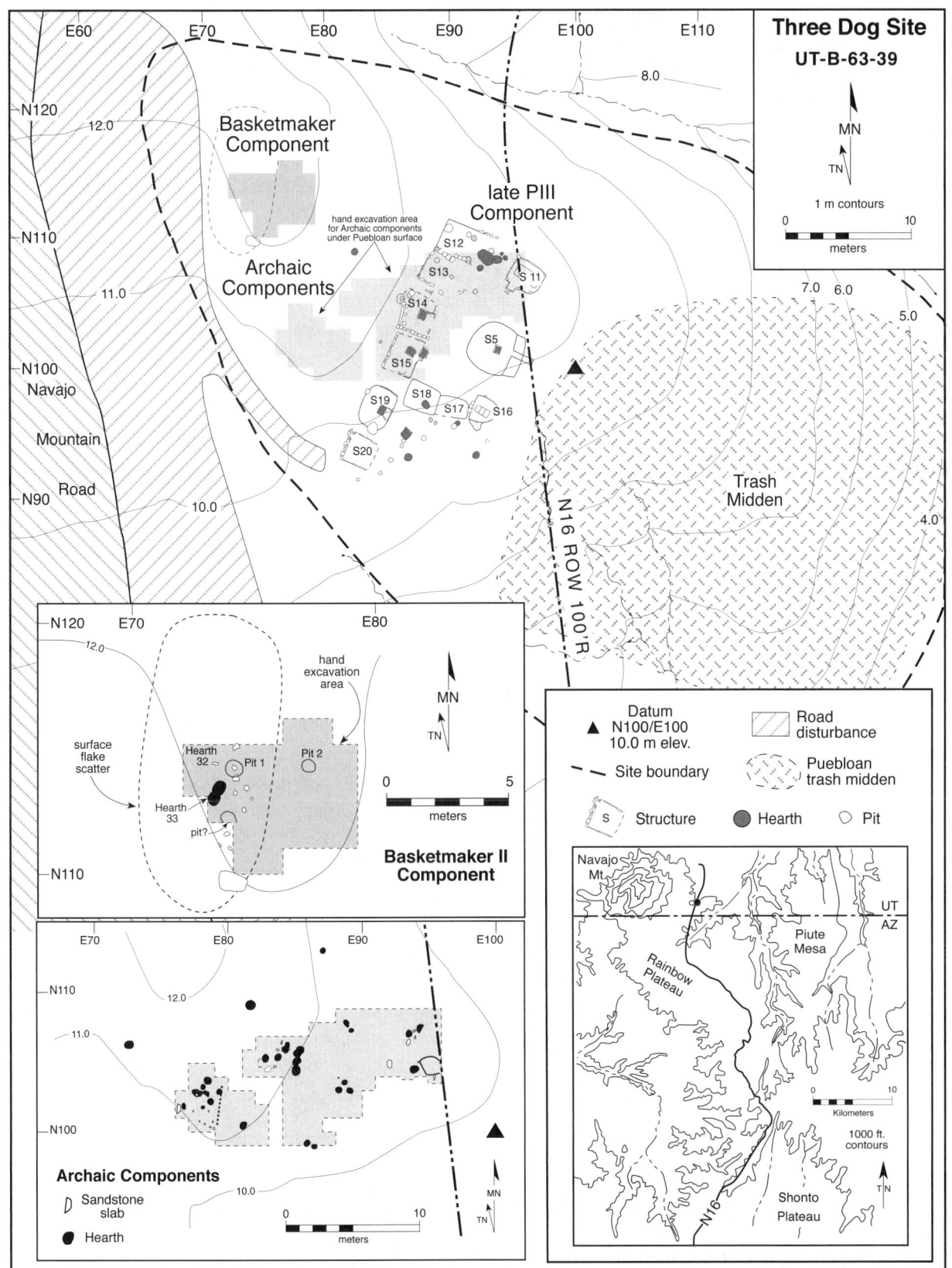

Figure 3.30. Plan map of Three Dog Site showing topography, work effort, and excavated features.

the middle Pueblo III component and both often intruding the underlying Archaic components, which consisted of upper and lower layers. In general the work progressed from west to east and north to south, with all excavation vertically controlled by natural strata and horizontally controlled by 1-×-1-m grid units. All hand-excavated sediment from the Archaic and Basketmaker cultural layers was screened using ⅛-in mesh to ensure recovery of small lithic debris and bone fragments. Though ¼-mesh was used to screen most Puebloan cultural deposits, structure floor fill, the primary fill of features, and a sample of trash layers filling a few structures were screened using ⅛-in mesh.

Excavation of the Pueblo III components at Three Dog Site began in the northern courtyard area and room block. Concurrent excavations in the western part of the site exposed late Archaic deposits and explored the Basketmaker remains that were visible on the surface. Each Puebloan room with surface evidence (usually masonry) was investigated by first clearing away the overlying eolian sand to define the wall alignments. After the room outline was defined, excavation removed the interior fill down to roughly 10 cm above the floor, working within halves or quadrants depending on the size of the room. This surface sediment was screened only if it appeared intentionally deposited, which was rare. The lower 10 cm of floor fill was excavated by half or quadrant and was screened through ⅛-in mesh. The large amount of hand excavation within and adjacent to the room block and courtyard ensured that no Pueblo III features went undiscovered. As excavation of the late Pueblo III room block was completed, the underlying middle Pueblo III structures were defined. During construction of the later room block, sterile sand was tossed into the earlier structures, which had been dismantled and scavenged for construction materials. This sterile fill presented challenges to the excavators, and the earlier structures were sometimes initially identified based only on the presence of rocks in sterile sand or by intrusive later floor features that extended into the lower fill of the earlier rooms. Mechanical stripping followed hand excavation of the preceramic components west and north of the main site area; several additional features from each component were exposed by this activity. Archaic deposits extended beneath a few of the Puebloan features at the north end of the room block, but time constraints prevented an extensive search for earlier features in this area. Backhoe stripping beneath Puebloan features eventually disclosed a few more Archaic hearths. Only a few units were hand excavated in the small portion of the midden that existed within the N16 ROW. The deposit was relatively shallow and deflated, but it produced an abundance of artifacts, primarily from the final occupation of the site. The entire midden within the ROW was eventually stripped to sterile sand to ensure that no burials or underlying features were overlooked. It is likely that the midden outside the ROW is quite thick and contains an even greater abundance of material. Rich deposits of Puebloan trash from the last occupation of the site occurred in two abandoned structures.

The Archaic components at Three Dog Site represent at least six episodes of activity, and perhaps more, each of which produced multiple thermal features ($n = 31$) associated with lithic debitage, faunal remains, and in some cases, grinding tools. I interpret the remains as deriving from short-term camps that foragers occupied over a span of some 1,000 years, from roughly 1600 to 500 cal. BC. At least one of the camping episodes may have occurred during cold weather, prompting the residents to construct a small brush shelter. Archaic features and artifacts were recovered from two distinct cultural components separated by a layer of sterile eolian sand. Radiocarbon dating demonstrates that much of the sand accumulated in very short order, probably less than 100 years. Each component was further differentiated horizontally into loci that contained somewhat distinctive lithic and faunal assemblages. The full extent of the late Archaic occupation at this site remains unknown because of ROW restrictions on the east side, destruction by the existing Navajo Mountain road on the west, and the heavy overlay of Puebloan structures and other features, which removed portions of the Archaic layers and limited full horizontal exposure. Nonetheless, from about 141 m², NNAD crews recovered almost 2,800 stone artifacts (2,688 unused flakes, 11 used flakes, 3 cores/nodular tools, 11 flaked facial tools, and 16 grinding tools), 3,255 bone fragments, and numerous flotation, radiocarbon, and pollen samples. Both Archaic components attest to large game hunting, chiefly of deer, as well as some procurement of rabbits and hares. Linked with this is evidence from the lithic assemblages for a heavy emphasis on the production and maintenance of hunting equipment and other formal bifacially thinned tools, including the presence of projectile point notching flakes. Abundant seeds of goosefoot, sparse seeds from a few other plants such as ricegrass, and the presence of manos and metates reveal that plant harvesting and processing also occurred. The numerous hearths of the components were probably used to process both animals and plants, both in roasting and to generate coals for parching seeds. Parching accidents could account for the numerous goosefoot seeds in some hearths. These seeds may signify fall occupancy, when they are mature, but the site might have been used in other seasons as well. Situated as it is in a small valley with perennial water at the eastern foot of Navajo Mountain, Three Dog Site provided an ideal camp location and offered relatively easy access to numerous microclimates and a variety of floral and faunal resources.

The Basketmaker II component was restricted to the far northwest edge of the site immediately adjacent the cut for the existing Navajo Mountain road. It is likely that road construction removed various features, including at least one structure; several lines of evidence suggest that the site functioned as a seasonal habitation during Basketmaker II. The small features that remained for excavation consisted of two hearths and two small pits. Flotation samples of the feature fill were relatively rich in macrobotanical remains, including corn, ricegrass, and goosefoot. Associated with the features was a lightly charcoal-stained sediment horizon, the residue of activity and trash deposition during the Basketmaker occupation. Hand excavation of the cultural stratum produced a collection of flaked-stone artifacts and grinding tools that represent a variety of activities. The average of statistically contemporaneous radiocarbon assays on ricegrass seeds and maize has a calibrated two-sigma range of AD 80–320, which places this component of Three Dog Site toward the later part of the Basketmaker II sequence for the project area.

The Puebloan components were similar in overall layout, consisting of two courtyard complexes, each containing living rooms, mealing facilities, and other rooms along with numerous extramural features. Both components date after AD 1200 and were probably immediately sequential in time, with the same families residing at the site. Rather than merely remodeled, nearly all of the early set of rooms were razed, and entirely new rooms were built in a more integrated and formal arrangement. The one notable exception to this was the main kiva, which remained in use for both occupations. The structures of the final late Pueblo III occupation were more numerous than those of the immediately preceding middle Pueblo III occupation, but there was one less kiva. The comprehensive remodel of the site bespeaks a formal, coordinated effort by the entire residential group, a cooperative undertaking that transformed the site into a more integrated architectural unit likely reflecting a more tightly knit social unit. The exact sequence of feature demolition and construction was only evident in a few cases, but the remodel must have been carefully planned to ensure that grinding facilities and shelter were available as needed during the process. A similarly coordinated effort took place when the site was finally abandoned and the last residents moved on.

The "complete" suite of architectural features associated with each courtyard suggests the presence of two extended families or related kin groups. The two site portions were evidently constructed at roughly the same time, suggesting that the two groups settled together. The orientation of architectural features toward contiguous courtyards is typical of the period just prior to and extending into the Tsegi phase in the Kayenta region, when multiple households began to coalesce into larger, more cohesive settlements (Dean 1969; Lindsay 1969). The structures and artifact assemblage associated with both components demonstrate a wide range of domestic activities. Economic pursuits clearly focused on maize agriculture; this is reflected in botanical remains, grinding tools, and mealing facilities. Other floral and faunal resources were used to a lesser extent, a pattern typical for this region in the Pueblo III period. The significance of large game hunting is shown by the faunal remains and the abundant arrowpoints. Deer and bighorn sheep were the principal game animals; rabbits and hares added to the table fare, but perhaps less significantly, with rodents making minor contributions. The lithic artifacts reflect local procurement of stone and relatively nonintensive tool production. The exception to this pattern is the large amount of pecking debris from ground stone manufacture that was recovered from trash deposits, from activity areas, and within mealing rooms. Nearly all of this debris is of sandstone that occurs locally in talus and wash deposits, having eroded from the upper slopes of Navajo Mountain. The residents may have produced far more grinding tools than necessary for their own use, perhaps for trade with communities to the south. Ceramic production also took place, indicated by the presence of processed clay and unfired vessel fragments.

The final use of Three Dog Site occurred during late Pueblo III between about AD 1235 and 1275 and partly overlapping with the Tsegi phase, the final florescence of the Kayenta Anasazi. During the Tsegi phase the population in the region coalesced into large communities that were abandoned after a relatively brief interval (Lindsay 1969; Lindsay et al. 1968). Small sites such as Three Dog Site and Sapo Seco were deserted in favor of the larger villages. When Three Dog Site was finally abandoned, the residents razed nearly all of the structures and scavenged most usable construction material. This behavior would be expected if the group was moving only a short distance, in that the effort to dismantle and move the material would be less than procuring new beams, rock for masonry, and large grinding tools. A large late Pueblo III habitation (UT-B-63-2) within a kilometer to the southwest is a potential candidate for where the occupants of Three Dog Site temporarily settled before vacating the region utterly. Ceramics on the surface of this unexcavated site include abundant Kayenta Black-on-white and whiteline polychrome types, suggesting that it slightly postdates Three Dog Site.

Hanging Ash (UT-B-63-14)

Hanging Ash is a multiple-component Puebloan residential site located on a moderately steep, sand-covered slope (falling dune) on the northeast side of a ridge at the eastern foot of Navajo Mountain (Figure 3.31). One of the components is a Pueblo II habitation that lies entirely outside the N16 ROW except for some erosional trash. Downslope is a middle Pueblo III habitation entirely within the ROW at an elevation of about 1,835 m (6,020 ft). Construction and maintenance of the existing N16 alignment had heavily damaged this component, bisecting three structures and removing nearly all of a trash deposit and likely an entire kiva. The peripheral, eroded edge of the trash midden lay on the east side of the road, with the damaged structures on the west. Also on the west side was an undamaged fourth structure, a hearth, and a large storage pit that likely originated from one of the structures. Structures and other features occurring in the main site area in the ROW were exposed by hand excavation of a total of 44 m². Sterile overburden was shoveled out, while the cultural stratum was screened through ¼-in mesh. The fill of all structures was screened through ¼-in mesh to 10 cm above the floor, when excavators switched to ⅛-in mesh. After recording all floor artifacts and features, the structures were subfloored to expose any hidden pits, buried artifacts, or second floors. Following all hand excavation, the backhoe was used to mechanically strip the remainder of the entire main site area within the ROW, an area of about 150 m². During this task, a concentration of sandstone slabs and trash was found northwest of Structure 1. It was not associated with any structure and was designated an extramural feature; no additional features were revealed. The peripheral and eroded portion of the midden that lay east of the road was surface collected to augment the artifact sample for the Pueblo III component.

Hanging Ash is a middle Pueblo III habitation that consisted of at least four unattached dwellings. The four dwellings were semisubterranean with jacal superstructures. Three had hearths, and the fourth probably did as well, judging from the ash and charcoal staining of the floor, so all served as living rooms. With four households to feed and no food-storage rooms (granaries), provisions for the occupants through the winter may have been stored in house pits. One structure had a large bell-shaped pit originating from its southern side, which had a storage capacity of just under 1 m³. Such subterranean storage features are a good means to secure field produce within detached jacal living structures. Other houses at Hanging Ash may have had such features, which were destroyed by the road. The main extramural activity area for this site was doubtless east of the houses and thus destroyed, but the occupation surface behind and around the structures contained a modest concentration of remains, including evidence of grinding tool production consisting of sandstone flakes, hammerstones, pecking stones, and unfinished manos and metates. There is considerable evidence from the site for the exploitation of corn; other plant remains consist of a squash seed, the seeds of weedy annuals and ricegrass, pinyon cone scales, and pollen from beeweed, cattail, and a few other taxa. Large and small game were hunted and consumed at the site. The occupation of Hanging Ash likely occurred during the early portion of the middle Pueblo III period, sometime after AD 1200 but before AD 1230. The site lacks any of the ceramic types that are diagnostic of the late Pueblo III Tsegi phase such as Kayenta Black-on-white, Kayenta Polychrome, and Kiet Siel Polychrome.

UT-B-63-19

UT-B-63-19 is a middle Pueblo III seasonal habitation or field house situated at an elevation of about 1,745 m (5,725 ft) at the eastern foot of Navajo Mountain on the northern portion of the Rainbow Plateau (Figure 3.32). The site occupies a gentle, sand-covered slope below Segazlin Mesa. Data recovery began with horizontal excavation of the main site area to expose features and recover associated artifacts. The crew excavated a contiguous set of 1-×-1-m units totaling 85 m², screening most sediment through ¼-in mesh but with ⅛-in mesh used to screen the sediment from units that included the small trash midden.

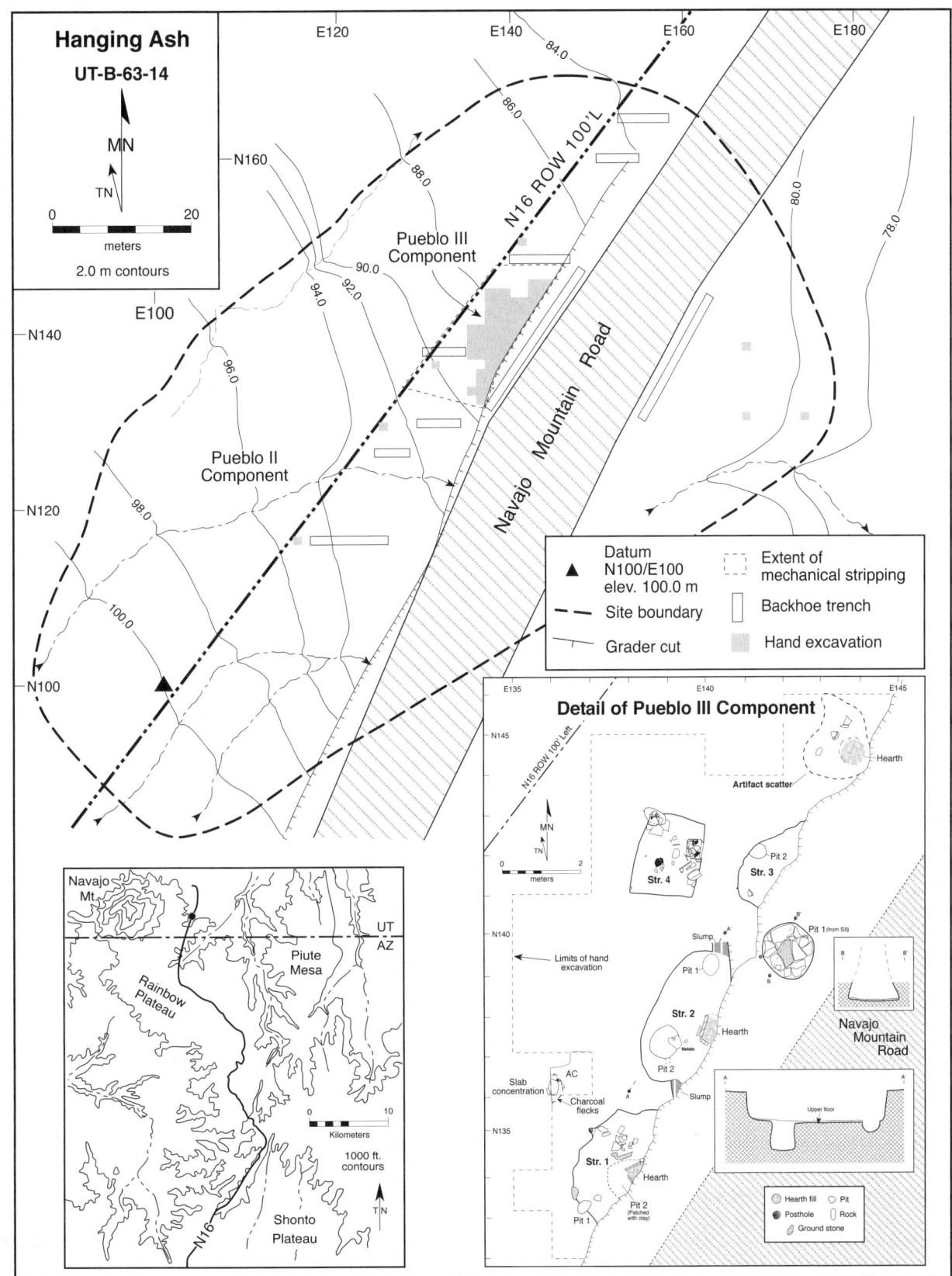

Figure 3.31. Hanging Ash site plan showing topography, work effort, and excavated structures.

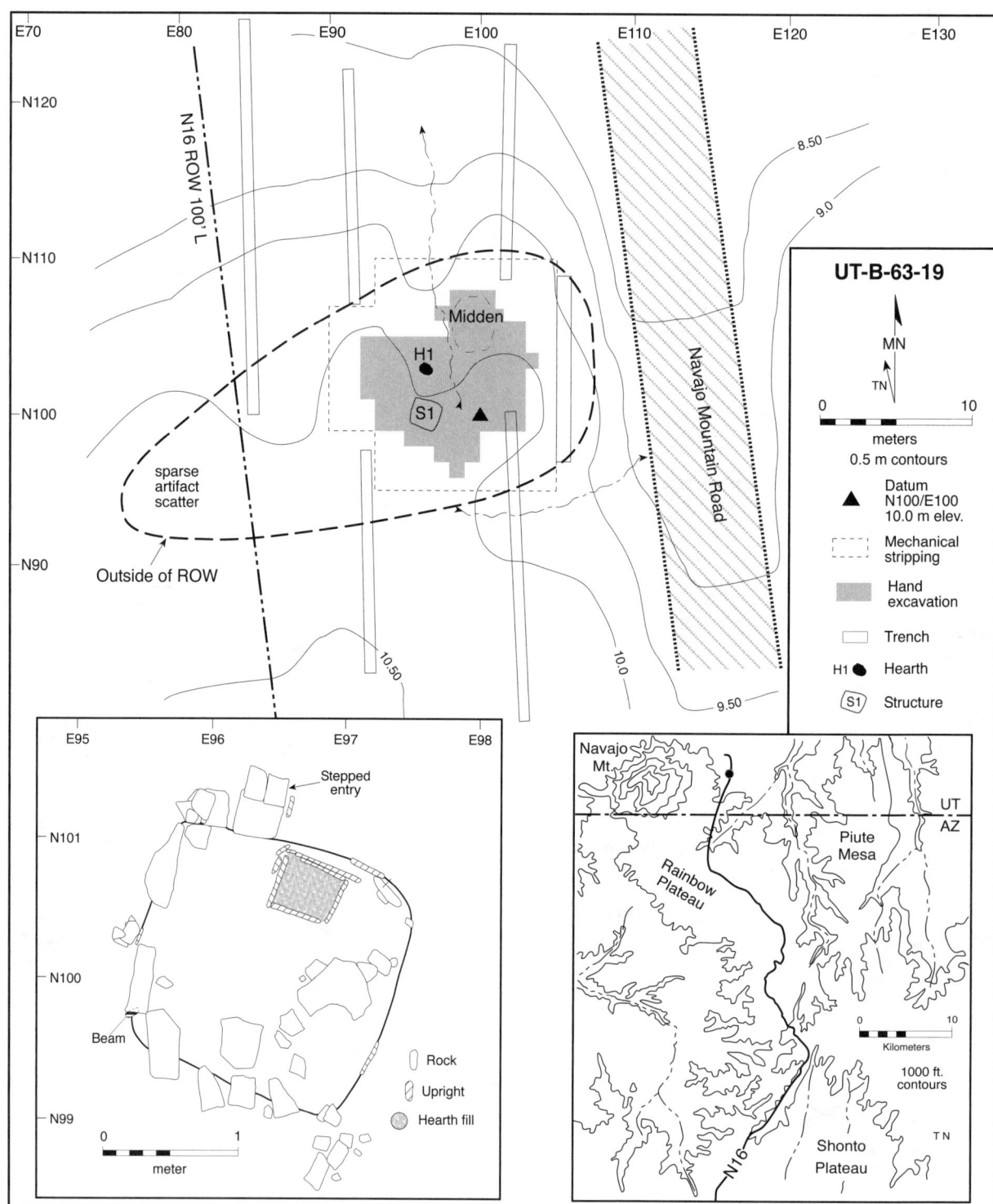

Figure 3.32. UT-B-63-19 site plan showing topography, work effort, and excavated structure.

This work exposed a structure and a slab-lined extramural hearth. The hearth was excavated following standard practice, but excavation of the structure was somewhat at variance with the usual procedure. By the time the crew had this small and shallow structure defined, its fill was essentially removed except for 10 cm or less of fill above the floor, all of which was excavated by grid unit and screened with ⅛-in mesh. After completing hand excavation the entire site area was mechanically stripped to a depth of roughly 1 m below the occupation surface, well into sterile sand. This tasked failed to reveal any additional features.

Thorough excavations at UT-B-63-19 revealed the remains of a small, shallow pit structure, a single slab-lined hearth, and a small trash midden. The structure was oriented with the general lay of the land and faced downslope to the northeast. Several paces to the northeast from the front door was the trash midden, but additional artifacts and sandstone slab fragments were scattered in an arc around the structure from northwest to southeast. The hearth lay 2 m directly north of the structure. Excavations recovered 355 sherds, mostly of various Pueblo III types, 458 stone artifacts, 66 bones, and a small sample of carbonized plants, principally corn and pinyon. The documented features and recovered remains made up virtually the entire site; sparse surface artifacts outside the ROW appear peripheral to the excavated remains and might be unrelated.

I interpret the site as a seasonal habitation that was probably occupied while tending fields. The site setting seems well suited to dry farming, with some potential for enhanced water from slope runoff in the drainage several hundred meters to the east. That the house was occupied seasonally is suggested by the lack of storage features and mealing facilities. The orientation of the site is also indicative of use in other than the winter months, as the door and the house face north. The presence of an interior hearth sets this house apart from most other NMRAP field houses, which lack these features. Moreover, the fill of the hearth was white ash like that seen in living rooms at more permanent habitations, which suggests that the structure was sometimes occupied when the weather was cool, likely during spring or autumn evenings. The pollen sample from the structure floor, which is dominated by disturbance species and contains low proportions of tree and sagebrush pollen, seems consistent with structure placement in or near a field. No maize pollen occurred in the sample, but burned corn kernels, cobs, and shanks occurred in the midden, providing circumstantial evidence for local harvests. This is especially true for the shank portions that probably would have been removed in shucking, which is likely to have occurred in or near a cornfield. Field hunting might be evidenced by the cottontail bones at the site. The procurement of larger game might be implied by the presence of arrowpoints, although the finding of just a single deer part does not suggest much success in this activity.

Given the presence of just a single structure, it is likely that only a single family or a portion of a family occupied UT-B-63-19. If the Hopi ethnographic tradition of men planting and cultivating fields (e.g., Bradfield 1971: 20; Kennard 1979:554) has any relevance to this prehistoric situation, then the occurrence of arrowpoints at the site might make sense, in that point production or arrow maintenance could have been crafts worked on while avoiding the heat of the day. The evidence for grinding tool production, consisting of pecking stones, sandstone flakes, and unfinished manos and metates, could well signify that women also occupied the site. The presence of women is perhaps also indicated by the used manos and metates at the site. The presence of an entire family perhaps is a better fit for the overall nature of the site—a place used for longer periods than simply a few hours each day, where people stayed overnight, cooked and consumed food, and carried out various domestic activities.

UT-B-63-38

The unnamed UT-B-63-38 consists of a small dense scatter of flaked-stone artifacts and several grinding tools on a moderately level sandy area near the crest of a ridge at the northeast foot of Navajo Mountain (Figure 3.33). The site is at an elevation of 1,728 m (5,670 ft) in a pinyon–juniper forest with an understory of abundant big sagebrush, snakeweed, and other shrubs. The remains occur on the surface and shallowly buried within a hard, clayey sand layer. This layer may have formed well after the artifacts were deposited, and it appears that they rested on the surface for a considerable time, perhaps as a lag deposit eroded from their original depositional context. Erosion is one likely reason that no intact features were found, even though at least one of the grinding slabs from the site was discolored from fire. The adjacent site of Tsé Haal'á (see below) reveals the extent to which wind erosion removes buried features and leaves artifacts scattered as a lag deposit.

Data recovery consisted of hand excavation of 55 m^2 within a 15-×-12-m area centered upon the surface lithic scatter. One-square-meter units provided maximum horizontal control, and all sediment was screened through $\frac{1}{8}$-in mesh. There was a single cultural stratum at the site, but flakes were also recovered from overlying loose eolian sand because of erosion of the cultural layer. The maximum depth of excavation was never more than about 30 cm below the modern ground surface, within the underlying sterile sand. Artifacts were concentrated below the surface in the same area where they appeared on the surface; units away from this concentration yielded few artifacts. Because of this tight clustering and the lack of any evidence of features, hand excavation soon reached a point of diminishing returns and was discontinued. As a final step, the entire site area was stripped with the

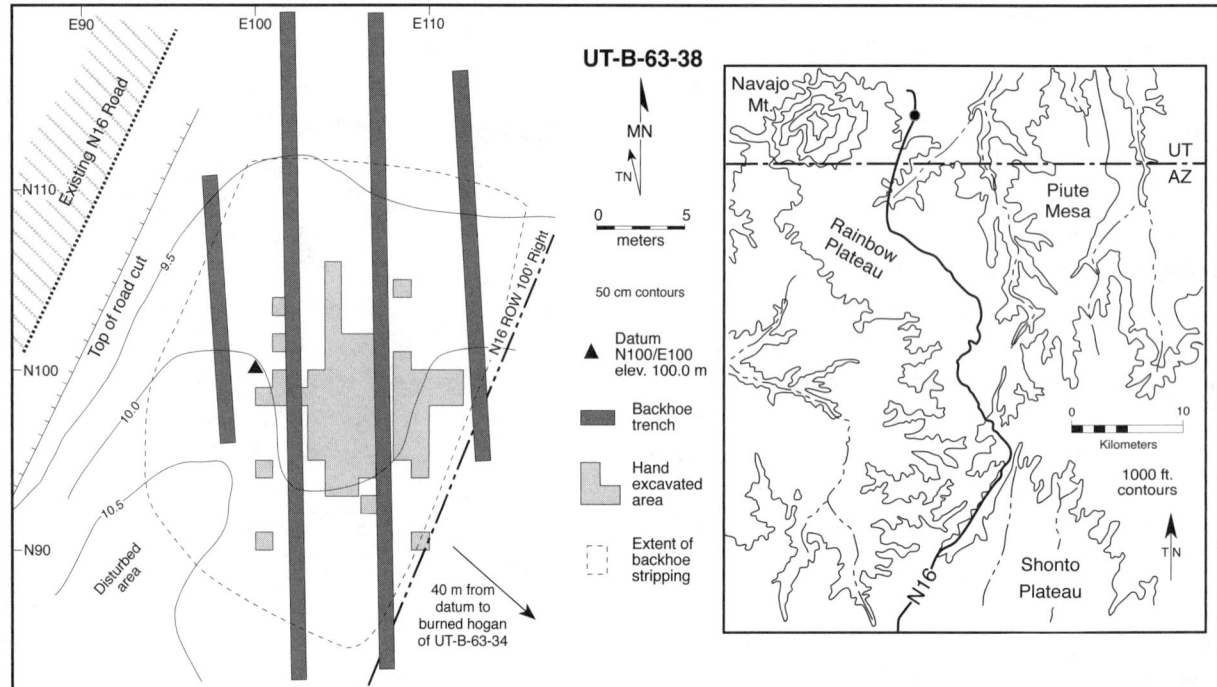

Figure 3.33. UT-B-63-38 site plan showing topography and work effort.

backhoe, a task that revealed no features, artifacts, or charcoal staining.

Excavation recovered a modest assemblage of flaked-stone artifacts (910 unused flakes, 11 used flakes, four flaked facial tools, one core/nodular tool) and eight grinding tools. The site perhaps served as a temporary residential camp, based on the presence of food-processing tools and the flaked-stone artifact assemblage. Grinding tools, but especially metates, are an important reason for classifying the site as a residential camp, given their role in daily food preparation and consumption. General camp activities of tool production and use are represented in the flaked-stone tool assemblage. The used flakes indicate a variety of general cutting and scraping tasks, such as might have occurred to process game or manufacture other tools. Biface reduction was clearly emphasized, and this appears to have involved early- through late-stage percussion thinning of bifaces but considerably less pressure finishing or modification of tools. The presence of notching flakes indicates that at least one projectile point was completed at the site. Virtually all of the debitage raw materials came from outside the immediate vicinity of the site, evidently from the Glen Canyon lowlands or even farther afield to the north. Given the small site size and dense concentration of remains, the locale might have been used just once by a single family or other small group.

UT-B-63-38 is assigned a generic Archaic temporal affiliation. It is one of just two Archaic sites excavated within the N16 ROW that could not be temporally placed based on radiocarbon dates. Lacking both hearths and diagnostic flaked-stone artifacts, the site is not definitively Archaic in age, although an Archaic affiliation is suggested by the one-hand beveled cobble manos, one of which is typical of early Archaic manos in the area. A serrated dart point tip also appears to be supportive of an Archaic affiliation; point serration is moderately common during the Archaic but poorly represented at Basketmaker II sites.

Tsé Haal'á (UT-B-63-30)

Tsé Haal'á, which in Navajo means "rocks scattered about in large numbers," is an extensive surface scatter of stone artifacts (chiefly metate fragments and debitage), along with some sherds (Figure 3.34). The site is situated on a gentle sand-covered slope at an average elevation of 1,719 m (5,640 ft) at the northeast foot of Navajo Mountain. The remains clearly derive from several different periods of prehistory, but the principal component dates to the late Archaic, roughly 3,000 radiocarbon years ago; it is likely that most of the recovered artifacts are from that time. The Puebloan artifacts scattered sparsely across the site are likely from the intensive use of the general area

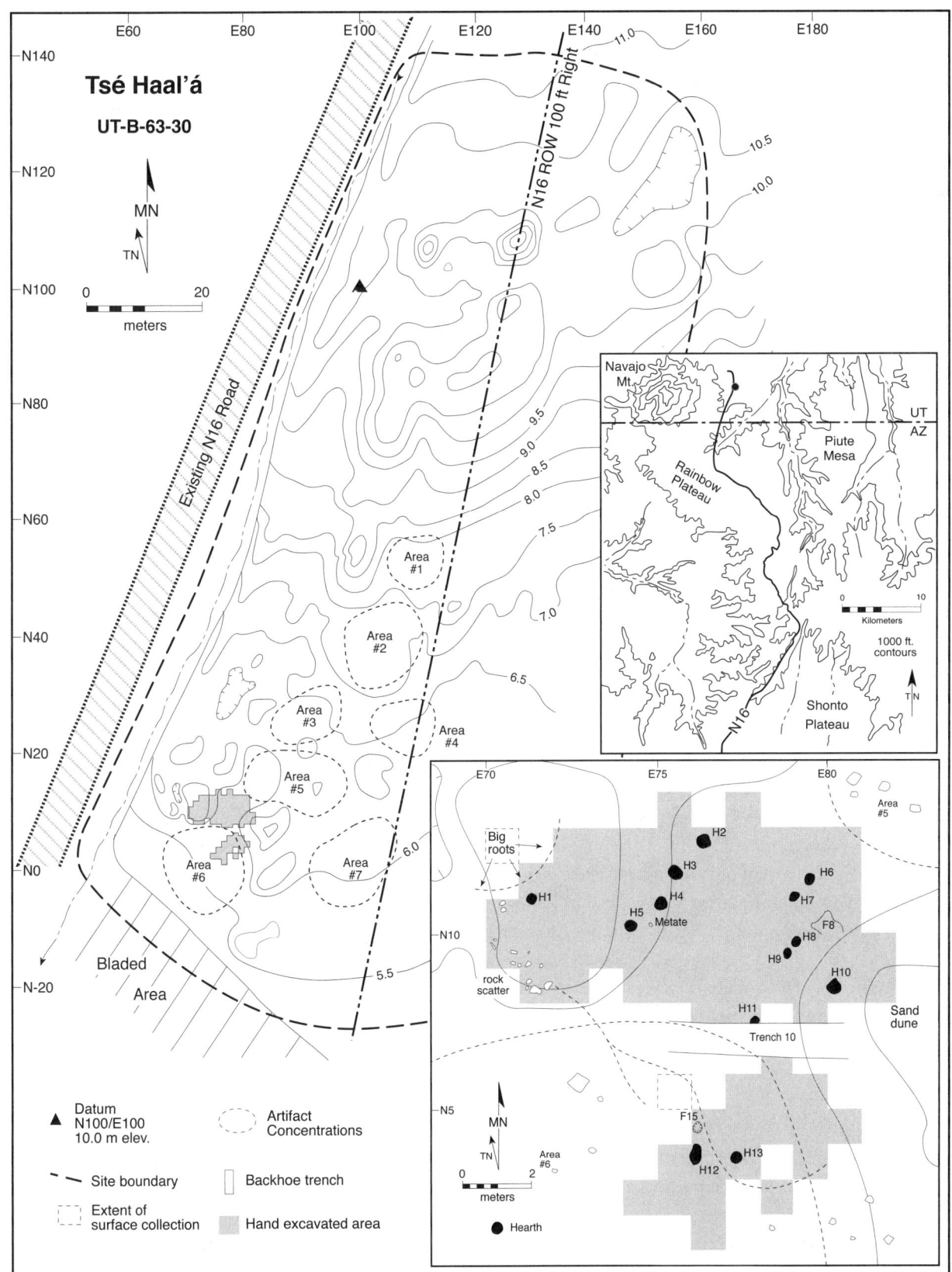

Figure 3.34. Tsé Haal'á site plan showing topography, work effort, and excavated features.

between late Pueblo II and late Pueblo III. Although much of the site is deflated, with the remains occurring as a lag deposit, a portion remained partially intact in the southern part of the site, buried beneath 30–40 cm of eolian sand. The buried portion of the site contained 13 basin hearths, as well as the same types of artifacts that characterized the site as a whole. A large but diffuse portion of the artifact scatter occurs outside of the N16 ROW. This area looks to be entirely deflated, with all artifacts occurring as a lag deposit on a veneer of sand over bedrock; thus it seems unlikely that this unstudied portion can contribute information different from what was obtained from the investigated portion.

Data-recovery excavations focused on a comparatively small portion of the overall site area as originally mapped, a portion in the southwestern part where a partially intact cultural stratum lay buried beneath 30–40 cm of eolian sand. Here a backhoe test trench exposed a probable hearth. Workers initially dug a series of units around the probable feature, which turned out to be a basin hearth (Hearth 11), and then expanded out both north and south following the cultural stratum until a maximum of 76 m² had been excavated. The overburden of eolian sand was shoveled out down to the upper boundary of the cultural stratum. This stratum was removed as a single layer using trowels and shovels, with all sediment screened through ⅛-in mesh and all remains provenienced by 1-×-1-m unit. Excavation usually stopped several centimeters into the underlying sterile sand, but in a few units work extended deeper to verify that no remains occurred lower. Horizontal exposure revealed a total of 13 basin hearths, a pit, and a small rock concentration. These were excavated following the standard procedure for small features. Another task was the excavation of nine 2-×-2-m blocks in areas of concentrated artifacts where the cultural stratum appeared deflated and the remains occurred as a lag deposit. The remains found in these units always occurred within the first 5 cm of loose surface sand. This effort was directed at providing comparative data on artifact frequency and type between excavation units where the cultural stratum was intact and portions of the site that were deflated. Two additional tasks included collecting formal stone artifacts on the surface and backhoe trenching of an eolian dune immediately east of the hand-excavation area to be certain that no cultural stratum remained intact. The trenching verified that the surface artifact concentrations were not "activity areas" in a behavioral sense but, rather, were products of postdepositional processes that differentially exposed remains.

Excavations in the southwestern part of the site recovered more than 3,000 stone artifacts, with almost 1,500 more recovered from the surface, in both the 5-×-5-m surface collection units and the 2-×-2-m shovel-skimmed and screened units. Detailed comparison of stone artifact data from subsurface and surface contexts reveals few differences, suggesting that nearly all remains, except for a few notable exceptions, can be assigned to the late Archaic component. Debitage accounts for the vast majority of the artifacts, with flakes from bifacial tool reduction by both percussion and pressure constituting the majority of the classifiable debris. The flaked-stone tool assemblage also reflects this emphasis on bifacially thinned forms, especially those in advanced reduction stages. More than 70 percent of the tools have been bifacially worked, with the majority of these ($n = 23$) being finished projectile points, mainly dart-sized bases snapped in the haft from impact. Fully thinned stage 4 and 5 bifaces outnumber those from earlier reduction stages. It is evident that rearming broken hunting equipment was an important activity at the site, with snapped point bases removed from foreshafts and replaced with newly produced points. The moderately high incidence of notching flakes at Tsé Haal'á is a key piece of evidence supporting this scenario. Classifiable dart points include Elko Corner-notched and Elko Eared, with a clear dominance of the former. There are five points classified as Elko Corner-notched and another five stem fragments snapped across the notches while in the haft, all probably from Elko Corner-notched points. Three corner-notched points with purposefully flaked basal indentations or notches are classified as Elko Eared. Faunal remains from the site, although poorly preserved on account of lengthy surface exposure, also attest to the role of hunting, particularly of large game. Food-processing tools consist of well over a hundred fragmented metates and three manos. Given the overall quantity of artifacts, the spatial extent of the scatter, and the vast number of individual cores or nodules represented by the flaking debris and tools (far more than is apparent in the raw material categories), it is likely that the site represents a composite of many separate use episodes.

Potential evidence in support of site reuse comes from the radiocarbon dates for the hearths. AMS dates on carbonized fuel from six hearths range from 2,910 to 3,180 radiocarbon years ago but are not statistically the same.

The burning of old wood might account for the date discrepancies because only a date on a small-diameter twig is unlikely to overestimate age. Nonetheless, the twig date is the second-oldest date for the site, so if some of the other assays overestimate age, then multiple use episodes are evident. Five of the six dates can be grouped to form two averages, one with a calibrated two-sigma age range of 1390–1130 BC (Hearths 3, 11, and 13) and another with a calibrated two-sigma age range of 1210–1000 BC (Hearths 1 and 7). Hearth 2 remains ungrouped and older than the rest: 1530–1320 cal. BC (two sigma).

Tsé Haal'á appears to have functioned as an important temporary residential camp during the late Archaic. One prime attraction of this location was the slickrock plunge pools in the adjacent drainage, which hold water throughout much of the year. This site is only about 2 km downstream from Sand Dune Cave (Lindsay et al. 1968), a site well used by early Archaic foragers but evidently lacking a recognized late Archaic component. Tsé Haal'á and the late Archaic components at Three Dog Site clearly indicate that the foot of Navajo Mountain was occupied during the late Archaic and that some locations saw rather intensive and repeated use.

Atlatl Rock Cave (AZ-J-14-41)

Atlatl Rock Cave is a large dry shelter with stratified cultural deposits located on the southeast edge of the Rainbow Plateau at an elevation of about 1,990 m (Figure 3.35). Named after an associated petroglyph panel depicting oversized atlatls, the shelter contains evidence of early Archaic, Basketmaker, and Puebloan occupancy. Unfortunately, large-scale looting in 1993 destroyed upward of 60 m³ of cultural deposit, prompting emergency backfilling of the massive looter holes, as well as limited study and sampling of intact deposits and features, which gleaned valuable information, artifacts, and samples. Although the site was not part of the NMRAP per se, NNAD's work there was conducted in conjunction with the NMRAP and is reported here because of its relevance to the project.

The symmetric and spacious cave measures about 24 m deep from the dripline and 15 m wide for most of this length. The floor at the cave mouth is moderately steep for a distance of about 6 m; it then gradually levels off so that the back half is essentially flat. The arched ceiling is 2–4 m high, providing ample headroom. It is nearly devoid of smoke blackening, apart from one large patch toward the back southeast portion. It was principally the early Archaic occupants who blackened the roof, and the entire ceiling was once heavily sooted. Active spalling about 3700–2500 cal. BC removed all traces except for the one remnant where the roof has remained stable for the last 8,000 years. Besides the grotto, the site consists of a rock art panel on the cliff face immediately south of the cave mouth and an area of features and sparse habitation refuse in the open area below the cave to the southeast. In all, the site encompasses about 9,600 m² (120 m north–south × 80 m).

NNAD archaeologists worked five days at the site, during which time they produced an overall plan map, cleaned up looter backdirt to expose intact deposits and damaged features, excavated a few test units to sample features and deposits from the major episodes of cultural use, profiled the stratigraphic sections provided by looter broadside cuts and test units, and backfilled the site, returning it close to its previous appearance. An overall site plan illustrated the spatial relationship between the cave and the open habitation area. The contours of this map are given in meters above mean sea level; these are internally consistent, but they might be off by several meters from true elevation because we could not accurately tie our transit readings to a benchmark. A central datum (N100/E100) for a metric grid system used for horizontal provenience control within the cave was established on a remnant of a probable structure floor (Feature 3) of clay. A steel spike sunk into the floor at this point was left in place upon backfilling. To profile cave strata, the field crew removed backdirt from the base of the looter broadside cuts, to the maximum depth of disturbance. The approximately meter-high cuts were essentially vertical but somewhat sinuous and in several places were undercut. The crew made no attempt to straighten the cuts to conform with the grid system or resemble clean vertical sections. This would have facilitated measuring and drawing the stratigraphic sections, but at the price of having to cut away intact deposits and features. Some 16 m² of area along the base of the broadside cuts was cleared to expose about 24 linear meters of stratigraphic section. This effort exposed numerous damaged features, some consisting only of cist floors.

Time and personnel were insufficient to draw all of the exposed broadside cuts; only those that provided the best information and were representative of the overall depositional sequence were recorded. The crew drew the profiles following standard practice, using a level line and

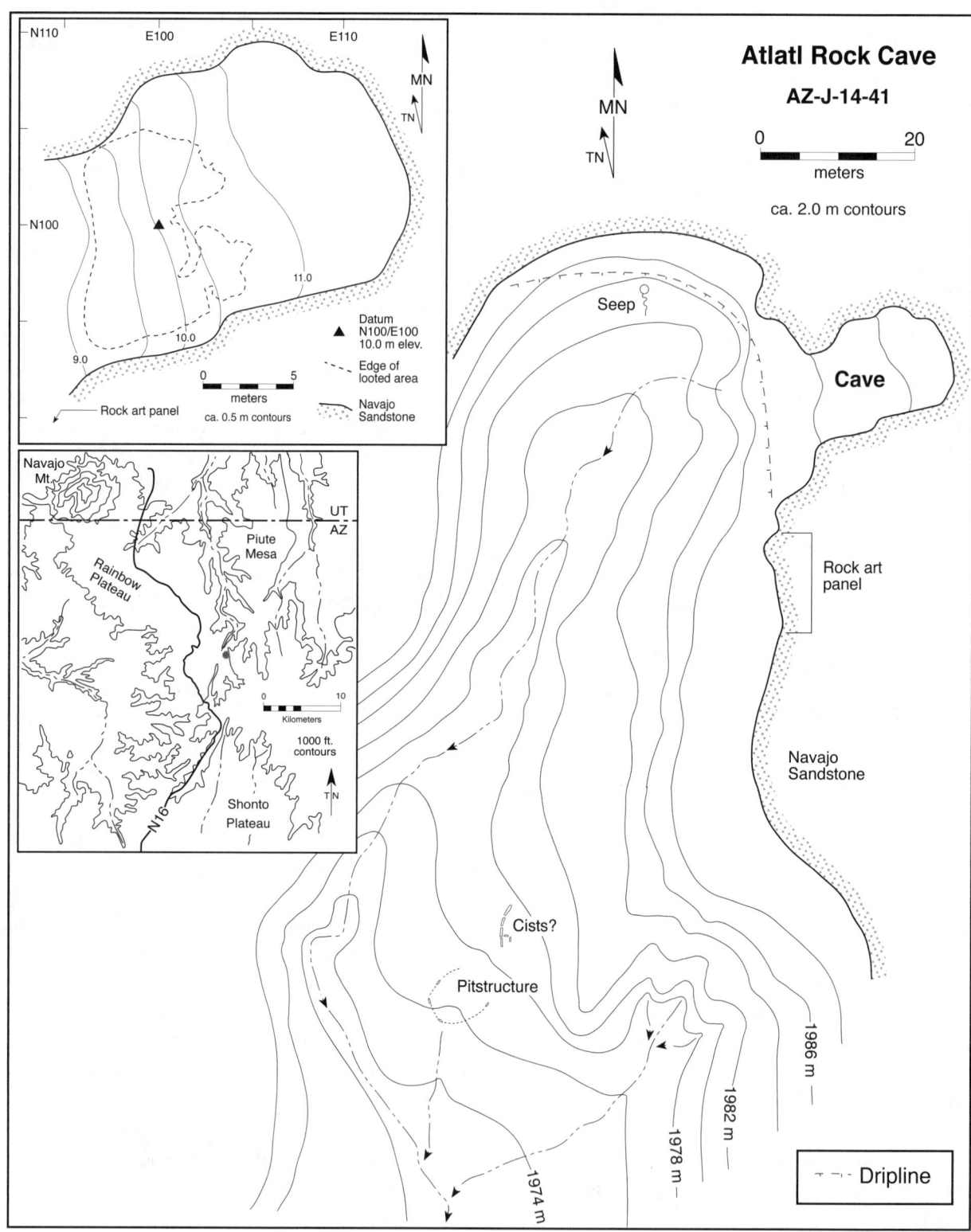

Figure 3.35. Atlatl Rock Cave site plan showing topography and exterior features, including the area damaged by looters where limited testing and stratigraphic sampling occurred.

measuring tape, but because the cuts varied by 50 cm or so on either side of our assumed sectional lines, some artistic license was necessary. After the profiles were drawn, exposed samples of organic remains such as corncobs and other artifacts were collected for possible radiocarbon dating or other forms of analysis; a flotation sample was also collected. The locations of all samples were recorded on the profiles, as well as on a detailed plan map showing features, the limits of disturbance, and the work effort.

Two test units were excavated to investigate the remaining depth of cultural and natural deposition. All excavation of intact deposits was by trowel, following natural strata, and all sediment from such work was screened through ⅛-in mesh. A 1-×-1-m test unit was placed at the very edge of the broadside cut in the northern disturbed area to augment the exposure of cave stratigraphy. In this area, looters had removed cave deposits down to the floors of two Basketmaker cists that had identical depths. Early Archaic deposits or a subsequent layer of rockfall lie directly under the cist floors. The test unit was excavated to a depth of about 1 m below the extent of looter disturbance, well within culturally sterile sand. The small remnant of a largely destroyed Basketmaker cist was completely excavated, and the floors of the two Basketmaker cists were removed. The fiber-tempered mortar used in construction was saved for ^{14}C dating. The second test unit, which measured 1.5 × 2 m, was placed at the southern edge of the southern looted area. The southeast corner of this unit was not excavated because the deposits there were intact for their full depth. Along the western and northern edges of the test unit the looters had removed all cultural deposition by pursuing their digging into the culturally sterile sand underlying the early Archaic deposits. Across the rest of the unit the looters had cut down into a rockfall layer under the Basketmaker deposits. The work here consisted of removing the remainder of the rockfall to expose the early Archaic deposit, excavating this, and sinking a portion of the unit into the underlying sterile sand. Removal of the rockfall revealed a whole grinding slab, several fragments of other grinding slabs, a few open-twined sandal portions, and other remains at the top of a thin early Archaic deposit. These remains were mapped in place prior to removal. These two test units provided a small sample of early Archaic remains within the cave but not of the later materials, which the looters had removed from these particular areas. A peninsular remnant of intact deposits separating the southern and northern cells of looter disturbance provided an opportunity to sample the more recent depositional units. This remnant measured about 2 m long, 1 m high, and from .5 to 1 m wide; the crew removed intact deposits from it by natural strata visible on both sides of the broadside cuts. Excavation for most of this sample area extended to the top of the rockfall layer that rested upon the early Archaic deposits, but at the south end of the peninsula it extended into the upper 10 cm of the culturally sterile sand below the early Archaic deposits. In this same area the remnants of two largely destroyed features, a cist and a pit, were totally excavated.

The final aspect of work was backfilling. The crew draped plastic window screen over the exposed broadside cuts, held in place by a line of rocks placed at the top of the cut. This was done to serve as demarcation between disturbed and undisturbed portions should future excavation ever be done at the site. Then the massive looter backdirt piles were moved back against the profile to stabilize it. Rock from outside the cave was brought in to help in backfilling and to provide something of a barrier to further digging. The looter pits were filled and recontoured to give the cave a more natural appearance. Unusual artifacts and other remains such as whole corncobs were collected during backfilling; these account for the quantity of nonprovenienced remains.

Atlatl Rock Cave joins Sand Dune and Dust Devil as examples of natural shelters on the Rainbow Plateau that were lived in during the early Archaic but little used by foragers during the subsequent five millennia. Not until the first farmers inhabited the region did the caves see renewed occupancy at levels that resulted in obvious cultural deposition. At Dust Devil Cave, a thick layer of eolian sand (Unit V) separated the roughly meter-thick early Archaic Unit IV from the Basketmaker accumulation of Unit VI (Ambler 1996). In contrast, the hiatus deposit at Atlatl Rock Cave was roof spall. Radiocarbon dating of oak leaves, blown into the cave and trapped within the spall layer, places the rockfall episode during an approximate 1,200-year interval centered on about 3100 cal. BC. Between about 3700 and 5500 cal. BC there was no deposition in the cave, cultural or natural, and the early Archaic cultural deposit lay exposed on the surface. This roughly 2,000 years of negligible deposition parallels Schroedl and Coulam's (1994) conclusions about deposit formation at Cowboy Cave. Three extended intervals of forager use of that cave, each separated by a few thousand years of nonuse, left cultural deposits resting one upon the other, with no matrix corresponding to the periods of abandonment. In geologic terms, the deposits are unconformable. Failure to recognize stratigraphic unconformities in situations where different-age cultural deposits rest directly upon each other can result in a badly garbled archaeological record (Schroedl and Coulam 1994:25). Fortunately, at Atlatl Rock Cave the rockfall deposit provided a clear unit of demarcation between the early Archaic and Basketmaker cultural units.

The rockfall deposit at Atlatl Rock Cave was also a fortunate occurrence because it served to partially insulate early Archaic deposits from Basketmaker activities in the shelter. Minus this protective barrier, it is likely that the early Archaic deposits would have been largely churned up and lost. A 10- to 15-cm layer of loose ash and organics on the surface of a shelter would not survive long under heavy foot traffic and the excavation of numerous pits and cists. It is easy to envision why some sites with abundant Basketmaker features and deposits, such as White Dog Cave or Turkey Pen Ruin, evidently lack intact Archaic deposits.

From the limited work I cannot exclude the possibility of late Archaic forager use of the Atlatl Rock Cave. There was not, however, an obvious late Archaic depositional unit. The problem is that any forager accumulations from this relatively recent interval would have rested on top of the rockfall layer and been directly exposed to Basketmaker disturbance. Excavations at both Sand Dune and Dust Devil caves produced Gypsum points, but not from a distinct depositional unit that was clearly produced by foragers, such as Unit IV at Cowboy Cave (Jennings 1980; Schroedl and Coulam 1994). Extensive and careful excavation would be necessary to ascertain whether late Archaic deposits are truly absent from Atlatl Rock Cave. Even during the period when farming was becoming established, deposits from the initial interval of crop use might have become thoroughly intermixed with those that date slightly later, after food production became more important and storage within caves intensified with the digging of pits and cists.

Basketmaker II use of Atlatl Rock Cave seems to have been principally for storage and not habitation or burial. The latter cannot be claimed with great certainty because so little of the site was studied in systematic fashion. Yet, while moving some 60 m³ of sediment to clear the profiles and backfill the looter holes, only a single cranial fragment was found. Given the amount of looter disturbance, we should have found more scattered human bone if burials had been present in any quantity. As to habitation use, there should have been considerably more charcoal and ash in Unit IV if the cave had actually been lived in. Indeed, one of the noticeable changes in the deposits was the increase in charcoal and ash above the Basketmaker II unit. Basketmaker II use of the cave is dated to the first several centuries AD; earlier occupancy by these first farmers is expected based on the age of nearby open sites. Kin Kahuna, a substantial Basketmaker residential site located less than 5 km away, is dated nearly to 400 cal. BC. Basketmaker use of caves farther east and southeast is dated substantially earlier (Smiley 1993; Smiley et al. 1986). There is reason to suspect that additional dating might eventually reveal that Basketmaker II use of Atlatl Rock Cave was similar in age to cultural strata in White Dog and Kinbiko caves, which were in use by about 600 cal. BC (Smiley et al. 1986); however, no evidence currently exists for corn this early on the Rainbow Plateau.

It was during the transition from Basketmaker II to Basketmaker III that there appears to have been a shift toward more residential use of the cave. In addition to the greater evidence of fire use, this shift is reflected by the less massive quality of the upper Basketmaker deposits, where cultural deposition seems to have resulted from a relatively fine accretion of living debris. The shift toward more residential use is correlated with the construction of at least one possible structure in the cave, which has a radiocarbon age within the transitional interval—ca. cal. AD 250–600. It is also possible that the pithouse and other habitation features in the open area below the cave also date to this interval; this is based on the use of sandstone slabs to entirely line the pithouse, something that is only seen at sites in the area that contain early pottery (Obelisk).

Atlatl Rock Cave is significant for its record spanning the Basketmaker II–Basketmaker III transition. This is evidenced by both the unbroken series of radiocarbon dates on high-quality materials that span the centuries from about cal. AD 150 to 650 and the continuous cultural deposits that correspond to this interval. So far, few sites are known that provide an uninterrupted record of human occupation for this time span. The cave record reflects the larger pattern of settlement history for Rainbow Plateau. The NMRAP excavations, coupled with recent radiocarbon dating of remains from previously investigated sites, have shown continuous settlement of the plateau during the transitional interval (Geib and Spurr 2000). Moreover, the record from the plateau reveals that the technological and biological innovations that provide the traditional hallmarks of Basketmaker III were adopted at various times by different households, probably for different reasons. Change from Basketmaker II to Basketmaker III took place over the span of several hundred years and did not involve a dramatic and sudden panregional adoption of a new trait complex.

Puebloan use of the cave seems to have been quite limited, because the corresponding depositional unit is thin and not uniformly present in the exposures available for study. Though minimally sampled, the Puebloan deposit is heavily ashy, and at least two basin hearths originate from the unit. Given the heavy amounts of ash, which indicates full combustion of fuel instead of smothering the coals as happens with pit roasting, it is possible that the hearths were campfires related to overnight stays in the cave. The cave continued to be used for storage of corn and other produce, as evidenced by a storage cist, dated ca. cal. AD 820–1030. This was the only storage feature that I could correlate with the Puebloan unit; thus, it seems that the cave was used considerably less for storage than during Basketmaker times.

Atlatl Rock Cave was a pristine cave site containing stratified cultural deposits from several thousand years of human occupancy. It was one of a handful of similar sites on the Colorado Plateau that seemed destined to make it into the twenty-first century without being ruined by looters or excavated by archaeologists. Then in 1993 the inevitable happened when criminals destroyed a major portion of the deposits and features, greatly reducing the scientific value of the site. This cave should have been preserved for posterity, but unfortunately, this is rarely achieved for sites of its caliber. It would be extremely difficult these days for archaeologists to justify permission to excavate 60 m^3 from a cave such as this. The basic objection would be the need to preserve in place the rich record for future study after field and laboratory techniques have both improved and theory has advanced. Even if sufficient cause could be made, it would be a daunting task to find the funding for both the fieldwork and the analyses of the great diversity of remains that would be recovered. The unfortunate truth is that looters have no such constraints. Sites like Atlatl Rock Cave are an endangered species, for without some extreme measures their days are numbered. It is becoming depressingly common for archaeologists to be relegated to cleanup and damage assessment in the wake of severe looting, salvaging vestiges of remains and data from sites that were previously off limits to study. Such was our fate with Atlatl Rock Cave. Although NNAD recovered valuable new information and artifacts and samples for future study, there is no way to recoup what was lost. Our ability to examine many important issues is greatly diminished every time a site like Atlatl Rock Cave is lost to science.

CHAPTER 4

Summary and Interpretation of Archaic Period Forager Remains

When Guernsey and Kidder (1921) presented their summary of Basketmaker remains from the Kayenta region of northeast Arizona, they described a preceramic farming culture that predated the Puebloan cliff dwellers. The origins of the Basketmakers were a mystery, because none of the numerous shelters that the researchers excavated produced evidence of a prior hunter-gatherer stage—they found no remains underlying those of the Basketmakers. Granted that excavation technique in the early 1900s was not what it is today and that the loose sands of the shelters where Guernsey and Kidder worked can challenge even the most meticulous modern excavator, still, had obvious cultural layers rested below those with Basketmaker materials, then these keen observers likely would have noted them. This absence of evidence was not, however, equated with evidence of absence, so Kidder (1962 [1924]) conjectured that the Basketmakers must have developed from a prior population of hunter-gatherers. Accordingly, the formulators of the Pecos classification left open a developmental stage (Basketmaker I) for the hypothetical forager ancestors of the Basketmaker II farmers (Kidder 1927). There was virtual agreement among the 1927 Pecos Conference participants that "agriculture was taken up by a previous resident...nomadic or semi-nomadic people" (Kidder 1927:489). The conceptual foundation for this view might have derived from an implicit assumption of continuous cultural development within single regions and areas (Berry and Berry 1986:255).

Today, of course, the first Basketmaker stage is known as the Archaic, and by slow degrees, especially since the 1960s, archaeologists have accumulated evidence for the preagricultural foragers on the Colorado Plateau. But the evidence produced has yet to accord with the apparent unanimous position in 1927 that farming was adopted by long-resident Archaic foragers. An initial finding in this regard, and indeed the first recognized discovery of demonstrable Archaic remains directly underlying Basketmaker materials, occurred in 1961 when J. Richard Ambler excavated Sand Dune Cave at the foot of Navajo Mountain and tested the nearby Dust Devil Cave (Lindsay et al. 1968). At both sites he recovered distinctive open-twined sandals from cultural deposits directly under those with typical Basketmaker artifacts. Unlike anything reported from Basketmaker sites, the sandals raised the possibility that ancestral remains had finally been unearthed.[1] Radiocarbon dates on three of the sandals from Sand Dune Cave came as a surprise: they were some 5,000 years older than the maximum postulated age of Basketmaker II—the sandals ranged in age from 7150 to 7700 BP (Lindsay et al. 1968:96). These sandals were thus not immediately ancestral to the Basketmaker culture. Indeed, given the age disparity, they perhaps had no affinity whatsoever with Basketmaker materials beyond occurring within the same grottos.

There are many reasons why the findings from a cave or two might not contain an accurate record of prehistoric use for an entire region—Thomas's (1989:426–430) "fallacy of the 'typical' site." No matter how deeply stratified and materially rewarding a site is, it can never serve as a model for past forager societies—it is merely another sample, albeit a rich one, of cultural variability. As Wills puts it, "We need to consider individual sites and artifacts as participants in and products of socioeconomic systems, not models for such systems" (1988:155). Although Sand Dune and Dust Devil caves were high-information sites of the kind that can provide about as detailed a glimpse of past lifeways as is possible for early foragers, they nonetheless represented single data points.

When the NMRAP began in 1991, Archaic prehistory for the Kayenta region remained little changed since the 1960s. Numerous large contract excavations had been conducted in the region for power plants, coal leases, and rights-of-way for roads, railroads, and transmission lines, thereby greatly increasing our understanding of Puebloan and Basketmaker periods, but the Archaic period remained mainly a blank slate. Even the largest undertaking in the region, the excavations conducted for the Peabody Western coal lease on northern Black Mesa, provided minimal information (Parry et al. 1994; Smiley 2002b). In all, that project identified just seven Archaic sites, and Smiley (2002b:30) recently reassigned many of these to the Basketmaker II period. As Smiley puts it, "Rarely have so many searched so intensively in an area of such limited size for so few old sites" (2002b:15). Virtually the same result came from the large sample survey of Cedar Mesa—abundant Basketmaker and Puebloan sites but no certain Archaic sites (Matson 1991:8): "The Basketmaker II culture...appears as if out of nowhere to begin the Anasazi cycle of occupations and abandonments on Cedar Mesa" (Matson 1991:10).

Thus, I had some degree of hope that the NMRAP would provide an opportunity to overcome the sampling deficiency for the Kayenta region by excavating a series of Archaic sites on the Rainbow Plateau and far-northern edge of the Shonto Plateau. One basic interest was what the NMRAP excavations would reveal about forager occupation of the area. Would there be a continuous record of forager occupancy culminating in Basketmaker II or one that was punctuated by hiatuses, a discontinuous record? Would the NMRAP excavations reveal a pattern similar to that evident for Sand Dune Cave and Dust Devil Cave—early Archaic occupancy followed by Basketmaker occupancy, but with no evident link between the two? These questions ultimately relate to evaluating two alternative, though not mutually exclusive, pathways to the agricultural transition: the diffusion of crops to in situ forager populations or the migration of farming groups from some southern source area (see review by Matson 1991, 2002). Moreover, what would be revealed about forager occupation during the middle Holocene (middle Archaic), a time that previous authors had recognized as one of greatly diminished population (Schroedl 1976) or outright regional abandonment (Berry and Berry 1986; cf. Geib 1996a). It seemed that the NMRAP excavations would make a solid contribution by providing an initial documentation of forager remains at open sites for this northern portion of the Kayenta Anasazi region.

THE NMRAP ARCHAIC SITE SAMPLE

The Archaic period denotes a socioeconomic adaptation of broad-spectrum gathering and hunting that developed during the early Holocene, beginning at around 8000 cal. BC or shortly thereafter, and lasted many thousands of years into the late Holocene until the introduction of Mesoamerican domesticates at about 2100 cal. BC. The 2,600 years from roughly 2100 cal. BC to cal. AD 500 is designated herein as the Archaic–Formative transition, during which two differing adaptive strategies are recognized. The NMRAP excavations recovered evidence for a continued hunter-gatherer lifestyle until slightly past 1000 cal. BC, with domesticates not appearing until about 400 cal. BC at the earliest. The remains from this continued foraging adaptation during the transitional interval are considered here as late Archaic, whereas those associated with maize and dating after about 400 cal. BC but prior to cal. AD 500 are designated as Basketmaker II. There is no evidence to suggest continuity between Paleoindian and Archaic populations in the Kayenta region—point types and other aspects of Archaic material culture differ markedly from those of the preceding Paleoindian period. The gathering of plant resources was more heavily emphasized than hunting by Archaic foragers, including the collection of low-ranking resources such as small seeds. Hunting continued to be important, but small game was emphasized.

Excavations within the N16 ROW disclosed Archaic remains at 14 sites, with multiple components at a few of these. A related undertaking involved the testing of Atlatl Rock Cave on the southeast edge of the Rainbow Plateau, which contained early Archaic deposits and features. Combined, this work contributed significant knowledge about Archaic foragers (pre-pottery and nonagricultural) for the Kayenta region. Some basic information about each of the Archaic sites is given in Table 4.1, with locations shown in Figure 4.1. This figure also shows two previously investigated caves known to have Archaic components: Dust Devil and Sand Dune. The sample consists mainly of temporary camps, likely used briefly and for specific purposes. At least some of them appear hunting related; others may have served in plant processing; and still others were perhaps the remains from simple overnight stays. At least three of the late Archaic components (two at one site) appear to have functioned as residential camps. Most of the Archaic sites date to the early portion of this period, before about 5000 cal. BC. At

TABLE 4.1. Summary of Archaic Sites Excavated During the Navajo Mountain Road Archaeological Project

Site Name/No.	Function	Temporal Assignment	¹⁴C Dating Dates	¹⁴C Dating Date Range (BP)	Visibility Degree	Visibility Cause
Tsé Haal'á, UT-B-63-30	residential camp	late Archaic	6	3180–2890	high	deflation
UT-B-63-38	residential camp	Archaic	0	unknown	partial	deflation
Three Dog Site, UT-B-63-39	residential camp	late Archaic	19	3390–2520	none	exposed in backhoe trenches
Bonsai Bivouac, AZ-J-2-55	temporary camp	Archaic	1	8180 & 4450	none	exposed by backhoe stripping
Sapo Seco, AZ-J-2-6	temporary camp	early Archaic	1	8230	none	exposed in backhoe trench
Dune Hollow, AZ-J-2-2	temporary camp	early Archaic	2	8270 & 8070	none	exposed in backhoe trench
Mouse House, AZ-J-3-7	temporary camp	early Archaic	2	7960 & 7930	none	exposed in backhoe trenches and stripping
Atlatl Rock Cave, AZ-J-14-41	residential camp	early Archaic	3	7900–7010	none	exposed in looter holes
Big Bend, AZ-J-14-13	temporary camp, processing	early and late Archaic	6	7530 & 3360–3070	partial	exposed by roadcuts, other disturbance, and backhoe trenches
Tres Campos, AZ-J-14-12	temporary camp, hunting emphasis	early Archaic	5	8260–5910	partial	exposed by roadcut and deflation
Polly's Place, AZ-J-14-31	temporary camp	early Archaic	3	7970–6940	none	exposed in backhoe trench
Windy Mesa, AZ-J-14-28	temporary camp, hunting emphasis	early Archaic	3	8270–5990	none	exposed in backhoe trench
Pee Wee Grande, AZ-J-14-26	temporary camp, processing	early Archaic	4	8230–7080	partial	drainage
Hólahéi Scatter, AZ-J-14-23	temporary camp, hunting emphasis	Archaic	0	unknown[a]	partial	exposed by roadcut
The Pits, AZ-J-14-17	temporary camp, hunting emphasis	late Archaic	1	3740[b]	partial	exposed by roadcut

Note: Sites are ordered from north to south.

[a] Natural burns of 2220 and 2020 BP provide a minimal age for the assemblage.

[b] Two other hearths unassociated with remains have ages of 9780 and 6030 BP.

least five components date to the late Archaic after about 1500 cal. BC but before 800 cal. BC; these sites lack domesticates. Volume 2 of the Web-posted supporting documentation provides detailed descriptions for the Archaic sites, including Atlatl Rock Cave, with chapter 3 of this report briefly characterizing all sites, the excavation effort at each, and their components.

Although the NMRAP sample includes both early and late Archaic remains, the sites/components dating to these intervals do not allow for a useful discussion of change through time. This is so because of the different nature of the components and their spatial distribution. For example, the only residential camps in the sample date to the late Archaic and occur near the foot of Navajo Mountain. There are several good examples of probable hunting camps dating to the early Archaic but few from the late Archaic. As such, I tend to treat the Archaic as a single unit and have not subdivided data into early and late Archaic groups for comparison purposes. In the future, after more Archaic sites have been excavated in the region, it should prove informative to examine change in forager lifeways across the Holocene.

The Archaic archaeological record of the N16 ROW and elsewhere across much of the Kayenta region is largely a buried phenomenon. Only three of the NMRAP Archaic sites (AZ-J-14-16, UT-B-63-30, and UT-B-63-38) were partially exposed on the surface from natural erosion; the other Archaic sites or components were buried and hidden from view. The buried Archaic sites were found either because prior road construction had sectioned and exposed them (three cases, AZ-J-14-12, -21, and -23) or because the Archaic remains fortuitously occurred under a Basketmaker or Puebloan site that was trenched. The Archaic archaeological record thus appears to be largely obscured from view, at least the portion of it containing intact features. Because the Archaic record was largely unknown prior to preparation of the data-recovery plan, few research topics were specifically

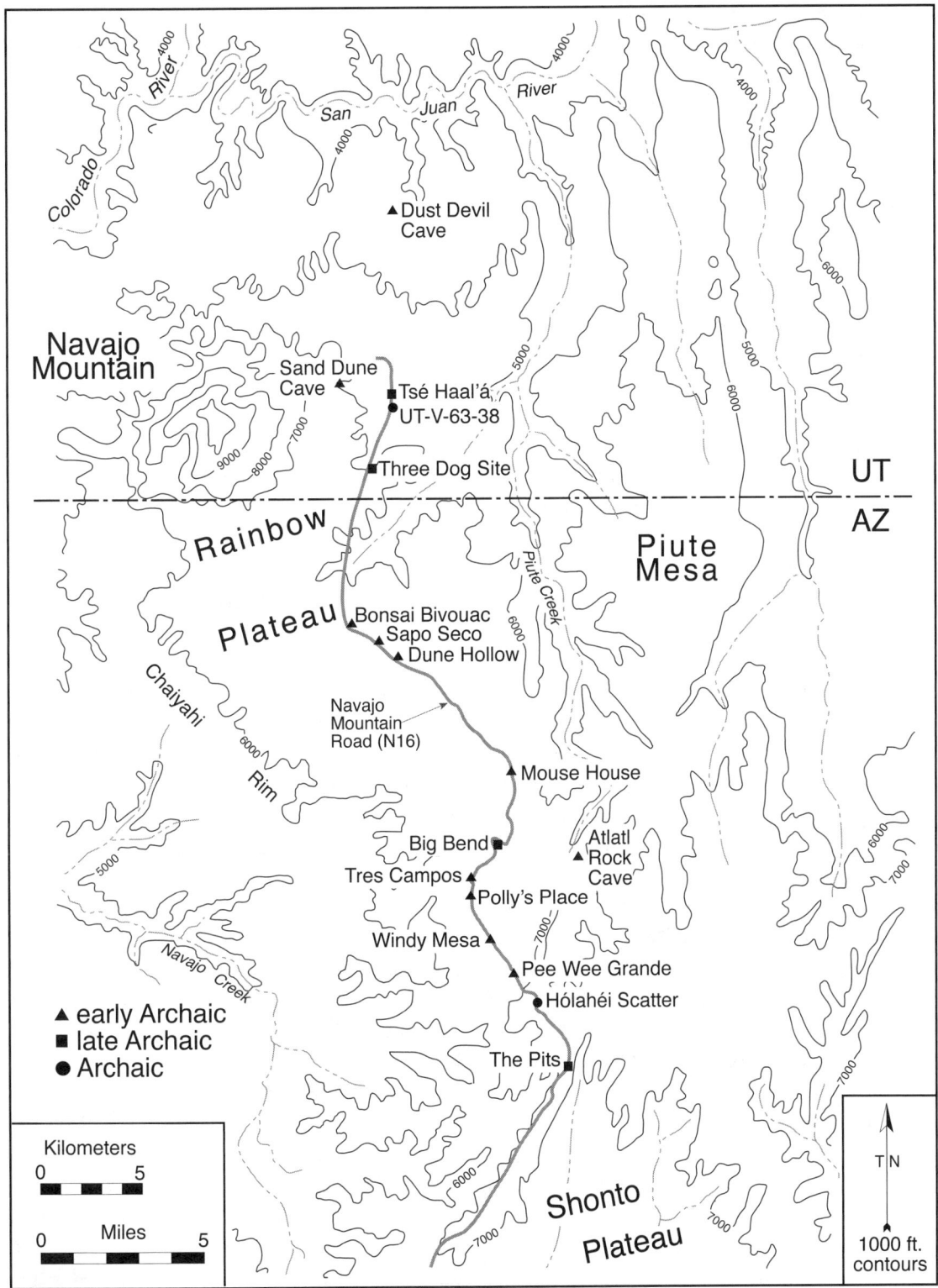

Figure 4.1. Distribution of Navajo Mountain Road Archaeological Project Archaic sites by principal temporal component; also shown are Dust Devil and Sand Dune caves, two previously investigated sites known to have early Archaic components.

focused on these resources, though the overall general approach was applicable. Providing basic documentation of chronology, lithic assemblage variability, and subsistence remains for the Archaic components is a significant contribution of the NMRAP, but I have also tried to use the findings to explore some broader issues.

For people who leave the remnants of their lives scattered across vast territories and in mostly low-density concentrations, archaeologists must work extra hard to assemble enough evidence to piece together a reasonably detailed picture of past life. Such is the nature of investigations into Archaic foragers on the Colorado Plateau. Even the richest of Archaic sites, such as Cowboy and Dust Devil caves, provide only a limited view, a paltry set of remains. This problem is compounded tenfold at open sites where the ravages of time run unchecked. The loss of perishables reduces an already meager forager trace to a mere fraction of its original content. Thousands of years of erosion and deposition and disturbance by rodents, roots, and other causes further eradicate remains and obscure spatial patterns. Erosion allows archaeologists to find Archaic remains, but usually at a cost: hundreds or thousands of years of accumulation are mixed together on a single surface, often without any datable features or subsistence remains. Burial has the benefit of some preservation and the potential for stratigraphic separation of discrete temporal intervals, but it imposes a harsh penalty: the remains are lost from view, thus rarely encountered, and costly to study if found.

The generally sparse and dispersed archaeological record left by hunter-gatherers of the distant past requires intensive investigation for what often seems like poor returns, especially when contrasted with the often abundant information and remains recovered from Puebloan sites. This was a common experience for NNAD excavators on this project. Weeks of excavation at an Archaic site might produce less than what was recovered in one day of excavation at a Puebloan site. Of course quantity is not the goal of science, but open sites have limitations to evidence that are worth recognizing.

One of the principal of these concerns subsistence information. Even when open Archaic sites contain hearths, such as nearly all of those reported in this volume, subsistence remains are usually in short supply, an evident preservation problem. This is especially true for the oldest sites, those of the early Archaic. The often sharp contrast in the types of evidence recovered from open and sheltered sites provides little doubt as to why archaeologists

TABLE 4.2. Comparison of Macrobotanical Recovery from Early Archaic Contexts of Navajo Mountain Road Archaeological Project Open Sites and Atlatl Rock Cave

Variable	Open Sites (n = 8)	Atlatl Rock Cave
Number of Samples	25	4
Liters of Sediment	97	4
% of Samples with Seeds	40.0	100.0
Number of Seeds	15	300+
Number of Taxa	6[a]	17

[a] Includes one case of an unidentified seed.

interested in forager subsistence might do better testing a single shelter than with excavating scores of open sites. NMRAP findings effectively illustrate this point by contrasting the early Archaic macrobotanical remains recovered from open sites with those from the limited test of Atlatl Rock Cave near to the N16 road ROW. An analysis of 25 flotation samples totaling 97 liters of sediment from hearths at eight early Archaic open sites resulted in the recovery of just 15 burned seeds from six taxa, with five of the seeds being Chenopodium and six being pinyon nut shells (Table 4.2). In contrast, just four 1-liter flotation samples from early Archaic deposits in Atlatl Rock Cave next to this road contained not just orders of magnitude more seeds but 17 plant taxa. Moreover, excavations of shelters often result in the recovery of human feces, thereby greatly increasing our understanding of subsistence (several feces were recovered from Atlatl Rock Cave).

The general lack of macrobotanical subsistence remains at open sites is best explained as a result of the mechanical breakdown of carbonized plant parts with time. The longer remains are buried in the ground, the greater the opportunity for degradation, but time is not the only variable. It appears that the depth and rapidity of burial also play an important role. This can be gauged by tabulating macrobotanical plant remains from NMRAP open sites dating to two different Archaic intervals—early and late—and by separating those of the late Archaic by shallowness of burial (Table 4.3). The late Archaic features of Three Dog Site were rapidly and deeply (up to 1.4 m) buried by eolian sand, and they remained buried until their excavation by NNAD. In contrast, the late Archaic features at Tsé Haal'á and Big Bend appear to have been shallowly buried until the time of excavation. Shallow burial leaves any carbonized macrobotanical remains exposed to alternating cycles of wet/dry and freeze/thaw as well as more intensive root and animal activity. The end

TABLE 4.3. Comparison of Macrobotanical Recovery from Early and Late Archaic Contexts of Navajo Mountain Road Archaeological Project Open Sites and from Buried Late Archaic Contexts

	Early Archaic Open Site	Late Archaic		
Variable		Open Site	Deeply Buried	Shallowly Buried
Number of Samples	25	46	27	19
Liters of Sediment	97	184	108	76
% of Samples with Seeds	40.0	32.6	28.3	5.3
Number of Seeds	15	1,024	1,023	1
Number of Taxa	6	6	6	1

result is the mechanical breakdown of nearly all carbonized plant portions, with seeds and like structures entirely lost; even charcoal becomes degraded, reduced to powder and minute flecks.

NMRAP Archaic Chronology
Radiocarbon Dating

Temporal placement for the NMRAP Archaic sites was based exclusively on radiocarbon dating, using both standard beta-decay counting and accelerator mass spectrometry. Obsidian-hydration dating was attempted at two Archaic sites early in the project, but the evident ambiguities of the technique, despite controlling for local soil temperature and relative humidity, led me to abandon it (see discussion that follows).

The radiocarbon method is well known and understood by archaeologists, so there is no reason to review the technique here (see Taylor 1987, 2000). A few words are in order though about sample selection and processing for the NMRAP. At open Archaic sites of the region, only hearths usually yield carbon samples for dating purposes. Bone is poorly preserved, if at all, especially on the earliest sites, and it often lacks datable collagen. The one attempt with bone dating for the project failed because both of the bone samples submitted (from Hólahéi Scatter) lacked a collagen fraction; the samples yielded only organics that had infiltrated the bone since burial.

Archaic hearths contain variable amounts of carbon, with age appearing to be the principal determinant in the degree of preservation—the older the feature, the less carbon it contains, especially in the easily recoverable form of charcoal chunks. Most of the excavated hearths were filled with black charcoal-stained sediment containing generally sparse charcoal flecks. The carbonized fuel of these features appears to have been reduced largely to charcoal dust by mechanical processes (alternating wet/dry, freeze/thaw, plus intensive root and animal activity), which made radiocarbon sampling a challenge, but NNAD crews nonetheless endeavored to recover radiocarbon samples in the field from every Archaic hearth. If carbonized remains could not be secured directly from features during excavation, they were sought in the ⅛-in mesh screening of feature fill, with a fallback strategy of using carbonized remains separated from flotation samples. The amount of charcoal collected in any specific case was dependent upon preservation, with the general goal always to collect enough for a standard beta-decay date (at least 2 g of clean charcoal but preferably 10 g). Given that I usually had to rely on wood charcoal for dating and that temporal accuracy is less important for the Archaic, there was every reason to submit sufficient charcoal to allow for beta-decay radiocarbon analysis rather than the more costly AMS analysis. By this means I reserved dating funds for Basketmaker II chronology, where AMS analysis had a far larger payoff. As it turned out, beta-decay counting was rarely possible for Archaic features except for the late Archaic hearths of Three Dog Site, where rapid burial and relatively recent age appear to have enhanced charcoal preservation. At most of the NMRAP Archaic sites, NNAD crews could only collect small to minute samples from each hearth, sometimes little more than a few tiny charcoal flecks that weighed less than .1 g. In no case did I want to rely on bulk sediment samples from hearths because of the chance for contamination from more recent carbon, especially humic acids.[2]

Prior to submitting samples to a dating laboratory, I inspected each one to see if any identifiable remains had been recovered that might provide a better age estimate than carbonized wood. Hearth charcoal routinely overestimates the age of cultural events because hundreds of years usually have elapsed between the death of woody materials and their use as fuel (Schiffer 1982, 1986; Smiley 1985, 1998b). Some of the Archaic hearths contained sagebrush charcoal along with that of trees; indeed, some Archaic hearths appear to have been fueled mostly with brush. Until late in this project I thought that the small-diameter twigs of sagebrush would be less likely than tree limbs to overestimate age and so submitted sagebrush samples whenever this material was found in hearth fill. Some early dating results initially supported the idea that sagebrush provided dates closely corresponding in time to the behavioral event, but the analysis of subsequent samples indicated that this is not necessarily true, a finding discussed further below. Other remains found on occasion in Archaic hearths and used for radiocarbon dating included juniper seeds and small twigs other than sagebrush, those less than 5 mm in diameter and usually less than 2 mm. These were preferentially submitted for dating under the assumption that they too would provide a better age estimate than the charcoal of larger-diameter tree limbs.

If hearth radiocarbon samples contained nothing other than wood charcoal, I sometimes delayed sample submission pending the results of flotation analysis in hopes of recovering carbonized annuals or other plant remains that would more accurately estimate the age of feature use. Almost invariably the macrobotanical analyst did not find any carbonized annuals from Archaic-age samples or at least none in sufficient quantity for a trustworthy date—i.e., there might be a single Cheno-Am seed fragment weighing less than .001 g. Thus many of the NMRAP Archaic hearths yielded nothing other than wood charcoal for radiocarbon analysis. In such cases I usually tried to submit as many individual charcoal pieces as possible. I could have dated a single charcoal piece from each hearth by AMS, but there is no reliable way of knowing beforehand which piece of charcoal most closely approximates the episode of burning, and the one chosen might be very ancient. Assaying numerous charcoal chunks results in a date that is an "average" for many separate individual ages (the age of each charcoal chunk), which reduces the relative contribution of extremely old wood (see Smiley 1985:72).

Relying on wood charcoal dates to provide temporal control for the Archaic period might not present insurmountable interpretive problems. Because of the overall coarse temporal resolution for the Archaic and the millennial intervals used for comparative and interpretive purposes, even a 1,000-year age discrepancy resulting from the burning of old wood is of minor consequence. The critical issue is not to overinterpret the dates from any single site as necessarily indicating overly long intervals of use or as evidence for multiple occupations. There is more concern with late Archaic sites that approach in time the interval when domesticates were introduced.

Beta Analytic was the primary contractor for radiocarbon dating services, performing in-house all of the standard beta-decay counting but pretreating and preparing into graphic targets all AMS samples for dating at one of its consortium accelerator laboratories. I requested that all AMS samples be analyzed at Lawrence Livermore National Laboratory to help reduce potential problems with interlaboratory comparability (see discussion of this issue in chapter 5). Prior to submitting them to Beta, I carefully inspected each sample under a binocular microscope and removed any roots or other foreign materials. Beta Analytic also performs physical pretreatment, but my initial cleaning seemed a useful step toward ensuring accurate results.

The NMRAP Archaic Dates

The N16 excavations produced a sizable sample of 59 radiocarbon dates for the Archaic period and another 75 radiocarbon dates from the following Basketmaker II period. This separation between Archaic and Basketmaker II dates is discussed in greater detail in chapter 5, which also presents and interprets the Basketmaker II dates. Suffice it to say here that maize was not found at NMRAP sites that dated before 2400 BP, yet nearly all sites that dated after 2400 BP contained maize, some in considerable abundance; the earliest direct date on maize for the project area is 2230 BP.

The 59 Archaic period dates, ranging from 9780 BP up to 2520 BP, are listed in Table 4.4 by site and then by conventional radiocarbon age in descending order. This table also provides information on the type of material dated, the initial pretreatment weight of the sample, the dating method used (beta decay or AMS), the measured or assumed δ^{13}C value, the feature, and the calibrated two-sigma age range. The latter were calculated using the OxCal program, Version 3.10 (Bronk Ramsey 1994, 1995, 1998). Figure 4.2 plots all but the oldest of the 59 dates according to calibrated age; included are both one-sigma ranges (solid black boxes) and two-sigma ranges (enclosing boxes).

The 59 Archaic period dates come from 13 sites, including Atlatl Rock Cave. All but two of the 14 open Archaic sites investigated during the project could be assigned a temporal placement based on radiocarbon dates, in most cases multiple dates. Of the two Archaic sites that could not be assigned, one (UT-B-63-38) lacked features and thus carbon samples altogether, whereas the other (Hólahéi Scatter) produced carbon samples from what I ultimately interpreted as natural burns unrelated to the nearby artifact and faunal assemblages. The test excavations at Atlatl Rock Cave produced numerous carbon samples; three of the 12 submitted for radiocarbon analysis were from the site's Archaic component.

The oldest date in Table 4.4 is from an isolated hearth

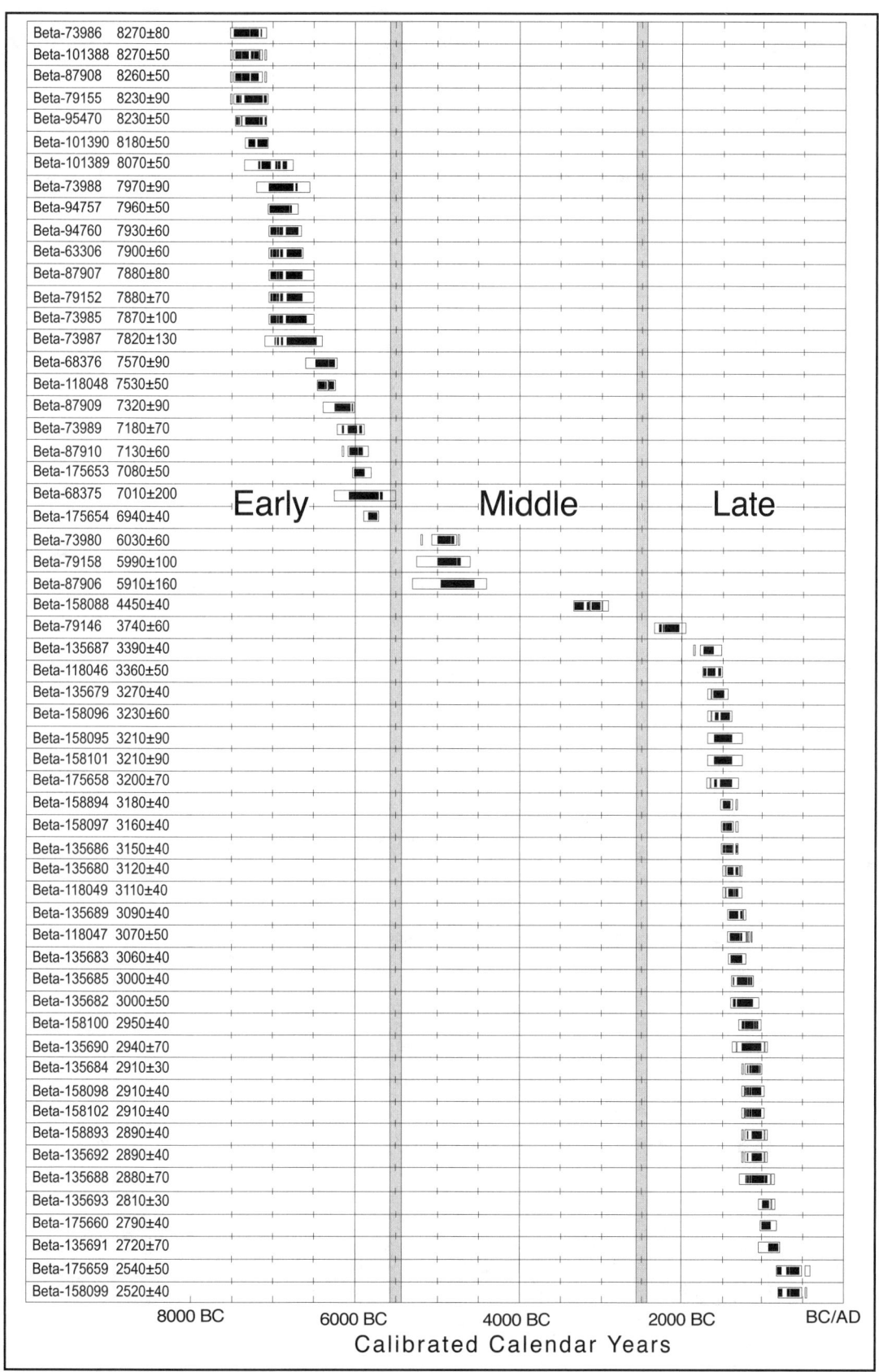

Figure 4.2. Array of all but the oldest of the 59 radiocarbon dates from Navajo Mountain Road Archaeological Project Archaic sites according to calibrated age (solid black boxes = 1σ ranges, enclosing boxes = 2σ ranges).

TABLE 4.4. List of Radiocarbon Dates from Navajo Mountain Road Archaeological Project Archaic Sites

SITE	^{14}C AGE (BP)	LAB NO.	MATERIAL	WEIGHT (g)	METHOD	δ^{13}C (‰)	FEATURE	CAL. 2σ RANGE (BC)
Atlatl Rock Cave	7900 ± 60	Beta-63306	grass	47.0	BD	−11.2	cultural layer	7050–6630
Atlatl Rock Cave	7570 ± 90	Beta-68376	yucca	45.0	BD	−24.2	cultural layer	6600–6220
Atlatl Rock Cave	7010 ± 200	Beta-68375	yucca	13.5	BD	−23	cultural layer	6250–5500
Big Bend	7530 ± 50	Beta-118048	charcoal	.034	AMS	−24.2	Hearth 5	6460–6240
Big Bend	3360 ± 50	Beta-118046	juniper seeds	.014	AMS	−20.1	Hearth 4	1750–1510
Big Bend	3270 ± 40	Beta-135679	twig	.02	AMS	−21.9	Hearth 1	1690–1440
Big Bend	3120 ± 40	Beta-135680	sagebrush	.031	AMS	−24.9	Hearth 7	1500–1260
Big Bend	3110 ± 40	Beta-118049	sagebrush	.04	AMS	−24.0	Hearth 8	1500–1260
Big Bend	3070 ± 50	Beta-118047	twigs	.016	AMS	−22.7	Hearth 2	1440–1130
Bonsai Bivouac	8180 ± 50	Beta-101390	sagebrush	.034	AMS	−24.0	Hearth 5	7340–7060
Bonsai Bivouac	4450 ± 40	Beta-158088	charcoal	.022	AMS	−23.6	Hearth 9	3340–2920
Dune Hollow	8270 ± 50	Beta-101388	sagebrush	.042	AMS	−23.1	Hearth 2	7520–7080
Dune Hollow	8070 ± 50	Beta-101389	charcoal	.044	AMS	−25.1	Hearth 1	7350–6750
Mouse House	7960 ± 50	Beta-94757	sagebrush	.171	AMS	−27.3	Hearth 8	7060–6690
Mouse House	7930 ± 60	Beta-94760	sagebrush	.091	AMS	−25.0	Hearth 9	7050–6650
Pee Wee Grande	8230 ± 90	Beta-79155	charcoal	8.26	BD	−25.0*	Hearth 5	7520–7060
Pee Wee Grande	7880 ± 70	Beta-79152	sap	.07	AMS	−19.8	Hearth 6	7050–6500
Pee Wee Grande	7870 ± 100	Beta-73985	charcoal	5.2	BD	−25.0*	Hearth 10	7050–6500
Pee Wee Grande	7080 ± 50	Beta-175653	charcoal	.1	AMS	−22.4	Hearth 8	6030–5810
Polly's Place	7970 ± 90	Beta-73988	charcoal	7.1	BD	−25.0*	Hearth 1	7200–6550
Polly's Place	7180 ± 70	Beta-73989	charcoal	.33	AMS	−22.6	Hearth 6	6220–5890
Polly's Place	6940 ± 40	Beta-175654	charcoal	.1	AMS	−21.7	Hearth 12	5900–5720
Sapo Seco	8230 ± 50	Beta-95470	charcoal	.0102	AMS	−24.0	Hearth 1	7460–7080
The Pits	9780 ± 100	Beta-79147	charcoal	3.93	BD	−25.0*	Hearth 3	9650–8800
The Pits	6030 ± 60	Beta-73980	charcoal	.0986	AMS	−22.8	Hearth 2	5200–4730
The Pits	3740 ± 60	Beta-79146	sagebrush	.02	AMS	−21.1	Hearth 1	2340–1950
Tres Campos	8260 ± 50	Beta-87908	sagebrush	.0584	AMS	−22.6	Hearth 1	7520–7080
Tres Campos	7880 ± 80	Beta-87907	charcoal	11.2	BD	−25.0*	Hearth 1	7050–6500
Tres Campos	7320 ± 90	Beta-87909	charcoal	3.8	BD	−25.0*	Hearth 3	6390–6010
Tres Campos	7130 ± 60	Beta-87910	charcoal	.7898	AMS	−22.1	Hearth 2	6160–5840
Tres Campos	5910 ± 160	Beta-87906	charcoal	1.6	BD	−25.0*	Hearth 4	5300–4400
Tsé Haal'á	3180 ± 40	Beta-158894	charcoal	.02	AMS	−23.0	Hearth 2	1530–1320
Tsé Haal'á	3060 ± 40	Beta-135683	twig	.022	AMS	−11.1	Hearth 13	1430–1210
Tsé Haal'á	3000 ± 50	Beta-135682	sagebrush	.023	AMS	−20.7	Hearth 3	1400–1040
Tsé Haal'á	3000 ± 40	Beta-135685	sagebrush	.033	AMS	−25.4	Hearth 11	1390–1110
Tsé Haal'á	2910 ± 30	Beta-135684	sagebrush	.035	AMS	−19.1	Hearth 1	1260–1000
Tsé Haal'á	2890 ± 40	Beta-158893	sagebrush	.12	AMS	−23.9	Hearth 7	1260–930

Site	Lab No.	Material	Size (g)	Method	δ13C	Provenience	Calibrated Range
Three Dog Site	Beta-135687	sagebrush twig	.02	AMS	−22.1	Hearth 4	1860–1520
Three Dog Site	Beta-158096	charcoal	4.2	BD	−25.0*	Hearth 1	1690–1390
Three Dog Site	Beta-158095	sagebrush	2.1	BD	−25.0*	Hearth 1	1690–1260
Three Dog Site	Beta-158101	charcoal	2.0	BD	−25.0*	Hearth 2	1690–1260
Three Dog Site	Beta-175658	charcoal	3.2	BD	−25.0*	Hearth 31	1690–1310
Three Dog Site	Beta-158097	juniper seed	.367	AMS	−22.9	Hearth 4	1520–1310
Three Dog Site	Beta-135686	juniper seeds	.03	AMS	−21.0	Hearth 6	1520–1310
Three Dog Site	Beta-135689	sagebrush	.066	AMS	−24.0	Hearth 13	1440–1210
Three Dog Site	Beta-158100	sagebrush	.013	AMS	−23.8	Hearth 2	1300–1010
Three Dog Site	Beta-135690	sagebrush	12.2	BD	−23.5	Hearth 20	1380–930
Three Dog Site	Beta-158098	twig	.01	AMS	−20.8	Hearth 27	1260–970
Three Dog Site	Beta-158102	juniper seed	.044	AMS	−18.9	Hearth 13	1260–970
Three Dog Site	Beta-135692	twig	.014	AMS	−22.5	Hearth 25	1260–930
Three Dog Site	Beta-135688	charcoal	19.8	BD	−25.0*	Hearth 13	1290–840
Three Dog Site	Beta-135693	sagebrush	.037	AMS	−21.9	Structure(?) 1	1050–840
Three Dog Site	Beta-175660	twig and juniper seed	<.1	AMS	−21.4	Structure(?) 1	1020–820
Three Dog Site	Beta-135691	charcoal	11.9	BD	−25.0*	Hearth 20	1050–780
Three Dog Site	Beta-175659	twigs	<.1	AMS	−22.7	Hearth 30	810–410
Three Dog Site	Beta-158099	twig	.01	AMS	−11.1	Hearth 29	800–450
Windy Mesa	Beta-73986	charcoal	7.2	BD	−25.0*	Hearth 4	7520–7080
Windy Mesa	Beta-73987	charcoal	4.8	BD	−25.0*	Hearth 2	7100–6400
Windy Mesa	Beta-79158	charcoal	3.26	BD	−25.0*	Hearth 3	5250–4600

Note: AMS = accelerator mass spectrometry; BD = beta decay.

Site	Lab No.	Age (BP)
Three Dog Site	Beta-135687	3390 ± 40
Three Dog Site	Beta-158096	3230 ± 60
Three Dog Site	Beta-158095	3210 ± 90
Three Dog Site	Beta-158101	3210 ± 90
Three Dog Site	Beta-175658	3200 ± 70
Three Dog Site	Beta-158097	3160 ± 40
Three Dog Site	Beta-135686	3150 ± 40
Three Dog Site	Beta-135689	3090 ± 40
Three Dog Site	Beta-158100	2950 ± 40
Three Dog Site	Beta-135690	2940 ± 70
Three Dog Site	Beta-158098	2910 ± 40
Three Dog Site	Beta-158102	2910 ± 40
Three Dog Site	Beta-135692	2890 ± 40
Three Dog Site	Beta-135688	2880 ± 70
Three Dog Site	Beta-135693	2810 ± 30
Three Dog Site	Beta-175660	2790 ± 40
Three Dog Site	Beta-135691	2720 ± 70
Three Dog Site	Beta-175659	2540 ± 50
Three Dog Site	Beta-158099	2520 ± 40
Windy Mesa	Beta-73986	8270 ± 80
Windy Mesa	Beta-73987	7820 ± 130
Windy Mesa	Beta-79158	5990 ± 100

at The Pits and is the one not included in Figure 4.2. This sample might provide evidence of late Paleoindian occupancy, but it lacks any associated remains. At 1,500 radiocarbon years older than all other Archaic assays, this date remains an intriguing anomaly that cannot be integrated with the current discussion.

The pattern immediately evident from Figure 4.2 is two main date clusters with little or nothing in between. The first cluster is during the early Archaic, prior to 5500 cal. BC, and is represented by 23 dates from 10 sites, including Atlatl Rock Cave. The second cluster is during the late Archaic, between 2500 and 500 cal. BC, and is represented by 31 dates from four sites. Although there are fewer sites, two of the late Archaic sites are of substantial size and complexity, far more than those of the early Archaic, representing many separate episodes of use. Except for Atlatl Rock Cave, the early Archaic sites appear to result from brief single-use episodes or at most just a few closely overlapping episodes. Atlatl Rock Cave showed no evidence of use during the late Archaic, although more research will be required at the site to be certain of this. Other caves of the region, such as Sand Dune, do have some evidence of late Archaic use (see discussion below).

Four dates occur between the date clusters; three are between about 5500 and 4500 cal. BC, and one is between about 3500 and 3000 cal. BC. The latter (4450 ± 40 BP) is suspect, in that the feature it came from might or might not be cultural and other possible hearths at the site (Bonsai Bivouac) produced early Archaic or Basketmaker II radiocarbon ages. Even if it were a cultural feature and the age could be verified as accurate, there were no associated remains, so the sample is largely devoid of meaning. The assay occurs during an interval that continues to be poorly documented on the Colorado Plateau, but this assay, like the 9780 BP date, is merely an intriguing anomaly, a hint that there might have been middle Archaic occupancy on the Rainbow Plateau (see further discussion of the middle Archaic below).

The three dates between about 5500 and 4500 cal. BC are from separate sites (Tres Campos, Windy Mesa, and The Pits), each of which has additional radiocarbon dates on other features that are in disagreement. At Tres Campos, the 5910 BP date for Hearth 4 is significantly later than the four other radiocarbon dates for the site, which range between 8260 and 7130 BP. Nonetheless, the more recent assay is consistent with stratigraphy because Hearth 4 overlaid the other features at the site, originating from the top of the cultural layer (Stratum VI) rather than at the bottom. Therefore, there is no apparent reason to dismiss the 5910 BP date; rather, it is taken as evidence of brief site use during the start of the middle Archaic. Unfortunately it is impossible to say what if any of the remains recovered from Tres Campos might be associated with Hearth 4. Most items from the site seemed clearly associated with the other hearths and therefore belonged to the early Archaic.

I am less willing to accept either of the other two dates. Hearth 3 at Windy Mesa produced a 5990 BP date, but there was no stratigraphic evidence suggesting that this feature was significantly more recent than the other nearby features at this site, which dated 8270 and 7820 BP. The 6030 BP date for Hearth 2 at The Pits is significantly older than a 3740 BP date on Hearth 1, which was the one feature clearly associated with the buried Archaic artifacts and other remains at the site (flakes of the same New Mexico obsidian occurred in the hearth fill and in the buried stratum). The feature that yielded the 6030 date was less certainly of cultural derivation, but even if it was truly the remains of a human fire, there were few if any remains in secure association. Foragers may have occupied both Windy Mesa and The Pits during the start of the middle Archaic, but this remains to be demonstrated by additional dating, and even then little else could be said given the lack of related materials.

Sample Quality

Sagebrush vs. Wood Charcoal. The radiocarbon data set for the Archaic period is not nearly as ideal as that available for the Basketmaker II period because a high percentage of the dates are based on samples of low material quality (see Smiley 1998b:39–40). Forty-one percent ($n = 22$) of the 54 dates are on wood charcoal from hearths. This is expectable given the open Archaic sites investigated for the NMRAP; Archaic hearths rarely produced carbonized plant remains other than charcoal. The charcoal was not identified prior to dating, but most was probably a mixture of juniper and pinyon, the two species most prevalent in the region and most commonly identified in the flotation samples from the dated features. Smiley's (1998c:Table 7-2) analysis of wood charcoal dates from Basketmaker II sites on Black Mesa showed that just 15 percent fell within the Lolomai phase occupation span as estimated by six corn dates, with a full 85 percent overestimating true site age; almost half of these were too old by 100 years or more, with 30 percent of them overestimating site age by 200 years or more. There is every reason to

TABLE 4.5. Comparison of Radiocarbon Determinations on Sagebrush and Wood Charcoal from Single Features at Navajo Mountain Road Archaeological Project Archaic Sites

Site	Feature	Material Dated	Sample No.	Conventional ^{14}C Age (BP)	Calibrated 2σ Range (BC)
Tres Campos	Hearth 1	sagebrush	Beta-87908	8260 ± 50	7520–7080
Tres Campos	Hearth 1	wood charcoal	Beta-87907	7880 ± 80	7050–6500
X^2 test fails at 5%: 15.881 (5% 3.8), df = 1; difference ^{14}C years = 380					
Three Dog Site	Hearth 1	sagebrush	Beta-158095	3210 ± 90	1690–1260
Three Dog Site	Hearth 1	wood charcoal	Beta-158096	3230 ± 60	1690–1390
X^2 test does not fail at 5%: .0 (5% 3.8), df = 1; difference ^{14}C years = 20					
Three Dog Site	Hearth 2	sagebrush	Beta-158100	2950 ± 40	1300–1010
Three Dog Site	Hearth 2	wood charcoal	Beta-158101	3210 ± 90	1690–1260
X^2 test fails at 5%: 7.120 (5% 3.8), df = 1; difference ^{14}C years = 260					
Three Dog Site	Hearth 4	sagebrush twig	Beta-135687	3390 ± 40	1860–1520
Three Dog Site	Hearth 4	juniper seed	Beta-158097	3160 ± 40	1520–1310
X^2 test fails at 5%: 16.526 (5% 3.8), df = 1; difference ^{14}C years = 230					
Three Dog Site	Hearth 13	sagebrush	Beta-135689	3090 ± 40	1440–1210
Three Dog Site	Hearth 13	wood charcoal	Beta-135688	2880 ± 70	1290–840
Three Dog Site	Hearth 13	juniper seed	Beta-158102	2910 ± 40	1260–970
X^2 test fails at 5%: 12.685 (5% 6.0), df = 2; difference ^{14}C years = 210 & 180					
Three Dog Site	Hearth 20	sagebrush	Beta-135690	2940 ± 70	1380–930
Three Dog Site	Hearth 20	wood charcoal	Beta-135691	2720 ± 70	1050–780
X^2 test fails at 5%: 4.937 (5% 3.8), df = 1; difference ^{14}C years = 220					

suspect that the wood used by Archaic foragers for fuel would result in similar discrepancies between the radiocarbon ages and the times of site use. There is also no necessary reason to suspect that charcoal dates from adjacent hearths at a single site used at the same time would result in statistically equivalent ages.

Many of the NMRAP Archaic hearths contained sagebrush charcoal along with that of trees; indeed some Archaic hearths appear to have been fueled mostly with brush. Thirty-three percent (n = 18) of the NMRAP Archaic dates are on sagebrush charcoal. Until the last session of the fieldwork on the project (1999), I considered sagebrush charcoal dates to be more accurate than those on wood charcoal and would submit sagebrush samples whenever this material was found in hearth fill. My presumption was that the small-diameter twigs of this shrub would be less likely than tree wood to survive in the open. Sagebrush charcoal, it seemed, would provide dates that more closely corresponded to the events of interest because shrubs should suffer less from the "old wood" problem—long-dead organics being collected and burned, resulting in ages several hundred years or more displaced from the actual time of the fires. The first hint that this might not be true came from separately analyzing wood and sagebrush charcoal from Hearth 1 at Tres Campos. The sagebrush assay was 380 radiocarbon years older than the wood charcoal assay. This result raised a red flag, but at the time it was but a single discrepancy, so I did not know what to conclude from the results. Excavation of the late Archaic components at Three Dog Site during the final season of NMRAP fieldwork presented an excellent opportunity to test the notion of age overestimation with sagebrush. The hearths at this site contained abundant carbonized remains, many containing both wood and sagebrush charcoal and a few with enough of both materials to obtain standard beta-decay dates.[3]

Table 4.5 and Figure 4.3 present a comparison of radiocarbon dates on sagebrush charcoal with dates on wood charcoal or juniper seeds from single features at two different sites. There are six different comparisons, and in all but one case (83%) the dates are statistically different with a 95 percent probability limit. In four of six cases (67%) the sagebrush charcoal returned ages significantly older than wood charcoal and juniper seeds: a 380-year difference between the two dates for Hearth 1 at Tres Campos, a 230-year difference between the two dates

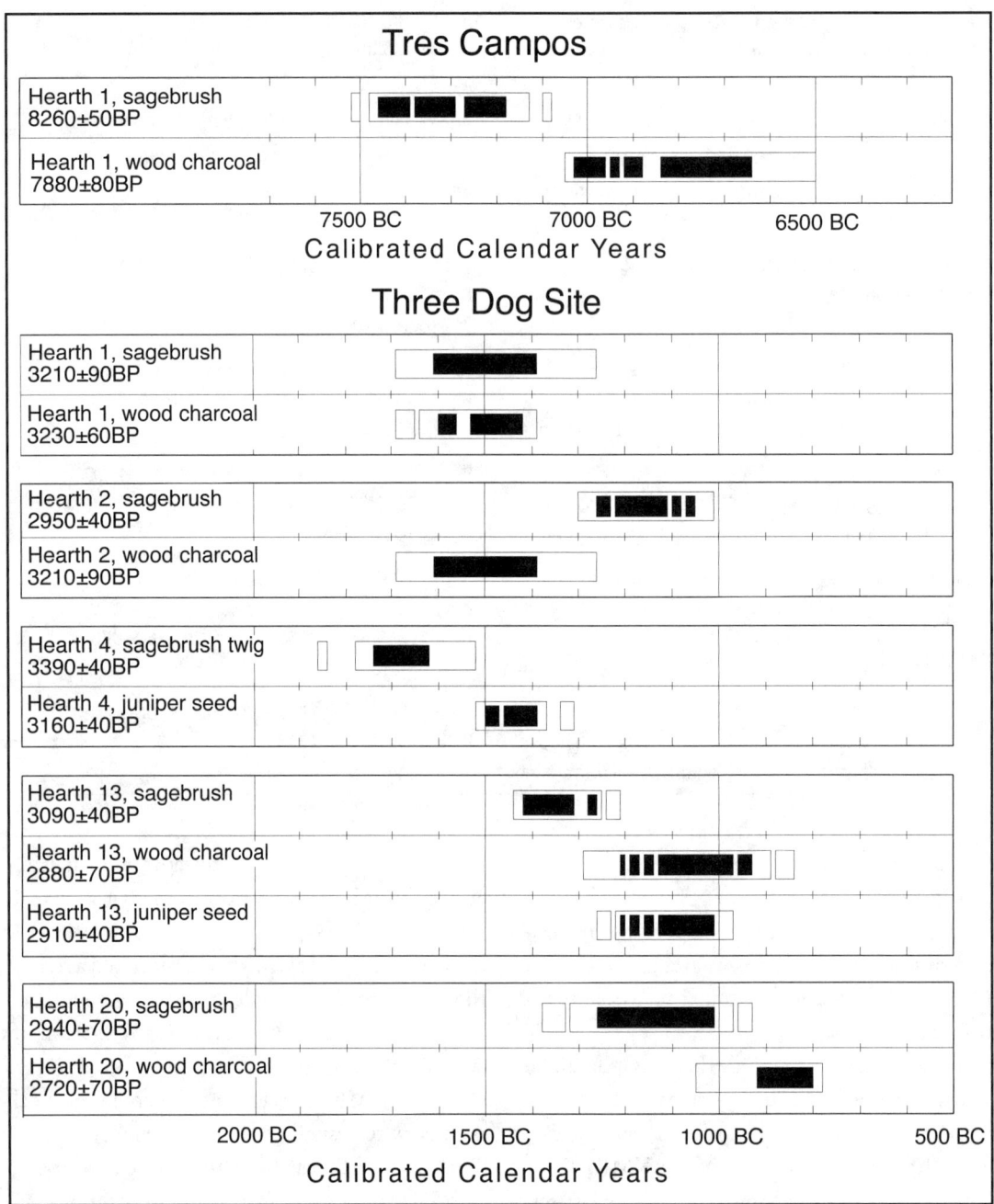

Figure 4.3. Comparison of radiocarbon determinations on sagebrush and wood charcoal from single features at Navajo Mountain Road Archaeological Project Archaic sites (solid black boxes = 1σ ranges, enclosing boxes = 2σ ranges).

for Hearth 4 at Three Dog Site, a 220-year difference between the two dates for Hearth 20 at Three Dog Site, and a 210- to 180-year difference between the sagebrush date and the other two dates for Hearth 13 at Three Dog Site. Two aspects of this are worth calling attention to. First, the Hearth 4 sagebrush date is on a tiny twig 2 mm in diameter, a seemingly improbable item to overestimate age. Second, the two nonsagebrush dates for Hearth 13 are statistically the same and produce an average (2903 ± 35 BP) with even less overlap with the sagebrush date given its smaller sigma.

In each of these four cases it is expectable that the wood charcoal assays are themselves offset from the true times of the fires—recall Smiley's (1998c) data cited above that fully 85 percent of the BMAP wood charcoal dates overestimated true site age. If true in these NMRAP instances, then the sagebrush dates are even more off the mark, in that they are compared against dates that are perhaps too old themselves. Comparison of sagebrush charcoal dates against maize and other remains at two Basketmaker sites also reveals discrepancies of a few hundred years (see chapter 5).

Although sagebrush commonly resulted in ages that were older than wood charcoal, this was not always true, as indicated by Hearth 1 at Three Dog Site, whose two dates are virtually identical. What remains unknown in this case is whether both material types equally overestimate the age of the fire—the wood charcoal in this instance is as bad as the sagebrush—or whether both samples represent the true antiquity of the feature. The Hearth 2 samples for Three Dog Site actually resulted in a reverse pattern, with the sagebrush charcoal producing a date significantly younger than the wood charcoal date. In this case the sagebrush date might be the best bet, but overall it appears safe to conclude that sagebrush is no better than wood charcoal when it comes to accurately estimating the age of past occupations, and indeed it is likely to be worse.

Sagebrush is not known to be a long-lived shrub; "it commonly reaches 40 to 50 years of age, and some plants may exceed 100 years" (www.fs.fed.us/database/feis/). Ferguson (1964) reported a maximum age of 217 years, but this is an extreme outlier; another study in Wyoming found a maximum age of 81 years, also an extreme outlier (Perryman et al. 2001). Cawker's (1980) study of 1,276 sagebrush sections showed that the vast majority are less than 20 years old, with a distinct grouping of "older" shrubs between 30 and 60 years of age and none past 85 (1980:Figure 3). Perryman et al. (2001:Table 1) found that sagebrush in various stands in Wyoming ranged in mean and median ages from between 14 and 50 years (total sample size was some 2,200 plants, with anywhere from 59 to 224 per stand). At a Nevada site the oldest sagebrush had fewer than 59 annual rings (Biondi et al. 2007). Even if rare individuals live more than 100 years, pinyon and juniper trees normally live for hundreds of years (Jeffrey Dean, personal communication 1996). Consequently, it is probably not the overall life span of sagebrush that causes age overestimation, in that carbon is fixed within a relatively short interval, especially compared to the common fuel wood species of the Colorado Plateau. Excluding longevity in life, then longevity after death is a plausible reason for age overestimation. One means to test this and to obtain a better handle on the extent of age overestimation possible using sagebrush as fuel was to directly date specimens of this plant present on the ground surface of the area today.

At any particular place on the Rainbow Plateau one sees sagebrush in various states of life and death—from flourishing to dying to badly decayed hulks. This shrub is hard to tear from the ground when alive, but dead shrubs are often easily yanked free owing to termite activity and rot of the roots. The more advanced the decay, the easier the shrub is to procure and tear asunder. Eventually shrubs fall over of their own accord and enter an even more advanced state of decay. In collecting sagebrush for fuel, the dead and down shrubs would seem to be natural choices since they require the least work (pick up pieces and move along). The question is, How long does it take for sagebrush to reach this state of optimal fuel: 50 years, 100 years, 200 years, more?

In an effort to answer this query, samples were collected from several sagebrush shrubs in various states of decay, and two of these samples were submitted to Beta Analytic for standard beta-decay radiocarbon dating. One was from a standing dead shrub that still retained most of its small twigs (Shrub A), and the other was from a bush that had rotted through at the base and fallen over, with small twigs gone and the wood somewhat decayed but in good condition to serve as fuel (Shrub C). The samples were soaked in distilled water and carefully scrubbed prior to submission to the dating laboratory in order to remove lichens and moss growing on the wood—modern contaminants that might not be eliminated in standard chemical pretreatment. The results of this experiment (Table 4.6) show that the standing dead shrub was alive and respiring carbon after the start of atomic bomb testing in the 1950s. The sample contained more ^{14}C than the 1950 reference standard. The fallen and partially decayed shrub was not enriched in radiocarbon, so it must predate 1950; it returned an assay of 120 ± 50 BP. The calibrated two-sigma range was AD 1670–1960.

The modern samples provide initial confirmation of the suspected reason behind the evident trend for sagebrush samples to overestimate the age of a cultural event, an overestimation that can exceed the estimate provided by samples of tree wood from the same context. Sagebrush might have a particularly long "shelf life" as fuel, in that it might take 50 years or more for a dead shrub to fall over and then hundreds of years before the wood is so sufficiently decayed and scattered that it would no longer be collected for burning. As a result, there is no reason to privilege carbonized sagebrush over that of tree wood for the radiocarbon dating of prehistoric features, and indeed the reverse might be true. The potential for

TABLE 4.6. Radiocarbon Dates on Two Samples of Sagebrush Collected in 2002

SAMPLE ID	CONDITION	LABORATORY NO.	CONVENTIONAL ^{14}C AGE	CALIBRATED 2σ RANGE
Shrub A	standing dead with small twigs intact	Beta-175492	120.92 ± .72 pMC[a]	modern
Shrub C	wood charcoal	Beta-175493	120 ± 50 BP	AD 1670–1960

Note: Samples were not corrected for fractionation but have an assumed δ^{13}C value of –25.0‰.

[a] pMC = percent modern carbon, which means that the sagebrush is less than 50 yeas old. It had more ^{14}C than did the AD 1950 reference standard; thus the sample must have been respiring carbon after this time and included extra ^{14}C from atomic bomb testing.

age discrepancy with short-lived shrubs that have a potentially long shelf life is to a large extent related to the local rate of fuel consumption. This is basically a density-dependent phenomenon, in that areas with sparse population and high residential mobility will have a far lower rate of fuel consumption than those with greater population density and substantial residential stability. The former was evidently true during the Archaic interval in the Southwest, whereas the latter characterizes the Puebloan period for this same region. As a result, sagebrush might provide more reliable results during more recent intervals, as was exemplified by the sagebrush sample from a Puebloan hearth reported in chapter 6 that closely corresponded to the tree-ring date for a charred log from the same feature. Further back in time during the Archaic period, when the radiocarbon technique has increased significance because reliable dating alternatives are lacking, relatively sparse population and dispersed settlement would allow dead sagebrush to accumulate such that the chances of age overestimation are increased.

Other Plant Remains. The only obvious high-quality samples in the Archaic radiocarbon dates are from Atlatl Rock Cave, where dry conditions preserved various plant remains. Two of the three Archaic age dates from this site are on yucca leaves, and the third is on grass. Yucca is not an annual plant, but it is moderately short lived with little chance for age overestimation when human harvesting of the leaves is evident—such as when used to make sandals.

Other NMRAP Archaic dates that may not overestimate age or perhaps not to a great extent include six on small-diameter twigs (exclusive of a dated sagebrush twig) and four on juniper seeds. There is also one date on sap, and although it represents the fluid of a living plant, once secreted this material can last for a considerable length of time in the open. As such it is difficult to know to what extent sap might overestimate age. Juniper seeds have the aura of being higher-quality samples than wood charcoal, perhaps somewhat deservedly so, but the Hearth 13 comparison in Table 4.5 shows no difference between dates on wood charcoal and a juniper seed. Moreover, comparisons between dates on corn and juniper seeds from a Basketmaker II site (see chapter 5) reveal the potential for modest discrepancies, with juniper seeds yielding ages that were 100–200 years older than maize dates.

Small-diameter twigs, like juniper seeds, are not necessarily as high quality as they might appear. The truth to this is revealed by the tiny sagebrush twig of Hearth 4 at Three Dog Site, which yielded a date 230 years older than wood charcoal from the same hearth (see Table 4.5). The species represented by the twig is probably quite important as to whether or not it will overestimate age and by how much. The six twig samples reported in Table 4.4 were not identified prior to dating, although it is certain that they were not sagebrush. One clue to identification is provided by the delta ^{13}C values. Two of the twigs have values of 11.1‰, which indicates that they are from a C4 shrub such as saltbush; the delta values for the other twigs are consistent with a C3 woody plant. Whether or not age overestimation will occur with the twigs of a specific species, either shrub or tree, will probably require individual study, like was done above for sagebrush. Small-diameter twigs might provide accurate dates, but, as with much about radiocarbon dating, there are no easy fixes, no simple solutions.

Obsidian-Hydration Dating

When Friedman and Smith (1960) first published their report on obsidian-hydration dating (OHD) it seemed that archaeologists had a simple, inexpensive, and reliable method for dating artifacts and associated sites. It was widely embraced in regions where obsidian was abundant, such as California, the Columbia Plateau, and the Great Basin of the western United States and in Mesoamerica. Almost 40 years later Ridings (1996) trenchantly questioned, "Where in the world does obsidian hydration work?" "Not in northeast Arizona" appears to be one answer. Samples of obsidian artifacts were submitted for hydration analysis as part of the NMRAP dating effort at Archaic sites. Appendix E of the online supporting documents presents the specialist's report on the results of this effort. Here I discuss the findings relative to what is known of the sites, including radiocarbon dates, obsidian sources, and reduction technology.

Background

This is not the place to review the history of OHD and its underlying working assumptions—readers should consult recent articles by Anovitz et al. (1999), Friedman et al. (1997), Hull (2001), and Stevenson et al. (2000)—but some description and a few comments are in order. Friedman and Smith (1960) recognized that exposed surfaces of prehistoric obsidian artifacts had absorbed water, resulting in a hydrated layer or rim seen as a birefringent line when observed in thin section under a microscope. The width of hydration rims seemed dependent upon time, temperature, and chemical composition (obsidian source). In the simplest of applications, hydration rims provide a relative ordering of artifacts or corresponding sites or components, and perhaps relative placement is the best we can hope for given various unresolved problems with OHD (e.g., Jackson 1984; Tremaine and Frederickson 1988). Absolute dates are often of greater archaeological utility, and researchers have taken two different approaches for converting hydration rim measurements into calendar age estimates by estimating the hydration rate of obsidian. Empirical rate determination uses independent chronometric data such as radiocarbon dates that are associated with analyzed obsidian artifacts (e.g., Kimberlin 1976; Meighan 1976). The other approach uses experimentally derived hydration rates, thereby eliminating the need for independent dates (e.g., Ambrose 1976; Friedman and Long 1976; Michels and Tsong 1980; Michels et al. 1983). Such "intrinsic rate dating" has many perceived advantages over the empirical method, but problems persist. Indeed, Anovitz et al. conclude "that the optical technique employed for standard OHD measurements is unsuited to providing data with the needed precision, and that the theoretical basis on which these data have been evaluated is incorrect" (1999:749). Doubtless some specialists in the field of OHD might take exception to this last statement and may find fault with the study by Anovitz et al. that led to their conclusion (see Hull 2001). Still, given such debate on basic fundamentals of the technique, it is perhaps no wonder that OHD has commonly proved unreliable.

NMRAP Analysis

The 25 obsidian flakes submitted for OHD analysis came from two Archaic sites within the southern portion of the road ROW: 10 flakes from The Pits and 15 flakes from Hólahéi Scatter. The samples were analyzed by Christopher Stevenson, then affiliated with the Diffusion Laboratory of Archaeological Services Consultants, Inc. Appendix E online presents his specific methods and results of the OHD analysis, so here just the main points are given. Stevenson's approach is to provide absolute dates based on experimentally derived hydration rates for a variety of obsidians. The rate of hydration varies based on intrinsic water content and not on obsidian source; intersource variability in water content means that source-specific rates may be unreliable (e.g., Stevenson et al. 1993; Stevenson et al. 1996; Stevenson et al. 1998). A proxy measure of intrinsic water content is provided by density measurements of each artifact using the Archimedes method (Ambrose and Stevenson 1995). Because hydration rate is also affected by soil temperature and relative humidity (e.g., Mazer et al. 1991), control over these variables should be obtained with local monitoring of these conditions. In this particular study saline-based temperature and humidity cells (Trembour et al. 1988) were buried for one year at the two sites that produced the OHD samples.

Table 4.7 presents the results of the OHD analysis along with values for effective hydration temperature and soil relative humidity. The hydration rate for each artifact takes into account intrinsic water content as derived from the density measurements. The calculated ages for each artifact take into account all of the currently identified relevant variables for converting a hydration rim measurement into an absolute date. Two of the flakes from Hólahéi Scatter did not have a visible hydration rim.

Discussion of Results

The Pits (AZ-J-14-17). The calculated ages for the 10 flakes from The Pits make up a disparate lot, ranging in age from 2390 BC to AD 1470. Table 4.8 presents these dates grouped according to obsidian source and organized from oldest to youngest. Had I lacked additional chronological information and depended on OHD alone for temporal placement, I might have made the ludicrous suggestion that the buried stratum identified as the Archaic component saw nearly continuous use from the late Archaic

TABLE 4.7. Obsidian-Hydration Results for 10 Flakes from The Pits and 15 Flakes from Hólahéi Scatter

Lab No.	Navajo Nation Archaeology Department No.	Rim (μm)	Density (g/cm³)	Intrinsic Water (wt. %)	Rate	Age	SD
The Pits (AZ-J-14-17); effective hydration temperature (EHT) = 10.83, % relative humidity (RH) = .98							
DL-95-437	516.1a	2.47	2.3418	.129	2.531	461 BC	199
DL-95-438	516.1b	1.99	2.3453	.126	1.934	98 BC	211
DL-95-439	526.1a	2.92	2.3402	.130	2.013	2285 BC	295
DL-95-440	528.1a	1.25	2.3617	.116	1.681	AD 1021	155
DL-95-441	530.1a	2.90	2.3451	.127	1.937	2392 BC	305
DL-95-442	545.1a	1.98	2.3498	.123	1.864	153 BC	218
DL-95-443	546.1a	1.43	2.3665	.113	1.609	AD 679	184
DL-95-444	556.1a	1.90	2.3433	.128	1.965	AD 113	198
DL-95-445	562.1a	.92	2.3556	.120	1.775	AD 1473	109
DL-95-446	568.1a	1.45	2.3611	.116	1.691	AD 706	177
Hólahéi Scatter (AZ-J-14-23); EHT = 12.34, % RH = .96							
DL-95-422	529.1a	.92	2.3614	.116	2.148	AD 1556	90
DL-95-423	529.1c	1.29	2.3612	.116	2.152	AD 1177	125
DL-95-424	527.2a	.92	2.3598	.117	2.179	AD 1562	89
DL-95-425	527.2b	.90	2.3616	.116	2.144	AD 1572	89
DL-95-426	512.1a	.94	2.3605	.116	2.165	AD 1542	91
DL-95-427	512.1b	3.27	2.3430	.128	2.507	2315 BC	265
DL-95-428	24.4a	.0	2.3710	.110	1.964	0	
DL-95-429	501.1a	1.31	2.3607	.116	2.162	AD 1156	126
DL-95-430	509.1a	1.31	2.3643	.114	2.092	AD 1130	130
DL-95-431	514.1a	.84	2.3594	.117	2.187	AD 1627	81
DL-95-432	516.1a	.0	2.3585	.118	2.204	0	0
DL-95-433	518.2a	.92	2.3605	.116	2.165	AD 1559	90
DL-95-434	535.1a	1.27	2.3587	.118	2.200	AD 1217	120
DL-95-435	542.1a	1.33	2.3591	.117	2.192	AD 1143	126
DL-95-436	548.1a	.88	2.3588	.118	2.198	AD 1598	85

through the late Prehistoric periods. Indeed, based on the proportion of dated flakes of Archaic age (two of 10), it would appear that about 80 percent of the recovered remains actually were Basketmaker and Puebloan, not Archaic. Fortunately, I avoided such lamentable confusion because additional information was available, including a radiocarbon date. Figure 4.4 plots the two-sigma range for the 10 OHD dates in chronological order and provides the two-sigma calibrated age range for the radiocarbon sample that represents the probable time of deposition of the artifacts. The date is on sagebrush charcoal from a shallow basin hearth that the flakes were scattered around and within; it has a two-sigma range of 2340–1950 cal. BC. It is possible that this material overestimates the true age of the feature by several hundred years, as discussed above, but even so the age is solidly within the late Archaic, likely prior to 1500 cal. BC. Two of the hydration dates have two-sigma ranges that coincide with the radiocarbon age, but the other eight samples are not even close, being minimally anywhere from 1,200 to 3,200 years outside the calibrated radiocarbon date range. Even the two samples that overlap with the radiocarbon date have poor precision, well below that of radiocarbon dating, which is sufficiently limiting in itself for some interpretations.

Two out of 10 samples falling within the expected date range is quite poor, but a defender of OHD might counter that the other eight dates cannot be dismissed based on the single radiocarbon sample. In this case there is stratigraphic cause to reject at least seven of the other eight samples. The obsidian flakes came from a buried cultural layer overlain by a sterile sand layer and then a Basketmaker II cultural layer. The Basketmaker component at The Pits is well dated at about 400 cal. BC to cal. AD 200 (see chapter 5), which means that the obsidian flakes should not date to this time or later. In a stretch to make the OHD results fit what is known of the site, one could

TABLE 4.8. Obsidian-Hydration Results for 10 Flakes from The Pits (AZ-J-14-17) Grouped by Obsidian Source and Arranged from Oldest to Youngest

Lab No.	Navajo Nation Archaeology Department No.	Rim (μm)	Age	1σ Age Range	2σ Age Range
Cerro del Medio Obsidian					
DL-95-441	530.1a	2.90	2392 BC	2697–2087 BC	3002–1782 BC
DL-95-439	526.1a	2.92	2285 BC	2580–1990 BC	2875–1695 BC
DL-95-437	516.1a	2.47	461 BC	660–262 BC	859–63 BC
DL-95-438	516.1b	1.99	98 BC	309 BC–AD 113	520 BC–AD 324
DL-95-444	556.1a	1.90	AD 113	85 BC–AD 311	283 BC–AD 509
Government Mountain Obsidian					
DL-95-442	545.1a	1.98	153 BC	371 BC–AD 65	589 BC–AD 283
DL-95-443	546.1a	1.43	AD 679	AD 495–863	AD 311–1047
DL-95-446	568.1a	1.45	AD 706	AD 529–883	AD 352–1060
DL-95-440	528.1a	1.25	AD 1021	AD 866–1176	AD 711–1331
DL-95-445	562.1a	.92	AD 1473	AD 1364–1582	AD 1255–1691

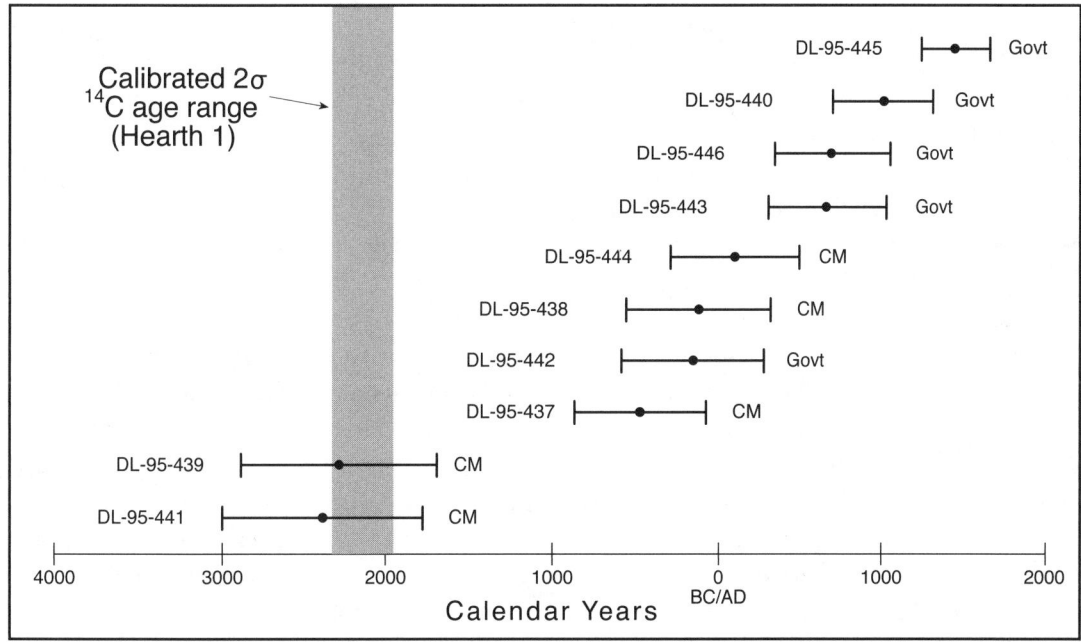

Figure 4.4. Plot of the 10 obsidian-hydration dates from the Archaic component of The Pits in chronological order showing the 2σ range along with the 2σ calibrated age range for the radiocarbon sample that represents the probable time of deposition of the artifacts.

argue that four of the dated obsidian artifacts are actually from the Basketmaker component (DL-95-437, -442, -438, and -444) and were intruded into the late Archaic layer. For this to be the case there had to have been two reduction events separated by about 2,000 years involving the same highly exotic obsidian. The information on obsidian source is also provided in Figure 4.4 (source identification based on X-ray fluorescence–energy-dispersive spectrometer [XRF-EDS] analysis by Richard Hughes; see SD, Appendix A). Five of the dated flakes are of Cerro del Medio glass from the Jemez Mountains source area of north-central New Mexico (Baugh and Nelson 1987) located some 400 km from the site. Basketmaker flintknappers rarely used obsidian for tool production, but even if they had, it is highly improbable that they would have been reducing glass from this distant source in exactly the same small area as did late Archaic knappers a few thousand years previous. More important, no flakes or tools of obsidian were recovered from or observed at the Basketmaker II component of The Pits. Based on the lithic analysis, I am certain that the flakes of Cerro del Medio obsidian are from a single tool flaked at a single point in time during the late Archaic. Even if one ignores the calculated ages, the rim widths for this single glass, which vary from 1.90 to 2.92 μ, are inconsistent with the highly probable single reduction event.

The other five analyzed flakes are of Government Mountain obsidian, a source in north-central Arizona that is considerably closer to the project area (ca. 230 km). The rim widths are almost equally diverse for the flakes of Government Mountain obsidian, although for this material the flakes may well be from several tools (at least I am not certain that they came from a single tool). Again, using the hydration layers alone as a means of relative dating suggests that the flakes were deposited during two or three intervals. These artifacts came from the same buried layer that produced the Cerro del Medio flakes, so a single event in prehistory is indicated. The calculated ages for the Government Mountain flakes show little overlap with those of the Cerro del Medio flakes except for sample DL-95-442. With the Government Mountain flakes we have to add the implausibility of Puebloan artifacts having been intruded into the Archaic cultural layer.

The other highly suspect aspect of these results is that the two different obsidian sources produced such incongruent results, with the Cerro del Medio glass older in almost all cases than the Government Mountain glass—there is very little overlap. Although there would be no statistically valid reason to average the dates from each source, if that was done, then they would be separated by almost 1,800 years (1025 BC vs. AD 745). This is from obsidian that I have every reason to believe was flaked at essentially the same time in prehistory. This suggests that there is probably some source-related variability in hydration rind development that is not being controlled or accounted for, perhaps by assuming that hydration varies based on intrinsic water content, or by the density measurements used as a proxy measure of intrinsic water content, or even by both or other factors.

My final conclusion is that OHD failed miserably for The Pits. Two of the samples seem to fall within the probable date range of the Archaic component, but whether this was by simple random chance or because the technique actually worked in these instances is impossible to say. The artificial creation of a long continuous series of dates from what was probably a single event in time should sound a loud siren that continuous occupational histories reconstructed by this method are likely as not spurious.

Hólahéi Scatter (AZ-J-14-23). At first glance the OHD results for Hólahéi Scatter appear far more reasonable than was true for The Pits. Thirteen of the 15 submitted flakes had measurable hydration rims, with all but one of these quite similar. The outlier has a rim measurement of 3.27 μ and a calculated age of 2315 BC; the other samples have rim measurements from .84 to 1.33 μ, with calculated ages between AD 1130 and 1627. The outlying sample is from the Wild Horse source located in the Mineral Mountains of central southwest Utah (Nelson 1984; Nelson and Holmes 1979). This is the single dated flake that is not of Government Mountain obsidian, and even though it occurred in a buried cultural layer along with the other dated flakes, it is conceivably from an earlier use of the site or a scavenged artifact.

Excluding this sample leaves the 12 flakes of Government Mountain obsidian. These 12 can be split into two moderately tight groups based on either rim measurements or calculated ages. There are five flakes with ages between AD 1130 and 1217 and a mean hydration rim of 1.3 μ and seven flakes with ages between AD 1542 and 1627 and a mean hydration rim of .9 μ. The 12 dates are plotted in chronological order in Figure 4.5. There is no overlap between these two group of dates at one sigma, but at two sigma there is some degree of overlap among most flakes of each group. Despite the two-sigma overlap, a chi-square test failed at less than a 5 percent chance, indicating statistically significant differences among the dates. If the dated flakes are treated as the by-products of two separate and brief occupations, then perhaps the sample ages of each group can be averaged with the means providing more precise temporal brackets around these events. Because the dates within each of the two groups are internally consistent, they were combined, resulting in an average of AD 1166 ± 56 for the oldest group and AD 1576 ± 33 for the youngest group (Figure 4.6). Based on these averages, there is a 410-year gap between the midpoints and a 220-year gap between the closest points of the two-sigma ranges.

Conceivably hunters used the site on two separate occasions as the hydration results suggest. Some support for the multiple-occupation scenario is perhaps provided by

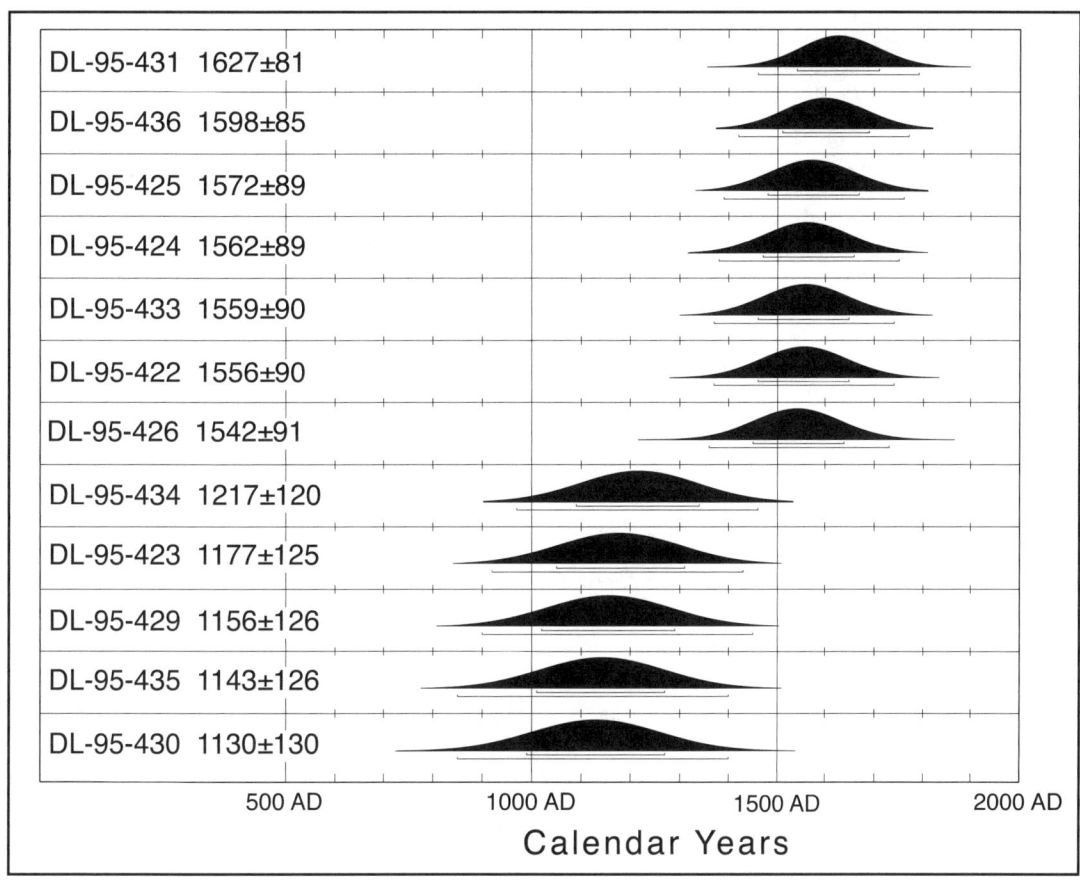

Figure 4.5. Plot of the 12 obsidian-hydration dates from Hólahéi Scatter in chronological order showing the 2σ range along with the 2σ calibrated age range for the radiocarbon sample that represents the probable time of deposition of the artifacts.

the spatial pattern of the dated flakes. The flakes of the AD 1166 group (or the 1.3 μ group) mostly occurred in the southeast portion of the main site area, whereas the flakes of the AD 1576 group (or the .9 μ group) occurred in the northwest portion. There is clearly some overlap, and in two instances where obsidian flakes from single proveniences were analyzed (PN512 and -529), discordant rim measurements were returned. There are also other reasons to doubt the scenario of multiple occupations. First, the scatter of debitage and bone is concentrated within a small area, perhaps too small to be the residue of occupations separated by what appears to be several hundred years (or ca. .4 μ in average hydration rim width). A wellnigh spatially coextensive scatter of remains from use episodes separated by hundreds of years is conceivable, but the occupants had to have had indistinguishable tool kits, made of virtually identical and exotic raw materials and produced in the same fashion. All of the obsidian debitage from the site is derived from the same reduction technology, and indeed flakes with different dates appear to come

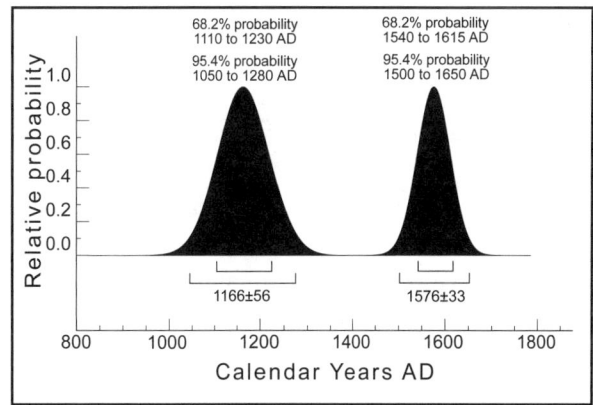

Figure 4.6. Averages of the two internally consistent groups of obsidian-hydration dates from Hólahéi Scatter.

from the same tools (although attempted refitting failed to produce any conjoins). There may well have been multiple uses of the site, but at a larger spatial scale than the small area where the dated obsidian came from. The remains of this area appear to have been deposited during a single use episode, probably of brief duration.

Although multiple use of the site area is a possibility that cannot be totally eliminated, there is an even more basic problem with the OHD results. The obsidian flakes all came from a cultural layer buried by a soil that has a minimum radiocarbon age of roughly 400–110 cal. BC, with perhaps soil formation continuing until sometime after cal. AD 130. This means that the artifacts were resting upon the ground surface for an undetermined period of time prior to when the soil started to form, sometime prior to 400 cal. BC. The nature of the lithic assemblage (abundant use of obsidian and heavy emphasis on bifacial technology) suggests a minimal age of late Archaic (ca. 1000 cal. BC). I attempted to radiocarbon date the small bone fragments associated with the stone artifacts, but this proved fruitless because of a lack of collagen. In any event, none of the calculated ages for the Government Mountain obsidian flakes make sense with regard to the site's depositional history. The late Archaic age of the Wild Horse flake potentially accords with the depositional history, but whether the date for this specimen is accurate is impossible to say.

Natural fires had burned over the site area at least once and perhaps several times. Many of the chert artifacts exhibited evidence of burning (potlids, crenated fractures). The obsidian artifacts lack any obvious signs of thermal alteration, but it is possible that fire might have affected the development of hydration rinds, at least partly explaining the confusing results. A symposium on fire's effects on obsidian at a Society for Conservation Archaeology meeting found that temperatures as low as 200°C "reset" the hydration layer back to zero or at least to a rim measurement that had no meaning (M. Steven Shackley, personal communication 2001; Steffen 2005). It seems plausible that the natural burn(s) of Hólahéi Scatter variably affected the hydration rims. In this regard it is interesting to note that a natural burn feature where the obsidian flakes were recovered has two stratigraphically consistent radiocarbon ages of 2220 ± 60 BP (lower) and 2020 ± 60 BP (upper). If this fire eliminated the hydration rinds, then they should have started to reform sometime during the first several centuries of the Christian era, well before the hydration dates indicate. A subsequent fire might have variably reset the hydration layers, but this remains speculative.

What About OHD?

The Pits and Hólahéi Scatter were among the first nine sites excavated for the NMRAP, and the original plan called for conducting OHD at several more Archaic sites with obsidian artifacts. The poor results obtained for these two sites were sufficient cause to abandon the technique for further application on this project, with funding instead shifted to the more reliable radiocarbon method. The unsatisfactory performance of OHD in this instance is just another example in a long catalog of failure throughout the world (see review in Anovitz et al. 1999:736–737). Anovitz et al. conclude that "at best, OHD as it currently exists is an inconsistent and unpredictable dating method; at worst, it is entirely unreliable" (1999:737). OHD results for The Pits appear to fit the "best"-case scenario, in that two of the 10 hydration dates fall within the expected time period (20% success!). Unfortunately, the technique alone provides no basis for knowing that these two dates were any better than the others. The results for Hólahéi Scatter appear to fit the "worst"-case scenario, in that 14 of the 15 hydration dates are unacceptable and the one outlier might also be wrong. In this case natural burns through the site area might have reset the hydration rinds to values that are meaningless with regard to the time of deposition.

It is perhaps telling that in a paper advocating the technique (Stevenson et al. 2000), the method fared essentially no better than reported here. The truth to this is especially evident in the hydration results for single features (Stevenson et al. 2000:Table 3) where rim measurements and calculated dates fluctuate wildly and the hydration dates show no correspondence with radiocarbon dates. But perhaps we ask too much of the technique (Hull 2001). There can be no doubt that our views of OHD's success depend upon our expectations of how the technique will perform, what it can achieve with temporal placement. If a one in five chance of correct temporal placement is acceptable—as well as the converse, a four in five chance of incorrect temporal assignment—then by all means use OHD. The trick is knowing which of the five dates, if any, to believe.

Archaic Settlement

The geographies of subsistence and settlement are intertwined and, among foragers, interdependent; home, whether transitory or permanent, tends to be located so as to enhance the efficiency of work spent acquiring resources, while the mix of resources actually exploited tends to be selected in part with reference to the benefits and costs inherent in transport and travel to and from the home base [Raven 1991:42].

Archaeologists have been interested in prehistoric settlement behavior for one reason or another ever since the pioneering work of Gordon Willey (1953) in the Virú Valley of Peru. Settlement data are important as a means for making inferences about other aspects of past lifeways, especially economic differentiation and integration at all levels of complexity, from a forager band that annually moves itself across regional space for various extractive purposes to a state-like polity with its differentiated parts scattered across the landscape and tied together by various economic and political means. Settlement behavior is a central topic of forager studies, and in a large sense this interest can be traced back to Julian Steward's (1938) ethnographic work among hunter-gatherers of the Great Basin and Columbia Plateau and his (1937a) own preliminary analysis of prehistoric settlement patterns around the Great Salt Lake. Steward's approach was essentially one of simple analogy, long used in archaeology but also criticized (e.g., Binford 1967). To eschew such criticism and associated ad hoc reasoning, studies of forager settlement can begin with theory and then make predictions about the settlement record, as seen in Thomas's (1983) work in Monitor Valley and Kelly's (1985) research in the Carson Desert. This approach is not infallible, as was dramatically shown by the flooding in the Carson Desert that exposed a plethora of forager habitations next to marshes, evidence of a limnosedentary (or semisedentary) adaptation (Raven and Elston 1991:5).

A beginning place for most settlement studies is with the locations in space at which past human activity left concentrations of artifacts or features, inferring what such sites were used for. Were they places of family residence, even if transitory? Or were they used on a more limited basis, such as a temporary resting place for hunters or a location of plant processing or lithic procurement? One basic issue concerns reconstructing or inferring the activity or behavior that generated the cluster of remains that we identify as sites. Foragers on the Colorado Plateau created some sites specifically for symbolic purposes. Good examples are the rock art panels widely scattered across the region, such as the impressive examples known as the Barrier Canyon style (Schaafsma 1971, 1986). Ritual sites for the deposition of split-twig figurines, often with extremely dangerous access (Coulam and Schroedl 2004; Emslie et al. 1987; Emslie et al. 1995), provide other good examples. There were probably other sites as well not directly related to acquiring and processing resources of one type or another or to general living, but none were recognized on the NMRAP, so the concern here is with sites easily accommodated within an ecological perspective.

Another interest in forager settlement has been describing how sites are distributed across a landscape and attempting to understand the reasons for any distributional regularities within the ecological framework implied by Raven's quote above. This can happen on one of two levels: trying to understand decisions of site location that are spatially general (why was this locality or region used?) and those that are spatially specific (why was this particular spot occupied?). General settlement decisions are principally made on the basis of one or more resource requirements, mainly those pertaining to subsistence, especially bulky staple foods. Specific settlement decisions follow those of general site location and may be predicated on a variety of factors that usually relate to convenience, efficiency, and comfort in daily activities. The former are critical to survival and take precedence over those of specific location, except perhaps during winter in temperate climates when shelter and fuel wood become significant variables. How foragers organized the procurement and consumption of food is another aspect of settlement behavior of interest to archaeologists. Variability in human organizational strategies is highly dependent on the nature of subsistence resource distributions (Ambrose 1984; Dyson-Hudson and Smith 1978).

Optimization theory in behavioral ecology—the desire to achieve maximum net gain from resource acquisition (e.g., Charnov 1976; Kaplan and Hill 1992)—is a key assumption underlying most archaeological studies of hunter-gatherer settlement behavior. The assumption of optimality for humans has been questioned as unrealistic since much human decision making seems to better accord with courses of action that are simply "good enough" but not necessarily optimal with respect to some objective measure (Simon 1957:198–199): "To the extent that human decisions are rational, they are rational with respect to a bounded view of the alternatives and consequences that affect the outcome of decisions" (Wood 1978:259). Although choices might not have maximized returns in some ultimate sense, humans tend to behave optimally when satisfying some predetermined need because of natural selection on the underlying determinants of behavior (e.g., Krebs and Davies 1984). Indeed, there are important fitness benefits to behaving in an optimizing manner (Smith 1979) even with "limited rationality," or constrained optimization (Foley 1985).

Since it is generally true that maximization is best achieved by residing close to the primary resources being used, especially if they are heavy or bulky relative to the energy provided (not nutrient dense), seasonal movement by foragers is expectable. Foragers create sites at different places on the landscape throughout a year principally because food availability is variable in both space and time. On the Rainbow Plateau, like most portions of the Southwest, critical resources rarely co-occur in the same location or time; the former is a problem of geographic placement, the latter is one of scheduling, yet both are tightly interwoven. For example, the northern part of the Rainbow Plateau is characterized by a shrub grassland that supports such economically important species as dropseed and ricegrass, but this area lacks nutritious pinyon nuts and is generally poor for hunting, at least for large game. Furthermore, the geographic location of food shifts as the seasons change—the productive ricegrass-covered flats of early summer offer little sustenance later in the year, and if the pinyon mast is heavy, the lower slopes of Navajo Mountain would be a preferable location during mid fall yet less ideal for winter, when cactus pads assume great importance and are limited in abundance there compared to lower elevations. Although food has been emphasized, water can also be a critical limiting resource during portions of the year, especially in drought conditions; settlement shifts can happen for this reason alone, with residential camps moved to reliable water sources and placement relative to energy sources taking second priority.

Hunter-gatherers coped with spatial and temporal differences in resource distributions by various forms of movement, either as entire family groups or in some subset thereof (Binford 1978, 1980; Kelly 1983; Thomas 1985). Binford's (1980) well-known forager–collector continuum is one common way of conceptualizing variability in mobility organization. Although called a continuum, and despite Thomas's claim that "any given group of hunter-gatherers can be characterized as residentially mobile, logistically mobile, or as some mix of the two" (1983:17), in a very real sense the two ends are mutually exclusive at any single point in time, because either consumers are moved to resources (residential mobility) or a small group of providers move resources to consumers back at home (logistic mobility). The continuum part refers to the temporal dimension, either annually or on larger temporal cycles, "since ecological requirements sometimes are such that a given group must shift seasonally and/or annually along the foraging–collecting continuum" (Thomas 1983:17).

It is highly doubtful that a strict collecting strategy with no or low residential mobility was a realistic possibility on the Colorado Plateau until the introduction of domesticates. Prior to this, subsistence resources were probably never sufficiently abundant, predictable, and concentrated to allow the establishment of long-term residential camps. Archaic populations probably used a largely foraging strategy of residential mobility with many temporary residential camps widely distributed across the landscape to effectively exploit critical bulky subsistence resources that were differentially distributed in both space and time.

General Considerations of Site Types

Foraging theory has nothing specific to say about how hunter-gatherers might structure and organize their settlement behavior, perhaps since animals other than humans have a very simple system—either an endless series of one-night stands or, for some species, the use of a temporary home base (nest or burrow) during the breeding season. Observations of chimps in the wild reveal that they operate under the principle of endless one-night stands all the time (e.g., Goodall 1986), and this may have been the original pattern for human ancestors as long as the environment stayed homogeneous rather than patchy in both space and time. Once resources became clumped in space or time, including water resources, then there may have been incentive to stay in one place for some duration before moving to the next patch. Male provisioning could have played an important role in this as well. The idea of male provisioning and repeatedly used home bases in human evolution was brought to the fore by Glynn Isaac (1978a, 1978b) to account for localized concentrations of early hominid artifacts and bones separated by relatively empty space. Assuming that natural forces have not concentrated the remains or created artificial partitions, the base camp inference was basically one of simple analogy to ethnographic descriptions of camps such as Yellen (1977) provided for the San of South Africa. Using such a modern analogue to interpret the remains of ancestral humans is potentially suspect, but even in more recent archaeological cases, where we are dealing with anatomically and behaviorally modern humans, simple analogues should be treated cautiously.

There are two basic ways of making site type assignments: (1) by proceeding inductively to group or cluster sites based on their characteristics (usually a partitioning of a continuum of variability) and then assigning such groups to settlement types (assigning behavioral meaning) or (2) by starting with statements about what the archaeological patterning should be for certain activities and settlement organization (logistic or forager) and then assessing the degree of fit for individual sites. Ethnographic observations on the range of behaviors observed in the world are critical to either approach, but in the former the information is used on more of an ad hoc basis to infer what the groups or data partitions might mean in terms of settlement behavior. In the latter approach, well exemplified by Thomas's (1983) research in Monitor Valley of the Great Basin, ethnographies help to inform what we might expect to see in the archaeological record for given activities. Either way there is a linkage problem, something that Thomas discussed at great length in his 1983 report. Because of this linkage problem, he cautions with regard to site types that "it seems preferable to exercise a degree of interpretive restraint than to blither on about what simply is not so" (1986:243). Although mindful of the need for circumspection, a site typology has utility for providing an initial basis for describing and perhaps understanding settlement behavior.

A key assumption when considering site types is the anticipated extent of settlement differentiation, which immediately brings to mind the now commonplace contrast between foragers and collectors (Binford 1980). Following Yellen's (1977:77–84) arguments about hunter-gatherer intercamp variability, and Binford's (1980:5–10) expectations about the archaeological remains produced by simple collectors, one might expect that most Archaic sites were base camps and that task-specific sites, other than lithic quarries, would leave few material remains, meaning that they would be largely invisible in the archaeological record because they get recorded as isolated occurrences. Vierra (1980) took this position in his analysis of Archaic sites for the Coal Gasification Project (CGP) in northwestern New Mexico. He reached different conclusions about Archaic settlement behavior compared to Reher (1977), who had analyzed sites of the same area. The differing interpretations of Vierra and Reher in this case can be traced to divergent theoretical views concerning Archaic settlement-subsistence organization. To Vierra, the Archaic people of the San Juan Basin were foragers, and as Binford (1980:5–10) argued, foragers generate basically two types of sites, the residential base and the largely invisible location. Reher's view of Archaic settlement-subsistence organization is not explicitly stated, but Vierra (1980) implies that Reher allowed more site variability than entailed by a foraging model.

Even if a forager strategy was pursued on a full-time basis throughout the year, there are reasons to expect that some task-specific sites might be less invisible than assumed. There are also good reasons to expect that hunter-gatherers on the Colorado Plateau used some level of logistic organization and hence had a slightly more differentiated system that resulted in other kinds of sites than simply base camps and quarries. Hunting big game is a principal reason to expect overnight camps well away from residential camps. These could occur in any season since residential camps might not be located in areas that were productive of game or such areas could have become resource depressed soon after arrival. Logistic hunting camps seem especially likely for the winter months, when forager groups are assumed to have been far less residentially mobile. Even during the growing season, camp movement might have been severely constrained by water availability, which could have resulted in gathering-related camps at some distance from the base camp. Moreover, some plant harvesting might have involved the use of hearths and even grinding tools at temporary camps away from residential bases in order to field process and thereby decrease transport weight (e.g., Barlow and Metcalfe 1996). Based on all of these issues, I expect Archaic foragers of the Kayenta region to have generated several different kinds of sites.

Three behavioral dimensions are implicated in the analysis of site function: occupation duration, activity diversity, and activity type. All are important separate considerations, though the three tend to be interrelated. For example, activity diversity can be directly related to occupation duration, and activity types are essential to any assessment of overall activity diversity, although diversity is not the same as function. Two sites could have similarly diverse lithic assemblages but different activity types (settlement roles), and the ability to diagnose such functional differences is essential to any regional study of settlement behavior. While acknowledging the many complexities involved in assemblage formation, archaeologists assume that the artifacts left at archaeological sites allow inferences about each of these three behavioral dimensions. Features also play an important role since feature type is commonly assumed to inform us about one or more of the dimensions. Furthermore, features represent on-site activity by definition, something that is not necessarily true of stone tools.

Occupation duration, activity diversity, and activity type are involved in the continuum of structural–functional variability that gets preserved in the archaeological record at sites. Measures of this variability are also usually arrayed as a continuum—from few artifacts and features to many, from single artifact or feature types to numerous types. This continuum is partitioned into groups that are thought to have behavioral meaning. At the simplest level, this continuum is dichotomized into two major groups and interpreted as distinct site types: habitation sites, or base camps, and limited-activity sites. Consensus among archaeologists at even this simple dichotomous level seldom exists, except in trivially obvious examples. This continuum of site variability can be split finer; for example, Tipps and Schroedl (1988:48) recognized four site groupings, designated as limited-activity sites, temporary field camps, extended field camps, and base camps. Tipps and Schroedl derived their four groups based on a principal components analysis of five archaeological measures of the behavioral dimensions of site function: tool assemblage diversity, maximum artifact density, debitage frequency, feature number, and site size.

Statistical manipulations do not guarantee useful or meaningful partitions of a data set any more than intuitive partitions. When Reher (1977:98) used a battery of statistical techniques on lithic assemblage attributes to distinguish between Archaic base camps and limited-activity sites for the CGP in northwestern New Mexico, he found a continuum of variation with no distinct breaks. Even upon considering hearths and the number and types of tool classes, "the overall continuum from one end of the range to the other was maintained" (Reher 1977:98). The lack of obvious breaks did not surprise Vierra (1980) in his later study of CGP Archaic sites. Because he considered the San Juan Basin Archaic groups as foragers in Binfordian terms, the existence of an unpartitionable continuum presented no conceptual dilemma since it supported the view that Reher was merely measuring variability within a single site type—the forager base camp. In this case, different notions about how societies organized their settlement behavior affected the perception of data variability and its meaning. What neither researcher fully addressed is how different occupational histories influenced the site content they interpreted. Reher admits that his inability to define distinct site types resulted from "several thousand years of small, overlapping settlement events followed by several thousand years of movement of aeolian sands" (1977:98). Deciphering the occupational histories of these sites might disclose that therein lies the underlying cause of the unpartitionable continuum, but this remains to be seen.

NMRAP Archaic Sites

During the course of the N16 project, NNAD archaeologists excavated 16 Archaic components at 14 open sites and tested Atlatl Rock Cave, which contains early Archaic deposits. The extent of excavation at each of the 15 sites varied from near minimal (the cave and a few open sites) to extensive, amounting to essentially 100 percent of what was preserved. The caveat that NNAD archaeologists studied what remained is important because several of the sites had been impacted by prior road construction. In each of these cases I assume that what was lost was just more of the same (redundant information) rather than something entirely different. In at least two cases (Tres Campos and Hólahéi Scatter), remains present along the old roadcut matched those recovered from the intact site portions, supporting the assumption that the lost information would not alter data patterning had we recovered all remains.

I did not begin the NMRAP with a predetermined settlement typology for classifying the N16 Archaic sites, but it is also true that working in the region for decades and grappling with the issue of site types leave one with predetermined notions or preconceptions as to what intersite patterning in material remains and features might mean with regard to settlement behavior. In the process of report writing, when all the data were in hand, the intuitive classification procedure continued, and the site type assignments essentially became formalized in the process of putting ideas to paper. It is important to realize the limitations of organizational schemes based on inferred functions and subjective pattern seeking, but this seems an appropriate approach given the limited number of sites considered here and the complications of factoring in the variable nature of the excavations at each site, the effects of time and differential burial on preservation, and factors of site formation. Furthermore, the approach does not preclude examining the data so that readers can reach their own conclusions or use them to group sites in other ways such as on descriptive attributes alone rather than functional inferences.

Table 4.9 summarizes basic descriptive data for each of the 15 NMRAP Archaic sites, which are organized geographically from north to south. As detailed previously under radiocarbon dating, all but two of the sites are assigned to a specific temporal interval of the Archaic period based on radiocarbon dates; the two exceptions were given a general "Archaic" designation in the temporal assignment column. The basic inferred roles of the sites in regional settlement-subsistence are also listed here based on the sum of all evidence, intuitively taking into account several independent behavioral dimensions such as inferred economic pursuit, group composition, and occupation duration. The four principal site types are residential camp, hunting camp, processing camp, and processing site. These generally track with decreasing quantity and diversity of remains, with processing sites having the fewest items or even none, consisting only of hearths.

Differences in the quantity of remains are perhaps best appreciated after controlling for variable recovery rates since the excavated areas varied greatly among sites. A simple yet informative way to do this is by excavated area—the square meters of cultural fill that were removed by hand and screened. Because the strata in all cases were essentially of the same thickness, usually no more than 10–15 cm of accumulation, an area figure is a useful way to standardize frequency (Table 4.10). The size of the excavation area cannot necessarily be equated with the degree of representation. For example, the 4-m² area hand excavated at Sapo Seco seems like a paltry amount, yet it was quite adequate because the site consisted of only a single hearth in a flat expanse of shrubs and grass. In effect, the work involved thorough excavation of the entire Archaic component, a claim bolstered by the fact that extensive backhoe stripping and trenching did not locate any additional Archaic features. In contrast, the roughly 2.5-m² area excavated at Atlatl Rock Cave might be poorly representative of the deposition in that shelter, not only because it is a small fraction of the overall site but also because foragers might have differentially used the interior sheltered space such that any one spot would likely be unrepresentative of shelter use overall. For example, full excavation of Dust Devil Cave revealed clear patterns in how early Archaic foragers used the interior space of the site (Ambler 1996).

Feature density cannot be gauged from the hand-excavation areas given in Table 4.9 since at many sites feature count is partially or wholly the result of mechanical stripping with a backhoe. In several cases, such as at Tsé Haal'á, features were documented only within the hand-excavated area. Hearth density may not be that informative anyway, since sites thought to have been residential, such as Three Dog, were no different in density and patterning than sites of limited activity such as Polly's Place—both had areas with dense clusters and areas with few hearths. Perhaps more telling was the presence, extent, and density of charcoal-flecked and -stained sediment, since this probably has a much greater bearing on the intensity of site use. To continue with the two previous examples, Three Dog Site was characterized by darkly charcoal-stained and -flecked Archaic layers, whereas at Polly's Place the hearths originated from a layer of sand that lacked charcoal staining and flecking (though it was organic stained from incipient A horizon development).

The density figures of Table 4.10 are sorted in order from greatest to least in Table 4.11, with each column treated individually. This allows easy appreciation of which sites have the most of each type of remains and which have the least or none. Some sites, for example, are mostly near the top of each list, whereas some are mostly near the bottom. Figure 4.7 plots the density values for the three remains that are the most revealing.

Residential Camps

Residential camps are thought to have served as the focal points of numerous activities necessary for the day-to-day maintenance of family groups. The duration of occupancy of these camps was probably quite variable but in general was probably less than a few months and most commonly just a few weeks or less. The notion of a relatively short length of stay at such camps is predicated on subsistence strategy and local ecology, which for the Colorado Plateau probably required a moderate to high degree of residential mobility (Binford 1978, 1980; Kelly 1983; Thomas 1983). As mentioned previously, the subsistence resources available to Archaic foragers on the Colorado Plateau in general and the Rainbow Plateau in this particular instance were probably never sufficiently abundant, predictable, and concentrated to allow the establishment of long-term residential base camps or what might be termed semipermanent residences. Archaic foragers of the region probably depended on moving consumers to the resources, thereby resulting in a series of residential camps, each situated in or near some seasonal resource patch and seldom used for long, though perhaps reoccupied repeatedly. The possible exception to this would have been during winter, when there were few plant foods to

TABLE 4.9. Summary Data for the Navajo Mountain Road Archaeological Project Archaic Sites or Components as well as the Inferred Settlement Role

Site Name	Site No.	Function	Excavated Area (m²)	Temporal Assignment	14C Dated	Living Structures	Pits	Hearths	Faunal Bone	Debitage	Flaked Tools	Cores/ Nodular Tools	Grinding Tools
Tsé Haal'á	UT-B-63-30	residential camp	76	late Archaic	+	0	1	13	1,402	3,532	38	1	70[a]
	UT-B-63-38	residential camp	57	Archaic	−	0	0	0	3	910	4	1	8
Three Dog Site	UT-B-63-39	residential camp	~171	late Archaic	+	1?	0	30	3,255	2,699	11	4	16
Bonsai Bivouac	AZ-J-2-55	processing site	0	early Archaic	+	0	0	8	0	0	0	0	0
Sapo Seco	AZ-J-2-6	hunting camp	4	early Archaic	+	0	0	1	1	56	0	0	0
Dune Hollow	AZ-J-2-2	processing camp	9	early Archaic	+	0	0	2	40	16	0	0	2
Mouse House	AZ-J-3-7	processing site	~1	early Archaic	+	0	0	2	0	0	0	0	0
Atlatl Rock Cave	AZ-J-14-41	residential camp	~2.5	early Archaic	+	0	0	+	71	14	1	0	10
Big Bend	AZ-J-14-13	processing camp	70	early and late Archaic	+	0	0	8	1	35	1	1	1
Tres Campos	AZ-J-14-12	hunting camp	56	early Archaic	+	0	0	4	107	873	7	0	1
Polly's Place	AZ-J-14-31	processing site	~21.5	early Archaic	+	0	0	13	0	6	0	0	0
Windy Mesa	AZ-J-14-28	hunting camp	~38	early Archaic	+	0	1?	4	11	281	3	0	1
Pee Wee Grande	AZ-J-14-26	processing site	27	early Archaic	+	0	0	11	0	302	3	2	0
Hólahéi Scatter	AZ-J-14-23	hunting camp	69	Archaic	−	0	0	0	50	851	13	2	0
The Pits	AZ-J-14-17	hunting camp	40	late Archaic	+	0	0	3	18	237	5	1	0

Note: Sites are ordered from north to south.

[a] This excludes 54 grinding tools from the surface that could be from later site use.

TABLE 4.10. Density of Various Remains Recovered from Navajo Mountain Road Archaeological Project Archaic Sites

SITE NAME	DENSITY (#/m²)				
	FAUNAL BONE	GRINDING TOOLS	DEBITAGE	FLAKED TOOLS	CORE/NODULAR TOOLS
Tsé Haal'á	18.45	.92	46.47	.50	.01
UT-V-63-38	.05	.14	15.96	.07	.02
Three Dog Site	19.04	.09	15.78	.06	.02
Bonsai Bivouac	.00	.00	.00	.00	.00
Sapo Seco	.25	.00	14.00	.00	.00
Dune Hollow	4.44	.22	1.78	.00	.00
Mouse House	.00	.00	.00	.00	.00
Atlatl Rock Cave	28.40	4.00	5.60	.40	.00
Big Bend	.01	.01	.50	.01	.01
Tres Campos	1.91	.02	15.59	.13	.00
Polly's Place	.00	.00	.28	.00	.00
Windy Mesa	.29	.03	7.39	.08	.00
Pee Wee Grande	.00	.00	11.19	.11	.07
Hólahéi Scatter	.72	.00	12.33	.19	.03
The Pits	.45	.00	5.93	.13	.03

Note: Sites are ordered from north to south. Excavated areas are given in Table 4.9.

TABLE 4.11. Ordering of the Archaic Sites by the Five Density Measures of Remains (#/m²) from Highest to Lowest

FAUNAL BONE		GRINDING TOOLS		DEBITAGE		FLAKED TOOLS		CORE/NODULAR TOOLS	
SITE NAME	DENSITY	SITE NAME	DENSITY	SITE NAME	DENSITY	SITE NAME	DENSITY	SITE NAME	DENSITY
Atlatl Rock Cave	28.40	Atlatl Rock Cave	4.00	Tsé Haal'á	46.47	Tsé Haal'á	.50	Pee Wee Grande	.07
Three Dog Site	19.04	Tsé Haal'á	.92	UT-B-63-38	15.96	Atlatl Rock Cave	.40	Hólahéi Scatter	.03
Tsé Haal'á	18.45	Dune Hollow	.22	Three Dog Site	15.78	Hólahéi Scatter	.19	The Pits	.03
Dune Hollow	4.44	UT-B-63-38	.14	Tres Campos	15.59	Tres Campos	.13	Three Dog Site	.02
Tres Campos	1.91	Three Dog Site	.09	Sapo Seco	14.00	The Pits	.13	UT-B-63-38	.02
Hólahéi Scatter	.72	Windy Mesa	.03	Hólahéi Scatter	12.33	Pee Wee Grande	.11	Big Bend	.01
The Pits	.45	Tres Campos	.02	Pee Wee Grande	11.19	Windy Mesa	.08	Tsé Haal'á	.01
Windy Mesa	.29	Big Bend	.01	Windy Mesa	7.39	UT-B-63-38	.07	Windy Mesa	.00
Sapo Seco	.25	Bonsai Bivouac	.00	The Pits	5.93	Three Dog Site	.06	Tres Campos	.00
UT-B-63-38	.05	Sapo Seco	.00	Atlatl Rock Cave	5.60	Big Bend	.01	Sapo Seco	.00
Big Bend	.01	Mouse House	.00	Dune Hollow	1.78	Bonsai Bivouac	.00	Polly's Place	.00
Bonsai Bivouac	.00	Polly's Place	.00	Big Bend	.50	Sapo Seco	.00	Mouse House	.00
Mouse House	.00	Pee Wee Grande	.00	Polly's Place	.28	Dune Hollow	.00	Dune Hollow	.00
Polly's Place	.00	Hólahéi Scatter	.00	Bonsai Bivouac	.00	Mouse House	.00	Bonsai Bivouac	.00
Pee Wee Grande	.00	The Pits	.00	Mouse House	.00	Polly's Place	.00	Atlatl Rock Cave	.00

collect except for cactus pads, and survival probably involved reliance upon stored seeds or meat that could have been efficiently brought back to base camps.

Four residential camps were identified in the NMRAP site sample: Atlatl Rock Cave and the three open sites Tsé Haal'á, Three Dog Site, and the unnamed UT-B-63-38 (Figures 4.8–4.9). The cave was occupied during the early Archaic, and its use was probably quite comparable to Sand Dune and Dust Devil caves, although Dust Devil evidently saw considerably more occupation because the early Archaic cultural accumulation was many times thicker (ca. 1 m) than at either of the other caves. The two largest of the open sites date to the late Archaic, while the third smaller example remains undated. Not too surprisingly, all residential camps are located near reliable water sources. The open sites all occur along the eastern base of

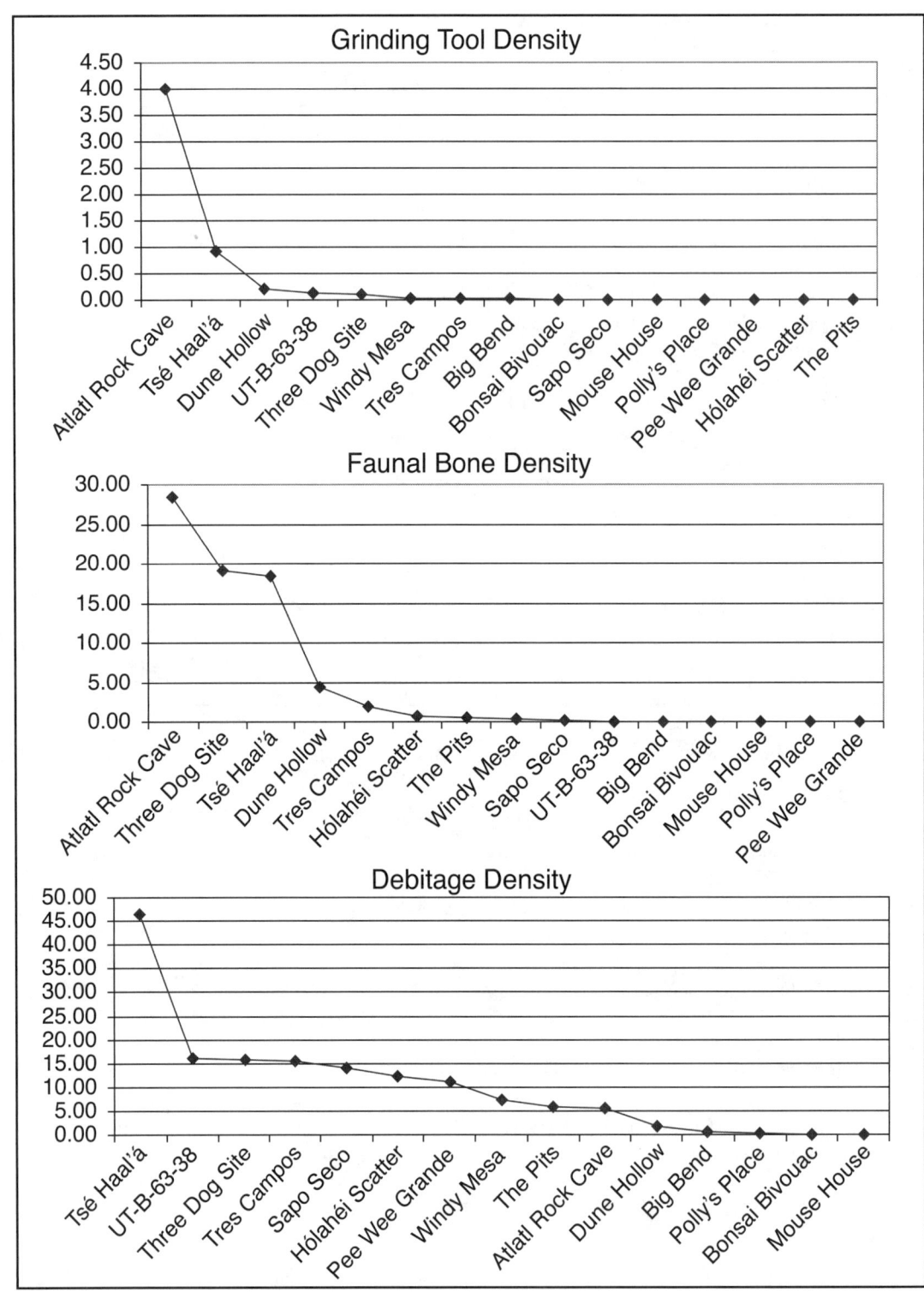

Figure 4.7. Plots of Navajo Mountain Road Archaeological Project Archaic sites organized by density (#/m²) of grinding tools, faunal bone, and debitage.

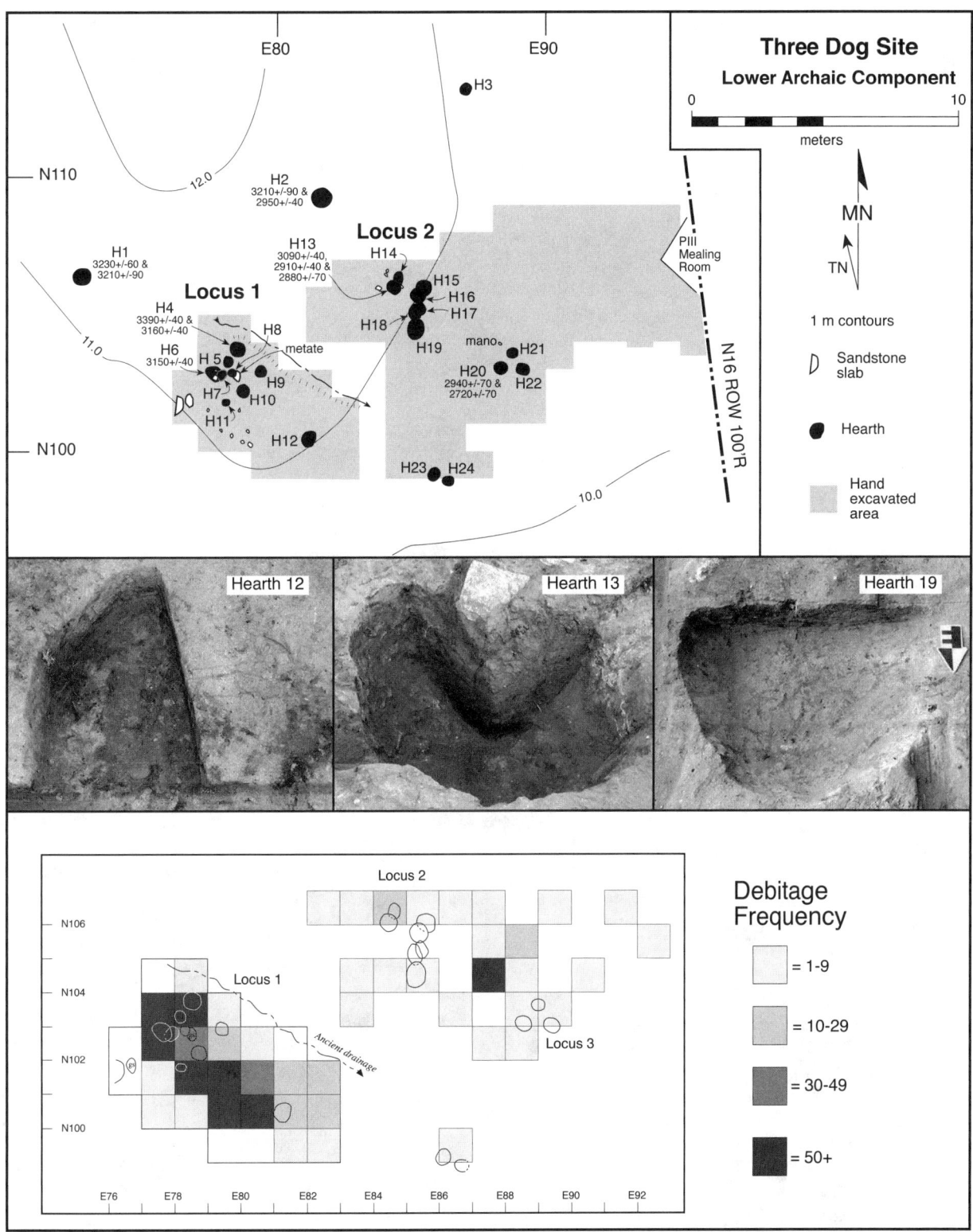

Figure 4.8. Plan map of the lower late Archaic component of Three Dog Site showing examples of the basin hearths and the density of debitage recovered from 1-x-1-m units.

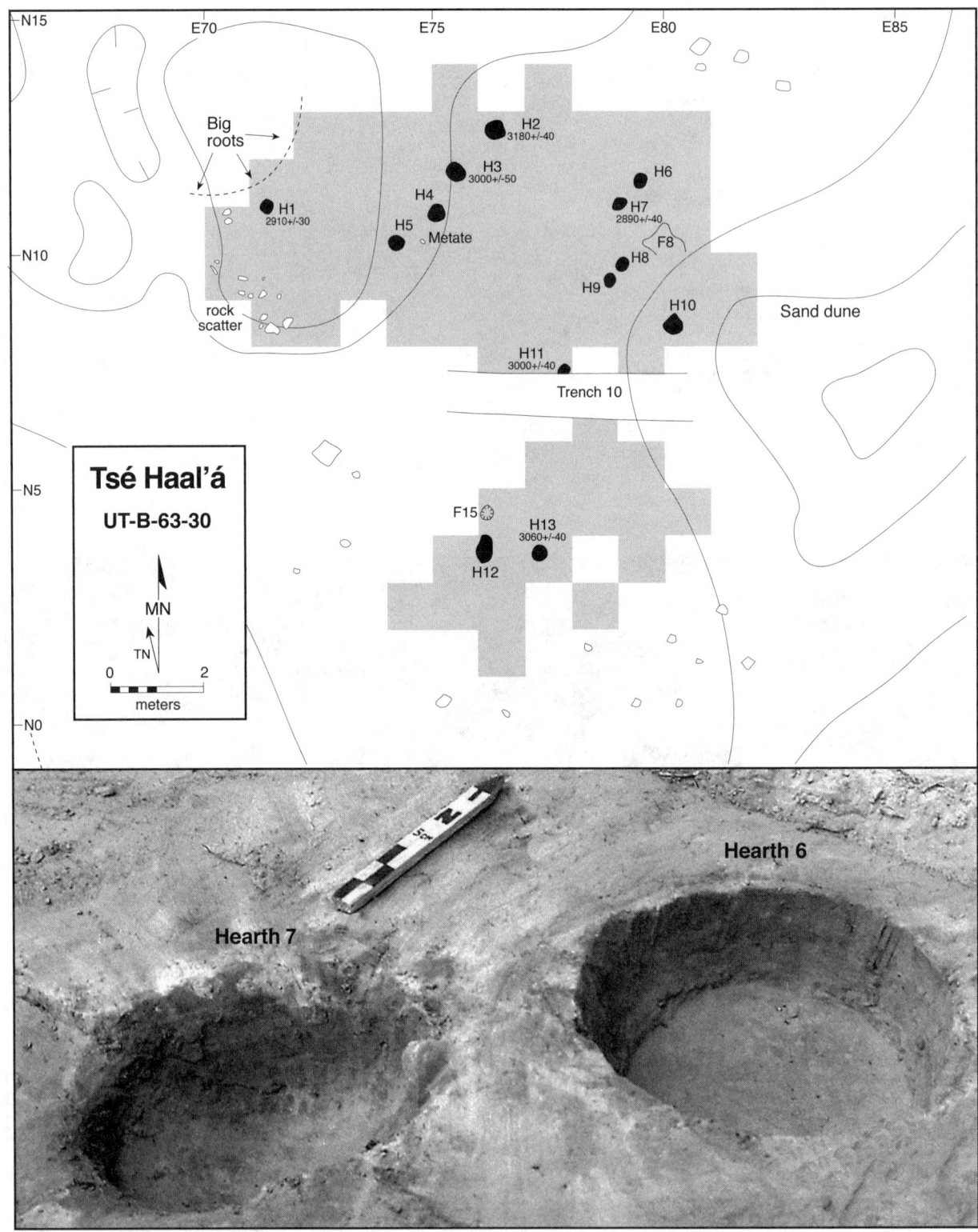

Figure 4.9. Plan map of the late Archaic component of Tsé Haal'á showing examples of the basin hearths.

Navajo Mountain next to drainages that head on the mountain slopes—a spring that often supports streamflow for a short distance occurs in the drainage by Three Dog Site, and in the drainage by Tsé Haal'á and UT-B-63-38 there is a large plunge pool that holds water throughout the year except for times of extreme drought. Atlatl Rock Cave has a seep that issues from its mouth just outside the dripline, a source augmented by several permanent springs within a few kilometers in Piute Canyon. Although other site types might also be located somewhat close to water, this may have been a less pressing concern given more transient use and probable smaller group size.

The important attribute for identifying sites as temporary residential camps is an abundant and diverse set of stone artifacts, with the presence of grinding tools of special significance, especially when co-occurring with hearths and charcoal-stained and -flecked sediment as previously mentioned. Assemblage diversity is linked to the notion that residential camps are the locus of most food processing and tool manufacture and maintenance. All of the diverse activities of camp life, such as seed grinding, hide scraping, tool production, and the like, ostensibly result in the accumulation of a diverse set of artifact classes. Part of this diversity includes the co-occurrence of tools commonly assumed to be associated with sex-differentiated subsistence tasks (hunting implements vs. grinding implements), with the implication that entire families occupied such camps. Assemblage diversity can be measured in several ways, such as simple class richness or the Shannon information statistic and derivatives (Pielou 1966; Zar 1974); I use an intuitive estimate. Because of sample size effects, no simple correlation necessarily exists between assemblage diversity and site functions (Thomas 1986:242). Sites with numerous artifacts may appear more diverse than sites with fewer remains simply because having more often results in greater variety; see Leonard and Jones (1989) for an extensive discussion of the diversity–sample size issue. But sample size variation can be a real attribute of past behavior and not merely an artifact of our methods (Plog and Hegmon 1993). Variation among sites likely results from some composite of factors relating to differences in function, occupation duration, group size, repetitive and nonrepetitive site reuse, and unobserved mixture of temporal components.

Grinding tools, but especially metates, are important criteria for inclusion in the residential camp class because few other stone artifacts have such a clear association with food preparation and daily consumption. This stands in marked contrast to most other stone artifacts at sites, which were used in the manufacture or maintenance of other technology (general domestic activity) or were the debris from manufacture and maintenance activities. Given the importance of seeds in Archaic diets on the Colorado Plateau (e.g., Van Ness and Hansen 1996), it is probable that families encamped for a day or two during most seasons would have needed some means for grinding. Grinding is seldom a useful processing step in preparation for storage because turning seed to flour hastens deterioration and the loss of nutrition and increases exposure to pests. Seeds for storage are best left whole and in their protective hulls. Grinding slabs and manos are therefore considered evidence of food preparation just prior to consumption. Manos are easily transported, and it is likely that these tools formed part of the mobile tool kit that forager groups carried from one location to another. Consequently, they could end up at sites where the tools were never used. Metates, on the other hand, are considered "site furniture" (Binford 1979:263–264); thus their recovery context is likely to have been their use context. As such, these tools provide a reliable means to infer in situ seed processing.

Features indicative of food processing (hearths and roasting pits) co-occurring with grinding tools helps to corroborate the residential camp inference. Since it is useful to parch most seeds prior to consumption—to increase their flavor, as a means to help reduce or eliminate chaff, and in some cases for adequate nutrition absorption—hearths are essential for creating the necessary hot coals. Hearths are also important for preparing prickly pear pads for consumption, both for singeing of spines and for cooking, to say nothing of their role in meat preparation. The repeated use of hearths over some length of time generates areas of charcoal-stained and -flecked sediment that is intermixed with bone, flaking waste, and occasional stone tools creating midden accumulations. These are not necessarily middens in the sense of secondary refuse disposal but, rather, are locations where debris accumulated in abundance while conducting various cooking, processing, and production tasks associated with living. This is also seen at occupied caves of the region, except that at these the organic debris from living has been preserved as well. Middens are unlikely to occur at short-term use locations, simply because of the nature of the activities and the brief stays, which tend not to generate such messy deposits.

Figure 4.10. The interior of Atlatl Rock Cave from its mouth prior to looting; Kathryn McCraley stands at the back. Note the patch of smoke blackening, which demarks a portion of the ceiling that has been relatively stable; the darkest portions probably date to the early Archaic, when the cave served as a residential base and many fires were built within its confines. A thick layer of roof spall, up to 80 cm deep, buried early Archaic deposits (photo by Dan Boone).

A Cave for All Seasons. Despite the small area investigated, I have good reason to believe that Atlatl Rock Cave (Figure 4.10) served as a forager residential base, something that is perhaps generally true of caves that are ideally situated relative to water and food resources as this one is. Such an ideal shelter was likely used for other purposes as well, but like Dust Devil Cave, its chief role was probably as a residential base, a key node for foragers who considered the Rainbow Plateau home for at least a portion of the year. Despite the very limited test, Atlatl Rock Cave contains the highest bone and grinding tool density among any of the Archaic sites considered here (Table 4.11 and Figure 4.7). The faunal bone reveals an emphasis on cottontail and jackrabbit, something that is also true for Dust Devil Cave (Gilbert 1984; Stroup 1972) and evidently for the early Archaic diet in the region generally (e.g., Van Ness and Hansen 1996). This site also yielded a great diversity and abundance of macrofloral remains (see Table 4.2) as well as discarded sandals.

Three flotation samples for the early Archaic layers in the cave contained a relatively high number of individual plant specimens ($n = 105-261$) and a high diversity ($n = 11-15$) of plant taxa (see SD vol. 2, Table 2.7). Pads and the burned and unburned spines of prickly pear cacti were well represented. Prickly pear is one of the common constituents of early Archaic feces and often accounts for the bulk of food residue therein (Van Ness and Hansen 1996). Ethnobotanical studies (e.g., Kelly 1964:45) have indicated that cacti were generally burned and eaten as starvation foods in early spring. Therefore, the presence of burned and unburned cacti spines may represent a late winter or early spring occupation of the cave. The common edible seeds in the early Archaic samples are from dropseed and Cheno-Am, the two taxa most frequently represented in early Archaic feces and evidently heavily relied upon for food (Van Ness and Hansen 1996). Grass seed processing at the site is also indicated by a pollen wash of a whole metate. Ricegrass is poorly represented in the early Archaic samples, paralleling the findings from other early Archaic sheltered sites.

In addition to cacti and seeds, the early Archaic matrix samples also contain several fruits that would have been available in the late summer or early fall, including pinyon (*Pinus edulis*), hackberry (*Celtis reticulate*), chokecherry (*Prunus virginiana*), and rose (*Rosa* sp.) The occurrence of pinyon in all of the early Archaic samples from Atlatl Rock Cave helps to confirm that this plant was present on the Colorado Plateau at the Utah-Arizona border at or shortly after 7000 cal. BC, a claim verified by the pack rat midden study around Navajo Mountain (see SD Appendix K). With pinyon unequivocally documented as a component of the Upper Sonoran flora from the early Holocene onward, this significant food resource must have played a role in structuring fall settlement behavior, especially during years of sporadic bumper harvests.

Contrasting Camps: Three Dog Site and Tsé Haal'á. Both of these sites (see Figures 4.8–4.9) date to the late Archaic and were perhaps used during roughly the same time. The suite of radiocarbon dates for both sites shows considerable overlap in the interval from about 1300 to 1000 cal. BC. Three Dog Site evidently saw slightly earlier use at ca. 1500–1300 cal. BC and also transient use at ca. 800–500 cal. BC. These two sites are interpreted as residential camps because of similarly high densities and diversities of remains, yet they have differences worth considering. The differences are especially noteworthy since, as essentially contemporaneous and within several kilometers of each other, these sites easily could represent the remains from the same general band of foragers.

Both sites have similar densities of faunal bone but significant differences in the density of grinding tools, debitage, and flaked-stone tools. The difference in grinding tool density is largely the result of fragmentation at Tsé Haal'á, where single grinding slabs were broken into many small pieces, greatly inflating the count, whereas at Three Dog Site whole grinding slabs or large portions were recovered. Ninety-six percent of the 70 Archaic grinding tools from Tsé Haal'á consisted of small fragments (average weight is 759 g), whereas 44 percent of these tools from Three Dog Site were whole, with another 13 percent as large fragments (average weight is 2,694 g). This contrast is no doubt the result of rapid and deep burial by eolian sand at Three Dog but a lack of such at Tsé Haal'á (Figure 4.11), which left the grinding tools exposed and subject to the destructive forces of nature. Bone is similarly far more fragmented at Tsé Haal'á than at Three Dog Site, although this is not readily apparent from the analysis results. A hint of this is apparent in how few of the specimens from Tsé Haal'á could be identified to at least the genus level (5/283 or 1.8%) compared to Three Dog Site, where almost 18 percent of the bone was identifiable to the genus level (51/286 or 17.8%; Table 4.12).

Although perhaps also related to differential preservation of faunal remains, another interesting difference between these two sites concerns bone artifacts. No worked bone came from Tsé Haal'á, but excavations at one portion of the late Archaic component of Three Dog Site recovered whole and fragmented beads along with other modified bone (Figure 4.12). Among the latter are the evident scraps from bead production, revealing the likely species and elements that the late Archaic foragers used to make their beads. The scraps consist of cottontail and jackrabbit articular ends of long bones, especially metatarsals, which were detached by score-and-snap incisions. Removal of articular ends created tubes or bead blanks that were finished by abrading smooth the irregularities of the scored and snapped cuts. These small tubular segments could then be strung and worn without further modification, with long wear providing use-polish and smoothing. Evidently the late Archaic foragers at Three Dog Site replaced old beads that were lost or discarded with new ones made from current kills, an activity that seems consistent with interpreting the site as a residential camp.

The contrast between Tsé Haal'á and Three Dog Site in debitage and flaked-stone tools cannot be accounted for by differential preservation. There is greater diversity in the flaked facial tool assemblage from Tsé Haal'á (eight of eight classes) than from Three Dog Site (four of eight), but this seems to be largely a sample size issue, since Tsé Haal'á produced more than three times as many tools (Table 4.13). Projectile points make up a large proportion of the flaked tools at Tsé Haal'á, almost 40 percent,

TABLE 4.12. Faunal Bone Recovered from the Late Archaic Components of Tsé Haal'á and Three Dog Site

TAXON	TSÉ HAAL'Á		THREE DOG SITE	
	n	%	n	%
Snake (Colubridae)	0	.0	1	.3
Perching bird (Passeriformes)	0	.0	1	.3
Pocket mouse (*Perognathus* sp.)	0	.0	1	.3
Kangaroo rat (*Dipodomys* sp.)	0	.0	3	1.0
Wood rat (*Neotoma* sp.)	2	.7	1	.3
Ground squirrel (*Spermophilus* sp.)	0	.0	1	.3
Cottontail (*Sylvilagus* sp.)	1	.4	22	7.7
Jackrabbit (*Lepus californicus*)	1	.4	6	2.1
Canids (Canidae)	0	.0	2	.7
Coyote (*Canis latrans*)	0	.0	2	.7
Artiodactyl (Artiodactyla)	41	14.5	1	.3
Deer (*Odocoileus* sp.)	1	.4	14	4.9
Tiny mammal	0	.0	1	.3
Small mammal	3	1.1	2	.7
Medium mammal	1	.4	6	2.1
Large mammal	9	3.2	21	7.3
Unidentified	224	79.2	201	70.3
Total	283	100.0	286	100.0

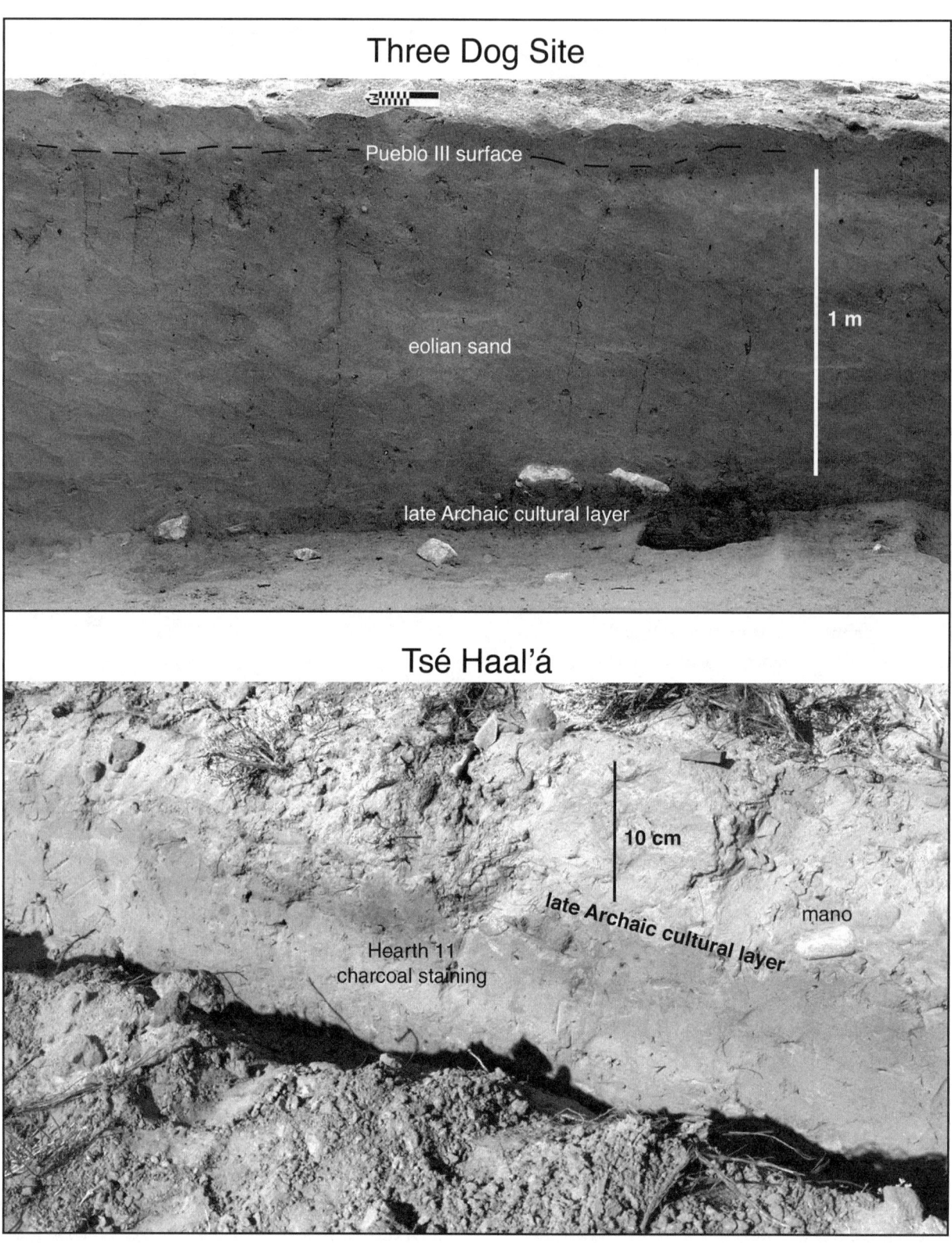

Figure 4.11. Stratigraphic exposures at Three Dog Site and Tsé Haal'á showing the vastly different depositional contexts; the late Archaic components of the former site were rapidly and deeply buried by eolian sand.

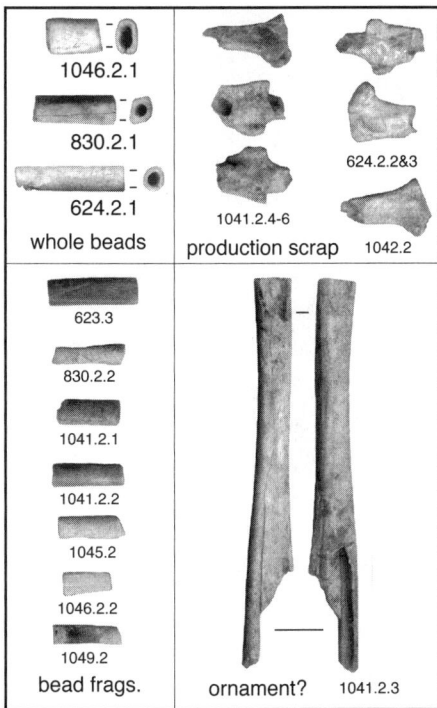

Figure 4.12. Bone beads and other artifacts recovered from the late Archaic component of Three Dog Site.

Figure 4.13. Projectile points recovered from Tsé Haal'á.

compared to less than 20 percent at Three Dog Site. The points at Tsé Haal'á consist largely of stem fragments (Figure 4.13), the sort of remains that hunters would deposit when they repaired gear, something that is expectable for a base camp. Although gear repair is less in evidence at Three Dog Site, faunal bone from large game was moderately abundant, attesting to the significance of hunting and game processing at that location. There is also evidence of smaller mammal procurement and consumption at Three Dog Site, especially at one portion of the camp that contains remains from lagomorphs to the near exclusion of deer or other large game (only a single identified large-mammal bone was recovered from that portion).

Unrelated to sample size is the contrast in the proportions of technological flake types (Table 4.14) and, even more notable, in the types of raw material used (Figure 4.14). Both assemblages are overwhelmingly dominated by debris from biface reduction, but with pressure flakes accounting for the majority from Tsé Haal'á and percussion thinning flakes accounting for the majority from Three Dog Site. Glen Canyon chert accounts for almost 75 percent of the Tsé Haal'á debitage raw material, but at Three Dog Site this material represents less than half of the assemblage, with quartzite accounting for 47 per-

TABLE 4.13. General Kinds of Flaked Facial Tools Recovered from the Late Archaic Components of Tsé Haal'á and Three Dog Site

	Tsé Haal'á		Three Dog Site	
Tool Class	n	%	n	%
Scraper	8	22.2	0	.0
Unifacial Knife	1	2.8	0	.0
Drill	1	2.8	2	18.2
Biface Stage 2	2	5.6	0	.0
Biface Stage 3	2	5.6	0	.0
Biface Stage 4	3	8.3	3	27.3
Biface Stage 5	5	13.9	4	36.4
Projectile Point	14	38.9	2	18.2
Total	36	100.0	11	100.0

cent, compared to the 9 percent quartzite debris at Tsé Haal'á. Because the quartzite at these sites was mostly obtained locally as cobbles eroded from the upper slopes of Navajo Mountain, the contrast in use of this material may relate to when either site was primarily occupied in an annual pattern of regional mobility. Groups recently arriving from the Glen Canyon lowlands where Glen Canyon chert is abundantly available should have had little need

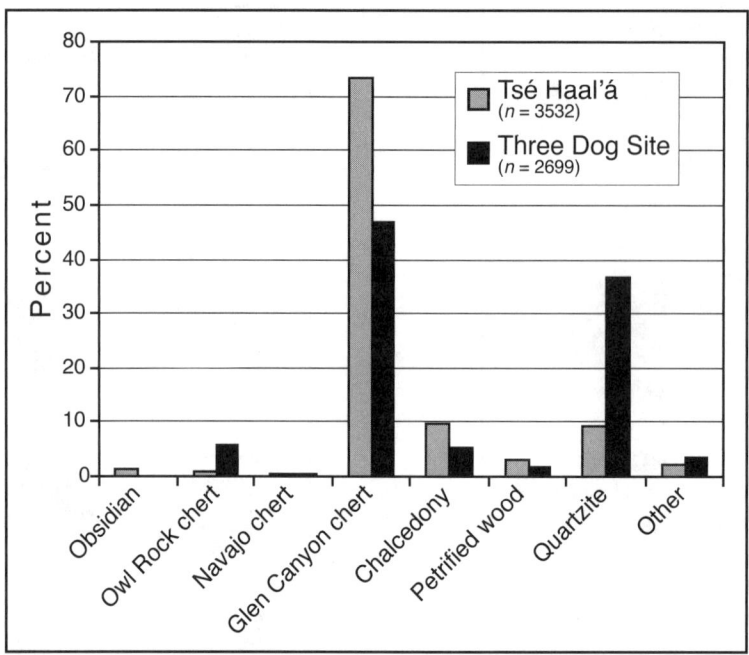

Figure 4.14. Frequency of debitage raw material for the late Archaic components of Tsé Haal'á and Three Dog Site.

Table 4.14. Technological Flake Types for the Late Archaic Components of Tsé Haal'á and Three Dog Site

Flake Type	Tsé Haal'á		Three Dog Site	
	n	%	n	%
Core	159	6.1	42	2.6
Bipolar	2	.1	0	.0
Biface	824	31.8	1,020	62.5
Pressure	1,328	51.2	459	28.1
Edge Preparation	220	8.5	109	6.7
Tool Spall	62	2.4	1	.1
Total	2,595	100.0	1,631	100.0
% Notching		4.3		1.3

to exploit the moderately coarse local quartzite (depending on required tasks), whereas groups having spent time on the Rainbow Plateau and to the south on the Shonto Plateau away from sources of the Glen Canyon chert may have needed to replenish their tool kits and had to make do with the "best" local material. The use of Owl Rock chert at Three Dog Site, a material virtually absent at Tsé Haal'á, seems to fit this pattern.

There is another aspect of these two sites that deserves mention because it implicates the problematical nature of treating sites as single units of analysis, at least in cases of unrecognized accretional accumulation. Three Dog Site was an active depositional environment during the late Archaic when the site was being occupied (see Figure 4.11). As a result, several discrete episodes of use were separated both vertically and horizontally, allowing recovery by components that could then be individually described and analyzed as detailed in chapter 14 of volume 2 of the Web-posted supporting documentation. The same is not true of Tsé Haal'á, where there was an evident lack of natural sediment deposition or soil formation during the late Archaic and indeed there might have been some deflation. As a result, there is no way of knowing whether the remains at this site represent a single episode of use or several. Given what we can tell from a site like Three Dog, and can assume based on knowledge about mobile hunter-gatherer disposal practices, it would seem likely that the materials at Tsé Haal'á accumulated during many different use episodes, perhaps even for different purposes. Radiocarbon dates on six of the hearths at the site might support the multiple-use scenario (see SD vol. 2, chap. 16), but given the low-quality samples (wood and sagebrush charcoal), it is impossible to know whether foragers camped at Tsé Haal'á for several nights or weeks over the span of several decades or intermittently like this across several centuries. With only a single cultural layer, and lacking a stratigraphic basis for segregating remains, they all become part of the same composite picture of late Archaic site use. This is by far the more typical case in Archaic period research, with the finer-resolution segregation of depositional/behavioral events at Three Dog Site representing an exception.

Temporary Camps

Special-purpose task groups, principally involved in the procurement and processing of faunal or floral resources, can create sites at temporary resting places and staging points (Binford 1980:10, 1982). Such logistical camps should normally occur when travel extends beyond the normal foraging range of home base. As the name implies, the sites are thought to have been used for a short duration, although this use could occur intermittently time and time again. The quantity and nature of artifact debris are likely to be variable, resulting from differences in the types of resources being exploited, the season, distances between these camps and residential bases, and other factors. Artifact diversity usually should be more limited than at residential camps, and certain tool types are more likely to be dominant, depending on the nature of the exploited resource. The two types of short-term camps identified here are those used principally for hunting and those used for nebulous processing tasks.

Hunting Camps. Logistical camps involved in game procurement are expectable almost regardless of the overall pattern of residential mobility. The one exception could be groups so heavily reliant on hunting that residential camp movements were governed by meat procurement (Folsom groups might be an example). The positioning of most forager residential camps on the Colorado Plateau was likely predicated upon the distribution and seasonal ripening of local floral resources. There are at least three important reasons that this was likely so: (1) floral resources constituted a major portion of the diet; (2) most plant foods are bulky with respect to nutritional value; and (3) most plant foraging was probably done by females whose travel range and length of absence from residential bases were minimized. The second point concerns transportation costs, which to be minimized require locating the consumers close to the resource. The opposites of these three points are commonly applicable to faunal resources, especially big game, and provide reasons that logistical hunting camps exist, even for foragers. Not only did meat likely make up less of an Archaic forager diet than plants, but meat comes in highly nutritious and comparatively low-bulk packages that can be moved to consumers. Hunting is also predominantly a male activity, so there are fewer constraints on making overnight forays well beyond the daily travel radius of the family camp.

Five examples of Archaic hunting camps were identified in the NMRAP sample (The Pits, Hólahéi Scatter, Tres Campos, Windy Mesa, and Sapo Seco) based prin-

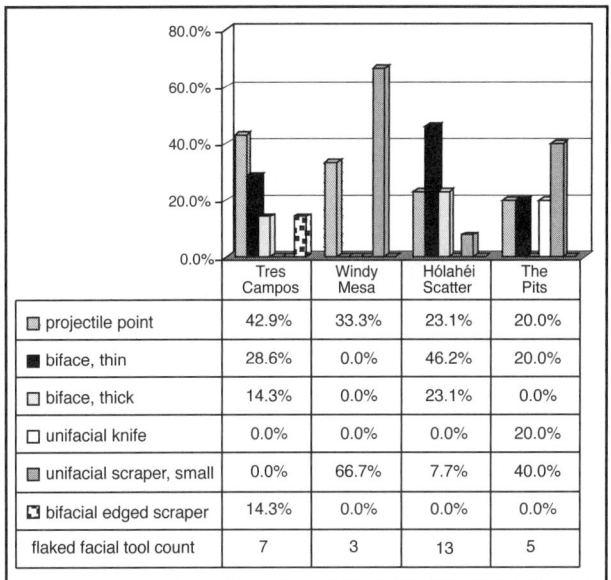

Figure 4.15. Frequency of general types of flaked facial tools for the Navajo Mountain Road Archaeological Project Archaic sites identified as hunting camps (excludes a site that lacked tools).

cipally upon the co-occurrence of modest assemblages of debitage and faunal remains, in conjunction with an absence of grinding tools. The negative evidence is significant since the previously discussed Archaic residential camps contained an abundance of bone, debris from late-stage biface reduction, and projectile points—game processing and the preparation and refurbishment of weaponry are not exclusive to hunting camps. Indeed, because more time would normally be available at residential camps than at transient sites to repair gear and rearm foreshafts by removing point fragments, it is perhaps more likely for point bases snapped across the notches (bending breaks) or larger portions with tip impact fractures to be more common at residential sites than hunting camps. This said, all but one of the five hunting camps have projectile points (Figures 14.15–14.16), and the exception (Sapo Seco) seems to have been occupied for the briefest interval based on scant remains around a single hearth. This site perhaps provides some indication of the temporal factor mentioned previously since brevity of stay would limit the activities conducted and tools discarded. Bifaces at various stages of reduction are also present at most of the hunting camps, but the range of tool forms overall is limited. The flaking debris at the five hunting camps was derived from a mixture of flake types (Table 4.15), sometimes with an almost exclusive emphasis on late-stage biface reduction, such as the 94 percent pressure

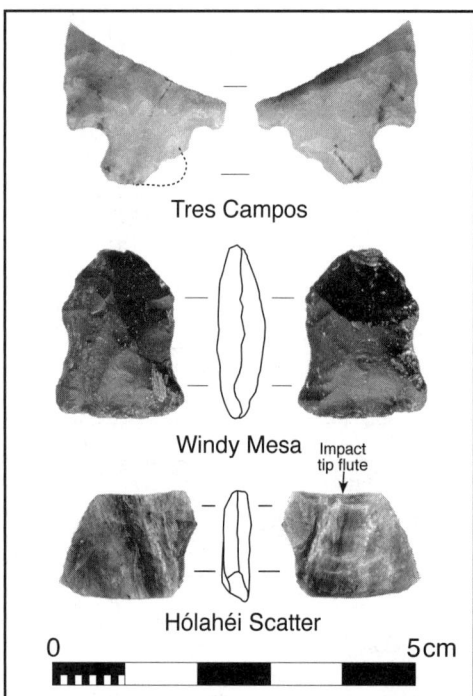

Figure 4.16. Projectile points recovered from several of the Navajo Mountain Road Archaeological Project Archaic hunting camps; Tres Campos and Windy Mesa are radiocarbon dated to the early Archaic.

Table 4.15. Proportions of Identified Technological Flake Types for the Navajo Mountain Road Archaeological Project Archaic Sites Identified as Hunting Camps

Flake Type	Sapo Seco	Tres Campos	Windy Mesa	Hólahéi Scatter	The Pits
Core	3.7	34.1	11.4	8.9	16.4
Bipolar	.0	2.8	.6	.5	.6
Biface	.0	18.3	45.5	18.4	23.9
Pressure	94.4	32.8	39.8	63.9	56.0
Edge Preparation	.0	11.3	.0	2.6	.0
Tool Spall	1.9	.6	2.8	5.5	3.1
Total %	100.0	100.0	100.0	100.0	100.0
n	54	469	146	380	159

flakes from Sapo Seco, but also including earlier reduction stages, perhaps reflecting variability in activity.

Several of the hunting camps had a moderately high incidence of obsidian, between 25 and 54 percent, an indication that the sites were probably situated well outside the normal annual foraging range of the groups involved. This inference is based on finding that probable residential sites of the project area have a very low incidence of obsidian (see discussion below), something that is also true for the early Archaic stratum (Unit IV) of Dust Devil Cave (Geib 1984). Obsidian use during the Archaic is discussed in greater detail below, but it is worth pointing out in passing that such evidence is consistent with the notion that logistical camps should normally occur when travel for subsistence pursuits extends outside the normal foraging range of a residential base. Obsidian provides a handy means for identifying such extensive travel, but in many cases a material indicator is unlikely to exist. For example, nearly all of the pressure flakes at Sapo Seco consist of Navajo chert, a material widely available across much of the Kayenta region including the Rainbow Plateau. The individual who left these flakes at the site may or may not have resided outside the Kayenta region, but the debitage raw material provides no means for knowing this.

Hearths were present at four of the five hunting camps and are to be expected for the preparation of game, with burned faunal bone indicative of meat preparation and consumption. Though it is likely that fires were used at hunting camps, hearth presence is not essential for inclusion in this class, since a lack of these features might be a preservation problem related to building fires directly upon the ground surface rather than within some sort of basin. Such surface fires are far more easily eliminated by deflation and other postdepositional processes, especially at sites many thousands of years old and shallowly buried. Testing of hearths on the Kaiparowits Plateau (Geib et al. 2001) provides sufficient cause to infer that surface heating fires at 1,000-year-old hunting camps, let alone those from anywhere from 3,000 to 8,000 years old, might not last the ravages of time.

Processing Camps. Six of the NMRAP Archaic sites were classified as processing camps based principally on scant remains (see Table 4.9). The potential for processing camps to exist as functionally distinct from residential camps is partially dependent upon the temporal period under investigation. Sites are more likely to have served as logistical processing camps during the Basketmaker and Puebloan periods than during the Archaic period. Groups during this earlier temporal interval were more likely to have operated using a foraging strategy wherein resources other than large game were gathered within close proximity to constantly shifting residential bases. Foragers generally have little need for logistical camps because if a desired resource occurs outside the daily travel distance from a residential base, then the base itself is relocated close to the resource. Farmer-foragers, in contrast, because they tend to maintain semipermanent residential bases close to farm fields, may well have used logistical camps for collecting floral resources, particularly if certain important plants were not readily available within the foraging radius of the primary habitation. This is typical for plants such as ricegrass, which flourish on lower-elevation sandy benches of the Glen Canyon lowlands well away from the primary residential sites of most Basketmaker and Puebloan farmers. Had Archaic foragers wanted to exploit such resources they would have established a residential base in the grass-harvesting area, which is perhaps partly why Dust Devil Cave, located as it is in a shrub grassland, was so heavily used during the early Archaic.

Such considerations aside, the limited abundance and diversity of remains recovered from some Archaic sites are such that classifying them as residential bases seems a far stretch. Take, for example, the early Archaic component at the site known as Polly's Place. Excavation of almost 22 m² exposed 13 basin hearths, but the associated remains consisted of just six flakes with no grinding tools or flaked-stone tools (see Table 4.9). Because of a lack of contemporaneity among some hearth radiocarbon dates and the spatial separation between several of the features, the site likely was occupied on a few different occasions during the early Archaic. Despite reuse, the nature of the occupation each time was such that almost no nonperishable remains were discarded; the principal undertaking that can be inferred from the surviving evidence involved fires within small, shallow basins. The transient use did not require stone tools or did not require them to be maintained or modified. Whether the hearths were used to process or cook certain foods or were merely campfires for heat and light during overnight stays remains unknown. A food-processing role seems intuitively likely, but evidence in support of such an interpretation was lacking. With a complete lack of bone and preservation bias unlikely, faunal processing and consumption seems improbable. If plants were processed or cooked, the flotation analysis of hearth fill revealed only a single carbonized *Corispermum* seed—hardly convincing evidence of subsistence pursuits. Plants such as prickly pear pads, banana yucca fruit, or onion and lily bulbs can be processed without leaving any macrobotanical trace; thus subsistence remains might not necessarily be expected in the features themselves. No matter the case, this site differs vastly in character from the previously discussed residential base and is unlikely to have served such a purpose.

The Archaic component of Pee Wee Grande presents another useful example; here excavations revealed a cluster of 11 basin hearths and a small flaked-stone assemblage from foragers who occupied the sandy ridge sometime during the first half of the seventh millennium BC. The number of basin hearths within such a small area likely resulted from several sequential short-term use episodes. Site use did not result in appreciable amounts of nonperishable artifact deposition; however, several nodules of local Navajo chert were brought in and reduced by both percussion and pressure flaking into several mainly bifacial tools. The facially flaked tools along with two tabular core chunks were subsequently used on some semi-resistant material such as wood and then discarded along with the debris within a small area. The production and use of the stone tools may have been incidental to use of the hearths, such as shaping wooden artifacts while waiting for some food to cook. As at Polly's Place, the function of the hearths remains a mystery since flotation samples provided no convincing trace of food processing. The lack of faunal remains from the flotation samples as well as the cultural stratum suggests that animals were not processed. The nature of the assemblage appears consistent with a foraging group local to the Rainbow or Shonto Plateau—a group that made do with the best siliceous stone immediately at hand for an expedient task.

While this site has more remains than Polly's Place and greater diversity, including tools and cores, it still seems appreciably different from the sites classified as residential bases. But the assumption that contrasting settlement roles is what underlies the distinctions need not be true. Instead such factors as the size of the occupying social group (one family vs. many), the composition of the social group (part of the family vs. the entire family), the length of stay (two nights vs. two weeks), the frequency of site reoccupancy (none vs. many), or some combination thereof could be involved. Consequently, although the separation of sites into the categories of residential and processing might monitor differences in the archaeological record, these differences may not relate to whether or not a site was used residentially (Geib et al. 2001:332–335, 367–368, discusses this issue with regard to Archaic residential bases and processing camps on the Kaiparowits Plateau).

Consider the record from Dune Hollow, which was classified as an early Archaic processing camp because of the comparative scarceness of remains—two small basin hearths and a small assemblage of bone ($n = 40$) and stone artifacts (16 flakes and two tiny grinding slab fragments) all within an excavation area of 9 m². The Dune Hollow artifact assemblage lacks facially flaked stone tools and used flakes. The sparse flake waste is mainly derived from cores or nodular core tools and not from bifacially flaked tools, as at many early Archaic lithic assemblages that seem oriented toward hunting and were found associated with large-mammal bone. The meager faunal remains from Dune Hollow did not include large-mammal bone, and much of the rodent-sized mammal bone seemed intrusive (fresh looking). The rabbit-sized remains seemed nonintrusive, and most of the unidentifiable bone fragments of this size group were burned; all identifiable bone came from desert cottontail, an animal more likely taken by traps or with sticks and not requiring the production and maintenance of projectile points. The two tiny grinding slab fragments, along with the occurrence of goosefoot seeds in the basin hearths, might support the conclusion that the site also served as a temporary camp related to seed collecting and processing, which would seem to accord well with the site setting in a shrub grassland.

The limited spatial extent of the remains and proximity of the two hearths might be taken as an indication of a single use episode, but this might have simply resulted because the site setting fostered repeated use of a small area. The recovery of artifacts and bone from the entire 85-cm thickness of the dune sand that comprised the Archaic stratum seems more consistent with multiple use episodes. The radiocarbon dates on the two hearths indicate that they are both more than 8,000 radiocarbon years old but are not contemporaneous, so these features also appear to have resulted from two successive uses of the site location. If there were two or more use episodes, there is no way to know which remains (artifacts and bone) are associated with them because the hearths had the same stratigraphic position. For interpretive purposes, therefore, there is but a single composite assemblage and set of features. In this sense, the site is no different from the late Archaic residential camp of Tsé Haal'á, which clearly seems to be the aggregate of many individual use episodes, yet there is a staggering difference in the abundance, diversity, and type of remains. The findings from Dune Hollow seem to accord with specialized transient use, but the presence of grinding tools indicates seed processing, implying food processing and consumption, something likely to occur at a residential camp. If true, then the limited nature of the Dune Hollow assemblage suggests that the site was a different sort of residential base than Tsé Haal'á, and distinguishing between these two still has utility, although interpretation of meaning will differ.

Settlement Pattern

Our understanding of Archaic settlement on the Rainbow Plateau—indeed the Kayenta region more broadly—is hampered by a lack of intensive regional survey coupled with a serious visibility problem. As mentioned previously, the Archaic archaeological record of the N16 ROW and elsewhere across much of the Kayenta region is largely a buried phenomenon. Only three of the Archaic sites were partially exposed on the surface from natural erosion. The other Archaic sites or components were buried and hidden from view and were found either because prior road construction had exposed them or because the Archaic remains fortuitously occurred under a Basketmaker or Puebloan site that was trenched. This same pattern was observed on other recent NNAD road excavation projects on the Kaibito Plateau (Bungart et al. 2004; Neff et al. 2004). The Archaic archaeological record thus appears to be largely obscured from view, especially the portion of it that is most informative, containing intact features and some preservation of subsistence remains. The problematical nature of trying to use the current record of Archaic remains to talk about settlement practices is perhaps illustrated by the fact that no Archaic sites are reported for the southern portion of the N16 ROW (Schroedl 1989). The upshot is that I cannot make any substantive claims about settlement patterning beyond a few generalizations that reflect little more than common sense based on the limited empirical patterns now known. It should go without saying that statements about Archaic settlement are subject to revision once substantial portions of both the Rainbow and Shonto plateaus have been surveyed and a greater number and diversity of Archaic sites have been excavated.

With these caveats in mind, it seems reasonable to look at where Archaic sites are concentrated and the possible environmental reasons for why this might be the case. In this regard it is important to state that I assume that the Archaic foragers of the region probably had several general criteria about where to locate their settlements—the same ones Jochim identified in his ethnographic overview of hunter-gatherer settlement behavior: "(1) proximity of economic resources; (2) shelter and protection from the elements; and (3) view for observation of game and strangers" (1976:46). Although sociocultural factors may also be a strong determinant of site placement on a landscape, environmental variables are especially appropriate for understanding hunter-gatherer site location preferences because of the close relationship that foragers have to their environments coupled with relatively low population densities and generally fluid and open social networks.

The distribution of the 14 NMRAP Archaic sites is shown in Figure 4.17 along with the locations of three caves. This figure provides the inferred settlement type for the sites and their temporal placement. Because the sites reported here occur within such a narrow swath, they are not highly informative of settlement patterns for the obvious reason that data from large blocks of terrain are needed to make strong inferences about this topic. Does the distribution of sites shown in this figure accurately reflect the overall patterning of how Archaic foragers distributed settlements across the area? For example, most of the sites specifically identified as hunting camps occur in the southern portion of the project area where the road ROW traverses the dissected slickrock divide between Piute and Navajo creeks. This is not to suggest that hunting was not being done around Navajo Mountain, since some of the best faunal evidence for deer procurement comes from sites at the base of this laccolith. However, these sites appear to have served as residential bases, so were not exclusively hunting related like the sites along the divide. Three of the four hunting sites situated along this divide have a moderately high proportion of obsidian debitage, as discussed in greater detail below, which suggests that this location lies well outside the annual foraging terrain for the groups. One of these sites dates to the early Archaic and one dates to the late Archaic (one remains undated), which hints at the continued significance of this area for hunting purposes throughout the Archaic sequence. This divide is still reputed to be a good area for deer hunting by local Navajos despite the greatly diminished forage from livestock and the presence of the Navajo Mountain road. At a regional scale, if the divide was less desirable for exploitive tasks other than hunting, then it is expectable that hunting camps might be differentially concentrated there.

The concentration of residential camps at the eastern foot of Navajo Mountain is perhaps also a pattern that is real and meaningful, although not necessarily a great surprise. This setting can be seen as optimally located relative to the environments that provided essential food, especially areas supporting late summer through fall resource abundance. Because of the great elevational differences compressed within a small area around this mountain, by locating residential bases around the foot of the mountain on the east and south sides, foragers had the potential to be situated where the foraging radius of a residential camp embraced the great environmental diversity that was critical to survival. This might be seen as an example of the vegetative diversity models of Archaic camp location as proposed by Reher and Witter (1977) for the San Juan Basin, except that the important factor is subsistence resource abundance and not general environmental diversity. Moreover, the diversity of important environmental zones within the daily foraging radius of a site at the foot of Navajo Mountain is on a completely different scale than that present in the San Juan Basin, where the daily foraging radius usually provides just more of the same. The Navajo Mountain location compresses the diversity of the entire San Juan Basin and surrounding mountains, a radial distance of 100–150 km, to a radius of less than 10 km. Proximity to highly diverse environments should have helped promote common site reuse and more extended stays, as many different resource opportunities were available with minimal residential movement, even over the span of an entire annual cycle. One limitation was perhaps a greater potential for resource depression since no environmental zone is highly extensive. This might also mean that only small groups could be supported locally.

The good examples of late Archaic residential camps excavated along the N16 ROW at the foot of Navajo Mountain provide an interesting contrast with the findings from Sand Dune Cave (Lindsay et al. 1968). These two open sites (Tsé Haal'á and Three Dog Site) provide ample evidence of repeated late Archaic occupation of the area that resulted in considerable accumulation of remains, especially at Tsé Haal'á, which is located less than 3 km downstream from this cave across easily traversed terrain. It is also worth mentioning that only small portions of much larger late Archaic components were excavated at both sites. The existing road removed unknown but perhaps extensive portions of both sites, and the ROW imposed another boundary; because of deflation at Tsé Haal'á, the area investigated was a small fraction of the main artifact scatter, on the order of about 5 percent. My point is that despite significant evidence for rather intensive use of the region by late Archaic foragers, they apparently left scant record of their presence at Sand Dune Cave, an excellent natural shelter. Two questions emerge: (1) Was a late Archaic component missed? and (2) Even so, did late Archaic foragers rarely use the cave anyway?

Lindsay et al. (1968) made no mention of a late Archaic component at Sand Dune Cave, although any deposition would have been included with Stratum V, which

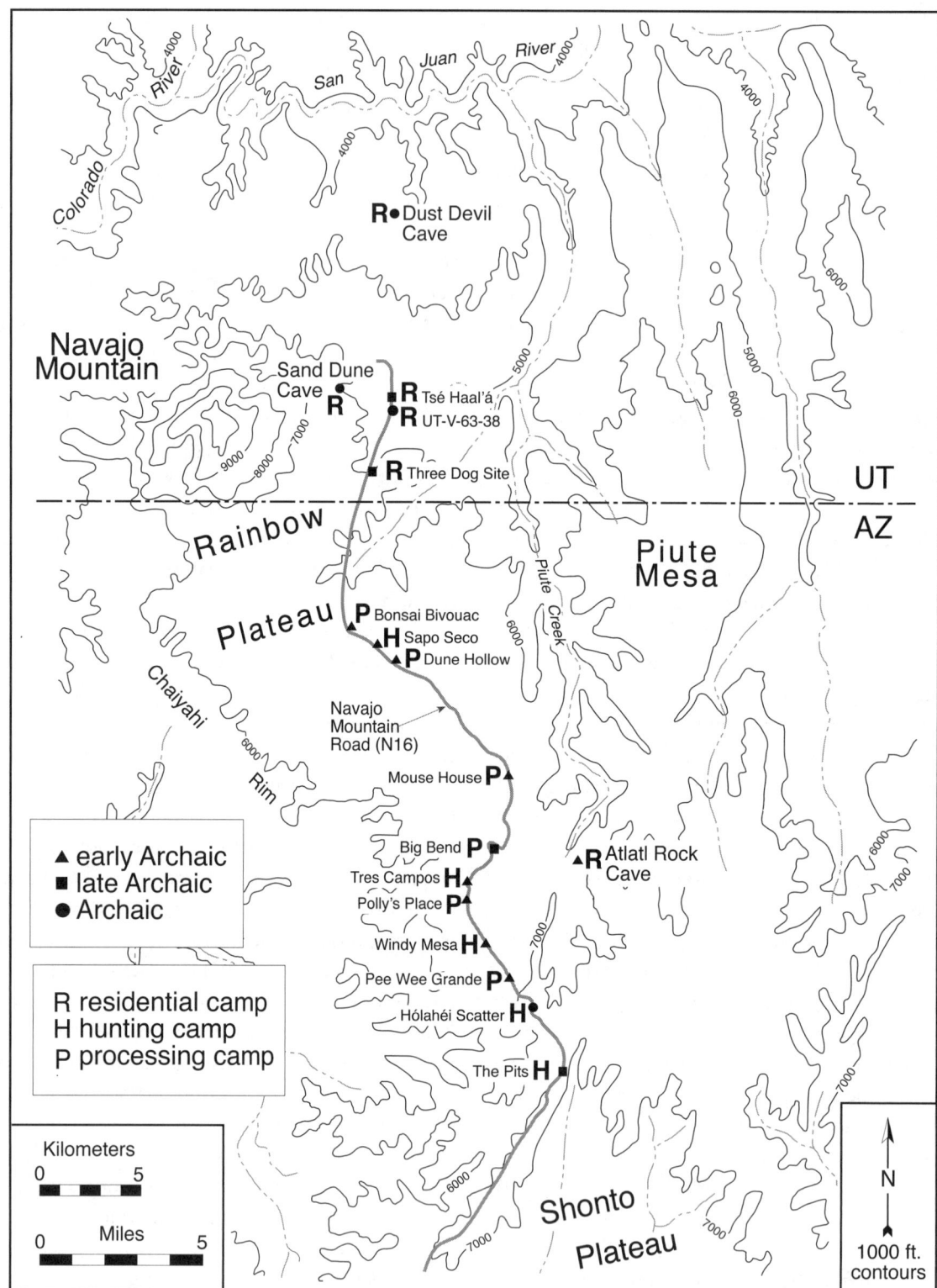

Figure 4.17. Distribution of inferred settlement types by temporal period for Navajo Mountain Road Archaeological Project Archaic sites and three caves with excavation data.

is interpreted as primarily a Basketmaker II and early Archaic (Desha complex) accumulation (1968:35). The presence of a Gypsum point at the site (Lindsay et al. 1968: Figure 23w) hints at some late Archaic use, as does the recovery of mountain sheep hyoid bone pendants (Lindsay et al. 1968:Figure 36n–o, 59–60). The latter artifacts, which are highly distinctive, were assigned to the Desha complex, but stratigraphically controlled excavations at Cowboy Cave also recovered examples of hyoid bone pendants from late Archaic layers (Lucius 1980:100, Figure 42). The secure recovery context at Cowboy Cave makes it highly probable that the pair of hyoid bone pendants from Sand Dune Cave also belong to the late Archaic. One further piece of evidence is provided by the direct dating of collagen from Burial 2, which produced a date of 4480 ± 60 BP (Coltrain et al. 2007:316). With these hints, a viable reinterpretation of the stratigraphy at this site is that Stratum V actually represents late Archaic deposits overlain and partially intermingled with subsequent Basketmaker II deposits, rather than being a composite of early Archaic (Desha complex) and Basketmaker II as claimed. In such a scenario, Stratum III would represent deposition during the early Archaic associated with the Desha complex and not pre-Desha as claimed in the excavation report (Lindsay et al. 1968:36). Likewise, Stratum IV would represent a largely sterile middle Holocene deposit of eolian sand like Stratum V at Dust Devil Cave. Late Archaic deposition at the site is represented by the lower portion of Stratum V, but the subsequent and intensive Basketmaker II use of the site and the creation of numerous cists greatly intermingled the pure forager deposit with the accumulation of these early farmers. Direct dating of specific remains would help to reveal the extent of the hidden late Archaic component and the validity of this reinterpretation. Key in this regard would be the single-rod basketry, fur cordage, and various types of fiber cordage. Direct dating of remains might well reveal that the cave was little used during the late Archaic, and if so, then it is reasonable to ponder why this was the case, given the common presence of foragers in the area. Was the confined space of this shelter too small for the late Archaic social groups who occupied the region?

Although speculative, one possible pattern is a shift in elevation zones favored for residential bases from grasslands during the early Archaic to pinyon–juniper uplands in the late Archaic. Examples of early Archaic residential camps were not revealed in the NMRAP site sample, although there were examples of early Archaic hunting and processing camps. The early Archaic residential bases known in the project area are all caves: Dust Devil at the lowest elevation (ca. 1,494 m), Sand Dune at somewhat higher elevation (1,780 m), and Atlatl Rock Cave at the highest elevation (1,978 m). Dust Devil Cave is well within a grassland environment, some 5 km or more from the lower fringe of pinyon–juniper forest. This site saw rather intensive early Archaic occupation, resulting in roughly 1 m of rich cultural deposition (Ambler 1996; Lindsay et al. 1968). Both of the higher-elevation caves saw more limited early Archaic use, as revealed by cultural layers reaching a maximum of 15 cm thick. The NMRAP excavations documented late Archaic residential sites around the foot of Navajo Mountain, and Sand Dune Cave also might have had late Archaic residential use. Dust Devil Cave, however, evidently had minimal late Archaic occupation. Environmental change and corresponding shifts in geographic distributions of key plants such as pinyon and grasses during the long Archaic sequence might have been responsible for this tentative pattern, if it holds up to further excavation data. The environment around Dust Devil Cave that was evidently so desirable during the early Archaic seems to have lost favor by the late Archaic, perhaps as a result of Holocene drying.

Subsistence Range and Territory

Given a study area of relatively small size such as that covered by the Navajo Mountain road, it is possible that the Archaic remains excavated within the ROW for any synchronous slice represent those of a single forager group or band. After all, the linear distance of the N16 ROW is only 43 km, and it includes just portions of two small plateaus (Rainbow and Shonto). Ethnographic data for hunter-gatherers living in the Great Basin and the Southwest indicate that annual subsistence territories easily exceed this distance, often greatly so (Kelly 1995:Table 4-1). In a Southwest example, Gifford (1936:254) reported that the northern Yavapai procurement range had a linear distance of more than 100 km north to south. A similar range can be inferred from Kelly's (1964) data on the Kaibab Band of the Southern Paiute. Consequently, one may be tempted to interpret the excavated NMRAP Archaic remains as parts of a single differentiated system. But what if the sample contains mixed portions of two or more different settlement systems? Paynter (1983:254) has considered this possibility from two perspectives: (1) that the region under investigation contains only part of a complete settlement system and (2) that it contains portions drawn from several different systems. Sampson's (1988) study of stylistic boundaries among mobile foragers in South Africa arose from an attempt not to conflate the archaeological records of several different independent forager groups since doing so could result in a fictive whole of unrelated parts for subsistence-settlement strategies. As he puts it, "Seasonal mobility systems cannot be properly delineated unless they are first circumscribed by the territorial boundaries within which they functioned" (1988:13).

I can readily accept, based on the nature of the environment coupled with ethnographic accounts of foragers for the Southwest, that the N16 project area may not have sustained populations on a yearly basis. In order to survive, Archaic foragers likely had to operate on a geographical scale far exceeding the size of the project area, especially over the span of several consecutive years. As many have observed, and Ford states emphatically, "calories were a limiting factor for hunters and gatherers in the pre-maize Southwest. Plant foods were not sufficiently abundant in any one location to support large populations or even the annual return of small bands" (1984:129). But if this is true for the N16 project area, which is admittedly quite ecologically diverse, given the close proximity of the Glen Canyon lowlands and Navajo Mountain, then it would be even more true for the relatively uniform expanses to the south, such as the Kaibito Plateau and Painted Desert. As such, the area traversed by the NMRAP may have included more than a single forager settlement system. Indeed, given the geography that separates the Shonto and Rainbow plateaus, it might be reasonable to postulate that this broken ridgeline could have served as one of those obvious physical markers of different territories (it works this way today for the Inscription House and Navajo Mountain communities).

If the NMRAP study area includes components of different subsistence-settlement systems, then the interpretation of the remains is vastly different than if the various synchronous sites are all part of one system. But how can we know this? Raw material use provides one means, especially obsidian because it comes from point-specific sources far away from the project area and artifacts can be chemically assigned to those sources. In an informative study, Shackley (1990) used geochemical sourcing of obsidian to reconstruct the procurement ranges of middle and late Archaic groups in southern Arizona (cf. Ingbar 1993). The interest here is slightly different, in that I start with the lithic assemblages from the sites of one relatively small area to see if the nature of the raw materials represented makes sense with regard to them being part of a single settlement system or parts of more than one.

One critical assumption for Shackley's interpretations is direct procurement of obsidian embedded within subsistence-related tasks. Under the same assumption and also using obsidian and the visually distinctive Washington Pass (Chuska) chert, Vierra (1994:124–131) used source distance to calculate the potential size of annual foraging ranges for Archaic foragers in the San Juan Basin of New Mexico. When obsidian proportions are low, the assumption of direct procurement is questionable, since casual exchange could have been the means for obsidian movement. For example, Brown (1988:315) has attributed the small quantities of obsidian from two Archaic sites on the Kaibab Plateau (.1% of the debitage at AZ B:8:7 and 1.1% at AZ B:12:2) as resulting from casual exchange relationships rather than direct procurement. An important part of his interpretation is the diversity of sources represented at the two sites, with obsidian derived from both Utah and northern Arizona. More will be said about the inference of procurement strategies later, but first we will look at what raw materials Archaic foragers used in the project area.

Table 4.16 shows the major raw material types represented at the NMRAP Archaic sites; some minor resources are lumped together as "other." The incidence of obsidian is clearly quite variable, ranging from none at several sites to more than 50 percent at Hólahéi Scatter, with two other sites having proportions above 20 percent. The extraordinary proportion of obsidian flakes at Hólahéi Scatter is the highest for any site investigated within the Kayenta region. One site with a somewhat similar proportion of obsidian is AZ D:11:3063, an early Archaic limited-activity site on northeastern Black Mesa radiocarbon dated to around 8100–7800 BP (Lebo and MacMinn 1984). At that site 40 percent of the flakes (68 of 169) were obsidian (Parry 1987a:Table 6-A-25; this material is misidentified as "burnout" in the site report [Lebo and MacMinn 1984:341]), and there were two projectile points and two bifaces of obsidian. Because only ¼-in mesh was used to screen site sediments, the number of obsidian flakes at AZ D:11:3063 may have been considerably higher, with a proportion perhaps even greater than for Hólahéi Scatter. For example, if NNAD excavators had not used ⅛-in mesh at Hólahéi Scatter, 35 percent of the obsidian flakes would have been left in the backdirt; of the 268 total flakes that would have been lost (all flakes smaller than ¼ in), 61 percent are obsidian.

TABLE 4.16. Proportions of Debitage Raw Material from Navajo Mountain Road Archaeological Project Archaic Sites

Site Name	Obsidian	Owl Rock Chert	Navajo Chert	Glen Canyon Chert	Chalcedony	Petrified Wood	Quartz	Other	Total %	n
Tsé Haal'á	1.3	.7	.4	73.2	9.7	3.2	9.1	2.4	100.0	3,532
UT-B-63-38	.0	.0	.1	77.4	19.3	.3	2.6	.2	100.0	910
Three Dog Site	.0	5.7	.3	46.7	5.2	1.8	36.8	3.5	100.0	2,699
Sapo Seco	.0	5.4	94.6	.0	.0	.0	.0	.0	100.0	56
Dune Hollow	6.3	43.8	37.5	.0	6.3	6.3	.0	.0	100.0	16
Big Bend	.0	2.9	74.3	17.1	.0	5.7	.0	.0	100.0	35
Tres Campos	32.5	12.7	12.1	22.1	4.0	11.3	.5	4.7	100.0	873
Polly's Place	.0	50.0	33.3	16.7	.0	.0	.0	.0	100.0	6
Windy Mesa	.7	5.3	59.8	24.2	1.8	5.3	.7	2.1	100.0	281
Pee Wee Grande	.0	1.7	91.7	2.6	.3	.3	.3	3.0	100.0	302
Hólahéi Scatter	54.3	.7	3.9	26.3	1.9	3.6	.6	8.7	100.0	851
The Pits	24.5	3.0	17.7	39.7	6.8	2.1	1.3	5.1	100.0	237

Note: Sites are ordered from north to south.

TABLE 4.17. Count and Weight (g) Representation of Technological Flake Types for Obsidian Debitage from Navajo Mountain Road Archaeological Project Archaic Sites

Flake Type	The Pits		Hólahéi Scatter		Windy Mesa		Tres Campos		Dune Hollow		Tsé Haal'á		Total	
	n	Weight	n	Weight	n	Weight	n	Weight	n	Weight	n	Weight	n	Weight
Core	1	.8	2	3.8	0	0	25	24.15	1	1.1	0	0	29	29.85
Bipolar	0	0	0	0	1	1.9	10	4.2	0	0	0	0	11	6.1
Biface	9	2.9	42	14.55	1	.2	41	11.95	0	0	6	.45	99	30.05
Pressure	34	3.4	170	12.05	0	0	50	3.6	0	0	32	1.95	286	21
Edge Preparation	0	0	10	1.3	0	0	17	1.2	0	0	4	.35	31	2.85
Tool Spall	0	0	16	5.65	0	0	0	0	0	0	0	0	16	5.65
Indeterminate	14	2.2	222	21.35	0	0	141	13.95	0	0	5	.25	382	37.75
Total	58	9.3	462	58.7	2	2.1	284	59.05	1	1.1	47	3	854	133.25
Mean Weight		.16		.13		1.05		.21		1.1		.06		.16

Note: Sites ordered left to right from south to north.

Although obsidian might be well represented at some sites, it generally occurs in relatively small size such that it accounts for just a tiny fraction of any assemblage by weight representation. For example, at Hólahéi Scatter the representation of obsidian declines from 54 percent by count to only 7 percent by weight. The small size of the obsidian debris at all sites is readily apparent by the mean weight of obsidian flakes presented in the bottom row of Table 4.17, where values range from less than a tenth of a gram to just over 1 g. The sites with the largest average obsidian flakes are Windy Mesa and Dune Hollow, but this is only because these sites have next to no obsidian (two pieces at the former, one at the latter), and in both cases the large obsidian flakes are likely to have been brought to the sites for use rather than resulting from on-site reduction. The minuteness of the obsidian debitage results from both how this material arrived at the sites—as finished or nearly finished tools or edged flake blanks—and how it was reduced—mainly by pressure flaking. Returning to Hólahéi Scatter as an example, of the 240 obsidian flakes classifiable as to technological "type" (excluding indeterminate), almost 70 percent were pressure flakes, less than 20 percent were percussion flakes from biface reduction, and less than 1 percent were percussion core flakes (Table 4.18). The large proportion of obsidian debitage that is represented by pressure flakes suggests that the primary lithic reduction activity of this material at Hólahéi Scatter consisted of the resharpening or rejuvenation of finished tools and reduction of preforms or edged flake blanks into finished tools (an edged flake blank fragment of obsidian

TABLE 4.18. Technological Flake Type Proportions and Mean Weights (g) for Obsidian Debitage from Navajo Mountain Road Archaeological Project Archaic Sites

Flake Type	The Pits		Hólahéi Scatter		Windy Mesa		Tres Campos		Dune Hollow		Tsé Haal'á	
	%	Mean Weight	%	Mean Weight	%	Mean Weight	%	Mean Weight	%	Mean Weight	%	Mean Weight
Core	2.3	.80	.8	1.90	0	0	17.5	.97	100.0	1.10	0	0
Bipolar	0	0	0	0	50.0	1.9	7.0	.42	0	.00	0	0
Biface	20.5	.32	17.5	.35	50.0	.2	28.7	.29	0	.00	14.3	.08
Pressure	77.3	.10	70.8	.07	0	0	35.0	.07	0	.00	76.2	.06
Edge Preparation	0	0	4.2	.13	0	0	11.9	.07	0	.00	9.5	.09
Tool Spall	0	0	6.7	.35	0	0	.0	.00	0	.00	0	0
Total %	100.0		100.0		100.0		100.0		100.0		100.0	

Note: Indeterminate debris is excluded.

broken by perverse fracture was recovered from the site). The minuteness of the obsidian debris was even more extreme at Tsé Haal'á, where the mean flake size was not even one-tenth of a gram. Indeed, the obsidian flakes were so small at that site that only six of the 47 recovered pieces (12.8%) could be chemically sourced, even when pushing the limits of analytical technique (Richard Hughes, personal communication 2002).

One interesting aspect of the obsidian debitage at the N16 Archaic sites is the evidence of abrasion on the arrises of some of the flakes (Figure 4.18). This wear closely matches that of obsidian biface blanks and preforms that have been carried around in a bag for many months, an observation that is based on the examination of prehistoric tools found cached in bags and of modern replicas of obsidian tools carried in bags. The motion of walking causes the tools to rub and jostle against one another, such that the areas of high relief become "abraded," rounded by numerous overlapping microfractures, damage that develops more quickly on the more brittle obsidian than on chert or quartzite. This form of wear is consistent with that resulting from transport rather than postdepositional modification because it only occurs on arrises and not on other flake surfaces or edges as would be the case with wind polish or abrasion from sediment transport. The wear on the N16 obsidian artifacts is consistent with transporting tools in bags as part of tool kits carried for long distances during many seasonal moves.

The spatial distribution of the sites with obsidian is shown in Figure 4.19. It is readily obvious that the sites with a high percentage of glass occur on the broken, high divide between the Shonto and Rainbow plateaus. To the north of this, out on the Rainbow Plateau proper, obsidian accounts for only a trace of the Archaic lithic assemblages. The 6 percent occurrence of obsidian at Dune Hollow results from but a single flake combined with very little reduction activity at this limited-use camp (16 flakes total). Indeed, given that this one flake is far larger (1.1 g) than most other obsidian flakes at other sites (Table 4.17), it may well have been brought in for use rather than being a by-product of on-site reduction. This also seems likely for the one large obsidian flake from Windy Mesa, which exhibited traces from use as a scraping tool. The question that comes to mind in examining Figure 4.19 is, How could the sites with moderately high proportions of obsidian be parts of the same settlement system that created the other sites of the project area where so little obsidian is represented?

One possibility is that the sites with obsidian represent logistic hunting camps where the assemblages are likely to appear somewhat specialized in raw material use, with obsidian preferentially used for dart points and knives or other cutting (butchery) implements. The fragmented and burned large-mammal bone found at each of the sites with abundant obsidian is consistent with the hunting camp hypothesis as detailed previously. Any residential camp that such hunters were based out of should likewise have obsidian represented at some modest level, especially in tool fragments because of the likelihood of tool kit repair at residential camps. In this regard, it is worth considering the residential camps of Three Dog Site and Tsé Haal'á at the foot of Navajo Mountain. Both sites contained abundant evidence of large mammal procurement (large-mammal bone), yet no obsidian was present in the thousands of flakes recovered from Three Dog Site, and the proportion from Tsé Haal'á was paltry (1.3%). Moreover, not one of the many projectile points or bifaces at either site was of obsidian. If these were the

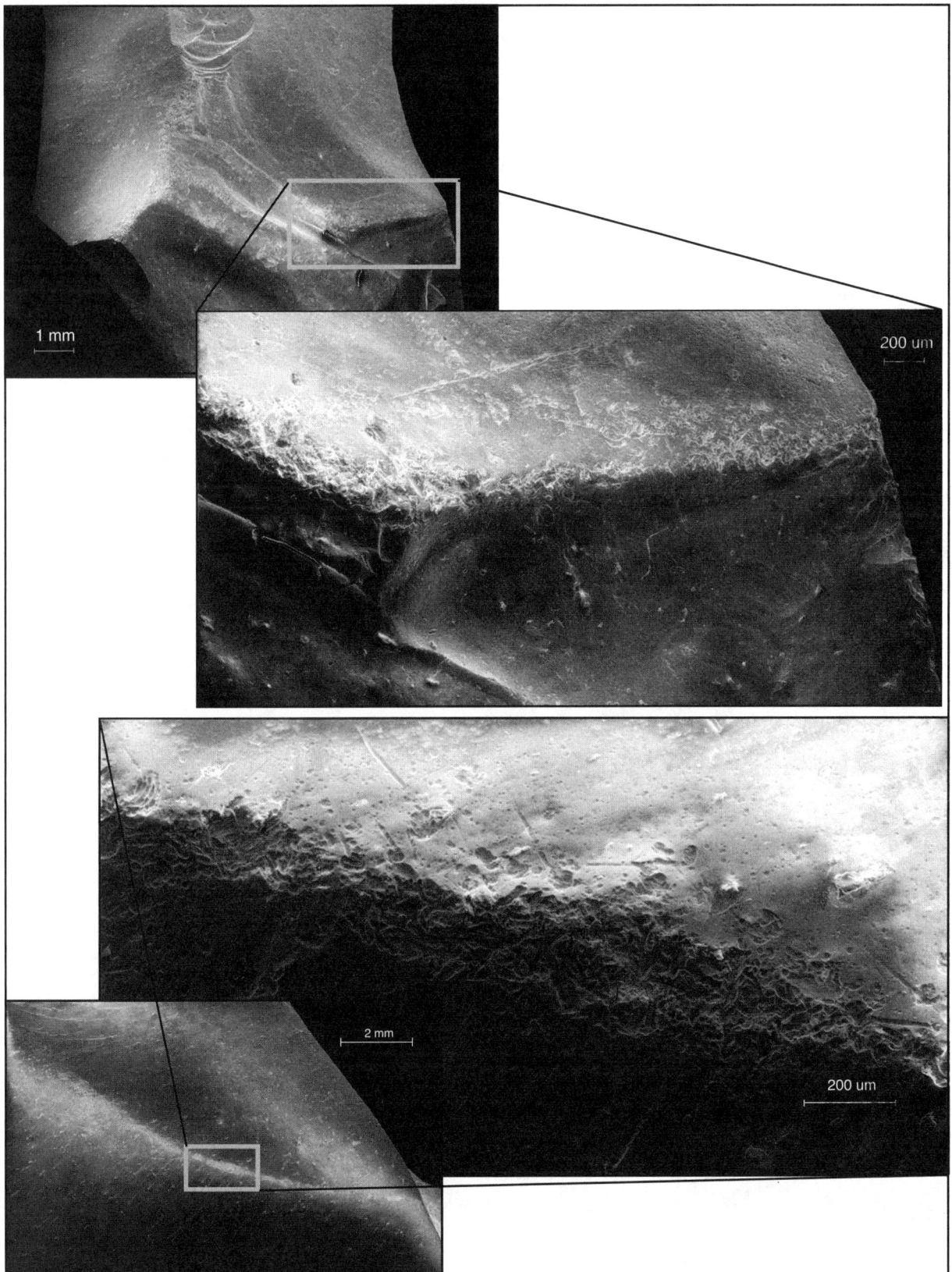

Figure 4.18. Scanning electron microscope images of transport wear on obsidian artifacts from Hólahéi Scatter.

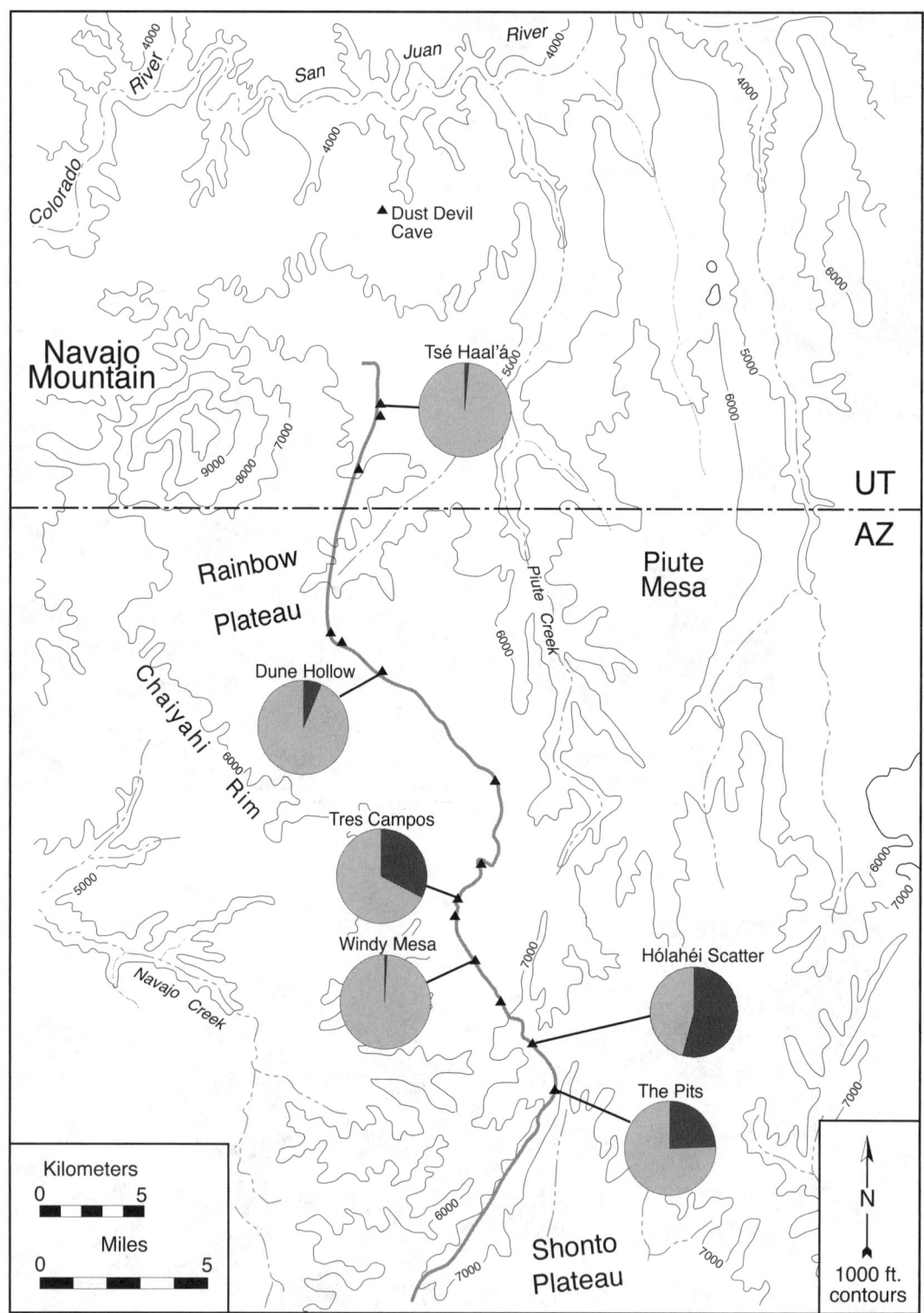

Figure 4.19. Frequency of obsidian debitage within the lithic assemblages of Navajo Mountain Road Archaeological Project Archaic sites.

TABLE 4.19. Summary Results for X-Ray Fluorescence Chemical Sourcing of Obsidian from Navajo Mountain Road Archaeological Project Archaic Sites

Obsidian Source	The Pits	Hólahéi Scatter	Windy Mesa	Tres Campos	Tsé Haal'á	Total	%
Government Mountain, AZ	19	66	2[a]	32	6	125	89.3
Black Tank, AZ	0	1	0	6	0	7	5.0
Presley Wash, AZ	0	1	0	1	0	2	1.4
Wild Horse, UT	0	1	0	0	0	1	.7
Cerro del Medio, NM	5	0	0	0	0	5	3.6
Total	24	69	2	39	6	140	100.0
% of Obsidian Analyzed	41.4	14.9	50.0	13.7	12.8	16.4	

[a] One of these analyzed items is a projectile point, and the other is a flake, so only one of the two obsidian flakes from this site was analyzed; the second flake was too small (visually it resembled glass from Cerro del Medio or some other source outside northern Arizona).

residential bases for hunters creating sites such as Hólahéi Scatter, then they were highly selective in their locations of obsidian tool reduction and disposal. The early Archaic layers of Dust Devil Cave, Stratum IV, likewise had almost no obsidian represented in the debitage (less than 1%) and none in the tools (Geib 1984). That this site served as an important residential base for foragers seems certain (Ambler 1996; Lindsay et al. 1968)—foragers for whom the Rainbow Plateau figured prominently in subsistence-settlement rounds, just like it did for the foragers who created Three Dog Site and Tsé Haal'á.

The differential incidence of obsidian in Archaic assemblages of the project area seems best explained as deriving from foragers with at least two different subsistence-settlement rounds, one of which was centered more in the Glen Canyon lowlands and represented by assemblages with infrequent or no use of obsidian and another centered elsewhere and represented by assemblages with moderately frequent use of obsidian. Foragers who circulated in the Glen Canyon lowlands acquired obsidian via down-the-line exchange because the source locations lay well outside their normal travel rounds, outside the area of embedded direct procurement. Direct procurement by one means or another is implicated by assemblages with moderately abundant obsidian, along with the inference that the normal foraging areas of the groups that created the sites lay considerably closer to the sources than the N16 project area. But direct procurement from where, and how does knowledge of source origin tie into the notion that the N16 Archaic site sample represents portions of at least two different general settlement systems?

Samples of obsidian from the Archaic sites were submitted to Richard Hughes (Geochemical Research Laboratory) for sourcing via XRF-EDS (SD, Appendix A). The samples consisted of all that appeared to be of sufficient size (ca. 1 cm^2 in area or larger) for chemical characterization. In the case of Tsé Haal'á this included flakes that were below this size limit, especially for several specimens of visually distinctive glass, because of the desire to obtain source information for this site at the foot of Navajo Mountain as a point of comparison with sites farther south. I attempted to visually identify all of the obsidian flakes submitted for XRF analysis using a binocular microscope with both transmitted and reflected light. This effort indicated that there was very little diversity, with one source comprising more than 90 percent of all flakes; most of the obsidian appeared to match glass from the Government Mountain source area of north-central Arizona. There were a few flakes that appeared to derive from other sources of northern Arizona (Black Tank, Partridge Creek, RS Hill, or Slate Mountain) and some quite translucent, high-quality glass that appeared to be from New Mexico or Utah sources. One of the reasons for the visual analysis was to obtain some gauge on whether the size threshold for XRF-EDS chemical analysis would bias some sources over others. The one clear example of this was with Tsé Haal'á, where all flakes that appeared to derive from a source other than Government Mountain were too small to analyze. One obsidian projectile point from Windy Mesa was also analyzed, resulting in a total of 140 chemically sourced artifacts.

Table 4.19 presents a summary of the XRF analysis, which confirms that nearly all of the obsidian (89.3%) came from the Government Mountain source (see SD,

Appendix A, for chemical data). Two other obsidian sources in north-central Arizona—Black Tank and Presley Wash—account for a small proportion of the debris and further support an inference of forager movement onto the Coconino Plateau. These two sources are located in the Mt. Floyd Volcanic Field about 80 km west of the Government Mountain source (Lesko 1989). A single flake was sourced to the Wild Horse locality in the Mineral Mountains of central Utah (Nelson 1984; Nelson and Holmes 1979). Five flakes of distinctive, almost clear, highly vitreous glass matched the trace element fingerprint characteristic of the Cerro del Medio locality in the Jemez Mountains source area of north-central New Mexico (Baugh and Nelson 1987). These five flakes were larger on average than those of Government Mountain obsidian from the same site and might well have come from percussion resharpening/modification of a single large biface.

The high proportion of obsidian in the assemblages of The Pits, Hólahéi Scatter, and Tres Campos, combined with the chemical source data, strongly suggest that the foragers using these sites directly procured the Government Mountain obsidian. The lesser-used other obsidian types might have been introduced through exchange. Under the assumption of direct procurement embedded within subsistence-related tasks, the occupants of these three sites would have traveled more than 200 km to obtain the glass and might have had an annual foraging range of more than 30,000 km^2 assuming a roughly circular-shaped territory, which is quite large, about three times larger than is evident for Southern Paiute bands as can be discerned from Kelly's (1934, 1964) records. Rather than being embedded within the annual pattern of overall band movement, obsidian procurement may have occurred on logistic hunting trips that diverted small task groups a considerable distance outside home territory. In such a scenario, the range of annual movement for subsistence by the band as a whole was far less than the range traveled by hunters on focal trips to distant areas. The result would be two different annual ranges that partly overlapped: a moderate-sized annual foraging territory for the entire band and a logistic hunting territory of far greater dimension (Figure 4.20). The raw material types used for hunting tools (projectile points and bifacial knives) are likely to reflect this entire logistic hunting territory and not just those sources available within the annual foraging territory. If this suggestion has merit, then it is possible to envision a hypothetical band centered on an area north of the Little Colorado River that could have directly procured obsidian from the north-central sources and reduced, resharpened, or modified tools of such material at hunting sites on the high divide between Piute and Navajo canyons. In such a scenario, hunters would have traveled to the forested highlands of the Coconino Plateau for large game; traveling there simply for stone seems unlikely given the local availability of chert in the Little Colorado River Pleistocene gravels and from various formations of the area (Chinle, Kayenta, Navajo). While on the Coconino Plateau, hunters would have quarried obsidian from the Government Mountain source and fashioned bifaces and projectile points. On another trip to a different forested highland for hunting, this time between the Shonto and Rainbow plateaus, the hunters used, resharpened, and modified their obsidian points and knives, resulting in the scatters reported here. As such, the annual logistic hunting range might have measured about 30,000 km^2, but the annual foraging range may well have been less than 8,000 km^2.

Figure 4.21 shows the same general idea but with the territories configured as ellipses, something that might be more realistic, at least for the specific region, so as to take advantage of elevation gradients. A somewhat circular foraging terrain might still apply to the Navajo Mountain region because of the vast differences in elevation compressed into such a relatively small area (top of Navajo Mountain and the Kaiparowits Plateau to the Colorado River in Glen Canyon). In both this figure and the previous one, a circular foraging area is depicted for bands local to the Navajo Mountain–Lower Glen Canyon region, one that partially overlaps with that used by foragers originating from "home bases" farther south. Regardless of the specifics of how the southern-based forager bands organized their procurement of obsidian, it is this sort of situation of overlapping territories that I think best accounts for the N16 Archaic sites with more than trace amounts of obsidian. Foragers local to the Navajo Mountain region might not have had logistic hunting camps within their annual residential range because in most cases such sites probably would have been unnecessary when home was so close at hand. The logistic hunting camps of groups local to Navajo Mountain would be expected to occur outside their annual foraging range, such as on Black Mesa or the Abajo Mountains.

In the account just given, the N16 Archaic sites with moderately abundant Government Mountain obsidian are part of the remains of more southerly focused forager bands who procured this material directly, either em-

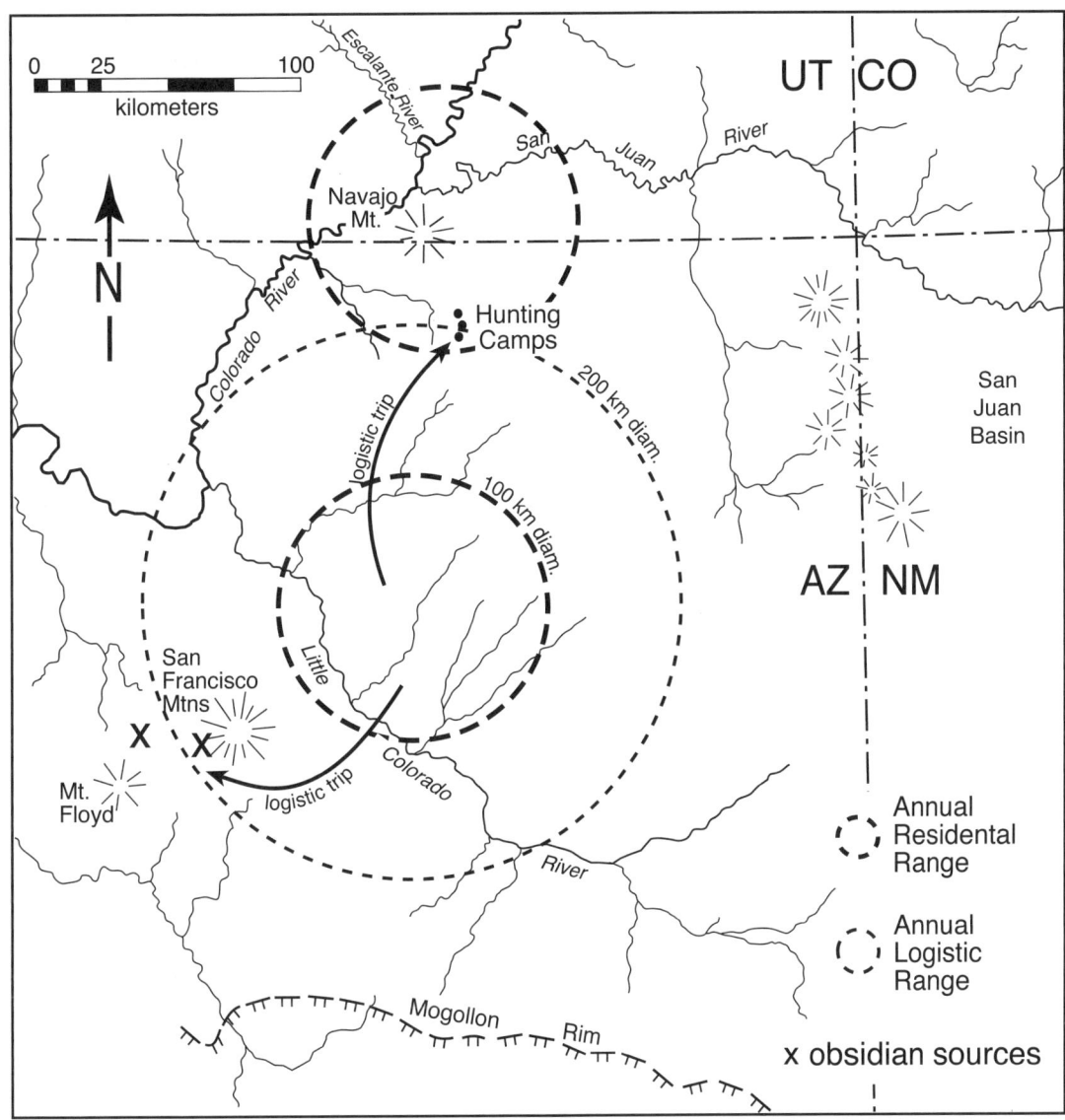

Figure 4.20. Hypothetical annual logistic range of Archaic foragers that could account for the proportion of obsidian in assemblages at probable hunting camps within the northern Kayenta region.

bedded within subsistence tasks of one sort or another (through residential or logistic hunting movements) or on specific raw material–procurement trips outside of normal annual movement for subsistence resources. Given this, I would expect certain other raw materials to be represented in the lithic assemblages of these sites, materials that would be less likely to be represented in the assemblages of foragers more local to Navajo Mountain. Such expectations provide a means to test my speculative scenario. Forager groups that were more centrally located along the Little Colorado River and adjacent localities would have regular access to raw materials such as Kaibab chert, Tolchaco chert (nodules in Pleistocene gravel of the Little Colorado River), agatized wood and brightly colored chert of the Chinle Formation, Navajo chert, and a brightly colored chert that is local to the Tuba City area. Of these materials, Navajo chert and various materials from the Chinle Formation are available within what might have been the common foraging range of foragers local to the Navajo Mountain area. Moreover, none of these other materials have a point-specific source like obsidian; they have extensive primary and secondary deposits occurring over vast areas. This, coupled with the problematic aspect of visual identification (is a white to pink chert from the Kaibab Formation or some other deposit?), precludes any confident statements. So, for example, lithic analysts did not identify any Kaibab chert or Tolchaco chert in the Tres Campos assemblage, which

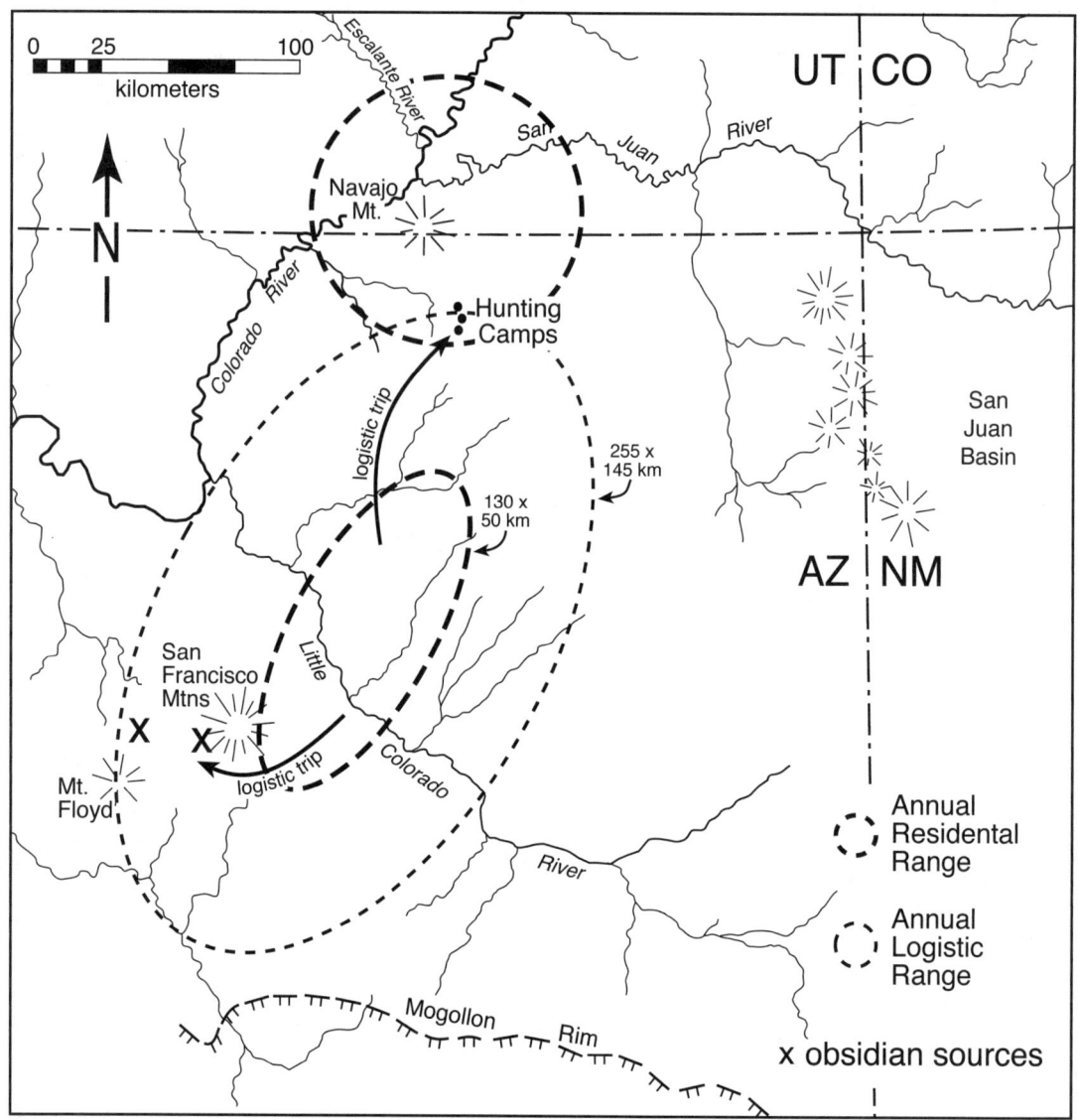

Figure 4.21. Hypothetical annual logistic range of Archaic foragers that could account for the proportion of obsidian in assemblages at probable hunting camps, with the foraging territories configured as ellipses.

has over 30 percent obsidian debitage, all of which comes from north-central Arizona sources. There are flakes of white chert in the Tres Campos assemblage, several of which might be Kaibab chert, but they were not specifically identified as such because of small size (nearly all were pressure flakes). The lack of Tolchaco chert might also result from an identification failure rather than true absence, but to make this case, sourcing techniques will have to be greatly improved.

Windy Mesa presents an interesting case, since the debitage, tools, and faunal bone recovered from there are similar in character to those at the three obsidian-rich hunting sites (The Pits, Hólahéi Scatter, and Tres Campos). The one marked difference between Windy Mesa and these three is with debitage raw material use. First, the former site has less than 1 percent obsidian representation in debitage, plus an exhausted (greatly resharpened) obsidian projectile point (see Figure 4.16). The two flakes at this site include a moderately large flake identified as bipolar that also exhibits traces of use and a small biface thinning flake. The former was chemically sourced to Government Mountain, as was the projectile point, but the latter was too small for XRF analysis, though visually it does not match any of the north-central Arizona sources. Second, unlike at the other hunting camp sites, Navajo chert makes up 60 percent of the debitage at Windy Mesa. The heavy exploitation of Navajo chert could indicate fairly local procurement, but this material is also common across a broad portion of the Kayenta region such that it might also fit the pattern expected for a nonlocal forager group from the south. For example, Archaic sites on the Kaibito Plateau have a high proportion of Navajo chert (Robins and Warburton 2004). I tend to favor the view that this site is the accumulation of a forager group local to the Kaibito or Shonto plateaus rather than the Rainbow Plateau; otherwise far more Glen Canyon chert would be represented in the assemblage, as is true of the Archaic residential camps near Navajo Mountain, which almost lack Navajo chert. Discarding an exhausted but still somewhat functional obsidian projectile point and large obsidian flake seems somewhat consistent with a group that anticipates returning to an obsidian source at some not-too-distant future time.

PALEOINDIAN REMAINS AND ARCHAIC BEGINNINGS

As reviewed in chapter 2, excavations at Dust Devil Cave revealed that Archaic foragers were living in the northern Kayenta region by around 8000 cal. BC. This is based on an 8830 ± 160 BP radiocarbon date on yucca leaves lining the bottom of a small storage pit originating from the bottom of Stratum IV (this assay has a calibrated two-sigma range of 8300–7550 BC). With such time depth there is the possibility for coexistence between Archaic and Paleoindian foragers or for securing evidence of continuity between the two. There are traces for a sparse late Paleoindian presence in the general Kayenta region such as the Badger Springs site on the Shonto Plateau (Hesse et al. 1996; Smiley 2002b:23–25) and Cody-like points from around Tuba City (seen by me in a private collection), but the ages of these remains are unknown.

Unfortunately, the N16 excavations shed no additional light on the earliest portion of the early Archaic period. The oldest Archaic features excavated during the NMRAP date to 8,200–8,300 radiocarbon years ago. One isolated hearth at The Pits produced an assay of 9780 ± 100 BP, which has a calibrated two-sigma range of 9650–8800 BC. This assay is within the expected time frame for late Paleoindian remains, but nothing else can be related to this date. No artifacts were recovered from the immediate vicinity of the feature, and because its age was not known until well after data recovery was over, work within its vicinity was quite limited. Consequently the date remains an enigma, a hint that late Paleoindian remains might eventually be uncovered in the area.

Had this date been obtained from Hearth 1 at Sapo Seco then I would have another story to report. During excavation of Locus B at this Tsegi phase (late Pueblo III) site on the Rainbow Plateau (see SD vol. 4, chap. 8) the

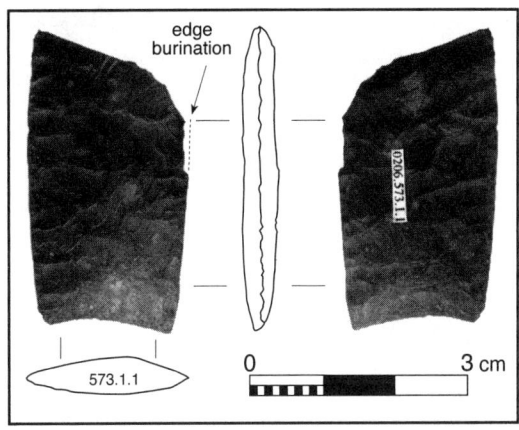

Figure 4.22. Plainview-like point base from the surface of Locus B at Sapo Seco.

NNAD crew recovered a Plainview-like point base from the surface (Figure 4.22). Because the point appeared to be within the edge of an eroded Puebloan trash midden, the field crew thought little of the find, until underneath the Puebloan component they uncovered a buried hearth containing pressure flakes. The hearth was only about 10 m from where the point was recovered, and the pressure flakes in the feature were of the same general material type as the point (Navajo chert). Radiocarbon dating of charcoal from this feature produced an age well within the local Archaic sequence (8230 ± 50 BP), so the point is unlikely to be associated with the hearth. Attempts to refit the pressure flakes to the point also failed, and indeed no flakes were sufficiently similar in color and micro-inclusions to have been from this tool. Indeed, it is improbable that any flakes detached from finishing this tool would have been recovered from where the broken, used point ended up. The projectile point might have been a Paleoindian hunting loss at the approximate find location, but Puebloans may have instead collected it as a curiosity and then discarded it in the midden.

SETTLEMENT CONTINUITY AND THE MIDDLE ARCHAIC

Archaeologists often divide things into three stages.... Afterwards, of course, they argue that the whole thing was continuous anyhow and that the divisions are arbitrary and for convenience [Leakey 1984:13].

There is a simple yet unanswered question concerning whether the Colorado Plateau was the setting of continuous cultural development during the Archaic period. There are advocates both for and against continuity in occupation (e.g., Berry and Berry 1986; Matson 1991; Wills 1988), with perhaps more in the former camp. Such a question may seem trivial, yet our attempts at describing and explaining culture change in the Southwest and throughout the world partly depend on whether we are studying autochthonous or allochthonous phenomena. As an influential advocate of the autochthonous view, Cynthia Irwin-Williams (1967, 1973, 1979) succinctly expressed its underlying assumption: "The northern Southwest was the focus of a long-term continuous development within the Archaic spectrum, which culminated ultimately in the formation of the central core of the relatively well-known sedentary Anasazi culture" (1979:35).

Claudia and Michael Berry (1986:321) argued that the notion of continuous cultural development during the Archaic as advocated by archaeologists such as Irwin-Williams was a self-fulfilling prophecy unsupported by facts. The key piece of evidence for them was the uninterrupted occupancy of the same area, referred to as settlement or population continuity. The significance of this is obvious, for without any observable trace of human existence within a region it is difficult to make a case for long-term in situ development. Measures of settlement continuity include regional chronometric records such as tree-ring or radiocarbon dates, as well as regional composite histories of site occupancy. Sample adequacy and bias loom large in arguments for a lack of continuity— Have we investigated enough of a given region? Have we systematically ignored a given class of evidence? Are the traces of some periods less obvious than those of other periods? Concerns that regional radiocarbon records might not accurately track the density of human populations in the past have been categorized by Rick (1987:55–58, Figure 1) as falling under one of three reasons: creation biases, preservation biases, and investigation biases. All might play a role and should be seriously evaluated.

Previous Date Summaries

In the first regional summary of preceramic radiocarbon dates for the northern Colorado Plateau, Schroedl (1976: 13–29) identified two major breaks during the Archaic period—a 1,000-year interval from ca. 6000 to 5000 BP and a 500-year interval from 3000 to 2500 BP. A decade later and working on a larger geographic scale, Berry and Berry (1986) analyzed the patterning of 152 radiocarbon dates prior to 1400 BP from 57 Colorado Plateau sites. Despite their larger data set, Berry and Berry recognized the same 1,000-year middle Archaic gap, from 6000 to 5000 BP, and postulated a major hiatus in forager occupancy (a lack of settlement continuity). They claimed that hunter-gatherer occupation of the Colorado Plateau was discontinuous, that the Archaic period was punctuated by a sequence of regional abandonment and reoccupation, resulting in a succession of new lifeways and material culture. Changes in projectile point styles roughly corresponding with reputed times of reoccupation provided evidence for cultural discontinuity.

In 1996, I summarized an even larger set of radiocarbon dates (180) but for a smaller region, one centered on Glen and Cataract canyons of the Colorado River and including the N16 project area—basically the Canyonlands Section of the Colorado Plateau. As illustrated and discussed in that summary (Geib 1996a:26–28, 31–34), the middle Archaic date gap was beginning to be filled, in part by dating materials from museum collections for the express purpose of trying to fill this gap (e.g., Geib 1996b). I thought that the new evidence did not support the notion of regional abandonment. As concerns the largest gap in the record, that of the middle Archaic, I suggested that "there may have been a reduction in population density owing to an expansion of foraging territories coupled with some migration" and that because of several factors, "middle Archaic remains might be far more dispersed than those of other Archaic intervals and thus less subject to archaeological discovery and investigation" (Geib 1996a:36).

My argument for greatly diminished forager populations rather than regional abandonment is ultimately an interpretation of evidence subject to different opinions. The middle Archaic is characterized by a significant reduction in radiocarbon dates, and there remain gaps in the record between about 6000 and 4000 BP, especially upon treating the dates critically rather than accepting them at face value. If only including assays on the high-quality materials most likely to represent the true times of human presence, then there are far fewer dates to work with, but this is perhaps too cautious of an approach. Beyond examining the overall trend, it is important to identify which particular areas of the Colorado Plateau might contain middle Archaic occupations, to compare the occupation histories within and between portions of the plateau.

Shelter Abandonment

It must be kept in mind that the middle Archaic reduction in date frequency is coupled with (partly a result of) the apparent long-term abandonment or diminished use of previously well-used shelters. Cowboy Cave provides perhaps the best-known example of middle Archaic cave abandonment (Jennings 1980). The 7,000-year occupation sequence at this site consists of layers of relatively clean eolian sand classified as "sterile" separated by trashy cultural deposits. This depositional sequence led Jennings (1980:20–26, Table 2) to conclude that there had been three significant occupational breaks during the Archaic use of the site, with the second and longest during the middle Archaic from roughly 6300 to 3700 BP (Strata IVa–IVb). Schroedl and Coulam (1994) reinterpreted this sequence doing away with the first hiatus, but they still find an extended interval between about 6300 and 3600 BP when foragers did not use the site and during which there apparently was virtually no cultural or natural deposition (see Figure 2.5; they also recognize a later hiatus between the late Archaic and terminal Archaic). The middle Archaic hiatus at Cowboy Cave is repeated on the Rainbow Plateau at two sites (Dust Devil Cave and Atlatl Rock Cave) and perhaps as well at a third (Sand Dune Cave). At Dust Devil Cave (Ambler 1996; Lindsay et al. 1968) there was a thick early Archaic trash accumulation (Stratum IV) buried beneath a middle Holocene layer of eolian sand about 1 m thick that yielded few cultural remains (Stratum V). The dating of Stratum V needs investigation, but the end of the early Archaic occupation is well fixed by the direct dating of plain-weave sandals from the top of Stratum IV (resting on IV–V contact) to around 6800 BP (Ambler 1996; Geib 1996b). Shortly after this time, the cave was little used for several thousand years. At Atlatl Rock Cave (see SD vol. 2, chap. 2), a massive layer of thin roof spalls (Unit III) separated early Archaic deposition dated between about 8000 and 7000 BP from Basketmaker II deposits dated from about 1900 to 1500 BP. The rock spall layer accumulated between 5000 and 4000 BP and contained no cultural remains; from 7000 to 5000 BP there appears to have been no cultural deposition in the shelter and negligible natural deposition. This interpretation parallels Schroedl and Coulam's (1994) conclusions about deposit formation at Cowboy Cave, where the deposits from three extended intervals of forager use, each separated by a few thousand years of nonuse, left cultural deposits resting one upon the other with no matrix corresponding to the periods of abandonment.

The case for Sand Dune Cave (Lindsay et al. 1968) seems less clear-cut because excavation by arbitrary levels precluded a definite statement. This cave apparently lacked middle Archaic deposits, although a recent radiocarbon assay on collagen from Burial 2 of this site returned an age of 4480 ± 60 BP (Coltrain et al. 2007), which is within the end of the middle Archaic. This date highlights the difficulties of making claims about the occupation histories of shelters without careful excavation by natural strata accompanied by numerous radiocarbon dates. In cases of stratigraphic excavation and abundant dates, the common pattern is one of repeated and at times even rather intensive use by foragers during the early Archaic followed by little or no use for several millennia. Old Man Cave (Geib and Davidson 1994) provides an example of this: forager use of this shelter started coming to a close some 6,800 radiocarbon years ago, with probable abandonment of the site for several thousand years from about 6000 to 3700 BP and sustained use not occurring again until after around 2300 BP with Basketmaker II farmers.

Based on current evidence, then, the middle Archaic for a significant portion of the Colorado Plateau was more than just a time of different point styles (e.g., Holmer 1980, 1986); the record also exhibits a significant reduction in radiocarbon dates and the abandonment or drastic reduction in use of sites that were once key nodes in annual subsistence rounds. There is a close linkage between these phenomena, in that shelters have provided a large proportion of Archaic period radiocarbon dates, hence the abandonment or drastic reduction in their use has a concomitant effect on date patterning, partially creating the reduction in frequency. Still, both factors appear to herald significant shifts in forager settlement and perhaps subsistence, or at least in the organization of subsistence tasks, and would seem to implicate climatic change. The start of this interval is placed at about 6000 BP (ca. 4800 cal. BC), with the realization that there appears to have been an extended transition from the early Archaic and that many cave sites were evidently abandoned before this time. And 4000 BP (ca. 2500 cal. BC) provides an approximate ending time for the middle Archaic, although many sites do not show use until several hundred years after that. Despite significant shifts in favored projectile point styles during this interval, sandals nevertheless reveal cultural continuity (Geib 1996b).

The Local Radiocarbon Record

Radiocarbon dates have a seemingly irreplaceable role not only in the temporal ordering of Archaic remains but also as a data set for examining inter- and intraregional patterns that can inform about changes in settlement, settlement organization, and perhaps population fluctuations. At the simplest of levels, because the number of radiocarbon

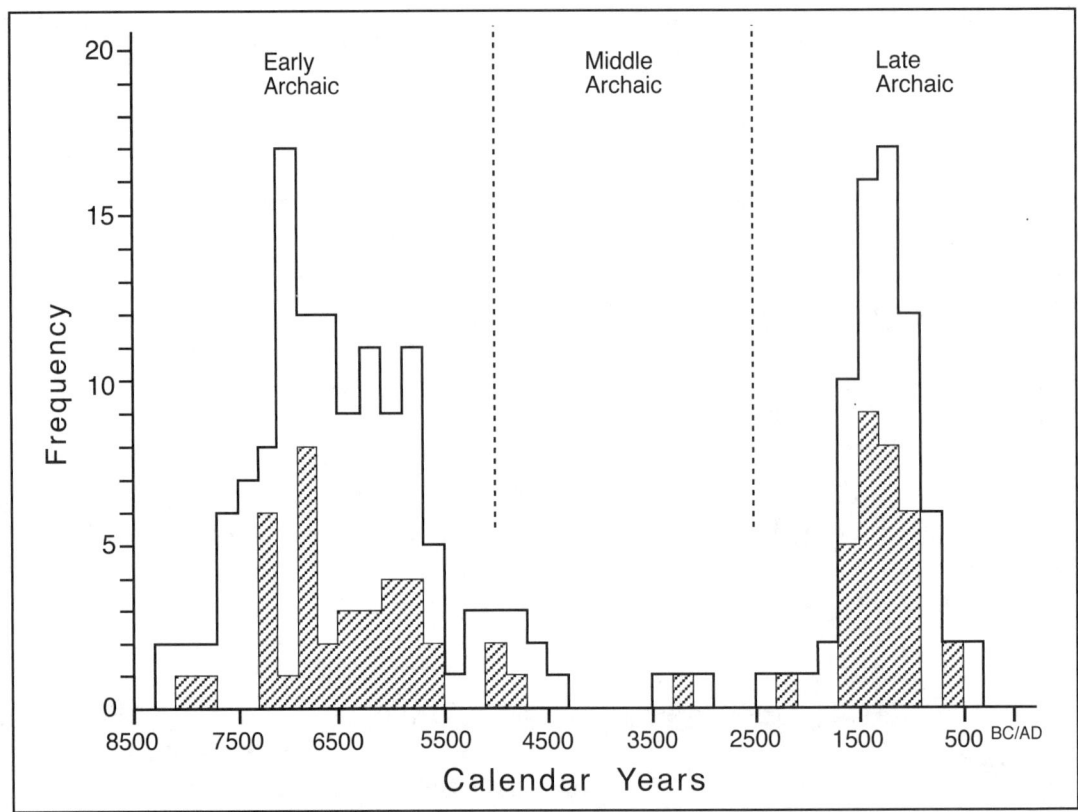

Figure 4.23. Frequency distribution of Archaic radiocarbon dates for the northern Kayenta region (Rainbow Plateau and far-northern Shonto Plateau); shaded area depicts the count of dates falling within a 200-year interval based on calibrated midpoints, whereas the larger distribution uses the count of dates falling within 200-year intervals based on calibrated 2σ age ranges.

dates can be interpreted as a reflection of the "magnitude of occupation,... it is possible to assess and compare, in a relative fashion, the occupation histories within and between regions" (Rick 1987:55). The NMRAP presented a wonderful opportunity to begin to assemble a detailed record of forager occupation for one particular portion of the Colorado Plateau and thereby test the notion of regional abandonment during the middle Archaic. This project did not select certain Archaic sites for excavation based on temporal diagnostics, prior dates, site characteristics, or the like; rather, it excavated what was presented. As discussed previously, most of the Archaic sites were discovered fortuitously while trenching Puebloan or Basketmaker II sites; a few were excavated because of exposures provided by previous road construction. In all cases, I had no prior knowledge as to the age of an Archaic site; crews simply excavated everything presented, and I diligently sent in samples for radiocarbon analysis.

The substantial number of NMRAP Archaic radiocarbon dates reported earlier in this chapter can be combined with 12 previous dates from the Rainbow Plateau to provide a record of forager occupancy for the northern Kayenta region. The previous dates, which are from Sand Dune Cave ($n = 3$) and Dust Devil Cave ($n = 9$), consist mainly of high-quality samples—yucca or grass from open-twined sandals.[4] The 70 dates, which range in age from 8830 to 2520 BP, are graphed in Figure 4.10; excluded in this figure is the one early outlier date of 9780 BP from The Pits. Many of the Archaic period radiocarbon dates are based on samples of low material quality, with 40 percent ($n = 28$) on wood charcoal and another 26 percent ($n = 18$) on sagebrush charcoal. There are, however, 24 dates (32%) that are unlikely to overestimate age—11 for certain and 13 not by much if at all. These dates on high-quality materials are scattered throughout the early and late portions of the sequence, thus adding credibility to the overall pattern.

The frequency distribution shown in Figure 4.23 has been compiled by two different methods that complement one another. The small pattern (shaded area) is based on counting up the number of dates within a given 200-year interval using the approximated midpoints of calibrated ages (calibrations based on the OxCal program, Version 3.5 [Bronk Ramsey 1994, 1995, 1998]). A 200-year interval seemed appropriate for taking into account the level of imprecision with the dates and for smoothing the results. The larger distribution takes into account the error term of each date by summing how many dates occur within each 200-year interval based on their calibrated two-sigma age range. For example, the date of 8180 ± 50 BP (Beta-101390) with a calibrated two-sigma range of 7340–7060 BC is counted in three 200-year intervals: 7500–7300, 7300–7100, and 7100–6900 cal. BC. As Berry and Berry (1986:284) have mentioned, this method can result in distortion because very imprecise dates have a greater impact on the pattern than precise dates, basically producing a leveling effect on trends and a filling of gaps. Overall the standard error is quite small for this data set, ranging from a low of 30 years to a high of 200 years with an average of 72 years. Precision in radiocarbon dating has generally improved with time; thus most of the imprecise dates are those processed prior to the NMRAP: 10 of the 15 dates with a standard error of 100 years or more (67%) were analyzed in the 1960s or 1970s. Fortunately, almost half of the most imprecise dates (seven of the 15) are on materials unlikely to overestimate age and indisputably of cultural origin (sandals and feces). Moreover, whatever distortion there is by factoring in the error term can be gauged against the core pattern based on date midpoints.

The frequency distribution of Archaic period radiocarbon dates for the project area is discontinuous, containing a major break between early and late Archaic; a shorter break between late Archaic and Basketmaker II is discussed in the next chapter. The middle Archaic date gap from about 4500 to 2500 cal. BC is unlikely to be the result of a biased selection of the sites for excavation. As explained previously, the NMRAP Archaic sites were not chosen according to some scheme that purposefully omitted those of the middle Archaic. Indeed, an Archaic component was not even suspected at most sites until excavation exposed the remains and in some cases not until radiocarbon dates were actually run. This is even true for the earlier excavations of Sand Dune Cave and Dust Devil Cave (Lindsay et al. 1968); MNA archaeologists had no suspicion that they would unearth Archaic remains from these sites, and it was not until radiocarbon dates were obtained on three sandals from Sand Dune Cave that the significance of their findings became obvious.

As cautioned previously, sample adequacy is critical for judging the significance of gaps in radiocarbon records. Sample adequacy can be figured with regard to both the total number of radiocarbon dates available and the total number of sites that yielded the samples. At 70, the total number of dates used to create Figure 4.23 is respectable considering the relatively small size of the study area, at least for an initial approximation of trends. However, it is worth pointing out that Stolk and colleagues (Stolk et al. 1989; Stolk et al. 1994) maintain that at least 40 dates per millennium are required to be certain that any trends have statistical reliability. It would be admittedly difficult to get any dates, let alone 40, for those millennia when there was no human occupation, but then perhaps this was never the case. Of far greater concern than sheer date number in this instance is the second aspect of sample adequacy—site count. With 15 sites providing the radiocarbon dates graphed in Figure 4.23 it is possible that simply too few have been studied to disclose the record of the middle Archaic. While conceivable, this is not highly credible. Again, the relatively small size of the region is an important consideration. Moreover, if the true history of forager occupancy of the study area did not closely resemble that shown by the radiocarbon distribution, the probabilities are exceedingly low that 15 sites chosen by happenstance would yield virtually no evidence for middle Archaic occupancy yet abundant remains for both the early and late Archaic. After all, the middle Archaic is not a brief time interval but, in fact, more than 2,000 years long, or over 100 generations.

An Expanded Record

Increased sample size is always welcome for a study like this, and one means to provide this is by adding in newly obtained Archaic radiocarbon dates from farther south in the Kayenta region. Two road excavation projects (N21 and N608) that NNAD conducted partially contemporaneously with the NMRAP produced 36 radiocarbon dates from 11 Archaic sites (Bungart et al. 2004; Neff et al. 2004). The N21 project actually processed many more dates from Archaic sites, 83 in all, but 57 of these were bulk sediment samples from hearths that systematically underrepresented the age of the features by anywhere from several hundred years to several thousand years. Because all of the bulk sediment dates are unreliable they cannot be used for chronological placement of sites and have been omitted from consideration here. Had one wanted to artificially eliminate the middle Archaic gap, then these unreliable bulk sediment dates were perfect since most fell into

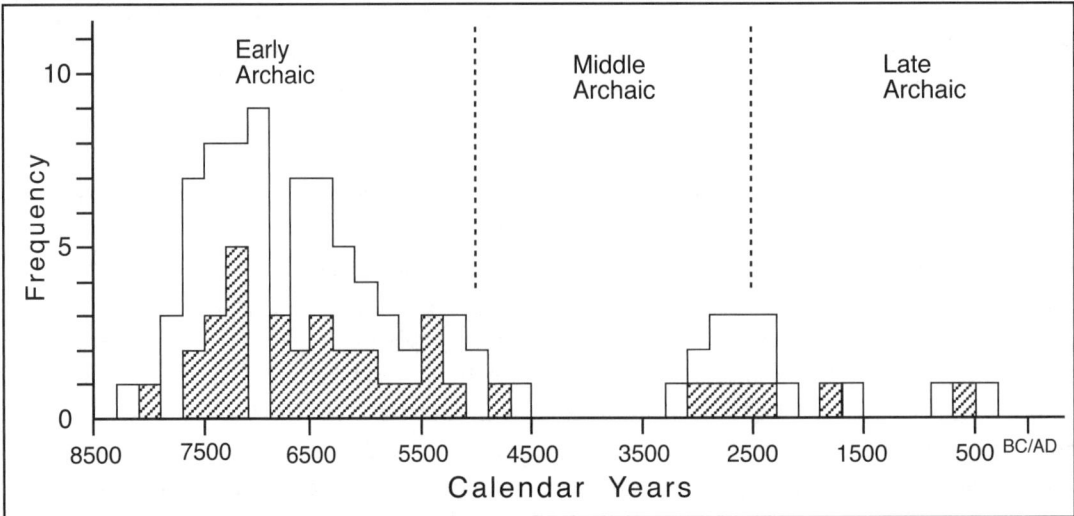

Figure 4.24. Frequency distribution of Archaic radiocarbon dates from the Kaibito Plateau (N21 and N608 projects); shaded area depicts the count of dates falling within a 200-year interval based on calibrated midpoints, whereas the larger distribution uses the count of dates falling within 200-year intervals based on calibrated 2σ age ranges.

this interval because of contamination of early Archaic charcoal by more recent carbon.

The 36 dates from these two projects (N21 and N608) are graphed in Figure 4.24 by the same method described above. This Kaibito Plateau radiocarbon record generally reproduces the record for the Rainbow Plateau (northern Kayenta region), with a significant cluster of dates in the early Archaic, a middle Archaic gap, and another cluster during the late Archaic. A chief difference is with the height (frequency) and placement of the late Archaic date cluster, with the Kaibito Plateau having fewer late Archaic dates that tend to be earlier than those of the Rainbow Plateau. Nonetheless, two separate excavation projects on the Kaibito Plateau produced essentially identical results.

Figure 4.25 plots the entire radiocarbon data set for the Rainbow and Kaibito plateaus to reveal the overall pattern. Based on 106 dates from 26 sites, this strongly bimodal pattern is far less likely to be the result of sampling bias. The lack of evidence for open sites dating to the middle Archaic within NNAD's road excavations parallels the declines and breaks in the use of natural shelters on the Colorado Plateau mentioned previously and closely accords with the middle Archaic date gap highlighted by Berry and Berry (1986) and initially by Schroedl (1976). Given that NNAD's road excavations uncovered both late and early Archaic components, sometimes at the same locations, it appears unlikely that the revealed patterning merely tracks a preservation or discovery bias. In other words, the patterning is unlikely to be unrepresentative because of removal by erosion, obstruction by burial, or other geomorphic processes. Rather, it seems a probable reflection of reality. And even though I doubt that foragers totally abandoned the Colorado Plateau because the date gap is beginning to disappear as more sites are studied (e.g., Geib 1996a, 1996b; Tipps 1998), nonetheless the date distribution for the Kayenta region is striking. But what does it signify?

Explaining the Pattern

There are two interrelated aspects as to the significance of the radiocarbon pattern: (1) Is the patterning telling us something about behavior in the past rather than merely preservation biases or the behavior of archaeologists, and what might this be? and (2) What has caused this pattern, why is it present? Obviously, if the answer to the first question has to do with biases of one sort or another, then the answer to the second question is moot. However, if biases are not the answer to the first question and some past behavior is reflected, then the second question has relevance, although the probable answer as to why appears highly constrained (environmentally determinist) given the nature of the hunter-gatherer adaptation in the Archaic.

Climatic Conditions

Almost 30 years ago when Schroedl (1976:64) created a frequency distribution of preceramic radiocarbon dates and first called attention to a middle Archaic date gap, he interpreted the pattern as evidence that forager pop-

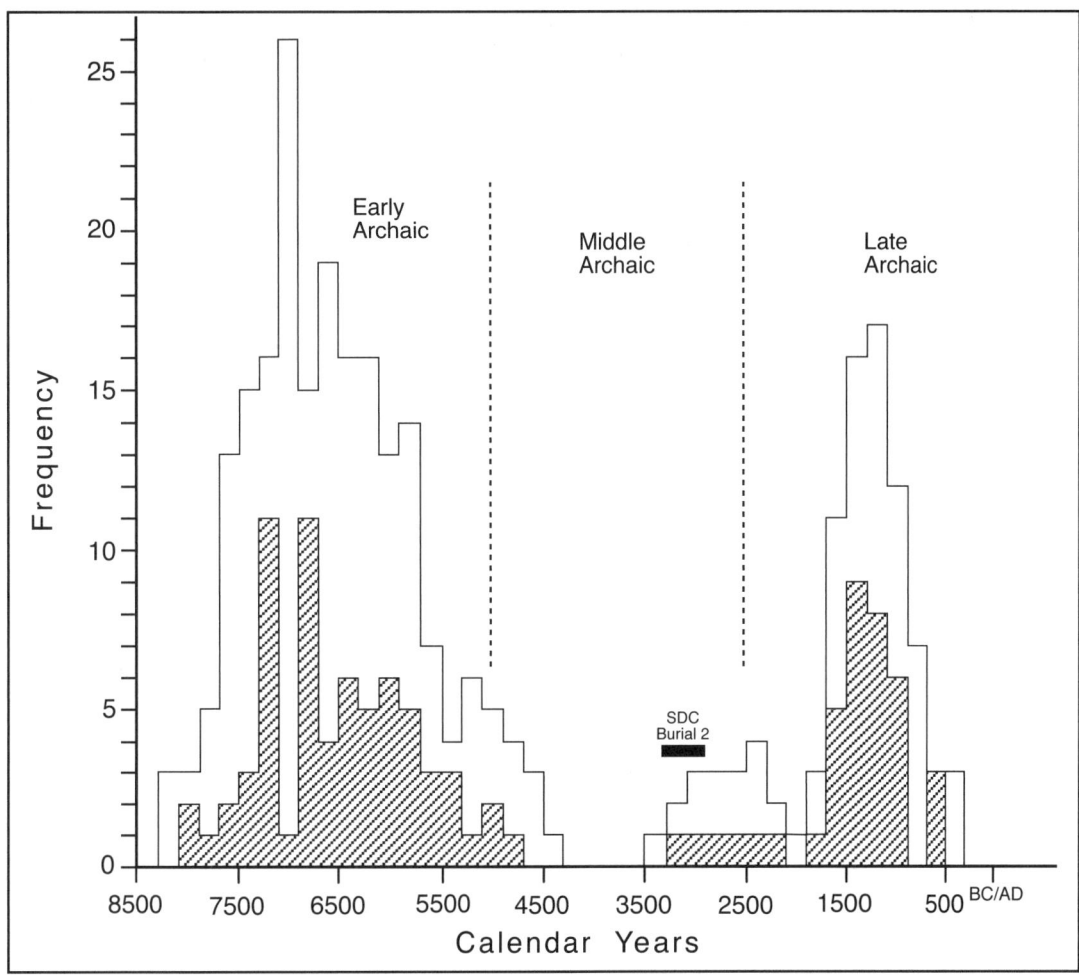

Figure 4.25. Frequency distribution of all Archaic radiocarbon dates for the northern Kayenta region and the Kaibito Plateau; shaded area depicts the count of dates falling within a 200-year interval based on calibrated midpoints, whereas the larger distribution uses the count of dates falling within 200-year intervals based on calibrated 2σ age ranges. Also shown is a recently obtained determination on Burial 2 from Sand Dune Cave (SDC [Coltrain et al. 2007]).

ulations declined to an all-time low relative to the early and late Archaic. The assumption was that more people result in more hearths and cultural deposits, which result in more radiocarbon dates: "All things being equal, more occupation produces more carbon dates" (Rick 1987:56). The converse of this is also assumed. When Berry and Berry graphed an even larger set of dates for the entire Colorado Plateau 10 years later, they concluded that the gap was not merely a population decline but an abandonment of the region. The bimodal pattern of radiocarbon dates for the Kayenta region closely matches Berry and Berry's (1986) date distribution for the Colorado Plateau, which they saw as evidence incompatible with the notion of continuous forager occupancy. Both Schroedl (1976) and Berry and Berry (1986) looked to the paleoenvironmental record as the causal factor behind the middle Archaic population decline or abandonment. It is clear that these authors took the radiocarbon record that they graphed as a reflection of human population trends in the past rather than as some spurious result of various biases.

Meltzer adopted a more cautious view with regard to the radiocarbon record (and site frequencies) for the Great Plains: "For now, evidence of Altithermal human population decline is unproven" (1999:413). As he sees it, the population decline inference is unsupported until we can effectively address preservation and discovery biases (removal and burial by geomorphic processes) and until we have considered how other behavioral responses might mistakenly lead us to believe that there was a population decline. As to the latter, I have previously argued that several responses might have resulted in a substantially less visible middle Holocene archaeological record for the region centered on Glen Canyon: "Middle Archaic populations could have increased the frequency of residential moves, greatly expanded the territory of seasonal rounds, and decreased the periodicity of residential reuse" (Geib 1996a:34). Some or all of this may well be true, but I still see Schroedl's conclusion that forager population declined to an all-time low as the best account of the Archaic period radiocarbon record for the Colorado Plateau. For the southern plains, Meltzer ultimately conceded this probability as well: "It seems reasonable to infer as well that these foragers were not permanent inhabitants of the area—in effect, there was local abandonment and a decline in the human population during this period" (1999:413). This statement, of course, begs the question as to where these foragers went to live on a more permanent basis. When the radiocarbon records for the Great Plains, the Colorado Plateau, and the Great Basin are considered in combination, it seems reasonable to ask, Where were these foragers surviving for most of the middle Holocene? The Rocky Mountains in Colorado is a plausible refuge (Benedict and Olson 1978), but could this region absorb all foragers if so much terrain was vacated? Perhaps so if the middle Holocene was a bottleneck, with forager populations being knocked back substantially from early Archaic levels. The middle Holocene could well have been a time of "die-off" from a combination of increased death rates and lowered fertility, such that forager populations on a panregional scale were rather sparse. Such speculation is, of course, well beyond the issue at hand, which now concerns the why of question 2 above given that various biases seem unable to account for the radiocarbon pattern.

Antevs's (1955) Altithermal drought appears to provide a ready-made account for why foragers would have experienced trouble making a living during the middle Holocene. As Jennings puts it: "If the archaeological record of the region was apparently locally blank, from 5000 to 3000 BC, the explanation was already in hand.... [A]rchaeologists created the equation: Altithermal = too hot for humans = abandonment" (1986:58). Antevs's controversial tripartite division of the climatic history of the western United States is now recognized as invalid, because "the periods of maximum warmth and moisture were time-transgressive, and the range of climatic conditions was much broader than the cool-wet versus warm-dry opposition seen by Antevs" (Thompson et al. 1993: 495, but cf. Haynes 1990). As an alternative for comparison with cultural events on the Colorado Plateau, both Schroedl and the Berrys used the Blytt-Sernander sequence of global climatic steady states and transitions. In this model, "the timing of the [climatic] transitions is thought to be applicable on a global scale, whereas the direction of change and the nature of any particular quasi-steady state vary from continent to continent and region to region" (Berry and Berry 1986:311). Hence, the sequence implies nothing about the particulars of the climatic transitions (i.e., the directions of change—cooler to warmer, wetter to drier, or vice versa) that might have been the external factor precipitating the systemic changes leading to the middle Archaic population decline or abandonment.

As to the climatic particulars for the Colorado Plateau during the middle Holocene, there seems little consensus, and unfortunately, there is no well-supported paleoenvironmental reconstruction specific to the plateau as a whole or its various geographic subdivisions that deals in detail with the early–middle Holocene transition and the middle Holocene (at least none that is compatible with the larger picture and which reconciles evident local discrepancies or contradictions). What can be offered at this time are small bits of information that combined seem to suggest that the climatic pattern for the middle Archaic period was both warmer and drier than during the early Archaic. This is certainly a simplification of what was probably a complex and variable situation, both spatially and temporally. Yet numerous and diverse data sets show that the middle Holocene between roughly 8,000 and 5,000 years ago was generally far warmer and drier than what came before or what followed. Increasing temperatures are thought to be driven by the changing nature of solar insolation, accompanied in many areas during the middle Holocene by decreased summer precipitation (Bartlein et al. 1998; Thompson et al. 1993). There are latitudinal variations to consider as well as significant differences in elevation (both affect temperature and evaporation rates), plus the orographic effects of mountains and high plateaus. The Southwest generally is characterized by aridity and drought, with the latter resulting from diminishment of one or both of the biseasonal precipitation sources—the summer monsoons out of the southern gulfs and the winter frontal systems from the northwest off the Pacific Ocean. The significance of these two precipitation sources diminishes in opposite directions, with monsoonal moisture decreasing in contribution to total precipitation from south to north and conversely for winter Pacific moisture, which accounts for less total precipitation from north to south.

Climatic modeling would suggest that middle Holocene warming in the Southwest would be accompanied by strengthened monsoonal incursions as more moisture-laden air masses were drawn from the Gulfs of Mexico and California. Van Devender (1990) finds evidence for just this pattern in the Sonoran Desert and argues that summer precipitation increased rather than diminished during the middle Holocene. Spaulding (1991) has suggested that any such monsoonal incursions did not penetrate significantly into the Great Basin, and there appears to be nearly unanimous opinion these days that the basin was both warmer and drier in the middle Holocene than before or after (e.g., summaries in Grayson 1993, 2000). Whatever mechanism of air mass circulation limited middle Holocene penetration of monsoonal moisture to the southern Great Basin where Spaulding's record comes from (see also Quade et al. 1998) would also have applied for most of the adjoining Colorado Plateau, especially those portions away from the Mogollon Rim. Even along this rim there appears to have been a drastic reduction in effective precipitation during the middle Holocene, as indicated by lake records that reflect desiccation, reduced sedimentation, and poorly preserved pollen (Anderson 1993; Hasbargen 1994; Jacobs 1985). So, perhaps there was an easterly shift in the monsoonal boundary, which left the Arizona and Utah portions of the Colorado Plateau deprived of summer moisture. Comparatively xeric conditions on the Colorado Plateau during the middle Holocene are indicated by various pieces of evidence. For example, based on the alluvial records of Black Mesa, T. Karlstrom (1988:69) documented a major postglacial drought that culminated about 6000–3500 BP (see also E. Karlstrom 1988; Karlstrom and Karlstrom 1986). Withers's (1989) study of late Quaternary macrobotanical remains from alcoves in the Glen Canyon area is interpreted as reflecting a warming and drying trend at the end of the late Pleistocene, culminating in hot xeric conditions by the middle Holocene (ca. 7000 BP). Following Cole (1981), Withers believes that shifts of the summer monsoon and polar jet stream could account for a dry middle Holocene in Glen Canyon.

It is important to point out that the evidence for reduced effective moisture in the Great Basin during the middle Holocene has an important bearing on the interpretation of precipitation patterns on the Colorado Plateau. Basin drying would have resulted from a reduction in the intensity or number of Pacific storm systems that moved through the area coupled with somewhat higher temperatures (increased evaporation). Decreases in summer precipitation are inferred (e.g., Grayson 1993), but to the extent that this was also true in winter, then much of the Colorado Plateau might have received a double whammy—a lessening of both summer and winter sources of moisture. The effects of such a condition would of course vary depending on which portion of the Colorado Plateau one examined. Arid low-elevation basins or river valleys might have been more severely affected than, say, high-elevation plateaus, especially those of broad aerial extent and adjoining the Rocky Mountains (e.g., the Uncompahgre Plateau). Dry plateaus at average elevation such as the Rainbow Plateau or the Kaibito Plateau might have been quite undesirable places during an extended drought interval. This would perhaps apply more to the Kaibito Plateau than the Rainbow Plateau, because the former is far more environmentally uniform. The Rainbow Plateau is adjacent to the Glen Canyon lowlands, with its permanent rivers, and also has the higher elevations of Navajo Mountain.

Less Food, Less Water

If the reconstructed middle Holocene climatic patterns are approximately correct, then the implications for foragers are not good. Judging from the dietary evidence contained in human feces and recovered from cave deposits, it is clear that early Holocene (early Archaic) foragers on the Colorado Plateau were already living close to the margin. This inference is based on the evidence for heavy reliance on prickly pear cactus pads and on various low-rank seeds such as dropseed, goosefoot, and sunflower (Van Ness and Hansen 1996). Thus, any factors that reduced the resource base further would have been significant, and this is precisely what lessened effective moisture is likely to have done. In times of drought on the Colorado Plateau there can be little or no harvest for many of the critical annual seed resources such as dropseed, goosefoot, and sunflower. Indeed these plants depend on the summer monsoon rains to generate and then reach maturity, so their productivity would have been impacted in a major way by any shift of the monsoonal boundary. Successive seasons of no or poorly developed monsoon rain could have reduced the abundance of annual plants such as goosefoot and sunflower, which generate anew each year from seeds of past growing seasons. The perennials such as dropseed could have survived for years and not been diminished in abundance, but prolonged drought could ultimately have reduced their frequency as well, especially under heavy herbivore grazing. Dropseed is a warm-season grass that depends on summer rains to be productive. Ricegrass (*Achnatherum hymenoides*), in contrast, is a cool-season grass that uses winter to mature and as such might have retained its productive potential during intervals of lessened summer moisture. Whether ricegrass continued to be productive during the middle Holocene remains to be demonstrated. Even if true, the overall reduced herbaceous plant cover would have had a negative impact on animals. Grasses are a principal source of food energy for many herbivores, although some also rely on browse (the foliage, fruits, and nuts of shrubs and trees). Even if cool-season grasses remained productive during the middle Holocene, there would have been a shortage of graze starting about July, such that forage might have been in limited supply in the latter half of the growing season.

The impact of less effective moisture (decreased precipitation accompanied by increased evaporation from solar insolation) results in a predictable chain reaction—less forage for both animals and humans and consequently fewer animals for predators, including humans. The lack or reduced incidence of middle Holocene pack rat middens was sometimes accounted for by the inferred decline in forage resulting from middle Holocene climatic conditions. Of course, it does not require too much of a jump in inference to think that if times were difficult for rodents, then they might have been even more dire for humans. In the context of trying to reconstruct the Holocene paleoenvironmental record for the N16 project area, Peter Koehler was contracted by NNAD to conduct an analysis of pack rat middens from the Navajo Mountain area. The hope was to better refine the ecological context of the local Archaic foragers, with a particular interest in the middle Holocene vis-à-vis the bracketing early and late Holocene. In short, is there any indication in pack rat midden data for decreased effective forage from climatic change?

His results, which are presented in Appendix K, of the supporting documentation, include 28 radiocarbon dates on middens, which document an essentially continuous series from almost 14,000 years ago to about 1,000 years ago. This includes 11 dates between 7000 and 4000 BP, a time poorly represented by assays with reliable cultural associations. Unlike the radiocarbon record for human presence on the Rainbow Plateau, the record for pack rats does not reveal any middle Holocene gap. It would seem that whatever the conditions were that led to a diminished human presence in the region did not result in a diminished presence of pack rats. It is important to consider the different elevations and settings of the middens, but not all of the dates between 7000 and 4000 BP come from mesic settings, although most do. The obvious difference in biomass needs coupled with the group living of humans seems to adequately account for why pack rats might persist in a region that humans found less desirable. The potential for decreased representation of dropseed relative to ricegrass during the middle Holocene owing to lessened summer precipitation cannot, unfortunately, be examined because of processing bias. As Koehler explains in his report, the sieve size used in midden macrofossil processing did not recover tiny seeds such as those of *Sporobolous* sp. He found a general trend within the midden record for an increase in the relative abundance and frequency of several other plant species important to humans (pinyon pine, yucca, cactus, and ricegrass) from the middle Holocene to recent times. Nonetheless, there is no reliable way to correlate surrounding plant density to the plant specimens contained in middens (cf. Dial and Czaplewski 1990).

A decline in precipitation also means that less water would be available for daily drinking needs—not only less overall but fewer sources to rely on. Seasonally filled potholes, which abound in many areas of the Colorado Plateau, especially where certain formations such as the Navajo Sandstone occur, could have become far less reliable. At Dust Devil Cave, for example, there is a large weathering basin on top of the sandstone knob that contains the shelter, one that holds water for days after a storm and was likely key to the role of the cave as a base camp during the early Archaic. If this source became unreliable, then the closest dependable water supply was several kilometers away in Desha Canyon, which limits the utility of the cave as a residential base. Seeps might have dried up completely, as might some springs; other springs could have been reduced in flow, down to seep status. The flow of the few streams in the region might have become intermittent, but even in the worst conditions, rivers such as the Colorado and San Juan would have been dependable sources because they originate in mountains outside the Colorado Plateau. Since "a lack of water, and not food resources or foraging efficiency, is the limiting factor in arid settings" (Meltzer 1991:259), it seems reasonable to expect that water sources were a critical variable in determining where middle Holocene foragers located their residential bases.

Behavioral Responses

With regard to middle Holocene behavioral responses it is informative to use what may have been the situation on the Great Plains as a point of contrast with the Colorado Plateau. Meltzer (1999:411–412) has identified an expansion of diet breadth as one significant behavioral response on the plains on account of reduced bison populations. It might well be true that low-ranked resources were not part of the daily Great Plains diet until the middle Holocene, but on the Colorado Plateau a small seed and cactus pad adaptation had already been in effect since the early Archaic (e.g., Van Ness and Hansen 1996). "Been down so long it seems like up to me" might reflect a realistic appraisal. Since the Archaic populations on the Colorado Plateau were already hardscrabble foragers (Meltzer 1991:237), how do we measure a shift in diet as a response to middle Holocene drought? Perhaps we can eventually document middle Holocene exploitation of the lowest ranked of the low, but any such analysis must realistically consider the early Archaic evidence. Sheehan (2002) was able to document changes in diet breadth on the Great Plains with faunal remains, leading him to conclude that hunter-gatherers may make rather minor adjustments in faunal exploitation in response to major climatic shifts. His analysis was possible because there actually are middle Holocene sites or components of sites. We would be hard pressed to conduct his sort of analysis on the Colorado Plateau with the current evidence, but perhaps eventually.

Meltzer (1991) likewise points to new technologies for coping with the diminished resources of the middle Holocene, with the creation of wells being the "most distinctive and novel technology" (1999:412). Although this may have occurred on the Colorado Plateau, well digging is perhaps less likely because springs and seeps usually emerge from bedrock contacts rather than in the alluvial fill of valleys; another common water source on the plateau not amenable to augmentation by well digging is bedrock catchments, either at pour-overs or in weathering basins. Meltzer also points to an increase in number and diversity of plant-processing artifacts and features such as grinding tools, roasting pits, and storage pits. On the Colorado Plateau, manos and metates were abundant and well developed in the early Archaic, so it would probably be impossible to make a case for some sort of adaptive shift with these tools. As to features, it is useful to consider this aspect using findings from Sudden Shelter (Jennings et al. 1980) because this single site contained many features that spanned much of the Archaic period (150 hearths, 114 fire pits, 53 pits, and 15 "special use" pits). Schroedl's (1980) description and analysis of these features showed that there was a significant decline in number during the middle Holocene and no greater diversity, not until conditions were probably on the upswing well after 5000 BP.

One behavioral response mentioned by Meltzer (1999:412) that is abundantly evident on the Colorado Plateau is settlement shifts. I have previously discussed this issue for the Glen Canyon region (Geib 1996a). The NMRAP findings as well as those from the Kaibito Plateau both attest to some significant change, otherwise both areas would have middle Archaic sites similar to those dating both earlier and later. I make no claim that either plateau was totally abandoned during the middle Archaic because this seems unlikely, at least not without far more investigation. What is plainly evident from the road ROW excavations is that foragers stopped using the plateaus in the same way that they had for millennia during the early Archaic such that their presence has yet to clearly register. The deposits of Atlatl Rock, Dust Devil, and Sand Dune caves on the Rainbow Plateau also attest to a profound shift in settlement—all show rather intensive early Archaic use ending between 7000 and 6500 BP, with negligible use during the middle Holocene.

Excavations along the Burr Trail in southeast Utah revealed three open sites dating to the middle Archaic (Tipps 1992). In a subsequent summary of the evidence, Tipps (1998:137–138) highlighted how these sites were concordant with her idea that middle Archaic foragers emphasized open sites for settlement rather than caves and that this practice coupled with the archaeologist's penchant for excavating shelters has created the evidence for regional abandonment or population decline. She has firm proof for middle Archaic open sites that probably functioned as residential bases and not just transient camps. Why they occur there and not on the Rainbow and Kaibito plateaus must be explained in broader terms than simply shifting settlement to open locations, since the latter two plateaus certainly offer plenty of open camp settings. Moreover, some of the best evidence for middle Archaic occupation comes from shelters along the Colorado River in Lower Glen Canyon (Geib 1996b), shelters that contain midden deposits. Tipps's (1998:138) suggestion that proximity to the extensive high-elevation settings of Boulder Mountain and the Aquarius Plateau was a prime attraction seems reasonable, not only because of the opportunities for serial foraging as she suggests but also because these high plateaus would have continued to support streamflow in various nearby creeks (Boulder, Deer, etc.) and also big-game populations. The lack of similar extensive high-elevation settings adjacent to the Rainbow and Kaibito plateaus might be a critical factor accounting for the evident lack of middle Archaic forager sites, either in the open or in shelters. Navajo Mountain is over 3,000 m in elevation, but it is a very small area, no more than a point compared to the Aquarius Plateau.

Accounting for what happened during the middle Holocene by localized adjustments in the organization of annual settlement and mobility patterns is at a far different scale than wholesale population movement over long distances to more favorable environments of adjacent regions—the Altithermal refugia hypothesis (e.g., Benedict 1979; Benedict and Olson 1978). A model of localized adjustment assumes that the highly diverse settings of the Colorado Plateau were sufficient to allow foragers to persist during the changed conditions of the middle Holocene. This is especially true if Archaic foragers also experienced a population crash at various scales. The specifics of how forager persistence occurred remain to be worked out. River corridors and other permanent water sources are likely to have figured prominently, as well as the numerous widely scattered high-elevation settings such as the Kaibab Plateau, Coconino Plateau, White Mountains, Chuska/Lukachukai Mountains, Abajo Mountains, La Sal Mountains, and more. A key benefit of settings above about 2,400 m, especially those of great areal extent, would have been their greater biotic productivity relative to lower-elevation settings during a protracted drought.

Along with changes in the locations of residential camps, middle Archaic populations perhaps increased the frequency of residential moves, greatly expanded the territory of seasonal rounds, and decreased the periodicity of residential reuse. All of these behaviors could have led to a substantially less visible archaeological record, one greatly diminished in cultural remains and more spatially diffuse. A middle Holocene population bottleneck would have added to this pattern by having fewer foragers around to create an archaeological record. Consequently, the middle Archaic material record might be far more dispersed than that of the early or late Archaic, so perhaps less subject to archaeological discovery and investigation. Even if foragers became more tethered to fewer secure water sources, expanded foraging territories, shorter stays at residential bases, longer lapses between residential reuse, and smaller groups sizes still could have resulted in a diffuse archaeological record. How changes in Archaic mobility and settlement strategies might affect patterning in radiocarbon dates has yet to be adequately addressed.

Macroscale patterns observable in Archaic period radiocarbon records for the entire North American Southwest or the Colorado Plateau are certainly instructive. Yet informative details are lost at this scale of comparison. The creation of detailed radiocarbon records for localized areas, as done by the NMRAP for the Rainbow Plateau or by two other road excavations for the Kaibito Plateau, is a significant contribution. These small-scale records enable a much better understanding of the processes and biases at work: past human behavior, postdepositional impacts, and archaeological predilections. By compiling data sets from small regions it is also easier to adequately evaluate the quality of dates and thereby eliminate chronological "slop" resulting from the inclusion of poor samples.

Conclusions

The highly visible and comparatively rich archaeological records left by Puebloan and Basketmaker farmers or farmer-foragers of the N16 ROW sharply contrast with the generally diffuse remains from ephemeral forager use of the project area. This is generally true all across the Colorado Plateau unless, perhaps, one has the good fortune to be working in a dry shelter where organics are preserved. The returns from studying Archaic sites in the Southwest usually appear scant by comparison with those from sites dating after the introduction of domesticates. For buried Archaic sites, great effort must be expended to expose a few basin hearths and recover a handful or two of small flakes, some bone, and rare tool fragments. Such is the fate of the archaeological study of foragers, and it is unfair to expect the debris scatters generated by such highly mobile groups to be the information troves generated by more sedentary and logistically organized groups. Given the vast expanse of time covered by the Archaic period coupled with the paltry nature of the record, there will be no time soon when the discipline has reached a point of diminishing returns. Indeed this provides good cause to work at trying to maximize the information return from forager sites and isolated occurrences as well as sufficient justification for what might seem to be comparatively high expense (per artifact or other remain recovered or per square or cubic meter of deposit or features excavated).

Although the Archaic period appeared to be a minor aspect of the NMRAP when the project began, it ultimately made a significant contribution to what little was known about the pre-pottery and nonagricultural foragers of the Kayenta Anasazi region. Fourteen open Archaic sites were excavated to varying extents by the project, with several of these being quite rewarding. In addition, the limited testing and damage assessment of Atlatl Rock Cave conducted in conjunction with the NMRAP provided another datum point for hunter-gatherer use of caves in the region. Much of the results came about because of fortuitously finding Archaic remains underlying those of Puebloans or Basketmakers or because of exposure by the existing road. In something of a twist on Smiley's (2002b: 15) quote about Archaic sites on Black Mesa, rarely have so many old sites been revealed in an area of such limited size by good fortune coupled with dogged determination to squeeze the most from what came to light.

The NMRAP compiled an impressive radiocarbon record of forager occupancy for the Rainbow Plateau and far-northern Shonto Plateau from what was likely an unbiased sample of preceramic sites. This data set revealed a discontinuous record of forager occupancy punctuated by a long hiatus during the middle Archaic and a possible brief hiatus just prior to the local introduction of domesticates. The N16 road excavations revealed a pattern similar to that documented by Berry and Berry (1986), which they interpreted as resulting from large-scale forager abandonment of the Colorado Plateau. I still doubt the regional abandonment scenario (Geib 1996a) because there are sites or components securely dated to the middle Archaic across various portions of the Colorado Plateau. Moreover, we have yet to adequately address how changes in Archaic mobility and settlement strategies might affect patterning in radiocarbon dates. Nonetheless, the data set assembled by the NMRAP strongly suggests a reduced forager presence in the northern Kayenta region from about 6000 to 4000 BP. The addition of recently obtained radiocarbon dates from the Kaibito Plateau further corroborates the overall pattern, showing that a large portion of the Kayenta region had a limited forager presence during the middle Archaic. Arguing that the patterning in dates was real and not the result of some bias, I have explored potential causes. The middle Holocene might have been a climatic bottleneck for portions of the Southwest, with forager populations knocked back substantially from early Archaic levels. Adequate explanations for this pattern will ultimately entail detailed study of sites well dated to the middle Archaic along with paleoenvironmental reconstructions at both large and small scales.

Notes

1. It is interesting to note that my examination of collections at the American Museum of Natural History in 2007 disclosed many examples of open-twined sandals from Basketmaker sites of Grand Gulch that had been recovered in the late 1800s; had such finds been reported, Ambler might not have suspected that the sandals he found at Sand Dune Cave and Dust Devil Cave were other than Basketmaker.
2. This turned out to be an especially wise choice as revealed by the N21 road excavation project, which relied primarily on bulk sediment samples from Archaic hearths for dating purposes. Invariably these samples underestimated the age of the features by anywhere from 1,000 to 4,000 years (Bungart et al. 2004).
3. The unusually good preservation in this case seems to be the result of rapid and deep eolian burial of the Archaic features.
4. Previously obtained dates, except those from Geib 1996b, were not corrected for isotopic fractionation. Nonetheless, only one of these requires such correction, that on the grass lining of a sandal from Sand Dune Cave (A-848). The prior dates on yucca are unlikely to require correction even though the plant has a crassulacean acid metabolism photosynthetic pathway because all prior measurements on yucca from early Archaic contexts on the Rainbow Plateau and northward have $\delta^{13}C$ values between –21‰ and –26‰; yucca used for early Archaic sandals from the southern Colorado Plateau has $\delta^{13}C$ values between –11‰ and –14‰, requiring correction (see Geib 2000:Table 4).

CHAPTER 5

Summary and Interpretation of Basketmaker II Remains

Archaeological study of the preceramic farming culture known as Basketmaker II within the Kayenta region spans nearly a century and includes such luminaries of Southwestern archaeology as Alfred Kidder. The rich bounty of perishable remains retrieved from dry caves of the Marsh Pass area early in the 1900s provided a detailed picture of the material culture of these initial farmers, as well as a sizable skeletal sample (Guernsey 1931; Guernsey and Kidder 1921; Kidder and Guernsey 1919). A focus on dry cave excavations continued into the early 1960s (Lindsay et al. 1968; Lockett and Hargrave 1953) and still has much to offer (e.g., Smiley and Parry 1992; SD vol. 2, chap. 2). Basketmaker research shifted direction during the 1970s toward an emphasis on open sites, with Lipe and Matson's research on Cedar Mesa leading the way (see review in Matson 2006b). Issues of settlement pattern and subsistence came into focus, and chronology became an important topic. Within the Kayenta region, BMAP's excavations on northern Black Mesa exemplified this trend. When that project ended in the early 1980s, excavation of 35 late Basketmaker II (Lolomai phase, ca. cal. AD 50–350) sites of various settlement types provided the first detailed documentation of this previously unstudied portion of the local archaeological record (see review in Smiley 2002a).

By excavating all or portions of 17 Basketmaker II sites within the N16 ROW, the NMRAP has greatly added to the database for the first farmers within the Kayenta region. This effort increased the excavated sample of open Basketmaker II sites to half again what it was based on prior research. Moreover, the NMRAP findings come from a portion of the Kayenta region that complements and augments the data for open Basketmaker II sites on northern Black Mesa both geographically and temporally. Indeed, NMRAP's contribution to our understanding of Basketmaker II was greater than initially suspected, in part because of more time depth and longer-duration use of a few favored locales than was true for northern Black Mesa. Furthermore, several of the open sites, as well as Atlatl Rock Cave, a site tested in conjunction with the road project, provide evidence for the Basketmaker II–Basketmaker III transitional interval (Geib and Spurr 2000), which is poorly known for the entire Four Corners region and not at all on northern Black Mesa.

The NMRAP research plan specifically addressed the Basketmaker II archaeological record with a research issue designated as the *agricultural transition*. The shift from a hunting-gathering economy to one based on farming has been a long-standing research topic throughout the world. In the early 1970s, Flannery (1973:271) bemoaned the fact that research on the origins of agriculture had become a bandwagon, and although there are perhaps fewer projects these days with this topic as a chief focus, there seems little letup in the volume of ink and paper devoted to the subject (e.g., Barker 2006; Cowan and Watson, ed. 1992; Ford 1985; Gebauer and Price 1992; Harris and Hillman 1989; Kennett and Winterhalder 2006; Piperno and Pearsall 1998; Price and Gebauer 1995; Smith 1998). The American Southwest, a region of *primary crop acquisition* (a secondary setting) rather than one of *pristine domestication* (Cowan and Watson 1992; Minnis 1992:122), has seen no shortage of research into the agricultural transition (see reviews in Huckell 1990, 1995; Mabry 1998, 2008; Matson 1991; Wills and Huckell 1994). An unprecedented increase in the excavation of early agricultural sites and the dating and restudy of old collections during the decades since 1980 has greatly increased our knowledge of this interval of profound change in prehistoric cultural development. Still, much remains to be learned.

The agricultural transition in the secondary setting of the Colorado Plateau may have transpired by the diffusion of crops and farming knowledge to in situ foragers or by the migration (demic diffusion) of farmers. These two alternative but not mutually exclusive pathways to the agricultural transition both may have operated on the Colorado Plateau (see review by Matson 1991, 2002), perhaps at different times and with somewhat differing consequences. Just having crops is the initial step toward greater subsistence specialization, but there is considerable debate about the extent of economic dependence on cultigens during the preceramic farming interval (see Wills and Huckell 1994:34–39). Matson (1991; Matson and Chisholm 1991) demonstrated that late Basketmaker II (ca. AD 100–400) populations on Cedar Mesa were nearly as dependent on maize as were the later Puebloan populations of this mesa (cf. Wills and Huckell 1994:38–39). But can this evidence be extrapolated to the Kayenta region? Moreover, did the shift to food production occur in the context of increased population density, or was that a consequence of that shift? I had these and many other questions in mind as NNAD began to excavate Basketmaker II sites within the N16 ROW during the mid-1990s.

The NMRAP Basketmaker Site Sample

Basketmaker II in this report has both adaptive and cultural meaning and is not a mere period designation for the interval during which agriculture was first practiced but ceramics were not in use. The general temporal interval overall is designated as the Archaic–Formative transition, with no necessary implications about what was eaten, what type of footwear was worn, or other details; it only specifies that a site belongs to a given time period during which domesticates may or may not have been used. Assignment to this transitional interval is best based on chronometric dates. Other issues such as degree of maize reliance and cultural affiliation can then be investigated in their own right without becoming embroiled in definitional debate. During the Archaic–Formative transition I recognize a Basketmaker II adaptation and cultural assemblage and an Archaic adaptation (continued foraging). The terminal Archaic lifeway lasted until about 800 cal. BC for the N16 project area, with the possibility for sporadic Archaic use until about 400 cal. BC. Basketmaker II in the northern Kayenta region appears to be no older than about 400 cal. BC. Farther south in this same region a Basketmaker II adaptation and cultural assemblage may be as old as 800 cal. BC (cf. Smiley 2002a). The definition of Basketmaker II is based foremost on adaptation—basically a reliance on domesticates, with the principal archaeologically recovered trace being maize. Judging from the subsistence remains recovered coupled with other less direct indicators, maize appears to have formed a substantial part of the Basketmaker diet for the project area (details follow). Evidence for the first use of agriculture on the Rainbow Plateau appears to be associated with Basketmaker II material culture as initially described by Guernsey and Kidder (1921; also Kidder and Guernsey 1919, 1922). Excavated caves on the Rainbow Plateau have produced assemblages of perishable artifacts that are no different from those of the classic Basketmaker II type sites, such as White Dog Cave and Kinboko Caves 1 and 2 (Lindsay et al. 1968; Schilz 1979; SD vol. 2, chap. 2). Open sites during this interval have yielded nonperishable remains that likewise typify the stone and bone artifacts found at the classic Basketmaker II rockshelters (discussed below). Consequently, there are both adaptive and cultural grounds for referring to the preceramic agricultural sites of the N16 ROW as Basketmaker II.

Seventeen of the 33 sites excavated within the N16 ROW have Basketmaker components, and Atlatl Rock Cave, which was tested in conjunction with the project, has a rich Basketmaker deposit that includes evidence of the Basketmaker II–III transition. Thus the total Basketmaker II sample for the project is 18 sites or components functionally classified as primary habitations, secondary (seasonal) habitations, and temporary camps (see site type discussion below). Table 5.1 provides some useful summary data about each of these sites or components, while Figure 5.1 shows their location within the project area. Prior to the NMRAP no open Basketmaker II habitations had been studied within 40 km of the project area, so the investigation of these sites provides important new information. One of the Basketmaker residential sites (Mountainview) has an assemblage of Obelisk Utility pottery and is well dated to between cal. AD 220 and 350, so it is a good example of a Basketmaker II–III transitional habitation. As shown in Figure 5.1, most of the 18 Basketmaker II sites occur in the southern portion of the project area where the road ROW traverses the dissected slickrock divide between Piute and Navajo creeks. This area appears to have been favored by these early farmers for seasonal residential sites. The largest and longest-duration habitation, known as Kin Kahuna, occurs next to a prime agricultural setting on the southeast edge of the Rainbow Plateau. The location is also within moderately close proximity to excellent farmland in Upper Piute Canyon. Based on reconnaissance and previous surveys that I participated in dating back to 1981, similar sites occur on the southeast edge of the Rainbow Plateau, around the foot

TABLE 5.1. Summary Data for the Navajo Mountain Road Archaeological Project Basketmaker Sites or Components as well as the Inferred Settlement Role

Site Name/No.	Site Type	¹⁴C Date Range	Living Structures	Storage Features	Other Pits	Hearths	Burials	Faunal Bone	Flakes	Used Flakes[a]	Flaked Tools	Cores/ Nodular Tools	Grinding Tools
Three Dog Site, UT-B-63-39	secondary habitation	AD 80–320	?[b]	0	2	2	0	347	1,796	16	11	1	8
Bonsai Bivouac, AZ-J-2-55	temporary camp	180 BC–AD 10	0	0	0	2	0	0	0	0	0	0	0
Kin Kahuna, AZ-J-3-8	permanent habitation	360 BC–AD 430	7	26	30	17	6	2,348	9,207	102	74	30	47
Mouse House, AZ-J-3-7	temporary camp	AD 80–340[c]	0	0	0	4	0	0	2	0	0	0	0
Sin Sombra, AZ-J-3-6	secondary habitation	AD 120–330	1	0	0	3	0	46	916	32	14	8	3
Mountain View, AZ-J-14-38	permanent habitation?	AD 220–350	1	0	0	15	0	175	4,240	112	73	38	18
Atlatl Rock Cave, AZ-J-14-41	permanent habitation?	AD 150–650	2+	22+	4	2	0	11	4	1	1	0	0
Scorpion Heights, AZ-J-14-37	secondary habitation? and temporary hunting camp	AD 80–390[d]	?[b]	0	0	5	0	11	769	20	11	13	12
Blake's Abode, AZ-J-14-36	secondary habitation	360–90 BC	1	0	0	3	0	70	748	42	13	3	8
Ko' Lanhi, AZ-J-14-35	secondary habitation?	350 BC–AD 10	?[b]	0	1	13	0	11	677	8	14	10	8
Big Bend,[e] AZ-J-14-13	permanent habitation	380–90 BC	2+	1+	?	+	?[f]	0	0	0	14	0	0
Panorama House, AZ-J-14-34	secondary habitation	AD 240–390	1	0	0	4	0	22	243	5	3	3	3
Tres Campos, AZ-J-14-12	secondary habitation	170 BC–AD 140	1	0	0	1	0	7	122	2	0	3	0
Polly's Place, AZ-J-14-31	secondary habitation	AD 250–440 & AD 410–600	2	0	2	5	0	7	213	8	0	16	7
Windy Mesa, AZ-J-14-28	temporary camp, hunting	None	0	0	0	0	0	23	3,731	9	17	3	2
Pee Wee Grande, AZ-J-14-26	temporary camp	AD 250–540[c]	0	0	0	1	0	0	0	0	0	0	0
Ditch House, AZ-J-14-21	secondary habitation	100 BC–AD 60	2	2	1	1	0	2	26	3	1	51	3
The Pits, AZ-J-14-17	permanent habitation	400–50 BC	1+	24+	0	7	?[a]	57	93	7	6	6	1

Note: Sites are organized from north to south. Some of these sites such as Atlatl Rock Cave and Big Bend have had minimal excavation, so counts of remains are unknown. Feature counts for Atlatl Rock Cave are high but still minimal estimates based on observed remnants.

[a] Used flakes are also tallied in the total flake count.
[b] Site disturbance appears to have removed structures, but these were likely present, based on remains that were recovered.
[c] Dates based on wood or sagebrush charcoal might overestimate true age.
[d] Dates based on a hearth associated with an evident temporary hunting camp component of this site and might not apply to the secondary habitation component.
[e] No data-recovery excavation was done at the Basketmaker component of this site, which lay outside the right-of-way, but a radiocarbon sample and projectile point recovered from a disturbed burned structure years before the N16 project were analyzed and reported.
[f] Burials seem likely given a primary residential function.

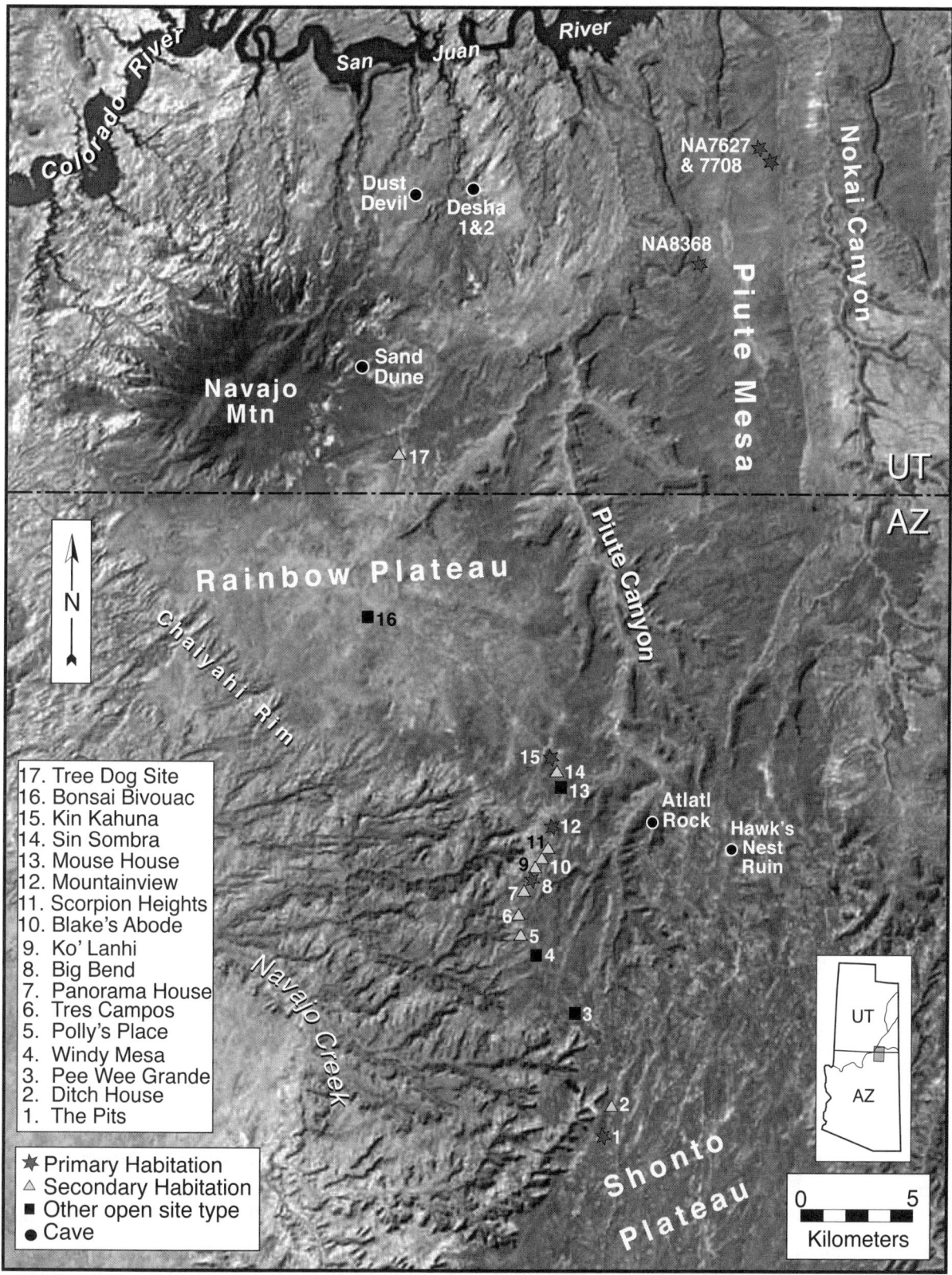

Figure 5.1. Distribution of Navajo Mountain Road Archaeological Project Basketmaker sites including Atlatl Rock Cave by inferred settlement type; also shown are other excavated or tested Basketmaker II sites mentioned in the text.

of Navajo Mountain, and on Piute Mesa. Figure 5.1 also gives the location of 10 previously excavated or tested Basketmaker sites, mostly caves, such as Desha Caves 1 and 2 excavated in 1930 (Geib and Robins 2003; Schilz 1979). I know of many other Basketmaker sites on the Rainbow Plateau and adjacent terrain that could have been plotted on this map, but I have illustrated only those with subsurface data. All of the previously tested or excavated sites are discussed in chapter 1, volume 3, of the supporting documentation. The Basketmaker components excavated for the NMRAP are reported in volume 3 except that Atlatl Rock Cave is reported in volume 2 because of its early Archaic component.

Northern Kayenta Region Basketmaker Chronology

Prior to 1990, chronological control for Basketmaker occupancy of the northern Kayenta region was provided by just three radiocarbon dates on wood charcoal from hearths at three sites: a large roasting pit at Roasting Pit Alcove (Long 1966:60), Hearth 3 at Dust Devil Cave (Lindsay et al. 1968:108), and Feature 2 at UT-V-13-72 (Geib et al. 1985:234). I dismiss all but the Dust Devil Cave assay as unlikely to have relevance for Basketmaker II chronology (SD vol. 3, chap. 1). In addition to these were the confounding tree-ring dates on charcoal chunks recovered from Hearth 9 of Sand Dune Cave. Of the 28 noncutting (vv) tree-ring dates, the youngest was AD 701 (the other dates ranged from 696 to 491 [Harlan and Dean 1968:381]). By linking the tree-ring dates with the Basketmaker II remains from the cave, Lindsay et al. (1968:3, 102, 364) argued for the continuation of a Basketmaker II lifeway in the Navajo Mountain area. The beginning of Basketmaker II in the northern Kayenta region remained unknown, but the Hearth 9 tree-ring dates extended the ending well into Basketmaker III. The purported persistence of a Basketmaker II lifeway past AD 700 in the Kayenta region had gained some acceptance (e.g., Dean 1996:29, 32; Gumerman and Dean 1989:111) but is now known to be baseless (see Geib 2004; Geib and Spurr 2000:178–179). Beginning in the early 1990s the number of Basketmaker radiocarbon dates for the northern Kayenta region mushroomed, due mainly to the NMRAP excavations. Although a few of the NMRAP Basketmaker sites produced tree-ring samples, unfortunately none could be dated; samples with an adequate number of rings may predate the local master chronology, which ends at AD 338, and might ultimately be assigned an age.

NMRAP Radiocarbon Dating and Basketmaker II Dates

Capitalizing on an expensive lesson learned by the BMAP, the NMRAP endeavored to avoid the chronological chaos created by radiocarbon dating of Basketmaker wood charcoal (see Smiley 1985, 1998a, 1998c) and therefore expended more effort in the field and laboratory on securing high-quality samples. My focus was on maize because it is a human-controlled annual plant with durable, large, and easily recognizable parts and because of its relevance for subsistence and for tracking the temporal spread of this domesticate. Maize remains were relatively abundant at several N16 Basketmaker sites, and many samples were retrieved directly from features or floor surfaces during excavation. This combined with the ⅛-in mesh screening of floor fill and in situ feature fill ensured the field recovery of maize kernels and cupules from many features and most Basketmaker II sites. In cases where maize was not recovered in the field, I delayed dating any samples pending the results of flotation analysis. Flotation almost invariably yielded maize remains or portions of other plants that provided more accurate estimates of feature and site age than afforded by wood charcoal.

As might be expected, the emphasis on maize and other quality materials meant that few Basketmaker samples were sufficiently large for conventional beta-decay counting ($n = 6$), with 92 percent of the samples requiring AMS analysis. Beta Analytic, the primary contractor for radiocarbon dating services for the project, processed the conventional dates in-house, with the AMS samples pretreated and prepared into graphic targets for dating at one of its consortium accelerator laboratories. Early in the project, I requested that all AMS samples be analyzed at Lawrence Livermore National Laboratory to limit potential problems with interlaboratory comparability. I did this after obtaining slightly different results for samples from the same sites processed at two different AMS facilities (discussed in detail below). At one point, the NSF-Arizona AMS Facility in Tucson analyzed several samples to assess interlaboratory comparability. Later in the project, I had Beta Analytic perform a further check of interlaboratory comparability using maize samples from two of the Basketmaker sites. In this final quality control study, both samples were sufficiently large that multiple graphic targets were prepared from each for submission to different laboratories (results discussed later).

The 75 Basketmaker radiocarbon dates obtained by the N16 excavations make up a sizable data set, one based almost entirely on high-quality samples, especially maize.

The dates are listed in Table 5.2 by site and then by conventional radiocarbon age in descending order. The dates come from 17 sites, including Atlatl Rock Cave, a few of which were evidently occupied for extended intervals, with Kin Kahuna the best example. Table 5.2 also provides information on the type of material dated, the initial pretreatment weight of the sample, the dating method (beta-decay or AMS), the measured or assumed delta ^{13}C value, the feature, and the calibrated two-sigma age range calculated using the OxCal program, Version 3.10 (Bronk Ramsey 1994, 1995, 1998). Spurr and I (Geib and Spurr 2000:Table 9.1) listed many of these dates, but others have been added since then; the calibrated age ranges presented in Geib and Spurr 2000 might differ from those given here because of using a different calibration program (CALIB, Version 3.0.3a [Stuiver and Reimer 1993]).

The 75 Basketmaker period dates range between 2230 BP and 1500 BP; Figure 5.2 plots all these according to their calibrated two-sigma age range. This figure also shows which of the dates are on maize. There is a continuous sequence of dates from around 400 cal. BC to cal. AD 650. This time span includes the interval during which pottery was introduced and became part of the local technology, sometime between cal. AD 220 and 350. The dating of pottery is detailed later in this chapter (also see SD vol. 3, chap. 10). The earliest direct date on maize for the project is 2230 BP (410–100 cal. BC); this is also the earliest date of the Basketmaker chronology. It is supported by six additional dates on maize from 2210 to 2180 BP; together these seven maize dates, seen at the top of Figure 5.2, span the interval from 400 to 100 cal. BC. These seven early maize dates come from the two largest and longest-occupied Basketmaker II open pithouse habitations: Kin Kahuna and The Pits. If we assume for the sake of argument that the dates represent a single temporal interval (they are statistically indistinguishable), they can be averaged in an attempt to provide a narrower temporal range. Doing this produces an average of 2199 ± 21 BP, but the calibrated two-sigma range is still quite wide: 360–170 BC. Because the fluctuations in atmospheric ^{14}C at this interval create a plateau and several small reversals (wiggles), temporal placement of an event will always be poorly resolved (Guilderson et al. 2005). Even with a standard deviation of one year, the two-sigma age range for a 2199 BP date is 360–200 BC (OxCal, v. 3.5). Therefore, we cannot know with any greater precision when the Basketmaker II interval started in the northern Kayenta region other than after about 400 cal. BC but before 200 cal. BC.

None of the NMRAP sites that produced radiocarbon dates earlier than 2300 BP contained maize plant portions, whereas nearly all sites dated after this yielded maize cupules and kernels, some in considerable abundance. This pattern was based on both the field recovery of plant remains and the analysis of numerous flotation samples. As detailed below, we recovered maize remains from nearly every Basketmaker II site of the N16 ROW, and a few Basketmaker habitations produced maize remains in an abundance equal to or exceeding that of Puebloan habitations of the project area. Of the numerous flotation samples analyzed from late Archaic sites, those dating earlier than 2300 BP, none contained maize or other domesticates.

All but one of the 17 open Basketmaker sites investigated during the project have a temporal assignment based on radiocarbon dates, in most cases multiple dates. The exception is Windy Mesa, which lacked Basketmaker features within the ROW and thus carbon samples altogether; excavations outside the ROW at this site might eventually uncover datable Basketmaker features. The presumed Basketmaker II component at Windy Mesa occurred within a stratum that overlay an early Archaic cultural stratum and underlay a Puebloan cultural stratum. Its temporal assignment is somewhat conjectural but is supported by the flaked-stone assemblage. In addition to the 17 open sites, the limited test of Atlatl Rock Cave recovered numerous carbon samples or other organic remains from many Basketmaker features and a thick cultural deposit; six of these returned assays within the Basketmaker chronology for the project area.

Material Quality

The NMRAP Basketmaker radiocarbon data set is not only robust but based on high-quality samples from excellent contexts. Almost 70 percent of the dates are on maize ($n = 51$). Other high-quality samples include grass and juniper bark extracted from mortar used in cist construction ($n = 3$, all from Atlatl Rock Cave), grass seed ($n = 1$), juniper twigs (annual growth) used as fire starter in a roasting pit ($n = 1$), and small twigs other than from sagebrush ($n = 1$). Samples that also appear to be of high quality are pinyon bark ($n = 3$) and a pinyon cone scale. Two samples from the outer rings of posts in burned structures appear to be lower quality, in that the post at one site was roughly 150 radiocarbon years older than dates on associated maize (discussed below). Also evidently of somewhat lower quality are dates on juniper seeds ($n = 2$). Just two of

TABLE 5.2. List of Radiocarbon Dates from Navajo Mountain Road Archaeological Project Basketmaker Sites

Site Name	Lab No.	^{14}C Age	^{13}C (‰)	Material	Weight (g)	Method	Feature	Cal. 2σ Range
Atlatl Rock Cave	Beta-68380	1810 ± 90	−25	juniper bark	22.9	BD	Feature 5, cist	AD 20–430
Atlatl Rock Cave	Beta-68379	1810 ± 70	−25	juniper bark	73.0	BD	Feature 24, pit	AD 60–400
Atlatl Rock Cave	Beta-68381	1710 ± 60	−11.3	maize	25.4	BD	Feature 16	AD 130–440
Atlatl Rock Cave	Beta-68383	1640 ± 70	−23.7	grass	40.0	BD	Feature 3	AD 240–570
Atlatl Rock Cave	AA-19526	1535 ± 65	−11.7	maize	.091	AMS	Feature 15, cist	AD 400–650
Atlatl Rock Cave	Beta-68382	1500 ± 60	−10.5	maize	18.8	BD	Feature 18, cist	AD 430–650
Big Bend	Beta-135681	2170 ± 40	−17.3	sagebrush	.027	AMS	Structure	380–90 BC
Blake's Abode	Beta-158090	2150 ± 40	−21.9	pinyon bark	.018	AMS	Structure	360–50 BC
Blake's Abode	Beta-158091	2150 ± 40	−21.4	pinyon bark	.0073	AMS	Hearth of structure	360–50 BC
Bonsai Bivouac	Beta-101391	2120 ± 50	−23.7	sagebrush	.06	AMS	Hearth 8	360 BC–AD 10
Bonsai Bivouac	Beta-158087	2040 ± 40	−22.9	charcoal	.103	AMS	Hearth 7	170 BC–AD 60
Ditch House	Beta-102489	2180 ± 40	−25.9	sagebrush	.16	AMS	Roasting Pit 2	380–110 BC
Ditch House	Beta-94765	2080 ± 40	−14.6	maize	.012	AMS	Structure 6, hearth	200 BC–AD 20
Ditch House	Beta-94766	2010 ± 60	−24.8	pinyon cone	.036	AMS	Structure 6, hearth	170 BC–AD 130
Ditch House	Beta-158089	1960 ± 40	−22.8	pinyon bark	.01	AMS	Storage Pit 1	50 BC–AD 130
Kin Kahuna	Beta-87905	2210 ± 50	−11.0	maize	.0987	AMS	Structure 5, Pit 1	400–110 BC
Kin Kahuna	Beta-87904	2210 ± 50	−11.0	maize	.0589	AMS	Structure 5, floor	400–110 BC
Kin Kahuna	Beta-87903	2190 ± 60	−11.6	maize	.0911	AMS	Structure 5, lower fill	390–90 BC
Kin Kahuna	Beta-156067, ETH	2180 ± 50	−12.8	maize	.6	AMS	Structure 5, Pit 1	390–90 BC
Kin Kahuna	Beta-87898	2140 ± 50	−11.0	maize	.1337	AMS	Pit 17, upper fill	360–40 BC
Kin Kahuna	Beta-156067, VERA	2110 ± 40	−10.1	maize	.6	AMS	Structure 5, Pit 1	350–0 BC
Kin Kahuna	Beta-156067, CAMS	2090 ± 40	−11.0	maize	.6	AMS	Structure 5, Pit 1	210 BC–AD 10
Kin Kahuna	Beta-94764	2090 ± 80	−14.7	maize	.056	AMS	Pit 10	360 BC–AD 70
Kin Kahuna	Beta-94763	2080 ± 50	−15.3	maize	.241	AMS	Pit 13	350 BC–AD 30
Kin Kahuna	Beta-94761	1990 ± 50	−11.4	maize	.015	AMS	Structure 1, floor fill	120 BC–AD 130
Kin Kahuna	Beta-87901	1960 ± 60	−12.4	maize	.0403	AMS	Structure 4, floor	110 BC–AD 220
Kin Kahuna	Beta-87902	1840 ± 50	−11.7	maize	.1514	AMS	Hearth 6, fill of Structure 5	AD 60–340
Kin Kahuna	Beta-87900	1780 ± 60	−11.2	maize	.1554	AMS	Structure 4, trashy fill	AD 80–410
Kin Kahuna	Beta-94762	1740 ± 50	−13.4	maize	.038	AMS	Hearth 10	AD 130–420
Kin Kahuna	Beta-87899	1730 ± 60	−12.4	maize	.0373	AMS	Structure 3, floor fill	AD 130–430
Ko' Lanhi	Beta-94767	2120 ± 60	−23.1	juniper seeds	.028	AMS	Hearth 1	360 BC–AD 10
Ko' Lanhi	Beta-94768	2080 ± 60	−12.9	maize	.044	AMS	Hearth 6	360 BC–AD 60
Mountainview	Beta-158094	1830 ± 40	−11.0	maize	.013	AMS	Midden	AD 80–320
Mountainview	Beta-87912	1810 ± 50	−10.8	maize	.0196	AMS	Midden	AD 80–350
Mountainview	Beta-87913	1770 ± 60	−12.6	maize	.0101	AMS	Structure 1, floor fill	AD 120–410
Mountainview	Beta-87914	1750 ± 60	−10.4	maize	.0765	AMS	Structure 1, floor fill	AD 130–420
Mountainview	Beta-158092	1730 ± 40	−11.7	maize	.03	AMS	Hearth 11	AD 220–420
Mountainview	Beta-158093	1700 ± 40	−11.1	maize	.013	AMS	Structure 1 ashpit	AD 240–430
Mouse House	Beta-94758	1820 ± 50	−17.7	twigs	.088	AMS	Hearth 4	AD 70–340
Mouse House	Beta-94759	1810 ± 60	−26.7	sagebrush	.123	AMS	Hearth 2	AD 70–390
Panorama House	Beta-101393	1890 ± 40	−21.4	post outer rings	.034	AMS	Structure, floor fill	AD 20–240
Panorama House	Beta-101394	1820 ± 50	−21.0	juniper seeds	.072	AMS	Structure, floor fill	AD 70–340
Panorama House	Beta-118050	1760 ± 50	−12.2	maize	.014	AMS	Hearth 1 of Structure	AD 130–400
Panorama House	Beta-101396	1730 ± 60	−10.8	maize	.111	AMS	Midden	AD 130–430
Panorama House	Beta-118051	1720 ± 50	−11.6	maize	.021	AMS	Hearth 2 of Structure	AD 170–430
Panorama House	Beta-101395	1710 ± 50	−11.0	maize	.027	AMS	Hearth 1	AD 210–440

TABLE 5.2. (cont'd.) List of Radiocarbon Dates from Navajo Mountain Road Archaeological Project Basketmaker Sites

Site Name	Lab No.	¹⁴C Age	¹³C (‰)	Material	Weight (g)	Method	Feature	Cal. 2σ Range
Pee Wee Grande	Beta-79153	1660 ± 50	−23.2	charcoal	.0464	AMS	Hearth 2	AD 250–540
Polly's Place	AA-19524	1750 ± 50	−12.3	maize	.056	AMS	Hearth 17	AD 130–410
Polly's Place	Beta-79159	1640 ± 60	−25.0*	sagebrush	7.57	BD	Structure 2, Hearth 2	AD 250–560
Polly's Place	Beta-79160	1610 ± 50	−20.5	maize	.022	AMS	Hearth 17	AD 260–570
Polly's Place	Beta-79161	1580 ± 50	−19.5	maize	.02	AMS	Structure 1, floor	AD 380–610
Polly's Place	AA-19523	1550 ± 65	−9.3	maize	.0144	AMS	Midden	AD 380–650
Scorpion Heights	Beta-94769	1800 ± 60	−25.6	sagebrush	.115	AMS	Hearth 4	AD 80–390
Sin Sombra	Beta-94754	1850 ± 60	−14.5	maize	.153	AMS	Midden	AD 20–340
Sin Sombra	Beta-94755	1840 ± 60	−14.4	maize	.022	AMS	Structure, floor fill	AD 20–350
Sin Sombra	Beta-94756	1820 ± 60	−11.9	maize	.008	AMS	Structure, Hearth 3	AD 60–390
Sin Sombra	Beta-94753	1750 ± 60	−14.3	maize	.088	AMS	Hearth 1	AD 130–420
The Pits	Beta-73979	2230 ± 60	−10.9	maize	.0357	AMS	Structure 1, Hearth 1	410–110 BC
The Pits	Beta-73984	2190 ± 60	−11.2	maize	.1275	AMS	Storage Pit 3, maize offering	390–90 BC
The Pits	Beta-73982	2180 ± 60	−11.5	maize	.08	AMS	Storage Pit 2, lower trashy fill	390–60 BC
The Pits	Beta-73983	2160 ± 60	−20.9	juniper twigs	.0862	AMS	Storage Pit 20, charcoal layer	380–50 BC
The Pits	Beta-156068, CAMS	2120 ± 40	−11.4	maize	1.88	AMS	Storage Pit 3, maize offering	360–40 BC
The Pits	Beta-156068, ETH	2100 ± 50	−12.2	maize	1.88	AMS	Storage Pit 3, maize offering	360 BC–AD 30
The Pits	Beta-156068, VERA	2100 ± 40	−12.1	maize	1.88	AMS	Storage Pit 3, maize offering	350 BC–AD 10
The Pits	Beta-73981	2070 ± 70	−24.9	sagebrush	.1924	AMS	Storage Pit 2, charcoal layer	360 BC–AD 80
The Pits	AA-19519	2035 ± 65	−11.1	maize	.0161	AMS	Structure 1 floor	210 BC–AD 130
The Pits	AA-19522	2005 ± 65	−10.4	maize	.2837	AMS	Storage Pit 3, maize offering	180 BC–AD 130
The Pits	AA-19521	1995 ± 65	−10.9	maize	.124	AMS	Storage Pit 2, lower trashy fill	180 BC–AD 140
The Pits	Beta-79145	1990 ± 60	−15.3	maize	.05	AMS	Structure 1, floor	170 BC–AD 140
The Pits	AA-19520	1940 ± 65	−12.2	maize	.0128	AMS	Storage Pit 13, lower trashy fill	100 BC–AD 240
The Pits	Beta-79148	1920 ± 50	−16.4	maize	.0087	AMS	Storage Pit 13, floor	40 BC–AD 230
Tres Campos	Beta-87911	1980 ± 60	−22.8	post outer rings	.0257	AMS	Structure 1	170 BC–AD 140
Three Dog Site	Beta-135694	2020 ± 40	−22.6	sagebrush	.134	AMS	Hearth 32/33	160 BC–AD 80
Three Dog Site	Beta-175655	1810 ± 40	−22.8	ricegrass	<.1	AMS	Hearth 33	AD 70–320
Three Dog Site	Beta-175656	1850 ± 40	−9.1	maize	<.1	AMS	Hearth 32/33	AD 80–340

Note: AMS = accelerator mass spectrometry; BD = beta decay.

the 75 dates are on tree charcoal from hearths, both from limited-activity sites; other low-quality samples include eight on sagebrush charcoal. The overall assessment is that more than 80 percent of the samples are on materials unlikely to overestimate site age, with less than 15 percent on materials that might overestimate age to a significant degree.

Sagebrush vs. Other Materials. As reported in chapter 4, the dating of sagebrush charcoal and wood charcoal from single features demonstrated that sagebrush commonly resulted in ages that were a few hundred years older than the ages provided by wood charcoal. The Basketmaker II radiocarbon data set provides two examples where sagebrush dates can be checked against those on

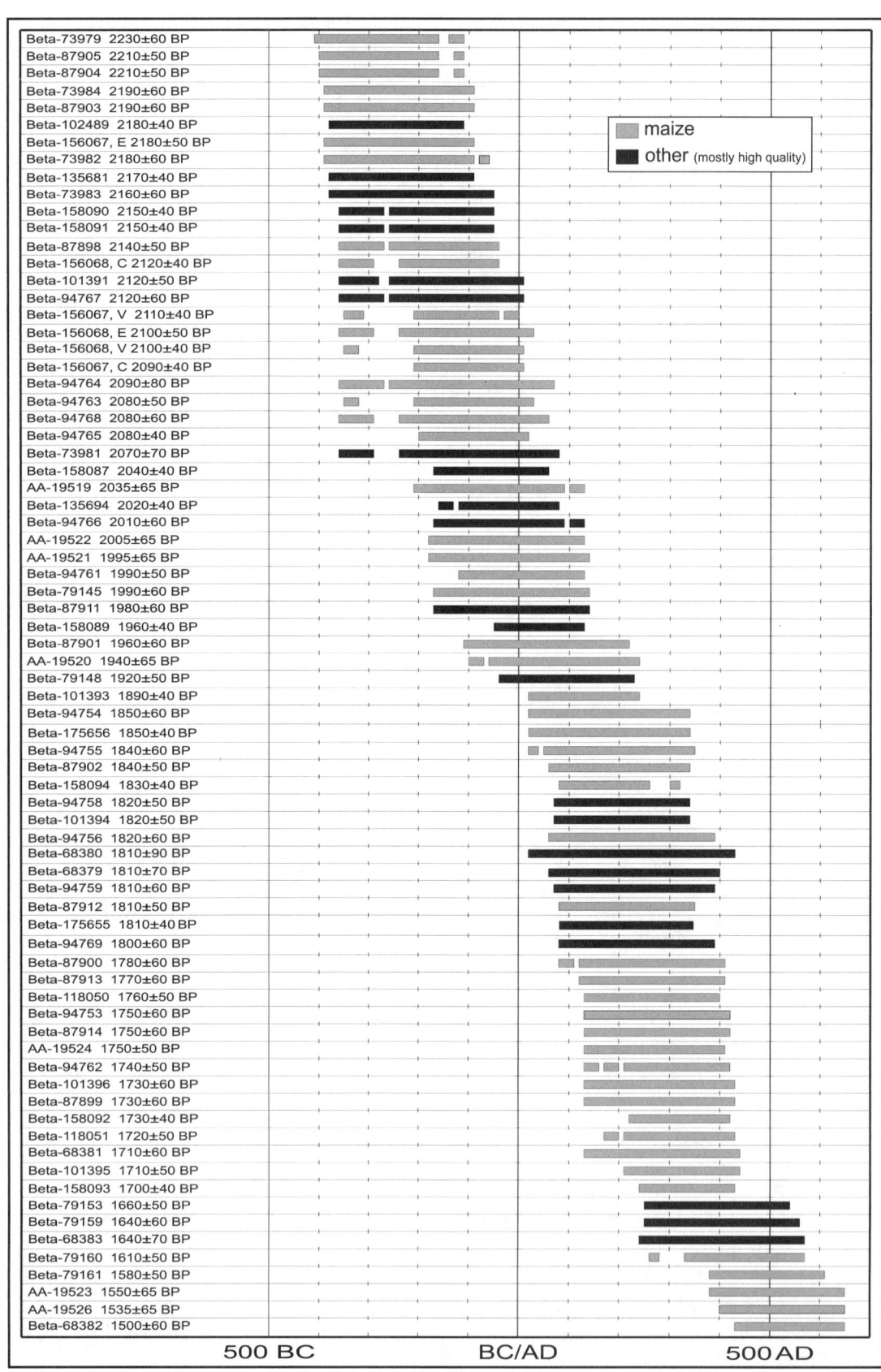

Figure 5.2. Array of all 75 of the Navajo Mountain Road Archaeological Project Basketmaker radiocarbon dates according to a calibrated 2σ age range; maize dates are designated by the lighter-colored bars.

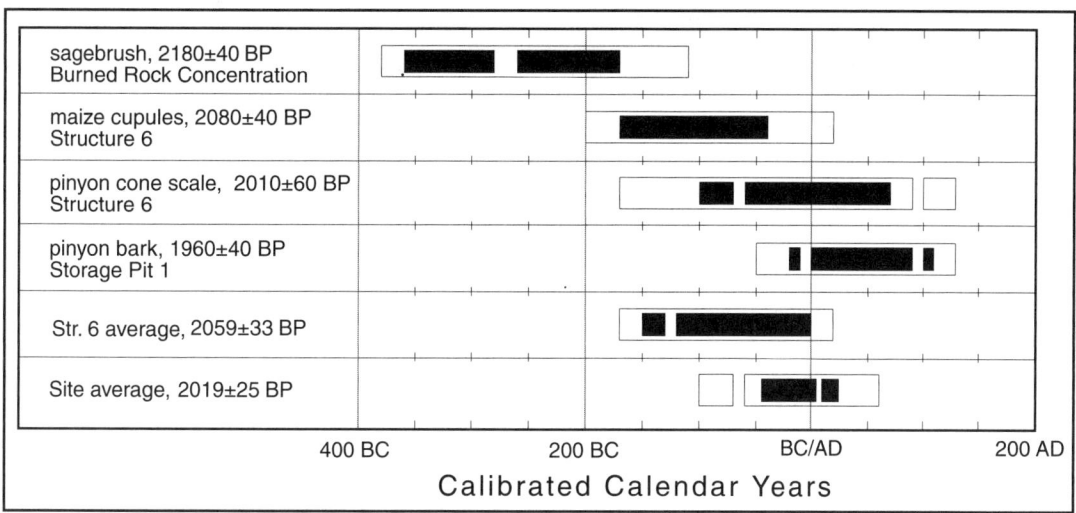

Figure 5.3. Comparison of radiocarbon determinations on sagebrush, maize cupules, a pinyon cone scale, and pinyon bark from various Basketmaker features at Ditch House (solid black boxes = 1σ ranges, enclosing boxes = 2σ ranges).

high-quality materials. One of these is for Ditch House, where there are four radiocarbon dates from three individual features. The dates are plotted in Figure 5.3. One date is on sagebrush from a burned rock concentration, whereas the other three dates are on other remains: maize cupules, a pinyon cone scale, and pinyon bark. The maize and cone scale came from the hearth of Structure 6 and produced similar assays that are statistically the same and can be averaged (2059 ± 33 BP). The spread on the four Ditch House dates extends from just under 400 cal. BC to just over cal. AD 100; the dates are significantly different ($T = 15.2$, $5\% = 6.0$ [$df = 3$]). The 2180 BP date from the burned rock concentration appears most at odds, and indeed a test shows that the Structure 6 date average and that for Pit 1 are statistically the same ($T = 3.6$, $5\% = 3.8$ [$df = 1$]). Given the small size of the Basketmaker component at Ditch House and the presence of only one true living structure, the Basketmaker remains at this location are more likely the residue of a moderately short-lived occupation rather than one of several hundred years or a few sequential use episodes. Because of the burning of dead sagebrush, the assay from the burned rock concentration could easily be 100–200 years too old. Indeed, as I learned, sagebrush charcoal is often older than wood charcoal from the same hearth. The sagebrush date supports assignment of the burned rock feature to the Basketmaker component but is not sufficiently accurate to be used as part of the temporal bracket for site occupation. Because the determinations for Structure 6 and Pit 1 are statistically the same, their average of 2019 ± 25 BP provides the best temporal estimate for the Basketmaker component at Ditch House, which has a two-sigma range of 100 cal. BC to cal. AD 60.

The Basketmaker II component at Three Dog Site is another case where an assay on sagebrush charcoal can be compared against assays on annual plant remains. The initial date for this component consisted of sagebrush charcoal from two overlapping hearths, which returned a date of 2020 ± 40 BP (Beta-135694). The subsequent processing and analysis of two flotation samples from the hearths recovered annual plant remains, including ricegrass seeds and a maize kernel fragment. These two samples returned statistically contemporaneous radiocarbon dates in the 1800s BP (Figure 5.4), with an average of 1830 ± 28 BP—almost 200 years more recent than the previous sagebrush date. With a calibrated two-sigma range of AD 80–320, this mean date places the Basketmaker occupation of Three Dog Site toward the later part of the Basketmaker II sequence for the N16 project area.

Juniper Seeds vs. Maize. Two of the NMRAP Basketmaker sites have radiocarbon dates on both maize and juniper seeds, allowing an assessment of age correspondence. Although juniper is not a culturally controlled annual plant, juniper seeds nonetheless represent annual growth. Moreover, juniper seeds are relatively large and durable; the substantial size means that a single seed or even seed half is more than sufficient for an AMS date, and they are noticeable when excavating and easily recovered when using ⅛-in mesh screens. Durability means that

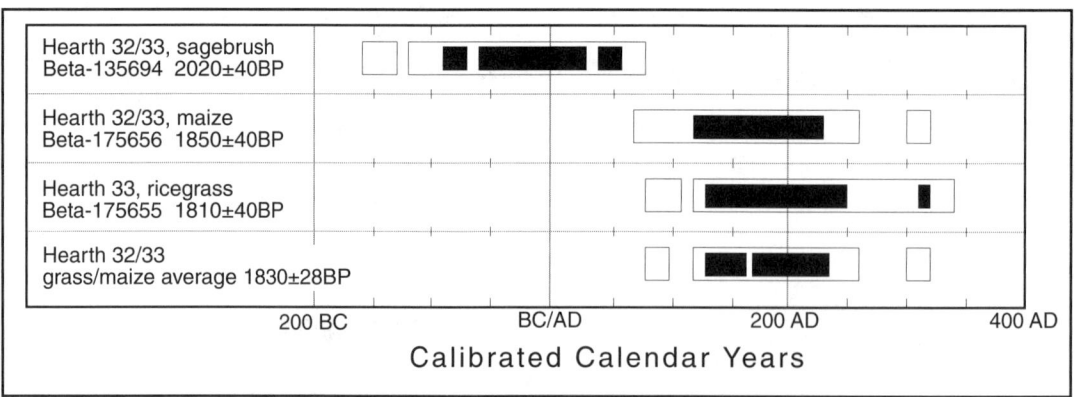

Figure 5.4. Comparison of radiocarbon determinations on sagebrush, maize cupules, and ricegrass seeds from Basketmaker hearths at Three Dog Site (solid black boxes = 1σ ranges, enclosing boxes = 2σ ranges).

carbonized seeds can survive the deleterious effects of wetting and drying, roots, other bioturbation, and the trauma of being unearthed and tossed onto a screen or floated from sediment in water. The one potential problem is that these hard woody items, after falling from a tree, can last for an unknown length of time on the ground surface or buried in a duff layer. Because the seeds are shed annually, their incorporation within the fill of a hearth is likely to result from either burning juniper twigs for fuel or use of the berry for food, and as such, little or no time should separate death of the organism from carbonization.

One of the sites with comparative maize and juniper seed dates is Ko' Lahni, a site with numerous hearths and a small midden but no house, although previous disturbance to a portion of the site may have removed a living structure. Excavation produced no high-quality radiocarbon samples, but the flotation analyst recovered maize kernels and juniper seeds from Hearths 6 and 1, respectively. In this case the juniper seed assay is slightly older than the maize date (see Table 5.2), but the 40–radiocarbon year discrepancy is of no consequence because the two dates are statistically the same and can be averaged (2100 ± 42 BP), resulting in a calibrated two-sigma range of 350 BC to AD 10.

Panorama House provides an even better test case because the comparative samples came from a single structure—juniper seeds from the burned roof fall of the floor fill and maize from the interior hearths; there are also dates on maize from the associated midden and an extramural hearth. Excavators speculated that the numerous carbonized juniper seeds that occurred within the burned roof fall layer of the structure's floor fill were derived from green boughs that helped to form the closing material for the superstructure. Any scavenged dead juniper trees or limbs used in the roof and walls would not have retained seeds. Thus, a juniper seed date in this case should closely correspond to the actual construction event. Nonetheless, there is a 60- to 110–radiocarbon year discrepancy between the maize dates and the juniper seed (see Table 5.2). The four maize dates form a tight group between 1,710 and 1,760 radiocarbon years ago, but the juniper seed yielded an assay of 1820 BP. The maize dates are statistically the same and can be averaged (1730 ± 26 BP), resulting in a calibrated two-sigma range of AD 240–390. Despite some overlap with the two-sigma calibrated range of AD 70–340 for the juniper seed, the maize is younger. One plausible account for the discrepancy is that the sediment used to cover the structure included duff from under juniper trees and thus old seeds, which became carbonized when the superstructure burned. The use of dead juniper trees for the superstructure is indicated by the 1890 ± 40 BP radiocarbon date on the outer rings of a burned timber from the floor, which is even more at odds with the maize dates but is statistically the same as the juniper seeds. The average of the timber and juniper seed is about 130 years older than the maize average, with no overlap at the calibrated two-sigma range (Figure 5.5).

Interlaboratory Comparisons

Following the first year of data-recovery excavations, Beta Analytic received an initial batch of radiocarbon samples, several of which came from the Basketmaker II habitation of The Pits. After pretreatment and preparation of graphic targets, Beta forwarded all AMS samples to Lawrence Livermore National Laboratory in California (CAMS), one of the consortium of laboratories that provides AMS dating for Beta. Upon receipt of the results for this first group (73000s Beta sequence), I submitted

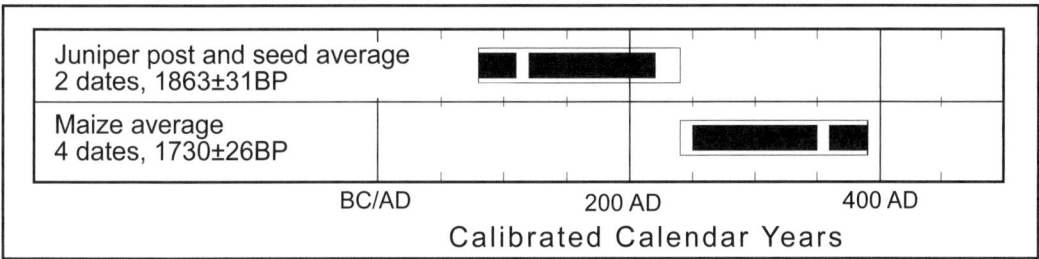

Figure 5.5. Comparison of averaged radiocarbon determinations on burned timber, juniper seeds, and maize from Panorama House (solid black boxes = 1σ ranges, enclosing boxes = 2σ ranges).

a second batch of samples, including several more from The Pits in order to date more of the site's numerous features. This time Beta forwarded the samples to the Eidgenössische Technische Hochschule in Zurich (ETH). This second batch of samples (79000s Beta sequence) had ages that appeared somewhat at odds with those of the previous samples from The Pits. The three dates on corn obtained by CAMS formed a tight group: 2230 ± 60 BP, 2190 ± 60 BP, and 2180 ± 60 BP (see Table 5.2). The two subsequent maize dates obtained by ETH were clustered together in the 1900s BP (1990 ± 60 and 1920 ± 50). Early farmers conceivably occupied the site for the length of time suggested by all five maize dates, but it seemed odd that the results from different laboratories would pattern as they did. Whereas the three CAMS maize dates are contemporaneous or statistically the same, as are the two ETH maize dates, together all five are significantly different. Moreover, two of the divergent samples are from the same surface structure (2230 ± 60 BP [CAMS] and 1990 ± 50 BP [ETH]), a feature with a probable use-life of about a decade.

At first glance there seemed a plausible explanation for the discrepancy because the delta ^{13}C values provided by ETH at −15.3‰ and −16.4‰ are well beyond the norm for maize (e.g., Bender 1968; Creel and Long 1986: Table 1; Stuiver and Polach 1977: Figure 1; Tieszen and Fagre 1993) and quite different from the delta ^{13}C measurements provided by CAMS, which had an average of −11.2‰ (normal for maize). An error in the measurement of the ^{13}C/^{12}C ratio by ETH could account for much of the interlaboratory difference in radiocarbon ages. Might different measurement techniques account for the variant delta values? ETH's measurements were made simultaneous with the actual counting of carbon isotopes for dating and might therefore include the effects of fractionation in the AMS beam or during sample preparation to graphite, whereas the CAMS's delta ^{13}C measurements were measured on the CO_2 derived from combustion of the original sample, thereby providing the more geochemically correct value. Ron Hatfield (personal communication 2001) of Beta Analytic explained that while the ETH delta values may appear incorrect, the reported conventional ages have been corrected for any additional fractionation effects using measurements of the ^{13}C/^{12}C ratio during the combustion to CO_2 (this has been done since 1994).

If the odd delta ^{13}C values for maize obtained by ETH had not affected the sample ages, then a lack of interlaboratory comparability seemed likely. Consequently, I submitted a third set of four maize samples from The Pits. This time the samples went to the NSF–Arizona AMS Facility at the University of Arizona. The rationale was to try a laboratory outside the Beta consortium as an independent means to arbitrate the evident discrepancies and to come to some resolution as to the age of this Basketmaker II site—was it around 2200 BP, between 1900 and 2000 BP, or perhaps the entire range from 2200 to 1900 BP? One of the four new samples consisted of more maize from the floor of the shallow structure that produced the previous two disparate assays.

Queue size, equipment breakdown, and other priorities at the NSF–Arizona AMS Facility meant that more than half a year passed before I received the results for this third set of radiocarbon samples from The Pits. In the meantime, NMRAP fieldwork continued, and more radiocarbon dating was required, especially during the second year of data recovery when many Basketmaker II sites were excavated. To circumvent the issue of interlaboratory disagreement, I requested that Beta Analytic submit all of the project AMS samples to the Lawrence Livermore National Laboratory. This facility had processed most of the AMS samples already submitted for the project at that time, except for several assayed by ETH. Moreover, CAMS's measured delta ^{13}C values for maize were normal, and the few cases of dates from stratigraphic sequence had

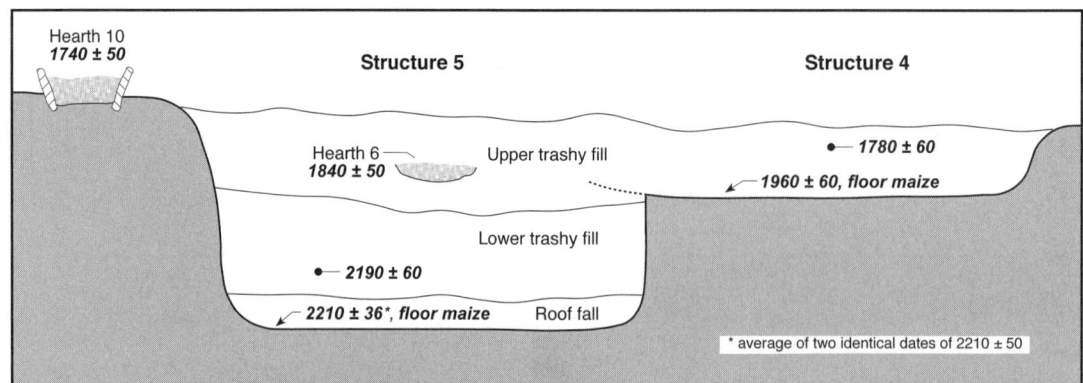

Figure 5.6. Stratigraphically consistent series of accelerator mass spectrometry radiocarbon assays on maize from superimposed features at Kin Kahuna.

the expected order. By the time that I received the NSF-Arizona AMS dates, CAMS had provided 35 additional AMS radiocarbon determinations for the project and an additional 18 more were in the queue, with results arriving shortly after those from NSF-Arizona. A sizable number of these new dates came from the complex Basketmaker II habitation of Kin Kahuna, including a series from superimposed houses and features. This series has excellent stratigraphic agreement as shown in Figure 5.6: identical 2210 BP dates for maize samples from Structure 5 (one from the floor surface and one from a floor pit, bottom of the sequence), a date of 2190 BP on maize from the lower trashy fill above the roof fall layer of Structure 5, a date of 1960 BP on maize from the floor of Structure 4 that overlay Structure 5, an 1840 BP date on maize from a hearth within the upper fill of Structure 5 that was part of the activity that formed the upper trashy fill of this structure, and a date of 1780 BP on maize within the upper trashy fill of Structure 4.

When the NSF-Arizona dates for The Pits finally arrived they tended to agree more with the ETH dates than those of CAMS, although the delta ^{13}C values for maize were similar to those of CAMS. Yet these results failed to provide much clarification largely because the samples were not from identical contexts or of assuredly contemporaneous material. Burned corn kernels from the trashy fill of a storage pit could easily have a true age discrepancy of several hundred years. The ultimate test of interlaboratory comparability comes from dating splits of single samples. Thus, as a final means to check for interlaboratory disagreement, Beta Analytic agreed to process at no cost two previously dated NMRAP samples as part of its audited quality assurance program (QA-494 and -495). These two samples consisted of additional maize kernels from an offering in Storage Pit 3 at The Pits and a corncob from a small bell-shaped floor pit (Pit 1) of Structure 5 at Kin Kahuna. CAMS had previously dated portions from both of these samples, and NSF-Arizona had assayed some of the Storage Pit 3 maize. In both cases the newly submitted portions were large enough for several independent AMS assays; three different AMS laboratories dated a split of the graphite from this sample. Two of the laboratories were CAMS and ETH, and the third was the Institut für Isotopenforschung und Kernphysik, Universität Wein, Austria.

Analysis results from three independent assays on splits of the graphite targets for both samples are given in Tables 5.3 and 5.4 along with previous dates on these same samples. In both cases the new dates show a high degree of consistency among themselves and generally good agreement with the previous assays. For Structure 5 at Kin Kahuna there are now four dates on a maize cob recovered from the fill of a small floor pit (Table 5.3). These four can be combined with another assay on corn from the floor of this structure (these five dates are statistically the same at the 95% level), providing an average of 2149 ± 20 BP, which has a calibrated two-sigma date range of BC 360–100. There are now five dates on the maize offering from Storage Pit 3 at The Pits (Table 5.4), with no significant difference among them at the 95 percent level, suggesting that all five can be averaged. The resulting age estimate of 2107 ± 21 BP has a calibrated two-sigma date range of BC 200–50. No interlaboratory error is evident in these results, though there remains the possibility of a slight degree of interlaboratory disagreement with the initial assays of The Pits. In answer to the question about the temporal duration of Basketmaker occupancy at The Pits, averaged determinations suggest use from about 200 cal. BC to cal. AD 220.

Building chronologies with radiocarbon dates is

TABLE 5.3. Comparison of Radiocarbon Dates on a Maize Cob (PN1045.3) from a Bell-Shaped Pit in the Floor of Structure 5 at Kin Kahuna

Lab No.	Conventional ^{14}C Age (BP)	^{13}C/^{12}C Ratio (‰)	Comment
Beta-87905, CAMS	2210 ± 50	−11.0 (CO_2 gas)	first submission
Beta-156067, CAMS	2090 ± 40	−11.9 (CO_2 gas)	Beta's QA-494
Beta-156067, VERA	2110 ± 40	−10.1 (graphite in beam)	Beta's QA-494
Beta-156067, ETH	2180 ± 50	−12.8 (graphite in beam)	Beta's QA-494

Note: CAMS = Lawrence Livermore National Laboratory in California; ETH = Eidgenössische Technische Hochschule University in Zurich; VERA = Institut für Isotopenforschung und Kernphysik, Universität Wein, Austria. The 156067 series is graphite splits of a single portion of this cob submitted years after the first submission. Maize cupules from the floor of the structure produced the same age as the 87905 series (2210 ± 50, −11.0‰, Beta-87904) for an average of 2210 ± 36 BP. Stratigraphically above the floor is a consistent series of maize dates: 2190 ± 60 BP (Beta-87903), 1960 ± 60 BP (Beta-87901), 1840 ± 50 BP (Beta-87902), and 1780 ± 60 BP (Beta-87900).

TABLE 5.4. Comparison of Radiocarbon Dates on Maize Kernels (PN623.4), Part of a Maize Offering in a Bell-Shaped Storage Pit at The Pits

Lab No.	Conventional ^{14}C Age (BP)	^{13}C/^{12}C Ratio (‰)	Comment
Beta-73984, CAMS	2190 ± 60	−11.2 (CO_2 gas)	first submission
AA-19522	2005 ± 65	−10.4	second submission
Beta-156068, CAMS	2120 ± 40	−11.4 (CO_2 gas)	Beta's QA-495
Beta-156068, VERA	2100 ± 40	−12.1 (graphite in beam)	Beta's QA-495
Beta-156068, ETH	2100 ± 50	−12.2 (graphite in beam)	Beta's QA-495

Note: AA= NSF–Arizona Accelerator Mass Spectrometry Facility at the University of Arizona; CAMS = Lawrence Livermore National Laboratory in California; ETH = Eidgenössische Technische Hochschule University in Zurich; VERA = Institut für Isotopenforschung und Kernphysik, Universität Wein, Austria. The 156068 series is graphite splits of a single portion of the kernels from this feature submitted years after the two prior submissions.

fraught with many difficulties, and despite the call more than 30 years ago to introduce quality control in dating (Waterbolk 1971), problematic dates are still generated by the score. One of the nine potentially problematic areas that Waterbolk addressed was interlaboratory pretreatment and measurement error. Dating laboratories around the world have since made great strides toward eliminating this concern and ensuring comparability among laboratories (Scott 2003a, 2003b), yet the results always show that there are some outliers, at times even extreme outliers. The results reported here of AMS assays by three different laboratories on splits of graphite from two different samples reveal a high degree of comparability. Despite this, were I to direct this project all over again, I would still insist on having a single laboratory assay all AMS samples. This way there is just one less variable to worry about, which, with radiocarbon dating, is a good thing. Even so, it is useful to split samples on occasion and submit them to an additional laboratory for comparative purposes.

Regional Date Distribution

The NMRAP provides the bulk of Basketmaker II radiocarbon dates for the northern Kayenta region, but a few other studies have added to the data set. These consist of the dating of maize and other remains from previously excavated shelters such as Dust Devil Cave (Geib 1996a), Desha Caves 1 and 2 (Geib and Robins 2003), and Sand Dune Cave (Geib 2004). These related studies have contributed to a refinement of Basketmaker chronology for the northern Kayenta region, especially as it relates to the use of caves vis-à-vis open settings. By adding in these 14 additional dates to those of the NMRAP, the sample size is expanded to 89. All but one of these additional dates are on materials that have clear cultural origin, have an unambiguous relationship to the event of interest, and do not overestimate age. Of these 14, four are on maize cobs, three are on juniper bark used as fiber temper for mortar in storage cists, two are on human feces, two are on hide bags, two are on artifacts of yucca, and one is on wood

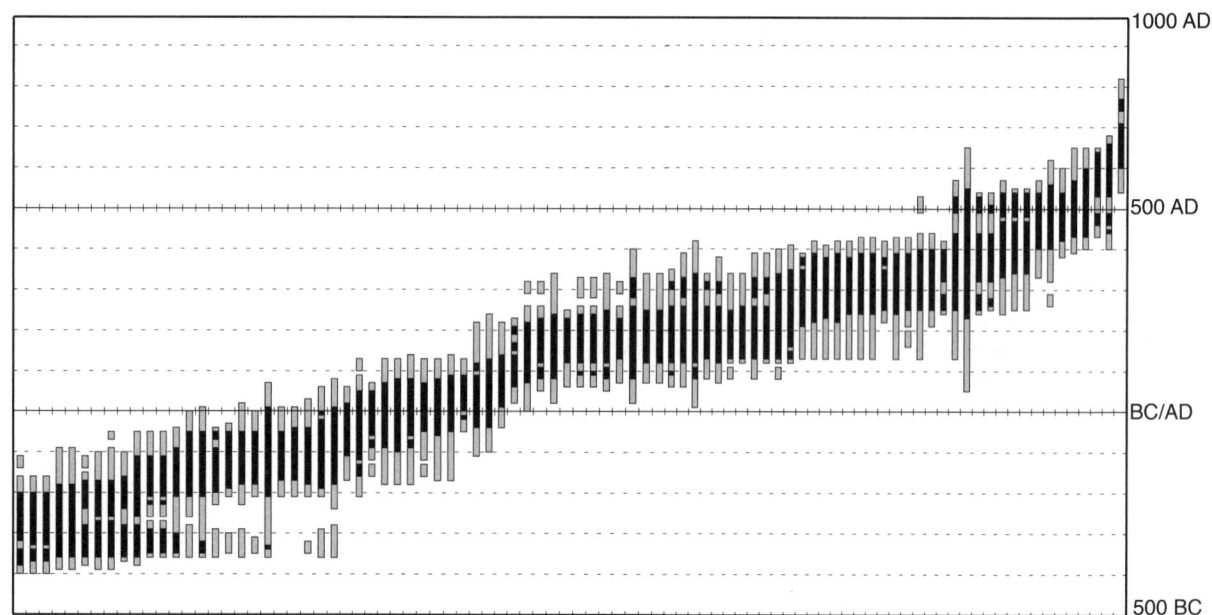

Figure 5.7. Array of 89 Basketmaker radiocarbon dates for the northern Kayenta region (solid black boxes = 1σ ranges, enclosing gray boxes = 2σ ranges).

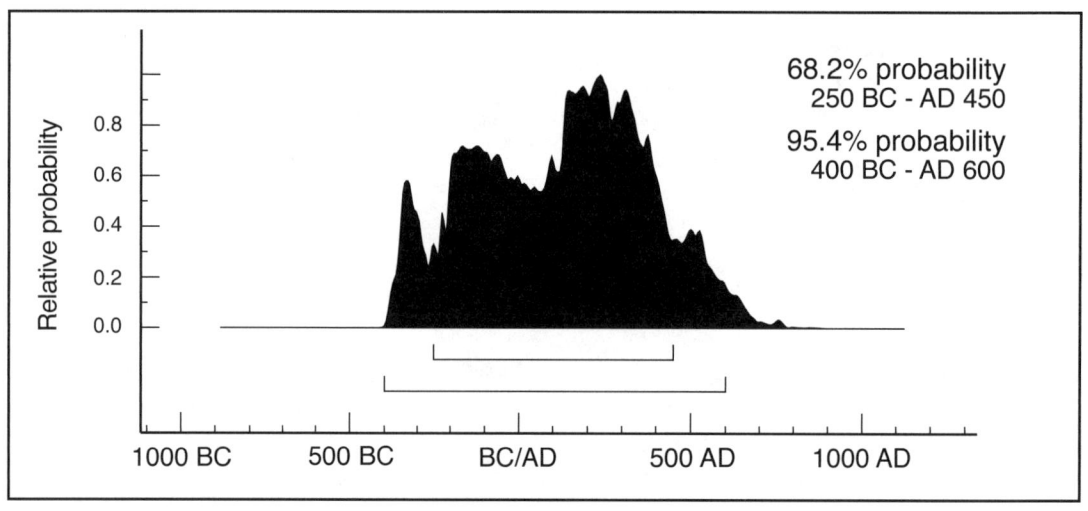

Figure 5.8. Sum of the probability distributions of all 89 Basketmaker dates for the northern Kayenta region.

charcoal from a hearth. The latter was obtained prior to 1970 (Lindsay et al. 1968:108). All nonwood dates have been corrected for ^{13}C fractionation based on measured values.

After calibration using the OxCal program (v. 3.5 [Bronk Ramsey 1994, 1995]), the 89 individual dates reveal a nearly continuous series spanning almost 1,200 years from roughly 400 cal. BC to cal. AD 820 (Figure 5.7). This temporal span is based on the calibrated two-sigma range of the youngest and oldest of the dates considered here, thus this might tend to exaggerate the range. The young end of the sequence is especially suspect since it includes a sample of probable Puebloan maize from Dust Devil Cave that returned an assay of 1370 ± 70 BP (B-47894 [Geib 1996a:Table 11]). Because dates on maize and other high-quality samples bracket lower and upper ends, this date range is likely a close approximation of the true time of Basketmaker presence in the region. A sum of the probability distributions of all 89 dates (Figure 5.8) provides one means to arrive at a best estimate for the chronological span of the Basketmaker presence in the northern Kayenta region—from 400 cal. BC to cal. AD 600. Pottery appeared during the later portion of this range, so this interval includes the start of Basketmaker III if ceramics are used as the prime criterion for this period designation.

Temporal patterning in the 89 radiocarbon dates may be better perceived as graphed in Figure 5.9. This frequency distribution has been compiled by the same method as used in chapter 4 for Archaic radiocarbon dates. The small pattern (shaded area) is based on summing the number of dates within a given 100-year interval using the approximated midpoints of calibrated ages. This interval width is roughly twice the mean of standard deviations for the Basketmaker II dates (56 years), which seemed a useful way for smoothing the results while factoring in the level of imprecision with the dates. Overall, the standard error is quite small for this data set, ranging from a low of 40 years to a high of 140 years with an average of 56 years and both a median and mode of 60 years. As noted, precision in radiocarbon dating has generally improved with time, even during the course of the NMRAP, with nearly all of the most recent AMS dates having an error term of 40 years. The larger distribution accounts for the error term of each date by summing how many dates occur within each 100-year interval based on the calibrated two-sigma age ranges. Whatever distortion there is from factoring in the error term can be gauged against the core pattern based on date midpoints, a benefit of plotting the frequency histograms of both procedures in a single graph.

There are no clear gaps in the distribution, but there is an obvious increase in dates between about cal. AD 200 and 300. This third-century spike may relate to a population increase, or it may simply be from biased sampling. Before graphs such as these can inform about population trends, we need considerably more dates from a larger sample of sites, from all portions of the northern Kayenta region. The falloff in dates after cal. AD 700 is an artifact of using 1300 BP as the upper limit for inclusion in this analysis, but it also appears to reflect a real population trend. As of yet, few sites are known from the northern Kayenta region that have ceramic assemblages containing Lino Black-on-gray and Kana-a Black-on-white (Ambler et al. 1964; Lindsay et al. 1968; Stein 1966; see summary of evidence in SD, Appendix F). Moreover, I know of no residential sites in the area that have Lino Black-on-white or Kana-a Black-on-white as the dominant decorated ceramic types, so no Basketmaker III or Pueblo I habitations. There are habitations with plain pottery (Obelisk) and then habitations with mainly Wepo Black-on-white

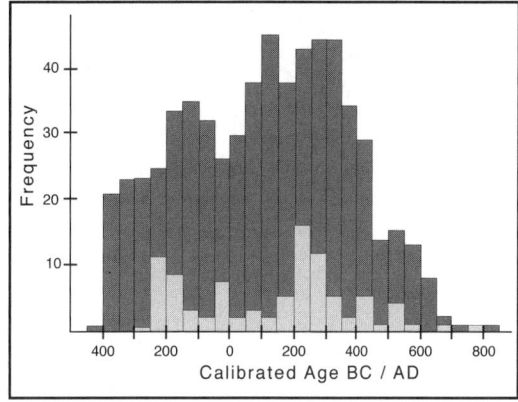

Figure 5.9. Frequency distribution of Basketmaker radiocarbon dates for the northern Kayenta region (Rainbow Plateau and far-northern Shonto Plateau); shaded area depicts the count of dates falling within a 100-year interval based on calibrated midpoints, whereas the larger distribution uses the count of dates falling within 100-year intervals based on a calibrated 2σ age range.

or Wepo and Kana-a combined—thus early Pueblo II or the Pueblo I–Pueblo II transition.

The distribution of Basketmaker dates for the northern Kayenta region stands in marked contrast to Michael Berry's summary of the Basketmaker chronometric data for the Colorado Plateau available in 1980 (see Berry 1982:Figure 10). He identified three discrete temporal clusters: Period I, or early Basketmaker II, from about 200 BC to the time of Christ; Period II, or late Basketmaker II, from about AD 200 to 400; and Period III, or Basketmaker III, from AD 500 to 700. Assuming that the patterning disclosed was not from sampling error, he argues "that occupation occurred in three discrete periods, each separated in time by significant hiatuses" (1982:87). The date distribution for the northern Kayenta region lacks breaks marking a natural line of separation between Basketmaker II and Basketmaker III or early and late Basketmaker II. If I wanted to subdivide this distribution, arbitrary cuts would be called for. Where, though, should such divisions be placed? Does the adoption of new material culture items such as pottery provide an answer? What about changes in subsistence or settlement? Each of these issues is examined in detail as this chapter unfolds. It is also worth pointing out that radiocarbon dating is too coarse a chronometric technique to disclose short-duration population breaks or changes.

Although the distribution of Basketmaker dates for the northern Kayenta region does not support Berry's tripartite temporal scheme, it supports his critique of

Glassow's (1972) proposed explanation of the Basketmaker II–III transition as a response to stress resulting from steady population increase. As noted by Berry, Glassow "set for himself the problem of explaining a series of events that probably never happened" (1982:89). With a 200-year gap separating the strong temporal clustering of Basketmaker II sites from Basketmaker III sites, Berry concluded that increasing population density could not be used as an independent variable in an explanatory model. There is no evidence for a 200-year gap in occupancy for the northern Kayenta region, but neither is there evidence for steady population increase. The cultural traits that serve as the traditional markers for Basketmaker III do not appear suddenly as a suite at all sites but, rather, seem to have individual temporal patterns and rates of acceptance.

The Basketmaker date distribution for the Rainbow Plateau will become informative for regional comparisons once robust chronologies are available for other areas. Unfortunately these are lacking at present for other areas of the Kayenta region. There is a large suite of dates available for Lolomai phase Basketmaker sites on northern Black Mesa, but nearly all of these (140) are on wood charcoal and have little or no relevance for dating the Basketmaker II occupation on the mesa (Smiley 1985, 1998c). The six dates on high-quality samples that are available suggest that the Lolomai phase is restricted to the interval of roughly AD 50–350 (1900–1600 cal. BP [Smiley 1998c: 117]). Unfortunately these six dates suffer from poor precision (standard deviations of 90–130 years). This plus their limited number raises the possibility that this phase might be somewhat longer in duration, having begun earlier than currently accepted.[1] Detailed Basketmaker chronologies are beginning to be assembled for other portions of the Colorado Plateau (e.g., Charles and Cole 2006) and should eventually allow useful interregional comparisons.

Farming and Foraging

Food production distinguishes Basketmaker II groups from the Archaic foragers who preceded them. This change does not appear to be one of degree but, rather, a profound alteration of the previously existing relationships on the Colorado Plateau between people and their natural environment and among different groups of people. Archaic foragers might have worked unintensively to artificially increase the spatial concentration of certain food plants (e.g., Winter and Hogan 1986), but the scale of any such efforts appears to have been minor and the impact negligible compared to what happened with the arrival of Mesoamerican domesticates. Likewise, Basketmaker II groups continued foraging as an important means of augmenting field produce, but the focus had shifted away from the high residential mobility and extensive adaptation of Archaic foragers to one that was far more intensive, emphasizing relatively small parcels of land for the production of a significant amount of plant food coupled with limited residential mobility, at least on an intra-annual basis.

As many have observed, and Ford stated emphatically, "calories were a limiting factor for hunters and gatherers in the pre-maize Southwest. Plant foods were not sufficiently abundant in any one location to support large populations or even the annual return of small bands" (1984: 129). The notion of the Colorado Plateau as marginal for foragers goes back at least to the time of Hugh Cutler, who in 1954 published an account of his experience of trying to subsist for several days on gathered resources in Glen Canyon, wherein he bemoaned, "This turned out to be a struggle even during the most favorable season of the year and...I gathered barely enough to keep from being hungry." Cutler correctly observed that "only a small population of hunters and gatherers could exist in the region" (1954:39). Farming changed this situation and not just because of the presence of domesticates but also by creating disturbed settings that allowed the proliferation of many useful weeds (e.g., Bye 1976, 1981; Ford 1984:129–130) and even the concentration of game, following Linares's (1976) garden hunting hypothesis.

The Age of Maize

The antiquity of farming on the Colorado Plateau and in the Southwest generally is a constantly moving target. Even before the ink is dry on a latest pronouncement about the initial use of domesticates, there is some new discovery that pushes the age of maize further back in time, with the Old Corn site (Huber 2005) being just the latest during the past few decades. There is, however, an absolute limit to the age of maize in the Southwest, set by the oldest corn in Mexico, which is currently dated at about 5,400 rcybp (Piperno and Flannery 2001). Squash (*Cucurbita pepo*) is even older in Mexico (Smith 1997), but this domesticate appears to have arrived in the Southwest contemporaneously with corn as part of the same cultural/adaptational package. Since corn is far more visible in the archaeological record (both macroscopically and microscopically) than squash, it serves as the marker for the spread of farming. In essence, the age of maize for a region equals the age of farming for that region. Of course the mere presence of a domesticate does not necessarily imply a farming-based economy, since foragers may have traded for corn ears or kernels from adjacent farmers. Moreover, as some have argued, domesticates may have initially been incorporated into existing forager subsistence/settlement strategies with minimal adjustment (e.g., Irwin-Williams 1973, 1979; Minnis 1985, 1992).

Despite recent revelations elsewhere, maize in the northern Kayenta region is not all that old, appearing no earlier than about 400 cal. BC. Several NMRAP sites date to between 1000 and 400 cal. BC, contemporaneous with domesticate use on other portions of the Colorado Plateau to the south and east. Even with diligent searches through the ⅛-in-mesh-screened fill of cultural strata and dozens of hearths at these sites, excavators never found any corn remains. Flotation analysis has verified the lack of macroremains for maize or domesticates. The analysis of 46 4-liter flotation samples from the sites dated between 1000 and 400 cal. BC revealed no corn or squash. In stark contrast, nearly all NMRAP preceramic sites dated after 400 cal. BC contained maize, sometimes in great abundance. Excavators recovered kernels, cupules, and occasional cobs in the field from most post–400 cal. BC sites. Flotation analysis has verified this pattern of the common recovery of maize: 56 percent of 174 samples from sites between 400 cal. BC and cal. AD 400 contain some portion of corn, with kernels represented in 25 percent (see summary below).

Maize first appears in the northern Kayenta region after an evident decline in date frequency between about 700 and 400 cal. BC and perhaps even a slight gap, although this will probably disappear with additional assays (Figure 5.10). Two hearths from a single NMRAP site (Three Dog) dated between about 800 and 400 cal. BC (two sigma), but neither contained maize; nor did the rest of the features from the component with these hearths. All sites on the older side of the date decline/gap lack maize, whereas most sites on the younger side contain maize, some in considerable abundance. Moreover, as discussed below (also Geib and Spurr 2002), there is an obvious change in the archaeological record that also coincides with this date decline/gap and the arrival of maize. As argued in chapter 4, I believe that the nonagricultural sites dating to before 400 cal. BC represent the trace of a continued forager adaptation on the Rainbow Plateau that lasted until perhaps 600 cal. BC and not the foraging and hunting camps of preceramic farmers. Besides a lack of domesticates, a principal reason for thinking this is that the projectile points and other remains are unlike those typical of Basketmaker II sites. I classify all sites on the older side of the date gap as late Archaic (or terminal Archaic), in that they appear to be the archaeological expression of a continued foraging lifestyle. The sites on the younger side of the date gap are classified as Basketmaker II.

The earliest direct maize date on the Rainbow Plateau is roughly 300 cal. BC (2230 ± 60 BP, Beta-73979), and there are no earlier dates for sites that produced corn. As more corn and squash from preceramic contexts on the Rainbow Plateau and elsewhere in the local area are directly dated it might well turn out that domesticate use in this portion of the Kayenta region matches that for Marsh Pass and Black Mesa (Smiley 1994; Smiley and Parry 1992; Smiley et al. 1986), where corn was definitely present by about 800 cal. BC (multiple corn dates in the 2500s BP), with the likelihood that it might date as early as 1000 BC (the 2880 BP date from Three Fir Shelter). Nonetheless, the current evidence for the age of domesticates on the Rainbow Plateau is based on a robust sample size of 55 direct dates on corncobs or kernels from a variety of site types, including rockshelters and caves that might have a greater chance of having been occupied during the earliest part of the Basketmaker II sequence. Furthermore, corn was not selected for dating based on some criteria that might have lowered the probabilities of including earlier specimens. Rareness alone could do this if early corn was poorly represented relative to later Basketmaker corn, but the sample size is beginning to be large enough to render this possibility moot.

This mutually exclusive pattern—corn at sites dating more recent than 400 cal. BC but no corn at sites dating older than this—does not seem to be the by-product of site setting or site preservation. Most of NNAD's excavation took place at open sites, which are ordinarily less likely to yield preserved organic materials than sheltered sites. This sampling problem has been offset to a large degree by the direct dating of corn from several caves on the Rainbow Plateau, including Desha Caves 1 and 2 (Geib and Robins 2003), Dust Devil Cave (Geib 1996a), and Atlatl Rock Cave (SD vol. 2, chap. 2). This effort has yet to produce a date earlier than the Christian era. Thus, there is currently no reason to suspect that the first farmers on the plateau preferred caves to open sites. This is important because Smiley (1998c:100) argued that the earliest evidence

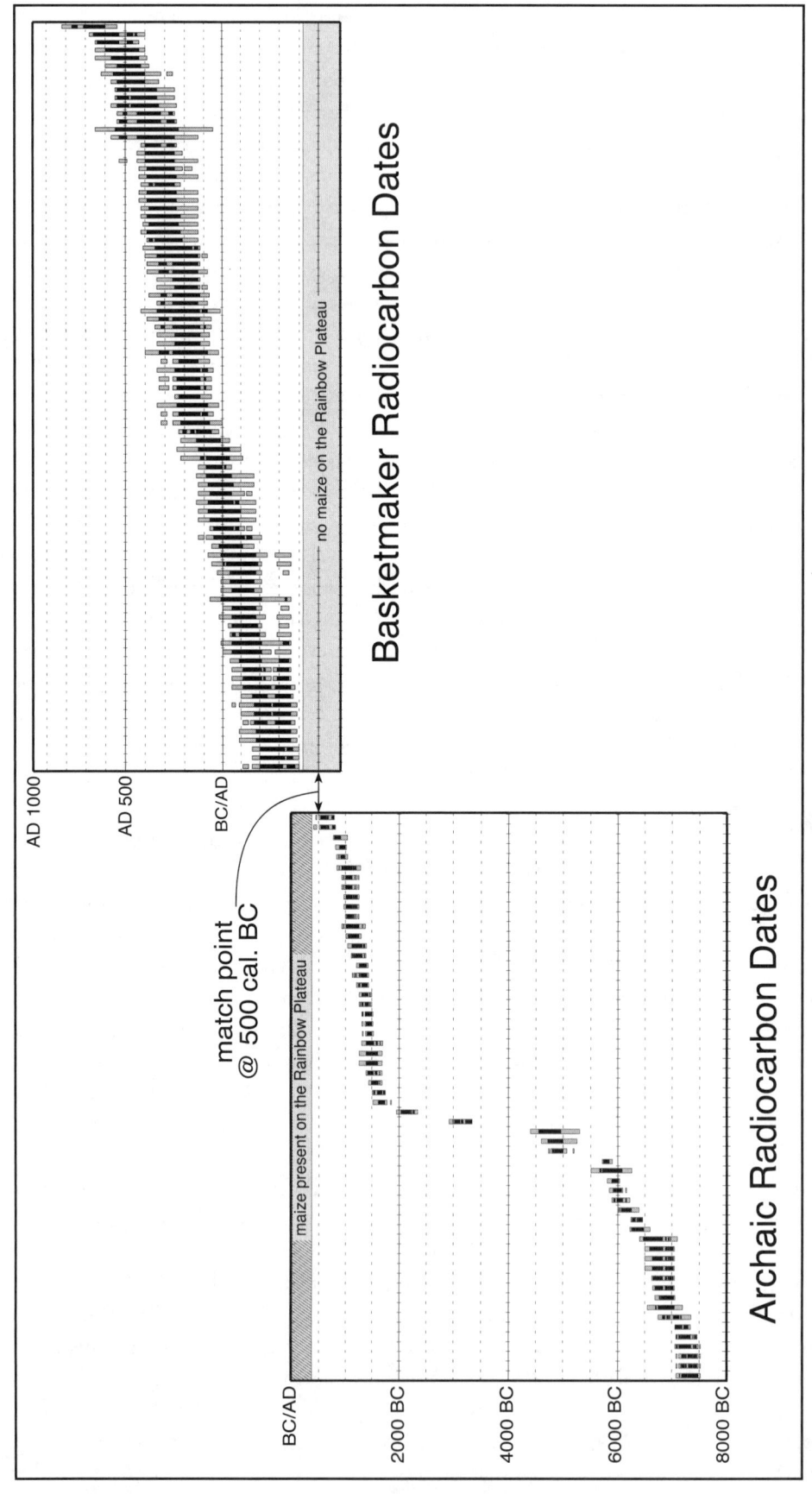

Figure 5.10. Archaic and Basketmaker radiocarbon date distributions for the northern Kayenta region highlighting the interval of date decline after which maize appears (Rainbow Plateau and far-northern Shonto Plateau).

for maize use in the Kayenta Anasazi region comes from caves and shelters that form part of the early Basketmaker II White Dog phase rather than from the open sites of the late Basketmaker II Lolomai phase (see also Matson 1991: 122–124). The link here is that floodwater farming preceded dry farming on mesa tops, as Matson (1991) argued in his model of maize adoption to the Colorado Plateau, and that suitable early planting locations often occurred in canyons that also provided dry shelters. The work on both Cedar Mesa and Black Mesa shows an early Christian-era expansion of open Basketmaker II residential sites across areas that previously lacked such settlements. Given the settings, such an expansion was presumably permitted by the use of dry farming, and the new land opened up by this technique resulted in population growth. Since open site locations also occur next to floodwater settings in many portions of the Colorado Plateau, there is no necessary reason to expect sheltered sites to produce maize any earlier than open sites. Indeed, current finds reveal just the opposite, with the best evidence for the earliest use of cultigens on the Colorado Plateau derived from open settings. The Lukachukai site, an open pithouse settlement in northeastern Arizona with maize dated to before 1000 cal. BC (Gilpin 1994:Table 4), once provided the earliest securely dated maize. The Old Corn site near Fence Lake, New Mexico, is the new standard-bearer, with numerous direct maize dates at around 2100 cal. BC (Huber 2005). In any event, it cannot be claimed that the NMRAP focus on open sites has precluded documentation of earlier maize. Admittedly, more corn (and squash) from both open and sheltered sites of the northern Kayenta region needs to be directly dated because revealing the rare among the more common usually requires large sample sizes, and early domesticates might be rare relative to those from about the time of Christ or later.

Agricultural Dependence

How archaeologists measure agricultural dependence is a complicated issue, made even more so these days because of the many separate lines of evidence that can be mustered, some of which may give conflicting results. One of the principal measures of agricultural dependence is provided by macrobotanical remains from both human feces and sediment samples (e.g., Gasser 1982; Minnis 1989; Stiger 1977). Macroremains in feces provide direct evidence of corn consumption but only for a single meal or two, leaving questions about the diet for the rest of a year. In addition, it is exceedingly difficult to infer the relative contributions of different fecal constituents, although the absolute abundance of a component and the number of feces with a given component provide some indication. The remains of maize in flotation samples provide an indirect measure of agricultural dependence, subject to multiple interpretations. Even when maize remains are exceedingly abundant, as at the Donaldson and Los Ojitos sites (L. Huckell 1995), the question remains, "Does an abundance of evidence necessarily translate into evidence of abundance?" (B. Huckell 1995:120). Pollen in both fecal and sediment samples can also be related to diet, but interpretation of pollen findings in terms of agricultural dependence seems even more problematic than for macrobotanical remains. Greater efficiency in maize kernel processing, as evidenced by mano and metate size, provides another indirect measure of increased dependency (Hard et al. 1996; cf. Adams 1999). Bone isotope ratios, though not without interpretive complications (see reviews in Ambrose 1993; Katzenberg and Pfeiffer 2000; Sealy 2001), provide perhaps the best evidence currently available for a signature of long-term diet, and several such studies are available for early farming groups on the Colorado Plateau (Chisholm and Matson 1994; Coltrain 1996, 1997; Coltrain et al. 2007; Martin 1999; Martin et al. 1991; Matson and Chisholm 1991). Unfortunately, this type of analysis was not possible for the NMRAP despite the discovery of Basketmaker burials at the site of Kin Kahuna.

Flotation samples from NMRAP sites provide useful information regarding Basketmaker subsistence in the northern Kayenta region, data that can be supplemented with limited findings from caves, including the analysis of a few human feces. One hundred ninety-four flotation samples from 14 of the NMRAP Basketmaker sites were processed and analyzed for macrobotanical remains (Table 5.5). Many samples came from the largest sites, Kin Kahuna and The Pits, two primary habitations (defined below) within the ROW. Secondary habitations (see site type discussions that follow) produced fewer samples each, but in aggregate this type of site accounts for nearly half of all Basketmaker flotation samples. Fecal analysis is represented by eight specimens from Desha Cave 1 (Geib and Robins 2003), two of which are directly dated. Probable Basketmaker II feces from Sand Dune and Dust Devil caves have received some level of analysis (J. Richard Ambler, personal communication 1996), but the results are not yet reported (Van Ness [1986] has an excellent study of the Archaic feces from Dust Devil Cave).

Maize recovery from the NMRAP flotation samples of Basketmaker and Puebloan sites offers a useful means for assessing the relative importance of maize in the

TABLE 5.5. Characteristics of the Flotation Analysis Sample for Navajo Mountain Road Archaeological Project Basketmaker and Puebloan Sites

VARIABLE	BASKETMAKER II		PUEBLOAN	
	n	%	n	%
Number of Samples	194	46.5	200	53.5
Total Liters	771	46.6	792	53.4
Number of Sites	14	42.4	19	57.6
Primary Habitations	3	21.4	10	52.6
Secondary Habitations	9	64.3	6	31.6
Temporary Camps	2	14.3	3	15.8
Samples from Primary Habitations	109	56.2	161	80.5
Samples from Secondary Habitations	81	41.8	32	16
Samples from Temporary Camps	4	2.1	7	3.5

Note: Samples were mostly 4 liters in size.

TABLE 5.6. Summary of *Zea mays* Remains Recovered from Flotation Samples of Navajo Mountain Road Archaeological Project Basketmaker and Puebloan Sites

MAIZE PORTION	BASKETMAKER II		PUEBLOAN	
	n	%	n	%
Cob	1	.5	13	6.5
Rachis Segment	3	1.5	0	0
Cupule	110	56.7	116	58
Glume	7	3.6	15	7.5
Kernel	49	25.3	62	31
Shank	0	0	1	.5
All Parts	118	60.8	125	62.5

Basketmaker diet. The sample sizes are quite good for the assemblages from these two general intervals—both the total number of samples analyzed (194 and 200, respectively) and the volume of sediment processed (771 and 792 liters, respectively). The number of sites analyzed is less robust, consisting of 14 for the Basketmaker sample and 19 for the Puebloan sample. More significantly, just three sites (21%) classified as primary habitations added to the Basketmaker float sample, accounting for 56 percent of all analyzed Basketmaker floats, whereas more than half of the sites adding to the Puebloan sample are primary habitations (53%), accounting for 80 percent of the analyzed Puebloan floats. Secondary habitations, which tended to have somewhat lower representation of maize and other macrobotanical remains than primary habitations, accounted for more than 60 percent of the Basketmaker site sample and 42 percent of the analyzed Basketmaker floats but just 16 percent of all Puebloan floats. Because there is a greater likelihood for maize to be represented at primary habitations, the differential representation of this site type and float samples therefrom is likely to make maize appear more ubiquitous in the Puebloan sample compared to the Basketmaker sample.

Table 5.6 presents a comparison of various *Zea mays* remains recovered from the numerous flotation samples of NMRAP Basketmaker and Puebloan sites, and Figure 5.11 graphs their ubiquity values. In both the figure and the table the heading of "all parts" denotes those samples that contained at least one type of maize remain, and this provides the best overall estimate for its representation. Based on all plant parts, maize ubiquity is high during the Basketmaker period. Indeed, other than goosefoot seeds, which have a ubiquity value of 64 percent, maize is the most common food remain in the flotation data set. At primary habitations, maize actually equals or exceeds the percent presence of goosefoot seeds. Although maize appears to be slightly more common within Puebloan flotation samples, this is likely a product of the comparative overrepresentation of float samples from primary habitations as mentioned previously. There is a significant difference in maize ubiquity between primary and secondary habitations in the Basketmaker sample, with the former having a value of just over 80 percent (83.5%), whereas the latter have a value of 32 percent (32.1%). There is good reason to believe that macrobotanical remains from places resided in for a substantial portion of a year provide a better approximation of overall subsistence orientation than macrobotanical remains from places of limited residence. Besides the high incidence of maize in flotation samples from primary habitations, maize is far more abundant at these Basketmaker sites than at secondary habitations, something that was unmistakable in the field during excavation. For example, NNAD excavators recovered maize from most features at Kin Kahuna and The Pits, whereas maize was rare and often had to be carefully searched for during the excavation of features at secondary habitations such as Panorama House and Sin Sombra. Quantification of this difference is best provided by Andrea Hunter's flotation results (SD, Appendix B) from the first year of data-recovery excavation. In 20 flotation samples (73 liters of sediment) from The Pits, a primary habitation site with abundant storage capacity, the quantity of maize was 20.8 parts per liter and 1.7 kernels per liter, whereas in 13 samples (47 liters of sediment) from Polly's Place, a secondary habitation lacking storage features, the quantity of maize was 2.7 parts per liter and .6 kernels per liter. These

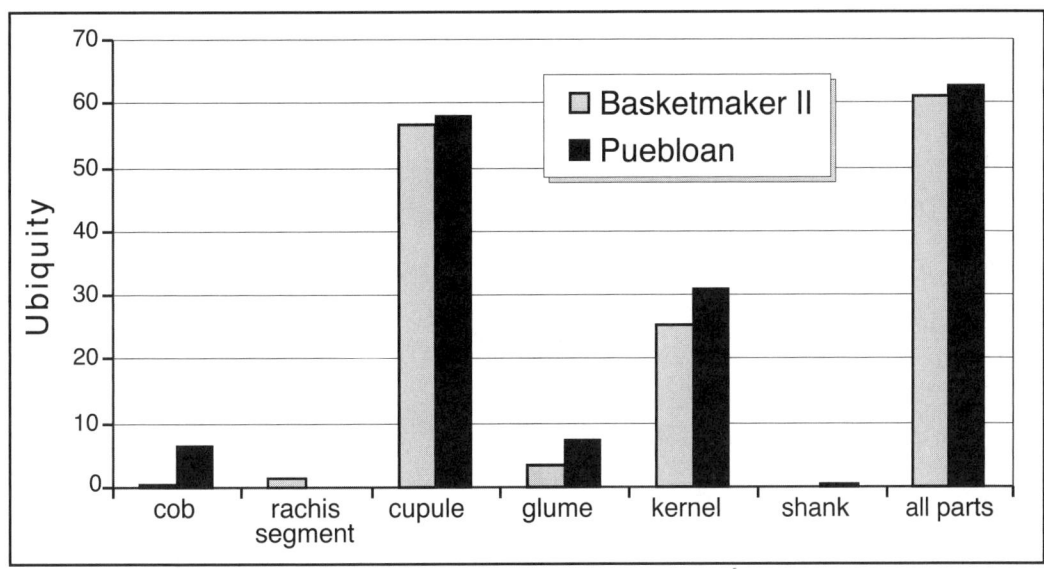

Figure 5.11. Maize ubiquity values for Basketmaker and Puebloan flotation samples of the Navajo Mountain Road Archaeological Project.

findings differ from those for northern Black Mesa, where Wills and Huckell (1994:44) reported a lack of clear correspondence between site type and maize occurrence.

Figure 5.12 presents a plot of maize ubiquity values through time for Basketmaker habitations excavated within the N16 ROW; primary habitations are depicted as squares, and secondary habitations, as circles. Sample size is also shown to provide a perspective on how robust the patterning might be. The blackened squares and circles are ubiquity values calculated using all maize parts (cupules, kernels, glumes, cob portions), whereas the open squares and circles represent ubiquity based only on maize kernels. Assessing kernels alone eliminates the possibility that purposeful burning of maize cobs for fuel or incidental disposal into hearths might greatly and differentially inflate the incidence of maize. In most cases, representation declines substantially when just kernels are used for calculating ubiquity values. In two instances this did not occur, but one of these (Ditch House) has a minuscule sample size, so it may simply be an aberration. Because it is based on 20 samples, the equal 75 percent ubiquity of kernels and cob portions at The Pits is notable, providing good evidence for the significance of maize during the last few centuries BC and the first few centuries AD.

For this presentation, I separated the lengthy Basketmaker occupancy of Kin Kahuna into two temporal components: early, from about 2200 to 1900 BP, and late, from about 1900 to 1700 BP. The late portion is viewed as potentially ceramic because of the Mountainview site (reviewed below and see SD vol. 3, chap. 10), although no pottery was actually recovered from Kin Kahuna. The significance of maize in the diet throughout the occupancy of Kin Kahuna is attested to by its presence in 66 of 72 analyzed flotation samples (92%; see SD vol. 3, chap. 2, and Appendix B). Maize kernels occurred in 21 of the 72 samples, or 29 percent. Based on radiocarbon dates and feature attributes, I assigned 43 of the flotation samples to the early component and 21 samples to the later component, with eight samples left unassigned. Some form of maize was present in 88 percent of the early component samples and 95 percent of the later component samples, whereas maize kernels occurred in 26 percent of the early component samples and 38 percent of the later component samples.

There is no clear temporal pattern in the ubiquity data supporting an increase in maize use during the Basketmaker chronology for the Rainbow Plateau. Moderately heavy maize dependence appears with the earliest of the open habitations with storage features, perhaps as early as 400 cal. BC and certainly by 200 cal. BC. With maize occurring in 75 to 90 percent of the samples from Kin Kahuna and The Pits, there is little room for an increase in maize representation. Indeed, maize is no more ubiquitous at Pueblo II and III habitations on the Rainbow Plateau, varying between 60 and 90 percent with a total value of 63 percent for the 200 NMRAP Puebloan flotation samples (see Table 5.6), nearly all of which came from primary habitations. Casto and I (Geib and Casto 1985) report a maize ubiquity of greater than 60 percent for Puebloan habitations at the northeast foot of Navajo

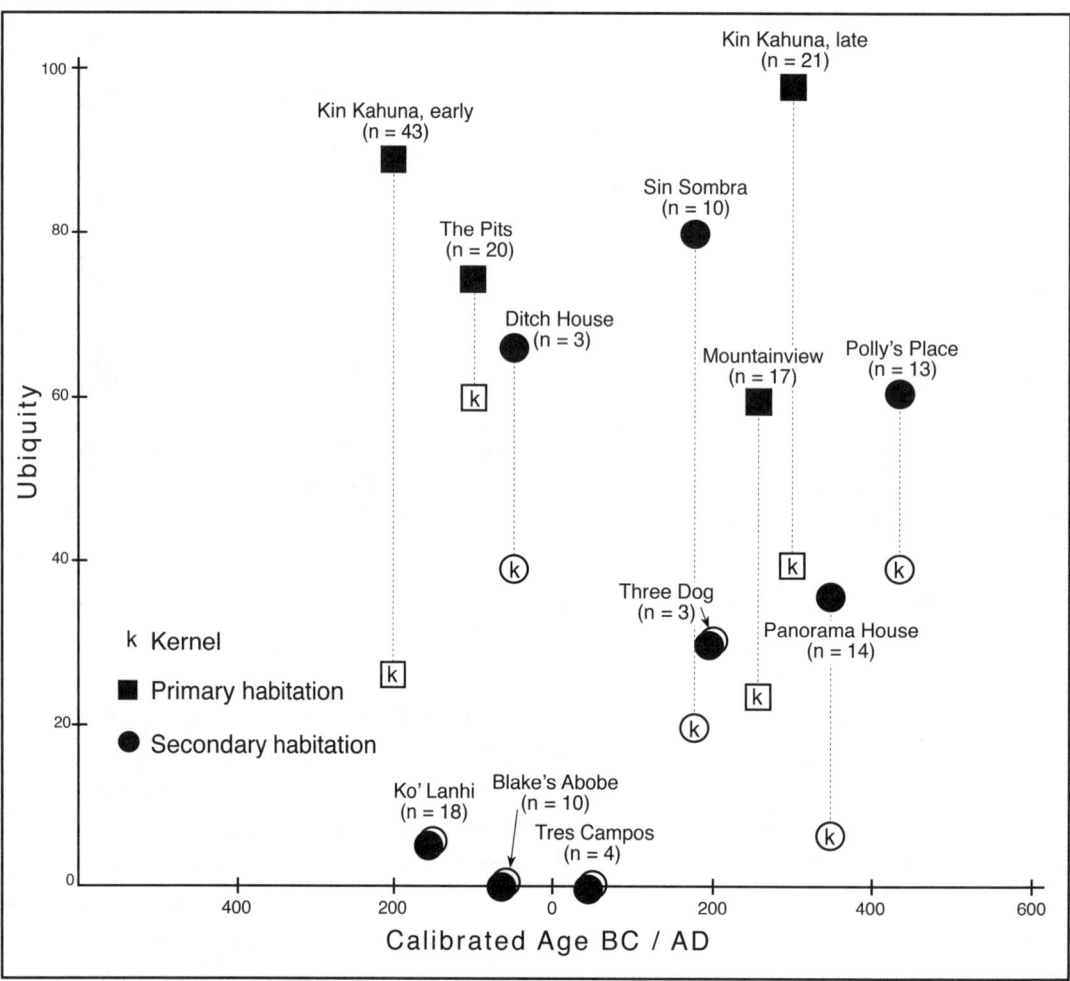

Figure 5.12. Maize ubiquity values through time for Navajo Mountain Road Archaeological Project Basketmaker habitations.

Mountain. Other quantification methods, such as ratios, might disclose patterns lost in this analysis, but at present it seems that farming remained consistently important from the start of the Basketmaker period to the end.

The truth to this claim for western Basketmaker II overall is borne out by recent isotope analysis and direct dating of Basketmaker burials from the Kayenta region. With delta ^{13}C values ranging from −5.9 to −13.7 and a mean of −8.0 ± 1.7 (Coltrain et al. 2007:Tables 1–2), it is clear that Basketmaker II people were heavily dependent on maize by 400 cal. BC, with a degree of dependence that was similar to that of Pueblo II and III farmers a thousand years later.

Basketmaker Maize

Maize may be equally common to preceramic and ceramic Basketmaker contexts on the Rainbow Plateau, but evidence from Atlatl Rock Cave indicates a significant change in kernel morphology that may have implications for the dietary significance of maize or the processing methods. The sample from this site is small but from well-controlled and -dated proveniences, both preceramic and early ceramic. The latter consisted of the floor fill of a slab-lined cist (Feature 18) that contained Obelisk Utility pottery, a common bean, an arrowpoint, abundant turkey feces, and maize kernels and cobs. A single corncob from this fill returned a radiocarbon date with a calibrated two-sigma age range of cal. AD 430–650. Immediately underlying this cist was a preceramic storage pit, the fill of which yielded maize kernels and cobs; juniper bark lining the bottom of this pit returned a radiocarbon date with a calibrated two-sigma age range of cal. AD 60–400.

Table 5.7 presents measurement data on kernels from these two contexts. The preceramic Basketmaker kernels tend to be squat and nearly equal in the three dimensions of height, width, and thickness (isodiametric). In contrast, the early ceramic Basketmaker kernels are comparatively thin in relation to their height and width. In

TABLE 5.7. Comparison of Measurements on Maize Kernels from Preceramic and Early Ceramic Basketmaker Contexts of Atlatl Rock Cave

VARIABLE	PRECERAMIC, FEATURE 24 (n = 12)				EARLY CERAMIC, FEATURE 18 (n = 26)				T-Test	Probability
	MINIMUM	MAXIMUM	MEAN	SD	MINIMUM	MAXIMUM	MEAN	SD		
Height (mm)	5.33	9.46	6.92	1.01	7.41	11.44	9.97	.93	8.847	.0
Width (mm)	5.18	8.82	6.77	1.08	6.04	10.12	8.36	1.16	4.143	.0
Thickness (mm)	4.1	6.22	5.13	.7	3.28	7.1	4.33	.92	−2.980	.006
Area (Height × Width)	33.83	74.17	46.85	10.63	46.09	115.67	83.98	17.14	8.159	.0
Area : Thickness	5.94	18.09	9.44	3.23	7.44	31.35	20.21	5.43	7.613	.0

Note: Karen Adams (personal communication 2007) determined that the preceramic kernels have a pop/flint endosperm texture whereas the early ceramic kernels have a flour endosperm.

addition to the alteration in kernel morphology, there is an abrupt shift in kernel color. Most preceramic kernels are reddish, commonly yellowish red (5YR5/6, 5/8) and reddish yellow (7.5YR7/8), with some that are dark red (10R2.5/2, 3/4, 3/6) and a few that are bright red (off the Munsell soil chart). In contrast, most of the early ceramic kernels are yellow (primarily 10YR7/8). Adams et al. (2006) have documented that the kernel color can have important implications with regard to the conditions of growth and productivity, and the color might thus serve as an easily monitored proxy indicator of this information. The change in kernel color and shape documented at Atlatl Rock Cave seemed like it might correspond to a shift from a popcorn endosperm (preceramic) to a flour endosperm (early ceramic [see Benz 1981 and Doebley and Bohrer 1983:32 for endosperm descriptions]). Karen Adams (personal communication 2007) sectioned some of the kernels and determined that the preceramic kernels have a pop/flint endosperm whereas the early ceramic kernels have a flour endosperm. To what extent this small sample is reflective of wider trends is unknown, but the abruptness of the changes suggests the introduction of a new maize type or landrace that was developed elsewhere, one that might have increased the nutritional value or energetic return of maize.

Continued Foraging

There is no doubt that foraged resources were an important supplement to domesticates, that Basketmaker II groups relied to varying extents on nature's bounty, fickle as it often is in the Southwest. That foraging was important to Puebloan farmers even during the recent past (e.g., Whiting 1939) reveals that there is every reason to expect the same during the interval when crops were initially used on the Colorado Plateau. Equally, though, the use of wild resources or nondomesticates says nothing necessarily about the extent of reliance on food production. Evoking Romer's rule, some authors have argued that farming was adopted so as to maintain a foraging lifestyle (Wills 1988:36)[2]—it was a means to continue a traditional way of life under altered circumstances. Part and parcel with this argument is the assumption that domesticates diffused to the Colorado Plateau and were adopted by foragers. Even if crops came to the plateau with migrant farmers (Berry and Berry 1986; Matson 1991, 2002), the migrants still would have been reliant to some extent on foraged resources, because ultimately, as many have observed, farming on the Colorado Plateau is a risky endeavor. Surviving through bad years no doubt hinged upon gathered and hunted resources, and even during good years crops alone would not have sufficed. If for no other reason than dietary diversity, Basketmaker groups would have sought out plants other than their own crops.

In any discussion of the role of foraged resources it is important to make the distinction between ecologically wild species whose abundance and productivity are basically outside the control or influence of humans and weedy or ruderal plants that thrive in farmed fields and around habitations (virtually any place disturbed by humans [Wetterstrom 1986:18–218]). The former include such critical economic resources as pinyon and ricegrass, whereas the latter include a host of annual plants such as amaranth, beeweed, goosefoot, purslane, and sunflower. Stiger (1977:47, Appendix B) was one of the earliest authors to point out that most of the wild plants common in the Anasazi diet came from disturbed areas such as fields, a pattern documented more fully by Minnis (1989), among others. Ford highlighted that one of the key benefits of farming on the Colorado Plateau was not just domesticates but the weeds that proliferated in the fields: "Cornfield agriculture, including the continued exploitation of old field perennials, increased the edible biomass of the area within the site catchment, increased the predictability of the yield, and improved the nutritional basis of the population" (1984:137). Bye's (1981) discussion of the dietary significance of field weeds among contemporary Mexican farmers can probably be projected backward in time to the Basketmaker occupants on the Colorado Plateau without much distortion.

Foraging in farm fields differed from foraging on the land as previously practiced by Archaic populations. Many of the resources might have been the same, but the high residential mobility needed to access these resources on an annual basis was greatly reduced since they were now concentrated in areas that were already residential focal points. Farming in effect lowered the search costs (see Bettinger 1980; Simms 1987) for exploiting many "wild" resources, and this may have been one of the principal side benefits and perhaps attractions of agriculture. Archaic populations on the Colorado Plateau may have practiced weed encouragement well before the introduction of agriculture (Winter and Hogan 1986), but for farmers, the encouragement of useful weeds would occur as a by-product of agriculture practices and would not require additional costs as it might for hunters and gatherers. Agriculture also may have resulted in the consumption of previously unused or underused plants in addition to the newly introduced crops. Also, some plants such as beeweed (*Cleome* spp.), ground-cherry (*Physalis* spp.), and wolfberry (*Lycium pallidum*) may have been introduced from Mexico along with farming and could thus have constituted new dietary additions (Yarnell 1965). Wetterstrom (1986:55–60) has provided various calculations on the potential productivity of field weeds around Arroyo Hondo, New Mexico, based on the unpublished collecting data of Richard Ford. She was interested simply in the total potential productivity within the "catchment area" of the site and therefore did not calculate return rates. There are plenty of unknowns in this exercise, but it drives home the point that there was far more of value in the Puebloan garden than simply the domesticates.

Flotation samples from NMRAP Basketmaker sites document the use of such weedy taxa as goosefoot (*Chenopodium* sp.), purslane (*Portulaca* sp.), bugseed (*Corispermum* sp.), and pigweed (*Amaranthus* sp.), among other taxa (Table 5.8). Goosefoot is by far the most common seed recovered in the samples and the most ubiquitous potential food item overall within all samples, although maize is equally or more common when just samples from primary habitations are considered. The consumption of these and other weedy taxa is confirmed by the contents of human feces from the Rainbow Plateau (Desha Cave 1; Table 5.9) and elsewhere (Aasen 1984; Androy 2003; Rob-

TABLE 5.8. Potential Subsistence Remains of "Wild" Plants Recovered from Flotation Samples of Navajo Mountain Road Archaeological Project Basketmaker Sites

CATEGORY	TAXON/ITEM	n	UBIQUITY (%)
Seeds	*Amaranthus*	7	3.6
	Cheno-Am	7	3.6
	Chenopodium	125	64.4
	Compositae	1	.5
	Corispermum	20	10.3
	Cycloloma	7	3.6
	Descurainia	1	.5
	Echinocereus	2	1.1
	Eragrostis	2	1.1
	Gramineae	17	8.8
	Poaceae, small	8	4.1
	Poaceae, medium	3	1.5
	Helianthus	2	1.0
	Juniperus	8	4.1
	Malva	2	1.0
	Malvaceae	4	2.1
	Achnatherum hymenoides	13	6.7
	Polygonum	1	.5
	Portulaca	24	12.4
	Sphaeralcea	2	1.0
	Unidentified	14	7.2
Other Remains	Cactaceae pad	1	.6
	Juglans major nutshell	1	.6
	Pinus umbo/scale	8	4.6
	Pinus nutshell	7	4.0
	Unidentified fruit/pericarp	7	4.0

ins 2000), which attest to the importance of bugseed, amaranth, goosefoot, sunflower, ground-cherry, and tansy mustard. Seeds are the most commonly identified constituents of feces and flotation samples, but the leaves and stems from many of these plants were probably commonly consumed as field greens. The absence of maize in the Rainbow Plateau feces is uncommon among Basketmaker II coprolite samples, where maize is present in significant quantities (see summary in Matson and Chisholm 2007), but these other samples came from sites that were likely used for winter habitation, which does not appear to have been the case for Desha Cave 1. This would appear to provide another example of how seasonally used sites (field stations) provide samples that can underrepresent the dietary significance of maize. The commonly used weedy species may have been cultivated or encouraged to grow in and around fields and gardens or simply tolerated and exploited as a useful by-product of the farming effort.

As for ecologically wild plants, ricegrass (*Achnatherum hymenoides*) and pinyon (*Pinus edulis*) are two that seem

TABLE 5.9. Rank Order (5 Highest, 1 Lowest) of Taxa from Eight Coprolites from Desha Cave 1

Taxon	Common Name	1	2	3	4[a]	5	6	7[b]	8	Score	Ubiquity (%)
Achnatherum hymenoides	Ricegrass	5	—	5	—	5	5	—	2	22	63
Fibers (dicotyledons)		3	—	1	2	—	—	—	—	6	38
Unidentified Plant Material		—	5	—	—	—	—	2	5	12	38
Chenopodium sp.	Goosefoot	2	—	2	—	2	—	—	—	6	38
Corispermum sp.	Bugseed	—	—	—	5	—	—	5	—	10	25
Cucurbita pepo	Squash/pumpkin	—	2	—	—	—	—	—	2	4	25
Bulb Epidermis		3	—	3	—	—	—	—	—	6	25
Helianthus sp.	Sunflower	—	—	—	1	—	—	1	—	2	25
Physalis sp.[c]	Ground-cherry	—	—	3	—	—	—	—	2	5	25
Amaranthus sp.	Amaranth	—	—	—	—	—	—	—	1	1	13
Descurania sp.	Tansy mustard	—	1	—	—	—	—	—	—	1	13
Cleome sp.	Beeweed	—	—	—	—	—	—	1	—	1	13
Insect		—	2	—	—	—	—	—	—	1	13
Small Bone Fragments		—	2	—	—	—	—	—	—	2	13

Note: Data are from Geib and Robins 2003.
[a] Portion dated, 1660 ± 60 BP (Beta-175650).
[b] Portion dated, 1640 ± 60 BP (Beta-175651).
[c] Seeds and fruit.

especially important for Basketmaker populations, with data from the Rainbow Plateau providing evidence for limited use (Tables 5.8–5.10). It is true that ricegrass can eventually proliferate in long-abandoned fields (e.g., Ford 1984:137; Stiger 1977:49), but across much of the Colorado Plateau the vast low-elevation, sand-covered benches and flats sustain a density of ricegrass that doubtless would have been preferred for gathering this resource. This is readily appreciated in any area today that is not overgrazed, such as in the portions of the Glen Canyon National Recreation Area that are closed to livestock. Prior to the arrival of cattle in the American Southwest, ricegrass formed almost pure stands, with "old-timers" telling of rangelands that resembled fields of grain (Forest Service 1937:G88). Ricegrass grows prolifically in sandy soils, and during years of good winter and spring precipitation it produces an abundant harvest of seeds in early summer (late June to early July depending on elevation). This grass will occasionally produce a second crop in fall if summer rains are good.

The dietary importance of grass seed to Native Americans on the Colorado Plateau is well documented. Nearly all hunting-gathering and agricultural societies at the time of initial ethnographic study relied to varying degree on one or more grass species (Bohrer 1975; Castetter 1935; Elmore 1944; Kelly 1964; Stevenson 1915; Whiting 1939). Grass seed was so essential for some groups, such as the Paiute, that historic stock overgrazing resulted in starvation and was one factor that led to cultural disintegration (Bohrer 1975:203, 206; but cf. Simms 1985:123–124). Analyses of archaeological samples of macrobotanical and pollen remains from feces, middens, and features have consistently shown that grass was an important dietary item for prehistoric agriculturalists of the Colorado Plateau (e.g., Aasen 1984; Bohrer 1975; Fry and Hall 1973, 1986; Gasser 1982; Geib and Casto 1985; Lepofsky 1986; Matson and Chisholm 1991; Minnis 1989; Stiger 1977). Ricegrass in particular is the one grass species of great relevance to farmers on the Colorado Plateau. Beyond the obvious benefits of its nutritious starchy seeds, the dietary significance of ricegrass can be attributed to its time of maturation. Bohrer (1975:199) has stressed that cool-season grasses such as ricegrass, which use winter and spring moisture to promote growth, provide a source of calories at a time when other food supplies are in short supply. She sees early summer as a critical time for both hunter-gatherers and agriculturalists since "stored food supplies descend to their lowest annual level [and] new crops are immature" (1975:199).

The dietary significance of ricegrass for Basketmaker populations is confirmed by the common occurrence of this resource in Basketmaker feces and flotation samples. In the Desha Cave feces, ricegrass had the highest ubiquity and rank order of all plant taxa, clearly indicating that its seeds were an important dietary item (Geib and Robins 2003). Desha Cave 1, which yielded the feces, is located on a low-elevation bench that would have provided an excellent area for harvesting ricegrass prior to recent

TABLE 5.10. Macrobotanical Remains Observed in Dry-Screened Matrix Samples from Basketmaker Layers at Atlatl Rock Cave

TAXON	PART	BURNED	BASKETMAKER II, UNIT IV	BASKETMAKER III, UNIT V
Amelanchier sp.	seed	+	—	1
Atriplex sp.	leaf	–	2	—
Atriplex sp.	seed	–	1	—
Cactaceae	2 spines/areolae	–	2	—
Cactaceae	3+ spines/areolae	+	1	1
Carex sp.	seed	–	2	—
Cercocarpus intricatus	leaf	+	1	—
Cercocarpus intricatus	leaf	–	1	—
Cheno-Am	seed	+	8	5
Cheno-Am	seed	–	14	5
Compositae	seed	–	1	1
Corispermum villosum	seed	–	23	7
Cucurbita moschata	rind (1 mm)	–	—	1
Cyperus sp.	seed	–	1	—
Gramineae	roots	–	1	—
Gramineae	seed	–	6	3
Gramineae	stems	–	100	—
Helianthus annus	seed	–	1	—
Helianthus petiolaris	seed	+	—	—
Helianthus petiolaris	seed	–	1	1
Juniperus osteosperma	seed	–	1	2
Juniperus osteosperma	twig	–	9	2
Juniperus sp.	bark	–	100	1
Juniperus sp.	cone	–	1	—
Nicotiana attenuata	seed	–	3	—
Phragmites australis	leaf	–	—	1
Pinus edulis	cone	–	2	—
Pinus edulis	needle	+	—	1
Pinus edulis	needle	–	8	1
Pinus edulis	seed	+	—	—
Pinus edulis	seed	–	13	10
Purshia tridentata	leaf	+	1	—
Quercus sp.	acorn	–	—	3
Rhus aromatica	leaf	–	—	1
Rosa sp.	seed	–	3	3
Sambucus sp.	seed	–	1	—
Sporobolus sp.	seed	+	1	—
Sporobolus sp.	seed	–	100	2
Achnatherum hymenoides	seed	–	11	2
Unknown	seed	–	1	1
Zea mays	kernel	–	—	2

Note: Analysis by Nancy Coulam. Counts of 100 denote samples with at least this many seeds.

overgrazing. The analyses of Basketmaker feces from Grand Gulch and Butler Wash also document the common consumption of ricegrass (Aasen 1984; Androy 2003; Robins 2000). Flotation samples from NMRAP Basketmaker sites contain some ricegrass seeds, but the samples did not adequately reflect the importance of this plant since the overall ubiquity was just 7 percent.

Jones and Madsen (1989:Table 1) took a preliminary stab at deriving quantitative estimates of the costs and benefits of transporting different resources including ricegrass. According to their calculations, ricegrass seed has a maximum transport distance of 85 km compared to 829 km for tansy mustard seeds or 812 km for pinyon nuts; this is because ricegrass is a low-ranked resource (high handling costs—calories expended relative to calories obtained [see Simms 1985, 1987]) compared to the other two. Rhode (1990:Tables 2–3) presented some refinements to Jones and Madsen's calculations while taking into account the returns of harvesting a local resource relative to harvesting and transporting a distant resource. He also factored in round-trip travel, which reduced the maximum transport distance of ricegrass to 48 km, and further added in the costs of moving a family group, which reduced the transport distance of any resource by almost a third—so about 14 km for ricegrass for a round-trip. Given the relative transport costs of various resources, Rhode concludes that "it is never profitable to transport distant resources that rank lower in return rate than local resources. For this reason, a group may sometimes be better off residing in a resource patch with a relatively low return rate and using other resource patches with higher return rates on a logistical basis" (1990:417). Essentially this same conclusion was also reached by Barlow and Metcalfe: "Given an array of resources in the diet, the processing characteristics of each [whether high or low ranked] may influence which resources are most effectively exploited through strategies of logistic procurement and long distance transport, and which are more likely to affect the locations of residential camps" (1996: 368). In the matrix of 10 resources that Rhode considered, ricegrass is at the bottom, meaning that it would make the most economic sense to live in a dense patch of ricegrass and move other resources to that location. When seasonality of harvest is also considered, there is even more incentive to locate in a dense stand of ricegrass, because, as observed by Bohrer (1975), few resources are available at the time that ricegrass seed is ripe. The few resources that might be available during the ricegrass harvest, such as the seeds of tansy mustard and peppergrass, can be profitably exploited on a logistic basis according to Rhode's calculations and transported to the location of ricegrass harvesting. Based on transport decay curves for two resources, one of which is far higher ranked than ricegrass (pinyon) and one that is even lower ranked (pickleweed), Barlow and Metcalfe conclude that

> it is always more efficient to move the consumer to the resource patch than it is to move the resource to the consumer.... [P]rocurement...from a base camp outside the resource patch is only expected when the choice of the camp location is a tradeoff between other competing demands, such as access to water, fuel, other foods, or perhaps previously stored foods [1996:365].

This finding appears to explain in no uncertain terms ethnographic accounts of Puebloan towns vacated during the ricegrass harvest (see Bohrer 1975).

Another point that comes out of Jones and Madsen's study concerns the storage of resources for future consumption—basically the generation of surpluses. They conclude that "a high return rate should be the best indicator of whether collection in excess of consumption is likely" (1989:533). Ricegrass is such a low-return resource relative to pursuit and processing costs that it is an unlikely resource for generating a storable surplus, especially if the harvest area occurred outside the distance of the foraging range around a habitation (roughly 3–5 km).

Pinyon pine is another wild resource of evident major importance in Basketmaker diet. This is not reflected in the feces from Desha Cave 1, which is below the elevation range of this species, but it is evident in the fecal and sediment samples from the Basketmaker II layers of Turkey Pen Cave (see summary in Matson and Chisholm 1991), a site situated in the pinyon zone on Cedar Mesa, Utah. Flotation samples from Atlatl Rock Cave and several of the NMRAP Basketmaker habitations also contain pinyon nuts and cone parts but with low overall ubiquity. Of course it is difficult to evaluate the reliance on this resource based on these data. Pinyon is, in Minnis's (1989: 548) terms, an erratic resource, such that, despite its high energy value (high rank [Simms 1985, 1987]), it cannot be depended upon. It will, however, be heavily used when available. The energetic value of pinyon makes it a likely candidate for long-distant transport back to a residential site (Jones and Madsen 1989; Rhode 1990), especially if the nonfood parts of the resource such as cones and hulls are removed (Barlow and Metcalfe 1996). As such, Minnis's statement should perhaps be qualified to read that pinyon is undependable in any one local area but that on a panregional basis it is far more reliable. Using Rhode's (1990:417–418) cost figure for a round-trip move of a family group to harvest pinyon, which yields a maximum transport distance of 136 km, a Basketmaker family from Navajo Mountain could have reached the Kaibab Plateau on the west, the Henry Mountains on the north, and almost to the Carrizo Mountains on the east. Included in this area at much closer distances are such prime yet diverse pinyon nut–harvesting areas as northern Black Mesa (80 km), the Kaiparowits Plateau (40 km), Cedar Mesa (90 km), and the Paria Plateau (90 km). Moreover, a family group harvesting pinyon nuts might quickly generate far more than they could ever carry as a group back to their home, caching the rest for later retrieval by an adult male in the group, which would then raise the maximum transport distance for a round-trip to 475 km (Rhode 1990:Table 3) or increase the "profit" margin if distance stayed the same. The ability to travel to where the nut mast for a given year is productive could have a leveling effect on the erratic nature of pinyon harvests. The key in all of this perhaps has more to do with the social environment than with counting calories spent in harvesting and travel. If territoriality and boundary defense became a concern during the early agricultural period, then how was travel through other people's terrain mediated or facilitated so as to exploit this resource? When available, the productivity of pinyon is such that the nut becomes a common good and it does not make much economic sense to keep others out. For example, Phillips (1909:220) reported a yield of 73 kg of pinyon nuts per hectare of New Mexico pinyon–juniper forest, and assuming roughly 6,340 calories per kilogram of nutmeats (Barlow and Metcalfe 1996:358), this weight of resource translates into 462,820 calories or 231 days of food (assuming a 2,000 calories/day diet). This yield per hectare might be high, but even if cut in half the productivity of pinyon is enormous given the vast tracks of pinyon–juniper forest on the Colorado Plateau.

Basketmaker Settlement

Early excavators implicitly recognized that Basketmaker II groups used different places on the landscape for certain purposes. Kidder and Guernsey (1919:206–207), for example, referred to some Basketmaker rockshelters as burial caves, some as a combination of both food storage and burial, and some as "dwelling places." Although believing that rockshelters were inhabited, they thought such use was for rather short periods and perhaps just during winter. In a speculative but perspicacious mode they state, "It seems probable, therefore, that the people lived during a large part of the year in the open, where they presumably erected temporary houses analogous to the summer shelters of the Navajo" (1919:207). Essentially this was as far as discussion went concerning Basketmaker II land use until the 1960s. By then, the discipline of archaeology had matured somewhat, and settlement studies had become almost de rigueur. Since settlement pattern studies depend on regional survey and excavation data, in the Southwest, large CRM projects were an excellent source of such data, with the Glen Canyon Project of the late 1950s and early 1960s an early example (Jennings 1966). The project provided the database for the first detailed reconstruction of Basketmaker II settlement-subsistence practices, by William Lipe (1967, 1970) in his Ph.D. dissertation.

Lipe's study area was the Red Rock Plateau, a large triangle of land in southeast Utah between the San Juan and Colorado rivers, west of the Red House Cliffs, and moderately close to the N16 project area. He identified 17 sites as having Basketmaker II components, all of which he classified as part of Colton's (1939) White Dog phase. Lipe's reconstruction involved several site types and their relationship to making a living, as well as the interrelationship between two site clusters—Moqui Canyon and Castle Creek—that he interpreted as contemporaneous communities. The site types consisted of habitations, camps, and storage shelters. The latter contained little or no evidence of use beyond cache pits and probable storage residue, and at least one appeared to be located away from known habitations. The open habitations in the site cluster along Castle Creek were the only ones to have living structures, with only one house excavated at the site of Lone Tree Dune. The habitations of the Moqui Canyon cluster consisted of shelters without obvious living structures; their identification as domiciles stemmed from the presence of "rather heavy midden deposits" (Lipe 1970:98). The camps contained grinding tools, projectile points, and abundant flaking debris; lacked structures or storage features; and were located in areas more suited to gathering than farming. Lacking direct dates, I have some doubt about the temporal assignment of the camps, at least those in the Camp Canyon tributary of Moqui Canyon, but I have no doubt that Basketmaker settlement did involve campsites.

Expanding upon his dissertation research, Lipe excavated three Basketmaker II habitations on Cedar Mesa that were similar to the Lone Tree Dune (Lipe 1978; Pollock 2001), and then, with R. G. Matson, he initiated the Cedar Mesa Project, explicitly designed to investigate settlement and subsistence patterns. Given the heavy Basketmaker II use of shelters in Grand Gulch, it is perhaps no wonder that Lipe and Matson documented more than 100 Basketmaker II open sites in their sample survey units. They assigned the sites to five different types: small limited-activity sites, limited-activity sites, camps, habitations, and lithic-reduction sites (Matson 1991:80–90). About half of the sites classified as habitations lacked surface evidence of structures, but they had tool assemblages similar to those with visible structures. The sites of this group were interpreted as playing a principal residential role for the Basketmaker occupants of Cedar Mesa, including winter dwelling. The spatial distribution of these sites led to the interpretation that they were grouped as "dispersed villages" (Matson 1991:82). Habitations were concentrated in areas of prime agricultural potential. Campsites were interpreted as places well away from habitations that were favorably situated for the exploitation of such principal wild resources as ricegrass, pinyon, and game animals; they were seasonally occupied for short duration but used repeatedly, resulting in considerable artifact accumulation (Matson 1991:82, 89). Limited-activity sites were interpreted mainly as "field stations," but with some related to hunting or other tasks.

BMAP is another project with data useful for the analysis of western Basketmaker II settlement. Susan Bearden (1984) presented the first detailed analysis of Basketmaker II sites (Lolomai phase) for the project. Originally written as a master's thesis in 1981, her study only included sites excavated through 1979 ($n = 7$); it thus omitted more than 80 percent of the Basketmaker II sites ultimately investigated. More detrimental, it labored under two fundamental problems: poor chronological control and an inappropriate ethnographic model. The former stems from a reliance on wood charcoal for radiocarbon dating, resulting in a vastly exaggerated overall time depth for the BMAP Basketmaker II occupation as well as erroneously long occupation spans for many sites. Smiley (1985, 1998a, 1998b) adroitly tackled this problem head-on, resulting in a greatly shortened overall time span for the Lolomai phase, restricted to the first several hundred years of the Christen era, which also vastly reduced the occupation spans of individual sites to no more than a few centuries. The ethnographic model came from Steward's study of the Paiute and western Shoshoni; notwithstanding the utility of the source, Matson (1991:104–105) rightly criticized this choice and some of the BMAP roots behind it. To be fair, a Southern Paiute model has deeper roots (Lipe 1970:97). This ethnographic record might not be applicable even for understanding the Archaic archaeological record of the region (Geib et al. 2001:369–373), let alone that of preceramic farmers. The intuitive site types recognized by Bearden (1984:Table 5) were large and small habitations and special-activity sites or camps. She provided useful data on the Basketmaker II lithic assemblages well above and beyond the original site reports.

A more useful summary of Basketmaker II site types for northern Black Mesa resulted from Smiley's (1985: 261–330, 1993:248–250) dissertation research, which included the full sample of 35 Basketmaker II sites excavated by the BMAP. His five general site types were open camps, nonstorage habitations, earthen pit storage habitations, bedrock pithouse settlements, and rockshelters. Smiley recently modified his scheme slightly by substituting the term *proto-villages* for bedrock pithouse settlements, redefining this category as "settlements with from six to twelve structures" (2002a:53). Eliminating the bedrock reference is a welcome change because it broadens the potential utility of the site type beyond the Peabody Coal Company mining area on northern Black Mesa. As demonstrated by the NMRAP site of Kin Kahuna, multiple structures at Basketmaker II sites do not necessarily equate with multiple families because few if any of the structures may be contemporaneous. As such, sites like this may fall far short of being a village or even a proto-village. Rockshelters are not comparable with the other site types because they can include sites functionally equivalent to the other types but occurring within naturally sheltered settings. Smiley (1993:250), among others, suggested that many rockshelters probably served as habitations, but some were used almost exclusively for storage—examples from the Rainbow Plateau include the Desha Caves (Geib and Robins 2003; Schilz 1979), and Lipe (1970:100–103) discusses similar sites from the Red Rock Plateau.

NMRAP Sites and Settlement Types

The NMRAP sample of Basketmaker II sites can be organized into groups that generally decrease in size and complexity from large sites with many and diverse structures and features to small sites with few and simple features and no structures. The presence or absence of dwellings provides a significant first-order split between sites designated as habitations and those considered as camps or sites of other limited purpose. It is, of course, essential to factor in at least two variables: (1) to what extent prior site disturbance has eliminated features and (2) whether ROW restrictions prevented disclosure of all features.

Most of the investigated Basketmaker II sites were residential in nature, containing at least one living structure and middens of various size with artifacts and an abundance of burned rock, both limestone and sandstone. Matson et al. (1988) note that burned limestone was a typical attribute of Basketmaker II habitations on Cedar Mesa, and the same is clearly true for the northern Kayenta region. Within the group of sites called habitations, some have large-volume storage features and others lack these. Indeed, the presence or absence of storage features at open habitations tends to correlate with other aspects of the archaeological record. As discussed below, I have designated structural sites with large-volume storage facilities as primary habitations and those lacking such features as secondary habitations (with one notable exception). I use these labels with some degree of uneasiness, and other names were considered, such as permanent vs. seasonal habitations or long-term vs. short-term residences. An initial summary of the N16 Basketmaker II sites (Geib and Spurr 2000) adopted Smiley's (1985, 1998c) designations of habitations with and without storage, which are more descriptive of content and less inferential of settlement role.

Although the presence or absence of structures and storage features was critical in making site type inferences, it was also important to consider other aspects of the archaeological record, such as the extent and nature of trash deposition and the artifact assemblage. For example, excavation located no storage features at the Mountainview site, but the abundant and diverse artifacts and moderately rich trash midden distinguish this site from other habitations lacking food-storage features. A primary residential role seems highly plausible for the Mountainview site, and in this instance prior disturbance might have removed storage features. There are also several cases where prior disturbance, either from natural causes or from construction activity, appears to have eliminated evidence of structures but a residential role is indicated by other evidence—at Scorpion Heights natural erosion appears to have eliminated a house that was once associated with a small midden, and at Three Dog Site prior road construction appears to have done the same thing. Artifact assemblages and other remains are also important for distinguishing among various nonhabitation sites used for a variety of more limited or specialized activities.

Primary Habitations

The largest and most complex Basketmaker sites for the N16 ROW are residential sites with pithouses, extensive midden deposits containing abundant and diverse artifact assemblages, and numerous large storage features. The NMRAP partially excavated two excellent examples—The Pits and Kin Kahuna (Figure 5.13). Both are aceramic, with initial occupancy during the third or fourth centuries BC. Kin Kahuna continued to be occupied up until about cal. AD 400, contemporaneous with the first appearance of pottery in the region, whereas The Pits had been abandoned by about cal. AD 200. Long-duration residential use of both locations is indicated based on numerous AMS radiocarbon assays on maize and other high-quality samples. These sites appear to have functioned as semipermanent residences for a few families—the primary home base from which annual settlement and subsistence tasks were based.

I was somewhat hesitant to apply the adjective *primary*, in that it implies that any single Basketmaker group had but one important settlement that they used on a yearly basis. It is possible that they had two such settlements or perhaps even more, but it is worth differentiating these places from those that appear to have been used seasonally and perhaps for relatively short intervals. Indeed, it is in the context of contrasting the records of these two different settlement types that there is a need for a term that encapsulates the differences. I have no qualms about labeling the group of sites discussed next as secondary habitations, but what are they subsidiary to if not a principal place of residence? Admittedly, I assume that the Basketmaker settlements excavated for the NMRAP form a cohesive whole, that they are the differentiated parts of an integrated settlement-subsistence strategy. If not, then some Basketmaker groups lived in the settlements here classified as secondary habitations using an annual sequence of one-month stands, whereas other Basketmaker groups lived in settlements for much of the year. Fundamental reasons for thinking of the one group of residences as secondary include their lack of storage facilities and their comparatively less substantially built houses, both of which suggest that occupation did not occur during the dead of winter.

An important aspect of a primary habitation is abundant food-storage capacity, enough to tide a group over through the winter and spring prior to the ready availability of plant foods, whether grown in fields (crops and weeds) or harvested from the wild. Storage occurred in deep bell-shaped pits, in shallower large pits that may have had domed roofs, and in slab-lined cists. There is an evident temporal order to the preference for deep bell-shaped pits followed by wider-mouthed pits lined with sandstone slabs (slab-lined cists), at least at open sites,

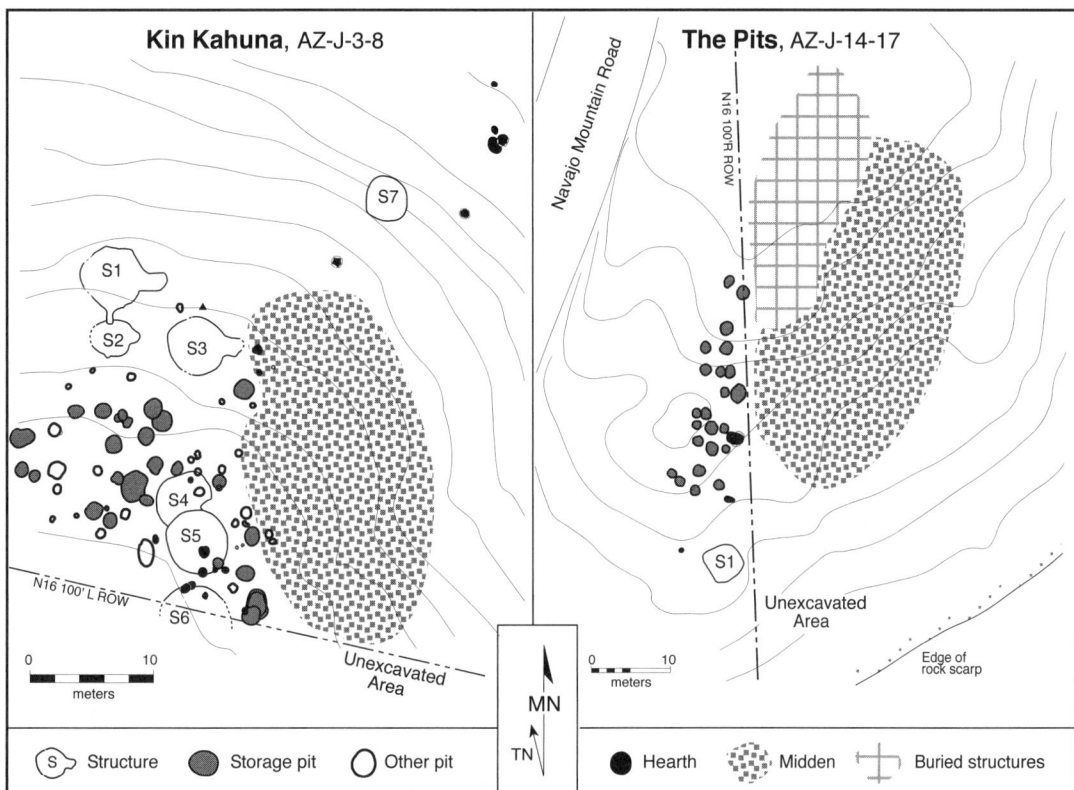

Figure 5.13. Examples of Basketmaker II primary habitations partially excavated by the Navajo Mountain Road Archaeological Project.

with the former being the earliest form. Slab-lined cists appear to have been used earlier in rockshelters than at open sites, or at least few Basketmaker II open sites of the N16 ROW have slab-lined storage features, whereas virtually all Basketmaker II shelters of the area have such features. As discussed in detail below, all direct dates on Basketmaker II shelters of the northern Kayenta region fall within the Christian era; thus dating of the slab-lined cists for the area is currently no older than about cal. AD 100. The only slab-lined cist at any of the open Basketmaker II sites of the NMRAP is at Big Bend, but the feature lies outside the ROW and remains undated. All of the other NMRAP Basketmaker II sites contain deep bell-shaped storage pits rather than shallow slab-lined storage cists. Undated open Basketmaker II habitations on Piute Mesa contain cists; whether they also have bell-shaped storage pits requires further excavation.

Large-Volume Storage: The Pits. The nature of storage facilities at early primary habitations for the northern Kayenta region is best illustrated by examples from the site known as The Pits. As described in chapter 3, this site is situated on a high bedrock ridge (elevation of 2,175 m) above two incised drainages. Surface evidence indicates that much of the habitation lies outside the N16 ROW, and excavation within the ROW appeared to confirm this. Within an area of about 300 m² at the eastern edge of the ROW, NNAD archaeologists excavated a cluster of 24 large, bell-shaped storage pits along with a surface structure almost 5 m in diameter and several hearths. These pits varied in size from .2 to 1.6 m³ (mean of .7 m³), with a combined storage capacity of almost 17 m³.[3] The storage pits are arranged along the crest of a sandy rise that extends outside the ROW, where additional storage pits, most structures, and other features certainly occur. The sandy rise was ideally suited for subterranean storage features: besides being well drained, the deep sand is easily excavated when damp but hardens upon drying to form stable walls. In addition, the Basketmaker II occupants used an intense but brief fire provided by brush and the like to bake the walls. The pits appear to have been purposefully laid out in rough north–south and east–west alignments, which may have simplified their relocation once sealed and buried.

B. Huckell (1995:120–121) has provided numbers for estimating how many kilograms of corn could have been stored in bell-shaped pits, how many calories this could represent, and how many person-days of food might be represented. Applying his figures to The Pits yields the following results. The 17 m³ of storage capacity provided by the 24 excavated pits could have held 312,800 maize ears (Huckell lists 9,200 ears per .5 m³). This number of ears yields 6,881.6 kg of kernels (Huckell lists 22 g of kernels per ear). This weight of corn provides 24,429,680 calories (based on the Food and Agricultural Organization [1953] figure of 3,550 calories per kilogram). Assuming a diet of 2,000 calories per day, the storage pits at the site could have held 12,215 person-days of maize or 33 years of surplus for one person. Obviously there are plenty of unknowns and assumptions in these calculations, but they are provocative, and they point to the inescapable conclusion that the occupants saved a large volume of food at this one location. These features may have held items other than corn, but that may not reduce the overall caloric figure that much, if at all, depending on the types of resource represented. Indeed, if pinyon nuts had been stored in the pits, a resource that yields about 7,140 calories per kilogram (Madsen 1986:Table 1), then the caloric yield of the pits would be vastly greater. Squash, if stored as whole fruits, is one resource that would have reduced the caloric yield of the pits.

The largest assumption about these figures is that the pits were all used at about the same time, something that is not the case based on the existing radiocarbon dates. More important, the effective use-life of these features remains a large unknown. Several years of use seem likely, but would the pits have remained functional for 10 years? If these features were usable for just five years, then 120 years of food storage could be represented. Assuming that only one pit was in use at a time and using the average size of .7 m³, it could have held 510 person-days of maize.

Given the abundant storage potential of these features, I believe that The Pits served as a winter residence. The nature of surface evidence outside the ROW is consistent with this interpretation. A midden of abundant burned rock, charcoal-stained soil, and artifacts covers the entire eastern slope of the site, an area 1,600 m² in size. Based on this accumulation I have no doubt that the excavated features represent just the storage component of a major residential site and that several pithouses lie buried in a level area just beyond excavation limits. Unfortunately, we could not excavate outside the ROW, so the number and nature of the likely pithouses at this site remain a matter of speculation. However, the project has an acceptable analogue for the types of features and other remains that the surface evidence is indicative of in the site known as Kin Kahuna.

A Pithouse Hamlet: Kin Kahuna. Considerably more of Kin Kahuna lay within the N16 ROW than was the case for The Pits, allowing about half of this Basketmaker II settlement to be excavated. NNAD archaeologists uncovered seven pithouses, 26 storage pits, 32 other pits, 17 hearths, extensive trash deposits, and human burials (see Figure 5.13). Because half or more of this site also lies outside the N16 ROW, its true size and complexity remain unknown.[4] Six of the houses were completely excavated, whereas the seventh, which lay mostly outside the ROW, was only sectioned along its northern edge. Surrounding the houses are numerous storage pits of various sizes. Eighteen pits are of the bell-shaped storage variety, like those at The Pits, whereas eight others are shallow with straight sides, but still large. The bell-shaped storage pits range in size from .2 to 1.6 m³ (average .6 m³), with a combined storage capacity of 10.4 m³. Estimating storage capacity of the eight other large pits is difficult because they might have had domed superstructures of sticks and mortar, as seen in certain sheltered sites (e.g., Guernsey and Kidder 1921:Plate 9); such domes would have added considerable volume.

Kin Kahuna has evidence for long-term occupancy based on the superpositioning of structures and other features and the filling of abandoned structures and storage pits with rich midden accumulations (see Figure 5.6). The oldest and deepest house (Structure 5), at slightly more than 1 m deep, had been totally trash filled, with another house partially superimposed over it, which was in turn trash filled (Structure 4). Although workers excavated only a relatively small fraction of the cultural stratum and midden, only about 10 percent or less, a large quantity of remains was recovered. This is perhaps most easily appreciated by debitage and faunal bone, with total counts for these of 9,207 and 2,380, respectively. The density of remains within the trashy fill of Structure 5 exceeds 200 per cubic meter for flakes and 100 per cubic meter for bone. With maize radiocarbon dates ranging from about 400 cal. BC to cal. AD 400, it is clear that Basketmaker occupancy of this one location, besides being intensive, was long lived. An obvious reason for the long-duration use of this location was the prime agricultural land that lay immediately north of the site at the confluence of two small drainages. The importance of maize for the occupants

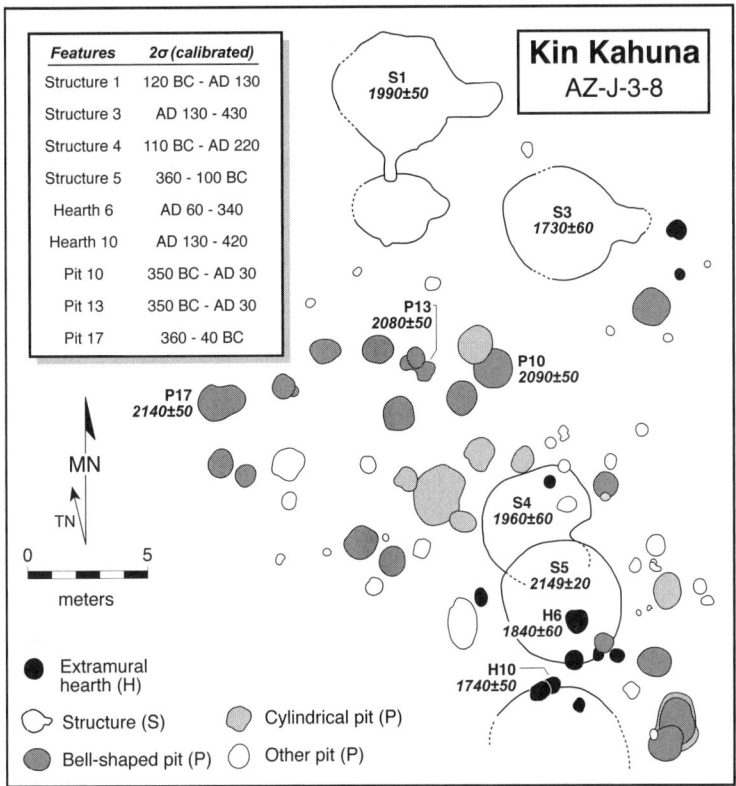

Figure 5.14. Distribution of dated features at Kin Kahuna illustrating feature accretion through time.

of Kin Kahuna seemed obvious during excavation, because workers found corn kernels and cupules (sometimes cobs) in most features, either while digging or in sediment screening (see previous subsistence discussion).

Kin Kahuna seems to fit Smiley's "proto-village" (2002a:53) site type, in that it contains more than six structures. Nonetheless, the term *proto-village* appears potentially misleading for a site like Kin Kahuna because extensive dating of maize samples has shown that few if any of the structures were contemporaneous (Figure 5.14). Indeed, based on radiocarbon dates, only Structures 1 and 4 have the potential to have been in use at the same time. Yet, given the hundreds of years commonly represented by radiocarbon dates, even these two houses may never have been in use simultaneously. Thus, no more than one or two families probably occupied the site at any one interval, making it considerably smaller than a village. The probable small group size of the site is underscored by the size of the houses, whose floor areas are less than 20 m².

A Habitation with Early Pottery: Mountainview. One of the more interesting sites excavated by the NMRAP is Mountainview, a Basketmaker habitation with early pottery. As reported in chapter 3, excavation of virtually the entire site revealed a shallow pit structure, a midden, 12 basin hearths, three slab-lined hearths, and four shallow pits (Figure 5.15). The pottery from this site consists of brownware identified as Obelisk Utility. Six statistically contemporaneous radiocarbon dates on maize from both the structure and midden place site occupancy sometime between cal. AD 220 and 350 (two-sigma range). The site provides evidence of pottery use on the Rainbow Plateau in the northern Kayenta Anasazi region several hundred years earlier than was previously thought.

The single structure occupied a slight level area on the crest of a narrow ridge, with its eastern entryway opening onto a moderately steep slope covered with a thin trash deposit. The structure was a shallow, roughly circular pithouse that probably had a superstructure of small logs and brush covered with earth. Interior features of the unprepared sandy floor comprised a central clay-rimmed hearth, an ashpit, four small pits, and eight postholes. In the southeast corner of the house was a storage area, separated from the main room by a low wall of upright sandstone slabs. A similar storage area was probably present in the northeast corner of the house, but machinery had cut

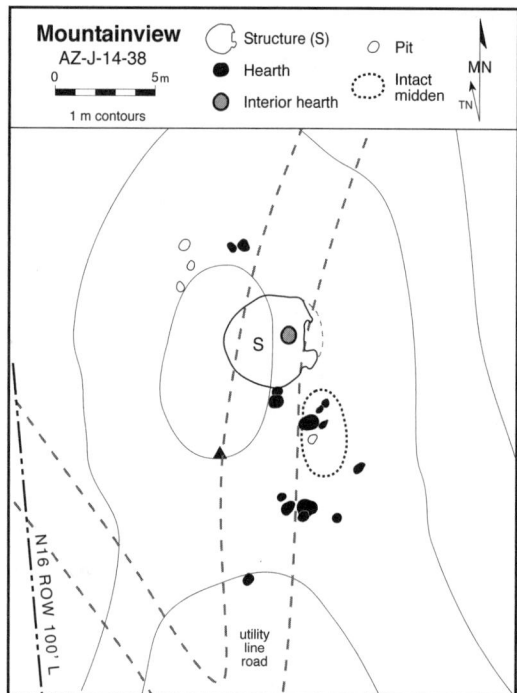

Figure 5.15. The Mountainview site, a Basketmaker primary habitation with Obelisk Utility.

through this portion of the structure during the construction of a nearby power line. The structure's interior measured 3.7 × 4.4 m, providing about 14 m² of floor space. The walled-off storage area(s) added additional use space. The occupants left behind part of their household assemblage upon abandonment; a large metate leaned against the lower wall in the southeast part of the structure, and three manos occurred elsewhere within the floor fill. The southeastern quadrant of the structure floor and floor fill yielded significantly more artifacts than any other area including several bone artifacts, projectile points, and mineral specimens. Artifacts from the storage area at the southeast edge of the structure included two partially reconstructible Obelisk Utility jars, heavily sooted from use in cooking. More fragments of Obelisk Utility came from the trash midden, contributing to the total of 393 sherds from the site. Lithic artifacts were especially abundant from the midden, with the total site assemblage consisting of more than 4,000 flakes; more than 200 used flakes, flaked-stone tools, and cores; 18 manos and metates; and 18 other stone artifacts (see Table 5.1).

Given the presence of just one small structure, the site was certainly occupied by no more than a single family. They probably used the site for perhaps several sequential seasons; more than one year is indicated by the amount of remains, the size of the midden, the number of hearths, and some feature superpositioning. The lack of storage features at this site raises a question about its settlement role—whether it should be classified as a primary or secondary habitation. The quantity, density, and diversity of remains certainly distinguish this site from those classified as secondary habitations. For example, the site known as Panorama House (discussed in greater detail below) produced less than 6 percent of the flakes and flaked-stone tools as Mountainview and less than 17 percent of the manos/metates and other stone artifacts. ROW restrictions to excavation limited midden sampling somewhat in this case, but not so with Sin Sombra (also discussed below), which produced less than 22 percent of the flakes and flaked-stone tools of Mountainview and less than 17 percent of the manos and metates. What cannot be known in the case of Mountainview is whether heavy machinery bladed away near-surface storage cists.

Located just 500–600 m upslope from Mountainview is a large Basketmaker habitation (AZ-J-14-54) with the same Obelisk Utility pottery assemblage (Figure 5.16). This site has surface evidence for at least five structures scattered on level portions of a sandstone ridge, and there could well be more along with probable storage cists. At least one of the houses is entirely lined with upright sandstone slabs. It is impossible to say whether all of the houses were contemporaneous, but the artifact assemblages associated with each are similar, including early brownware pottery along with arrow- and dart points. This is just one of several Basketmaker habitations with storage features and early pottery that are located on the southeast edge of the Rainbow Plateau and are known from surface evidence alone. They range in size from a single residential structure with five or more associated storage cists, such as site AZ-D-2-355 (NAU) on the west rim of Upper Piute Canyon (Fairley 1989), to sites like AZ-J-14-54, with multiple residential structures.

Secondary Habitations

In contrast to the sites previously discussed are single-family habitations with modest artifact assemblages and lacking bulk food-storage facilities that appear to have been occupied for far less duration and perhaps not during the winter. NMRAP excavated six Basketmaker habitations of this type: Blake's Abode, Ditch House, Polly's Place, Panorama House, Tres Campos, and Sin Sombra. Sites that likely also belong to this class include Ko' Lahni, a portion of Scorpion Heights, and Three Dog Site, but in each case past disturbances preclude certain classification.

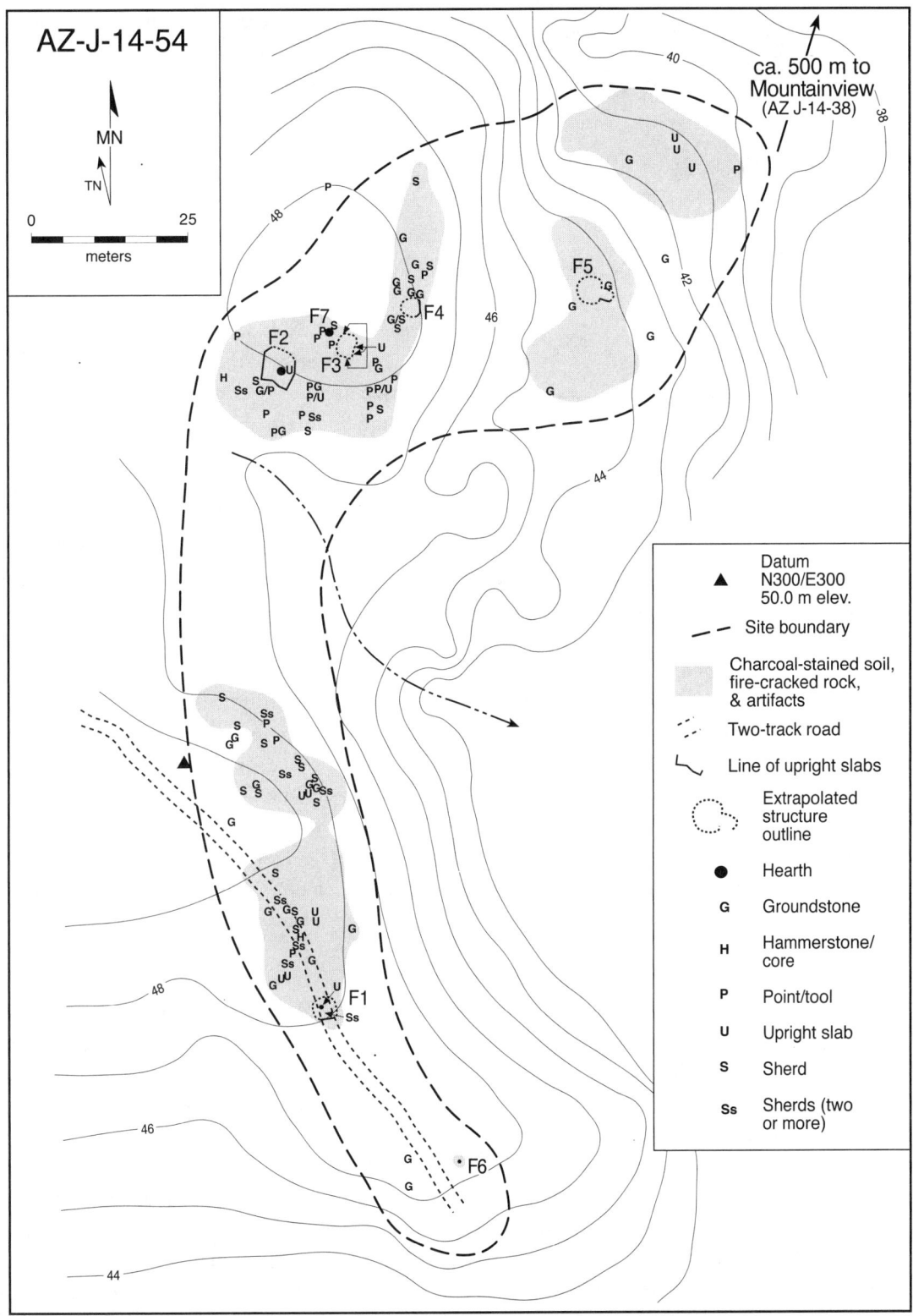

Figure 5.16. Map of a large unexcavated primary habitation outside the N16 right-of-way that has an artifact assemblage similar to Mountainview, including early brownware pottery.

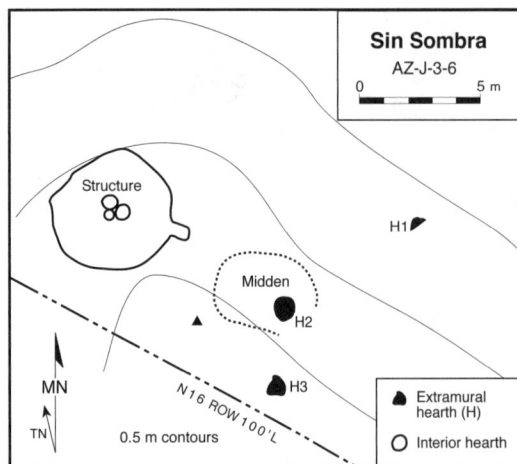

Figure 5.17. Sin Sombra, a Basketmaker II secondary habitation.

The sites of this class are characterized by a structure or two associated with a small trash midden and extramural hearths; small pits may also be present. The middens are never more than a few paces in front of the houses, immediately east or southeast of the entryways. They are relatively artifact poor, characterized mainly by abundant burned rock in a matrix of charcoal-stained and -flecked soil. The small size of the middens and comparative scarcity of artifacts seem to indicate temporary habitation, yet the presence of moderately formal structures suggests that the occupants envisioned more than a brief, single-use episode. It is possible that this type of site was sequentially occupied over several seasons or occupied for a month or more during a single season. Because they lack storage features, the likely time of site occupancy was summer or fall, when survival would not depend upon stored foods. The inference seems supported by the less substantial nature of house construction, especially when compared with the houses at Kin Kahuna. Polly's Place contains two structures, but this need not imply multiple families, just single families at different times; and radiocarbon dating demonstrates a lack of contemporaneity between them. It seems likely that Panorama House also has more than a single structure, with one or more located outside the ROW, but in this case, too, the houses are probably not contemporaneous.

Seasonal habitation is another potential name for this type of site, but I ultimately avoided this term because it seemed that the name might imply use during a certain season when we lack such information and indeed there may never have been a specific season of use but, rather, short-term use during several seasons or different examples of this site type being used during different seasons. The common denominator among them was the suggestion based on features and remains that they never served as a principal abode but, rather, as a less permanent residential node—satellite sites of sorts that were tied to more permanent residential bases.

Single-Structure Sites: Sin Sombra and Blake's Abode. Sin Sombra is a good example of a secondary habitation in its simplest form (Figure 5.17). It was characterized by a single, relatively small dwelling facing east, three extramural basin hearths to the east and southeast of the house, and a small trash midden located a few steps away from the house door. The calibrated two-sigma date range for the site is AD 120 to 330 based on the average of four statistically contemporaneous radiocarbon dates on maize from the structure, midden, and one extramural hearth. The semicircular house at Sin Sombra was 4.8 × 4.6 m in size, 70 cm deep, and accessed through its east side by a narrow stubby ramp 85 cm long and 45 cm wide. A series of probable shallow postholes along the perimeter of the structure may have marked the position of logs leaned toward the center to provide a roof similar to that of a forked-stick hogan. Near the center of the basin-shaped and slightly irregular floor was a cluster of three partially overlapping shallow basin hearths. A small deflector constructed of two upright slabs lay between the hearths and the ramp entry. A few meters southeast of the house was a trash midden up to 20 cm thick, whose main area measured 3 m in diameter, with a lighter density of material covering an area about 5 m in diameter. The midden consisted of charcoal-stained sand, charcoal, ash, burned rock, flakes, and bone. The density of artifacts was not great, fewer than nine flakes on average per square meter and fewer than one bone per square meter. For the entire site, excavations yielded 916 flakes, 22 flaked tools and cores, three manos and metates, and six other stone artifacts (Table 5.1).

Another good example of a seasonal habitation in its most basic form is Blake's Abode. This site consisted of a single structure (Figure 5.18; see Figure 3.15), three extramural hearths, and a surface artifact scatter mainly to the southeast of the house a few meters. The calibrated two-sigma date range for this site is 360–90 BC based on the average of two identical radiocarbon dates on pinyon bark from the structure, showing that it was a few hundred years earlier than Sin Sombra. The structure measured about 4.5 m in diameter and was up to 30 cm deep;

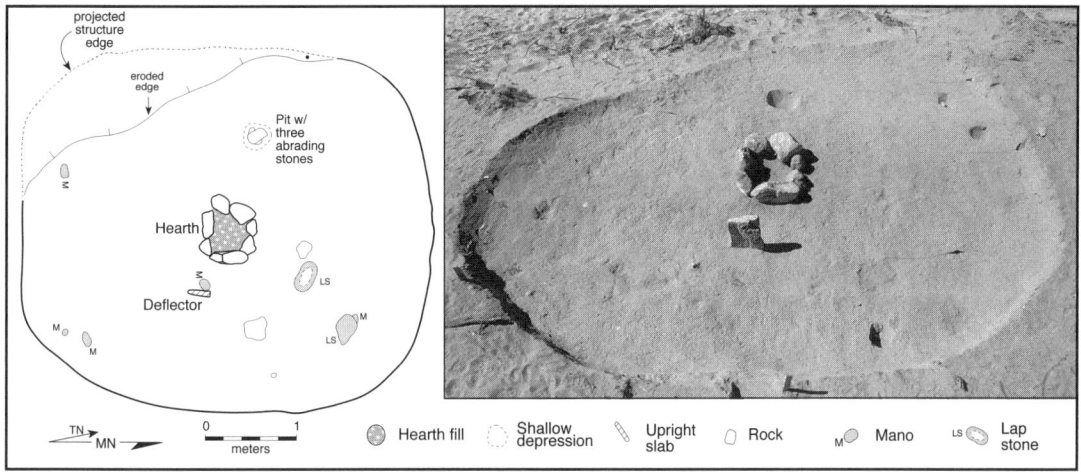

Figure 5.18. Blake's Abode, a Basketmaker II secondary habitation.

the far west edge of the house had been removed by erosion following construction of the existing N16 road. The few interior features consisted of a rock-outlined surface hearth, a low slab deflector, and a small floor pit containing abrading stones. The house lacked the ramp entryway common to other Basketmaker II habitations in the area, but this may be the result of deflation. The location of the deflector relative to the hearth reveals that egress was through the east wall. Lacking posts or obvious postholes, the superstructure was probably constructed, like that of the house at Sin Sombra, by leaning in timbers from the perimeter of the shallowly excavated basin. The floor or floor fill contained several manos and lap stones and both bone beads and worked bone fragments. About 9 to 10 m northeast of the house were three extramural hearths, one of which was slab lined. The trash deposit outside the structure at Blake's Abode appeared deflated and compressed, with most of the charcoal-stained sediment eroded away. Although the number of stone artifacts was modest and quite similar to Sin Sombra (748 flakes, 16 flaked tools and cores, eight manos/metates, and 21 other stone artifacts; Table 5.1), there was great diversity, including several nonutilitarian items such as a pipe fragment, gaming pieces (also some of these of bone), and ornaments. The bone count at 70 was slightly higher than at Sin Sombra.

Multiple-Structure Sites: Polly's Place and Panorama House. Larger versions of secondary habitations contain more than one house clustered together but without any obvious spatial integration of the separate dwelling units. Rather than being contemporaneous multifamily residences, they appear like examples of single-family compounds, each with separate middens and extramural features, sharing the same approximate space. One completely excavated example of this is Polly's Place (Figure 5.19), which consisted of two structures, one associated with a small trash midden and a slab-lined hearth and the other associated with a small group of extramural features—two small storage pits, three shallow basin hearths, and a possible roasting pit. The midden for the second structure probably eroded away because of the slope. Both structures had partial slab-lined entryways, interior hearths, and small interior storage pits. Structure 1 measured about

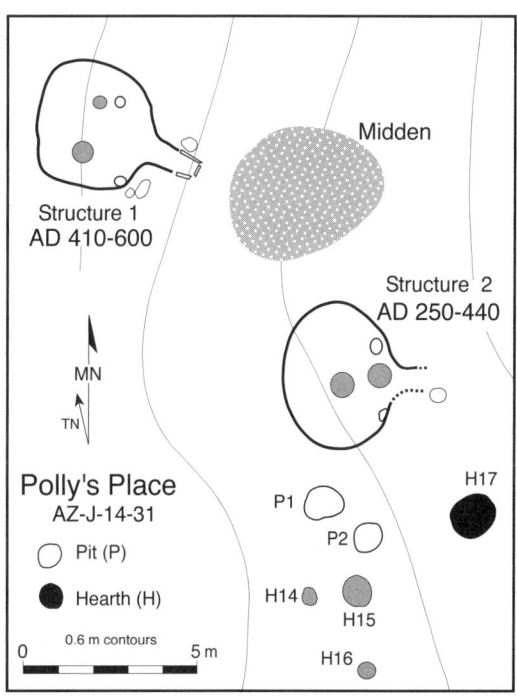

Figure 5.19. Polly's Place, a Basketmaker II secondary habitation with two noncontemporaneous structures.

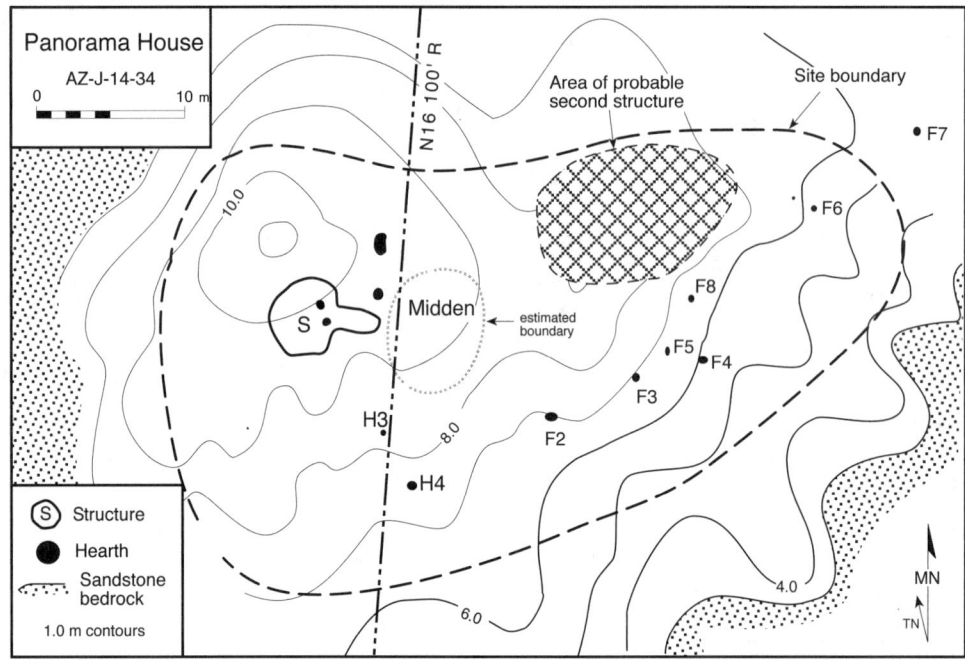

Figure 5.20. Panorama House, a Basketmaker II secondary habitation with two noncontemporaneous structures.

3.8 m in diameter and 50 cm deep below the occupation surface. A 1.5-m-long ramp accessed the structure through its east wall; the exterior end of the ramp was slab lined. A small trash midden about 4 m in diameter occurred just a few meters east of the Structure 1 entry ramp. The midden deposit consisted of charcoal-stained sediment containing abundant burned rock, which constituted up to 10 percent of the midden deposit by volume. Artifacts were rare in the midden, approximately one flake per square meter. Structure 2 was essentially a surface house that measured about 4.3 × 3.4 m. An entryway defined by slabs and clay extended roughly 2 m to the east. A midden was not identified for this structure, but this may be a consequence of slope erosion.

The clustering of radiocarbon dates for each structure and its associated features strongly suggests that the site was used sequentially on two separate occasions, with Structure 2 occupied first sometime between cal. AD 250 and 440 and Structure 1 subsequently occupied sometime between cal. AD 410 and 600. It is important to point out that in this particular case radiocarbon dating was able to temporally differentiate between these two houses, but this might not always be possible with this technique. Indeed, the error term of radiocarbon and the wide interval commonly resulting from calibration make it more likely than not that this method will fail to temporally sort sequentially used structures at a single site.

Another site probably like this is Panorama House, located just a few kilometers north of Polly's Place, on a narrow ridge of eolian sand (Figure 5.20). The N16 ROW clipped the west edge of the site boundary, but this small area contained a burned living structure, a few extramural hearths, and part of a small midden. Four statistically contemporaneous AMS assays on maize fix the time of occupancy at cal. AD 240–390 (two-sigma range). The single structure was a shallow pithouse a little more than 5 m in diameter, with an eastern ramp entry partially defined by small sandstone slabs. The entry was remodeled at least once with a slight change of orientation from east-southeast to east. The house had two interior hearths, each likely corresponding with one of the entries. Burned posts from a superstructure occurred around the house perimeter and toward its center. Two central posts might have supported a single north–south primary beam for the roof, as seen at a few of the Kin Kahuna houses. A few meters directly east of the structure entry (roughly two–three steps) was a small midden deposit, up to 20 cm thick. As at similar Basketmaker II secondary habitations, the midden was rich with burned rock and charcoal but comparatively artifact poor. Artifacts from the site as a whole are limited to 243 flakes, six flaked-stone tools and cores, three fragments of a single metate, and three other stone artifacts; faunal bone was limited to 22 fragments (see Table 5.1). Overall recovery would have been greater had the entire midden been excavated such as at other secondary habitations, but still probably fewer than 1,000 items total (artifacts and bone combined).

The density of burned rock in the core portion of the midden averaged 337 pieces and 13.9 kg per square meter and consisted of both limestone (67%) and sandstone (33%). This, along with the density of charcoal pieces and charcoal staining, indicates considerable processing of some sort, either pit roasting with heated stones or stone boiling or both. I tend to believe that much of the rock was used for stone boiling, both because no roasting pits were found in or around the structure and because most of the burned limestone had been reduced into small chunks. Informal experiments using the local limestone for pit cooking and stone boiling showed that the latter technique greatly fractures the rock, reducing it into increasingly smaller pieces. This can happen after just one or two boilings. Indeed, it is possible that limestone chunks would be discarded after just a single use because there is a greatly increased chance of adding stone debris to the food with repeated use. Pit baking with limestone can also fracture the rock, but far less severely and usually at different fracture angles than for stone boiling. Another obvious difference between the two methods is that the pit baking results in rock chunks that are heavily sooted, whereas stone boiling cleans much of the soot from the stones, though they are still usually identifiable as having been heat altered.

To the east of the excavated structure at Panorama House and outside the ROW occur other features, all of which are exposed on the eroded slope. These features, along with a light scatter of artifacts, are probably associated with a buried structure that occupies a level area of the sand ridge. The features exposed on this slope are only likely to be located here if there is indeed another house to the east of the excavated example. The ridge provides an ideal setting for a house because of the level deep sand, and it may have been used several times for this propose over the span of a few hundred years.

Secondary habitations appear to have served as the domicile of a single residential unit, which judging from structure size and number was a nuclear family or some portion thereof. In the one excavated case with two living structures, Polly's Place, the structures were not contemporaneous, just grouped together based on spatial proximity (although there may well have been a generational family connection). If there was some larger social grouping of multiple families residing in secondary habitations, then it existed above the level of a single site and is not yet spatially obvious because we lack thorough survey coverage. It is easy to envision several related families occupying their own secondary habitations but placing these all within a kilometer or so of one another as a means to maintain their social bond and for mutual protection. Numerous Basketmaker II sites that appear to qualify as secondary habitations are grouped together around the rim of Piute Canyon in the area where most of the excavated examples occurred. Clustered residential sites might well form larger communities—examples of what Matson (1991:82) designated as dispersed villages with regard to a similar pattern on Cedar Mesa.

Open Camps

The open camp class of site is poorly represented in the NMRAP sample, in part perhaps as an indirect result of the numerous Basketmaker habitations along the ROW. Camps are unnecessary when home is nearby. The probable ecological reason behind this pattern is that the N16 ROW traverses an area well suited to farming and semipermanent settlement. A greater concentration of camps might be expected in places more suited to gathering, yet at a distance from residential sites, such as the grass-covered benches of the Glen Canyon lowlands. Based on the few examples of the N16 excavations, there are camps that consist of little more than a hearth or two with next to no artifactual remains (Mouse House, Pee Wee Grande), camps with numerous hearths and moderate densities of remains (Ko' Lahni, although this might be a secondary habitation), and camps with hundreds or thousands of flakes and biface production fragments (Windy Mesa and a portion of Scorpion Heights). The latter seem to be the locations of intensive biface reduction and can include dart point bases snapped across the notches. Maize occurs in some hearths at some camps but is not common. Sites of this kind with early ceramics have yet to be identified, but there are hearths dated by radiocarbon assays to the interval when early pottery was in use.

Hunting-Related Camps. Some of the Basketmaker camps lacked sufficient material remains for making a reliable inference as to function, other than knowing that they served some very limited purpose. Scorpion Heights and Windy Mesa stand out because of their abundant flaking debris, almost all derived from biface reduction, and the occurrence of flaked facial tools such as projectile points. Scorpion Heights is perhaps the clearest case. Excavations here exposed a small midden, five hearths, and two pits and recovered a moderate assemblage of stone artifacts along with a few bones and minerals. Although extensively impacted by eolian and alluvial erosion, the extant pattern of features and artifacts allowed reconstruction of the site layout and use. The site appears to have been a composite of at least two separate use episodes that occurred during late Basketmaker II. The southern site area included a remnant of a small burned rock midden along with a hearth or two. The nature of the midden and the artifacts it contained is wholly consistent with this part of the site having served as a secondary habitation but with extensive erosion having removed all evidence of the structure (see SD vol. 3, chap. 16). The northern portion of Scorpion Heights may contain slightly overlapping remains from two functionally distinct use episodes or one episode with spatial division of activities. The quantity and type of debitage in the eastern part of the northern site area are indicative of intensive late-stage biface production (percussion thinning and pressure flaking), including the reduction of initially thinned bifaces of white baked siltstone from northern Black Mesa. In this area, too, occurred a whole projectile point and five point bases, four of them broken across the notches and the fifth with its tip removed by an impact bending fracture. This evidence is the signature of hunters removing the broken proximal ends of points from foreshafts and rearming them with new points. This northeast portion of the site therefore would seem to have served as a temporary camp for hunters. The age of the remains in the northern site area can be approximated based on the presence of Basketmaker II–style projectile points.

What makes Scorpion Heights stand out as unusual and provides a perfect fit with the hunting camp interpretation—above and beyond the evidence that dart foreshafts were rearmed—is that part of this activity involved the reduction of bifaces of white siltstone, a material type that originates on northern Black Mesa (Green 1985; Parry 1987b). This material occurs in low frequency at Basketmaker II sites of the Rainbow Plateau but is the most widely used tool stone by Basketmaker II occupants on northern Black Mesa (Parry 1987b:25), to the extent that flaking debris of this material is a useful temporal marker if occurring on an aceramic site. Based on the quantity of this siltstone at Scorpion Heights, it is plausible that Basketmaker hunters from Black Mesa created the concentrated scatter of flaking debris and discarded point bases at Scorpion Heights, having traveled to the rugged canyon country in pursuit of deer or bighorn sheep. However, given that the broken dart point bases from the site were of Glen Canyon chert, petrified wood, or other materials not available on Black Mesa, it is more likely that the hunters were local to the northern Kayenta region and acquired the siltstone through direct procurement while visiting Black Mesa. In this case the raw material supports the idea of a logistic foray outside the northern Kayenta region, one that hunters were likely to make in pursuit of large game.

Intensive biface reduction was also documented at the Basketmaker component of Windy Mesa, where excavations recovered a substantial assemblage of stone artifacts numbering close to 4,000 items but did not disclose any Basketmaker features. The small area investigated represents just part of the Basketmaker II remains at this site, and outside the ROW there are a few upright slabs that are candidates for features perhaps associated with this component. Also, because a portion of this component within the ROW was eroded and disturbed by road construction, some features may have been lost. Features or not, a central activity for the Basketmaker II occupants was biface reduction, apparently beginning midway in the reduction sequence (partially thinned blanks were brought to the site) and directed at the production of projectile points or point preforms. Reduction activity was quite intensive and mainly involved locally occurring Navajo chert (outcrops occur within 1 km); petrified wood that may have been procured less than 10 km away in Piute Canyon was also reduced. A large proportion of the debitage was identified as derived from percussion biface thinning, with pressure flaking accounting for much of the remainder. Eighteen bifaces, all in late stages of reduction, were recovered, with six of these being projectile points. Based on the proportions of bifaces at various stages and the nature of the debitage assemblage, it appears that the goal of reduction was to produce projectile points, or at least point preforms such as the group of 16 found together in a hunter's tool kit (Cache 1) at Sand Dune Cave (Geib 2004; Lindsay et al. 1968:Figure 23). The six projectile points are fragmentary, and only one could be confidently classified as a Basketmaker II Corner-notched point. A stem fragment of nearly identical dimensions and shape is also likely derived from a similar Basketmaker point.

The Basketmaker II lithic assemblage of Windy Mesa, like that of Scorpion Heights, is quite different from that of the Basketmaker II habitations of the immediate area, especially the secondary habitations, which are characterized by an emphasis on simple core reduction apparently for the production of flakes for expedient use and for the preparation and maintenance of core tools such as pecking stones and choppers. These contrasts in flaked-stone assemblages clearly reflect different sets of activities and settlement roles. Windy Mesa was the location of rather intensive reduction, but this was probably done by hunters in the context of using the place as a temporary logistic camp, who, while out on their foray, replenished their tool kits with projectile point preforms if not finished points.

Other Camps. A few of the Basketmaker II camps identified in the N16 ROW consisted simply of hearths with few or no associated artifacts (Bonsai Bivouac, Mouse House, and Pee Wee Grande). The features were not exposed on the surface but discovered while backhoe trenching or stripping; temporal assignment was based on radiocarbon dating. Most of these features did not produce any remains indicative of what they might have been used for. They might have been used for some sort of food processing, or they might have simply been the brief campfires of transient groups, with the fires used principally for warmth. The latter seems especially true for exceedingly shallow hearths, which is what most of these features were. At one camp that contained several hearths (Mouse House), two of them produced a few macrobotanical remains other than wood charcoal: a maize cupule and a few goosefoot seeds from one hearth and a purslane seed from another. Not much can be said about this sparse set of remains, except that corn was present in minimal quantity. The few seeds might merely have come from the incidental charring of weeds growing on the site. The presence of corn and late summer–fall seeds might be taken as evidence of occupancy during the late growing season. In this particular case the features were situated next to a likely farming area, so these features may have been associated with tending fields. At one other Basketmaker camp (Bonsai Bivouac) some unidentified seeds were observed in the light fraction from floated fill of a hearth, and these remains may relate to foraging activities (use of the hearths in seed parching). This last case was on the central portion of the Rainbow Plateau and might represent a satellite foraging camp used for a few hours by a small group based out of a Basketmaker residential site.

Other Basketmaker Sites of the Northern Kayenta Region

Findings that complement the NMRAP results and allow for a fuller understanding of Basketmaker II site types and settlement patterns in the northern Kayenta region come from previous excavations, chiefly sheltered settings on the northern portion of the Rainbow Plateau, and from open sites on Piute Mesa, settings and areas not represented by the excavations reported here. The list of sites includes all that belong to the chronological interval outlined previously and for which there is enough information in published reports, file reports, or field notes to make a site type assignment. MNA archaeologists excavated many of these sites as part of the Glen Canyon Project, including Sand Dune Cave (Lindsay et al. 1968) and a few open pit-house settlements on Piute Mesa that are unreported and thus little known. Dust Devil Cave was tested as part of that project, but most information comes from complete excavation in 1970, which was a separate undertaking directed by J. Richard Ambler. At that same time, Ambler tested a half dozen other shelters in the general area, two of which had significant Basketmaker II use. Added to this list are the Desha Caves excavated by Irwin Hayden in 1930 (Geib and Robins 2003; Schilz 1979) and Atlatl Rock Cave, which NNAD archaeologists tested in 1993. The latter site is a large dry shelter with stratified cultural deposits dating back to the early Archaic (see SD vol. 2, chap. 2). The significance of these additional Basketmaker sites is that they add to the variability documented by the NMRAP, thereby providing a more complete characterization of Basketmaker II settlement.

Piute Mesa Habitations

As part of the Glen Canyon Project, MNA archaeologists excavated several sites on Piute Mesa, including the Tsegi phase habitations of Pottery Pueblo (Stein 1984) and Neskahi Village (Hobler 1964, 1974). Unreported and therefore essentially unknown was the partial excavation of two open Basketmaker II habitations located north of Pottery Pueblo (NA7627 and -7708) and a third open Basketmaker II site (NA8368) that might also have been a habitation. My knowledge of these sites comes from field notes and preliminary reports on file at MNA (site files and library archives). Ambler directed the excavations at both of the habitations near Pottery Pueblo. "Coffin-like" arrangements of upright sandstone slabs (Figure 5.21) were the features of interest at both of the Basketmaker habitations, with two examples excavated at NA7708 and three at NA7627. At the time, Ambler was interested in discovering what these unusual constructions had been used for, but he was unable to provide a satisfactory answer. Had he expanded his effort only slightly the truth likely would have been revealed—they are the slab-lined

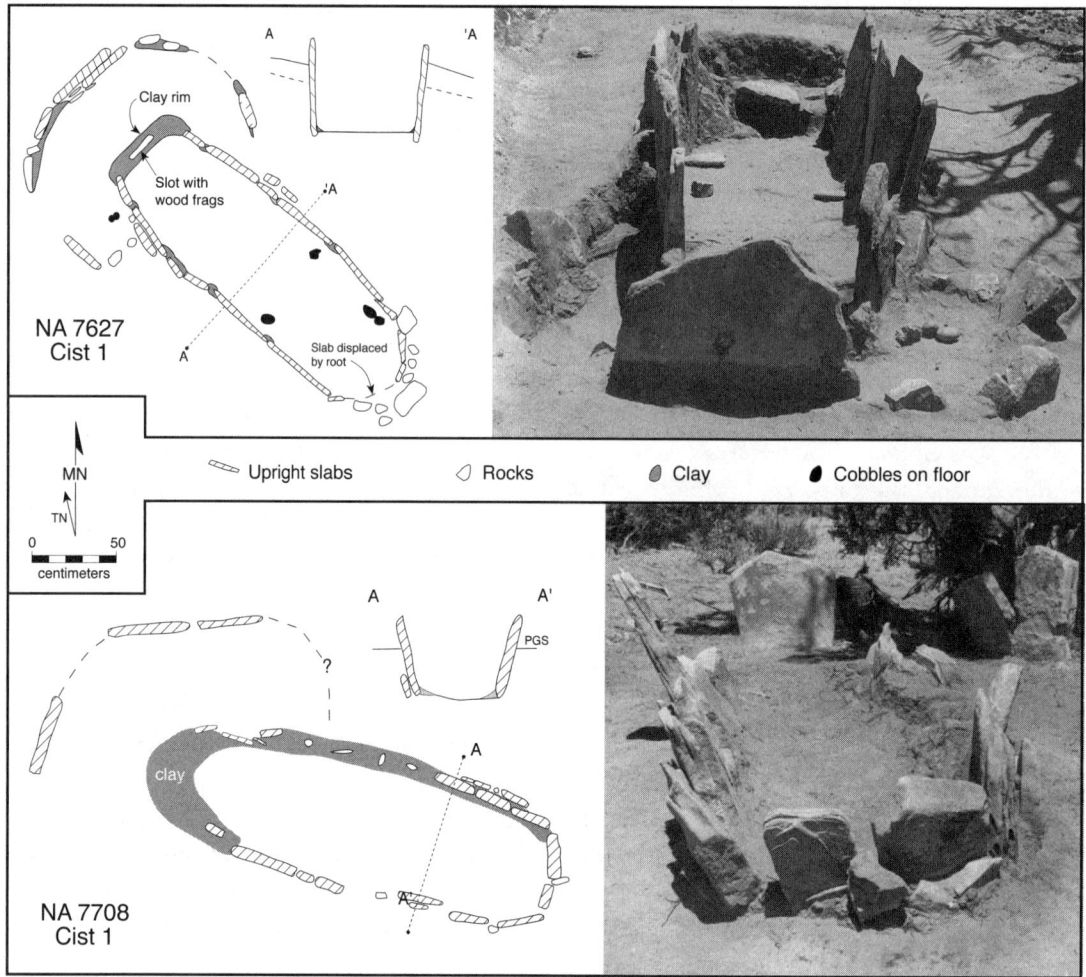

Figure 5.21. Slab-lined ramp entryways to probable Basketmaker II houses on Piute Mesa (excavation photos courtesy of the Museum of Northern Arizona; feature plans drawn from sketches by J. Richard Ambler on file at the Museum of Northern Arizona).

entries to shallow pithouses. This is obvious today given the excavation of Lone Tree Dune (Sharrock et al. 1963: 151–161) by University of Utah archaeologists during the Glen Canyon Project and Lipe's subsequent excavation of Basketmaker II structures at the Pittman and Veres sites on Cedar Mesa (Matson 1991:Figure 1.3; Pollock 2001). The slab-lined entries on Piute Mesa averaged about 3 m long and 75 cm wide. Other slab-lined features, both hearths and cists, were also excavated at these Cedar Mesa sites. Ambler suggested a Basketmaker II temporal assignment for the Piute Mesa sites based on the lack of surface pottery, an inference supported by the subsurface recovery of only stone artifacts, including manos and projectile points similar to those found at dated Basketmaker II sites. At NA7708 there were at least two cists with clay plastered floors and small sandstone slabs pushed into the clay. Similar features occur at the Desha Caves and Atlatl Rock Cave, where they have been radiocarbon dated to the late Basketmaker II period (first half-millennium of the Christian era), which is likely the age for both of these habitations on Piute Mesa. One of the interesting aspects of these two sites is how similar the entryway architecture is to the Basketmaker sites north of the San Juan River on Cedar Mesa and the Red Rock Plateau, yet such slab-lined ramps are poorly represented in the NMRAP sample of Basketmaker II sites, suggesting some degree of geographic variability in house construction within relatively close distance.

NA8368 is the third Basketmaker II site on Piute Mesa, excavated by MNA during the Glen Canyon Project. Philip Hobler directed the excavations and prepared the preliminary descriptive report that is on file at MNA. Excavated features consisted of six slab-lined hearths and what appears to have been a slab-lined cist, the roof of which burned. Tree-ring samples submitted from this site did not return a date. Given the presence of a probable food-storage feature it is possible that this site also functioned as a habitation, but it may have instead functioned as some specialized collecting and processing location such as for pinyon nuts. Only further investigation of this site can resolve this issue, but a habitation role seems likely given the presence of a cist.

Natural Shelters and Settlement Roles

The natural shelter provided by a cave or alcove was important throughout Anasazi prehistory, but with heavy use during Basketmaker II, Basketmaker III, and late Pueblo III. Both Matson (1991:117) and Smiley (1994:182) have argued that shelters were preferred for habitation and storage during the early portion of the Basketmaker stage, with open locations not widely used for residential settlement until around the Christian era. Although this might be true in some areas, in the northern Kayenta region there is no evident temporal priority of shelter use over open settlements. All radiocarbon dating of Basketmaker II remains from caves on the Rainbow Plateau have returned assays with no greater antiquity than about cal. AD 100: two dates from Dust Devil Cave (Geib 1996a:Table 11), three dates from Sand Dune Cave (Geib 2004:Table 1), six dates from Atlatl Rock Cave (SD vol. 2, chap. 2), and eight dates from the Desha Caves (Geib and Robins 2003). Shelter use appears to be no more than a component of overall Basketmaker II settlement organization, wherein open pithouse habitations figured prominently from the beginning of Basketmaker II occupation of the northern Kayenta region at around 300 cal. BC or slightly before.

Rockshelters are not a site type per se since they may include sites functionally equivalent to other types mentioned previously. Many shelters probably served as habitations, as Kidder and Guernsey (1919:206–207) originally suggested; Smiley (1993:250), among others, has further championed this view. On the Rainbow Plateau, shelters such as Sand Dune Cave appear to have been used this way, but there are also examples used almost exclusively for storage, such as the Desha Caves (Geib and Robins 2003; Schilz 1979); Lipe (1970:100–103) discusses similar sites from the Red Rock Plateau. Consequently, Spurr and I (Geib and Spurr 2000) subdivided the rockshelter class into sheltered habitation and sheltered storage, a distinction that still seems useful. Some sheltered storage sites appear closely associated and functionally linked with adjacent open habitations (e.g., Atlatl Rock Cave [SD vol. 2, chap. 2; also Geib and Spurr 2000:188]). Rockshelters formed a key part of the earliest phase of Basketmaker II settlement in the Kayenta region, the White Dog phase, but they were also central to later Basketmaker II occupation, at least for the northern Kayenta region and perhaps farther south as well.

Sheltered Habitation. Sand Dune Cave is the best-known example of a natural shelter on the Rainbow Plateau that Basketmakers evidently used for both habitation and storage. Excavation of this cave uncovered numerous storage cists, five sleeping beds, hearths, and a substantial accumulation of living refuse, leading Lindsay et al. to conclude that the cave "was used largely as a habitation and storage area rather than for interment of the dead" (1968:101). The cave yielded a wealth of Basketmaker II artifacts and other remains, with most artifacts closely resembling those from White Dog Cave (Guernsey and Kidder 1921) and similar sites of the Kayenta region (Guernsey 1931; Kidder and Guernsey 1919). Among the notable finds from the site was a whole, beautifully preserved atlatl and a dog-skin bag that contained a hunter's tools and other paraphernalia (Cache 1).

The Basketmaker occupation of Sand Dune Cave was assumed by the excavators to correspond in age to the then-postulated antiquity of these preceramic farmers elsewhere in the Four Corners region of the Colorado Plateau (roughly AD 0–500). None of the Basketmaker remains from the cave were directly dated in the 1960s, but recent radiocarbon dating firmly demonstrates that the hunter's bag from Cache 1 was made and used late in Basketmaker II times (cal. AD 80–330 based on the average of three statistically contemporaneous dates [Geib 2004]). The dating of this one bag is an important contribution, but it would be ill-advised to assume that the AD 80–330 span applies to all Basketmaker remains from the site. Far more assays need to be run on the collections from this site.

Another site of this class is Atlatl Rock Cave on the southeast edge of the Rainbow Plateau (SD vol. 3, chap. 2). One important aspect of this cave is that it appears to have been continuously occupied during the Basketmaker II–III transitional interval and it contains Obelisk Utility, an early brownware pottery. This site is also notable because a slab-lined pithouse and other slab-lined features occupy a small flat below the cave. Based on the use of upright slabs to line the entire circumference of the house,

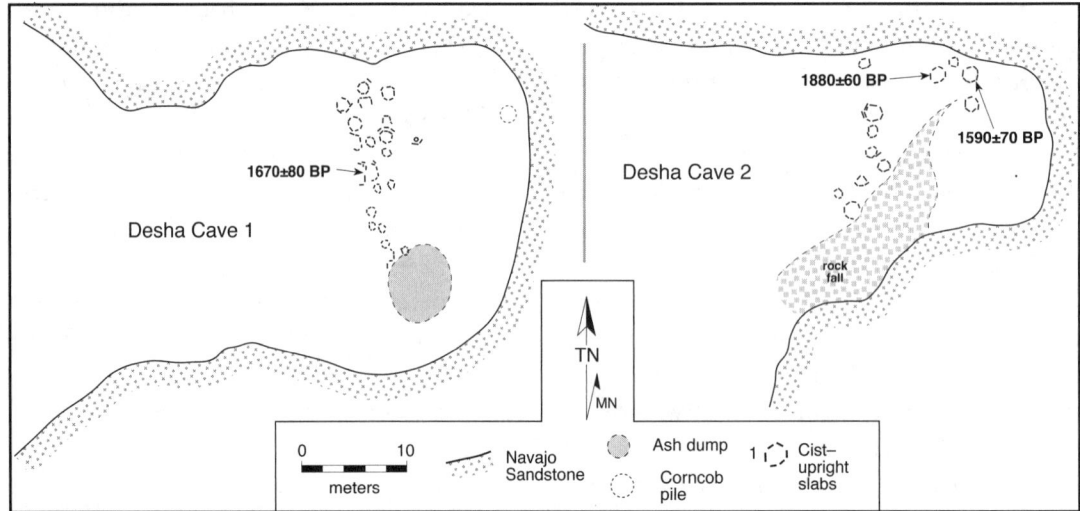

Figure 5.22. Maps of the Desha Caves as drawn by Irwin Hayden (1930; redrawn from Schilz 1979) showing the excavated cists and recently obtained ^{14}C dates (see Geib and Robins 2003).

I believe that this feature dates to the time that Obelisk Utility was in common use. In the cave proper, Basketmakers constructed numerous storage cists and pits. Six radiocarbon dates on maize and construction materials from several of these features indicate rather intensive use of the cave between about cal. AD 100 and 600. One of the more interesting finds from the site came from excavation of a small remnant of a cist formed of slabs plastered over with clay. Resting upon the floor were 10 cm of turkey feces mixed with some feathers, a small amount of sediment, organic remains, and a few artifacts. The organic remains included maize cobs and kernels and a single whole bean. The artifacts included portions of a polished brownware seed jar and a whole small arrowpoint of chert. A radiocarbon date on a corncob from the floor of the cist has a calibrated two-sigma range of AD 430–650.

Sheltered Storage. These are sites that appear to have been principally used for storage, though most also likely served on occasion as temporary resting or camp locations. These sites lack substantial living debris. There are at least two dozen examples of Basketmaker storage sites on the northern portion of the Rainbow Plateau, but as yet most are known from survey evidence alone. Three excavated sites of this class include Desha Caves 1 and 2 (Schilz 1979) and Dust Devil Cave (Lindsay et al. 1968). All are located on the northern portion of the plateau at elevations of 1,410–1,500 m in a grassland setting well below where dry farming is feasible, yet all three sites contained numerous storage cists and abundant corn remains. Irrigated farmland occurs less than 2 km away from the caves along Desha Creek (Lindsay et al. 1968:136–137); this is likely the area where Basketmakers raised the produce stored at the sites—the Desha Caves are on the east side of Desha Canyon, with Dust Devil Cave on the west.

Excavation of the Desha Caves in 1930 revealed 33 slab-lined storage cists—21 cists in Cave 1 and 12 in Cave 2 (Figure 5.22). Based on Irwin Hayden's notes, Schilz (1979:Tables 1–2) reports that eight of these features had no mortar or other caulking between the upright slabs but the rest had some material sealing the spaces. Juniper bark or other vegetation was packed between slabs for 18 cists, fiber-tempered mortar sealed the spaces for three cists, mortar without fiber was used for another three cists, and one had slab fragments as chinking. The cists from these two sites have a combined storage capacity of about 12 m³ (this excludes two cists of Cave 1 for which no measurements were provided). The few cists in these caves constructed with fiber-tempered mortar were recently dated by extracting the juniper bark from the clay for radiocarbon analysis (Geib and Robins 2003). This, plus the dating of two maize cobs, two human feces, and a Basketmaker II–style four-warp wickerwork sandal, demonstrates that both caves were used from roughly AD 0 to AD 630, or during the latter part of the Basketmaker II chronology for the northern Kayenta region.

Dust Devil Cave was tested in 1961 during the Glen Canyon Project (Lindsay et al. 1968), with full excavation occurring nearly a decade later. A full report on the site has yet to appear, but Ambler (1996) provides a preliminary description, though one focused on the rich Archaic deposits at the site. Judging from the field notes, there were at least 21 storage features in the cave that can be assigned to the Basketmaker II period, nearly all of which were storage cists. The capacity of these features is less than for the Desha Caves, probably about 3–4 m^3, but still sizable. Dust Devil Cave is along a route that runs from the higher elevations around the foot of Navajo Mountain to the canyon lowlands of the San Juan River and beyond; thus it provides an excellent resting place or way station for groups traveling back and forth between these settings. As such, this site likely served as a camp as well as for storage since it was well situated for both. Certainly the cave was used this way by Puebloan hunters, who left a considerable amount of biface flaking debris at the site (Geib 1984). One question is, How do we differentiate repeated camp use of a shelter like this (and repeated use is to be expected) from habitation use? This is not the place to attempt an answer. All shelters made excellent larders, but some also made excellent places to stop and rest; they were fixed places on the landscape that people would return to time and time again. Lipe (1970:102) also identified an alcove along Castle Wash on the Red Rock Plateau as a Basketmaker II camp and storage site.

It is worth cautioning that some shelters may appear to fit the sheltered storage class when in fact they are part of a habitation that contains structures and trash situated in the open near to the shelter. *Near* is of course a relative term, and a shelter might not be close enough to a poorly visible open site to register. What is the spatial extent that allows for probable association? Atlatl Rock Cave is an example of where storage cists in the shelter were probably associated with an unexcavated habitation structure in front of the cave (see SD vol. 2, chap. 2). I observed a similar pattern at the site of Hawk's Nest Ruin in Sage Valley west of the NMRAP study area on the northern portion of the Shonto Plateau (see Figure 5.1). Storage features in the dry alcove of Hawk's Nest appear to have been used by residents living in the open at least twice in prehistory, first during Basketmaker II and then again during Pueblo II; most recently a Navajo family stored trunks of clothes in the shelter. Several hundred meters separated the shelter from the actual Basketmaker and Pueblo II habitations, both of which remain unrecorded by the Navajo Nation. Looking farther afield it may be instructive to ponder Cave du Pont (Nusbaum 1922), long considered a classic example of an isolated Basketmaker II storage site—true enough, the site itself is north facing and cold,

not an ideal setting for habitation, but the canyon that it occurs within is well suited for living, and there is every probability for an open pithouse settlement close to the shelter yet buried and thus unknown to archaeologists.

Settlement Pattern: Where Are Sites Distributed?

A linear project such as the NMRAP is poorly suited to the study of settlement patterns for the obvious reason that the data come from such a narrow swath, when what is needed is information for large blocks of terrain. A natural question is whether the strongly clustered distribution of Basketmaker sites in the N16 ROW as shown in Figure 5.1 is merely some sampling fluke or whether it is a true reflection of reality. Most of the 17 NMRAP Basketmaker sites occurred in the southern portion of the project area where the road ROW traverses the dissected slickrock divide between Piute and Navajo creeks. This area appears to have been favored by these early farmers for their residential sites. One could simply proceed trying to explain why this is so, but if it is totally the result of sampling bias, then such an account might well be wrong or at least not fully informed. Therefore, it is important to bring in whatever other relevant data are available, as limited as these may be.

Our understanding of Basketmaker settlement on the Rainbow Plateau is hampered by a lack of intensive regional survey and the problem of positively identifying Basketmaker sites based on surface evidence. I consider the second problem first, because without positive identification all else is futile, no matter the amount of survey. Most of the sites that can be assigned with certainty to the Basketmaker period are those reported above, for which there are radiocarbon dates and excavation data. Nearly all of these sites were excavated to varying extent, most for the NMRAP. Minus chronometric dates, the few sites reliably assigned to this interval include several excavated caves that produced typical western Basketmaker perishable remains and a few open sites with diagnostic projectile points or other remains or distinctive architecture. The temporal placement of open sites known from surface evidence alone is more problematic. Aceramic sites with quantities of burned limestone have a good chance of a Basketmaker affiliation, but Puebloans or Archaic foragers on hunting and gathering forays may have created such sites as well. Identification problems extend to Basketmaker sites with early brownware pottery. Not only do these sites appear similar to aceramic Basketmaker sites, but the pottery is often unobtrusive and may occur in such low quantities that it can be overlooked. Earlier surveys also may not have recognized the early pottery for what it is, instead considering it unidentified and undiagnostic.

Survey coverage on the Rainbow Plateau is relatively more thorough north of the Utah state line, but none has been intensive over broad areas, so I am in a poor position to make any substantive claims about settlement patterning. For the Arizona portion of the plateau, survey coverage is limited to small parcels for modern homes and the like and linear transects for the N16 road and a power line. Even though MNA and NAU archaeologists have recorded more than 360 sites on the plateau in Utah (Ambler et al. 1985; Lindsay et al. 1968:16–30), none were positively identified as Basketmaker. A few dozen sites lacking masonry architecture and pottery were considered as probable evidence of Basketmaker II occupation, but a lack of diagnostics precluded positive identification.[5] Many of the probable Basketmaker sites are shelters, some with cists exposed on the surface, but there are also a number of open aceramic sites with burned rock and charcoal-stained soil. Current knowledge of Basketmaker settlement remains sketchy and subject to revision once a substantial portion of the plateau has been surveyed and a greater number and diversity of Basketmaker settlement types have been excavated.

With these caveats in mind, it seems reasonable to look at where Basketmaker sites are concentrated and the possible environmental reasons for why this might be the case. The concentration of secondary habitations on the divide between Piute and Navajo canyons is real and meaningful. There are simply too many sites located here, both within the NMRAP sample and known from personal reconnaissance in the area, for this pattern not to be significant. Having hiked extensively in the area and participated in a survey of Upper Piute Canyon (Fairley 1989), I know that the NMRAP sample along this divide is quite representative and that small Basketmaker residential sites abound in the area. The specific locations of these secondary habitations were probably selected for such factors as view quality, proximity to water, and well-drained level sand for house construction, factors that relate to convenience, efficiency, and comfort. At a larger scale though, it is worth considering why it was important to locate so many similar sites along the high divide between Piute and Navajo canyons. How do the secondary habitations fit into the larger pattern of Basketmaker II settlement organization for the area? What was their subsistence-settlement role, and if used seasonally, during what season or seasons? The dissected high divide between the canyons of Piute and Navajo creeks must have been favorably placed relative to Basketmaker II subsistence pursuits, otherwise secondary habitations would not be so numerous.

Some secondary habitations, such as Sin Sombra, are situated on the southeast edge of the Rainbow Plateau close to arable land, allowing for the possibility that they served as summer field residences. On the dissected divide, however, arable land appears to be in short supply, raising the possibility that these habitations were located here for access to other resources, although what these might have been remains speculative. Smiley (1985:264–267, 1993:248–249) suggested that similar Basketmaker sites on Black Mesa (small, nonstorage habitations) were associated with specific economic tasks such as pinyon nut harvesting. The divide would have provided access to pinyon nuts, and certainly this nutritious nut was an important food resource for these early farmers (e.g., Aasen 1984). Nonetheless, the lack of direct evidence for pinyon exploitation at any of the secondary habitations makes this suggestion less plausible. Moreover, if this site type was linked in an important way to pinyon exploitation, then I would also expect to find sites like this located in other areas with dense pinyon growth but poor farming opportunities such as on the lower flanks of Navajo Mountain, yet reconnaissance in this area has not disclosed these. Another good location to examine whether Basketmaker II secondary habitations might be related to pinyon nut collecting is Skeleton Mesa, which has a dense cover of pinyon but is too high for successful farming during normal years (>2,134 m, or 7,000 ft). This mesa is reputed to be covered with Navajo pinyon camps, the modern analogue for Basketmaker II pinyon camps.

On northern Black Mesa, the Basketmaker sites that appear analogous to the NMRAP secondary habitations are designated as nonstorage habitations. Six of these were excavated by the BMAP, and three lacked any maize remains (Smiley 1985:311). These were the only three Basketmaker II sites excavated by the project that lacked evidence of cultigens; even limited-activity Basketmaker camps yielded maize. Perhaps because of this absence it seemed reasonable to suggest that this class of site may have been foraging related. For the NMRAP, nearly all of the Basketmaker secondary habitations produced maize macroremains or pollen. These remains were far less abundant than at primary habitations, but their occurrence nonetheless hinted that this site type also may have been related to agricultural pursuits despite the setting. Key in this respect is the proximity to the lush Upper Piute Canyon, with its excellent farming potential. The tributaries of Navajo Creek, such as Segito and Far End, also offer excellent farming opportunities. Secondary habitations could have been occupied while tending canyon fields because the distance is not great, just 3–6 km horizontally and about 240 m vertically from any one of the excavated sites, something easily covered in a few hours. Although field tending from temporary homes located within canyons may seem more plausible, if multiple fields in various canyons on both sides of the divide were being farmed, it might make sense to have a temporary residential site midway between. The high proportion (over 60%) of Owl Rock chert in the debitage assemblages from most of the secondary habitations provides evidence for frequent travel into Upper Piute Canyon, which is the closest source for this material. There may have been other reasons to travel into the canyon, including the simple need to obtain flakeable stone, but Navajo chert is more immediately available on the divide and could have sufficed for most chipped-stone tools. The occurrence of Owl Rock chert is probably related to embedded procurement—obtaining nodules and large flakes while in the canyon tending fields.

While discussing the settlement role of secondary habitations vis-à-vis Piute Canyon it is perhaps worth considering an annual settlement strategy much like that documented for the Havasupai (Spier 1928:99–100; Weber and Seaman 1985:7–10), at least as a way to generate expectations to test against the record provided by the Basketmaker II residential sites. In times past, the Havasupai farmed and lived in Cataract Canyon during the growing season but then retreated to the surrounding plateau highlands during the winter:

> As winter approached, they broke up into small family bands and wandered off by themselves to establish winter camps. Often several families settled within a short distance of each other. Here they built conical huts covered with brush and earth.... From these semi-permanent camps individuals or groups of men from several households would go off on hunting expeditions.... As food ran low, occasional trips would be made back to the vicinity of the fields and storehouses [Weber and Seaman 1985:10].

If Basketmaker II groups of the northern Kayenta region followed a similar yearly cycle, might this account for the structural sites sampled by the NMRAP on the high divide between Piute and Navajo canyons? Might the secondary habitations be the winter residences where Basketmaker II families scattered themselves on favorable settings of the high divide after spending the growing and harvest season within Piute and Navajo canyons? In such a scenario, crops would have been left cached in pits or cists in the open near the fields or within shelters in the canyons. As such, the lack of storage pits at the sites classified here as secondary habitations does not necessarily count against an overwintering role.

There are two problems, however, with such a picture. One concerns the nature of remains at the secondary habitations, and the other has to do with the existence of residential sites that seem a far better fit as winter residences—sites such as Kin Kahuna and The Pits. The trash middens at the secondary habitations are inconsistent with an overwinter occupation, in that they are small and contain a low density of remains. These deposits are charcoal stained, but the burning of fuel for warmth during the winter months should generate an abundance of charcoal and ash, creating extensive deposits of blackened sediment such as were documented at Kin Kahuna or on the surface of The Pits outside the ROW. The density of remains and their total abundance at secondary habitations are also inconsistent with overwintering. Since such a site would be occupied for several months during a season when time is not overly committed to subsistence pursuits, there would be plenty of opportunity for various arts and crafts, with producing and using flaked-stone tools accounting for a significant contribution of artifacts to any midden. The quantity, density, and diversity of stone artifacts from Kin Kahuna stand out as what I would expect for a winter residence, but not the paltry lithic assemblages from any of the secondary habitations. Another issue along these lines concerns the recovery of macrobotanical remains. Even if corn was not stored directly at a winter residence, it would have been consumed there because survival during this lean season depended in large part on stored field produce. As such, corn remains should accumulate at any winter residence, especially since cobs probably would be burned as fuel for warmth or for cooking. Although corn was present at most of the secondary habitations, it occurred in moderately low rates, tending to be found in flotation samples rather than field screening. In contrast to this situation is the high ubiquity of corn remains at The

Pits and Kin Kahuna, including the common recovery of kernels and cobs, or portions thereof, during excavation.

In sum, it seems highly unlikely that the secondary habitations could have served as winter residences like those of the Havasupai; rather, they were likely used during another season (or seasons) and for a shorter duration than the several-month span of an average winter. The only probable candidates for winter residences are the sites classified as primary habitations, which brings me back to the assumption stated earlier, that the Basketmaker habitations excavated for the NMRAP are the differentiated parts of a settlement-subsistence strategy that together with camps and other site types formed an integrated whole. When Kidder and Guernsey speculated that Basketmakers "lived during a large part of the year in the open, where they presumably erected temporary houses analogous to the summer shelters of the Navajo" (1919:207), it is almost as if they had foreseen the secondary habitations excavated by the NMRAP. What Kidder and Guernsey had not foreseen was that many Basketmakers also spent their winters in the open within pithouses. Although secondary habitations were evidently used for only a small part of a year, the presence of moderately formal structures suggests that more than a brief single-use episode was envisioned; thus it seems probable that this type of site was intended for sequential occupancy over several seasons. Internal modifications to structures such as the multiple entryways and hearths at the Panorama House structure are consistent with nonsequential use across several seasons and perhaps the refurbishment of a house after a several-year lapse in use.

The N16 swath across the central part of the Rainbow Plateau lacks Basketmaker habitations of any type, and although this could merely be a sampling problem, there are reasons to believe otherwise. First, habitations of later farmers are well represented on this part of the plateau, so the area was inhabitable by farmers. Unlike in the area of the high divide to the south where almost any brief walk will encounter a small Basketmaker II habitation, no Basketmaker II sites were discovered during reconnaissance walks in the central portion of the Rainbow Plateau. Plenty of sites occur in this area, but invariably they are Puebloan in age, especially middle to late Pueblo III. Finally, the few surveys of this area that have been conducted, though limited in scope, also have not found Basketmaker II habitations. This does not mean that none occur in the area, but certainly far fewer than either on the southeast edge of this plateau or at its northwest edge around the foot of Navajo Mountain. One reason for this could be that settlement of this area would have relied almost exclusively on dry farming. There are small runoff-enhanced settings in a few drainages, but these do not appear to be as optimal as those elsewhere. The Basketmaker population density was perhaps low enough for the area that families could concentrate in more optimal settings, which meant along the southeast edge of the Rainbow Plateau and the foot of Navajo Mountain.

The remnants of one Basketmaker II habitation along the east side of Navajo Mountain included in the N16 ROW poorly represents what seems to have been an important area of settlement for these initial farmers of the region. Survey coverage and personal reconnaissance in this area have been sufficient to demonstrate that Basketmaker II sites are quite common. Moreover, this is where there are six excavated or tested Basketmaker II caves. This area is generally lower in elevation than the central portion of the Rainbow Plateau, but here there are drainages that head on the mountain slopes, drainages that carry abundant runoff during summer rain showers, thereby providing good farming opportunities. Moreover, this area is close to prime well-watered low-elevation settings in Lower Piute Canyon, Desha Creek, and Cha Canyon, settings that provided excellent farming areas complementary to those around the foot of the mountain. In this sense the area around Navajo Mountain is similar to that on the southeast edge of the Rainbow Plateau, where two different types of farming opportunities are available. The Navajo Mountain area might be even more preferable, in that the spring-fed low-elevation fields such as along Desha Creek (Lindsay et al. 1968) have a much longer growing season and earlier harvest than in Upper Piute Canyon.

It appears that primary residential sites with storage facilities for overwintering occur in areas of maximum agricultural potential from the earliest part of the Basketmaker period for the Rainbow Plateau. This is best illustrated by the long-lived Basketmaker hamlet of Kin Kahuna, which occupies a ridge on the southeast edge of the Rainbow Plateau above the confluence of two drainages that collect runoff from the high divide to the south. A Navajo family living nearby still farms the area where these two drainages come together. Basketmakers built at least one substantial pithouse and several deep storage pits on this ridge sometime around 300 BC. Other structures and storage pits followed, providing evidence for intensive occupancy of the ridge for some 600 years. The long-term stability in Basketmaker settlement of this one location appears to reflect an underlying concern for situating primary residential sites next to prime agricultural land. Not only does this keep transportation costs of produce relatively low (Bradfield 1971), but the proximity of houses provides a direct marker of land tenure. Matson and Chisholm's conclusion about Basketmaker II settlement on Cedar Mesa seems most apt to the Rainbow Plateau: "The overall Basketmaker II settlement pattern is consistent with dependence on maize agriculture because it is so similar to later Anasazi settlement patterns" (1991: 448). Situating a primary habitation in this area probably had the additional benefit of being proximate to the farmland in the adjacent canyons, especially Upper Piute Canyon. From this one setting, the Basketmaker occupants could farm the drainages immediately in front of the site and also tend fields in the closely adjoining canyons.

The primary habitation with a large volume of storage known as The Pits occurs on the far northeast edge of the Shonto Plateau, also in an area with good agricultural potential but different from that of Kin Kahuna. The setting is high in elevation, somewhat over 2,164 m (7,100 ft). In this setting it seems that farming would have been dependent upon rainfall but with limited potential to concentrate water in drainages because this is where drainages actually begin. The elevation is such that precipitation is more than adequate for farming most years, and there is also the potential for high water table or irrigation farming in the adjacent canyons.

In the southern portion of the N16 ROW two primary habitations bracket the southern and northern ends of the high divide between Piute and Navajo canyons, with a string of secondary habitations in between. There is also at least one primary habitation located among the secondary habitations (the Big Bend site), but the Basketmaker component remains largely unstudied because it lay outside the N16 ROW. The question becomes, Why would an occupant of, say, Kin Kahuna need a secondary residence so close to home? After all, most of the secondary habitations excavated by the NMRAP lie within 6 km of this site or The Pits and even closer to the Big Bend, and none are in an environment much different from that of primary habitations. Also, none are really much closer to the farmland of Piute Canyon or other canyons. One reasonable possibility is that the secondary habitations were used by Basketmaker II families who had their principal place of dwelling much farther afield, such as at the foot of Navajo Mountain some 20–25 km away. Maintaining structures on the divide between Piute and Navajo canyons might have been one means of ensuring a claim to resources of the area for families who did not live in the immediate vicinity.

Architecture

Houses

Pithouses have a long history of use in the Southwest (Wills 1995:Table 8.2), and in the mountains of Colorado substantial houses containing subfloor storage pits came into use more than 6,000 years ago (Metcalf and Black 1991). Although pre-farming hunter-gatherers used pithouses, widespread use of these features on the Colorado Plateau is correlated with the adoption of agriculture. The presence of pithouses with substantial investment in construction has implications for the relative stability and longevity of a residential location, as well as the resource base and settlement patterns. Gilman's (1987) examination of the conditions surrounding the pit structure–to–pueblo transition in the prehistoric Southwest focused on subsistence, especially agricultural dependency. It would be equally informative to study changes in the nature and construction of pithouses from Basketmaker II to Basketmaker III to see if patterning relates to changes in agricultural dependency, restrictions in residential mobility, or other factors. The NMRAP has gone far toward assembling a data set on Basketmaker structures for the northern Kayenta region, but it is still inadequate for broad generalizations. The presence on Piute Mesa of Basketmaker houses with long slab-lined ramp entries like those common to Cedar Mesa (Matson 1991; Pollock 2001), a rare feature in the NMRAP sample, indicates that there is spatial or temporal variability not yet adequately covered. Nonetheless a discussion of excavated Basketmaker houses will help document general trends in construction for the northern Kayenta region and enable comparisons with other areas. Temporal changes in construction details and interior features are evident, but how these relate to other variables is yet unknown. One important consideration is that we lack an equal sample of houses from functionally equivalent sites. Houses dating to the same time might be different because one was built as a long-term winter residence with a planned use-life of a decade or more, whereas another was built as a short-term summer residence with a brief use-life.

Figure 5.23 depicts all completely excavated Basketmaker houses for the NMRAP ordered by time. Temporal placement for the structures is based on radiocarbon

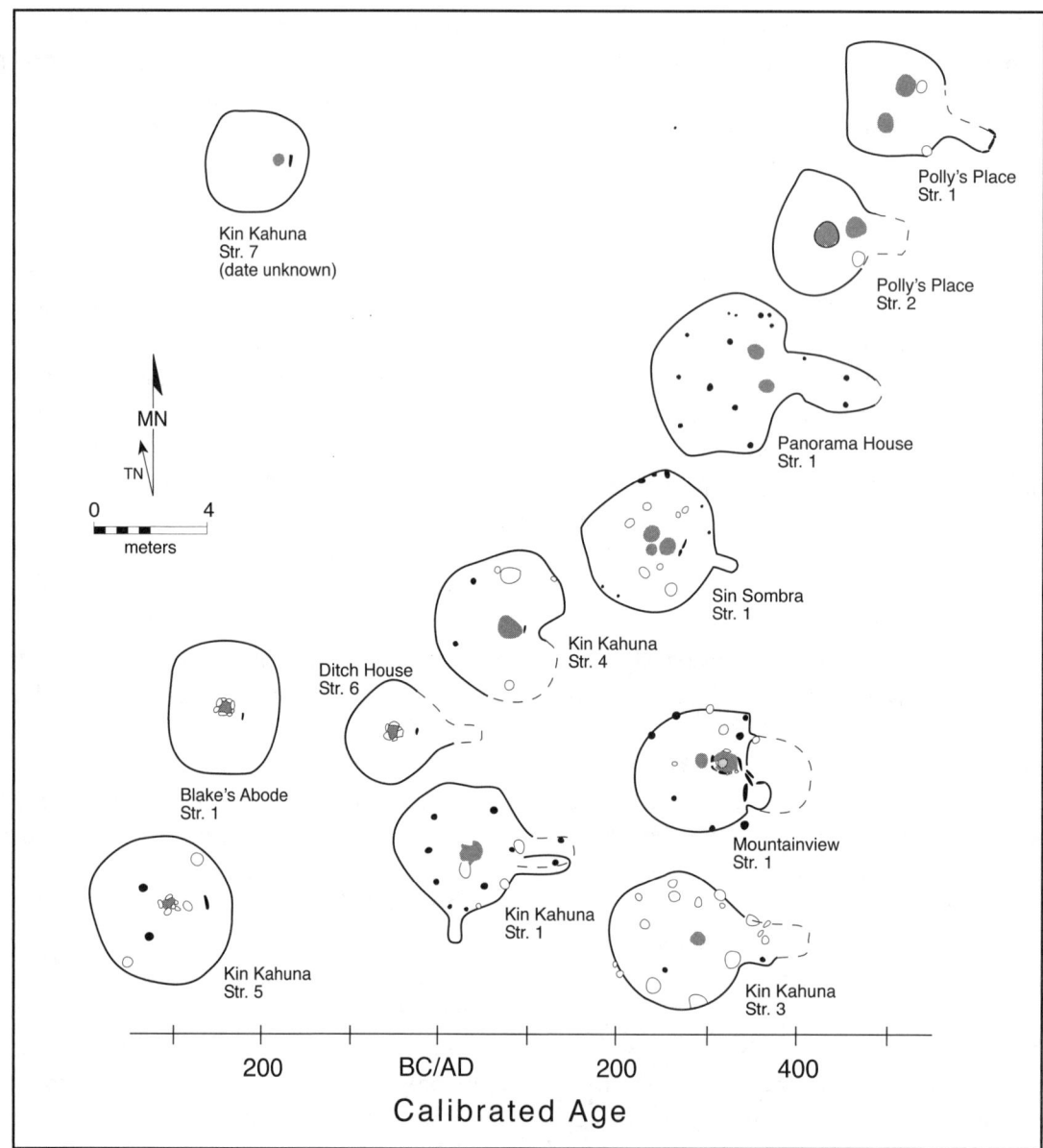

Figure 5.23. Comparison of Navajo Mountain Road Archaeological Project Basketmaker house configurations through time; houses are sized and oriented the same and ordered by calibrated ^{14}C age based on date averages.

dating of maize or other high-quality remains from hearth and floor contexts. Structure 7 at Kin Kahuna is undated because of a lack of high-quality organic remains. All structures are shown at the same scale and orientation. Basketmaker houses are generally circular, usually about 4 to 5 m in diameter, and from .2 to 1 m deep below the prehistoric occupation surface. The oldest house was also the deepest, and it had straight walls meeting a level floor with a neat right angle. Most houses, however, had sloping pit walls and saucer-shaped floors. Houses had eastern or southeastern ramp entries when evident. All had at least one centrally located interior hearth. Deflectors commonly occurred between the hearth and the entry;

most consisted of small unshaped slabs that seem oddly disproportionate to the task (Figure 5.24; and see Figure 5.18). In the oldest structure, the deflector consisted of a large trough metate (a basin-shaped trough) set upright in the floor; this tool had a crack running through it, which might have been the reason it was recycled as an architectural stone.

Changes in the nature of superstructure construction are difficult to evaluate because the evidence is dependent upon several factors such as whether a structure burned or was scavenged and whether the substrata helped or hindered preservation of construction details (e.g., clay vs. loose sand). Some houses had no obvious interior post-

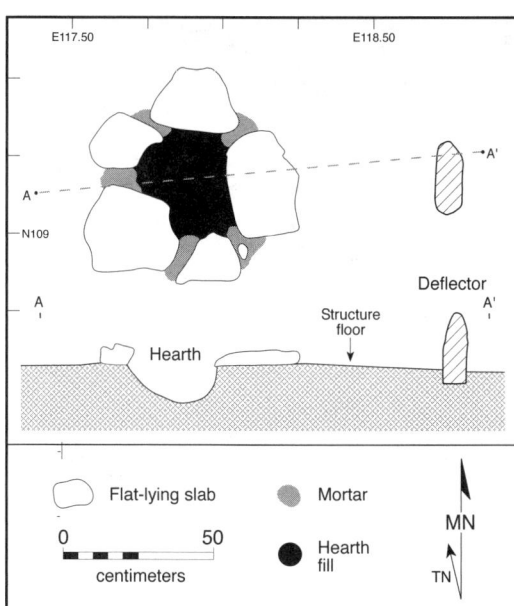

Figure 5.24. Typical example of a deflector in a Basketmaker II house of the N16 project area; this instance is from Structure 6 of Ditch House, AZ-J-14-21 (see also Figure 5.18).

holes; these may have been roofed by leaning in timbers and linking them together at the top somehow, much like a forked-stick hogan. Several houses at Kin Kahuna had just two posts that would have supported a single north–south primary beam offset to the west from the center of the structure so as to allow creation of a smoke hole directly over the hearth. This type of roof support is most clearly exemplified by Structure 5 of Kin Kahuna, shown in Figure 5.25. The floor of the 1-m-deep house was well preserved and plastered with a reddish clayey sand. Despite a careful and thorough search for additional postholes across the entire floor and especially along the east side in anticipation of a four-post support system, only the two postholes shown in the photo were found. A two-post support system is clearly quite different from the quadrilateral method so often discussed for Basketmaker houses. Structures 3 and 4 at this site also have what appears to have been a two-post support system. A typical four-post arrangement is evident at Structure 1 at Kin Kahuna (Figure 5.26), so at least two different roof-support methods are evident at this site (actually a third method, that of leaners, is indicated by Structure 7 at this site).

One of the most obvious temporal trends, although it is not clear in Figure 5.23, concerns the use of sandstone slabs in construction. In all houses dating before AD 200, upright slabs were used only as deflectors. At some point after AD 200, slabs began to be used in the construction of entry ramps, such as at Panorama House and Polly's Place.

In these examples the entry slabs tended to be quite small, especially compared with those of the late Basketmaker II houses on Cedar Mesa (Matson 1991:Figure 1.3; Pollock 2001), which date to the Grand Gulch phase, ca. AD 200–400. Several undated Basketmaker II houses on Piute Mesa also have large slabs lining the entries (see Figure 5.21). The entry ramps of these Piute Mesa houses are so similar to those on Cedar Mesa that I would expect that they have a similar temporal placement, so sometime between AD 200 and 400. The NMRAP Basketmaker structure with the most use of upright slabs is at Mountainview, where they formed a low partition across the front of the house and helped to define at least one storage bin (Figure 5.27). Given the steep east slope, the entry had eroded, so its construction remains conjectural. This house appears most similar to Basketmaker III houses of the Klethla Valley with tree-ring dates in the AD 500s (e.g., Pit House 1 of NA11,058 [Swarthout et al. 1986:426–430]). Nonetheless, the Mountainview structure is securely dated to sometime between cal. AD 220 and 350. Structures fully outlined by upright slabs occur at the large early ceramic habitation of AZ-J-14-54 described previously and at AZ-D-2-355 (NAU), which has a single living structure and multiple storage cists. In the open out in front of Atlatl Rock Cave there is a structure totally outlined by upright slabs, along with associated slab-lined cists (SD vol. 2, chap. 2). None of these slab-lined houses are dated, but I anticipate that they were built sometime between AD 400 and 600. The increased use of slabs probably entailed somewhat of an increase in construction investment, but this may not necessarily imply greater permanency. Lining the entire circumference of houses may have resulted because the slabs were a useful way to provide stable vertical walls within loose surface sand. The deepest of the Basketmaker houses in the northern Kayenta region reach depths of up to 1 m. These were excavated into hard stable sand so that the walls could be vertical without a lining. Increased use of upright sandstone slabs in house construction appears time dependent, and this is also evident for storage features, a topic discussed below.

Interior hearths of Basketmaker houses show an interesting pattern. Some of the NMRAP Basketmaker houses had shallow basins excavated for the hearth, but in many pithouses the hearths consisted of no more than a fire built directly on the floor surface with no prior preparation. In several cases, stones were placed on the floor surface to help contain the accumulating ashes, but these were loose rather than embedded within the floor and would have allowed for constant rearrangement of the hearth. At the

Figure 5.25. The earliest pithouse at Kin Kahuna (Structure 5) showing the twin postholes that supported the roof (view to the west); the structure is dated to ca. 360–100 cal. BC based on the average of five statistically contemporaneous maize assays. The deflector consists of a recycled trough metate.

Figure 5.26. Structure 1 at Kin Kahuna showing a four-post roof-support arrangement (view to the south); the structure is dated to ca. 120 cal. BC–cal. AD 130. The south entry accesses a small structure that might have functioned like an antechamber.

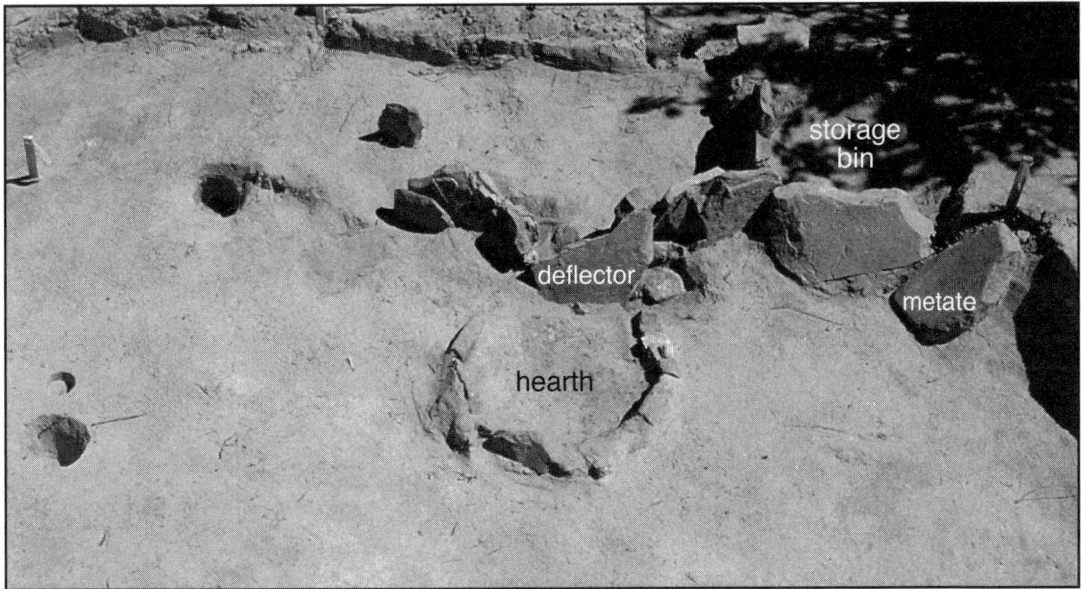

Figure 5.27. Close-up of the hearth and low partition of upright slabs in the house at Mountainview (view to the east); slabs were partially damaged by heavy machinery. A metate leans against the pit wall of the house on the south side adjacent to a small bin that contained portions of an Obelisk Utility vessel.

oldest structure at Kin Kahuna the floor surface under the stones was ash stained, indicating use of the central hearth before placing the stones or movement of the stones during use. This type of hearth results in an accumulation of ash and charcoal with topographic expression above the floor rather than below it, filling a basin. Consequently, unless an excavator is paying careful attention and anticipates such a situation, it is possible to remove the evidence of a hearth during the process of excavating fill to expose the floor surface. This may well be why many of the Basketmaker II pithouses on northern Black Mesa appear to lack hearths (e.g., AZ D:7:3107 [Lebo et al. 1983] and D:11:3133 [Leonard et al. 1984]). Such an absence led the excavators of AZ D:7:3107 to argue that the site was not a winter habitation (Lebo et al. 1983:148), though Smiley (1998c:110) subsequently concluded that it was.

With time, interior hearths became more formalized, consisting of an excavated basin with a clay collar. Hearths of this sort occurred in Structure 2 at Polly's Place and the Mountainview structure. This type of hearth typifies later Basketmaker III structures of the Klethla Valley (Ambler and Olson 1977; Swarthout et al. 1986). This change in the nature of interior hearths does connote greater formalization and functional differentiation of interior space—a trend carried forward in Basketmaker III structures with the creation of partitioning walls or ridges and interior bins. The start of this spatial partitioning and more formal features is seen in the Mountainview house.

Storage Features

The introduction of domesticates to the Southwest seems strongly correlated with a vast increase in the number and size of storage features (Wills 1995:231). Abundant storage, in the form of large bell-shaped pits, is an important part of the earliest Basketmaker sites excavated by the NMRAP. This is well exemplified by the site known as The Pits, where excavations uncovered 24 such features distributed along the crest of a sand-covered ridge (Figure 5.28). Because of right-of-way limits to excavation, the full size and complexity of this site, including the total count of storage features, remain to be determined. With almost 17 m^3 volume represented by the 24 storage pits, this site has the largest storage capacity and most storage features of any open Basketmaker residential site currently known in the Kayenta region. By comparison, the BMAP Basketmaker II site with the largest amount of storage in bell-shaped pits is AZ D:11:449 (Leonard et al. 1985), where 20 pits provided close to 11 m^3 (Smiley 1985). Moreover, that site is an extreme outlier in the BMAP sample, having several times more storage pits than other Basketmaker II sites excavated on that project.

Most of the storage features at The Pits have shapes exemplified by the profiles of two examples shown in Figure 5.29, and these are typical of such features throughout the Kayenta region and beyond. The few exceptions at this site include pits that had been reused for roasting purposes, and these were likely once bell shaped, but the neck

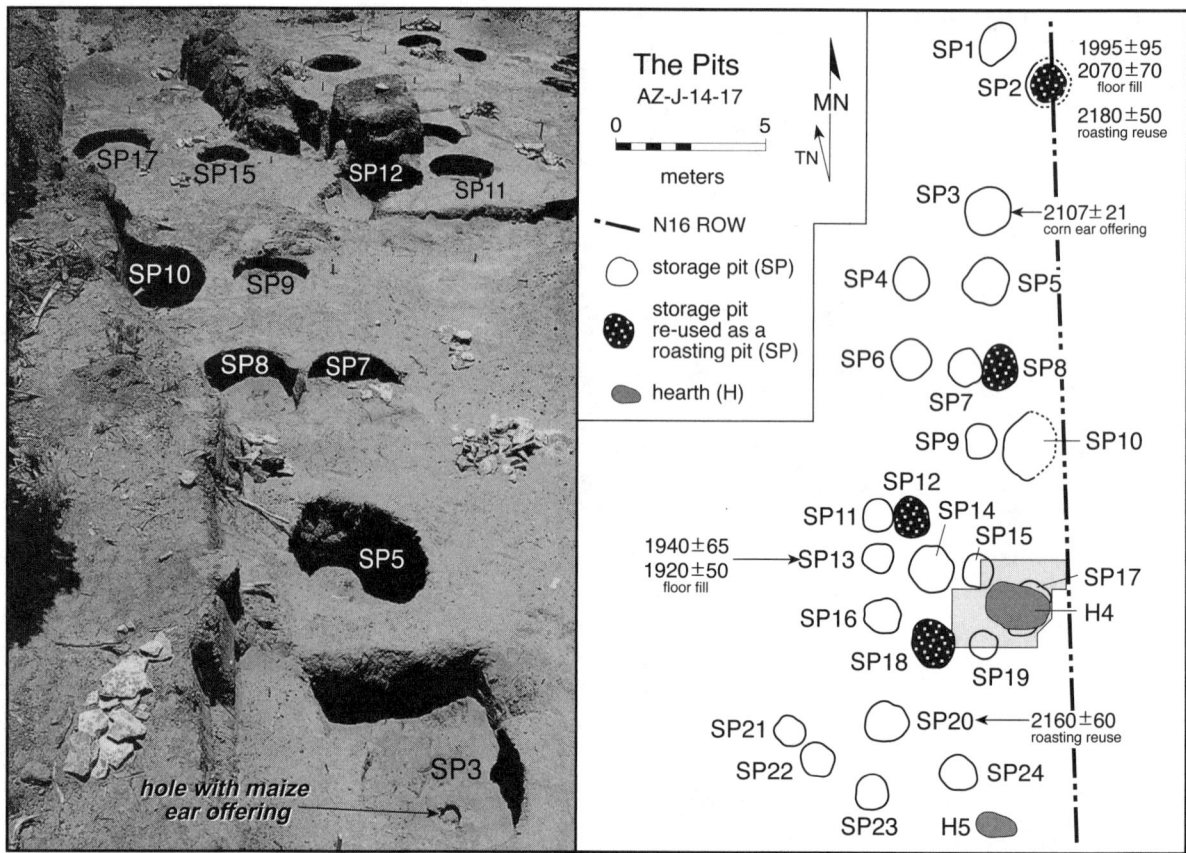

Figure 5.28. Array of large bell-shaped storage features at The Pits (view to the south), with Storage Pit 3 in the foreground and Storage Pits 21 and 22 in the background. The average of five statistically contemporaneous assays on kernels from an offering of maize ears within a small hole of Storage Pit 3 has a calibrated 2σ date range of 200–50 BC.

had been cut away to prepare them for their new cooking role. The storage pits are generally circular in outline and tend to have closely comparable measurements of length and width. Maximum dimensions, which usually occur at or just above the floor, can be as large as 2 m (the average maximum interior diameter of the 24 pits at The Pits is 1.3 m [mean length = 1.36 m, mean width = 1.29 m]). There is an obvious relationship between pit diameter and depth: the larger the diameter, the deeper the pit. Depths below the Basketmaker II occupation surface at The Pits ranged from approximately .6 to 1.7 m (1.1 m was the average depth for the 24 pits). The size of pit openings was in part a function of pit depth and maximum diameter, but evidently there was a minimal size because of the equal-sized openings, roughly 90 cm, for one of the shallowest pits and one of the deepest pits—basically large enough to crawl in and out.

Approximate contemporaneity among all or most pits at The Pits is suggested by their systematic layout along approximate cardinal directions and the lack of superposition (see Figure 5.28). Variable amounts of trash fill and the reuse of some pits for roasting purposes indicate that some storage features had been abandoned earlier than others. An estimate of when these features were used is provided by an unusual maize offering at the bottom of Storage Pit 3. In the center of the fire-hardened floor of this pit were three identical siltstone pendants laid out around a small hole 7 cm in diameter and 29 cm deep that contained three partially carbonized maize ears. My interpretation of the evidence is that it represents part of a dedication ceremony that involved placing dry corn ears within the hole and arranging pendants around it. This was done prior to fire hardening the pit. The subsequent burning partially carbonized the corn ears. The mean of five statistically contemporaneous independent radiocarbon dates on kernels from this offering is 2107 ± 21 BP, with a calibrated two-sigma date range of 200–50 BC. Maize from the floor fill of Pits 2 and 20 produced radiocarbon dates with similar age ranges, but maize from the lower fill of Pit 13 was some 170 years more recent, which is sufficiently different to suggest that some of these storage features had different periods of use.

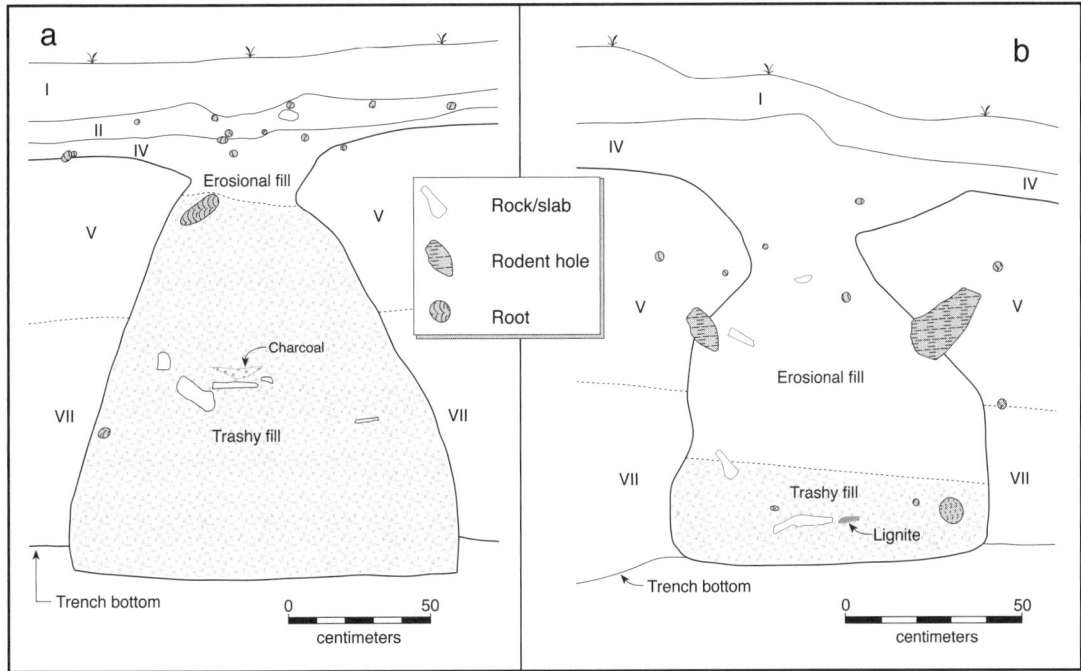

Figure 5.29. Typical cross sections of large bell-shaped storage pits at Basketmaker sites: (a) Storage Pit 14 and (b) Storage Pit 24, The Pits.

The early abundance of bell-shaped storage pits is also exemplified by Kin Kahuna, where NNAD archaeologists documented 18 such features with a capacity of just over 10 m³. Radiocarbon dating of maize from the floor fill of these features indicates that all predate AD 100. These storage features were not laid out in such a systematic way as at The Pits, and there were cases of pit superpositioning, indicating that probably only a limited number of these features were in use at any one time. Moreover, Kin Kahuna had a longer history of use than The Pits, extending well into the Christian era, and there was another type of probable storage feature at the site that might well correspond to this later interval. These other storage features consisted of large oval to circular pits with straight sides and flat bottoms; these add an uncalculated amount of additional storage capacity for the site. Given the lengthy Basketmaker occupancy of this one location (potentially 600–800 years), the total amount of storage at any one time might have been low, but since much of the Basketmaker II component at Kin Kahuna lies unexcavated outside the ROW the total amount of storage at this one location remains unknown.

An important unknown is the use-life of storage pits. Were they serviceable for a decade or two or merely a year or two? Pit use-life may well be limited compared to slab-lined cists, especially at open sites, but this is a topic needing experimental research. There is ethnographic data for the Southwest (Hill 1938; Jett and Spencer 1981; Kluckholm et al. 1971) about how such storage or cache pits were used, which foods were secured in them, and how they were prepared and packed, but there is little information about the longevity of such features. For the Hidatsa, Ahler et al. note that "after a period of use, the pit would 'sour' or become moldy" (1991:33), but they do not elaborate on what this interval of use might have been. No doubt it probably varied considerably depending on local setting, type of sediment, and climatic conditions, and pits on the plains perhaps had briefer use than those in the arid Southwest. B. Huckell claims that the pits "are also known to have relatively short use lives" (1995:43), but Buffalobird-woman of the Hidatsa tribe recounted that "a cache pit lasted for a long time, used year after year" (Wilson 1917:95). Buffalobird-woman's statement of use-life comes in the context of her very detailed account of storage pit use that comprises an entire short chapter of Hidatsa agricultural practices; thus it should not be dismissed lightly.

Also, it is worth considering if a "stale" pit might be refurbished since that might be far more time efficient than digging a whole new feature. In this regard it is possible that the burning commonly observed in Southwestern storage pits, including most of those in the N16 ROW, had to do with efforts to renovate these features by driving out moisture, mold, insect pests, and other vermin. Such burning may have been done on the first creation and use of these features, as several Navajo ethnographies report (Kluckholm et al. 1971:112–113), but also as well after some interval of use. Perhaps only after this strategy was no longer effective were the features then abandoned, especially if they had been penetrated by rodents or with slumping of the pit walls. Knowing the average use-life of such storage features is not an idle question, because it has ramifications for how many pits might have been in use at any one time and thus what the potential momentary storage capacity of a single site such as The Pits might have been. This capacity relates to the potential size of the group that the produce was being saved for as well as a measure of local productivity.

Ethnographically in both the Southwest and the Great Plains the use of storage pits appears to be linked with seasonal shifts in residential location and the need to hide food stores from other humans: "Where mobility is important, subsurface storage may be required because of an inability to monitor the stored resource" (Wills 1988: 39).[6] Concerning storage pit use for the Ramah Navajo, Kluckholm et al. claim that "they were hidden as well as possible and sometimes located in out-of-the-way places away from the hogan. Just one family would know where its own corn was stored" (1971:111). For other Navajo, as noted by Kluckholm et al., "Hill's informants confirmed the careful concealment of the pits" (1971:112). The reasons for Navajo seasonal movement are doubtless somewhat more relevant to the Basketmaker II situation than those on the Great Plains, where they have much to do with village abandonment during buffalo hunts (Forde 1963; Weltfish 1965). For the Navajo, seasonal movement related to the two principal economic pursuits—herding and farming—and annual movement was between summer habitations located near fields (except for families more dependent on herding) and winter habitations located where fuel wood was plentiful (Jett 1978). According to the Franciscan Fathers, "The winter supply of corn, wheat, melons, squashes, pinyon nuts, and the like, is stored in pits of the shape of a wicker bottle. These are dug near the summer residences, or in the field" (1968:267 [1910]). In the case of Kin Kahuna it would appear that the Basketmakers followed a similar practice because this residence is located adjacent to a farming area, so the presence of storage pits here is expectable, but in this case the site is not simply a transitory summer residence. The same probably applies as well for The Pits, another residence with abundant storage and farmland nearby. Both of these sites with numerous storage facilities also appear to be winter habitations, the implication being that they were probably lived in during much of the year—the winter and much of the growing season.

In this case, then, given the existence of sites like Kin Kahuna and The Pits, what type of seasonal mobility for Basketmaker II populations necessitated the use of hidden food caches? If they were already living next to good farmland that was also densely wooded for winter fuel, then why have residential mobility at all? Wouldn't it have been better to exploit other areas for resources on a logistic basis? Yet the presence of food cache pits implies residential abandonment and concern over securing food stores while no one was around to protect them. Further corroboration of this inference is provided by the presence of numerous secondary habitations, ones that obviously did not serve the role of long-duration and multiseason residences and which lacked storage pits. The existence of these sites strongly suggests that for some portions of the year people lived away from their food caches. Given the evidence in feces for the dietary importance of ricegrass seed and pinyon nuts, these two resources could have exerted sufficient draws that Basketmaker groups would have temporarily abandoned their permanent sites located next to prime farmland. The ricegrass harvest occurs during an interval of the growing season that is somewhat of a downtime—after crops have been planted yet before there is serious predation and weed competition (before the monsoon), usually during June depending on elevation and climatic conditions (i.e., spring moisture and warmth). Family groups or some component thereof might be gone for a month or so to harvest ricegrass and forage for other resources or to hunt. This would in many cases be well away from the habitations situated next to prime farmland because the best ricegrass stands occur on dry sandy benches and flats below the normal elevation that is farmable. Key exceptions to this are such low-elevation fields as occur along Desha Creek and elsewhere in the Glen Canyon lowlands, but these areas are not suitable for overwintering because of a lack of fuel wood, so food resources, whether it was field produce or the seeds of wild plants, had to be transported from such locations. Harvesting pinyon nuts could also result in residential mobility as groups relocated to densely wooded areas where the nut mast was high. Even if a primary residential site was located in an area of thick pinyon cover, such as at Kin Kahuna, mobility could result because of low or no yields in local areas during many years (Lanner 1981) necessitating temporary residence on distant mesas where nut production was higher.

Slab-lined storage cists became common during the interval in which pottery was adopted, apparently replacing deep, bell-shaped pits. Some unexcavated early ceramic habitations, such as AZ-D-2-355 (NAU), have clustered slab-lined storage cists. All direct dates on slab-lined cists constructed with fiber-tempered mortar holding the slabs in place or sealing interstices place them during the interval of about AD 100 to 600. The form and construction of storage features seem to have changed through time, but it remains to be demonstrated whether or not storage volume increased. A lack of excavation of early ceramic Basketmaker habitations with storage features hinders discussion of this topic. There was, however, a clear change from concealed to unconcealed storage, from deep pits that are easily hidden from view to shallower slab-lined cists that are not so easily hidden (see discussion in Wills and Windes 1989:357–359). There also may have been a corresponding increase in facility use-life. The initial step from concealed to unconcealed storage might be seen in the shallow storage pits at Kin Kahuna, where pits perhaps had domed covers of sticks and sediment that would have protruded above the ground surface. The change to this sort of storage feature, which would have allowed for more ready access but at the price of visibility, suggests an alteration of residential mobility, at least for some portion of the population, such that food stores were never left unattended. Part of this might have to do with multiple trusted family groups living together or in close proximity, thereby allowing stores to be monitored even when portions of the families were absent.

Basketmaker Origins

One research issue that came to the fore at the start of the NMRAP concerned the origins of Basketmaker II populations in the Kayenta region (see review by Matson 1991, 2002). Were they in situ forager groups transformed by the adoption of domesticates or farmer migrants from some southern source area? Would the N16 excavations reveal a continuous record of forager occupancy culminating in Basketmaker II or one punctuated by hiatuses, a discontinuous record? Moreover, what about continuity in material culture?

Kidder and Guernsey's (1919; Guernsey 1931; Guernsey and Kidder 1921) excavations and others such as those by Earl Morris across the Four Corners region of the Colorado Plateau unearthed an impressive inventory of Basketmaker II remains but did not disclose unequivocal evidence for earlier hunter-gatherer occupation. This finally occurred in 1961 at Sand Dune Cave on the Rainbow Plateau when distinctive open-twined sandals were recovered from cultural deposits directly under those with typical Basketmaker artifacts (Lindsay et al. 1968). Radiocarbon dates on three of the sandals demonstrated great antiquity (7150 to 7700 BP [Lindsay et al. 1968:96]), confirming the long-held suspicion that foragers had existed in the region long before the Basketmakers. Research since then, especially at open sites, has greatly added to the descriptive details of Archaic period foragers (see reviews in Huckell 1996; Matson 1991; Vierra 1994), but it has not necessarily supported the notion that hunter-gatherers had a developmental relationship to subsequent Basketmaker farmers in the sense originally envisioned by formulators of the Pecos classification. Sequential use of the same site or area does not qualify as a descendant relationship, and the assumption of continuous cultural development within regions should be a matter of empirical study rather than being taken as a given (Berry and Berry 1986). Archaic populations of the Four Corners region may have been predecessors in lifeway only and not ancestral.

For the northern Kayenta region, evidence relevant to Basketmaker origins at the start of the NMRAP seemed to strongly support the notion that it was an allochthonous process. On the Rainbow Plateau, excavations at both Sand Dune and Dust Devil caves suggested a considerable hiatus between Archaic foragers and Basketmaker II farmers, with the caves abandoned for thousands of years prior to Basketmaker reoccupation. The potential biases of single sites are well known, yet the breaks in site use appeared to be a microcosm of a regional pattern highlighted by Berry and Berry (1986), of a discontinuous radiocarbon record that preceded the spread of domesticates across the Southwest (cf. Geib 1996a). Breaks in occupation seemed to be accompanied by other abrupt changes in material culture that did not accord well with the notion of autochthonous development as championed by Irwin-Williams (1973) and others. Focusing on material remains rather than regional chronologies, Matson (1991) called attention to the lack of Basketmaker II cultural unity and suggested multiple origins and processes to account for this patterning—transformation of in situ foragers in some cases and migrant farmer-foragers in others.

Continuity vs. Discontinuity

Two aspects of the archaeological record are relevant for examining continuity during the agricultural transition on the Rainbow Plateau: continuity in settlement and continuity in material culture. Genetic continuity is another crucial line of evidence, although even if DNA analysis or nondestructive cranial morphometric or dental trait analyses could be undertaken, the sample of Archaic skeletal remains from the Colorado Plateau is unlikely to be sufficient to make a strong case either for or against genetic relatedness. Quite promising in this regard is the recovery of DNA from human feces (Poinar 2002; Poinar et al. 2001), something that might eventually allow Archaic–Basketmaker genetic continuity to be examined in detail (research on this front is currently under way by Brian Kemp). The feces of Archaic foragers are not a rare find on the Colorado Plateau.

Continuity of settlement refers to the uninterrupted occupation of the same region. The significance of this is obvious, for without any observable trace of humans it is difficult to make a case for long-term continuous development (Berry 1982; Berry and Berry 1986). Measures of settlement continuity include regional chronometric records provided by tree-ring or radiocarbon dates as well as regional composite histories of site use. Sample adequacy and bias loom large in arguments for lack of settlement continuity (see Geib 1996a:28; Meltzer 1999). Have we investigated enough of a given region? Have we systematically ignored a given class of evidence or type of site? Are the traces of some periods less obvious or less well preserved than those of other periods?

Continuity in culture refers to a clearly linked temporal sequence of cultural traits. This is an inherently subjective endeavor no matter what quantitative techniques are used, for it involves judgments as to the degree of relatedness among objects from slices of time. Moreover, even when there appears to be unprecedented change in artifact style or production technology, it is difficult to be sure that we have not merely missed an intermediate stage, especially if the interval of morphological or technological change occurred during a very brief period preceded and followed by long intervals of little or no change. The basic question is whether there are Archaic prototypes for the impressive inventory of Basketmaker II material remains from the Kayenta region first described in detail by Guernsey and Kidder (1921; Guernsey 1931; Kidder and Guernsey 1919). Unfortunately, the open sites excavated by the NMRAP have not yielded the most distinctive portions of Basketmaker II material culture, which are the perishable artifacts. This problem can be partially offset because of the perishable artifacts recovered from caves in the northern Kayenta region and by examining certain classes of nonperishable artifacts that were recovered from the NMRAP sites as well as from the caves. Even with an abundance of perishables, temporal control for specific Basketmaker artifact types such as sandals and bags is an additional problem. Detailed chronologies are required to document temporal sequences of change within artifact types. When making comparisons between Basketmaker and Archaic technology it will be important to know whether remains come from the late portion of the Basketmaker II period, the earliest part, or somewhere in between.

Settlement Continuity and the Radiocarbon Record

As reviewed earlier in this chapter and in chapter 4, the current sample of radiocarbon dates for the Archaic and Basketmaker periods of the northern Kayenta region is quite substantial, due in large part to the recent NMRAP excavations but including additional dates from caves (Ambler 1996; Geib 1996b, 2004; Geib and Robins 2003; Lindsay et al. 1968). As of this report, there are 154 dates ranging from almost 8000 cal. BC up to 700 cal. AD, with somewhat over half of these from the Basketmaker II period ($n = 89$). Given that most of the Basketmaker radiocarbon assays are on high-quality samples from all types of sites, both open and sheltered, this robust data set may accurately reflect the time of Basketmaker occupancy for the northern Kayenta region.

The frequency distribution of all radiocarbon dates currently available for Archaic and Basketmaker sites in the study area (Figure 5.30) is hardly continuous, containing a major break between early and late Archaic and a possible short gap between late Archaic and Basketmaker (see also Figure 5.10). Though I doubt that foragers totally abandoned the region during the interval of the middle Archaic period date gap (see discussion in chapter 4), even if they had it might be immaterial to the issue of Basketmaker origins. With domesticates now known to be present in the Southwest at around 4000 BP, the late Archaic spike in radiocarbon dates beginning at about this time may well result from an increase in the population of pure foragers and the initial appearance of farmer-foragers.

The possible small gap on the tail end of the date distribution from ca. 800 to 400 cal. BC has relevance for

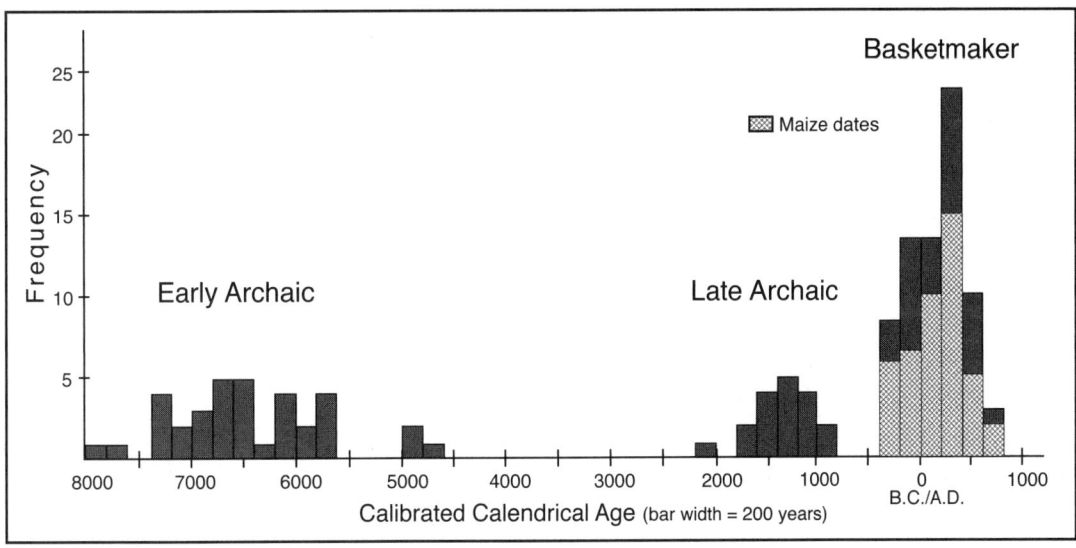

Figure 5.30. Frequency distribution of all Archaic and Basketmaker radiocarbon dates available from the northern Kayenta region with direct dates on maize remains highlighted.

examining the issue of settlement continuity for the Rainbow Plateau. This gap was discussed earlier in this chapter where I concluded that it may result from limited sample size, and certainly the number of excavated sites at present is inadequate to effectively argue for complete forager abandonment of the Rainbow Plateau. The gap is provocative, sampling problems aside, but I nonetheless believe that searching for a hiatus misses an important point about Basketmaker origins—namely, that there can be cultural discontinuity without any evident break in occupation as indicated by radiocarbon dates or other proxies of settlement history. Obviously the coarse resolution offered by radiocarbon must be considered, since it could fail to differentiate sequential occupations, but even if dating was based on tree-rings, a temporal gap is not necessary for a discontinuity in cultural to occur. A marked example of this is with European colonization of the Americas—no break in settlement, but the introduction of completely new material remains. Abandonment or not, the nature of the archaeological record in the northern Kayenta region after 400 cal. BC is markedly changed both adaptively and culturally, and it is these discontinuities that are of import.

Adaptive Continuity

Regardless of what the radiocarbon record indicates about settlement continuity during the Archaic–Formative transition, to what extent is there adaptive continuity? Does the record produced by populations living in the region after the appearance of maize differ by slight degree from that produced by the foragers on this plateau prior to the appearance of maize, or was there an immediate and radical change? The former scenario would seem to better accord with the idea of in situ foragers adopting domesticates as an adjunct to their hunter-gatherer adaptation, the "monumental nonevent" (Minnis 1985:310) advocated by Irwin-Williams (1973, 1979), among others. A dramatically different postdomesticate archaeological record would, however, seem to better accord with the idea that there was no "transition" to domesticate use in the usual sense within the northern Kayenta region but, rather, there was adaptive replacement or displacement. At a larger scale it is worth considering whether the changes in the archaeological record of the N16 project area coincident with the introduction of agriculture paralleled some of the trends indicated by Wills and Huckell (1994; also Huckell 1996) for the American Southwest as a whole.

The sites at which maize first occurs were characterized earlier in this chapter. In part they consist of the primary residential sites of Kin Kahuna and The Pits, with their extensive trash deposits, pithouses, numerous bell-shaped storage pits and other pits, and human burials. The capacity of the large storage pits allowed a considerable surplus of food to be cached for future use. The 24 such features at The Pits had a combined capacity of almost 17 m^3, and the total storage potential was even greater because the number of pits in the core portion of the settlement (outside the ROW) remains unknown. Maize kernels and cupules occurred in most features at both habitations, with

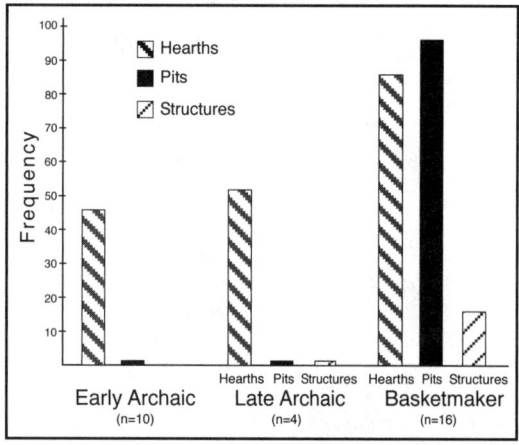

Figure 5.31. Frequency of feature types on early Archaic, late Archaic, and Basketmaker sites. The number of excavated sites that provided these data is given in parentheses.

corncobs obtained from several of the best-preserved contexts. Ninety-five percent of the 72 flotation samples from Kin Kahuna contained maize, with almost 40 percent containing kernels. Maize had a 75 percent ubiquity in the 20 flotation samples from The Pits and a 60 percent occurrence based on kernels. These findings strongly suggest subsistence dependence on maize, which is exactly what stable isotopic data from Basketmaker burials of the Kayenta region document (Coltrain et al. 2007).

The late Archaic sites of the northern Kayenta region are vastly different in character from those associated with maize. As summarized in the previous chapter and described in detail in volume 2 online, they consist of hearths in association with lithic debitage and occasional grinding tools, and they lack storage features entirely. The most impressive late Archaic sites consisted of small clusters of hearths surrounded by variable amounts of flaking debris, grinding tools, and bone. At Three Dog Site these concentrations of remains were both horizontally and vertically separated from one another following sequential use of a dune ridge over the span of several hundred years. At most, this and other late Archaic sites functioned as temporary camps used by small social groups; none appear to have had the substantial, long-lived residential occupations that are evident for Kin Kahuna and The Pits. Indeed, none of the late Archaic sites on the Rainbow Plateau appeared similar to the Basketmaker II seasonal residences excavated by the NMRAP, summarized above, even though the late Archaic sites contained considerably more artifacts.

Figure 5.31 shows the increase in feature abundance from Archaic to Basketmaker and hints at the contrast in feature diversity. The late Archaic sites consist of hearths of various types and one possible burned brush structure. In contrast, the Basketmaker sites contain a great abundance and diversity of features. The dramatically different nature of the Basketmaker sites compared with those of the immediately preceding late Archaic strongly suggests a lack of adaptive continuity. The distinct records seem more in accordance with an adaptive disjuncture than an autochthonous transformation from a foraging economy to that of a farmer-forager economy. Relevant to this inference is the relatively brief interval on the larger time scale of prehistory that separates these contrasting archaeological records. At most there are about 300–400 years of separation, and the interval might actually be just a few hundred years. Change during the preceding 7,000 years of the Archaic period appears glacial by comparison to what transpired during the brief gap in the radiocarbon record for the northern Kayenta region.

Continuity in Culture

Basketmaker II material culture is best known from the wonderful array of perishable artifacts recovered from caves and dry shelters in the late 1800s and early 1900s. Much of this material lingers unstudied and unreported to this day, but fortunately Kidder and Guernsey (1919; Guernsey 1931; Guernsey and Kidder 1921) set a high standard for analysis and reporting with the sizable collection of Basketmaker II artifacts they amassed from the Marsh Pass–Monument Valley area of northeast Arizona. The wealth of perishables provided a glimpse into prehistoric life that archaeologists in few places of the world are privileged to see. Years later, Kidder along with Cosgrove made a "survival survey" of the vast collection recovered from the Basketmaker caves—determining what would have remained had the collection been recovered from an open site:

> We found that of the hundreds of objects, filling five large display cases and many storage drawers, there would have remained no more than a score or so of chipped flints, a handful of bone awls, and a few beads of stone and shell. The whole lot would have gone into a good-sized soup plate. That pitiful residue would have told us nothing of how the Basket-makers cradled and diapered their babies, how they dressed, how they wore their hair, what crops they grew or—what is more important—what plants they had not yet learned to cultivate. It would have given us no inkling of their extraordinary skill

as weavers and wood-workers. As it is, we have intimate knowledge of all these and many other details of Basket-maker life, knowledge which in the case of the overwhelming majority of ancient cultures is lost beyond recall [Kidder 1947:vii].

Among other things, one aspect of life that Basketmaker material remains have informed about, especially the perishable artifacts, is the extent of commonality or uniformity of culture among the first farming populations on the Colorado Plateau. In reviewing this evidence Matson (1991, 2002) concluded that there was a basic east–west division that was ethnic in nature, resulting from different origins for Basketmaker II populations: "The Western or 'Classic' Basketmaker II [BMII] have affinities with the San Pedro Cochise, as recognized by the Berrys. The Durango, or Los Pinos [eastern] BMII, however, have affinities with local Archaic cultures, as argued by Cynthia Irwin-Williams" (2002:346–347). Matson (2002:Table 27.1, Figure 27.4) pointed to such aspects of technology as basketry, cordage (cf. Haas 2003), sandals, cradleboards, and dart points as well as house construction techniques.

Early archaeologists, most notably Byron Cummings and Irwin Hayden, unearthed Basketmaker remains in the northern Kayenta region, but not until MNA's excavation of Sand Dune Cave in 1961 were any Basketmaker II artifacts for the area adequately described and published (Lindsay et al. 1968). In his write-up of the site, Ambler concluded that "although substantially increasing our knowledge of the Basketmaker II period, most of the items fall within the established range of artifacts for that period" (Lindsay et al. 1968:101). This statement basically refers to Kidder and Guernsey's findings, the benchmark for Basketmaker II artifacts. Ambler's conclusion about the essential similarity of Basketmaker II artifacts around Navajo Mountain to those of the Marsh Pass area was borne out by Schilz's (1979) analysis of artifacts recovered from Desha Caves 1 and 2. Again the assemblage consisted of standard western Basketmaker II items such as four-warp wickerwork (plain-weave) sandals, close-twined bags, Z-twist cordage, two-rod and bundle basketry, and hafted dart points with wide side or corner notches. A heel fragment of a four-warp wickerwork sandal from Desha Cave 1 has an AMS radiocarbon age of 1800 ± 40 BP (Figure 5.32; Geib and Robins 2003:Table 1), confirming the Basketmaker II typological assignment of this artifact. Additional western Basketmaker II diagnostics such as this type of sandal have been observed or collected from other sites of the region (e.g., Lipe 1960:200–202,

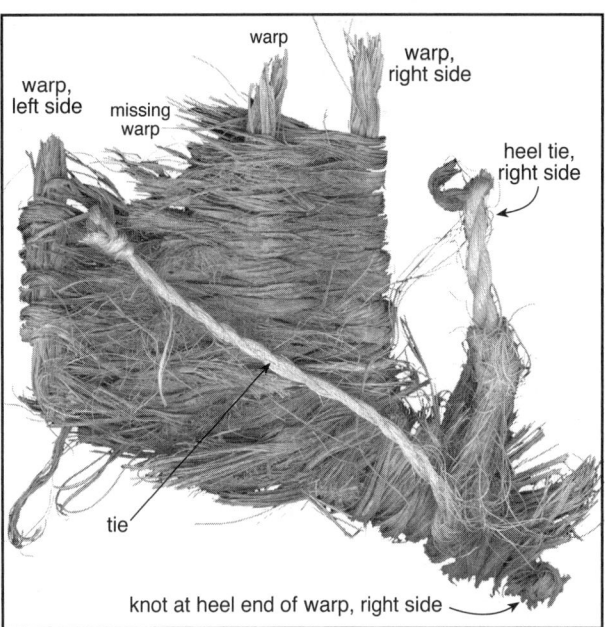

Figure 5.32. A heel fragment of a four-warp wickerwork sandal from Desha Cave 1 with an accelerator mass spectrometry radiocarbon age of 1800 ± 40 BP (from Geib and Robins 2003: Figure 5).

Figure 62, Table 18; Long 1966:Figure 56; MNA collections I observed). The limited work at Atlatl Rock Cave (SD vol. 2, chap. 2) also recovered a few artifacts that appear typical of western Basketmaker II remains, most notably a mountain sheep horn flaker (Geib 2002) and an elaborate feather object of probable ceremonial use.

As observed by Kidder, few remains would have been left for archaeological recovery had he and Guernsey worked at open sites instead of dry shelters. The rich diversity of perishable artifacts would have been totally lost, leaving just stone and bone. The NMRAP excavations attest to this fact, because no perishables were recovered, even from burned structures. Lacking this most highly diagnostic set of remains, what can be said about the cultural affiliation of open Basketmaker sites? Are there sufficiently distinctive imperishable artifacts that a western Basketmaker II cultural affiliation can be supported? At the very least it should prove useful to review the most formal and high-input artifacts such as projectile points, ornaments, and gaming pieces found at open Basketmaker sites so as to facilitate future comparisons.

Dart-Sized Points

Most stone artifacts are mundane and likely have little value with regard to examining cultural relatedness. Some nonutilitarian items such as stone pipes, pendants, and atlatl weights may have relevance, but low recovery rates

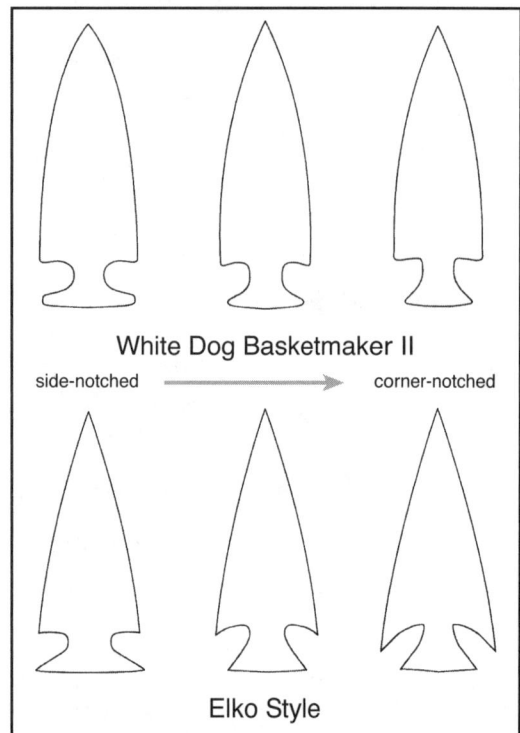

Figure 5.33. Idealized outlines for western Basketmaker and Elko dart points (from Geib 1996a:Figure 19).

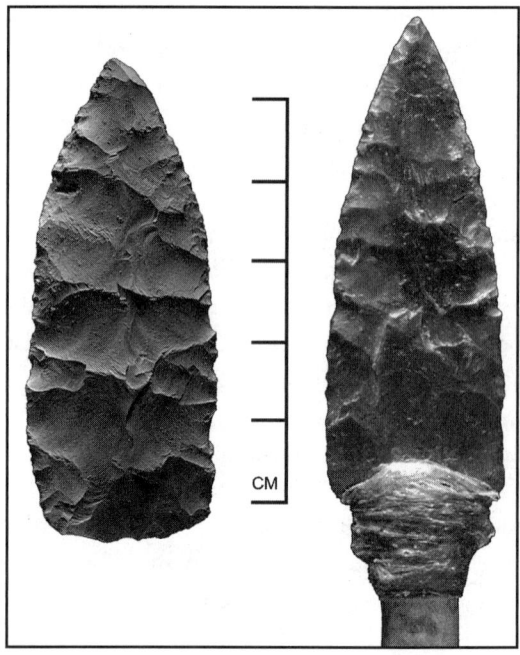

Figure 5.34. A western Basketmaker dart point preform and hafted dart point from Cache 1 of Sand Dune Cave showing important characteristics including flake scars; the preform is coated to enhance flake scars.

limit their utility. Projectile points are the one class of stone artifacts recovered in sufficient number that they may have some value in cultural identification, but this is no easy matter (see Geib 1996a:62–64) because dart points during the interval of initial corn use were grossly similar across the entire Colorado Plateau, being principally characterized by low side-notched to corner-notched forms. This said, there are important aspects of morphology and production technology that characterize western Basketmaker II points and serve to distinguish them from Archaic Elko points and perhaps from points made by contemporaneous early farmers on the Colorado Plateau.

Berry and Berry (1986:319) maintained that the points from Basketmaker II sites, which they called San Pedro/Basketmaker II, bore only faint similarity to Elko points. Previously, C. Berry (1984:71) named points of this kind as western or San Juan Basketmaker II following Morris and Burgh (1954:56, Figure 29), who first used the term *San Juan Basketmaker* with reference to the common, though numerically limited kind of dart point recovered from Kayenta-region caves by Kidder and Guernsey (1919; Guernsey 1931; Guernsey and Kidder 1921). Morris and Burgh saw little similarity between the San Juan Basketmaker points and many of the more than 200 dart points they recovered from Talus Village and the Falls Creek rockshelters near Durango, Colorado. Matson (1991:45, sidebar) noted that the corner-notched forms from the Durango Basketmaker II sites, especially those with parallel, moderately narrow notches, are what many archaeologists today would type as Elko Corner-notched. Matson (1991:46, sidebar) suggests that there is more overlap than Morris and Burgh would lead one to expect, yet with such a large assemblage of points it is perhaps meaningful that so few resemble the typical dart point from White Dog Basketmaker contexts.

Primary Point Form. Western Basketmaker points can be distinguished from earlier (or contemporaneous?) Elko points using the specifics of notch placement, size, and shape (Figure 5.33), as Morris and Burgh intimated, but also how the notches were produced, along with overall blade shape and size and production technology. The latter aspects are best perceived on finished dart points hafted onto foreshafts and the often numerous preforms recovered from some western Basketmaker sites—items usually found together within hide bags, such as Cache 1 of Sand Dune Cave (Geib 2002, 2004). The preforms and hafted points as whole and unreworked items provide an accurate reflection of cultural objectives for finished projectile points (Figure 5.34). Without going into too much detail here, the important characteristics include (1) an outline that has gently curved margins resulting in a general lanceolate rather than triangular shape; (2) a maximum blade width that is usually achieved roughly one-third from the base with the margins more or less parallel but often slightly constricting toward the base (observable on preforms); (3) a relatively great length to width, often with a length-to-width ratio of around 2.5:1; (4) a finishing with very broad collateral percussion flake scars; and (5) an edge-on profile that is markedly sinuous for finished points, the result of wide bending-initiated flakes being removed alternately from one face and then the other (for details, see Geib 2002:287–293, Figures 18.9–18.12).

Guernsey and Kidder first described the notching of western Basketmaker points: "Almost all our finished points are notched at right angles to their long axes, the notches having a depth equal to about one-third of the total width of the base" (1921:87). Each notch is equal to about one-third of the width; thus the final width across the notches is just one-third of the point width. The notches are not only relatively deep but broad; indeed the notches on some specimens are as broad as they are deep, making for a very delicate-looking stem (see Parry and Christenson 1987:Plates 6–9). The evident common practice for western Basketmakers to tightly bind their points to foreshafts (see below) must have led to frequent breaks across the notches. Deep notching may have created a purposeful failure area, intended to prevent damage to the foreshaft and provide a large fragment easily recycled into a usable point by renotching above the break. The elongated nature of Basketmaker preforms would have easily allowed for at least one recycling.

In addition to side notching, many points from western Basketmaker II contexts have a corner-notched appearance. There appears to be a continuum between side and corner notching for western Basketmaker points, similar to what Holmer (1980:67) quantitatively demonstrated for Elko points. Nevertheless, the corner-like notching on western Basketmaker points is distinctive from the type of corner notching seen on most points from the Durango Basketmaker sites or on Elko points from the northern Colorado Plateau (see Geib 1996a:62–64). The distinctions appear to result from the different origin of the notch and perhaps the size of the notching tool or method of notching. The notches on western Basketmaker points appear to begin on the side rather than the corner per se, at a distance above the base similar to the side-notched variety. During the process of notching the bottom part is extended down to the bases, removing some of the basal width. The top of the notch (toward the tip) is generally straight, parallel to the base (no barb), whereas the bottom angles back toward the original corner of the preform, removing some of it, thereby resulting in a corner-notched appearance. This contrasts with the corner notches of Elko points and many Durango points, which, when executed without a production mistake, extend diagonally and often quite narrowly from the actual corner of the preform, leaving the side margins mostly intact, resulting in a pronounced barb.

The notches on the Elko series points from late Archaic sites on the Rainbow Plateau are commonly narrow and deep and appear to have been made chiefly (perhaps exclusively) by the "edge of tool" technique as described by Titmus (1985:248–249), which results in widely expanding, lunate-shaped notching flake scars. This is quite different from the common type of notching seen on Basketmaker II points of the Rainbow Plateau, which seems consistent with an "end of tool" technique. The moderately high incidence of notching flakes in the late Archaic debitage assemblage from Tsé Haal'á accords well with the evidence on the points for use of an edge-of-tool notching technique, since it produces more readily identifiable notching flakes than does the end-of-tool technique. Notching flakes were rarely identified at NMRAP Basketmaker II sites, and the overall incidence was markedly lower than from Archaic sites: just 14 notching flakes were identified out of a total of 22,783 flakes from Basketmaker sites (.1%) compared to 145 notching flakes out of a total of 9,798 flakes from Archaic sites (1.5%).

Horn Flakers and Point Morphology. To produce projectile points and large bifaces, western Basketmaker II flintknappers employed rods made of mountain sheep horn (Geib 2002, 2004). Excellent examples of these tools formed part of a hunter's tool bag cached at Sand Dune Cave at the foot of Navajo Mountain (Geib 2004; Lindsay et al. 1968:42). Eight such mountain sheep horn rods or dowels were contained within a small bag made from the skin of a prairie dog, which was in turn within the overall dog-skin bag. Detailed study of these specimens, including examination under a scanning electron microscope, has conclusively demonstrated that they had been used to fabricate flaked-stone tools (Geib 2002). All but one of the eight tools from the cache contained minute fragments of silica embedded in their use-worn ends. The two size classes of horn flakers in the cache correspond with two distinct methods of stone tool reduction: robust

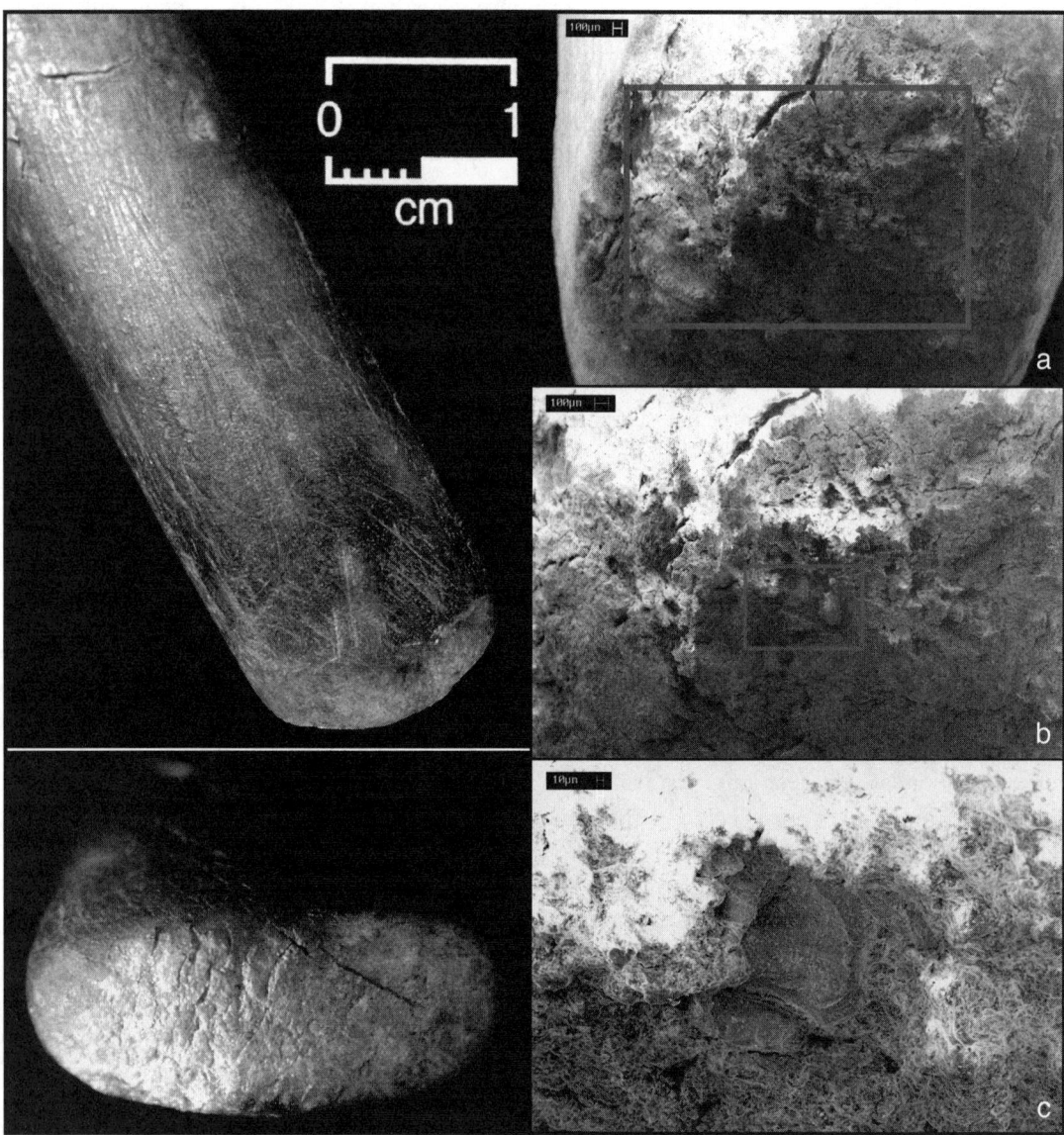

Figure 5.35. A mountain sheep horn flaking tool thought to have been used as an indirect percussion punch recovered from Atlatl Rock Cave; scanning electron microscope images at increasing magnification show silica fragments embedded in the used end.

horn flakers were used as punches for indirect percussion, and smaller horn flakers, once hafted to sticks with sinew and hide, functioned as composite pressure flakers.

The limited work conducted at Atlatl Rock Cave in conjunction with this project also recovered an example of a Basketmaker horn flaker (Figure 5.35). This particular stubby rod (7.3 cm long, 1.6 cm wide, and 1.1 cm thick) is shaped like a flattened dowel in cross section with a slight curve in long section that follows the original arc of the horn it was made from. This item is stained brown and exhibits a polish from handling, and both ends exhibit extensive use-wear consisting of pitting, grooves, and scratches. The use-wear evident on the Atlatl Rock Cave specimen is consistent with using the flaker as an indirect percussion punch. Minute fragments of siliceous stone are embedded within pits on each worked end—certain evidence for use of the tool in working stone. The embedded silica fragments are visible under a light microscope but are most clearly viewed and imaged with a scanning electron microscope as shown in Figure 5.35. The horn flaking tool from Atlatl Rock Cave differs from the flakers of the Sand Dune Cave cache, which have a freshly worked appearance, exhibiting both a natural color and abrasion marks but lacking polish; most are also much longer in length. The differences result because the Atlatl Rock Cave flaker is worn down in size from use and may have

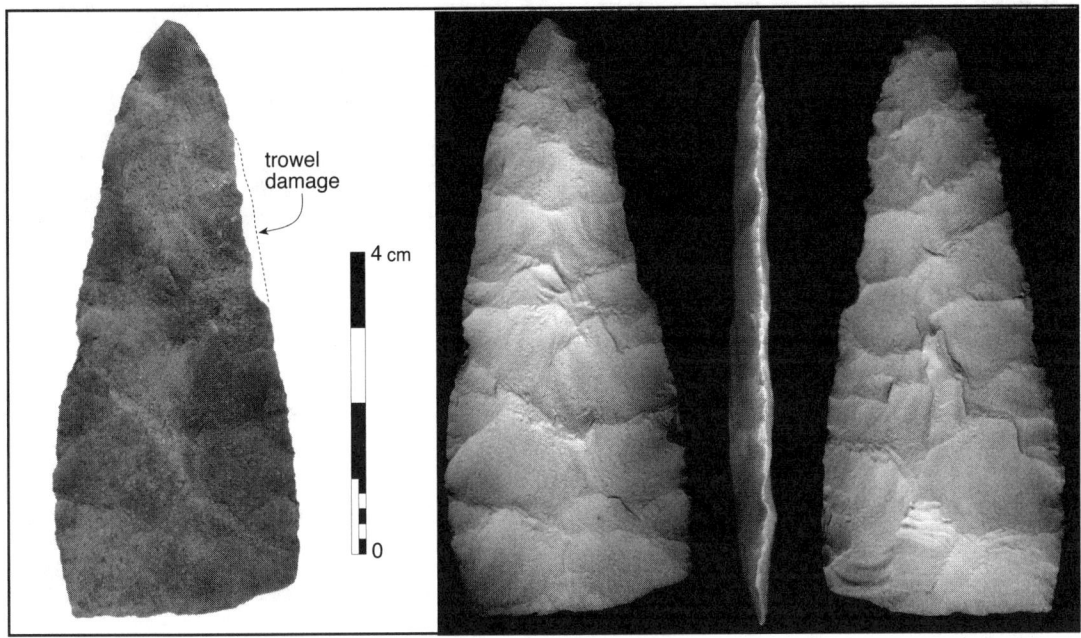

Figure 5.36. A western Basketmaker dart point preform recovered from Structure 3 of Kin Kahuna, AZ-J-3-8. The tool on the left is shown naturally; in the other views the preform is coated to enhance flake scars.

been discarded because it was no longer serviceable as an indirect percussion punch.

Basketmaker II horn flakers created the distinct flaking pattern seen on western Basketmaker II projectile points (Figure 5.36). The horn flakers, whether used as indirect punches or for pressure flaking, produced wide flake initiations and corresponding wide flakes because of their large and somewhat soft contact areas. The resulting broad flake scars are readily appreciated on the six hafted points and 16 dart point preforms from the Sand Dune Cave cache (see Figure 5.34; also Geib 2002:Figures 18.9–18.12), bifaces doubtless made with the horn flakers from the same bag. The original production flake scars are best seen on points in primary condition, those that occur in caches and burial contexts and are evidently little used. As points are resharpened or morphologically changed through use for tasks other than as projectile tips, the original production scars become obscured. But the flake scars observed on western Basketmaker II points in primary form appear to be principally from percussion flaking, likely indirect percussion, and these scars are from flakes that simultaneously thinned and shaped, such that finished points appear different from most Archaic corner-notched and side-notched dart points of the same region. The latter were usually finished by pressure flaking and have narrow flake scars and far more extensive edge trimming (see discussion in Geib 2002). An excellent example of western Basketmaker flake scars is provided by the biface (point preform) shown in Figure 5.36, which came from a floor pit of Structure 3 at Kin Kahuna, a structure with a radiocarbon age of cal. AD 130–430.

Resharpened and Use-Modified Points: The NMRAP Assemblage. Unlike the preform shown in Figure 5.36, none of the finished projectile points recovered from NMRAP Basketmaker sites can be considered to be in "primary form," all having been broken, resharpened, or otherwise use modified (Figure 5.37). This is the usual state of affairs when dealing with collections other than cached artifacts or those placed with the dead. Even the two whole points in the upper left (a–b) appear to have been resharpened to their current small size, and b exhibits use-wear from extensive cutting use. Those two and c, despite being small in size, exhibit the classic morphology of western Basketmaker II side-notched points. Points d–f, on the other hand, can be considered corner notched; the two whole examples appear to have been resharpened at least once. Point i is another good example of a western Basketmaker corner-notched point, and in this case it is made of white siltstone from Black Mesa, a material type that was preferred by local Basketmaker groups on this mesa (see Parry 1987a:209, Table 6-3, 1987b:25). This point along with those that flank it on both sides in the figure (g–k) came from the site of Sin Sombra and reflect the range of variability that might be expected in a late Basketmaker II assemblage (Sin Sombra was occupied sometime between

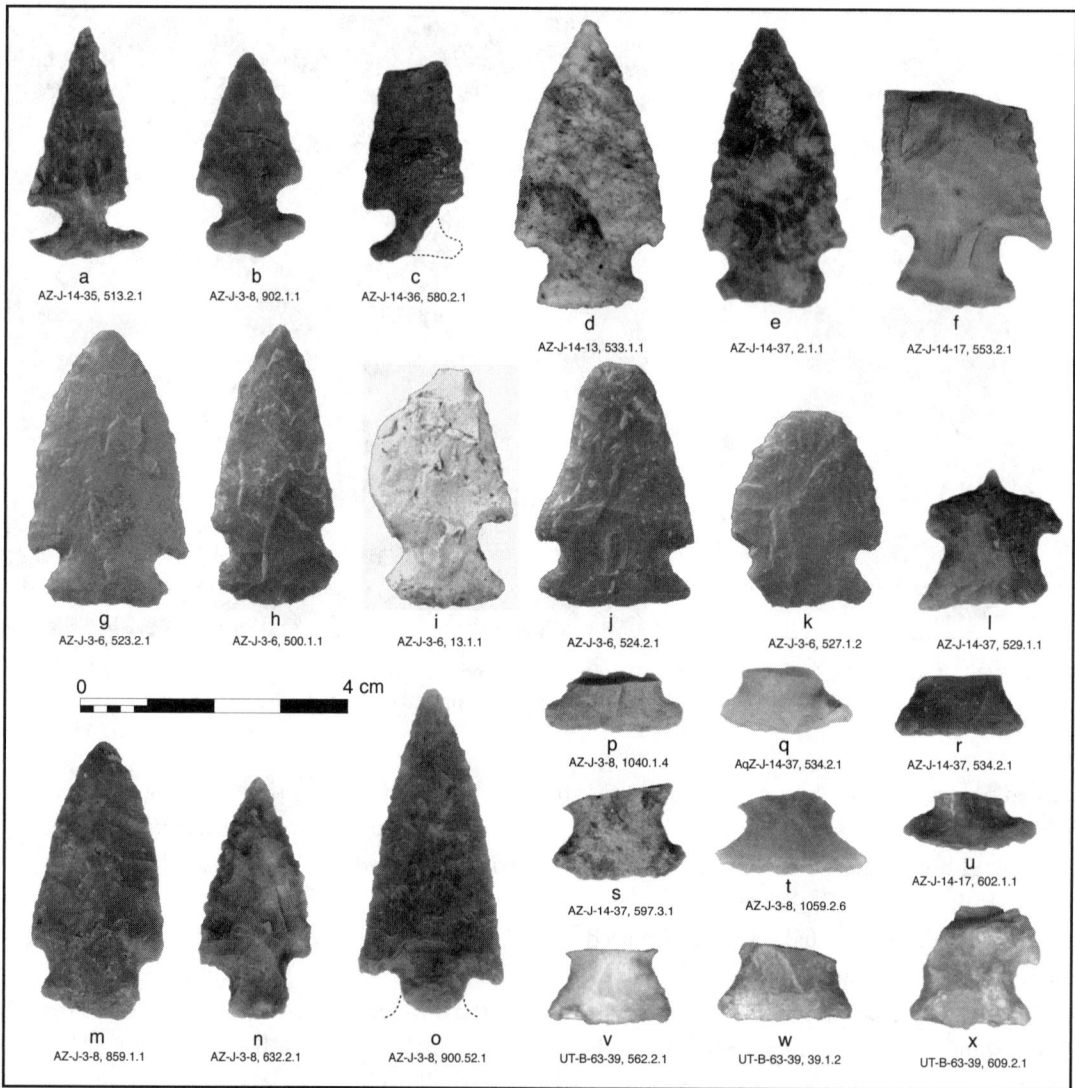

Figure 5.37. Dart points recovered from Navajo Mountain Road Archaeological Project Basketmaker II sites, including points heavily reworked or use modified; none can be considered in "primary form."

cal. AD 120 and 330). Although all of these tend to have the wide side to corner notches, most are not as deep as often occur. All retain portions of the wide percussion flake scars that are so characteristic of Basketmaker II dart points of the region, scars from flakes that simultaneously thinned and shaped the projectile points (see Geib 2002). Reflaking and reuse have obliterated many of these flake scars, but they are still evident on the bases and lower portions of the blades.

These five points plus m also exemplify the Basketmaker II penchant for extensive use of projectile points for tasks other than or subsequent to their use as weapon tips. All exhibit traces of extensive use, probably while they were hafted to foreshafts or other handles. The tip of point g exhibits extensive edge polish from cutting use; this tip had broken and then been refashioned, but with a small remnant of the break surface still evident. The three points with fractured tips (i–k) all have use-wear extending over the breaks, indicating continued use in capacities other than as projectile tips. A good example of what these tools probably looked like when hafted is provided by one of the hafted dart points from Cache 1 at Sand Dune Cave, a point that had been used extensively as a cutting tool (Geib 2002:Figure 18.10 left, n. 7). Guernsey and Kidder (1921:Plate 35e, 95) illustrated and described a dart point that had been hafted onto a short handle for use. The recycled point i has a large impact break that removed the tip and burinated one margin down to the notch, but it shows use rounding and a small flake or two removed from the broken edge, and the intact margin ex-

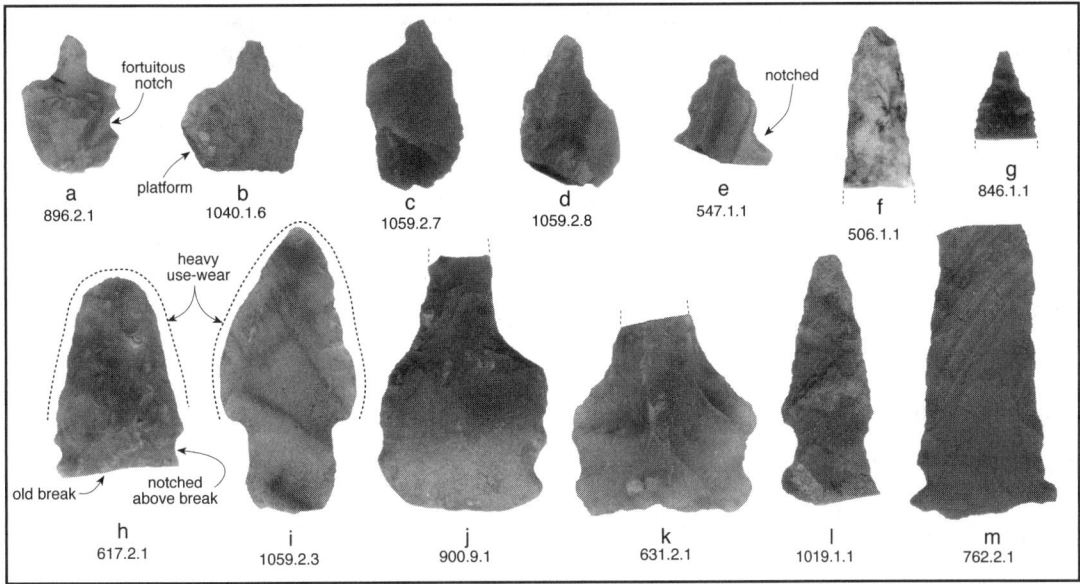

Figure 5.38. Examples of drills recovered from Kin Kahuna, a Basketmaker II primary habitation dated between ca. 360 cal. BC and cal. AD 430. Many of the drills vary from those found in Archaic contexts, if not in overall morphology, then in use-wear.

hibits edge rounding and polish from use, so evidently the item continued to be used as a hafted knife or cutting tool.

The tool shown in Figure 5.37l is so extensively modified that it no longer resembles a projectile point tip except for the obviously notched base. Given the presence of the upper part of both notches, this point evidently snapped transversely like f, with the basal portion then being reflaked to fashion the stubby drill tip. A more common way for this type of point to break is straight across the notches, as represented by the eight bases p–w and by the one tip and midsection portion o (point x was snapped by a bending break above the notches). In most cases these artifacts appear to have broken in the haft from bending forces, likely during impact; these are the sorts of items that would be cleaned from foreshafts to be replaced with new points. This sort of breakage leaves large tip and midsection portions like those shown in o, which could have been collected for recycling (this example came from the floor of Structure 4 at Kin Kahuna). This point portion was snapped across the notches by bending forces exerted parallel to the long axis of the tool, something that could have resulted when the tool was deeply embedded, such as in an animal carcass. A large tip portion like this could be rebased by extending the notch farther and perhaps tapering the square broken edge. This would result in a point much like that shown as n from the same site. Such a fragment could also be readily modified into a drill or many other tools.

Drills

The discussion of projectile points opened with the statement that few stone artifacts other than projectile points are of much value for examining cultural relatedness but mentioned such nonutilitarian items as stone pipes, pendants, and atlatl weights as having potential relevance. The problem with these items concerns their generally low recovery rates, which limit their utility. Another way to examine the issue of continuity/discontinuity is with tools such as drills that were potentially used in the fabrication of pipes, ornaments, or other distinctive artifacts. These tools might well be represented in numbers that are meaningful because disposal was more frequent than long-term retention and it commonly occurred in the production context rather than as specialized discard.

Examples of various types of Basketmaker II drills are shown in Figure 5.38, all from Kin Kahuna. The drills appear to have been used for a variety of different tasks judging from their morphology and use-wear, from boring bowls in stone pipes to creating deep sockets in dart shafts. Many Basketmaker II drills were bifacially thinned and shaped, and many of these probably began their use-life as a projectile point or knife, with subsequent transformation into a drill. In some cases this is obvious, such as several of the points shown in Figure 5.37. In other cases the obvious characteristics of projectile point morphology have been lost to breakage, retouch, or use modification. Basketmaker II groups also made and used more expedient drills, usually fashioned from small single flakes with minimal edge modification.

Perhaps the most distinctive form of drill within Basketmaker assemblages, one that is not observed in Archaic assemblages, is that used to fashion pipes. Pipe drills are exemplified by those of Figure 5.38h and i and by the recycled dart points of Figure 5.37h and j. All four have relatively wide bits that exhibit heavy rotational abrasion and striations; the use-wear extends from the tip down the margins to the haft element (notches) on three specimens and two-thirds of the distance to the notches on the recycled point shown in Figure 5.37j. The use-wear facets on the edges of these drills are up to 1 mm wide, and the striations are plainly visible in good light without the aid of magnification. The nature of the use-wear is consistent with rotational motion within hard and abrasive substances. Given bit length and width and the extent of wear along the edges it is clear that these tools were used to create deep, wide holes: at least 20 mm deep and 17 mm wide for 5.38h; 25 mm deep and 19 mm wide for 5.38i; 26 mm deep and 23 mm wide for 5.37h; and 22 mm deep and 20 mm wide for 5.37j, where the use-wear does not extend the full distance of the blade. The one item of Basketmaker II material culture that required such deep and wide holes was the stone pipe, and given the nature of the use-wear this is likely what these drills had been used for. Drills I used to bore pipe bowls in siltstone and scoria exhibit comparable use-wear. All four items compare favorably with the pipe drill described by Guernsey and Kidder (1921:95), except that their specimen had more pronounced use-wear. Their tool was hafted to a short wooden handle (Guernsey and Kidder 1921:Plate 35e), as probably were the NMRAP examples when in use. A handle would have been useful for efficient use of these drills, especially for working stone. The dart points recycled as pipe drills might have been used within their original foreshafts, since these would have provided a useful handle. The pipe drill of Figure 5.38h is made from a recycled tip portion of a dart point with shallow notches placed above the break for hafting purposes.

To my knowledge, stone pipes are unknown from Archaic contexts of the Colorado Plateau. Equally, Archaic sites lack the drills used to create the bowls of such pipes, including the large late Archaic assemblages of the Rainbow Plateau investigated by the NMRAP. The occurrence of pipe drills in Basketmaker II assemblages, even those from secondary habitations such as Sin Sombra, which yielded the two examples of Figure 5.37, is but one example of a cultural discontinuity between the Archaic and Basketmaker II periods. Other kinds of drills may also be significant in this regard, and indeed the overall number and diversity of drills from NMRAP Basketmaker sites vastly exceed those from NMRAP Archaic sites (see discussion in chapter 4).

Aside from the pipe drills, the other boring tools from Kin Kahuna pictured in Figure 5.38 are a diverse lot, with bit length ranging from long to short and from delicate to robust and with use-wear indicating a range of substances from soft to very hard. The drills with stubby, robust tips such as 5.38a–e have use-wear suggestive of drilling semihard material such as green wood or fresh bone. They are made on thin flakes or flake fragments, usually with minimal edge modification (bidirectional, noninvasive pressure flaking). The bits are 3 to 5 mm long and about 2 mm thick; use-wear indicates a depth of penetration of no more than 3 mm. Given the shallow depth of penetration, these tiny tools could have been handheld, but a haft would have been quite practical; drill 5.39e was notched for hafting. The occurrence of drills like this in Basketmaker II assemblages could result from the proliferation of ornaments and other aspects of Basketmaker material culture that were not seen during the Archaic period.

Drills that may well have been used for socketing dart shafts, among other tasks, are those with long and narrow bits such as shown in Figure 5.38f and j–l. One is whole (l), but the rest are represented by two bases and one tip. The breaks on these tools appear to be the result of bending, something that could happen when the tip was embedded to full depth and the tool was flexed off the rotational axis. The use-wear, which is best seen on the tip fragment (f) and whole example (l), is consistent with drilling a semihard material such as wood. These tools are exactly what would be needed for creating the socket on dart shafts to receive the foreshaft. In describing Basketmaker atlatl dart main shafts, Guernsey and Kidder state that "in the distal or large end of the shaft is drilled a cone-shaped hole 5/16 of an inch in diameter at the mouth and 1 inch to 1.5 inches in depth" (1921:84). The drill bit shown in Figure 5.38f measures 9 mm (6/16 of an inch) wide and just under 21 mm (an inch) long to the break, with use-wear extending along the entire length. The two base fragments and the whole example have shallow notches that were probably used for hafting; 5.38l has notches above an old break and is probably a recycled portion of a dart point tip. The two base fragments also exhibit rather intensive handling polish, including over the notch scars, and they are sufficiently large that there would have been no problem exerting sufficient force without handles. It is interesting that both of theses bases exhibit the same production characteristics as do western Basketmaker II dart points and preforms such as those from Sand Dune Cave, which were finished by a series of wide percussion flakes. Indeed, both are of sufficient width and thinness to have been point preforms, but instead their tips were reworked by pressure flaking into long narrow bits for use as drills. Archaic hunters also used atlatls and darts and would have needed to bore the dart main shaft to accommodate a foreshaft, so this kind of drill might not provide evidence of cultural discontinuity. Yet only a single example of these long-bit drills was recovered from NMRAP Archaic sites, one from the upper late Archaic component at Three Dog Site (see SD vol. 2, Figure 14.19b).

Corner-Notched Knives

Ever since Guernsey and Kidder's 1921 report, corner-notched knife blades have been known to be part of the western Basketmaker II tool assemblage (Guernsey and Kidder 1921:93–95, Plate 35j–l). These large, thin, well-made artifacts (up to 18 cm long and 7 cm wide but just .6 cm thick) were doubtless such highly valued artifacts and so readily recycled into smaller tool forms that they are seldom recovered in regular archaeological deposits. The two whole examples described by Guernsey and Kidder came from burials, and the hafted but broken specimen came from the fill of a storage cist. A heat-spalled example of such a knife blade came from a Basketmaker II site on northern Black Mesa (AZ D:7:103) along with small heat spalls from at least three or four additional bifaces (Parry 1987a:238, Plate 6-7; Parry and Christenson 1987:Plate 15). These latter tools came from the fill of a hearth along with beads and thus also represent some special depositional context. No Basketmaker II knives were found by the NMRAP excavations, although there are numerous examples of bifaces at various stages of reduction, mostly fragments broken during production or use that never made it to the fully thinned or finished stage.

Bone, Shell, and Stone Ornaments and Miscellaneous Objects

Despite being relatively rare finds, ornaments and other less mundane objects such as gaming pieces are still useful measures of the degree of Archaic to Basketmaker cultural continuity. Ornaments of any sort were nearly nonexistent at NMRAP Archaic sites, with only one of the late Archaic components at Three Dog Site yielding bone beads (see Figure 4.12). These small tubular beads, made from cottontail and jackrabbit metatarsals and similar elements, are quite different from the bone beads typical of Basketmaker II contexts, which are usually made of larger-diameter bones and are frequently ground on the exterior surface to produce a somewhat football-shaped long section, fatter in the middle than on the ends. In contrast to the NMRAP Archaic assemblages, many of the Basketmaker sites produced ornaments or the unfinished portions or production scraps therefrom as well as other special items such as gaming pieces and atlatl weights. Figure 5.39 shows some examples of the diverse objects recovered from Basketmaker sites. These include objects made of obvious exotic materials such as the siltstone pendants (k–n), whose material is derived from Black Mesa, and the fossil shell pendant (j), which may also come from one of the Cretaceous formations of this geographic feature. These may come from direct procurement or contact with adjacent groups, but the abalone shell pendants (a) are evidence of extensive trade networks that reached the Pacific coast of California. Other objects such as the shaped pieces of iron/manganese (f–g) demonstrate considerable production effort given how hard and dense this material is.

The limited evidence from NMRAP Archaic sites of nonutilitarian objects must be qualified by Burial 2 from Sand Dune Cave, which had a necklace of three abalone shell pendants and a pouch containing four pendants made from coal along with projectile points (Lindsay et al. 1968:44). This burial, which is directly dated to 2938–3360 cal. BC (Coltrain et al. 2007:316), shows that some Basketmaker II ornaments and distant trade contacts for exotic materials had Archaic precedent. Yet the frequency and type of nonutilitarian objects found at Basketmaker sites suggest something of a cultural discontinuity from the Archaic period in the northern Kayenta region.

Manos and Metates

Grinding tools are worth considering here, though they likely have more to say about subsistence than cultural continuity; perhaps as a result they reveal something of a gradational sequence, especially for manos. Probably the first published account of Basketmaker manos for the Kayenta region comes from Guernsey and Kidder, who, foreshadowing much of the recent discussion about mano size and agricultural dependency (e.g., Hard 1990; Hard et al. 1996), state that manos "are intimately related to the

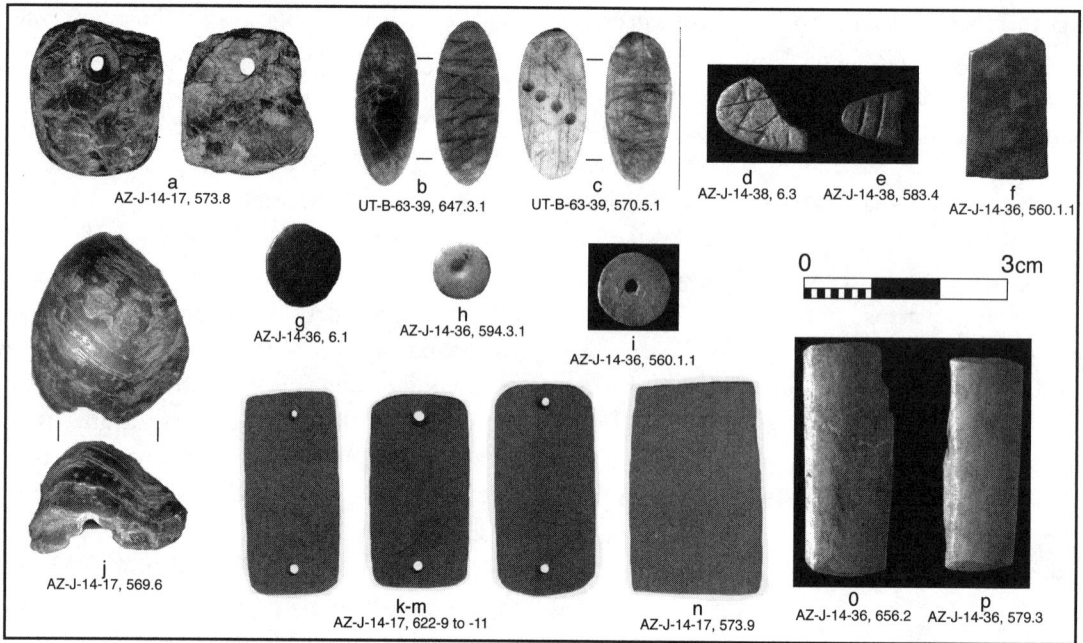

Figure 5.39. Examples of ornaments, gaming pieces, and other miscellaneous artifacts recovered from Navajo Mountain Road Archaeological Project Basketmaker sites but not from Archaic sites: (a) abalone shell pendants; (b–e) bone gaming pieces; (f–g) probable pendant and bead blank of iron/manganese; (h) bone disk; (i) bone disk bead; (j) fossil shell pendant; (k–m) siltstone pendants; (n) probable pendant blank of siltstone; (o–p) large bone beads.

domesticate life of corn-growing Indians, and in a measure furnish an index to their progress as agriculturalists" (1921:93, see Plate 38d–f). Guernsey and Kidder characterize the oval Basketmaker manos that they recovered as being of the type "used by people of less firmly established corn-eating habits" (1921:93). Basketmaker manos have both oval and rectangular plan views, a distinction that may have little significance beyond description of form.

As Figure 5.40 illustrates, Basketmaker manos differ from those of the early Archaic period in being larger and having more regularized plans and sections that derive from greater production input. The early Archaic examples in this figure come from Stratum IV of Dust Devil Cave because the NMRAP excavations did not recover a sufficient sample of manos from early Archaic sites. A sandstone cobble was the starting point for both early Archaic and Basketmaker manos, but besides somewhat different preferences for cobble size and shape (longer, wider, and somewhat thinner during the Basketmaker period), Basketmakers tended to shape their manos (regularization of the outline), whereas early Archaic foragers simply used the cobbles as is without plan shaping. Moreover, the use surfaces of Basketmaker manos tend to be gently convex and lack the pronounced rocker bevels of the early Archaic manos. The presence of a rocker bevel with the early Archaic manos suggests that even when an early Archaic and Basketmaker mano are the same size and have the same grinding surface area, a smaller portion of the Archaic mano was regularly contacting the metate than was true with the Basketmaker mano because of its flatter cross section (on any given stroke the Basketmaker mano had more surface area contacting the metate). The late Archaic manos are more similar to those of the Basketmaker II period, tending to be larger in surface area than those of the early Archaic, although still less on average than Basketmaker manos, and having their outlines purposefully shaped to an oval or rectangular form. They tend to be thicker than the Basketmaker II manos and have a rocker bevel, but not like the pronounced ones seen on the early Archaic manos.

Using a length measurement of 16 cm as an arbitrary dividing point between small and large manos, all of the Archaic examples are small. The longest whole mano from an Archaic site measures 12.5 cm, with the next largest two measuring 11.6 and 10.1 cm. These are all from late Archaic sites at the foot of Navajo Mountain. Manos in the early Archaic assemblage from Dust Devil Cave averaged less than 10 cm in maximum dimension. In the Basketmaker assemblage there are three large manos, with one measuring 19.7 cm long, well over the 16-cm interval of separation

Summary and Interpretation of Basketmaker II Remains

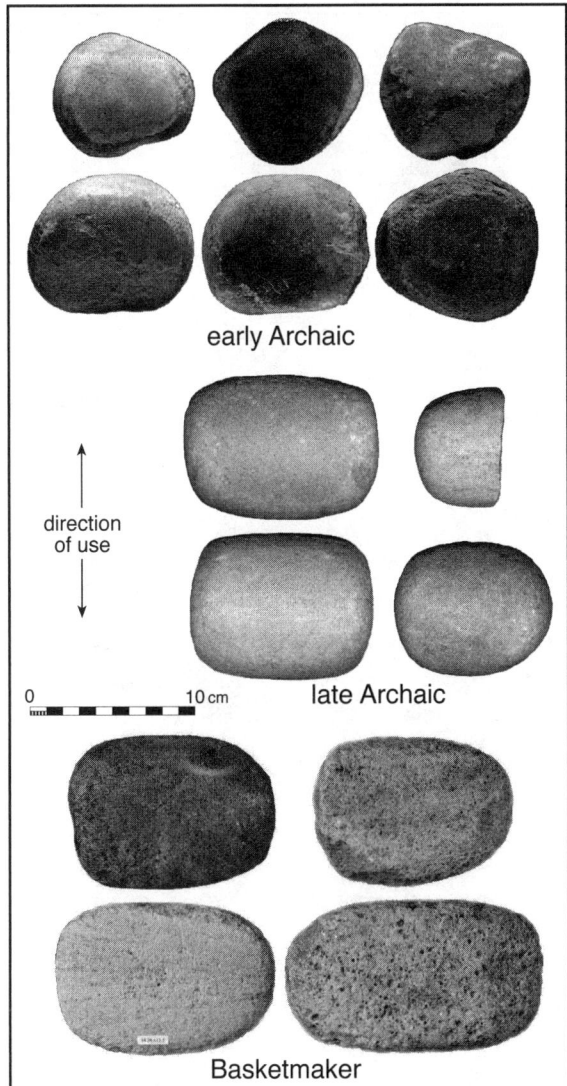

Figure 5.40. Examples of manos recovered from Archaic and Basketmaker sites showing the change through time in size and general morphology; small size and "rocker bevels" are typical of early Archaic manos for the region.

TABLE 5.11. Grinding Area (cm²) for Whole Archaic and Basketmaker Manos Recovered by the Navajo Mountain Road Archaeological Project

Variable	Archaic	Basketmaker
Mean	52.0	67.8
Standard Deviation	21.3	32.8
Minimum	23	26
First Quartile	44	40
Median	47	56
Third Quartile	72	92
Maximum	74	172
N	5	33

Note: This only includes the primary or largest surface if used on both faces.

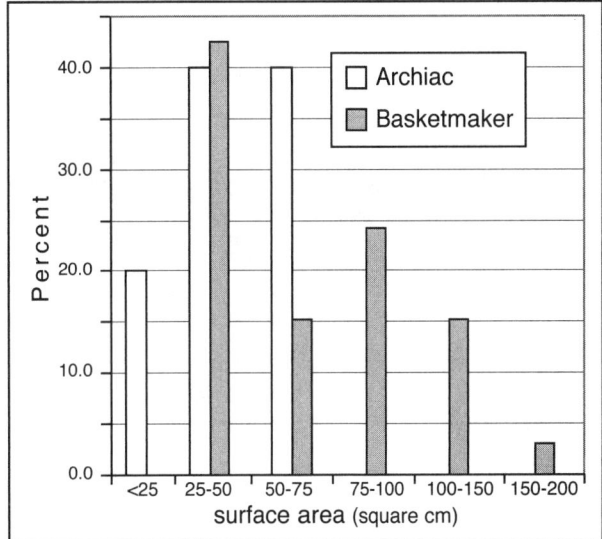

Figure 5.41. Grinding surface area recorded as an approximate square-centimeter value for Archaic and Basketmaker manos.

between small and large forms. The other two manos classified as large are fragments, but portion length suggests that both may have measured more than 16 cm long when whole. There were three Basketmaker manos between 15 and 16 cm in length straddling the line between small and large forms and seven between 12 and 14 cm, but the mode ($n = 11$) is manos 8–10 cm long. Mano grinding surface area recorded as an approximate square-centimeter value (Table 5.11, Figure 5.41) reveals the expected trend of greater use area after the introduction of agriculture. With just five whole Archaic manos the central tendency values of Table 5.11 must be considered cautiously, but Basketmaker manos nonetheless average almost 16 cm² larger than those of the Archaic. The change is even more obvious in the frequency histogram of Figure 5.41, with the long right tail of the Basketmaker assemblage. Still, the difference between Archaic and Basketmaker is dwarfed by the vast increase in surface area size from Basketmaker to Puebloan. The latter occurs even though there is little evidence in support of a major increase in the dietary intake of maize from the Basketmaker to Puebloan periods.

Unlike manos, metates reveal a more significant change, not so much in size as in the conformation of the grinding slick. Archaic examples recovered by the NMRAP and for the northern Kayenta region generally are basically flat sandstone slabs that might have a very shallow oval basin from repeated reciprocal grinding in the central portion. In contrast, the usual Basketmaker II metate has a grinding slick that consists of a well-defined

Figure 5.42. Examples of metates recovered from Basketmaker sites. The specimen on the right had been recycled as a deflector in the oldest house at Kin Kahuna, one with a radiocarbon age of 360–100 cal. BC.

trough with a basin-like conformation from reciprocal grinding (Figure 5.42). The whole example shown in Figure 5.42 had been recycled as the deflector in the oldest house at Kin Kahuna, one with an age of 360–100 cal. BC. Because the manos were not the long, flat varieties typical of Puebloan times but, rather, shorter and often somewhat concave in long section, the basin-like trough resulted. Since the manos are generally less than 15 cm long, the grinding troughs are relatively narrower, more so than those of Puebloan metates and far more concave. The Basketmaker metates provide a distinct contrast with those found at Archaic sites of the region, but this is more reasonably explained as a consequence of having to process maize.

Conclusion for "Origins"

The natural question with this evidence is whether it merely constitutes the expected effects of increasing sedentism (Wills 1995:217). The elaboration of material remains that played an important role in public display and ceremony, items involved in the active expression of social messages (Wiessner's [1983, 1989] emblemic and assertive styles), might be wrongly mistaken as a signal of cultural discontinuity when in fact all that changed was the nature of social relationships and the need for or intensity of social signaling. Although this is possible, the rapidity of such change in the northern Kayenta region seems excessive. Moreover, there are other shifts in material culture that appear more consistent with a population influx coincident with the appearance of maize on the Rainbow Plateau. These include mundane items of material culture with low visibility such as the mountain sheep horn flaking tools used in the fabrication of projectile points. Flintknapping tools and the resultant flake scars on bifacial tools are unlikely to change because of increasing sedentism or intensified social interaction and the need to actively display social identity. Yet the Basketmaker II dart points of the Rainbow Plateau differ from those of the late Archaic, not just in general plan view morphology but also in production features. The latter can be linked to the use of different types of stone flaking tools, which arose from differences in enculturation. When considering the whole suite of material remains that may serve to track the history of cultural transmission, both the artifacts that passively monitor or reflect social groups because of learned patterns of production and those that might be used to actively express identity, all suggest a significant disjuncture in the cultural remains of the northern Kayenta region, a lack of continuity that coincides with the arrival of food production to the local area. This patterning is most consistent with a migration of farming populations rather than an in situ transformation.

Local discontinuity during the agricultural transition in the northern Kayenta region does not imply a lack of continuity elsewhere on the Colorado Plateau. This study concerns one modest-sized area, and just as a single site can never inform about the prehistory of some local area, likewise the archaeological record of one area does not inform about macroscale patterns for an entire region. Spatial scale clearly becomes a factor in the analysis of continuity/discontinuity and the question of farmer migration. Basketmaker occupation of the Rainbow Plateau might represent little more than the expansion of farmer-foragers from an adjacent area within the Kayenta region, and on this slightly larger spatial scale continuity in occupation and culture may well exist. To the southeast of the Rainbow Plateau, directly dated burials and other Basketmaker remains (Coltrain et al. 2007; Smiley and Parry 1992; Smiley et al. 1986) demonstrate the earlier presence, by a few hundred years, of agricultural dependence and associated cultural diagnostics. Whether the Kayenta Valley–Long House Valley–northern Black Mesa locality is the source area for the Basketmaker II groups who settled the northern Kayenta region remains to be demonstrated by future research.

Basketmaker II–III Transition

The cultural sequences recognized for Cedar Mesa and northern Black Mesa are characterized by a significant hiatus in occupation following Basketmaker II (Matson 1991; Smiley 2002b), with a short-lived reoccupation during late Basketmaker III on Cedar Mesa but no permanent reoccupation on northern Black Mesa until Pueblo I. These sequences seem to reflect a larger trend for a greater-than-two-century gap between the Basketmaker II and III stages as documented by Berry (1982:117), something that other Southwest archaeologists have also mentioned (e.g., Rohn 1989:154). Evidence obtained by the NMRAP suggests that the northern Kayenta region has a record that spans the gap between Basketmaker II and III—that the occupation of this region was continuous from about 400 cal. BC up to about cal. AD 700. More important, the findings shed some light on the processes of this transition, revealing that change was more piecemeal than sweeping, without "suites" of newly introduced traits; the change that occurred is poorly captured or characterized by phase or stage schemes that presuppose or impose steplike shifts.

How to best subdivide a continuum of cultural development within a region is a common problem for archaeologists (e.g., Lyman et al. 1997; O'Brien et al. 2002). The advent of pottery manufacture traditionally seemed an unambiguous and useful marker for dividing the continuum of Basketmaker cultural development, and it was explicitly incorporated into the Pecos classification for such purposes (Kidder 1927). Most archaeologists working on the Colorado Plateau use ceramics to differentiate between Basketmaker II and III (cf. Berry 1982:88). Pottery occurs on open as well as sheltered sites, making it a more widely documented trait than the many perishable remains (e.g., sandals and feather blankets) that may also serve as markers of this transition. Pottery also seems to have made a rather sudden sweeping appearance across the Four Corners region, so that by AD 500 or shortly thereafter it was found nearly everywhere.

The situation appears different on the Rainbow Plateau, where the persistence of a Basketmaker II lifeway past AD 700 was inferred from the findings of Sand Dune Cave: "Development of the Basketmaker tradition into a later manifestation characterized by ceramics, the bow and arrow, and a different settlement and community patterning is not evidenced on the plateau" (Lindsay et al. 1968:364). This notion gained some acceptance (e.g., Dean 1996:29, 32; Gumerman and Dean 1989:111), but the findings reported here and in Geib and Spurr 2000 and Geib 2004 refute this idea. Indeed, in the context of current knowledge it is reasonable to question what a continuation of Basketmaker II lifeways means. Basketmaker II groups can no longer be considered as modified hunter-gatherers, for evidence indicates that they were nearly as dependent upon maize as were Basketmaker III and later Puebloan populations (Chisholm and Matson 1994; Coltrain et al. 2007; Matson and Chisholm 1991, 2007; cf. Wills 1992:159). Increased reliance on cultigens, therefore, is not a distinguishing characteristic of Basketmaker III. Also there is no absence of ceramics, beans, and the bow and arrow prior to AD 700. These traits did not appear as a suite at a single point in time in the northern Kayenta region, nor were these items equally adopted by all contemporaneous households of the region, but, as is detailed below, pottery and the bow and arrow predate AD 500, with beans occurring at about that time.

Initial Pottery

Basketmaker II populations, like Archaic foragers before them, manipulated clay to make small artifacts, especially human figurines. Such a practice dates back to the early Archaic for the portion of the Colorado Plateau that includes the northern Kayenta region (Coulam and Schroedl 1996). However, if we restrict the definition of pottery to the creation of purposefully fired vessels used for cooking or storage, then this practice is comparatively recent. For the Kayenta area, like the Four Corners region generally, the advent of pottery production has traditionally been placed at around AD 500 based on tree-ring dates associated with pottery.[7] Evidence accumulated in the past two decades has tended to push the starting date for pottery back several hundred years (see review in Reed et al. 2000), with NMRAP findings providing part of the case for this revision, principally the site of Mountainview (Geib and Spurr 2000; see SD vol. 3, chap. 10).

The earliest pottery for the Kayenta region is a plain utilitarian ware usually brownish in color and varyingly burnished. A number of traits distinguish this material from Lino Gray. Early pottery on the Rainbow Plateau is classified as Obelisk Utility (SD vol. 5, chap. 2). It resembles the pottery recovered from Obelisk Cave but differs from much of the pottery previously identified as Obelisk Gray in the Kayenta region—pottery that fits the type description of Lino Gray except for being polished. The primary criterion distinguishing Obelisk Utility from Lino Gray, polished or not, is the use of iron-rich clay containing abundant fine sand and other particles, in addition to poorly sorted quartz and multilithic sand. Lino Gray is made from iron-poor clay, lacks abundant fine sand, and is tempered with well-sorted, usually subrounded quartz grains.

The count of known early pottery sites is currently low, a likely result of both limited survey coverage and identification problems. I have firsthand knowledge of the latter because the site that currently provides the best-dated assemblage of this early pottery, Mountainview, was initially identified as aceramic. It took close inspection of the surface remains during a second visit to notice a few sherds and actual excavation to convince me that the pottery was indeed associated with the structure and other features. Except for sparse sherds, the surface appearance of early ceramic habitations may be no different from the surface appearance of aceramic Basketmaker habitations. The most obvious evidence for both is abundant burned rock and darkened soil, along with flaking debris and occasional upright slabs that mark the locations of structures, cists, or hearths.

The currently known examples of early pottery sites are clustered at the southeast edge of the Rainbow Plateau and in Upper Piute Canyon. Several of these are not yet recorded, and for only three is there excavation information: Mountainview, Atlatl Rock Cave, and Polly's Place. Recorded but unexcavated early pottery sites in the area include AZ-J-14-54, the largest example currently known (see Figure 5.16), and NAU sites AZ-D-2-174, -200, and -355. All of the early pottery sites thus far documented have evidence for one or more living structures, with upright slabs forming the entryways and at times lining house perimeters. Whether early pottery occurs at nonhabitation sites remains to be seen, but it is absent from Dust Devil Cave and the Desha Caves—sites that likely did not function as habitations but were used during the interval that pottery was present in the area.

The best sample of early pottery thus far comes from Mountainview, where excavation of virtually the entire site recovered a small assemblage of Obelisk Utility from a shallow pit structure and associated trash midden. Based on rim sherds, the Mountainview assemblage consists of a minimum of a straight-necked jar and two seed jars from the structure, with at least two more seed jars and two possible bowls or seed jars from the midden. Jar sherds from the structure refit with midden sherds. Several body sherds from the structure do not appear to belong to any of the rims. The vessels from the unburned structure are heavily sooted, indicating use for cooking. The average of six statistically contemporaneous maize assays fixes the occupation of Mountainview between cal. AD 220 and 350 (two-sigma range). The implication of this evidence is that pottery was in use on the southeast edge of the Rainbow Plateau by the middle of the fourth century AD at the very latest and possibly before the middle of the third century AD.

Excavation of a cist remnant filled with turkey feces at Atlatl Rock Cave yielded portions of a polished Obelisk Utility seed jar (SD vol. 2, chap. 2). This vessel is quite similar to a polished brown seed jar found by Kidder and Guernsey (1919: Plate 59, see Figure 35 and p. 95 for discussion of recovery location) at Sunflower Cave.[8] There are portions of at least two other Obelisk Utility vessels from the limited testing of Atlatl Rock Cave. A corncob from the cist with the Obelisk Utility seed jar returned a radiocarbon assay of cal. AD 430–650, more in line with the traditional dating for pottery use. The Atlatl Rock Cave seed jar may be a few hundred years younger than the Mountainview pottery, and it is notably better crafted than the vessels at Mountainview, having a harder and more consistent polish, a more even thickness to the vessel walls, and a quite regular rim lip.

Excavation of Polly's Place also recovered pottery, but in this case just a single vessel fragment. This is sparse evidence for ceramic use, but the sherd was clearly not intrusive as there was no pottery on the surface of this site or any ceramic site in the vicinity. The small Obelisk Utility sherd came from a buried occupation surface just outside a structure. This house was occupied sometime between cal. AD 250 and 440 (SD vol. 3, chap. 7), quite similar to the date range of Mountainview.

A detailed description of the Mountainview assemblage and Obelisk Utility in general occurs in chapter 2, volume 5, of the supporting documentation (see also SD vol. 3, chap. 10). Mountainview provides the largest sample of well-dated early pottery from the northern Kayenta region and indeed most of northeast Arizona and all of southeast Utah. Examination of sherds from other early ceramic sites on the Rainbow Plateau leads me to conclude that the Mountainview assemblage captures the distinctive essence of this early pottery while at the same time well representing its variability. In brief, this early pottery is a crumbly plain ware with abundant fine sand, surface textures ranging from well polished to rough, and variable surface colors that are most frequently reddish yellow to reddish brown, reflecting a high-iron clay with an uncontrolled firing atmosphere and lack of vessel protection from fuels. The nature of the clay and the temper indicates that early potters used self-tempered alluvial clays. Locally in the northern Kayenta region such material is available in abundance from Piute Canyon, where, after a storm, clay with the perfect moisture content for vessel production can be collected from damp settling basins. As might be expected, vessel forms appear to parallel gourd or squash shapes and include seed jars (apparently the most common), straight-necked jars with globular bottoms, and bowls. Based on sooting and interior surface pitting and spalling it is evident that all jars were used over fires, probably for boiling food.

By the fourth century AD, and perhaps as early as the third century, some Basketmaker occupants of the northern Kayenta region were using pottery. Yet many of the NMRAP sites dating to this interval, even long-term residential sites, lack pottery. Panorama House, for example, is quite similar in character to Mountainview, consisting of a single pit structure, a few hearths, a small midden, and no storage facilities. Occupancy of this site occurred between cal. AD 240 and 390 (two-sigma range) based on an average of four maize radiocarbon dates. Kin Kahuna provides an example of a more substantial habitation with abundant trash and storage features that likewise lacks ceramics. There was considerable trash deposition at the site during the interval represented by Mountainview, with one excavated structure (Structure 3) dated by maize at cal. AD 130–430 (two-sigma range). Extensive excavation of this site, including the screening of tens of cubic meters of refuse accumulation, recovered not a single sherd of Obelisk Utility. At nonhabitation sites, I expect an even lower probability for pottery to be represented. This seems to be borne out by the findings from Dust Devil Cave and Desha Caves 1 and 2, sites that, as argued earlier, appear to have been used principally for storage. Dating of maize and bark from cist construction reveals that these three sites were occupied during the time that pottery was in use on the Rainbow Plateau, yet no early brownware pottery was recovered. The maize dates from Dust Devil Cave are late enough (ca. AD 400–800 [Geib 1996a]) that pottery was in general wide use and Lino Gray was being produced in the Kayenta region.[9]

Arrow-Sized Points

Traditional culture history holds that the bow was a Basketmaker III addition across the Four Corners region of the Colorado Plateau, being adopted after about AD 500 (Cordell 1984:102; McGregor 1965:213; Plog 1979:114). Excavation of Basketmaker II remains from numerous dry caves uncovered abundant and varied evidence of atlatl use (dart points and preforms, dart foreshafts and main shafts, foreshafts with dart points, atlatls, atlatl weights) but no evidence of bow use (e.g., Guernsey 1931; Guernsey and Kidder 1921; Kidder and Guernsey 1919; Lindsay et al. 1968; Lockett and Hargrave 1953; Schilz 1979). Given the time depth of the Basketmaker II period (e.g., Smiley 1993; Smiley et al. 1986), the lack of evidence for bow use from caves may result because most remains from these sites date from the first millennium BC. Yet findings from excavations at late Basketmaker II (ca. AD 1–400) open sites on Cedar Mesa and Black Mesa follow the traditional framework—plenty of dart points but no arrowpoints (R. G. Matson, personal communication 1991; Parry 1987a).

Based on Earl Morris's finding of a Basketmaker II burial from Battle Cave in Canyon del Muerto with an arrowpoint and foreshaft imbedded between the ribs, Wormington concludes that "although the Basketmakers did not use the bow and arrow, they apparently were in contact with people who did" (1961:55). This was an initial indication that bow technology may have been present in the Four Corners region earlier than generally supposed. Excavation of the Tamarron site in southwest Colorado led to the first general claim that some Basketmaker II groups used the bow (Reed and Kainer 1978). This site remains undated and was assigned to the Basketmaker II period based on architectural similarities between a pithouse and the tree-ring-dated structures of Talus Village and the Falls Creek shelters (Dean 1975; Morris and Burgh 1954). The excavation of 5DL896 provided additional evidence for potential early bow use in southwest Colorado (Reed and McDonald 1988). Here excavations recovered eight arrowpoints from a stratum radiocarbon dated between AD 130 and 430, but the dates are on wood charcoal. Nevertheless, evidence continues to trickle in, especially from northern sites, for the appearance of bow technology during the first several centuries AD. On the northern Colorado Plateau it is generally accepted that the bow and arrow began to replace the atlatl and dart by at least AD 300 (Holmer 1986:106; Holmer and Weder 1980:60). Closer to the Four Corners region, arrowpoints were recovered from a nonhabitation site in Glen Canyon radiocarbon dated to the first few centuries AD (Geib and Bungart 1989), and Richens and Talbot (1989) recovered arrowpoints from a temporary residential site with a 5-m-diameter pithouse that was also radiocarbon dated to the first few centuries AD. The dating for this latter site is quite good because it is based on the average of three statistically contemporaneous assays on burned roof beams.

Of the NMRAP Basketmaker sites with arrowpoints, Mountainview provides the best evidence for early bow and arrow use for the northern Kayenta region, from a site that also contained early pottery. The unexcavated large habitation site AZ-J-14-54 with the same cultural assemblage as Mountainview—Obelisk Utility and arrowpoints—reveals that Mountainview is not unique and provides ample opportunity to obtain chronometric dates to check NMRAP findings with regard to the age of both arrowpoints and pottery. NMRAP sites yielding corroborative data about the early presence of arrowpoints include Kin Kahuna and The Pits, and in these cases without associated pottery.

The Mountainview site provides fairly conclusive evidence for early bow use on the southeast edge of the

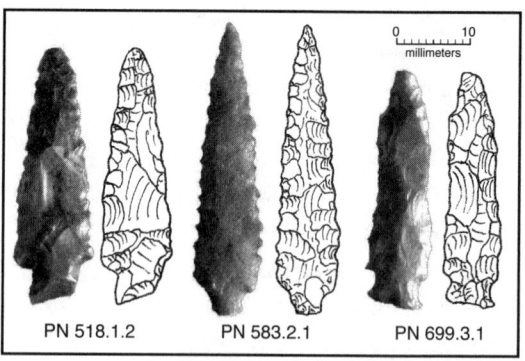

Figure 5.43. Arrow-sized projectile points recovered from Mountainview, a site with a radiocarbon age between cal. AD 220 and 350 based on the average of six statistically contemporaneous maize assays.

Rainbow Plateau sometime between cal. AD 220 and 350 (two-sigma range). From the shallow pithouse and associated midden described earlier, excavators retrieved three whole or nearly whole arrow-sized points (Figure 5.43), a few arrowpoint fragments, and several small pressure-flaked biface fragments that are probably arrowpoint preforms broken in production (Figure 5.44). The dating for this site is based on the average of six statistically contemporaneous maize assays processed in two separate batches of three samples, each separated by several years. This date range fits quite closely with that for the Sandy Ridge site (Richens and Talbot 1989) of southeast Utah.

The points shown in Figure 5.43 are classified as arrow sized based on their overall small proportions: from left to right the illustrated points measure 3.3 × 1.1 × .4 cm, 3.8 × .9 × .3 cm, and 3.0 × .9 × .5 cm. Points of this size intuitively fit the arrow class. Statistical verification comes from Shott's (1997) expansion of Thomas's (1978) study of hafted darts and arrowpoints. According to Shott's (1997: Table 2) summary metric data, the Mountainview points are below the arrowpoint mean for length, shoulder width, and neck width. Shott's (1997:98) threshold value for distinguishing between darts and arrowpoints is a shoulder width of 20 mm, which is about twice or more the width of the Mountainview points. Neck width, a variable that other researchers have emphasized (e.g., Corliss 1972; Fawcett and Kornfeld 1980; cf. Shott 1997: 98), also indicates that the Mountainview points are arrow sized, given that they measure 6 mm or less.

The Mountainview assemblage contains small pressure-flaked bifaces from what appears to be the entire sequence of arrowpoint production (Figure 5.44), starting with a flake blank and ending with a preform finished except for the notches. Whole finished arrowpoints from the site have poorly executed corner notches, thus I assume that the preforms at the bottom of Figure 5.44 were also ultimately going to be notched. It appears to have been common for Basketmaker knappers to fabricate projectile points up to the notching stage, postponing this last finishing touch until just before hafting. Guernsey and Kidder first recognized this, concluding that the preforms "are dart heads completed up to the final step of flaking out the deep notches on the lower sides, a step deferred until just before mounting them in the foreshafts" (1921:87).

Most of the arrowpoints from Mountainview, both unfinished and finished, are made of local Navajo chert, whereas the dart points from this site are of other materials generally procured at a moderate distance from the site. The common small size of Navajo chert nodules would have been an impediment when it comes to dart points but far less so for arrowpoints. Indeed one of the unintended benefits of shifting to the use of bows and arrows was the ability to make do with the local Navajo chert for projectile points with less need for more distantly procured stone.

One of the most interesting aspects of the Mountainview assemblage is the evidence that it straddles the transition from dart points to arrowpoints. Both darts and arrowpoints are present in the collection, and there is also an atlatl weight, additional evidence for the use of the atlatl. Two distinct trajectories for point production are apparent—one for dart points that follows the standard western Basketmaker II approach and a new strategy for arrowpoints. The dart points from the site exhibit the production traces (flake scars) that are characteristic of western Basketmaker II points of the area, with wide flakes that achieved both the final thinness (section symmetry) and most of the plan symmetry and are believed to have been detached mainly by percussion flaking including indirect percussion with punches (Geib 2002). In contrast, the arrowpoints were made solely by pressure flaking, starting with narrow and often thin flake blanks and using narrow-tipped flaking tools. Figure 5.45 shows examples of both dart and arrowpoint preforms from the site at similar stages of reduction. The readily apparent contrast in flake scars results from using different tools and techniques in reduction.

The first indication for early bow and arrow technology at an NMRAP Basketmaker site came in 1994 from excavation of The Pits. Quite unexpectedly NNAD

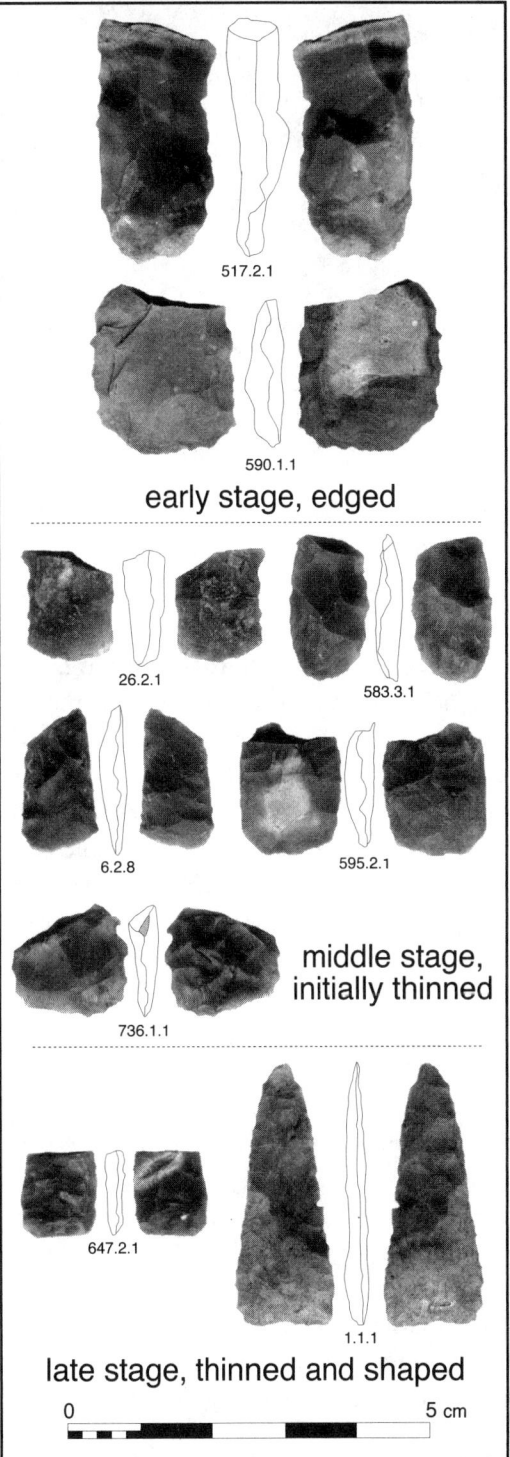

Figure 5.44. Production sequence of arrow-sized projectile points as reconstructed by pressure-flaked bifaces recovered from Mountainview.

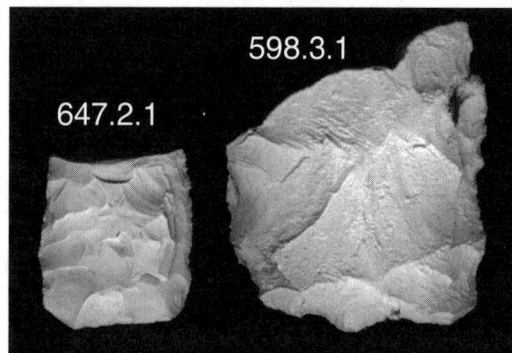

Figure 5.45. Dart and arrowpoint preforms from Mountainview at similar stages of reduction showing the contrast in flake scars that result from different reduction tools and techniques; preforms are coated with ammonium chloride to highlight the flake scar details.

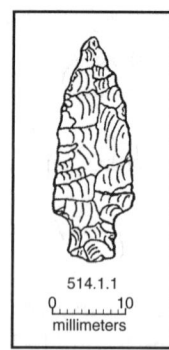

Figure 5.46. Arrow-sized projectile point recovered from the floor of a shallow structure at The Pits.

archaeologists recovered a whole stemmed arrow-sized projectile point (Figure 5.46) from the floor of a shallow structure. A maize kernel from what was thought to be the principal hearth of this house dated to the first several centuries cal. BC. Extensive root and rodent disturbance in the area of the point find limited confidence in the actual association between the artifact and the house; additional dating of maize recovered from the floor surface and closer to where the point was actually recovered returned statistically contemporaneous dates, the average of which has a calibrated two-sigma range of 160 BC to AD 90.

At Kin Kahuna, the youngest structure is dated by maize at cal. AD 130–430 (two-sigma range). No early pottery was recovered in or near this house, or indeed from the site as a whole, but an arrowpoint came from the floor fill of the structure, and a small pressure-flaked arrowpoint preform fragment was recovered from the occupation surface just outside the house. The radiocarbon date indicates that this structure was perhaps contemporaneous with Mountainview, and other radiocarbon dates from hearths and trash deposits at Kin Kahuna document substantial use of the site during the first several centuries AD.

Atlatl Rock Cave yielded a single arrowpoint (see SD vol. 2, Figure 2.13) in association with Obelisk Utility, but in this case the associated maize has an age in the AD 425–660 range. Nevertheless, because the cave was occupied during the first several centuries AD, it may contain perishable components of early bow technology (e.g., nocked ends of arrowpoints, bow fragments, bow string) that could be directly dated.

Based on NMRAP findings, it appears that arrow-sized points, and bows by implication, were being used by some occupants of the northern Kayenta region by the third to fourth centuries AD. The evidence from The Pits gives cause for speculating that bow technology might have been in limited use even earlier, perhaps around the time of Christ. The early arrowpoints are for the most part crudely produced, consisting of flakes trimmed to shape with noninvasive, marginal pressure flaking. The same also appears true for the early points from the Sandy Ridge site of southeast Utah (Richens and Talbot 1989:Figure 4). A few examples from the Rainbow Plateau, however, are much better made and exhibit overall pressure flaking scars.

Many late Basketmaker sites excavated by the NMRAP lack evidence for bow technology. The list of excavated structural sites dated to the first several centuries AD that lack arrowpoints includes Blake's Abode, Panorama House, Polly's Place, Sin Sombra, and all but Structure 3 at Kin Kahuna. Most of these sites yielded corner- and side-notched dart points, including typical examples of western Basketmaker II points.

Agricultural Dependence

Many archaeologists have characterized the subsistence change from Basketmaker II to III as an increased reliance on domesticates (Glassow 1972:298; Gumerman and Dean 1989:114; LeBlanc 1982; Minnis 1989:546). Part and parcel of this view is the notion that new, larger corn varieties were grown, greater efficiency was obtained in corn processing, and storage capacity increased. Storage capacity is one potentially indirect measure of changing agricultural dependence. To the extent that agricultural dependence increased from Basketmaker II to Basketmaker III, I might also expect increasing reliance on storage as part of the Basketmaker II–III transition. The NMRAP excavation data do not clearly support such a case, in that high-volume storage dates to the start of Basketmaker II. The evident temporal shift from the use of pits to cists might support this, in that cists would appear to have a longer use-life, although the suspected short use-life of pits needs experimental verification, including study of pit refurbishment.

Although I have data for numerous flotation samples from aceramic habitations with abundant storage, I lack a sample from analogous early ceramic sites. Mountainview—the best example of an early ceramic habitation excavated to date—appears to lack storage features. Several caves in the area apparently had continuous Basketmaker use during the interval in which pottery first appeared, but only Atlatl Rock Cave has been sampled for macrobotanical remains. Unfortunately, the sample size ($n = 3$) for this site is not sufficient to be informative.

There is no clear temporal pattern in the ubiquity data to support an increase in maize use during the Basketmaker chronology for the Rainbow Plateau. Moderately heavy maize dependence appears with the earliest of the open habitations with storage features, sometime around 300 BC. With maize occurring in 75 to 90 percent of the samples from Kin Kahuna and The Pits, there is little room for an increase in maize representation. As discussed previously, maize is no more ubiquitous at Pueblo II and III habitations of the northern Kayenta region. It seems that farming remained consistently important from the start of the Basketmaker period to the end, with no increase in dependency corresponding to the interval during which ceramics were introduced. Moreover, although the incorporation of ceramics seems to have been an individual household decision, maize is no more abundant at early ceramic sites than at contemporaneous households without ceramics. This is best illustrated by the late component of Kin Kahuna, where maize ubiquity was 95 percent but no pottery was recovered.

Maize may be equally common to preceramic and ceramic Basketmaker contexts on the Rainbow Plateau, but the maize kernels recovered from well-dated contexts of Atlatl Rock Cave indicate a significant change in kernel morphology and color between cal. AD 430 and 650 that may have implications for the dietary significance of maize or the processing methods (see Table 5.7). The sample from this site is small but from well-controlled and -dated proveniences. A shift to larger-kernel flour maize is indicated—something that also may have impacted environmental tolerances of growth and perhaps susceptibility to damage or nutritional loss in storage.

Introduction of Beans

Part of the argument for increased reliance on domesticates during Basketmaker III is the evidence that beans were added to the list of cultigens during this stage. Today we know that beans provided an important source of protein, but prehistoric cognizance of this may have been limited; simply the satiated feeling one gets with eating beans may have been reason enough for their adoption. Perceived or not, one additional benefit of incorporating beans within subsistence practices may have been their role in maintaining soil fertility by fixing nitrogen. If Wormington's anecdotal account is true, then beans might provide another indirect measure of residential permanence. She relates that "such a crop also indicates a more settled life, for, while corn may be planted and then left for long periods of time, beans require almost constant attention" (1961:55).

The earliest evidence of beans on the Rainbow Plateau comes from Atlatl Rock Cave. A single whole bean was recovered from the previously mentioned cist used to pen turkeys. This item may be classified as Kaplan's (1956) type CII. The radiocarbon date on a corncob in association with the bean suggests an age between AD 425 and 660. Cutler (1968:377) reported wads of bean strings containing pod tips and stem ends assigned to the Basketmaker II deposits of both Sand Dune and Dust Devil caves. The age of these wads must be verified by direct dating.

Some see an obvious functional link between what has seemed to be the contemporaneous introduction of beans and pottery. Linton first expounded upon this, stating that "the relationship of this important protein source [beans] to pottery boiling is of the closest sort" (1944: 377). The earliest direct dates on beans from the Southwest deserts (Tagg 1996:Table 2; Wills 1995:Table 8.1) indicate that this cultigen was in use at or shortly before the adoption of pottery (Deaver and Ciolek-Torrello 1995; summary in Mabry 1998). The role of beans is little considered in various recent explanations as to why pottery production began in the Southwest (e.g., Crown and Wills 1995; Glassow 1972:297; but see Skibo and Blinman 1999). Arguments for labor efficiency and improved nutrition for women and children are not at odds with a functional relationship between pottery and bean cooking. Beans cooked and mashed into a soupy pulp make an excellent weaning food, something prehistoric women may have found quite useful. Beans clearly fit the expectations of a model outlined by James Brown (1989) for the origins of pottery, wherein one of the motivating factors was the addition of new processing requirements such as long-term boiling.

If pottery was adopted principally for cooking beans, then I expect that this domesticate should first appear on the Rainbow Plateau at the approximate same time as ceramics. So far this is not the case. Flotation samples from excavated early pottery sites have not yielded any bean remains. In particular, the analysis of 19 flotation samples (76 liters) from the Mountainview site did not reveal any beans. These samples came from virtually every feature at the site, including the structure hearth and ashpit, extramural hearths ($n = 9$), and the midden ($n = 6$ from different portions of the deposit). Observed floral remains included maize kernels and cupules along with seeds from grasses and several weedy species. It is worth mentioning that analysis of a considerable number of flotation samples ($n = 119$) and a large volume of dirt (470 liters) from aceramic Basketmaker habitations has yielded no evidence for beans. Extensive pollen sampling has likewise resulted in negative results, from both aceramic and early ceramic sites. I must caution that discovering evidence of beans at open sites is a low-probability event. Even at open Puebloan sites, beans are exceedingly rare finds, with the NMRAP results bearing this out since only 1 of 200 Puebloan flotation samples yielded a bean.

Conclusions

Excavations for the N16 ROW have made a significant contribution to our understanding of the Basketmaker II period in the Kayenta region and the Colorado Plateau more generally. I hope that the truth to this claim is apparent in the information summarized in this chapter, even given the limited research topics that I explored. The detailed site descriptions, volume 3 online, and the data generated by the various analyses should provide a useful reference point for some time to come. The NMRAP has provided the second-largest sample of excavated open Basketmaker II sites within the Kayenta region, complementing and augmenting both geographically and temporally the data obtained by the BMAP for northern Black Mesa. This effort also provided evidence for the Basketmaker II–Basketmaker III transitional interval (see Geib and Spurr 2000), which is poorly known for much of the Four Corners region.

The NMRAP excavation data, along with other evidence from the northern Kayenta region, inform about continuity during the agricultural transition. The robust radiocarbon record provided by the project for the Archaic and Basketmaker periods appears inconsistent with the notion of continuous settlement of the Rainbow Plateau during the interval when domesticates were introduced to the area. There is a several-hundred-year gap in the available dates, with no evidence of maize before the gap and abundant maize remains after the gap. The Basketmaker presence on the Rainbow Plateau appears shortly after about 400 cal. BC and evidently lacks local precedent. Some may see this as another strong case for a lack of continuity, whereas others might dismiss the evidence as inconclusive because of sample size limitations and other concerns. Sample size gives sufficient cause to be circumspect, in terms of both total number of sites and types of sites excavated; this is especially true for the late Archaic, but the sample of studied Basketmaker sites is quite good in both respects. Because of small sample size, it is conceivable that the project missed a large portion of late Archaic adaptive variability as well as remains that could show more continuity in settlement and adaptation during the agricultural transition than currently indicated. Yet the current evidence in favor of discontinuity from Archaic to Basketmaker II is compelling and is backed by the findings from caves of the area.

The nature of the archaeological record after the date gap reveals a profound change, one that is difficult to reconcile with autochthonous transformation of the local forager population in the northern Kayenta region. The nature of the change might be considered merely the expected effects of the increased sedentism that domesticates afforded, but evidence for the transitional interval has yet to be found in the northern Kayenta region and would need to be compressed into an exceedingly brief temporal window. Compared to late Archaic sites lacking corn (those before the date gap), the Basketmaker II sites considered here reflect a marked departure in facilities investment, storage capacity, and building for permanence. This change appears to be more than one of degree; it seems to reflect an entirely new set of concerns or priorities that lay outside those of preagricultural late Archaic foragers in the region.

The pattern documented by NMRAP is part of the puzzle that needs to be explained, part of the variability that informs about the processes at work in the past. Local discontinuity does not imply a lack of continuity elsewhere on the Colorado Plateau. Just as a single site can never serve as a model for the occupational history of some local area, the archaeological record of one locality likewise does not inform about macroscale patterns for an entire region. Discontinuity at the scale of the N16 project area does not equate with discontinuity for the entire Kayenta region. The Basketmaker occupants of the northern Kayenta region might represent the expansion of farmer-foragers from an adjacent portion of the Kayenta region. Continuity in occupation and culture may well exist at this larger spatial scale.

The Basketmaker occupation of the northern Kayenta region is demonstrably related culturally to the Basketmaker occupation of the Marsh Pass–Monument Valley area in northern Arizona as well as the Grand Gulch–Cottonwood Wash area of southeast Utah. This chapter attempted to show this and to also make the case for cultural discontinuity between the Archaic and Basketmaker periods, focusing on nonperishable artifacts rather than the distinctive perishables that have so frequently been the focus of discussion about Basketmaker cultural distinctiveness. Tools used to fabricate such low-recovery objects as stone pipes or other artifacts can be quite informative since they are more likely to have higher recovery rates and to be disposed of in less specialized contexts and also because they are less likely to be used in social messaging but, rather, reflect learning traditions.

Domesticates appear no earlier than about 400 cal. BC in northern Kayenta region, but both corn and squash have an earlier history of use in both the Marsh Pass–Monument Valley area in northern Arizona and the Grand Gulch–Cottonwood Wash area of southeast Utah. Smiley's (1994; Smiley et al. 1986) dating of maize from the White Dog phase type sites excavated by Kidder and Guernsey (White Dog Cave and Kinboko Caves 1 and 2) as well as from Three Fir Shelter (Smiley and Parry 1992) establishes that this domesticate was in common use by at least 600 cal. BC, with earlier use indicated by a single corn date at about 1000 cal. BC from Three Fir Shelter. Even earlier use at almost 2000 cal. BC is possible if the outlier date from Three Fir Shelter is confirmed (see Smiley 1994: 173), which is possible given the age of maize at the Old Corn site in New Mexico (Huber 2005). The dating of maize and squash from sites along Butler Wash (e.g., Smiley and Robins 1997; Michael R. Robins, personal communication 2000) also demonstrates domesticate use by at least 600 cal. BC. With an earlier agricultural transition in evidence to the southeast and east of the northern Kayenta region, it seems plausible that the first farmers on the Rainbow Plateau represented a local expansion of nearby groups shortly after 400 cal. BC.

On northern Black Mesa, the earliest open-air Basketmaker habitations are dated to the first few centuries of the Christian era and are designated as the Lolomai phase. Smiley and Ahlstrom have argued that this early village manifestation "assumes a basal position on the scale of Anasazi development providing examples of some of the first villages in the northern Southwest" (1998:219). The evidence reported here (also Geib and Spurr 2000) indicates a somewhat earlier period for the open-air Basketmaker habitations in the Kayenta region, beginning by at least 300 cal. BC. This is during the White Dog phase, according to the currently proposed temporal spans of early agricultural phases for the Kayenta region (Matson 1991: 122–124, Figure 2.42; Smiley and Ahlstrom 1998:219, Figure 13-1), well prior to the Lolomai phase on northern Black Mesa. Given that the Basketmaker occupation of the northern Kayenta region appears to be an expansion of a phenomenon from the southeast and east rather than a local development, then there should be even earlier open-air early agricultural settlements waiting to be identified somewhere in the greater Kayenta region. The Marsh Pass–Klethla Valley–Red Lake area is a likely place to look for evidence of the earliest farming villages. Lolomai phase settlements on northern Black Mesa might ultimately prove to be an expansion of Basketmaker populations or settlement-subsistence practices from the adjoining valleys to the west. Gilpin's (1994) findings from limited testing of two sites in the Upper Chinle Valley reveal that early agricultural pithouse settlements in this area date back to at least 1600 cal. BC. At present it is difficult to evaluate how this finding fits within the larger picture because of the limited nature of the work, but it suggests that much remains to be learned by future excavations throughout the region, especially ones that can compile detailed radiocarbon records on high-quality samples for defined areas. Certainly the time depth provided by the acceptable dates for maize on the Colorado Plateau is sufficiently great for there to have been a local development of farming adaptations by about 400 cal. BC, such that local discontinuities as represented by the Rainbow Plateau need not involve distant population intrusions.

The NMRAP findings provide evidence that helps bridge the greater-than-two-century gap between the Basketmaker II and III stages perceived by Berry (1982:117). The northern Kayenta region is perhaps not exceptional with its record of the Basketmaker II–III transition but, instead, will be just one of several localities with sites dating to the transitional interval, once sufficient research is done. The characteristics of these areas, such as the Upper San Juan River from the La Plata Valley (Toll and Wilson 2000) to the Navajo Reservoir District (Eddy 1966; Wilson and Blinman 1993, 1994) and the middle Little Colorado River area around Petrified Forest National Park (Burton 1991; Wendorf 1953), need to be compared in order to understand what these regions share that other places such as Cedar Mesa and northern Black Mesa lack.

In the northern Kayenta region pottery was not widely adopted within a short time frame by all households; rather, it took several hundred years to become a ubiquitous item of material culture (ca. AD 200–500). This appears to be the case elsewhere on the Colorado Plateau. Consequently, ceramics do not provide a hard and fast marker for distinguishing between Basketmaker II and Basketmaker III even if we restrict our definition of pottery to true vessels and not figurines and other "nonutilitarian" items. Changing the Basketmaker III criterion from pottery in the generic sense to the advent of grayware production provides some degree of temporal specificity. With the advent of grayware it seems that virtually every household on the Colorado Plateau used pottery, with sherds occurring even at seasonal residences and some temporary camps. So, should the Basketmaker III designation be restricted to sites with grayware, and should sites with brownware alone be classified as Basketmaker II or as Basketmaker II–III transitional? For the simple sake of communication I prefer the latter, but explicit recognition of intermediate stages, especially those with fuzzy boundaries, does not allow greater understanding as to how and why cultures change (e.g., Lyman et al. 1997; O'Brien et al. 2002).

In this chapter I have attempted to graph and discuss change in Basketmaker culture for the northern Kayenta region using the culturally independent dimension of time furnished by chronometric dates rather than by phases or stages. In this way it is possible to see that changes from preceramic to ceramic times, or from Basketmaker II to Basketmaker III, took place over the span of several hundred years, or many generations. There was no dramatic or sudden panregional adoption of a new trait complex that ushered in the Basketmaker III stage. Even within a small area such as the N16 project it is apparent that some households adopted pottery and others did not. On a larger regional scale, it is evident that pottery was more widely accepted earlier in some areas than in others. For example, no early pottery is reported from the AD 200–400 Grand Gulch phase of Cedar Mesa (Matson 1991; Matson et al. 1988). Whatever advantage or benefit that pottery provided was not equally perceived or acted upon in the short run.

Pottery was but one of the technological or biological innovations during the early centuries of the Christian era (ca. AD 200–600) that individual households apparently decided whether or not to use according to their own cost/benefit calculations. Some of these new traits may have been directly linked, such as pottery and beans, but apparently not as a trait complex. Innovations were adopted at various times by different households for different reasons and with different temporal and spatial patterns to acceptance (bow technology also apparently entered the Southwest from the north rather than the south [Blitz 1988] as was true for many traits such as beans). Attempts to provide a single explanation embracing all or most aspects of change in Basketmaker culture (e.g., Glassow 1972) do not hold up once better temporal control shows that changes in various aspects of culture and adaptation are not necessarily coextensive. Indeed, the notion of temporally coincident changes in multiple traits from Basketmaker II to Basketmaker III may be in large part a by-product of the stage concept. Intra- and interregional variability in the adoption of new traits likely stems from many different sources, including variations in information flow mediated by kinship or other social forms, proximity to longstanding travel/exchange routes, generational differences in the acceptance of novelties, community/household conservatism, and variable perceptions as to the costs vs. benefits of innovation, concerning both the practicalities of energy expenditure and social concerns. To investigate these and more substantive issues it may help to treat each aspect of culture or each archaeological measure of behavior as a separate variable plotted against the dimensions of time and space.

To examine the Basketmaker II–III transition I have relied upon radiocarbon dating for temporal ordering but would have preferred the precision of tree-ring dating (the poor success with this method for the Basketmaker sites of the N16 excavations is probably typical for this early time). Reliance on radiocarbon dates is unlikely to change anytime soon, and unfortunately, this technique imposes its own limitations in the form of broad temporal ranges for even the best samples. Because temporal resolution in an ideal case is on the order of about six generations (see Smiley 1985:86–92), we must be circumspect about our ability to describe change, let alone explain it.

Our concept of Basketmaker III seems to be the outcome of the adoption and successful incorporation of technological and biological innovations during the Basketmaker II–III transitional interval. These innovations stimulated subsequent developments, the most important and interesting of which seem to have been social in nature. Rather than population growth being a cause for the adoption of new traits (as per Glassow 1972), the reverse may have happened. Prior adoption of traits that provide the traditional hallmarks of the Basketmaker III stage may have resulted in population growth during Basketmaker III. This growth would have precipitated experimentation with new social forms, as evidenced by multifamily settlements and integrative structures, laying the foundation for future developments.

Notes

1. The sum of probabilities for the six maize dates reported by Smiley (1998c:Table 7-1) is AD 0–390 at 1σ and 200 BC–AD 650 at 2σ; individually the oldest and youngest dates of the group cover spans of time from 350 BC to AD 400 and AD 240–670, respectively.

2. The rule is named after Alfred S. Romer, a zoologist who first articulated it in 1933 with regard to the emergence of the land-dwelling animals (amphibians) from fish (Hockett and Ascher 1964). When considering the domestication process or the subsequent spread of domesticates, as in all aspects of evolutionary change, it can be useful to divorce present or latter-day utility from past function.

3. Storage capacity was calculated using a version of Smiley's (1985:295–297) formula for deriving a conservative estimate for pit volume (see SD, vol. 3, chap. 2).

4. The site boundary for Kin Kahuna was based on Puebloan remains not the buried Basketmaker II remains, so the true size of the Basketmaker II component remains unknown; I assume that a substantial part of the component lies outside the ROW because at the limit of excavation the Basketmaker II cultural stratum was thickest and features were far more concentrated and superimposed, implying that this was near the core site area.

5. This is a conservative interpretation of the evidence in several cases, especially based on what we currently know about the surface appearance of Basketmaker sites. The presence of four-warp wickerwork sandals (Lindsay et al. 1968:27) provides fairly conclusive proof for Basketmaker occupancy of several shelters.

6. Besides being able to hide food from thieves, storage pits can allow families to protect their larders from heavy borrowing since this is one means from preventing relatives or neighbors from knowing how much food you have stored (how much might be available for them to "borrow").

7. The earliest tree-ring-dated pottery is a polished brownware recovered by Earl Morris from Obelisk Cave in the Prayer Rock District of far-northeast Arizona; the available dates indicate that pottery was in use at this site by AD 480 (Berry 1982:68; Morris 1980:Table 2). This finding is supported by Breternitz's (1986:263) report of brownware sherds from a pit structure in Mancos Canyon with tree-ring dates in the early AD 470s. Specific to the Kayenta region, the earliest tree-ring-dated pottery comes from two sites in the Klethla Valley, NA8163 at AD 555 (Ambler and Olson 1977) and NA11,058 in the mid–AD 530s (Swarthout et al. 1986:426).

8. The Sunflower Cave seed jar is interesting, for it provides the first indication of early pottery within the Kayenta region. Kidder and Guernsey state that "the position in which this pot was discovered renders it certain that it is of an earlier period than the main sunflower cliff-house. As Basket Maker remains were noted in the same cave, and as this vessel is unlike any normal Cliff-house product with which we are familiar, it is possible that it may have belonged to that culture" (1919:144).

9. To be certain that no early pottery occurred in the collections from Dust Devil Cave, Kim Spurr and I examined the entire ceramic assemblage but observed no Obelisk Utility or even Lino Gray.

CHAPTER 6

Summary and Interpretation of Puebloan Remains

with Jim Collette

In early September 1859, Lt. John George Walker, leading a military expedition out of Fort Defiance, reached a "plateau on the summit" of Black Mesa's north rim (what Walker called Mesa de la Vaca [Bailey 1964:83]). Scanning the countryside to the west and north, Walker was unimpressed: "We obtained a view of a vast range of as desolate and repulsive looking country as can be imagined" (Bailey 1964:83). He could see as far as what he called Sierra Pinoche, or Navajo Mountain, including the Shonto and Rainbow plateaus traversed by the N16 ROW. The desolate and repulsive country that he referred to once sustained prehistoric farmers in considerable numbers, a population denoted by archaeologists as the Kayenta Anasazi. Later that same day, Walker and his troops made camp on a hill covered with an "ancient ruin," one of the "same form and appearance as those met with in the Cañon of Chelly and other parts of New Mexico" (Bailey 1964:84). A prominent masonry room block backed the ruin, walls still standing. Toward sunset, Walker and several members of his party entered this room block and chiseled their names on the interior walls. To his name, J. G. Walker, the lieutenant added the date, "Sept 12 1859" (Knipmeyer 2002). Walker and his men had signed their names to the site known today as Long House (NA897), perhaps "the largest-known Kayenta site" and "one of the most complex of the plaza pueblos…which probably has more than three hundred rooms" (Dean 2002:146, Figure 6.13).

Perceptions vary, and Walker's snap judgment of the region reflected his military training and perhaps the eyes of someone accustomed to Midwestern lushness. Many visitors to the Kayenta region today see it as beautiful and inviting, and it seems probable that the Kayenta Anasazi found the region neither repulsive nor desolate, for they managed to thrive there for more than a few thousand years, from at least 600 BC up until about AD 1300. The site noted by Walker represented just the culmination of this long-term successful adaptation to the region, for it was one of the aggregated communities that appeared during late Pueblo III, or the Tsegi phase, just prior to Puebloan resettlement southward to the Hopi Mesas and beyond. Southwestern archaeologists, like early explorers and the public at large, have an enduring fascination with large pueblos—witness the attention lavished on the ruins of Chaco Canyon. Since the masonry pueblos of aggregated communities are generally restricted to the late Pueblo III period in the Kayenta region, habitations such as Long House have received considerable research interest, and more is known or has been written about the Tsegi phase compared to most other temporal periods (e.g., Dean 1969, 1970, 2002; Haas and Creamer 1993, 1995; Hobler 1974; Lindsay 1969; Lindsay et al. 1968; Stein 1984).[1] Even so, much remains to be learned or examined in greater detail about this interval, and if true for late Pueblo III, then this statement applies even more to the many centuries leading up to this time of rather abrupt and profound transformation (see Dean 2002).

Perhaps because the Kayentan pottery sequence seems so straightforward, with sherds easily classified into well-described types (Colton 1955, 1956, 1958) that have moderately tight and well-supported temporal intervals (e.g., Ambler 1985a; Christenson 1994), there is an assumption that the archaeology of the region is equally straightforward and well understood. The evident lack of significant sociocultural complexity in the region until the final Tsegi phase might also add to this impression. Missing are the Chacoan great houses and aggregated Pueblo I and Pueblo II communities seen in the San Juan Basin and Mesa Verde region.[2] Despite some degree of aggregation during Basketmaker III in a few localities (e.g., Gilpin and Benallie 2000), for centuries the Anasazi population of the Kayenta region lived in unit-type pueblos (Prudden 1903, 1914), settlements no larger than what could accommodate several households consisting of a large extended family. Material culture and architecture evolved, but without any significant alteration of an overall simple-looking social fabric, and across a large region there appears to be the evident uniformity of a strong cultural tradition. Despite centuries of comparative social "simplicity," the Kayenta Anasazi ultimately ended up forming aggregated communities at the very end of Pueblo III, communities that set the stage for an even more profound change that resulted in what might be termed a convergence of settlement form between western and eastern Puebloan traditions in Pueblo IV, well represented by the Homolovi ruins of the Little Colorado River (E. Adams 2002). The Kayenta Anasazi are important as an alternative pathway in Puebloan social development and evolution, differing in several key respects from that of the eastern Anasazi tradition as represented by the record in the San Juan Basin, the Mesa Verde region, and the Upper Little Colorado River Basin (cf. Plog 1979:Figure 1).

THE NMRAP PUEBLOAN SITE SAMPLE

Sites/components dating from middle Pueblo II to late Pueblo III were the most numerous archaeological remains investigated by the NMRAP and comprised a significant proportion of the field and laboratory budget on account of their size, their often numerous and sometimes complex large features, and the frequent abundance of recovered remains. In all, the project investigated 25 distinct Puebloan components at 22 sites during data recovery; a few score Puebloan components were surface documented or tested within the ROW but were avoided or determined to be ineligible to the National Register and thus not subject to the final phase of research reported herein. Volume 4 of the Web-hosted supporting documentation provides detailed descriptions of the architecture, artifacts, and other remains for the 25 diverse Puebloan sites/components. All but one of these date to an interval between about AD 1050 (probably shortly thereafter) and 1270 (probably shortly before). The exception might date as early as about AD 780 but might not be any older than about AD 950. Table 6.1 provides useful summary information about each of these sites or components, with Figure 6.1 showing their locations within the project area.

Given the number of investigated Puebloan sites, a project the size of the NMRAP invariably adds in a significant way to what is currently known about local prehistory. That the area traversed by the N16 ROW on the northern Shonto and Rainbow plateaus was poorly known from excavation makes this claim all the more true, especially when the NMRAP findings are combined with those from the data-recovery project for the southern portion of this road (Schroedl 1989), which excavated 16 Puebloan sites/components (Segments 1–2 of N16). The sites described here come from the approximately 43-km stretch of N16 that traverses the broken divide connecting the northwestern tip of the Shonto Plateau with the Rainbow Plateau and then crosses this tableland to the northeastern foot of Navajo Mountain (Segments 3–6). Unlike the Basketmaker sites discussed in the previous chapter, which tended to be clustered in the southern portion of the project area along the dissected slickrock divide between Piute and Navajo creeks, the Puebloan sites are distributed all along the road but with some notable clumping. Any grouping of sites on the map is purely illusory since all evident gaps in the distribution, especially on the Rainbow Plateau, are merely a sampling problem of the narrow ROW. Nearly the entire project area is densely peppered with Puebloan settlements. The only portion that appears to contain fewer sites, or at least fewer permanent habitations, is the divide between Piute and Navajo creeks. Yet even here there are primary residential sites such as Windy Mesa or sites of more limited activity, a few of which, such as The Slots and Tres Campos, contained interesting artifact assemblages.

Road ROW excavations are unlike those of a coal lease where entire sites can be studied in toto; rather, the sample consists of what happens to be in the corridor. Unfortunately, this can sometimes result in a midden with no architecture or vice versa, a situation well represented by the sites excavated in the southern two segments of N16 (Schroedl 1989). Moreover, the existing road has often damaged the properties under investigation to varying degrees, sometimes substantially so. The damage done by previous road construction or other developments was one reason that several Puebloan sites/components in the N16 ROW were eliminated from data recovery. Of those not eliminated, some were squarely within the ROW and undamaged, others were undamaged or minimally so yet only partially in the ROW, and still others were within the ROW to varying extents and damaged but still seemingly informative. In one case (AZ-J-2-55), what initially

TABLE 6.1. Summary Information for the Navajo Mountain Road Archaeological Project Puebloan Sites

Site No.	Site Name	Temporal Affiliation	Site Type	Structures	Exterior Features	Middens	Ceramics	Debitage	Flaked Tools	Cores/Nodular Tools	Grinding Tools	Miscellaneous Stone	Bone Artifacts	Bone	Animal Burials	Eggshell	Marine Shell
UT-B-63-19	—	late Pueblo III	secondary habitation	1	1	1	355	413	6	9	28	2	1	66	0	0	0
UT-B-63-14	Hanging Ash	mid Pueblo III	primary habitation	4	1	1	2,609	520	9	6	5	2	0	4	0	0	0
UT-B-63-39	Three Dog Site	mid Pueblo III	primary habitation	9	4	1	1198	22	0	3	1	0	0	10	0	0	0
UT-B-63-39	Three Dog Site	late Pueblo III	primary habitation	11	34	1	20,923	860	30	22	42	15	4	215	0	0	0
AZ-J-2-55	Bonsai Bivouac	mid Pueblo III	secondary habitation	1	0	0	568	11	0	0	1	0	0	0	0	0	1
AZ-J-2-6	Sapo Seco	late Pueblo III	primary habitation	18	26	3	9,510	827	5	81	127	31	13	319	2	20	0
AZ-J-2-58	Water Jar Pueblo	late Pueblo III	primary habitation	9	13	1	5,699	194	3	6	18	0	0	19	0	0	0
AZ-J-2-5	Modesty House	mid Pueblo III	secondary habitation	1	1	1	1,093	135	2	8	9	0	0	2	0	0	0
AZ-J-2-5	Modesty House	late Pueblo II	secondary habitation	1	1	0	9	55	1	1	1	0	0	0	0	0	0
AZ-J-2-3	Hymn House	mid Pueblo III	primary habitation	3	7	0	1,586	985	9	53	23	2	3	40	0	0	1
AZ-J-2-2	Dune Hollow	mid Pueblo III	secondary habitation	1	4	1	203	586	12	53	89	27	8	70	0	0	3
AZ-J-3-8	Kin Kahuna	Pueblo III	secondary habitation	1	2	0	183	310	6	30	23	5	0	18	0	0	0
AZ-J-3-14	Hillside Hermitage	mid Pueblo II	primary habitation	4	1	1	1,514	68	2	10	16	4	0	0	0	0	0
AZ-J-3-14	Hillside Hermitage	late Pueblo II	secondary habitation	2		1	268	1	0	0	0	0	0	0	0	0	0
AZ-J-3-7	Mouse House	late Pueblo II–early Pueblo III	secondary habitation	1	1	0	27	2,210	6	103	48	16	10	359	1	0	0
AZ-J-14-16	Hammer House	mid Pueblo II	primary habitation	3	7	1	2,566	377	11	41	42	11	3	39	0	0	0
AZ-J-14-52	Camp Dead Pine	late Pueblo II	secondary habitation	0	3	1	425	538	50	14	11	1	0	202	1	6	0
AZ-J-14-12	Tres Campos	late Pueblo II	secondary habitation	2	2	0	413	1,239	6	12	5	19	5	133	0	0	0
AZ-J-14-11	Naaki Hooghan	late Pueblo II	secondary habitation	3	6	1	930	740	4	12	9	12	4	69	0	0	0
AZ-J-14-30	The Slots	late Pueblo II	secondary habitation	1	17	1	30	299	5	17	21	3	0	25	0	0	0
AZ-J-14-28	Windy Mesa	early Pueblo III	primary habitation	0[a]	4	1	1,498	243	0	11	1	3	0	2	0	0	0
AZ-J-14-26	Pee Wee Grande	Puebloan	temporary camp	0	2	0	0	1,476	35	20	36	26	63	531	0	26	0
AZ-J-14-20	Wolachii Bighan	Pueblo I	temporary camp	0	2	0	122	5	0	0	0	0	0	0	0	0	0
AZ-J-14-21	Ditch House	late Pueblo II–early Pueblo III	secondary habitation	2	2	?	1,475	34	1	6	0	3	0	1	0	0	0
AZ-J-14-21	Ditch House	middle Pueblo III	primary habitation	7	8	?	317	160	2	9	3	0	0	1	0	0	0
AZ-J-14-17	The Pits	Puebloan	temporary camp	0	1	0	8	6,768	168	94	337	131	18	2,507	2	900	0
Total				85	150	17	53,529	19,076	373	621	896	313	132	4,632	6	952	6

Note: Sites are ordered from north to south.
[a] Structures lie unexcavated outside the N16 ROW

Summary and Interpretation of Puebloan Remains 293

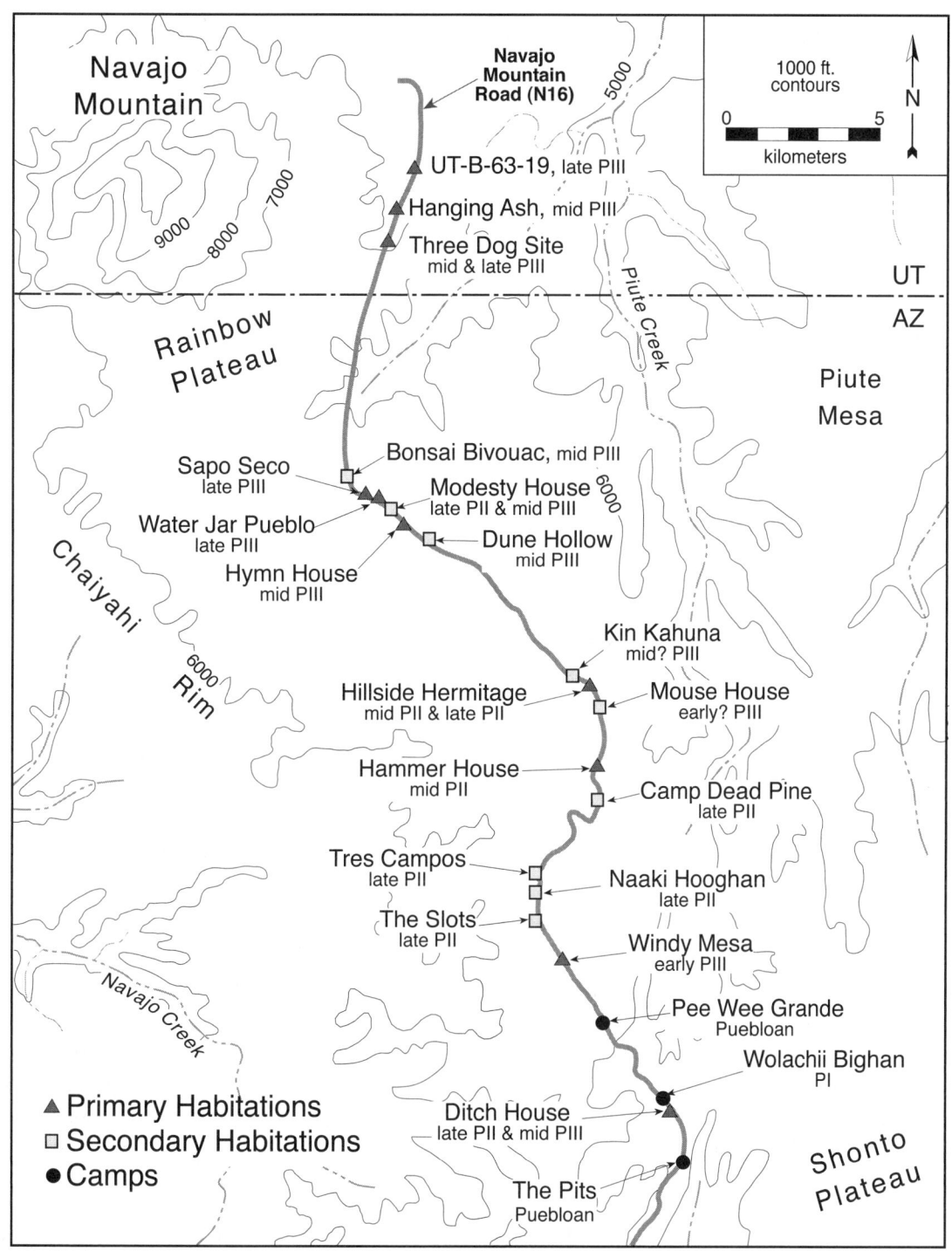

Figure 6.1. Distribution of Navajo Mountain Road Archaeological Project Puebloan sites by inferred settlement type; temporal periods are also listed after each site name.

seemed like a worthwhile site proved disappointing since full excavation eventually revealed that past roadwork had largely destroyed the settlement. Fortunately, the N16 ROW at times strayed across "virgin" terrain where sites in their entirety lay unimpacted, allowing thorough investigation. The two most notable examples in the current sample are Sapo Seco (AZ-J-2-6) and Water Jar Pueblo (AZ-J-2-58). Even some Puebloan sites partially in the ROW were troves of information, with Three Dog Site (UT-B-63-39) a notable standout in this regard; Schroedl (1989) reports on a few examples like this from the southern portion of N16.

TABLE 6.2. Tree-Ring Dates for Navajo Mountain Road Archaeological Project Puebloan Sites

SITE NAME/NO.	PROVENIENCE	LAB NO.	SPECIES	OUTER DATE
Hammer House, AZ-J-14-16	ramada	NMR-39	pinyon	987vv
		NMR-38	pinyon	1047++vv
Ditch House, AZ-J-14-21	Structure 1	NMR-17	juniper	1213++B
		NMR-16 (a–b)	juniper	1217++B
		NMR-21	juniper	1225+r
		NMR-19 (a–b)	pinyon	1227+vv
		NMR-13	juniper	1227+r
		NMR-20 (a–b)	juniper	1228r
		NMR-14	juniper	1228r
	Structure 2	NMR-27	juniper	928vv
	Structure 3	NMR-10 (a–b)	juniper	1166vv
		NMR-12 (a–b)	juniper	1180vv
		NMR-11 (a–b)	juniper	1193vv
		NMR-9 (a–f)	juniper	1200vv
	Structure 4	NMR-23	pinyon	1222+vv
	Structure 8	NMR-26	pinyon	1161+vv
Windy Mesa, AZ-J-14-28	Hearth 6	NMR-28 (a–b)	juniper	1132+r

Note: B = bark present; r = less than a full section but outermost ring is continuous; vv = there is no way of estimating how far the last ring is from the true outside ring; + = one or more rings perhaps missing but indeterminate; ++ = a ring count is necessary since beyond a certain point the specimen could not be dated.

CHRONOLOGY

Tree-Ring Dating

At the start of work on Puebloan sites there is potential for the dreamed-about fine temporal resolution provided by tree-ring dating, the ability to specify the year or even the season when timbers were procured and a structure was built—the charting of cultural change on a scale that few archaeologists in the world can imagine. We thus had high hopes for the NMRAP excavations when testing revealed structural burning at several sites, including those with ceramic assemblages from important temporal intervals, such as the middle Pueblo II sites of Hammer House and Hillside Hermitage or the middle Pueblo III sites of Ditch House and Hymn House. These were sites that, if they could be dated by dendrochronology, had great potential to help refine ceramic chronology. Such hopes were heightened when some excellent-looking samples were recovered, such as the solid timbers from the kiva and habitation room at Hammer House, specimens that had complete cross sections, bark, and lengths of up to 1 m; indeed, at least one sample had to be sawed in half just to ease boxing and transport. However, the eventual finding of erratic juniper was the unfortunate verdict that is all too frequent across much of the Kayenta region. Only two inferior-looking samples of the 18 submitted from Hammer House could be dated, both from a ramada with highly eroded outer rings that returned noncutting dates of AD 987 and 1047 (Table 6.2).

Sample problems aside, few of the NMRAP Puebloan sites actually presented the opportunity to attempt tree-ring dating at all. Just seven Puebloan sites produced samples, and in all but three cases these consisted of just a few isolated specimens. The exceptions were Ditch House, Hammer House, and the middle Pueblo III component of Three Dog Site. The lack of suitable timbers appears to have been largely the result of orderly site abandonments and the extensive scavenging of usable wood, either for rebuilding elsewhere or for fuel wood. The timbers of Hammer House were never scavenged, and the structures did not burn; but the posts had been partially carbonized prior to placement in the ground (a preservative measure?), so they were well preserved but unfortunately of no chronological value. The several carbonized timbers recovered from Three Dog Site came from middle Pueblo III structures that had been torn down in a renovation project for an expanded late Pueblo III settlement and probably represent the burning of waste to clear the ground for the new construction. None of these samples contained sufficient rings to be dated. Ditch House is the single Puebloan site that had thoroughly burned soon after abandonment while the structures still stood intact (perhaps in a forest fire), but even in this case it did not seem "catastrophic," in that the site appears to have been largely closed down, with most usable goods removed from the households, including the metates from mealing bins. Sites like this might represent rather firm evidence of residential mobility: a settlement cleaned and temporarily shut down while the occupants took up residence at another location, but without the structures being dismantled because a return was anticipated and the presence of intact houses prevented encroachment.

In the end, the NMRAP excavations obtained a paltry 17 tree-ring dates from the 83 submitted, a 21 percent "success" rate. Worse still, only seven of the 17 dates can be considered to have any real value, with just two being cutting dates, and these from a single structure at Ditch House. This is the one NMRAP site where dendrochronology proved useful (Table 6.2), leaving the other 25 Puebloan sites/components to be assigned a temporal affiliation using other means, mainly ceramic cross dating. Excavations for the southern portion of the N16 ROW obtained similar results, in that few sites produced samples and of the 28 specimens submitted only 10 dated (36%), with no cutting dates (Schroedl and Blinman 1989:54, Table 8). The latest noncutting dates for a structure or site can at times be informative and should not be dismissed out of hand. Plog and Hantman (1986:Table 20, 1990) have shown that 80 percent of the latest noncutting dates are within 20 years of the latest cutting dates at a site. Single or paired noncutting dates such as those of Hammer House and Windy Mesa have far less utility than various-sized date distributions (see Ahlstrom 1985, 1998b).

In the case of Ditch House, burned structures from the principal component yielded 31 samples that appeared to represent individual charred roof and wall timbers. Out of this batch, 14 samples could be dated (45%), and half of these came from the deepest pithouse (Structure 1). The tight cluster of noncutting, near-cutting, and cutting dates at 1225–1228 places wood procurement for Structure 1 in AD 1228. The two ++B dates in the 1210s probably represent dead or dying trees cut in the same year as the others. In his letter report, Dean (SD, Appendix D) observed that incomplete and complete terminal rings indicate that the two AD 1228 beams were cut during and after the juniper growing season of that year, which suggests that Structure 1 was built in the late summer or fall of 1228 or shortly thereafter. In Ahlstrom's (1998b:153) assessment of dating quality, this structure is at Level II (construction event based on three–eight dates), which he considers "reliable." A series of noncutting dates indicate that Structure 3 at Ditch House was built after AD 1200, while a noncutting date indicates some construction or use in Structure 4 in or after AD 1222. When taking the entire suite of tree-ring dates into consideration along with structure layout and ceramic associations, we concluded that Structures 1 through 4 and 9 (the latter being almost attached to Structure 1 and clearly associated) were constructed at essentially the same time, during or shortly after AD 1228. In essence, the cutting dates for Structure 1 are applied to the other structures, which, except for the mealing room (Structure 2) and Structure 9, have noncutting dates in the early 1200s. Structure 1 is the deepest structure at the site, and at the depth where most beams occurred, the sediment was relatively dry and root disturbance was minimal. This is likely why the Structure 1 samples were both easier to collect and better preserved than those of the shallower structures, such as 2–4, where postdepositional erosion surely removed outside rings from the samples.

The dating of this one component at Ditch House is something of a contribution because, as Dean observes, "barely half a dozen tree-ring dated sites provide the absolute chronological structure for the interval from AD 1150 to 1250" (2002:121). Still, the partial destruction of this component by previous road construction, including what were certainly several additional structures, limits the utility of the site for understanding change in settlement size and configuration just prior to the Tsegi phase (see Dean 1996, 2002). Moreover, the absence of a trash midden for sampling, accompanied by partial admixture of ceramics from a late Pueblo II component, limits the utility of the dates in this instance for refining ceramic chronology. It is also true that we have a far better handle on ceramic dating for this immediately pre–Tsegi phase interval than, say, middle Pueblo II, the time when Hammer House and Hillside Hermitage were occupied. Still, every dated construction event is welcome. Even for the BMAP there is no sense of data redundancy with the 642 dated tree-ring samples from 32 construction events between late Pueblo I and late Pueblo II (AD 840–1149 [Ahlstrom 1998b, 1998c]).

Radiocarbon Dating

Radiocarbon dating generally has poor utility for the chronological ordering of Puebloan sites on the Colorado Plateau. Given the counting error inherent to the technique, and the wide temporal ranges after calibration, pottery types usually provide more precise and accurate estimates of temporal placement. This is especially true in an area like the Kayenta region, where pottery types are distinct and well defined, are easily recognized, and have relatively tight periods of manufacture established by dendrochronology (e.g., Breternitz 1966, with recent adjustments by Ambler [1985b] and Sullivan et al. [1995]). More likely than not, radiocarbon assays either will provide no new information from what was already known based on pottery types or will be inconsistent and therefore need to be reconciled. There is no gain in either case, with money and time wasted. Support for this assertion comes from many site reports for the Colorado Plateau, but locally the attempted radiocarbon dating of Puebloan sites in the southern portion of the N16 ROW provides a handy example (Schroedl and Blinman 1989; this should not be seen as a criticism of the authors, who were exploring all options and may have been directed to try radiocarbon by contract administrators). Even the samples from this project that produced the best results provided no information that was not evident based on the ceramic assemblages from these sites, assemblages that allowed for quite precise estimates of occupation spans by either multiple regression, ceramic seriation, or subjective assessment (Schroedl and Blinman 1989:Table 19). For example, four statistically identical assays from AZ-J-31-5 were averaged to provide a one-sigma calibrated date range of AD 1222–1279 (Schroedl and Blinman 1989:Table 10), while the ceramic assemblage indicated an AD 1250–1285 date range (Schroedl and Blinman 1989:86). While the ^{14}C dates certainly are supportive in this instance, the two-sigma calibrated range for the average, which is appropriate for interpretive purposes to avoid error, is AD 1180–1300 (based on OxCal v. 3.10), outside the time of occupation. This is the best case on that project. The fifth radiocarbon date from site AZ-J-31-5 has a two-sigma calibrated date range of AD 610–970 (OxCal v. 3.10), well out of line by hundreds of years. Such inconsistency was a common finding.

The utility of radiocarbon dating for the Puebloan period depends on what portion of it is being investigated. As portrayed in Figure 6.2, radiocarbon analysis has increasing utility as one moves backward in time from Pueblo II to Pueblo I and into the Basketmaker period. This figure shows the calibration curve based on atmospheric data from Reimer et al. (2004) as graphed by OxCal v. 3.10 (Bronk Ramsey 2005), to which we have added other information such as ceramic-defined periods for the northern Kayenta region and Christenson's (1994:307) point of demarcation for markedly different accuracies in mean ceramic dates. We have also highlighted portions of the calibration curve that are flat and exhibit marked reversals; in these portions the calibrated ranges of dates are greatly lengthened, thereby lessening their utility for chronological placement. Note that the ceramic-based temporal periods toward the more recent end of the temporal range are on the order of about 50 years, which is the accuracy that an experienced ceramic analyst can obtain with relative ease. As such, there is scant possibility for radiocarbon to have much utility unless perhaps for wiggle matching (see Kojo et al. 1994), but the chronological question has to be quite significant to merit such an approach.

In early Pueblo II, the approximate time for which Wepo Black-on-white (late Kana-a) is a predominant decorated type, the ceramic-defined periods begin to lengthen, a trend that continues into Pueblo I and Basketmaker III, accompanied by a loss of temporal specificity based on ceramic types (in part because of fewer types). Consequently, the radiocarbon technique increases in value as a chronological tool, such that the dating of high-quality samples like maize from any Basketmaker III and Pueblo I site may provide useful temporal information. It is still important to be cognizant of the wide temporal spans that can be obtained after calibration and to resist the urge to ignore the error term and treat the results like they were tree-ring dates. As a realistic example, a date of 1250 ± 40 BP, which is a believable assay for maize from a late Basketmaker III site, has a calibrated two-sigma range of AD 670–880. This range includes over half of the late Basketmaker III period and half of the Pueblo I period shown in Figure 6.2. Even with a counting error of just 25 years, something that could be obtained by averaging several statistically identical dates on high-quality materials, the span remains virtually unchanged because of the large reversal at this interval. However, a maize cob with an age of 1400 ± 40 BP would provide a calibrated temporal span of AD 570 to 680 at two sigma, just 110 years; an error term of 25 years for a 1400 BP date, achievable by averaging or high-precision dating, would narrow this range to AD 600–665. Sixty-five years is a far more precise temporal estimate than would be possible with ceramics at this interval, so the choice for using the technique is obvious. Of course this whole discussion assumes high-quality samples; if wood charcoal is being assayed, then all bets are off since the results are likely to be useless. Not all wood assays are necessarily too old, but many are, and this doubt alone renders them valueless for the Puebloan and

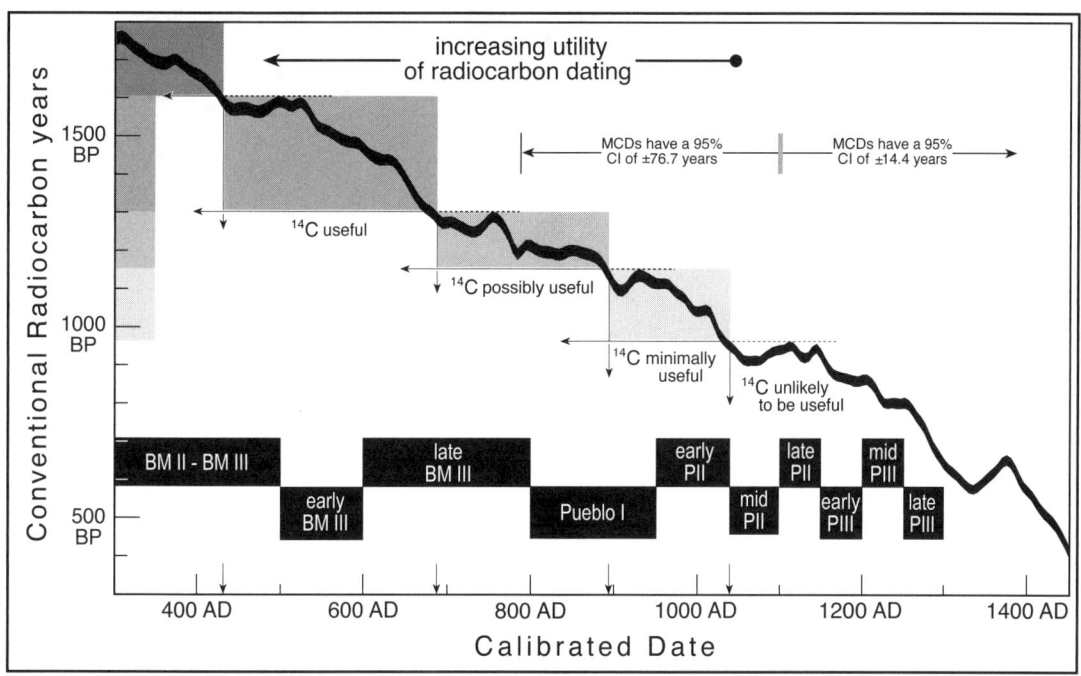

Figure 6.2. Graphic representation of the utility of radiocarbon dating for the Puebloan period, which increases with age but is virtually nil after about AD 1050 (more recent than ca. 960 BP): (1) the radiocarbon calibration curve (atmospheric data from Reimer et al. 2004 as graphed by OxCal v. 3.10 [Bronk Ramsey 2005]), highlighting portions that are flat and exhibit marked reversals; (2) ceramic-defined temporal periods for the northern Kayenta region; (3) Christenson's (1994:307) point of demarcation for markedly different accuracies in mean ceramic dates (MCDs).

Basketmaker periods since there is no way of determining which ones accurately correspond with the target event.

Needless to say, radiocarbon dating was not formally pursued as a means of chronological placement for NMRAP Puebloan sites. Had the project area included many Basketmaker III and Pueblo I settlements the story would be different, but the northern Kayenta region is well known as lacking habitations from these intervals (e.g., Ambler et al. 1983; see SD, Appendix F). Nonetheless, several radiocarbon dates were ultimately obtained, and these are presented in Table 6.3. In all cases these came from multicomponent sites, and the dating was done because the temporal affiliation of the sampled feature was not known and was thought to have been earlier, such as for two hearths at Windy Mesa that excavators suspected to be Basketmaker II in age but which turned out to have a Puebloan affiliation. The Windy Mesa assays are worth considering further because one of the hearths from this site also contained a large charred log submitted for tree-ring analysis. This specimen returned a "near-cutting" date of AD 1132+r, which, given the probable burning of a scavenged timber or a dead tree, accords well with the ceramic-based temporal assignment. Pottery types suggested an occupation medium of AD 1170, with a range of 1133–1188, but likely occurring sometime after AD 1150, during early Pueblo III (see SD vol. 5, chap. 2). This case seems to provide a useful outcome for the technique since the radiocarbon dates from the two hearths appear to closely agree with the tree-ring date and the ceramic cross-dating assignment. Yet, upon considering the calibrated two-sigma range for the dates (AD 970–1190 and 980–1220), even when averaged to lower the error term (AD 990–1160), the temporal span is too great to be informative, with the bulk of the indicated range predating the Puebloan occupation of the site (Figure 6.3).

A somewhat more optimal outcome is provided by the Ditch House results. In this case, radiocarbon dating was done in an attempt to isolate a suspected Basketmaker II component that was not recognized during excavation (see SD vol. 3, chap. 5, and vol. 4, chap. 4). Multiple dates on plant remains such as maize from two Basketmaker-looking structures and other features at the site confirmed a preceramic temporal assignment, although two of the hearths returned Puebloan period assays. These two features were within an extramural activity area that contained a mixture of Pueblo II and Pueblo III ceramic types

TABLE 6.3. Radiocarbon Determinations for Navajo Mountain Road Archaeological Project Puebloan Sites

SITE NAME/NO.	FEATURE	SAMPLE NO.	MATERIAL DATED	CONVENTIONAL ^{14}C AGE (BP)	δ^{13}C (‰)	CAL. 1σ RANGE (AD)	CAL. 2σ RANGE (AD)
Ditch House, AZ-J-14-21	Pit 3, Extramural Area	Beta-102490	sagebrush twigs	910 ± 50	−23.4	1030–1190	1020–1230
	Roasting Pit 3	Beta-102491	maize cupule	910 ± 50	−11.2	1030–1190	1020–1230
Windy Mesa, AZ-J-14-28	Hearth 5	Beta-79157	sagebrush charcoal	980 ± 50	−25.1	1000–1160	970–1190
	Hearth 6	Beta-79156	sagebrush charcoal	960 ± 60	−22.4	1010–1160	980–1220
Pee Wee Grande, AZ-J-14-26	Hearth 1	Beta-79154	wood charcoal	1250 ± 70	−25.0[a]	680–870	650–960
Kin Kahuna, AZ-J-3-8	Hearth 18	Beta-101392	sagebrush charcoal	810 ± 50	−25.6	1190–1280	1040–1300
Three Dog Site, UT-B-63-39	Pit 4	Beta-175657	maize cupule	870 ± 50	−11.8	1060–1230	1030–1270

Note: Calibrated date ranges are based on OxCal v. 3.10 (Bronk Ramsey 2005).

[a] Value is assumed.

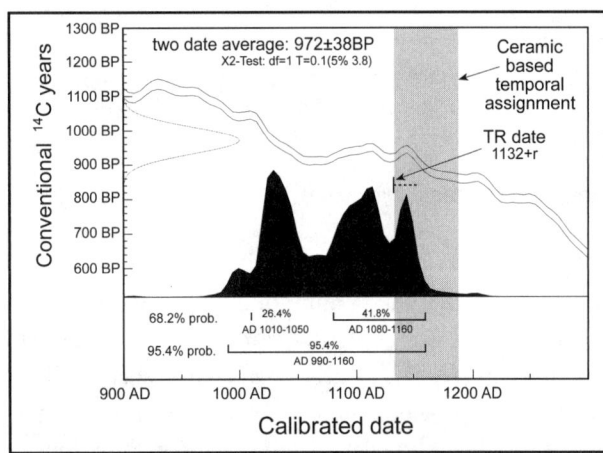

Figure 6.3. Calibration results for the average of two statistically equivalent dates from the Puebloan component at Windy Mesa in relation to a tree-ring date and the ceramic-based temporal assignment.

initially interpreted as evidence that the site spanned the transition between these two periods. As just discussed above, several structures to the north of the activity area were eventually tree-ring dated to the middle Pueblo III period (see Table 6.2), and these features contained a "purer" middle Pueblo III ceramic assemblage than the rest of the site. This led to the suspicion that the remains from two discrete Puebloan occupations were blended together as a palimpsest—one late Pueblo II and the other middle Pueblo III—and that the site was in no way "transitional," merely containing a mixed ceramic assemblage and thus a temporal average that misinformed about the true situation. The two hearth assays fortuitously support this scenario since both are younger than the likely time that the middle Pueblo III structures were built—at or shortly after AD 1228. The calibrated two-sigma range of the average (910 ± 35 BP) of these two identical assays is AD 1030–1220, with little overlap with the likely time of the middle Pueblo III component. Because the samples consisted of a maize cupule in one instance and small twigs in another, this result is credible, and the likelihood of a mixed assemblage from temporally discrete components is supported. Radiocarbon dating in this case proved informative because the results could be juxtaposed against highly precise tree-ring dates, which, fortunately, were just far enough removed in time from the assays to support separate occupations. The slight value of radiocarbon dating in this one particular instance should not be generalized for the Kayenta region at large or other Puebloan sequences with fine-gained ceramic dating, but it serves to highlight that dates on high-quality samples such as maize can prove informative in specific instances.

The date on the Puebloan feature of Three Dog Site was obtained in an effort to identify potential Basketmaker II features that originated from the same occupation surface as the Puebloan structures. Mechanical stripping west of the room block exposed two small pits (Pits 3–4) of uncertain temporal affiliation. The presence of a Basketmaker-style bone gaming piece in the lower fill of Pit 4 suggested that they might relate to features of a Basketmaker II component to the northwest, although there was a single corrugated sherd from the upper part of the pit. The intact portion of this feature measured 60 cm in diameter and nearly 25 cm deep, and its lightly charcoal-flecked fill contained hundreds of Chenopodium and Oryzopsis seeds and at least 10 small fragments of maize cupules, one of which returned a radiocarbon assay of 870 ± 50 BP (cal. AD 1030–1270 at two sigma). This date demonstrates contemporaneity with one of the Pueblo III components at the site. Nearly the exact same scenario applies to the one date from a slab-lined hearth at Kin Kahuna, while for Pee Wee Grande radiocarbon dating was the only means for estimating what the target date might be.

Before moving on it is worth mentioning the one NMRAP Puebloan site that might have benefited the most from radiocarbon dating—Wolachii Bighan (AZ-J-14-20). The sparse ceramic assemblage from this limited-activity site consisted of 122 sherds of which just 17 were typable; most consisted of plain gray utilitarian jar sherds or unpainted whiteware. The three named types represented were Kana-a Gray, Lino Gray, and Kana-a Black-on-white. This sparse assemblage is typical of Pueblo I, with occupation perhaps occurring sometime after about AD 750 but before AD 900. The mean ceramic date is AD 779 based on sherd count or AD 781 based on sherd weight (see SD vol. 5, chap. 2), with mean date ranges of AD 725–834 (count) and AD 728–835 (weight). This interval is admittedly a tricky one for radiocarbon analysis to resolve owing to the reversals and general flatness of the calibration curve. However, Wolachii Bighan might also have been used during early Pueblo II (Wepo phase on Black Mesa), since the types recovered would not necessarily be out of place in such an assemblage. Moreover, there are a few substantial early Pueblo II habitations in Upper Piute Canyon (Fairley 1989; designated as late Pueblo I in her temporal scheme—AD 950–1000), ones with Wepo Black-on-white as the predominant whiteware, some Kana-a Black-on-white, and abundant Kana-a Gray. It is easy to envision the occupants of such settlements creating limited-activity sites in the adjacent countryside, such as the highland setting of Wolachii Bighan. If true in this case, the sherd-based temporal assignment of this site might well be 200 years off, more like AD 979 than 779. No high-quality organic remains were recovered in the field, but the float analyst found maize cupules in the sediment from one of the two hearths excavated at the site. Radiocarbon analysis of the maize was not pursued in this case because the payoff seemed limited given the extent of prior site disturbance and because the dating of the many NMRAP Basketmaker II and Archaic sites had greater priority.

Ceramic Cross Dating

Ultimately the temporal placement for virtually all NMRAP Puebloan sites was based on ceramic types. Relative quantities of specific Kayentan pottery types are very sensitive time indicators. Conservatively, simple seriation allows a Pueblo II and Pueblo III period site or component to be placed within a 50-year interval if there are at least 1,000 total sherds or more than 300 typable sherds (Ambler 1985b). About 100-year intervals might be obtained for earlier periods, although in the northern Kayenta region there are few if any Basketmaker III and Pueblo I habitations.

The methods and results of ceramic dating of the N16 sites are detailed in chapter 2, volume 5, of the supporting documentation, so there is no need to repeat much of that discussion here. Suffice it to say that the basic data are provided by classifying all sherds according to the traditional ware/type system for the Kayenta region (Colton 1955, 1956, 1958; Colton and Hargrave 1937; Hargrave 1935). There are methods that do not involve traditional types (e.g., Plog and Hantman 1986, 1990), but these may not be any more accurate and ceramic typing is inexpensive, has a proven track record, and integrates new data with old (e.g., Ambler 1985b; Christenson 1994). Tables with sherd counts for each site are presented in the Puebloan site descriptions of volume 4 of the supporting documentation, tabulations that cannot be repeated here because of space limitations. With type counts in hand there are several different methods for actually deriving estimates for the occupation of a settlement or a component thereof. All depend on knowing the temporal span for when a given type was manufactured or in common use, information derived from clear associations between pottery types and tree-ring dates (e.g., Breternitz 1966), such as floor assemblages of vessels from burned houses with well-established construction dates and short intervals of use; a good example is AZ I:1:17 (ASM) reported in Sullivan 1986 (also Sullivan et al. 1995). With experience, one can make a fairly educated estimate of the time of occupation by examining the relative frequencies of types within each of the three wares of the Kayenta ceramic tradition: Tusayan White Ware, Tsegi Orange Ware, and Tusayan Gray Ware. This is what archaeologists routinely do in survey

TABLE 6.4. Mean Date and Mean Date Range by Sherd Count and Weight for Navajo Mountain Road Archaeological Project Puebloan Sites, Along with Occupation Median as Derived by Seriation and Geib's Subjective Temporal Assignment

SITE NAME	MEAN DATE (AD)		MEAN DATE RANGE (AD)[a]		OCCUPATION MEDIAN (AD)	SUBJECTIVE ASSIGNMENT (AD)
	COUNT	WEIGHT	COUNT	WEIGHT		
Wolachii Bighan	779	781	725–834	728–835	—	900–1000
Hammer House	1060	1061	1032–1087	1034–1089	1050	1050–1070
Hillside Hermitage, Mid–Pueblo II	1067	1064	1036–1098	1034–1093	1065	1060–1080
Camp Dead Pine	1102	1101	1066–1138	1065–1136	1100	1100–1140
The Slots	1115	1115	1083–1148	1083–1148	—	1100–1150
Mouse House	1115	1115	1083–1148	1083–1148	—	1150–1200
Naaki Hooghan	1115	1113	1085–1145	1083–1143	1120	1100–1160
Hillside Hermitage, Late Pueblo II	1124	1122	1088–1161	1086–1158	1128	1100–1150
Modesty House, Pueblo II	1125	1120	1088–1163	1085–1155	—	1100–1150
Tres Campos	1126	1126	1092–1159	1091–1160	1130	1100–1150
Windy Mesa	1160	1162	1133–1188	1135–1189	1170	1140–1200
Ditch House, Mixed	1180	1226	1147–1214	1203–1249	1190	1115–1240
Ditch House, Mid–Pueblo III	1194	1194	1159–1229	1158–1230	1220	1220–1240
Kin Kahuna	1189	1242	1161–1218	1223–1261	—	1200–1240
Three Dog Site, Mid–Pueblo III	1194	1203	1167–1221	1179–1227	1215	1220–1250
Dune Hollow	1202	1200	1177–1228	1173–1227	—	1180–1210
Hanging Ash	1215	1221	1184–1246	1190–1252	1217	1200–1230
Bonsai Bivouac	1225	1214	1192–1258	1178–1251	1230	1200–1240
Hymn House	1235	1237	1206–1265	1207–1267	1235	1200–1240
Sapo Seco	1238	1240	1209–1266	1212–1268	1255	1220–1260
Modesty House, Pueblo III	1241	1242	1216–1267	1217–1267	1255	1200–1250
Water Jar Pueblo	1244	1242	1216–1271	1215–1268	1260	1230–1270
UT-B-63-19	1247	1249	1222–1271	1224–1273	1240	1220–1260
Three Dog Site, Late Pueblo III	1252	1257	1233–1272	1238–1275	1250	1240–1260

Note: Sites are ordered from oldest to youngest using the mean date range based on sherd count.

[a] This is the 50 percent portion of the range closest to the mean following Reed and Hensler (1999:56).

situations, although usually from mental accounting of frequencies noted rather than actual tabulation. More replicable approaches, some of which provide temporal ranges with confidence intervals, include judgmental seriation (e.g., Ambler 1985b), what Schroedl (1989:74–79) termed absolute seriation, mean ceramic dating (e.g., Christenson 1994), and multiple regression (Schroedl and Blinman 1989:58–74).

Using date ranges for pottery types (see SD vol. 5, Table 2.7), the NMRAP ceramic analysts (Kelly Hays-Gilpin and Janet Hagopian) computed mean ceramic dates and mean ceramic date ranges using both sherd counts and weights; they also plotted assemblages on seriation curves. All Puebloan sites and components were included in the mean ceramic date calculations, but only sites or components with 45 or more typable sherds were considered for seriation, which allowed 18 components to be included. The production date ranges of diagnostic types were derived from Breternitz (1966) as amended by recent projects in the Kayenta Anasazi region (Ambler 1985b; Christenson 1994; Schroedl and Blinman 1989; Sullivan et al. 1995). Only types with a time span of less than 300 years were used in the calculations. The results are presented in Table 6.4 and depicted in Figure 6.4. The relative chronological order of each site or component in Table 6.4 is based on the mean date range calculated using sherd count; comparing both count and weight within the same assemblage can help control for factors such as trampling and the influence of partial vessels. That this approach is fallible is indicated by the temporal mean and range of the middle Pueblo III component at Ditch House, which was constructed around AD 1228 (shown in Figure 6.4 with the dot and dashed line to the right indicating the probable occupation span). This site is discussed in greater detail below.

NMRAP ceramic analysts also placed sites/com-

Summary and Interpretation of Puebloan Remains 301

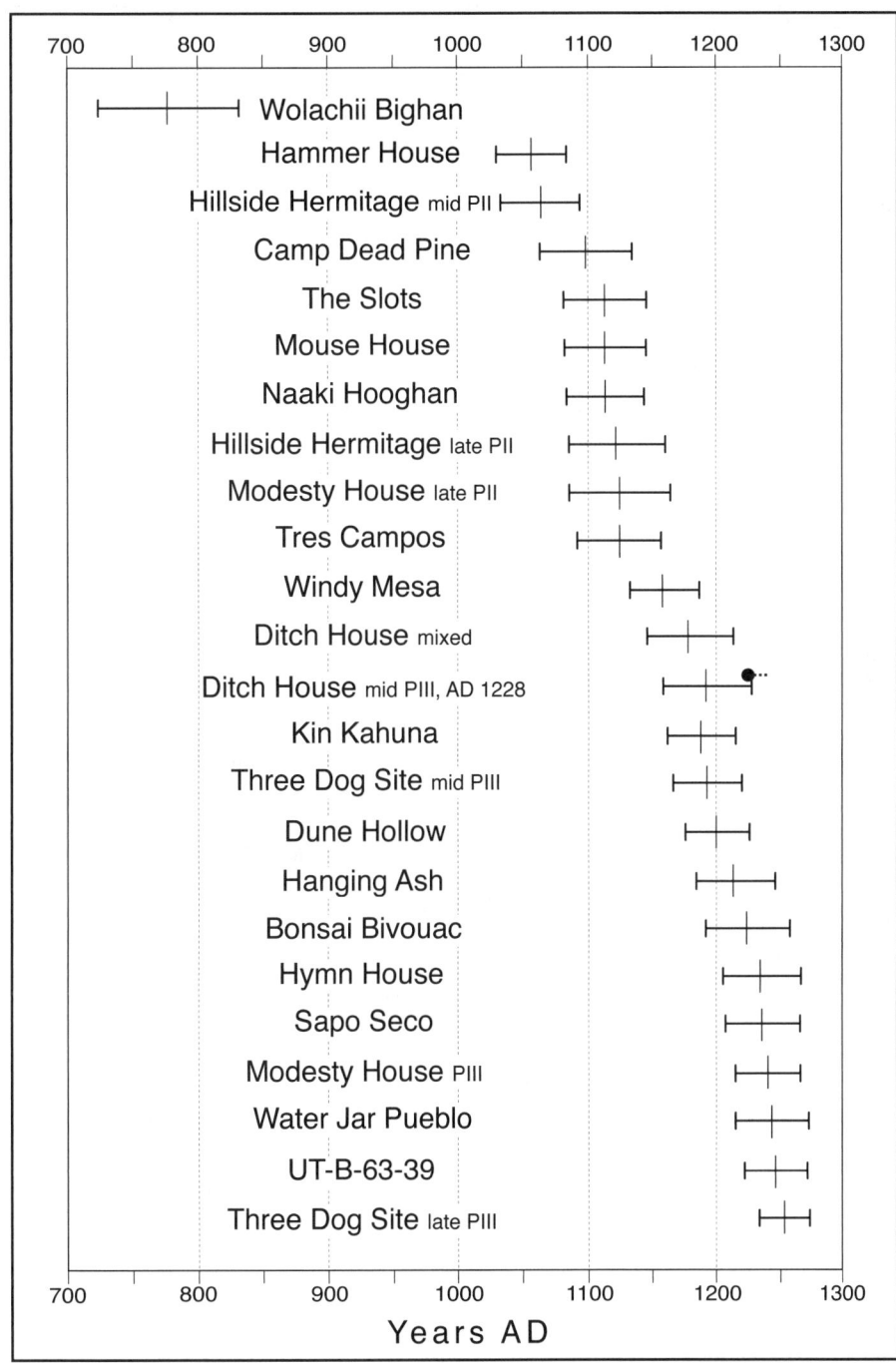

Figure 6.4. Mean ceramic dating of the Navajo Mountain Road Archaeological Project Puebloan sites organized from oldest to youngest; results are based on sherd count. Also shown is the one tree-ring-dated construction event of the middle Pueblo III component at Ditch House (see Supporting Documents vol. 5, chap. 2, for methods and ceramic date ranges).

ponents in relative chronological order using Ambler's (1985b) seriation curves for Tusayan White Ware, Tsegi Orange Ware (includes San Juan Red Ware), and Tusayan Gray Ware. This method employs type frequencies calculated as percentages within ware, not as a percentage of the total assemblage. The percentages within each ware for a site or component are plotted on a bar graph, using the same scale as the seriation curve, and these bar graphs are moved along the temporal axis of Ambler's seriation curves until a "best fit" is approximated. Examples for

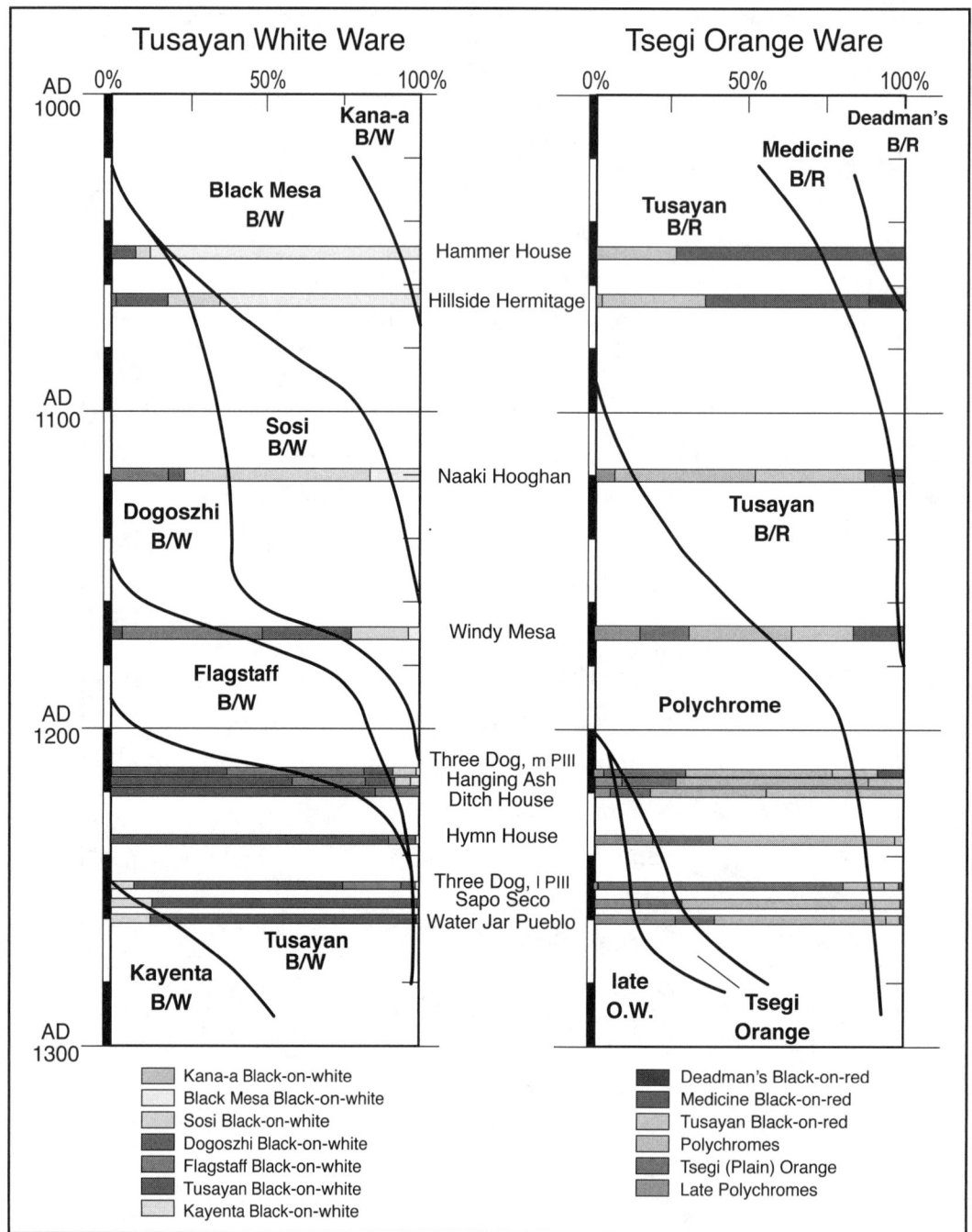

Figure 6.5. Dating of Navajo Mountain Road Archaeological Project Puebloan sites with large ceramic assemblages (mainly primary habitations) using Ambler's (1985b) seriation curves for Tusayan White Ware and Tsegi Orange Ware.

NMRAP primary habitations using Tusayan White Ware and Tsegi Orange Ware are shown in Figure 6.5. Ambler created these curves to date excavated sites at Navajo Mountain (Geib et al. 1985) that all postdated AD 1000. Consequently, his curves begin at about AD 1025. Since he used assemblages from Black Mesa, Klethla Valley, Shonto Plateau, Piute Mesa, and the Rainbow Plateau, the curves should be applicable throughout the core area of the Kayenta region. Outside of this area, such as in the Hopi Buttes or Grand Canyon, the curves might not give accurate results.

Ambler's method defines a point in time called the occupational median "where equal numbers of person-days of occupation are represented on both sides of the

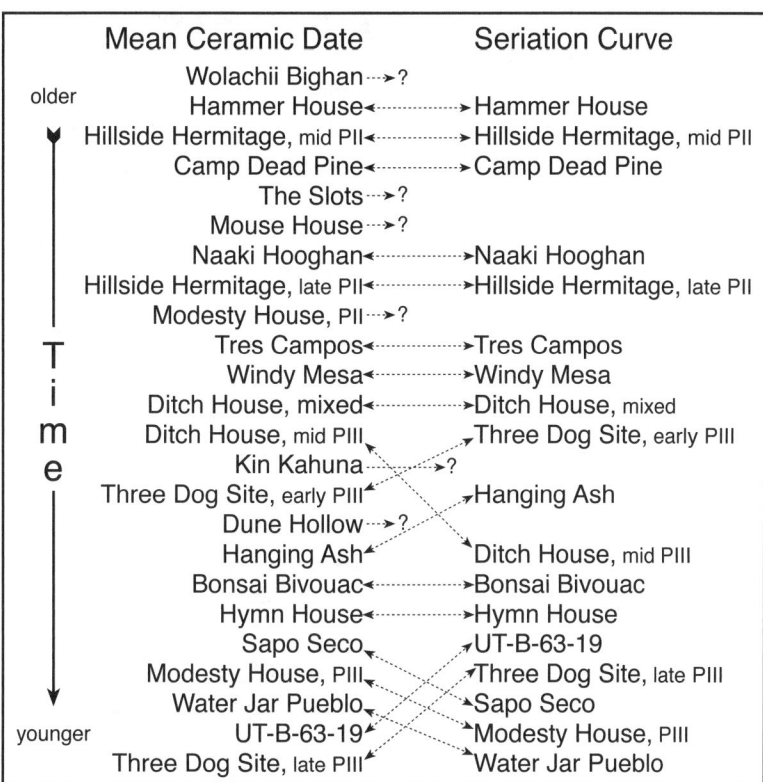

Figure 6.6. Temporal ordering of Puebloan sites from oldest to youngest based on mean ceramic dating and the seriation curve; fewer sites could be assigned a temporal span with the seriation method on account of too few typable sherds. Note that this figure does not chart the scale of change in temporal order.

median; thus, half of the vessels recovered in sherd form would have been broken prior to that time, and half after" (1985b:36). Since sherd frequencies and the relative proportions of ceramic types can change rapidly, the occupational median can be estimated to within a few years. This is especially true when there is a correlation between all three wares and the seriation curve (Ambler 1985b:53). Because only sites or components with 45 or more typable sherds were considered, six NMRAP sites with small assemblages could not be included. These occupation medians are listed in Table 6.4, and they generally correspond to the mean date calculations. The difference in the chronological ordering of the NMRAP Puebloan sites by mean ceramic dating and seriation is shown in Figure 6.6, but not the scale of the change in temporal assignment. It is noteworthy that the seriation method performed much better at representing the occupation of the tree-ring-dated middle Pueblo III component of Three Dog Site by providing an occupation median of AD 1220 instead of a mean date of AD 1194. The ceramic analysts provide their reasoning for the occupational medians for each site or component in Tables 2.10 and 2.11 of volume 5 online, discussing which of the three seriation curves was given most weight. In theory the "best fit" takes into account the three different wares, but the more temporally sensitive white and orange/red wares often take precedence.

Site Occupation Spans and Use Histories

The sample of Anasazi sites excavated within the N16 ROW appears largely representative of the temporal distribution of Puebloan occupation in the northern Kayenta region. The first residential sites date to middle Pueblo II, at or shortly after AD 1050, with only a single temporary camp dating earlier than this. This parallels earlier findings for the region that suggested a virtual absence of classic Basketmaker III and Pueblo I. Unlike portions of the Kayenta region such as the Klethla Valley and Red Lake area where single sites can have very long and complex histories of use (e.g., Clark 1993b), the more truncated temporal span of settlement in the northern Kayenta region tends to simplify matters such that many sites were occupied just once and briefly, with no superpositioned features or complex remodeling of structures. Sites that were occupied for a few generations exist, however, such as Neskahi Village (Hobler 1974), and several of the NMRAP sites contained features and structures from distinct temporal components. In most cases of multicomponent Puebloan sites, NNAD field crews were able to identify structures and other features from separate times of occupancy. The combined evidence from architectural patterning, debris accumulation, stratigraphy, ceramic dates, and other data allows conjectures about the use histories of each site and estimates of occupation spans that sometimes are more restricted than ceramic dates alone.

Basketmaker III

As discussed in the previous chapter (also Geib and Spurr 2000, 2002), the NMRAP documented an excellent record of Basketmaker II settlement for the northern Kayenta region, including the transition to the Basketmaker III period as evidenced by sites with Obelisk Utility, arrowpoints, and other characteristics. The region then appears to have been abandoned during what might be considered classic Basketmaker III, when Lino Black-on-white (Black-on-gray) was the predominant decorated type; at least, no habitations are known that date to this interval, and none were found within the N16 ROW.

Pueblo I

Late Pueblo I habitations have been documented within canyons of the northern Kayenta region where water table or irrigation farming was possible, such as Piute Canyon (Fairley 1989) and parts of the Navajo Canyon system (Miller and Breternitz 1958b:5–6), but it appears that the plateaus and mesas surrounding these canyons were not favored for habitation during this interval. Wolachii Bighan (AZ-J-14-20) may provide limited evidence for use of the highlands for other than habitation purposes during Pueblo I, a time period that is poorly documented in the area, but this evidence must be viewed with caution. The temporal assignment of Wolachii Bighan (no tree-ring samples were recovered, and radiocarbon dating was not attempted) is based on a small ceramic sample, with only three named types represented: Kana-a Gray ($n = 13$), Lino Gray ($n = 3$), and Kana-a Black-on-white ($n = 1$). The other 105 recovered sherds consisted of plain gray body portions, unpainted whiteware, and one that was unidentifiable. Although this assemblage is typical of Pueblo I, with a calculated mean ceramic date prior to AD 800, there is the possibility that the site corresponds with a later period of use as discussed previously under radiocarbon dating. Upper Piute Canyon contains several substantial early Pueblo II habitations (Wepo phase on Black Mesa) that are characterized by abundant plain gray but with Kana-a Gray as the chief utilitarian type, Wepo Black-on-white as the predominant whiteware, and Kana-a Black-on-white in lesser abundance (Fairley 1989; designated as late Pueblo I in her temporal scheme—AD 950–1000). It is easy to envision the inhabitants of such settlements creating limited-activity sites such as Wolachii Bighan in the highlands that surround Upper Piute Canyon, and the ceramic types recovered from the site would not be out of place for an assemblage from an early Pueblo II encampment. Consequently, the sherd-based temporal assignment of this site might well be 200 years off, with occupation occurring in the late 900s rather than the late 700s. Whether this is the case might be determined by radiocarbon dating, but either way the NMRAP excavations support previous conclusions regarding the lack of Pueblo I residential settlement of the northern Kayenta region. The meager remains documented at Wolachii Bighan seem consistent with deposition from a single use episode or two episodes within the span of a few years. The role of the site within regional settlement remains conjectural, but a temporary camp for some extractive purpose is indicated.

Middle Pueblo II

The initial Puebloan habitations within the N16 ROW date to middle Pueblo II or the Black Mesa ceramic period, sometime after about AD 1050 but before AD 1100. This is a time when Black Mesa Black-on-white was the predominant whiteware, Tsegi Orange Ware had replaced San Juan Red Ware, and utilitarian jars were typically corrugated, especially by neatly done corrugation but also on occasion exuberant corrugation and various tooled or appliqué designs. San Juan Red Ware was produced in the western Mesa Verde region (e.g., Hegmon et al. 1997) and imported to the Kayenta region during Pueblo I and early Pueblo II, but once redware production started in the Kayenta region, sometime after AD 1000, San Juan Red Ware stopped being imported. As a result, the ratio of San Juan Red Ware to Tsegi Orange Ware quickly dropped during the 1000s, such that by AD 1100 Tsegi Orange Ware makes up 100 percent of the redware on nearly all Kayentan sites.

The two NMRAP sites that characterize the middle

TABLE 6.5. Comparison Among Several Middle and Late Pueblo II Sites of the N16 Project Area Using Ratios of Black Mesa Black-on-white to Sosi and Dogoszhi Black-on-white Combined and Medicine Black-on-red to Tusayan Black-on-red

Site	Black Mesa Black-on-white : Sosi + Dogoszhi Black-on-white	Medicine Black-on-red : Tusayan Black-on-red	Tree-Ring Date (Latest Noncutting, AD)
AZ-J-3-13	25.1 : 1	0 : 0[a]	none
Hammer House, Mid–Pueblo II	11.2 : 1	3.9 : 1	1047++vv
AZ-J-19-12	3.3 : 1	.4 : 1[b]	1075vv
Hillside Hermitage, Mid–Pueblo II Component	1.9 : 1	1.6 : 1	none
Naakai Hooghan, Late Pueblo II	.3 : 1	.4 : 1	none
Camp Dead Pine, Late Pueblo II	.2 : 1	.5 : 1	none
AZ-J-19-3	.2 : 1	.4 : 1	none
UT-V-13-19	.2 : 1	.3 : 1	none
Hillside Hermitage, Late Pueblo II Component	.1 : 1	0 : 15	none
Small Jar Pueblo (NA7537)	.05 : 1	.1 : 1	1110+vv

Note: Known latest tree-ring dates are given: vv = there is no way of estimating how far the last ring is from the true outside ring; + = one or more rings perhaps missing but indeterminate; ++ = a ring count is necessary since beyond a certain point the specimen could not be dated. Ratios are calculated from data in this report, Geib et al. 1985, Lindsay et al. 1968, and Schroedl 1989.

[a] 100 percent San Juan Red Ware.

[b] There were three polychrome sherds from this assemblage, but from surface and random units not feature contexts or middens.

Pueblo II interval are Hammer House and Hillside Hermitage; a late Pueblo II component was also present at the latter site, but it occurred more than 10 m to the northeast with a separate midden, so it was easy to separate remains from both occupations (see Figure 3.22). Key temporally sensitive ceramic types suggest that Hammer House was occupied slightly earlier than Hillside Hermitage. The predominant whiteware type for both sites is Black Mesa Black-on-white, with lesser amounts of Sosi and Dogoszhi Black-on-white; the ratio of the former to the latter two types combined is 8.8 for Hammer House but 1.9 for Hillside Hermitage (Table 6.5). Such ratios should reflect temporal order, given that Black Mesa Black-on-white has an earlier start date for manufacture and appears to have developed out of the preceding Wepo Black-on-white style. Sites from the early portion of the middle Pueblo II interval should have more Black Mesa Black-on-white relative to Sosi and Dogoszhi than habitations established toward the end of this interval. Supportive of this pattern based on similar logic is the ratio of Medicine Black-on-red to Tusayan Black-on-red. Medicine is the earliest type of Tsegi Orange Ware and was evidently inspired by the earlier Deadmans (La Plata) Black-on-red of the San Juan Red Ware tradition, whereas Tusayan Black-on-red is most characteristic of late Pueblo II extending into Pueblo III. For Hammer House the Medicine to Tusayan Black-on-red ratio is 3.9, whereas for Hillside Hermitage it is 1.6. Slightly at odds with this result, but perhaps not overly important, is the higher proportion of San Juan Red Ware to Tsegi Orange Ware at Hillside Hermitage (.17) compared to Hammer House (.02), where only four San Juan Red Ware sherds were recovered.

Type frequencies for Hammer House suggest a best fit in Schroedl and Blinman's "Period 2" (1989:62), AD 1050–1080, a dating scheme that assumes a start date of AD 1050 for Dogoszhi Black-on-white. If Ambler's start date of AD 1040 is used, together with the fact that Hammer House has more Medicine Black-on-red than Tusayan Black-on-red, a date range closer to AD 1040–1060 is possible. Ambler's (1985b:Figures 11 and 13) frequency distributions for the Navajo Mountain area support this range as well, with a best fit at AD 1050. Hillside Hermitage, with its higher proportion of slightly later types, has a best fit at about AD 1065, with abandonment before 1080. It is conceivable that they were sequentially used rather than contemporary. Mean ceramic dating suggests occupation spans that are certainly too long for both sites, with a span of AD 1032–1087 for Hammer House and AD 1036–1098 for Hillside Hermitage. Given a subjective assessment of all information we would eliminate the early end of the ceramic mean date ranges for both sites—initial use probably postdated AD 1050. Both sites appear to have been occupied for short intervals given the relatively sparse trash, certainly less than a generation and perhaps not even 20 years. The total sherd count for Hammer House is 2,566, with Hillside Hermitage yielding 1,514; debitage counts are 2,210 and 985, respectively. These frequencies of the rapidly accumulating debris suggest greater longevity of occupancy at Hammer House (group size appears equivalent based on area of enclosed and roofed structures), something that seemed evident in the field based on the nature of the trash middens—the Hammer House deposit was both thicker and richer in charcoal and artifacts compared to the Hillside Hermitage midden. The Hammer House kiva exhibited extensive remodeling of loom holes and some patching of the floor, something not in evidence at Hillside Hermitage, although the jacal living structure there had been reconfigured into a storage and activity room containing a mealing bin.

Schroedl (1989) reported two habitations excavated in the southern portion of the N16 ROW on the northern Shonto Plateau that were designated as early Pueblo II in the temporal scheme used for that report. Only the midden lay within the ROW at one of these sites (AZ-J-31-3), so findings were limited to an artifact assemblage, two burials, a pot cache, and a few small pits. The other site (AZ-J-19-12) lay totally within the ROW, so findings were comparable to those of the NMRAP Pueblo II sites, and indeed the site appears quite similar in character. This site has an assemblage that we would characterize as middle Pueblo II, and the site would have been so designated had it been excavated by the NMRAP. The assemblage appears later than that of Hammer House based on the ratio of Black Mesa to Sosi and Dogoszhi Black-on-white combined (see Table 6.5) but perhaps earlier than Hillside Hermitage. The redware ratios suggest the opposite, as does the presence of three polychrome sherds; moreover, AZ-J-19-12 lacks San Juan Red Ware. If not strictly contemporaneous, Hillside Hermitage and AZ-J-19-12 are perhaps so close in time that ceramics cannot differentiate them unless one ware is weighted more than another in making such a determination.

Site AZ-J-31-3 has a ceramic assemblage that presents an interesting contrast with the sites just considered because it is clearly earlier based on several important distinctions, as Blinman describes (in Schroedl 1989:95–98): an absence of Tsegi Orange Ware with a relatively high proportion of San Juan Red Ware (12% of the entire collection) and a high proportion of late neck-banded types (Coconino and Medicine). Despite this, the Tusayan White Ware consists almost entirely of Black Mesa Black-on-white with nearly no Kana-a (Wepo was not identified in this analysis [Schroedl 1989:34]). Schroedl and Blinman assigned this assemblage to their "Period 1" (1989:Table 12), which they estimate as having an approximate temporal span of AD 1020–1050. Given the high incidence of Black Mesa Black-on-white we would place this assemblage within the middle Pueblo II ceramic period, but much of the Black Mesa might well be classified as Wepo Black-on-white, hence an early Pueblo II designation could be warranted. The one vessel design that is illustrated (Schroedl 1989:Figure 18) is an unmistakable example of Black Mesa Black-on-white, so perhaps Wepo is poorly represented at this site. In any event, this assemblage is significant with regard to Sullivan et al.'s (1995:185) proposed shifting of the production start date for Black Mesa Black-on-white upward from AD 875 to AD 1058. They admit not being surprised if "unambiguous examples of Black Mesa Black-on-white are recovered that date prior to AD 1050" (1995:185 n. 2), and AZ-J-31-3 might well provide just such evidence. All in all, the Pueblo II sites considered here suggest that relatively fine parsing of the eleventh century is possible in the Kayenta region for single-component habitations.

Late Pueblo II

The next ceramic period is characterized by a preponderance of Sosi and Dogoszhi Black-on-white, the ascendance of Tusayan Black-on-red as the dominant type within Tsegi Orange Ware, and the initial production of polychromes, usually those made with black hachure over bands of red slip or over unslipped bands of orange paste. This late Pueblo II interval was a time of Puebloan expansion throughout the Kayenta region and beyond. Ambler et al. (1983) suggested, like many authors before, that the proliferation of late Pueblo II habitations across the northern Kayenta region (Rainbow Plateau, Piute Mesa, and Cummings Mesa) resulted from migration rather than simple population growth, an inference based on the number of settlements that appeared within a fairly brief interval and the evident lack of local antecedents. Dean et al. (1985) have characterized the late AD 1000s and early AD 1100s as a relatively warm and wet interval favorable to farmers, a time that might have encouraged population movement into areas near the lower fringe of the present pinyon–juniper zone.

The NMRAP excavations included six late Pueblo II sites, all of which are classified as secondary habitations or otherwise limited-use sites rather than primary residencies like the middle Pueblo II sites just discussed. As an example of how late Pueblo II ceramic assemblages differ from those of middle Pueblo II, consider the same type ratios for whiteware and redware presented earlier. Table 6.5 lists these for the NMRAP late Pueblo II sites with the largest ceramic assemblages—Naakai Hooghan, Camp Dead Pine, and the late Pueblo II component of Hillside Hermitage, along with those from a few previously excavated late Pueblo II primary habitations. For Naakai Hooghan the ratio of Black Mesa Black-on-white to Sosi and Dogoszhi Black-on-white combined is .3, while the ratio of Medicine Black-on-red to Tusayan Black-on-red is .4. Moreover, the Naakai Hooghan ceramic assemblage contains polychromes and a few sherds of Flagstaff Black-on-white, types unrepresented in the middle Pueblo II assemblages.

Hillside Hermitage presents a useful comparison because the assemblages from the late Pueblo II component at this site can be contrasted with that of the middle Pueblo II component. The late Pueblo II assemblage is quite small, but with sufficient typable sherds to provide a reliable temporal estimate, especially when looking at the composition of the overall assemblage and the within-ware types. Dogoszhi Black-on-white and Sosi Black-on-white are the preponderant identifiable types of Tusayan White Ware; Black Mesa Black-on-white, the only other whiteware type, accounts for just two sherds (the ratio of the latter to the former two types is .1, compared to 1.9 for the middle Pueblo II component). Regarding Tsegi Orange Ware at the late Pueblo II component, Medicine Black-on-red is absent, and there are almost as many polychrome sherds ($n = 12$) as Tusayan Black-on-red ($n = 15$), with several different polychrome types represented. Tusayan White Ware and Tsegi Orange Ware sherds combined indicate that occupation probably occurred well after the middle Pueblo II structures had been abandoned, with perhaps several decades intervening. The sherd assemblage is certainly consistent with occupancy after AD 1100, perhaps after AD 1130, but likely before AD 1160.

The ceramic assemblages from the late Pueblo II sites are too small to place great confidence in fine parsing of this interval. Naaki Hooghan has the largest assemblage at 930 sherds, but just 112 could be typed; Tres Campos is next with 83 typable sherds out of 413, and Camp Dead Pine has 62 typable out of 425. With every such decrease in the number of typed sherds the estimates of temporal placement become less precise or more generalized. What this means is that the dating of any of the late Pueblo II sites is perhaps only accurate in the sense of placement into the overall late Pueblo II interval, with any relative ordering therein highly speculative. That all of the sites evidently functioned as seasonal residences or for other limited activities might also make temporal assignment by ceramic cross dating more error prone because of the potential for the recycling of old vessels or vessel fragments (would the newest and best cooking and serving vessels be used at a seasonal habitation?). Mean ceramic dating suggests a temporal ordering of the late Pueblo II sites with Camp Dead Pine potentially the oldest (range of AD 1066–1138 by sherd count) and Tres Campos potentially the youngest (range of AD 1092–1159). Anything before AD 1100 can probably be eliminated from these sites, and only Naakai Hoogan has evidence of two separate use episodes, but even so its occupation span was likely to have been less than 30 years.

Structural simplicity and seasonal occupation do not necessarily mean that secondary habitations had short durations of use—shorter than, say, the middle Pueblo II primary residential sites previously considered. Standards of what is acceptable or tolerable at a seasonal settlement might be lower, and minimal repairs might be more easily done such that a shade structure could be serviceable for 20 years. Debris might not accumulate rapidly at such sites either. The largest and structurally most substantial of the late Pueblo II NMRAP sites was Naaki Hooghan, with two living structures (see Figure 3.10). The site yielded a low number of artifacts, including those with a relatively high discard rate (930 sherds and 199 flakes), but whether this is indicative of a short occupation length is hard to say. In this case the site appears to consist of two separate structural suites, each consisting of a shallow jacal living room with an attached ramada/activity area. Sequential use accounts for between-structure differences in abandonment scenarios and the placement of Structure 3 immediately in front of Structure 2. Two separate uses means that the total assemblage derived from any one episode should perhaps be halved. The degree of investment in the living structures, which exceeds that at the other late Pueblo II sites, suggests that the occupants planned on using the location more than once. The intended and actual use of the site (Kent 1992), therefore, may have been as a seasonally reoccupied, short-duration habitation associated with some essential annual extractive task(s). The structures at the other late Pueblo II sites are even less substantially built and lack hearths, or they consist of simple brush enclosures or shades. These other sites also tend to have even fewer remains than Naaki Hooghan, all consistent with the seasonal use interpretation (see site type discussion later in this chapter).

The clearest case of a briefly occupied late Pueblo II structure is provided by Modesty House on the sagebrush flats of the central Rainbow Plateau. Here there was an oval brush structure with a floor area of only about 2 m². It lacked an interior hearth, but there was an exterior hearth a few meters from the structure. The total artifact assemblage consisted of 11 flakes and nine sherds, with all the sherds coming from decorated vessels. The sherds represent portions of at least five vessels—two bowls and three jars—with the sherds relatively large and perhaps representing vessel portions brought in for use as containers and eating utensils. Recycling vessel fragments makes sense at briefly occupied sites. The pottery types represented (Sosi Black-on-white, Dogoszhi Black-on-white, Tusayan Black-on-red, and Cameron/Tusayan Polychrome) are consistent with a late Pueblo II temporal assignment, certainly after AD 1100, perhaps even after AD 1120, and likely before AD 1160. Even though the site was probably used but a single brief season or two, without a tree-ring date temporal specificity will always remain in the ca. half-century range.

Problematic Late Pueblo II–Early Pueblo III Assemblages

Two sites present difficulties in dating that deserve individual attention here. One of these is Ditch House, touched upon in the previous discussion of radiocarbon dating. The other is the small site of Mouse House. Ditch House, which is the more significant of the two sites (Figure 6.7), was problematic not just because of having two partially overlapping and intermingled Puebloan components but also because of an intermingled Basketmaker II component that had to be isolated by postexcavation analysis and radiocarbon dating (see SD vol. 3, chap. 5). Impacts to the site from previous road construction doubtless complicated matters by preventing full assessment of structural relationships. Ditch House was initially interpreted as a small settlement of lengthy occupation from late Pueblo II to middle Pueblo III based on a mixture of types that in the whiteware ranged from Sosi to Tusayan Black-on-white (Table 6.6). Full excavation combined with tree-ring dating and the segregation of sherd assemblages from specific structures allowed a temporally discrete middle Pueblo III component to be recognized, one with likely construction near the close of the AD 1220s (see previous tree-ring dating discussion). Features of this component were intermixed with those from

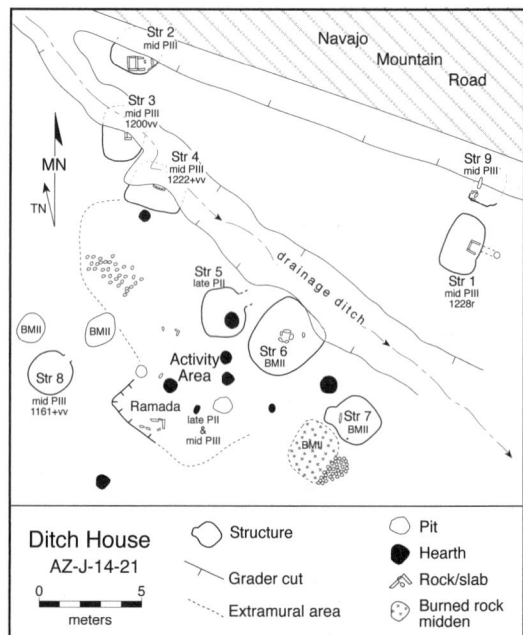

Figure 6.7. Plan map of Ditch House showing the structures and other features derived from three separate occupations of this single location; tree-ring-dated middle Pueblo III structures occur along the northern part of the site, with most primary habitations excavated within the N16 right-of-way impacted by previous road construction and maintenance.

earlier Puebloan use, including warm-season structures or ramadas. There was no area of the site that provided a "clean" ceramic assemblage of this earlier component, only one badly mixed with sherds from the middle Pueblo III component. There was no obvious vertical separation and little horizontal separation except for isolating the pottery from the structures in the northern portion of the site area (Structures 1–4 and 9) associated with the AD 1200s tree-ring dates. In addition, even though a somewhat "pure" middle Pueblo III assemblage could be obtained by tabulating sherds from just the burned structures that could be confidently assigned to the last occupation, this too contained admixture of earlier types such that the mean ceramic date was neither accurate nor precise, overestimating the temporal span and placing it prior to the time of actual construction.

Mean ceramic dating suggested a range of AD 1147–1214 based on sherd count for the assemblage from the earlier component, while the seriation curve indicated an occupation median of AD 1190. Both of these results would be consistent with an initial occupation of Ditch House during early Pueblo III, but is this credible? The radiocarbon dates reported above support the idea that Puebloans initially occupied the site prior to middle

TABLE 6.6. Count and Weight of Identified Ceramic Types by Ware for the Middle Pueblo III and Mixed Ceramic Assemblages at Ditch House

Ceramic Type	Middle Pueblo III		Mixed	
	n	Weight (g)	n	Weight (g)
Tusayan White Ware				
Sosi Black-on-white	0	0	6	101
Dogoszhi Black-on-white	0	0	13	79
Flagstaff Black-on-white	1	39	39	367
Tusayan Black-on-white	6	50	14	181
Tsegi Orange Ware				
Medicine Black-on-red	0	0	6	64
Tusayan Black-on-red	18	216	51	684
Citadel Polychrome	0	0	1	77
Tsegi Red-on-orange	1	3	10	91
Tsegi Black-on-orange	0	0	2	174
Tsegi (Plain) Orange	5	58	11	2,276
Tusayan A Polychrome	10	135	44	414
Tusayan B Polychrome	5	141	9	162
Kiet Siel Black-on-red	1	23	1	15
Citadel/Tusayan A Polychrome	8	56	62	452
Cameron/Tusayan B Polychrome	1	14	16	72
Tusayan Gray Ware				
Tusayan Corrugated	37	595	342	3,003
Moenkopi Corrugated	88	1,118	86	612
Kiet Siel Gray	28	387	95	1,890

Pueblo III, but these dates are not sufficiently precise to differentiate between late Pueblo II and early Pueblo III. The frequency of Pueblo II types in the mixed assemblage (Sosi and Dogoszhi Black-on-white, Medicine and Tusayan Black-on-red, and Tusayan Corrugated) seems most consistent with being derived from an occupation dating between AD 1100 and 1150 rather than between AD 1150 and 1200. In this instance, mean ceramic dating appears to have produced a phantom occupation by averaging the manufacturing spans for pottery assemblages derived from two separate site use episodes that perhaps never overlapped in time—one was late Pueblo II and another was middle Pueblo III. This said, it is also possible that the site saw continual occupation from late Pueblo II through middle Pueblo III, and such a scenario is presented in the site description (see SD vol. 4, chap. 4).

The Puebloan component at Ditch House appears to have had a more complex history of formation and use than originally envisioned based on survey evidence and limited testing. In assessing the patterning of known features while considering the spatial distribution of datable ceramics, tree-ring dates, and radiocarbon dates, Ditch House seems to have had at least two separate phases of construction. The site definitely served as a primary habitation during middle Pueblo III, with several living rooms being constructed toward the end of the AD 1220 decade. These include three living structures (1, 3, and 4) and a possible fourth (Structure 9), along with a mealing room (Structure 2). No doubt other structures, including a kiva, were likely associated with this habitation, but these features along with an associated midden were destroyed by the existing alignment for the Navajo Mountain road. Other features of the middle Pueblo III occupation of Ditch House were located south of the structures intermixed with earlier Puebloan features. The nature of these earlier features and the lack of formal living rooms suggest that the site was used as a temporary residence during late Pueblo II, perhaps associated with tending fields in the flats to the southeast of the site. There is no indication that the site functioned as a primary habitation at this earlier interval, and it seems unlikely that late Pueblo II living structures or a kiva were lost to road construction because the identifiable remains from this component were located sufficiently far from the existing Navajo Mountain road. It is easy to envision how a field camp might evolve into a more permanent residential site, as occurred with the Hopi village of Moenkopi (Connelly 1979:542, 553), but whether the middle Pueblo III occupants of Ditch House were descendants of those who used the area previously is impossible to say. There is no evidence that the middle Pueblo III structures were remodeled versions of earlier houses.

Another problematic ceramic assemblage came from Mouse House, perhaps in large part because previous road construction had destroyed a portion of the living structure at this seasonal habitation and also removed any associated trash midden; consequently the ceramic assemblage consisted of just 27 sherds. There were 14 sherds from decorated vessels, but only three had designs, and these had elements that suggested the Pueblo II styles of Black Mesa Black-on-white and Sosi Black-on-white. However, there were issues with the classification of these sherds (see SD vol. 4, chap. 18), and the utility wares included locally produced pottery made from iron-rich clay with a rough exterior surface treatment (cf. Rainbow Gray). This material, and to a lesser extent Moenkopi Corrugated, suggests an early Pueblo III temporal assignment. Utility pottery made with iron-rich clay appears at other early Pueblo III sites of the project area but not Pueblo II period sites (see Fairley and Callahan 1985).

Therefore, the presence of this utility ware is most consistent with a date in the late AD 1100s (early Pueblo III). The sherds with problematic Black Mesa designs make more sense with this information in hand, since in early Pueblo III there was some experimentation with designs including dots and ticks that hearken back to the Black Mesa style. Even if these particular vessel fragments were true Pueblo II productions, their value in temporal assignment for a seasonal habitation is limited (they could easily represent recycled sherds) and not sufficient to outweigh the more numerous utilitarian sherds in this instance. Although mean ceramic dating suggests an occupation range from AD 1083 to 1148 based on sherd count, the site was likely occupied sometime between AD 1150 and 1200, which here is considered an early Pueblo III site, the time period examined next.

Early Pueblo III

Early Pueblo III is characterized by the predominance of Flagstaff Black-on-white, a style that appears to have developed out of Sosi Black-on-white, though perhaps with influence from designs of a more "southern" origin (Beals et al. 1945:109, 133), such as seen on textiles from south of the Mogollon Rim (see SD vol. 5, chap. 3). Ceramics aside, this interval is often characterized by the abandonment of certain areas (northern Black Mesa being a prime example) and perhaps even population reduction, occurrences thought to be directly related to environmental conditions inimical to farmers (e.g., Dean 1988a, 1988b; Dean et al. 1985). Dislocation of people is evident enough, but there was continuous occupation of several localities in the Kayenta region from late Pueblo II to late Pueblo III, including the Shonto and Rainbow plateaus. Such continuity of settlement is barely evident in the NMRAP site sample since this interval is poorly represented. This sample is, however, unrepresentative of the regional pattern. For example, excavations for the southern portion of N16 documented three primary habitations ceramically dated to the early Pueblo III period (Schroedl 1989), with one (AZ-J-19-9) providing three noncutting tree-ring dates, the youngest being AD 1189vv. Work was confined to the trash middens at two of these sites, one of which produced 10 burials, a sizable number; a kiva and mealing room were excavated at the site with the tree-ring dates.

In the NMRAP sample there is but a single early Pueblo III primary habitation (Windy Mesa), and it was avoided during data recovery except for a few peripheral hearths encountered while excavating earlier components at this site (early Archaic and Basketmaker II). Testing of this site acquired a large enough ceramic sample to be certain of its temporal placement, and surface evidence of a room block, a kiva depression, and abundant trash indicate a substantial habitation. Aside from Windy Mesa the previously discussed Mouse House, a probable field house or secondary habitation, is the only other NMRAP site occupied during early Pueblo III. Ditch House might have been seasonally occupied at this time, as the ceramic types suggest, but the evidence in this case is equivocal, as discussed previously.

The early Pueblo III sites that Schroedl (1989) reported from the southern portion of the N16 ROW on the Shonto Plateau have ceramic assemblages that well represent this interval. The site with structures and the noncutting date of AD 1189 contained no sherds classified as Tusayan Black-on-white but almost 500 Flagstaff Black-on-white and a sizable number of Dogoszhi Black-on-white (Schroedl 1989:Table 97). Sosi Black-on-white is virtually absent (four sherds total) since this design had "morphed" into Flagstaff Black-on-white. Six sherds were classified as Kayenta Black-on-white, but all came from the upper fill of the kiva and are doubtless intrusive. The absence of Tusayan Black-on-white in this ca. AD 1190 assemblage is significant, especially given the number of sherds recovered (over 9,000). At the other two early Pueblo III sites, the ratio of Flagstaff to Tusayan Black-on-white ranges from 12.2:1 (AZ-J-19-13) to 6.4:1 (AZ-J-19-6), far greater than the ratio of these types for sites dating after AD 1200.

Middle to Late Pueblo III

Twelve of the NMRAP Puebloan sites were occupied after AD 1200, corresponding to the middle to late Pueblo III ceramic periods, including the transition to the Tsegi phase. The key diagnostic types for this interval are Tusayan and Kayenta Black-on-white, with the latter used as an indicator of the Tsegi phase, along with Kayenta and Kiet Siel polychromes, often given the shorthand designation of "whiteline" polychromes. Kayenta Black-on-white should be absent from settlements occupied prior to AD 1260 (Ambler 1985b; Breternitz 1966) or perhaps even 1270 (Dean 2002:131). Ditch House provides a useful example because of its AD 1228 cutting dates. The ceramic assemblage contains both Flagstaff and Tusayan Black-on-white but no Kayenta Black-on-white and no whiteline polychromes (see Table 6.6). Given that the structures of the middle Pueblo III component at Ditch House may have been occupied for 10 years after construction, the lack of Tsegi phase ceramic hallmarks is significant. The ratio of Flagstaff Black-on-white (earlier) to Tusayan Black-on-white (later) at Ditch House is 2:1, but this might be influenced by the presence of an earlier component (the ratio using sherds within certain middle Pueblo III structures is .2:1 but based on a total of just seven sherds). Hymn House and Hanging Ash are other useful examples of middle Pueblo III ceramic assemblages, although lacking associated tree-ring dates; as at Ditch House both sites lack Kayenta Black-on-white and whiteline polychromes. The identifiable whitewares at Hymn House consist almost entirely (91%) of Tusayan Black-on-white, with only a single sherd classified as Flagstaff Black-on-white (the ratio of Flagstaff to Tusayan is .02:1). More Flagstaff Black-on-white was recovered from Hanging Ash, where the ratio of Flagstaff to Tusayan is .3:1. The higher proportion of Flagstaff Black-on-white at Hanging Ash (also sherds with designs that appear intermediate between Flagstaff and Tusayan) and a greater proportion of Moenkopi Corrugated than Kiet Siel Gray suggest that this site was perhaps constructed and abandoned before Hymn House.

Ditch House, Hymn House, and Hanging Ash were primary residential sites that had been abandoned prior to the late Pueblo III Tsegi phase. However, three of the NMRAP primary habitations—Sapo Seco, Water Jar Pueblo, and Three Dog Site—have ceramic assemblages indicative of continuous occupancy from middle Pueblo III into late Pueblo III, making them at least partially contemporaneous with the well-known large aggregated pueblos of the area such as Segazlin Mesa and Upper Desha Pueblo on the Rainbow Plateau (Lindsay et al. 1968) and Neskahi Village and Pottery Pueblo on Piute Mesa (Hobler 1974; Stein 1984). Mean ceramic dating suggests temporal ranges of AD 1209 to 1266 for Sapo Seco, AD 1216 to 1271 for Water Jar Pueblo, and AD 1233 to 1272 for Three Dog Site, excluding its middle Pueblo III component (see Table 6.4).[3] Even though these sites had complex use histories, including the dismantlement and redesign of rooms or, in the case of Three Dog Site, the entire pueblo, each was probably occupied for less than 40 years. The early end of the ranges for Sapo Seco and Water Jar Pueblo can probably be truncated by 20 years or more, and the seriation-based occupation medians for all three sites are between AD 1250 and 1260. Dean (1969:196) temporally restricted the Tsegi phase to the 50 years between AD 1250 and 1300 (also Colton 1939:55). Lindsay (1969:117) argued that by AD 1250 the phase was fully developed but that AD 1240 was a more realistic beginning date for the phase in order to allow inclusion of the poorly documented transition. The end of late Pueblo III settlement in the northern Kayenta region was perhaps around AD 1280, based on the lack of tree-ring dates after AD 1275 (Bannister et al. 1969) and the generally low level of trash accumulation at most late Pueblo III sites relative to their large size.

By either Dean's or Lindsay's reckoning, Sapo Seco, Water Jar Pueblo, and Three Dog Site are partially if not fully within the Tsegi phase, but these sites likely correspond primarily to the transitional interval and not the full development. All three sites appear to have been abandoned prior to the end of Puebloan occupation in the area, indeed prior to the full-blown aggregation of households into villages that are a hallmark of this phase (e.g., Dean 1969, 1970; Lindsay 1969). Our inference that these sites were abandoned prior to the full expression of the Tsegi phase in the northern Kayenta region hinges upon two separate lines of evidence—the ratio of key ceramic types and the scavenging of usable materials.

A Tsegi phase assignment for all three sites certainly accords well with the recovery of Kayenta Black-on-white and Kayenta or Kiet Siel polychromes. Based on these ceramic types, there can be little doubt that site occupancy extended after about AD 1260; hence the sites are given a late Pueblo III temporal assignment. But such a placement obscures the reality of what was probably continual habitation from pre–Tsegi phase into Tsegi phase, but with abandonment during the interval of population aggregation that formed such pueblos as Segàzlin Mesa and Upper Desha Pueblo (Lindsay et al. 1968). Table 6.7 compares several late Pueblo III sites on the Rainbow Plateau using the ratio of Tusayan Black-on-white to Kayenta Black-on-white and the ratio of Tusayan Polychrome to Kayenta and Kiet Siel polychromes. Tree-ring cutting dates are added for calibration purposes. The interpretive logic behind these ratios follows that presented earlier for Pueblo II types; in this particular case they should be higher for a site occupied during the AD 1250s than one occupied during the AD 1270s since through time Kayenta Black-on-white should increase at the expense of Tusayan

TABLE 6.7. Comparison Among Several Late Pueblo III Sites on the Rainbow Plateau of the Ratio of Tusayan Black-on-white to Kayenta Black-on-white and Tusayan Polychrome to Kayenta and Kiet Siel (Whiteline) Polychromes

Site	Tusayan Black-on-white : Kayenta Black-on-white	Tusayan Polychrome : Whiteline Polychromes	Tree-Ring Date (Cutting and Latest, AD)
Three Dog Site (UT-B-63-39)	9.5 : 1	62.3 : 1	none
Sapo Seco (AZ-J-2-6)	7.2 : 1	12.3 : 1	none
Water Jar Pueblo (AZ-J-2-58)	7.0 : 1	4.8 : 1	none
Upper Desha Pueblo (NA5815)	2.0 : 1	15.5 : 1	1261B, 1261r, 1265++vv
Guardian Pueblo (NA4075)	4.1 : 1	2.5 : 1	1269B
Tcamahia Pueblo (NA7519A)	1.9 : 1	12.4 : 1	1262r, 1263+r, 1271rB, 1274r, 1275v
NA7520B	1.1 : 1	8.0 : 1	1268c, 1268r, 1270v

Note: Known latest tree-ring dates are given: B = bark present; c = outermost ring in continuous around full section; r = less than a full section but outermost ring is continuous; v = subjective assessment that the date is within a few years of being a cutting date; vv = there is no way of estimating how far the last ring is from the true outside ring; + = one or more rings perhaps missing but indeterminate; ++ = a ring count is necessary since beyond a certain point the specimen could not be dated.

Black-on-white and whiteline polychromes should increase at the expense of Tusayan Polychrome.

The ratio of late whiteware types clearly differentiates the NMRAP late Pueblo III sites from several tree-ring-dated late Pueblo III pueblos on the Rainbow Plateau reported by Lindsay et al. (1968), which are thought to be some of the last occupied in the local area. The latter are characterized by construction in defendable positions on small mesas or outcrops. These settlements contained whole grinding tools and other usable artifacts; thus they fit the expected pattern of final area-wide abandonment (long-distance migration that precluded the movement of heavy and bulky objects). The whiteware ratios for the NMRAP sites are consistent with the idea that these settlements had been abandoned at a slightly earlier time, probably prior to around AD 1270 and perhaps even as early as 1260. Unlike the whiteware, the polychrome ratios reveal no clear pattern. It is difficult to know why this might be the case. Whiteline polychromes are temporally meaningful on a presence/absence basis, but the proportion within an assemblage appears to have no temporal significance; this might not be true elsewhere on the Colorado Plateau, but it appears to be the case for the Rainbow Plateau.

The other key piece of evidence concerning abandonment of NMRAP late Pueblo III sites prior to the end of the Tsegi phase is the extensive scavenging of usable materials. For example, all mealing bins at late Pueblo III NMRAP sites had been dismantled, and all whole usable metates were removed. This is not the case at the Tsegi phase sites reported by Lindsay et al., as exemplified by the whole metates recovered (e.g., 1968:Figures 140, 197, and 219). Relinquishment of high-input metates is particularly noteworthy since this behavior contrasts with the previous centuries when metates were virtually always removed from abandoned sites, with large fragments commonly being recycled into other tool forms such as manos and mauls. Added to this is the infrequent finding of whole or reconstructible vessels from the NMRAP sites compared with sites reported by Lindsay et al. (1968: e.g., Tables 57, 61, 67), at which many whole large vessels had been left (most subsequently broken as structures collapsed). There is also the evident scavenging of construction materials from the NMRAP sites by removing kiva roofs and living room wall and roof timbers and even robbing stones from some masonry structures (e.g., Structures 1–2 at Water Jar Pueblo). The removal of large vessels, heavy grinding tools, and construction timbers from late Pueblo III NMRAP sites suggests that the occupants did not move far, indeed perhaps just to one of the nearby aggregated pueblos that started to be built in the AD 1260s and 1270s. With the abandonment of these larger pueblos, the distance moved was on a scale that precluded the transport costs of heavy and bulky items.

This contrast in abandonment signatures, like the ratio of Tusayan to Kayenta Black-on-white, supports the inference that the late Pueblo III sites excavated within the N16 ROW were occupied prior to and during the start of the Tsegi phase but then were abandoned as the dynamic of late Pueblo III population reorganization played out. The occupants of these sites were probably part of the family units that banded together to form the larger pueblos on

TABLE 6.8. Summary of the 83 Structures Excavated at Navajo Mountain Road Archaeological Project Puebloan Sites

Variable	Classification	n	%	Floor Area (m²)	Floor Area Range (m²)
Site Type	Primary habitation	67	80.7	5.47	1.6–14.0
	Secondary habitation	16[a]	19.3	4.28	2.0–9.6[b]
	Total	83	100.0		
Temporal Period	Mid–Pueblo II	10	11.9	7.20	2.7–10.2
	Late Pueblo II	7	8.3	4.58	2.0–9.6[c]
	Early Pueblo III	1	1.2	?	—
	Mid–Pueblo III	27[d]	32.1	5.56	2.6–14.0
	Late Pueblo III	39[e]	46.4	5.15[f]	1.6–14.0
	Total	84	100.0		
Structure Type	Kiva	6	7.2	8.02	4.5–14.0
	Living	33	39.8	5.65	3.5–11.3[g]
	Mealing	16	19.3	3.79	1.6–5.3
	Miscellaneous/storage	13	15.7	4.61	2.0–9.6
	Granary	5	6.0	4.74	2.7–7.3
	Ramada	8	9.6	5.52	5.0–12.2
	Unknown	1	1.2	?	—
	Unfinished	1	1.2	3.60	—
	Total	83	100.0		

[a] Structure 10 at Sapo Seco is counted here though the site overall is classified as a primary habitation; this structure seems to have functioned as a field house and is unrelated to the other remains at the site.

[b] 9.6 m² is an outlier; the next highest is 5.0 m².

[c] 9.6 m² is an outlier; the next highest is 5.5 m².

[d] A probable ramada at Kin Kahuna is counted here although temporal assignment is not quite that accurate.

[e] A kiva at Three Dog Site is also part of the late Pueblo III component, so it is counted here as well as in the mid–Pueblo III row.

[f] This includes the 14 m² of floor area of the kiva at Three Dog that is also listed under mid–Pueblo III.

[g] 11.3 is an outlier; the next highest are 8.6 m² and 8.4 m².

the Rainbow Plateau, and indeed, each site is relatively close to an aggregated Tsegi phase settlement: Sapo Seco and Water Jar Pueblo next to Gray House and its associated complex of ruins, and Three Dog Site just downstream from a Tsegi phase pueblo (UT-B-63-2) within the compound for the old Navajo Mountain school.

Puebloan Architecture

The remains of 83 structures were excavated at NMRAP Puebloan sites, far more than occurred at the project Basketmaker sites. This sizable sample is characterized in a basic way in Table 6.8 by listing the structures according to some major data divisions: site type (primary vs. secondary, see following discussion), temporal period, and structure type (kiva, mealing room, etc.). Structures were generally classified according to long-standing criteria for the Kayenta region as detailed by Dean (1969:27–33) and Lindsay (1969:141–156; Lindsay et al. 1968:4–5) but with minor loosening of the granary criteria and some modification of what had been termed storage rooms, herein designated as activity/storage rooms, in part to accommodate some of the structures at secondary habitations.

Living Rooms

Living rooms are identified as structures that contain a hearth, one that was often rectangular and slab lined, though this seems partly a temporal pattern. Thirty-three examples of living rooms were fully excavated by the project; Figure 6.8 illustrates about half of these, all to the same scale and oriented north, with Figure 6.9 showing two representative examples excavated to floor. Table 6.9 provides some basic measurements and data for each of

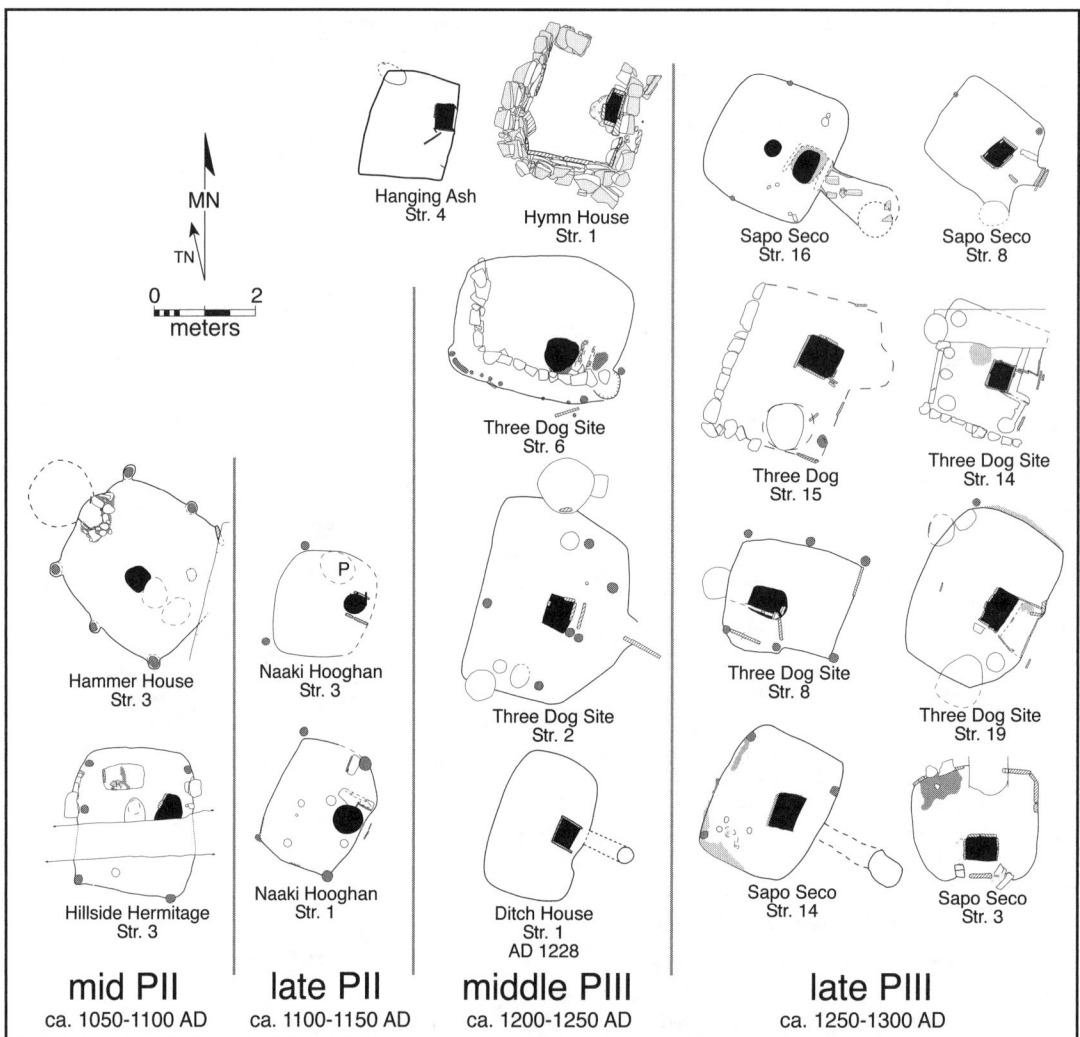

Figure 6.8. Examples of excavated Puebloan living rooms ordered by temporal interval.

these structures. In all cases living rooms are rectangular or subrectangular, with the long dimension usually parallel to the wall breached by the door or in the case of full subterranean houses, the ventilator. There are a few exceptions to this, including rooms that are essentially square, such as the bottom example of Figure 6.9. The long dimension usually follows the general orientation of most structures on a site, which is southwest to northeast, so that the door (or ventilator) faces southeast. The exceptions to this are generally because the living room was incorporated within a room cluster or courtyard complex/plaza pueblo (see below) that imposed a larger orientation logic or set of constraints. So, for example, the south-facing living room of Sapo Seco (Structure 3) shown in the lower right of Figure 6.8 was oriented this way because it was embedded within and helped to define a small plaza compound at the main residential locus of this site.

In like fashion, the south/southwest-facing Structure 8 of Three Dog Site formed part of the north side of a courtyard complex that was paired with another courtyard complex to form the middle Pueblo III component at this site. In the case of the living structure shown at the bottom of Figure 6.9, which faces north/northeast, this is a single house that probably functioned as a summer field station, so the door was probably situated in the direction of the field and it was occupied during the portion of the season when shade was more desirable than sunlight. One could say that door orientation often follows the natural slope of the terrain but the terrain selected for sites commonly slopes to the east (sort of like observing that American houses commonly face the street).

Living rooms ranged in length from 1.9 to 3.75 m and in width from 1.75 to 3 m, providing an average floor area of just over 5.6 m^2 with a range between 3.5 and 11.3 m^2. The

Summary and Interpretation of Puebloan Remains   315

Figure 6.9. Two Puebloan living rooms excavated to floor: (a) Structure 4 at Hanging Ash (hearth not yet cleaned out); (b) Structure 1 at UT-B-63-19.

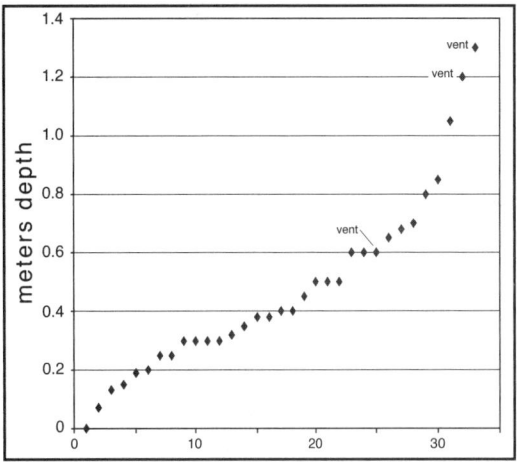

Figure 6.10. Scatter plot of Puebloan living room depths from shallowest to deepest.

latter is an outlier represented by Structure 2 of the middle Pueblo III component at Three Dog Site (shown in Figure 6.8), with the next largest living room over 2.5 m² smaller. The average size of the NMRAP living structures backs Dean's claim that "there is hardly enough space in the average [Kayenta] living room for one family, let alone two or more" (1969:37). When it comes to tight family quarters, the Kayenta appear to have excelled, perhaps excessively so. Based on Naroll's (1962) cross-cultural average of roofed house space per individual, the typical Kayenta living room would have housed about half a person. With houses this small, mechanical trenching as an archaeological discovery technique can be disastrous, such as shown by Structure 3 at Hillside Hermitage in the lower right of Figure 6.8. A standard backhoe bucket can remove one-quarter or more of a house in just a few scoops. The structure shown at the top of Figure 6.9 measures 2.1 × 1.8 m, providing just 3.8 m² of floor space, with about 15 percent of this taken up by the entry and hearth. In many cases it is clear that such small structures form part of a larger complex of rooms—Lindsay's (1969:156–157) room cluster—making the living space of a family considerably larger, but this was not obvious for this house, Structure 4 at Hanging Ash (see Figure 3.31).

There is no standard depth of Kayenta living rooms, and it is difficult to guess what the controlling parameters might have been, but it seems quite evident that excavation of a pit to accommodate a house had the benefit not only of defining the footprint but also of generating enough sediment to cover the superstructure, which was almost always of jacal. The NMRAP living rooms vary from surface or near-surface phenomena to those considered fully subterranean at greater than 1 m deep. Depths range from 0 to 1.3 m as shown in Figure 6.10. The deepest structures have ventilators and were accessed via a roof hatch and ladder. There are three examples, including one (Structure 14 at Sapo Seco) that had a depth of just 60 cm. Entry to this house would have involved climbing the earth-covered mound of the superstructure before descending a ladder. Other living rooms were accessed via short steps or in some cases ramps. The "entrybox" complex (Lindsay et al. 1968:Figure 204) is evident in fully developed form in late Pueblo III structures, perhaps as early as AD 1240, and in incipient form as early as AD 1200. Pueblo II houses have entries but not the Pueblo III entrybox complex (cf. Powell 2002:98, Figure 5.10).

A few fully subterranean houses were excavated, including Structure 1 at Ditch House (tree-ring dated to AD 1228) and Structure 16 at Sapo Seco. The latter is the one example of the N16 ROW that is closely similar to an uncommon type of pithouse found widely distributed

TABLE 6.9. Summary Data for Puebloan Living Structures Excavated Within the N16 Right-of-Way

Site No.	Structure No.	Site Type	Temporal Affiliation	Construction	Floor Area (m²)	Length (m)	Width (m)	Depth (m)	Type of Hearth	Vents	Pits	Storage Pits
AZ-J-14-11	1	secondary habitation	late Pueblo II	jacal	4.6	2.35	1.95	.19	basin	0	5	0
AZ-J-14-11	3	secondary habitation	late Pueblo II	jacal	4.0	2	2	.13	basin, with slabs	0	1	0
AZ-J-14-21	1	primary habitation	mid–Pueblo III	earthen	5.0	2.8	1.8	1.3	slab lined, rectangular	1	0	0
AZ-J-14-21	3	primary habitation	mid–Pueblo III	jacal	5.5	2.6	2.1	.6	slab lined, rectangular	0	0	0
AZ-J-14-21	4	primary habitation	mid–Pueblo III	jacal	5.9	2.7	2.2	.3	slab lined, rectangular	0	0	0
AZ-J-14-16	3	primary habitation	mid–Pueblo II	jacal	8.4	3	2.8	.65	basin	0	3	1
AZ-J-3-14	1	secondary habitation	late Pueblo II	jacal and masonry	4.2	2.1	2	.3	—	0	4	0
AZ-J-3-14	3	primary habitation	mid–Pueblo II	jacal and masonry	6.6	2.8	2.35	.6	basin, subrectangular, one slab	0	2	0
AZ-J-2-3	1	primary habitation	mid–Pueblo III	masonry	5.5	2.4	2.3	.35	slab lined, rectangular	0	0	0
AZ-J-2-6	3	primary habitation	late Pueblo III	jacal	5.5	2.5	2.2	.5	slab lined, rectangular	0	0	0
AZ-J-2-6	8	primary habitation	late Pueblo III	jacal	4.4	2.3	1.9	.32	slab lined, rectangular	0	0	1
AZ-J-2-6	12	primary habitation	late Pueblo III	jacal	7.2	3	2.4	.8	basin	0	2	0
AZ-J-2-6	14	primary habitation	late Pueblo III	jacal	5.8	2.7	2.15	.6	rectangular clay-lined basin	1	3	0
AZ-J-2-6	16	primary habitation	late Pueblo III	earthen	3.5	1.9	1.85	1.2	circular clay-lined basin and rectangular clay-lined basin	1	6	0
AZ-J-2-6	17	primary habitation	late Pueblo III	jacal	3.5	2	1.75	.45	circular basin partially clay and slab lined	0	0	0
AZ-J-2-6	18	primary habitation	late Pueblo III	jacal	4.1	2.05	2	.7	slab lined, rectangular	0	0	1
AZ-J-2-58	3	primary habitation	late Pueblo III	jacal	4.6	2.2	2.1	0	slab lined	0	0	0
AZ-J-2-58	9	primary habitation	late Pueblo III	jacal	5.0	2.25	2.2	.07	slab lined, rectangular	0	0	0
UT-B-63-39	2	primary habitation	mid–Pueblo III	jacal	11.3	3.75	3	.15	slab lined, rectangular	0	4	1
UT-B-63-39	6	primary habitation	mid–Pueblo III	jacal and masonry	6.4	2.9	2.2	1.05	basin	0	0	0
UT-B-63-39	8	primary habitation	mid–Pueblo III	jacal	5.3	2.4	2.2	.5	slab, rectangular	0	0	1
UT-B-63-39	14	primary habitation	late Pueblo III	jacal and masonry	7.4	2.95	2.5	.25	slab, rectangular	0	6	0
UT-B-63-39	15	primary habitation	late Pueblo III	jacal and masonry	7.4	3.1	2.4	.25	slab, rectangular	0	0	1
UT-B-63-39	18	primary habitation	late Pueblo III	jacal	6.4	2.9	2.2	.5	basin, oval	0	0	0
UT-B-63-39	19	primary habitation	late Pueblo III	jacal and adobe	8.6	3.45	2.5	.38	slab, rectangular	0	3	1
UT-B-63-14	1	primary habitation	mid–Pueblo III	jacal	.0	?	?	.4	slab, rectangular	0	2	0
UT-B-63-14	2	primary habitation	mid–Pueblo III	jacal	.0	3.5	?	.85	slab, rectangular	0	2	0
UT-B-63-14	3	primary habitation	mid–Pueblo III	jacal	.0	?	?	.2	?	0	1	1
UT-B-63-14	4	primary habitation	mid–Pueblo III	jacal	3.8	2.1	1.8	.3	slab, rectangular	0	1	0
AZ-J-2-2	1	secondary habitation	mid–Pueblo III	jacal	3.7	2	1.85	.38	slab, rectangular	0	1	0
UT-B-63-19	1	secondary habitation	late Pueblo III	jacal	3.6	2	1.8	.3	slab, rectangular	0	0	0
AZ-J-2-6	5	primary habitation	late Pueblo III	jacal	5.0	2.4	2.1	.68	basin	0	1	1
UT-B-63-39	12	primary habitation	late Pueblo III	jacal attached to masonry	7.5	3	2.5	.4	basin, subrectangular	0	3	0

Summary and Interpretation of Puebloan Remains 317

Figure 6.11. Floor of Structure 16 at Sapo Seco after excavation, a 1.3-m-deep square pithouse with a pair of recessed roof-support posts, a clay-rimed hearth with a deflector, and paired loom holes.

within the Kayenta region at sites postdating AD 1200 and in the Hopi Buttes at a slightly earlier date (see Ambler 1994). These distinctive deep, square, small structures have roof supports consisting of two posts recessed into opposing walls just slightly off center on the northeast and southwest sides (Figure 6.11). In addition to a clay-rimmed fire pit and deflector or slot therefrom (two each because of a remodel), the floor features of Structure 16 consisted of three sets of paired loom anchors in different locations. Ambler (1994:460–462) believes that similar paired holes in a comparable late Pueblo III structure in the Klethla Valley were used as anchors for sash looms. Structures like this one not only might have had a somewhat special function associated with weaving narrow fabrics (craft specialization) but might also be indicative of migrant groups in the Kayenta region from the south, as Ambler (1994:468–469) speculated.

Living room hearths show a pattern of increasing formalization through time until Pueblo III, when they are virtually all slab-lined rectangular boxes. Slab lining started in Pueblo II if not before, but as circular, oval, or pentangular arrangements. The squaring of these features allowed for more efficient placement within rectangular houses, such as against walls as in Figure 6.9, and it might have made them easier to clean. The fill of interior hearths was usually reduced to white or gray ash with little charcoal content because of full combustion of the fuel. This contrasts with the charcoal-rich fill of exterior hearths indicative of smothered fires such as occur when pit baking foods. As such, flotation samples from living structure hearths often contained scant macrobotanical remains related to subsistence, but with a few notable exceptions. The size of many hearths relative to floor space is notable, often more than 10 percent and when combined with an entrybox, then up to 20 percent.

In addition to hearths, most living rooms had floor pits of various size. In most cases these were small or medium sized and relatively shallow, likely used to store artifacts. There were, however, a few examples of large storage pits such as that at the middle Pueblo II site of Hammer House shown in Figure 6.12. The capacity of these features can be enormous, at some sites reaching 2 m or more below the floor (e.g., the pit in Room 1 at Small Jar Pueblo [Lindsay et al. 1968:123–125, Figure 98] or the pits in Structures 3–4 at AZ-D-10-17 [Callahan 1985]). The example illustrated here from Hammer House is estimated at roughly

Figure 6.12. Photo and illustration of Structure 3 at Hammer House, namesake for the site; a storage pit with a volume of roughly 1.4 m³ extends off on the side of the structure floor.

1.4 m³ in volume, which could have held a considerable amount of maize on the cob (see Huckell et al. 2002:145–146, Table 11.1) or even more kilocalories as kernels in bags or baskets. This particular room, with its shallow basin hearth, was evidently also used for grinding corn; at least, the dozens of pecking stones and debris therefrom that covered the floor evince considerable mano and metate maintenance in the room.

The Hammer House room also serves to illustrate the most common construction method for living rooms, that of jacal. The postholes, some with posts, can be clearly seen recessed into the corners of the room and midway along the walls of the long axis. These would have supported a cross frame of roof timbers, with the superstructure finished by leaning other timbers against the roof frame and weaving willows or other plants to form the wattle frame for the sediment. For this particular structure, unlike most examples in the N16 ROW, the superstructure had been left intact upon abandonment, so the fill contained a thick layer of wall and roof fall that consisted of clayey sand.

The NMRAP sample has but a single living room built totally of masonry. Thirty living rooms had jacal superstructures in whole or in part: 23 of only jacal, one of jacal attached to masonry, five of jacal and masonry (different walls), and one of jacal with a 10-cm-thick layer of clay lining one wall. Full-height adobe walls have been documented in the Kayenta region (e.g., Ward 1975), even at open sites (e.g., Schroedl 1989:481–482, Figures 167–171), but this was the single limited example of a thick clay wall found at an NMRAP site. The two fully subterranean houses had earthen walls and were probably flat roofed. With shallower rooms more of the superstructure would have projected above the occupation surface, with greater use of jacal construction. Since nearly all structures had been dismantled in prehistory, direct evidence for construction method was usually absent, such that the use of jacal is an inference usually supported by a lack of masonry wall fall and the finding of postholes or in some cases rotted or burned posts. Because so few structures had burned, preserved mortar (Figure 6.13) was rare.

Kivas

Six of what we refer to as kivas were excavated within the N16 ROW. This label is applied because of architectural features and placement relative to other structures, and classification as such does not preclude an important domiciliary role (Geib et al. 1985:198).

Brew (1946) and Smith (1990) have eloquently summed up the dilemma of defining pit structures as either kivas or secular habitations. In the process of describing the problems involved in distinguishing kivas from habitation rooms at Alkali Ridge and the range of architectural variation that occurred among both types of structures, Brew (1946:204–205) discussed the lack of cohesive and consistent trait complexes to characterize kivas in the San Juan and Kayenta Anasazi regions. By quantifying the presence and form of architectural traits such as benches, pilasters, deflectors, ventilators, hearths, niches, and plaster, as well as size and depth, Brew (1946:Table

Figure 6.13. Stick-impressed mortar chunks from Structure 8 at Sapo Seco.

5) showed that a clear division was not present among kivas and domestic structures. Smith summarizes the problem by stating that "there is not one architectural feature that is either universally present in all kivas or universally absent from all non-kivas, or vice-versa" (1990:70) in the San Juan and Kayenta areas. There is similar variability in structure morphology within the N16 corridor. Suites of traits are probably more useful in defining a kiva, but it may not always be possible to separate structures into kiva/nonkiva categories based on trait lists.

The term *pithouse* (or *pit structure*) simply does not suffice in the Kayenta region to denote the kind of structure considered here because of the abundance of rectangular living rooms in the region that are also commonly referred to as pithouses or pit structures but which lack the architectural characteristics of what Kayenta archaeologists have commonly called kivas. In the eastern Pueblo area, those wanting to restrict usage of the kiva designation to a very specific kind of structure that is evidenced by room/kiva ratios rather than distinctive architectural traits per se (e.g., Lekson 1988, 1989) could apply the term *pit structure* without risking confusion between qualitatively different structure "types" because there tends to be only one form of subterranean structure in use in that area. The same is not true for the Kayenta region, or the larger western Pueblo area, where many of the previously described living rooms are also commonly referred to as pithouses or pit structures. If the more generic term was adopted, then additional qualifiers would need to

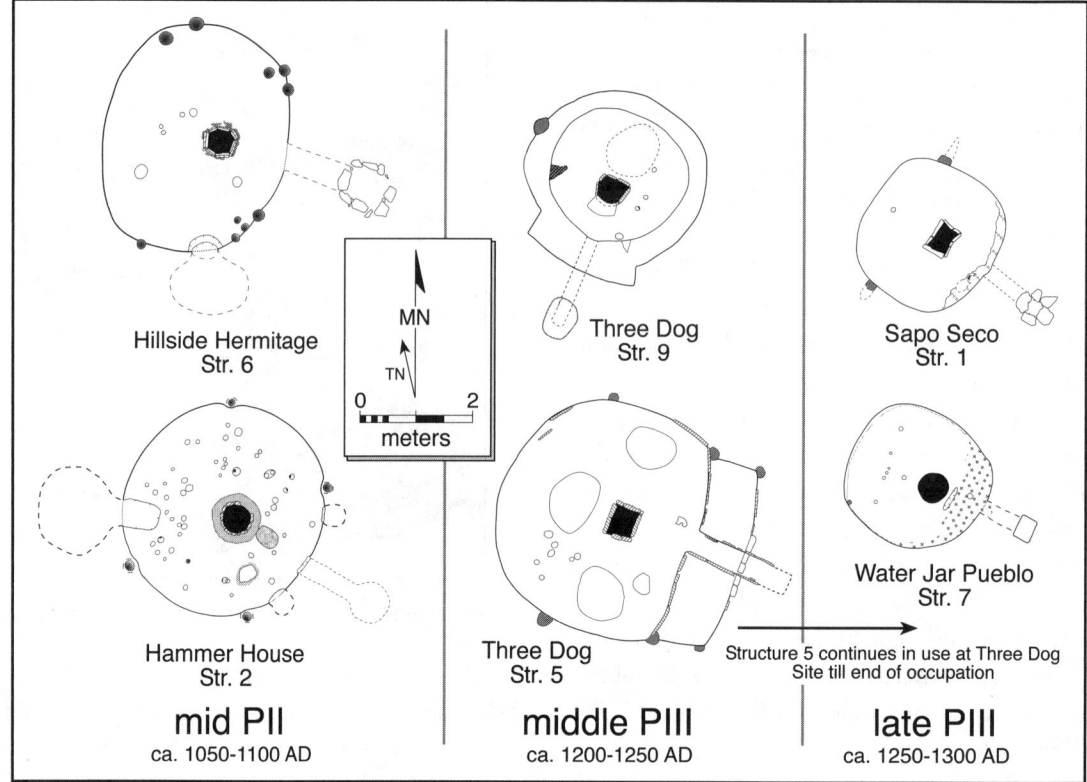

Figure 6.14. All excavated Puebloan kivas ordered by temporal interval.

be added in order to be precise in reports and discussion. Simply adding *round* and *square* to *pithouse* (or *pit structure*) would not suffice, since there are also square kivas in the Kayenta region (e.g., Lindsay et al. 1968:218–220, Figures 171–172) and the Ramp site in the Hopi Buttes had a square kiva surrounded by square pithouses (Gumerman 1988). We use the term *kiva* as a simple and useful shorthand that captures the distinctive characteristics of these structures when compared to the living rooms previously considered. Although Kayenta kivas were likely lived in, ceremonies also doubtless occurred there as well, and the evidence of loom holes suggests that weaving was done in at least some of the NMRAP kivas, and this craft is ethnographically documented to be the domain of men. We readily accept that Kayentan kivas did not lose their domestic functions and take on their largely ceremonial role until the late Pueblo III aggregated pueblos, and perhaps not until the even larger Pueblo IV sites (Lekson 1988, 1989; Steward 1937b). These "true" kivas had their genesis in the structures considered here and represent an evolved form of a long-standing architectural tradition and its important social concomitants.

As can be seen from Figure 6.14, the six NMRAP structures classified as kivas represent a diverse lot, which is partly a temporal by-product but not totally, since the Pueblo III group was also highly variable. Indeed, there appears to have been greater diversity in kiva form during Pueblo III in the Kayenta region than during Pueblo II. The diversity found on the NMRAP might be a consequence of different populations migrating to the Rainbow Plateau during Pueblo III (Ambler et al. 1983; see SD, Appendix F), since kivas seem more variable at that time than during Pueblo II, prior to evidence for the in-migration of populations from outside the Kayenta region proper. Although the Pueblo III kivas are variable in form, there is one aspect that is similar, which has to do with the simplification of floor features. Pueblo II and early Pueblo III kivas can have numerous and diverse floor features, such as the example from Hammer House, but by late Pueblo III the diversity and number of features had been reduced to certain essentials. This issue, which seems to relate to the functional role of kivas, is examined in greater detail below.

Kivas are fully subterranean, the deepest structures at any of the NMRAP Puebloan sites; all had ventilators and roof entries. Table 6.10 provides some basic measurements and data for each of these structures. They range in depth from 1.1 to 2.1 m, with the shallowest example being

Figure 6.15. The kiva at Sapo Seco, excavated during its construction up to 35 cm into Navajo Sandstone. The ventilator runs across the top of the sandstone and is thus not flush with the floor as is common; the sandstone forming the walls has been battered smooth and exhibits dimples from pecking.

something of an outlier since the next value is 1.4 m and the mean kiva depth is 1.61 m. Sometimes the occupants had to work extra hard to ensure that adequate depth was obtained. Both of the small late Pueblo III kivas in the NMRAP sample were cut into the underlying sandstone bedrock, up to 35 cm at Sapo Seco and almost 60 cm at Water Jar Pueblo. Figure 6.15 shows the interior of the Sapo Seco kiva looking across the hearth at the ventilator shaft, which entered the structure on a slant at the top of the bedrock. Navajo Sandstone formed the lower wall of the structure, its surface dimpled from pecking; alongside the vent opening, the sandstone that formed the floor exhibited drill holes and a grinding slick from using the bedrock as a work surface. In their desire to achieve a certain minimum depth, the Kayenta were seldom stopped; at Pottery Pueblo there are kivas cut entirely into bedrock, with the sandstone then ground smooth (Stein 1984: 110–128).

Two of the NMRAP kivas have a recess, both at Three Dog Site (Figure 6.16). The lack of a recess on the middle

Table 6.10. Summary Data for Puebloan Kivas Excavated Within the N16 Right-of-Way

Site Name	Structure No.	Site Type	Temporal Affiliation	Floor Area (m²)	Diameter (m)	Depth (m)	Hearth Type	Deflectors	Ashpits	Loom Holes	Sipapus	Pits/Holes	Storage Pits
Hammer House	2	primary habitation	mid–Pueblo II	10.2	3.60	2.1	circular basin, clay and rock rim	0	1	1	1	56	1
Hillside Hermitage	6	primary habitation	mid–Pueblo II	10.2	3.60	1.1	circular basin, clay and rock rim	0	0	1	1	5	1
Sapo Seco	1	primary habitation	late Pueblo III	4.7	2.45	1.56	slab lined, rectangular	0	0	0	1	1	0
Water Jar Pueblo	7	primary habitation	late Pueblo III	4.5	2.40	1.6	bedrock basin	1	0	1	1	8	0
Three Dog Site, Mid–Pueblo III	9	primary habitation	mid–Pueblo III	4.5	2.40	1.4	slab, rectangular	0	1	1	0	4	0
Three Dog Site, Late Pueblo III	5	primary habitation	mid–Pueblo III	14.0	3.80	1.9	slab, rectangular	0	0	1	0	7	0

Figure 6.16. The Structure 5 kiva at Three Dog Site, associated with both the middle and late Pueblo III components. Many of the slabs that lined the front of the recess had been removed in prehistory along with three oval-circular sandstone slabs that once surrounded the hearth on three sides. Slabs leaning against the back wall are probably a hatch cover and a ventilator cover.

Pueblo II kivas is to be expected since this feature appears to have been adopted after these sites were abandoned. Late Pueblo II kivas commonly have a recess—indeed, it is unusual for them not to have such features. Nearly all other previously excavated kivas built after AD 1100 in the Kayenta area have this feature, and in the Navajo Mountain area they are nearly always partially, if not completely, lined with masonry (e.g., Small Jar Pueblo and Upper Desha Pueblo [Lindsay et al. 1968:128–130, 168–171]; see also sites AZ-J-19-3, AZ-J-19-9, AZ-J-31-8, AZ-J-31-2, and AZ-J-31-5 [Schroedl 1989:153–159, 228–240, 340–349, 407–411, 465–467, 471–476]). The BMAP excavation reports provide many examples, as does the excavation report for the Navajo Generating Station coal haul railroad (see summary in Germick 1989). This is partly what distinguishes the examples from Sapo Seco and Water Jar Pueblo (Figure 6.17) as outside the norm. Indeed, given their small size and lack of recess they appear like a throwback to an earlier form of pithouse. Yet similar structures were in use into the start of Pueblo III at sites north and west of the Kayenta region, such as Coombs Village (Lister et al. 1960). It is not total speculation to imagine migrant groups from such outlying communities establishing settlements on the Rainbow Plateau and retaining some previous construction patterns. The similarity of the kivas at Water Jar Pueblo and Sapo Seco, and their dissimilarity from other kivas of the Kayenta region, hints that the same group or related individuals built both. Perhaps indicative of this is the refitting of a trough metate fragment from the Sapo Seco kiva with the two other fragments of this same tool recovered from the Water Jar Pueblo kiva. The largest portion of this tool came from within the ventilator of the Sapo Seco kiva, where it appears to have been placed to block or seal off the opening. The smaller fragments came from the fill of the Water Jar Pueblo kiva, including one portion from floor fill. The refit tool exhibits an impact blow to the nonwork face that split the artifact into the three pieces, an activity that evidently occurred at Water Jar Pueblo when the kiva was abandoned. Whether struck to purposefully "kill" the tool or simply to split it in two because the whole slab was not needed to cover the ventilator opening at Sapo Seco, the tool provides a link between the two sites.

The middle Pueblo II kivas exhibit the roof-support

Figure 6.17. Small kivas at the late Pueblo III sites of Water Jar Pueblo (top) and Sapo Seco (bottom).

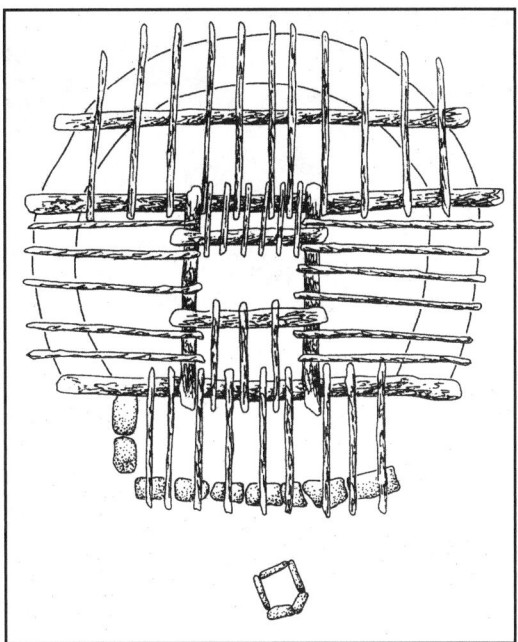

Figure 6.18. Hypothetical roof construction method for Kayenta Anasazi kivas (from Geib et al. 1985:Figure 57; drawn by Debra K. Meier).

pattern common to the Kayenta region of four posts partially recessed into the walls and "framing" the hearth. Two posts are placed along the wall where the ventilator enters, one to the southeast and one to the northeast. In later kivas with a recess these posts occur at the interior corners of this feature, as seen for Structure 5 at Three Dog Site. The other two posts are along the interior wall past the midline as defined by a southwest–northeast line of bisection orthogonal to the ventilator-hearth-sipapu axis. This type of post arrangement allowed placement of southwest–northeast primary beams, in combination with large southeast–northwest secondaries to create a frame centered over the hearth and thereby an appropriately placed smoke hole. Setting the posts within the walls helped conserve valuable floor space, a practice that was common to Kayenta living rooms as well. Note that the Hillside Hermitage kiva had several postholes in a few positions along the wall, including two slightly within

the room interior, which suggests that the kiva roof was redone at one point, with the wall expanded northward by about 50 cm. The posts and roof had been removed from all of the NMRAP kivas except for the Hammer House example. Because the Hammer House kiva had not burned, the roof was not preserved; the posts, however, were solid because their exteriors were carbonized, something that happened prior to placement in the kiva perhaps purposefully as a preservative measure. The posts were all of juniper, which is also typical of Kayenta sites, perhaps because the wood is far less subject to insect damage and rot. The posts varied from 10 to 15 cm in diameter and had been sunk 34 to 55 cm below the kiva floor; the postholes for other kivas had similar depths. Unfortunately none of the posts in the Hammer House kiva could be dated because of moderately erratic growth.

By extrapolating from examples of Kayenta kivas with preserved roofs, it is safe to assume that the four posts supported two large horizontal beams laid southwest to northeast as shown in Figure 6.18. Across these beams, and at right angles to them (southeast to northwest), would have been a series of secondary beams or poles, creating a square framework to support the roofing material. There would have been an entryway centered over the hearth to provide access via an interior ladder and to vent smoke. Sandstone slabs might have framed the entryway to provide additional support; several slabs in the lower fill of

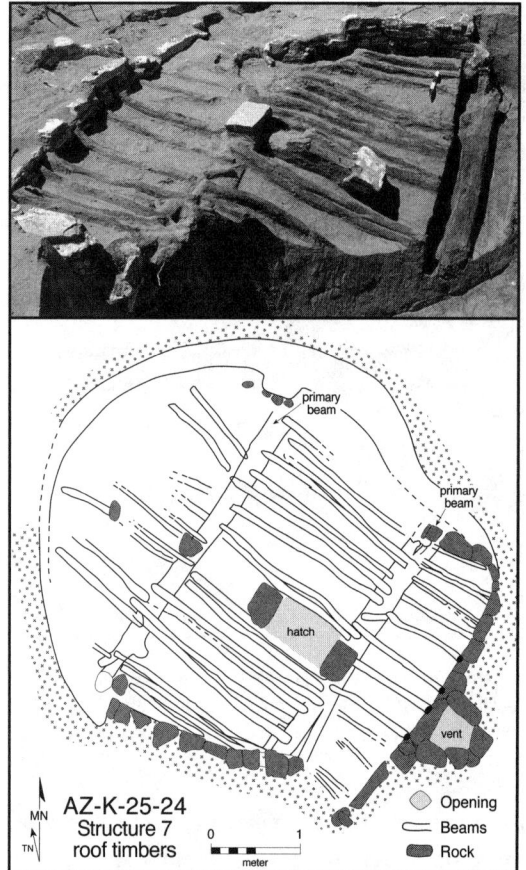

Figure 6.19. Well-preserved roof of a kiva at the late Pueblo II site of AZ-K-25-24 (after Bungart et al. 2004: Figures 4.20–4.21); photo looks south.

the Hammer House kiva above the hearth may have once served this function. Over the beam and pole framework would have been a layer of thatch, with grass, juniper bark, and brush over willows or reeds having been commonly used, covered with earth. The roof reconstruction figure is based on a late Pueblo II kiva excavated at Navajo Mountain originally presented in Geib et al. 1985:Figure 57 and reproduced here. A kiva excavated within the N21 ROW on the Kaibito Plateau at site AZ-K-25-24 presents an unequaled example of kiva roof construction for an open site (Figure 6.19). Here the roof had never been dismantled or burned, but the hatch was left open, allowing the interior to fill with eolian sand such that the roof did not collapse inward but was gradually "let down" onto the fill, leaving the beams in their original placement.

The kivas at Water Jar Pueblo and Sapo Seco may have served a predominantly utilitarian role, especially when compared to their counterparts at other sites such as the much larger and more formal version at Three Dog Site. Yet both contain loom holes and sipapus, and their placement as the focal point of small plazas ringed by rooms of diverse functional roles tracks with Smith's (1990) argument for kiva identification. Moreover they, like most Pueblo III kivas of the Kayenta region, have very simple floor features compared to those of the Pueblo II structures. If kivas were being used for utilitarian as well as nonutilitarian purposes, it is perhaps expectable that they might have numerous floor features, reflecting the necessary modification of space for constantly changing roles. This is perhaps best reflected by the kiva at Hammer House, which contained a large array of floor features (Figure 6.20), 72 in all, including a hearth, an ashpit, a large-volume storage pit, three possible sipapus, at least six loom holes that were in use at abandonment, more than 40 "closed" loom holes, a metate/anvil set in the floor, and ladder rests. There is also evidence for reuse and remodeling, including the patching of floor pits and depressions, sealing of abandoned pits, construction of new pits into old pits, reconfiguration of loom anchors, and possible remodeling of the ashpit. This indicates that the residents of Hammer House were highly dependent on the kiva as a dedicated living area and not just a ceremonial retreat and that it acted as a sustained but evolving focal point for site activities.

The Hammer House kiva might seem like it has an anomalously high number of floor features for a Pueblo II Kayenta kiva, but it is not without precedent, at least for more recent excavations. The kiva at site AZ-J-19-9, an early Pueblo III habitation (AD 1160–1200) on the Shonto Plateau, had 52 floor features (Schroedl 1989), including ladder rests; seven pot rests; three basin-shaped storage pits; 33 small, generally cylindrical pits; three "paho" holes; and a "foot drum." A kiva (Structure 11) at site AZ-K-40-7 on the Kaibito Plateau contained even more floor features, 65 in all (Bungart et al. 2004), including many storage pits and much evidence for feature reuse and remodeling like at Hammer House. Tree-ring dates for the kiva at AZ-K-40-7 place construction at AD 1130, probably more than two generations after the kiva at Hammer House. A kiva at site AZ-J-55-39 on north-central Black Mesa contained 49 floor features that consisted of the usual suite (hearth, ashpit, sipapu, foot drum, ladder rests, etc.), two storage pits, one of modest size, and many loom holes, most cleaned and filled but with several that had been in use at the time of structure abandonment (Collette et al. 2009). The quantity of features found at recently excavated Kayenta kivas is perhaps because of extensive subfloor excavation, something seldom practiced,

Summary and Interpretation of Puebloan Remains 325

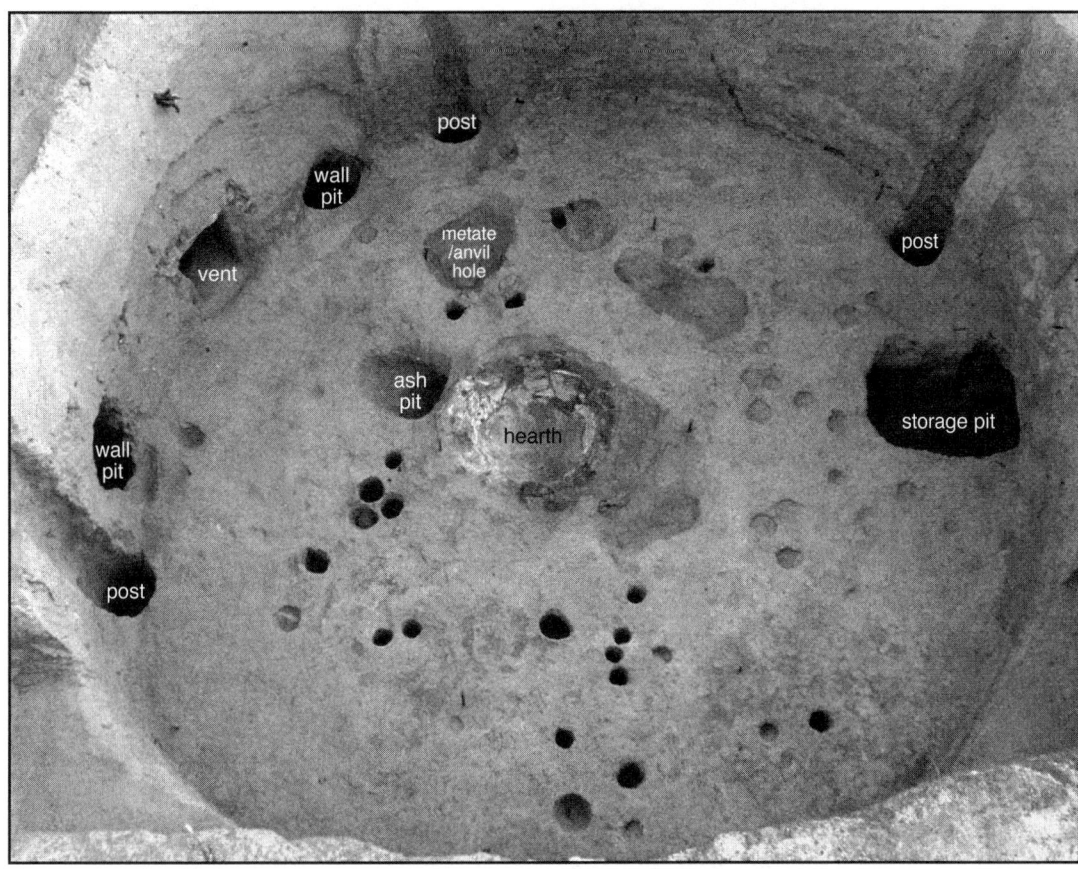

Figure 6.20. Kiva at the middle Pueblo II site of Hammer House showing its numerous floor features, including a large-volume storage pit; also present are two wall niches that extend below the floor exterior to the kiva.

at least not to the exhaustive extent done on recent road excavation projects. Of the 65 features at AZ-K-40-7 mentioned previously, only a few (the principal large ones located along the central axis) were apparent upon exposure of the floor surface, the rest having been filled in and patched over. It took complete removal of the floor surface in a systematic fashion to locate all the floor features; this was also true for the Hammer House kiva.

The importance of so many features is, we believe, related to two aspects of the Kayenta lifeway that changed between Pueblo II and late Pueblo III, such that Tsegi phase kivas lack the numerous floor features of their predecessors. One of these has to do with less general domestic activity in this sort of structure through time, along with increased specialized use of them for both weaving and perhaps other men's crafts as well as for ceremonial purposes. The other aspect that is perhaps related has to do with changes in residential mobility. We believe that reduced residential mobility through time and increasing differentiation and specialization of residential space (hence less domestic use of kivas) are both reflected in the reduction in the number and diversity of kiva floor features.

Both of the Pueblo II kivas have large-volume storage pits (ca. 1.5 m³ at Hammer House and 1.1 m³ at Hillside Hermitage)—features not seen in the NMRAP Pueblo III kivas or other Pueblo III kivas of the Kayenta region. A Pueblo II kiva at site AZ-J-19-12 on the Shonto Plateau comparable in age to the ones at Hammer House and Hillside Hermitage also contained a storage pit, labeled as a floor vault in the report (Tipps et al. 1989:116–119). This kiva does the Hammer House structure one better by having a pair of metates/anvils embedded in the floor on either side of the ashpit rather than the single example at Hammer House (in Figure 6.20 the anvil has been removed for shipment back to the lab).

The numerous loom holes in the floors point to the constant setting up and taking down of looms, with new hole placements established and old holes closed by being filled in and plastered over. There are two likely reasons for this. Looms had to be moved during certain seasons, such as in the winter when more people had to crowd into the structures to keep warm; kivas doubtless offered the best protection from the elements during winter and were the warmest places to be, especially at night. Residential mobility would be another reason that looms could get moved, shifting from one habitation to another perhaps because fields in an alternative area proved more productive for a few years or perhaps because of some more or less scheduled shifting around the landscape, not necessarily truly swidden-like but similar. Setting up another loom after moving back in, a few years later, would entail new loom anchors and, hence, a proliferation of holes. The finding of just a few sets of loom holes in Pueblo III kivas suggests that looms were set up and left in place and that there was not a lot of reshuffling of the interior space to make room for new projects or activities. This trend toward formalization of space is extended even further in Pueblo IV kivas, where loom holes are found within immovable floor slabs (see Smith 1972). The trend toward more dedicated space that was not reconfigured can be traced architecturally in the changing frequencies and types of floor features in Kayenta kivas through time.

Kivas seem likely to have been used more strictly for habitation during colder months because of their greater ability to retain a certain constant temperature compared to a surface or shallow structure. Warmer weather would have encouraged greater use of exterior space and surface structures, thereby freeing up kiva floor space for the more specialized and space-demanding activity of weaving and perhaps ritual devotion (this could have assumed the form of a ceremonial cycle). Weaving seems like a good activity for the winter, when field tasks are at their lowest, and perhaps the presence of looms would not have been too limiting of family space, so possibly the difference was simply in the number of looms that could be accommodated: one in winter and two in summer.

Likely one of the significant factors contributing to a need for more specialized space was the spread of cotton farming across the Colorado Plateau sometime around AD 1000 or so and with it the weaving of textiles. Cotton production and the manufacture of garments for trade are documented to have been of great economic importance among Puebloan groups during the historic period (see review in Wright 2000) and doubtless were an aspect of Puebloan life with great time depth. The textiles woven by Puebloans (see Kent 1983) required dedicated space of a special type, because of both the time required to produce cloth and the need for a protected area sufficiently large for an upright loom. Deep pithouses were uniquely suited to fill these requirements, especially if space could be found elsewhere in other living quarters for routine daily activities and family members who might interfere. The desire to produce cotton cloth, whether for home use or in social negotiations, could have been a driving force behind shifting much family living to other rooms and activity spaces for a significant portion of the year, thereby transforming pithouses into a more specialized architectural form.

The addition of a recess, often masonry lined, to Kayenta kivas might be seen as another aspect of increased ceremonial uses of kivas through time. The middle Pueblo II NMRAP examples lack these features, but most kivas that are late Pueblo II or later in age have them; the lack of these recesses in the Sapo Seco and Water Jar Pueblo examples is notable in this regard. Recesses might have been places for storage of ceremonial (or utilitarian) items when not in immediate use or for the creation of alters.

Structure 6 at Hillside Hermitage is classified as a kiva because its size, shape, ventilator, and certain floor features make this structure more typical of kivas. Its depth also sets it apart from typical Pueblo II pit structures; at 1.1 m deep, the feature was two to three times as deep as most pithouses of this period. Structure 6 was not, however, fully subterranean, as is typical for kivas in this area. It also contains a large storage pit, the only potential food-storage feature at the site. Moreover, it had an unusual placement behind other structures.

Small Jar Pueblo, at the northeast foot of Navajo Mountain, has a more typical layout for Pueblo II sites in the Kayenta region, with a row of jacal structures facing southeast toward a kiva (Lindsay et al. 1968:128–130). The circular kiva contained a southern recess lined with masonry, and the main chamber walls were plastered. The kiva floor was also prepared, coated with layers of clayey sand. The hearth was unlined and less formal than the one in Structure 6 at Hillside Hermitage, but it had a more formal set of other floor features: in order of occurrence from southeast to northwest, ladder rests, a stick and mud deflector, an ashpit, a hearth, and a foot drum or some other special pit. Posts set into the walls were reminiscent of those in Structure 6 but less numerous. The kiva was nearly 3 m deep, and presumably its roof was flush with the ground surface. Small Jar Pueblo was occupied at least a generation later than the Locus B habitation of Hillside Hermitage. The temporal span between these two sites points to the change that occurred within a given class of structure during the Pueblo II period, becoming less of a domestic structure through time. In this sense, Structure 6 might be considered a "proto-kiva."

Brew (1946:208) noted that changes in architectural styles seldom appear at exactly the same time through space and that new and old architectural details often occur within a single structure, as new traits are adopted and others are retained. He correctly noted that retention of old styles concurrent with the adoption of new ones is a universal aspect of human behavior and that models of behavior that do not consider this reality will certainly fail to provide adequate explanation of the archaeological record. The variable use and combination of architectural traits, however, can cause difficulties in classification, as in the kiva/pithouse debate. In later periods, kiva architecture was more regular, but single architectural traits were still subject to great variation (Smith 1972). Such a situation should not necessarily surprise the archaeologist familiar with historic and recent Hopi kivas. Brew notes that Hopi workers at Alkali Ridge did not find the variation in sipapu presence odd, because "some kivas and societies hold ceremonies involving the use of sipapus while others do not" (1946:211).

According to Lekson (1988), the attempt to trace kivas further back in time and to find antecedents in the Basketmaker pithouses was based on a political trend in archaeology rather than on sound archaeological or ethnographic research. He argued that the pithouse-to-pueblo transition, generally attributed to the Basketmaker III–Pueblo I transition, actually took place during Pueblo IV. He stated that structures commonly identified as kivas were used as habitations throughout the Pueblo II and III periods and that the range of architectural features that appear through time represent changes in style rather than changes in function from secular to ceremonial. Thus the presence of pilasters, loom holes, or masonry-lined antechambers reflects changes in interior design rather than conversion of the structure to a sacred realm that has all the connotations of an early Hopi kiva. To support this view he noted that few archaeologists agree on which, if any, architectural features "define" a kiva, which are optional, and which are irrelevant to the function of the structure. As Brew's Hopi fieldworkers pointed out, uniformity should not be expected since this assumes some sort of uniform belief system or set of ceremonies. Having diverse ceremonial practices could help bind a community together since one key to integration can be differentiation and secret knowledge, with the common good requiring access to and maintenance of such diversity.

Calling something a kiva does not necessarily get in the way of appreciating how the "functional" role of this structure changed over time or that such structures had different functions at a single point in time (large and small versions). A Pueblo II kiva is not comparable to a Pueblo IV kiva except perhaps for a Pueblo II great kiva, but giving them a different label does not recognize the historical trajectory of cultural change. Pueblo IV kivas would not have sprung from nowhere as fully formed ceremonial chambers but, rather, from modification of a long-standing construction pattern that had for centuries been used for ceremonial purposes in addition to living. A hogan is a home, but it is also a ceremonial structure; one does not preclude the other. Kivas are simply another aspect of the Kayenta archaeological record that documents a process of social and economic differentiation and specialization—the creating of specialized space for specific activities and practices that were originally conducted in more generalized space, which can also lead to their elaboration. As kivas became more special purpose and less residential, perhaps driven in large part by a need for weaving space, living rooms became more established and well built as small rectangular rooms with comparatively large hearths. As residential size increased, with more numerous separate households at a site, it is perhaps expectable that the ritualized aspects of kivas became more evident, but multihousehold habitations that probably contained more than a single extended family are not apparent in the record of the Kayenta region until late Pueblo III. At habitations as small as those represented by Hammer House and Water Jar Pueblo a kiva could satisfy both habitation and ceremonial needs for a single family, but there was no need for social integration, which is a point made by Lekson: "It's hard to understand exactly what was being integrated—an extended family?" (1989:161). This seems like a good question, but then place it in the context of Navajo families who live in small extended-family homesteads—the ceremonies held in the hogan at such homesteads commonly involve a social component that draws in many surrounding families, with most of the social aspect occurring in the open rather than in the ceremonial structure per se.

Mealing Rooms

Sixteen of the excavated Puebloan structures were identified as mealing rooms, special-purpose rooms used to grind corn. Figure 6.21 shows various examples of these through time, from Pueblo II to late Pueblo III, with

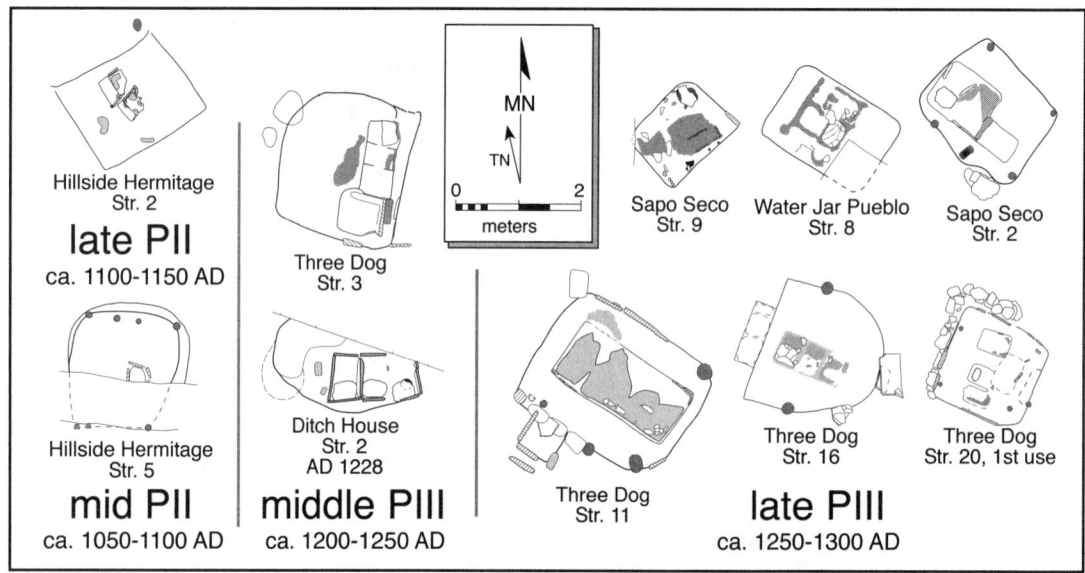

Figure 6.21. Examples of excavated Puebloan mealing rooms ordered by temporal interval.

Table 6.11 providing some basic descriptive data. Contrary to the claim made by Mobley-Tanaka (1997:439, 446), mealing rooms did not "disappear in the Southwest" between AD 1100 and 1150, at least not in the Kayenta region, where they persisted until the final abandonment shortly before AD 1300. Functional classification was based on the presence of mealing bins that occupy much of the floor area and the absence of hearths. Within the Kayenta region at large, mealing rooms are often detached pit structures most commonly situated on the north side of a kiva, but they can also occur elsewhere within a site, as the NMRAP sample illustrates. In depth they vary from surface and near surface to almost 1 m, with an average depth of 44 cm; 10 of the 16 have a depth of 40 cm or greater. These structures were smaller on average than living rooms, with the NMRAP examples ranging from 1.4 to 2.8 m in length and 1.1 to 2.3 m in width. Floor areas ranged from 1.6 to 5.7 m² with an average of 3.8 m², about 2 m² less than living rooms. Moreover, much of the floor area in nearly all cases was taken up by mealing bins such that they could be used for little else other than food processing and tasks that were directly related, such as the maintenance of mano and metate use surfaces. The constrained nature of the work area is easily appreciated by observing one of the late Pueblo III mealing rooms from Three Dog Site shown in Figure 6.22, and this was the largest mealing room excavated by the project. As if the quarters do not looked cramped enough, just imagine four women, even four young girls, at work, kneeling side by side facing the doorway (top right), and the daylight it afforded.

Figure 6.22. Mealing room (Structure 11) at the late Pueblo III component of Three Dog Site, largest example in the Navajo Mountain Road Archaeological Project sample. The central floor area is filled with the remnants of four dismantled mealing bins, with only the mortar used to hold the metates in place still somewhat intact. Two exhausted manos rest against the side wall near the lower right corner.

Mealing rooms are the most specialized structures for the Kayenta Anasazi besides granaries, but the latter are designed for simple secure storage rather than being an activity space. Mealing rooms represent the creation of highly specialized space for a single activity and perhaps largely for a single subsistence item—maize. Other seeds were doubtless processed in mealing rooms, but none re-

TABLE 6.11. Summary Data for Puebloan Mealing Rooms Excavated Within the N16 Right-of-Way

Site No.	Structure No.	Habitation Type	Temporal Affiliation	Floor Area (m²)	Length (m)	Width (m)	Depth (m)	Pits	Mealing Bins
AZ-J-14-21	2	primary	mid–Pueblo III	4.0	2	2	.6	1	3
AZ-J-3-14	2	secondary	late Pueblo II	3.0	2	1.5	0	0	2
AZ-J-3-14	5	primary	mid–Pueblo II	2.7	1.75	1.55	.8	0	1[a]
AZ-J-2-6	2	primary	late Pueblo III	3.5	2	1.75	.95	0	3
AZ-J-2-6	9	primary	late Pueblo III	1.6	1.4	1.13	.26	0	2
AZ-J-2-6	11	primary	late Pueblo III	5.3	2.5	2.1	.15	2	1[b]
AZ-J-2-6	13	primary	late Pueblo III	3.0	1.85	1.6	.7	1	3
AZ-J-2-6	15	primary	late Pueblo III	2.6	1.75	1.5	.75	0	3
AZ-J-2-58	5	primary	late Pueblo III	5.0	2.5	2	0	0	3
AZ-J-2-58	8	primary	late Pueblo III	2.5	1.9	1.3	.2	0	3
UT-B-63-39	7	primary	mid–Pueblo III	2.6	1.7	1.5	.45	0	3
UT-B-63-39	10	primary	mid–Pueblo III	5.0	2.8	1.8	.2	0	3
UT-B-63-39	11	primary	late Pueblo III	5.7	2.7	2.1	.8	0	4
UT-B-63-39	16	primary	late Pueblo III	4.5	2.6	1.85	.4	0	3
UT-B-63-39	3[c]	primary	mid–Pueblo III	4.7	2.3	2.05	.4	2	4
UT-B-63-39	20[d]	primary	late Pueblo III	5.3	2.3	2.3	.4	0	3

[a] The backhoe trench likely removed at least one additional bin.

[b] Erosion and road maintenance may have removed at least one additional bin; otherwise this structure is more like an activity/storage room.

[c] This was initially a mealing room and then transformed into a living room.

[d] This was initially a mealing room and then transformed into a living room and ultimately a storage room.

quired the "staged" processing implicated by the side-by-side bins. If the time estimates of three hours per day spent grinding for every Hopi woman (see references cited in Christenson 1987b:48) have any relevance to the Pueblo II and Pueblo III situation, then it is perhaps no wonder that adjacent bins were adopted—these installations might indeed be more efficient as many have suspected, but they also would go far toward alleviating the boredom of such a repetitive daily activity by grouping workers together for discussion, idle talk, and simple camaraderie.

As Figure 6.21 clearly shows, the orientations of mealing rooms are quite variable, a product of where on a site they are located and how this relates to a kiva. In nearly all cases the mealing rooms are oriented such that the bins face the kiva no matter what direction that is. "Facing the kiva" means that the bins were situated such that women/girls would have faced this direction when grinding, according to the placement of the metates and catch basins. Almost invariably catch basins were on the side closest to the kiva, with the sloping metate rests inclined back away from the kiva. Entries, when these could be positively identified, opened toward the kiva; entries were difficult to identify for the shallow mealing rooms, but for those with any depth the entry consisted of a step or ramp as in the example of Figure 6.22. Posts to support the roof and superstructure were recessed within or placed next to the walls so as to conserve the limited interior space. Construction methods for roofs and superstructures are easily conjectured and similar to the jacal superstructures of living rooms. The only cases of masonry being used in mealing rooms were a few that represented modified structures, such as a living room transformed into a mealing room.

The 16 mealing rooms had a total of 44 individual bins; additional bins occurred at many sites in activity/storage rooms, ramadas, and exterior spaces such as courtyards. The number of bins per mealing room ranged from one to four, with an average of 2.75, but three bins was the mode. Indeed, 10 of the mealing rooms had three bins, and two had four bins. One of the two structures with a single bin is probably simply the result of disturbance—it is the middle Pueblo II example shown in Figure 6.21 bottom left; the backhoe trench more likely than not removed a second bin from this room (there is not enough space for a third bin, but a third metate might have simply rested on the floor surface to the north of the one intact bin). Ethnographic data (Bartlett 1933; Hough 1915:23, 62–63) describe the Puebloan corn-grinding process as involving several steps, beginning with the initial cracking of the kernels and coarse grinding and ending with fine grinding, each of which might involve manos and metates of different textures (sandstone coarseness but also perhaps vesicularity [but see discussion in Adams 1999]). The occurrence of three bins or more in most of the NMRAP mealing rooms matches the ethnographic description of the process. Even two bins would be sufficient for staged processing. Corn can certainly be reduced to flour upon a single metate, but efficiency might be increased using a staged process, and having a space that facilitates cooperative work also helps with training daughters. For several of the rooms with multiple bins, the catch basins had variable depths and thus variable slopes for the metates that would have been placed within them. Such instances of increasing depth and metate slope from one side of a bin group to the other may well relate to sequenced corn grinding from coarse to fine and the metates used for each stage. It is easy to imagine that whole kernels or large cracked pieces would too easily roll from a steeply sloped metate such that one with a relatively flat placement would be desirable during initial processing. As the kernels were reduced to finer meal, more steeply angled metates might have been useful, ones that naturally allowed the fine flour to collect in the catch basins.

None of the mealing bins excavated during the project, whether in mealing rooms or elsewhere, contained metates, all having been removed upon feature/structure/site abandonment. In general few artifacts were recovered from most mealing rooms, and this applies especially to grinding tools, which were exceedingly rare. This is doubtless a result of the systematic dismantlement of these features and removal of high-cost tools such as metates and two-hand manos. The tools that often were left behind were pecking stones and flakes, the latter frequently derived from the flaking of pecking stones to refurbish battered edges or as fortuitous spalls from pecking stone use. Some of the large sherds recovered from mealing rooms might have functioned as flour catch receptacles, as seen at intact mealing bins (Geib 2006 presents an example from Black Mesa). The treatment of mealing bins seems excessive for simple scavenging alone, in that slab partition walls and even catch basins were often removed—effort above and beyond simple scavenging of useful tools. This treatment, which verges on "destruction," might be a form of ritual closure (Schlanger and Wilshusen 1993).

Mealing bins first appear in middle to late Pueblo II contexts within the Kayenta region, so the example from Hillside Hermitage (ca. AD 1060–1080) is an early form. This does not mean that staged processing using side-by-side metates did not occur earlier in time, just that formal bins were not constructed for that purpose. A hint of this is seen at Structure 3 at Hammer House (ca. AD 1050 and 1070), the structure for which the site was named (shown in Figure 6.12). The occurrence of more than 50 pecking stones in this structure along with debris from their use and refurbishment gives strong indication of use of the room for mealing activities; moreover, a two-hand mano from the floor perfectly matched a whole trough metate in the floor fill of the adjacent kiva. On the structure floor next to the central basin hearth were two side-by-side shallow, oval depressions in the living surface. These easily could have been the rests for metates, such as the trough example found in the kiva. Hammer House appears to have been occupied slightly before Hillside Hermitage, so the absence of true bins might be a temporal issue. Perhaps also relevant to when the use of mealing bins and formalized mealing rooms began is the issue of residential mobility. If there was a higher degree of residential mobility during middle Pueblo II than later, then constructing facilities with expensive metates fixed into place might make little sense since leaving them risked thievery. Loose metates could be easily moved to a secure hiding place, even to a new settlement.

In all but one case, mealing rooms occur on primary habitations. The single exception is the small mealing room appended to a living structure at the late Pueblo II component of Hillside Hermitage, shown in the upper left of Figure 6.21. This may have been a preliminary step toward establishing a primary residential habitation at this location, one that never came to fruition. A single mealing bin was found at two other secondary habitations (Camp Dead Pine and the Puebloan component at Kin Kahuna), but in general this sort of formal processing facility would seem to be unnecessary at a seasonally used site, especially one that was not occupied by a full family unit.

Two of the mealing rooms listed in Table 6.11 started out in this role but were then transformed, with the mealing bins dismantled and filled in and hearths installed so that the rooms could be used for living purposes. One of these, Structure 20 at Three Dog Site, was subsequently modified again when its floor was paved with slabs, probably so that it could be used for storage purposes (Figure 6.23). These examples, especially the latter, serve to illustrate the dynamic nature of room function, something that can be difficult to infer archaeologically.

There may well have been social issues involved with the appearance of mealing rooms, as some have argued; Mobley-Tanaka suggests that "they represent important aspects of ritual and social integration that surround the importance of corn in Anasazi society, reflecting the importance of the female role in Pueblo II ritual and social integration" (1997:446). Such reasons seem less in play in the Kayenta region since mealing rooms first appear in the context of sites that housed a nuclear or extended family but probably not more than that. Rather than social underpinnings, mealing bins and rooms seem to be efficiency related and tied to a general trend toward specialized use of space and reduced residential mobility; mealing rooms certainly would have helped with mother–daughter training. This does not mean that mealing rooms had no integrative role to play in the multifamily habitations established during the Tsegi phase, such as the example (Pit House 11) from Neskahi Village (Hobler 1974), ultimately carrying forward and perhaps elaborating during Pueblo IV with the establishment of piki rooms.

Granaries

Specialized storage rooms were identified only at NMRAP Pueblo III sites, but this is not a general pattern for the Kayenta region. Granaries or their equivalent are known to have a much longer span of use in the Kayenta region than this, dating back to Pueblo I when they evidently "evolved" from Basketmaker III slab-lined cists. The lack of granaries at the middle Pueblo II habitations excavated within the N16 ROW might relate to issues of residential mobility and the initial spread of Puebloan populations onto the plateaus of the northern Kayenta region. Food storage at both of the middle Pueblo II primary habitations was within pits attached to structures. Well-built masonry granaries are typical of Pueblo I and Pueblo II sites on northern Black Mesa, where they form the back set of rooms for unit pueblos (see virtually any of the BMAP site reports or the summary of site plans in Ahlstrom 1998a).

Granaries are identified by the lack of interior features and by construction efforts to prevent food loss from rodents, other vermin, or spoilage. Lindsay (1969:146–152; Lindsay et al. 1968:5) restricted the granary definition to structures with sufficiently intact walls to allow entry identification, which had to be small and capable of being tightly sealed from the outside, such as with grooved door jambs to allow secure placement of slab covers (see Lindsay et al. 1968:Figure 209). Structures that looked like granaries but lacked intact doors, or at least sufficient portions thereof, were classified more generally as storage rooms. As Lindsay (1969:149) observed, the emphasis on

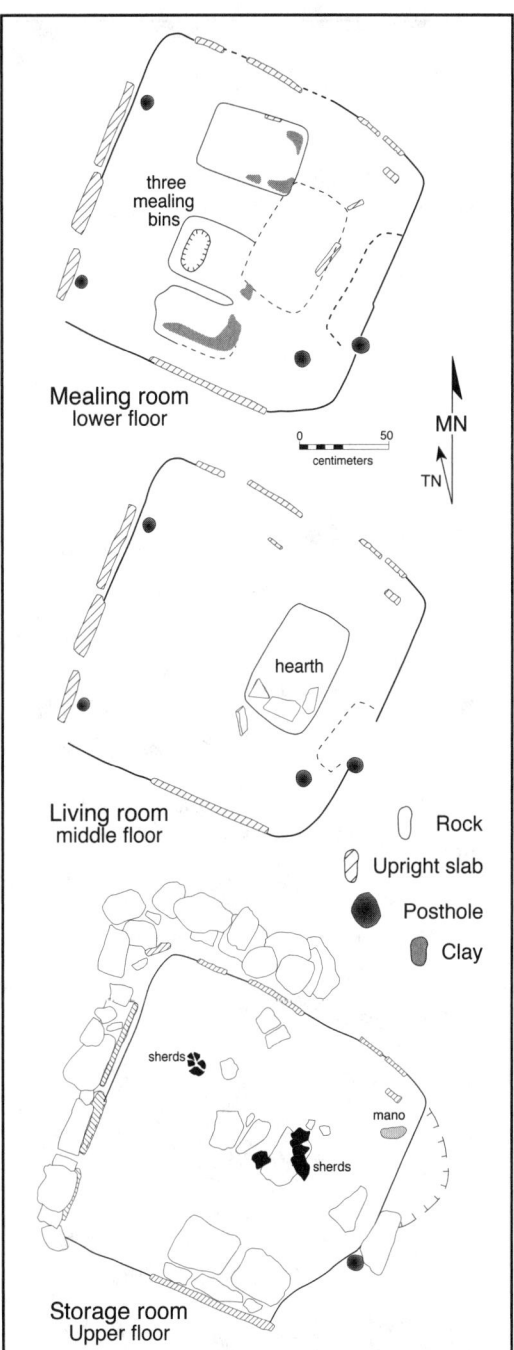

Figure 6.23. Examples of changing room function for Structure 20 at Three Dog Site: initially a mealing room with three bins, then a living room, and finally for storage.

wall preservation in this definition can bias the representation of granaries between open and sheltered sites owing to differential preservation of walls. We opted for a somewhat less restrictive definition of granaries—one that does not require intact doorways, only sufficient evidence of floor and wall construction.

Figure 6.24. Examples of excavated Puebloan granaries: (a) Structure 17 at Three Dog Site; (b) Structure 7 at Sapo Seco.

Two examples of NMRAP granaries are shown in Figure 6.24, a subterranean structure at Sapo Seco fully lined with masonry (Structure 7) and a surface jacal structure with an entirely slab-lined floor, the slabs set within abundant mortar. As described by Lindsay et al. (1968; also Lindsay 1969), granaries can be the most solidly built structures on a Kayenta site except perhaps for kivas. The effort expended is a reflection of content value—the food reserves. Structure 7 at Sapo Seco well represents this effort, though it is unusual in being subterranean, since most granaries are surface or near-surface features. The jacal granary is also somewhat unusual, in that jacal construction was mainly reserved for living structures, activity rooms, and general partitions, but in this case the tight slab floor is consistent with a concern over preventing food loss, especially from rodent intrusion. An example of a jacal granary that burned with ears of corn in storage occurs at site AZ-D-5-8 on the Shonto Plateau (Fairley 1987). Lindsay et al. (1968:270–271) also described two jacal granaries (Rooms 9–10) at Tcamahia Pueblo (NA7519A), though by their more restrictive granary definition they are classified as simple storage rooms.

The NMRAP granaries have a mean floor area of 4.7 m^2, ranging from 2.7 to 7.3 m^2. Except for the subterranean Structure 7 at Sapo Seco, the storage volume for these rooms is impossible to calculate with any accuracy because it would depend on estimating roof height. For Structure 7 a simple calculation based on preserved masonry yields a volume of 5 m^3, but since the roof probably was 1.4 m above the floor, judging from wall fall, the volume was perhaps around 5.8 m^3. It is unlikely that the occupants stacked corn to the rafters, so full capacity was probably less. It is worth mentioning that Structure 7 appears to have been constructed initially as a living structure, but the unfinished and unused hearth was plastered over and the floor was paved with slabs for its revised role.

Activity/Storage Rooms

The types of structures that we refer to here as activity/storage rooms partially overlap with granaries and are identified by Lindsay (1969) as storage rooms. We added *activity* to explicitly recognize that they were evidently used for daily activities, at least on occasion, and were not just "dead storage" space, like granaries. When occurring at primary habitations, rooms of this type appear similar to granaries in their lack of interior hearths but are usually larger and have features indicative of nonstorage activities, especially mealing bins. A good example is shown in Figure 6.25. This room had full-height masonry walls on three sides, with the front wall, facing the plaza, made of jacal. It lacked a slab floor as is typical of structures that were used solely for secure food storage and was larger than most storage rooms (floor area of 7.8 m^2). It was more like a living room in size but lacked an interior hearth or other features, except for two mealing bins that occupied a small front portion of the room, with plenty of space for other activity or goods.

The above example is a formal construction at a primary habitation, integrated within or juxtaposed to other rooms of a pueblo. Other examples of rooms placed within this class were of more expedient design and usually isolated, or if occurring on a multistructure site, they were not integrated within the larger architectural arrangement. Many of these occur at secondary habitations (Figure 6.26) and were perhaps houses used while tending fields, ones that lack interior hearths, but others occur at sites that perhaps had other purposes such as the structure at The Slots (see discussion below).

PUEBLOAN SETTLEMENT TYPES AND PATTERNING

To search for patterning in settlement types, the 25 Puebloan sites are first separated according to the presence or absence of dwellings. Three sites with no structures are designated as temporary camps, and the remaining 23 sites are considered habitations. Structural sites are further subdivided (see below), but no matter how one partitions the continuum of site variability into potentially meaningful groups, it is essential to factor in at least these two variables: (1) the extent to which prior site disturbance has eliminated features and (2) whether ROW restrictions have prevented disclosure of all associated features.

Primary Habitations

The NMRAP sample of Puebloan habitations seems to consist of those occupied on a relatively permanent basis and those occupied seasonally, if repeatedly, and perhaps by less than the entire social group represented at a more permanent residential site. Our separation of habitations into two general classes called primary and secondary was based on an assessment of architectural permanence, the presence and nature of interior hearths, and food-storage capacity. As discussed in the previous Basketmaker chapter, in applying the terms *primary* and *secondary* to habitations we recognize potential problems and that such a simple dichotomy may not accurately characterize

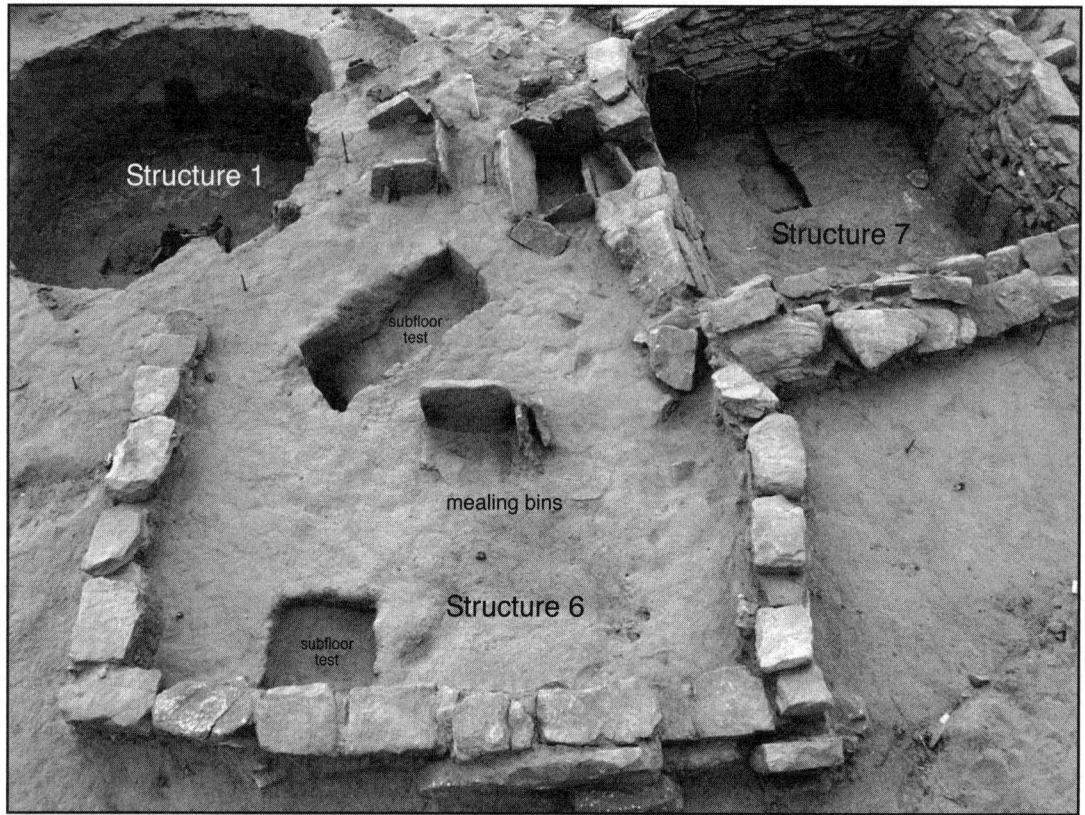

Figure 6.25. Structure 6 at Sapo Seco, an example of an activity/storage room. This building had full-height masonry walls on three sides and jacal across the front (southeast) side; it lacked a hearth or other floor features except for two dismantled mealing bins, which occupied a relatively small area of the floor.

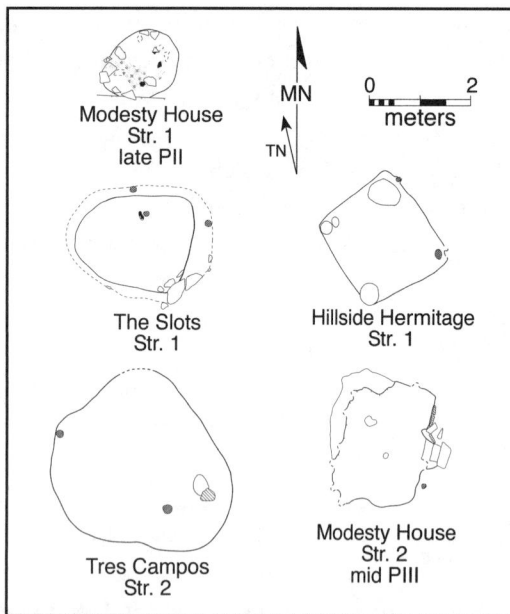

Figure 6.26. Examples of excavated Puebloan activity/storage rooms at secondary habitations, many of which may have served as field houses for temporary resting and storage.

settlement variability. *Primary* implies, perhaps erroneously, that any single Puebloan group had but one important settlement that they used on a yearly basis, the principal domicile for a social unit. It is quite possible that they had two such settlements or perhaps even more, but it seems worth differentiating these places from those that appear to have had a more limited settlement role both seasonally and functionally. Indeed, it is in the context of contrasting the records of these two different settlement types that there is a need for terms that encapsulate the differences. If it is possible to recognize sites as "secondary" habitations, which seems quite evident for the bulk of examples considered next, what are they subsidiary to if not a principal place of residence? The issue is tied up both with theory and with how we recognize or measure patterned differences in the archaeological record. There are identifiable distinctions among sites in construction details or other attributes—whether the structures were built for permanent use (Kent's [1992] "anticipated mobility" or immobility), storage volume or lack thereof, measures of occupation duration and activity diversity, and so

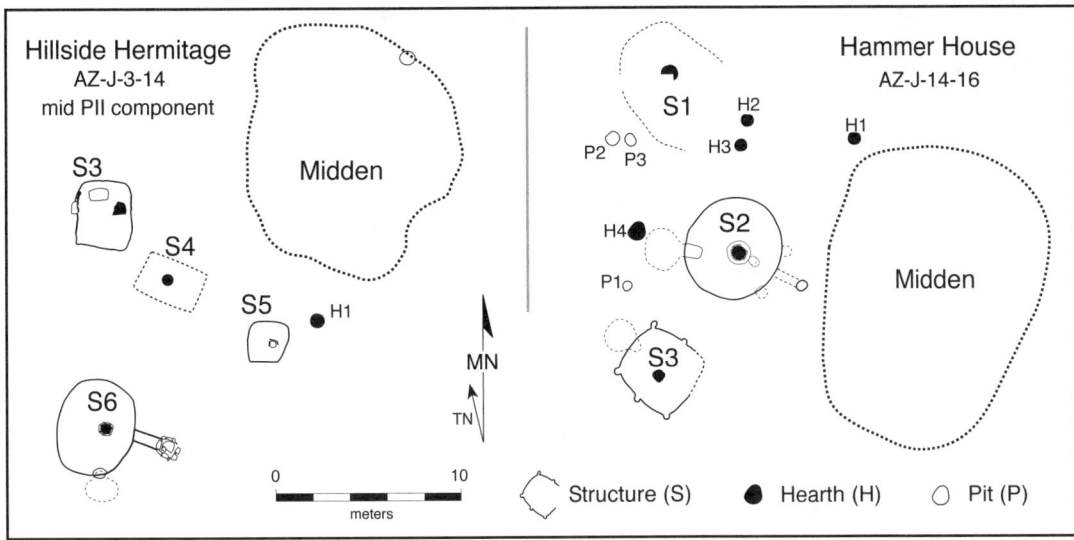

Figure 6.27. Middle Pueblo II primary habitations excavated within the N16 right-of-way.

forth—but what one makes of these differences is directly tied to preconceived notions as to how societies organized their subsistence-settlement strategies. As Kelly has observed, "There are no Gardens of Eden on earth, no single locales that can provide for all human needs. Mobility—residential, logistical, long-term, and migration—was the first means humans used to overcome this problem" (1992:60). The Kayenta Anasazi used all of these strategies and far more variably than is often assumed or presented in summary characterizations that emphasize modal or typical behavior.

The 10 Puebloan primary habitations excavated within the N16 ROW range from single household affairs with relatively simple histories of construction, use, and abandonment (such as Hammer House and Hymn House) to those with multiple households and more complex settlement histories, perhaps best typified by Three Dog Site. In all cases these residential sites have structures of diverse type and functional roles, midden deposits containing abundant and diverse artifact assemblages, and storage capacity of varying size. Primary habitations were identified for all of the ceramic periods found within the project area except Pueblo I, which is represented by a single temporary camp. Table 6.12 presents some basic data for seven of the 10 primary habitations. Three sites are excluded from this comparison because of limited excavation (Windy Mesa), disturbance and mixture from other components (Ditch House), and lack of sampled trash (the middle Pueblo III component of Three Dog Site). The table presents counts of various artifact classes and bones, counts standardized by number of structures (quantity per structure), and ratios of various artifact classes such as sherds to flakes and debitage to facial flaked tools. This table shows some important differences especially in debitage and bones per structure, which range from less than 46 to more than 436 for flakes and from 6 to just under 228 for faunal bone.

Middle Pueblo II

The earliest primary residential sites within the NMRAP sample date to the middle Pueblo II period or Black Mesa ceramic phase sometime after about AD 1050 but before AD 1100. The two NMRAP sites that characterize the middle Pueblo II interval are Hammer House and Hillside Hermitage (Figure 6.27); at the latter site there is also a late Pueblo II component, but only the earlier component is relevant here. Both are characterized by an architectural suite of a single small household, one that likely was no larger than a nuclear family or perhaps a very small extended family. The inference of small group size is based on the total area of enclosed roofed space, which is less than 20 m^2 (18.6 m^2 for Hammer House and 19.5 m^2 for the middle Pueblo II component of Hillside Hermitage). At each of these primary residences the enclosed roofed space consists of a single semisubterranean jacal living room and a subterranean kiva or pithouse; at Hillside Hermitage there is also a largely subterranean mealing room, something lacking at Hammer House, although Structure 3 appears to have served this purpose but lacked mealing bins (the room may well have had two side-by-side metates placed within shallow basins on the floor). Both sites also have probable ramadas or semiprotected

TABLE 6.12. Comparison Among Navajo Mountain Road Archaeological Project Primary Habitations with Comparable Levels of Investigation Using Overall Artifact and Bone Counts, Counts per Structure, and Ratios of Certain Artifact Classes

Site Name	Sh	Sh/Str	Mod Sh	% Mod Sh	Deb	Deb/Str	Deb/Sh	FT	FT/Str	Deb/FT	C&N	C&N/Str	Deb/C&N	Deb/FT+C&N	GT	GT/Str	GT/FT	Sh/GT	Misc	Misc/Str	Total Tools	Bone	Bone/Str	Bone Artifacts
Hanging Ash	2,609	652.3	27	1	860	215	.3	30	7.5	28.7	22	5.5	39.1	16.5	42	10.5	1.4	62.1	15	3.8	109	215	53.8	4
Three Dog Site, Late Pueblo III	20,923	1,902.1	91	.4	6,768	615.3	.3	168	15.3	40.3	94	8.5	72	25.8	337	30.6	2	62.1	131	11.9	730	2,507	227.9	63
Sapo Seco	9,510	528.3	67	.7	827	45.9	.1	5	.3	165.4	81	4.5	10.2	9.6	127	7.1	25.4	74.9	31	1.7	244	319	17.7	13
Water Jar Pueblo	5,699	633.2	29	.5	586	65.1	.1	12	1.3	48.8	53	5.9	11.1	9	89	9.9	7.4	64	27	3	181	70	7.8	8
Hymn House	1,586	528.7	6	.4	310	103.3	.2	6	2	51.7	30	10	10.3	8.6	23	7.7	3.8	69	5	1.7	64	18	6	0
Hillside Hermitage, Middle Pueblo II	1,514	378.5	15	1	985	246.3	.7	9	2.3	109.4	53	13.3	18.6	15.9	23	5.8	2.6	65.8	2	.5	87	40	10	3
Hammer House	2,566	855.3	28	1.1	2,210	736.7	.9	6	2	368.3	103	34.3	21.5	20.3	48	16	8	53.5	16	5.3	173	359	119.7	10
Total	44,407	5,478.4	263	5.1	12,546	2,027.6	2.6	236	30.7	812.6	436	82	182.8	105.7	689	87.6	50.6	451.4	227	27.9	1,588	3,528	442.9	101
Average	6,343.9	782.6	37.6	.7	1,792.3	289.7	.4	33.7	4.4	116.1	62.3	11.7	26.1	15.1	98.4	12.5	7.2	64.5	32.4	4	226.9	504	63.3	14.4

Note: Sites are organized from north to south. Sh = sherds; Str = structure; Mod Sh = modified sherds; Deb = debitage; FT = flaked facial tools; C&N = cores/nodular tools; GT = grinding tools (manos and metates); Misc = other stone artifacts.

outdoor work and activity areas (Structure 1 at Hammer House and Structure 4 at Hillside Hermitage). The jacal living room at Hillside Hermitage (Structure 3) was eventually transformed into a more general-purpose activity and storage room by eliminating the hearth and installing a mealing bin. This may have happened after the kiva-like Structure 6 was built, which assumed the role of winter shelter.

That these middle Pueblo II habitations are located within 3 km of each other on the southeastern portion of the Rainbow Plateau within close proximity to Upper Piute Canyon might not be a coincidence. Residential sites of this temporal interval are few in the northern Kayenta region and are chiefly known from Upper Piute Canyon (Fairley 1989) and immediately adjacent highlands such as Dzil Nez/Sage Valley (Ambler et al. 1983; SD, Appendix F). Habitations from the immediately preceding ceramic period (Wepo) are known only from Upper Piute Canyon, where a few modest-sized (multiple-household) settlements occur on the eastern rim (Fairley 1989). Farther north on the Rainbow Plateau there are few residential sites with ceramic assemblages as early as Hammer House and Hillside Hermitage; in this area the earliest sites, such as Small Jar Pueblo, appear to date to the late Pueblo II interval or Sosi-Dogo ceramic period, placed at ca. AD 1100 to 1150. Small Jar Pueblo has an estimated temporal span of roughly AD 1100–1115, supported by noncutting tree-ring dates (Harlen and Dean 1968:381; Lindsay et al. 1968:134).

It is perhaps from the early Pueblo II "founding" communities of Piute Canyon that the occupants of the middle Pueblo II settlements of Hammer House and Hillside Hermitage are descended; consequently they are situated within relatively close proximity. A simple shift in settlement organization from several multihousehold early Pueblo II residencies to more numerous single nuclear household examples might account for sites like the two reported here. Whether or not such societal reorganization occurred, residential site location close to Upper Piute Canyon may also have been prompted by a desire to farm in diverse locations, both on the canyon floodplain using irrigation or subirrigation (high water table moisture) and in the washes and sand flats on the southeast portion of the Rainbow Plateau, thereby reducing the risks inherent with relying on food produced from a single field setting. The extensive use of Owl Rock chert for flaked-stone tools and debitage at both settlements seems indicative of frequent movement in and out of Piute Canyon, where outcrops of this material are located (at Hammer House 90% of the debitage and 85% of the core/nodular tools are of Owl Rock chert). These sites could have been part of a settlement-subsistence strategy that involved cyclical movement at some periodicity between canyon habitations and fields and habitations and fields on adjacent plateaus.

This said, these two primary residential sites occupy different environmental niches. Hillside Hermitage not only is farther away from Piute Canyon but is situated at the confluence of two important washes that drain the highlands on the southeast edge of the Rainbow Plateau, a location that is still farmed today by Navajo families and which Basketmaker farmers had initially exploited more than 2,000 years ago (the Basketmaker II site of Kin Kahuna is located at this place [see chapter 5]). Hammer House, in contrast, is situated far closer to Piute Canyon and not adjacent to such an ideal farm setting. Both aspects could account for the lower incidence of Owl Rock chert at Hillside Hermitage.

The nature of the food-storage facilities at both of these middle Pueblo II habitations is worthy of comment because in both cases there were no obvious food-storage rooms or granaries. This does not preclude the use of other structures for food storage, but specially designed structures for this purpose were absent at these sites. This seems significant since the Kayenta Anasazi have a much longer tradition of constructing granaries, going back at least to Pueblo I (Dinnebito phase on northern Black Mesa) and even earlier if Basketmaker III slab-lined cists are considered. The specialized storage features at the NMRAP sites are large subfloor pits (the kivas at both sites and the jacal living room at Hammer House). Although these features cannot be considered "hidden" to the same extent that exterior Basketmaker II cache pits were hidden, they still suggest a concern for secreting away food stores to avoid their plunder when no one was around (see Gilman 1987). This seems to imply more residential mobility by the occupants of Hammer House and Hillside Hermitage than was true at some other Kayenta sites during middle Pueblo II, such as those on northern Black Mesa, an occurrence that might fit a "frontier" situation where families are expanding out and diversifying their landholdings (experimenting) but not fully committed or restricted to living in a single location. If the groups using these sites originated from Piute Canyon, then perhaps the smaller volume of storage at the more distantly located Hillside Hermitage (ca. 1 m^3) makes sense relative to the considerably larger storage volume at Hammer House (ca. 3 m^3), in that only seed for next year's planting might have been secured in the former, whereas the latter also included storage of food for overwintering (more will be said about Kayentan mobility later).

Tipps et al. (1989) reported a primary habitation (AZ-J-19-12) in the southern portion of the N16 ROW, essentially contemporaneous with Hammer House and Hillside Hermitage, that is remarkably similar in overall layout and size. The report designates the site as early Pueblo II, but the ceramic assemblage is herein designated as middle Pueblo II. The site consists of two living rooms, a subterranean circular storage room, and a kiva, providing a total roofed space of about 21 m². The kiva exhibits numerous floor features, including a storage pit (a vault in the report), but with nowhere near the capacity of the NMRAP sites. However, AZ-J-19-12 had a subterranean, masonry-lined room with a potential volume of 2.7 m³, considerably greater capacity than Hillside Hermitage but comparable to Hammer House. This subterranean storage feature is of a type that could easily have been concealed while still being more rodent and insect secure than a storage pit. Located on the high divide between Gishi Canyon on the west and the upper reaches of an arm of Begashibito Wash on the east, this site also occupied a setting conducive to a settlement strategy that might have involved seasonal cycling between canyons and plateau rim, with primary habitations perhaps maintained in both settings.

Late Pueblo II
Late Pueblo II is an interval of Puebloan population expansion throughout the Kayenta region and beyond. Ambler et al. (1983) suggested, like many authors before, that the proliferation of late Pueblo II habitations across the northern Kayenta region (Rainbow Plateau, Piute Mesa, and Cummings Mesa) resulted from migration rather than simple population growth, an inference based on the number of settlements that appeared within a fairly brief interval and the evident lack of local antecedents for extensive populations during prior ceramic periods. In the Red Lake area, for example, one can point to Basketmaker III, Pueblo I, and early Pueblo II settlements, but this is not the case for the northern Kayenta region. Early Pueblo II settlements of modest size occur in Piute Canyon, followed by small scattered hamlets in middle Pueblo II such as those considered previously, but these alone seem inadequate to account for the late Pueblo II habitations that are distributed across the entire northern Kayenta region—a migratory influx seems implicated. The relatively warm and wet climatic optimum of the late AD 1000s and early AD 1100s (Dean et al. 1985; Gumerman 1988) might have encouraged farming populations to move into areas near the lower fringe of the present pinyon–juniper zone. Such a change could well have promoted the use of regions previously considered too marginal for settlement.

The NMRAP sample does not adequately reflect the late Pueblo II population increase and spread since all sites dating to this period are classified as seasonal or otherwise limited-use habitations rather than primary residencies, such as represented by the middle Pueblo II sites previously discussed. Several late Pueblo II primary habitations lay partially within the N16 ROW but were excluded from data recovery either by avoidance or because no work was warranted. Primary habitations from this interval are well known from the northern Kayenta region, with two examples excavated, both at the northeast foot of Navajo Mountain—Small Jar Pueblo (Lindsay et al. 1968) and UT-V-13-19 (Geib et al. 1985). Hewitt et al. (1989) reported a late Pueblo II primary habitation (AZ-J-19-3) lying largely within the southern portion of the N16 ROW on the Shonto Plateau. This site consisted of a mealing room, a kiva, and a surface activity area that may have been covered by a ramada; other structures might have existed outside the ROW.

Early Pueblo III
Early Pueblo III is characterized by the abandonment of certain areas such as northern Black Mesa and perhaps even population reduction, occurrences thought to be directly related to a worsening environment for farmers (e.g., Dean 1988a, 1988b; Dean et al. 1985). Dean has characterized the start of this interval as a "second-order interruption of the depositional trend...which was centered on AD 1150, [when] alluvial water tables dropped, and floodplains ceased accreting...[and] erosion, in the form of surface stripping and moderate channel incision, dissected the floodplain deposits" (2002:122–123). Dislocation of people is evident enough, but there was continuous occupation of several localities in the Kayenta region from late Pueblo II to middle Pueblo III across the early Pueblo III environmental downturn, including the Shonto and Rainbow plateaus.

Such continuity of settlement is barely evident in the NMRAP site sample since this interval is poorly represented. This sample is, however, unrepresentative of the regional pattern. For example, excavations for the southern portion of N16 documented three primary habitations ceramically dated to the early Pueblo III period (Schroedl 1989). Work was confined to the trash middens at two of these sites, one of which produced 10 burials, a sizable number for a pre–Tsegi phase site in the Kayenta region; at the third site a kiva and mealing room were excavated. The site with excavated structures produced noncutting tree-ring dates, the latest of which was AD 1189+vv.

In the NMRAP sample there is but a single early Pueblo III primary habitation (Windy Mesa), and it was avoided during data recovery except for a few peripheral hearths. Testing acquired a large-enough ceramic sample from this site to be certain of its temporal placement; a primary residential role is indicated by surface evidence of a room block, a kiva depression, and abundant and diverse trash. Aside from this there is a probable field house (secondary habitation) that was likely used during this interval (Mouse House). The site of Ditch House also might have been seasonally occupied at this time as the ceramic types suggest, but the evidence in this case is equivocal because the ceramic assemblage might well result from the mixing of types from two temporally discrete occupations—late Pueblo II and middle Pueblo III. The latter is confirmed by tree-ring dates on several burned structures, and the late Pueblo II component appears substantiated by two radiocarbon dates.

Middle to Late Pueblo III

Many of the NMRAP Puebloan sites were occupied after AD 1200, corresponding to the middle or late Pueblo III ceramic periods. This includes all of the largest primary habitations excavated during the project, several of which appear to span the transition to the Tsegi phase. The NMRAP sample is a true reflection of what was clearly a Pueblo III population surge in the northern Kayenta region, one that is evident on all of the local highlands—Cummings Mesa, Rainbow Plateau, and Piute Mesa (Ambler et al. 1964; Ambler et al. 1983; Lindsay et al. 1968; Stein 1966, 1984). Population growth is represented not just by the number of middle to late Pueblo III sites present in the area but also by the increase in their size and room count, a trend that is seen in the NMRAP sample, since the latest sites are the largest (Figure 6.28). Excavations for the southern portion of N16 also documented an increase in site size and structure count leading into late Pueblo III (Schroedl 1989).

Six NMRAP sites are primary habitations occupied during middle or late Pueblo III. One of these, Three Dog Site, had both a middle Pueblo III component and a late Pueblo III component that were stratigraphically distinct, at least for the structures. Like Three Dog Site, Sapo Seco and Water Jar Pueblo were two primary residential sites with complex histories of use that evidently spanned the middle to late Pueblo III intervals, although without the obvious structural modifications and reorganization seen at Three Dog Site. Unlike these sites, three other primary habitations—Ditch House, Hymn House, and Hanging Ash—were built and abandoned during middle Pueblo III, prior to the Tsegi phase.

Hymn House is an appropriate site to consider first in greater detail since it is a classic example of a *room cluster* (Dean 1969:34–35; Lindsay 1969:156–157), the distinctive grouping of architectural units that were combined like building blocks to form the larger Tsegi phase pueblos, whether in the open or as cliff dwellings (Figures 6.29–6.30). This habitation consisted of a small room block situated on a low bedrock ridge rising above the rolling sagebrush plain of the central Rainbow Plateau. The room block consisted of three masonry structures attached in cloverleaf fashion and connected to a courtyard partially enclosed by a low masonry retaining wall. The one room with a hearth evidently served for living purposes; another, for storage (a granary); and the third, for general activity, including mealing. The latter opened onto an exterior courtyard and provided an access buffer between the outside and the adjoining rooms, which could only be entered via this interior courtyard room. The exterior space contained a hearth, mealing bin, and pit; two additional hearths occurred to the northeast (off the map), perhaps so that smoke and charcoal dust could be kept away from the main living area. Based on architectural investment, functionally specialized rooms, artifact diversity and type, and subsistence remains, we believe that Hymn House functioned as a primary residential site. The absence of a kiva in this particular case might relate to construction of the settlement on bedrock and perhaps to an all-too-brief occupation span.

Occupancy of Hymn House occurred toward the end of the middle Pueblo III period, probably sometime between AD 1230 and 1250. The site lacks any of the ceramic types that are exclusive diagnostics of the late Pueblo III Tsegi phase, so abandonment before about AD 1260 is probable. The near absence of Flagstaff Black-on-white and the low proportion of Moenkopi Corrugated indicate a lower temporal bracket of roughly AD 1230 (see Ambler 1985b:59). Even with a probable 30-year time bracket, we

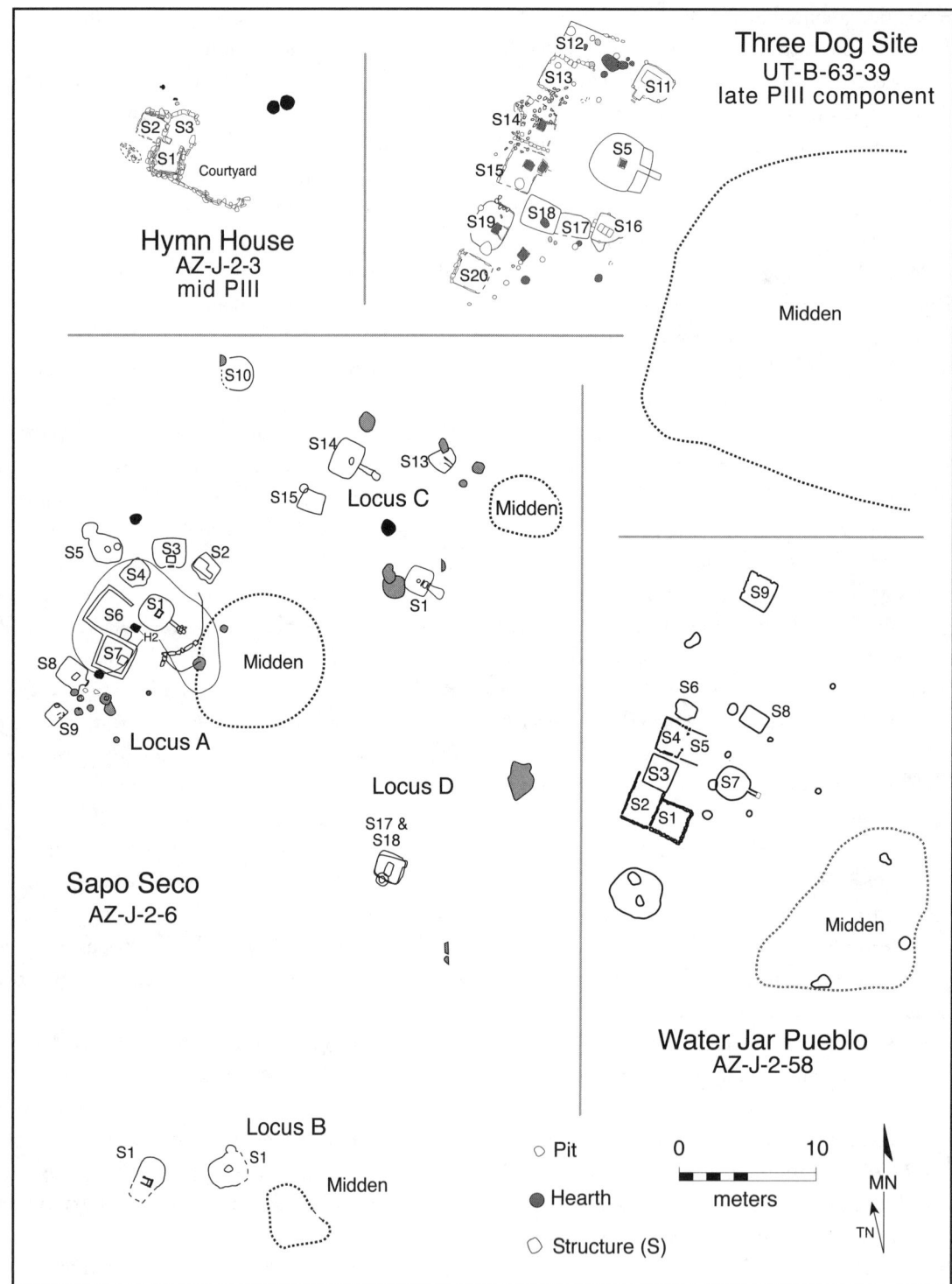

Figure 6.28. Examples of middle to late Pueblo III primary habitations excavated within the N16 right-of-way.

doubt that Hymn House was occupied for more than about 10 years. This inference is based on the comparatively small amount of domestic refuse recovered from the site, coupled with a lack of midden accumulation, especially dense charcoal-stained sediment. With less than 1,600 sherds, 300 flakes, and 100 stone tools, 30 years of site use seems unlikely. Though artifacts do not occur in great quantity, there is considerable diversity, more than would be expected for a temporary residence. Furthermore, with a storage room that had a potential volume

Summary and Interpretation of Puebloan Remains   341

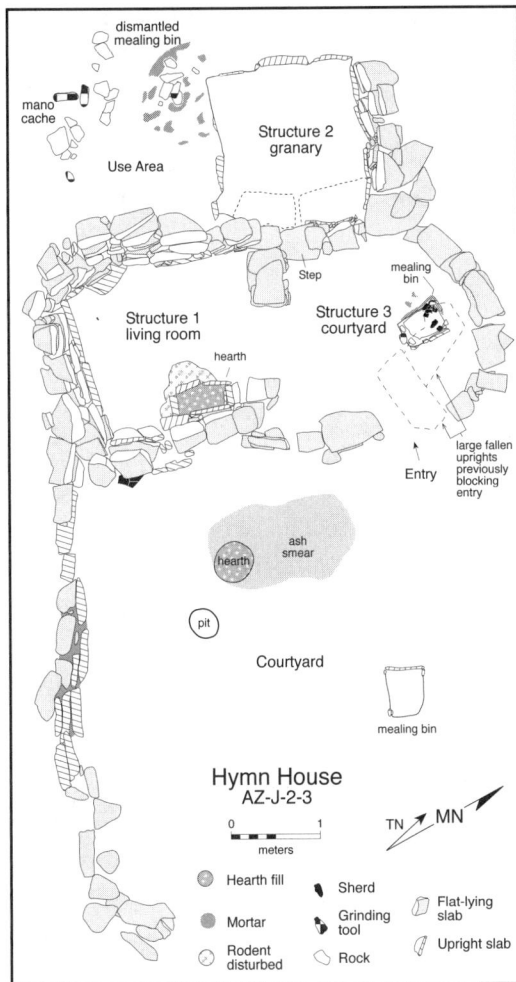

Figure 6.29. Plan map of Hymn House, a middle Pueblo III primary habitation that illustrates a room cluster, the "basic structural component of most excavated Tsegi Phase sites" (Dean 2002:143).

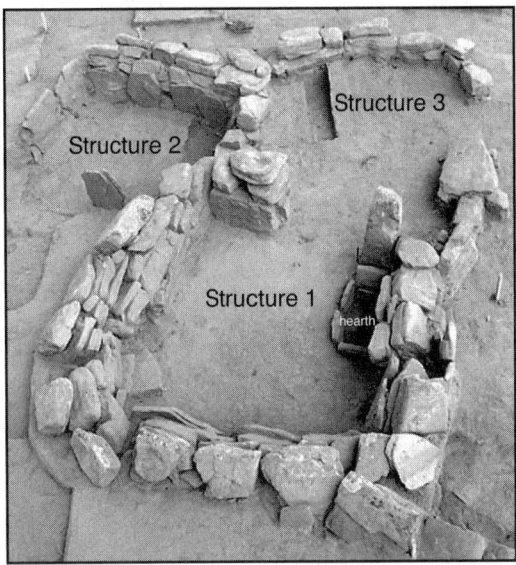

Figure 6.30. The structures at Hymn House after full excavation (view to the north).

of more than 3 m³ (this assumes a conservative 1.2 m estimate of ceiling height), Hymn House had plenty of food-storage capacity for overwintering.

The Hymn House room cluster probably represents the physical manifestation of a household consisting of a single nuclear family. In Dean's terms, "An architectural unit of residence corresponds to a social unit of residence" (1969:37), and in this case, given the limited space, the social unit was doubtless a nuclear family. As he (1969:37) has pointed out, and Structure 1 at Hymn House well exemplifies, the average Kayenta living room provides cramped quarters for one family. The single living room had a floor area of just 5.5 m². Hymn House reflects the modularization of architectural space that facilitated the creation of large Tsegi phase pueblos. Family units of various size could be attached together to form larger aggre-

gates, much like building blocks. Occupation of scattered settlements such as Hymn House by single small families suggests that the social and environmental forces that resulted in the reorganization of Kayenta social structure during the Tsegi phase were at play during the middle Pueblo III period. The social group occupying Hymn House could have been incorporated into a larger architectural grouping through some form of crosscutting social structures, as outlined by Kroeber (1917). Whatever ties existed to unite diverse families also would have served as the social glue to attach segments into the courtyard-oriented sites of the Tsegi phase (see Lindsay 1969:163, 360–373). Hymn House was abandoned just prior to the Tsegi phase, and the family that moved on would have participated in the formation of a Tsegi phase village by one of the processes that Dean recognized—"the apparent independent movement of single households" (1969:190). Given the evident scavenging of useful tools from Hymn House, the occupants probably did not move far, perhaps to one of the many Tsegi phase villages sprinkled across the Rainbow Plateau.

Hymn House lay undisturbed, so its architectural configuration was clear; unfortunately, the same was not true for the other Pueblo III primary habitations of Ditch House and Hanging Ash, both of which seem to differ from typical Pueblo III room clusters in several respects. Both sites clearly contain multiple households. Four living rooms are evident at Hanging Ash, with three of these adjacent to each other in a southwest-to-northeast line (see Figure 3.31). The presence of at least four different houses implies multiple families, but the total number of households remains unknown, as does whether a kiva and mealing room were present. Multiple families are also in evidence at Ditch House since there were three living rooms preserved and possibly a fourth, with the rooms occurring in side-by-side pairs, one pair with an associated mealing room (see Figure 6.7). The overall arrangement of these structures remains unknown, but paired or otherwise grouped houses are seen at other Pueblo III pithouse sites such as AZ-D-10-17 (Callahan 1985). Also unknown for Ditch House and Hanging Ash is the treatment of food stores—Was storage organized above the level of the household, or did each residential unit maintain its own facilities? The large pit of Structure 3 at Hanging Ash suggests the latter, something seen in other Pueblo III communities such as Dog Town (Callahan 1985). If storage was controlled at the level of individual households rather than multiple households, then the configuration of Hanging Ash also differs from plaza-oriented villages such as Surprise Pueblo on Cummings Mesa (Ambler et al. 1964:53–83) or Neskahi Village on Piute Mesa (Hobler 1974), which appear to have communal storage rooms.

Ditch House and Hanging Ash also differed from Hymn House in being semisubterranean to subterranean pithouse settlements rather than masonry constructions, which might have implications for the degree of planned permanence or anticipated short occupation (see Kent 1992). The effort that went into constructing Hymn House seems consistent with building for a long occupation, even though the modest amount of remains at the site and lack of evidence for structure remodeling and additions suggest that site tenancy was cut short. The structures at Ditch House and Hanging Ash were perhaps far easier to build, requiring less time and effort, especially in the quarrying and hauling of stone. Thus, they seem more in line with Kent's (1992) notion of anticipated short occupation, with both sites also appearing to have had rather short actual occupations as well, probably less than 20 years. Anticipated short occupation does not mean that the sites were not principal places of residence, just that the stay was not envisioned as sufficiently long to merit substantial construction investment, even for a settlement that served as the only domicile for several years. The changes in architectural construction as a site transitions from one of anticipated short occupation to one of anticipated long occupation is perhaps evidenced by the architectural reconfiguration at Three Dog Site.

Lindsay's term *courtyard pueblo* (1969:243–246) describes a specific form of late Pueblo III aggregated pueblo in the Kayenta region where room clusters are grouped together to form *courtyard complexes* and these in turn are further grouped to form pueblos (see Dean 2002:143–146). Three Dog Site appears to exemplify the architectural reconfiguration that marks the transition to this type of village and in a way that seems consistent with anticipated greater longevity of use, though occupancy ultimately was not all that long. The structural remains of a middle Pueblo III habitation lay beneath those of a late Pueblo III habitation (Figure 6.31). The late Pueblo III structures of Three Dog Site were built on the same spot and generally following the same ground plan established by the residents just a decade or two earlier but organized into a larger and more formal pueblo that included additional rooms, probably more people, and a greater investment in architectural permanence. The middle Pueblo III structures were razed and filled in, but the larger central kiva of the earlier component was maintained (Structure 5) and serves as a handy reference point in Figure 6.31 for how the architectural units from the two time periods relate to each other. It is probably not wild speculation to claim that the final residents of this site were descendants of and perhaps some of the same people who initially built two courtyard complexes during middle Pueblo III. The nearly identical footprint and continued use of the one large kiva seem to support this argument. Moreover, the site occupied a sheltered drainage with permanent water and farmable alluvium at the foot of Navajo Mountain—just the sort of prime location that is likely to have been "owned" by some social unit.

The middle Pueblo III component at Three Dog Site consisted of two courtyard complexes, each containing living rooms, mealing facilities, and a kiva. The layout of the middle Pueblo III component and the "complete" suite of architectural features associated with each courtyard imply the presence of two extended families or related kin groups, each being somewhat autonomous with regard to food-storage, food-processing, and ceremonial space. The two site portions were evidently constructed at roughly the same time, suggesting that the two groups settled together. The orientation of architectural features toward contiguous L-shaped courtyards is typical of the period just prior to and extending into the Tsegi phase in the Kayenta region, when large sites began to form through the coalescence of multiple households into more cohesive settlements (Dean 1969; Lindsay 1969). Occupa-

Summary and Interpretation of Puebloan Remains   343

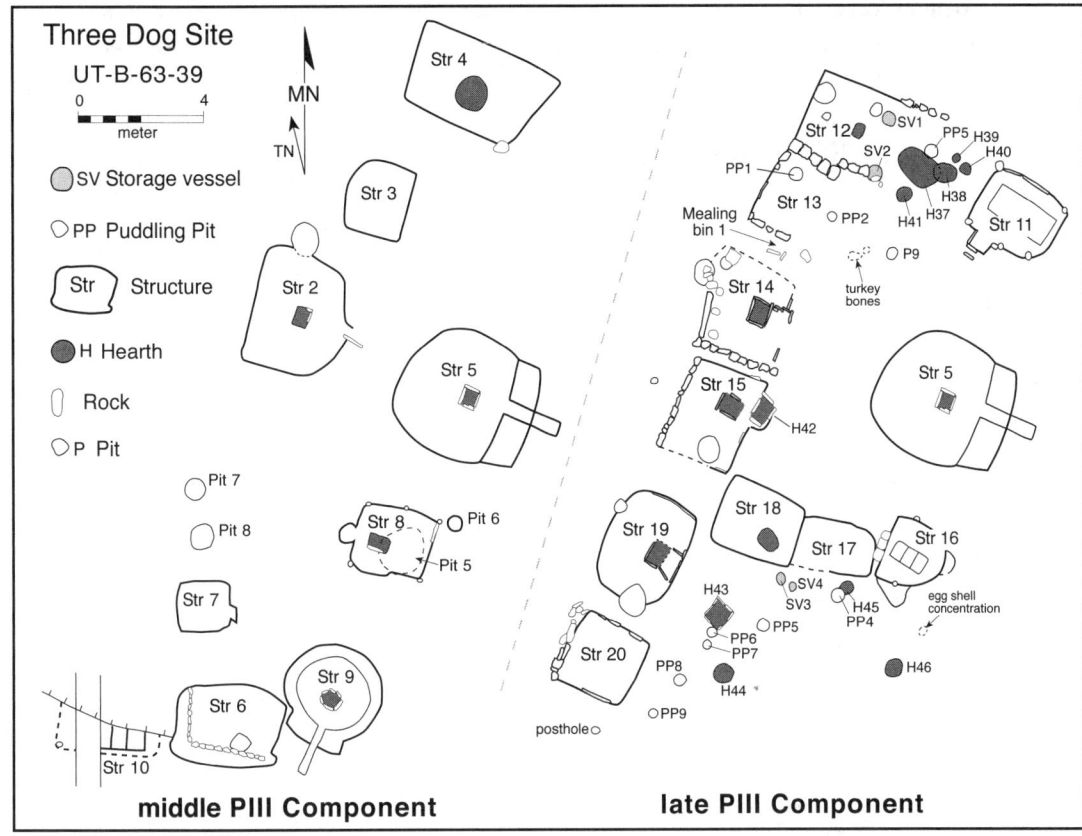

Figure 6.31. Plan map of the two superimposed architectural units at Three Dog Site, one from the middle Pueblo III ceramic period and the other from the late Pueblo III period. Structure 5, a kiva, was used during both times and serves as an orientation reference point; two "courtyard complexes" are evident during both periods, and the site can be considered as an incipient form of a "courtyard pueblo" (Lindsay 1969:243–246).

tion of Three Dog Site during middle Pueblo III probably lasted just 10–20 years, based on the amount of domestic trash generated and the general lack of remodeling within structures associated with that component. Only Structure 6 showed evidence of major remodeling, with the construction of a masonry wall inside the original structural basin. All of these middle Pueblo III structures except the principal kiva (Structure 5) were dismantled and scavenged for construction materials. Structural basins were filled with trash or sediment produced by the excavation of new rooms, and most of the new rooms were situated partially or completely over earlier rooms.

The late Pueblo III component continued to be organized as two residential units, each comprising a courtyard surrounded by living rooms, mealing rooms, and storage rooms. Each courtyard also exhibited several extramural hearths, puddling pits, and other small features. The most obvious difference between the earlier and later site layouts was the presence of a single kiva (Structure 5) in the later period. The smaller kiva in the southern court-

yard of the middle Pueblo III component was abandoned, and its roof was removed, with the depression then used as a trash dump. Six rooms made up the southwest- to northeast-trending spine of rooms that structured the two courtyards during late Pueblo III. The back walls of all six rooms formed an approximately straight line, although discrete square or rectangular shallow basins were excavated for each room. Some rooms had masonry foundations or rear walls, while others were built almost entirely of jacal. In at least two cases the walls of rooms abutted but were not shared (i.e., there was not a single wall). Two rooms at the apex of the room block (Structures 12–13) shared a single masonry wall, although Structure 12 was clearly enclosed after Structure 13 was occupied. The three rooms dividing the two courtyards (Structures 16–18) were constructed separately, although all were probably used simultaneously.

The comprehensive remodel of the site speaks of a coordinated effort by the entire group that transformed the site into a more integrated architectural unit. The exact sequence of feature demolition and construction was only evident in a few cases, but the remodel must have been planned to ensure that grinding facilities and shelter were available as needed during the process. The use of a single kiva and what appears to have been the organized group construction of a more formal room block implies integration of the two families or kin groups, a pattern noted throughout the Kayenta region during the Tsegi phase (Dean 1969; Lindsay 1969). There are no indications that the remaining kiva (Structure 5) was enlarged to accommodate more site residents, and the two separate courtyards of the late Pueblo III component retained separate food-storage and -preparation space.

As discussed earlier, the final occupation of Three Dog Site extended into the Tsegi phase, but the residents appear to have moved prior to full abandonment of the northern Kayenta region, as usable timbers, construction material, and whole artifacts appear to have been scavenged from the structures. This behavior would be expected if the occupants relocated only a short distance since the effort to dismantle and move the material would be less than procuring new beams, rocks for masonry, and large grinding tools. A large Tsegi phase habitation (UT-B-63-2) lies within a kilometer to the southwest of Three Dog Site, next to the old Navajo Mountain school. This site has not been excavated, so its total size and configuration are unknown, but ceramics on the surface, including abundant Kayenta Black-on-white and whiteline polychromes, imply that it slightly postdates Three Dog Site. The Three Dog residents may have simply moved upstream, perhaps to be closer to the source of permanent water of their drainage, where they combined with other families to build a larger pueblo.

Another form of late Pueblo III settlement configuration is Lindsay's (1969:243–246; Dean 2002:143–144) *plaza pueblo*, an inward-looking community organized around a plaza containing a kiva. These should not be confused with what Adams (1989:156) refers to as *plaza-oriented villages*, the large aggregated communities that appeared in western Puebloan refuge areas at the close of the thirteenth century. The term *village* is a key distinction to keep in mind (plaza pueblo vs. plaza village) since it emphasizes the large scale of the residential populations at the sites that Adams discusses: hundreds of people vs. a few dozen. Lindsay's Pueblo III plaza pueblos appear to be scaled-up versions of Pueblo II unit pueblos, with Surprise Pueblo (NA7498) on Cummings Mesa (Ambler et al. 1964:53–83) and Neskahi Village (NA7719) on Piute Mesa (Hobler 1974) providing the typical examples and also illustrating the two standard forms—square/rectangular and D shaped, respectively. Surprise Pueblo had a roughly square plaza defined by a linear room block on the northwest side and masonry walls on the other three sides. The room block consisted of seven contiguous masonry rooms for storage and general activity. The living rooms for the site consisted of five contiguous pithouses accessed by entries through the masonry wall that defined the northeast side of the plaza. The plaza had an entrance through its southeast wall in the direction of the trash midden. Surprise Pueblo showed signs of accretionary room construction, and, in fact, there was an earlier, inner plaza wall along the northeast side of the pueblo that was abandoned as the room block grew in length. A kiva with a masonry bench and recess occupied the middle of the plaza. Ambler et al. (1964:82) estimated that Surprise Pueblo had about 20 but no more than 30 residents.

Neskahi Village had a D-shaped plaza defined in like fashion by a linear room block on the northwest side but then an arched wall of masonry. The back room block consisted of seven contiguous masonry rooms for storage and general activity, with the actual living rooms (up to 11 in use at one time) consisting of semisubterranean pithouses arrayed around the arched masonry wall of the plaza on both its northeast and southwest sides. The pithouses opened onto the plaza and were accessed through the plaza wall, creating an inward-looking community like at Surprise Pueblo. As Hobler describes it, "The pit houses were integrated into an organized village plan first by means of a single jacal enclosing wall and later by means of a pair of parallel curved masonry enclosing walls which meet the straight row of masonry rooms and impart to the village its characteristic 'D' shape" (1974:1). The pueblo went through several phases of construction before it reached its ultimate configuration. Hobler did not provide a population estimate for Neskahi Village, but at its largest it was probably only double that of Surprise Pueblo.

Two of the late Pueblo III habitations excavated by the NMRAP—Sapo Seco Locus A and Water Jar Pueblo—can be characterized as scaled-down versions of plaza pueblos or late Pueblo III unit pueblos (Figures 6.32–6.33). Both of these sites occupy the broad, open sagebrush plain of the central Rainbow Plateau, and they lie only about 100 m apart, with Water Jar on a slight rise. The main compounds of both settlements have very similar architectural configurations, consisting of a suite of

Summary and Interpretation of Puebloan Remains   345

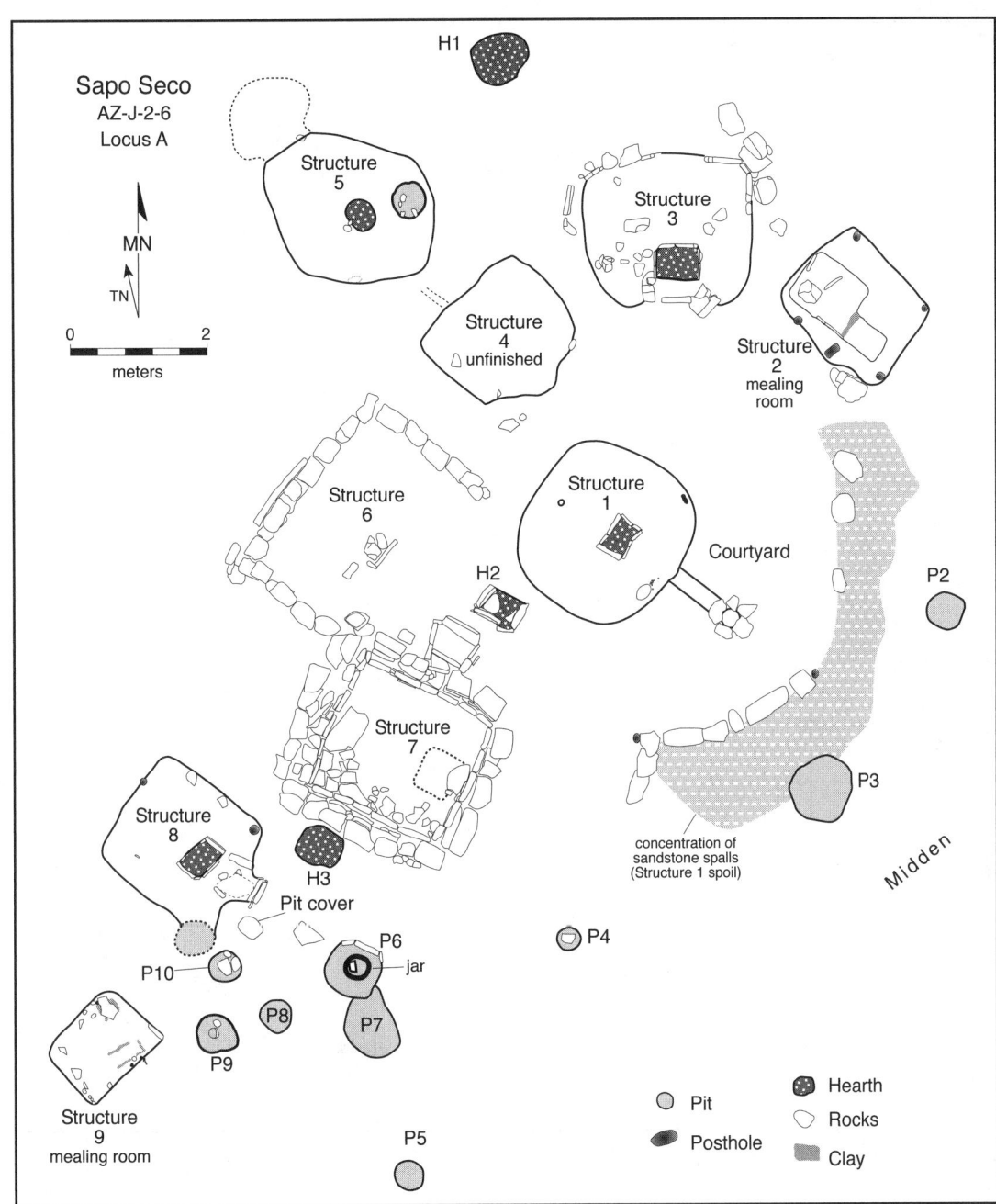

Figure 6.32. Plan map of the main architectural unit (Locus A) at Sapo Seco, a late Pueblo III primary habitation that illustrates a unit pueblo type of arrangement.

differentiated rooms—living, mealing, storage, and general purpose—that face and open upon a small plaza space containing a simple kiva that at both sites resembles more of an early Puebloan pithouse (see previous kiva discussion). The superstructures of the surrounding buildings would have helped to define the plaza on the northwest and southwest sides. At Sapo Seco evidence for an enclosing wall on the east and south side consisted of postholes along with an arch of sandstone slabs, remnants of a prob-

able jacal wall that tied in with the rooms to close off the space around the kiva. An apron of rocky spoil from excavation of the kiva (which, like the version at Water Jar Pueblo, was cut into sandstone bedrock) lay just outside the postholes and sandstone alignment, demarking where the plaza enclosing wall once stood. The wall was evidently in place prior to the kiva excavation because the rock spall seemed to have been dumped against this feature. An enclosing plaza wall was not in evidence at Water

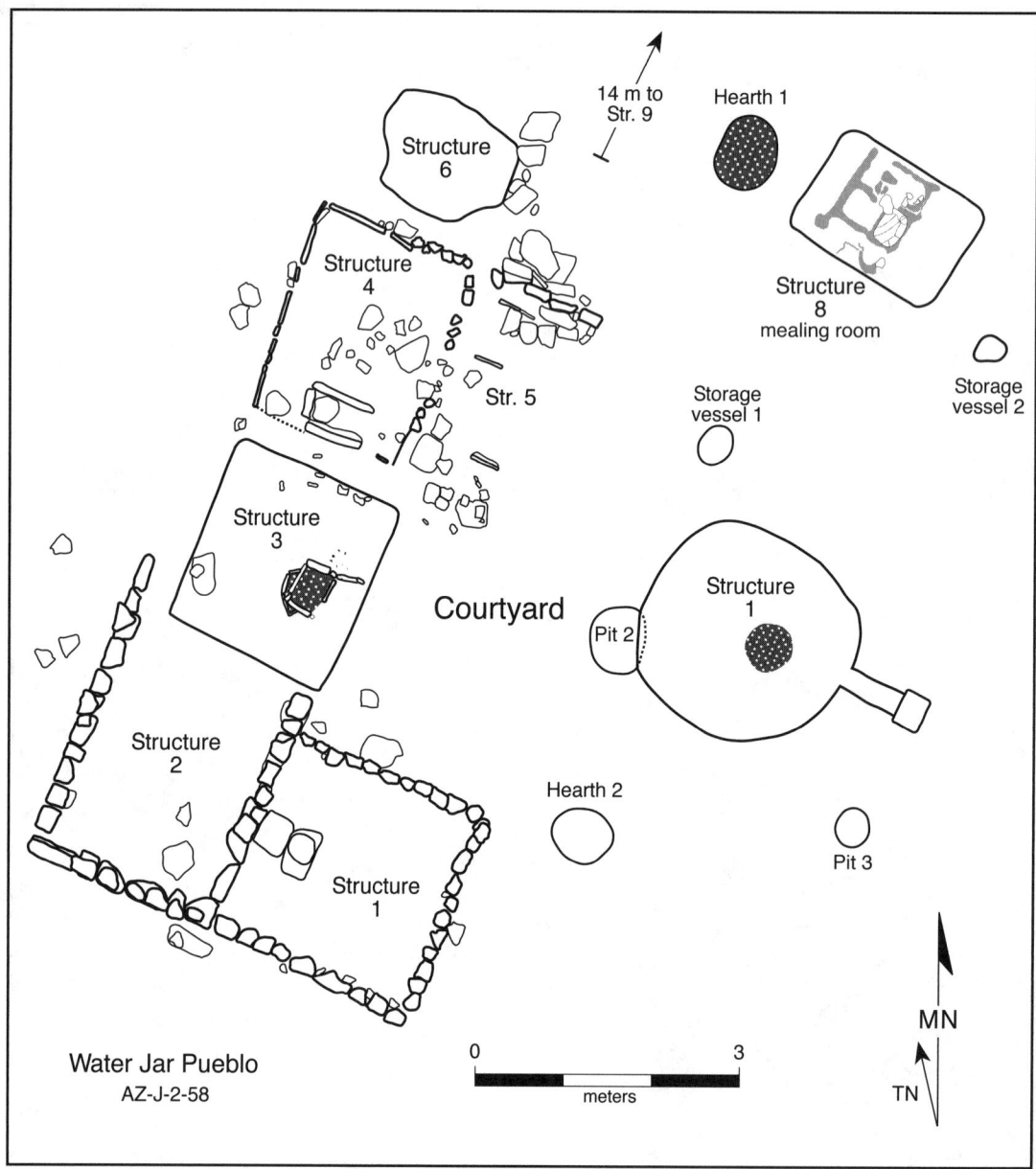

Figure 6.33. Plan map of the main architectural unit at Water Jar Pueblo, a late Pueblo III primary habitation.

Jar Pueblo but probably was present given the arrangement of the rooms around the kiva. Both of these small unit pueblos probably housed single extended families. There were no more than two living rooms in use at both sites at any one time, and the total roofed space is quite modest, around 30 m² for Sapo Seco and 33 m² for Water Jar. Much of this was storage and general-activity space for the group at large, and the lack of household-specific food stores seems an important difference from some late Pueblo III settlements (Structure 3 at Hanging Ash just considered or the structures at Dog Town, AZ-D-10-17 [Callahan 1985]). Given the small size of both Sapo Seco and Water Jar Pueblo there would not have been a significant trust issue about separate households excessively using the common food stores. The same is not necessarily true at large plaza pueblos such as Neskahi Village and Surprise Pueblo; how a "tragedy of the commons" was avoided at these sites is worth pondering.

At the time of excavation during the early 1960s, Neskahi Village and Surprise Pueblo offered new insights into Kayenta settlement configuration and architectural diversity during Pueblo III. In particular, the excavators noticed the continuing reliance on pithouses, previously thought to have "died out" during earlier time periods

(Hobler 1974:41). Pithouses not only were in use at the two pueblos but formed an "integral part of the social unit" (Ambler et al. 1964:82). Researchers also concluded that the formalized village plan had "social concomitants if not social causes" (Hobler 1974:42). It is easy to envision the formal configurations of Surprise Pueblo and Neskahi Village developing out of Pueblo II unit pueblos with palisades. Black Mesa provides some good examples of these (see summary maps in Ahlstrom 1998a:Figure 12-1, especially p. 212; also Spurr 1993). Documentation of these features requires broad horizontal exposure during excavation and conditions that support wood preservation or the definition of postholes, something favored by silty soils on Black Mesa. If sufficient care is taken at horizontal exposure, palisades are likely to be revealed at most Kayentan Pueblo II sites such as Small Jar Pueblo on the Rainbow Plateau, where only limited trenching for rooms was done. Palisades are simple fences or screens that in combination with the attached rooms helped to define the residential space. The masonry plaza wall at Neskahi Village clearly grew out of an earlier palisade since workers found postholes of a wooden wall that originally defined the plaza space. The jacal wall that once ringed the plaza was later converted into two parallel masonry walls.

The social underpinnings of the enclosed plaza pueblo, both small and large, were likely identical—strong family ties such as parents and their offspring with spouses and children, perhaps several generations deep. The accretional growth of a slowly expanding plaza pueblo is easily envisioned as the result of increasing family size as children reached adulthood and married, with spouses of one sex or another moving in (matrilocal residence is often assumed based on western Puebloan ethnographic analogy [Eggan 1950; Titiev 1944], supported somewhat by richer-than-average elderly female graves, e.g., the burials at RB568 [Crotty 1983]). Neskahi Village would seem to be at the potential upper size range for a community organized on such direct kin relationships where food stores were centralized rather than under individual household control. Also, beyond the inward-looking insularity of plaza pueblos, they have an inherent physical limit to their growth that can only be overcome by rebuilding on an ever larger scale. When there is no longer any room within the plaza for newcomers, they must simply be appended to the outside, something that is in evidence at Neskahi Village and perhaps also as well in Structures 8 and 9 at Sapo Seco.

Prior to late Pueblo III, the unit pueblo (small plaza pueblo) appears to have been the largest architecturally represented social formation in the Kayenta region (this excludes the Basketmaker III site of Juniper Cove). This does not mean that these unit pueblos might not have been organized at some higher level, but there is scant architectural manifestation of such a practice (see Klesert 1982 for a possible exception, although the evidence provided for a "redistributive center" can be accounted for by other means). Much larger social formations are in evidence during the Tsegi phase, as the pueblos that were built at that time contained dozens or more separate households. The modular architectural arrangement of the room cluster and courtyard complex is inherently more useful for creating ever-larger pueblos by appending new households. Plaza pueblos were also evidently combined together to form multiplaza pueblos such as Long House (Dean 2002:144, Figure 6.13), although whether the individual plaza units of these larger sites were organized like those of single-plaza sites like Neskahi Village is debatable.

Village size evidently could be increased as long as there was some means of social integration or some force that exceeded the strains of ever-larger social groups—war and fear of others according to Haas and Creamer (1993, 1995), though direct evidence of violence is nearly nonexistent in the Kayenta region (Haas and Creamer 1993:Figures 4-27–4-28) compared to the Mesa Verde and Chaco regions (e.g., LeBlanc 1999; Turner and Turner 1999). It is plausible that plaza sites like Neskahi Village, which occupy prime settlement locations, represent a single large kin group with long-standing kinship or communal ties to an area, holding onto an older pattern of residence (Lindsay 1969:367); whereas nearby courtyard pueblos such as Pottery Pueblo were built by people experimenting with new means of social integration, perhaps a previously dispersed community of unrelated families but also including transients or newcomers, allowing ever-larger architectural configurations that more easily incorporated individual households without direct family ties. The courtyard format of residential construction allowed this to occur far more easily than the plaza format. New residential groups might have been welcomed because of special knowledge or skills that they offered, either practical or ritual, or perhaps simply because they added to the numerical strength of a settlement.

The main habitation area of Sapo Seco previously characterized (Locus A) seems to have been the residential site of an extended household situated for efficient food production and processing, but the site overall shows a considerably more complex settlement pattern than that of a small unit pueblo, as it is surrounded by scattered pithouses and therefore has the appearance of a small *pithouse village*. There were three other residential loci at this site, all of which were located in a northeast-to-south arc 10–30 m from Locus A (Figure 6.34). Overall the site had a total of 18 living or communal structures and 32 primary features (such as pits and hearths). Locus B, to the south of Locus A, had a mealing room and a living room with two burials in a wall chamber. The existing road here might have removed additional structures, but they were few, judging from the trash. Locus C, northeast and east of Locus A, was a loose configuration of two living rooms, two mealing rooms, and associated pits. A seasonally used structure, possibly a field house, occurred nearby but seems unrelated (Structure 10). Since the N16 ROW defined our area of work there is no way to know how many other structures might exist to the north of this locus. Locus D to the southeast of Locus A consisted of two superimposed pithouses both intruded by a burial; nearby is a possible unfinished pithouse and two pits. The enclosed unit pueblo of Locus A presents a marked contrast to the pithouses of the other loci, which are more loosely configured and lack formal communal areas.

As opposed to Locus A, the structures at the other loci appear to have been occupied on a short-term, seasonal, or intermittent basis. The principal reason for this conjecture is the lack of adequate food-storage facilities for overwintering. The four loci are from the same general time period but may not have been strictly contemporaneous. In fact, the lack of Kayenta Black-on-white and whiteline polychrome outside of Locus A may indicate that the other loci were occupied prior to Locus A. If so, it is unlikely that the residents of the other loci would have gone on to construct the Locus A pueblo given its architectural integration. Given the possible lack of contemporaneity, it may be mere coincidence that Loci B–D are located in proximity to Locus A.

The smattering of late Pueblo III types at Locus A alone may be accounted for by having a slightly longer duration of use; thus all four loci may have been largely contemporaneous. If so, the occupants of each likely had some form of social or economic association with the Locus A residents. The inhabitants of Loci B–D likely resided there on a temporary basis, affiliating themselves with the more permanent Locus A households as the need arose and then splitting off when that need was fulfilled. Among the three loci are several cases where habitation structures were abandoned, and later structures or primary features intruded into the walls and fill (e.g., the superimposition of Structures 17 and 18 at Locus D). There is also evidence for the reuse or remodeling of structures (e.g., the multiple floors of Structure 14 at Locus C; changing of the hearth and deflector locations in Structure 16 at Locus C), implying that inhabitants returned to previously occupied structures or that loci were reoccupied by new tenants. This kind of "recombinant" residency has been noted elsewhere in the Kayenta region at the Tsegi phase sites of Betatakin and Kiet Siel (Dean 1969). The historic Raramuri (Tarahumara) of northern Mexico provide an ethnographic example as well as details of the social and economic motivations behind such moves (Graham 1994). The motivations for residential clustering are probably numerous and nearly impossible to extract from the archaeological record, at least at Sapo Seco. Likely reasons would include participation in social and ceremonial activities, communal work efforts such as gathering and processing crops or other resources, defensive alliances, economic alliances—particularly during times of stress—and the event-specific kind of on-again/off-again co-residency of familial members that has been observed by various ethnographers.

It is worth mentioning that the scale of mechanical trenching and stripping is what afforded the unprecedented view of the Pueblo III settlement at Sapo Seco. This site contained only one small hint of a structure at Locus A, based on surface evidence (masonry rubble of Structure 6); little could anyone know that scattered Pueblo III pithouses lay buried beneath the sand in this sagebrush flat. Had NNAD archaeologists focused their efforts on the partially visible masonry component at Locus A, the remainder of the site would have gone undetected, greatly simplifying the potential complexities of settlement history and social organization. Haas and Creamer (1993:78–85) had a similar find at Kin Klethla: trenching to defensive locate walls that they thought might be present at this open Tsegi phase pueblo located defenselessly in the valley bottom managed to section through numerous scattered pithouses but failed to locate any fortification features. Broad horizontal exposure around such Tsegi phase settlements as the Thief site (NA11,047 [Swarthout et al. 1986]), Kin Klethla (Haas and Creamer 1993), or Mud Wallow (Clark 1993b) would

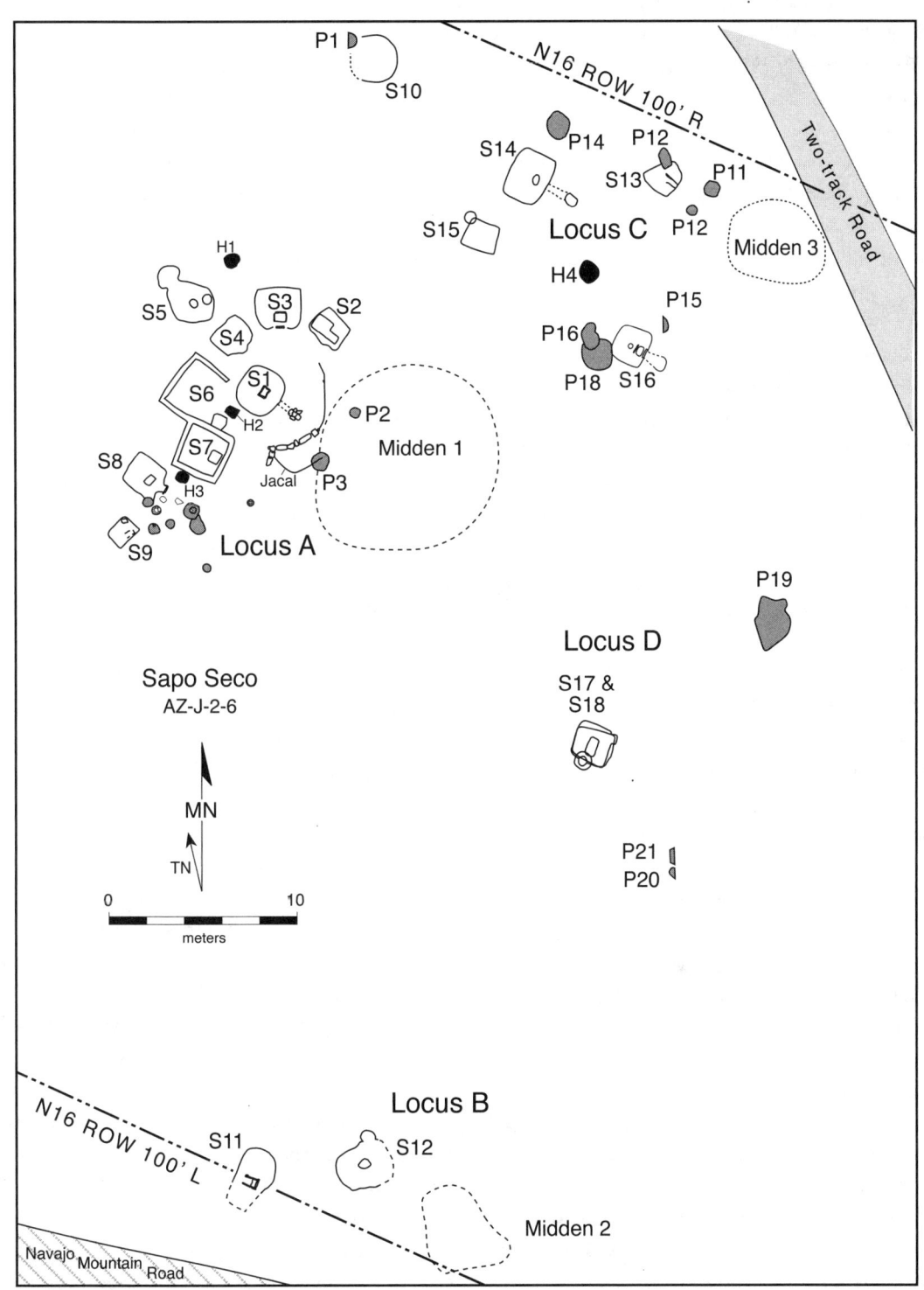

Figure 6.34. Plan map of Sapo Seco showing all loci at a late Pueblo III primary habitation.

be most illuminating. A residential core such as Locus A at Sapo Seco or the masonry room block at Kin Klethla or the Thief site might have served to attract "loose" households, those either new to an area or wanting to be part of a larger population aggregate. These "newcomers" built temporary residences in the form of pithouses clustered around an established residential core; they built in an efficient fashion because the duration of stay was not necessarily anticipated to be long, given that much was in flux during the thirteenth century.

Secondary Habitations and the Field House Conundrum

As mentioned earlier, we separated the NMRAP sample of Puebloan habitations into those thought of as the anchor point(s) of annual settlement (primary habitations) and those occupied on a more seasonal or limited basis. The term *secondary* implies that a habitation served as a subsidiary domicile for a social unit, indeed, in a subordinate or supporting role relative to the settlements considered previously. To distinguish between primary and secondary habitations we focused on architectural permanence, the presence and nature of interior hearths, and food-storage capacity or lack thereof and to a much lesser extent on artifact or faunal/floral measures of occupation duration and activity diversity. Despite some rather clear-cut distinctions in the NMRAP sample, there are at least two issues that need to be considered individually to the extent possible. One relates to the annual duration of site use: Was the site lived in seasonally or year-round? The other relates to the subsistence role for which seasonally used residences were created: Are they field houses, as is often assumed, or something else?

The concepts of site seasonality and duration of occupation are intertwined, as sites on the "short" end of actual occupation are, by definition, seasonal. Evidence for seasonality is difficult to muster and comes principally from assessments of how structures were built, the presence of storage features, and the occurrence and type of interior hearths. Basically these concern whether sites were occupied during warm weather as "summer" habitations. A confounding issue with any assessment of seasonality is the intended (anticipated) and actual number of seasons that a secondary habitation was used (Kent 1992). As Kent argued, anticipated reuse of a place over many seasons could result in greater investment in feature construction from the start, while actual reuse over many seasons could result in much accumulation of debris and modification of features. Ethnographic descriptions of summer sites such as those used while tending fields are often used to model archaeological expectations or to build a simple interpretive framework. What Lightfoot and Jewett call the "use duration of an archaeological place" is defined as the "total aggregate of time that a specific location is used regardless of the functional nature of that site"; a variation of occupation duration is "residential stability," described as "the length of time spent at any one settlement during the annual cycle" (1984:49). Evidence for site duration is primarily limited to the accumulation of various artifact classes with perhaps the greatest weight given to items with the quickest rates of deposition and smallest tendency to be recycled. Grinding tools should in theory be good indicators because they require some time to become exhausted unless expedient tools are used, but grinding tools also have a high rate of recycling and reuse.

Southwestern archaeologists frequently use the functionally specific term *field house* for secondary habitations (e.g., Kohler 1992; chapters in Ward 1978; see Colton 1918 and Colton and Colton 1918 for an early reference to field houses on Sinaguan sites in and around Flagstaff). This term is an archaeological inference linked to ethnographic descriptions, an inference that conjures up Mindeleff's (1891:Figures 111–113) images of Native Americans huddled in the shade of "rude shelters" (1891:217). Mindeleff (1891:217–219) described "field shelters" (*kis*; *ki'si* in Beaglehole 1937:39) that the farmers used on a limited basis while tending their crops. His comparatively brief descriptions along with those of other ethnographers (e.g., Beaglehole 1937; Bradfield 1971; Ellis 1974; Hack 1942; Hill 1938; Stephen 1936; Titiev 1944) defined what archaeologists would come to commonly call field houses (or field stations, field camps, farm shelters, or any number of like terms). The ethnographic accounts served to create expectations of material patterns in the archaeological record that would allow for the "proper" identification of the permanent (pueblos) and nonpermanent (field shelters) aspects of Puebloan settlement and also the interpretive conventions for how these different sites fit within subsistence and settlement organization.

The term *field house* implies proximity to a field, perhaps land use and ownership (see Kohler 1992; Lambert 2006; Moore 1978; Preucel 1990), but it also implies reliance on food production, sedentism, and residential stability, issues that are themselves worthy of study. Obviously the NMRAP was in no position to resolve these thorny issues, though the collected data do allow some inferences. Subsistence base is key because the field house category presumes that farming (food production) provided a substantial proportion of the diet. This is something that Powell (1983), for one (see also Seward 1983), questioned based on the macrobotanical remains recovered from BMAP Anasazi sites as well as ethnographic data of how certain societies such as the Pai and the Navajo survived on the Colorado Plateau. A field house designation is perhaps warranted for some of the NMRAP secondary habitations; indeed, we have employed this term at several places earlier in this chapter. Yet some of the NMRAP secondary habitations seem to have functioned for purposes other than tending fields, and a generic term such as *secondary* acknowledges that possibility from the start, which is perhaps why other generic terms are used, such as *limited-activity/occupation site, satellite site,* or *seasonal habitation*. Designating a site as a field house might seem to accord with intuitive, commonsense notions of site and land relationships, but today we might want to be more precise (see Sutton's [1977:30] remark concerning Pilles 1969). Not all secondary habitations are necessarily field houses, although all field houses are presumable secondary habitations.

More than three decades after the Small Sites Conference (Ward 1978) there are still no agreed-upon methods to reliably discern prehistoric field houses from other small site types or to test alternative interpretations of use (McAllister and Plog 1978). Site descriptions and interpretations continue to rely on ethnographic inference to define field house form and function (e.g., Ward 1978). For this reason McAllister and Plog (1978) rued the lack of interpretive models for small sites (including field houses) and performed tests of site type–artifact association that highlight the problems inherent in more intuitive approaches. Since then, however, there have been several studies regarding small site function and duration (Stone 1993), interior vs. exterior feature patterning (Sobolik et al. 1997), and the relationship between artifacts–ecofacts and room function–duration (Clark 1998; Nelson and Lippmeier 1993; Schlanger 1991), among others, that are not so dependent on historic analogy.

In an interesting study of small Hohokam sites, Stone concludes that "there is no consistent, clear-cut relationship between site types and material culture in the northern Hohokam periphery" (1993:79). Site types, in this case, consisted of limited-activity loci, field houses, farmsteads, and hamlets, each of which was defined by an expected set of artifacts and features that presumably reflected differences in site function. Such was not the case, however; rather than functional differentiation, "the… site typology appears to represent varying levels of occupational permanency" (Stone 1993:79)—i.e., duration. In other words, a farmstead is simply a field house writ large, and a hamlet is just a farmstead occupied that much longer. In each case the habitation is a response to a need for more efficient farming or food gathering. We have not partitioned NMRAP sites along the lines of Stone, and the Hohokam study did not include anything above the level of a hamlet, but we wonder if there isn't a similar phenomenon happening for the Kayenta region. Is site variability primarily due to differences in site function or to differences in duration of use? Since the ethnographic record provides the touchstone for archaeological "recognition" of field houses or the identification of seasonal habitations no matter their actual function, it is worth a brief consideration of this literature.

Ethnographic Accounts

In Beaglehole's "Notes on Hopi Economic Life" (1937:39) he described a typical scene on the first day of planting, usually conducted in late April or May. A small working party gathers at the appointed field, digging sticks and corn in hand. Before starting they "smoke and breathe prayers" for rain under a *ki'si*, what the author translates as a "field hut"; then the real work begins. The "hut" probably looked similar to those illustrated by Mindeleff (1891:Figures 112–113), based on observations made during the 1880s. Mindeleff (1989:217–219) referred to "field shelters" collectively as *kisi* but distinguished between two types: the *tuwahlki*, or watch house, and the *kishoni*, or uncovered shade. The *kishoni* is the simplest form, consisting of an arc of upright cottonwood saplings and attached boughs. The *tuwahlki* can range from a covered ridgepole supported by a forked stick (not illustrated by Mindeleff) to the roofed, mostly open-sided, four-post arrangement that may correspond with Beaglehole's field hut. Perhaps publishing the first examples of Puebloan field structures, Mindeleff lamented not having "an opportunity of making an examination of all the field shelters used in these pueblos" (1891:217). His comparatively brief descriptions continued to be the standard well into the twentieth century, as ethnographic accounts of what archaeologists now commonly call field houses were relegated to a few lines subsumed within the more social, ritual, or ecological aspects of agricultural planting, harvesting, and processing (e.g., Beaglehole 1937; Bradfield 1971; Ellis 1974; Hack 1942; Hill 1938; Stephen 1936; Titiev 1944; for more comprehensive listings see "Appendix: Summary of Data" in Sutton 1977 and Appendixes A and B in Moore 1979). One early exception is Cosmos Mindeleff's treatise *Navaho Houses* (1898), which set the stage for later studies of Navajo dwellings (Jett and Spencer 1981; Russell 1978; Spencer 1969).

One could imagine that a field-tending locus close to home need be little more than a tree with shade, whereas locations farther "afield" would require the full complement of domestic items. The comment that "on very hot days…I took a nap in the shade of a bush" (Talayesva 1942:206, in Moore 1979:263) reflects the former situation, and the latter might correspond with Bandelier's claim that Cochiti Pueblo was "almost depopulated in summer, nearly everybody going out to the ranchos" (1966:265, in Moore 1979:270). But are the Cochiti summer homes "field houses" in the traditional sense? Or are the ranchos the summer quarters of a biseasonal round? If so, they are on the extreme end of what Moore calls the "full set of potential analogs" (1979:119) within the class of ethnographic phenomena known as field houses. Such sites may appear in the archaeological record simply as small, self-contained habitations, clearly related to agriculture but lacking the hallmarks of a humble field house.

Ethnographic accounts of field houses also vary in the identity of the occupants. Beaglehole (1937) noted the following division of labor among Hopi of the mid–twentieth century—men: planting, hoeing, cultivating, harvesting, roasting, and gardening; women: preparing food, husking, grinding, storing foodstuffs, cooking, baking, and collecting wild foods. Both sexes would sometimes participate in planting, harvesting, and gardening, depending on the need, and boys were known to do some of the hoeing. Hill (1938) observed that weeding with a hoe was usually a man's work, unless the individual who normally did it was otherwise occupied. During the use-life of a field house, it is probable that more than one family member tended to some aspect of field work. "He stays here constantly," said Stephen of a Hopi man tending his peach orchard in the 1890s, "*or some of his family*, from the time the fruit gets large enough to eat till the crop is gathered, to guard against Navajo and other depredators" (1936:284–285, emphasis added). Stephen called the structure an "outlook house" and added that one *woman* built her outlook "right on the edge of the orchard" (1936:285); thus both men and women could be involved in field house construction and use. This is not surprising when one notes Stephen's earlier description of spring house repair and construction as involving both genders, with men doing the "heavy lugging" of stone and timber and women doing the roof and wall thatching and plastering (1936:284).

In his dissertation Moore (1979) went to great lengths to report the ethnographic range in field house architecture, associated artifacts and activities, seasonality, function, location, and social makeup. These included the lengths and periods of use for field houses of various cultures during each growing season, termed temporal patterns of use (Moore 1979:268). Of particular interest was just how intensively some field houses (or "ranchitos," as they were known in the Eastern Pueblos [Moore 1979:270]) were used. Reference upon reference have some variation of the following: "A generation ago and earlier, almost every family occupied a ranchito for extended periods, if not for the entire growing season" (Lange 1959:42, speaking of Cochiti Pueblo, in Moore 1979:270). It is possible that the "ranchito" was more analogous to Moore's "summer village" (1979:135), but consider Hack's (1942:28) comment that Hopi field houses at distant fields were used during the entire summer or Hoover's observation that "someone goes out to the fields every day, or some go and stay out for a number of weeks but return to the villages for dances and for the winter" (1930:434, in Moore 1979:269). At the very least, field houses are occupied continuously during the period between crop maturation and harvest—"these huts were often occupied by the entire family during the period of roasting green corn and during the main harvest" (Forde 1931:391, on the Hopi, in Moore 1979:269).

Navajo field structures can also serve as analogs for potential prehistoric counterparts. The works by Spencer (1969) and Jett and Spencer (1981) focused on the architecture of Navajo dwelling types, with an emphasis on diagnostic, major, and minor features such as construction materials and techniques, walls, floors, doorways, and the like. Under the category of "Temporary and Summer Dwellings" they listed the following: windbreaks, conical forked-pole shades, lean-to shades, and flat-roofed shades (ramadas). Of interest to the present study are their descriptions of ramadas and, perhaps, forked-pole shades: A conical forked-pole shade is essentially the Navajo version of the northern Athapaskan "conical, pole-and-bark-covered hut with a tripod foundation" (Jett and Spencer 1981:36–37), which might elsewhere be termed a wickiup. Small poles, or leaners, are placed between the main tripod poles and covered with brush, boughs, bark, and such. The shade forms a circular, oval, or possibly D-shaped plan. Meanwhile, "the ramada or flat-roofed shade consists of a flat roof of poles or boughs supported on stringers running between four vertical posts" (Jett and Spencer 1981:41). The structure can be unwalled or walled with almost any available material, but typically poles and brush or boughs are used. It is generally rectangular in plan, but other shapes are known. The roofs are not usually earth covered but can be used for drying and storage. Ramadas are used both for summer living and as shelters for guests at ceremonials.

Russell (1978:35) identified three types of Navajo field houses in the Klethla Valley of northern Arizona based principally on differences resulting from length of occupation: (1) occupied during an entire field season, (2) occupied during periods of peak agricultural labor, and (3) occupied for perhaps a week or less at harvest time. Structural variation correlated with the length of time a field house was occupied (or was intended to be occupied), which has a direct bearing on the permanence of the structure. As might be expected, "the longer a site is to be occupied, the more labor is expended on the construction of its structures and the sturdier they are" (Russell 1978:36). This parallels Kent's (1992) model about anticipated mobility. Ramadas, circular brush shades, and even hogans belong to the first type—structures occupied for an entire growing season. Circular brush shades constitute the primary shelter for intermittent occupations, and lean-tos, windbreaks, and camps without structures are used for only occasional visits.

Regarding associated remains, Russell identified two aspects of field house use that can produce unexpected patterns in the archaeological record. The first is year-to-year reoccupation such that field houses, even comparatively humble dwellings, can have associated trash areas (Russell 1978:37–38). Tools and materials, however, are usually few, and most usable items are returned to the winter residence; in some cases, items are cached, often in trees. Broken and worn-out tools are discarded at the field house. The second pattern is that corn-roasting pits and storage pits (for shelled or whole-ear corn and squash) are often associated with field houses or located next to the field itself (Russell 1978:38), with each family using from one to four storage pits (Hill 1938:42–43). The pits are hidden but unobtrusively marked to aid in relocating them. The storage pits are visited several times during the winter to restock food supplies. Thus preserved, stored goods can last up to two years if kept dry (Hill 1938:45).

Placement on the landscape is also worth mentioning. The Navajo ideally located field houses within 100 m of the field, preferably on top of a low rise, ridge, or knoll (although sometimes in or immediately adjacent to the field itself [Russell 1978:38; see also Hill 1938; Spencer 1969]). And "summer sites [tend] to be located near arable, unforested, alluvial, flood-plain lands along valleys" (Rocek 1988:525). This pattern of locating field houses immediately adjacent to, if not within, agricultural fields is predictable on the basis of foraging theory since a transitory home established for the purpose of food production needs to be located so as to enhance the efficiency of the associated work; otherwise why bother? A good answer is to legitimize claims of ownership or use rights to fields, as Kohler (1992) has argued.

Since field houses should thus be explicitly located next to farmable land, secondary habitations situated in other than farmable places are not likely to be field houses. Depending on the environment, making such a judgment might be easy or hard. In the Kayenta region, including on the NMRAP, archaeologists are perhaps encouraged in making the field house inference when the site under consideration overlooks a modern Navajo field. Several examples of this were observed. Of course propinquity to modern fields does not necessarily have implications for past situations, although such an inference is almost impossible to avoid. Yet traditional farmers are few and far between these days, and even so, past practices may have been different, such that retrodicting what was farmable based on current evidence is suspect. The well-used and favored farming situations today were likely similarly so in the past, but what about the areas less used or unused today?

Besides making simple analogies for the functional role of settlements, the ethnographic record can also serve as a source of information for modeling expectations for the archaeological record concerning site seasonality and residential mobility more generally. Shirley Powell (1983) and Susan Kent (1992), among others, have done this, and their two studies will provide a useful background context before delving into the NMRAP sample of secondary habitations.

Powell's Black Mesa Study

Powell (1983) was concerned with the issue of residential mobility, which entails the seasonality of small sites rather than with field houses per se. The ethnographic foundation for her analysis included the Pai and Navajo from Arizona, forager-farmers and herder-farmers, respectively, but excluded the Hopi or other Puebloan groups, whom, she explained, "live in very large villages—relative to the size of northeastern Black Mesa settlements—and for this reason are an inappropriate analog" (1983:54). Although the scale of Kayenta Anasazi habitations, even at their largest, is miniscule compared to modern-day Hopi or Zuni villages, aspects of *field sites* old and recent are probably comparable. But Powell's more central concern with using the Hopi/Zuni analog was perhaps their degree of reliance on farming and evident long-term sedentism, both aspects that she doubted were applicable to the Pueblo I and Pueblo II Kayenta Anasazi on Black Mesa. Yet one does not preclude the other: the Kayenta Anasazi could have been heavily reliant on field produce (which is what stable isotope analysis reveals [e.g., Coltrain et al. 2007]) and still have had a modest degree of residential mobility, perhaps not intra-annually but at least interannually or on some larger time scale, one perhaps largely dependent on the unpredictable vagaries of climate. Powell's conclusions regarding prehistoric cultural change on Black Mesa were later criticized by Plog (1986), but the data on Navajo field houses may still be useful for modeling some expectations for the patterning of prehistoric remains.

Powell (1983:Table 42) presented several expected material culture patterns for Anasazi *summer habitations* that could easily be seen as applying to NMRAP secondary habitations generally or to field houses specifically: less interior habitation area, more exterior habitation area, more total site area, smaller structures, located near arable upland, fewer interior hearths, more exterior hearths, and lower artifact density. Powell determined that some of the variables covaried to a greater or lesser degree with site type and season of use. We generally agree that structures used in the summer while tending fields should usually have less interior space than winter houses, but not for the reasons that Powell suggests—group size is a critical variable as well as the intended uses of interior space and the frequency of such use. Field houses might well have been occupied by smaller groups—portions of families—compared to winter houses, and a smaller range of activities likely took place in summer houses simply because one could comfortably work outdoors. Her values for Navajo sites ("sites with interior areas less than 25 m^2 are likely to be summer-occupied" [1983:77]) have little relevance for Kayenta sites, where all interior space tends to be quite small. The total interior space for the NMRAP primary habitation of Hymn House is just 12 m^2 (see Figures 6.29–6.30). Still, this floor area is far more than those seen at secondary habitations because they generally consist of single structures, whereas Hymn House, as the smallest sort of primary habitation, comprises three rooms of different functional type, something not generally true of secondary habitations. Naakai Hooghan, the largest NMRAP secondary habitation, has 13.6 m^2 of floor space, but since the structures at this site are probably not all contemporaneous, the floor area in use at any one time was probably less than 9 m^2. The floor area of the Pueblo II component at Hillside Hermitage, a secondary habitation with two functionally differentiated rooms (living and mealing), is just 7.2 m^2.

Plog disputed Powell's suggestion that winter-occupied dwellings tend to be larger than summer-occupied dwellings (1986:192–193), citing mean sizes for winter homesteads (17.3 m^2) and sheep camps (13.8 m^2) that are comparable with that of summer field houses. On the other hand, his average size of homesteads occupied year round (25.5 m^2) was, interestingly, nearly identical with the figure Powell used to demarcate summer field sites from other site types.

Powell's expectation that summer habitation sites could have more exterior and total site space than winter habitation sites is suspect on several grounds, and indeed, we would anticipate just the opposite pattern. Longer duration of use, larger group size, and greater activity diversity at primary habitations should result in larger scatters of remains (greater exterior site areas) than comparatively briefly occupied and more task-specific field houses. The issue has to do with the visibility of remains in the archaeological record; those at a primary residence cover more area than those at a secondary residence in almost all cases. This said, Powell's expectation did not pan out for Anasazi sites: "The pattern of occurrence of exterior area on sites was counter to the expectations.... [S]ites with great amounts of interior area also [tend] to have large amounts of exterior space" (1983:111).

Powell's expected pattern for site location, defined as winter sites having proximity to hunted and gathered resources (uplands) and summer sites having proximity to potential farm parcels (lowlands), proved wrong, but then the expectation was too simplistic to start with and extension of the underlying Pai ethnographic model to the Black Mesa Anasazi case is dubious. As Powell (1983:42–43) herself has observed, the upland/lowland dichotomy was poorly defined and any site on the BMAP lease is within a few hundred meters of both zones. That issue aside, the economics of food movement alone (Barlow and Metcalfe 1996; Jones and Madsen 1989; Rhode 1990) suggest that primary habitations will be located next to the bulky and comparatively low-return resources of fields (this includes maize [Barlow 2002]), with high-return resources such as hunted game and pinyon nuts transported as needed to the residential sites. In other words, there would be no reason to locate a winter residence in the uplands to be near pinyon nuts and game, especially in a setting where these "uplands" are less than a few minutes' walk away. Unless there is some critical compelling reason otherwise, such as need for a defendable location, residential sites should be situated next to food resources that are bulky relative to their net energy gain or to patches that provide such resources when these constitute a spatially and temporally predictable source.

In this context it is worth recalling Bradfield's observations about maize transportation at Hopi, where 120–144 bushels of corn per household had to be moved annually from the field to the village: "Given…the size of crop required by each household, the physical labor of carrying in that weight of corn (on the cob) *must*…have precluded the use of any considerable acreage of farm land sited more than four miles from the parent village" (1971:22). If two adults transported this amount from fields 4 mi distant, for example, it would take at least six weeks to bring in the harvest. Perhaps not coincidentally, the 4-mi radius essentially delimited the historic "clan lands" of Old Oraibi. Although he perhaps grossly underestimates how much weight an adult male can carry daily over long distances (Malville 2001), Bradfield's insights are probably generally right. More important, his observations and conclusions can be turned on their head and applied in the other direction to the earlier periods of Puebloan prehistory: villages would not be sited more than 4 mi from the primary fields so as to reduce the transport of heavy low-return resources, and maize is low return despite accounting for a large proportion of the daily calories (see Barlow 2002). The returns on pinyon are so much higher than for maize and it is so much more nutrient dense that it could easily be transported great distances to residences situated next to abundant low-return resources. This is one of Barlow and Metcalfe's (1996) main points, which is easily extended to the situation of Puebloan farmers who lived close to their maize fields but traveled far and wide for pinyon nuts and deer. The tethering of habitations to productive field locations makes great sense in the Pueblo I and Pueblo II period that Powell considered since there were no compelling reasons for settlement in just a few select locations away from fields as was true at Hopi, whether for social factors or mutual defense.

Powell (1983) examined the frequently used assumption that hearth location indicates the season of occupation. For example, "hearths will be located out-of-doors in the summer to avoid overheating shelter interiors" (Powell 1983:79). In her comparison, none of the Black Mesa pinyon camps had exterior hearths (all had a single interior hearth), but 60 percent of the field houses had exterior hearths. Her conclusion that "fall–winter sites are characterized by interior hearths, whereas spring–summer sites are characterized by exterior hearths" (1983:81) is perhaps a tad simplistic. Indeed, 67 percent of the summer Navajo field houses examined by Powell (1983:Table 15) had interior hearths. Since field house use can range from late spring through early fall, regarding them as "summer" residences is perhaps misleading. Climatological data from the Coppermine Trading Post at 1,946 m (6,380 ft) show a mean minimum temperature of 44.3°F for May, when planting is likely to begin, and 50.1°F for September, the peak of harvest (Sellers and Hill 1974:166). The record low for the five-month period between May and September was 25°F. Dissipating tropical disturbances can also bring tremendous rain, usually in September. The implication is that field house residents may well have needed occasional interior fires for warmth and to "take the edge off" of chills following intense downpours. What seems safe to conclude is that structures lacking hearths were not winter residences and indeed were perhaps briefly occupied; those with small and little-used basin hearths were also probably not winter residences but perhaps saw more seasons of use and longer durations of use. It is also important to note in passing that hearth use might have nothing to do with cooking and keeping warm—Navajo sweat baths can generate considerable quantities of charcoal and burned rock.

Several of the NMRAP secondary habitations lacked interior hearths, but several contained them. Most were unlined basins rather than the formal slab-lined affairs of living rooms at primary residential sites, but there were a few of those as well. Exterior hearths were present at most of the sites; The Slots provides numerous examples. This mix of interior and exterior hearths may be more typical of field house situations than previously assumed and is perhaps a simple reflection of the climatic variability of the seasons during which secondary habitations were occupied, especially if they had roles in activities such as pinyon nut harvesting, which occurs in the cooler fall months.

Kent's Mobility Model

Kent's (1992) ethnoarchaeological study, like that of Powell, was concerned not with field houses per se but with developing a model for distinguishing between short-term (seasonal) and long-term (year-round) Puebloan occupations. Based on research among Kalahari Desert communities in Botswana, she deduced that "anticipated mobility appears to be the strongest predictor of various facets of site structure" (1992:641). In other words, how long a group *plans* to inhabit a site has a greater bearing on site variables such as site size, size of habitation structures, presence or absence of certain features, and material abundance or diversity than actual length of stay. When comparing anticipated occupation with actual occupation, four outcomes are possible: (1) long anticipated occupation–long actual occupation (long/long), (2) long anticipated occupation–short actual occupation (long/short), (3) short anticipated occupation–long actual occupation (short/long), and (4) short anticipated occupation–short actual occupation (short/short). Thus, application of Kent's ethnographic model, theoretically, not only can discriminate between occupations of short and long duration (seasonal vs. year round) but can also identify sites where "occupants planned one thing and actually did another" (1992:652). This feature adds some verisimilitude to the study of short- and long-term occupations.

The results of Kent's work in the Kalahari indicate that "anticipated length of occupation…is a stronger predictor of site size, square meters per person, and the diameter of huts than are the other variables tested"; she adds that "the presence/absence of formal storage loci also is dependent on how long inhabitants plan to reside at a camp" (1992:639). Furthermore, people tend to dispose of trash in formal middens when they anticipate a longer stay and, likewise, disperse trash in unconcentrated scatters on the margins of sites when they anticipate a short stay. Finally, "people who plan to stay a short time will bring less objects to a site than those who plan to stay a long time" (Kent 1992:641). The only variable that accounts for more variance in the amount of cultural remains is "site type."

Using her "mobility model," Kent compared aspects of five prehistoric Pueblo II sites excavated during the Dolores Archaeological Project (DAP) in southwestern Colorado. The aspects were site size, architecture and site structure, formal storage loci, and material culture abundance and diversity. Site size is simply "the absolute extent of the site as inferred from the distribution of surface artifacts/features" (Kent 1992:644; see also Yellen 1977:103), with anticipated length of occupation being a strong predictor of size (Kent 1992:639). Of interest to this study is that the smaller the site, the shorter the anticipated duration of occupation. The full sizes of some of the NMRAP sites are unknown because of prior disturbance or ROW limits, but for several sites the size is well known, as the sites were entirely excavated. Liberal calculations for the largest of the N16 secondary habitation sites results in a size of 400 m^2 (Naaki Hooghan), considerably smaller than even the smallest DAP settlement that Kent studied, at a little over 1,000 m^2, and the only one considered to have a "short/short" occupation. By this measure, the N16 secondary habitations appear to reflect short anticipated occupations.

Architecture and site structure are relative measures of the range and size of architectural features at a site, specifically size of habitation structures and presence or absence of a midden. Kent believes that "site population influences the *number* of habitation structures at a site but does not determine their *size*, which is instead influenced by anticipated mobility" (1992:639, emphasis added; see also Kent and Vierich 1989). In other words, "structures are larger when occupants anticipate a long rather than a short habitation, regardless of the number of people living in the dwellings" (Kent 1992:639). Curiously, Kent was reluctant to compare "specific number and size of rooms" of DAP sites, due to concerns about comparability between "ethnoarchaeological camps" and Pueblo II sites (1992:643). Her discussion of Pueblo II architecture and site structure was, for this reason, mostly a qualitative comparison without reference to the ethnoarchaeological model.

As Kent pointed out, all but the smallest of the DAP sites had rooms or room blocks, kivas, and middens. The smallest (Paintbrush House) had only a small, shallow kiva. Except for Naaki Hooghan and Hillside Hermitage, the NMRAP secondary habitations each had just one habitation structure. None of the structures were more than 8 m^2 in size. Using an estimate of 4 m^2 of floor area per person (following Anyon and LeBlanc 1984), each structure could have reasonably housed from one to two individuals.[4] This is considerably less than a household unit of five people, defined here as two adults and three subadults (Wills and Windes 1989:363), suggesting short-term or sporadic use by individual family members. Warm-weather sites, of course, can support extramural activity areas that elevate the numbers of concurrent residents. Such areas were identified at some but not all of the secondary habitations and might be an important variable. For example, the numerous hearths at The Slots attest to considerable extramural activity involving fire, but the small structure there still could have housed only a few people, and then not very comfortably. The size and limited number of structures at NMRAP secondary habitations appear to reflect both short anticipated occupations and small populations per structure.

Nearly all of the NMRAP secondary habitations had middens. At sedentary Basarwa camps, "refuse at anticipated medium- and long-term habitations tends to be disposed of at formal loci more often than at short-term sites" (Kent 1992:641), although small sites can have middens if residents *anticipate* a long occupation. We suspect that the association of middens with structures at Puebloan sites was conditioned more by social mores than by intended length of stay, but this assumption may not hold with smaller, more expedient constructs such as field houses.

Kent (1992:639) found that formal storage facilities such as granaries or cache pits were absent from sites of anticipated short occupation regardless of how long such sites were ultimately used. This is also true of all the NMRAP secondary habitations. As mentioned earlier, the presence of storage features has sometimes been a defining attribute of field house or farmstead sites and is a common component of Navajo and Hopi field-tending sites. A brief review of the literature concerning prehistoric field houses suggests that—like middens—there is much more variability in storage presence or absence than assumed. An example of "storage-free" field houses from the Cave Creek area is found in Rodgers 1978; excavated structures had no storage features and revealed "a total absence of any economic, micro- or macrobotanical remains" (1978:155). But it is conceivable that some groups might maintain storage pits of sufficient capacity to hold seed for next year's planting in or near field houses.

Material culture abundance and diversity offer several avenues of inquiry regarding duration of site occupation. According to Kent's model, "anticipated and actual short occupations should have fewer artifacts and more homogeneous assemblages than…longer occupations" (1992:647). Kent focused primarily on the quantity and diversity (richness) of ceramic, lithic, faunal, and micro- and macrobotanical remains. The number of ceramic types cannot be compared across regions and across significantly different temporal periods, e.g., DAP Pueblo I sites with Pueblo II and Pueblo III sites of the Kayenta region. Through time there is an increase in the number of types represented in a region regardless of site function or different recovery methods and sample sizes, and in the Kayenta region there are three ware traditions with many different identified types, far more than for the Mesa Verde area. By dividing the total number of sherds by the number of ceramic types, Kent arrived at an "abundance index…to hold sample size constant" (1992:646–647). To control for the increase in type number through time one would also need to make comparisons only within given temporal intervals.

There is risk in placing too much emphasis on any one of the artifacts and nonartifactual remains, as the data come from several projects across different regions and time periods that used, presumably, somewhat idiosyncratic methods and analysis techniques. Still, Kent notes that "attributing all differences to sampling error…is not a very productive way to view the archaeological record" (1992:653), and we agree.

General inferences are possible if one views the results as a *relative set* of contrasts. There has also been one study, coincidently utilizing data from Pueblo I sites excavated during the Dolores project, that simulated the effects of occupation duration on artifact assemblages; the simulation was then tested on a subset of excavated DAP sites (Schlanger 1990). The author concluded that "total artifact number appears to be a good indicator of occupation duration and intensity. This comforting result holds for individual artifact type totals, including sherds, debitage, and projectile points" (Schlanger 1990:114–115). Also useful, as a diversity measure, was "the number of artifact types present in an assemblage" (Schlanger 1990:119), although what constituted an artifact type was not defined. As Kent suggested, diversity increases with occupation length. Measures of proportions and ratios, however, are generally less useful, especially for sites occupied for a short time. Vessels or portions thereof (sherds as tools and containers) as well as stone tools may have been brought into secondary habitations rather than being made there, but in part this depends on the length of occupation. The longer a place is occupied, the greater the chance for debris to accumulate as old tools are refurbished or replaced by new ones produced on-site.

The NMRAP Sample

Figure 6.35 illustrates examples of secondary habitations excavated by NMRAP—eight of the 13 such sites excavated. In this figure late Pueblo II examples occur in the upper two rows, with Pueblo III examples in the bottom row. The NMRAP sample includes six from late Pueblo II, with a possible seventh occurring at Ditch House but poorly differentiated from the middle Pueblo III primary habitation at that location; one from early Pueblo

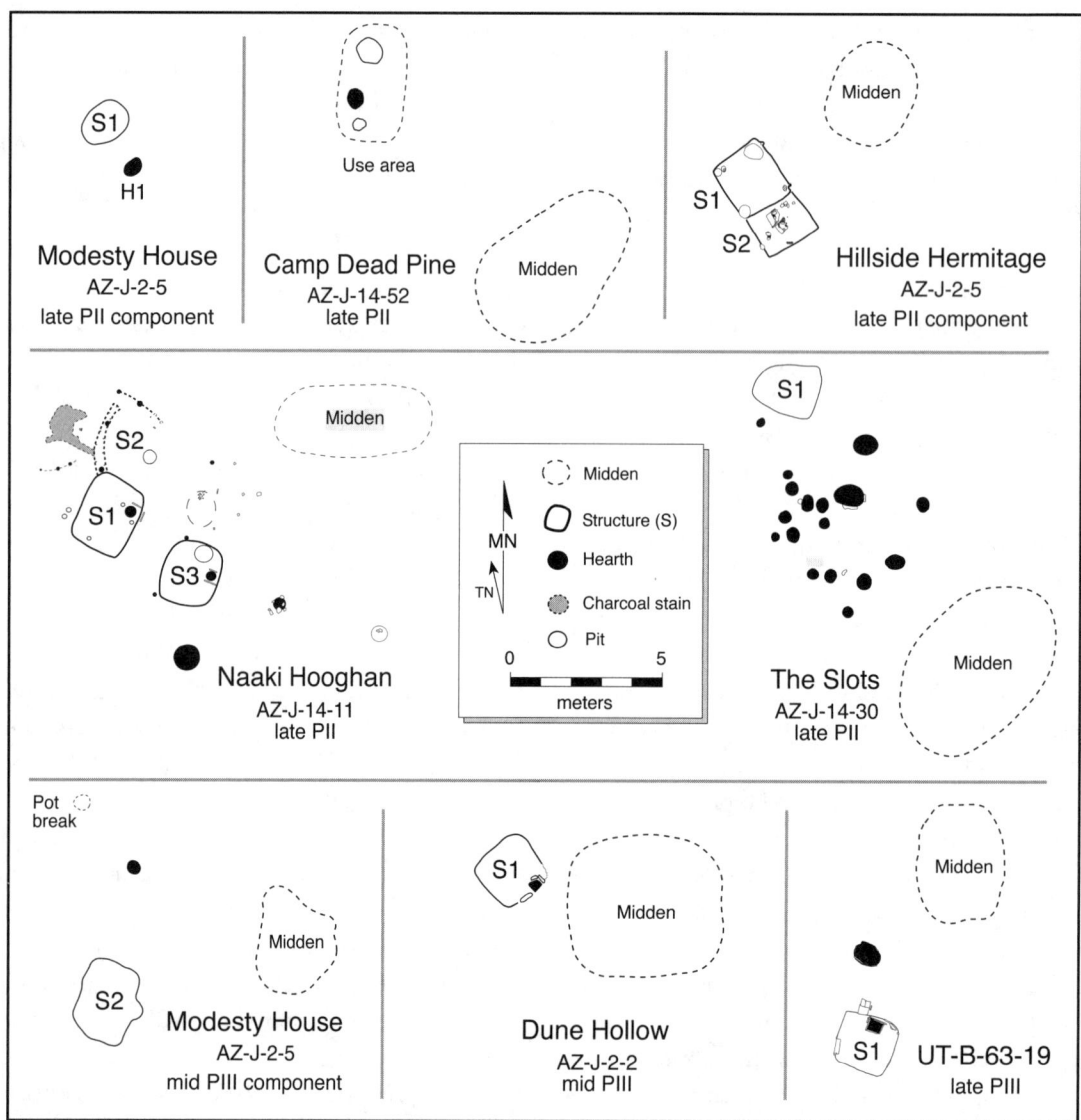

Figure 6.35. Examples of Puebloan secondary habitations excavated within the N16 right-of-way.

III (Mouse House) that was badly damaged; three from middle Pueblo III; one from either middle or late Pueblo III; and one from late Pueblo III. No secondary habitations were identified from middle Pueblo II or earlier; the single Pueblo I site lacked a structure and is thought to have functioned as a temporary camp. Although the secondary habitations are generally distinct as a group from those classified as primary habitations, there is considerable variability among them, both in architecture and in artifacts (abundance, type, and diversity). This variability likely results from many factors, such as different settlement roles (i.e., not all are field houses), differing group sizes or compositions (one individual vs. many, an entire family vs. some portion, both sexes vs. a single gender), diverse seasons, differences between intended and actual use-lives, and others. Some of the variability is cap-

tured in Table 6.13, which presents some basic data for 10 of the 13 secondary habitations. Three sites are excluded from comparison because of disturbance (Mouse House) or mixture from other components (Kin Kahuna and Ditch House). The table presents counts of various artifact classes and bones, counts standardized by number of structures (quantity per structure), and ratios of various artifact classes such as sherds to flakes and debitage to facial flaked tools. As this table shows there are some marked differences: with total sherd counts and sherds per structure ranging from 9 to 1,093, total flake counts and flakes per structure ranging from 11 to 1,239, and total bone counts and bones per structure ranging from 1 to 133.

Overall the NMRAP sample of Puebloan residential sites generally reveals little gray area between those classified as primary habitations and those classified as

TABLE 6.13. Comparison Among Navajo Mountain Road Archaeological Project Secondary Habitations with Comparable Levels of Investigation Using Overall Artifact and Bone Counts, Counts per Structure, and Ratios of Certain Artifact Classes

Site Name	Sh	Sh/Str	Mod Sh	% Mod Sh	Deb	Deb/Str	Deb/Sh	FT	FT/Str	Deb/FT	C&N	C&N/Str	Deb/C&N	Deb/FT+C&N	GT	GT/Str	GT/FT	Sh/GT	Misc	Misc/Str	Total Tools	Bone	Bone/Str	Bone Artifacts
UT-B-63-19	355	355.0	0	—	413	413.0	1.2	6	6.0	68.8	9	9.0	45.9	27.5	28	28.0	4.7	12.7	2	2.0	45	66	66.0	1
Bonsai Bivouac	568	568.0	6	1.1	194	194.0	.3	3	3.0	64.7	6	6.0	32.3	21.6	18	18.0	6.0	31.6	0	0.0	27	19	19.0	0
Modesty House, Late Pueblo II	9	9.0	0	—	11	11.0	1.2	0	0	—	0	.0	—	—	1	1.0	—	9.0	0	0.0	1	0	.0	0
Modesty House, Middle Pueblo III	1,093	1,093.0	6	.5	135	135.0	.1	2	2	67.5	8	8.0	16.9	13.5	9	9.0	4.5	121.4	0	0.0	19	2	2.0	0
Dune Hollow	203	203.0	0	—	22	22.0	.1	0	0	—	3	3.0	7.3	7.3	1	1.0	—	203.0	0	0.0	4	10	10.0	0
Hillside	268	134.0	1	.5	160	80.0	.6	2	1	80.0	9	4.5	17.8	14.5	3	1.5	1.5	89.3	0	0.0	14	1	.5	0
Hermitage, Late Pueblo II	425	425.0	1	.2	243	243.0	.6	0	0	—	11	11.0	22.1	22.1	1	1.0	—	425.0	3	3.0	15	2	2.0	0
Camp Dead Pine	413	206.5	0	—	740	370.0	1.8	4	2	185.0	12	6.0	61.7	46.3	9	4.5	2.3	45.9	12	6.0	37	69	34.5	4
Tres Campos	930	310.0	0	—	299	99.7	.3	5	1.7	59.8	17	5.7	17.6	13.6	21	7.0	4.2	44.3	3	1.0	46	25	8.3	0
Naaki Hooghan	30	30.0	0	—	1,239	1,239.0	41.3	6	6	206.5	12	12.0	103.3	68.8	5	5.0	.8	6.0	19	19.0	42	133	133.0	5
The Slots	4,294	3,333.5	14	2.3	3,456	2,806.7	47.5	28	21.7	732.3	87	65.2	324.9	235.2	96	76.0	24.0	988.2	39	31.0	250	327	275.3	10
Total																								
Average	429.4	333.4	1.4	.2	345.6	280.7	4.8	2.8	2.2	104.6	8.7	6.5	36.1	26.1	9.6	7.6	3.4	98.8	3.9	3.1	25	32.7	27.5	1.0

Note: Sites are organized from north to south. Sh = sherds; Str = structure; Mod Sh = modified sherds; Deb = debitage; FT = flaked facial tools; C&N = cores/nodular tools; GT = grinding tools (manos and metates); Misc = other stone artifacts.

secondary habitations. Both contain at least one living structure, but the structures at secondary habitations tend to be small, are less substantially built, and frequently lack hearths, suggesting warm-season use. There is also a general lack of functionally differentiated rooms at secondary residential sites such as mealing rooms, kivas, and those for storage aside from those for living and general activities, yet such specialized rooms are ubiquitous at primary residential sites. Plog observes in his criticism of Powell that "a diversity of different functional types of structures also is characteristic of more permanent settlements among Pueblo and Great Basin groups" (1986:193). There is but a single NMRAP site—Naaki Hooghan, which is the largest and structurally most substantial of any secondary habitation—that comes close to straddling the line between primary and secondary habitations. This late Pueblo II settlement along the divide between Piute and Navajo canyons had two subrectangular jacal living rooms, both containing hearths, a ramada attached to one of these houses, an extramural activity area with a dismantled mealing bin that might represent the remnants of a ramada attached to the second house, a few outside hearths and pits, and a shallow, eroded midden (see Figure 6.35). Three significant aspects of this site suggest that it was not a primary residence: (1) the lack of a deep pit structure or kiva, (2) the lack of large-volume storage features, and (3) the presence of rather informal and little-used basin hearths in the structures accompanied by scant charcoal accumulation in the small midden. Each of these speaks to behavior that presumably tracks with the degree of residential permanence and a lack of occupancy through the long cold months of winter.

Moreover, since the structures appear to have been used sequentially rather than being contemporaneous, the site actually housed only one social group at a time. This greatly simplifies the appearance of the site, and the remains recovered should be roughly apportioned half to each occupation (the artifacts per structure in Table 6.13 are based on a structure count of three because of the ramada attached to Structure 1). The lack of specially prepared, large-volume storage features, such as cists or bell-shaped pits, is significant. The two houses may have provided storage using large jars, but the sherd assemblage suggests few storage jars at the site. This lack of storage suggests that the site was occupied during a time when food surpluses were unnecessary, such as during the growing season. Occupation during warmer times of the year is evidenced by the comparatively small, less formalized, and little-used hearths within the structures as well as by the rather charcoal-poor midden. The absence of a kiva is also a significant factor in suggesting a seasonal occupation. The low number of artifacts from the site, including those with a relatively high discard rate, such as sherds ($n = 930$) and debitage ($n = 299$), is indicative of a moderately short occupation length. The total of 21 grinding tools from the site (mostly manos) seems like quite a few and certainly indicates daily food processing, but this assemblage is relatively expedient and recycled, with the tools made of local Navajo Sandstone slabs that were minimally shaped. The extent of investment in two living structures indicates that the occupants planned on using the site more than once. The intended and actual use of the site, therefore, may have been as a seasonally reoccupied, short-duration habitation associated with some essential annual extractive task(s). The natural question is what such a task was (or tasks were), a topic covered later.

Only one other NMRAP secondary habitation—the late Pueblo II component at Hillside Hermitage—contained two rooms, which consisted of a shallow living room and an attached mealing room (see Figure 6.35). The presence of rooms with distinct functions is notable, especially since one contains two mealing bins, which indicates a moderate amount of food processing for domestic purposes, an interpretation supported by the recovery of maize in all four flotation samples along with other likely food items such as the seeds of ground-cherry, purslane, and grass. A shallow pit in the living structure appears to have served as a heating basin, but the lack of a true interior hearth, along with sparse charcoal accumulation in the tiny midden, suggests use of this settlement during the warm months. The lack of food-storage facilities is also consistent with use during the growing season. The sparse trash (268 sherds, 160 flakes) and small midden argue for a limited occupation span, with use perhaps lasting for just a few seasons. Other than a small segment of masonry along the back wall of Structure 1, the architecture was insubstantial. Jacal probably formed most of the Structure 1 walls and perhaps part of Structure 2 as well; brush probably completed the Structure 2 enclosure. Interior features were limited to a few small pits and the two mealing bins. As it happens, Hillside Hermitage is located next to a probable field area at the confluence of two drainages, an area still farmed today by Navajo families. As a result it is difficult not to assume that this component functioned as a field house. The two rooms provide a roofed floor area of just over 7 m², which is not much, but by Kayentan standards perhaps sufficient for a nuclear family, especially for limited summer use. Construction of a somewhat formal and moderately durable structure in this location perhaps had as much to do with providing seasonal shelter with an anticipated long use-life as marking ownership or use rights to a coveted farm parcel.

At the other end of the spectrum is the late Pueblo II component at Modesty House, which consisted of a small brush enclosure and an adjacent extramural hearth. The oval structure, which had burned, measured just 1.7 × 1.3 m, providing about 2 m² of floor area. It may have been cleaned out prior to abandonment, but likely few utensils were ever present; the total artifact yield for this component was nine sherds, 11 flakes, and one grinding tool. The shallow basin floor was unprepared, and there were no interior features. A scattering of rocks within the structural depression and around its perimeter likely served to stabilize the brush walls. The structure probably served as both a shade and a windbreak, and it may have been comparable to the simple uncovered shade described and illustrated by Mindeleff (1891:217–218, Figure 111), which was created by placing a dozen or so branches into the ground to create a slightly curved enclosure against which brush was stacked and interwoven. Whereas the late Pueblo II component at Hillside Hermitage was perhaps used as a family residence for some portion of the growing season, the late Pueblo II component at Modesty House was a day-use facility for a family member who probably resided nearby and went home every night. Had the Pueblo II brush structure not burned, then it likely would have gone unrecognized.

The later component at Modest House, which dates to middle Pueblo III, perhaps 100 years after the initial shade house, presents another facet of variability. The midden of this secondary habitation was small but moderately concentrated, and the nature of deposits indicated discontinuous site use. Numerous charred corncobs, kernels, and stalk fragments in the deposit demonstrated that some burning took place within the midden, either deliberately or through the addition of live coals to the organic trash; some of the sherds in the midden were burned. The two midden flotation samples both contained maize (cob portions and a kernel fragment) but no other carbonized subsistence remains. The site setting seemed well suited to tending fields, and the recovered macrobotanical remains are consistent with such an inference. The structure at this component was a roughly square room with a floor area of 4.2 m², which is small compared to the average for living

Figure 6.36. Structure 2 of the middle Pueblo III component of Modesty House, excavated during its construction up to 32 cm into the Navajo Sandstone bedrock, which represents considerable effort for a probable field house.

rooms at primary habitations. The room lacked a hearth; interior features were limited to postholes and two shallow pits. The lower walls of the structure were created by excavating 70 cm below the prehistoric occupation surface, including cutting 32 cm into sandstone bedrock, no easy task without metal picks (Figure 6.36). The lack of storage features or an interior hearth is consistent with seasonal occupancy, yet despite this the effort represented in construction would seem to imply some degree of building for anticipated long-term use, even though the intended interval of occupancy was seasonal. Greater investment in the architecture of field houses might be related to greater emphasis on the control of field ownership, as argued by Kohler (1992), which on the Rainbow Plateau could have become an important issue after AD 1200 as the Anasazi population reached an all-time high and large villages began to form. There is clearly an abundance of sites resembling field houses on the Rainbow Plateau that are ceramically dated to the middle to late Pueblo III interval. Dry farming in the thirteenth century may have been a risky business and quite variable (see Dean 1988a, 1988b; Dean et al. 1985), such that it might have benefited families to have diverse field settings to take advantage of microclimatic fluctuations, soil conditions, and changing social responsibilities or networks. The consolidation of the population into large villages meant that farmers had to travel farther to their fields than previously when habitations were scattered and adjacent to farm parcels. This alone could increase the number of field houses but not necessarily change how they were constructed—greater labor investment, increased longevity/durability of construction—which seems more in line

Figure 6.37. View of the divide between Piute and Navajo canyons looking north from The Slots, with Navajo Mountain in the distance peaking out from behind the high ridge center top.

with Kohler's argument about marking field ownership or use rights.

Modesty House, like most of the NMRAP secondary habitations, appears analogous to Russell's (1978) description of Navajo field houses, situated in proximity to farmable land in the form of drainages, basins, and sandy flats and often located on adjacent higher slopes or rises about 1–3 m above the surrounding landscapes. In some cases the potential field association is obvious at sites such as Hillside Hermitage and Mouse House, which are within 100 m of currently used Navajo fields along a drainage. Dune Hollow, Modesty House, and Bonsai Bivouac are located in the sagebrush flats of the central Rainbow Plateau, settings that were likely dry-farmed just as Navajos continue to do today, although currently in-use fields are not close at hand to these sites. UT-B-63-19 is situated in the flats at the foot of Navajo Mountain in a similar setting—one potentially farmed but without a close-by currently in-use field. But not all of the NMRAP secondary habitations are within 100 m of obvious arable land, with three on the divide between Navajo and Piute canyons being obvious examples—Naaki Hooghan, The Slots, and Tres Campos. Camp Dead Pine would also seem to fit this scenario, though it is situated closer to the southeast edge of the Rainbow Plateau, where there are areas that appear more conducive to farming.

Were They All Field Houses?

Propinquity to some resource or environment is potentially shaky ground for assignment of site function, but it provides the principal piece of evidence for the field house designation. Although we are convinced that sites like Naaki Hooghan were occupied seasonally, their role within an overall settlement-subsistence system is somewhat enigmatic. A seasonal habitation associated with field tending seems unlikely given the apparent lack of obvious arable land within the immediate vicinity. As just mentioned, this site was situated on the divide between Piute and Navajo canyons along with The Slots and Tres Campos, within several hundred meters of one another. With little soil and large slickrock exposures (Figure 6.37), this divide seems an unlikely setting for agricultural fields. Indeed, the forested upland appears better suited to foraging and hunting, and the divide provides a natural travel corridor between the Rainbow and Shonto plateaus. There are currently no Navajo fields anywhere along this divide. Numerous Basketmaker II secondary habitations are also located along this divide around the three Puebloan sites considered here (see discussion in chapter 5). Settlement patterns of course may have changed between Basketmaker II and Pueblo II, but still it is worth considering what might have been the potential commonality. Prime farmland is located not too far away in Upper

Piute Canyon, where deep alluvium coincides with abundant flowing water from springs for irrigation or subirrigation farming. To efficiently exploit canyon fields, camps should be located within the canyon proper rather than several kilometers away and more than 200 m higher in elevation. Furthermore, there are many primary residential settlements in Piute Canyon, perhaps obviating the need for any field houses in the canyon and certainly those located on the canyon rim.

Although the presence of in-use or recently used fields colors our perceptions of where farming is practicable and encourages a field house designation for secondary habitations adjacent to historic field areas, this might be stacking the deck against areas like the divide considered here. We may have a poor notion of how Anasazi farmers rated areas as to agricultural potential. Scattered pockets of deep dune sand on the divide might have afforded small but important microniches for deep-sand dry farming, similar to the falling dune field locations ethnographically documented for the Hopi (e.g., Hack 1942:26–32). The generally east-facing falling dunes along the prominent ridgeline of the site area could have provided an opportunity to diversify food production by using settings quite different from those elsewhere. If Pueblo II farmers planted in scattered parcels of deep dune sand around Naaki Hooghan as a means to diversify their field locations, then what might be the evidence that would help confirm such an inference? Domesticates were found in analyzed flotation samples, but these could have been brought in from elsewhere, especially since the remains consisted of maize cob portions and kernels, with no shanks, husks, stalks, or roots. Only a single pollen sample contained maize pollen, and this was represented by a grain. We would expect maize pollen to be represented at field houses because of direct contact with tasseling plants during the growing season and the likely stripping and discard of leaves and husks from corn ears at harvest time to enable drying (see discussion of experimental maize pollen washes in Geib and Smith 2008). The single grain from a single provenience thus seems inadequate evidence. The presence of squash pollen, including aggregates, is a better indication that crops were grown in close proximity to the site. Other plant remains found at the site included plants most likely obtained from agricultural fields and other humanly disturbed habitats, as well as wild plants such as prickly pear and pinyon. Pinyon nut harvesting is a possible additional reason for occupation at Naaki Hooghan, since the site area is forested, but locations with denser pinyon stands would seem to offer better potential in this regard.

Nineteen features were excavated at The Slots: 16 small, shallow basin hearths, a large slab-lined hearth, a small midden, and a small pit structure (see Figure 6.35). The 16 basin hearths, all clustered together, were each probably used just once, but the slab-lined hearth appears to have been used on numerous occasions, and repeated cleaning could account for the abundant charcoal and burned rock in the midden. The semisubterranean structure provided just over 3 m² of floor area, without a hearth or other features. The informal nature of the structure, with just a log and brush superstructure and no interior hearth, suggests that the dwelling, and the site as a whole, was occupied during the warm months of the year. That a structure was built at all, however, indicates that the occupants planned on using the site for longer than one brief episode. More than transitory use is also indicated by the presence of a trash midden and the number and density of small basin hearths. The very practice of moving debris from living and activity space to a dump area implies some degree of occupation longevity (e.g., Graham 1994; various chapters in Kent 1987). The artifact assemblage is distinctive for its low quantity of sherds and comparatively high frequency and diversity of stone artifacts. Sherds were few in number, significantly lower than at most other secondary habitations (see Table 6.13) and evidently derived from just four vessels. The portions of these vessels were so small as to raise doubts about whether whole pots were ever present at the site; instead, jar fragments may have been brought in for use as plates or other utensils. In contrast, stone artifacts were comparatively numerous, including the highest count of debitage, flaked facial tools, and cores/nodular tools of any of the secondary habitations. Grinding tools were comparatively scarce, but miscellaneous stone artifacts were common, including a few unusual items such as fragments of two cloud blowers made of scoria (a nonlocal raw material) and a pendant of limestone. Subsistence remains consisted of maize (fragmentary cobs and kernels), seeds from weedy annuals (especially goosefoot), and a modest amount of small-mammal bone (rabbits and hares), much of it burned. Though seemingly low, the count of bone ($n = 133$) exceeds the amount recovered from three of the NMRAP primary habitations, and the count per structure exceeds those at all but one of the primary habitations (Three Dog Site, with 228). Despite the presence of corncobs and kernels there was a lack of artifacts associated with intensive

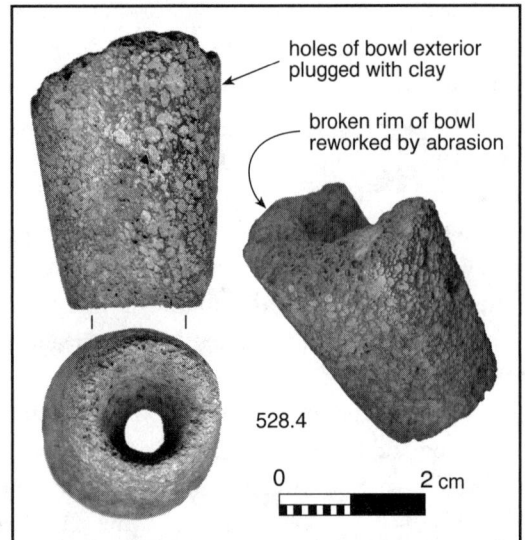

Figure 6.38. Recycled pipe fragment of black scoria from Tres Campos similar to portions of two other pipes found at The Slots.

maize processing and consumption, specifically the scarcity of ceramics; near absence of grinding tools, including a lack of two-hand manos and trough metates; and absence of mealing bins or mealing areas. The general site setting seems poorly suited for agriculture, so perhaps the recovered maize was brought to the site. An absence of shanks and husks and maize pollen perhaps supports this notion, suggesting that the site was not related to tending fields.

Tres Campos lay nearby The Slots and seemed functionally similar, in that it had an informal structure lacking a hearth, an exterior slab-lined hearth, abundant evidence of fire use, an unusual assemblage of stone artifacts, and carbonized plant remains including maize. One major difference was the greater abundance of pottery at Tres Campos, but the artifact assemblage was still distinctive because of its comparatively high frequency and diversity of stone artifacts. The most unusual find was yet another pipe made of exotic black scoria. This specimen was a recycled fragment of a once larger artifact (Figure 6.38). The pipe was still used after the upper portion of the bowl broke, as evidenced by the abrasion and smoothing of the broken edge; the original mouth is still intact, and the exterior of the pipe is polished from extensive handling (vesicles on the exterior have been purposefully plugged with light-colored clay). Other seemingly unusual finds for a seasonal habitation were three possible bead blanks (one of obsidian) and 10 stone disks. As with The Slots, the informal nature of the structure, the presence of just a log and brush superstructure that likely was not earth covered, and the lack of an interior hearth led us to believe that the dwelling, and indeed the site as a whole, was occupied during the warm months of the year. Seasonal short-term use is also evidenced by the general scarcity of remains associated with food preparation and consumption, specifically the near absence of grinding tools and low proportion of utility ceramics, with few being sooted. The construction of at least one structure, and possibly a second, as well as a ramada, indicates that the occupants planned on using the site for longer than one brief episode. That this actually occurred is suggested by the accumulation of artifacts, burned rock, and charcoal within what amounts to a trash midden. Fragmentary corncobs, cupules, and kernels were recovered from flotation samples from the fill of the structure and the cultural stratum; cobs were also collected in the field while screening the cultural stratum. As with The Slots, maize pollen was absent from the structure, and we would expect maize pollen to be represented at temporary structures associated with field tending. The problem with the pollen evidence is that sampling was perhaps inadequate to be certain that corn pollen was truly absent, both here and at The Slots.

The settlement role of these two sites remains a mystery. In our rush to accord every site a functional role in some annual subsistence strategy we might be overlooking an important aspect of the past—humans do not live by bread alone. The pipes at both of these sites along with abundant burned rocks and hearths for heating seem to hint at an alternative purpose. Perhaps the sites were used for sweat baths and ceremonial cleansing, hence the cloud blowers, and the divide might have offered an enticing secluded retreat for contemplation, along with stunning vistas.

Table 6.14 presents different orderings of the secondary habitations based on the counts of certain artifacts: total sherds, total flakes, total formal stone tools (excluding used flakes), and total grinding tools (manos and metates). Site sequence generally changes from one column to the next, sometimes markedly so because artifact counts such as sherds and flakes do not always covary. For example, The Slots goes from second to last place for sherds (few) to the top of the list for debitage (the most) and also has a high number of stone tools, but few of which are grinding tools. Hence, occupation duration as evidenced by sherds substantially differs from that indicated by stone artifacts, and in this instance we have sided

TABLE 6.14. Changing Order of Secondary Habitations According to the Frequency of Recovered Sherds, Debitage, Formal Flaked Tools (Excludes Used Flakes), and Grinding Tools

SHERDS		FLAKES		TOTAL TOOLS		GRINDING TOOLS	
SITE	n	SITE	n	SITE	n	SITE	n
Modesty House, Late Pueblo II	9	Modesty House, Late Pueblo II	11	Modesty House, Late Pueblo II	1	Modesty House, Late Pueblo II	1
The Slots	30	Dune Hollow	22	Dune Hollow	4	Dune Hollow	1
Dune Hollow	203	Modesty House, Mid Pueblo III	135	Hillside Hermitage, Late Pueblo II	14	Camp Dead Pine	1
Hillside Hermitage, Late Pueblo II	268	Hillside Hermitage, Late Pueblo II	160	Camp Dead Pine	15	Hillside Hermitage, Late Pueblo II	3
UT-B-63-19	355	Bonsai Bivouac	194	Modesty House, Mid–Pueblo III	19	The Slots	5
Tres Campos	413	Camp Dead Pine	243	Bonsai Bivouac	27	Tres Campos	9
Camp Dead Pine	425	Naaki Hooghan	299	Tres Campos	37	Modesty House, Mid–Pueblo III	9
Bonsai Bivouac	568	UT-B-63-19	413	The Slots	42	Bonsai Bivouac	18
Naaki Hooghan	930	Tres Campos	740	UT-B-63-19	45	Naaki Hooghan	21
Modesty House, Mid–Pueblo III	1,093	The Slots	1,239	Naaki Hooghan	46	UT-B-63-19	28
Total	4,294	Total	3,456	Total	250	Total	96

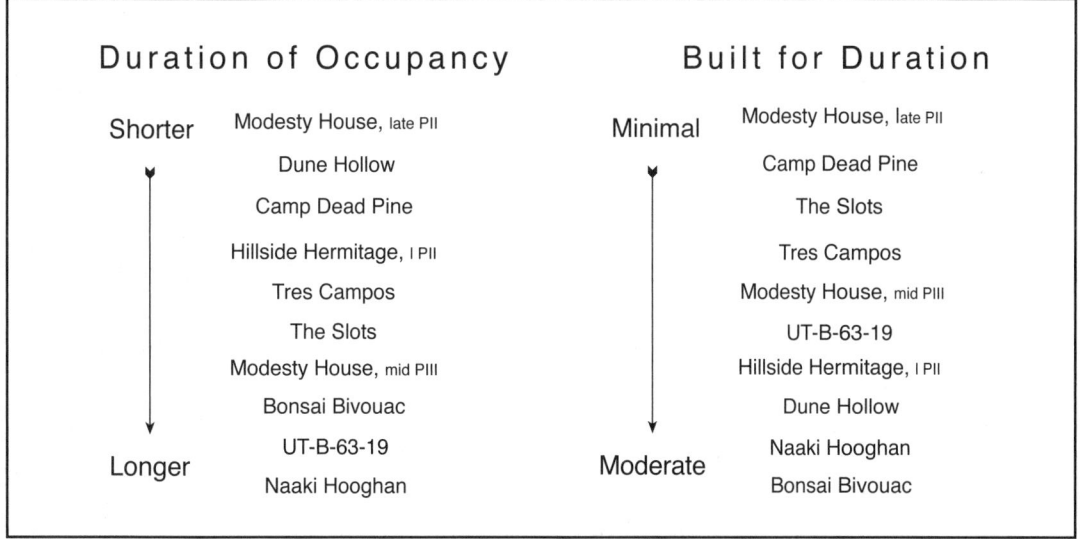

Figure 6.39. Navajo Mountain Road Archaeological Project Puebloan secondary habitations (those with the most complete information; see Table 6.13) ordered according to an assessment of occupation duration and building for duration (anticipated length of occupancy).

with the stone evidence (plus our subjective knowledge about the site) rather than the ceramics. In some cases, best exemplified by the Pueblo II component at Modesty House, the order remains unchanged, in this case at the bottom. The architectural evidence for this site is clearly in agreement since the brush structure here was the flimsiest of the lot, suggesting construction for an anticipated brief stay. The information from this table was used along with subjective knowledge about the nature of each site to provide a relative ordering of these 10 sites according to duration of occupancy as shown in Figure 6.39. We tended to give slightly more weight to the grinding tool totals since these are involved in food processing and this is taken to be an indicator of occupation length.

Scavenging of ground stone is well documented in the ethnographic and archaeological literature (e.g.,

Schlanger 1991), but it is our guess that some manos and metates were cycled from small sites to large sites and back again as needed. This is not scavenging in the usual sense, but the end result is the same: we may not be seeing the full complement of grinding tools used at the site. There may also have been scavenging or at least a returning of ground-stone tools to primary residential sites upon *final* abandonment of a secondary site (which would explain the "absence" of whole metates). The two processes—cycling and scavenging—would be most effective at removing items with high replacement costs, such as formalized trough metates, especially when transport distance is low. There was virtually no evidence for formalized trough metates at the field house sites. This could indicate that the occupation or reoccupation of any small site was never long enough to outlast the use-lives of most grinding tools: "When occupations…last longer than tools, discarded tools begin to accumulate in fill, trash, and other contexts" (Schlanger 1991:467). In a study of highland Maya ground-stone technology, Hayden (1987:Table 5.3) estimated average use-lives of 32.9 years for metates and 21.5 years for manos. The Mayan ground stone is probably more formal and long-lasting than that observed on N16, but even halving the figures far exceeds the estimated duration of use of all of the field house sites.

Many other measures could be used for discriminating between short and long site duration, such as the numbers of diagnostic ceramic types, the numbers of different vessel categories, and the diversity of lithic raw material types, and more might be better, although any of these will have their issues, such as how much natural raw material variability occurs in an area and whether some sites are located right next to outcrops whereas others are not. For vessel types and forms, much of the pottery at secondary habitations might arrive there not as whole items but as recycled portions. Some sites might have all jar sherds, all of which were being used as plates and bowls rather than as jars. Other measures, such as tool–flake ratios, macrobotanical and faunal frequencies, and variety of identified faunal species, appear to have widely variable results and may better reflect differences in site function, preservation, and the like.

Several of the structures at the NMRAP secondary habitations appear to be more substantial than the ethnographic examples of field houses, especially the rectangular structures at sites such as Hillside Hermitage, Naakai Hooghan, Dune Hollow, and UT-B-63-19. Indeed, some of these structures contained hearths of the type used for interior heat, which suggests that walls were more substantial than simple brush or poles. They were classified as living rooms in the structure typology considered previously, and the rooms were comparable to those that occurred on primary residential sites. This type of structure would have been suitable for the better part of a growing season and would represent a higher order of permanence than shades, lean-tos, windbreaks, or ramadas. The very fact of excavating a rectangular pit to serve as the base for a structure, whether an interior hearth is added or not, is consistent with a need to generate sediment in order to cover the superstructure, which implies a modest degree of building for permanence and therefore perhaps use throughout the growing season.

As for associated remains, none of the NMRAP secondary habitations have evidence for long-term storage. Some structures have pits, but these are all small and unlikely to have been used for food. One of the problems with site- and feature-centered data recovery is that isolated, buried features—like storage pits—are not likely to be found except as occasional "discoveries" during development. Yet it is worth mentioning that NNAD archaeologists performed extensive backhoe stripping around all sites, and if storage pits had been present, they would have been found; but there were none. This said, the occupants may have used storage pits located near fields, which would have been outside the immediate vicinity of these sites, thus outside the N16 ROW and not subject to discovery. More than likely, food may have been transported directly to the primary, year-round residence. "In the old days," reports Bradfield of the pre-mechanized Hopi, "the [corn]cobs were carried back to the village, either in deep baskets or in large woven blankets on the backs of villagers" (1971:22).

One possibility is that the field houses themselves were used for storage, particularly those without interior features such as hearths (Sutton 1977:54–58). Woodbury (1961) described field structures with sealed doorways, presumably used for storage. Within such structures foodstuffs could be stored in large ceramic jars; quantities of jar sherds, in fact, are often used as a field house criterion (Pilles 1969). This approach could be effective under certain circumstances but leaves the stored goods susceptible to depredation. Storage within a field house perhaps more likely involved seed for next year's planting, but loss from thieves seems too high a risk for even this convenience.

All but two of the NMRAP secondary habitations

have just a single structure *in use at one time*. (Naaki Hooghan had two structures in use concurrently—a living room attached to a ramada, a pattern evidently repeated twice at this single location—and Hillside Hermitage also had two—a living room and attached mealing room.) The degree of investment in the houses varied greatly from what appear to have been expedient, brush constructions that might not have been totally enclosed (Pueblo II component at Modesty House) to fully enclosed semisubterranean jacal constructions suitable for use during all or part of a growing season. The latter often had interior basin hearths. Nearly all of the NMRAP secondary habitations have middens (as do the large sites). The exception is the tiny brush shelter at the late Pueblo II component of Modesty House. Middens ranged from 5 to 30 cm in depth, were concentrated in areas less than 5 m in diameter, and typically had maximum artifact counts of less than 30 items per 1 m².

Final Thoughts About NMRAP Secondary Habitations
It is clear from all of the preceding that the field house interpretation does not end with a finding of "seasonality" or dichotomies that partition occupations into short and long term. Various results indicate that small sites, such as field houses, must also be evaluated in light of duration of occupation (including time of occupation), function, and the site's relationship to associated settlement systems. The rank order of field house duration presented earlier is based on qualitative and quantitative differences in site use. We believe that the order is primarily related to differing site durations (or perhaps intensity of use), with variability in function playing a minor role. The functional role of some secondary habitations such as The Slots still eludes us, perhaps because we lack a nuanced understanding of settlement organization and mobility among the Kayenta Anasazi. When we ask ourselves, "What do we mean by field house?" we have set ourselves a challenge—a challenge, as Graham says, "to develop the means by which we can interpret…settlement pattern[s] accurately" (1994:106). Only then will we be able to explain what the "little" sites mean and what the "big" sites mean in relation to them.

Temporary Camps
Just three of the NMRAP Puebloan sites were designated as temporary camps. At two of these the Puebloan component was discovered while excavating a buried Basketmaker or Archaic component and consisted simply of a single hearth with several artifacts. The third site consisted of a Pueblo I artifact scatter around two basin hearths at Wolachii Bighan. Puebloans clearly had a need for temporary camps, but perhaps less so within the region of intensive land use, which is what the N16 ROW mostly represents. The Glen Canyon lowlands adjacent to the project area contain a profusion of Puebloan temporary camps (Adams and Adams 1959; Adams et al. 1961; Geib 1989; Long 1966). The NMRAP sites with single hearths produced too few remains to get any indication of settlement function, and the flotation samples from the features were equally uninformative.

The meager remains documented at Wolachii Bighan easily fit the deposition of a single use episode or perhaps a few episodes within the span of a few years. The role of the site within regional settlement remains conjectural, but a lack of faunal remains and hunting-related tools and production debris would seem to preclude faunal procurement or processing. The occurrence of a moderately well-used metate fragment along with certain macrobotanical remains, most notably abundant fragments of pinyon nutshell and cone scales within a hearth flotation sample, may support an interpretation of the site use as a pinyon nut–harvesting camp (alternatively, the pinyon remains may have entered the record by burning cones for fuel). The site today is located within a dense pinyon and juniper forest that produces abundant nut masts during good years, and there is no reason to believe that the situation was any different during Pueblo I times. Habitat proximity is admittedly an inadequate basis for inferring subsistence practices (e.g., Madsen 1981), but upon considering locational data in conjunction with the flotation results and the presence of a metate, pinyon exploitation takes on a degree of plausibility. Excavations at Wolachii Bighan uncovered two use areas, each with a basin hearth surrounded by small scatters of sherds and stone artifacts, mostly chipped-stone debris, along with unworked sandstone and limestone chunks. The hearths seem to have been used just once, as there was no evidence that the occupants had emptied the fill of either. Excavations recovered 122 sherds from a maximum of just five ceramic vessels or portions thereof, all jars. If the Kana-a Gray jars were used at the site as whole vessels, rather than as reused pieces, it is probable that they were the only whole vessels ever used at the site. Due to their scarcity and degree of fragmentation, it seems likely that the one Kana-a Black-on-white sherd and the few Lino Gray sherds were brought in as pieces for reuse as some other tool form. The stone artifact assemblage was equally skimpy, with only four lithic tools and 54 pieces of debitage. These meager remains could easily have been deposited during a single use episode or perhaps a few episodes over the course of a few years.

Puebloan Mobility

Robert Kelly's (1992:60) quote presented earlier about humans using mobility to overcome the fact that no single locale can provide for all human needs occurs in an article where he cites archaeological research from the American Southwest (e.g., Gilman 1987; Powell 1983; Preucel 1990) to make a case that mobility patterns in prehistory had been unappreciated until recently. This is certainly true for residential mobility of the type that Binford (1980) explicated, since Puebloans were seen as largely sedentary, staying in places for long durations of time. Yet logistical mobility and migration both seem to have always been part of the conceptual tools of Southwestern archaeologists. Early ethnographic accounts of Puebloans described large aggregated communities (towns) where people lived most of the year but also field shelters that the farmers used on a limited basis while tending their crops. The ethnographic accounts served to create expectations of material patterns in the archaeological record that would allow identification of permanent and nonpermanent aspects of Puebloan settlement. Prehistoric Puebloans were assumed to have been largely sedentary like their ethnographic counterparts (cf. Parsons [1939:14], who characterized Puebloans as seminomadic), but their lifeway also involved considerable movement in the context of trips to and from the fields, usually involving only certain segments of a population (males and children). Recognition of nonpermanent habitations such as field houses did not necessarily challenge the prevailing view that Puebloan groups were residentially immobile, staying put in one place for extended intervals—deep sedentism, as Lekson (1990) termed it.

Mobility in the sense of migration also has a long pedigree in Southwestern archaeology, at least back to the late 1800s with Fewkes (see review in Downum 1988). Interest in migration waned during the processual fervor of the late 1960s and 1970s, but interest in the topic never fully died, and by the 1990s it had returned full force (e.g., Cameron 1995; Clark 2001; Lyons 2003). Mobility at this scale presents no real challenge to traditional conceptions of residential permanence, since it does not necessarily involve any increase in annual residential moves beyond the "singular" major relocation of residence from one setting to another. Periodic dislocations of small spatial scale, usually attributed to environmental factors (boom-and-bust cycles), also present no necessary challenge to a general assumption of a sedentary existence.

Persuasive evidence from the Kayenta region of Puebloan mobility levels exceeding the ethnographic norm, if you will, came from the MNA's investigations for the Glen Canyon project. The evidence recovered supported the inference that significant population movement had occurred on an interannual basis between the canyon lowlands and the surrounding highlands. Archaeologists on that project argued that the small transient-looking habitations and camps that they recorded in Glen Canyon were seasonally used during the summer by Anasazi populations living permanently in the surrounding highlands (Adams and Adams 1959; Adams et al. 1961; Ambler et al. 1964; Lindsay 1961; Long 1966:61, 65–68). Movement of course occurred in the context of farming as the primary subsistence strategy, and a chief corollary assumption was that populations resided permanently in the highlands, where farming was optimal. Lipe (1967, 1970; Lipe and Lindsay 1983:29–31) provided a somewhat different account for the archaeological remains, one that embraced the residential mobility of populations living in the lowlands alone but also assumed subsistence based on food production. He suggested that the transient quality of the Pueblo II settlements in Glen Canyon, as characterized by their lack of well-made living structures and generally scant artifactual remains, reflected an adaptive strategy of relatively mobile and dispersed small family groups living in favorable locales of the lowlands where mild winters did not necessitate substantial structures (cf. Geib 1996a). Lipe might have been the first to suggest that the Kayenta were residentially mobile, at least those groups occupying Glen Canyon, but other researchers soon added their voices.

Another case of Kayentan residential mobility concerns research findings in the Grand Canyon, where survey and excavation in the lowlands and highlands documented residential settlements in both settings (e.g., Schwartz et al. 1979; Schwartz et al. 1980; Schwartz et al. 1981). Here, the situation seems to be the reverse of that in Glen Canyon, with permanent residential sites built in the canyon lowlands and somewhat less substantial structures built in the surrounding highlands. Schwartz et al. (1981:129–132) argued for a biseasonal movement of populations from winter residential sites in the lowlands to summer residential sites in the highlands. Unlike the situation in Glen Canyon, the distinction between lowland and highland sites was far less marked, and it is easy to envision that in other settings the sites might both be considered equivalent in terms of residential permanence. The case for biseasonal movement in Grand Canyon has not been accepted by all, and there are competing alternatives that all involve residential mobility to one degree or another (see review in Fairley 2003), more so than indicated by the notion of deep sedentism (Lekson 1990). The great environmental contrasts compressed within such relatively small areas here and in Glen Canyon make scenarios of residential mobility appear not only feasible but reasonable given the vast elevation change within short horizontal distances and attendant great differences in the possibilities of and limitations to crop production and timing and availability of other resources. This does not mean that areas with more gradual ecological zones and evident large-scale uniformity in environments might not also have been effectively exploited by residential mobility, just that making a case for such a pattern might be more difficult.

Powell (1980, 1983) accepted this challenge when she examined the issue of residential mobility for the Kayenta Anasazi who lived on northern Black Mesa. Powell thought that the Hopi were an "inappropriate analog" (1983:54) for understanding Kayenta Anasazi settlement because the villages that they occupied were so much larger and more permanent compared to the Kayenta settlements of northern Black Mesa. Instead, she turned to ethnographic descriptions of settlement practices for the Pai and Navajo from northern Arizona. Urging her in the direction of analogies drawn from farmer-foragers rather than more fully sedentary Puebloan farmers was the floral and faunal evidence accumulated by the BMAP, which indicated a greater subsistence role for hunting and gathering than was commonly assumed for the Kayenta Anasazi. She thought the evidence indicated that the Kayenta had a mixed economy, that they were part-time horticulturalists and part-time foragers and therefore had to be residentially mobile: "Groups practicing a mixed hunting, gathering, and horticultural subsistence strategy are not fully sedentary in these general environmental conditions [on the Colorado Plateau]. Rather, they occupy sites on a seasonal basis in order to procure the foods necessary for survival" (1983:69). She (1983:136) concluded that few Kayenta sites on northern Black Mesa were permanently occupied until after AD 1050.

Plog (1986) subsequently criticized Powell's study and her conclusions regarding prehistoric cultural change on Black Mesa on a number of cogent grounds. It is easy to envision that the mobility practices of the Navajo with their herding lifeway might have less relevance for understanding Kayenta Anasazi settlement than the Hopi, Zuni, or other Puebloan groups. In large part the issue boils down to expectations about the natural productivity of the environment and how the Anasazi could have survived in the region if they were in fact less reliant on agriculture than commonly supposed. Powell's (1983) mobility argument partly hinges on the assumption that the Kayentans were far less dependent on farmed produce than indicated in the ethnographic accounts of Puebloan farmers. The recovery of diverse plants and animals from BMAP sites was thought to signify this aspect of subsistence diversity, even though the potential productivity of the preagricultural landscape on the Colorado Plateau appears quite limited (e.g., Ford 1984) and most of the diverse subsistence remains were those characteristic of disturbed areas and thus likely a direct side benefit of agricultural fields—i.e., not wild land foraging but foraging in the garden, something likely true for many game animals as well (e.g., Semé 1984, following Linares 1976). More important, stable isotope analysis has now adequately demonstrated that maize agriculture was a focal aspect of Anasazi subsistence in the Kayenta region since Basketmaker II times (Coltrain et al. 2007), so whatever residential mobility existed should be considered in terms of this aspect, not by overemphasizing the foraging of wild resources (cf. Sullivan 1987, 1992) and downplaying farming. Despite problems with Powell's theoretical approach and expectations, she rightly called attention to the need to question traditional assumptions about Puebloan mobility strategies; at the very least we should explicitly acknowledge what these assumptions are.

Perhaps it would behoove us to eschew the assumption that there exists an ideal adaptive pattern that all members of society strive to follow. We should all heed Kelly's admonition to avoid typological thinking and attend to "the many different dimensions of mobility—individual mobility, group residential movements, territorial shifts, and migration—each of which can vary independently of the others" (1992:50). Key is recognizing that it is individual people and families who made decisions about where, when, and how frequently to move in order to survive. The average or mode of any behavior does not express what an individual will do or how variable the behaviors are around some measure of central tendency. Biseasonal movement in the Grand Canyon from summer highland settlements to inner canyon winter settlements might indeed characterize some portion of the population but perhaps not all, and some might have practiced the reverse strategy or one totally different. In any analysis of residential mobility it is also important to factor in the transport costs of different resources (e.g., Barlow and Metcalfe 1996; Jones and Madsen 1989) since some are more affordably moved great distances (e.g., deer and pinyon nuts) than others (maize) and dependence on abundant but bulky and low-return resources, especially those stored for winter subsistence, should markedly constrain residential placement.

The NMRAP provided a few pieces of evidence that are relevant to the issue of residential mobility in the Kayenta region, ones worth considering for future projects and in the analysis of existing data. The first of these concerns differential abandonment modes. It is most common for Kayenta habitations, except for terminal Tsegi phase villages, to be thoroughly scavenged of artifacts and usable wood. That is why Hammer House and the middle Pueblo III component of Ditch House are notable since both had intact roofs and superstructures at the time that the structures started to enter the archaeological record, although in the case of Ditch House the rooms thoroughly burned while the structures stood intact, perhaps in a forest fire. The fire in this latter case does not seem to have been catastrophic (not Pompeii like), in that the site appears to have been largely closed down, with most usable goods removed from the households, including the metates from mealing bins, although the bins themselves were left intact, an important distinction from most NMRAP sites. Hammer House also seems closed down, with most but not all useful tools removed. Sites like these seem to represent settlements that were cleaned and temporarily shut down while the occupants took up residence at another site, but without the structures being dismantled because a return was anticipated and the presence of intact houses discouraged encroachment. Valuables like whole metates might have been removed to the new residence or placed in hiding; thus the whole and heavy trough metate from the floor fill of the kiva at Hammer House might have been buried in the sediment that covered the roof of this structure. We have already discussed how the numerous floor features of this kiva might also be indicative of residential mobility. Such temporarily closed sites might represent rather firm evidence of residential mobility and are worth being examined in this light.

The nature of the food-storage facilities at both of the middle Pueblo II habitations is also worth considering with regard to residential mobility. The specialized storage features at these sites are large subfloor pits that emanate off the kivas (both sites) and the jacal living room at Hammer House. Although such cache pits are not as easily concealed as those exterior to houses, they are far less obvious than food-storage rooms or granaries and may thus have been more secret and secure (see Gilman 1987). This seems to imply more residential mobility by the occupants of Hammer House and Hillside Hermitage than was true at some other Kayenta sites during middle Pueblo II, such as those on northern Black Mesa, where granaries were common occurrences at many Kayenta habitations, dating back to at least Pueblo I (Dinnebito phase). Storage in pits is common at Pueblo III Kayenta sites as well, especially those that employ pithouses or semisubterranean jacal living rooms (e.g., Callahan 1985; and Hanging Ash reported herein). These might also be indicative of the need to secure food stores while structures were left unoccupied for some extent of time. That such storage facilities occur in what might have been more expediently constructed houses rather than, say, masonry pueblos might not be a coincidence.

REGIONAL SETTLEMENT HISTORY AND POPULATION TRENDS

A few areas of the Kayenta region appear to have been continuously occupied by Puebloan farmers from Basketmaker III through late Pueblo III. Examples include Long House Valley (Dean et al. 1978), the area around Red Lake (Tonalea) on Lower Begashibito Wash, the Klethla Valley, and the greater area around the modern town of Kayenta (Beals et al. 1945). A few of these areas are quite small, such as Long House Valley and Red Lake, yet, despite this, they maintained food producers for hundreds of years without evident break in settlement. Nonetheless, most of the Kayenta region, like many portions of the Colorado Plateau, was characterized by boom-and-bust cycles (e.g., Matson and Lipe 1978; Matson et al. 1988), with periods of abandonment or hiatuses interrupting the record of ceramic-era farmer settlement. On northern Black Mesa there is a gap of several hundred years between late Basketmaker II and late Pueblo I (ca. AD 400–840), followed by total abandonment of the area by the close of late Pueblo II (ca. AD 1150 [see summary in Powell and Smiley 2002; Smiley and Ahlstrom 1998]). Settlement history for the northern Kayenta region begins somewhat similarly, since there is a virtual absence of late Basketmaker III and

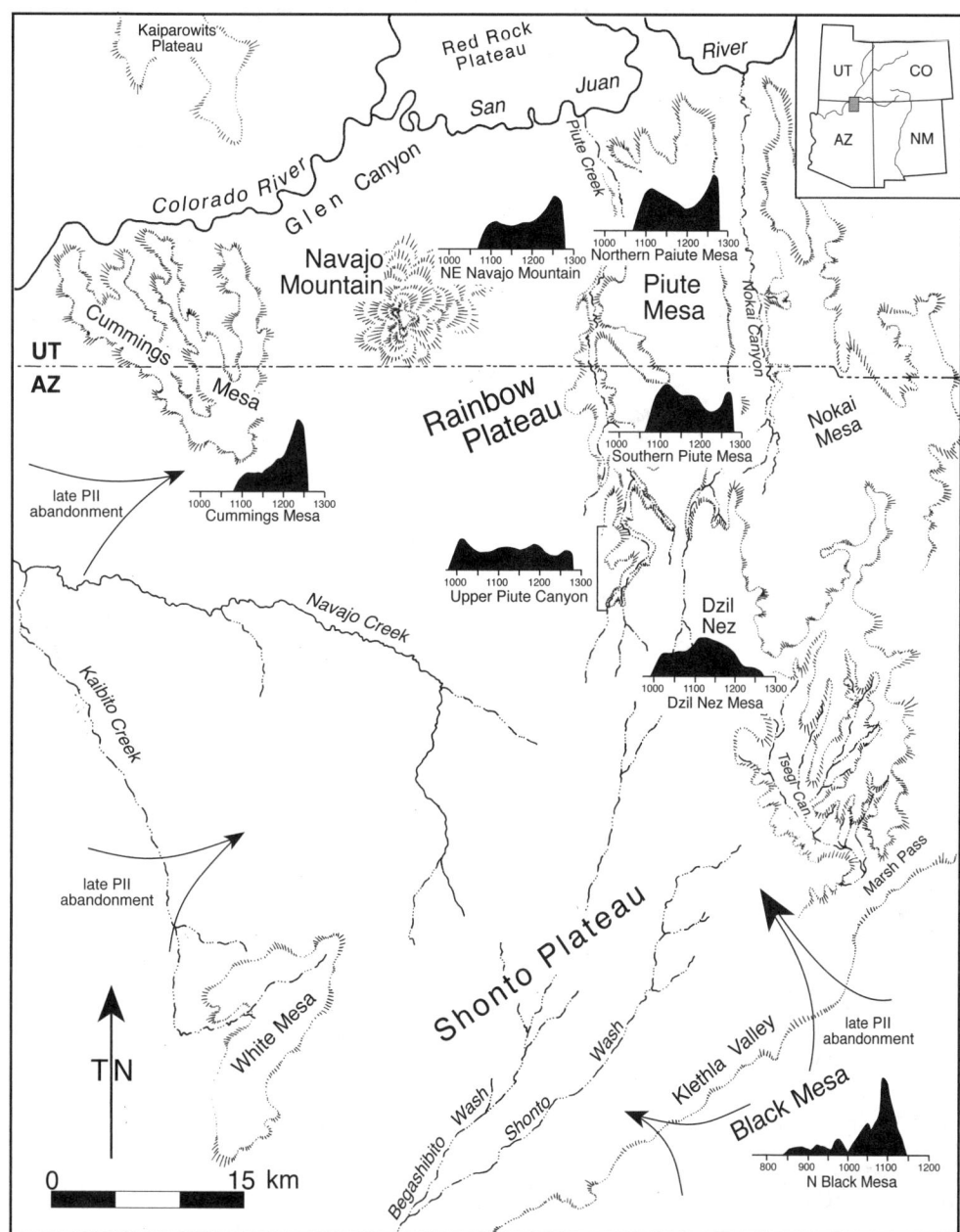

Figure 6.40. The relative population trends of Figure 2.8 placed in approximate geographic position, along with a general depiction of population trends for northern Black Mesa after Ahlstrom 1998b:Figure 9-5.

Pueblo I, but then ends quite differently because there was continued population increase from Pueblo II through Pueblo III, up until about AD 1280 (Ambler et al. 1983; Lindsay et al. 1968; Stein 1966; SD, Appendix F).

Figure 2.8 shows the reconstructed population trends for six different localities of the northern Kayenta region from Ambler et al. (1983; SD, Appendix F). Figure 6.40 places these relative population curves upon a map focused on the northern Kayenta region so that trends can be seen in spatial relationship to each other. Also included in this figure is a general depiction of population trends for northern Black Mesa as derived from Figure 9-5 of Ahlstrom 1998b (see also Plog, ed. 1986:Figure 43; cf. Hantman 1983; Layhe 1977, 1981; Swedlund and Sessions 1976). This helps to visualize that the late Pueblo II population abandonment of northern Black Mesa, something evidently under way before AD 1100 and precipitous thereafter, may have been a significant source of families who settled the northern Kayenta region beginning at about AD 1100. It is also important to point out that after AD 1150 most of the Kaibito Plateau except for right around White Mesa had been abandoned, as had the Paria

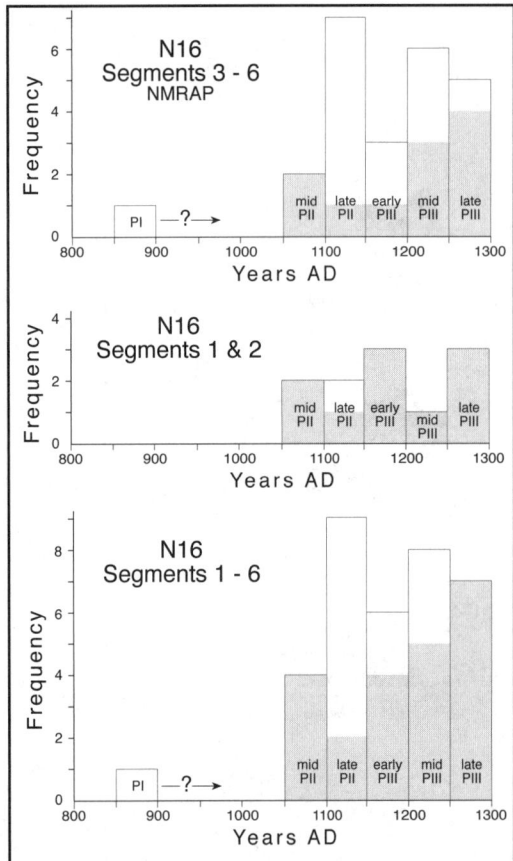

FIGURE 6.41. Frequency of Puebloan residential components by temporal interval for the N16 right-of-way as represented by the Navajo Mountain Road Archaeological Project (Segments 3–6), earlier work (Segments 1–2), and both combined. Shading indicates primary residential sites, and unshaded portions represent field houses or other limited-activity sites.

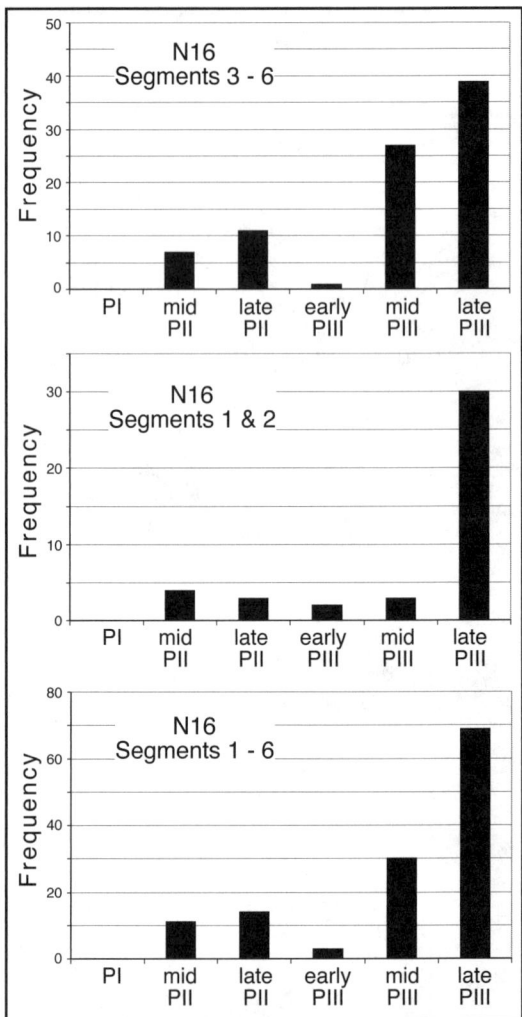

Figure 6.42. Frequency of Puebloan structures by temporal interval for the N16 right-of-way as represented by the Navajo Mountain Road Archaeological Project (Segments 3–6), earlier work (Segments 1–2), and both combined.

Plateau and the Grand Canyon region (reviews in Fairley 1989, 2003; Lyneis 1996); thus the Pueblo III population surge evident in the northern Kayenta region need not be accounted for by internal growth alone.

The sample of residential sites excavated for the N16 ROW reveals a pattern of settlement history that appears remarkably consistent with the trend in population for the northern Kayenta region. Figure 6.41 shows a simple frequency histogram of sites/components by general ceramic period as represented by 50-year intervals. This figure excludes sites that could not be confidently placed within these time slots. The NMRAP sample is at the top (N16 Segments 3–6), followed by the previously reported sites excavated within Segments 1 and 2 of this ROW (Schroedl 1989) and the sum of both projects. The shaded bars are primary residential sites, with the unshaded portions representing field houses or other limited-activity sites. The previous chapter documents the excellent record of Basketmaker II habitation in the northern Kayenta region including sites that span the Basketmaker II–III transition as represented by the occurrence of Obelisk utility ware. The area appears to have been abandoned during what might be considered classic Basketmaker III, when Lino Black-on-white (Black-on-gray) was the predominant decorated type. There is also an absence of Pueblo I habitations; the one site assigned to this interval in the NMRAP sample appears to have served as a limited-activity camp and might even date to the early Pueblo II period as discussed previously. Evidence of residential settlement begins during middle Pueblo II, at or shortly after AD 1050. This is represented by four primary residences—two of the NMRAP sample and two within Segments 1 and 2 (designated early Pueblo II in Schroedl 1989). The overall pattern shows an increase in primary residential sites through late Pueblo III. What is not evident in the graph is that besides an increase in site number, there is a corresponding increase in site size and therefore probably population as well.

Figure 6.42 shows frequency histograms for structure counts according to the same general temporal breaks as in Figure 6.41. This is a count of all structures rather than just those that are living rooms, and it includes all settlement types. This simplistic handling of data is used merely to indicate the overall general trend for the N16 sample, which shows an overall increase in room counts through time. The small dip in early Pueblo III is likely just a sampling problem; indeed, had we been able to excavate the early Pueblo III habitation of Windy Mesa, this dip probably would have disappeared. For the time span considered here there is not a major differentiation in room function that could account for the increase in room number since the same overall suite of room types is found at settlements of each interval—living rooms, mealing rooms, kivas, storage/general-activity rooms, granaries, and ramadas. At full-blown Tsegi phase habitations such as Segazlin Mesa there may well be an increased ratio of specialized grain-storage rooms to other room types, but this does not appear true for the sites excavated in the N16 ROW. More so than the simple enumeration of sites per period, the graph of room counts might reflect a real increase in population along the N16 ROW into late Pueblo III, mirroring the overall regional population trend for the Rainbow Plateau and the northern Kayenta region generally.

Notes

1. The exception to this might be the Toreva phase or late Pueblo II on northern Black Mesa; not only have many Toreva phase habitations been excavated within the coal lease (see Ahlstrom 1998a; Powell 2002; Spurr 1993), but the standardization of site layout adds to a perception of redundancy.
2. But see Gilpin 1989 for such great house sites along the eastern and southern fringe of the Kayenta region.
3. Contrary to the ceramic mean date, the middle Pueblo III component of Three Dog Site was probably occupied sometime after AD 1230 but before AD 1250, perhaps for less than 10 years.
4. Selecting a relevant population density factor (e.g., x individuals per floor area or household) is notoriously difficult. Using another figure of one individual per 10 m^2 (based on a cross-cultural logarithmic figure by Naroll [1962]) results in structure use by just a single individual. Either estimate is far below the threshold of a household unit of five individuals.

CHAPTER 7

Conclusion

Writing the conclusions to NMRAP would have been an easier task had I been able to complete it back in 1999, soon after our last season of fieldwork. Unfortunately, other projects intervened, and the analyses and specialists' reports were not done, some until just recently. The state of the discipline is not what it was back in 1991 when the project started or in early 1993 when the research plan was finalized. Moreover, my perspectives on archaeology have changed, in no small part by the very process of having worked on this project but also due to other developments. The very act of directing a project of this scale and thinking about its findings can change one's outlook, and often as not it is with the hindsight that comes in the write-up stage that one can better see what should have been done to answer certain questions or indeed what some of the useful questions would have been. But that too is progress, to arrive at a different, more informed place.

The NMRAP was not a big project, but it was the largest archaeological excavation undertaken in the Kayenta region of northeast Arizona and southeast Utah since BMAP, the fieldwork of which ended in 1983 (see Powell and Smiley 2002). One useful measure of the value of an undertaking is whether knowledge has been advanced, even if slightly. To this I can offer an unqualified yes. The NMRAP made numerous significant contributions to our understanding of prehistory and lifeways for the northern portion of the Kayenta region, providing a nice bookend to the BMAP findings and extending that study's results in a few key areas. The most important contributions concern the Basketmaker and Archaic periods, although this may largely reflect my predilections. An archaeologist with greater research leanings toward the ceramic interval might conclude that the contributions to the Puebloan occupation of the region were at least equal to those of preceramic times.

The area traversed by the N16 ROW consists of three main environments that seem to have influenced prehistoric settlement patterns and site types. The southernmost consists of the dissected ridgeline that connects the northwestern part of the Shonto Plateau to the southeast edge of the Rainbow Plateau and separates the upper reaches of Piute Canyon from the eastern tributary canyons of Navajo Creek. This portion, which ranges in elevation from about 2,240 to 2,100 m, is characterized by a dense pinyon–juniper forest but with vast exposures of Navajo Sandstone slickrock. Well-watered alluvium for farming is available within adjacent canyons, especially the upper portion of Piute Canyon. The middle portion of the ROW, at about 1,900–1,800 m, consists of the sagebrush-covered flats of the Rainbow Plateau, an area generally sparse in tree cover. Anasazi settlement of this portion would have depended upon dry farming, with the enhanced moisture in drainages offering the best opportunities. The final portion of the ROW is the lowest in elevation, from about 1,800 to 1,700 m. It runs along the eastern foot of Navajo Mountain, which rises to a height of 3,166 m in elevation, about 1,200 m above the Rainbow Plateau. This area consists of sagebrush-filled sandy drainages separated by pinyon- and juniper-covered ridges that are mantled with talus boulders. Proximity to the Glen Canyon lowlands may have been an additional benefit/attraction of this setting.

With 33 excavated sites dating from the early Archaic, more than 8,000 years ago, up until the final Anasazi abandonment of the area at about AD 1300, the NMRAP provided an informative sample from a cross section of the prehistoric occupation of the region. Fourteen of the sites had two or more components, so in all NNAD-NAU excavated 58 components. Atlatl Rock Cave adds to this tally with its lengthy history of use. Although outside the ROW and tested in an unrelated undertaking, the site is reported in volume 2 online because of its direct relevance to the study area. The NMRAP sample included 16 sites/components from forager use of the area during the early and late Archaic periods, 17 sites/components from the initial farmer presence in the area known as Basketmaker, and 25 sites/components from later Puebloan use of the area.[1] This sample allowed NNAD-NAU archaeologists to examine a number of topics regarding long-term human adaptive responses to the changing environment of the Colorado Plateau, including changes wrought by humans themselves or resulting from social elaboration and differentiation that stemmed from food production.

The Archaic sample (SD vol. 2) mainly consisted of temporary camps, likely used briefly and for specific purposes such as hunting, plant processing, and perhaps simple overnight stays. Several late Archaic components (including two at one site) appear to have functioned as residential camps. Most of the Archaic sites date to the early portion of this period, before about 5000 cal. BC. At least five components date to the late Archaic, after about 1500 cal. BC but before ca. 800 cal. BC; these sites lack domesticates. The Basketmaker sites/components include greater diversity in site function, with several primary habitations, more secondary habitations, and a few temporary camps. The Basketmaker sites (SD vol. 3) all date to an interval between about 400 cal. BC (shortly thereafter) and 500 cal. AD, overlapping the introduction of pottery. One Basketmaker site with an assemblage of Obelisk Utility pottery is well dated to between cal. AD 220 and 350 and appears to represent a good example of a Basketmaker II–III transitional habitation (see SD vol. 3, chap. 10). The numerous Puebloan sites/components (SD vol. 4) include many primary habitations that range in age from middle Pueblo II to late Pueblo III but also several secondary habitations or field houses and limited-activity camps, including one from the Pueblo I period, which is virtually unknown for the Rainbow and Shonto plateaus. The Pueblo III sites in the N16 ROW are single- or extended-family habitations, reflecting the generally low level of social complexity that characterizes the Kayenta area throughout most of the Puebloan period. Eight of the sites are middle Pueblo III in age and are especially important because they date to the interval just before the larger pueblos started to form in the Tsegi phase and thus are critical to understanding organizational changes leading to late Pueblo III aggregation. At one, pithouses were loosely grouped together to form a hamlet that might herald the larger social aggregations seen in the Tsegi phase. At another, the building sequence appears to document the transformation of structures into a more integrated architectural unit that implies a more tightly knit social unit consisting of two extended families.

Research Issues

The NMRAP had six broad and overlapping research issues subsumed under the domains of economic specialization and social differentiation. The economic issues were those of agricultural transition, subsistence specialization, and craft production and exchange, and the issues of social differentiation were those of social organization, social status, and gender. These issues served as guiding principles for the NMRAP research effort but not as a straightjacket, and some issues received considerably more attention than others because of both the types of remains and information that were ultimately recovered and the predilections or interests of participating researchers, including myself. The overarching research domains are intertwined, and the processes involved can be mutually reinforcing. Without food production, the possibilities for either economic specialization or social differentiation would have been exceedingly limited on the Colorado Plateau since Archaic foragers of the area seem to have lived more of a hardscrabble existence. The adoption of maize and other domesticates allowed these processes to come into play as families became more residentially stable and especially as population density increased and social groups expanded in size. Accordingly one of the primary interests of this project concerned the agricultural transition, an issue relevant to the Archaic and Basketmaker records documented by the NMRAP. In this conclusion I touch on a few of the salient findings but by no means all of them.

A Middle Holocene Bottleneck?

Although the Archaic period appeared to be a minor aspect of the NMRAP when the project began, it ultimately made a significant contribution to what little was known about the pre-pottery and nonagricultural foragers of the Kayenta Anasazi region. Most of the results came about because of fortuitously finding Archaic remains underlying those of Puebloans or Basketmakers or because of exposure by the existing road. In something of a twist on Smiley's (2002b:15) quote about Archaic sites on Black Mesa, rarely have so many old sites been revealed in an area of such limited size by good fortune coupled with dogged determination to squeeze the most from what came to light.

The highly visible and comparatively rich archaeological records left by Puebloan and Basketmaker farmers or farmer-foragers of the N16 ROW sharply contrast with the generally diffuse remains from transient forager use of the project area. This is generally true all across the Colorado Plateau unless one has the good fortune to be working in a dry shelter where organics are preserved. The returns from studying Archaic sites in the Southwest usually appear scant by comparison with those from sites dating after the introduction of domesticates. For buried Archaic sites, great effort must be expended to expose a few basin hearths and recover a handful or two of small flakes, some bone, and rare tool fragments. Such is the fate of the archaeological study of foragers—the debris scatters generated by such highly mobile groups pale against the information troves generated by more sedentary and logistically organized groups. Given the vast expanse of time covered by the Archaic period coupled with the paltry nature of the record, there will be no time soon when the discipline has reached a point of diminishing returns. Indeed, this provides good cause for extra effort to maximize the information return from forager sites and isolated occurrences as well as sufficient justification for what might seem to be comparatively high expense (cost per artifact or other remain recovered or per square or cubic meter of features/deposits excavated).

The NMRAP excavations compiled an impressive radiocarbon record of forager occupancy for the Rainbow Plateau and far-northern Shonto Plateau from what amounted to an unbiased sample of preceramic sites. The project obtained 59 radiocarbon dates for the Archaic period from 13 sites, including Atlatl Rock Cave. When combined with 12 previous dates from Dust Devil and Sand Dune caves, these 71 dates, which range from 9780 BP up to 2520 BP, reveal a record of forager occupancy for the northern Kayenta region that is discontinuous, containing a major break between early and late Archaic and a shorter break between late Archaic and Basketmaker II. Sample adequacy is critical for judging the significance of gaps in radiocarbon records, both the total number of radiocarbon dates available and the total number of sites that yielded the samples. Seventy-one dates is a respectable number considering the relatively small size of the project area. Site count, the second aspect of sample adequacy, is of greater concern than sheer date quantity in this instance, but again, the relatively small size of the region is an important consideration. Moreover, if the true history of forager occupancy of the study area did not closely resemble that shown by the radiocarbon distribution, probabilities are exceedingly low that the 15 dated sites would yield virtually no evidence for middle Archaic occupancy from about 4500 to 2500 cal. BC yet abundant remains both earlier and later. After all, the middle Archaic is not a brief time interval but, in fact, more than 2,000 years long, or over 100 generations.

The addition of radiocarbon dates from the Kaibito Plateau further corroborates the overall NMRAP pattern, showing that a large portion of the Kayenta region had limited forager presence during the middle Holocene. NNAD conducted two road excavation projects (N21 and N608), contemporaneous with the NMRAP, that produced 36 radiocarbon dates from 11 Archaic sites, resulting in an increased sample size and expanded geographic coverage for the Kayenta region (Bungart et al. 2004; Neff et al. 2004). These additional 36 dates closely match the record for the NMRAP project area, with a significant cluster in the early Archaic, another cluster during the late Archaic, and a middle Archaic gap. A chief difference is with the frequency and placement of the late Archaic date cluster, with the Kaibito Plateau having fewer late Archaic dates that tend to be earlier than those of the Rainbow Plateau. Nonetheless, two separate excavation projects on the Kaibito Plateau produced essentially identical results that in turn parallel those for the Rainbow and northern Shonto plateaus.

Combined, the strongly bimodal pattern revealed by 107 dates from 26 sites is even less likely to result from simple sampling biases. The lack of evidence for open sites dating to the middle Archaic within these road excavations parallels the declines and breaks in the use of natural shelters on the Colorado Plateau and closely accords with the middle Archaic date gap highlighted by Berry and Berry (1986) and initially noted by Schroedl (1976). Because the road excavations uncovered both late and early Archaic components, sometimes at the same locations, it appears unlikely that the gap is the result of preservation or discovery biases such as removal by erosion or obstruction by burial. Given that the patterning does not seem to result from preservation biases or the behavior of archaeologists, it strongly suggests that a large portion of the Kayenta region had limited forager presence during the middle Holocene from about 6000 to 4000 BP. The cause of this discontinuous record of forager occupancy surely lies in environmental constraints, ones that perhaps made the middle Holocene a population bottleneck for Archaic foragers on the Colorado Plateau. Both Schroedl (1976) and Berry and Berry (1986) looked to the paleoenvironmental record as the causal factor behind what was a middle Archaic population decline to the former author and regional abandonment to the latter authors. No doubt people did leave, but sites or components securely dated to the middle Archaic across various portions of the Colorado Plateau (e.g., Geib 1996b; Tipps 1998) argue against plateau-wide abandonment. It seems probable that forager populations on the Colorado Plateau were unstable during the Holocene, with cycles of slow growth and more precipitous declines. If the end of the early Holocene was one of net decline, which is what the radiocarbon evidence hints at, either from increased death rates or decreased birthrates or both, then there was not necessarily any sizable forager population that had to move somewhere. With populations knocked back substantially from early Archaic levels, the thinned ranks of foragers would have faced less competition and as a result more ready access to whatever prime locations still existed. Increased residential mobility and different settlement strategies might have affected the patterning of radiocarbon dates. As explored in chapter 4, the specifics remain to be worked out, including the environmental aspects of the middle Holocene. Adequate explanations for the date pattern will ultimately entail study of sites well dated to the middle Archaic along with detailed paleoenvironmental reconstructions at both large and small scales.

Forager Territories

With a data set spanning more than 5,000 years it seems reasonable to ask what changes there were during this span in site types, settlement patterns, subsistence, and the like. My evident lack of attention to this aspect should not be construed to mean that I view the Archaic as the "long, static prelude to the ceramic-producing Southwestern cultures" (Huckell 1996:306). Rather, it reflects caution because the information in hand, although now vastly more than what previously existed, is still insufficient to the task. Not only are there too few sites and too much time, but there is inadequate coverage of site "types" through time or, rather, inadequate sampling of the variability for any single chunk of time such that what might seem like change might merely reflect the sampling of different seasonal or functional aspects. Moreover, the sample might actually contain portions of two or more different settlement systems, and conflating the archaeological records of different independent forager groups could result in a fictive whole of unrelated parts. I think that a case can be made that the NMRAP sample contains portions drawn from at least two subsistence-settlement strategies and that tool stone provides the evidence for this.

The use of exotic stone for tool production is well represented by several of the NMRAP Archaic sites, which have moderately high proportions of obsidian. Although many of the NMRAP sites lack obsidian or have low proportions, Hólahéi Scatter had over 50 percent, with two other sites having proportions above 20 percent. In these cases, the evidence is not indicative of specialized production in the sense used for later Puebloan assemblages, and the high proportions are consistent with an interpretation of direct procurement rather than exchange. With low proportions of obsidian, such as the small quantities (1% or less) at some of the NMRAP Archaic sites, direct procurement is doubtful, since casual exchange could account for the raw material movement.

Flake attributes indicate that the volcanic glass was used at NMRAP Archaic sites almost exclusively for high-input bifacial tools. This is a specialized use of the raw material related to evident site function—camps associated with hunting. Although obsidian is well represented at some sites, it generally occurs in relatively small size such that this material accounts for just a tiny fraction of any assemblage by weight representation: at Hólahéi Scatter obsidian representation declines from 54 percent by count to only 7 percent by weight. Minute debitage resulted from both how this material arrived at the sites—as finished or nearly finished tools or edged flake blanks—and how it was reduced—mainly by pressure flaking. Some of the obsidian flakes exhibited "transport wear" on dorsal arrises, which is consistent with tools in bags carried for long distances during many seasonal moves.

Chemical analysis (XRF-EDS) of the Archaic site obsidian revealed little diversity, with almost 90 percent (89.3%) derived from the Government Mountain source located in north-central Arizona more than 180 km from the NMRAP study area. Two other north-central Arizona obsidian sources—Black Tank and Presley Wash—account for several more obsidian flakes, further supporting an inference of forager movement onto the Coconino Plateau. The other two sources are located in the Mt. Floyd Volcanic Field about 80 km west of the Government Mountain source. A single flake was sourced to the Wild Horse locality in the Mineral Mountains of central

Utah, and five flakes matched the Cerro del Medio locality in the Jemez Mountains source area of north-central New Mexico but came from a single site and likely came from a single large biface.

The sites with moderate proportions of obsidian occurred on the broken divide between the Shonto and Rainbow plateaus. To the north of this, on the Rainbow Plateau proper, obsidian accounted for just a trace of the Archaic lithic assemblages. The sites on the divide with abundant obsidian may have served as logistic hunting camps where dart points and knives were resharpened and modified; the fragmented and burned large-mammal bone found at each of the sites is consistent with the hunting camp interpretation. A case is made in chapter 4 that logistic hunting camps with moderately high proportions of obsidian would be unrelated to residential sites on the Rainbow Plateau that have sparse amounts of obsidian or none at all and therefore that the NMRAP sample of Archaic sites includes portions of at least two different settlement systems. The Archaic sites with moderately abundant Government Mountain obsidian are thought to be derived from more southerly focused forager bands who procured this material directly, either embedded within subsistence tasks of one sort or another (through residential or logistic hunting movements) or on specific raw material–procurement trips outside of the normal annual movement for subsistence resources. Foragers whose subsistence-settlement rounds were centered more in the Glen Canyon lowlands had assemblages with infrequent or no use of obsidian and acquired this material via down-the-line exchange because the source locations lay well outside their normal travel rounds, outside the area of embedded direct procurement. Direct procurement by one means or another is implicated by assemblages with moderately abundant obsidian, along with the inference that the normal foraging areas of the groups that created these sites lay considerably closer to the Government Mountain source than the N16 project area.

Some of the implications of these possibilities are explored in chapter 4 along with figures that graph the possible configurations of territory and movement. These speculations can be tested in several ways and are worth considering on future projects within the region. The important point here is that project areas may include components of different subsistence-settlement systems and assuming otherwise can profoundly affect interpretations if various synchronous sites are *not* differentiated parts of one strategy but actually from two or more. A small project area may contain only part of a complete settlement system, which is one problem, but even a project area as limited in size as the NMRAP may contain site types drawn from several different systems. This becomes less of a concern as residential mobility declines after the start of food production because of a great reduction in the spatial scale of residential movement, but for the Archaic it is an important consideration. Since the linear distance of the N16 ROW is only 43 km and includes just portions of two small plateaus (Rainbow and Shonto), it is easy to envision that the N16 project area may have been inadequate to sustain forager populations on a yearly basis. In order to survive, Archaic foragers likely operated on a geographical scale far exceeding the size of the project area, especially over the span of several consecutive years. Ethnographic data for hunter-gatherers living in the Great Basin and the Southwest indicate that annual subsistence territories easily exceed this distance, often greatly so (Kelly 1995:Table 4-1). For example, the northern Yavapai procurement range had a linear distance of more than 100 km north to south (Gifford 1936:254); a similar range can be inferred from Kelly's (1964) data on the Kaibab Band of the Southern Paiute. Although tempted to interpret the excavated NMRAP Archaic remains as parts of a single differentiated strategy, I think that raw material use is indicative of forager groups that operated on different spatial scales and had different geographic centers.

Agricultural Transition

The shift from a hunting-gathering economy to one based to some extent on food production, or farming, has been a long-standing research topic throughout the world. Fully domesticated plants spread from Mesoamerica to the North American Southwest by one means or another; thus the processes of the agricultural transition are unlike those of pristine centers of food production where forager populations became food producers as they developed maize or other crops. Throughout portions of Mesoamerica, Archaic foragers slowly became Formative food producers as the subsistence contribution of crops increased at the expense of wild resources, in part because of improvements in the yield of domesticates. In the secondary setting of the Colorado Plateau and the Southwest more generally, the agricultural transition may not have followed Romer's rule (Hockett and Ascher 1964), at least not everywhere. This is clearly an important concept when it comes to considering sociocultural or evolutionary change:

> The rule implies that incorporation of domesticated plants into hunter-gatherer economies sustains the ongoing system instead of changing it.... In this view, domesticates were first adopted not for food production itself, as some anthropologists have suggested (e.g., Cohen 1977), but rather for their contribution to the success of existing foraging strategies [Wills 1988:36].

Although some Archaic foragers of the Southwest probably acquired maize and squash and farming knowledge via diffusion, doing so to continue with their foraging lifeways, there also may have been a demic diffusion of farmer-foragers—Berry and Berry's (1986) San Pedro migration—to account for Basketmaker populations on the Colorado Plateau. If food production spread into the Southwest with migrant farmers, then Romer's rule does not apply. Indeed, in such a scenario, foragers within the same area as the migrant farmers may have adopted domesticates not so much to continue with their foraging lifestyle but out of necessity in the face of economic competition from farmer-foragers (see Wills 1995). The economically viable options for foragers facing the loss of many prime settlement locations and a reduction in high-return resources might have been limited to either moving on or adopting food production to stay within a region yet avoid extinction.

A critical part of interpreting the agricultural transition is thorough documentation and understanding of what came before—knowledge of Archaic foragers prior to the advent of food production. The NMRAP presented this opportunity, given the number of preceramic sites or components studied that lacked corn and those that contained corn. A basic question at the start of the project was what the excavations would reveal about the long-term history of forager occupation of the area—Would there be a continuous record of forager occupancy culminating in Basketmaker II or a discontinuous record punctuated by hiatuses? Would the NMRAP excavations reveal a pattern similar to that evident for Sand Dune and Dust Devil caves—Archaic use followed by Basketmaker use, but with no evident link between the two? Moreover, beyond simple continuity in population, was there cultural continuity? These questions ultimately track with coming to grips with the possibility that the agricultural transition on the Colorado Plateau, and in the Southwest more generally, may have transpired by two alternative, though not mutually exclusive, pathways (see review in Matson 1991, 2002).

As reviewed above, the NMRAP excavations produced a sizable sample of radiocarbon dates for sites that lacked corn or other domesticates. Following the evident reduction in population represented by the middle Archaic date gap, the Kayenta region started to see a renewed forager presence beginning around 2500 BC. By about 1800 BC the spike in the radiocarbon dates suggests that population levels were perhaps back to what they had been during the early Archaic. This increase did not result simply because groups of farmer-foragers were present on the Colorado Plateau at this time. The population upswing is also apparent on the northern Colorado Plateau, where maize and food production was not commonly practiced until after about cal. AD 100. The late Archaic sites in the northern Kayenta region and on the Kaibito Plateau lack maize or other domesticates; thus they appear to be the remains from a continued hunter-gatherer existence and not just the foraging components associated with groups who were food producers elsewhere.

As detailed in chapter 5, the NMRAP obtained a large sample of dates from sites that contained corn ($n = 75$), sites designated as Basketmaker II. Despite recent revelations (e.g., Huber 2005), maize is not all that old in the northern Kayenta region, appearing no earlier than about 400 cal. BC (the earliest direct corn date for the area is 2230 ± 60 BP). Additional dating of corn and squash might eventually demonstrate earlier use approximating that in Marsh Pass and Black Mesa to the south, where corn is well represented by about 800 cal. BC (multiple corn dates in the 2500s BP [Smiley 1994; Smiley and Parry 1992; Smiley et al. 1986]). If early corn was poorly represented relative to later Basketmaker corn, then rareness alone will lower the probabilities of being dated, but the sample size for the northern Kayenta region is beginning to be large enough to render this possibility moot. The current sample is a robust count of 55 direct dates on corncobs or kernels from a variety of site types, including dry rockshelters.

In the radiocarbon chronology for the area there is an evident decline in date frequency between about 700 and 400 cal. BC, and maize first appears after then. The hint of a gap will probably disappear with additional assays, but even so this interval may well remain a low point in the date histogram of this area. All sites on the older side of the date decline lacked maize, whereas most sites on the younger side contained maize, some in considerable abundance. Moreover, a pronounced change in the archaeological record coincides with the arrival of maize (chapter 5). I have classified all sites on the older side of the date decline as late Archaic (or terminal Archaic), in that they appear to be the archaeological expression of a continued foraging lifestyle. The sites on the younger side of the date decline are classified as Basketmaker II.

This mutually exclusive pattern—corn at sites dating more recent than 400 cal. BC but no corn at sites dating older than this—does not seem to be the by-product of site setting or site preservation. Most of NNAD's excavation took place at open sites, but this potential sampling bias is offset to a large degree by the direct dating of corn from several caves on the Rainbow Plateau. This effort failed to produce a date earlier than the Christian era, so there is currently no reason to suspect that the first farmers on the plateau preferred caves to open sites. Since the earliest maize on the Colorado Plateau is from open sites, there is no necessary reason to expect that open sites in the Kayenta region would not contain early maize.

NMRAP field and laboratory findings reveal an absence of maize at sites dating after about 1000 cal. BC but before 400 cal. BC, a time when domesticates were in use on portions of the Colorado Plateau to the south and east. Diligent searches of the ⅛-in mesh screened fill from cultural strata and dozens of hearths at late Archaic sites failed to produce any corn or squash remains. Subsequent flotation analysis verified this lack since none of 46 4-liter samples from late Archaic sites contained corn or squash. In stark contrast, nearly all preceramic sites dated after 400 cal. BC contained maize, sometimes in great abundance. Excavators recovered kernels, cupules, and occasional cobs in the field from most Basketmaker sites, and 61 percent of 194 Basketmaker flotation samples yielded some corn part, with kernels represented in 25 percent. As argued in chapter 4, I believe that the nonagricultural sites dating to before 400 cal. BC represent the trace of a continued forager adaptation on the Rainbow Plateau that lasted until perhaps 600 cal. BC and not the foraging and hunting camps of preceramic farmers. Besides the lack of domesticates, a principal reason for thinking this is that the projectile points and other remains are unlike those typical of Basketmaker II sites.

This latter aspect concerns continuity in material culture, a key piece of evidence regarding the agricultural transition in the northern Kayenta region or elsewhere on the Colorado Plateau. Continuity in culture refers to a clearly linked temporal sequence of cultural traits, which involves subjective judgments as to the degree of relatedness among objects from slices of time. The basic question is whether there are Archaic prototypes in the Kayenta region for the impressive inventory of Basketmaker II material remains first described in detail by Guernsey and Kidder (1921; Guernsey 1931; Kidder and Guernsey 1919). The open Basketmaker sites of the NMRAP did not yield perishable artifacts, the most distinctive portions of the Basketmaker II material culture. Yet the cave assemblages of the area combined with certain classes of nonperishable artifacts from both open and sheltered sites strongly indicate a significant disjuncture in stylistic and technological aspects of the archaeological record for the northern Kayenta region. This is seen when considering the whole suite of material remains that may serve to track the history of cultural transmission, both the artifacts that passively monitor or reflect social groups because of learned patterns of production and those that might be used to actively express identity.

Just having crops is the initial step toward greater subsistence specialization, but the extent of economic dependence on cultigens during the preceramic interval is a matter of debate. Matson (1991; Matson and Chisholm 1991) made a case that late Basketmaker II (ca. AD 100–400) populations on Cedar Mesa were nearly as dependent on maize as were the later Puebloan populations of this mesa (cf. Wills and Huckell 1994:38–39). Maize recovery from flotation samples of NMRAP Basketmaker and Puebloan sites offers one means for assessing the relative importance of maize in the Basketmaker diet, especially after controlling for whether a site was a primary or secondary habitation, since maize remains are less likely to occur in flotation samples from the latter type. Based on all plant parts (kernels, cupules, cobs, and other), maize ubiquity was high during the Basketmaker period, being the most common food remain in the flotation data set other than goosefoot seeds. At primary habitations, maize actually equals or exceeds the percent presence of goosefoot seeds. Although maize appears to be slightly more common within Puebloan flotation samples, this is likely a product of the comparative overrepresentation of float samples from primary habitations (80% for Puebloan, 56% for Basketmaker). Maize ubiquity significantly differs between primary and secondary Basketmaker habitations: almost 80 percent vs. 32 percent, respectively. Based on 20 flotation samples (73 liters of sediment), maize recovery from the Basketmaker primary habitation of The Pits was 20.8 parts per liter and 1.7 kernels per liter. With maize occurring in 90 percent of the samples from this site and 75 percent from the primary habitation of Kin Kahuna, there is little room for an increase in maize representation. Maize is no more ubiquitous at Pueblo II and III habitations of the northern Kayenta region, varying between 60 and 90 percent with a total value of 63 percent for the 200 NMRAP Puebloan flotation samples, nearly all of which came from primary habitations (also Geib and Casto 1985).

Measuring agricultural dependence is a complicated issue for archaeologists, made even more so these days because of the many separate lines of evidence that can be mustered, some of which may give conflicting results. Even when maize remains are exceedingly abundant, as at the Donaldson and Los Ojitos sites (L. Huckell 1995), the question remains, "Does an abundance of evidence necessarily translate into evidence of abundance?" (B. Huckell 1995:120). An answer to this question for the study area is provided by a recent isotope analysis of Kayenta-region Basketmaker burials (Coltrain et al. 2007). With delta ^{13}C values ranging from −5.9 to −13.7 and a mean of −8.0 ± 1.7 (Coltrain et al. 2007:Tables 1–2), the results demonstrate that Basketmaker II people were heavily dependent on maize by 400 cal. BC to the extent that their isotope values were similar to those of Puebloan farmers a thousand years later. The flotation results and the common field recovery of maize from nearly all Basketmaker features at primary habitations reflect this heavy emphasis on food production.

This does not mean that foraged resources did not provide an important supplement to domesticates. The most important ecologically wild resources seem to have been pinyon and ricegrass. Other "wild" plants consisted mostly of field weeds, which were largely a side benefit of agricultural disturbance and hence should not be treated as foraging in the sense practiced by Archaic groups of the local area thousands of years prior. That foraging was important to Puebloan farmers even during the recent past (e.g., Whiting 1939) reveals that there is every reason to expect the same during the interval when crops were initially used on the Colorado Plateau. Equally, though, the use of wild resources or nondomesticates says nothing necessarily about the extent of reliance on food production or about which is supplemental to which. Whereas food production might have been initially adopted so as to maintain a foraging lifestyle, as a means to continue a traditional way of life under altered circumstances, foraging was also an essential way to mitigate the economic risk associated with farming in an environment where crop losses from frost, inadequate rain, insect and animal predation, or other problems were inevitable. Foraging as a means to buffer crop loss was perhaps most practicable during Basketmaker II, when regional population density was apt to have been relatively low. Surviving through bad years no doubt hinged upon gathered and hunted resources, and even during good years crops alone would not have sufficed. If for no other reason than dietary diversity, Basketmaker groups would have sought out plant foods other than their crops; more important, they are a source of basic nutrients (Bye 1981:114–116). Yet the carbon isotope data when coupled with the evidence from feces and flotation samples strongly indicate that the Basketmaker economy was focused around maize production (Matson and Chisholm 2007).

The nature of the Archaic and Basketmaker settlements documented by the NMRAP reveals a marked difference suggestive of a profound alteration in adaptive strategy. The Archaic sites of the project area summarized in chapter 4 (and see SD vol. 2) consisted of hunting and processing camps along with several residential camps. The late Archaic residential camps consisted of hearths in association with lithic debitage, faunal bone, and occasional grinding tools; they lacked storage features entirely, and only one had a possible small structure that was no more than a wickiup. Radiocarbon dates along with vertical separation in one instance indicate that these sites accumulated from sequential reuse of locations over the span of several hundred years, which renders the sites all the less impressive. At most, these late Archaic sites represent the temporary camps for small social groups, perhaps just nuclear families. None of the Archaic sites appear to have had the substantial, long-lived residential occupations that are evident for the NMRAP Basketmaker settlements of Kin Kahuna and The Pits. Indeed, even though the late Archaic sites contained a considerable number of artifacts, none appeared even closely similar to the Basketmaker II seasonal residences, which contained easily identified shallow pithouses and small middens.

As summarized in chapter 5 and detailed in volume 3 of the supporting documentation, the sites at which maize first occurs are distinctly different from the NMRAP Archaic sites; the Basketmaker sites evince greater residential permanence, sequential reuse across many seasons, and a concern for securing large volumes of produce. Basketmaker residential sites are clearly differentiated between those that served as primary residential locations and those with a secondary role. The former, if not lived in permanently, were occupied for substantial portions of the year including winter. Primary residential sites contained extensive trash deposits, well-built pithouses, numerous bell-shaped storage pits and other pits, and human burials. The capacity of the large storage pits allowed for considerable surplus of food to be cached for future use: The Pits had a total capacity of almost 17 m³ in 24 storage pits (and this for just the portion within the ROW). Secondary residential sites contained single structures, small middens, and hearths but lacked storage features; these structures were perhaps used for a variety of seasonal extractive tasks made more efficient by temporary family resettlement to locations close to the resources being exploited.

It is interesting to observe that the changes seen in the archaeological record between Archaic and Basketmaker times transpired during the several hundred years of the decline in radiocarbon dates that locally separates these two intervals. Change during the preceding 7,000 years of the Archaic period appears glacial in comparison to what transpired between about 800 and 400 cal. BC in the northern Kayenta region. The dramatically different nature of the Basketmaker sites compared with those of the immediately preceding late Archaic strongly suggests a lack of adaptive continuity and seems more in accordance with a disjuncture than with an autochthonous transformation from a foraging economy to a farmer-forager economy.

Local discontinuity during the agricultural transition in the northern Kayenta region does not imply a lack of continuity elsewhere on the Colorado Plateau. The NMRAP excavations concern a modest-sized area, and just as a single site can never inform about the prehistory of some local area, likewise the archaeological record of one area does not inform about macroscale patterns for an entire region. Spatial scale clearly becomes a factor in the analysis of continuity/discontinuity and the question of farmer migration. Basketmaker occupation of the study area might represent little more than the expansion of farmer-foragers from an adjacent area, and on this slightly larger spatial scale continuity in occupation and culture may well exist. To the southeast of N16, directly dated burials and other Basketmaker remains demonstrate the earlier presence, by a few hundred years, of agricultural dependence and associated cultural diagnostics.

It is clear that much remains to be learned about the agricultural transition in the Kayenta region.

Puebloan Craft Production and Exchange

Central to any prehistoric economy is the acquisition and processing of resources into tools, containers, ornaments, and other items. Craft production is also closely tied to the transfer of material items among individuals or social groups. All societies interact with their neighbors to varying degrees and through various culturally structured mechanisms. Exchanges of materials, information, and marriage partners are common forms of socioeconomic interaction. Even when the focus of interaction lacks a material basis, such as with intergroup ceremonies, artifact exchange is often involved or serves as a mediating device. The unequal distribution of particular resources is a common reason for the rise of craft specialization and exchange (cf. Arnold 1980, 1985). Craft specialization might also be fostered by social reasons, such as to promote intercommunity dependency or to maintain alliances (Cordell and Plog 1979:421). Whatever the underlying causes, the unequal availability of natural resources provides an initial point of departure for examining the issue of craft production and exchange, and the raw material for artifacts such as pottery and stone tools is quite accessible to archaeological study.

In 1960, Turner and Cooley argued for extensive trade of flaked-stone tools or raw materials within the Kayenta region. They argued that most Kayenta Anasazi did not have ready access to material sources for producing flaked lithic tools such as bifaces (knives and projectile points). Yet groups residing close to the San Juan and Colorado rivers such as around Navajo Mountain had access to nodules of high-quality chert and other siliceous material. As a result, these groups exchanged either the raw materials or the finished products to populations living to the south, such as those of Tsegi Canyon (Turner and Cooley 1960). Exploitation of these sources was seen as a principal reason for Kayentan use of the Glen Canyon lowlands, where sites contained abundant evidence of flaked-stone tool reduction (e.g., Adams et al. 1961:54; Long 1966:66).

Today we know that siliceous rock sources are not so limited in the Kayenta region as Turner and Cooley supposed. Navajo chert is available from outcrops throughout most of the region. Less widely distributed, but occurring in great abundance in several localities, is Owl Rock chert. Chert and quartzite are also obtainable from the ancient river gravels that cap White Mesa and occur as a vast lag pavement north of Tuba City and in several other locations. Despite the occurrence of these other siliceous stones, most are poorly suited to the production of bifaces due to small nodule size and poor fracture qualities. As a result, it is still reasonable to hypothesize that Kayentans close to sources of good-quality stone for flaked implements might have specialized in tool production, which means the populations living at the foot of Navajo Mountain adjacent to the Glen Canyon lowlands, as Turner and Cooley suggested.

The NMRAP indeed documented an emphasis on the production of arrowpoints and bifaces at Pueblo III habitations clustered around the foot of Navajo Mountain. The number of arrowpoints alone from the Pueblo III habitation of Three Dog Site was remarkable for the Kayenta region ($n = 89$). At this site and the habitation of Hanging Ash the number of flakes per structure was 615 and 215, respectively, and the number for flaked tools per structure was 7.5 and 15.3, respectively. This stands in marked contrast to the flaked-stone assemblages at the Pueblo III habitations of Sapo Seco and Water Jar Pueblo just 8 km farther south, which produced 46 and 65 flakes per structure and .8 and 1.3 flaked tools per structure, respectively. Perhaps more important, the identifiable flake waste at the latter two sites consisted almost entirely of core and bipolar flakes (89 and 96%, respectively), whereas biface and pressure flakes constitute a significant proportion of the debris at Three Dog Site and Hanging Ash (more than 50%). This might be seen as dramatic and strong support for semispecialized production of high-input, facially thinned tools such as knives and projectile points by groups living in close proximity to the Glen Canyon lithic sources, and indeed this clearly seems to be the case, but was the motivation to exchange tools or something else?

By considering the flaked-stone artifacts alone the tool exchange interpretation seems well supported. But the story does not end there because faunal remains strongly suggest that large game hunting of deer and mountain sheep was an important activity for the inhabitants at the foot of Navajo Mountain. The count of bones from Three Dog Site is a few thousand, with a few hundred per structure, compared to just 70 bones total from Water Jar Pueblo, less than eight per structure, and 319 from Sapo Seco, with just under 17 per structure. Of the identifiable bone from Three Dog Site, excluding intrusive remains and a dog burial, more than 40 percent is from large mammals including mule deer, bighorn sheep, pronghorn, and perhaps even elk. Identifiable faunal remains from the other sites, excluding animal burials and intrusive materials, consist mostly of cottontail and jackrabbit; remains from deer or other large game are scant. The implication for me is that the numerous points and evidence of biface production at Three Dog Site and Hanging Ash, which also had relatively abundant faunal remains, had more to do with stone tool production for hunting than with stone tool production for tool exchange per se. Meat or hides from large game probably had far more value as exchange items to populations farther south in the Kayenta region than arrowpoints, knives, or other tools did. The occupants of Three Dog might have had ready access to stone for making points, but the significant issue is that they were in proximity to the Glen Canyon lowlands and benches and plateaus farther away to the north and west, such as the Kaiparowits, that had been depopulated and thus provided an area that would not have been resource depressed like the core Kayenta region, with its many centuries of intensive habitation and ever-increasing population. Protein is a far more vital resource and potentially more limited in supply in the core Kayenta region than stone or stone tools; thus if something was exchanged, it was more likely to have been meat, hides, or the products therefrom.

The unequal distribution of particular resources is also relevant to potential specialization in grinding tool production during the Puebloan period. While the Kayenta region has no shortage of sandstone, much of it is poorly suited to grinding hard maize kernels, due either to friability (Navajo and Wingate sandstones) or fine grain size (sandstones of the Kayenta Formation). Quality stone for maize-grinding tools comes from various Upper Jurassic and Cretaceous formations, with those that crop out on Navajo Mountain and occur as talus boulders and cobbles on its slopes and in washes being an excellent stone for manos and metates (and also mauls). This material is well cemented and comes in a variety of grain sizes and textures, with abundant natural vesicles. Beals et al. (1945:79) first reported on this material, learning of it from their Navajo workers when they identified the tool stone for several mauls from a site in the Kayenta Valley as deriving from "somewhere near Navajo Mountain." These workers specifically stated how the stone was prized for manos. As of 2002, a Navajo woman (Mrs. Holgate) living at the foot of this mountain still produced manos and metates of this stone, the last person doing so on the western reservation.

Evidence for prehistoric production of grinding tools in the Navajo Mountain area consists of the common recovery of mano and metate blanks at most sites (e.g., Geib et al. 1985:379, Table 98; Lindsay et al. 1968:292–293). In contrast, only a single mano blank was found at one of the excavated sites within the portion of the N16 ROW on the Shonto Plateau (Russell 1989). Even more telling is the abundant flaking and pecking debris at some habitations at the foot of Navajo Mountain (Geib et al. 1985:192, Figure 65). The NMRAP excavations found that grinding tool production debris increases from absent or very low as one moves northward from the Shonto Plateau and onto the Rainbow Plateau, not becoming significant until nearing the foot of Navajo Mountain. The rock fraction of flotation samples should be even more informative of this activity. The NMRAP Puebloan habitations near the base of the mountain also produced unused manos in various stages of completion, further evidence of local production that was not found at habitations farther south (see SD vol. 5, chap. 6, and the site descriptions of SD vol. 4). The production activity might have been all for local use, but there are several reasons to think not. First is the fact that manos, metates, and mauls of Navajo Mountain sandstone occur at sites well away from the source, sites that lack any production debris. The finds of Beals et al. (1945) are just one notable example. Exchange thus seems likely. Also, given the use-life of manos and metates, the amount of debris noted at Navajo Mountain sites seems far in excess of the needs of small households.

The production scale was likely that represented by Mrs. Holgate—part-time on a catch-as-catch-can basis in between the other daily chores of life. This seems to be the scale of all craft activity in the Kayenta region and is likely a factor in why it is so difficult to detect and why Kayenta households are sometimes portrayed as autonomous. But as anthropologists have learned, all societies interact with their neighbors to varying degrees and through various culturally structured mechanisms, and material exchange is one of them. Grinding tools highly suitable for intensive maize processing represented a real need across much of the Kayenta region, a need that some families living around Navajo Mountain appear to have willingly met by producing more manos and metates than were required at home.

I started this discussion of craft production and exchange by talking about stone tools rather than ceramics, which so frequently figure prominently. This does not mean that the NMRAP recovered no evidence for ceramic production—quite the contrary, as chapters 2 and 4 of volume 5 of the online documents demonstrate. Part of the effort on this project involved further exploration for clay resources in the Kayenta region as a means to help shed light on potential production areas (Geib and Callahan 1987), the results of which are summarized online in Appendix H3.

The trend noted by Fairley and Callahan (1985; also Callahan and Fairley 1983) for greatly increased localized production of utility ware on the Rainbow Plateau during Pueblo III has been confirmed by the NMRAP findings. Prior to Pueblo III, virtually all utility ware of the northern Kayenta region appears to have been imported from the core Kayenta area to the south such as the Klethla or Long House valleys, since the utility ware is made from light-firing clays tempered with a nonlocal sandstone and is a perfect match for typical Tusayan Gray Ware. Puebloans on the Rainbow Plateau during Pueblo III increasingly experimented with local production, using a wide variety of local clays with higher iron content, local sandstone for temper, and surface treatments that varied from those of Kiet Siel Gray. By at least AD 1200 inhabitants on the Rainbow Plateau had established a local utility ware tradition (Rainbow Gray) based on the use of crushed sandstone temper and iron-rich clays (Callahan and Fairley 1983). Production of utility ware on the Rainbow Plateau appears to have been only for local use rather than exchange, at least not outside of the northern Kayenta region, as sites on the Shonto Plateau lack Rainbow Gray. None was found at the Pueblo III sites on the southern portion of the N16 ROW (Blinman 1989), including the middle Pueblo III habitation of Ditch House excavated by the NMRAP.

Despite the localized production of utility ware during Pueblo III, some utilitarian vessels were imported to habitations of the northern Kayenta region from the south since typical examples of Moenkopi Corrugated and Kiet Siel Gray occur in Pueblo III assemblages on the Rainbow Plateau. Importation of Tusayan White Ware also continued, with much of it taking the form of volcanic ash–tempered Tusayan and Kayenta Black-on-white, the production of which appears to have become increasingly specialized in the Klethla Valley. Chemical analysis of volcanic ash in sherds from the project area and elsewhere indicates that two different ash sources were being used and that movement of vessels with this temper may have followed along kinship lines (see SD vol. 5, chap. 4).

One production area for Tsegi Orange Ware was the northern Kayenta region, and the finding of a tiny fragment of an unfired polychrome bowl sherd at Three Dog Site clearly indicates that items of potential high social value were produced there as well, along with the almost utilitarian form of orange ware known as Tsegi Orange. To what extent Tsegi Orange Ware vessels made in the local Navajo Mountain area were traded south to other populations of the Kayenta region remains to be determined. No sites of the NMRAP project area seem to have specialized in pottery production per se, and indeed this will be hard to demonstrate given that it, like mano and metate production, was probably a low-level activity but one of even less visibility since so little "debris" is left behind. Having a better idea as to where pottery was fired might help (e.g., Fuller 1984; Heacock 1995).

Social Issues

Inferences or speculations on various social issues are presented throughout this document but are kept to a minimum in this conclusion. Treatment of the dead is one of the best avenues for approaching the topic of social differentiation that the NMRAP research plan identified, but it was ultimately outside the mandated purview of this project, and in the end so few burials were discovered that it would not have mattered.

For nearly the entire sequence of occupation in the project area, from the early Archaic up until middle Pueblo III, nuclear or small extended families appear to have been the principal units of residence. Organization above the household doubtless existed, but an archaeological trace for this does not become obvious until after AD 1200, when settlements such as Three Dog Site clearly accommodated multiple households, evidently separated into two kin groups. It is quite possible that the multiple Basketmaker II secondary habitations grouped closely together along the divide between Piute and Navajo canyons represented a dispersed community, but demonstrating this is not possible at present. Even the NMRAP Basketmaker II site with the largest number of structures, Kin Kahuna, apparently housed no more than one or perhaps two families at a time. Although it contained a minimum of at least six structures and doubtless several more outside the road ROW, and therefore clearly fits Smiley's (2002a:53) "proto-village" site type, extensive dating of maize samples demonstrated that few if any of the structures were contemporaneous, and indeed only two have the potential to have been in use at the same time. Yet, given the hundreds of years commonly represented by radiocarbon dates, sequential occupation of even these two houses is highly probable. With no more than one or two families probably occupying the site at any one interval, it was considerably less than a village or even a proto-village, not even qualifying as a small hamlet. The probable small group size of the site is underscored by small house size, with floor areas less than 20 m^2. If true in this case, then it also may apply to other Basketmaker II and III sites where numerous structures hint at social units of residence beyond single extended families. For example, Schurr and Gregory (2002) demonstrated at the early Agricultural period village of Los Pozos in southeastern Arizona that the site comprised an agglomeration of features from many temporal intervals. In this and likely many other cases the sum of the parts can misinform about social scale.

Community size is an important variable when it comes to discussions about social differentiation, for in small groups there is little opportunity and perhaps little incentive for demarcation to occur. Thus the processes of social differentiation likely started coming more into play by late Pueblo III, when the Kayenta Anasazi began to aggregate into communities of many households, perhaps unrelated ones. Yet even then there is no solid evidence in the Kayenta region overall for ranking beyond that which is achieved with age, with elderly female burials some of the richest. The possibility exists that certain lineages or clans had the richest burials according to some degree of social position based on family connections, perhaps tied to ritual significance, but this remains speculative. Certainly there are no obvious differences in the ceramic assemblages at small and large Pueblo III habitations in terms of the "more expensive" fine decorated vessels (type distributions) or in terms of vessel forms and specific stylistic and iconographic features. The same extends to other items of material culture.

Despite a brief experiment with a great kiva at Juniper Cove (Gilpin and Benallie 2000), there is a lack of evidence for significant sociocultural complexity in the region until the final Tsegi phase, after about AD 1240. There are no aggregated Pueblo I and Pueblo II communities such as occur in the Mesa Verde and Chacoan regions. For centuries the Anasazi population of the Kayenta region lived in settlements no larger than what could accommodate several households consisting of a large extended family (Prudden units). Material culture and architecture evolved, but without any significant alteration of an overall simple-looking social fabric. The centuries of comparative social "simplicity" came to a close in the 1200s; several of the NMRAP sites date to this interval of profound change when aggregated communities began to form, setting the stage for an even more profound change that resulted when populations abandoned the core Kayenta region, many of which evidently settled in the Hopi area to the south, where they formed true villages in the 1300s, such as represented by the Homolovi ruins of the Little Colorado River area (E. Adams 2002).

The processes at work in this "transformation" no doubt included the "increasing subsistence and social stresses resulting from greater population densities, caused by settlement relocations, and severe environmental degradation" highlighted by Dean (2002:157). The role that warfare played (Haas 1989, 1990; Haas and Creamer 1993) remains mostly conjectural and based largely on the defendable positions of many Tsegi phase pueblos, which the northern Kayenta region is well endowed with. Unprecedented high population density is a critical variable, and in the northern Kayenta region population clearly peaked in the 1200s. One important aspect of the population peak is not that the increase occurred but the implications of how it occurred—from possible influxes of people who had little or no history of residence in the region. This need not have been a migration of complete outsiders, since places like Cummings Mesa started to be abandoned in the early to mid-1200s (Ambler et al. 1964), prior to late Pueblo III, and some of these families likely settled around Navajo Mountain or elsewhere on the Rainbow Plateau. The important point is that newcomers would have created land-allocation issues not faced before on such a scale or without defined social mechanisms for resolution. The maxim that "possession is nine-tenths of the law" is an old commonsense concept (Lawson and Rudden 1984:49–50) that may have been put to a crucial test as populations crowded onto the Rainbow Plateau and other portions of the Kayenta region during the 1200s. If primacy of residence in an area and kin relations were the means of preventing a state of anarchy concerning use rights and ownership, then one other means of doing so or of "enforcing" one's position was by consolidating into larger social aggregates, visibly expressed as Pueblo III villages. This could also be done by loose family units trying to gain access to land, even if by leverage. Note that this does not necessarily entail physical conflict, since social group size can intimidate or persuade without overt action simply by the fact of village size and membership.

When aggregated pueblos appear in the northern Kayenta region in the middle 1200s, several diverse settlement layouts are evident. Some, such as Neskahi Village (NA7719) on Piute Mesa (Hobler 1974) or Surprise Pueblo (NA7498) on Cummings Mesa (Ambler et al. 1964:53–83), appear to be larger versions of the architecturally (and presumably socially) integrated Pueblo II and early Pueblo III "unit pueblos" that Lindsay (Lindsay 1969; Lindsay et al. 1968) classified as plaza sites/pueblos. These two sites illustrate the two standard forms of plaza pueblos—D-shaped (Neskahi) and square/rectangular (Surprise). It is important to point out that Tsegi phase plaza pueblos are different from what Adams (1989:156) referred to as plaza-oriented villages—the large aggregated communities that appeared in western Puebloan refuge areas at the close of the thirteenth century. The term *village* provides an important distinction (plaza pueblo vs. plaza village) since it emphasizes the key difference in social scale between the two: a few dozen people vs. hundreds. Plaza pueblos contrast with the Segazlin Mesa community at the foot of Navajo Mountain, which is a loose affiliation of small extended-family courtyard complexes (Lindsay et al. 1968) all occupying the same small mesa top. Pottery Pueblo on Piute Mesa (Stein 1984) several kilometers from Neskahi Village appears to be a similar architecturally nonintegrated agglomeration of family courtyard units, but ones that are more physically compacted by the consequence of occupying a small rock prominence. These latter two sites are a specific form of late Pueblo III aggregated pueblo that Lindsay (1969: 243–246) termed a courtyard pueblo, where room clusters are grouped together to form courtyard complexes and these in turn are further grouped to form pueblos (see Dean 2002:143–146). Lindsay (1969:367) noted that these variations in Tsegi phase village patterning could be a reflection of the arrival of different traditions in the Navajo Mountain district, but both could also have been homespun, although perhaps engendered by the arrival of outside families.

An example of this is provided by Three Dog Site, excavated by the NMRAP, which appears to exemplify the architectural reconfiguration that marks the transition to the courtyard pueblo type of village. At this site the structural remains of a middle Pueblo III habitation lay beneath those of a late Pueblo III habitation. The late Pueblo III structures were built on the same spot and generally followed the same ground plan established by the residents just a decade or two earlier but were organized into a more formalized and tightly integrated pueblo that included additional rooms, probably more people, and a greater investment in architectural permanence.

The middle Pueblo III structures were razed and filled in, but the large central kiva of the earlier component was maintained. It is probably not wild speculation to claim that the final residents of this site were descendants of and perhaps some of the same people who initially built two courtyard complexes during middle Pueblo III. The nearly identical footprint and continued use of the one large kiva seem to support this argument. Moreover, the site occupies a prime piece of real estate in what was a very crowded area along the foot of Navajo Mountain—a sheltered drainage with permanent water and farmable alluvium—just the sort of setting that is likely to have been "owned" by some social unit such as a localized lineage. The comprehensive remodel of the site bespeaks a cooperative effort by the entire residential group that transformed the site into a more integrated architectural unit that implies a more tightly knit social unit. The exact sequence of feature demolition and construction was only evident in a few cases, but the remodel must have been planned to ensure that grinding facilities and shelter were available as needed during the process. A similarly coordinated effort took place when the site was finally abandoned and the last residents moved on. The use of a single kiva and what appears to have been the organized group construction of a more formal room block signaled integration of the two families or kin groups, a pattern noted throughout the Kayenta region during the Tsegi phase (Dean 1969; Lindsay 1969). There are no indications that the remaining kiva was enlarged to accommodate more site residents, and the two separate courtyards of the late Pueblo III component retained separate food-storage and -preparation space.

The final use of Three Dog Site occurred during late Pueblo III, partly overlapping with the Tsegi phase, but the residents moved from the site prior to full abandonment of the northern Kayenta region since usable timbers, construction material, and whole artifacts were scavenged from the structures. This behavior would be expected if the occupants moved only a short distance, in that the effort to dismantle and move the material would be less than procuring new beams, rocks for masonry, and large grinding tools. A large Tsegi phase habitation lies within a kilometer to the southwest (UT-B-63-2). This site has not been excavated, so its total size and configuration are unknown, but ceramics on the surface, including abundant Kayenta Black-on-white and whiteline polychrome types, imply that it slightly postdates Three Dog Site. The residents of Three Dog may have simply moved upstream, perhaps to be closer to the source of permanent water of their drainage, where they combined with other families to build a larger pueblo. By such an effort they took on the appearance of being physically larger and thus more able to defend/negotiate their claims to what was likely to have been a coveted location.

The social underpinnings of the enclosed plaza pueblo were likely identical—strong family ties such as a mother and father and their direct descendants with spouses and children, perhaps several generations deep. It is possible to envision the accretional growth of a slowly expanding plaza pueblo as the result of increasing family size as children reached adulthood and married, with spouses of one sex or another moving in. Neskahi Village would seem to be at the potential upper size range for a community organized on such direct kin relationships, where food stores were centralized rather than under individual household control. Also, beyond the inward-looking insularity of plaza pueblos, they have an inherent physical limit to their growth that can only be overcome by total redesign and rebuilding on an ever-larger scale. When there is no longer any room within the plaza for newcomers they must simply be appended to the outside, something that is in evidence at Neskahi Village. Nonetheless plaza pueblos such as Neskahi Village eventually needed to be "reformatted" if, as a means of equalizing social relations with larger, potentially competing neighbors such as at Pottery Pueblo, they were to grow any larger through "outsider" recruitment. It is plausible that plaza sites like Neskahi Village, which occupy prime settlement locations, each represent a single large kin group with long-standing kinship or communal ties to an area that held onto an older pattern of residence (Lindsay 1969:367). Courtyard pueblos such as Pottery Pueblo were built by people experimenting with new means of social integration, perhaps a previously dispersed community of unrelated families but also including transients or newcomers, that allowed ever larger architectural configurations, ones that more easily incorporated individual households without direct family ties. The courtyard format of residential construction allowed this to occur far more easily than the plaza format. New residential groups might have been welcomed because of special knowledge or skills that they offered, either practical or ritual, or perhaps simply because they added to the numerical strength of a settlement.

The key element in this is the social fluidity that appears evident in the Kayenta region from the movement of single nuclear and extended families. Dean (1969) first documented this in detail in his dissertation research in Tsegi Canyon, where he showed how larger sites such as Kiet Siel were constantly in flux with families moving in and out—"the apparent independent movement of single households" (1969:190). The NMRAP also documented this with the excavation of small nuclear-family residential units such as Hymn House, a classic example of a room cluster (Dean 1969:34–35; Lindsay 1969:156–157), the distinctive grouping of architectural units that were combined like building blocks to form the larger Tsegi phase pueblos, whether in the open or as cliff dwellings. Occupancy of Hymn House occurred toward the end of the middle Pueblo III period, probably sometime between AD 1230 and 1250. That this site probably housed a nuclear family is suggested by its small size, whether one considers the total roofed space or just that of the one living room (5.5 m^2). As Dean points out, and Hymn House well exemplifies, "there is hardly enough space in the average [Kayenta] living room for one family, let alone two or more" (1969:37). Hymn House represents the modularization of architectural space for a family that facilitated the creation of large Tsegi phase pueblos. Family units of various size could be attached together to form larger aggregates. Occupation of scattered settlements such as Hymn House by single small families suggests that the social and environmental forces that resulted in the reorganization of Kayenta social structure during the Tsegi phase were at play during the middle Pueblo III period. Key in this may have been the environmentally caused fragmentation and dislocation of residential groups that caused nuclear families to attempt fending for themselves. Although always a potential "option," it perhaps became a major factor with the drought of the middle twelfth century AD. Whatever ties existed to unite scattered households also would have served as the social glue to attach segments into the courtyard-oriented sites of the Tsegi phase (see Lindsay 1969:163, 360–373). Hymn House was abandoned just prior to the Tsegi phase, and the family that moved on would have participated in the formation of a Tsegi phase village. Given the evident scavenging of useful tools from Hymn House, the occupants probably did not move far, perhaps to one of the many Tsegi phase villages sprinkled across the Rainbow Plateau.

One speculative final aspect of the social organization was brought to mind upon reading Graham's (1994) research on Rarámuri settlement mobility while contemplating the late Pueblo III site of Sapo Seco, located in the sagebrush flats on the central portion of the Rainbow Plateau. Concerning the Rarámuri, Graham states that each family "is part of an established network whose members pool their labor to accomplish the task at hand" (such as harvesting crops [1994:21]). Visiting households are "put up" in temporary abodes near the main residence, a form of residential mobility that is the hallmark of that culture. The main habitation area of Sapo Seco (Locus A) consisted of a small unit pueblo, the residential site of an extended family situated for efficient food production and processing. However, the site overall shows a considerably more complex settlement pattern, with three other residential loci of scattered pithouses in a northeast-to-south arc 10–30 m from Locus A. Overall the site had a total of 18 living structures of various types, principally living rooms and mealing rooms, and therefore the site has the appearance of a larger pithouse hamlet. The enclosed unit pueblo of Locus A presents a marked contrast to the pithouses of the other loci, which are more loosely configured and lack formal communal areas; the only kiva occurred at Locus A. As opposed to Locus A, the structures at the other loci appear to have been occupied on a short-term, seasonal, or intermittent basis. The principal reason for this conjecture is the lack of adequate food-storage facilities for overwintering. It may be mere coincidence that the structures of other loci are located in proximity to Locus A, but partially contemporaneous occupancy seems probable, at least initially; and although the occupants of all four loci may have been related by kin, clan, or some other form of social or economic association, the other loci are expressly not part of the Locus A pueblo core. The inhabitants of the other loci apparently resided at the site on a temporary basis, affiliating themselves with the more permanent Locus A households as the need arose and then splitting off when that need was fulfilled. Superpositioning and remodeling of structures imply that inhabitants returned to previously occupied structures or that loci were reoccupied by new tenants. This kind of "recombinant" residency has been noted elsewhere in the Kayenta region at the Tsegi phase sites of Betatakin and Kiet Siel (Dean 1969). The motivations for residential clustering are probably numerous and nearly impossible to extract from the archaeological record, at least at Sapo Seco, but the Rarámuri example presents some plausible scenarios, including details as to the social and economic motivations behind such moves (Graham 1994). Temporary residence and mutual assistance in social and ceremonial activities or communal work efforts such as planting or harvesting crops may have provided an initial basis for creating the larger architectural configurations of aggregated pueblos.

Final Thoughts

The brief summary of certain research issues presented here incorporates just some of the topics covered in the overall NMRAP report, the bulk of which is devoted to presenting the descriptive details of what the project excavated, described, and analyzed. There is no way that a chapter authored by a single individual could do justice to the diversity of topics covered in the entire report. I only hope that I touched on some aspect that either piqued the interest or sufficiently galled the reader to dig deeper into this report or the supporting documentation posted on the Web.

The future of archaeological research in the Kayenta region remains a large unknown. CRM projects are still likely to arise on occasion, but as of yet there are few large undertakings that promise to make substantial contributions. Developments are often limited in extent, and projects are redesigned such that impacts to cultural resources appear negligible, although cumulative long-term effects are seldom considered. Most progress in understanding the past will depend on taking small steps and working on rather confined interests or around the margins of larger topics. Even with a project the size of the NMRAP, providing sufficient data to address complex issues is difficult, and testing models of culture change is all the more problematic. Many basic issues of chronology and culture history remain to be documented in the Kayenta region, and we are far from fully comprehending them, let alone the larger concerns of arriving at some understanding of why cultures change. If work can continue, I look forward to what will be learned in the next several decades.

Notes

1. The NMRAP excavated 14 Archaic sites in the N16 ROW, with two of these having multiple Archaic components.

APPENDIX

Contents of Supplemental Documents

The following contents page represents the four volumes and the appendixes of the original contract report on which this book is based. The documents may be accessed free of charge at the University of Utah Press website www.UofUpress.com. Please look for the link on the book's main page.

Volume 2: Archaic Site Descriptions
1. "Introduction to the Archaic Period," Phil R. Geib
2. "Atlatl Rock Cave," Phil R. Geib, Nancy Coulam, Victoria H. Clark, and Kelley A. Hays-Gilpin
3. "The Pits," Phil R. Geib and Victoria H. Clark
4. "Hólahéi Scatter," Phil R. Geib
5. "Pee Wee Grande," Victoria H. Clark and Phil R. Geib
6. "Windy Mesa," Jim Collette and Phil R. Geib
7. "Polly's Place," Kimberly Spurr and Phil R. Gei
8. "Tres Campos," Phil R. Geib
9. "Big Bend," Phil R. Geib
10. "Mouse House," Victoria H. Clark and Phil R. Geib
11. "Dune Hollow," Victoria H. Clark and Phil R. Geib
12. "Sapo Seco," Phil R. Geib
13. "Bonsai Bivouac," Victoria H. Clark and Phil R. Geib
14. "Three Dog Site," Kimberly Spurr and Phil R. Geib
15. "UT-B-63-38," Phil R. Geib
16. "Tsé Haal'á," Phil R. Geib

Volume 3: Basketmaker Site Descriptions
1. "Introduction to Basketmaker II," Phil R. Geib

Open Habitations with Storage Features
2. "Kin Kahuna," Phil R. Geib and Kimberly Spurr
3. "The Pits," Phil R. Geib
4. "Big Bend," Phil R. Geib

Open Habitations without Storage Features
5. "Ditch House," Phil R. Geib and Victoria H. Clark
6. "Polly's Place," Kimberly Spurr and Phil R. Geib
7. "Tres Campos," Phil R. Geib
8. "Panorama House," Phil R. Geib
9. "Blake's Abode," Jim Collette and Phil R. Geib
10. "Mountainview," Kimberly Spurr, Phil R. Geib, and Kelley A. Hays-Gilpin
11. "Sin Sombra," Jim Collette and Phil R. Geib
12. "Three Dog Site," Kimberly Spurr and Phil R. Geib

Other Site Types
13. "Pee Wee Grande," Victoria H. Clark and Phil R. Geib
14. "Windy Mesa," Jim Collette and Phil R. Geib
15. "Ko' Lanhi," L. Theodore Neff and Phil R. Geib
16. "Scorpion Heights," Kimberly Spurr and Phil R. Geib
17. "Mouse House," Victoria H. Clark and Phil R. Geib
18. "Bonsai Bivouac," Victoria H. Clark and Phil R. Geib

Volume 4: Puebloan Site Descriptions
1. "Introduction to the Formative Period," Jim Collette and Phil R. Geib

Semipermanent Habitations
2. "Hammer House," Jim Collette and Phil R. Geib
3. "Hillside Hermitage," Kimberly Spurr and Phil R. Geib
4. "Ditch House," Victoria H. Clark and Phil R. Geib
5. "Windy Mesa," Jim Collette and Phil R. Geib
6. "Naaki Hooghan," Jim Collette and Phil R. Geib
7. "Hymn House," Victoria H. Clark and Phil R. Geib
8. "Sapo Seco," Jim Collette and Phil R. Geib
9. "Water Jar Pueblo," Kimberly Spurr and Phil R. Geib
10. "Three Dog Site," Kimberly Spurr and Phil R. Geib
11. "Hanging Ash," Phil R. Geib and Kimberly Mangum

Other Site Types
12. "The Pits," Phil R. Geib
13. "Wolachii Bighan," Victoria H. Clark and Phil R. Geib
14. "Pee Wee Grande," Victoria H. Clark and Phil R. Geib
15. "The Slots," Kimberly Spurr and Phil R. Geib
16. "Tres Campos," Phil R. Geib
17. "Camp Dead Pine," Victoria H. Clark and Phil R. Geib
18. "Mouse House," Victoria H. Clark and Phil R. Geib
19. "Kin Kahuna," Phil R. Geib
20. "Dune Hollow," Victoria H. Clark and Phil R. Geib
21. "Modesty House," Kimberly Spurr and Phil R. Geib
22. "Bonsai Bivouac," Victoria H. Clark and Phil R. Geib
23. "UT-B-63-19," Phil R. Geib

Volume 5: Analyses and Interpretation
1. "Project Summary," Phil R. Geib
2. "Ceramic Analysis," Kelley Hays-Gilpin and Janet Hagopian
3. "Painted Pottery: Analysis and Interpretation," Kelley Hays-Gilpin
4. "Microprobe Analysis of Volcanic Ash Tempered Tusayan White Ware," Kimberly Spurr, Phil R. Geib, and James Wittke
5. "Patterns in Stone Tool Raw Materials, Production, and

Use: Analysis of the N16 Lithic Artifacts," Phil R. Geib and Miranda Warburton

6. "Grinding Tools and Miscellaneous Stone Artifacts," Stewart Deats
7. "Minerals and Pigments," Kimberly Spurr and Phil R. Geib
8. "Faunal Remains from the N16 Sites," Kari M. Schmidt
9. "Shell Artifacts," Arthur W. Vokes
10. "Flotation Analysis," Meredith Matthews
11. "Pollen Analysis," Susan J. Smith
12. "Special Pollen Studies from the N16 Project: Bridging the Inferential Gap Between Pollen Analysis and Past Behavior," Susan J. Smith and Phil R. Geib
13. "Summary and Interpretation," Phil R. Geib
14. "The First Kayenta Farmers: Summary and Interpretation of Basketmaker II," Phil R. Geib
15. "Summary and Interpretation of Puebloan Remains," Phil R. Geib and Jim Collette
16. "Conclusions: The Research Design and Beyond," Phil R. Geib

Appendix Volume

"Appendix A: Source Analysis of Obsidian Artifacts from Archaeological Sites in the Navajo Mountain Road Archaeological Project, Northeastern Arizona," Richard E. Hughes

"Appendix B: Flotation Analysis Data," Meredith H. Matthews

"Appendix C1a: Navajo Mountain (N16) Pollen, Raw Counts," Susan Smith

"Appendix C1b: Navajo Mountain (N16) Taxa Frequency," Susan Smith

"Appendix C2: Navajo Mountain (N16) Detailed Pollen Sample Provenience," Susan Smith and Phil Geib

"Appendix C3: Navajo Mountain (N16) Pollen Washes of Seeds and Metates from Seed Grinding," Susan Smith

"Appendix C4: Navajo Mountain (N16) Corn Husks Pollen Wash Data," Susan Smith

"Appendix D: Results of Tree-Ring Data," Jeffery S. Dean

"Appendix E: Analysis of Obsidian Artifacts from Sites AZ-J-14-17 and AZ-J-12-23, Arizona," Christopher M. Stevenson

"Appendix F: The Ebb and Flow of Kayenta Population in the Navajo Mountain District," J. Richard Ambler, Helen C. Fairley, and Phil R. Geib

"Appendix G: Geological Investigations Along N16," Kirk C. Anderson

"Appendix H1: A Strength Analysis of Kayenta Area Ceramics for the Navajo Mountain Road Project," Mark A. Neupert

"Appendix H2: Comments on Selected White Ware and Gray Ware Ceramics from Hymn House, Sapo Seco, Water Jar Pueblo, Hanging Ash and Three Dog Site, N16 Road Project," Winston Hurst

"Appendix H3: Raw Material Data," Kelley Hays-Gilpin

"Appendix H4: Ceramic Analysis Format," Kelley Hays-Gilpin

"Appendix I: Radiocarbon Results for N16," no author, who obtained is self explanatory

"Appendix J: Research Design," Phil Geib, Miranda Warburton, and Kelley Hays-Gilpin

"Appendix K: Vegetation Changes on the Rainbow Plateau Since the Last Glacial Stage," Peter Koehler

References Cited

Aasen, D. K.
1984   Pollen, Macrofossil and Charcoal Analysis of Basketmaker Coprolites from Turkey Pen Ruin, Cedar Mesa, Utah. Unpublished M.A. thesis, Department of Anthropology, Washington State University.

Adams, E. C.
1989   Changing Form and Function in Western Pueblo Ceremonial Architecture from AD 1000 to 1500. In *The Architecture of Social Integration in Prehistoric Pueblos*, edited by W. D. Lipe and M. Hegmon, pp. 155–160. Occasional Paper No. 1. Crow Canyon Archaeological Center, Cortez, Colorado.
1996   The Pueblo III–Pueblo IV Transition in the Hopi Area, Arizona. In *The Prehistoric Pueblo World, AD 1150–1350*, edited by M. A. Adler, pp. 48–58. University of Arizona Press, Tucson.
2002   *Homol'ovi: An Ancient Hopi Settlement Cluster*. University of Arizona Press, Tucson.

Adams, J. L.
1999   Refocusing the Role of Food-Grinding Tools as Correlates for Subsistence Strategies in the U.S. Southwest. *American Antiquity* 64:475–498.

Adams, K. R., C. M. Meegan, S. G. Ortman, R. E. Howell, L. C. Werth, D. A. Muenchrath, M. K. O'Neill, and C. A. C. Gardner
2006   MAÍS (Maize of American Indigenous Societies) Southwest: Ear Descriptions and Traits That Distinguish 27 Morphologically Distinct Groups of 123 Historic USDA Maize (*Zea mays* L. spp. *mays*) Accessions and Data Relevant to Archaeological Subsistence Models. Available at http://farmingtonsc.nmsu.edu/documents/maissouthwestcopyrightedmanuscript1.pdf.

Adams, W. Y.
1951   *Archaeology and Culture History of the Navajo Country: Report on Reconnaissance for the Pueblo Ecology Study, 1951*. MS on file, Museum of Northern Arizona, Flagstaff.
1960   *Ninety Years of Glen Canyon Archaeology, 1869–1959*. Museum of Northern Arizona Bulletin No. 33. Northern Arizona Society of Science and Art, Flagstaff.
1963   *Shonto: A Study of the Role of the Trader in a Modern Navajo Community*. Bureau of American Ethnology Bulletin 188. Washington, D.C.

Adams, W. Y., and N. K. Adams
1959   *Inventory of Prehistoric Sites on the Lower San Juan River, Utah*. Museum of Northern Arizona Bulletin No. 31. Northern Arizona Society of Science and Art, Flagstaff.

Adams, W. Y., A. J. Lindsay Jr., and C. G. Turner II
1961   *Survey and Excavations in Lower Glen Canyon, 1952–1958*. Museum of Northern Arizona, Bulletin 36. Flagstaff.

Ahler, S. A., T. D. Thiessen, and M. K. Trimble
1991   *People of the Willows: The Prehistory and Early History of the Hidatsa Indians*. University of North Dakota Press, Grand Forks.

Ahlstrom, R. V. N.
1985   The Interpretation of Archaeological Tree-Ring Dates. Unpublished Ph.D. dissertation, Department of Anthropology, University of Arizona, Tucson.
1998a Black Mesa's Ceramic Period Occupation: Chronology as Chronicle. In *Archaeological Chronometry: Radiocarbon and Tree-Ring Models and Applications from Black Mesa, Arizona*, by F. E. Smiley and R. V. N. Ahlstrom, pp. 203–214. Center for Archaeological Investigations Occasional Paper No. 16. Southern Illinois University, Carbondale.
1998b Dating Individual Structures and Sites. In *Archaeological Chronometry: Radiocarbon and Tree-Ring Models and Applications from Black Mesa, Arizona*, by F. E. Smiley and R. V. N. Ahlstrom, pp. 149–167. Center for Archaeological Investigations Occasional Paper No. 16. Southern Illinois University, Carbondale.
1998c The Black Mesa Tree-Ring Date Distribution. In *Archaeological Chronometry: Radiocarbon and Tree-Ring Models and Applications from Black Mesa, Arizona*, by F. E. Smiley and R. V. N. Ahlstrom, pp. 137–147. Center for Archaeological Investigations Occasional Paper No. 16. Southern Illinois University, Carbondale.

Aikens, C. M.
1970   *Hogup Cave*. Anthropological Papers No. 93. University of Utah Press, Salt Lake City.

Allen, V. T.
1930   Triassic Bentonite of the Painted Desert. *American Journal of Science* 19:283–288.

Ambler, J. R.
1983   Kayenta Craft Specialization and Social Differentiation. In *Proceedings of the Anasazi Symposium 1981*, edited by J. E. Smith, pp. 75–82. Mesa Verde Museum Association, Mesa Verde National Park, Colorado.
1985a *Navajo National Monument: An Archaeological Assessment*.

Northern Arizona University Archaeological Series 1. Flagstaff.

1985b Northern Kayenta Ceramic Chronology. In *Archaeological Investigations Near Rainbow City, Navajo Mountain, Utah*, edited by P. R. Geib, J. R. Ambler, and M. M. Callahan, pp. 28–68. Northern Arizona University Archaeological Report No. 576. Flagstaff.

1994 The Shonto Junction Doghouse: A Weaver's Field House in the Klethla Valley. *Kiva* 59:455–473.

1996 Dust Devil Cave and Archaic Complexes of the Glen Canyon Area. In *Glen Canyon Revisited*, by P. R. Geib, pp. 40–52. Anthropological Papers No. 119. University of Utah Press, Salt Lake City.

Ambler, J. R., H. C. Fairley, M. A. Davenport, and P. R. Geib

1985 Survey. In *Archaeological Investigations Near Rainbow City, Navajo Mountain, Utah*, edited by P. R. Geib, J. R. Ambler, and M. M. Callahan, pp. 241–258. Northern Arizona University Archaeological Report 576. Flagstaff.

Ambler, J. R., H. C. Fairley, and P. R. Geib

1983 *Kayenta Anasazi Utilization of Canyons and Plateaus in the Navajo Mountain District*. Second Anasazi Symposium, Farmington, New Mexico.

Ambler, J. R., A. J. Lindsay Jr., and M. A. Stein

1964 *Survey and Excavations on Cummings Mesa, Arizona and Utah, 1960–1961*. Museum of Northern Arizona, Bulletin 39. Flagstaff.

Ambler, J. R., and A. P. Olson

1977 *Salvage Archaeology in the Cow Springs Area*. Museum of Northern Arizona Technical Series No. 15. Flagstaff.

Ambrose, S. H.

1984 *Holocene Environments and Human Adaptations in the Central Rift Valley, Kenya*. Ph.D. dissertation, University of California, Berkeley. University Microfilms, Ann Arbor.

1993 Isotopic Analysis of Paleodiets: Methodological and Interpretive Considerations. In *Investigations of Ancient Human Tissues: Chemical Analyses in Anthropology*, edited by K. Sandford, pp. 1–37. Gordon and Breach, Langhorne, Pennsylvania.

Ambrose, W. R.

1976 Intrinsic Hydration Rate Dating of Obsidian. In *Advances in Obsidian Glass Studies*, edited by R. E. Taylor, pp. 81–105. Noyes, Ride Park, New Jersey.

Ambrose, W. R., and C. M. Stevenson

1995 *Estimation of Hydration Rates from Obsidian Density Measurements*. Report on file, Diffusion Laboratory, Archaeological Services Consultants, Inc., Columbus, Ohio.

Anderson, B. A. (compiler)

1990 *The Wupatki Archaeological Inventory Survey Project: Final Report*. Cultural Resources Center Professional Paper No. 35. Division of Anthropology, National Park Service, Santa Fe.

Anderson, K.

1992 Geoarchaeological Investigations Along N16, Segment 3. In *Phase I Testing of Prehistoric Sites Along Segment 3 of N16, the Road to Navajo Mountain*, by P. R. Geib, pp. A1–A17. Navajo Nation Archaeology Department Report No. 91-19. Navajo Nation Historic Preservation Department, Window Rock, Arizona.

Anderson, R. S.

1993 A 35,000 Year Vegetation and Climatic History from Potato Lake, Mogollon Rim, Arizona. *Quaternary Research* 40: 351–359.

Androy, J.

2003 Agriculture and Mobility During the Basketmaker II Period. Unpublished M.A. thesis, Department of Anthropology, Northern Arizona University, Flagstaff.

Anovitz, L. M., J. M. Elam, L. R. Riciputi, and D. R. Cole

1999 The Failure of Obsidian Hydration Dating: Sources, Implications, and New Directions. *Journal of Archaeological Science* 26:735–752.

Antevs, E.

1955 Geologic-Climatic Dating in the West. *American Antiquity* 20:317–335.

Anyon, R., and S. LeBlanc

1984 *The Galaz Ruin: A Prehistoric Mimbres Village in Southwestern New Mexico*. University of New Mexico Press, Albuquerque.

Arnold, D. E.

1980 Localized Production: An Ethnoarchaeological Perspective. In *Models and Methods in Regional Exchange*, edited by R. E. Fry, pp. 147–150. SAA Papers No. 1. Society for American Archaeology, Washington, D.C.

1985 *Ceramic Theory and Cultural Process*. Cambridge University Press, New York.

Axtell, R. L., J. M. Epstein, J. S. Dean, G. J. Gumerman, A. C. Swedlund, J. Harburger, S. Chakravarty, R. Hammond, J. Parker, and M. Parker

2002 Population Growth and Collapse in a Multiagent Model of the Kayenta Anasazi in Long House Valley. *PNAS* 99(3):7275–7279.

Baars, D. L.

2000 *The Colorado Plateau: A Geologic History*. University of New Mexico, Albuquerque.

Bailey, L. R.

1964 *The Navajo Reconnaissance: A Military Exploration of the Navajo Country in 1859*. Westernlore Press, Los Angeles.

Baker, A. A.

1936 *Geology of the Monument Valley–Navajo Mountain Region, San Juan County, Utah*. Bulletin 865. U.S. Geological Survey, Washington, D.C.

Bannister, B., J. S. Dean, and W. J. Robinson

1969 *Tree-Ring Dates from Utah S-W, Southern Utah Area*. Laboratory of Tree-Ring Research, University of Arizona, Tucson.

Barker, G.

2006 *The Agricultural Revolution in Prehistory: Why Did Foragers Become Farmers?* Oxford University Press, Oxford.

Barlow, K. R.

2002 Predicting Maize Agriculture Among the Fremont: An Economic Comparison of Farming and Foraging in the American Southwest. *American Antiquity* 67:65–88.

Barlow, K. R., and D. Metcalfe

1993 *1990 Archaeological Excavations at Joe Valley Alcove*. Reports of Investigations 93-1. University of Utah Archaeological Center, Salt Lake City.

1996 Plant Utility Indices: Two Great Basin Examples. *Journal of Archaeological Science* 23:351–371.

Bartlein, P. J., K. H. Anderson, P. M. Anderson, M. E. Edwards, C. J. Mock, R. S. Thompson, R. S. Webb, T. Webb III, and C. Whitlock

1998 Paleoclimate Simulations for North America over the Past 21,000 Years: Features of the Simulated Climate and Comparisons with Paleoenvironmental Data. *Quaternary Science Reviews* 17:549–585.

Bartlett, K.

1933 *Pueblo Milling Stones of the Flagstaff Region and Their Relation to Others in the Southwest: A Study in Progressive Efficiency.* Museum of Northern Arizona Bulletin 3. Northern Arizona Society of Science and Art, Flagstaff.

Baugh, T. G., and F. W. Nelson Jr.

1987 New Mexico Obsidian Sources and Exchange on the Southern Plains. *Journal of Field Archaeology* 14:313–329.

Beaglehole, E. O.

1937 *Hopi Economic Life.* Yale University Publications in Anthropology 15. New Haven.

Beals, R. L., G. W. Brainerd, and W. Smith

1945 *Archaeological Studies in Northeastern Arizona.* University of California Publications in American Archaeology and Ethnology 44:1–177. Berkeley.

Bearden, S. E.

1984 *A Study of Basketmaker II Settlement on Black Mesa, Arizona: Excavations 1973–1979.* Research Paper No. 44. Center for Archaeological Investigations, Southern Illinois University Press, Carbondale.

Benedict, J. B.

1979 Getting Away from It All: A Study of Maw Mountains, and the Two Drought Altithermal. *Southwestern Lore* 45(3):1–12.

Benedict, J. B., and B. L. Olson

1978 *The Mount Albion Complex: A Study of Prehistoric Man and the Altithermal.* Center for Mountain Archaeology Research Report No. 1. Ward, Colorado.

Bender, M. M.

1968 Mass Spectrometric Studies of Carbon 13 Variations in Corn and Other Grasses. *Radiocarbon* 10:468–472.

Benz, B. F.

1981 Five Modern Races of Maize from Northeastern Mexico: Archaeological Implications. Unpublished M.A. thesis, Department of Anthropology, University of Colorado, Boulder.

Berry, C. F.

1984 *Coronado Project Archaeological Investigations. A Description of Lithic Collections from the Railroad and Transmission Line Corridors.* Coronado Series 6, MNA Research Paper 29. Museum of Northern Arizona Press, Flagstaff.

1987 *A Reassessment of the Southwestern Archaic.* Ph.D. dissertation, Department of Anthropology, University of Utah. University Microfilms, Ann Arbor.

Berry, C. F., and M. S. Berry

1986 Chronological and Conceptual Models of the Southwestern Archaic. In *Anthropology of the Desert West. Essays in Honor of Jesse D. Jennings*, edited by C. J. Condie and D. D. Fowler, pp. 253–327. Anthropological Paper No. 110. University of Utah Press, Salt Lake City.

Berry, M. S.

1982 *Time, Space, and Transition in Anasazi Prehistory.* University of Utah Press, Salt Lake City.

1985 The Age of Maize in the Greater Southwest: A Critical Review. In *Prehistoric Food Production in North America*, edited by R. I. Ford, pp. 279–307. Anthropological Papers No. 75. Museum of Anthropology, University of Michigan, Ann Arbor.

Berry, M. S., and C. F. Berry

1976 *An Archaeological Reconnaissance of the White River Area, Northeastern Utah.* Antiquity Section Selected Papers No. 4. Utah State Historical Society, Salt Lake City.

Bettinger, R. L.

1980 Explanatory-Predictive Models of Hunter-Gatherer Behavior. *Advances in Archaeological Theory and Method* 3:189–255.

Binford, L. R.

1967 Smudge Pits and Hide Smoking: The Use of Analogy in Archaeological Reasoning. *American Antiquity* 32:1–12.

1978 Dimensional Analysis of Behavior and Site Structure: Learning from an Eskimo Hunting Stand. *American Antiquity* 43:330–361.

1979 Organizational and Formation Processes: Looking at Curated Technologies. *Journal of Anthropological Research* 35(3):255–273.

1980 Willow Smoke and Dog's Tails: Hunter-Gatherer Settlement Systems and Archaeological Site Formation. *American Antiquity* 45:4–20.

1982 The Archaeology of Place. *Journal of Anthropological Archaeology* 1:5–31.

Biondi, F., S. D. J. Strachan, S. Mensing, and G. Piovesan

2007 Radiocarbon Analysis Confirms the Annual Nature of Sagebrush Growth Rings. *Radiocarbon* 49:1231–1240.

Black, K. D., J. M. Copeland, and S. M. Horvath Jr.

1982 An Archaeological Survey of the Central Lisbon Valley Study Tract in the Moab District, San Juan County, Utah. In *Contributions to the Prehistory of Southeastern Utah*, assembled by S. G. Baker. Cultural Resource Series No. 13, Part 2, pp. 1–188. Bureau of Land Management, Utah State Office, Salt Lake City.

Blackburn, F. M., and R. A. Williamson

1997 *Cowboys and Cave Dwellers: Basketmaker Archaeology in Utah's Grand Gulch.* School of American Research Press, Santa Fe.

Blinman, E.

1989 Pottery. In *Kayenta Anasazi Archaeology and Navajo Ethnohistory on the Northwestern Shonto Plateau: The N-16 Project*, edited by A. R. Schroedl, pp. 599–629. P-III Associates, Salt Lake City.

Blitz, J. H.

1988 Adoption of the Bow in Prehistoric North America. *North American Archaeologist* 9:123–145.

Bohrer, V. L.
1975 The Prehistoric and Historic Role of the Cool-Season Grasses in the Southwest. *Economic Botany* 29:199–207.

Bolton, H. E.
1950 Pageant in the Wilderness: The Story of the Escalante Expedition into the Interior Basin, 1776, Including the Diary and Itinerary of Father Escalante. *Utah Historical Quarterly* 18(1–4):1–265.

Bradfield, M.
1971 *The Changing Pattern of Hopi Agriculture*. Occasional Paper No. 30. Royal Anthropological Institute, London.

Breternitz, D. A.
1966 *An Appraisal of Tree-Ring Dated Pottery in the Southwest*. University of Arizona Anthropological Papers 10. Tucson.
1986 Notes on Early Basketmaker III Sites in Mancos Canyon, Colorado. *Kiva* 51:263–264.

Brew, J. O.
1946 *Archaeology of Alkali Ridge, South-Eastern Utah*. Papers of the Peabody Museum of American Archaeology and Ethnology, Vol. 21. Harvard University, Cambridge.

Bronk Ramsey, C.
1994 Analysis of Chronological Information and Radiocarbon Calibration: The Program OxCal. *Archaeological Computing Newsletter* 41:11–16.
1995 Radiocarbon Calibration and Analysis of Stratigraphy: The OxCal Program. *Radiocarbon* 37(2):425–430.
1998 Probability and Dating. *Radiocarbon* 40(1):461–474.
2005 OxCal Progam v3.10. Available at http://www.rlaha.ox.ac.uk/O/oxcal.php.

Brown, D. E. (editor)
1982 Biotic Communities of the American Southwest—United States and Mexico. *Desert Plants* 4(1–4).

Brown, G. M.
1988 Raw Materials Analysis. In *Cultural Resource Investigations on the Kaibab Plateau, Northern Arizona: The Highway 67 Data Recovery Project*, complied by A. R. Schroedl, pp. 307–320. P-III Associates, Inc., Salt Lake City.

Brown, J. A.
1989 The Beginning of Pottery as an Economic Process. In *What's New: A Closer Look at the Process of Innovation*, edited by S. E. van der Leeuw and R. Torrance, pp. 203–224. Unwin Hyman, London.

Brown, T. L.
1969 Low Grade Metamorphism in the Chinle Clays of Northern Arizona. Unpublished M.A. thesis, Department of Geology, Arizona State University, Tempe.

Brugge, D. M.
1983 Navajo Prehistory and History to 1850. In *Handbook of North American Indians, Vol. 10: Southwest*, edited by A. Ortiz, pp. 489–501. Smithsonian Institution Press, Washington, D.C.

Brush, S. B., H. J. Carney, and Z. Huaman
1981 Dynamics of Andean Potato Agriculture. *Economic Botany* 35:70–88.

Bungart, P. B., J. Collette, and K. Spurr
2004 *A Better Road Ahead: Archaeological Excavations Along Navajo Route 21 Near White Mesa, Arizona*. Navajo Nation Archaeology Department Report No. 01-237. Navajo Nation Historic Preservation Department, Window Rock, Arizona.

Bunte, P. A., and R. J. Franklin
1987 *From the Sands to the Mountain: Change and Persistence in a Southern Paiute Community*. University of Nebraska Press, Lincoln.

Burton, J. F.
1991 *The Archaeology of Sivu'ovi: The Archaic to Basketmaker Transition at Petrified Forest National Park*. Western Archaeological and Conservation Center, National Park Service, Publications in Anthropology 55.

Bye, R. A., Jr.
1976 Ethnoecology of the Tarahumara of Chihuahua, Mexico. Unpublished Ph.D. dissertation, Anthropology Department, Harvard University, Cambridge.
1981 Quelites—Ethnoecology of Edible Greens—Past, Present, and Future. *Journal of Ethnobiology* 1:109–123.

Byers, D. S.
1959 An Introduction to Five Papers on the Archaic Stage. *American Antiquity* 24:229–232.

Cadigan, R. A.
1972 Sedimentary Petrology. In *Stratigraphy and Origin of the Chinle Formation and Related Upper Triassic Strata in the Colorado Plateau Region*, edited by H. H. Stewart, F. G. Poole, and E. R. Wilson, pp. 60–63. U.S. Geological Survey Professional Paper 690.

Callahan, M. M.
1985 Excavations at Dogtown: A Pueblo III Pithouse Village in the Klethla Valley. Unpublished M.A. thesis, Department of Anthropology, Northern Arizona University, Flagstaff.

Callahan, M. M., and H. C. Fairley
1983 Rainbow Gray: A Distinctive Utility Ware in the Northern Kayenta Region. *Pottery Southwest* 10(2):1–6.

Cameron, C. M. (editor)
1995 Migration and the Movement of Southwestern Peoples. *Journal of Anthropological Archaeology* 14(2).

Castetter, E. F.
1935 *Ethnobiological Studies in the American Southwest I: Uncultivated Native Plants as Sources of Food*. University of New Mexico Bulletin 266, Biological Series 4(1). Albuquerque.

Cawker, K. B.
1980 Evidence of Climatic Control from Population Age Structure of *Artemisia tridentata Nutt.* in Southern British Columbia. *Journal of Biogeography* 7:237–248.

Chapin, N.
2005 Hunter-Gatherer Technological Organization: The Archaic Period in Northern New Mexico. Unpublished Ph.D. dissertation, Department of Anthropology, University of New Mexico, Albuquerque.

Charles, M. C., and S. J. Cole
2006 Chronology and Cultural Variation in Basketmaker II. *Kiva* 72:167–216.

Charnov, E. L.
1976 Optimal Foraging: The Marginal Value Theorem. *Theoretical Population Biology* 9:129–136.

Chisholm, B., and R. G. Matson
1994 Carbon and Nitrogen Isotopic Evidence on Basketmaker II Diet at Cedar Mesa, Utah. *Kiva* 60:239–256.

Christensen, D., S. M. Chandler, K. Kreutzer, and J. Jennings
1983 *Results of the 1982 Class II Archaeological Survey of the Alton and Kolob Tracts in Northwestern Kane County, Utah*. Nickens and Associates, Montrose, Colorado. MS on file, Bureau of Land Management, Kanab, Utah.

Christenson, A. L.
1983 The Archaeological Investigations of the Rainbow Bridge–Monument Valley Expedition, 1933–1938. In *Honoring the Dead: Anasazi Ceramics from the Rainbow Bridge–Monument Valley Expedition*, by H. K. Crotty, pp. 9–23. Monograph Series No. 22. Museum of Cultural History, University of California, Los Angeles.
1987a Projectile Points: Eight Millennia of Projectile Change on the Colorado Plateau. In *Prehistoric Stone Technology on Northern Black Mesa, Arizona*, by W. J. Parry and A. L. Christenson, pp. 143–198. Occasional Paper No. 12. Center for Archaeological Investigations, Southern Illinois University Press, Carbondale.
1987b The Prehistoric Tool Kit. In *Prehistoric Stone Technology on Northern Black Mesa, Arizona*, by W. J. Parry and A. L. Christenson, pp. 43–93. Occasional Paper No. 12. Center for Archaeological Investigations, Southern Illinois University Press, Carbondale.
1994 A Test of Mean Ceramic Dating Using Well-Dated Kayenta Sites. *Kiva* 59:297–317.

Clark, J. J.
2001 *Tracking Prehistoric Migrations: Pueblo Settlers Among the Tonto Basin Hohokam*. Anthropological Papers No. 65. University of Arizona Press, Tucson.

Clark, T. C.
1998 Assessing Room Function Using Unmodified Faunal Bone: A Case Study from East-Central Arizona. *Kiva* 64(1):27–51.

Clark, V. H.
1993a *Significance Testing of 11 Prehistoric Sites Along Segments 4–6 of N16, the Navajo Mountain Road*. Navajo Nation Archaeology Department Report No. 92-29. Navajo Nation Historic Preservation Department, Window Rock, Arizona.
1993b *The Mud Wallow Site: An Archaeological Discovery at an Indian Health Service Water Line Project, Red Lake, Arizona*. Navajo Nation Archaeology Department Report No. 92-145. Navajo Nation Historic Preservation Department, Window Rock, Arizona.

Cleland, C. E.
1966 *The Pleistocene Animal Ecology and Ethnozoology of the Upper Great Lakes Region*. Anthropology Papers No. 9. Museum of Anthropology, University of Michigan, Ann Arbor.

Clemen, R. T.
1976 Aspects of Prehistoric Social Organization on Black Mesa. In *Papers on the Archaeology of Black Mesa, Arizona*, edited by G. J. Gumerman and R. C. Euler, pp. 113–135. Southern Illinois University Press, Carbondale.

Cohen, M. N.
1977 *The Food Crisis in Prehistory*. Yale University Press, New Haven.

Cole, K. L.
1981 Late Quaternary Environments in the Eastern Grand Canyon. Vegetational Gradients over the Last 25,000 Years. Unpublished Ph.D. dissertation, University of Arizona, Tucson.

Collette, J., K. C. Anderson, J. S. Edwards, J. Hagopian, K. Mangum, J. Nez, M. R. Robins, S. J. Smith, K. Spurr, N. Tsosie, and T. Wilcox
2009 *Data Recovery of Three Prehistoric Sites Along Navajo Route 8066, Black Mesa*. Navajo Nation Archaeology Department Report No. 00-38. Navajo Nation Historic Preservation Department, Window Rock, Arizona.

Collier, M.
1951 Local Organization Among the Navajo. Unpublished Ph.D. dissertation, University of Chicago.

Colton, H. S.
1918 The Geography of Certain Ruins Near the San Francisco Mountains, Arizona. *Geographical Society of Philadelphia, Bulletin* 16(2):37–60.
1939 *Prehistoric Culture Units and Their Relationships in Northern Arizona*. Museum of Northern Arizona Bulletin 17. Flagstaff.
1955 *Pottery Types of the Southwest: Wares 8A, 9A, 9B, Tusayan Gray and White Ware, Little Colorado Gray and White Ware*. Museum of Northern Arizona Ceramic Series 3A. Flagstaff.
1956 *Pottery Types of the Southwest: Ware 5A, 5B, 6A, 6B, 7A, 7B, 7C*. Museum of Northern Arizona Ceramic Series 3C. Flagstaff.
1958 *Pottery Types of the Southwest: Wares 14, 15, 16, 17, 18*. Museum of Northern Arizona Ceramic Series No. 3D. Northern Arizona Society of Science and Art, Flagstaff.

Colton, H. S., and L. L. Hargrave
1937 *Handbook of Northern Arizona Pottery Wares*. Museum of Northern Arizona Bulletin 11. Northern Arizona Society of Science and Art, Flagstaff.

Colton, M. R. F., and H. S. Colton
1918 *The Little-Known Small House Ruins in the Coconino Forest*. Memoirs of the American Anthropological Association 4(4).

Coltrain, J. B.
1996 Stable Carbon and Radioisotope Analysis. In *Steinaker Gap: An Early Fremont Farmstead*, by R. K. Talbot and L. D. Richens, pp. 115–122. Museum of Peoples and Cultures Occasional Papers No. 2. Brigham Young University, Provo.
1997 Fremont Economic Diversity: A Stable Carbon Isotope Study of Formative Subsistence Practices in the Eastern Great Basin. Unpublished Ph.D. dissertation, Department of Anthropology, University of Utah, Salt Lake City.

Coltrain, J. B., J. C. Janetski, and S. W. Carlyle
2007 The Stable- and Radio-Isotope Chemistry of Western Basketmaker Burials: Implications for Early Puebloan Diet and Origins. *American Antiquity* 72:301–321.

Condie, K. C.
1964 Crystallization Po2 of Syenite Porphyry from Navajo Mountain, Southern Utah. *Geologic Society of America Bulletin* 75:359–362.

Connelly, J. C.
1979 Hopi Social Organization. In *Southwest*, edited by A. Ortiz, pp. 539–553. Handbook of the North American Indians, Vol. 9, W. C. Sturtevant, general editor. Smithsonian Institution Press, Washington, D.C.

Cooley, M. E.
1960 Analysis of Gravel in Glen–San Juan Canyon Region, Utah and Arizona. *Arizona Geological Society Digest* 3:19–24.
1965 *Stratigraphic Sections and Records of Springs in the Glen Canyon Region of Utah and Arizona*. Technical Series No. 6. Museum of Northern Arizona, Flagstaff.

Cooley, M. E., J. W. Harshbarger, J. P. Akers, and W. F. Hardt
1969 *Regional Hydrogeology of the Navajo and Hopi Indian Reservations, Arizona, New Mexico, and Utah*. U.S. Geological Survey Professional Paper 521-A. Government Printing Office, Washington, D.C.

Cordell, L. S.
1984 *Prehistory of the Southwest*. Academic Press, Orlando.
1997 *Prehistory of the Southwest*. 2nd ed. Academic Press, Orlando.

Cordell, L., and F. Plog
1979 Escaping the Confines of Normative Thought: A Re-Evaluation of Puebloan Prehistory. *American Antiquity* 44:405–429.

Corliss, D. W.
1972 *Neck Width of Projectile Points: An Index of Culture Continuity and Change*. Occasional Paper No. 29. Idaho State University Museum, Pocatello.

Coulam, N. J.
1988 Intermountain Archaic Subsistence and an Archaeobotanical Analysis of Swallow Shelter and Remnant Cave. Unpublished Ph.D. dissertation, Arizona State University, Tempe.

Coulam, N. J., and A. R. Schroedl
1996 Early Archaic Clay Figurines from Cowboy Cave and Walters Caves in Southeastern Utah. *Kiva* 61:401–412.
2004 Late Archaic Totemism in the Great American Southwest. *American Antiquity* 69:41–62.

Cowan, C. W., and P. J. Watson
1992 Some Concluding Remarks. In *The Origins of Agriculture: An International Perspective*, edited by C. W. Cowan and P. J. Watson, pp. 207–212. Smithsonian Institution Press, Washington, D.C.

Cowan, C. W., and P. J. Watson (editors)
1992 *The Origins of Agriculture: An International Perspective*. Smithsonian Institution Press, Washington, D.C.

Creel, D., and A. Long
1986 Radiocarbon Dating of Corn. *American Antiquity* 51:826–837.

Crotty, H. K.
1983 *Honoring the Dead: Anasazi Ceramics from the Rainbow Bridge–Monument Valley Expedition*. Monograph Series No. 22. Museum of Cultural History, University of California, Los Angeles.

Crown, P. L., and W. H. Wills
1995 Economic Intensification and the Origins of Ceramic Containers in the American Southwest. In *The Emergence of Pottery: Technology and Innovation in Ancient Societies*, edited by W. Barnett and J. W. Hoopes, pp. 241–254. Smithsonian Institution Press, Washington, D.C.

Cutler, H. C.
1954 Food Sources in the New World. *Agricultural History* 28:39–41.
1968 Appendix I: Plant Remains from Sites Near Navajo Mountain. In *Survey and Excavation North and East of Navajo Mountain, Utah 1959–1962*, by A. J. Lindsay Jr., J. R. Ambler, M. A. Stein, and P. M. Hobler, pp. 371–378. Museum of Northern Arizona Bulletin No. 45. Northern Arizona Society of Science and Art, Flagstaff.

Cummings, B.
1953 *First Inhabitants of Arizona and the Southwest*. Cummings Publication Council, Tucson.

Davis, W. E.
1985 The Montgomery Folsom Site. *Current Research in the Pleistocene* 2:11–12.
1989 The Lime Ridge Clovis Site. *Utah Archaeology* 2:66–76.

Dean, J. S.
1969 *Chronological Analysis of Tsegi Phase Sites in Northeastern Arizona*. Papers of the Laboratory of Tree-Ring Research, University of Arizona 3. Tucson.
1970 Aspects of Tsegi Phase Social Organization: A Trial Reconstruction. In *Reconstructing Prehistoric Pueblo Societies*, edited by W. A. Longacre, pp. 140–174. University of New Mexico Press, Albuquerque.
1975 *Tree-Ring Dates from Colorado W, Durango Area*. Laboratory of Tree-Ring Research, University of Arizona, Tucson.
1988a Dendochronology and Paleoenvironmental Reconstruction on the Colorado Plateaus. In *The Anasazi in a Changing Environment*, edited by G. J. Gumerman, pp. 119–167. School of American Research Advanced Seminar Series. Cambridge University Press, Cambridge.
1988b A Model of Anasazi Behavioral Adaptation. In *The Anasazi in a Changing Environment*, edited by G. J. Gumerman, pp. 25–44. School of American Research Advanced Seminar Series. Cambridge University Press, Cambridge.
1996 Kayenta Anasazi Settlement Transformations in Northeastern Arizona. AD 1150–1350. In *The Prehistoric Pueblo World, AD 1150–1350*, edited by M. A. Adler, pp. 29–47. University of Arizona Press, Tucson.
2002 Late Pueblo II–Pueblo III in Kayenta Branch Prehistory. In *Prehistoric Culture Change on the Colorado Plateau: Ten Thousand Years on Black Mesa*, edited by S. Powell and F. E. Smiley, pp. 121–157. University of Arizona Press, Tucson.

Dean, J. S., R. C. Euler, G. J. Gumerman, F. Plog, R. H. Hevly, and T. N. V. Karlstrom
1985 Human Behavior, Demography, and Paleoenvironment on the Colorado Plateaus. *American Antiquity* 50:537–554.

Dean, J. S., G. J. Gumerman, J. M. Epstein, R. Axtell, A. C. Swedlund, M. T. Parker, and S. McCarroll
2000 Understanding Anasazi Culture Change Through Agent-Based Modeling. In *Dynamics of Human and Primate*

Societies: Agent-Based Modeling of Social and Spatial Processes, edited by T. A. Kohler and G. J. Gumerman, pp. 179–205. Santa Fe Institute Studies in the Sciences of Complexity. Oxford University Press, Santa Fe.

Dean, J. S., A. J. Lindsay Jr., and W. J. Robison
1978 Prehistoric Settlement in Long House Valley, Northeastern Arizona. In *Investigations of the Southwestern Anthropological Group: An Experiment in Archaeological Cooperation—The Proceedings of the 1976 Conference*, edited by R. C. Euler and G. J. Gumerman, pp. 25–44. Museum of Northern Arizona, Flagstaff.

Dean, J. S., and W. J. Robinson
1978 *Expanded Tree-Ring Chronologies for the Southwestern United States*. Chronology Series 3. Laboratory of Tree-Ring Research, University of Arizona, Tucson.

Deaver, W. L., and R. Ciolek-Torrello
1995 Early Formative Period Chronology for the Tucson Basin. *Kiva* 60:481–529.

DeBloois, E. I., D. F. Green, and J. Wylie
1979 *Joes Valley Alcove: An Archaic–Fremont Site in Central Utah*. MS on file, Manti-La Sal National Forest, Price, Utah.

Del Bene, T. A., and D. Ford
1982 *Archaeological Excavations in Blocks VI and VII, Navajo Nation Irrigation Project, San Juan County, New Mexico*, Vols. 1 and 3. Navajo Nation Papers in Anthropology 13. Window Rock, Arizona.

Deutchman, H. L.
1979 Interregional Interaction on Black Mesa Among the Kayenta Anasazi: The Chemical Evidence for Ceramic Exchange. Unpublished Ph.D. dissertation, Department of Anthropology, Southern Illinois University.
1980 Chemical Evidence of Ceramic Exchange on Black Mesa. In *Models and Methods in Regional Exchange*, edited by R. E. Fry, pp. 119–133. SAA Papers No. 1. Society for American Archaeology, Washington, D.C.

Dial, K. P., and N. J. Czaplewski
1990 Do Woodrat Middens Accurately Represent the Animals' Environment and Diet? In *Packrat Middens*, edited by J. L. Betancourt, T. R. Van Devender, and P. Martin, pp. 43–58. University of Arizona Press, Tucson.

Dick, H. W.
1954 The Bat Cave Pod Corn Complex: A Note on Its Distribution and Archaeological Significance. *El Palacio* 61:138–144.

Diggs, R. D.
1982 Ten Thousand Years of Land Use at the Hall Ranch Locality Near Springerville, Arizona. Unpublished M.A. thesis, Department of Anthropology, Northern Arizona University, Flagstaff.

Doebley, J., and V. Bohrer
1983 Maize Variability and Cultural Selection at Salmon Ruin, New Mexico. *Kiva* 49:19–37.

Dodd, D.
1979 The Wear and Use of Battered Tools at Armijo Rockshelter. In *Lithic Use-Wear Analysis*, edited by B. Hayden, pp. 231–242. Academic Press, New York.

Downum, C. E.
1988 Grand History: A Critical Review of Flagstaff Archaeology, 1851 to 1988. Unpublished Ph.D. dissertation, Department of Anthropology, University of Arizona.

Durrenberger, R. W.
1976 *Climatic regions of Arizona*. Arizona Resources Information Systems Cooperative Publication No. 8. Office of Arizona State Climatologist, Arizona State University, Tempe.

Dyson-Hudson, R., and E. A. Smith
1978 Human Territoriality: An Ecological Assessment. *American Anthropologist* 80:21–42.

Eccles, C., and B. A. Walling-Frank
1998 Stone Implement Analysis. In *Excavation/Mitigation Report. Three Sites Near Hildale, Utah, 42WS2195, 42WS2196, AZ B:1:35 (BLM) (Reservoir Site)*. Baseline Data, Inc., Orem, Utah. MS on file, U.S. Department of the Interior, Bureau of Land Management, Cedar City District, Utah.

Eddy, F. W.
1966 *Prehistory of the Navajo Reservoir District, Northwestern New Mexico*. Museum of New Mexico Papers in Anthropology 15(1–2). Santa Fe.

Effland, R. W., Jr.
1979 *A Study of Prehistoric Spatial Behavior: Long House Valley, Northeastern Arizona*. Ph.D. dissertation, Arizona State University. University Microfilms, Ann Arbor.

Eggan, F.
1950 *Social Organization of the Western Pueblos*. University of Chicago Press, Chicago.

Ellis, F. H.
1974 The Hopi: Their History and Use of Lands. In *Hopi Indians*, edited by F. H. Ellis and H. S. Colton, pp. 25–277. Garland Publishing, New York.

Elmore, F. H.
1944 *Ethnobotany of the Navajo*. University of New Mexico and School of American Research, Albuquerque.

Emslie, S. D., R. C. Euler, and J. I. Mead
1987 A Desert Culture Shrine in Grand Canyon, Arizona. *National Geographic Research* 3:511–516.

Emslie, S. D., J. I. Mead, and L. Coats
1995 Split-Twig Figurines in Grand Canyon, Arizona: New Discoveries and Interpretations. *Kiva* 61:145–173.

Euler, R. C.
1966 *Southwestern Paiute Ethnohistory*. University of Utah Anthropological Paper 78. Salt Lake City.

Fairley, H. C.
1987 *Archaeological Testing of Four Sites on the Shonto Plateau Near Inscription House, Arizona*. Northern Arizona University Archaeological Report No. 378. Flagstaff.
1989 Prehistoric Settlement Dynamics in Upper Paiute Canyon, Northeastern Arizona. Unpublished M.A. thesis, Department of Anthropology, Northern Arizona University, Flagstaff.
2003 *Changing River: Time, Culture and the Transformation of Landscape in the Grand Canyon*. Technical Series 79. Statistical Research, Tucson.

Fairley, H. C., and M. M. Callahan
1985 Ceramics. In *Archaeological Investigations Near Rainbow City, Navajo Mountain, Utah*, edited by P. R. Geib,

J. R. Ambler, and M. M. Callahan, pp. 259–310. Northern Arizona University Archaeological Report 576. Flagstaff.

Fawcett, W. B., and M. Kornfeld
1980 Projectile Point Neck-Width Variability and Chronology on the Plains. *Wyoming Contributions to Archaeology* 2:66–79.

Ferguson, C. W.
1964 *Annual Rings in Big Sagebrush*. Papers of the Laboratory of Tree-Ring Research, No. 1. University of Arizona Press, Tucson.

Fernstrom, K.
1980 The Effect of Ecological Fluctuations on Exchange Networks, Black Mesa, Arizona. Unpublished M.A. thesis, Department of Anthropology, Southern Illinois University, Carbondale.

Finnell, T. L., P. C. Franks, and H. Hubbard
1963 *Geology, Ore Deposits, and Exploratory Drilling in the Deer Flat Area, White Canyon District, San Juan County, Utah*. U.S. Geological Survey Bulletin 1132. U.S. Government Printing Office, Washington, D.C.

Flannery, K. V.
1973 The Origins of Agriculture. *Annual Review of Anthropology* 2:271–310.

Foley, R.
1985 Optimality Theory in Anthropology. *Man* 20:222–242.

Food and Agricultural Organization
1953 *Maize and Maize Diets: A Nutritional Survey*. FAO Nutritional Studies 9. U.N. Food and Agricultural Organization, Rome.

Ford, R. I.
1984 Ecological Consequences of Early Agriculture in the Southwest. In *Papers on the Archaeology of Black Mesa, Arizona, Vol. II*, edited by S. Plog and S. Powell, pp. 127–138. Southern Illinois University Press, Carbondale.

Ford, R. I. (editor)
1985 *Prehistoric Food Production in North America*. Anthropological Papers No. 75. Museum of Anthropology, University of Michigan, Ann Arbor.

Forde, C. D.
1931 Hopi Agriculture and Land Ownership. *Journal of the Royal Anthropological Society* 61:357–412.
1963 *Habitat, Economy and Society*. E. P. Dutton and Co., New York.

Forest Service
1937 *Range Plant Handbook*. U.S. Government Printing Office, Washington, D.C. Available at http://www.archive.org/details/rangeplanthandbooounitrich.

Foust, R. D., Jr., J. R. Ambler, and L. D. Turner
1989 Trace Element Analysis of Pueblo II Kayenta Anasazi Sherds. In *Archaeological Chemistry IV*, edited by R. O. Allen, pp. 125–143. American Chemical Society, Washington, D.C.

Fowler, D. D., and C. S. Fowler (editors)
1971 *Anthropology of the Numa: J. Wesley Powell's Manuscripts on the Numic Peoples of Western North America, 1868–1880*. Smithsonian Contributions to Anthropology No. 14. Smithsonian Institution, Washington, D.C.

Franciscan Fathers
1968 [1910] *An Ethnologic Dictionary of the Navajo Language*. St. Michael's Press, St. Michael's, Arizona.

Freestone, I. C.
1982 Applications and Potential of Electron Probe Micro-Analysis in Technological and Provenance Investigations of Ancient Ceramics. *Archaeometry* 24(2):99–116.

Friedman, I., and W. Long
1976 Hydration Rate of Obsidian. *Science* 159:347–352.

Friedman, I., and R. L. Smith
1960 A New Dating Method Using Obsidian: Part I, the Development of the Method. *American Antiquity* 25:476–522.

Friedman, I., F. W. Trembour, and R. E. Hughes
1997 Obsidian Hydration Dating. In *Chronometric Dating in Archaeology*, edited by R. E. Taylor and M. J. Aitken, pp. 297–321. Plenum Press, New York.

Frison, G. C.
1978 *Prehistoric Hunters of the High Plains*. Academic Press, New York.
1992 The Foothills–Mountains and the Open Plains: The Dichotomy in Paleoindian Subsistence Strategies Between Two Ecosystems. In *Ice Age Hunters of the Rockies*, edited by D. J. Stanford and J. S. Day, pp. 323–342. Denver Museum of Natural History and University Press of Colorado, Niwot.

Frison, G. C., and B. A. Bradley
1980 *Folsom Tools and Technology at the Hanson Site, Wyoming*. University of New Mexico Press, Albuquerque.

Fry, G. F., and H. J. Hall
1973 *The Analysis of Human Coprolites from Inscription House*. MS on file, National Park Service, Tucson.
1986 Human Coprolites. In *Archaeological Investigations at Antelope House*, by D. P. Morris, pp. 165–188. National Park Service, Washington, D.C.

Fuller, S. L.
1984 *Late Anasazi Pottery Kilns in the Yellowjacket District, Southwestern Colorado*. CASA Papers No. 4. Complete Archaeological Service Associates, Cortez, Colorado.

Gasser, R. E.
1982 Anasazi Diet. In *The Coronado Project Archaeological Investigations. The Specialists' Volume: Biocultural Analysis*, edited by R. E. Gasser, pp. 8–95. Museum of Northern Arizona Press, Flagstaff.

Gebauer, A. B., and T. D. Price (editors)
1992 *Transitions to Agriculture in Prehistory*. Monographs in World Prehistory 4. Prehistory Press, Madison, Wisconsin.

Geib, P. R.
1984 *Early Archaic Lithic Artifacts from Dust Devil Cave*. Paper presented at the 19th Biennial Great Basin Anthropological Conference, Boise.
1985 Lithic Artifacts. In *Archaeological Investigations Near Rainbow City Navajo Mountain, Utah*, edited by P. R. Geib, J. R. Ambler, and M. M. Callahan, pp. 311–414. Northern Arizona University Archaeological Report No. 576. MS on file, Archaeology Laboratory, Northern Arizona University, Flagstaff.

1989 *Archaeological Survey of Lower Glen Canyon Benches and a Descriptive Model of General Site Location.* Northern Arizona University Archaeological Report No. 1011. MS on file, Rocky Mountain Regional Office, National Park Service, Denver.

1992 *Phase I Testing of Prehistoric Sites Along Segment 3 of N16, the Road to Navajo Mountain.* Navajo Nation Archaeology Department Report No. 91-19. Navajo Nation Historic Preservation Department, Window Rock, Arizona.

1996a *Glen Canyon Revisited.* Anthropological Papers No. 119. University of Utah Press, Salt Lake City.

1996b AMS Dating of Plain Weave Sandals from the Central Colorado Plateau. *Utah Archaeology* 9:35–53.

2000 Sandal Types and Archaic Prehistory on the Colorado Plateau. *American Antiquity* 65(3):509–524.

2002 Basketmaker II Horn Flakers and Dart Point Production: Technological Change at the Agricultural Transition. In *Traditions, Transitions and Technologies: Themes in Southwest Archaeology,* edited by S. H. Schlanger, pp. 272–306. University Press of Colorado, Boulder.

2004 AMS Dating of a Basketmaker II Hunter's Bag (Cache 1) from Sand Dune Cave, Utah. *Kiva* 69:271–282.

2006 *Additional NAGPRA Excavations for Prehistoric Human Remains from Archaeological Sites Within the Peabody Western Coal Company Leasehold, Black Mesa, Arizona.* Navajo Nation Archaeology Department Report No. 05-059. Navajo Nation Historic Preservation Department, Window Rock, Arizona.

Geib, P. R., and J. R. Ambler

1983 Late Pueblo III in the Navajo Mountain Area, Southern Utah. Paper presented at the 56th Pecos Conference, Bluff, Utah.

1985 Environment. In *Archaeological Investigations Near Rainbow City, Navajo Mountain, Utah,* edited by P. R. Geib, J. R. Ambler, and M. M. Callahan, pp. 15–27. Northern Arizona University Archaeological Report 576. Flagstaff.

Geib, P. R., J. R. Ambler, and M. M. Callahan (editors)

1985 *Archaeological Investigations Near Rainbow City, Navajo Mountain, Utah.* Northern Arizona University Archaeological Report 576. Flagstaff.

Geib, P. R., and J. M. Bremer

1988 *Prehistory of the Orange Cliffs Tar Sands Triangle and a Descriptive Model of General Site Location.* Northern Arizona University Archaeological Report No. 997. MS on file, Rocky Mountain Regional Office, National Park Service, Denver.

Geib, P. R., and P. W. Bungart

1989 Implications of Early Bow Use in Glen Canyon. *Utah Archaeology* 2:32–47.

Geib, P. R., and M. M. Callahan

1987 Ceramic Exchange Within the Kayenta Anasazi Region: Volcanic Ash-Tempered Tusayan White Ware. *Kiva* 52:95–112.

Geib, P. R., and B. Casto

1985 Macrobotanical Remains from Seven Archaeological Sites Near Navajo Mountain, Utah. In *Archaeological Investigations Near Rainbow City, Navajo Mountain, Utah,* edited by P. R. Geib, J. R. Ambler, and M. M. Callahan, pp. 450–469. Northern Arizona University Archaeological Report 576. Flagstaff.

Geib, P. R., J. H. Collette, and K. Spurr

2001 *Kaibabitsinüngwü: An Archaeological Sample Survey of the Kaiparowits Plateau.* Cultural Resource Series No. 25. Bureau of Land Management, Salt Lake City.

Geib, P. R., and D. Davidson

1994 Anasazi Origins: A Perspective from Preliminary Work at Old Man Cave. *Kiva* 60:191–202.

Geib, P. R., and M. R. Robins

2003 The Desha Caves: Radiocarbon Dating and Coprolite Analysis. *Utah Archaeology* 16:81–94.

Geib, P. R., and S. J. Smith

2008 Palynology and Archaeological Inference: Bridging the Gap Between Pollen Washes and Past Behavior. *Journal of Archaeological Science* 35:2085–2101.

Geib, P. R., and K. Spurr

2000 The Basketmaker II–III Transition on the Rainbow Plateau. In *Foundations of Anasazi Culture: The Basketmaker–Pueblo Transition,* edited by P. F. Reed, pp. 175–200. University of Utah Press, Salt Lake City.

2002 The Forager to Farmer Transition on the Rainbow Plateau. In *Traditions, Transitions and Technologies: Themes in Southwest Archaeology in the Year 2000,* edited by S. H. Schlanger, pp. 224–244. University Press of Colorado, Boulder.

2007 *Prehistory of the Northern Kayenta Anasazi Region: Archaeological Excavations Along the Navajo Mountain Road (N16).* 5 vols. Edited and assembled by P. R. Geib and K. Spurr. Navajo Nation Archaeology Department Report No. 02-48. Navajo Nation Historic Preservation Department, Window Rock, Arizona.

Geib, P. R., and M. Warburton

1991 *A Class 1 Cultural Resources and Ethnographic Overview of the Glen Canyon–Shiprock Transmission Line Corridor.* Navajo Nation Archaeology Department Report No. 91-016. Navajo Nation Historic Preservation Department, Window Rock, Arizona.

Geib, P. R., M. Warburton, and K. A. Hays-Gilpin

1993 *Economic Specialization and Social Differentiation in the Northern Kayenta Region: A Data Recovery Plan for Prehistoric Sites Along the Navajo Mountain Road.* Navajo Nation Archaeology Department Report No. 92-31. Navajo Nation Historic Preservation Department, Window Rock, Arizona.

Germick, S., Jr.

1989 Form and Function of the Kayenta Anasazi Kiva, AD 1300 to 800. Unpublished M.A. thesis, Department of Anthropology, Northern Arizona University, Flagstaff.

Gifford, E. W.

1936 *Northeastern and Western Yavapai.* University of California Publications in American Archaeology and Ethnology, Vol. 29, No. 3. University of California Press, Berkeley.

Gilbert, B. M.

1984 *A Re-Examination of the Faunal Material from Dust Devil Cave: Old Data, New Interpretations.* Paper presented at the 19th Biennial Great Basin Anthropological Conference, Boise.

Gile, L. A., F. F. Peterson, and R. B. Grossman
1966 Morphological and Genetic Sequences of Carbonate Accumulation in Desert Soils. *Soil Science* 101:347–360.

Gilman, P. A.
1983 *Changing Architectural Forms in Prehistoric Southwest*. Ph.D. dissertation, Department of Anthropology, University of New Mexico, Albuquerque. University Microfilms, Ann Arbor.
1987 Architecture as Artifact: Pit Structures and Pueblos in the American Southwest. *American Antiquity* 52:538–564.

Gilpin, D.
1989 *The Salina Springs Discoveries: Archaeological Investigations at the Western Edge of the Chinle Valley, Apache County, Arizona*. Navajo Nation Cultural Resource Management Program Report No. 85-469/86-027, addendum. Navajo Nation Historic Preservation Department, Window Rock, Arizona.
1994 Lukachukai and Salina Springs: Late Archaic/Early Basketmaker Habitation Sites in the Chinle Valley, Northeastern Arizona. *Kiva* 60:203–218.

Gilpin, D., and L. Benallie Jr.
2000 Juniper Cove and Early Anasazi Community Structure West of the Chuska Mountains. In *Foundations of Anasazi Culture: The Basketmaker–Pueblo Transition*, edited by P. F. Reed, pp. 161–173. University of Utah Press, Salt Lake City.

Gladwin, W., and H. S. Gladwin
1934 *A Method for Designation of Cultures and Their Variations*. Medallion Papers No. 15. Gila Pueblo, Globe, Arizona.

Glassow, M. A.
1972 Changes in the Adaptation of Southwestern Basketmakers: A Systems Perspective. In *Contemporary Archaeology: A Guide to Theory and Contributions*, edited by M. P. Leone, pp. 289–302. Southern Illinois University Press, Carbondale.

Goodall, J.
1986 *The Chimpanzees of Gombe: Patterns of Behavior*. Harvard University Press, Cambridge.

Gooding, J., and W. L. Shields
1985 *Sisyphus Shelter*. Cultural Resource Series 18. State Office, Colorado Bureau of Land Management, Denver.

Graham, M.
1994 *Mobile Foragers: An Ethnoarchaeological Approach to Settlement Organization Among the Rarámuri of Northwestern Mexico*. International Monographs in Prehistory, Ethnoarchaeology Series 3. Ann Arbor.

Grayson, D. K.
1984 *Quantitative Zooarchaeology: Topics in the Analysis of Archaeological Faunas*. Academic Press, New York.
1993 *The Desert's Past: A Natural Prehistory of the Great Basin*. Smithsonian Institution Press, Washington, D.C.
2000 Mammalian Responses to Middle Holocene Climatic Change in the Great Basin of the Western United States. *Journal of Biogeography* 27:181–192.

Green, M.
1982 Chipped Stone Raw Materials and the Study of Interaction. Unpublished Ph.D. dissertation, Department of Anthropology, Arizona State University, Tempe.
1985 *Chipped Stone Raw Materials and the Study of Interaction on Black Mesa, Arizona*. Center for Archaeological Investigations Occasional Paper No. 11. Southern Illinois University, Carbondale.
1986 The Distribution of Chipped Stone Raw Materials at Functionally Nonequivalent Sites. In *Spatial Organization and Exchange. Archaeological Survey on Northern Black Mesa*, edited by S. Plog, pp. 143–168. Southern Illinois University Press, Carbondale.

Gregory, H. E., and R. C. Moore
1931 *The Kaiparowits Region: A Geographic and Geologic Reconnaissance of Parts of Utah and Arizona*. Geological Survey Professional Paper 164. U.S. Government Printing Office, Washington, D.C.

Guernsey, S. L.
1931 *Explorations in Northeastern Arizona*. Papers of the Peabody Museum of American Archaeology and Ethnology Vol. 12, No. 1. Harvard University, Cambridge.

Guernsey, S. L., and A. V. Kidder
1921 *Basket Maker Caves of Northeastern Arizona*. Papers of the Peabody Museum of American Archaeology and Ethnology Vol. 8, No. 2. Harvard University, Cambridge.

Guilderson, T. P., P. J. Reimer, and T. A. Brown
2005 The Boon and Bane of Radiocarbon Dating. *Science* 307:362–364.

Gumerman, G. J.
1988 *The Archaeology of the Hopi Buttes District, Arizona*. Research Paper No. 49, Center for Archaeological Investigations. Southern Illinois University, Carbondale.

Gumerman, G. J. (editor)
1988 *The Anasazi in a Changing Environment*. Cambridge University Press, Cambridge.

Gumerman, G. J., and J. S. Dean
1989 Prehistoric Cooperation and Competition in the Western Anasazi Area. In *Dynamics of Southwest Prehistory*, edited by L. S. Cordell and G. J. Gumerman, pp. 99–148. Smithsonian Institution Press, Washington, D.C.

Gumerman, G. J., and R. C. Euler (editors)
1976 *Papers on the Archaeology of Black Mesa, Arizona*. Southern Illinois University Press, Carbondale.

Gumerman, G. J., D. Westfall, and C. S. Weed
1972 *Archaeological Investigations on Black Mesa: The 1969–1970 Seasons*. Prescott College Press, Arizona.

Haas, J.
1989 The Evolution of the Kayenta Regional System. In *The Sociopolitical Structure of Prehistoric Southwestern Societies*, edited by S. Upham, K. G. Lightfoot, and R. A. Jewett, pp. 491–508. Westview Press, Boulder.
1990 Warfare and the Evolution of Tribal Polities in the Prehistoric Southwest. In *The Anthropology of War*, edited by J. Haas, pp. 171–189. Cambridge University Press, Cambridge.

Haas, J., and W. Creamer
1993 *Stress and Warfare Among the Kayenta Anasazi of the Thirteenth Century AD*. Fieldiana, Anthropology New Series 21. Field Museum of Natural History, Chicago.
1995 The Role of Warfare in the Pueblo III Period. In *The Prehistoric Pueblo World, AD 1150–1350*, edited by M. Adler, pp. 205–213. University of Arizona Press, Tucson.

Haas, W. R., Jr.
2003 The Social Implications of Basketmaker II Cordage Style Distribution. Unpublished M.A. thesis, Department of Anthropology, Northern Arizona University, Flagstaff.

Hack, J. T.
1942 *The Changing Physical Environment of the Hopi Indians of Arizona*. Papers of the Peabody Museum of American Archaeology and Ethnology, Vol. 35, No. 1. Harvard University, Cambridge.

Hantman, J. L.
1983 *Stylistic Distributions and Social Networks in the Prehistoric Plateau Southwest*. Ph.D. dissertation, Arizona State University. University Microfilms, Ann Arbor.

Hard, R. J.
1990 Agricultural Dependence in the Mountain Mogollon. In *Perspectives on Southwestern Prehistory*, edited by P. E. Minnis and C. L. Redman, pp. 135–149. Westview Press, Boulder.

Hard, R. J., R. P. Mauldin, and G. R. Raymond
1996 Mano Size, Stable Carbon Isotope Ratios, and Macrobotanical Remains as Multiple Lines of Evidence of Maize Dependence in the American Southwest. *Journal of Archaeological Method and Theory* 3:253–318.

Hargrave, L. L.
1935 *Report on Archaeological Reconnaissance in the Rainbow Plateau Area of Northern Arizona and Southern Utah*. University of California Press, Berkeley.

Harlan, T. P., and J. S. Dean
1968 Tree-Ring Data for Several Navajo Mountain Region Sites. In *Survey and Excavation North and East of Navajo Mountain, Utah 1959–1962*. Museum of Northern Arizona Bulletin No. 45. Northern Arizona Society of Science and Art, Flagstaff.

Harrill, B. G.
1982 *Prehistoric Agricultural Adaptation and Settlement in Long House Valley, Northeastern Arizona*. Ph.D. dissertation, Department of Anthropology, University of Arizona, Tucson. University Microfilms, Ann Arbor.

Harris, D. R., and G. C. Hillman (editors)
1989 *Foraging and Farming: The Evolution of Plant Exploitation*. Unwin Hyman, London.

Hasbargen, J.
1994 A Holocene Paleoclimatic and Environmental Record from Stoneman Lake, Arizona. *Quaternary Research* 42:188–196.

Hassan, F. A.
1981 *Demographic Archaeology*. Academic Press, New York.

Hauck, F. R.
1979a *Cultural Resource Evaluation in Central Utah, 1977*. Cultural Resource Series No. 3. Bureau of Land Management, Utah State Office, Salt Lake City.
1979b *Cultural Resource Evaluation in South Central Utah 1977*. Cultural Resource Series No. 4. Bureau of Land Management, Utah State Office, Salt Lake City.

Hayden, B. (editor)
1987 *Lithic Studies Among the Contemporary Highland Maya*. University of Arizona Press, Tucson.

Hayden, I.
1930 *Preliminary Report on Two Caves in Southeastern Utah Explored in July and August, 1930, by the Van Bergen–Los Angeles County Museum, Los Angeles Field Party*. MS on file, Los Angeles County Museum, Los Angeles.

Haynes, C. V., Jr.
1990 The Antevs–Bryan Years and the Legacy for Paleoindian Chronology. In *Establishment of a Geological Framework for Paleoanthropology*, edited by L. F. LaPorte, pp. 55–68. Special Paper 242. Geological Society of America, Boulder.

Hays-Gilpin, K.
1994 *Ceramic Analysis Manual: Navajo Mountain Road Archaeology Project*. MS on file, Navajo Nation Archaeology Department, Window Rock, Arizona.

Hays-Gilpin, K. A., A. C. Deegan, and E. A. Morris
1998 *Prehistoric Sandals for Northeastern Arizona: The Earl H. Morris and Ann Axtell Morris Research*. Anthropological Papers of the University of Arizona No. 62. University of Arizona Press, Tucson.

Heacock, L. A.
1995 Archaeological Investigations of Three Mesa Verde Anasazi Pit Kilns. *Kiva* 60:391–410.

Hegmon, M., J. R. Allison, H. Neff, and M. D. Glascock
1997 Production of San Juan Red Ware in the Northern Southwest: Insights into Regional Interaction in Early Puebloan Prehistory. *American Antiquity* 62:449–463.

Hesse, I. S., W. J. Parry, and F. E. Smiley
1996 *A Unique Late Paleoindian Site Near Inscription House, Northeastern Arizona*. Paper presented at the Society for American Archaeology Meetings, New Orleans.
1999 Badger Springs: A Late-Paleoindian Site in Northeastern Arizona. *Current Research in the Pleistocene* 16:27–30.

Hewitt, N. J.
1980 Fiber Artifacts. In *Cowboy Cave*, by J. D. Jennings, pp. 49–74. University of Utah Anthropological Papers No. 104. University of Utah Press, Salt Lake City.

Hewitt, N. J., B. L. Tipps, and J. M. Brisbin
1989 Site AZ-J-19-3. In *Kayenta Anasazi Archeology and Navajo Ethnohistory on the Northwestern Shonto Plateau: The N-16 Project*, edited by A. R. Schroedl, pp. 148–184. P-III Associates, Salt Lake City.

Hill, W. W.
1938 *The Agricultural and Hunting Methods of the Navaho Indians*. Yale University Publications in Anthropology No. 18. New Haven.

Hobler, P. M.
1964 The Late Survival of Pithouse Architecture in the Kayenta

Anasazi Area. Unpublished M.A. thesis, Department of Anthropology, University of Arizona, Tucson.

1974 The Late Survival of Pithouse Architecture in the Kayenta Anasazi Area. *Southwestern Lore* 40(2):1–44.

Hockett, C. F., and R. Ascher
1964 The Human Revolution. *Current Anthropology* 5:135–168.

Hogan, P.
1994 Foragers to Farmers II: A Second Look at the Adoption of Agriculture in the Northern Southwest. In *Archaic Hunter-Gatherer Archaeology in the American Southwest*, edited by B. J. Vierra, pp. 155–184. Contributions in Anthropology, Vol. 13, No. 1. Eastern New Mexico University, Portales.
1996 *Time-Space Systematics of the San Juan Basin*. Paper presented at the Conference on the Archaic Prehistory of the North American Southwest, Albuquerque.

Holmer, R. N.
1978 *A Mathematical Typology for Archaic Projectile Points of the Eastern Great Basin*. Ph.D. dissertation, Department of Anthropology, University of Utah, Salt Lake City. University Microfilms, Ann Arbor.
1980 Projectile Points. In *Sudden Shelter*, edited by J. D. Jennings, A. R. Schroedl, and R. N. Holmer, pp. 63–83. Anthropological Papers No. 103. University of Utah Press, Salt Lake City.
1986 Common Projectile Points of the Intermountain West. In *Anthropology of the Desert West. Essays in Honor of Jesse D. Jennings*, edited by C. J. Condie and D. D. Fowler, pp. 90–115. Anthropological Papers No. 110. University of Utah Press, Salt Lake City.

Holmer, R. N., and D. G. Weder
1980 Common Post-Archaic Projectile Points of the Fremont Area. In *Fremont Perspectives*, edited by D. B. Madsen, pp. 55–68. Antiquities Section Selected Papers Vol. 3, No. 16. Utah State Historical Society, Salt Lake City.

Horn, J. C.
1990 *Archaeological Data Recovery at the Down Wash Site (42WN1666), Canyonlands National Park, Utah*. MS on file, Rocky Mountain Regional Office, National Park Service, Denver.

Hough, W.
1915 *The Hopi Indians*. Torch Press, Cedar Rapids.

Huber, E. K.
2005 Early Maize at the Old Corn Site (LA 137258). In *Fence Lake Project: Archaeological Data Recovery in the New Mexico Transportation Corridor and First Five-Year Permit Area, Fence Lake Coal Mine Project, Catron County, New Mexico, Vol. 4: Synthetic Studies*, edited by E. K. Huber and C. R. Van West, pp. 36.1–36.14. SRI Technical Series 84. Statistical Research, Tucson.

Huckell, B. B.
1977 *The Hastqin Site: A Multicomponent Site Near Ganado, Arizona*. Contribution to Highway Salvage Archaeology in Arizona 61. Arizona State Museum, Tucson.
1990 *Late Preceramic Farmer-Foragers in Southern Arizona: A Cultural and Ecological Consideration of the Spread of Agriculture in the Arid Southwestern United States*. Ph.D. dissertation, Arid Land Resource Sciences, University of Arizona, Tucson. University Microfilms, Ann Arbor.
1995 *Of Marshes and Maize: Preceramic Agricultural Settlements in the Cienega Valley, Southeastern Arizona*. Anthropological Papers of the University of Arizona No. 59. University of Arizona Press, Tucson.
1996 The Archaic Prehistory of the North American Southwest. *Journal of World Prehistory* 10(3):305–372.

Huckell, B. B., L. W. Huckell, and K. K. Benedict
2002 Maize Agricultural and the Rise of Mixed Foraging-Farming Economies in Southern Arizona During the Second Millennium B.C. In *Traditions, Transitions and Technologies: Themes in Southwest Archaeology in the Year 2000*, edited by S. H. Schlanger, pp. 137–159. University Press of Colorado, Boulder.

Huckell, L. W.
1995 Farming and Foraging in the Cienega Valley. Early Agricultural Period Paleoethnobotany. In *Of Marshes and Maize: Preceramic Agricultural Settlements in the Cienega Valley, Southeastern Arizona*, by B. B. Huckell, pp. 74–97. Anthropological Papers of the University of Arizona No. 59. University of Arizona Press, Tucson.
2006 Ancient Maize in the Southwest: What Does It Look Like and What Can It Tell Us? In *Histories of Maize: Multidisciplinary Approaches to the Prehistory, Linguistics, Biogeography and Evolution of Maize*, edited by J. Staller, R. Tykot, and B. Benz, pp. 97–107. Elsevier Academic Press, Boston.

Huffman, J.
1993 Navajo Mountain Road Archaeological Project Field Manual. In *Economic Specialization and Social Differentiation in the Northern Kayenta Region: A Data Recovery Plan for Prehistoric Sites Along the Navajo Mountain Road*, by P. R. Geib, M. Warburton, and K. A. Hays-Gilpin, Appendix A. Navajo Nation Archaeology Department Report No. 92-31. Navajo Nation Historic Preservation Department, Window Rock, Arizona.

Hull, K. L.
2001 Reasserting the Utility of Obsidian Hydration Dating: A Temperature-Dependent Empirical Approach to Practical Temporal Resolution with Archaeological Obsidians. *Journal of Archaeological Science* 28:1025–1040.

Hunt, C. B.
1967 *Physiography of the United States*. W. H. Freeman, San Francisco.

Ingbar, E. E.
1993 Lithic Material Selection and Technological Organization. In *The Organization of North American Prehistoric Chipped Stone Tool Technologies*, edited by P. J. Carr, pp. 45–56. International Monographs in Prehistory, Archaeological Series 7. Ann Arbor.

Irwin-Williams, C.
1967 Picosa: The Elementary Southwestern Culture. *American Antiquity* 32:441–457.
1973 *The Oshara Tradition: Origins of Anasazi Culture*. Contributions in Anthropology 5(1). Eastern New Mexico University, Portales.

1979 Post-Pleistocene Archaeology 7000–200 BC. In *Southwest*, edited by A. Ortiz, pp. 31–42. *Handbook of North American Indians*, Vol. 9, W. C. Sturtevant, general editor. Smithsonian Institution, Washington, D.C.

1994 The Archaic of the Southwestern United States: Changing Goals and Research Strategies in the Last Twenty Years 1964–1989. In *Archaic Hunter-Gatherer Archaeology in the American Southwest*, edited by B. J. Vierra, pp. 566–653. Contributions in Anthropology Vol. 13, No. 1. Eastern New Mexico University, Portales.

Irwin-Williams, C., H. Irwin, G. Agogino, and C. V. Haynes Jr.
1973 Hell Gap Paleo-Indian Occupation of the High Plains. *Plains Anthropologist* 18:40–53.

Isaac, G.
1978a Food Sharing and Human Evolution: Archaeological Evidence from the Plio-Pleistocene of East Africa. *Journal of Anthropological Research* 34:311–325.
1978b The Food Sharing Behavior of Protohuman Hominids. *Scientific American* 238:90–108.

Jackson, R. J.
1984 Current Problems in Obsidian Hydration Analysis. In *Obsidian Studies in the Great Basin*, edited by R. E. Hughes, pp. 103–115. Contributions to the University of California Archaeological Research Facility No. 45. Berkeley.

Jacobs, B. F.
1985 A Middle Wisconsin Pollen Record from Hay Lake, Arizona. *Quaternary Research* 24:121–130.

Jennings, J. D.
1956 The American Southwest: A Problem in Cultural Isolation. In *Seminars in Archaeology, 1955*, edited by R. Wauchope, pp. 59–127. Memoirs of the Society for American Archaeology 11. Salt Lake City.
1957 *Danger Cave*. University of Utah Anthropological Papers 27. University of Utah Press, Salt Lake City.
1966 *Glen Canyon: A Summary*. Anthropological Papers No. 81. University of Utah Press, Salt Lake City.
1968 *Prehistory of North America*. McGraw-Hill, New York.
1973 The Short Useful Life of a Simple Hypothesis. *Tebiwa* 13(1):1–9.
1980 *Cowboy Cave*. Anthropological Papers No. 104. University of Utah Press, Salt Lake City.
1986 American Archaeology, 1930–1985. In *American Archaeology Past and Future: A Celebration of the Society for American Archaeology 1935–1985*, edited by D. J. Meltzer, D. D. Fowler, and J. A. Sabloff, pp. 53–62. Smithsonian Institution, Washington, D.C.

Jennings, J. D., A. R. Schroedl, and R. N. Holmer
1980 *Sudden Shelter*. Anthropological Papers No. 103. University of Utah, Salt Lake City.

Jett, S. C.
1978 Navajo Seasonal Migration Patterns. *Kiva* 44:65–75.

Jett, S. C., and V. E. Spencer
1981 *Navajo Architecture*. University of Arizona Press, Tucson.

Jochim, M. A.
1976 *Hunter-Gatherer Subsistence and Settlement: A Predictive Model*. Academic Press, New York.

Jones, G. T., and C. Beck
1999 Paleoarchaic Archaeology in the Great Basin. In *Models for the Millennium: Great Basin Archaeology Today*, edited by C. Beck, pp. 83–95. University of Utah Press, Salt Lake City.

Jones, K. T., and D. B. Madsen
1989 Calculating the Cost of Resource Transportation: A Great Basin Example. *Current Anthropology* 30:529–534.

Judge, W. J.
1982 The Paleo-Indian and Basketmaker Periods: An Overview and Some Research Problems. In *The San Juan Tomorrow: Planning for the Conservation of Cultural Resources in the San Juan Basin*, edited by F. Plog and W. Wait, pp. 5–57. National Park Service, Southwest Region, Santa Fe.

Kaplan, H., and K. Hill
1992 The Evolutional Ecology of Food Acquisition. In *Evolutionary Ecology and Human Behavior*, edited by B. Winterhalder, pp. 167–202. Aldine de Gruyter, New York.

Kaplan, L.
1956 The Cultivated Beans of the Prehistoric Southwest. *Annals of the Missouri Botanical Gardens* 43:189–249.

Karlstrom, E. T.
1988 Rates of Soil Formation on Black Mesa, Northeastern Arizona: A Chronosequence in Late Quaternary Alluvium. *Physical Geography* 9(4):301–327.

Karlstrom, E. T., and T. N. V. Karlstrom
1986 Late Quaternary Alluvial Stratigraphy and Soils of the Black Mesa–Little Colorado River Areas in Northern Arizona. In *Geology of Central and Northern Arizona*, edited by J. D. Nations, C. M. Conway, and G. S. Swann, pp. 71–92. Rocky Mountain Section Guidebook, Geological Society of America.

Karlstrom, T. N. V.
1988 Alluvial Chronology and Hydrologic Change of Black Mesa and Nearby Regions. In *The Anasazi in a Changing Environment*, edited by G. J. Gumerman, pp. 45–91. Cambridge University Press, Cambridge.

Katzenberg, M. A., and S. Pfeiffer
2000 Stable Isotope Analysis: A Tool for Studying Past Diet, Demography and Life History. In *Biological Anthropology of the Human Skeleton*, edited by M. A. Katzenberg and S. R. Saunders, pp. 305–328. Wiley-Liss, New York.

Kearns, T. M.
1982 *The Escalante Project: A Class II Cultural Resources Inventory of Preference Right Coal Lease Tracts in South Central Utah*. 2 vols. MS on file, Bureau of Land Management, Kanab, Utah.

Kelley, K. B.
1986 *Navajo Land Use*. Academic Press, New York.

Kelley, K. B., and H. Francis
1994 *Navajo Sacred Places*. Indiana University Press, Bloomington.

Kelly, I. T.
1934 Southern Paiute Bands. *American Anthropologist* 36:548–560.
1964 *Southern Paiute Ethnography*. Anthropological Papers No. 69. University of Utah Press, Salt Lake City.

Kelly, I. T., and C. S. Fowler
1986 Southern Paiute. In *Great Basin*, edited by W. L. D'Azevedo, pp. 368–397. *Handbook of North American Indians*, Vol. 11, W. C. Sturtevant, general editor. Smithsonian Institution, Washington, D.C.

Kelly, R. L.
1983 Hunter-Gatherer Mobility Strategies. *Journal of Anthropological Research* 39:277–306.
1985 Hunter-Gatherer Mobility and Sedentism: A Great Basin Study. Unpublished Ph.D. dissertation, Department of Anthropology, University of Michigan, Ann Arbor.
1992 Mobility/Sedentism: Concepts, Archaeological Measures, and Effects. *Annual Review of Anthropology* 21:43–66.
1995 *The Foraging Spectrum: Diversity in Hunter-Gatherer Lifeways*. Smithsonian Institution Press, Washington, D.C.

Kennard, K.
1979 Hopi Economy and Subsistence. In *Handbook of North American Indians, Vol. 9: Southwest*, edited by A. Ortiz, pp. 554–563. Smithsonian Institution, Washington, D.C.

Kennett, D. J., and B. Winterhalder (editors)
2006 *Behavioral Ecology and the Transition to Agriculture*. University of California Press, Berkeley.

Kent, K. P.
1983 *Prehistoric Textiles of the Southwest*. School of American Research, Santa Fe.

Kent, S.
1987 Understanding the Use of Space—An Ethnoarchaeological Perspective. In *Method and Theory for Activity Area Research—An Ethnoarchaeological Approach*, edited by S. Kent, pp. 1–60. Columbia University Press, New York.
1992 Studying Variability in the Archaeological Record: An Ethnoarchaeological Model for Distinguishing Mobility Patterns. *American Antiquity* 57:635–660.

Kent, S., and H. Vierich
1989 The Myth of Ecological Determinism: Anticipated Mobility and Site Organization of Space. In *Farmers as Hunters: The Implications of Sedentism*, edited by S. Kent, pp. 97–130. Cambridge University Press, Cambridge.

Kidder, A. V.
1927 Southwestern Archaeological Conference. *Science* 66:489–491.
1947 Foreword. In *Caves of the Upper Gila and Hueco Areas in New Mexico and Texas*, by C. B. Cosgrove, pp. vii–ix. Papers of the Peabody Museum of American Archaeology and Ethnology Vol. 24, No. 2. Harvard University, Cambridge.
1962 [1924] *An Introduction to the Study of Southwestern Archaeology*. Rev. ed. Yale University Press, New Haven.

Kidder, A. V., and S. L. Guernsey
1919 *Archaeological Explorations in Northeastern Arizona*. Bureau of American Ethnology Bulletin 65. Washington, D.C.
1922 Part II. Notes on the Artifacts and on Foods. In *A Basket-Maker Cave in Kane County, Utah*, by J. L. Nusbaum, pp. 64–150. Indian Notes and Monographs, Museum of the American Indian, New York.

Kimberlin, J.
1976 Obsidian Hydration Rate Determinations on Chemically Characterized Samples. In *Advances in Obsidian Glass Studies*, edited by R. E. Taylor, pp. 63–79. Noyes Press, Park Ridge, New Jersey.

Klesert, A. L.
1982 Standing Fall House: An Early Puebloan Storage and Redistribution Center in Northeastern Arizona. *Kiva* 48:39–61.

Kluckholm, C., W. W. Hill, and L. W. Kluckholm
1971 *Navajo Material Culture*. Harvard University Press, Cambridge.

Knipmeyer, J. H.
2002 *Butch Cassidy Was Here: Historic Inscriptions of the Colorado Plateau*. University of Utah Press, Salt Lake City.

Kohler, T. A.
1992 Field Houses, Villages, and the Tragedy of the Commons in the Early Northern Anasazi Southwest. *American Antiquity* 57:617–635.

Kojo, Y., R. M. Kalin, and A. Long
1994 High-Precision "Wiggle-Matching" in Radiocarbon Dating. *Journal of Archaeological Science* 21:475–479.

Krebs, J. R., and N. B. Davies (editors)
1984 *Behavioral Ecology: An Evolutionary Approach*. Blackwell Scientific, Oxford.

Kroeber, A. L.
1917 *Zuni Kin and Clan*. Anthropological Papers of the American Museum of Natural History, Vol. 18, Pt. 2:41–204. New York.

Lambert, R. E.
2006 *Investigations of Small Structures in the Citadel District of Wupatki National Monument*. Ph.D. dissertation, Department of Anthropology, University of New Mexico. University Microfilms, Ann Arbor.

Lanner, R. M.
1981 *The Piñon Pine: A Natural and Cultural History*. University of Nevada Press, Reno.

Lawson, F. H., and B. Rudden
1984 *The Law of Property*. Oxford University Press.

Layhe, R. W.
1977 A Multivariate Approach for Estimating Population Change: Black Mesa, Northeastern Arizona. Unpublished M.A. thesis, Department of Anthropology, Southern Illinois University, Carbondale.
1981 *A Locational Model for Demographic and Settlement System Change: An Example from the American Southwest*. Ph.D. dissertation, Southern Illinois University. University Microfilms, Ann Arbor.

Leakey, M. D.
1984 *Disclosing the Past: An Autobiography*. Doubleday, Garden City, New York.

LeBlanc, S. A.
1982 Temporal Change in Mogollon Ceramics. In *Southwestern Ceramics: A Comparative Review*, edited by A. H. Schroeder, pp. 107–128. The Arizona Archaeologist No. 15. Arizona Archaeological Society, Phoenix.
1999 *Prehistoric Warfare in the American Southwest*. University of Utah Press, Salt Lake City.

Lebo, C. J., B. M. Estes, and J. E. Belser
1983 Arizona D:7:3107. In *Excavations on Black Mesa, 1981: A Descriptive Report*, edited by F. E. Smiley, D. L. Nichols,

and P. P. Andrews, pp. 138–151. Center for Archaeological Investigations Research Paper No. 36. Southern Illinois University, Carbondale.

Lebo, C. J., and M. MacMinn
1984 Arizona D:11:3063. In *Excavations on Black Mesa, 1982: A Descriptive Report*, edited by D. L. Nichols and F. E. Smiley, pp. 339–345. Center for Archaeological Investigations Research Paper No. 39. Southern Illinois University, Carbondale.

Lekson, S. H.
1988 The Idea of the Kiva in Anasazi Archaeology. *Kiva* 53:213–234.
1989 Kivas? In *The Architecture of Social Integration in Prehistoric Pueblos*, edited by W. D. Lipe and M. Hegmon, pp. 161–167. Occasional Papers, No. 1. Crow Canyon Archaeological Center, Cortez, Colorado.
1990 Sedentism and Aggregation in Anasazi Archaeology. In *Perspectives on Southwestern Prehistory*, edited by P. Minnis and C. Redman, pp. 333–340. Westview Press, Boulder.

Leonard, R. D.
1986 *Patterns of Anasazi Subsistence: Faunal Exploitation, Subsistence Diversification and Site Function in Northeastern Arizona*. Ph.D. dissertation, Department of Anthropology, University of Washington. University Microfilms, Ann Arbor.
1989 *Anasazi Faunal Exploitation: Prehistoric Subsistence on Northern Black Mesa, Arizona*. Center for Archaeological Investigations Occasional Paper No. 13. Southern Illinois University, Carbondale.

Leonard, R. D., J. E. Belser, D. A. Jessup, and J. Carucci
1984 Arizona D:11:3133. In *Excavations on Black Mesa, 1982: A Descriptive Report*, edited by D. L. Nichols and F. E. Smiley, pp. 370–394. Center for Archaeological Investigations Research Paper No. 39. Southern Illinois University, Carbondale.

Leonard, R. D., and G. T. Jones
1989 *Quantifying Diversity in Archaeology*. Cambridge University Press, Cambridge.

Leonard, R. D., P. H. McCartney, M. Gould, J. Carucci, and G. D. Glennie
1985 Arizona D:11:449. In *Excavations on Black Mesa, 1983: A Descriptive Report*, edited by A. L. Christenson and W. J. Parry, pp. 124–154. Center for Archaeological Investigations Research Paper No. 46. Southern Illinois University, Carbondale.

Lepofsky, D.
1986 *Preliminary Analysis of Flotation Samples from the Turkey Pen Ruin, Cedar Mesa, Utah*. MS on file, Laboratory of Archaeology, University of British Columbia, Vancouver.

Lesko, L. M.
1989 A Reexamination of Northern Arizona Obsidians. *Kiva* 54:385–399.

LeTourneau, P. D.
2000 Folsom Toolstone Procurement in the Southwest and Southern Plains. Unpublished Ph.D. dissertation, Department of Anthropology, University of New Mexico, Albuquerque.

Lightfoot, K. G., and G. M. Feinman
1982 Social Differentiation and Leadership Development in Early Pithouse Villages in the Mogollon Region of the American Southwest. *American Antiquity* 47:64–86.

Lightfoot, K. G., and R. A. Jewett
1984 The Occupation of Duncan. In *The Duncan Project: A Study of the Occupation Duration and Settlement Pattern of an Early Mogollon Pithouse Village*, by K. G. Lightfoot, pp. 47–82. Anthropological Field Studies 6. Arizona State University, Tempe.

Linares, O. F.
1976 "Garden Hunting" in the American Tropics. *Human Ecology* 4:331–349.

Lindsay, A. J., Jr.
1961 The Beaver Creek Agricultural Community on the San Juan River, Utah. *American Antiquity* 27:245–249.
1969 *The Tsegi Phase of the Kayenta Cultural Tradition in Northeastern Arizona*. Ph.D. dissertation, University of Arizona. University Microfilms, Ann Arbor.

Lindsay, A. J., Jr., and J. R. Ambler
1963 Recent Contributions and Research Problems in Kayenta Anasazi Prehistory. *Plateau* 35(3):86–92.

Lindsay, A. J., Jr., J. R. Ambler, M. A. Stein, and P. M. Hobler
1968 *Survey and Excavation North and East of Navajo Mountain, Utah 1959–1962*. Museum of Northern Arizona Bulletin No. 45. Northern Arizona Society of Science and Art, Flagstaff.

Linton, R.
1944 North American Cooking Pots. *American Antiquity* 9:369–380.

Lipe, W. D.
1960 *1958 Excavations, Glen Canyon Area*. Anthropological Papers No. 44. University of Utah Press, Salt Lake City.
1967 *Anasazi Culture and Its Relationships to the Environment in the Red Rock Plateau Region, Southeastern Utah*. Ph.D. dissertation, Department of Anthropology, Yale University. University Microfilms, Ann Arbor.
1970 Anasazi Communities in the Red Rock Plateau, Southwestern Utah. In *Reconstructing Prehistoric Pueblo Societies*, edited by W. A. Longacre, pp. 84–139. University of New Mexico Press, Albuquerque.
1978 Archaeological Work in the Grand Gulch Region, Southeastern Utah, 1969. In *National Geographic Society Research in 1969*, edited by P. H. Oehser and J. S. Lea, pp. 389–397. National Geographical Society, Washington, D.C.
1993 The Basketmaker II Period in the Four Corners Area. In *Anasazi Basketmaker: Papers from the 1990 Wetherill–Grand Gulch Symposium*, edited by V. M. Atkins, pp. 1–10. Cultural Resource Series No. 24. Bureau of Land Management, Salt Lake City.
1994 Comments. *Kiva* 60:337–344.

Lipe, W. D., and A. J. Lindsay Jr.
1983 *Pueblo Adaptations in the Glen Canyon Area*. Paper presented at the 2nd Anasazi Symposium, Farmington, New Mexico.

Lipe, W. D., and B. L. Pitblado
1999 Paleoindian and Archaic Periods. In *Colorado Prehistory:*

A Context for the Southern Colorado Basin, edited by W. D. Lipe, M. D. Varien, and R. H. Wilshusen, pp. 95–131. Colorado Council of Professional Archaeologists, Denver.

Lister, R. H., J. R. Ambler, and F. C. Lister
1960 *The Coombs Site, Part II*. Anthropological Papers No. 41. University of Utah Press, Salt Lake City.

Lockett, H. C., and L. L. Hargrave
1953 *Woodchuck Cave, a Basketmaker II Site in Tsegi Canyon, Arizona*. Museum of Northern Arizona Bulletin No. 26. Northern Arizona Society of Science and Art, Flagstaff.

Long, P. V., Jr.
1966 *Archaeological Excavations in Lower Glen Canyon, Utah–Arizona 1959–1960*. Museum of Northern Arizona Bulletin No. 42. Northern Arizona Society of Science and Art, Flagstaff.

Lucius, W. A.
1980 Bone and Shell Material. In *Cowboy Cave*, by J. D. Jennings, pp. 97–107. Anthropological Papers No. 104. University of Utah Press, Salt Lake City.
1983 *An Alternative Speculative History of San Juan County, Utah*. Paper presented at the 56th Pecos Conference, Bluff, Utah.

Lyman, R. L., M. J. O'Brien, and R. C. Dunnell
1997 An Introduction. In *Americanist Culture History: Fundamentals of Time, Space, and Form*, edited by R. L. Lyman, M. J. O'Brien, and R. C. Dunnell, pp. 1–13. Plenum Press, New York.

Lyneis, M. M.
1996 Pueblo II–Pueblo III Change in Southwestern Utah, the Arizona Strip, and Southern Nevada. In *The Prehistoric Pueblo World, AD 1150–1350*, edited by M. A. Adler, pp. 11–28. University of Arizona Press, Tucson.

Lyons, P. D.
2003 *Ancestral Hopi Migrations*. Anthropological Papers No. 68. University of Arizona, Tucson.

Mabry, J. B.
1998 Conclusion. In *Archaeological Investigations of Early Village Sites in the Middle Santa Cruz Valley: Analyses and Synthesis*, edited by J. B. Mabry, pp. 757–792. Anthropological Papers No. 19. Center for Desert Archaeology, Tucson.
2005 Diversity in Early Southwestern Farming and Optimization Models of Transitions to Agriculture. In *The Late Archaic Across the Borderlands: From Foraging to Farming*, edited by B. J. Vierra, pp. 41–83. University of Texas Press, Austin.

Madsen, D. B.
1981 The Emperor's New Clothes. *American Antiquity* 46:637–640.
1986 Great Basin Nuts: A Short Treatise on the Distribution, Productivity, and Prehistoric Use of Pinyon. In *Anthropology of the Desert West: Essays in Honor of Jesse D. Jennings*, edited by C. J. Condie and D. D. Fowler, pp. 21–41. Anthropological Paper No. 110. University of Utah Press, Salt Lake City.

Malville, N. J.
2001 Long-Distance Transport of Bulk Goods in the Pre-Hispanic American Southwest. *Journal of Anthropological Archaeology* 20:230–243.

Martin, D. L., A. H. Goodman, G. J. Armelagos, and A. L. Magennis
1991 *Black Mesa Anasazi Health: Reconstructing Life from Patterns of Death and Disease*. Center for Archaeological Investigations, Occasional Paper No. 14. Southern Illinois University, Carbondale.

Martin, S. L.
1999 Virgin Anasazi Diet as Demonstrated Through the Analysis of Stable Carbon and Nitrogen Isotopes. *Kiva* 64:495–514.

Matson, R. G.
1991 *Origins of Southwest Agriculture*. University of Arizona Press, Tucson.
1999 The Spread of Maize to the Colorado Plateau. *Archaeology Southwest* 13(1):10–11.
2002 The Spread of Maize Agriculture into the U.S. Southwest. In *Examining the Farming/Language Dispersal Hypothesis*, edited by P. Bellwood and C. Renfrew, pp. 341–356. McDonald Institute for Archaeological Research, Cambridge.
2006a What Is Basketmaker II? *Kiva* 72:149–166.
2006b Basketmaker II and Cedar Mesa. In *Tracking Ancient Footsteps: William P. Lipe's Contributions to Southwestern Prehistory and Public Archaeology*, edited by R. G. Matson and T. Kohler, pp. 46–62. Washington State University Press, Pullman.

Matson, R. G., and B. Chisholm
1991 Basketmaker II Subsistence: Carbon Isotopes and Other Dietary Indicators from Cedar Mesa, Utah. *American Antiquity* 56:444–459.
2007 *Basketmaker II Subsistence*. Poster presented at the 72nd Annual Meeting of the Society for American Archaeology, Austin.

Matson, R. G., and W. D. Lipe
1978 Settlement Patterns on Cedar Mesa: Boom and Burst on the Northern Periphery. In *Investigations by the Southwestern Anthropological Research Group: An Exercise in Archaeological Cooperation*, edited by R. Euler and G. J. Gumerman, pp. 1–12. Museum of Northern Arizona, Bulletin 50. Flagstaff.

Matson, R. G., W. D. Lipe, and W. R. Haase IV
1988 Adaptational Continuities and Occupational Discontinuities: The Cedar Mesa Anasazi. *Journal of Field Archaeology* 15:245–264.

Mayo, E. B.
1956 Copper. In *Mineral Resources, Navajo–Hopi Indian Reservations, Arizona–Utah: Vol. 1: Metalliferous Minerals and Mineral Fuels*, by G. A. Kiersch, pp. 19–32. University of Arizona Press, Tucson.

Mazer, J. J., C. M. Stevenson, W. Ebert, and J. K. Bates
1991 The Experimental Hydration of Obsidian as a Function of Relative Humidity and Temperature. *American Antiquity* 56:504–513.

McAllister, S. P., and F. Plog
1978 Small Sites in the Chevelon Drainage. In *Limited Activity and Occupation Sites: A Collection of Conference Papers*,

edited by A. E. Ward, pp. 17–23. Contributions to Anthropological Studies No. 1. Center for Anthropological Studies, Albuquerque.

McGregor, J. C.
1965   *Southwestern Archaeology*. University of Illinois Press, Urbana.

McNitt, F.
1966   *Richard Wetherill: Anasazi*. University of New Mexico Press, Albuquerque.

McPherson, R. S.
1988   *The Northern Navajo Frontier 1860–1900: Expansion Through Adversity*. University of New Mexico Press, Albuquerque.

Meighan, C. W.
1976   Empirical Determination of Obsidian Hydration Rates from Archaeological Evidence. In *Advances in Obsidian Glass Studies*, edited by R. E. Taylor, pp. 106–119. Noyes Press, Park Ridge, New Jersey.

Meltzer, D. J.
1991   Altithermal Archaeology and Paleoecology at Mustang Springs, on the Southern High Plains of Texas. *American Antiquity* 56:236–267.
1999   Human Response to Middle Holocene (Altithermal) Climates on the North American Great Plains. *Quaternary Research* 52:404–416.

Metcalf, M. D., and K. D. Black
1991   *Archaeological Excavations at the Yarmony Pit House Site, Eagle County, Colorado*. Cultural Resource Series No. 31. Bureau of Land Management, Denver.

Michels, J. W., and I. S. T. Tsong
1980   Obsidian Hydration Dating: A Coming of Age. In *Advances in Archaeological Method and Theory, Vol. 3*, edited by M. B. Schiffer, pp. 405–444. Academic Press, New York.

Michels, J. W., I. S. T. Tsong, and G. A. Smith
1983   Experimentally Derived Hydration Rates in Obsidian Dating. *Archaeometry* 25:107–117.

Miller, W. C., and D. A. Breternitz
1958a   1957 Navajo Canyon Survey: Preliminary Report. *Plateau* 30:72–74.
1958b   1958 Navajo Canyon Survey Preliminary Report. *Plateau* 31:3–7.

Mindeleff, C.
1898   *Navaho Houses*. 17th Annual Report of the Bureau of Ethnology, Smithsonian Institution, Pt. 2:469–518. Government Printing Office, Washington, D.C.

Mindeleff, V.
1891   *A Study of Pueblo Architecture in Tusayan and Cibola*. 8th Annual Report of the Bureau of Ethnology, pp. 3–228. Government Printing Office, Washington, D.C.

Minnis, P. E.
1980   Prehistoric Puebloan Food and Fuel: The Macroplant Evidence from Dead Valley, Arizona. In *Prehistory in Dead Valley, East-Central Arizona: The T&E Springerville Project*, edited by D. E. Doyel, pp. 371–387. Archaeological Series 144. Arizona State Museum, Tucson.
1985   Domesticating People and Plants in the Greater Southwest. In *Prehistoric Food Production in North America*, edited by R. I. Ford, pp. 309–339. Anthropological Papers No. 75. Museum of Anthropology, University of Michigan, Ann Arbor.
1989   Prehistoric Diet in the Northern Southwest: Macroplant Remains from Four Corners Feces. *American Antiquity* 54:543–563.
1992   Earliest Plant Cultivation in the Desert Borderlands of North America. In *The Origins of Agriculture: An International Perspective*, edited by C. W. Cowan and P. J. Watson, pp. 121–141. Smithsonian Institution Press, Washington, D.C.

Mobley-Tanaka, J. L.
1997   Gender and Ritual Space During the Pithouse to Pueblo Transition: Subterranean Mealing Rooms in the North American Southwest. *American Antiquity* 62:437–448.

Moore, B. M.
1978   Are Pueblo Field Houses a Function of Urbanization? In *Limited Activity and Occupation Sites: A Collection of Conference Papers*, edited by A. E. Ward, pp. 9–16. Contributions to Anthropological Studies No. 1. Center for Anthropological Studies, Albuquerque.
1979   Pueblo Isolated Small Structure Sites. Unpublished Ph.D. dissertation, Department of Anthropology, Southern Illinois University, Carbondale.

Moore, R. A.
1994   Archaic Projectile Point Typology/Chronology in Northern New Mexico and the Four Corners. In *Archaic Hunter-Gatherer Archaeology in the American Southwest*, edited by B. J. Vierra, pp. 456–477. Contributions in Anthropology, Vol. 13, No. 1. Eastern New Mexico University, Portales.

Morris, E. A.
1980   *Basketmaker Caves in the Prayer Rock District, Northeastern Arizona*. University of Arizona Anthropological Papers No. 35. University of Arizona Press, Tucson.

Morris, E. H., and R. F. Burgh
1954   *Basket Maker II Sites Near Durango, Colorado*. Carnegie Institution of Washington Publication 604. Washington, D.C.

Morss, N.
1931   *Notes on the Archaeology of the Kaibito and Rainbow Plateaus in Arizona*. Papers of the Peabody Museum of American Archaeology and Ethnology Vol. 12, No. 2. Harvard University, Cambridge.

Nabhan, G. P., A. M. Rea, K. L. Reichhardt, E. Mellink, and C. F. Hutchinson
1977   Living Fencerows of the Rio San Miguel, Sonora, Mexico: Traditional Technology for Floodplain Management. *Human Ecology* 5:97–111.

Nabhan, G. P., and T. E. Sheridan
1982   Papago Influences on Habitat and Biotic Diversity: Quitovac Oasis Ethnoecology. *Journal of Ethnobiology* 2:124–143.

Naroll, R.
1962   Floor Area and Settlement Population. *American Antiquity* 27:587–589.

Neff, L. T., K. Anderson, L. Huckell, and M. Robins
2004   *Archaic Period Occupation, Chronostratigraphy, and Soil Geomorphology on the Southern Kaibito Plateau: Results*

of Geoarchaeological Investigations Along N608–Arizona Boulevard, Tuba City, Arizona. Navajo Nation Archaeology Department Report No. 02-167. Navajo Nation Historic Preservation Department, Window Rock, Arizona.

Nelson, F. W., Jr.
1984 X-Ray Fluorescence Analysis of Some Western North American Obsidians. In *Obsidian Studies in the Great Basin*, edited by R. E. Hughes, pp. 27–62. Contributions of the University of California Archaeological Research Facility, No. 45. Berkeley.

Nelson, F. W., Jr., and R. D. Holmes
1979 *Trace Element Analysis of Obsidian Sources and Artifacts from Western Utah.* Antiquities Section Selected Papers No. 15. Utah State Historic Society, Salt Lake City.

Nelson, M. C., and H. Lippmeier
1993 Grinding-Tool Design as Conditioned by Land-Use Pattern. *American Antiquity* 58:286–305.

Newton, V., D. Gilpin, and D. Ortiz
1995 *The Navajo Mountain Road: An Ethnographic Survey of Navajo Route 16, Segments 3 Through 6, Navajo and Coconino Counties, Arizona and San Juan County, Utah.* SWCA Archaeological Report 94-15. Window Rock, Arizona.

Nichols, Deborah L.
2002 Basketmaker III: Early Ceramic-Period Villages in the Kayenta Region. In *Prehistoric Culture Change on the Colorado Plateau: Ten Thousand Years on Black Mesa*, edited by S. Powell and F. E. Smiley, pp. 66–75. University of Arizona Press, Tucson.

NOAA
1975 *Climate Atlas of the United States*, Vol. 2. Asheville, North Carolina.

Nusbaum, J. L.
1922 *A Basket Maker Cave in Kane County, Utah.* Indian Notes and Monographs, Miscellaneous Series No. 29. Museum of the American Indian, Heye Foundation, New York.

O'Brien, M. J., R. L. Lyman, and J. M. Cogswell
2002 Culture-Historical Units and the Archaeological Record of Southeastern Missouri, 500 BC–AD 700. In *The Woodland Southeast*, edited by D. G. Anderson and R. L. Mainfort Jr., pp. 421–443. University of Alabama Press, Tuscaloosa.

O'Connell, J. F., K. T. Jones, and S. R. Simms
1982 Some Thoughts on Prehistoric Archaeology in the Great Basin. In *Man and Environment in the Great Basin*, edited by D. B. Madsen and J. F. O'Connell, pp. 227–240. SAA Papers No. 2. Society for American Archaeology, Washington, D.C.

Odum, E. P.
1969 The Strategy of Ecosystem Development. *Science* 164: 262–270.

Parry, W. J.
1987a Technological Change: Temporal and Functional Variability in Chipped Stone Debitage. In *Prehistoric Stone Technology on Northern Black Mesa*, by W. J. Parry and A. L. Christenson, pp. 199–256. Center for Archaeological Investigations Occasional Paper No. 12. Southern Illinois University Press, Carbondale.

1987b Sources of Chipped Stone Material. In *Prehistoric Stone Technology on Northern Black Mesa*, by W. J. Parry and A. L. Christenson, pp. 21–43. Center for Archaeological Investigations Occasional Paper No. 12. Southern Illinois University Press, Carbondale.

Parry, W. J., and A. L. Christenson
1987 *Prehistoric Stone Technology on Northern Black Mesa, Arizona.* Center for Archaeological Investigations Occasional Paper No. 12. Southern Illinois University, Carbondale.

Parry, W. J., and F. E. Smiley
1990 Hunter-Gatherer Archaeology in Northeastern Arizona and Southeastern Utah. In *Perspectives on Southwestern Prehistory*, edited by P. E. Minnis and C. L. Redman, pp. 47–56. Westview Press, Boulder.

Parry, W., F. E. Smiley, and G. Burgett
1994 The Archaic Occupation of Black Mesa, Arizona. In *Archaic Hunter-Gatherer Archaeology in the American Southwest*, edited by B. J. Vierra, pp. 185–230. Contributions in Anthropology, Vol. 13, No. 1. Eastern New Mexico University, Portales.

Parsons, E. C.
1939 *Pueblo Indian Religion.* University of Chicago Press, Chicago.

Paynter, R. W.
1983 Expanding the Scope of Settlement Analysis. In *Archaeological Hammers and Theories*, edited by J. A. Moore and A. S. Keene, pp. 233–275. Academic Press, New York.

Pearsall, D. M.
1989 *Paleoethnobotany: A Handbook of Procedures.* Academic Press, New York.

Pepper, G. H.
1902 *The Ancient Basket Makers of Southeastern Utah.* American Museum of Natural History Journal 2(4), Supplement. New York.

Perryman, B. L., A. M. Maier, A. L. Hild, and R. A. Olson
2001 Demographic Characteristics of 3 *Artemisia tridentata* Nutt. Subspecies. *Journal of Range Management* 54:166–170.

Phillips, D. A., Jr.
1972 Social Implications of Settlement Distribution on Black Mesa. In *Archaeological Investigations on Black Mesa: The 1969–1970 Seasons*, by G. J. Gumerman, D. Westfall, and C. S. Weed, pp. 199–210. Prescott College Press, Prescott, Arizona.

Phillips, F. J.
1909 A Study of Pinyon Pine. *Botanical Gazette* 48:216–223.

Pielou, E. C.
1966 The Measurement of Diversity in Different Types of Biological Collectives. *Journal of Theoretical Biology* 13:131–144.

Pierson, L. M.
1981 *Cultural Resource Summary of the East Central Portion of the Moab District.* Cultural Resource Series No. 10. Bureau of Land Management, Salt Lake City.

Pilles, P. J., Jr.
1969 Habitation and Field Houses Near Winona and Angell, Arizona. *Kiva* 34:90–102.

1981 A Review of Yavapai Archaeology. In *The Protohistoric Period in the Northern American Southwest, AD 1450–1700*, edited by D. R. Wilcox and W. B. Masse, pp. 163–182. Anthropological Research Papers 24. Arizona State University, Tempe.

Piperno, D. R., and K. V. Flannery
2001 The Earliest Archaeological Maize (*Zea mays L.*) from Highland Mexico: New Accelerator Mass Spectrometry Dates and Their Implications. *Proceedings of the National Academy of Sciences* 98:2101–2103.

Piperno, D. R., and D. M. Pearsall
1998 *The Origins of Agriculture in the Lowland Neotropics*. Academic Press, San Diego.

Pitblado, B. L.
1994 Paleoindian Presence in Southwest Colorado. *Southwestern Lore* 60(4):1–20.

Plog, F.
1979 Prehistory: Western Anasazi. In *Southwest*, edited by A. Ortiz, pp. 108–130. *Handbook of the North American Indians*, Vol. 9, W. C. Sturtevant, general editor. Smithsonian Institution Press, Washington, D.C.

Plog, S.
1980 *Stylistic Variation in Prehistoric Ceramics: Design Analysis in the American Southwest*. Cambridge University Press, Cambridge.
1986 Group Mobility and Locational Strategies: Tests of Some Settlement Hypotheses. In *Spatial Organization and Exchange: Archaeological Survey on Northern Black Mesa*, edited by S. Plog, pp. 187–223. Center for Archaeological Investigations, Southern Illinois University Press, Carbondale.

Plog, S. (editor)
1986 *Spatial Organization and Exchange: Archaeological Survey on Northern Black Mesa*. Center for Archaeological Investigations, Southern Illinois University Press, Carbondale.

Plog, S., and J. L. Hantman
1986 Multiple Regression Analysis as a Dating Method in the American Southwest. In *Spatial Organization and Exchange: Archaeological Survey on Northern Black Mesa*, edited by S. Plog, pp. 87–113. Southern Illinois University Press, Carbondale.
1990 Chronology Construction and the Study of Prehistoric Culture Change. *Journal of Field Archaeology* 17:448–451.

Plog, S., and M. Hegmon
1993 The Sample Size–Richness Relation: The Relevance of Research Questions, Sampling Strategies, and Behavioral Variation. *American Antiquity* 58:489–496.

Plog, S., and S. Powell (editors)
1984 *Papers on the Archaeology of Black Mesa, Arizona, Vol. II*. Center for Archaeological Investigations, Southern Illinois University Press, Carbondale.

Poinar, H. N.
2002 The Genetic Secrets Some Fossils Hold. *Accounts of Chemical Research* 35:676–684.

Poinar, H. N., M. Kuch, K. D. Sobolik, I. Barnes, A. B. Stankiewicz, T. Kuder, W. G. Spaulding, V. M. Bryant, A. Cooper, and S. Paabo
2001 A Molecular Analysis of Dietary Diversity for Three Archaic Native Americans. *Proceedings of the National Academy of Science* 98:4317–4322.

Pollock, K. H.
2001 Pits Without Pots: Basketmaker II Houses and Lithics of Southeastern Utah. Unpublished M.A. thesis, Department of Anthropology, Washington State University, Pullman.

Ponczynski, J.
1995 Appendix A: Geomorphological Studies in Support of Site Excavations Along Segment 3 of N16, the Navajo Mountain Road. In *Excavations at Nine Sites Along Segment 3 of N16: An Interim Report of Data Recovery Findings*, by P. R. Geib, V. H. Clark, J. Huffman, K. Spurr, M. Warburton, and K. A. Hays-Gilpin. Navajo Nation Archaeology Department Report No. 95-130. Navajo Nation Historic Preservation Department, Window Rock, Arizona.

Popelish, L.
1984 *An Archaeological Traverse of the Shonto and Rainbow Plateaus, Arizona and Utah: The N-16 Road Survey*. Navajo Nation Cultural Resources Management Program Report 83-355. Navajo Nation Historic Preservation Department, Window Rock, Arizona.

Powell, S.
1980 *Material Culture and Behavior: A Prehistoric Example from the American Southwest*. Ph.D. dissertation, Department of Anthropology, Arizona State University, Tempe. University Microfilms, Ann Arbor.
1983 *Mobility and Adaptation. The Anasazi of Black Mesa, Arizona*. Center for Archaeological Investigations, Southern Illinois University, Carbondale.
2002 The Puebloan Florescence and Dispersion: Dinnebito and Beyond. In *Prehistoric Culture Change on the Colorado Plateau: Ten Thousand Years on Black Mesa*, edited by S. Powell and F. E. Smiley, pp. 79–117. University of Arizona Press, Tucson.

Powell, S., P. P. Andrews, D. L. Nichols, and F. E. Smiley
1983 Fifteen Years on the Rock: Archaeological Research, Administration, and Compliance on Black Mesa, Arizona. *American Antiquity* 48:228–252.

Powell, S., and F. E. Smiley (editors)
2002 *Prehistoric Culture Change on the Colorado Plateau: Ten Thousand Years on Black Mesa*. University of Arizona Press, Tucson.

Preucel, R. W.
1990 *Seasonal Circulation and Dual Residence in the Pueblo Southwest: A Prehistoric Example from the Pajarito Plateau, New Mexico*. Garland Publishing, New York.

Price, T. D., and A. B. Gebauer (editors)
1995 *Last Hunters First Farmers: New Perspectives on the Prehistoric Transition to Agriculture*. School of American Research Press, Santa Fe.

Prudden, T. M.
1897 An Elder Brother to the Cliff-Dweller. *Harper's Monthly Magazine* 95(5):56–63.
1903 The Prehistoric Ruins of the San Juan Watershed in Utah, Arizona, Colorado, and New Mexico. *American Anthropologist* 5:224–288.

1914 The Circular Kivas of Small Ruins in the San Juan Watershed. *American Anthropologist* 16:33–58.

Quade, J., R. M. Forester, W. L. Pratt, and C. Carter
1998 Black Mats, Spring-Fed Streams, and Late-Glacial-Age Recharge in the Southern Great Basin. *Quaternary Research* 49:129–148.

Quanbeck, K.
1995 Appendix D: Analysis of Faunal Remains from Prehistoric Sites Along the Navajo Mountain Road. In *Excavations at Nine Sites Along Segment 3 of N16: An Interim Report of Data Recovery Findings*, by P. R. Geib, V. H. Clark, J. Huffman, K. Spurr, M. Warburton, and K. A. Hays-Gilpin. Navajo Nation Archaeology Department Report No. 95-130. Navajo Nation Historic Preservation Department, Window Rock, Arizona.

Raven, C.
1991 Settlement Patterns and Foraging Strategies. In *Looking for the Marsh. Past, Present, and Future Archaeological Research in the Carson Desert*, by C. Raven and R. G. Elston, pp. 42–15. Intermountain Research, Silver City, Nevada.

Raven, C., and R. G. Elston
1991 *Looking for the Marsh. Past, Present, and Future Archaeological Research in the Carson Desert*. Intermountain Research, Silver City, Nevada.

Rea, A. M.
1978 The Ecology of Pima Fields. *Environment Southwest* 484:8–13.
1997 *At the Desert's Green Edge. An Ethnobotany of the Gila River Pima*. University of Arizona Press, Tucson.

Reed, A. D., and R. E. Kainer
1978 The Tamarron Site, 5LP326. *Southwestern Lore* 44:1–47.

Reed, A. D., and S. A. McDonald
1988 *Archaeological Investigations at Three Lithic Scatters and Eight Culturally Peeled Tree Sites Along the West Dolores Road, Montezuma and Dolores Counties, Colorado*. Report on file, National Park Service, Interagency Archaeological Service, Denver.

Reed, A. D., and M. D. Metcalf
1999 *Colorado Prehistory: A Context for the Northern Colorado Basin*. Colorado Council of Professional Archaeologists, Denver.

Reed, L. S., C. D. Wilson, and K. A. Hays-Gilpin
2000 From Brown to Gray: The Origins of Ceramic Technology in the Northern Southwest. In *Foundations of Anasazi Culture*, edited by P. F. Reed, pp. 203–229. University of Utah Press, Salt Lake City.

Reed, P. F., and K. N. Hensler
1999 *Anasazi Community Development in Cove-Redrock Valley: Archaeological Investigations Along the N33 Road in Apache County, Arizona*. Navajo Nation Papers in Anthropology No. 33. Navajo Nation Archaeology Department, Window Rock, Arizona.

Reher, C. A.
1977 Settlement and Subsistence Along the Lower Chaco River. In *Settlement and Subsistence Along the Lower Chaco River: The CGP Survey*, edited by C. A. Reher, pp. 7–112. University of New Mexico Press, Albuquerque.

Reher, C. A., and D. C. Witter
1977 Archaic Settlement and Vegetative Diversity. In *Settlement and Subsistence Along the Lower Chaco River: The CGP Survey*, edited by C. A. Reher, pp. 113–126. University of New Mexico Press, Albuquerque.

Reimer, P. J., M. G. L. Baillie, E. Bard, A. Bayliss, J. W. Beck, C. J. H. Bertrand, P. G. Blackwell, C. E. Buck, G. S. Burr, K. B. Cutler, P. E. Damon, R. L. Edwards, R. G. Fairbanks, M. Friedrich, T. P. Guilderson, A. G. Hogg, K. A. Hughen, B. Kromer, G. McCormac, S. Manning, C. B. Ramsey, R. W. Reimer, S. Remmele, J. R. Southon, M. Stuiver, S. Talamo, F. W. Taylor, J. van der Plicht, and C. E. Weyhenmeyer
2004 IntCal04 Terrestrial Radiocarbon Age Calibration, 0–26 cal kyr BP. *Radiocarbon* 46(3):1029–1059.

Reinhard, K. J., J. R. Ambler, and M. McGuffie
1985 Diet and Parasitism at Dust Devil Cave. *American Antiquity* 50:819–824.

Rhode, D.
1990 On Transportation Costs of Great Basin Resources: An Assessment of the Jones–Madsen Model. *Current Anthropology* 31:413–419.

Rhode, D., D. B. Madsen, and K. T. Jones
2006 Antiquity of Early Holocene Small-Seed Consumption and Processing at Danger Cave. *Antiquity* 80:328–339.

Richardson, G.
1986 *Navajo Trader*. University of Arizona Press, Tucson.

Richens, L. D., and R. K. Talbot
1989 Sandy Ridge: An Aceramic Habitation Site in Southeastern Utah. *Utah Archaeology* 2:77–88.

Rick, J. W.
1987 Dates as Data: An Examination of the Peruvian Preceramic Radiocarbon Record. *American Antiquity* 52:55–73.

Ridings, R.
1996 Where in the World Does Obsidian Hydration Dating Work? *American Antiquity* 61:136–148.

Robins, M. R.
2000 *Coprolite Analysis from Boomerang Shelter: Implications for Mobility and Site Function*. Paper presented at the 65th Annual Meeting of the Society for American Archaeology, Pittsburgh.

Robins, M. R., and M. Warburton
2004 N21 Lithic Analysis. In *A Better Road Ahead: Archaeological Excavations Along Navajo Route 21 Near White Mesa, Arizona*, by P. B. Bungart, J. H. Collette, and K. Spurr, pp. 23.1–23.13. Navajo Nation Archaeology Department Report No. 01-237. Navajo Nation Historic Preservation Department, Window Rock, Arizona.

Rocek, T. R.
1988 The Behavioral and Material Correlates of Site Seasonality: Lessons from Navajo Ethnoarchaeology. *American Antiquity* 53:523–536.

Rodgers, J. B.
1978 The Fort Mountain Complex, Cave Buttes, Arizona. In *Limited Activity and Occupation Sites: A Collection of Conference Papers*, edited by A. E. Ward, pp. 147–163. Contributions to Anthropological Studies No. 1. Center for Anthropological Studies, Albuquerque.

Roessel, R.
1983 Navajo History, 1850–1923. In *Handbook of North American Indians, Vol. 10: Southwest*, edited by A. Ortiz, pp. 506–523. Smithsonian Institution Press, Washington, D.C.

Rohn, A. H.
1989 Northern San Juan Prehistory. In *Dynamics of Southwest Prehistory*, edited by L. S. Cordell and G. J. Gumerman, pp. 149–177. Smithsonian Institution Press, Washington, D.C.

Romer, A. S.
1933 *Vertebrate Paleontology*. University of Chicago Press, Chicago.

Ruhe, R. V.
1974 Holocene Environments and Soil Geomorphology in Midwestern United States. *Quaternary Research* 4:487–495.

Russell, K. W.
1989 Groundstone. In *Kayenta Archaeology and Navajo Ethnohistory on the Northwestern Shonto Plateau: The N-16 Project, Vol. 2*, edited by A. R. Schroedl, pp. 649–689. P-III Associates, Inc., Salt Lake City.

Russell, S. C.
1978 The Agricultural Field House: A Navajo Limited Occupation and Special Use Site. In *Limited Activity and Occupation Sites: A Collection of Conference Papers*, edited by A. E. Ward, pp. 35–40. Contributions to Anthropological Studies No. 1. Center for Anthropological Studies, Albuquerque.

Sampson, C. G.
1988 *Stylistic Boundaries Among Mobile Hunter-Foragers*. Smithsonian Institution Press, Washington, D.C.

Schaafsma, P.
1971 *The Rock Art of Utah*. Papers of the Peabody Museum of Archaeology and Ethnology Vol. 65. Harvard University, Cambridge.
1986 Rock Art. In *Great Basin*, edited by W. L. D'Azevedo, pp. 215–226. Handbook of the North American Indians, Vol. 11, W. C. Sturtevant, general editor. Smithsonian Institution, Washington, D.C.

Schaefer, P. D.
1969 Prehistoric Trade in the Southwest and the Distribution of Pueblo IV Hopi Jeddito Black-on-Yellow. *Kroebar Athropological Papers* 41:54–77.

Schiffer, M. B.
1982 Hohokam Chronology: An Essay on History and Method. In *Hohokam and Patayan: Prehistory of Southeastern Arizona*, edited by R. H. McGuire and M. B. Schiffer, pp. 299–344. Academic Press, New York.
1986 Radiocarbon Dating and the "Old Wood" Problem: The Case of the Hohokam Chronology. *Journal of Archaeological Science* 3:13–30.

Schilz, A. J.
1979 *The Desha Caves: Two Basketmaker Sites in Southeast Utah*. M.A. thesis, California State University, Long Beach. University Microfilms, Ann Arbor.

Schlanger, S. H.
1990 Artifact Assemblage Composition and Site Occupation Duration. In *Perspectives on Southwestern Prehistory*, edited by P. Minnis and C. Redman, pp. 103–121. Westview Press, Boulder.
1991 On Manos, Metates, and the History of Site Occupations. *American Antiquity* 56(3):460–473.

Schlanger, S. H., and R. H. Wilshusen
1993 Local Abandonment and Regional Conditions in the North American Southwest. In *Abandonments of Settlements and Regions: Ethnoarchaeological and Archaeological Approaches*, edited by C. M. Cameron and S. Tomka, pp. 85–98. Cambridge University Press, Cambridge.

Schroeder, A. H.
1965 A Brief History of the Southern Utes. *Southwestern Lore* 30:53–78.

Schroedl, A.
1976 *The Archaic of the Northern Colorado Plateau*. Ph.D. dissertation, University of Utah, Salt Lake City. University Microfilms, Ann Arbor.
1977 The Grand Canyon Figurine Complex. *American Antiquity* 42:254–265.
1980 Cultural Features. In *Sudden Shelter*, by J. D. Jennings, A. R. Schroedl, and R. N. Holmer, pp. 31–61. Anthropological Papers No. 103. University of Utah Press, Salt Lake City.
1991 Paleo-Indian Occupation in the Eastern Great Basin and Northern Colorado Plateau. *Utah Archaeology* 4:1–15.
1992 Culture History. In *Burr Trail Archaeological Project: Small Site Archaeology on the Escalante Plateau and Circle Cliffs, Garfield County, Utah*, by B. L. Tipps, pp. 5–20. P-III Associates Cultural Resources Report 439-01-9102. MS on file, Bureau of Land Management, Kanab Resource Area, Kanab, Utah.

Schroedl, A. (editor)
1989 *Kayenta Anasazi Archeology and Navajo Ethnohistory on the Northwestern Shonto Plateau: The N-16 Project*. P-III Associates, Salt Lake City.

Schroedl, A. R., and E. Blinman
1989 Dating and Site Chronologies. In *Kayenta Anasazi Archeology and Navajo Ethnohistory on the Northwestern Shonto Plateau: The N-16 Project*, edited by A. R. Schroedl, pp. 53–87. P-III Associates, Salt Lake City.

Schroedl, A. R., and N. J. Coulam
1994 Cowboy Cave Revisited. *Utah Archaeology* 7:1–34.

Schultz, L. G.
1963 *Clay Minerals in Triassic Rocks of the Colorado Plateau*. U.S. Geological Survey Bulletin 1147-C. U.S. Government Printing Office, Washington, D.C.

Schurr, M. A., and D. A. Gregory
2002 Fluoride Dating of Faunal Materials by Ion-Selective Electrode: High Resolution Relative Dating at an Early Agricultural Period Site in the Tucson Basin. *American Antiquity* 67:281–299.

Schwartz, D. W., R. C. Chapman, and J. Kepp
1980 *Unkar Delta*. Grand Canyon Archaeological Series. School of American Research Press, Santa Fe.

Schwartz, D. W., J. Kepp, and R. C. Chapman
1981 *The Walhalla Plateau*. Grand Canyon Archaeological Series. School of American Research Press, Santa Fe.

Schwartz, D. W., M. P. Marshall, and J. Kepp
1979 *Archaeology of Grand Canyon: The Bright Angel Site.* Grand Canyon Archaeological Series. School of American Research Press, Santa Fe.

Scott, E.
2003a The Fourth International Radiocarbon Intercomparison (FIRI). *Radiocarbon* 45:135–291.
2003b The Third International Radiocarbon Intercomparison (TIRI). *Radiocarbon* 45:293–328.

Sealy, J.
2001 Body Tissue Chemistry and Palaeodiet. In *Handbook of Archaeological Sciences*, edited by D. R. Brothwell and A. M. Pollard, pp. 269–279. J. Wiley and Sons, Chichester.

Sellers, W. D., and R. H. Hill
1974 *Arizona Climate, 1932–1972.* University of Arizona Press, Tucson.

Semé, M.
1984 The Effects of Agricultural Fields on Faunal Assemblage Variation. In *Papers on the Archaeology of Black Mesa, Arizona*, Vol. 2, edited by S. Plog and S. Powell, pp. 139–157. Southern Illinois University Press, Carbondale.

Seward, G. L.
1983 You Can't Keep Them Down on the Farm. In *Proceedings of the Anasazi Symposium 1981*, edited by J. E. Smith, pp. 155–160. Mesa Verde Museum Association, Mesa Verde National Park, Colorado.

Shackley, M. S.
1990 *Early Hunter-Gatherer Procurement Ranges in the Southwest: Evidence from Obsidian Geochemistry and Lithic Technology.* Ph.D. dissertation, Department of Anthropology, Arizona State University, Tempe. University Microfilms, Ann Arbor.

Shaffer, B. S.
1992 Interpretation of Gopher Remains from Southwestern Archaeological Assemblages. *American Antiquity* 57(4): 683–691.

Sharrock, F. W., K. C. Day, and D. S. Dibble
1963 *1961 Excavations, Glen Canyon Area.* Anthropological Paper 63. University of Utah, Salt Lake City.

Sheehan, M. S.
2002 Dietary Responses to Mid-Holocene Climatic Change. *North American Archaeologist* 23:117–143.

Shepardson, M., and B. Hammond
1970 *The Navajo Mountain Community: Social Organization and Kinship Terminology.* University of California Press, Berkeley.

Shott, M. J.
1997 Stones and Shafts Redux: The Metric Discrimination of Chipped-Stone Dart and Arrow Points. *American Antiquity* 62:86–101.

Simmons, A. H.
1982 *Prehistoric Adaptive Strategies in the Chaco Canyon Region, Northwestern New Mexico.* 3 vols. Navajo Nation Papers in Anthropology 9. Window Rock, Arizona.
1986 New Evidence for the Early Use of Cultigens in the American Southwest. *American Antiquity* 51:73–89.

Simms, S. R.
1985 Acquisition Cost and Nutritional Data on Great Basin Resources. *Journal of California and Great Basin Anthropology* 7:117–126.
1987 *Behavioral Ecology and Hunter-Gatherer Foraging.* BAR International Series 381. BAR, Oxford.

Simon, H. A.
1957 *Models of Man: Social and Rational.* John Wiley and Sons, New York.

Skibo, J. M., and E. Blinman
1999 Exploring the Origins of Pottery on the Colorado Plateau. In *Pottery and People: A Dynamic Interaction*, edited by J. M. Skibo and G. M. Feinman, pp. 171–183. University of Utah Press, Salt Lake City.

Smiley, F. E.
1985 *The Chronometrics of Early Agricultural Sites in Northeastern Arizona: Approaches to the Interpretation of Radiocarbon Dates.* Ph.D. dissertation, Department of Anthropology, University of Michigan. University Microfilms, Ann Arbor.
1993 Early Farmers in the Northern Southwest: A View from Marsh Pass. In *Anasazi Basketmaker: Papers from the 1990 Wetherill–Grand Gulch Symposium*, edited by V. M. Atkins, pp. 243–254. Cultural Resource Series No. 24. Bureau of Land Management, Salt Lake City.
1994 The Agricultural Transition in the Northern Southwest: Patterns in the Current Chronometric Data. *Kiva* 60: 165–189.
1998a Black Mesa: Time, Place and Chronometry. In *Archaeological Chronometry: Radiocarbon and Tree-Ring Models and Applications from Black Mesa, Arizona*, by F. E. Smiley and R. V. N. Ahlstrom, pp. 13–21. Center for Archaeological Investigations Occasional Paper No. 16. Southern Illinois University, Carbondale.
1998b Wood and Radiocarbon Dating: Interpretive Frameworks and Techniques. In *Archaeological Chronometry: Radiocarbon and Tree-Ring Models and Applications from Black Mesa, Arizona*, by F. E. Smiley and R. V. N. Ahlstrom, pp. 25–48. Center for Archaeological Investigations Occasional Paper No. 16. Southern Illinois University, Carbondale.
1998c Applying Radiocarbon Models: Lolomai Phase Chronometry on Black Mesa. In *Archaeological Chronometry: Radiocarbon and Tree-Ring Models and Applications from Black Mesa, Arizona*, by F. E. Smiley and R. V. N. Ahlstrom, pp. 99–134. Center for Archaeological Investigations Occasional Paper No. 16. Southern Illinois University, Carbondale.
2002a The First Black Mesa Farmers: The White Dog and Lolomai Phases. In *Prehistoric Culture Change on the Colorado Plateau: Ten Thousand Years on Black Mesa*, edited by S. Powell and F. E. Smiley, pp. 37–65. University of Arizona Press, Tucson.
2002b Black Mesa Before Agriculture: Paleoindian and Archaic Evidence. In *Prehistoric Culture Change on the Colorado Plateau: Ten Thousand Years on Black Mesa*, edited by S. Powell and F. E. Smiley, pp. 15–34. University of Arizona Press, Tucson.

Smiley, F. E., and R. V. N. Ahlstrom
1998 *Archaeological Chronometry: Radiocarbon and Tree-Ring*

Models and Applications from Black Mesa, Arizona. Center for Archaeological Investigations Occasional Paper No. 16. Southern Illinois University, Carbondale.

Smiley, F. E., and P. P. Andrews
1983 An Overview of Black Mesa Archaeological Research. In *Excavations on Black Mesa, 1981: A Descriptive Report,* edited by F. E. Smiley, D. L. Nichols, and P. P. Andrews, pp. 45–60. Southern Illinois University, Center for Archaeological Investigations, Research Paper No. 36. Carbondale.

Smiley, F. E., and W. J. Parry
1990 *Early, Intensive, and Rapid: Rethinking the Agricultural Transition in the Northern Southwest.* Paper presented at the 55th Annual Meeting of the Society for American Archaeology, Las Vegas.
1992 *Rethinking the Agricultural Transition in the Northern Southwest: Evidence from Three Fir Shelter.* MS on file, Navajo Nation Historic Preservation Department, Window Rock, Arizona.

Smiley, F. E., W. J. Parry, and G. J. Gumerman
1986 *Early Agriculture in the Black Mesa/Marsh Pass Region of Arizona: New Chronometric Data and Recent Excavations at Three Fir Shelter.* Paper presented at the 51st Annual Meeting of the Society for American Archaeology, New Orleans.

Smiley, F. E., and M. R. Robins
1997 *Early Farmers in the Northern Southwest: Papers on Chronometry, Social Dynamics, and Ecology.* Animas-LaPlata Archaeological Project Research Paper No. 7. Bureau of Reclamation, U.S. Department of the Interior, Denver.

Smith, B. D.
1992 *Rivers of Change: Essays on Early Agriculture in Eastern North America.* Smithsonian Institution Press, Washington, D.C.
1997 The Initial Domestication of *Cucurbita pepo* in the Americas 10,000 Years Ago. *Science* 276:932–934.
1998 *The Emergence of Agriculture.* Scientific America Library, New York.
2001 Low-Level Food Production. *Journal of Archaeological Research* 1:1–43.

Smith, E. A.
1979 Human Adaptation and Energetic Efficiency. *Human Ecology* 7:53–74.

Smith, W.
1972 *Prehistoric Kivas of Antelope Mesa, Northeastern Arizona.* Papers of the Peabody Museum of Archaeology and Ethnology Vol. 39, No. 1. Report of the Awatovi Expedition 9. Harvard University, Cambridge.
1990 When Is a Kiva? In *When Is a Kiva? and Other Questions About Southwestern Archaeology,* edited by R. H. Thompson, pp. 59–75. University of Arizona Press, Tucson.

Sobolik, K. D., L. S. Zimmerman, and B. M. Guilfoyl
1997 Indoor Versus Outdoor Firepit Usage: A Case Study from the Mimbres. *Kiva* 62:283–300.

Spaulding, G. W.
1991 A Middle Holocene Vegetation Record from the Mojave Desert of North America and Its Paleoclimatic Significance. *Quaternary Research* 35:427–437.

Spencer, V. E.
1969 The Geography of Navajo Dwelling Types, with Special Reference to Black Creek Valley, Arizona–New Mexico. Unpublished M.A. thesis, University of California, Davis.

Spier, L.
1928 Havasupai Ethnography. *Anthropological Papers of the American Museum of Natural History* 29(3):81–392. New York.

Spurr, K.
1993 *NAGPRA and Archaeology on Black Mesa, Arizona: Compliance for Peabody Western Coal Company in Navajoland.* Navajo Nation Publications in Anthropology No. 30. Window Rock, Arizona.

Stebbins, S., B. Harrill, W. D. Wade, M. V. Gallagher, H. Cutler, and L. Blake
1986 *The Kayenta Anasazi: Archaeological Investigations Along the Black Mesa Railroad Corridor.* Research Paper 30(1). Museum of Northern Arizona, Flagstaff.

Steffen, A.
2005 *The Dome Fire Obsidian Study: Investigating the Interaction of Heat, Hydration, and Glass Geochemistry.* Ph.D. dissertation, Department of Anthropology, University of New Mexico. University Microfilms, Ann Arbor.

Stein, M. A.
1966 An Archaeological Survey of Paiute Mesa, Arizona. Unpublished M.A. thesis, Department of Anthropology, University of Oklahoma.
1984 Pottery Pueblo: A Tsegi Phase Village on Paiute Mesa, Utah. Unpublished Ph.D. dissertation, Department of Anthropology, Southern Methodist University, Dallas.

Stephen, A. M.
1936 *Hopi Journal of Alexander M. Stephen.* 2 vols. Edited by E. C. Parsons. Columbia University Contributions to Anthropology, No. 23. Columbia University Press, New York.

Stevenson, C. M., M. Gottesman, and M. Macko
2000 Redefining the Working Assumptions of Obsidian Hydration Dating. *Journal of California and Great Basin Anthropology* 22:223–236.

Stevenson, C. M., E. Knaus, J. J. Mazer, and J. K. Bates
1993 Homogeneity of Water Content in Obsidian from the Coso Volcanic Field: Implications for Obsidian Hydration Dating. *Geoarchaeology* 8:371–384.

Stevenson, C. M., P. J. Sheppard, D. G. Sutton, and W. R. Ambrose
1996 Advances in the Hydration Dating of New Zealand Obsidian. *Journal of Archaeological Science* 23:233–242.

Stevenson, M. C.
1915 Ethnobotany of the Zuni Indians. *Annual Report of the Bureau of American Ethnology* 30:31–102. Smithsonian Institution, Washington, D.C.

Steward, Julian H.
1937a *Ancient Caves of the Great Salt Lake.* Bureau of American Ethnology Bulletin 116. Smithsonian Institution, Washington, D.C.
1937b Ecological Aspects of Southwestern Society. *Anthropos* 32:87–104.
1938 *Basin–Plateau Aboriginal Sociopolitical Groups.* Bureau of American Ethnology Bulletin 120. Smithsonian Institution, Washington, D.C.

Stewart, G. R., and M. Donnelly
1943 Soil and Water Economy in the Pueblo Southwest. *Scientific Monthly* 56:31–44, 134–144.

Stewart, O. C.
1942 Culture Element Distributions: XVIII: Ute Southern Paiute. *University of California Anthropological Papers* 6(4):231–356.

Stiger, M. M.
1977 Anasazi Diet: The Coprolite Evidence. Unpublished M.A. thesis, Department of Anthropology, University of Colorado, Boulder.

Stolk, A., K. Hogervorst, and H. Berendsen
1989 Correcting ^{14}C Histograms for the Non-Linearity of the Radiocarbon Time Scale. *Radiocarbon* 31:169–178.

Stolk, A., T. E. Törnqvist, K. P. V. Hekhuis, H. J. A. Berendsen, and J. van der Plicht
1994 Calibration of ^{14}C Histograms: A Comparison of Methods. *Radiocarbon* 36:1–10.

Stone, T.
1993 Small Site Function and Duration of Occupation in the Hohokam Northern Periphery. *Kiva* 59:65–82.

Stroup, A.
1972 *Faunal Analysis of Dust Devil Cave, Utah*. MS on file, Department of Anthropology, Northern Arizona University.

Stuart, D. E., and R. P. Gauthier
1981 *Prehistoric New Mexico: Background for Survey*. Historic Preservation Bureau, Santa Fe.

Stuiver, M., and H. A. Polach
1977 Reporting of ^{14}C Data. *Radiocarbon* 19:355–363.

Stuiver, M., and P. J. Reimer
1993 Extended ^{14}C Data Base and Revised CALIB 3.0 ^{14}C Age Calibration Program. *Radiocarbon* 35:215–230.

Sullivan, A. P., III
1986 *Prehistory of the Upper Basin, Coconino County, Arizona*. Archaeological Series 167. Cultural Resource Management Division, Arizona State Museum, Tucson.
1987 Seeds of Discontent: Implications of a "Pompeii" Botanical Assemblage for Grand Canyon Anasazi Subsistence Models. *Journal of Ethnobiology* 7:137–153.
1992 Investigating the Archaeological Consequences of Short-Duration Occupations. *American Antiquity* 57:99–115.

Sullivan, A. P., III, M. E. Becher, and C. E. Downum
1995 Tusayan White Ware Chronology: New Archaeological and Dendrochronological Evidence. *Kiva* 61:175–188.

Sutton, M. Q.
1977 The Archaeological Concept of Field House. Unpublished M.A. thesis, Department of Anthropology, California State University, Sacramento.

Swarthout, J., S. Stebbins, P. Stein, B. Harrill, and P. J. Pilles Jr.
1986 *The Kayenta Anasazi: Archaeological Investigations Along the Black Mesa Railroad Corridor, Vol. 2*. Museum of Northern Arizona Research Paper 30. Flagstaff.

Swedlund, A., and S. D. Sessions
1976 A Developmental Model for Prehistoric Population Growth on Black Mesa, Arizona. In *Papers on the Archaeology of Black Mesa, Arizona*, edited by G. J. Gumerman and R. Euler, pp. 136–148. Southern Illinois University Press, Carbondale.

Tagg, M. D.
1996 Early Cultigens from Fresnal Shelter, Southeastern New Mexico. *American Antiquity* 61:311–324.

Taylor, R. E.
1987 *Radiocarbon Dating: An Archaeological Perspective*. Academic Press, Orlando.
2000 The Contribution of Radiocarbon Dating to New World Archaeology. *Radiocarbon* 42:1–22.

Taylor, W. W.
1958 *Two Archaeological Studies in Northern Arizona*. Museum of Northern Arizona Bulletin 30. Flagstaff.

Thaden, R. E., A. F. Trites Jr., and T. L. Finnell
1964 *Geology and Ore Deposits of the White Canyon Area, San Juan and Garfield Counties, Utah*. Geological Survey Bulletin 1125. U.S. Government Printing Office, Washington, D.C.

Thomas, D. H.
1978 Arrowheads and Atlatl Darts: How the Stones Got the Shaft. *American Antiquity* 43:461–472.
1983 *The Archaeology of Monitor Valley 1. Epistemology*. Anthropological Papers 58, Pt. 1. American Museum of Natural History, New York.
1985 *The Archaeology of Hidden Cave, Nevada*. Anthropological Papers Vol. 61, Pt. 1. American Museum of Natural History, New York.
1986 Contemporary Hunter Gatherer Archaeology in America. In *American Archaeology: Past and Future*, edited by D. J. Meltzer, D. D. Fowler, and J. A. Sabloff, pp. 237–276. Smithsonian Institution Press, Washington, D.C.
1989 *Archaeology*. 2nd ed. Holt, Rinehart and Winston, New York.

Thompson, R. S., C. Whitlock, P. J. Bartlin, S. P. Harrison, and W. G. Spaulding
1993 Climate Changes in the Western United States Since 18,000 yr BP. In *Global Climates Since the Last Glacial Maximum*, edited by H. E. Wright Jr., J. E. Kutzbach, T. Webb III, W. F. Ruddiman, F. A. Street-Perrott, and P. J. Bartlin, pp. 468–513. University of Minnesota Press, Minneapolis.

Tieszen, L. L., and T. Fagre
1993 Carbon Isotopic Variability in Modern and Archaeological Maize. *Journal of Archaeological Science* 20:25–40.

Tipps, B. L.
1988 *The Tar Sands Project: An Inventory and Predictive Model for Central and Southern Utah*. Cultural Resource Series No. 22. Bureau of Land Management, Utah State Office, Salt Lake City.
1992 *Burr Trail Archaeological Project: Small Site Archaeology on the Escalante Plateau and Circle Cliffs, Garfield County, Utah*. P-III Associates Cultural Resources Report 439-01-9102. MS on file, Bureau of Land Management, Kanab Resource Area, Kanab, Utah.
1995 *Holocene Archaeology Near Squaw Butte, Canyonlands National Park, Utah*. Selections from the Division of Cultural Resources No. 7. Rocky Mountain Region, National Park Service, Denver.

1998 Archaeology in the Grand Staircase–Escalante National Monument: Research Prospects and Management Issues. In *Learning from the Land—Grand Staircase–Escalante National Monument Science Symposium Proceedings*, edited by L. M. Hill, pp. 133–150. Bureau of Land Management, Salt Lake City.

Tipps, B. L., N. J. Hewitt, and J. M. Brisbin
1989 Site AZ-J-19-12. In *Kayenta Anasazi Archeology and Navajo Ethnohistory on the Northwestern Shonto Plateau: The N-16 Project*, edited by A. R. Schroedl, pp. 112–148. P-III Associates, Salt Lake City.

Tipps, B. L., and A. R. Schroedl
1988 Site Typology and Function. In *The Tar Sands Project: An Inventory and Predictive Model for Central and Southern Utah*, by B. L. Tipps, pp. 45–51. Cultural Resource Series No. 22. Bureau of Land Management, Utah State Office, Salt Lake City.

Titiev, M.
1944 *Old Oraibi: A Study of the Hopi Indians of the Third Mesa*. Papers of the Peabody Museum of American Archaeology and Ethnology, Vol. 22, No. 1. Harvard University, Cambridge.

Titmus, G. L.
1985 Some Aspects of Stone Tool Notching. In *Stone Tool Analysis: Essays in Honor of Don E. Crabtree*, edited by M. G. Plew, J. C. Woods, and M. G. Pavesic, pp. 243–263. University of New Mexico Press, Albuquerque.

Toll, H. W., and C. D. Wilson
2000 Locational, Architectural and Ceramic Trends in the Basketmaker III Occupation of the La Plata Valley, New Mexico. In *Foundations of Anasazi Culture: The Basketmaker–Pueblo Transition*, edited by P. F. Reed, pp. 19–43. University of Utah Press, Salt Lake City.

Towner, R. H., and M. Warburton
1990 Projectile Point Rejuvenation: A Technological Analysis. *Journal of Field Archaeology* 17:311–321.

Tremaine, K. J., and D. A. Frederickson
1988 Induced Obsidian Hydration Experiments: An Investigation in Relative Dating. *Materials Research Society Symposium Proceedings* 123:271–278.

Trembour, F., F. L. Smith, and I. Friedman
1988 Diffusion Cells for Integrating Temperature and Humidity over Long Periods of Time. In *Materials Issues in Art and Archaeology*, edited by E. V. Sayre, P. B. Vandiver, J. Druzik, and C. Stevenson, pp. 245–251. Materials Research Society Symposium Proceedings 123. Reno.

Trites, A. F., and G. A. Hadd
1958 *Geology of the Jomac Mine, White Canyon Area, San Juan County*. Bulletin 1046-H. U.S. Geological Survey, Washington, D.C.

Turner, C. G., and M. Cooley
1960 Prehistoric Use of Stone from the Glen Canyon Region. *Plateau* 33(2):46–53.

Turner, C. G., II, and J. A. Turner
1999 *Man Corn: Cannibalism and Violence in the Prehistoric American Southwest*. University of Utah Press, Salt Lake City.

Van Devender, T. R.
1990 Late Quaternary Vegetation and Climate of the Chihuahuan Desert, United States and Mexico. In *Packrat Middens*, edited by J. L. Betancourt, T. R. Van Devender, and P. S. Martin, pp. 104–133. University of Arizona Press, Tucson.

Van Ness, M. A.
1986 Desha Complex Macrobotanical Fecal Remains: An Archaic Diet in the American Southwest. Unpublished M.A. thesis, Northern Arizona University, Flagstaff.

Van Ness, M. A., and E. Hansen
1996 Archaic Subsistence in the Glen Canyon Region. In *Glen Canyon Revisited*, by P. R. Geib, pp. 117–125. Anthropological Papers No. 119. University of Utah Press, Salt Lake City.

Vierra, B. J.
1980 A Preliminary Ethnographic Model of the Southwestern Archaic Settlement System. In *Human Adaptations in a Marginal Environment: The UII Mitigation Project*, edited by J. L. Moore and J. C. Winter, pp. 351–357. Office of Contract Archaeology, University of New Mexico, Albuquerque.

Vierra, B. J. (editor)
1994 *Archaic Hunter-Gatherer Archaeology in the American Southwest*. Contributions in Anthropology, Vol. 13, No. 1. Eastern New Mexico University, Portales.

Warburton, M., and R. M. Begay
2002 The Navajos and Black Mesa. In *Prehistoric Culture Change on the Colorado Plateau: Ten Thousand Years on Black Mesa*, edited by S. Powell and F. E. Smiley, pp. 164–181. University of Arizona Press, Tucson.

Ward, A. E.
1975 *Inscription House: Two Research Reports*. Technical Series 16. Museum of Northern Arizona, Flagstaff.

Ward, A. E. (editor)
1978 *Limited Activity and Occupation Sites: A Collection of Conference Papers*. Contributions to Anthropological Studies No. 1. Center for Anthropological Studies, Albuquerque.

Warren, R. E., C. K. McDaniel, and M. J. O'Brien
1981 Soils and Settlement in the Southern Prairie Peninsula. *Contract Abstracts and CRM Archaeology* 2(3):36–49.

Waterbolk, H. T.
1971 Working with Radiocarbon Dates. *Proceedings of the Prehistoric Society* 37:15–33.

Weber, S. A., and P. D. Seaman (editors)
1985 *Havasupai Habitat: A. F. Whiting's Ethnography of a Traditional Indian Culture*. University of Arizona Press.

Weltfish, G.
1965 *The Lost Universe*. University of Nebraska Press, Lincoln.

Wendorf, F.
1953 *Archaeological Studies in the Petrified Forest National Monument*. Bulletin 27. Museum of Northern Arizona, Flagstaff.

Werner, D., N. M. Flowers, M. L. Ritter, and D. R. Gross
1979 Subsistence Productivity and Hunting Effort in Native South America. *Human Ecology* 7:303–315.

West, G. A.
1927 Notes on the Museum's Collecting Expeditions in 1925: Exploration in Navajo County, Arizona. *Yearbook of the Public Museum of the City of Milwaukee* 5:7–39.

Wetterstrom, W.
1986 *Food, Diet, and Population at Prehistoric Arroyo Hondo Pueblo, New Mexico*. Arroyo Hondo Archaeological Series Vol. 6. School of American Research, Santa Fe.

Whiting, A. F.
1939 *Ethnobotany of the Hopi*. Bulletin 15. Museum of Northern Arizona, Flagstaff.

Wiessner, P.
1983 Style and Social Information in Kalahari San Projectile Points. *American Antiquity* 48:253–276.
1989 Style and Changing Relations Between the Individual and Society. In *The Meanings of Things: Material Culture and Symbolic Expression*, edited by I. Hodder, pp. 56–63. One World Archaeology 6. Unwin Hyman, London.

Wilcox, D. R., and W. B. Masse (editors)
1981 *The Protohistoric Period in the Northern American Southwest, AD 1450–1700*. Anthropological Research Papers 24. Arizona State University, Tempe.

Willey, G. R.
1953 *Prehistoric Settlement Patterns in Virú Valley, Peru*. Bulletin No. 55. Bureau of American Ethnology, Washington, D.C.

Willey, G. R., and P. Phillips
1958 *Method and Theory in American Archaeology*. University of Chicago Press, Chicago.

Wills, W. C., and T. C. Windes
1989 Evidence for Population Aggregation and Dispersal During the Basketmaker III Period in Chaco Canyon, New Mexico. *American Antiquity* 54:347–369.

Wills, W. H.
1988 *Early Prehistoric Agriculture in the American Southwest*. School of American Research Press, Santa Fe.
1992 Plant Cultivation and the Evolution of Risk-Prone Economies in the Prehistoric American Southwest. In *Transitions to Agriculture in Prehistory*, edited by A. B. Gebauer and T. D. Price, pp. 153–176. Monographs in World Prehistory 4. Prehistory Press, Madison, Wisconsin.
1995 Archaic Foraging and the Beginning of Food Production in the American Southwest. In *Last Hunters First Farmers: New Perspectives on the Prehistoric Transition to Agriculture*, edited by T. D. Price and A. B. Gebauer, pp. 215–242. School of American Research Press, Santa Fe.

Wills, W. H., and B. Huckell
1994 Economic Implications of Changing Land-Use Patterns in the Late Archaic. In *Themes in Southwest Prehistory*, edited by G. J. Gumerman, pp. 33–52. School of American Research Advanced Seminar Series, Santa Fe.

Wilson, C. D., and E. Blinman
1993 *Upper San Juan Region Pottery Typology*. Archaeology Notes 80. Museum of New Mexico Office of Archaeological Studies, Santa Fe.
1994 Early Anasazi Ceramics and the Basketmaker Tradition. In *Proceedings of the Anasazi Symposium 1991*, compiled by R. Hutchinson and J. E. Smith, pp. 199–214. Mesa Verde Museum Association, Mesa Verde, Colorado.

Wilson, G.
1917 *Agriculture of the Hidatsa Indians: An Indian Interpretation*. University of Minnesota Studies in Social Sciences, No. 9. Reprinted as Reprints in Anthropology Vol. 5. J&L Reprints, Lincoln, Nebraska.

Winter, J. C., and P. F. Hogan
1986 Plant Husbandry in the Great Basin and Adjacent Northern Colorado Plateau. In *Anthropology of the Desert West: Essays in Honor of Jesse D. Jennings*, edited by C. J. Condie and D. D. Fowler, pp. 119–129. Anthropological Papers No. 110. University of Utah Press, Salt Lake City.

Withers, K.
1989 Late Quaternary Vegetation and Climate of Forty-Mile Canyon and Willow Gulch, in Central Colorado Plateau. Unpublished M.A. thesis, Quaternary Studies, Northern Arizona University, Flagstaff.

Witkind, I. J., and R. E. Thaden
1963 *Geology and Uranium-Vanadium Deposits of the Monument Valley Area, Apache and Navajo Counties, Arizona*. U.S. Geological Survey Bulletin 1103. U.S. Government Printing Office, Washington, D.C.

Wood, J. J.
1978 Optimal Location in Settlement Space: A Model for Describing Location Strategies. *American Antiquity* 43:258–270.

Woodbury, A. M.
1965 *Notes on the Human Ecology of Glen Canyon*. University of Utah Anthropological Papers No. 74. University of Utah Press, Salt Lake City.

Woodbury, R. B.
1954 *Prehistoric Stone Implements of Northeastern Arizona*. Papers of the Peabody Museum of American Archaeology and Ethnology, Vol. 34. Harvard University, Cambridge.
1961 *Prehistoric Agriculture at Point of Pines, Arizona*. Society for American Archaeology, Memoir No. 17.

Wormington, H. M.
1961 *Prehistoric Indians of the Southwest*. Popular Series No. 7 (Fifth Printing). Denver Museum of Natural History, Denver.

Wright, K. A.
2000 Archaeobotanical Evidence of Cotton, *Gossypium Hirsutum var. Punctatum*, on the Southern Colorado Plateau. Unpublished M.A. thesis, Department of Anthropology, Northern Arizona University, Flagstaff.

Yarnell, R. A.
1965 Implications of Distinctive Flora on Pueblo Ruins. *American Anthropologist* 67:662–674.

Yellen, J. E.
1977 *Archaeological Approaches to the Present*. Academic Press, New York.

Zar, J. H.
1974 *Biostatistical Analysis*. Prentice Hall, Englewood Cliffs, New Jersey.

Index

abandonment: of Colorado Plateau in middle Archaic, 194–95, 198, 205, 377; of Ditch House, 74, 294–95, 370; of Hammer House, 370; of Kayenta region in late Pueblo II, 370; of NMRAP sites in later years of Pueblo III, 312–13; of primary habitations in early Pueblo III, 338; of secondary habitations at Puebloan sites, 366; of Three Dog Site, 128, 387

activity diversity, and site types, 163, 164. *See also* limited-activity occupation sites

activity/storage rooms, and Puebloan architecture, 333, *334*

Adams, E. C., 344, 386

Adams, Karen R., 229

Adams, William Y., 24, 25

aggregation, and Pueblo III villages in Kayenta region, 312–13, 386

agriculture and agricultural transition: and Basketmaker II–III transition, 284–86; and environment of Kayenta region, 55–57; and Kin Kahuna site, 114; and markers for end of Archaic period, 36–37; and Naaki Hooghan site, 87; and NMRAP Basketmaker II sites, 38, 39, 206–7, 222–34, 378–82; and Oshara sequence, 31–32; and Rainbow Plateau, 264; and research design of NMRAP, 8–9; and Three Dog Site, 127. *See also* beans; cotton; field houses; maize; squash; turkey

Ahler, S. A., 261

Ahlstrom, R. V. N., 287, 295, 371

Alkali Ridge, 319, 327

alluvial cobbles, in Glen Canyon, 57

Altithermal refugia hypothesis, 204

Ambler, J. Richard, 7, 24, 25, 33, 43, 45, 46, 57, 140, 205n1, 247–48, 250–51, 267, 301, 306, 317, 338, 347, 371

American Museum of Natural History, 205n1

Anasazi: and Formative period, 43; soil characteristics and distributions as central to adaptation of, 56. *See also* Kayenta region

Anderson, Ettie, 5

Anderson, Kirk, 5

Anderson, R. Scott, 19

Anderson, Tonia, 5

Andrews, P. P., 44

animal life, and environment of Kayenta region, 54. *See also* faunal remains; pack rat middens

Anovitz, L. M., 155, 160

Antevs, E., 200

Archaic-formative transition, and previous archaeological research in Kayenta region, 36–43

Archaic period: and Atlatl Rock Cave, 135, 137, 138; and Big Bend site, 92, 94; and Bonsai Bivouac, 124; and chronology of NMRAP sites, 145–60; climate during middle years of, 198–204; and Dune Hollow site, 114–15, 116; evidence of continuity from Paleoindian period, 193; and Hólahéi Scatter site, 77; and middle Holocene bottleneck, 375–77; and Mouse House, 107–9; and NMRAP site sample, 6, 141–45; and obsidian in lithic assemblages, 377–78; and origins of Basketmaker cultures, 263, 381–82; overview of literature on settlement patterns in, 160–62; and Pee Wee Grande, 77–79; and Polly's Place site, 83, 85; and previous archaeological research in Kayenta region, 28–36; and radiocarbon dates for NMRAP sites, 145–54, 194, 195–97, 376; and settlement patterns for NMRAP sites, 164–83, 193–205; subsistence range and territory for NMRAP sites, 183–93; summary and interpretation of forager remains from NMRAP sites, 140–45; and The Pits site, 71; and Three Dog Site, 124, 126, 135; and Tres Campos site, 87, 89; and Tsé Haal'á, 132, 135; and UT-B-63-19, 132; and Windy Mesa site, 79, 81

architecture: and NMRAP Basketmaker II sites, 255–63; and NMRAP Puebloan sites, 313–33. *See also* houses; kivas; pueblos

Atene, Shirlene, 5

Atlatl Rock Cave: and ceramic assemblage, 280–81; and cultivation of beans, 285; description of, 135, *136*, 137–39; and elevation zone, 183; and evidence for bow-and-arrow use, 285; excavation of, 5–6; and feature density, *167, 168*; and horn flakers, 270–71; and maize samples, 228, 229, 285; and natural shelters in Basketmaker II, 249–50, 251; plant remains from, *232, 233*, 285; and radiocarbon dates, 146, *148*, 150, 154, *212*; as residential camp, *166, 167*, 171, 172–73; and separation between Archaic and Basketmaker II deposits, 195; and storage during Basketmaker II, 251; summary of information on, *142, 208*; and variability in recovery rates, 165

AZ-D-2-174, 280

AZ-D-2-200, 280

AZ-D-2-355: as early pottery site, 280; and slab-lined construction methods, 257, 263

AZ-D-5-8, 333

AZ-D-10-17, 342

AZ-J-2-6, 16

AZ-J-3-8, 16

AZ-J-3-13, *305*

AZ-J-14-54: as early pottery site, 280; as primary habitation, 240, *241*; structure of houses, 257

419

AZ-J-19-3: and ceramic cross dating, *305*; and primary habitations, 338
AZ-J-19-9: and kivas, 324; and tree-ring dating, 310
AZ-J-19-12: and ceramic cross dating, *305*, 306; and primary habitations, 338
AZ-J-31-3, 306
AZ-J-55-39, 324
AZ-K-40-7, and kivas, 324, 325
azurite, 61

bag numbers (BN), and field methods, 17
Bajada phase, of Archaic period, 30, *31*
Baker, A. A., 61
Barlow, K. R., 233, 355
Barrier Canyon style, of rock art panels, 161
Bartlett, K., 106
Basketmaker I: characteristics of, 38; debate on evidence for origins of, 140
Basketmaker II: and agricultural transition, 8–9, 222–34, 378–82; and architecture of NMRAP sites, 255–63; and Atlatl Rock Cave, 138, 195, 249–50, *251*; and Big Bend site, 92, 94–95; and Blake's Abode, 97; and Bonsai Bivouac, 124; and burials, 275, 381; chronology for NMRAP sites, 210–22; and continuation of foraging, 222–34; contributions of NMRAP to database on, 206; and Ditch House, 72–74; and Kin Kahuna, 112, 114; and Ko' Lanhi site, 95, 97; location of NMRAP sites, *209*; and Mouse House, 107; origins of, 263–79; and Panorama House, 90, 92; and Polly's Place site, 83, 85; and previous archaeological work in Kayenta region, 37–43; and Scorpion Heights, 100, 101; separation between dates for Archaic sites and, 146, 197, 381–82; and settlement patterns at NMRAP sites, 234–55, 385; and Sin Sombra site, 109, 110; and site sample of NMRAP, 6–7, 207–10; and The Pits, 71–72; and Three Dog Site, 124, 126, 127; transitional period between Basketmaker III and, 44, 279–89; and Tres Campos site, 87, 89–90; and Windy Mesa site, 79, 81
Basketmaker III: and Atlatl Rock Cave, 138–39; characteristics of in Kayenta region, 38, 44, 304; and Mountain view site, 102; and Pee Wee Grande, 79; and Polly's Place site, 83; and Rainbow Plateau sites, 43; transitional period between Basketmaker II and, 44, 279–89
Beaglehole, E. O., 351, 352
Beals, R. L., 59, 383, 384
beans, and Basketmaker II–III transition, 285–86
Bearden, Susan E., 235
Beck, G. T., 28
Begay, Judy, *5*
Begay, R. M., 48
Begay, Robert, *5*
Begay, Roxanne, *5*
Begay, Wilson N., *5*
behavior: dimensions of in analysis of site function, 163–64; and responses to climate of middle Holocene, 203–4
behavioral ecology, and optimization theory, 161
Benally, G. Stewart, *5*
bentonite, 60

Berry, Claudia F., 32, 33, 36, 37, 194, 197, 198, 199, 200, 205, 263, 268, 376, 377, 379
Berry, Michael S., 8, 9, 31, 32, 33, 36, 37, 194, 197, 198, 199, 200, 205, 221–22, 263, 268, 279, 376, 377, 379
Beta Analytic, 5, 19, 20, 146, 210, 216–19
Betatakin: and Tsegi phase site, 388; and weather station, 49, 52, *53*, *54*
Big Bend (AZ-J-14-13): description of, *66*, 92, *93*, 94–95; and feature density, *167*, *168*; and Panorama House, 91; as processing camp, *166*; and radiocarbon dates, *148*, *212*; and storage features, 237; summary of information on, *142*, *208*
Binford, Lewis R., 162, 163, 171, 368
Bitsinnie, Erickson, *5*
Black, Lee, Jr., *5*
Black, Lee, Sr., *5*
Black Mesa: agricultural methods and Basketmaker II sites on, 225, 287; and architecture of storage features, 259; and Kayenta region, 22; and Lolomai phase of Basketmaker II, 41; and secondary habitations, 353–55; settlement patterns and distribution of Basketmaker II sites on, 252–53; and social organization in Kayenta region, 12; and Toreva phase, 373n1
Black Mesa Archaeological Project (BMAP), 7, 25, 206, 235, 321
Black Mesa Black-on-white, 45, 305, 306
Black Mesa–Lake Powell railroad corridor, 25
black scoria, and pipe fragments, 364
Black Tank (Arizona), as obsidian source, 190, 377
Blake, John H., *5*, 97
Blake's Abode (AZ-J-14-36): description of, *66*, 97, *98*; and radiocarbon dates, *212*; as secondary habitation, 242–43; summary of information on, *208*
Blinman, E., 305, 306
Bohrer, V. L., 231, 233
bone beads, 275
Bonsai Bivouac (AZ-J-2-55): and ceramic cross dating, *300*, *301*, *303*; description of, *67*, 122, *123*, 124; and feature density, *167*, *168*; as processing site, *166*; and radiocarbon dates, *148*, *150*, *212*; and secondary habitations, *359*, *365*; summary of information on, *142*, *208*, *292*
Boone, Dan, *5*
Boston, Richard, *5*
bow-and-arrow technology, 282–84
Bradfield, M., 355, 366
Breen, Judith, *5*
Breternitz, D. A., 289n7, 300
Brew, J. O., 319, 327
Brown, G. M., 184
Brown, James A., 286
Brugge, D. M., 48
Bungart, Peter, *5*
Bureau of Indian Affairs (BIA), 1, 2, 4
Burgh, R. F., 38–39, 268
burials: field methods and disposition of, 16, 20n2; at Kin Kahuna, 112; and dependence of Basketmaker II populations on maize, 381; and origins of Basketmaker II, 275; at Sapo Seco site, 121; and social differentiation, 385; and storage pits, 261–62
burning: and abandonment of Ditch House, 74, 294–95; and Big

Bend site, 95; and Panorama House, 91; and thermal alteration of obsidian artifacts, 160
Burt Trail (Utah), 203
Butler Wash, 232, 287
Bye, R. A., Jr., 230

CALIB, Version 3.0.3a, 211
Callahan, M. M., 384
Camp Dead Pine (AZ-J-14-52): and ceramic assemblage, 307; and ceramic cross dating, *300, 301, 303, 305*; description of, *66*, 101, *102*; and secondary habitations, *358, 359, 365*; summary of information on, *292*
Castle Creek site cluster, 234
Casto, B., 227–28
Cataract Canyon, 253
Cave du Pont, 251
caves, use of during Basketmaker II period, 138. *See also* natural shelters
Cawker, K. B., 153
Cedar Mesa, and Basketmaker II sites, 41, 225, 234–35
ceramics: adoption of in northern Kayenta region, 288; and Basketmaker II–III transition, 279–81; and Camp Dead Pine, 101; and cooking of beans, 286; and cross dating of NMRAP Puebloan sites, 299–303; and Hammer House, 106; and markers for end of Archaic period, 36; and NMRAP laboratory methods, 18; and sources of pottery-quality clays in Kayenta region, 11, 60, 63; and Tres Campos, 90; and Water Jar Pueblo, 121. *See also* Obelisk Utility pottery; Tsegi Orange Ware; Tusayan White Ware
Cerro del Medio (Jemez Mountains), as source of obsidian, 157, 158, 190, 378
chert, and sources of raw materials in Kayenta region, 57–58. *See also* Navajo chert; Owl Rock chert
Chinle Formation, 60, *62*, 191
Chisholm, B., 40, 255
Christenson, A. L., 24, 30, 296, *297*
chronology: of NMRAP Archaic sites, 145–60; of NMRAP Basketmaker II sites, 210–22; of NMRAP Puebloan sites, 294–313. *See also* cultural-temporal framework; obsidian-hydration dating; radiocarbon analysis; tree-ring dating
chrysocolla, 61
Clark, Victoria H., *5*
clay, sources of for sites in Kayenta region, 11, 60, 63
climate: and field houses, 355; and middle Archaic date gap, 198–204; of NMRAP project location, 4, 49, 52, *53, 54*. *See also* drought; environment
Clovis point style, 26
coal, sources of and artifacts made from, 61, 63n2, 275
Coal Gasification Project (CGP), 162, 164
Cochiti Pueblo, 352
Coconino Plateau, 190, 377
Cole, K. L., 201
Collette, Jim, *5*
Collette, Lanita, *5*
color, and changes in maize samples, 229, 285
Colorado Plateau: and abandonment or reduction in use of sites during middle Archaic, 195, 198, 205, 377; and agricultural transition, 8, 9, 206–7; characteristics of Archaic sites on, 32–33, 194; and Paleoindian sites, 27
Colton, H. S., 21, 40, 43, 234
community size, and social differentiation, 385
Coombs Village, 322
Cooley, M., 11, 57, 61, 382
Coppermine Trading Post, 355
corner-notched knives, 275
cotton, cultivation of and Puebloan textiles, 326
Cottonwood Wash (Utah), 287
Coulam, Nancy J., 19, 33, 137, 195
courtyard pueblos, and courtyard complexes, 342, 386, 387
Cowboy Cave: abandonment of in middle Archaic, 194–95; and Archaic remains, 33, *34*, 137, 138, 183
craft production, and research design of NMRAP, 10–11, 382–85
Creamer, W., 347, 348
cultural-temporal framework: and Archaic period, 29–33, *35*; and Basketmaker II, 40–43; for Kayenta region, *26*
Cummings, Byron, 24, 267
Cummings Mesa, 47, 386. *See also* Surprise Pueblo
Cutler, Hugh, 222, 285

Danger Cave, 28
Dean, Jeffrey S., 12, 25, 47, 290, 295, 306, 311, 313, 315, 338, 341, 386, 387–88
Deats, Stewart, *5*, 19
deflectors, and Basketmaker II houses, 256, 278
dendrochronology, and laboratory methods, 19. *See also* tree-ring dating
Desha Caves, 33, 249, 250
diet: and behavioral responses to climate change in middle Holocene, 203–4; importance of grass seed on Colorado Plateau, 231–33; importance of maize for Basketmaker II, 225–27. *See also* faunal remains; food preparation and processing; plant remains; subsistence
Ditch House (AZ-J-14-21): burning and abandonment of, 74, 294–95, 370; and ceramic cross dating, *300, 301, 302, 303*, 308–9, 310–11; and dendrochronology, 295; description of, *65*, 72–74; and living rooms, 342; and mealing rooms, *328*; and radiocarbon dates, *212, 215*, 298; summary of information on, *208, 292*; tree-ring dates for, *294*
Dixon, Chris, *5*
Dodd, D., 106
Dogoszhi Black-on-white, 45, 305, 307
Dog Town, 342
Dolores Archaeological Project (DAP), 356, 357
Downer, Alan, *5*
drills, and Basketmaker II sites, 273–75
drought: and Altithermal during middle Archaic, 200; and Pueblo III population decline, 47. *See also* climate
Dune Hollow (AZ-J-2-2): and ceramic cross dating, *300, 301, 303*; description of, *66*, 114–16; and feature density, *167, 168*; obsidian in lithic assemblage of, 185, *186*; as processing camp, 166, 179–80; and radiocarbon dates, *148*; and secondary habitations, *358, 359, 365*; summary of information on, *142, 292*

Dust Devil Cave: and Archaic remains, 28–29, 33, 138, 140, 193, 195, 196, 197; chronology of Basketmaker II features, 210, 220, 249; and elevation zone, 183; and grinding tools, 276; location of, *143*; and natural shelters, 137, 250; as processing camp, 179; as residential camp, 167, 172; and storage during Basketmaker II, 250–51; and variability in recovery rates, 165
Dyer, Anderson, 5

Eidgenössiche Technische Hochschule (ETH), 217–18
elevation zones, and early Archaic residential camps, 183
Elko points, 134, 268, 269
entryways, slab-lining of in Basketmaker II houses, 248
environment: of Colorado Plateau in middle Holocene, 377; and description of Kayenta region, 48–63. *See also* climate
ethnography: and descriptions of secondary habitations, 350, 351–53; and mobility of Puebloan sites, 368; and Puebloan corn-grinding process, 329–30; and subsistence territories in Great Basin and Southwest, 378; and use of storage pits, 261, 262. *See also* Havasupai; Hopi; Navajo; Paiute; Yavapai
Euler, R. C., 48
excavation strategy, and field methods of NMRAP, 12, 13–15
exchange, and research design of NMRAP, 10–11, 382–85. *See also* ceramics; exotic materials; obsidian
exotic materials: and Basketmaker II sites, 275; and pipe fragments at Puebloan sites, 364; and tool production at NMRAP Archaic sites, 377

Fairley, Helen C., 25, 75, 304, 384
Falls Creek (Colorado), 268, 282
faunal remains: animal consumption and subsistence specialization, 10; and Dune Hollow site, 116; and importance of hunting at Puebloan sites, 383; and residential camps, 173; and Tsé Haal'á site, 134. *See also* animal life; fish; turkey
feature density: and NMRAP Archaic sites, *167, 168, 169, 170*; and variability in recovery rates, 165
Ferguson, C. W., 153
field houses: and Hillside Hermitage, 110; and Puebloan sites, 350–67
field methods, and methodology of NMRAP, 12–17
figurines, and Archaic through Basketmaker II, 280
Finnell, T. L., 63
fish, and San Juan River and tributaries, 54
Flagstaff Black-on-white, 45, 310
Flagstaff ceramic period, 43–44
Flannery, K. V., 206
floor features: and field methods, 15–16; and Puebloan living rooms, 317–18
Foley, R., 161
Folsom point style, 26, 27
food preparation and processing, evidence for at residential camps, 171. *See also* diet; processing camps and sites; stone boiling
foraging: and Archaic period on Colorado Plateau, 28; continuation of at NMRAP Basketmaker II sites, 222, 229–34, 381; and forager-collector continuum, 162; NMRAP data on territories for, 377–78; subsistence range and territory for NMRAP Archaic sites, 183–93. *See also* plant remains

Ford, Richard I., 184, 222, 229–30
Formative period: temporal framework of in Kayenta region, 43–47; and transition from Archaic, 36–43
Fowler, C. S., 48
Francis, H., 48
Friedman, I., 154, 155
Frison, G. C., 27

gaming pieces, 275, *276*
Gasser, R. E., 10
Geib, Phil R., 5, 19, 24, 41, 57, 151, 194, 200, 203, 205n4, 211, 227–28, 249, 279, 324
generalist/specialist continuum, and subsistence specialization, 9
genetic continuity, and relationship between Archaic and Basketmaker populations, 264
geography, of Kayenta region, 48–49, *50*
geology: and intraregional variability of Kayenta region, 11; of NMRAP research area, 4, 57–63. *See also* alluvial cobbles; chert; clay; gypsum points; obsidian; quartzite; sandstone
geomorphic study, and NMRAP research plan, 19–20
Gifford, E. W., 183
Gilman, P. A., 255
Gilpin, D., 287, 373n2
Gladwin, W. & H. S., 40
Glassow, M. A., 222
Glen Canyon: Kayentan presence in, 21; as source of flakeable stone, 11, 57
Glen Canyon National Recreation Area, 231
Glen Canyon Project, 25, 247–49, 368
goethite, 63
Goodman, John, 5, 19
goosefoot (*Chenopodium* sp.), 230, *231*
Government Mountain: and obsidian-hydration dating, *157*, 160; as source of obsidian, 77, 89, 158, 189, 190, 377
Graham, M., 367, 388
granaries, and Puebloan architecture, 331–33
Grand Canyon, and Kayentan residential mobility, 368–69, *370*
Grand Gulch, and Basketmaker II sites, 41, 232, 234, 287
Graymountain, Virginia, 5
Gregory, D. A., 385
Grey, Sarah, 5
grinding tools: and abandonment of sites, 312; and Archaic period on Colorado Plateau, 28; and Blake's Abode site, 97; and Camp Dead Pine, 101; and origins of Basketmaker II, 275–78; and residential camps, 171, 173; and Scorpion Heights, 101; sources of raw materials for, 11, 59; specialization in production of at Puebloan sites, 383–84; and UT-B-63-19, 131, *132*
Guardian Pueblo, *312*
Guernsey, S. L., 9, 24, 37, 38, 39, 40, 140, 207, 234, 249, 254, 263, 264, 266, 267, 268, 269, 272, 274, 275, 276, 283, 287, 289n8, 380
Gumerman, G. J., 12
gypsum points, 36, 138, 183

Haas, J., 347, 348
Hack, J. T., 56
Hadd, G. A., 61
Hagopian, Janet, 5, 18, 300

Hammer House (AZ-J-14-16): abandonment of, 370; and ceramic cross dating, *300, 301, 302, 303, 305*; description of site, *66*, 103, *105*, 106–7; and kivas, 106–7, *306, 320, 321*, 323, 324, *325*; and living rooms, 317–18; and primary habitations, 46, 335, *336*, 337–38; summary of information on, *292*; tree-ring dates for, *294, 305*

Hanging Ash (UT-B-63-14): and ceramic assemblage, 311; and ceramic cross dating, *300, 301, 302, 303*; description of, *67*, 128, *129*; and faunal remains, 383; and lithic assemblage, 383; and living room, 315; and primary habitations, *336*, 341–42; summary of information on, *292*

Hantman, J. L., 295

Hardy, Veronica, *5*

Havasupai, and secondary habitations, 253

Hawk's Nest Ruin, 251

Hayden, Irwin, 247, 250, 267, 366

Hays-Gilpin, Kelley A., *5*, 18, 300

hearths: basin hearths and feature density at Tsé Haalá, *170*; basin hearths and feature density at Three Dog Site, *169*; and field houses, 355; and food preparation, 171; and hunting camps, 178; and Puebloan living rooms, 317; and radiocarbon dating for Archaic sites, 145–46, 150–54; and structure of Basketmaker II houses, 257, 259. *See also* thermal features

Henderson, Roger, *5*

Henry, Jacqueline, *5*

Hewitt, N. J., 338

Hidatsa, and use-life of storage pits, 261

Hill, W. W., 352

Hillside Hermitage (AZ-J-3-14): and activity/storage rooms, *334*; and ceramic assemblage, 307; and ceramic cross dating, *300, 301, 302, 303, 305*; description of site, *66*, 110–11; and kivas, *320, 321*, 325, *326*; and living rooms, 315; and mealing rooms, *328, 330*; and primary habitations, 46, 335, *336*, 337–38; and secondary habitations, *358, 359*, 360–61, *365*; summary of information on, *292*

Hisatsinom phase, 39

historic record, for Colorado Plateau, 48

Hobler, Philip, 248–49, 344, 347

Hogan, P., 32

Hohokam sites, and secondary habitations, 351

Hólahéi Scatter (AZ-J-14-23): description of, *65*, 75–77; and feature density, *167, 168*; as hunting camp, *166*; and obsidian-hydration dating, 155, *156*, 158–60; obsidian in lithic assemblage at, 77, 184–85, *187*, 190, 377; and radiocarbon dating, 146; summary of information on, *142*

Holbrook Black-on-white, 79

Holiday, Gregory, *5*

Holmer, R. N., 29, 30, 32, 269

Holocene, and population bottleneck in middle Archaic on Colorado Plateau, 375–77

Holter, Louella, *5*

Homolovi ruins, 291, 386

Hopi: and field houses, 352; and Post-Formative period, 48; and soils for floodwater farming, 56

horizontal provenience, and field methods, 13–14

horn flakers, 269–71

houses, and architecture of Basketmaker II sites, 255–59. *See also* field houses; pithouses

Huckell, Bruce B., 28, 33, 37, 106, 225, 227, 237–38, 261, 265, 377, 381

Hughes, Richard, 19, 157, 189

Hull, K. L., 155

Hunt, Alice, 32

Hunter, Andrea, *5*, 19, 226

hunting. *See* faunal remains; hunting camps; subsistence

hunting camps: and NMRAP Archaic sites, *166*, 177–78, 181; and NMRAP Basketmaker II sites, 245–47; and obsidian in lithic assemblages, 186; as site type, 165

Hurst, Winston, 18

Hymn House (AZ-J-2-3): and ceramic assemblage, 311; and ceramic cross dating, *300, 301, 302, 303*; description of, *66*, 116–18; and primary habitations, *336*, 339–41; and room clusters, 388; summary of information on, *292*

intrinsic rate dating, 155

iron/manganese, 60–61, 275

Irwin-Williams, Cynthia, 9, 27, 29–30, 31, 32, 194, 263, 265

Isaac, Glynn, 162

jacal, and Puebloan architecture, 318–19, 333

Jay points, and Oshara tradition, *31*

Jeddito Yellow Ware, 48

Jemez Mountains. *See* Cerro del Medio

Jennings, Jesse D., 9, 32, 36–37, 195, 200

Jett, S. C., 352

Jewett, R. A., 350

Jochim, M. A., 180

Johnson, Vicky N., *5*

Jones, G. T., 28, 171

Jones, K. T., 232–33

Juniper Cove site, 385

juniper seeds, and radiocarbon dates, 154, 215–16

Kaibab chert, 192, 193

Kaibito Plateau: and Kayenta region, 22; and radiocarbon record for middle Archaic gap, 198, 376

Kalahari Desert (Botswana), 356

Kana-a Black-on-white, 221

kaolinite, 60

Kaplan, L., 285

Karlstrom, E. T., 201

Kayenta Black-on-white, 45, 384

Kayenta branch, 21, 22

Kayenta region: adoption of pottery in northern, 288; and background information for NMRAP, 21–24; contributions of NMRAP to understanding of prehistory and lifeways of, 206, 374–75; overview of previous archaeological work in, 24–48; regional settlement history and population trends in, 370–73; and settlement patterns at Basketmaker sites, 247–51

Kayenta Sandstone, 60

Kelley, K. B., 48

Kelly, I. T., 183, 190, 378

Kelly, R. L., 161, 335, 368, 369

Kent, S., 334, 342, 350, 353, 355–57

Ketchum, Alexandra, *5*

Kidder, Alfred V., 9, 21, 24, 37, 38, 39, 40, 140, 206, 207, 234, 249,

254, 263, 264, 266–67, 268, 269, 272, 274, 275, 276, 283, 287, 289n8, 380
Kiet Siel site, 388
Kinbiko Cave, 138
King, Geraldine S., 5
King, Keith, 5
King, Leander, 5
King, Leonard B., 5
Kin Kahuna (AZ-J-3-8): agricultural setting of, 207; Basketmaker II component and site boundary of, 289n4; and bow-and-arrow technology, 284; and ceramic cross dating, *300, 301, 303*; description of, *66*, 112, *113*, 114; and drills, 273, 274; and grinding tools, 278; as primary habitation, 236, 238–39, 254, 385; and radiocarbon dates, *212, 218, 219, 298*, 299; and storage features, 261, 262; and structure of houses, 257, *258*, 259, 278; summary of information on, *208, 292*; and temporal components of Basketmaker II occupation, 227
Kin Klethla, 348, 349
kisi and *kishoni*, and field houses, 351
kiva(s): and Hammer House, 106–7, 306; and Puebloan architecture, 319–27, 329; and Sapo Seco, 121; and seasonal occupation of sites, 360; and sociocultural complexity, 385; and Three Dog Site, 127; and Water Jar Pueblo, 120, 121
Klitso, Kilroy, 5
Kluckholm, C., 262
Koehler, Peter, 5, 20, 202
Kohler, T. A., 353, 361
Ko' Lanhi (AZ-J-14-35): description of, *66*, 95, *96*, 97; and radiocarbon dates, *212*, 216; summary of information on, *208*
Kroeber, A. L., 341

laboratory procedures, and NMRAP methodology, 17–20
Laboratory of Tree-Ring Research, 5
Lawrence Livermore National Laboratory, 19, 146, 210, 216–19
Lawson, F. H., 386
Leakey, M. D., 193
Lefthand, Nathan, 5
Lekson, S. H., 327, 368
Leonard, R. D., 10, 171
Lightfoot, K. G., 350
limited-activity occupation sites, and secondary habitations, 351
limonitic clay, 60, *62*, 63
Lindsay, Alexander J., Jr., 12, 24, 25, 47, 122, 181, 210, 249, 279, 311, 312, 313, 315, 331, 333, 342, 344, 386
Lino Black-on-white, 221, 304
Lino Gray, 280
Linton, R., 285
Lipe, William D., 38, 41, 206, 234–35, 248, 249, 251, 368
lithic assemblages: and Archaic point styles, 28, *31*, 32, 36; and Basketmaker II–III transition, 281–84; and Dune Hollow site, 116; and exchange of raw materials, 11; and Hammer House, 106; and Hóláhéi Scatter site, 76, 77; and hunting camps, 177–78, 245–47; and Ko' Lanhi site, 95; and laboratory methods, 18–19; and markers of late Prehistoric and Protohistoric periods, 48; and origins of Basketmaker II, 267–75; and Paleoindian point styles, 26–27; and Pee Wee Grande, 77–79; and residential camps, 171, 173, 175–76; and Scorpion Heights site, 100–101; and The Pits, 71; and The Slots, 81, 83; and Three Dog Site, 126; and Tres Campos, 89; and Tsé Haal'á, 134; and UT-B-63-19, 132. *See also* chert; grinding tools; obsidian; projectile points
Little, Calvin, 5
living rooms, and Puebloan architecture, 313–19, 341
Livingstone, Alfred, 5
Lolomai phase, 41, 235, 287
Lone Tree Dune site, 234, 248
Long House site (NA897), 290, 347
Long House Valley, 25
looting, at Atlatl Rock Cave, 135, 137, 139
Los Pozos (Arizona), 385

Madsen, D. B., 232–33
maize: and agricultural transition in Kayenta region, 8–9, 379–81; and agriculture at NMRAP Basketmaker II sites, 222–29; and Basketmaker II–III transition, 285; and Ditch House, 74; introduction of to Colorado Plateau in late Archaic, 36; and Kin Kahuna site, 114; as marker for beginning of Basketmaker II, 39, 40; and radiocarbon dating of Basketmaker II sites, 210, 211, 215–16; and Three Dog Site, 127
malachite, 61
Mangum, Kim, 5
Manheimer, Elaine (Smith), *5, 13*
manos. *See* grinding tools
manual, for laboratory procedures, 17
mapping, and field methods of NMRAP, 12–13
Marek, Ora, 5
Marsh Pass–Monument Valley (Arizona), 287
Masayesva, Esther, 5
masonry, and Puebloan living rooms, 319
material culture, and origins of Basketmaker II, 266–67
Mathews, Meredith, 19
Matson, R. G., 9, 38, 39, 40, 41, 42, 206, 207, 225, 234–35, 236, 245, 249, 255, 263, 267, 380
Matthews, Meredith, 5
Maya, and ground-stone technology, 366
McAllister, S. P., 351
McGregor, J. C., 38
mealing bins and rooms: and Hillside Hermitage, 110, 111; and Puebloan architecture, 327–31; and Water Jar Pueblo, 120
Medicine Black-on-red, 305
Meltzer, D. J., 199, 202, 203
Mesoamerica, domesticates and food production in late Archaic period, 37. *See also* Maya; Mexico
metates. *See* grinding tools
Metcalfe, D., 233, 355
methodology, and field methods of NMRAP, 12–20
Mexico, and origins of maize, 222. *See also* Maya; Mesoamerica
migration, and Puebloan mobility, 368
Mindeleff, V., 350, 351, 361
mineral(s): samples of and laboratory methods, 19; and sources of raw materials, 60–61, 275
Mineral Mountains. *See* Wild Horse
Minnis, P. E., 9, 10, 229, 233
Mizell-Begay, Cheryl, 5

mobility: and changes in locations of residential camps in middle Archaic, 204; and domestic use of Puebloan kivas, 325, 326; and forager-collector continuum during Archaic, 162; and NMRAP Puebloan sites, 368–70, 388; and secondary habitations, 355–57; and storage pits, 262–63. *See also* occupation spans; seasonality

Mobley-Tanaka, J. L., 328, 330–31

Modesty House (AZ-J-2-5): and activity/storage rooms, *334*; ceramic assemblage and occupation span at, 308; and ceramic cross dating, *300, 301, 303*; description of site, *67*, 118, *119*; excavation of, *13*; and secondary habitations, *358, 359*, 361–62, 365; summary of information on, *292*

Moenkopi (Hopi village), 309

Moenkopi Corrugated, 384

Moore, B. M., 352

Moqui Canyon site cluster, 234

Morris, Earl A., 24, 38–39, 263, 268, 281–82, 289n7

Morss, N., 24

mountain sheep horn rods, 269–71

Mountainview (AZ-J-14-38): and Basketmaker II–III transitional interval, 44; and bow-and-arrow technology, 282–83; and ceramic assemblage, 280, 281; description of site, *66*, 102–3, *104*; as primary habitation, 236, 239–40; and radiocarbon dates, *212*; structure of houses, 257; summary of information on, *208*

Mouse House (AZ-J-3-7): and ceramic assemblage, 308, 309–10; and ceramic cross dating, *300, 301, 303*; description of, *66*, 107–9; and feature density, *167, 168*; as processing site, *166*; and radiocarbon dates, *148, 212*; summary of information on, *142, 208, 292*

Mud Wallow, 348

Museum of Northern Arizona (MNA), 25

Naaki Hooghan (AZ-J-14-11): and ceramic assemblage, 307; and ceramic cross dating, *300, 301, 302, 303, 305*; description of, *65*, 85–87; and secondary habitations, *358, 359*, 360, 362, *365*; summary of information on, *292*

NA75208, *312*

NA8368 (Piute Mesa), 248–49

Naroll, R., 315

natural shelters: and Basketmaker II settlement patterns, 249–51; examples of from early Archaic on Rainbow Plateau, 137. *See also* caves

Navajo: and field structures, 352–53; and historic occupation of Kayenta region, 48; and mobility practices, 369; and use of storage pits, 262

Navajo, Willie, *5, 13*

Navajo chert, 57–58, 191, 192, 193, 283, 382

Navajo Houses (Mindeleff 1898), 351

Navajo Mountain, and sources of sandstone, 59

Navajo Mountain Boarding School, 5

Navajo Mountain Road Archaeological Project (NMRAP): and agricultural transition at Basketmaker II sites, 8–9, 222–34, 378–82; and architecture of Basketmaker II sites, 255–63; and architecture of Puebloan sites, 313–33; background information on, 1, 21–24; and Basketmaker II–III transition, 44, 279–89; and chronology for Archaic sites, 145–60; and chronology for Basketmaker II sites, 210–22; and chronology for Puebloan sites, 294–313; and continuation of foraging at Basketmaker II sites, 222–34; contributions to understanding of prehistory and lifeways of Kayenta region, 206, 374–75; and description of project, 4–6; and description of individual sites, 64–139; and environment of Kayenta region, 48–63; field methods and methodology of, 12–17; and forager territories, 377–78; laboratory procedures and methodology of, 17–20; and location of project, 1–4; and mobility at Puebloan sites, 368–70; and origins of Basketmaker II, 263–79; personnel and consultants for, 5; and previous archaeological work in Kayenta region, 24–48; and question of middle Holocene bottleneck at Archaic sites, 375–77; research design and issues of, 7–12, 375–89; and settlement patterns for Archaic sites, 164–83, 193–205; and settlement patterns for Basketmaker II sites, 234–55; site sample of, 6–7, 141–45, 207–10, 291–93; subsistence range and territory for Archaic sites, 183–93

Navajo Mountain Trading Post, and weather station, 49, 52, *53, 54*

Navajo Nation Archaeology Department (NNAD), 1. *See also* Navajo Mountain Road Archaeological Project

Navajo Nation Historic Preservation Department (NNHPD), 4, 16, 20n2

Navajo Nation Policy for the Protection of Jishchaa': Gravesites, Human Remains, and Funerary Items, 16

Navajo Quartz, 58

Navajo Sandstone, 59–60

Neff, L. Theodore, *5, 51*

Neskahi Village (Piute Mesa): and mealing rooms, 331; and plaza pueblos, 342, 344, 346–47, 386, 387; and site occupation span, 304

Neupert, Mark, 18

Nez, Laura, *5*

notching flakes, at Tsé Haal'á site, *134*

NSF-Arizona Mass Spectrometry Laboratory, *5*, 19, 217–18

Nusbaum, Deric, 25

Obelisk Cave (Arizona), 280, 289n7

Obelisk Utility pottery: and Atlatl Rock Cave, 249, 250; and Basketmaker II radiocarbon dates for Kayenta region, 221; and Basketmaker II–III transition, 43, 304; and Mountainview site, 103, 207, 239, 240, 280–81

obsidian: and Hólahéi Scatter site, 77, 184–85, *187*; and lithic assemblages at Archaic sites, 178, *188*, 189, 377–78; and Tres Campos site, 89; and Tsé Haal'á site, 186; transport and wear of, 186

obsidian-hydration dating, for Archaic sites, 154–60

occupation spans: and concept of anticipated short occupation, 342, 350; of NMRAP Puebloan sites, 303–13; seasonality and duration of secondary habitations, 350. *See also* mobility

Old Oraibi, 355

Old Corn Site (New Mexico), 39, 222, 287

Old Man Cave, 195

open camps, as site type, 245

optimization theory, and behavioral ecology, 161

orientation, and Puebloan architecture, 314, 329

ornaments: and coal pendants, 61; and origins of Basketmaker II, 275, *276*

Ortiz, David, *5*
Oshara sequence, and Archaic period, 29–32
Owl Rock chert, 58, 101, 253, 382
OxCal program, Version 3.10, 146, 211, 220, 296, *297*

pack rat middens: and climate of middle Holocene, 202; and geomorphic methods of NMRAP, 20
Paiute: and historic period, 48; importance of grass seed in diet of, 231. *See also* Southern Paiute
Paiute Canyon, and Petrified Forest Member, 60, *62*
Paleoarchaic, use of term, 28
Paleoindian period: characteristics of in Kayenta region, 26–28; evidence for continuity into Archaic period, 193
palisades, and Pueblo II sites, 347
Panorama House (AZ-J-14-34): description of, *66*, 90–92; and radiocarbon dates, *212*, 216, *217*; and secondary habitations, 242, 243–45; summary of information on, *208*
Parry, W., 30
Paynter, R. W., 183
pecking stones, 106, 330. *See also* grinding tools
Pecos Classification, 21, 263, 279
Pecos Conference, 21, 140
Pee Wee Grande (AZ-J-14-26): description of, *65*, 77–79; and feature density, *167, 168*; as processing site, *166*, 179; and radiocarbon dates, *148, 213, 298*, 299; summary of information on, *142, 208, 292*
Pepper, G. H., 37
Perryman, B. L., 153
Petrified Forest Member, of Chinle Formation, 60, *62*
petroglyphs, 5, 135, 161
Phillips, D. A., Jr., 234
pigments, and sources of raw materials, 60–61
Pinto points, 30
pinyon (*Pinus edulis*), 230–31, 233–34, 262–63, 381
pipes and pipe drills, 274, 364
pit baking, 245
Pitblado, B. L., 27
pithouses: at Hanging Ash site, 128; at Kin Kahuna, 112, 114, 238–39; and Puebloan kivas, 319–20. *See also* houses
pithouse village, 348
pit structure, 319
Piute Mesa, and Basketmaker II habitations, 247–49
plant remains: and Atlatl Rock Cave, *232*; and biota of Kayenta region, 55; and Camp Dead Pine, 101; and Ditch House, 72; and forager subsistence during Archaic, 144–45; and Hanging Ash site, 128; and laboratory methods, 19; and The Pits, 72; and radiocarbon dates from Archaic sites, 154; and residential camps, 172; and Three Dog Site, 126–27. *See also* beans; foraging; goosefoot; juniper seeds; maize; pinyon; ricegrass; sagebrush; squash; vegetation; yucca
plaza pueblos, and plaza-oriented villages, 344, 347, 386, 387
Plog, S., 295, 351, 354, 360, 369
plunge pools, as water sources, 55
pollen samples, and field methods, 17
Polly's Place (AZ-J-14-31): and ceramics, 281; description of, *65*, 83, *84*, 85; and feature density, 165, *167, 168*; as processing site, *166*, 179; and radiocarbon dates, *148, 213*; as secondary habitation, 242, 243–45; summary of information on, *142, 208*
Ponczynski, John, *5*
population: and diminished forager density in middle Archaic, 194, 199, 200; middle to late Pueblo III sites and growth of, 339; settlement history of Kayenta region and trends in, 370–73, 386; and trends in Formative period, 45–47
Poseyesva, Lanell T., *5*
Post-Formative period, definition of, 48
postholes, and field methods, 15
Pottery Pueblo: and courtyard pueblos, 347, 386, 387; and kivas, 321; and settlement patterns in Pueblo III, 47
Pottery Types of the Southwest (Colton), 21
Powell, Shirley, 350, 353–55, 369
precipitation, and environment of Rainbow Plateau, 49
Presley Wash (Arizona), as obsidian source, 190, 377
primary crop acquisition, 206
primary habitations: and NMRAP Basketmaker sites, 236–40, *241*, 255; and NMRAP Puebloan sites, 333–49
pristine domestication, 206
processing camps and sites: and NMRAP Archaic sites, *166*, 178–80; as site types, 165
projectile points, and origins of Basketmaker II, 268–73. *See also* bow-and-arrow technology
Protohistoric interval, 48
provenience numbers, and field methods, 17
P-III Associates, 2
pueblo(s), and Sapo Seco site, 121, 122. *See also* courtyard pueblos; plaza pueblos; unit pueblos
Pueblo I: and architecture of sites, 313–33; chronology of NMRAP sites, 294–313; craft production and exchange as research issue for NMRAP, 382–85; and mobility at NMRAP sites, 368–70; and NMRAP site sample, 7, 291–93; occupation span and use history of sites, 304; and prehistory of Kayenta region, 22–24, 44; settlement types and patterns of NMRAP sites, 333–68; and Wolachii Bighan site, 75
Pueblo II: and architecture of sites, 313–33; and Camp Dead Pine, 101; and chronology for NMRAP sites, 294–313; craft production and exchange as research issue for NMRAP, 382–85; and Ditch House, 74; and Hammer House, 106; and Hanging Ash site, 128; and Hillside Hermitage, 110–11; and mobility at NMRAP sites, 368–70; and Modesty House, 118; and Mouse House, 107; and Naaki Hooghan, 85, 87; and NMRAP site sample, 7, 291–93; occupation span and use history of sites, 304–10; and Pee Wee Grande, 79; and prehistory of Kayenta region, 22–24, 44–45; settlement types and patterns of NMRAP sites, 333–68; and The Slots, 82; and Tres Campos, 87, 89, 90
Pueblo III: and abandonment of sites, 312–13; and architecture of sites, 313–33; and chronology for NMRAP sites, 294–313; craft production and exchange as research issue for NMRAP, 382–85; and Ditch House, 74; and Dune Hollow site, 116; and Hammer House, 103; and Hymn House, 118; and Kin Kahuna, 112, 114; and mobility at NMRAP sites, 368–70; and Modesty House, 118; and Mouse House, 107; and NMRAP site sample, 7, 291–93; and prehistory of Kayenta region, 22–24, 45; and Sapo Seco, 121–22; settlement types and patterns of NMRAP

sites, 333–68; and social organization, 11; and The Slots, 81; and Three Dog Site, 124, 126, 127–28; and UT-B-63-19, 128; and Water Jar Pueblo, 118, 121; and Windy Mesa, 79, 81
Pueblo IV, and Homolovi Ruins, 291

Quanbeck, Karen, 5, 19
quartzite, and lithic assemblage at Three Dog Site, 175–76

radiocarbon analysis: and laboratory methods, 19; of maize samples, 224; and NMRAP Archaic sites, 145–54, 194, 195–97, 376; and NMRAP Basketmaker II sites, 210–22; and NMRAP Puebloan sites, 295–99; and origins of Basketmaker cultures, 264–65
Rainbow Gray, 384
Rainbow Plateau: and agricultural transition, 264; Basketmaker II sites on, 40, 42–43; and Basketmaker II–III transition, 279–80; earliest maize date on, 223; late Archaic dates from, 198; and location of NMRAP sites, 1, 3, 4; and natural shelters during early Archaic, 137; and precipitation, 49
ramadas, and secondary habitations, 352–53
Ramp site (Hopi Buttes), 320
Rarámuri (Mexico), 348, 388
Raven, C., 161
recesses, in kivas, 321–22, 326
Red Rock Plateau, 234
Reed, Phillip J., 5
Reher, C. A., 163, 164, 181
Reimer, P. J., 296, 297
research issues, and design of NMRAP, 7–12, 375–89
residential camps, and settlement patterns at NMRAP Archaic sites, 165, 166, 167, 171–73, 175–76, 181, 183
Rhode, D., 233
ricegrass (*Achatherum hymenoides*), 230–33, 262, 381
Richardson, Hubert, 2
Richens, L. D., 282
Rick, J. W., 196, 199
Ridings, R., 154–55
ritual sites, and Archaic settlement patterns, 161
Roasting Pit Alcove, 210
Robins, Michael R., 5, 19
Rocek, T. R., 353
rockshelters. *See* caves; natural shelters
Rodgers, J. B., 357
Roessel, R., 48
Romer, Alfred S., 289n2
roof: of Basketmaker II houses, 256–57, 258; and Puebloan architecture, 322–24
room blocks and room clusters: and Bonsai Bivouac, 124; and Hymn House, 117–18, 388; and primary habitations at Puebloan sites, 339; and Three Dog Site, 126; and Water Jar Pueblo, 120
Rudden, B., 386
Russell, S. C., 353, 362
Ryan, Darsita, 5

sagebrush, and radiocarbon dates, 150–54, 213, 215
Salt, Jocelyn, 5

Samples, Terry, 5
sandals: and Archaic sites, 33, 140, 196, 197, 205n1, 263, 267; as evidence of Basketmaker occupancy of sites, 289n5. *See also* yucca
Sand Dune Cave: chronology of Basketmaker II features, 210, 249; evidence of late Archaic use, 150, 183; as example of natural shelter use during Archaic and Basketmaker II, 137, 249; and Gypsum points, 138; and horn flakers, 270; location of, 143; and lack of remains from middle Archaic, 195; as residential camp, 167, 181; and sandals from Archaic, 33, 140, 196, 197, 263; and Tsé Haal'á site, 135
Sanders, Sharon, 5
Sandoval, Harriett, 5
sandstone, and sources for raw materials in Kayenta region, 58–60
Sandy Ridge site (Utah), 284
San Jose phase, of Archaic period, 30, 31
San Juan Basketmaker, and projectile points, 268
San Juan Paiute, 48
San Juan Red Ware, 45, 304, 305
Sapo Seco (AZ-J-2-6): and activity/storage rooms, 334; and ceramic assemblage, 311; and ceramic cross dating, 300, 301, 302, 303, 312; description of, 67, 121–22; and faunal remains, 383; and feature density, 167, 168; and granaries, 332, 333; as hunting camp, 166, 178; and kivas, 320, 321, 322, 323, 324; and lithic assemblage, 383; and living rooms, 314, 315, 317; and mealing rooms, 328; and mobility, 388; and Paleoindian remains, 193; and plaza or unit pueblos, 344–46; and primary habitations, 336, 340, 348, 349; Puebloan component of, 293, 336, 339, 348; and radiocarbon dates, 148; summary of information on, 142, 292; and variability in recovery rates, 165
satellite sites, and secondary habitations, 351
Schilz, A. J., 250, 267
Schlanger, S. H., 357, 366
Schmidt, Kari, 5, 19
Schroedl, A., 27, 32, 33, 36, 137, 164, 195, 198, 200, 203, 293, 305, 306, 310, 376, 377
Schurr, M. A., 385
Schwartz, D. W., 368–69
Scorpion Heights (AZ-J-14-37): description of, 66, 97, 99, 100–101; as hunting-related camp, 245–46; and radiocarbon dates, 213; summary of information on, 208
screening, and field methods, 14
Seaman, P. D., 253
seasonality: and secondary habitations during Basketmaker II, 242, 253–54; and secondary habitations at Puebloan sites, 350, 351, 354, 362; and settlement patterns during Archaic, 162, 204; and use of storage pits, 262. *See also* mobility
secondary habitations: and Basketmaker sites, 240, 242–45; and durations of use in middle Pueblo II, 307; and Puebloan sites, 350–67
sedentism, concepts of deep sedentism and mobility at Puebloan sites, 368, 369
Segazlin Mesa, and Pueblo III community, 47, 311, 386
settlement patterns: and general considerations for site types, 162–64; and NMRAP Archaic sites, 164–83, 193–205; and NMRAP Basketmaker II sites, 234–55; and NMRAP Puebloan sites, 333–70; overview of literature on Archaic

period and, 160–62; Paleoindian remains and question of continuity into Archaic, 193; and population trends in Kayenta region, 370–73; summary of NMRAP research on, 385–89. *See also* aggregation; mobility; seasonality

Shackley, M. S., 184

Sheehan, M. S., 203

shell, and Basketmaker II sites, 275

Shonto Plateau, and location of NMRAP, 1, 3

Shott, M. J., 282

silicified wood, 58

Simmons, A. H., 30

Simon, H. A., 161

Sin Sombra (AZ-J-3-6): description of, *66*, 109–10; and radiocarbon dates, *213*; as secondary habitation, 242; summary of information on, *208*; as temporary residential site, 107

site(s): location of, *69*; names and Navajo Nation site numbers, 64; and NMRAP site sample, 6–7, 141–45, 207–10, 291–93; settlement patterns and distribution of during Basketmaker II, 251–55; settlement patterns and types of during Archaic, 162–64; summary of information on, *65–67, 68–69*. *See also specific sites*

Skeleton Mesa, 252

slab-lined storage cists, 237, 250, 263

small features, and field methods, 15

Small Jar Pueblo, *305*, 326–27, 337, 338

Small Sites Conference, 351

Smiley, F. E., 36, 39, 41, 44, 141, 150, 205, 223, 225, 235, 236, 249, 252, 259, 287, 289n1, 289n3, 385

Smith, Alfred, 5

Smith, R. L., 154, 155

Smith, Susan, 5, 19

Smith, W., 319, 324

social issues, and research design of NMRAP, 11–12, 384–85. *See also* settlement patterns

soils, and agriculture in Kayenta region, 55–57

Sosi Black-on-white, 45, 307

Southern Paiute: and Post-Formative period, 48; and subsistence territories, 190, 378. *See also* Paiute

Spaulding, G. W., 201

Spencer, V. E., 352

springs, as water sources, 54–55

Spurr, Kimberly, 5, 19, 41, 211, 249, 279

squash, and agricultural transition in Southwest, 222–23

standardized documentation, 12

Stash, Roger, 5

Stein, M. A., 25

Stevenson, Christopher M., 19, 155

Steward, Julian H., 161, 235

Stiger, M. M., 10, 229

Stolk, A., 197

Stone, T., 351

stone boiling, 92, 245

stone pipes, 274

storage features: and architecture of Basketmaker II sites, 259–63; and Big Bend site, 95; and borrowing, 289n6; calculation of capacity, 289n3; and Hanging Ash site, 128; and Kin Kahuna, 114; and natural shelters in Basketmaker II, 250–51; and primary habitations, 236–38, 337–38; and Pueblo II kivas, 325, 326; and residential mobility, 370; and secondary habitations, 357, 360, 366; and The Pits, 71–72. *See also* activity/storage rooms; granaries

stratigraphic control, and field methods, 14

structures, and field methods, 15–16

subsistence: and research design of NMRAP, 9–10; and settlement patterns at NMRAP Archaic sites, 183–93. *See also* agriculture and agricultural transition; diet; foraging

Sudden Shelter, 203

Sullivan, A. P., 299, 306

summer habitations, 354

Sunflower Cave, 63, 289n8

Surprise Pueblo (Cummings Mesa), 342, 344, 346–47, 386

Talbot, R. K., 282

Talus Village (Colorado), 268, 282

Tamarron site (Colorado), 282

Taylor, Walter W., 25

Tcamahia Pueblo, *312*, 333

temporary camps: and NMRAP Archaic sites, 177–80; and NMRAP Puebloan sites, 367–68

textiles. *See* sandals; weaving

Thaden, R. E., 61, 63

The Pits (AZ-J-14-17): description of, 64, *65, 70*, 71–72; and early bow-and-arrow technology, 283–84; and feature density, *167, 168*; as hunting camp in Archaic, *166*; and obsidian-hydration dating, 155–58, 160; obsidian in lithic assemblage of, 190; as primary habitation in Basketmaker II, 236, 255; and radiocarbon dates, *148*, 150, *213*, *219*; and storage features, 237–38, 259–60, 262, 382; summary of information on, *142, 208, 292*

The Slots (AZ-J-14-30): and activity/storage rooms, *334*; and ceramic cross dating, *300, 301, 303*; description of, *65*, 82–83; and secondary habitations, *358, 359*, 363–64, *365*; summary of information on, *292*

thermal features, at Big Bend site, 94. *See also* burning; hearths

Thief site, 348, 349

Thomas, D. H., 140, 161, 163, 282

Thompson, Kerry, 5, 19

Three Dog Site (UT-B-63-39): abandonment of, 128, 387; and ceramic assemblage, 311; and ceramic cross dating, *300, 301, 302, 303, 312*, 373n3 ; and courtyard pueblo type of village, 386–87; description of, *67, 124, 125, 126*–28; and faunal remains, 383; and feature density, 165, *167, 168, 169*; and granaries, *332*; and kivas, *320, 321*, 323; and living rooms, *314, 315*; and mealing rooms, 328, 330, *331*; and lithic assemblage, 383; and ornaments, 275; and primary habitations, *336, 340*, 342–44; Puebloan component of, 293, 294, 298–99, *336*, 339, 342–44; and radiocarbon dating, 145, *149, 151, 152*, 153, 154, *213*, 215; as residential camp during Archaic, *166, 167*, 171, 173–76; summary of information on, *142, 208, 292*; and time frame of Paleoindian remains, 193

Three Fir Shelter (Black Mesa), 9, 39–40, 287

Till, Jonathan, 5

Tipps, B. L., 38, 39, 164, 203–4, 338

Titmus, G. L., 269

Todia, Nathaniel, 5

Tolchaco chert, 192

Tomasiyo, Rory T., Sr., 5

Toreva phase, on northern Black Mesa, 373n1
trash middens: and field methods, 16; and Hammer House, 106; and Scorpion Heights, 100; and secondary habitations, 367. *See also* pack rat middens
travertine, 61, 63
tree-ring dating, for NMRAP Puebloan sites, 294–95. *See also* dendrochronology
Tres Campos (AZ-J-14-12): and activity/storage rooms, *334*; and ceramic assemblage, 307; and ceramic cross dating, *300, 301, 303*; description of, *65*, 87, *88*, *89*–90; and feature density, *167, 168*; as hunting camp, *166*; obsidian and white chert in lithic assemblage of, 190, *192*; and radiocarbon dates, *148*, 150, *151, 152*, 213; and secondary habitations, *359*, 364, *365*; summary of information on, *142*, 208, 292
Trites, A. F., 61
Tsegi Orange Ware: and ceramic cross dating, 299, 301–3; and iron/manganese paint, 61; and limonitic clay, 60, 63; and Pueblo II sites in Kayenta region, 45; and Three Dog Site, 384–85
Tsegi phase: and abandonment of Pueblo III sites, 312–13; and Pueblo III sites in NMRAP, 7, 23; research interest in, 24; and Three Dog Site, 127; warfare and defensible positions of pueblos, 386
Tsé Haal'á (UT-B-63-30): description of, *67*, 132, *133*, 134–35; and feature density, 165, *167, 168, 170*; obsidian in lithic assemblage of, 186, *189*; and radiocarbon dates, *148*; as residential camp, *166*, 167, 171, 173–76, 181; summary of information on, *142*; and wind erosion, 131
Tsinnijinnie, Leo, 5
Tsosie, Carissa, 5
Tsosie, Neomie, 5
turkey (*Meleagris gallopavo*), 10
Turkey Pen Cave, 233
Turner, C. G., 11, 382
Tusayan Black-on-red, 305
Tusayan Black-on-white, 45
Tusayan Gray Ware, 299, 301–3
Tusayan White Ware, 43, 299, 301–3, 384
tuwahlki, and field houses, 351

unit pueblos, 344, 347
University of Arizona. *See* NSF-Arizona Mass Spectrometry Laboratory
Upper Chinle Valley, 287
Upper Desha Pueblo, 311, *312*
Upper Paiute Canyon: and early Pueblo II habitations, 304; geography of, *51*; population trends in Formative period, 46; previous research in, 25; Pueblo I sites in, 75
use histories, of NMRAP Puebloan sites, 303–13
use-life, of storage pits, 261–62
UT-B-63-2, 387
UT-B-63-19: and ceramic cross dating, *300*; description of site, *67*, 128, 130–31; and secondary habitations, *358, 359*, 362, *365*
UT-B-63-38: description of site, *67*, 131–32; and feature density, *167, 168*; and radiocarbon dating, 146; as residential camp, 171; summary of information on, *142*
UT-B-63-39. *See* Three Dog Site

UT-V-13-19: and ceramic cross dating, *305*; and primary habitations, 338
UT-V-13-72, 210

Van Devender, T. R., 201
vegetation: and climate during middle Archaic, 201–2; and description of NMRAP project location, 4, 52–54. *See also* plant remains
ventilators, and Puebloan architecture, 315, 322
vertical control, and field methods, 14
Vierra, B. J., 163, 164, 184
village: and concept of proto-village, 235, 239, 385; increase in size of in Pueblo III, 347; use of term, 344, 386
Vokes, Arthur W., 5, 19

Walker, Lt. John George, 290
wall features, and field methods, 15, 16
Warburton, Miranda, 5, 19, 24, 48
warfare, and settlement patterns in Kayenta region, 386
Waterbolk, H. T., 219
Water Jar Pueblo (AZ-J-2-58): and ceramic assemblage, 311; and ceramic cross dating, *300, 301, 302, 303*; description of, *67*, 118–21; and faunal remains, 383; and kivas, *320*, 321, 322, *323*, 324; and lithic assemblage, 383; and mealing rooms, *328*; and plaza or unit pueblos, 344–46; and primary habitations, *336, 340*; Puebloan component of, 293, *336*; summary of information on, 292
water sources: and climate during middle Archaic, 202–3; and description of environment of Kayenta region, 54–55; and residential camps, 167, 171
weathering basins, as water sources, 55
weaving, and Puebloan architecture, 317, 320, 325–26
Weber, S. A., 253
Wepo Black-on-white, 221, 296
Wepo phase, of Pueblo II, 44–45
Wesley, Yolanda, 5
Wetherill, Richard, 37
Wetterstrom, W., 230
White Dog Cave, 138
White Dog phase, of Basketmaker II, 39, 40, 41, 42, 138, 287
Whitehat, Bruce, 5, *13*
Wilcox, Tim, 5
Wild Horse (Mineral Mountains), as source of obsidian, 158, 160, 190, 377–78
Willey, Gordon R., 161
Willie, Rachael, 5
Wills, W. H., 29, 140, 227, 262, 265, 379
Wilson, C. D., 261
Windy Mesa (AZ-J-14-28): Basketmaker II component of, 211; and ceramic assemblage, 310; and ceramic cross dating, *300, 301, 302, 303*; description of, *65*, 79, *80*, *81*; and feature density, *167, 168*; as hunting camp, *166*, 245, *246*–47; obsidian in lithic assemblage of, 185, *186*, 192–93; as primary habitation in early Pueblo III, 339; Pueblo I component of, 304; and radiocarbon dates, *149*, 150, 211, 298; summary of information on, *142*, 208, 292; tree-ring dates for, *294*
Withers, K., 201
Witkind, I. J., 63

Witter, D. C., 181
Wolachii Bighan (AZ-J-14-20): and ceramic cross dating, *300, 301, 303*; description of, *65, 74–75*; and radiocarbon dates, 299; summary of information on, *292*; and temporary camps, 367
Wood, J. J., 161
Woodbury, A. M., 54, 366
Wood charcoal, and radiocarbon dates, 150–54
Wormington, H. M., 282, 285

X-ray fluorescence-energy-dispersive spectrometer (XRF-EDS), 157, 189–90, 377

Yavapai, and subsistence territories, 378
Yazzie, Natasha, *5*
Yazzie, Olivia, *5*
Yazzie, Orlinda, *5*
Yellen, J. E., 162, 163
yucca, and radiocarbon dates from plant remains, 154, 205n4. *See also* sandals

E 99 .N3 G355 2011
Geib, Phil R.
Foragers and farmers of the
 northern Kayenta region

DEC 1 2 2011